In Memory of

Richard E. Duprey

Howard W. Foltz

Virginia Leonard

Doyt Mohler

Richard C. Pollock

From

The Van Wert

Men's Garden Club

1999

———•———

About the Author

A lifelong Seattle resident, Lee has been fascinated by nature since high school. He earned his B.A. in history from the University of Washington. He feels that history embraces philosophy, anthropology, sociology, psychology, and more. In addition to being a tree expert, he is equally enthusiastic about edible plants, both wild and cultivated. Some of his salads feature more than 100 different kinds of plants, and he has written 100 *Weed of the Month* columns.

Lee only grows plants in his garden that are *useful,* which he defines as fragrant, edible, medicinal, or of remarkable ecologic benefit. He does not drive a car, and has bicycled thousands of miles. To support his passion, he writes, lectures, teaches, and does consulting.

Cover photographs

(dates indicate time of year photographs were taken)

Serviceberry trees
Amelanchier arborea
10/20
Fine textured, small trees prized for white spring flowers, summer berries, and autumnal splendor.

Blue Colorado Spruce
Picea pungens f. *glauca*
7/-
Much-loved and overplanted; many cultivars exist.

California Redbud
Cercis occidentalis
3/26
Shrubby and small, it is drought-tolerant and usually has a plain fall color.

Cistena Plum
Prunus × *cistena*
9/26
The most dwarf of all Purpleleaf Plums; very cold-hardy.

Sargent Magnolia
Magnolia Sargentiana
3/13
Floral splendor and an easy garden constitution make this popular.

Momi Fir
Abies firma
3/27
Native in Japan, where it is called *Momi*.
(Also shown on back cover.)

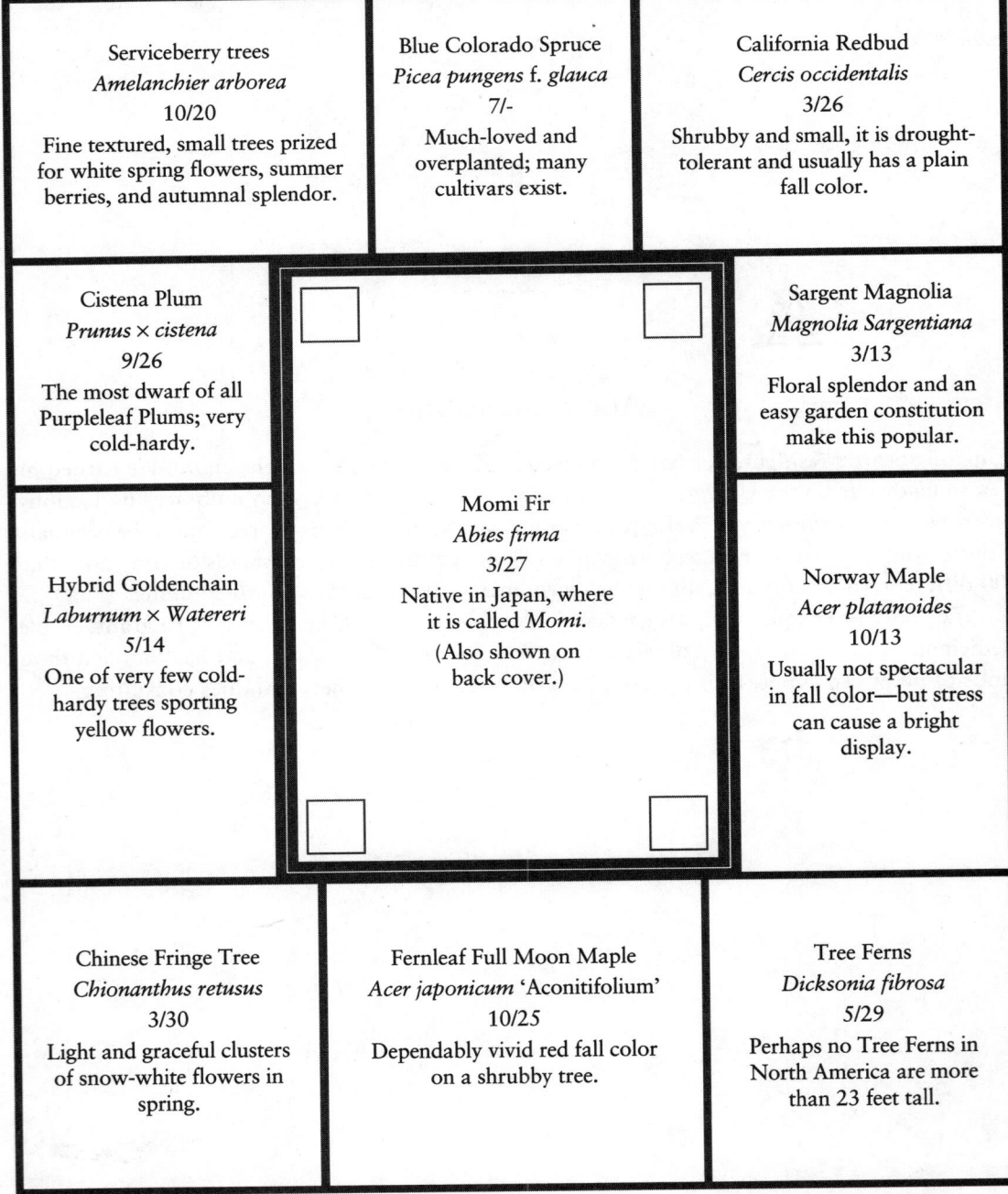

Hybrid Goldenchain
Laburnum × *Watereri*
5/14
One of very few cold-hardy trees sporting yellow flowers.

Norway Maple
Acer platanoides
10/13
Usually not spectacular in fall color—but stress can cause a bright display.

Chinese Fringe Tree
Chionanthus retusus
3/30
Light and graceful clusters of snow-white flowers in spring.

Fernleaf Full Moon Maple
Acer japonicum 'Aconitifolium'
10/25
Dependably vivid red fall color on a shrubby tree.

Tree Ferns
Dicksonia fibrosa
5/29
Perhaps no Tree Ferns in North America are more than 23 feet tall.

NORTH AMERICAN LANDSCAPE TREES

by Arthur Lee Jacobson

Drawings by Michael C. Lee

Ten Speed Press
Berkeley, California

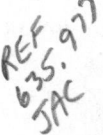

Ten Speed Press
Post Office Box 7123
Berkeley, California 94707

Distributed in Australia by E. J. Dwyer Pty. Ltd., in Canada by Publishers Group West, in New Zealand by Tandem Press, in South Africa by Real Books, and in the United Kingdom and Europe by Airlift Books.

Cover and book design by Victor Ichioka

Library of Congress Cataloging-in-Publication Data

Jacobson, Arthur Lee
        North American landscape trees / Arthur Lee Jacobson.
                p.   cm
        Includes index.
        ISBN 0-89815-813-3
        1. Ornamental trees—United States. 2. Ornamental trees—Canada.

        3. Ornamental trees—Pictorial works. I. Title.

        SB435.5.J335 1996
        635.9'77—dc20   95-40814
                                                    CIP

First printing, 1996
Printed in Canada

1 2 3 4 5 — 00 99 98 97 96

This book is affectionately dedicated to Brian O. Mulligan, former director (1947–1972) and selfless worker at the Washington Park Arboretum in Seattle. His devotion is consummate, as he retired from his job in 1972 but has volunteered at least two days a week since then. In doing so he has patiently endured conditions that would cause some of us hot-tempered people to revolt. I greatly admire Brian, and have benefited as much as anyone from his labor.

Acknowledgments

Friendly encouragement, expert feedback, hospitality, funds, and information were generously supplied by a host of people. Without such assistance, this book would not be as thorough. My whole existence is blessed by my supportive family and friends—but I will try to limit acknowledgments here to help given specifically towards this book.

Gerry Chaster set a world record for patience as we raced around looking at trees on Vancouver Island and in southern California. Warren Roberts has been constantly hospitable and generous, even while disagreeing with my taste for Capitalization and other matters. Mai Arbegast and Scot Medbury made my bookwormish life at Berkeley a joy.

For tree measurements my chief collaborators were Al Carder, Maynard Drawson, Alan Mitchell, Randy Stoltmann, and Bob Van Pelt.

For biographical information I am indebted to Evelyn Roehl.

Experts who took time to make suggestions for certain genera were George Argus (*Salix*), John den Boer (*Malus*), Ron Brightman (*Magnolia*), Scot Medbury (*Cupressus*), Virginia Morell (*Ilex*), Brian Mulligan (*Acer, Sorbus*), J.B. Phipps (*Cratægus*), and Stan Scher (*Taxus*).

Patrons who contributed financially enabled me to pay for preliminary editing and the illustrations. These include Leroy "Rip" Collins, Anne Gould Hauberg, Gretchen Hull, Marianna Price, Wells Medina Nursery, Bagley Wright, and Virginia Wyman. In addition, the many people who ordered pre-publication copies made possible still more illustrations.

Madelon Bolling edited the book. It was humbling to see how many errors she caught. Madelon, like myself and my illustrator, works for enjoyment first and money secondarily. So we are all cash-strapped, but manage to get by with our good humor.

Librarians of accommodating nature have made my long hours in their domain much easier and less draining than it might have been. Thanks to Barbara Pitschel at the Helen Crocker library in San Francisco, to Valerie Easton, Martha Ferguson and Laura Lipton at the Miller library in Seattle, and to John Skarstad at the Shields library in Davis.

For preliminary book design, production and computerization, my mentor and fellow tree lover Steve Herold has been priceless. If he had not intervened way back when I began writing books, my first title (*Trees of Seattle*) would not have been a success.

Thank you to my sister, Joy Jacobson, for drawing the map of USDA zones 1–11.

CONTENTS

INTRODUCTION

Basis for inclusion

This book is a concise account of most of the cold-hardy ornamental trees that have been or are grown in temperate North America north of Mexico.

My curiosity about ornamental trees has prompted me to spend time observing, growing, photographing, thinking about, and discussing them. Being of bookish inclination, I spend as much time reading about trees as I do studying them in the field. The enormous number of cultivated varieties causes confusion, but also enriches and improves our landscapes.

I did not wish to write a local gardener's guide to trees, or a book about the trees presently popular in commercial nurseries. This book's scope is our past and present, and it is wider in coverage than any other single volume on trees, with close to 5,000 different kinds included. However, it started as a much less encyclopedic project.

Initially, my goal was to include only major landscape trees; a list of about 1,500 was generated. Then a list was made of the availability of trees at North American nurseries. Many more varieties were offered than I had been aware of. I expanded these notes to include authors of the scientific names, synonyms, English names, dates of introduction, prevalence in the nursery trade, etc. I acquainted myself with the majority of the available literature, and in addition looked at, measured, and photographed many specimens.

Several personal biases must be acknowledged. Most of the populace live eastward: the Arnold Arboretum in Boston, and U.S. National Arboretum in Washington, D.C., have both been of major influence in developing tree awareness. However, I live in Seattle, and that fact helped in preparing a better-balanced book. Secondly, my background in the liberal arts, rather than science, has resulted in a warmer approach—though some might fault me for interjecting a strong personal element into a book of this nature. Finally, my love of history accounts for the emphasis on dates of discovery, introduction and naming.

This book should enable readers to look up virtually any tree and find:

- Where the tree came from and when it was introduced to cultivation.
- Who named it, and why, for both scientific and vernacular names.
- What makes the tree desirable, or what made it lose favor.
- How common it was and is.
- A description of its appearance, including its reported maximum size.
- Any remarkable facts about it.

Often information is simply not available, so entries are incomplete. Additional data will be received gratefully.

The focus is ornamental trees, rather than wild native ones, or those grown only for timber. The question of what qualities in a tree make us judge it "ornamental" is one that must be considered in a regional context. Clearly, a severe climate or troublesome soil conditions will force people to grow whatever trees will survive there, even though those same trees might be considered weedy or coarse elsewhere. In addition, public opinion of which trees are ornamental changes as availability of trees and information about them increases. Presently a resurgence of interest in native species is enabling certain trees to sell well even if they are considered homely.

Excluded are cold-tender trees successful only in the Deep South and much of California, where subtropical, largely frost-free conditions allow numerous acacias, eucalypts, palms, pittosporums, citrus, ficus, and many similar non-hardy trees to thrive.

Excluded are shrubby varieties such as dwarf conifer or bonsai selections, although in most tree books, some shrubby tree species are inevitably included or excluded according to individual judgement. If a genus is usually shrublike, the fact that one or two of its species may sometimes be treelike may not justify inclusion in a tree book. I do not use an arbitrary definition of a tree—unlike the U.S. Forest Service, which states that "trees are woody plants having one erect perennial stem or trunk at least 3 inches in diameter at 4 ½ feet, a more or less definitely formed crown of foliage, and a height of at least 13 feet." The Forest Service definition is liberal, and results in many shrubs being called trees.

Excluded are most fruit tree varieties, because there are already books devoted entirely to them. For example, I have a general entry for the common apple tree (*Malus* × *domestica*)—but no information on its more than seven thousand cultivars.

Excluded are most obscure species unknown outside of botanic gardens, specialist collections and arboreta. Still, many little-known trees are mentioned. Some of them have recently been promoted by major nurseries. But this work records primarily what has been planted rather than what may be desirable.

Since no other book does justice to numerous rare cultivated varieties—such as the cultivars of ROCKY MOUNTAIN JUNIPER (*Juniperus scopulorum*) and FLOWERING PEACH (*Prunus Persica*)—I chose to include ones that are inadequately documented elsewhere. I believe even the rare garden varieties must be recorded, somewhere, if only because a nursery naming a novel tree must be able to give it a name that has not been conferred already.

Ornamental trees sometimes have very utilitarian roles as windbreaks, as screens, to combat soil erosion, or to yield honey. In some cases, a tree is grown primarily because it is useful, and the fact that it is beautiful is secondary. Such trees are usually included, but their primary value from the human perspective is clearly stated.

Ultimately, the choice of trees and data to be included here is based on what I know of the tree and its role in North American horticulture. Admittedly, some of the choices are purely subjective. Some of the factors that weighed in favor of inclusion are:

- Personal familiarity.
- To offer original data.
- To correct inaccurate or incomplete portrayals found in the literature.
- Presence in the nursery trade.
- My ignorance of a tree, whereby I give it the benefit of my doubt.

The result is a descriptive reference book rather than a planting guide. It includes trees old and new, in hope of providing some sense of overall perspective, and to account for the names in existence.

A serious need exists for tools and expertise in the field of tree identification. At nurseries, arboreta, herbaria, and in books, at least 10 percent of the material tends to be inadequately or incorrectly identified. Some major wholesale tree nurseries send out tens of thousands of misidentified trees every year. One reason for this is simply that profit margins are sometimes more important than fact-checking and accurate labeling. Also, nursery label software is in its pioneering stage and is rife with errors.

This is not a guide to propagating or growing trees. It does not tend to mention a tree's preference for soil pH, or its pest or disease problems. Whenever such information is supplied, it should be understood as a generalization, and exceptions to the rule may well exist.

Cold-hardiness zones are not included, partly because substantial differences exist in the hardiness findings of researchers around the continent. There are many factors to consider: heat, humidity, rainfall, soil, temperature fluctuations, exposure, genetics, means of propagation, and the specific site of the tree. I look forward to the day when plant adaptability-zone maps will exist. Meanwhile, the trees included in this book are known to be more or less frost tolerant. My general rule for trees of questionable hardiness was: "will it survive in Seattle?" Seattle gets freezing weather nearly every winter, and is classed in the USDA cold-hardiness zone 8b, that is: average annual minimum temperature between 20 and 15°F (-6.7 to -7.4°C). According to the less accurate Arnold Arboretum hardiness map, Seattle is also zone 8. Trees for USDA zones 9–11 are not in this volume—except in a few cases where the text clearly notes their status and justifies their inclusion. Some trees simply require more testing before we will be sure of their cold-hardiness.

Relative rarity notes

A tree can be "common" in one area, yet still be described fairly as "exceedingly rare" if it is judged in the broad context of Canada and the United States. Some books about trees supply too little indication in the descriptions as to whether a species is abundant or rare. This book usually supplies some such commentary, but it must be viewed in the proper context. Generally, the context is restricted to a genus level. For example, there are common BIRCHES (genus *Betula*) and rare BIRCHES—and it is understood that BIRCHES as a group are common and thrive in the North, and are rare and weak in the South. The relative abundance must also be recognized in terms of time. Many trees in this volume were once readily available from nurseries, but are now commercially extinct. The presence or absence of trees in contemporary commerce is a fluctuating matter.

Nurseries

For most people, nurseries are the preferred way to obtain trees. Here are the names of a few present-day firms offering a diversity of rare species and varieties. From the following retail mail-order nurseries one could purchase dozens of trees so rare that they were excluded from this book—and available only in small sizes, in very limited quantities.

Arborvillage Farm of Holt, MO

Camellia Forest of Chapel Hill, NC

Colvos Creek of Vashon, WA

Forest Farm of Williams, OR

Foxborough of Street, MD

Kristick of Wellsville, PA

Louisiana of Opelousas, LA

Oikos of Kalamazoo, MI

Roslyn of Dix Hills, NY

Woodlanders of Aiken, SC

Yucca Do of Waller, TX

Some nurseries specialize in one group of trees, such as conifers, JAPANESE MAPLES, HOLLIES, natives, or nut trees. For contemporary plant sources and nurseries (including addresses), consult the *Andersen Horticultural Library's Source List of Plants and Seeds*, edited by Richard T. Isaacson (3rd ed., 1993), or *The Canadian Plant Sourcebook* by Anne and Peter Ashley (2nd ed.,1992).

Until recently, most landscape trees were raised from seed. Now most landscape trees, as well as fruit trees, are mass-produced, vegetatively propagated clones. For genetic diversity, it would seem prudent to plant a balance of diverse seedlings and clones. A few large wholesale tree nurseries mass-produce the majority of clonal trees, and introduce the majority of patented, trademarked cultivars. These nurseries (or introducers) include:

Bailey of St Paul, MN

L.E. Cooke of Visalia, CA

Davey of Wooster, OH

Discov-Tree Research of Oquawka, IL

Duncan & Davies of New Plymouth, New Zealand (they market globally)

Handy of Portland, OR

Iseli of Boring, OR

Lake County of Perry, OH

Monrovia of CA

Princeton of Princeton, NJ

Schmidt of Boring, OR

Siebenthaler of Dayton, OH

Simpson of Vincennes, IN

Arboreta, botanic gardens, and research stations

Landscape trees are often introduced, displayed, evaluated and promoted by non-commercial institutions. A few of note are singled out here. Each has publications documenting its accomplishments.

U.S. Plant Introduction Stations:

- at Chico, CA; established in 1904
- at Savannah, GA; established in 1919
- at Glenn Dale, MD; established in 1919–20

Notable State or Provincial research stations:

- Brookings, SD
- Morden, Manitoba

Some major arboreta:

- Arnold, at Jamaica Plain, MA
- Dominion, at Ottawa, Ontario
- Holden, at Mentor, OH
- Huntington, at San Marino, CA
- Longwood Gardens, at Kennett Square, PA
- Los Angeles State and County, at Arcadia, CA
- Minnesota Landscape, at Chanhassen, MN
- Missouri Botanical Garden, at St. Louis, MO
- Montreal Botanical Gardens, at Montreal, Québec
- Morris, at Philadelphia, PA
- Morton, at Lisle, IL
- New York Botanical Garden, at Bronx, NY
- North Carolina State University, at Raleigh, NC
- Strybing, at San Francisco, CA
- U.S. National, at Washington, D.C.
- Washington Park, at Seattle, WA

Other noteworthy organizations:

- Saratoga Horticultural Foundation, presently of San Martin, CA, was established in 1952, and has introduced 49 cultivars (through 1994), and "assisted with" 65 others. Not all are trees, but some of the trees are of great importance.
- Brookside Gardens of Montgomery County, MD, has introduced many cultivars from Japan since 1977.
- Center for Development of Hardy Landscape Plants. Started in 1990, an international cooperative plant introduction project based at Chanhassen, MN.
- Chicagoland Grows, Inc.®. Started in 1968, a cooperative plant introduction project based in Illinois.
- USDA. Continually engaged in plant introduction from overseas, but especially strong on ornamental plants (as opposed to economic crops) from 1955 to 1972.

For data on such organizations, consult *North American Horticulture: A Reference Guide* (2nd ed., 1992), edited by Thomas M. Barrett.

Dates and measurements

Except for eastern North American species known before about 1850, this book usually gives dates of introduction to cultivation in the Western World. The "Western World" in this sense can vary widely, being not a geographic place so much as the Eurocentric culture. (For example: St. Petersburg, Vienna, Paris, London, Australia, or the New World.) The dates that trees were discovered by Westerners are sometimes given, as are dates of publication of scientific or nursery names. This can help us sort tree varieties.

For every species, the goal in measuring was to provide the maximum recorded dimensions, whether it was recorded yesterday or in a primeval forest 200 years ago. But often included also are observations as to what can be expected of the tree in cultivation. Size varies according to many factors, including genetics, environment, and human intervention. The maximum height and trunk size of any given tree may be fully twice as much as its average mature size.

In the U.S. and Canada, attention to record-size trees has often been restricted to native species. For example the American Forests *National Register of Big Trees* excludes non-native species unless they are naturalized. Thus we are given no data on the memorable Chinese *Ginkgo*—planted in nearly every state and province. Fortunately, tree measuring in North America is carried out by many people, and some measure deserving non-natives. In the U.K., thousands of different species are measured, even when they're small. Yet the work there is done essentially by a couple of people running the non-profit Tree Register of the British Isles. A balance seems desirable. I prefer to supply for each species the tallest, the stoutest, and sometimes the widest recorded dimensions. This is the first book that attempts to do such a thing for the "champion trees" of our landscapes. The measurements are from many sources, including some of doubtful accuracy. I measured hundreds of trees myself. Readers are welcome to submit records for future editions.

Feet and inches are used rather than metric, because the metric system, as used in measuring trees, is less precise. (Meters are usually rounded off.) To determine how many meters tall a tree is, multiply the feet figure cited by .3048 (for example, 79' × .3048 = 24m).

A formula is used to cite tree measurements in this book: height followed by trunk girth (circumference), sometimes followed by crown spread (how wide the branching extends), followed by the measurement's known or supposed date. The crown spread is usually only important when the species tends to grow as wide or wider than it is tall. Where known, the planting date is often supplied, abbreviated as "*pl.*" In the case of most trees cited from botanic gardens or arboreta, the year cited is the accession date, meaning that seeds, cuttings or full sized nursery trees were acquired that year—not necessarily planted that year.

People measure trunks differently. Foresters and nurserymen tend to prefer trunk diameter, called caliper. That, frequently rounded-off, is a commodity viewpoint, measuring size as it relates to monetary value. On the other hand, measuring a specific trunk circumference obtains a personal and exact "waistline"—such as has been employed historically by most "big tree seekers." Persons preferring trunk diameter need only divide the circumference by 3.1416. Often the abbreviation DBH (Diameter at Breast Height) is used. Unfortunately, sometimes people confuse circumference measurements as diameter measurements, or vice-versa.

There is no international standard for selecting the height from the ground at which the measurment is taken. Generally, in the U.S., it is at four and a half feet. In any case, responsible tree measurers strive to obtain the smallest possible reading between the ground level and the accepted height. They pull their measuring tape tightly.

Numerals enclosed in parentheses refer to "normal" versus "exceptional" range, so that both extremes and averages are presented. Similarly, in giving dates of flowering or fruiting, the text may give ranges within parentheses.

Names

Scientific names are the international currency in plant information exchange. This book contains many alternate names, but even those are but a small fraction of the total. Some names have been long out of use, but are vital for consulting old sources (for example, as needed in researching historic landscapes). Others reveal the history of our understanding of plant classification.

The equal sign (=) is used in citing synonyms, but in actuality very few are literally equal—most are invalid for one reason or another. Some were not the oldest, or were misapplied by botanists or horticulturists, or were never widely accepted in the literature. This book records usage, and usage often breaks rules.

A great number of vernacular names are included. All English names are typeset in small capitals; all foreign ones are italicized. Derivations of both scientific and common names are usually supplied.

Names are not necessarily apt or literal. For example, many plants whose specific name is *japonica* are actually not natives of Japan, but rather of China—but long cultivated in Japan. Other names are often fanciful—like the POTATOCHIP TREE.

Every scientific name has an author. This book does not credit the authors of either the family or generic names, only of the specific and infraspecific names (subspecies, varietates, and formæ). Usually the botanists' names are abbreviated.

Scientific judgement is not uniform. Sometimes, one expert's species can be another's subspecies, or one scholar's concept of "valid publication" may fail to meet the criteria of another's. Readers familiar with standard tree works will find that some of the names I prefer are not in agreement with the judgement of other authors. This is inevitable. Unfortunately the oft-repeated phrase "there is only one true scientific name for each plant" is untrue. It is true that for any particular rank (such as species or subspecies) there is only one valid combination (the oldest that fulfills the requirements of valid publication). In any case, with the thousands of cross references in this book, readers will be able to locate a tree by one name or another. In some cases, I found that the oldest name was not the most familiar one, so I bowed to custom and conserved the familiar name, citing the older but obscure name as a synonym. This is patently incorrect, but I am by no means alone in the usage. There has evolved recently a gratifying trend in botany of minimizing disruptive name changes.

Nonetheless, there are names in the literature that should not be maintained. For example, the MOUNTAIN ASH called *Sorbus tianshanica* Red Cascade™ is clearly a variety of *Sorbus americana,* and to call it by another species' name is indefensible. On the other hand, I defer to the majority of authors in the case of the ATLAS CEDAR (*Cedrus atlantica*). This is only a subspecies of CEDAR OF LEBANON (*Cedrus libani*), but many feel that a change would be unnecessary and troublesome.

Since I believe that nomenclature should serve humanity, not vice-versa, this book has few new combinations of names. These are indicated by the words "stat. nov.," or "comb. nov." after the scientific name. Readers are free to reject any names I have given preference to, if an equally valid proposal is available. It is often difficult to know which synonymous names are outdated, and which are legitimate alternatives. I sometimes make parenthetical notes explaining my stance.

There is still a great deal of work to be done in plant classification. Currently, the different genera are divided into species according to chance, and by botanists of varying judgement. If a rigidly applied system of taxonomic uniformity were somehow imposed, the result would be a turmoil of name changes: certain species sunk into synonymy, numerous varietates elevated to species status, genera shattered and recombined.

Capitalization of selected specific names puzzles many people. Some professors, perhaps to make life simpler, tell students to always capitalize generic names and never capitalize specific ones. The international rules, however, allow capitalization for specific names which fall into one of the following categories:

1) derived directly from a person's name. (e.g., *Picea Breweriana*—after William Henry Brewer);

2) from a vernacular name. (e.g., *Picea Omorika*—the Balkan vernacular for SPRUCE);

3) from a generic name. (e.g., *Picea Abies).*

Sometimes people use capitals incorrectly, particularly with geographic names. Even though Pennsylvania and Washington are named after William Penn and George Washington, the plants recorded with the geographic terms *pennsylvanica* or *washingtonensis* remain uncapitalized because they are not directly named after a person.

Below, ranked from broader categories to narrower, are the levels of scientific plant-classification used in this book.

Family (plural families)

- A group of related genera.
- Always fully capitalized and ending in the ligature Æ in this book (e.g., ACERACEÆ; the Maple Family).
- 72 families are represented in this book.

Genus (plural genera)

- A group of related species.
- Always initially capitalized, and italicized in this book (e.g., *Acer*, the MAPLE).
- 198 genera are represented in this book.
- For each genus, the approximate number of species is indicated, and the figures cited often reflect scientific disagreement or uncertainty; new species are still being described every year.

Species (plural species; abbreviated sp. in the singular and spp. in the plural)

- The basic unit of classification.
- Usually uncapitalized, and always italicized in this book (e.g., *saccharum*). For example, *Acer saccharum* (SUGAR MAPLE) is one of the species in the genus *Acer*.
- 950 species are represented in this book.

Subspecies (plural subspecies; abbreviated subsp. or ssp.)

- A significant geographic race of a species.
- 36 subspecies are represented in this book.

Varietas (plural varietates; abbreviated var.)

- A minor race not deserving subspecies status; considered interchangeable with subspecies by some botanists.
- 159 varietates are represented in this book.

Forma (plural formæ; abbreviated f.)

- A seedling variation; used when a percentage of seedlings exhibit a distinctive characteristic.
- 95 formæ are represented in this book.

Hybrids
(indicated by × or, for graft-hybrids, +)

These are often treated as equal in rank to species and included in lists of species. Ideally, the parentage is cited with the female parent placed first, the male second. Since the direction of the cross is often unknown, some authors prefer always listing the two parental species alphabetically. The international rules prefer squeezing the multiplication sign right next to the name: *Photinia ×Fraseri;* I insert a space: *Photinia × Fraseri.*

The many hybrids in this book are designated in one of three different ways:

1) *Photinia × Fraseri* Dress

   A botanical epithet covering all crosses between *P. glabra* and *P. serratifolia.*

2) *Juglans Hindsii × J. regia*

   Direct indication of parentage (useful where no specific epithet has yet been given).

3) *Malus* 'Ferrill's Crimson'

This third method is inconsistent in that it does not use the multiplication sign (×). It is used in any of the following cases:

- Known to be a hybrid, but parentage is not known, nor is there a specific botanical epithet for the cross.

- Parentage is known, but there is no specific botanical epithet for the cross.

- Parentage is unknown, but the tree may be a hybrid.

Cultivars

To horticulturists, the vital category cultivar (abbreviated cv.) is, in regard to trees, almost invariably used to indicate a clone. This term is an abbreviation of "cultivated variety." Older books generally used the term "variety" for what we now call cultivars. The problem with that usage is that it did not differentiate between naturally occurring wild varietates of scientific nomenclature, and the genetically identical cultivated varieties named by nurseries and gardeners. Here, cultivars are indicated by single quotation marks: 'Sunburst'. Unfortunately, some nursery catalogs and other publications use the same marks for common names—a confusing practice.

Ilex opaca (AMERICAN HOLLY) has more than 1,000 cultivars (79 are in this volume). *Magnolia grandiflora* has about 175 (51 are in this volume). All told, this book treats 3,540 cultivars, and mentions in passing another 167. Some cultivar names are formally registered with various organizations here or abroad. Such registrars attempt to watch over a certain genus, to help ensure order. For a cultivar to be considered registered, usually there must be documentation of its origin and distinguishing attributes. If a nursery begins selling a plant as a cultivar, but does not contact the registration authority, or publish a "legitimate" description, the authority may proclaim the name invalid. But just because the name is invalid in this sense does not mean the cultivar is not worthy of recognition, or that it cannot be validated later. Registration is a good policy, but since it is strictly voluntary, few nurseries participate in the process.

For a listing of international cultivar registration authorities, see *HortScience,* June, 1990. Some are:

- *Acer* (MAPLE): Dr. Thomas M. Antonio, Chicago Botanic Garden, P.O. Box 400, Glencoe, IL 60022.
- *Amelanchier* (SERVICEBERRY): R.G. St. Pierre, Dept. of Horticultural Science, Univ. of Saskatchewan, Saskatoon, Saskatchewan, S7N 0W0.
- *Cornus* (DOGWOOD): Dr. Stephen A. Spongberg, Arnold Arboretum, Jamaica Plain, MA 02130.
- *Fagus* (BEECH): Dr. Stephen A. Spongberg, Arnold Arboretum, Jamaica Plain, MA 02130.
- *Gleditsia* (HONEYLOCUST): Dr. Stephen A. Spongberg, Arnold Arboretum, Jamaica Plain, MA 02130.
- *Ilex* (HOLLY): Holly Society of America, U.S. National Arboretum, 3501 New York Ave NE, Washington, D.C. 20002.
- *Lagerstrœmia* (CRAPEMYRTLE): U.S. National Arboretum, 3501 New York Ave NE, Washington, D.C. 20002.
- *Magnolia:* Dorothy J. Callaway, P.O. Box 3131, Thomasville, GA 31799.
- *Malus* (ORNAMENTAL CRABAPPLE): Dr. Stephen A. Spongberg, Arnold Arboretum, Jamaica Plain, MA 02130.
- *Populus* (POPLAR, ASPEN, COTTONWOOD): International Poplar Commission, Via della Terme di Caracalla, 00100 Rome, Italy.
- *Syringa* (LILAC): Mr. Freek Vrugtman, Royal Botanical Gardens, Box 399, Hamilton, Ontario, L8N 3H8.
- *Ulmus* (ELM): Dr. Stephen A. Spongberg, Arnold Arboretum, Jamaica Plain, MA 02130.
- Conifers: Piers Trehane, Hampreston Manor, Wimborne, Dorset, England, BH21 7LX.
- Other genera: Steven E. Clemants, Brooklyn Botanic Garden, 1000 Washington Avenue, Brooklyn, NY 11225–1099.

A cultivar will usually be described according to its performance in its place of origin, but the same cultivar, when propagated and grown in different regions, sometimes exhibits notably different characteristics. For example, a tree selected for bright, early, fall color in New Hampshire may prove a flop in Florida. This book repeats whatever the nursery catalogs recorded for their cultivars, so the location of the original selection needs to be taken into consideration.

There is a Cultivar Code that regulates cultivar naming. To qualify for valid publication, cultivar names cannot be published exclusively in nursery catalogs—there must be an account in a botanical or horticultural periodical or book. Therefore, certain cultivar names that have been used only in nursery catalogs will be "officially" validated by appearing in this book. The cultivar Code also designated 1958 as the last year in which Latinized names were acceptable for cultivers. Any cultivar names used after that time must be in modern languages to be valid. This is a reasonable effort to help people differentiate betwen scientific names and nursery names.

Patents and trademarks

Since the Plant Patent Act of 1930 (and since 1990 in Canada) anyone has been able to patent a tree—indicated in this book as "PP," which means Plant Patent. The first ornamental tree to receive a patent was a FLOWERING DOGWOOD, assigned in 1941 to Stark nursery of Louisiana, MO, for *Cornus florida* 'Stark's Giant' PP 442. This book includes 257 trees designated PP, and notes both the patent number and the year. Additional trees are in the process of being patented; these are indicated as PAF (Patent applied for). A patent means that for 17 years after the date indicated, only the patent holder or licensees may raise and sell the tree.

Major wholesale nurseries also are increasingly using trademark (™) or registered trademark (®) names. In such cases, the usage of the *names* is legally controlled. Unfortunately, catalogs sometimes list the same name differently: as a cultivar (' ') as a ®, and as a ™! I try to use the designation favored by the company that originated the variety in question, or that controls its propagation rights. If I have not seen the catalog of the originator, I use what seems to be the prevailing designation. Usage of trademarks can also vary from state to state. The rapidity with which such names are being changed is a source of confusion and a hotly disputed subject.

Although this book includes every name (cultivar or trademark, registered or not) the descriptive account is placed after whichever name is thought to be the one most likely to be consulted first. Doubtless, some of the names given in this edition as cultivars will shortly become trademarked, and replaced by new cultivar names. Examples:

Genus/species	original cv name	present cv	name trademark
Acer rubrum	'Red Sunset'	'Franksred'	Red Sunset®
Magnolia	'Majestic Beauty'	'Monlia'	Majestic Beauty™
Malus	'Centurion'	'Centzam'	Centurion®
Tilia cordata	'Green Mountain'	'PNI 0285'	Green Mountain®

This trend, ballooning since the early 1980s, is maddening but legal. Trademarked names last indefinitely, so a wholesale nursery, by making an obnoxious cultivar name and an attractive trademark name, gains financially: it can demand that other wholesalers or retailers pay a fee if they wish to use the trademark name for sales.

The recent flood of trademark names has caught academics, the public, and many nurseries off guard. Several tree books published in the 1990s accidentally describe the exact same tree in two places—under its cultivar name and under its trademark name. It would be almost miraculous if the present volume doesn't have a few such cases also.

ABBREVIATIONS AND SYMBOLS

1) Used in conjunction with tree names

auct.	(*auctor*) authors of plant names
comb. nov.	(*combinatio nova*) new name combination; e.g., saying a cultivar is in fact a hybrid
emend.	(*emendatio*) emended or corrected by
ex	used between the botanist who proposes a name, and the one who publishes it
f.	forma—see the outline of scientific and horticultural nomenclature on page xvi
fil.	(*filius*) son; for example Michx. fil. means François Michaux, son of André Michaux
hort.	(*hortulanorum*) of gardens or horticulture, as opposed to botanic science
L.	Carl Linnaeus, whose binomial names of 1753 began modern nomenclature
nom. ambig.	(*nomen ambiguum*) name ambiguous and must be disregarded as it is too confusing
nom. nud.	(*nomen nudum*) name invalidly published because it has no description
nom. subnud.	(*nomen subnudum*) name invalidly published yet frequently accepted anyway
non	not (used when botanists or horticulturists have misapplied names)
P.A.F.	Plant Patent applied for
PP	Plant Patent (valid for 17 years from date indicated in parentheses)
p.p.	(*pro parte*) in part, but not wholly
®	Registered trademark, its usage controlled by owner
sensu	in the sense of
s.l.	*sensu lato*—in a wide sense; a broad interpretation of a species' limits
ssp.	subspecies—see the outline of scientific and horticultural nomenclature on page xvi
stat. nov.	(*status novus*) new status of a name, such as changing a var. to a ssp.
™	Trademark, registered or not, the usage of such names controlled by the owner
var.	varietas—see the outline of scientific and horticultural nomenclature on page xvi
×	sexual hybrid (most crosses are of this kind). see page xvii
+	graft hybrid (only two in the book: *Cratægomespilus* and *Laburnocytisus*)

2) Miscellaneous

æ	indicates a silent a (as in Julius Cæsar)
a.k.a.	also known as
C	central
ca.	(*circa*) about
cf.	(*confer*) compare; see also
COPF	Canadian Ornamental Plant Foundation
E	east or eastern
e.g.	(*exempli gratia*) for example
fl.	flower or floral; or (in reference to a person), flourished
i.e.	(*id est*) that is; namely
m	meter(s)
mt.	mountain or mount
N	north or northern
n.d.	no date known
œ	indicates a silent o (as in Phœnix)
P.I.	Plant Introduction (a number follows)
pl.	planted (used with some tree-measurements to let one relate tree size to age)
q.v.	(*quod vide*) see
S	south or southern
sp.	species (singular)
spp.	species (plural)
syn.	synonym
USDA	United States Department of Agriculture
USNA	United States National Arboretum
W	west or western
?	possibly
°	degrees of temperature
±	more or less
'	feet
"	inches
≤	means before or during when used with a year
<	before
×	means "by" referring to different measurements (e.g., length × width of leaf; height ×trunk circumference ×branch spread of trees)

This white areas on the above map indicate the USDA Plant
Hardiness Zones 1–8. In these zones are the numerous cold-
hardy species listed in this book. The shaded areas indicate zones
9–11, in which tropical and subtropical trees can be found.
None of the trees native to zones 9–11 are listed here.

Abies

[PINACEÆ; Pine Family] 38–55 spp. of resinous, coniferous evergreens. Name of an Old World species used by the Roman naturalist Pliny ca. A.D. 77, its derivation variously interpreted. FIR trees, in a word, are "Christmas trees"—that is, usually narrowly conical rather than irregular and heavily branched like many PINES (*Pinus*). For the most part the needles are short and bluntish. Their cones are erect, colorful, jewelled with pitch, lovely to view in summer, but they turn brown and fall to pieces at maturity in fall (as those of *Cedrus*); moreover they are usually far out of sight and reach, near the tops of older specimens. July is an ideal time to admire the cones, while they are freshly colored and full size, before they dry and disintegrate. This genus is essentially of cool northern or mountainous regions, and needs moist, cool conditions to thrive, so relatively few species flourish under diverse conditions. In this respect they are similar to *Picea*, the SPRUCES.

A. alba Mill.

= *A. pectinata* (Lam.) Lam. & DC.

EUROPEAN SILVER FIR. COMMON SILVER FIR. From mountainous C and SE Europe. Grown in North America since ≤1847, overall, it is inferior in insect-resistance, strength and endurance to *A. Nordmanniana*, so has been comparatively little planted in recent years, but its cultivars offer special opportunities. Both the English name SILVER FIR, and the Latin name *alba*, white, allude to the tree's gray bark, strikingly pale against its rich green foliar backdrop. Needles flat; dark green and glossy on top, narrowly banded whitish beneath, ½"–1⅓" long. Buds not resinous. Twigs usually with minute hairs. Cones 4½"–6" (8") long, green, then reddish-brown; bract tips projecting and recurved. Records: Europe's largest evergreen, to 225' × 31'6" in the wild; 186' × 20'6" Kilbride, Inveraray, Argyllshire, Scotland (1964); 144' × 29'11" Strone, Cairndow, Argyllshire, Scotland (1982); in North America, *A. alba* has grown to upwards of 100' tall in some places, the stoutest trunks more than 10'0" around.

A. alba 'Columnaris'

Originally found in a forest on Mt. Pila, France. Described by the French horticulturist Carrière in 1859. To North America ≤1868. Tall and very slender but not fastigiate; branches short, of equal length, upturned with short thick branchlets. Needles shorter and broader than usual. Probably more than one clone is now cultivated under this name. Much rarer than *A. alba* 'Pyramidalis'.

A. alba 'Fastigiata'

Found by the botanist Reynier of Avignon in the forests of the Grande Chartreuse, France. Put into cultivation in 1846 by French gardener and dendrologist A. Sénéclauze. Rare; may not exist in North America. Fastigiate, like LOMBARDY POPLAR (*Populus nigra* 'Italica'). Needles short, narrow, evenly whorled around the twigs.

A. alba 'Green Spiral'

An old clone, but only named in 1979 by conifer specialist H. Welch. The original specimen was received by Secrest Arboretum of Wooster, Ohio in 1916 as a 1' tall grafted plant from Biltmore nursery of North Carolina, under the name 'Tortuosa' (which is a dwarf, properly). 'Green Spiral' is a twisted, narrowly pendulous, semi-dwarf (30' tall), coneless tree. Conifer specialist nurseries propagate it.

A. alba 'Pendula'

WEEPING SILVER FIR. More than one pendulous *A. alba* sport exists in Europe, but the first widely propagated clone arose ca. 1835 as a seedling at M. Godefroy's nursery at Ville d'Avray, near Paris. In North American nurseries since ≤1891, it is still commercially available. It can be a floppy little dwarf for years, but can also eventually attain 80' in height, making a narrow spire of fountain-like effect. The needles on the strong shoots are often recurved.

A. alba 'Pyramidalis'

SENTINEL SILVER FIR. Of German origin; cultivated in England by 1851. In North America ≤1870, and ever since continuously offered by at least one nursery or another. By far the most common of the narrow, compact cultivars, although maybe 'Columnaris' or 'Fastigiata' have been distributed under its name. An ascending-branched tree, fastigiate when young, compactly conical in age with short needles and drooping twigs.

A. Alcoquiana—see *Picea bicolor* and *P. jezoensis*

A. amabilis (Dougl. *ex* Loud.) Forbes

PACIFIC SILVER FIR. LOVELY FIR. BEAUTIFUL FIR. CASCADES FIR. RED FIR. From mountains (for the most part), extreme SE Alaska to extreme NW California. In Latin *amabilis* means pleasing or attractive, referring to the dark, dense, beautiful pyramidal or spire form of this FIR in comparison with the usually dome-like crown of its associates NOBLE FIR (*A. procera*) and GRAND FIR (*A. grandis*). First cultivated in 1830–31 when David Douglas sent seeds to London; grown in the U.S. ≤1862. Planted in lowland maritime B.C. into Oregon, it tends to enjoy a brief spurt of attractive youthful growth, followed by decline, thus old and large planted specimens are rare. Foliage much flattened on the twigs, the needles dark, very glossy above; vividly white beneath, ¾"–1½" long. Buds globular and pitch-enveloped. Cones 4"–6" long, massive, purplish. Records: to 268' tall in the wild; 245' × 26'3" Olympic National Park, WA (1960).

A. arizonica—see *A. lasiocarpa* ssp. *arizonica*

A. baborensis—see *A. numidica*

A. balsamea (L.) Mill.

BALSAM FIR. BALM-OF-GILEAD FIR. BALSAM. From a vast territory in the NE part of the continent; the widest range of any *Abies* in North America. A slender species of small stature, usually short-lived in cultivation, but widely planted anyway. Valued for its pleasing spicy fragrance, neat shape and bluish-green color. Needles blunt and short, ½"–1½". Cones 2"–4" long; purple, or olive-green tinged purple. Several plants, including other trees (e.g., *Liquidambar orientalis*), have been called BALM OF GILEAD. The fragrant resin Canada *balsam* obtained from this FIR was used medicinally for pulmonary complaints; a varnish for water-colors was prepared from it; it was used to seal birchbark canoe seams, and to glue microscope slide coverslips. Records: to 125' tall in the wild; 117' × 8'6" north of Wanganui, New Zealand (≤1982); 116' × 7'0" Porcupine Mts. State Park, MI (1962); 100' × 12'4" Fairfield, PA (1992); 92' × 6'6" Kilkenny, NH (1968).

A. balsamea 'Cree's Blue'

An outstandingly blue-colored seedling discovered in a Christmas tree plantation in the nursery of Leighton G. Cree of Colebrook, NH. Seldom grown.

A. balsamea var. *macrocarpa* Sarg.

Needles and cones longer (*macrocarpa* from Greek *macro-*, large, and *karpos*, fruit) than normal; a transition phase to *A. lasiocarpa*. Discovered in 1866 near Omro, WI, by nurseryman John Wilcox. Introduced to cultivation ca. 1884. Reported superior as an ornamental in the northeastern U.S. At least into the 1920s, this variety was grown, from seeds rather than as a clone, but in recent decades var. *macrocarpa* has been considered a phase within the species' normal variation, not deserving nominal status. The cones are often 4½" long.

A. balsamea f. *phanerolepis* (Fern.) Rehd.

= *A. balsamea* var. *phanerolepis* Fern.
= *A. × phanerolepis* (Fern.) Liu

Cones a little smaller (¾"–2¼") than on typical *A. balsamea*, their bract-scales ordinarily as long or longer than the fertile scales, with awns projecting. Not a hybrid with *A. Fraseri*. Generally not distinguished in either forestry or horticulture, but the name (from Greek *phaner-*, conspicuous, and *lepis*, a scale) is useful for botanical precision.

A. bifolia—see *A. lasiocarpa*

A. × Bornmuelleriana Mattf.

= *A. Nordmanniana* ssp. *Bornmuelleriana* (Mattf.) Coode & Cull.
(*A. cephalonica* × *A. Nordmanniana*)

TURKEY FIR. From mountains in NW Turkey. Named after Prof. Joseph Friedrich Nicolaus Bornmüller (1862–1948), of Weimar, Germany, a keen student of the eastern Mediterranean flora, and botanical explorer, who collected this species on Mount Olympus in Bithynia sometime <1894. BORNMÜLLER'S FIR may not be a hybrid of the parentage reported; it is partly intermediate between *A. cephalonica* and *A. cilicica*. As it is little studied in nature, and extremely rare in cultivation, dispute attends its actual placement in *Abies* classification. Being almost nonexistent in the nursery trade, it would be far too rare to include in this book, except that it shows great promise, being vigorous and more tolerant of lowland, warmer regions than most *Abies*. Needles blunt, densely upswept, 1"–1¾". Twigs hairless. Buds usually resinous. Cones 4¾"–5⅞" long; purplish-brown; bract tips projecting, recurved. Records: 115' × 10'7" Penrhyn Castle, Gwynedd, Wales (1959); 94' × 8'6" Mercer Island, WA (1989); 82' × 11'3" Cairnsmore, Kirkcudbrightshire, Scotland (1970).

A. brachyphylla—see *A. homolepis*

A. bracteata (D. Don) D. Don *ex* Poit.

= *A. venusta* (Dougl.) K. Koch

SANTA LUCIA FIR. BRISTLECONE FIR. From a few isolated groves in the Santa Lucia mountains of Monterey and

San Luis Obispo Counties in coastal California, on moist canyon bottoms. Discovered by T. Coulter in 1831. Introduced to cultivation when Wm. Lobb sent seeds to Veitch nursery of England in 1852–53. Little offered in U.S. nurseries, although attempted in the East early in this century. Primarily limited to West Coast cultivation, but even in California most specimens are young. It makes a lush spire of immense appeal, featuring bold, very sharp needles and uniquely showy cones. Needles among the longest and widest of all *Abies*, to 2¾" × ⅛". Buds ¾" long, spindle-shaped. Cones 2¾"–4" long, squat, first green, then purplish-brown, fringed with unique needle-like bracts or bristles to 2". Records: 182' × 13'6" Los

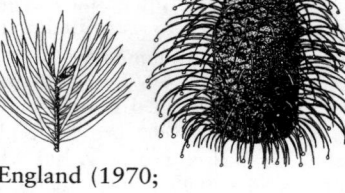

P a d r e s National Forest, CA (1976); 122 × 15'9" E a s t n o r C a s t l e , Herefordshire, England (1970; *pl.* 1865).

A. *cephalonica* Loud.

GREEK FIR. CEPHALONIAN FIR. BLACK MOUNTAIN FIR. MT. ENOS FIR. From mountains of Greece, S Albania, and the isles of the Ægean Sea. Seeds collected on Mt. Enos of the Ionian Island Cephalonia were sent to England by Sir Charles Napier (governor of Cephalonia at the time) in 1824. So named because it formerly formed an extensive forest on Cephalonia—the largest of the Ionian Islands. To North America ≤1850. An immense species, combining hardiness, drought-tolerance, and insect-resistance. Its very strengths make its horticultural drawback: it grows to such size as can rarely be allotted it. Needles ½"–1⅛" long, usually sharp, flushing early and subject to damage from late frosts in some locales. Twigs hairless. Buds resinous. Cones (4½") 5"–7" (9") long; brownish; bract tips projecting, recurved. Records: 136' × 11'5" Bodnant, Denbighshire, Wales (1981; *pl.* 1876); 110' × 17'0" Cortachy Castle, Angus, Scotland (1962).

A. *cephalonica* var. *Apollinis*—see
A. *cephalonica* var. *græca*

A. *cephalonica* var. *græca* (Fraas) Liu
= *A. cephalonica* var. *Apollinis* (Link) Beissn.
= *A. cephalonica* ssp. *Apollinis* (Link) Fukarek
= *A. Equi-Trojani* Asch. & Sint.

= *A. Nordmanniana* ssp. *Equi-Trojani* (A. & S.) Coode & Cull.

APOLLO FIR. MOUNT PARNASSUS FIR. From Greece to W Turkey—the latter population since 1925 often designated TROJAN FIR, *A. Equi-Trojani*. The APOLLO FIR variety, from Mount Parnassus in S Greece, was described in 1838. It was introduced to English cultivation <1876, and was in the U.S. nursery trade by the 1880s. Some botanists view the supposed distinctiveness of this variety as merely part of the natural variation of *A. cephalonica*, unworthy of naming separately. Be that as it may, nurseries long offered APOLLO FIR separately from regular GREEK FIR, and some horticulturists think APOLLO FIR makes a hardier and better tree. The differences, real or imagined, are that this variety bears needles that are denser, thicker, usually blunt (or at any rate more abruptly pointed), and crowded on the upper sides of the twigs. Record: 116' × 15'2" Tacoma, WA (1993).

A. *cilicica* (Ant. & Kotschy) Carr.

CILICIAN FIR. From the Taurus Mountains of S Turkey, NW Syria, and N Lebanon. The epithet *cilicica* refers to the southern region of Asia Minor, where this species was discovered in 1853 by the Austrian botanical explorer T. Kotschy. It was introduced to cultivation by him in 1854. In the U.S. since ≤1870. A tall, narrow tree, with markedly slender bright green needles, ¾"–1½" long. Twigs slightly hairy. Buds not resinous, or slightly so. Cones 6"–8" (12") long; usually markedly cylindric; reddish-brown. Specimens so called are often really *A. Nordmanniana*, which flushes much later in spring, is hardier and has always been planted more. Records: trunks to 20'3" around in the wild; planted specimens measured are taller than any noted in the wild: 121' × 13'2" Great River, NY (1981); 102' × 11'10" Wellesley, MA (1984).

A. *concolor* (Gord. & Glend.) Lindl. *ex* Hildebr.

WHITE FIR. COLORADO FIR. From much of western North America. The Latin epithet *concolor* refers to the uniform needle color—pale bluish green on both sides whereas most FIR needles are much paler beneath. Discovered in 1847 by August Fendler near Santa Fe, NM. Cultivated by 1867. By far the most amenable of the native FIRS to cultivation in the eastern U.S. Very popular and widely planted. Needles 1½"–3¼" long. Cones 3"–5" (6") long; olive-green, canary yellow, or purplish. Records (see *A.*

concolor ssp. *Lowiana*, too): 157' × 12'3" Cragside, Northumberland, England (1974); 110' × 17'8" Timpanogos Mountain, UT (≤1923); 94' × 18'11" Uinta National Forest, UT (1993).

A. concolor 'Candicans'

Needles strikingly vivid blue-gray to silvery white. The word *candicans* means whitish; from Latin *candidus*, bright white or hoary-white. Originated at the Arboretum des Barres, south of Paris. Described in 1929. Rare, but in North American commerce ≤1965.

A. concolor 'Conica'

From Durand Eastman Park in Rochester, NY. Discovered by B. Slavin. First described in 1923. Semidwarf, conical or narrowly pyramidal, with short needles, only ¾"–1½" long. The original, by 1938, was 11' tall and 8' wide. Very little grown until the late 1980s.

A. concolor 'Glenmore'

Selected <1955 by Robert E. More, of Glenmore Arboretum at Buffalo Creek, CO. Exceptionally pale bluish needles, to 3¼" long. Very rare, at least under this name.

A. concolor ssp. *Lowiana* (Gord.) E. Murray

= *A. concolor* var. *Lowiana* (Gord.) Lemm.
= *A. Lowiana* (Gord.) A. Murr.
= *A. Parsonsii* Fowler, non Séné.
= *A. Parsonsiana* McNab

PACIFIC WHITE FIR. CALIFORNIA WHITE FIR. SIERRA WHITE FIR. From mid-Oregon to S California mountains. Introduced to cultivation in 1851 when Wm. Lobb sent seeds to Veitch nursery of England. In the eastern U.S. nursery trade ≤1870. Named after Hugh Low (1794–1863), nurseryman of Great Britain. The *Parsonsii* name likely refers to the New York nursery of Samuel Bowne Parsons (1819–1906). Subspecies *Lowiana* differs from typical *A. concolor* in growing much larger, its needles are less bluish and more arranged like those of *A. grandis*, and it is less hardy. It is much less commonly grown. Botanically it might be regarded as intermediate between GRAND FIR and WHITE FIR. Records: 246' × 15'3" Yosemite, CA (1982); 192' × 27'11" Sierra National Forest, CA (1972).

A. concolor 'Rochester'

Sold ≤1994 by Girard nursery of Geneva, OH. "A very tight and robust wide pyramidal. Good blue, exceptionally long needles."

A. concolor 'Select Blue'

Vermeulen nursery of New Jersey, since ≤1980, has sold a selection of "outstanding color and habit" under this name. The International Conifer Register condemns the name as illegitimate because the description is inadequate.

A. concolor f. *violacea* (A. Murr.) Beissn.

= *A. concolor* var. *violacea* A. Murr.

PURPLECONE WHITE FIR. First used in 1875, this name has come to be used as a group name, whereby any markedly pale-bluish specimen, whether a seedling or a named cultivar, can be so designated. The name thus embraces 'Candicans', 'Glenmore' and 'Select Blue'. However, some authors insist 'Violacea' is, or at least was originally a clone, featuring both pale foliage and attractive purple cones. In any case, trees under the *violacea* name have been grown in North America since ≤1890, but most nurseries have not used the name, even if trees being sold fit the bill. Nurseries such as Biltmore, Bobbink & Atkins, and Kohankie did sell *violacea*, but whether the stock represented a single clone is highly doubtful.

A. concolor 'Wattezii'

Raised by D. Wattez, nurseryman at Bussum, Holland. Name published in 1900. Exceedingly rare, if present at all in North America. Needles pale yellow when young, becoming yellowish-white, and finally assuming a pale blue color. Pretty in May and June. Slower than normal but not a dwarf.

A. Delavayi (van Tiegh.) Franch., non Mast.

DELAVAY FIR. From NE India, N Burma, SE Tibet, and SW China, in mountains subject to monsoon rains. Essentially from high mountains, it has greater altitudinal and latitudinal range than any other Chinese *Abies* species. Named after a French Jesuit, Abbé Pierre Jean Marie Delavay (1834–1895), who traveled extensively in China in 1887 and discovered this species on the summit of Tsang-shan, near Tali, in NW Yunnan in April 1887. It was named after him in 1891. DELAVAY FIR is variable (with as many as five distinct forms), little understood, and scarcely ever planted in North America. Generally it has been a failure when planted in the British Isles. There is a remote possibility that one of its variations may perform well somewhere in North America. As for size, 200' × 20'3" was recorded in the wild by George Forrest, but he said "I think" as to its specific identification.

A. Equi-Trojani—see *A. cephalonica* var. *græca*

A. excelsa—see *Picea Abies*

A. firma S. & Z.

MOMI FIR. JAPANESE FIR. From S Japan. Japanese: *Momi*. The most widely distributed, and largest of 5 species of *Abies* in Japan. Introduced to Western cultivation in 1861 by Siebold to Holland, and J.G. Veitch to England. In 1862 G.R. Hall sent seeds to the U.S. The name *firma* refers to the stout habit of the tree, or to the thick and firm needles. MOMI FIR is characterized by its broad crown of strongly horizontal branching, bold sharp needles and yellow-green color. The needles, ⅝"–1½" long, on young specimens are tipped by two spines. Cones 3"–5" (6") long; green, then brown; bract tips projecting, not recurved. Records: 150' × 20'0" in Japan; 111' × 10'7" Tregrehan, Cornwall, England (1971); 95' × 8'0" Longwood Gardens, PA (ca. 1981); 94' × 12'1" Christchurch, New Zealand (1970); 71' × 6'1" Tacoma, WA (1990); 67' × 7'8" Ft. Lewis, WA (1990).

A. firma 'Halgren'

Sold ≤1994 by Buchholz & Buchholz nursery of Gaston, OR. "Named after Mr. Halgren. Vigorous. Best color."

A. Fraseri (Pursh) Poir.

FRASER FIR. SOUTHERN BALSAM FIR. MOUNTAIN BALSAM FIR. DOUBLE BALSAM FIR. SHE BALSAM. From a few of the highest slopes of the S Appalachians in Virginia, Tennessee, and North Carolina. Rare. On Mt. Mitchell, at 6,684'. The wild population has been suffering much, and the species is usually short-lived in cultivation. Named after John Fraser (1750–1811), its Scottish discoverer, who sent it to Lee's nursery at Hammersmith, London ca. 1807. Notable for its crowded needles, rich, luxuriant foliage, and for bearing cones while still a young specimen. Needles ½"–1" long, dark glossy green above, with two white bands separated by a prominent raised green midrib beneath. Cones 1½"–2½" (3") long; purple; bract tips much projecting, recurved, pale and pretty.

Records: to 100' tall in the wild; 94' × 10'0" × 58' High Hampton Inn, Cashiers, NC (1989).

A. grandis (Dougl. *ex* D. Don) Lindl.

= *A. Parsonsii* Séné., non Fowler

GRAND FIR. LOWLAND WHITE FIR. GIANT (SILVER) FIR. VANCOUVER FIR. YELLOW FIR. From SW British Columbia to coastal N California, essentially in lowlands rather than mountains; east into Montana. Introduced to cultivation by D. Douglas in 1830–31. Needles ¾"–2½" long, arranged in thin layers, as if ironed or pressed in a book; smelling of tangerines when bruised. Cones 2"–4½" (7") long, yellowish-green, rarely greenish-purple. The Latin name *grandis* means large. It grows extremely fast but is not long-lived compared to many of its associates, 400 years being the maximum. After the tree reaches about 100' tall, its top is often domed, with multiple leaders, rather than narrowly spired. Records: to 300' tall; 267' × 16'3" Glacier Peak Wilderness, WA (1993); 234' × 20'10" Chilliwack River, B.C. (1985); 170'× 22'11" Balmacaan, Drumnadrochit, Invernesshire, Scotland (1987; *pl.* 1850).

A. grandis 'Johnsonii'

Discovered in June 1897 by John A. Johnson (d. ca. 1956) on the lower Columbia River ca. 4 miles below Rainier, OR. Mr. Johnson grafted and traded or sold specimens to his neighbors. After his tree first coned in 1941, it was described and named in 1942. Needles shorter than those of typical *A. grandis*, to 1" long, less plane (more whorled), on shorter twigs, on shorter branches that are more upswept to form a very narrow tree. The largest at Portland's Hoyt Arboretum, grafted in 1944, planted in 1949, is 65' × 2'6" × 10' wide (1993). Larger ones exist elsewhere in the Portland area. Some conifer specialist nurseries stock it.

A. grandis 'Parsonsii'—see *A. concolor* ssp. *Lowiana*

A. holophylla Maxim.

MANCHURIAN FIR. NEEDLE FIR. From Korea, SE Manchuria, and adjacent Russia; disjunct in N Hopeh (Hebei) province of China. Introduced by the botanist V.L. Komarov to Russian cultivation in 1898; in December 1904 the Arnold Arboretum got seeds of Korean plants from the Japanese botanist T. Uchiyama. Although in some parks and arboreta, it has been offered little in the nursery trade. The specific epithet means leaves *not* divided at their apex; from Greek *holo*, whole or undivided, and *phyllon*, a leaf. Needles 1"–1¾" long, flushing early in spring. Cones 4"–6" long; green, then pale-brown. Records: 150' × 12' in the wild; 77' × 4'3" Borde Hill, Sussex, England (1981; *pl.* ca. 1925); 61' × 6'2" Philadelphia, PA (1980).

A. homolepis S. & Z.
= *A. brachyphylla* Maxim.

NIKKO FIR. From Japan. Found most abundantly on mountains around Nikko, of Honshu. *Nikko momi* is one of its Japanese names. The name *homolepis* means cone scales (Greek *lepis*) of the same kind and size. First introduced to cultivation in 1859–60 by Siebold to Holland. First planted in North America ≤1870. Needles ½"–1⅛" long. Cones 3"–4¾" long, purple; borne lower on the crown than on most species. As with another Japanese FIR, *A. firma*, this shares a distinctive broad-spreading silhouette. It is more common, and indeed is one of the commonest non-native FIRS planted in North America. Records: to 130' × 16'0" in Japan; 111' × 11'9" Taymouth Castle, Perthshire, Scotland (1983); 88' × 5'0" Rochester, NY (ca. 1981); 75' × 9'8" Arnold Arboretum, MA (ca. 1981).

A. homolepis 'Tomomi'
= *A. homolepis* var. *Tomomi* (Bobbink & Atkins) Rehd.

Originated ≤1907 in the northeastern U.S., and was sold by nurseries such as Hicks of Long Island, and Bobbink & Atkins of New Jersey. Slender, more sparingly branched; needles only ⅓"–⅝" (¾") long.

A. koreana Wils.

KOREAN FIR. From Korea, largely in alpine areas. Discovered by U. Faurie on Quelpaert Island in 1907; seeds were sent that year to Vilmorin nursery in France. First grown in North America by 1908. E. Wilson collected seeds from mainland Korea in October 1917. Most specimens are dwarf trees, remarkable for their stubby foliage and bearing a profusion of ornamental cones even while they are very young—even at 1' tall! The cones are 1½"–2¾" long, bluish-purple (in Korea, some are green); the bract tips much projecting, recurved, first pale green, then red-brown. Needles short and broad, ½"–¾" long,

dark green above, whitish beneath. Records: to 75' × 6' in the wild; 50'+ tall Arnold Arboretum, MA (ca. 1981); 43' × 2'3" Wind River, WA (1990); 42' × 5'6" Durris House, Kincardine-shire, Scotland (1987); 38' × 3'6" Hergest Croft, Herefordshire, England (1978; *pl.* 1927).

A. japonica—see A. Veitchii

A. koreana 'Aurea'

GOLDEN KOREAN FIR. Light golden-yellow; best in partial shade. Originated in 1956 in a batch of seedlings at the Victoria, B.C., nursery of the late Ed H. Lohbrunner. The name is of questionable legitimacy—being Latin for golden, it had to have been used <1959. Since at least 1975–76, conifer nurseries in Oregon have grown it in quantity. It can begin life by being prostrate, developing a leader only with age.

A. koreana 'Horstmann's Silberlocke'
= *A. koreana* 'Silberlocke' or 'Silverlocke'

Originated in Germany <1983, named and introduced in 1986–87 by Günter Horstmann (d. 1993), nurseryman of Schneverdingen, Germany. Iseli nursery of Oregon offered it in 1992. Strongly recurved needles, showing their silvery-whitish undersides. Slow growth. Similar to *A. koreana* 'Silver Show'.

A. koreana 'Silver Show'

Strongly recurved needles, showing their silvery-whitish undersides. Originated in Germany in 1969, named and introduced in 1976; Mitsch nursery of Oregon offered it ca. 1991–92. Similar to *A. koreana* 'Horstmann's Silberlocke'.

A. koreana 'Silberlocke' or 'Silverlocke'—see A. koreana 'Horstmann's Silberlocke'

A. lasiocarpa (Hook.) Nutt.
= *A. bifolia* A. Murr.

ALPINE FIR. SUBALPINE FIR. WESTERN BALSAM FIR. ROCKY MOUNTAIN FIR. From western North American mountains, to 12,000' elevation. Introduced to cultivation in 1863 when D. Lyall sent seeds to England. The specific epithet, derived from Greek *lasios*, hairy, and *karpos*, fruit, refers to the very hairy cone-scales—more noticeably hairy than in any other species then known. All *Abies* cones except those of *A. bracteata* are hairy. *Abies lasiocarpa* is a close cousin of the eastern *A. balsamea*, and is usually similarly short-lived in lowland gardens. It has luxurious foliage, is fragrant, and makes a handsome narrow spire. Needles 1"–1½" long. Cones 2"–4" long, dark purple to nearly black. Records: 172' × 11'0" Icicle Creek, WA (1988); 124' × 21'0" Cream Lake, Olympic National Park, WA (1992). In cultivation few if any are more than 75' × 6'0".

A. lasiocarpa ssp. arizonica (Merr.) E. Murr.

= *A. lasiocarpa* var. *arizonica* (Merr.) Lemm.
= *A. arizonica* Merr.

CORKBARK FIR. ARIZONA FIR. From central and SE Arizona, Colorado, and southwestern New Mexico (in the San Francisco Mts.). Introduced to cultivation at the Darmstadt Botanic Gardens, Germany, by Dr. Purpus ca. 1900; grown in the eastern U.S. ≤1903. Overall, a more adaptable, and prettier version of *A. lasiocarpa*. Bluer-needled, with very pale, thick, corky bark, and smaller cones. Records: 115' × 10'0" Santa Fé National Forest, NM (1968); 111' × 13'9" Lincoln National Forest, NM (1969).

A. Lowiana—see A. concolor ssp. Lowiana

A. magnifica A. Murr.

CALIFORNIA RED FIR. From SW Oregon and N California to W Nevada. Introduced to cultivation by J. Jeffrey in 1851, and Wm. Lobb in 1852. The epithet *magnifica* in Latin means magnificent, referring to the immense cones. Closely related to NOBLE FIR (*A. procera*), this species has laxer foliage, and takes its name RED FIR from the dark, often reddish-brown bark. This species is the SILVERTIP FIR of the Christmas-tree trade. Needles 1"–1¾" long, luxuriously upswept, more or less glaucous. Cones (4") 6"–8" (9") long, pale golden-green to dark purplish-brown. Records: to 300' × 37'8½" says E. Sheldon; 252' × 15'9" Sequoia National Park, CA (1994); 180' × 26'8" Fresno County, CA (1972).

A. magnifica 'Glauca'

AZURE FIR. Described in 1891. In North America since ≤1899; in the U.S. nursery trade since ≤1907. Rare. Needles decidedly bluish.

A. magnifica var. shastensis Lemm.

= *A. shastensis* (Lemm.) Lemm.
= *A. × shastensis* Lemm., *emend.* Liu

SHASTA FIR. SHASTA RED FIR. From Lassen Peak (N California) to Crater Lake (SW Oregon). First named

in 1885, SHASTA FIR is practically indistinguishable from typical *A. magnifica* except its cones bear conspicuously protruding bracts recalling those of NOBLE FIR (*A. procera*). Even without cones it can be distinguished from NOBLE FIR, as its needles are ridged above, not grooved as in NOBLE FIR. Cones 5½"–8" long, purple; bract tips projecting, recurved. Records: to 250' tall; 228' × 20'5" Rogue River National Forest, OR (1983); 176' × 27'1" near Horse Creek, CA (1971).

A. marocana—see A. Pinsapo ssp. marocana

A. mexicana—see A. Vejari

A. Nordmanniana (Stev.) Spach

CAUCASIAN FIR. NORDMANN FIR. CRIMEAN FIR. From the Caucasus area east of the Black Sea. Alexander Davidovic von Nordmann (1803–1866), Finnish botanist and professor at Odessa, discovered this species in the Adzhar Province of the Caucasus in 1836–37. Introduced to cultivation in 1840 by Lawson's nursery of Edinburgh, Scotland, and in 1848 by von Humboldt to the Berlin Botanic Garden. In North America ≤1860. The 1862 catalog of Parsons nursery of Long Island lists it. One of the most common and successful of foreign FIRS grown in Canada and the U.S. Needles ¾"–1½" long, dark green. Bark hard and gray, remaining smooth a long time. Twigs gray above, generally brown; hairy. Buds not or only slightly resinous. Cones 5"–6" (8") long; green, then reddish-brown; bract tips projecting, recurved. Records: to 225' × 20'6" in the wild, living to 700 years; 152' × 11'6" Cragside, Northumberland, England (1984); 115' × 15'6" Endsleigh, Devonshire, England (1977); 93' × 9'7" Rochester, NY (1976); 93' × 8'1" Victoria, B.C. (1989); 74' × 9'3" Fairview, MD (1972).

A. nobilis—see A. procera

A. Nordmanniana ssp. Bornmuelleriana—see A. × Bornmuelleriana

A. Nordmanniana ssp. Equi-Trojani—see A. cephalonica var. græca

A. Nordmanniana 'Pendula'

WEEPING NORDMANN FIR. Originated by nurseryman M. Young of Milford, Surrey, England; listed in his 1874 catalog. Also raised by Courtois, nurseryman at Clamart, France in 1869. Sold by Cottage Gardens nursery of Long Island in the late 1920s and early 1930s.

A. numidica De Lann. ex Carr.

= *A. baborensis* Coss.

= *A. Pinsapo* var. *baborensis* Coss.

ALGERIAN FIR. From mountainous NE Algeria, confined to Mounts Babor and Tababor of the Kabylie Range. An associate of ATLAS CEDAR (*Cedrus atlantica*). Discovered in 1861 by Captain de Guibert. Then M. Davout, Conservator-General of the Algerine forests, sent seeds to France in 1862. Introduced in 1865 to England. In North America ≤1897, and in the nursery trade ≤1907. It is still being sold here, but is comparatively rare. There may be a mixup, with misidentified stock prevailing. According to descriptions of actual Algerian trees, the needles are flattish, dark shining green above, whitish beneath, and more or less pectinate, ½"–1" long. Buds not- or only slightly-resinous. Cones 5"–8" long, narrow; green tinged lilac, then brown; bract scales hidden or their tips slightly exposed. Whether or not the trees being sold are purebred, or labeled correctly, they do make thrifty, desirable landscape specimens. Records: to 110' × 11'0" in British cultivation; 72' × 7'10" Rochester, NY (1977); 70' × 8'1" Great River, NY (1981).

A. Parsonsii—see A. concolor ssp. Lowiana and A. grandis

A. pectinata—see A. alba

A. × phanerolepis—see A. balsamea f. phanerolepis

A. Picea—see Picea Abies

A. Pindrow (Lamb.) Royle

PINDROW FIR. WEST HIMALAYAN FIR. WEST HIMALAYAN LOW LEVEL FIR. From the Himalayas, Afghanistan to Bhutan. Introduced to cultivation when Dr. J. Forbes imported cones to Britain in 1837. To North America by 1850, and in the nursery trade here since ≤1907. Rarely grown. The epithet *Pindrow* is of obscure origin, likely a common name in India referring to the growth being tall and cylindrical. This tree flushes early in spring, so can be injured by late frosts. Needles dark green, slender, remarkably long, to 3½" but usually ≤2½". Cones 4½"–7" long; bluish or deep purple. Records: to 250' × 26'0" in the wild; 117' × 13'3" Castle Leod, Ross, Scotland (1966; *died* 1978); 56' × 4'3" and 43' × 6'4" Seattle, WA (1988).

A. Pinsapo Boiss.

SPANISH FIR. BOTTLEBRUSH FIR. HEDGEHOG FIR. Spanish: *Abeto*. From S Spain (& N Morocco—ssp.

marocana). The epithet *Pinsapo* is short for *pinus saponis* or SOAP PINE, as the twigs crushed in water yield a kind of soap. In 1837 the Swiss botanist E. Boissier sent seeds of the species he had discovered to the French nurseryman Vilmorin; introduced to Britain in 1839 by Captain S.E. Widdrington. To North America by 1850. Needles plump, dense, rigid, pointy, whitish with powder, ½"–¾" long. Buds very resinous. Cones 4"–6" long; pale greenish, then purplish-brown. Records: in Spain the largest trunks are over 25'0" around; 120' × 13'4" Balaine near Villeneuve sur Allier, France (1973); 108' × 7'0" Rhinefield Drive, Hampshire, England (1980; *pl.* 1861); 80' × 12'0" Lydhurst, Sussex, England (1980); 78' × 6'10" Seattle, WA (1988); 46' × 8'9" Great River, NY (1981).

A. Pinsapo 'Aurea'

GOLDEN SPANISH FIR. Found in the nursery of French gardener and dendrologist A. Sénéclauze; described in 1868. Rare in North America, but in the nursery trade. Young branchlets and needles golden yellow, the needles quite cream-colored on their upper sides. Slow and shrubby.

A. Pinsapo var. baborensis—see A. numidica

A. Pinsapo f. glauca (Carr.) Beissn.

BLUE SPANISH FIR. First recorded <1867 by Desfossé & Thuillier in Orléans, France. SPANISH FIR seedlings vary from olive green to pale blue, much in the same way as COLORADO SPRUCE (*Picea pungens*). The bluest seedlings can be selected or grafted. Most SPANISH FIR specimens are more or less bluish.

A. Pinsapo ssp. marocana (Trab.) Emb. & Maire

= *A. Pinsapo* var. *marocana* (Trab.) Ceb. & Bol.

= *A. marocana* Trab.

MOROCCAN FIR. MAROC FIR. From mountains S of Tetuan, in north Morocco. Discovered in 1905 by A. Joly, professor of Arabic in Algeria, and collector of North African plants. Named in 1906. Compared to typical *A. Pinsapo*, this subspecies has flatter, wider needles, with few lines of stoma above (rather than equally stomatic on both sides). Buds slightly resinous, not much so as in *A. Pinsapo*. Cones larger, to 7" long. Intermediate between *A. numidica* and *A. Pinsapo*. Rare: essentially confined to arboreta and botanic gardens both in Europe and North America. At least some trees cultivated under the name MOROCCAN FIR are really hybrids or may be some other species. For example, the trees in Seattle's arboretum are very vigorous, uniform, and fertile, showing superb promise as ornamentals to be encouraged. Twigs brown and hairless. Needles rigid, not sharp, blue, sometimes recurved. Buds caramel-colored, resinous. Cones to 7" long. Records: to 100' × 15'8" in the wild; 67' × 3'11" Seattle, WA (1989; *pl.* 1954).

A. procera Rehd.

= *A. nobilis* (Dougl. *ex* D. Don) Lindl.,
   non A. Dietr.

NOBLE FIR. OREGON LARCH (from wood resemblance). FEATHERCONE FIR (from the cone scale bracts). From the Cascade Mountains and some coastal mountains of Washington, Oregon, and N California. Introduced to cultivation in 1830–31 when D. Douglas sent seeds to Britain. Grown in North America as an ornamental since ≤1850. Needles crowded on upper sides of twigs, upswept, grooved above, more or less bluish, ½"–1½" long. Cones 4"–6" (10") long; massive—up to 4" wide; green, then purplish-brown; bract tips much projecting, recurved, yellow-green. The Latin name in use since 1940, *procera*, means tall. Fittingly so, for it has the world height record in *Abies*: 325' tall at Harmony Falls, WA (<1967); 295'×19'9" Mt. St. Helens, WA (1989); 278' × 28'4" Gifford Pinchot National Forest, WA (1964); trunks once existed 34'7" around says E. Sheldon.

A. procera 'Aurea'—see *A. procera* 'Sherwoodii'

A. procera 'Fastigiata'

Sold ≤1994 by Buchholz & Buchholz nursery of Gaston, OR. "A unique seedling found growing in a Christmas tree plantation in what is now a nursery." The cultivar name, being Latin yet post-1959, is invalid.

A. procera 'Glauca'

= *A. procera* f. *glauca* (Ravenscr.) Rehd.

BLUE NOBLE FIR. Named in 1863 in England; grown in North America ≤1907. NOBLE FIR varies in the blue-gray color of its foliage, and the best blue form is grafted. It cones freely.

A. procera 'Sherwoodi'

= *A. procera* 'Aurea Sherwoodi'
= *A. procera* 'Aurea'

GOLDEN NOBLE FIR. Discovered in 1933 as a lightning-struck tree on Mt. Hood, OR, by Sherwood nursery of Portland, OR. Named officially in 1948. Oregon nurseries have continuously propagated it since then, but overall it has remained rare. Golden throughout the year.

A. religiosa (H.B.K.) Schlecht. & Cham.

MEXICAN FIR. SACRED FIR. Spanish names include: *Arbol de Navidad, Oyamel*. From C and S Mexico to high mountains of N Guatemala. Discovered by Von Humboldt in 1799, or possibly 1803. Introduced to cultivation in 1838 when T. Hartweg sent seeds to England. Seeds available in U.S. nurseries since ≤1879–80. Nonetheless, until the 1960s SACRED FIR has been virtually nonexistent in cultivation, and even since the 1960s has remained very rare—mostly in arboreta and botanic gardens. It may not survive in colder zones, and in warmer areas may not be sufficiently attractive. But it is interesting. The name comes from its branches being used for religious festivals. As an ornamental, it has been likened in appearance to both WHITE SPRUCE (*Picea glauca*) and DOUGLAS FIR (*Pseudotsuga Menziesii*). For a close cousin, see *A. Vejari*. Needles 1"–1½" (2¾") long. Twigs hairy when young. Cones 4"–6¼" long; blue to brown; bract tips projecting, recurved. Records: to 200' × 18'10" in Mexico; 67' × 4'1" Puketei, New Zealand (≤1982); 44' × 3'1" Berkeley, CA (1993; *pl.* 1974); 42' × 2'10" Hillier Arboretum, Hampshire, England (1987; *pl.* 1968).

A. sachalinensis (Schmidt) Mast.

SAKHALIN FIR. SACHALIN FIR. SAGHALIN FIR. Japanese: *Aka-todo-matsu*. From Sakhalin, the S Kuriles, and N Japan. Discovered and collected by F. Schmidt in Sakhalin 1866. In 1878–79, C. Maries sent seeds to Veitch nursery of England. In North America ≤1899; in nurseries since ≤1907. Rare. Flushing very early in spring, it can be damaged by late frosts. Nor is it a great beauty. Needles very slender, 1"–1¾" long. Cones 2"–3½" long; pinkish-purple; bract tips projecting, recurved. Records: to 130' × 11'0" in the wild; 78' × 4'8" Portland, OR (1993); 66' × 5'3" Headfort, County Meath, Ireland (1980; *pl.* 1928).

A. shastensis—see A. magnifica var. shastensis

A. spectabilis (D. Don) Spach
= *A. Webbiana* (Wall. *ex* Lamb.) Lindl.

HIMALAYAN FIR. WEST HIMALAYAN HIGH LEVEL FIR. From the Himalayas, NE Afghanistan through Bhutan. The Latin epithet *spectabilis* means worth seeing, notable or remarkable. Discovered by Captain William Spencer Webb (1784–1865), a surveyor and officer in service of the East India Company. Introduced in 1822 by Dr. Wallich to Britain. In North American cultivation since ≤1850, but has remained extremely rare, being ill-suited to our climate. Trees under the name *Abies spectabilis* in cultivation, may really be partly *A. Mariesii* Mast. or *A. densa* Griff. *ex* Parker (neither species in this volume). Needles dark bluish-green above, whitish beneath, 1"–2½" long. Cones 4"–8" long, deep violet-blue or violet-purple. Records: to 230' × 35'0" in the wild; 110' × 8'9" Powerscourt, Ireland (1980; *pl.* 1867); 87' × 12'1" Castle Leod, Ross, Scotland (1966; *died* 1978).

A. squamata Mast.

FLAKY FIR. From mountainous W China, setting the altitude record for trees—to 15,420' elevation. Introduced in 1910 by E. Wilson. Exceedingly rare in North American cultivation. Promoted since ≤1993 by some conifer nurseries. The Latin name *squamata* means furnished with scales, in reference to the bark, which is flaky and exfoliates like that of the RIVER BIRCH (*Betula nigra*). Cones 2"–2½" long; dark blue-purple; bract tips projecting, recurved. Growth is very slow in cultivation. Records: to 131' × 16'5" in the wild; 59' × 4'1½" Durris House, Tayside, Scotland (1987).

A. Veitchii Lindl.
= *A. japonica* hort.

VEITCH FIR. VEITCH SILVER FIR. JAPANESE ALPINE FIR. From central Japan on high mountains. Discovered by John Gould Veitch (1839–1870) on Mt. Fuji in 1860, but he failed to obtain seeds; introduced to cultivation when Siebold sent seeds to Holland in 1862. In cultivation in the U.S. (as *A. japonica*) ca. 1865. Needles ½"–1⅜" long, dark green on top, bluish-white underneath. Buds small, purple, rounded and completely enveloped in pitch. Twigs very dark brown, hairy. Trunk often fluted; bark smooth silvery-gray. Cones 2"–3" long, purplish; bracts slightly projecting and reflexed. Short-lived in cultivation. Records: to 100' tall in Japan; 93½' × 10'0" Hawkes Bay, New Zealand (≤1982; *pl.* ca. 1880); 92' × 6'3" Hopetoun House, West Lothian, Scotland (1984); 83' × 3'5" Seattle, WA (1988); 77' × 9'9" Dochfour House, Scotland (1982); 60' × 6'0" Rochester, NY (1981).

A. Vejari Mart.
= *A. mexicana* Mart.

VEJAR FIR. From NE Mexico, SE Coahuila to Tamaulipas. First collected, and its name published, in 1942. Named in honor of Octavio Véjar Vázquez, then Minister of the Public Education. Introduced to cultivation late, in the early 1960s. Closely related to *A. religiosa*. Still found almost only in collections, but shows great promise and is worthy of much testing. Needles gray-green or bluish, sharp, ½"–1" long, on olive-colored, minutely hairy shoots. Cones 2"–3½" long (to 7⅞" long in var. *macrocarpa* Martínez), purple when young, turning greenish-brown. Recorded to 130' tall in Mexico.

A. venusta—see A. bracteata

A. × Vilmorinii Mast.
(*A. Pinsapo* × *A. cephalonica*)

Raised in 1868 from an 1867 intentional cross by M. Henri Lévêque de Vilmorin (1843–1899) at Verrières-le-Buisson, near Paris. Only one fertile seed was produced. Likely the first intentional conifer hybrid. The clone, propagated by grafting, is said to bear fertile seeds freely. It is extremely rare in cultivation, but has been in the U.S. since at least 1913, and has appeared in the nursery trade, albeit to a minor degree. Records: 56' × 2'8" Westonbirt, England (1970; *pl.* 1923); 52' × 5'8" Bedgebury, Kent, England (1970; *pl.* 1925).

A. Webbiana—see A. spectabilis

Acacia

[LEGUMINOSÆ; Pea Family] 800–1,200 spp. of mostly tropical trees and shrubs. Ancient Latin, from Greek *akakia* (applied to the Egyptian species *A. Nilotica*), from *akis*, a sharp point, referring to the thorns. Most *Acacia* species are Australian, where the name WATTLE is used. WATTLE is Australia's national emblem. The name arose because early settlers used the pliable saplings of some species to make "wattle-and-daub" structures. Yet E. Lord reports the tree most used as wattle was not a true *Acacia* at all, but *Callicoma*. As for North American cultivation, André Michaux's Charleston nursery offered ACACIAS sometime between 1787 and 1796. Very few species are frost-tolerant. They tend to grow rapidly, and to bloom while young, providing dramatic landscape impact quickly. Most have a short lifespan of 15–30 years. Those included below are the ones to try growing in zones where frosts are light or infrequently severe; they are among the hardiest, and all have evergreen foliage. *Acacia* foliage is of two kinds: leaf-like phyllodes, and finely compound feathery or ferny true leaves (like those of *Albizia*). Some species bear both kinds of foliage, others bear only one or the other kind.

A. Baileyana F.v. Muell.

COOTAMUNDRA WATTLE. BAILEY ACACIA. FERNLEAF ACACIA. GOLDEN MIMOSA. From the Cootamundra and Wagga districts of New South Wales. Naturalized elsewhere in Australia, as well as parts of California. Introduced to Europe in 1873, and to California by 1900. Named after Frederic Manson Bailey (1827–1915), Queensland botanist. A small tree, to 30' tall and wide, of ferny, dusty-blue foliage and brilliant, fragrant, golden-yellow flowers in late winter or earliest spring. Drought-tolerant, it is best kept unwatered, and pruned heavily. The seed-pods, 2"–4" long, are an attractive purplish color when young. Variable cold-hardiness. Some can barely tolerate frost. Some established trees show little harm at 20° F, and can recover from 12°F freezes.

A. Baileyana f. *purpurea* hort.

PURPLELEAF ACACIA. A strain grown from selected seedlings, that first arose in L. Coates' nursery of California in the 1920s. New growth and pods lavender to purple, maturing to blue-gray. It may be more cold-hardy than the typical form.

A. dealbata Link
= *A. decurrens* var. *dealbata* (Link) F.v. Muell.

SILVER WATTLE. From E New South Wales, Victoria, and Tasmania. Naturalized in the Mediterranean region, as well as parts of California. Introduced to cultivation as early as 1792, to England in 1818, to France in 1824; in the California nursery trade by 1853. In France it was first thought exclusively a greenhouse subject; its immense appeal made it popular, but its vigor kept putting it literally "through the roof," so by the 1840s it was tested outdoors and was found surprisingly frost-hardy. Outside, in three years it can attain 16' in height, and blossom. Its flowers, highly scented, are the "golden mimosa" of florists. The name MIMOSA is from Greek *mimos*, a mimic or imitator: the leaflets mimic a wilted leaf by closing down when touched. Compared to *A. Baileyana*, this species is much larger, hardier, later-blooming, longer-lived, and not so pale-bluish. It is more closely related to *A. decurrens*, differing primarily in color of foliage: Latin *dealbatus* means covered with a white powder—referring to the whitish-hairy young shoots and leaves. The clusters of small ball-like golden flowers appear from February into May. Seedpods pale, 2"–4" long. As an ornamental, it is not without blemishes, being liable to fall over, to send forth root-suckers, and to be killed occasionally by freezing. Above all, it grows awkwardly large in a hurry. Records: 147' × 15'0" in Australia; to 70' tall in 22 years at Woodside, CA; 42' × 12'6" × 47' Berkeley, CA (1994).

A. decurrens (Wendl.) Willd.
= *A. decurrens* var. *normalis* Benth.
= *A. normalis* hort.

EARLY BLACK WATTLE. SIDNEY BLACK WATTLE. GREEN WATTLE. SIDNEY GREEN WATTLE. QUEEN WATTLE. From New South Wales. Introduced to cultivation in 1790; in California's nursery trade by 1858. Named *decurrens* because narrow "wings" run down the stems from the leaf bases. Foliage ferny, dark green and hairy; flowers spectacular, profuse, perfumed clear lemon-yellow balls in elongated clusters, March–June. Seedpods 2"–4" long. Tree dark-barked, round-crowned, often top-heavy, brittle; short-lived. Best grown unirrigated. Records: to 60' tall in 25 years at Redwood City, CA; usually only 30'–50' tall. Confusion in identity exists in cultivation. Many trees called *A. decurrens* are really *A. Mearnsii* DeWild., the BLACK WATTLE (also known as *A. decurrens* var. *mollis* Lindl., *A. mollissima* auct., non Willd.).

A. floribunda (Vent.) Willd.
= *A. longifolia* var. *floribunda* (Vent.) F.v. Muell.
= *A. rhetinodes* var. *floribunda* hort.

WHITE SALLOW. SALLY WATTLE. GOSSAMER WATTLE. CATKIN ACACIA. From E Victoria, New South Wales, Queensland. Introduced to cultivation in the late 1700s or early 1800s; to California by 1853. Names derived from Latin *flos, floris*, a flower, and *abundare*, to over-flow, to abound in. *Longus*, long, and *folium*, a leaf. Called SALLOW WATTLE for its willow-like habit. Bushy, or a tree to 25', of brittle, weeping habit. Foliage dark green, leafy, not ferny. Flowers prolific, light creamy-yellow, in loose elongated clusters ¾"–1" (3") long. Seedpods 2"–4" (5") long. Confusion in identity exists in California. Some trees called *A. floribunda* are really *A. rhetinodes*.

A. Julibrissin—see Albizia Julibrissin

A. melanoxylon R. Br.
BLACKWOOD. AUSTRALIAN BLACKWOOD. TASMANIAN BLACKWOOD. BLACKWOOD ACACIA. BLACK ACACIA. From SE Australia, and Tasmania. Introduced to cultivation in 1808; to California by 1858, and naturalized in some places there. Name derived from Greek *melas*, black, and *xylon*, wood. The bark is rough, dark gray, and the highly valued wood is dark. Compared to the other ACACIAS in this account, BLACKWOOD is more of a long-lived shade tree, less of a short-lived "flowering" tree. Root-suckering is a problem. Bears dense billowy masses of comparatively dark, leafy foliage, tinted silvery-purplish in winter. Ferny foliage is borne only on saplings. Flowers creamy-whitish to very pale yellow, in short clusters primarily in March. Seedpods 2"–5" long, markedly twisted or coiled, and slightly constricted between the seeds. Overall, a tough species; severe freezes kill it. It tolerates wet conditions better than most ACACIAS. Records: 120' × 31'0" recorded in Australia; 72' × 6'5" Berkeley, CA (1995); 67' × 11'11"

× 48' Berkeley, CA (1993); 71' × 14'5" × 90' Poverty Bay, New Zealand (≤1982).

A. Nemu—see Albizia Julibrissin

A. pravissima F.v. Muell.
SCREWPOD ACACIA. OVENS WATTLE. WEDGE-LEAF WATTLE. ALPINE WATTLE. TUMUT WATTLE. From NE Victoria, New South Wales, and A.C.T. Named in 1853. Introduced to California by 1897; less well-known than many ACACIAS. Its specific epithet means "very twisted"—from Latin *pravus*, crooked, and the superlative *-issima*, very crooked or twisted. A shrubby little tree with slender whiplike twigs bearing highly distinctive sage-green, dull, dryish-feeling ½" "leaves" (phyllodes) of broadly triangular shape. The branches are somewhat pendulous, so the foliage rustles as it sways. Bright clear yellow flowers in February-March. Seedpods 3"–4" long. Records: to 42' tall in Australia; to 30' tall in 22 years at Palo Alto, CA; 26' × 3'3" × 29' Davis, CA (1994; *pl.* 1969).

A. pycnantha Benth.
GOLDEN WATTLE. BROAD-LEAVED WATTLE. SOUTH AUSTRALIAN WATTLE. From S and E Australia. Introduced to cultivation ca. 1850; to California by 1871, but although naturalized in some places there, overall it is uncommon and little known. A shrubby, slender small tree, in Australia well-known, much cultivated and valued highly for its floral display (and its bark as a tannin source). Its juvenile "leaves" (phyllodes) can be sometimes 6" long and 4" wide and are shiny rich green. The epithet *pycnantha* is from Greek *pyknos*, dense, and *anthos* flower—the bright yellow flowers are dense-headed and comparatively large. Seedpods 2"–4¾" long. Rapid growing but frost-sensitive. Suckers freely from its base. Record: 35' tall in 25 years in San Mateo, CA.

A. rhetinodes Schlecht.
(*retinodes*)
= *A. floribunda* hort., non Willd.

EVERBLOOMING ACACIA. WIRILDA. SWAMP WATTLE. WATER WATTLE. From Tasmania, Victoria, and S Australia. Introduced to California in 1871; naturalized in some places there. The specific epithet from Greek *rhetine*, resin, meaning resinous, refers to its gum-yielding properties. A shrub or small open-crowned tree 20'–33' tall, with long, pale green, narrow "leaves" (phyllodes) 6" × ½". Notable for bearing flowers nearly all year around, but mostly in the summer and autumn. Flowers small, pale yellow, less showy than those of most cultivated species. Seedpods 1¼"–5½" (8") long, only ⅓" wide. Fast-growing, but brittle and short-lived; rarely more than 20 years old.

Acanthopanax ricinifolius—see *Kalopanax septemlobus*

Acanthopanax ricinifolius var. Maximowiczii—see *Kalopanax septemlobus* f. *Maximowiczii*

Acanthopanax septemlobus—see *Kalopanax septemlobus*

Acer

[ACERACEÆ; Maple family] 115–150 spp. of widely distributed trees and shrubs. From Latin *acer*, MAPLE tree. MAPLES are of great horticultural importance and accordingly comprise a major portion of this book. Most are prized for attractive fall leaf color. The species range from large shade-trees to small accent shrubs. All bear their leaves in opposite fashion along the twigs, and reproduce by distinctive paired, winged seeds. For more MAPLE information, consult the 1994 book *Maples of the World* by D.M. van Gelderen et al. The only closely related genus is *Dipteronia*.

A. argutum Maxim.

DEEP VEINED MAPLE. POINTED-LEAF MAPLE. Japanese: *Asa-no-ha-kaede*. From Japan. Introduced to cultivation in 1881 when C. Maries sent seeds to Veitch nursery of England; introduced to North America in 1889 when Veitch sent seeds to the Arnold Arboretum. Here it has remained exceedingly rare. *Argutum* in Latin means sharply toothed, referring to the five-lobed, 2"–4¾" wide leaves, ruggedly veined, with pronounced drip-tips, red stems, and yellow fall color. Male and female flowers borne on separate trees. A small, shrubby tree. Record: 36' × 3'11" Hollycombe, Surrey, England (1984).

A. barbatum—see A. saccharum ssp. floridanum

A. barbatum 'Caddo'—see A. saccharum 'Caddo'

A. Buergerianum Miq.
(*Buergeranum*)
= *A. trifidum* H. & A., non Th.

TRIDENT MAPLE. From China, Korea, and a variety in Taiwan. Named after Heinrich Buerger (1804–1858), German botanical explorer and collector in the Orient. Introduced to cultivation in 1890. C. Sargent collected seeds in Japan and sent them to the Arnold Arboretum in 1892. Until after WW II, TRIDENT MAPLE was very rarely grown in North America. A tree of dense foliage, its three-lobed ivy-like 1½"–3½" long leaves turn dark red or sometimes orange in fall. The bark is shreddy. Most specimens mature at about 35' tall and wide. Records: to 100' × 14'2" in China; 60' tall at Philadelphia, PA (ca. 1980); 52' × 8'4" × 52' Beaver College, PA (1980).

A. campestre L.

ENGLISH MAPLE. COMMON MAPLE. FIELD MAPLE. HEDGE(ROW) MAPLE. SMALL LEAVED MAPLE. ENGLISH CORK MAPLE. From Europe, N Africa, and the Near East. Long grown in North America, and common; naturalized in some locales. Its fall color ranges from pure butter-yellow (the usual in Seattle, WA) to dark red and purple, or orange to red-orange. Widely adaptable; a strong tree that can be used in many landscape situations. In stressful sites it bears enough seeds to be unsightly during winter. Its basal suckers, and less commonly its regular twigs, can be corky-ridged. Leaves bluntly lobed, 2"–4¾" wide; the stem with milky sap. Seed wings spread at 180° angles. Commonly, but wrongly, thought to be exclusively a bushy little tree. Records: 90' × 14'0" recorded in Europe; 83' × 11'2" × 64' Tacoma, WA (1987); 64' × 6'3" × 40' East Lansing, MI (<1979); 55' × 7'7" × 25' Montgomery County, PA (1980).

A. campestre 'Compactum'—see A. campestre 'Nanum'

A. campestre 'Evelyn'—see A. campestre Queen Elizabeth™

A. campestre Leprechaun™
Described in the 1976 catalog of Scanlon nursery of Ohio as a selection from a parent specimen some 18 years old, of excellent branching habit, making an

upswept, compact globe. Rarely sold; listed in 1994–95 catalog of Arborvillage nursery, Holt, MO.

A. campestre 'Nanum'

= A. campestre 'Compactum'
= A. campestre 'Globosum'

Described in 1839 as a rounded bush with smallish, 3-lobed leaves. The Arnold Arboretum distributed stock to 5 nurseries in 1943. Some nurseries sell it topgrafted on a straight trunk to produce a GLOBE ENGLISH MAPLE of naturally dwarf size.

A. campestre 'Postelense'

From Postel, Silesia; in commerce ca. 1896. Leaves golden yellow when young, becoming pale green. Tree of reduced size. Rare in North America; sold by Greer nursery of Oregon during the 1970s and '80s.

A. campestre 'Pulverulentum'

= A. campestre 'Variegata' (in part)

Introduced in Germany in 1859. Leaves heavily dotted and flecked with white. In Latin, *pulverulenta* means covered with powder. Rare in North America but here since ≤1896; sold by Greer nursery of Oregon during the 1970s and '80s.

A. campestre Queen Elizabeth™ PP 4392 (1970)

= A. campestre 'Evelyn'

Discovered as a seedling of unknown origin in Gresham, OR. Introduced in 1981–82 by Schmidt nursery of Boring, OR. This selection offers uniformity of habit, providing a better choice for street-planting than random seedling stock.

A. campestre 'Schwerinii'

Of German origin ca. 1895. Likely some connection with Graf Fritz Kurt Alexander von Schwerin (1856–1934), who lived near Berlin. Young leaves purplish. Very rare in North America, but here ≤1928.

A. campestre 'Variegata'—see A. campestre 'Pulverulentum'

A. capillipes Maxim.

RED STRIPEBARK MAPLE. RED SNAKEBARK MAPLE. HAKKODA MAPLE. Japanese: *Hoso-e-kaede. Ashibosouri-noki*. From Japan. Introduced to cultivation in 1892 when C. Sargent collected seeds in Japan and sent them to the Arnold Arboretum. The specific epithet *capillipes* is from Latin *capillus*, hair, and *pes*, foot—slender-footed, perhaps in reference to the delicate ⅓"–⅝" flower-stalks. Prized for its attractive reddish young growth, whitish-striped trunk, and red or orange-red fall color. Leaves usually three-lobed, sometimes unlobed or five-lobed; 3"–7½" long; stem often red. Like other STRIPEBARK MAPLES, it is lovely but comparatively short-lived, and best in cool, partly shady conditions. M. Dirr suggests it is the most heat-tolerant of the STRIPEBARK group. It certainly has a more elegant bearing than A. *Davidii*, let alone the bigleaf STRIPEBARKS A. *pensylvanicum* and A. *tegmentosum*. Rare in North America overall, yet relatively common for a STRIPEBARK species; grown by a few major nurseries since the 1950s. Records: to 82' × 7'3" in the wild; 56' × 3'3" × 33' Seattle, WA (1990); 38' × 4'1" × 43' Seattle, WA (1992).

A. cappadocicum Gledit.

= A. *lætum* C.A. Mey.
= A. *pictum* hort. (in part; cf. *Acer pictum*)
= A. *colchicum* hort.

COLISEUM MAPLE. CAPPADOCIAN MAPLE. CAUCASIAN MAPLE. COLCHICAN MAPLE. From east Asia Minor, the Caucasus, through the Himalayas to W China. It was named CAPPADOCIAN MAPLE in 1785 because the species was discovered by botanists in Cappadocia (NE Turkey). Introduced to cultivation in 1838; to North America in 1878 when the Arnold Arboretum got seeds from a French arboretum. Little grown here except in its cultivar 'Rubrum'. This species can be considered an Asiatic counterpart to the well known NORWAY MAPLE (A. *platanoides*). A shade tree, with leaves 3"–6¼" wide, of five lobes untoothed on the edges; clear yellow fall color. The leaf stem has milky sap. Root-suckers can be a nuisance, but are usually colored a lovely deep red. Records: 91' × 7'10" Tacoma, WA (1987); 78' × 11'0" Ladner, B.C. (1994); 73' × 9'0" Lima, NY (1980); 62' × 11'5" (at 1') Rochester, NY (ca. 1980; *pl.* 1902); 55' × 10'10" Washington, D.C. (1976).

A. cappadocicum 'Aureum'

Introduced in 1914 by Hesse nursery of Germany. Leaves emerge reddish but quickly turn yellow, except remain reddish or bronze on their veins and tips. Then they age to green, and finally turn yellow again in autumn. Scanlon nursery of Ohio sold 'Aureum' beginning in 1963–64, but warned that its delicate foliage sunburned badly in the Midwest climate. The tree performs better in the maritime Pacific Northwest, and has been sold sparingly by nurseries there.

A. cappadocicum 'Horticola'—see A. cappadocicum 'Rubrum'

A. cappadocicum ssp. Lobelii (Ten.) E. Murr.

= A. Lobelii Ten.

From S and C Italy. Named after Mathias de l'Obel (1538–1616), Flemish botanist, physician to King James I of England. Introduced to cultivation in 1683 in Italy; grown in Germany, France, England, etc. by 1838. First widely available in North American nursery trade when Scanlon nursery of Ohio offered it in 1957–58. Most specimens sold are grafted, but it can be raised from seeds. This subspecies differs much from typical A. cappadocicum. It is naturally fastigiate, its twigs are coated with a whitish powder, and its 4"–7" wide leaves are less lobed. The fall color is plain yellow. Records: 98' × 12'4" Eastnor Castle, Herefordshire, England (1989); 57' × 4'7" Seattle, WA (1993; pl. 1958).

A. cappadocicum 'Rubrum'

= A. cappadocicum 'Horticola'

Originated in Germany in 1838. In the U.S. nursery trade since ≤1880s. Young leaves dark red, maturing green, then yellow in fall. The most commonly grown variant of A. cappadocicum.

A. carpinifolium S. & Z.

HORNBEAM MAPLE. From Japan. Japanese: Chidorinoki. Yama-shiba-kaede. Introduced in 1879 when C. Maries collected seeds for Veitch nursery of England. C. Sargent collected seeds for the Arnold Arboretum in 1892. First widely available in North American nursery trade when Scanlon nursery of Ohio offered it in 1957–58. The specific epithet is from genus Carpinus, HORNBEAM tree, and Latin folium, a leaf. Leaves elongated, unlobed, with numerous parallel veins—utterly unlike those of familiar MAPLES. The largest leaves are 8" × 3¼" and bear 18–25 pairs of veins. Fall color usually dull golden-brown, at best yellow, orange and red. Only the seeds make it a MAPLE. HORNBEAM MAPLE is bushy, broad, and well-suited for woodland gardens. Male and female flowers borne on separate trees. Records: 50' × 5' in the wild; 39' × 3'10" Westonbirt, Gloucestershire, England (1989); 34' × 3'10" × 35¼' Seattle, WA (1994; pl. 1953); 34' × 2'6" × 30' Vancouver, B.C. (1993; pl. 1978).

A. carolinianum—see A. rubrum var. trilobum

A. carpinifolium 'Esveld Select'

A fastigiate, dwarfish selection from C. Esveld's nursery of Boskoop, Holland. Introduced in 1978. Not yet known in N America.

A. circinatum Pursh

VINE MAPLE. From SW British Columbia to N California. Introduced in 1826–27 when D. Douglas sent seeds to Great Britain. Rarely cultivated outside of its native range. An 1852 account extolling its virtues is still valid: "when its leaves unfold, they are preceded by long crimson leaf-scales, from two to four each twig; the leaves when they first come are thin, . . . a clear light green; at the same time peep out little tufts of purple flowers, with white petals." In form, VINE MAPLE is a small slender tree or very lanky shrub. Bark smooth, greenish, and easily injured by much exposure to sun. Leaves roundish, 3"–7", with 7–9 lobes that recall the species' affinities to the JAPANESE MAPLES A. japonicum, A. palmatum, A. pseudosieboldianum, A. Shirasawanum and A. Sieboldianum. In shade the fall color is yellow, in the sun reddish. Records: 63' × 1'9" × 12' Vancouver, B.C. (1992); 62' × 2'11" × 31' Olympic National Park, WA (1988); 46' × 5'7" × 35' Tillamook County, OR (1992); 42' × 2'1" × 52' Everett, WA (1991).

A. circinatum 'Elegant'

A selection made ca. 1954 in Skagit Valley, B.C. by Hubert Rhodes. Named at the Dominion Arboretum of Ottawa. Leaf margins slightly more incised. The Seattle arboretum specimen bears seven-lobed leaves of smaller size, on a small seedy plant.

A. circinatum 'Glen-Del'

Originated in 1976 at Del's Lane County nursery of Oregon. Propagated in 1978; introduced in 1982. Named after nurserymen Glen Handy (1916–1993) and Delbert L. Loucks. Of narrow, compact, upright habit, with deeply-cut lacy five-lobed leaves—the center of the five lobes longer than the other four. The lobes are not serrated as in A. circinatum 'Monroe'.

A. circinatum 'Monroe'

Discovered by Dr. Warner Monroe of Portland in 1960 at the headwaters of the McKenzie River in the Oregon Cascades, ca. 65 miles east of Eugene.

Propagated by 1965, registered in 1974, and in the general nursery trade by 1977. It is a cutleaf variant with extremely finely sharp-toothed and dissected leaves, not merely deeply-lobed as in *A. circinatum* 'Elegant'. Slower-growing than average specimens of *A. circinatum*, but not a dwarf (as is 'Little Gem'). It may reach 6' in ten years.

A. cissifolium (S. & Z.) K. Koch

VINELEAF MAPLE. TREFOIL MAPLE. IVY LEAVED MAPLE. JAPANESE BOXELDER. From Japan. Japanese: *Mitsude-kaede*. The specific epithet *cissifolium* is from Latin *cissus* (from Greek *Kissos*), vine, and *folium*, a leaf. Introduced by Siebold to Holland in 1860. To North America in 1878 when the Arnold Arboretum got seeds from a French arboretum. Until the 1960s scarcely in the nursery trade here; still rare. An elegant species with trifoliate leaves, the largest leaflet 2"–3½" long, and exquisitely dainty flowers (males and females borne on separate trees) in airy, narrow clusters to 4¾" long. In woodland gardens it is slim; in sunny, open sites broad and low. Fall color red and yellow. Records: to 80' tall in Japan; 42' × 9'8" × 53' Philadelphia, PA (1980).

A. cissifolium ssp. Henryi (Pax) E. Murr.
= *A. Henryi* Pax

From C China. Discovered in 1888 by Augustine Henry (1857–1930); introduced in 1903 by E. Wilson for Veitch nursery of England. Extremely rare in North America; scarcely ever offered in commerce. Differs from typical *A. cissifolium* in that its leaflets (the largest 2½"–4½" long) are usually untoothed or comparatively little-toothed, at least on older specimens. Fall color varies from a good red or adequate pastel mix including red, to simply dreadful. Record: 47' × 9'7" × 52' Philadelphia, PA (1980; *pl.* 1907).

A. colchicum—see A. cappadocicum

A. cratægifolium S. & Z.

HAWTHORN LEAF MAPLE. From Japan. Japanese: *Uri-kaede. Me-uri-no-ki*. Introduced in 1862 by C. Maximowicz to St. Petersburg; in 1879 C. Maries introduced it to England; in 1880 the Arnold Arboretum got seeds from England's Veitch nursery. Very rarely offered by North American nurseries until ca. 1960. Still a scarce tree overall. The name *cratægifolium* is from genus *Cratægus*, HAWTHORN, and Latin *folium*, a leaf. Leaves small (2"–3½" long) and dark, shaped vaguely like those of WASHINGTON HAWTHORN (*Cratægus Phænopyrum*) but not as glossy; finer-toothed, with delicate rusty hairs on the under-

sides. The tree is bushy, slender, with weakly-striped trunks. Male and female flowers borne on separate plants. Fall color can be a pale yellow, or, as E. Wilson writes, can go "from yellow to crimson or black-purple—no other maple is so dark." Records: to 40' tall in the wild; 36' × 1'6" Westonbirt, Gloucestershire, England (1967); 24' × 1'2" × 19' Seattle, WA (1994; *pl.* 1954).

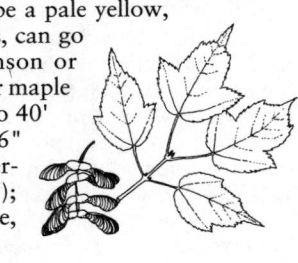

A. cratægifolium 'Beni-uri'—see A. cratægifolium 'Veitchii'

A. cratægifolium 'Hillieri'—see A. cratægifolium 'Veitchii'

A. cratægifolium 'Meuri-kaede-no-fuiri'—see A. cratægifolium 'Veitchii'

A. cratægifolium 'Meurikofuba'—see A. cratægifolium 'Veitchii'

A. cratægifolium 'Veitchii'

Leaves variegated white and pink. From Veitch nursery of England in 1881. Exceedingly rare in North America. Has been sold incorrectly as *A. cratægifolium* 'Beni-uri'. One was obtained in 1966 by Seattle's arboretum; curiously, its seedlings are often variegated also. Greer nursery of Oregon sold this cultivar during the 1970s. Variegated cultivars similar to 'Veitchii' are 'Hillieri' and 'Meuri-kaede-no-fuiri' ('Meurikofuba').

A. creticum—see A. sempervirens

A. dasycarpum—see A. saccharinum

A. Davidii Franch.

(PÈRE) DAVID'S MAPLE. From China. Discovered in 1869 by the Basque Jesuit, Jean Pierre Armand David (1826–1900). In U.S. nurseries since at least the late 1920s. It is a STRIPEBARK MAPLE, doubtless the most variable species, its fall color yellow, red-orange or purple. The nomenclaturally typical form of this species may not be in cultivation. Yet besides the subspecies *Grosseri*, several cultivars exist, which in commerce have usually been sold simply as *A. Davidii*. The record specimens cited below surely consist of different cultivars. Much study is needed before the comparative abundance and attributes of the various *A. Davidii* named forms can be documented conclusively. Records: 62' × 4'6" Winkworth Arboretum, Surrey, England (1988); 51' × 7'10" Wanganui, New Zealand (≤1982); 57' × 3'4" Richmond Beach, WA (1993); 46' × 5'0" Trewithen, Cornwall, England (1985).

A. Davidii 'Ernest Wilson'

Introduced to cultivation in 1879 when C. Maries sent seeds to Veitch nursery of England; Ernest Henry Wilson (1876–1930) obtained more seeds in 1902; seeds were sent in 1906 to the Arnold Arboretum from Veitch. A seed-propagated cultivar. Habit compact. Leaves light green, to 4½" × 3" with a short pink stem, and small, shallow lobes. Fall color orange to scarlet. Not sold in North America under this name (which dates from 1957).

A. Davidii 'George Forrest'
= A. Forrestii hort., non Diels

Introduced by the plant explorer George Forrest (1873–1932) from Yunnan in 1921–22. A seed-propagated cultivar. Notable for its dark, large leaves, to 8" × 5" with dark red stems, and few, shallow lobes. Fall color late and poor. Tree vigorous, open and arching. Probably the most common variant in cultivation.

A. Davidii ssp. Grosseri (Pax) de Jong
= A. Grosseri Pax

GROSSER'S STRIPEBARK MAPLE. Discovered ca. 1894 by G. Giraldi. Named in 1902 after the German botanist Wilhelm Carl Heinrich Grosser (1869–1942). Introduced as seeds from J. Hers to the Arnold Arboretum ca. 1919. GROSSER'S MAPLE was regarded as an independent species until 1988. However, Acer Davidii has proved so variable that the supposed specific distinctions between it and A. Grosseri don't suffice. Generally, Grosseri leaves are comparatively small and finely toothed. But they can be large, and either lobed or unlobed. The fall color is usually a pleasing orange, rosy or clear bright yellow. In the maritime Pacific Northwest, nurseries have sold GROSSER'S MAPLE since the 1970s, but elsewhere in North America it seems practically unheard of commercially. Seattle, WA's tallest is 56' and 22' wide (1994).

A. Davidii 'Hersii'
= A. Grosseri var. Hersii (Rehd.) Rehd.
= A. Hersii Rehd.

HERS' STRIPEBARK MAPLE. Discovered in 1919 by Joseph Hers (1884–1965), a Belgian railroad manager in China, who in the '20s sent seeds of plants to the West. He sent seeds of this MAPLE in 1921 to the Arnold Arboretum, and in 1922 A. Rehder named the species after him. Time has shown that far from being a separate species, the Hersii maple is a mere variant of Grosseri, which itself is a mere variant of Davidii. A. Hersii is said to have more prominently lobed leaves than A. Grosseri, turning darker colors earlier in autumn. HERS' STRIPEBARK-MAPLE has been sold to a very limited degree in the U.S. since the 1960s.

A. Davidii 'Horizontale'

Originated <1959 at Villa Taranto, Italy. Extremely rare if it exists at all in North American cultivation. C. Esveld's nursery of Boskoop, Holland, sold it during the 1970s and '80s. Tree sparse, of elegantly arching branches, forming a very wide, spreading crown. Confusion is likely with the botanical var. horizontale Pax. (of no horticultutal role).

A. Davidii 'Serpentine'

Originated in Holland; named in 1976; imported to North America ≤1978. Offered in Washington and British Columbia nurseries since ≤1990. Selected for its excellent white-striped purple or brown twigs. Tree arching, somewhat weeping, shrubby; branches slender and long; leaves usually small (at most 5⅞" × 2⅜"), with red stems. It recalls HAWTHORN LEAF MAPLE (A. cratægifolium). Record: 14' × 1'3" Seattle, WA (1994; pl. 1978).

A. Davidii "Slender-Leaved"

Tree expert A. Mitchell of England describes this variant as fairly common in British cultivation, but not named officially. It bears unlobed, long-pointed leaves 6" × 3⅛" or 5⅛" × 2"; autumn color yellow-brown to a good orange.

A. Davidii "Small-Leaved"

Alan Mitchell of England describes this variant, not officially named. It bears unlobed, small elliptic leaves 2⅜" × 1³⁄₁₆" of good orange in autumn.

A. diabolicum Bl. ex K. Koch

HORNED MAPLE. DEVIL MAPLE. From Japan. Japanese: Kaji-kaede. Oni-momiji. Introduced to cultivation in 1880 when C. Maries sent seeds to Veitch nursery of

England. Rare in North America; grown commercially since ≤1954. The name *diabolicum* means devilish; from the Japanese name *oni-momiji* (DEVIL MAPLE). The Japanese called it so because of the "wild and violent appearance of the leaves." Westerners, unaware of the reason behind the name *diabolicum*, imagined it was derived from the "stinging" bristles on the seeds, and/or the two tiny hornlike styles (like devil's horns) on them. Besides its fascinating name, this diabolical MAPLE's main attraction is its springtime flowers, which are as lovely (up close) as its summer foliage is heavy and dull to behold. Capable of a good yellow fall color, it usually has none worth noting, turning tawny late in autumn. The canopy is plain, the trunk clumsily stout. Leaf five-lobed, hairy on both sides, 4"–7½" wide, stem to 3¾" long. Bark dark gray, pebbled in "elephantine" fahion. Records: 65' tall in the wild; 50' × 3'6" Westonbirt, Gloucestershire, England (1980); 49' × 1'8" Seattle, WA (1993; *pl.* 1948); 44' × 5'6" Beauport, Sussex, England (1983).

A. *diabolicum* f. *purpurascens* (Franch. & Sav.) Rehd.
= A. *diabolicum* 'Purpurascens'
Introduced to North American cultivation in 1878 when the Arnold Arboretum got it from Lavallee's Arboretum Segrez in France. *Acer diabolicum* bears its flower sexes on separate trees; the flowers can be pale green, salmon-pink, coral or purplish. Clones of both sexes have been selected and grown under the name 'Purpurascens'. Such clones bear (variously) purplish flowers, reddish young seeds (if female), purplish-red emerging leaves, and red fall color. These pigmented trees are more valued than typical *Acer diabolicum* and yet are no more often cultivated.

A. *distylum* S. & Z.
LIMELEAF MAPLE. LINDEN LEAVED MAPLE. From Japan. Japanese: *Hitotsuba-kaede. Maruba-kaede*. The name *distylum*, given in 1845, translates "two styles" and seems meaningless since all *Acer* species bear two styles. Introduced to cultivation in 1879 when C. Maries sent seeds to Veitch nursery of England. Unknown in North American commerce until the 1960s. Still extremely rare. A small tree of graceless aspect and slow growth, best in woodland

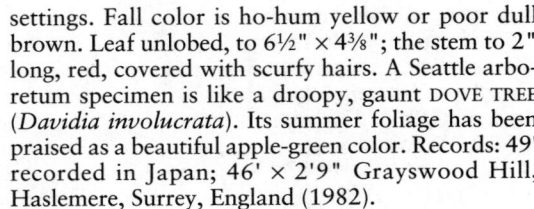

settings. Fall color is ho-hum yellow or poor dull brown. Leaf unlobed, to 6½" × 4⅜"; the stem to 2" long, red, covered with scurfy hairs. A Seattle arboretum specimen is like a droopy, gaunt DOVE TREE (*Davidia involucrata*). Its summer foliage has been praised as a beautiful apple-green color. Records: 49' recorded in Japan; 46' × 2'9" Grayswood Hill, Haslemere, Surrey, England (1982).

A. *Douglasii*—see A. *glabrum*

A. *eriocarpum*—see A. *saccharinum*

A. *floridanum*—see A. *saccharum* ssp. *floridanum*

A. *Forrestii* Diels—see A. *pectinatum* ssp. *Forrestii*

A. *Forrestii* hort.—see A. *Davidii* 'George Forrest'

A. *fraxinifolium*—see A. *Negundo*

A. × *Freemanii* E. Murr.
(A. *rubrum* × A. *saccharinum*)
FREEMAN MAPLE. HYBRID RED MAPLE. This hybrid was first raised in 1933 at the U.S. National Arboretum by Oliver M. Freeman (b. 1891). The name commemorating Mr. Freeman was only given in 1969. Only clones are sold. Often nurseries ignore the *Freemanii* designation and sell cultivars as if they were purebred RED MAPLES (A. *rubrum*).

A. × *Freemanii* 'Armstrong'
= A. *rubrum* 'Armstrong'
The original specimen was bought for $5 from a farmer near Hartgrove, OH, by Newton G. Armstrong (d. 1963) of Armstrong Tree Service, Windsor, OH. Mr. Armstrong in 1948 told his friend Ed Scanlon about it. Propagated by Scanlon nursery in 1949, but only offered in quantity by 1955–56. ARMSTRONG MAPLE is broadly columnar, female, its leaf obviously intermediate in form between RED and SILVER MAPLES. But its fall color is erratic—usually late, and fair at best. Therefore Armstrong Two™ has superseded it in nurseries, and has largely been sold under its name. Records: 71' × 4'4" × 21' and 69' × 5'0" × 25' Tacoma, WA (1990).

A. × *Freemanii* Armstrong Two™
= A. × *Freemanii* 'Armstrong II'
Around 1960 Scanlon nursery found a tree that had the tough dark foliage of the northern strain of A.

rubrum, that colored beautiful orange-red in fall. Since this tree had even tighter form as well as superior fall color compared to 'Armstrong', it was introduced by Scanlon in 1965. It may be a purebred RED MAPLE instead of a hybrid.

A. × *Freemanii* Autumn Blaze® PP 4864 (1982)
= *A. rubrum* Autumn Blaze®
= *A.* × *Freemanii* 'Jeffersred'

Selected in the late 1960s by nurseryman Glenn A. Jeffers (deceased) of Fostoria, OH, from a group of seedlings of putative RED MAPLE × SILVER MAPLE parentage. Much sold since its introduction ca. 1980. The tree forms a dense, broad oval. Leaf deeply lobed, turning brilliant, long-lasting orange-red in fall.

A. × *Freemanii* Autumn Fantasy® PP 7655 (1991)
= *A.* × *Freemanii* 'DTR 102'

Originated <1986 by W. Wandell of Urbana, IL. The original tree is a female in central Illinois. Of oval shape and upright branching. Leaf deeply lobed, turning red or crimson in fall. Grown by several major wholesale nurseries since 1991–92.

A. × *Freemanii* Celebration® PP 7279 (1990)
= *A.* × *Freemanii* 'Celzam'

Selected by Lake County nursery of Perry, OH. Introduced in 1987. Much grown. Compact, perhaps smaller than most FREEMAN MAPLE cultivars; strong branch crotches; male. Leaf deeply lobed; its fall color varies from yellowish-green to red and gold.

A. × *Freemanii* 'Celzam'—see *A.* × *Freemanii* Celebration®

A. × *Freemanii* 'DTR 102'—see *A.* × *Freemanii* Autumn Fantasy®

A. × *Freemanii* 'Indian Summer'—see *A.* × *Freemanii* 'Morgan'

A. × *Freemanii* 'Jeffersred'—see *A.* × *Freemanii* Autumn Blaze®

A. × *Freemanii* 'Lee's Red'
Selected in southern Ontario. Introduced ≤1987 by Sheridan nursery of Ontario. Brilliant red fall color.

A. × *Freemanii* 'Marmo'
The original specimen (probably planted in the mid-1920s, from a Wisconsin source) grows at the west end of Lake Marmo in the Morton Arboretum of Lisle, IL. It was a broad column (75' tall and 35' wide) when registered in 1985. Major wholesale nurseries began offering it in quantity in 1992–93. Fall color deep blood-red mottled with some yellow and green. Leaves deeply lobed. Seedless.

A. × *Freemanii* 'Morgan'
= *A.* × *Freemanii* 'Indian Summer'
= *A. rubrum* 'Indian Summer'
= *A. rubrum* 'Morgan'
?= *A. rubrum* Embers®
   (which see)

Selected at Morgan Arboretum of MacDonald College, Quebéc. Registered January 1971. Introduced ≤1972–73 by Sheridan nursery of Ontario. Much grown during the 1980s. Tree very fast and vigorous, of open habit, becoming broad as well as tall. Leaves large, deeply lobed; with consistent, brilliant red and purple, red, scarlet, or pale orange fall color. Female.

A. × *Freemanii* Scarlet Beauty™
Named and introduced ≤1986 by Boyd nursery of McMinnville, TN.

A. × *Freemanii* Scarlet Sentinel™ PP 3109 (1972)
= *A.* × *Freemanii* 'Scarsen'
= *A. rubrum* 'Scarlet Sentinel'
= *A. rubrum* 'Scarsen'

The original specimen was found by I-90 in Ashtabula, OH, by Schichtel nursery of Orchard Park, NY. Introduced in 1972 by Schmidt nursery of Boring, OR. Much grown. A male clone. Leaves large. Fall color inconsistent: varies from poor yellow-green, to good gold, to bright red. Vigorous; extended growing season. Broadly columnar, to at least 40' tall.

A. × *Freemanii* 'Scarsen'—see *A.* × *Freemanii* Scarlet Sentinel™

A. 'Gingerbread'—see *A. griseum* Gingerbread™

A. Ginnala—see *A. tataricum* ssp. *Ginnala*

A. Ginnala 'Bailey Compact'—see *A. tataricum* ssp. *Ginnala* 'Bailey Compact'

A. Ginnala var. *Semenowii*—see *A. tataricum* ssp. *Semenowii*

A. glabrum Torr.
= *A. Douglasii* Hook.

DWARF MAPLE. ROCKY MOUNTAIN MAPLE. SIERRA MAPLE. ROCK MAPLE. From SE Alaska and British Columbia, south to New Mexico. Introduced to cultivation in 1882. A slender species, sometimes shrubby, often tightly upright even in exposed sites. Leaves reminiscent of those of RED MAPLE (*A. rubrum*), 3"–5" long, but markedly longer-stemmed (to 6") and on basal sucker shoots actually compounded into three leaflets. Some sucker leaves are quite reticulate and strongly lobed, almost like a *Vitis* or *Parthenocissus* leaf. Fall color red and yellow. Comparatively little grown, but likely to become more cultivated in the West at least because of its drought-tolerance. Records: 80' × 4'5" × 33' Sandpoint, ID (1989); 70' × 2'4" Anacortes, WA (1987); 65' × 5'2" Ahsahka, ID (1985); 50' × 5'6" Birch Bay, WA (<1945).

A. glabrum 'El Dorado'
Named by B. LeRoy Davidson of Washington for a cut-leaved selection found <1976 in El Dorado Canyon of Colorado Springs State Park. Not in commerce.

A. grandidentatum—see *A. saccharum* ssp. *grandidentatum*

A. grandidentatum 'Schmidt'—see *A. saccharum* ssp. *grandidentatum* Rocky Mt. Glow™

A. griseum (Franch.) Pax
PAPERBARK MAPLE. From W China. Introduced to cultivation in 1901 when E. Wilson sent seeds to Veitch nursery of England. Introduced to the U.S. in 1907 by the Arnold Arboretum. Its specific epithet *griseum* is Latinized from the French *gris*, gray— referring to the grayish-glaucous leaf underside. Leaves trifoliate; the 1½"–4" long leaflets are pink beneath as they fall in November, but turn gray. Prized highly for its smooth, peeling cinnamon-colored bark (R. Lancaster reports some in China have dark, close bark). Its red fall color is also lovely. Difficulty in propagation has kept the species from becoming very common. A small tree; the largest dimensions recorded in cultivation are 40'–50' tall, and trunks 4'–5' around.

A. griseum Gingerbread™
= *A. griseum* 'Ginzam'
= *A.* 'Gingerbread'

Introduced in 1995 by Lake County nursery of Perry, PH. Vigorous upright habit ideal for use as a street tree. Twombly nursery of Monroe, CT, says *A.* 'Gingerbread' is a hybrid of *A. griseum* × *A. Maximowiczianum*.

A. griseum 'Ginzam'—see *A. griseum* Gingerbread™

A. griseum 'Girard's Selection'
= *A. griseum* 'Girard's'

Girard nursery of Geneva, OH, sold under this name since ≤1980 what may be a hybrid between *A. griseum* and *A. Maximowiczianum*; it is grafted on SUGAR MAPLE (*A. saccharum*) stock. Originally raised from a seed collected in Rochester, NY.

A. Grosseri—see *A. Davidii* ssp. *Grosseri*

A. Grosseri var. *Hersii*—see *A. Davidii* 'Hersii'

A. Heldreichii Orph. *ex* Boiss.
GREEK MAPLE. From SE Europe, including the slopes of Mount Parnassus. Introduced to cultivation in 1879. In North America ≤1896; in commerce ≤1910; still extremely rare here. Named after the Greek botanist Theodor von Heldreich (1822–1902). In nature, and perhaps also in cultivation, it often hybridizes with SYCAMORE MAPLE (*A. Pseudoplatanus*). Leaf 4"–9⅜" wide, deeply, bluntly five-lobed; golden in fall; stem to 7" long. Drought-tolerant. Records: to 98' tall in the wild; 75' × 8'11" Hergest Croft, Herefordshire, England (1985); 64' × 5'8" × 38' Arnold Arboretum, MA (1990); 55' × 5'0" × 41' Sidney, B.C. (1993; *pl.* 1914).

A. Heldreichii ssp. *Trautvetteri* (Medw.) E. Murr.
= *A. Trautvetteri* Medw.
= *A. insigne* hort.

REDBUD MAPLE. CAUCASIAN MAPLE. From the Caucasus, and SW Asia. Named after Ernest Rudolph von Trautvetter (1809–1889), Russian botanist.

Introduced to cultivation in 1866 in Belgium. Exceedingly rare in North America. Closely related to, and often hybridizes with *A. Pseudoplatanus*; the 4"–8" wide leaves are similar but more elegant, with deep lobes; the canopy is less dense, the bark smooth. The buds are brown in winter despite the name REDBUD MAPLE. But when the tree blooms, its leaf bud bracts are bright red; the flowers honey-scented. It is late to flush, looks dead for a while, then bursts forth when most MAPLES are already leafy and setting seeds. It also goes bare early— usually by late September, its yellow leaves are already on the ground. By far the earliest MAPLE to defoliate in the Seattle arboretum. In summer the seeds are an attractive pink or red, and stand out for their size, being as much as 2¾" long. Records: 70' × 17'4" Turkey (1992); 69' × 6'4" Edinburgh (1983); 41' × 3'6" × 31' Sidney, B.C. (1994; *pl.* 1914).

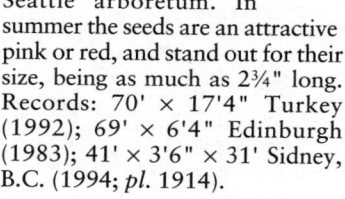

A. Henryi—see *A. cissifolium* ssp. *Henryi*

A. Hersii—see *A. Davidii* 'Hersii'

A. heterophyllum—see *A. sempervirens*

A. hyrcanum Fisch. & Mey.
= *A. tauricum* hort.
BALKAN MAPLE. From SE Europe, SW Asia. Introduced to cultivation in 1865. Exceedingly rare in North America. The specific epithet refers to its being from the Caspian Sea area—Hyrcania being an old name for that area. Leaves 2"–5⅛" wide, resembling those of *A. campestre* and *A. Miyabei*. Buds notably slender and closely imbricated, ¼"–⁵⁄₁₆" long. Bark can flake off like SHAGBARK HICKORY (*Carya ovata*). Specimens seen on Vancouver Island, B.C. are very slow-growing, suffer from insects, and give no indication of being worth cultivation. Records: to 82' tall in the wild; 74' × 6'3" Westonbirt, Gloucestershire, England (1982); 40' × 4'3" × 36' Sidney, B.C. (1993; *pl.* 1914).

A. insigne—see *A. Heldreichii* ssp. *Trautvetteri*

A. insigne var. *Van Volxemii*—see *A. velutinum* var. *Van Volxemii*

A. japonicum Th. *ex* Murr.
FULL MOON MAPLE. DOWNY JAPANESE MAPLE. Japanese: *Hauchiwa-kaede*. From Manchuria, Japan, and Korea. Introduced by Siebold to Holland in 1844. A treelike shrub, to 30' × 5'0" or rarely to 50' tall. Leaf roundish, (7) 9–11 (13) lobed; red or sometimes yellow in fall. Rarely cultivated, except in its cultivar 'Aconitifolium'. Distinguished from the very common JAPANESE MAPLE (*A. palmatum*), in having its leaf stem hairy, and the leaf has more lobes and is larger.

A. japonicum 'Aconitifolium'
= *A. japonicum* 'Laciniatum'
FERNLEAF (FULL MOON) MAPLE. CUTLEAF (FULL MOON) MAPLE. Japanese: *Maiku-jaku*. Introduced to cultivation ≤1888 by Parsons nursery of Flushing, NY. The cultivar name is from genus *Aconitum*, MONK'S HOOD, and Latin *folium*, a leaf. So named because the leaf is deeply divided into narrow, ferny lobes of refined elegance. Rich red in fall. The Japanese name means dancing peacock. The most widely grown *A. japonicum* variant. More cold-hardy than most cultivars of *A. japonicum* or *A. palmatum*.

A. japonicum 'Aureum'—see *A. Shirasawanum* 'Aureum'

A. japonicum 'Filicifolium'
= *A. japonicum* 'Parsonsii'
= *A. palmatum* var. *dissectum* 'Filicifolium'
First sold in the U.S. ≤1892. Filicifolium means fernleaved; from Latin *filix*, fern, and *folium*, a leaf. 'Filicifolium' may be simply an alternate name for *A. japonicum* 'Aconitifolium'. But the late J.D. Vertrees, JAPANESE MAPLE expert, found 'Filicifolium' differed in details such as having a slightly smaller leaf, with usually 9 instead of 11 lobes. In other words, separate clones, but not differing in a horticulturally significant way.

A. japonicum 'Green Cascade'
A gracefully mounded shrub of weeping habit; to 4' tall in ten years. Leaves also smaller and more delicately cut than those of typical *A. japonicum*. Raised

as an *A. japonicum* 'Aconitifolium' seedling in 1958 by Arthur Wright of Canby, OR. Registered in 1972.

A. japonicum 'Itaya'

= *A. palmatum* 'Itaya'

Leaf unusually large, 3"–6" wide, of (7) 9 (11) lobes. *A. japonicum* 'Macrophyllum' is the same, or practically identical. Offered in U.S. nurseries during the 1940s through '60s.

A. japonicum 'Junihitoye'—see A. Shirasawanum 'Junihitoye'

A. japonicum 'Laciniatum'—see A. japonicum 'Aconitifolium'

A. japonicum 'Lovett'

'Lovett' is a name dating from ≤1967 (when listed by Fred W. Bergman's Raraflora nursery of Feasterville, PA), but not well understood. Edward Murray thought it a synonym of *A. japonicum* 'Filicifolium'. Probably it applies to a small-leaved seedling of *A. japonicum* 'Aconitifolium'. A passage from the catalog of Greer nursery of Eugene, OR: "smallest leaved *A. japonicum* cultivar. An airy, gentle appearance as the leaves wave in soft breezes. Orange-red fall color. Grows 12' in ten years."

A. japonicum 'Macrophyllum'—see A. japonicum 'Itaya'

A. japonicum var. microphyllum—see A. Shirasawanum

A. japonicum 'O isami'

= *A. japonicum* 'Taiyu'

A vigorous small tree to 30' tall, with large leaves, measuring to 6¾" long and 7½" wide, divided about halfway. Fall color yellow, scarlet and red. Rarer than the other *A. japonicum* cvs. treated in this book.

A. japonicum 'Parsonsii'—see A. japonicum 'Filicifolium'

A. japonicum 'Taiyu'—see A. japonicum 'O isami'

A. japonicum 'Vitifolium'

Introduced to Western cultivation ca. 1863. A robust clone, with large leaves of dazzling fall color. "Vitifolium" means leaves like a grapevine; from genus *Vitis*, GRAPEVINE, and Latin *folium*, a leaf. Leaf usually 11-lobed; commonly to 5⅛" long × 6⅝" wide, exceptionally to 8⅝" long × 9½" wide. Much praised in Great Britain, where it has reached 49' in height. Scarcely known in North America, but here since ≤1939.

A. lætum—see A. cappadocicum

A. Lobelii—see A. cappadocicum ssp. Lobelii

A. macrophyllum Pursh

BIGLEAF MAPLE. BROADLEAF MAPLE. LARGELEAF MAPLE. PACIFIC MAPLE. OREGON MAPLE. From SW British Columbia through California, always within 200 miles of salt water. Name from Greek *macro*, large, and *phyllon*, a leaf. Introduced to cultivation in 1812. First grown in North American nursery trade ≤1854, primarily within its native range.

In overall size and in its parts, the largest *Acer*. Leaf deeply 5–7 lobed, to 22¼" wide, golden in autumn. Flower clusters to 8½" long with as many as 176 flowers, producing seeds to 3⅛" long. Records: 158' × 14'1" × 61' Mt. Baker National Forest, WA (1989); 105' × 37'1" × 102' Hemlock, OR (1993); 101' × 34'11" × 90' Jewell, OR (1977).

A. macrophyllum 'Kimballiae'

= *A. macrophyllum* var. *Kimballi* Sudw. *ex* Harrar
= *A. macrophyllum* f. *Kimballiæ* (Sudw. *ex* Harrar) E. Murr.

From western Washington, in several counties. Leaves much more deeply lobed, smaller—to 16" wide. Proportional in its deep lobing to *A. saccharum* 'Sweet Shadow'. Floral / fruit parts often in trios instead of in the typical pairs. First noticed ca. 1912; cultivated <1927; named officially in 1940, after Mrs. Frank Kimball of Seattle, WA. Not in the nursery trade.

A. macrophyllum f. rubrum E. Murr.

Named in 1969, after botanist Edward Murray noticed it in 1968 at the Anson Blake garden near Berkeley, CA; it also grows on Berkeley University campus and nearby in the San Francisco Bay area. Perhaps cultivated to a minor extent in its region. Also reported sporadically in the Puget Sound region of Washington. Emerging leaves in late March and April are variably dark reddish or greenish-red, vividly contrasting with the yellow flowers, in the same manner as *Acer platanoides* f. *Schwedleri*.

A. *macrophyllum* 'Seattle Sentinel'

A fastigiate street-tree found in Seattle, noticed and named in 1951 by B. Mulligan. It has been grafted and distributed to some gardens but has not been available commercially to any noticeable degree. Records: 80' × 4'4" × 27' and 60' × 6'6" × 22' Seattle, WA (1988).

A. *mandshuricum* Maxim.

MANCHURIAN MAPLE. From E Siberia, Manchuria, and Korea. Introduced to North American cultivation in 1903 when the Arnold Arboretum got seeds from St. Petersburg. Very rare, but in the nursery trade since the 1940s. A close cousin of NIKKO MAPLE (*A. Maximowiczianum*), and similar in being a small tree (to ca. 30' tall) with trifoliate leaves, but the leaves are much less hairy to nearly hairless. Leaflets 2"–4" long. It flushes early, in some locales suffering from late spring frosts, and colors early in fall, turning pink or red. The bark is a major attraction, attractively peeling, pale brown. Mostly the tree grows markedly low and broad.

A. *Matsumuræ*—see A. *palmatum* ssp. *Matsumuræ*

A. *Maximowiczianum* Miq. *ex* Koidz.
≠ *A. Maximowiczii* Pax
= *A. nikoense* auct., non Maxim.

NIKKO MAPLE. From central China, and Japan. Discovered in Japan ca. 1862 by Carl Johann Maximowicz (1827–1891); collected in 1881 by C. Maries for Veitch nursery of England; C. Sargent sent seeds to the Arnold Arboretum in 1892. This species has remained rare in the nursery trade. The name NIKKO MAPLE refers to the town of Nikko in central Japan. Leaves trifoliate, bold and fuzzy, turning pink to orange or spectacular red in fall; leaflets 2"–6½" long. Male and female flowers usually on separate trees. Records: to 80' × 7'3" in the wild; 62' × 5'0" Sheffield Park, Sussex, England (1989); 32' × 3'¼" × 26½' Vancouver, B.C. (1994).

A. *Miyabei* Maxim.

From N Japan; rare. Japanese: *Kurobi-itaya*. Discovered by the Japanese botanist Kingo Miyabe (1860–1951). Cultivated in Germany by 1888 (the year it was named). C. Sargent introduced it to North America in 1892. Extremely rarely offered by nurseries. A small shade tree with an obvious resemblance to *A. campestre*, but much larger and pointier leaves (to 8" wide; stem to 7" long, with milky sap), hairy on both sides. Fall color varies from an unappealing golden to ordinary yellow. The gray, raggedly flaky bark is not closely chinky like that of *A. campestre*. Seeds hairy, spreading horizontally, borne on drooping terminal panicles. Records: to 82' × 10'4" in Japan; 69' tall and 51' wide at Lisle, IL (1986; *pl.* 1929); 59' × 6'0" Bedgebury, Kent, England (1986; *pl.* 1944); 36' × 3'6" × 38' Spokane, WA (1993).

A. *Miyabei* 'Morton'—see A. *Miyabei* State Street™

A. *Miyabei* State Street™
= *A. Miyabei* 'Morton'

Introduced in 1993 by the Morton Arboretum. Excellent habit and branching character.

A. *Mono*—see A. *pictum*

A. *monspessulanum* L.

MONTPELIER MAPLE. From S & C Europe, N Africa and the Near East. In North American commerce ≤1854. More grown in the early 1900s than in the last 60 years. In general this is like ENGLISH MAPLE (*A. campestre*) but has darker, smaller (1½"–3⅛"), less lobed, and glossier leaves. The seed wings are borne in parallel pairs instead of at 180° alignment. Its leaf stem is not milky unlike that of *A. campestre*. The dense foliage is so dark it looks evergreen; the leaves drop late without bright color. Records: 65' × 5'8" Paris (1982; *pl.* 1895); 57' × 4'7" × 43' Tacoma, WA (1988); 48' × 6'8" × 48' Seattle, WA (1988; *pl.* ca. 1916); 46' × 9'3" Greece (1994); 46' × 6'4" × 54' Tacoma, WA (1992); 42' × 7'11" × 46' Bellingham, WA (1992).

A. *montanum*—see A. *spicatum*

A. *morrisonense*—see A. *rubescens*

A. *Negundo* L.
= *A. fraxinifolium* (Raf.) Nutt.
= *Negundium fraxinifolium* Raf.
= *Negundo aceroides* Moench
= *Negundo fraxinifolium* (Raf.) DC.
= *Rulac Negundo* (L.) Hitchc.

BOX ELDER. MANITOBA MAPLE. ASH LEAVED MAPLE. PLAINS MAPLE. STINKING MAPLE. MAPLE ASH. SUGAR ASH. From much of the U.S., much of Canada, northern Mexico and Guatemala. The most widely distributed native *Acer*, in every contiguous state but Washington, Oregon and Maine—and naturalized there now. *Negundo* from the Sanskrit and Bengali vernacular *Nirgandi* or *Nirgundi* of *Vitex Negundo*, transferred to *Acer Negundo* because of the general leaf similarity. The name BOX ELDER refers to the tree having leaves reminiscent of those of ELDER (*Sambucus*), and that its soft, weak wood is used for making boxes. Leaf compound, with 3–7 (9) leaflets, the terminal one 2"–5" long. Flower sexes on separate trees. Seedling BOX ELDERS were once widely planted as fast-growing shade trees. Now mostly grafted cultivars are sold. The species is tolerant of difficult conditions, but does not age well in cultivation, posing problems such as breaking limbs. Still, the whole-sale condemnation with which some people dismiss it is unfair and narrow-minded. Records: 110' × 16'11" × 120' Lenawee County, MI (1976); 75' × 19'11" × 102' White Plains, NY (1951); 98' × 18'0" × 112' Livingston County, MI (1984).

A. Negundo 'Argenteo-variegatum'—see *A. Negundo* 'Variegatum'

A. Negundo 'Auratum'
GOLDEN BOX ELDER. First sold in 1891 by Späth nursery of Germany. In North American commerce ≤1911, yet still rare overall. Tree female; twigs green; leaves wholly golden-yellow. First rate: one of the best golden trees. Smaller than typical *A. Negundo*.

A. Negundo 'Aurea Elegantissima'—see *A. Negundo* 'Elegans'

A. Negundo 'Aureo-marginatum'
≠ *A. Negundo* 'Elegans'
Originated at Dieck's nursery in Germany <1885—the gold equivalent of *A. Negundo* 'Variegatum' in that its leaflets are bordered yellow-gold. A male clone. Very rare.

A. Negundo 'Aureo-variegatum'
= *A. Negundo* 'Goldspot'
Origin unknown; name published in 1859 in Belgium. First listed commercially in 1887 by Späth nursery of Germany. In Canada ≤1898; possibly not present in the U.S. until 1960 when the Arnold Arboretum imported it from England. Leaflets spotted yellow.

A. Negundo 'Baron'
Name registered in 1970. An exceptionally cold-hardy, seedless selection from Morden research station of Manitoba. Sold by Bailey nursery of Minnesota in the late 1980s.

A. Negundo 'Californicum Aureum'—see *A. Negundo* 'Odessanum'

A. Negundo 'Elegans'
= *A. Negundo* 'Elegantissimum'
= *A. Negundo* 'Marginatis Elegans'
= *A. Negundo* 'Aurea Elegantissima'
≠ *A. Negundo* 'Aureo-marginatum'
Of French origin <1885 (B.K. Boom says 1701). In Canada ≤1897; possibly not present in the U.S. until 1939 when the Arnold Arboretum imported it from England. Very rare here. Leaflets large, glossy, edged with yellow. Twigs with powdery bloom. Record: 47' × 7'4" × 48' Woodinville, WA (1992).

A. Negundo 'Elegantissimum'—see *A. Negundo* 'Elegans'

A. Negundo 'Flamingo'
Raised in Holland and introduced there <1977. In the U.S. trade by 1984–85. Young leaves bright pink, aging to green with showy white and pink variegation. A small tree or large shrub.

A. Negundo 'Foliis Albo-variegatis'—see *A. Negundo* 'Variegatum'

A. Negundo 'Goldspot'—see *A. Negundo* 'Aureo-variegatum'

A. Negundo 'Kelly's Gold'
Introduced in 1989 by Duncan & Davies nursery of New Zealand. Twigs glaucous; leaves gold, hairy beneath.

A. Negundo 'Marginatis Elegans'—see *A. Negundo* 'Elegans'

A. Negundo 'Odessanum'
= *A. Negundo* 'Californicum Aureum'
= *A. Negundo* 'Odessanum Foliis Aureis'
Introduced by H. Rothe's nursery of Odessa, Russia, in 1890. Young twigs densely white hairy. Leaflets light golden in the sun, green in the shade. Extremely rare in North America. Listed in 1993–94 catalog of

Arborvillage nursery of Holt, MO: "bright orange/ yellow foliage fading to light green as summer wanes on."

A. Negundo 'Odessanum Foliis Aureis'—see A. Negundo 'Odessanum'

A. Negundo 'Rubescens'

Known since 1893. In the U.S. since ≤1929, but extremely rare. A female clone whose young leaves are reddish. Twigs brownish-green when young, becoming violet and powdery-bloomed.

A. Negundo 'Sensation'

Introduced in 1989 by Schmidt nursery of Boring, OR: "brilliant red fall color; more controlled growth; improved branch structure."

A. Negundo 'Variegatum'

= A. Negundo 'Argenteo-variegatum'
= A. Negundo 'Foliis Albo-variegatis'

THE GHOST TREE. VARIEGATED BOX ELDER. This originated as a sport in M. Fromant's Tolouse nursery in 1845. Widely cultivated: by far the commonest BOX-ELDER cultivar. A female clone with the leaflets creamy-white variegated, sometimes wholly white. It reverts to normal green with age. Record: 48' × 6'0" × 49' Woodland, WA (1990).

A. Negundo var. violaceum (Kirchn.) Jäg.

Common in the Midwest and prairie regions. Twigs usually purplish and covered with a white bloom, instead of the typical dark green. A male clone sold as 'Violaceum' has handsome purplish flowers.

A. nigrum—see A. saccharum ssp. nigrum

A. nigrum 'Greencolumn'—see A. saccharum ssp. nigrum 'Greencolumn'

A. nigrum 'Morton'—see A. saccharum ssp. nigrum 'Morton'

A. nigrum 'Slavin's Upright'—see A. saccharum ssp. nigrum 'Slavin's Upright'

A. nikoense—see A. Maximowiczianum

A. oblongum Wall. ex DC.

EVERGREEN MAPLE. From the Himalayas, and SW China. Introduced first in 1824; then in 1831 Siebold imported it from Nepal to Holland; next in 1901 E. Wilson sent seeds to England. It was being grown in California <1900, and mostly has remained there as far as North American cultivation goes. Dryness, as well as extreme cold, hurt it. Leaves elliptic, unlobed but often 3-veined from the base, to 7" × 3"; thick, evergreen or semi-deciduous, dark and shiny above, pale beneath—pinkish-bronze when young in spring. Overall the leaves recall those of SWEETBAY, Magnolia virginiana. Flowers greenish-white to yellowish-green. Seeds sprout readily in California. Compare Acer Paxii. Records: to 80' × 6'3" in the wild; 41' × 5'4" × 39½' Los Angeles Arboretum (1993; pl. 1954; now dead).

A. oblongum var. biauritum—see A. Paxii

A. Oliverianum Pax

From China, and a subspecies in Taiwan. Presumably named after Daniel Oliver (1830–1916), one-time Keeper of England's Kew Herbarium. Discovered by A. Henry in 1888; introduced in 1901 by E. Wilson for Veitch nursery of England. Introduced to the U.S. in 1936 by the Arnold Arboretum. Virtually never in the North American trade, except recently offered in limited quantity and small sizes, as both seedlings and grafts. It has been likened to a slender, vigorous version of A. palmatum. Leaf 2½"–5⅜" wide, with five shallow lobes (sometimes two tiny basal lobes as well), sharply but subtly toothed; covered beneath with fine silky hairs. The greenish bark, and young foliage, have a bronze tinge. M. Dirr praises its tolerance of Georgia heat. It is late to flush in spring, and its fall color is late, turning clear yellow, orange, red or purplish. Records: to 80' tall in the wild; 46' × 4'3" Endsleigh, Devon, England (1990); 43' tall × (multitrunked) Seattle, WA (1994; pl. 1949).

A. Opalus Mill.

= A. opulifolium Vill.

ITALIAN MAPLE. From SW and C Europe, Italy to Spain. Introduced in 1750 when M. Richard brought it from Corsica to Paris. Then P. Miller introduced it from Paris to England in 1752, and named it in 1768. To North America ≤1863, it has remained very rare. "Opalus" is a misspelling of Opulus, an old generic name. Notable for its beautiful yellow flowers in March-April before the leaves emerge. Leaf 3–5 lobed, 2½"–5" wide, often hairy beneath; lemony to pale orange in autumn. Records: 88' × 7'3" Westonbirt, Gloucestershire, England (1988); 74' × 10'6" Balloon, Castletown, Isle of Man (1978).

A. Opalus var. obtusatum (Waldst. & Kit. ex Willd.) Henry

= A. Opalus ssp. obtusatum (Waldst. & Kit. ex Willd.) Gams

= A. obtusatum Waldst. & Kit. ex Willd.

NEAPOLITAN MAPLE. BOSNIAN MAPLE. From C & SE Europe. Introduced ca. 1805. Less rare than the typical version in cultivation; in Canada ≤1897; in the U.S. nursery trade ≤1900. Leaves hairier (felty beneath), usually larger, with short and rounded rather than acute lobes. The leaves can be as wide as 9¾" and tend to stay green until very late in autumn. The foliage has a droopy aspect. Fall color is mixed green, yellow and pink pastels, or murky gold and pale purple. Record: 62' × 10'3" Kew, England (1984).

A. opulifolium—see A. Opalus

A. obtusatum—see A. Opalus var. obtusatum

A. orientale—see A. sempervirens

A. palmatum Th. ex Murr.

= A. polymorphum S. & Z., non Spach

(SMOOTH) JAPANESE MAPLE. From SW China, Korea, and Japan. One of 21 species of Acer native in Japan. Reportedly introduced to England, "based on Loudon," in 1820. Certainly present in England by 1832, brought by J. Reeves. Offered by a California nursery by 1854. G.R. Hall brought dozens of cultivars to the U.S. in 1862. No tree species has been more variable in cultivation. Although the following 14 pages fully treat 126 cultivars and mentions 5 more, many are extremely rare. The present volume mostly excludes especially dwarf cultivars, as well as those for which no evidence or likelihood of commercial availability is known. A handful of nurseries specialize in these trees, and sell limited quantities of small specimens. Comparatively few cultivars are mass-produced by major nurseries. For more details, see the book *Japanese Maples* by J.D. Vertrees. *Acer palmatum* generally can be described as a shrub or small tree, with roundish 2"–3" leaves, 5–7 (9) lobed, that suggested the Japanese name "frog paws" (i.e., *Kaede*, from *Kaeru-de*—frog paws). Records: 56' × 4'6" Muncaster Castle, Cumbria, England (1984); 50' × 1'8" × 25' Seattle, WA (1988; now dead); 45' × 10'1" × 59' Riverside, CT (1987); 42½' × 10'10" Japan (1994); 42' × 8'1"

× 46' Seattle, WA (1988); 38' × 10'2½" × 55' Waikato, New Zealand (1970); 28' × 7'8" × 50' Ashton, MD (1972).

A. palmatum 'Afterglow'

Studebaker nursery of New Carlisle, OH, lists this in their 1991–92 catalog.

A. palmatum 'Aka Shigitatsu Sawa'—see A. palmatum 'Beni Shigitatsu Sawa'

A. palmatum 'Akaji Nishiki'—see A. palmatum 'Seigai

A. palmatum 'Akegarasu'

Known since <1882. Rare. Leaves large, deep purple-red, fading to bronze in summer. Tree strong, upright, broad yet short, only 12' tall. The name means "crows at dawn."

A. palmatum 'Albo-marginatum'—see A. palmatum 'Higasayama' and 'Matsugae'

A. palmatum ssp. amœnum (Carr.) Hara

= A. palmatum var. amœnum (Carr.) Ohwi

= A. palmatum var. heptalobum Rehd.

= A. palmatum var. septemlobum Koidz., non K. Koch, non Th.

= A. palmatum f. euseptemlobum Schwer.

SEVENLOBE JAPANESE MAPLE. This subspecies or variant was described first in 1853. Although botanists have disagreed over its proper designation, they are united in understanding what is meant by their names. Nurseries have scarcely employed any of the names, but trees fitting the description are seen labeled in arboreta, and unlabeled in landscapes. The trees are stocky and bear bold, broadly 7 (9) lobed leaves, with consistently rich fall color. The seeds, like the leaves, are larger than typical for *A. palmatum*. Many cultivars are referrable to this subspecies. The epithet *amœnum* is Latin for beautiful or charming. Seven lobes is indicated by Greek (*hepta-*) or Latin (*septem-*).

A. palmatum 'Aoba Fuke'—see A. palmatum 'Volubile'

A. palmatum 'Aoba No Fuye'—see *A. palmatum* 'Volubile'

A. palmatum 'Aocha Nishiki'—see *A. palmatum* 'Seicha'

A. palmatum 'Aokii'—see *A. palmatum* 'Versicolor'

A. palmatum 'Aoyagi'

Grown in North America since the 1950s, but rare. Normal shaped seven-lobed leaves; bright green attractive young bark. Yellow fall color. Dense twiggy habit, 6'–15' tall. The name means "the green coral"—referring to its bark being as notable in its greenness, as is the bright coral color of the common CORALBARK MAPLE, *Acer palmatum* 'Sango Kaku'.

A. palmatum 'Arakawa'
= *A. palmatum* 'Ganseki Momiji'

ROUGHBARK JAPANESE MAPLE. Very rare. Typical green leaves. Bark corky, rough. Vigorous, upright to 15' tall or more.

A. palmatum 'Argenteo Maculatum'—see *A. palmatum* 'Versicolor'

A. palmatum 'Argenteo-marginatum'—see *A. palmatum* 'Higasayama' and 'Matsugae'

A. palmatum 'Asahi Juru'—see *A. palmatum* 'Asahi Zuru'

A. palmatum 'Asahi Kaede'—see *A. palmatum* 'Asahi Zuru'

A. palmatum 'Asahi Zuru'
= *A. palmatum* 'Asahi Juru'
= *A. palmatum* 'Asahi Kaede'

Grown since ≤1938. One of the more common and dependable variegated cultivars. Emerging leaves red, becoming green variegated with with fiery pink or bright scarlet and white. Poor in full sun. To 10'–12' or eventually 25' tall. The name means "rising sun maple" or "morning sun interpreted in tapestry."

A. palmatum 'Atrolineare'
= *A. palmatum* 'Filifera Purpurea'
= *A. palmatum* 'Linearilobum Atropurpureum'

PURPLE RIBBON-LEAF JAPANESE MAPLE. Dark, nearly blackish-red spring foliage turns bronze, finally yellow-gold in fall. Uncommon, but in Western cultivation for more than 100 years. Being discarded in favor of the absolutely bushy **'Red Pygmy'** cultivar.

A shrub 5'–10' tall. Smaller than its greenleaf counterpart *A. palmatum* 'Scolopendrifolium'. Very similar to 'Scolopendrifolium Rubrum'. These are FINGERLEAF or RIBBONLEAF cultivars of *A. palmatum* f. *linearilobum*. The leaf lobes are very deeply divided, very narrow, scarcely toothed, and widely separated, thus appearing like five slender straps, often twisted at the end.

A. palmatum f. *atropurpureum* (van Houtte) Schwer.
= *A. palmatum* var. *nigrum* hort. *ex* Rehd.
(see also *A. palmatum* 'Nigrum')

REDLEAF, PURPLELEAF, or BLOODLEAF JAPANESE MAPLE. This is a group name applicable to any seedling or cultivar with markedly reddish or purplish leaves. More than 40 such cultivars exist. They are very popular and common. The most prized retain their color well without fading to dull bronze in summer. REDLEAF JAPANESE MAPLES were cultivated in Europe in 1857, and were introduced to the U.S. by Thomas Hogg sometime between 1862 and 1875. Records: 39' × 4'9" × 45' Tacoma, WA (1990); 35' × 8'11" × 48' Ambler, PA (1980); 30' × 6'11" × 49' Tacoma, WA (1990).

A. palmatum 'Aureo-variegatum'

Sold during the 1950s and '60s, but scarcely since then, because it is not well marked. Five-lobed leaves are barely variegated with indefinite markings of yellow or gold in the green background color.

A. palmatum 'Aureum'

SUNRISE MAPLE. Known since <1881; in the U.S. nursery trade by 1892. Uncommon. Leaves of normal shape, 5 (7) lobed, small, golden tinged (light green if grown in shade), pink edged in spring. Bright yellow in fall. Leaf stems and twigs red. A small, slender bushy tree 15'–20' tall.

A. palmatum 'Azuma Murasaki'
= *A. palmatum* 'Toshi'

Cultivated ≤1882. Rare. An *atropurpureum* cultivar. Leaf deeply divided, purple in spring, gradually bronzing, then greening, and in fall turning yellow, deep red and purple. Strong upright growth, forming an 18'–25' broadly rounded tree. Name means "purple of the East."

A. palmatum 'Beni Kagami'

Cultivated ≤1930. Very rare. An *atropurpureum* cultivar. Deeply divided, reddish leaf. Strong upright spreading to weeping growth, to 15' tall. Name means "red mirror."

A. *palmatum* 'Beni Kawa'

Introduced ≤1986 in Oregon. To 10' tall; a CORALBARK MAPLE, with twigs more intensely colored than on A. *palmatum* 'Sango Kaku'.

A. *palmatum* 'Beni Otake'

Introduced ≤1980. Greer nursery of Oregon offered this ≤1987: "10' tall; outstanding; new; upright, with unique bamboo-like appearance. Purple-red, narrow-leafed."

A. *palmatum* 'Beni Shichihenge'

('Beni Schichihenge', 'Beni Shishihenge')

Grown since ≤1960s. Less common and less lively than other variegated cultivars such as 'Butterfly' and 'Karasugawa.' Leaves blue-green, deeply 5–7 lobed, lobes narrow and often twisted, edged pink-white or nearly entirely bright orange-pink. Fall color can be that of a dried-up orange skin, or shades of yellow and lavender. A twiggy shrub or little upright tree to 12' tall. Name means "seven red apparitions."

A. *palmatum* 'Beni Shigitatsu Sawa'

= A. *palmatum* 'Aka Shigitatsu Sawa'

SAMURAI MAPLE. Sold by maple specialist nurseries. The red-tinted counterpart of the much more common (but utterly bushy) A. *palmatum* 'Shigitatsu Sawa'. Leaves variegated murky red, cream and green. Shrub or very small tree, 12' tall.

A. *palmatum* 'Beni Tsukasa'

Very rare; sold since ≤1980s by maple specialist nurseries. Leaves variegated: at first yellow-red to peach or pink with mottled green tones; in summer darker and partly variegated. A semidwarf, and slender, willowy shrub or small tree to 10' tall. Name means "officer in red uniform."

A. *palmatum* 'Bill Dale's Red'

An 'Osakazuki' seedling raised ca. 1980 by Wm. A. Dale of Sidney, B.C. Named in 1995. Noted for superior scarlet fall color. To be introduced by Island Specialty nursery of Chemainus, B.C.

A. *palmatum* 'Bloodgood'

Like its foliage, the history of this cultivar is shadowy. Probably it originated in the Bloodgood nursery of Long Island (established 1798). The name 'Bloodgood' has been in American nursery commerce since ≤1936. This clone has become one of the most widely grown and popular of the REDLEAF- or PURPLELEAF JAPANESE MAPLES (that is, of the *atropurpureum* cultivars). It features deep, fade-proof purple color, fiery red in fall. Grows 15'–25' tall.

A. *palmatum* 'Bonfire'—see A. *palmatum* 'Seigai'

A. *palmatum* 'Boskoop Glory'

Greer nursery of Oregon, since ≤1985, has sold this *atropurpureum* cultivar. It grows 15'–25' tall. Named after Boskoop, Holland, a region known for its many nurseries.

A. *palmatum* 'Burgundy Flame'

Millane nursery of Avon, CT, since ≤1991, has sold this *atropurpureum* cultivar, saying it grows 15' tall. It may be A. *palmatum* 'Sherwood Flame' renamed.

A. *palmatum* 'Burgundy Lace'

Distributed as early as 1947; sold commercially ≤1955, the year Vermeulen nursery of New Jersey listed it. Very common and popular. An *atropurpureum* cultivar with deeply divided purplish leaves. Twigs greenish. A small wide tree, 10'–20' tall.

A. *palmatum* 'Butterfly'

= A. *palmatum* 'Kocho Nishiki'
= A. *palmatum* 'Kocho No Mai'

First sold in 1938 by K. Wada nursery of Japan. A variegated cultivar, very popular and widely grown. Leaves smaller than typical, deeply divided, gray-green with much creamy white (and while young some pink) trim, giving a bright cheery appearance. Twigs purple. A shrubby little tree 7'–12' tall.

A. *palmatum* 'Chikuma No'

Extremely rare. An *atropurpureum* cultivar. Leaves deeply divided, large (to 7" wide), red-purple, turning greenish. Tree to 20' tall, of spreading habit.

A. *palmatum* 'Chikushigata'—see A. *palmatum* 'Tsukushigata'

A. palmatum 'Chishio'
= A. palmatum 'Shishio'
= A. palmatum 'Mosen'

Rare. Sold in the late 1950s by Kingsville nursery of Maryland, but superseded by 'Chishio Improved.' Leaves intense, brilliant red in spring as they emerge, routine bright green in summer. In this respect it is like the original *A. palmatum* 'Sanguineum'. A rounded shrubby 10' tree of slow growth. Name means "color of blood."

A. palmatum 'Chishio Improved'
= A. palmatum 'Shishio Improved'

Introduced ≤1965. Shocking fluorescent or neon pink young growth in spring. It really stands out in a collection. Shrubby and slow, but can make a petite 10' tall tree. Similar cultivars include 'Corallinum', 'Deshojo', 'Sanguineum', 'Seigai' and 'Shindeshojo'.

A. palmatum 'Chisio'—see A. palmatum 'Okushimo'

A. palmatum 'Chitoseyama'

Known in Japan ≤1882. Rare in North America; grown by maple specialist nurseries only. An *atropurpureum* cultivar. Leaves deeply divided, purplish in spring, then dark bronzy-green; bright red in fall. A mounding shrubby tree 7'–10' tall and wide.

A. palmatum 'Christie Ann'

Introduced ≤1991–92 by Handy nursery of Portland, OR. An *atropurpureum* cultivar, broader than 'Bloodgood'; leaf more finely cut. One of five new cultivars introduced by Bob Vandermoss of Portland, OR.

A. palmatum 'Coralliformis'—see A. palmatum 'Corallinum'

A. palmatum 'Corallinum'
= A. palmatum 'Coralliformis'

Introduced by Hillier nursery of England in 1900. Very rare. Emerging spring leaves thrilling shrimp pink or peach pink. Slow growing shrubby tree, 6' tall. The name 'Corallinum' is wrongly applied to 'Sango Kaku'.

A. palmatum var. coreanum—see A. palmatum 'Koreanum'

A. palmatum 'Crimson Prince' PP 7217 (1990)

Princeton nursery, New Jersey, calls this the hardiest *atropurpureum* cultivar; more vigorous than 'Bloodgood' and deeper red.

A. palmatum 'Crispa'—see A. palmatum 'Okushimo' and 'Shishigashira'

A. palmatum 'Crispum'—see A. palmatum 'Okushimo' and 'Shishigashira'

A. palmatum 'Cristata'—see A. palmatum 'Okushimo' and 'Shishigashira'

A. palmatum 'Cristata-variegatum'—see A. palmatum 'Higasayama'

A. palmatum 'Dalton'

Louisiana nursery of Opelousas, LA, 1992–93 catalog: "a selected, greenleaf strain that has exceptional fall color."

A. palmatum 'Decompositum'—see A. palmatum 'Hagoromo' and 'Koshimino'

A. palmatum 'Deshojo'

Rare; grown by maple specialist nurseries. Brilliant carmine-red young growth. A shrub or tiny tree 5'–10' tall. Superseded by 'Shindeshojo' (q.v.).

A. palmatum 'Discolor Versicolor'—see A. palmatum 'Versicolor'

A. palmatum var. dissectum (Th.) Miq.
= A. palmatum f. palmatifidum van Houtte
= A. palmatum var. multifidum Koch

LACELEAF MAPLE. THREADLEAF MAPLE. SPIDERLEAF MAPLE. Grown for centuries in Japan, first named *dissectum* by Western botanists in 1784, and cultivated after 1844 when Siebold introduced some to Holland. The varietal name *dissectum* includes more than two dozen cultivars, nearly all of them low, broad shrubs (and therefore not individually described in this volume). All have the leaves so finely lobed or dissected that the names THREADLEAF or LACELEAF are right on target. As a group they are extremely popular and common, but certain clones much more so than others. Their colors are as variable as those of regular *A. palmatum* cultivars. After decades, some become small trees. Record: 10' × 2'3" × 25' Cos Cob, CT (1988).

A. *palmatum* var. *dissectum* f. *atropurpureum* Vertrees

RED LACELEAF MAPLE. This name has been applied in a clonal sense, but is best used as a group name to indicate generally any red, purple or bronzy-colored *dissectum* seedling or cultivar. These selections are more common than green LACELEAF cultivars. Popular clones in this group are 'Crimson Queen', 'Ever Red', 'Garnet', and 'Ornatum'. Records: 15' × 3'1" × 20' Montgomery Co, PA (1980); 13' × 1'10" × 21' Tacoma, WA (1993).

A. *palmatum* var. *dissectum* 'Filicifolium'—see A. *japonicum* 'Filicifolium'

A. *palmatum* var. *dissectum* 'Seiryu'

= A. *palmatum* 'Seiryu'

Known since ≤1882; much grown since ≤1960s. Common. The only LACELEAF cultivar of upright rather than mounded or weeping shrub-like habit. Green in spring and all summer; in fall brilliant gold, or orange-yellow splashed crimson. Name means "green dragon."

A. *palmatum* 'Elegans'

Cultivated in the West ≤1874. Rare; grown by maple specialist nurseries. Leaves deeply divided, large, seven-lobed; yellowish in spring, green all summer; superb orange-red to yellow in fall. A short, broad tree 6'–10' tall.

A. *palmatum* 'Elegans Atropurpureum'—see A. *palmatum* 'Hessei'

A. *palmatum* 'Emperor One'

An *atropurpureum* chance seedling found by D.G. Wolff of Red Maple nursery, Media, PA. Observed for 30 years before being introduced in 1992. Perhaps as strong a grower as 'Bloodgood'.

A. *palmatum* f. *euseptemlobum*—see A. *palmatum* ssp. *amœnum*

A. *palmatum* 'Fascination'

Originated by Bob Vandermoss of Portland, OR. Introduced ≤1992–93 by Handy nursery of Portland, OR. Leaf finely divided, gold in spring, light green in summer, rich orange in late summer. Of rapid growth and tiered, spreading habit, to 15'–20' tall × 15' wide.

A. *palmatum* 'Filifera Purpurea'—see A. *palmatum* 'Atrolineare'

A. *palmatum* 'Fireglow'

Originated ca. 1977 by Fratelli Gilardelli, Omate Brianza, Milan, Italy. Introduced to North American commerce ≤1982–83. Being propagated by several major wholesale nurseries. An *atropurpureum* cultivar. To 20'–25' tall.

A. *palmatum* 'Ganseki Momiji'—see A. *palmatum* 'Arakawa'

A. *palmatum* 'Green Mist'

A seedling selected in 1949 by Prof. William H. Wolff. Registered in 1991. Introduced by Red Maple nursery of Media, PA. A sturdy weeping tree, light green in spring. Fall color bright chrome yellow mixed with intense red and some green.

A. *palmatum* 'Green Trompenburg'

An *Acer palmatum* 'Trompenburg' seedling selected by the late J.D. Vertrees, JAPANESE MAPLE expert. Registered in 1988.

A. *palmatum* 'Hagoromo'

= A. *palmatum* 'Sessilifolium'
= A. *palmatum* 'Decompositum' (in part; cf. 'Koshimino')
= A. *palmatum* 'Kakuremino'

Described in 1845, but still very rare; grown in the U.S. since ≤1938, but scarcely sold, and only by maple specialist nurseries. A weak, dwarf version of A. *palmatum* 'Koshimino' in effect. Leaf highly distinctive: small, dark green, essentially stemless, with five deeply divided featherlike lobes. Name means "dress of angels."

A. *palmatum* 'Hanaizumi Nishiki'—see A. *palmatum* 'Kasen Nishiki'

A. *palmatum* 'Harusame'

Grown since 1938 but extremely rare; offered by specialist maple nurseries. Leaf normal green all summer, but variegated subtly in autumn with yellow and red. Very inconspicuous usually. A large shrub 7' tall, at most a small 20' tree. The name means "spring rain."

A. *palmatum* var. *heptalobum*—see A. *palmatum* ssp. *amœnum*

A. *palmatum* var. *heptalobum* 'Elegans Atropurpureum'—see A. *palmatum* 'Hessei'

A. *palmatum* var. *heptalobum* 'Elegans Purpureum'—see A. *palmatum* 'Hessei'

A. palmatum 'Hessei'
= A. palmatum var. heptalobum 'Elegans
(Atro)Purpureum'

An atropurpureum selection cultivated in Europe
≤1893. Named for Hesse nursery of Germany. Leaves
deeply divided. A large shrub or small tree. Its color
is not pure enough (too much bronze and green), and
its propagation not easy, so it has not become common.

A. palmatum 'Higasayama'
= A. palmatum 'Hikasayama'
≠ A. palmatum 'Albo-marginatum'
≠ A. palmatum 'Argenteo-marginatum'
≠ A. palmatum 'Cristata-variegatum'
≠ A. palmatum 'Rosa-marginalis'
≠ A. palmatum 'Roseo-marginatum'
≠ A. palmatum 'Shinn's #2'

Known since the early 1800s. Rare; sold mostly by
maple specialist nurseries (often wrongly called by the
various names as cited above). An ugly variegated
little tree usually less than 12' tall. Looks like weed-
killer was applied to it. Leaves small, usually deformed, deeply divided into 5–7 lobes, of green, pink
and cream. Name means "Mt. Higasa: mountain to
the east."

A. palmatum 'Hogyoku'
Rare; in North America ≤1940; sold
mostly by maple specialist nurseries.
A compact stocky large bush, or
20' tall tree prized for deep
orange or pumpkin-yellow fall
color. Leaves seven-lobed. Name
means "precious stone."

**A. palmatum 'Hubb's Red
Willow'**

An atropurpureum cultivar named after Elwood
Hubbs, an outstanding grower of Riverton, NJ. Introduced ca. 1992 by Red Maple nursery of Media,
PA. The leaf is long, red and willowy, holding its
color well all summer. The growth habit is fastigiate.

A. palmatum 'Ibo Nishiki'

Very rare; in North American commerce ≤1960s;
sold only by maple specialist nurseries. A 20' tree
with regular-shaped bright green leaves; fall color
orange to crimson. Prized for its cork-like bark, noticed on older branches. Name means "attractive
warts."

A. palmatum 'Ichigyoji'
('Ichijoji')

Originated in the 1800s. Very rare; in North American commerce ≤1960s; sold only by maple specialist
nurseries. A broad, sturdy tree to 20' tall, looking like
A. palmatum 'Osakazuki' in the summer, but with
spectacular yellow-orange fall color. Leaf to 7" wide.
Name means "superlative conduct."

A. palmatum 'Iijima Sunago'

Extremely rare; in North American commerce
≤1970s; sold only by maple specialist nurseries. An
atropurpureum cultivar with weakly variegated,
deeply divided leaves. Leaves large, to 7" wide; in
spring red; in summer dark bronzy, sprinkled with
tiny green spots; in fall reddish-green, the veins
remaining green. A large shrub or small, rounded 15'
tree.

A. palmatum 'Inazuma'

Originated in Japan <1882. Very rare; in North
American commerce ≤1960s; sold only by maple specialist nurseries. An atropurpureum cultivar. Leaves
deeply divided, in spring intense purple red, in summer dark green; crimson in fall. A large shrub or
small, rounded 12' tree. Name means "the thunder."

**A. palmatum var. involutum—see A.
palmatum 'Okushimo'**

**A. palmatum 'Iseli Tobiosho'—see A.
palmatum 'Tobiosho'**

A. palmatum 'Itaya'—see A. japonicum 'Itaya'

**A. palmatum 'Kageori Nishiki'—see A. palm.
'Shikageori Nishiki'**

A. palmatum 'Kagiri Nishiki'
= A. palmatum 'Roseo-marginatum'—cf. A.
palmatum 'Higasayama'
= A. palmatum 'Roseo-variegatum'

Imported in 1860 by Siebold from Japan to Holland.
In North American nursery trade ≤1892. Common
for a variegated cultivar. Leaves small, often deformed; green, narrowly edged creamy-white and (in
spring especially) pink. A slow-growing tree to 15'–
18' tall.

**A. palmatum 'Kakuremino'—see A. palmatum
'Hagoromo'**

A. *palmatum* 'Karasugawa'

First sold ≤1930; rare; grown mostly by specialist maple nurseries. Leaf small, 5–7 lobed. Variegated pink and white, appearing in spring a very pronounced pink that creates a light, cheery effect. Good white and green summer aspect. Tree very small and upright, to 12'–25' tall.

A. *palmatum* 'Kasagiyama'

Origin unknown; very obscure, extremely rare; grown only by specialist maple nurseries. An *atropurpureum* cultivar, its leaves brick-red with subtle, reticulated greenish-brown markings; seven deep lobes. A shrub or small tree, perhaps to 20' tall. Name means "in shadow of mountain."

A. *palmatum* 'Kasen Nishiki'

= A. *palmatum* 'Hanaizumi Nishiki'

Extremely rare; grown only by specialist maple nurseries. Leaves small, deeply (5) 7 lobed, often deformed; pink or orange-red in spring, becoming green with indistinct creamy white and pink variegation. A shrub or small tree 5'–20' tall. Name means "layers of variegation."

A. *palmatum* 'Katsura'

Introduced ≤1970s. Uncommon. Semidwarf of shrubby, dense habit, to 10'–20' tall. Leaf five-lobed, bright yellow-orange in spring, becoming greener in summer; fall color yellow or orange to rose. Leaf stems red. Name means "a wig."

A. *palmatum* 'Ki Hachijo'

First sold ≤1960s; rare; grown only by specialist maple nurseries. Leaves (7) 9 lobed, green, with long, elegantly pointed finely toothed lobes; prominent white hair tufts beneath. Fall color yellow-golden with rosy tones. On older branches, its green bark has broken stripes of white. Large shrub or very small tree 12'–15' tall. Name means "Hachijo Island: yellow silk."

A. *palmatum* 'Killarney'

('Kilgarney')

Sold since ≤1987 by Greer nursery of Eugene, OR: "vigorous, to 10' tall; exceptionally bright green in spring; one and two-year twigs light green; like a green A. *palmatum* 'Burgundy Lace'."

A. *palmatum* 'Kingsville Red'

An *atropurpureum* cultivar from H. Hohman's Kingsville nursery of Maryland. Sunburn-resistant. Dates of distribution unknown. Extinct commercially.

A. *palmatum* 'Kocho Nishiki'—see A. *palmatum* 'Butterfly'

A. *palmatum* 'Kocho No Mai'—see A. *palmatum* 'Butterfly'

A. *palmatum* 'Koreanum'

= A. *palmatum* var. *coreanum* hort., non Nakai

Under this name, W.J. Marchant nursery of England sold selected seedlings from the 1930s into the '50s, which were characterized by excellent red fall color, even better, it was asserted, than that of A. *palmatum* 'Osakazuki'. Hillier nursery of England also sold the tree(s). The Arnold Arboretum obtained specimens from England in 1960. Greer nursery of Oregon sold specimens in the 1970s. The leaves are deeply (5) 7 lobed. The twig bark is notably dark.

A. *palmatum* 'Koshimino'

= A. *palmatum* 'Koshininu'

= A. *palmatum* 'Decompositum' (in part; cf. 'Hagoromo')

Rare; grown since the 1950s by specialist maple nurseries. Very similar to 'Hagoromo' but vigorous, 12'–20' tall—even 50' tall in ideal conditions and with great age. Each leaf consists of five "feathers" separate to the center; very short stemmed or stemless; pale bronze when young; green all summer; gold or red in fall.

A. *palmatum* 'Koshininu'—see A. *palmatum* 'Koshimino'

A. *palmatum* 'Koto No Ito'

Extremely rare; sold only by maple specialist nurseries. Classed as "almost" a *linearilobum* cultivar, with 5 (7) narrow segments, briefly red in spring, green all summer, yellow in fall. Shrubby, twiggy, to 12' tall. Name means "harp of string."

A. *palmatum* 'Kurabeyama'

Known since ≤1882. Extremely rare; sold since ≤1938 only by maple specialist nurseries. Leaf thicker and heavier-textured than most A. *palmatum* cultivars; deeply divided into seven lobes; rusty red in spring, deep green in summer, crimson in fall. Vigorous, broad, to 8'–10' tall and wide.

A. *palmatum* 'Laciniatum'—see A. *palmatum* 'Tsuri Nishiki'

A. palmatum f. linearilobum (Miq.) Vertrees
= A. palmatum var. linearilobum Miq.

STRAPLEAF MAPLE. FINGERLEAF MAPLE. RIBBONLEAF MAPLE. Cultivated in Europe since 1860. Far less popular than the *dissectum* cultivars. A group name that embraces about 10 cultivars, distinguished by leaf lobes extraordinarily narrow, long, widely spaced, little tapered, and scarcely toothed. Most make upright shrubby little trees, at most 17' tall. The most common cultivars are 'Atrolineare' (purple) and 'Scolopendrifolium' (green). A scarcely linear one is 'Koto No Ito'. A mere dwarf shrub is **'Red Pygmy'**. See also 'Scolopendrifolium Rubrum' and 'Villa Taranto'.

A. palmatum 'Linearilobum Atropurpureum'—see A. palmatum 'Atrolineare'

A. palmatum 'Lozito'
('Lozita')

An *atropurpureum* cultivar similar to 'Bloodgood'. Origin unknown. Grown in New England ≤1980; still in the trade. To 15' tall.

A. palmatum 'Lutescens'
Selected and introduced in 1928 by Hillier nursery of England. Very rare; grown since ≤1970s by North American specialist maple nurseries. A subspecies *amœnum* cultivar. Leaves large, seven-lobed, yellowish-green in spring, glossy green in summer, outstandingly yellow or gold in fall. Tree 12'–20' tall.

A. palmatum 'Machi Kaze'—see A. palmatum 'Matsu Kaze'

A. palmatum 'Marakumo'
('Marakum')

Rare; grown by specialist nurseries. In North American commerce ≤1950s. Leaves variegated, in spring bright pink to pale apricot, becoming pale green and translucent, dotted with creamy flecks. A bushy little tree to 15' tall. Name means "concealing cloud."

A. palmatum 'Matsugae'
('Matsugai')
= A. palmatum 'Albo-marginatum'
= A. palmatum 'Argenteo-marginatum'
Cultivated in Europe since 1869. Extremely rare; it

was offered in the 1960s by one maple specialist. Leaves small, deformed, deeply 5–7 lobed, variegated white and pink. Prone to reverting to pure green. A small shrubby tree to 13' tall. Completely superseded by better variegated cultivars.

A. palmatum 'Matsu Kaze'
= A. palmatum 'Machi Kaze'
Known in Japan in the early 1700s. Rare; grown mostly by specialist maple nurseries. Leaves deeply divided; stems to 2½" long. Spring leaves bronzy-red with greenish veins; in summer green; in fall golden and red. A stout 15'–19' tree, of broad, somewhat pendulous aspect. Name means "wind among the pine cones."

A. palmatum ssp. Matsumuræ Koidz.
= A. palmatum var. Matsumuræ (Koidz.) Mak.
= A. Matsumuræ (Koidz.) Koidz.

A botanical name not used horticulturally. Named after Jinzo Matsumura (1856–1928). One of three major A. palmatum subspecies, the others being: the bold-leaved ssp. *amœnum* (*heptalobum*), and typical A. palmatum. Subspecies *Matsumuræ* gives rise to more cultivars than the other two. It has larger leaves than typical A. palmatum, and they are prominently incised serrated and usually deeply lobed—in a word, more elegant. The undersides are conspicuously shiny and often feature white tufts of hairs.

A. palmatum 'Matsu Yoi'
Extremely rare; grown only by specialist maple nurseries. Leaf large (4"), twisted, seven-lobed; yellowish-green in spring, bright green in summer, pale yellow or orange in fall. A 20' tall vigorous weeping tree. Name means "elegant pine."

A. palmatum 'Minus'—see A. palmatum 'Shishigashira'

A. palmatum 'Moonfire'
An *atropurpureum* cultivar selected by Richard P. Wolff of Red Maple nursery, Media, PA. It was a chance seedling at the nursery. Registered in 1978. Leaves large, of rare darkness, persisting even into September. Growth slower and not as strong as 'Bloodgood'. To 8' tall or more.

A. palmatum 'Mosen'—see *A. palmatum* 'Chishio'

A. palmatum 'Mt. Lelman S.'

Origin unknown. In the trade ≤1990s. Extremely rare. Possibly not purebred *A. palmatum*, but a hybrid or another species. Leaves roundish, extremely fine toothed, nine-lobed, silvery-hairy in spring. The lowermost lobes point straight down parallel with the leaf stem, which is hairy at least in spring.

A. palmatum var. *multifidum*—see *A. palmatum* var. *dissectum*

A. palmatum 'Murogawa'

Very rare; in North American cultivation ≤1940. An *atropurpureum* cultivar. Young leaves striking orange-red, then rusty green, finally deep green. Fall color pure yellow to orange-red to crimson. A short broad tree, 10' tall.

A. palmatum 'Musashino—see *A. palmatum* 'Nomura'

A. palmatum var. *nigrum* —see *A. palmatum* f. *atropurpureum*

A. palmatum 'Nigrum'

An *atropurpureum* cultivar, marketed in the U.S. between ≤1915 and 1949, but scarcely since then. Leaves seven-lobed, very dark before fading to bronze, then becoming bright red or crimson in fall.

A. palmatum "Nishiki Sho"—see *A. palmatum* 'Arakawa'

A. palmatum 'Nomura'
= *A. palmatum* 'Musashino'

An *atropurpureum* cultivar, grown in Japan since the 1600s. Some nurseries have listed 'Mushashino' and 'Nomura' as separate clones, but the late J.D. Vertrees, JAPANESE MAPLE expert, found the two names properly refer to only one clone. Leaves deeply lobed, purple-red, with sparse silvery hairs while young; crimson fall color. Tree to 24' tall, broad.

A. palmatum 'Nomura Nishiki'

Dissimilar cultivars have been sold under this name. The name dates from ≤1896 when it described a variant with "leaves green, blotched yellow." But in North America, 'Nomura Nishiki' has been applied to a different cultivar since the 1950s. According to the late J.D. Vertrees, JAPANESE MAPLE expert, 'Nomura Nishiki' of the U.S. nursery trade is an *atropurpureum* cultivar with a deeply divided leaf, red in spring, green in summer, orange and red in fall. It can be a mere 4' shrub or reach 18' eventually. Name means "beautiful tapestry."

A. palmatum 'Novum'

An *atropurpureum* cultivar dating from 1914, when listed by Koster nursery of Holland. Sold sparingly in North America, and scarcely at all since the 1950s. Light purple-red in spring, gradually becoming bronzy-green, then scarlet in fall. Fast to 25' tall or more.

A. palmatum 'Nuresagi'

An *atropurpureum* cultivar from Japan ≤1882. Grown in North America since ≤1966. Leaves large, seven-lobed, deeply cut, very dark purplish, veins red. It can be as lovely red as *A. palmatum* 'Osakazuki' in autumn. Makes a short broad 18' tree. Name means "wet heron."

A. palmatum 'Ogi Nagashi'—see *A. palmatum* 'Ogino Nagare'

A. palmatum 'Ogino Nagare'
= *A. palmatum* 'Ogi Nagashi'

Very rare; grown in 1950s and '60s by specialist nurseries. Weakly variegated green and pale green to cream. Leaves five-lobed. Fall color yellow or gold. Vigorous small tree to 15' tall or more.

A. palmatum 'Ogon Sarasa'
('Ogona Sarasa')

Rare; grown by specialist maple nurseries. Leaves in spring colored brick-red with greenish veins; in summer green; in fall wan yellow to orange and crimson. A shrub, or small, wide 18' tree. The name means "gold calico cloth."

A. palmatum 'Ohsakazuki'—see *A. palmatum* 'Osakazuki'

A. palmatum 'O Kagami'

Known since ≤1930. Rare; offered primarily by maple specialist nurseries. An *atropurpureum* cultivar. Leaves are seven-lobed, blackish purple in spring, greener by late summer; red or scarlet in fall. The lobes are nearly overlapping near the leaf stem. A small tree of outstanding vigor and hardiness. Name means "big mirror."

A. palmatum 'Okushimo'

= A. palmatum 'Crispa'
= A. palmatum var. involutum hort.
≠ A. palmatum 'Chisio'
≠ A. palmatum 'Crispum'
≠ A. palmatum 'Cristata'
≠ A. palmatum 'Shishio'

Known since 1700s; uncommon, highly distinctive. Leaf small, dark, 5–7 lobed, with edges curled up, giving the plant a thirsty appearance. Fall color yellow or gold. Tree narrowly upright, to 30' tall or more. Name means "Chinese" or "the pepper and salt leaf."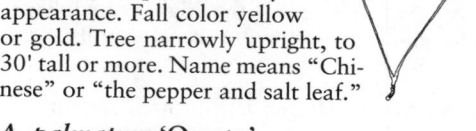

A. palmatum 'Omato'

Rare; grown by specialist maple nurseries. In North American commerce ≤1940s. A subspecies amœnum cultivar recalling 'Osakazuki', with large 5–7 lobed leaves coloring fiery red in fall. A stout tree to 20' tall. Name means "a fine target."

A. palmatum 'Omurayama'

('Omuroyama')

Uncommon; grown mostly by specialist maple nurseries. In commerce ≤1938. Leaf deeply divided, green in summer, gold or red in fall, hanging down laxly. Tree very gracefully pendent, 10'–18' tall and still wider. Name means "village on a mountain."

A. palmatum 'Orido Nishiki'

= A. palmatum 'Oridono Nishiki'

Dating from ≤1896; uncommon. Leaves small, often deformed, variegated green, pink and white. A 10' shrub, or eventually small rounded 18' tree. Name means "folding tapestry screen."

A. palmatum 'Osakazuki'

= A. palmatum 'Ohsakazuki'
= A. palmatum 'Taihai'

Dating from ≤1861; pitifully uncommon. A subspecies amœnum cultivar with fall color as good, or better than, any tree. Leaves large, to 8¼" wide, (5) 7 lobed, coloring intense brilliant crimson in fall. A short, stout tree to 18' tall. Name means "a wine cup; a toast."

A. palmatum 'Oshio Beni'

= A. palmatum 'Oshoi bani'

An atropurpureum cultivar. Introduced in 1898 by Yokohama nursery of Japan. Common. Leaves deeply seven-lobed, very bright orange-red in spring but sunburning or fading to dull bronze; bright scarlet in fall. To 15' tall or more. Name means "great red tide."

A. palmatum 'Oshu Beni'

('Oshyu Beni', 'Oshiu Beni', 'Osyu Beni')

An atropurpureum cultivar easily confused nominally with 'Oshio Beni'. Sold in the U.S. since ≤1918, into the 1950s but rarely listed thereafter. Leaves 7 (9) lobed, at first bright red, then maroon, bronzy in summer, bright red in fall. Lobes scarcely toothed and very narrow. A short, rounded 12' tree.

A. palmatum f. palmatifidum—see A. palmatum var. dissectum

A. palmatum 'Purple Splendor'

An atropurpureum cultivar offered in 1985–86 by Handy nursery of Oregon. Compared to A. palmatum 'Bugundy Lace', it is "brighter red and less serrated."

A. palmatum 'Red Select'

This name has been applied to atropurpureum selections by various nurseries. It signifies that the nursery in question has either choosen superior redleaf seedlings, or has selected one to graft.

A. palmatum 'Redspray'

An atropurpureum cultivar offered in 1991–92 by Handy nursery of Oregon. Selected for superior habit. Thick branches form an upright, well-balanced crown. Fall color bright red-orange, superior to that of 'Bloodgood'. Grows to 20' tall and 15' wide.

A. palmatum 'Ribesifolium'—see A. palmatum 'Shishigashira'

A. palmatum 'Rosa-marginalis'—see A. palmatum 'Higasayama'

A. palmatum 'Roseo Maculatum'—see A. palmatum 'Versicolor'

A. palmatum 'Roseo-marginatum'—see A. palmatum 'Higasayama' and 'Kagiri Nishiki'

A. palmatum 'Roseo-variegatum'—see A. palmatum 'Kagiri Nishiki'

A. palmatum 'Rubrum'

An *atropurpureum* cultivar. This name is used in two ways. In the narrow sense 'Rubrum' refers to an *A. palmatum* ssp. *amœnum* clone with seven-lobed large leaves, dark maroon-red, fading to bronze, with a finale of strong crimson fall color. But in broad usage the name is equivalent to *A. palmatum* f. *atropurpureum* 'Red Select'—i.e., used by nurseries to designate whatever clone of *atropurpureum* is deemed best. The latter usage of 'Rubrum' (Latin for red) was sanctioned, as it were, when *Standardized Plant Names* (1923) suggested that any REDLEAF JAPANESE MAPLE could be so named.

A. palmatum 'Rufescens'

An *atropurpureum* cultivar originally described in 1888. More grown in Europe than in North America. Overall it is very rare here. Leaves deeply (7) 9 lobed, brownish-red, then greener; orange and crimson in fall. A large shrub, possibly a broad small tree.

A. palmatum 'Saku'—see A. palmatum 'Shigarami'

A. palmatum 'Samidare'

Known since 1882. Extremely rare; grown only by specialist maple nurseries. Leaf large (to 5½"), (5) 7 (8) lobed; conspicuously hairy in spring; orange, red and green in fall. A shrub or little tree 7'–12' tall and much broader. Name means "long rain in June."

A. palmatum 'Sango Kaku'

= *A. palmatum* 'Senkaki'
≠ *A. palmatum* 'Corallinum'

CORALBARK MAPLE. Grown increasingly since ≤1940s; becoming common. Leaf small, pale green in spring, green in summer, plain yellow-gold in fall. Twigs bright coral-red, especially showy on young vigorous growth; less ornamental as the tree ages and the twigs become short and thin. Name means "coral pillars." (It may be that 'Senkaki' is an old cultivar, and 'Sango Kaku' a newer, improved version.) Record: 27' × 2'2" × 25' Tacoma, WA (1993).

A. palmatum 'Sanguineum'

The original usage of this name applied to a clone Siebold imported from Japan to Holland <1864. It had five-lobed leaves that emerged blood-red and later turned green. There are reports that 'Sanguineum' was imported to the U.S. in March 1862. Yet the name was not published until 1867. A California nursery listed it in 1892. By and by, an *atropurpureum* cultivar (likely 'Rubrum') with seven-lobed leaves that remained purplish all summer was much grown under the name 'Sanguineum'. This usage has prevailed in North American commerce, especially since the 1970s. Since it is practically impossible now to identify a single clone as 'Sanguineum', perhaps the name should be discontinued.

A. palmatum 'Scolopendrifolium'

STRAPLEAF MAPLE. FINGERLEAF MAPLE. RIBBONLEAF MAPLE. The least rare greenleaf cultivar of the *linearilobum* group. Leaves deeply divided into five long narrow fingerlike lobes. In early summer the red seeds are very lovely against the bright green foliage. Fall color golden to dark red. Vigorous shrub or 17' tree.

A. palmatum 'Scolopendrifolium Rubrum'

Extremely rare; sold in North America since ≤1892, but since the late 1950s scarcely listed even by maple specialist nurseries. A cultivar of the *linearilobum* group, very similar to and doubtless confused with 'Atrolineare' (which has narrower lobes). Leaves deeply divided into five (seven) long narrow fingerlike lobes. Red in spring and early summer, becoming bronzy later. Fall color red. A shrub 10' tall.

A. palmatum 'Seicha'

= *A. palmatum* 'Aocha Nishiki'

Old, but extremely rare, and deservedly so, because so weakly variegated. Creamy-white variegation, tinted rose when young. Often the variegation is nonexistent or weak, such as limited to the midrib. A short, broad little tree, to 6' tall.

A. palmatum 'Seigai'

= *A. palmatum* 'Bonfire'
= *A. palmatum* 'Seigai'
= *A. palmatum* 'Akaji Nishiki' *sensu* Vertrees

An old, well known cultivar featuring glowing bright red spring leaf color, from a distance recalling the effect of a red-flowering CRABAPPLE tree, or looking like fall color in April and early May. The summer foliage is subdued bronzy green, and again erupts into red in autumn. Large shrub or small tree, 15' tall. Leaves small, mostly with five deep lobes.

A. palmatum 'Seiryu'—see A. palmatum var. dissectum 'Seiryu'

A. palmatum 'Senkaki'—see A. palmatum 'Sango Kaku'

A. palmatum var. septemlobum—see A. palmatum ssp. amœnum

A. palmatum 'Sessilifolium'—see *A. palmatum* 'Hagoromo'

A. palmatum 'Sherwood Flame'

An *atropurpureum* 'Burgundy Lace' seedling originated ca. 1950 by Will J. Curtis of Sherwood, OR. Registered in 1972. Vigorous, upright. Purple color lasts well even in full sun. To 15' tall.

A. palmatum 'Shigarami'

= *A. palmatum* 'Saku'

Known since 1700s. Extremely rare; grown only by specialist maple nurseries. Leaf seven-lobed; yellow-green with lobe tips purplish during spring; pure green in summer; yellow, orange and red in fall. A 12' tall small tree. A similar clone, 'Tana' has broader, shallower lobes. Name means "boat posts."

A. palmatum 'Shikageori Nishiki'

= *A. palmatum* 'Kageori Nishiki'
≠ *A. palmatum* 'Kagiri Nishiki'

Known since 1700s. Very rare in North America; present since ≤1941; grown by maple specialist nurseries only. Leaves bronzy in spring, with indistinct variegation of greenish margins and veins. By fall a brown, red and pastel carmine variegation pattern can become noticeable; or, in shade, it can be a nondescript green. Leaf seven-lobed. A large shrub or very small tree to 10' tall.

A. palmatum 'Shikishigata'—see *A. palmatum* 'Tsukushigata'

A. palmatum 'Shindeshojo'

Rare; grown mostly by maple specialist nurseries. An improved, brighter 'Deshojo' variant that tends to be more dwarfed but has been recorded to 12' tall. Leaves small, 5–7 lobed, in spring pure bright crimson scarlet or fire-engine red. Name means "new 'Deshojo'."

A. palmatum 'Shinn's #2'—see *A. palmatum* 'Higasayama'

A. palmatum 'Shishigashira'

= *A. palmatum* 'Ribesifolium' ('Ribescifolium')
= *A. palmatum* 'Minus'
≠ *A. palmatum* 'Crispa'
≠ *A. palmatum* 'Crispum'
≠ *A. palmatum* 'Cristata'

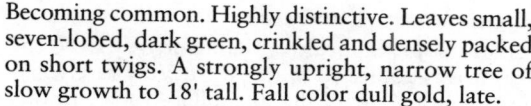

CRESTED MAPLE. LION'S MANE MAPLE. Cultivated in Europe ≤1871. Imported to the U.S. ≤1940. Rare here until the late 1950s.

Becoming common. Highly distinctive. Leaves small, seven-lobed, dark green, crinkled and densely packed on short twigs. A strongly upright, narrow tree of slow growth to 18' tall. Fall color dull gold, late.

A. palmatum 'Shishio'—see *A. palmatum* 'Chishio' and 'Okushimo'

A. palmatum 'Shishio Improved'—see *A. palm.* 'Chishio Improved'

A. palmatum 'Shojo'

An *atropurpureum* cultivar. In commerce ≤1930 but rare. Leaves five-lobed, very dark, holding their color well. A broad small tree.

A. palmatum 'Shojo Nomura'

Very rare; grown since the 1970s, mostly by maple specialist nurseries. An *atropurpureum* cultivar with deeply divided leaves which are mottled orange-red. Fall color brilliant crimson. A shrub or 6'–12' somewhat weeping tree.

A. palmatum 'Sinuatum'—see *A. palmatum* 'Yezo Nishiki'

A. palmatum 'Suminagashi'

In commerce since ≤1930 but uncommon. An *atropurpureum* cultivar. Leaves deeply divided, large, purple-red and hairy in spring, changing to deep maroon, fading bronzy-green, becoming crimson in fall. A vigorous shrub or broad tree, to 12'–20' tall. Name means: "the art of marbling: a butterfly."

A. palmatum 'Superbum'

An *atropurpureum* cultivar dating from ≤1938, the year Japanese nurseryman K. Wada described it as "bright red, vivid and semi-transparent, turning deep purple in summer." Scarcely known in North America ≤1968. Leaves primarily seven-lobed. To 20' tall and as broad.

A. palmatum 'Taihai'—see *A. palmatum* 'Osakazuki'

A. palmatum 'Tana'

Grown since 1960s, only by maple specialist nurseries; very rare. Leaf (5) 7 (9) lobed, bright green with reddish tips in spring. Gold to red in fall. Similar to 'Shigarami' but less deeply and narrowly lobed. A broad tree 15'–25' tall. Name means "shelves" or "layers."

A. palmatum 'Tanabata'

An *atropurpureum* cultivar dating from <1911, the year it was published in the West. Very rare. Confused routinely with the dissimilar 'Tana'. Leaves dark purple, deeply seven-lobed. Tree small and rounded, to 10'–15' tall.

A. palmatum 'The Bishop'

An *atropurpureum* cultivar from H. Hohman's Kingsville nursery of Maryland. Likely offered until the 1960s; now commercially extinct. Lasting purplish color, not bronzing until late summer.

A. palmatum 'Tobiosho'

= A. palmatum ' Iseli Tobiosho'

Selected in 1982 by Milt Tobie, production manager at Iseli nursery of Boring, OR. Typical *A. palmatum* habit and foliage, but fall color of "unmatched electric scarlet."

A. palmatum 'Toshi'—see A. palmatum 'Azuma Murasaki'

A. palmatum 'Trompenburg'

An *atropurpureum* cultivar from 1965 at Trompenburg arboretum in Rotterdam, Holland. Offered since ≤1976 in North America. Leaves deeply divided, purplish, each narrow lobe rolled under. A large shrub or small tree 8'–25' tall.

A. palmatum 'Tsukushigata'

= A. palmatum 'Chikushigata'
= A. palmatum 'Shikishigata'

An *atropurpureum* cultivar from Japan ≤1882. Very rare. Leaves seven-lobed, deep purple. Chartreuse-colored seeds. A broad low tree, to 20' tall only after 50 years.

A. palmatum 'Tsuma Beni'

= A. palmatum 'Tsumebeni'

Known since 1882. Very rare; grown since the 1940s, only by specialist nurseries. Leaves 5–7 lobed, light green with *reddish tips* in spring. Red fall color. Similar to 'Shigarami', 'Tana' and 'Tsuma Gaki' but only a twiggy 7' shrub. Name means "red nail."

A. palmatum 'Tsuma Gaki'

('Tsuma Gari')

Uncommon; grown since 1882. Leaves 5 (7) lobed, drooping, bright green with reddish tips in spring (looking like they were dipped in blood). Bright red in fall. A small tree 6'–12' tall. Name means "nails of the prankster or devil."

A. palmatum 'Tsumebeni'—see A. palmatum 'Tsuma Beni'

A. palmatum 'Tsuri Nishiki'

= A. palmatum 'Laciniatum'

Very rare; sold since the 1880s, but only by maple specialist nurseries. Leaves conspicuously roughly toothed, with (5) 7 (9) narrow dark green lobes, whitish tufts of hairs beneath. Fall color brilliant yellow, orange-gold, and sometimes crimson. A broad shrub or small 12' tree.

A. palmatum 'Ueno Yama'

Very rare; grown only by maple specialist nurseries. Leaf small, five-lobed, dark yellow to bright orange in spring, settling down to bright green in summer. A 24' tree. Name means "mountain top."

A. palmatum 'Ukigumo'

Very rare; grown only by maple specialist nurseries. Leaf small, five-lobed, variegated white and pink. A 10'–12' shrub. Name means "floating clouds."

A. palmatum 'Ukon'

Very rare; sold since the 1940s, only by maple specialist nurseries. Leaves 5–7 lobed, bright yellow, becoming yellow-green in spring, bright green in summer. Deep yellow and gold in fall. A large shrub 6'–9' tall. Name means "yellowish." Some plants so called are *A. palmatum* 'Aoyagi'.

A. palmatum 'Utsu Semi'

Known since 1882. Very rare; grown since the 1960s, only by maple specialist nurseries. Leaves shallowly seven-lobed, bright green; edges of young leaves tinted purple or red. Crimson and purple in fall. A large shrub or small 10' tree as wide as tall.

A. palmatum 'Variegatum'—see A. palmatum 'Versicolor'

A. palmatum 'Versicolor'

= A. palmatum 'Aokii'
= A. palmatum 'Argenteo Maculatum'
= A. palmatum 'Discolor Versicolor'
= A. palmatum 'Roseo Maculatum'
= A. palmatum 'Variegatum'

PINKEDGE MAPLE. Imported ca.1860 by Siebold from Japan to Holland. Sold in North America ≤1892.

One of the more widely distributed cultivars in North American nurseries. The leaves are variegated pink, cream and white; (5) 7 lobed, often deformed. A large shrub or small tree to 21' tall.

A. palmatum 'Villa Taranto'

Originated in Italy's Villa Taranto botanic garden; introduced in 1967 by C. Esveld's nursery of Boskoop, Holland. A *linearilobum* cultivar, shrubby to 12' tall. Young growth in spring bronzy-pink, turning green, then yellow in fall. Leaf divided into 5 linear lobes.

A. palmatum 'Volubile'

= A. palmatum 'Aoba No Fuye'
= A. palmatum 'Aoba Fuke'

Grown since ≤1893. Very rare; offered chiefly by specialist maple nurseries. Leaf 5–7 lobed, small, in spring light yellow-green, later darker; teeth exceptionally delicate. Markedly brilliant yellow to crimson fall color. A small dainty tree 8'–18' tall.

A. palmatum 'Waka Momiji'

Since ≤1966, this name has been used variously as a synonym of the CORALBARK MAPLE 'Sango Kaku', and to denote a variegated cultivar practically identical to 'Orido Nishiki'.

A. palmatum 'Whitney Red'

An *atropurpureum* cultivar sold since ≤1980 by in Oregon. Described as: to 20' tall; vigorous; outstanding deep red color; five-lobed, deeply divided leaves.

A. palmatum 'Wou Nishiki'

Rare; sold by specialist nurseries ≤1940s. Leaf deeply divided, (5) 7 lobed; reddish at first in spring, quickly turning green with bronzy-rose margins; then green all summer. Fall color red or pastel orange. A slender small tree to 12' tall. Name means "special brocade."

A. palmatum 'Yezo Nishiki'

= A. palmatum 'Sinuatum'

An *atropurpureum* cultivar from Japan before 1882. Rare. Leaves deeply seven-lobed, rich, bright reddish-purple in spring; fading to bronze, or greenish in shade. Either green and rosy, or at best brilliant carmine and red in fall. Fast when young, then very slow to 16'–20' tall or more, and as broad.

A. palmatum 'Yubae'

Registered in 1979 by the late J.D. Vertrees, JAPANESE MAPLE expert. An *atropurpureum* cultivar with deep red or purple leaves variegated light red to pink. Dense, upright; holds its color well. Since the variegation is not dependable and usually scantily produced, this cultivar has been offered very sparingly by nurseries.

A. palmatum 'Yugure'

Recorded in 1710 Japanese literature; grown rarely in North America since ≤1960s. An *atropurpureum* cultivar. Leaves deeply divided, seven-lobed; crimson in spring, rusty green in summer, magenta in fall. Upright round-topped tree 6'–12' tall.

A. Paxii Franch.

= A. oblongum var. biauritum W.W. Sm.

EVERGREEN MAPLE. From SW China. Discovered by P. Delavay in 1883. Named in 1887 after Ferdinand Albin Pax (1858–1942), a German botanist who published an *Acer* monograph in 1885–86. G. Forrest sent seeds to England but maybe he wasn't first to do so. In any case, compared to its close relative *Acer oblongum*, PAX'S MAPLE bears 2½" leaves prevailingly three-lobed, reminiscent of those of TRIDENT MAPLE, *A. Buergerianum*. It is also fully evergreen and more tender. Its seeds are reluctant to germinate. California nurseries have offered it since ≤1954–55. Record: 49' × 6'5" × 46½' Los Angeles, CA (1993; *pl.* 1955).

A. pectinatum Wall. ex Pax ssp. Forrestii (Diels) E. Murr.

= A. Forrestii Diels

From W China. *Acer pectinatum* is a variable species consisting of 5 subspecies. George Forrest (1873–1932) discovered this one in 1905, introduced it in 1906, and it was named after him in 1912. Some trees called *A. Forrestii* are really *A. Davidii* 'George Forrest'. The real FORREST MAPLE is indeed a STRIPEBARK MAPLE, somewhat tender, holding its leaves very late into autumn, then dropping them without flamboyant color. But this species is prized for its poise and summer color. Its leaf is strongly (rarely weakly) three-lobed, to 7" long, very finely toothed, at first rusty-hairy beneath, and its stems a lovely rhubarb-red. Exceedingly rare, but present in West Coast cultivation, and at least nominally, has been sparingly in the small-scale nursery trade since ≤1976–77. Records from Caerhays Castle, Cornwall, England (1984): 50' × 6'0" and 46' × 6'9".

A. pensylvanicum L.
= A. striatum Du Roi

MOOSEWOOD. STRIPED MAPLE. STRIPEDBARK MAPLE.
GOOSEFOOT MAPLE. WHISTLEWOOD. MALEBERRY. From
eastern North America—essentially the NE U.S. It is
an understory forest species; not just shade tolerant,
it suffers in full sunshine. Named MOOSEWOOD because deer, caribou and moose relish the opportunity
to browse it. George Emerson explained the name in
1850: "In Maine, it is called Moose Wood, the bark
and tender branches being the favorite food of the
moose, and, in their winter *beats*, it is always found
completely stripped." Its leaves turn bright yellow
early in autumn, and are soon shed. They are large
for the STRIPEBARK MAPLE clan, 5"–8⅝", similar in size
to those of *A. tegmentosum*. This tree has been much
planted, but is short-lived. Records: 77' × 4'2" Locust Valley, NY (1991); 65' × 4'6" Harlan County,
KY (1984).

A. pensylvanicum 'Erythrocladum'
First sold in 1904 by Späth nursery of Germany. Exceedingly rare in North America; in commerce here
≤1954. Its name derives from Greek *erythros*, red,
and *klados*, a branch—because its twigs in winter are
reddish-pink with white stripes.

A. pentaphyllum Diels
From Szechuan, China; very rare. Discovered in 1929
by J. Rock. In North American cultivation since
1938. Offered since 1993–94 by Buchholz &
Buchholz nursery of Gaston, OR. An elegant small
tree, ultimately vase-shaped. Young foliage (late to
appear in spring), pale bronzy-green; leaf stems red.
Leaves divided into (4) 5 (7) slender leaflets (hence
the name—from Greek *penta*, five, and *phyllon*, a
leaf). Fall color yellow or rarely orange. Not very cold
hardy. Record: 35' × 2'1" Occidental, CA (1995).

A. pictum Th. ex J.A. Murr.
= A. truncatum ssp. Mono (Maxim.) E. Murr.
= A. Mono Maxim.

PAINTED MAPLE. From much
of NE Asia. The name *Mono*
is a Japanese name. The name
Acer pictum was first
applied to a cultivar with
variegated leaves—hence the
name PAINTED MAPLE. That the
"variant" is nature's norm has no
bearing. In any case, this species was
introduced to Western cultivation by
Siebold to Holland in 1860. W.S.

Bigelow sent seeds in 1891 from Japan to the Arnold
Arboretum. The species and its varieties have remained very rare in North America. The leaves color
yellow in fall. The yellow varies from dirty to brilliant, and can color early or late. Tree varies from
slender and upright to mushroom-shaped. Bark taut,
smooth, gray or beige. Leaf highly variable, but primarily shallowly five-lobed, 3"–6" wide, stem to 3¾"
long and containing milky sap. The leaf can be wholly
hairless or quite hairy beneath. Seed wings vary from
horizontal to parallel. Records: 82' × 10'4" recorded
in Japan; 82' × 7'8" Hergest Croft, Herefordshire,
England (1985); 63' × 2'8" Seattle, WA (1994); 30'
× 4'11" × 35' Tacoma, WA (1990).

A. platanoides L.
NORWAY MAPLE. From Europe, to beyond the
Caspian Sea. William Bartram of Pennsylvania had
NORWAY MAPLE by 1756, but credit for its introduction to North America is attributed usually to 1784
and William Hamilton, also of Pennsylvania. One of
our most widely cultivated trees, its aggressive reseeding in parts of the continent has alarmed some native-
plant societies. The name "*platanoides*" is from genus
Platanus, PLANETREE or SYCAMORE, and Greek *-oides*,
resemblance. Still, scarcely anyone with general tree
familiarity could look at NORWAY MAPLE and thereby
be reminded of a SYCAMORE. Its leaves are broad and
thin, 5-lobed, rather "sharper-looking" than those of
SUGAR MAPLE (*A. saccharum*). Leaves measure 4"–7"
(10½)" wide, the longest stems 8½", containing
milky sap. Normal fall color is
yellow to golden; a few
cultivars turn orange
and reddish. The
seeds bear their
big thin wings at
180°. Records:
137' × 19'7" ×
116' New Paltz,
NY (1991); 102'
× 11'3" × 85'
Wayne County, MI
(1979); 98' × 25'3" Oslo,
Norway (1992); 65' × 24'0"
× 74' Lebanon County, PA
(1985).

A. platanoides Alberta Park™
Introduced ≤1989, said to be exceptionally cold-
hardy, as well as straight-trunked, vigorous, with a
well-balanced oval crown. Resists frost cracking.

A. platanoides 'Albo-variegatum'—see *A. platanoides* 'Variegatum'

A. platanoides Almira™
Discovered on a street in Cleveland by nurseryman Ed Scanlon in 1947; described in 1951; sold in 1955–56. A flat-topped, loose-umbrella form low tree to 16' in 30 years, eventually to 25' tall. Compared to *A. platanoides* 'Globosum' it is informal, sheds its leaves earlier, and makes seeds.

A. platanoides 'Argentea Variegata'—see *A. plat.* 'Drummondii'

A. platanoides 'Ascendens'—see *A. platanoides* 'Erectum'

A. plat. 'Atropurpureum Globosum'—see *A. plat.* 'Faassen's Black'

A. platanoides 'Bloodleaf'—see *A. platanoides* 'Reitenbachii'

A. platanoides Cavalier™ PP 2973 (1970)
Introduced in 1969 by Scanlon nursery of Ohio. Described as "very compact, roundish 32' tall and wide; the finest grower of any."

A. platanoides Chas. F. Irish™
Introduced in 1951–52 by Scanlon nursery of Ohio. Named for Mr. Irish (d. 1960), an arborist of Cleveland. Scanlon chose this as representative of the larger-growing NORWAY MAPLE selections, with a somewhat open, rounded crown of upswept branches, the leaf slightly smaller than average.

A. platanoides 'Clarkei'
Hortus III (1976) says this is similar to *A. platanoides* 'Drummondii'.

A. platanoides 'Cleveland'
= *A. platanoides* 'Columnar Pyramidalis'
This was the first of many trees selected by Ohio nurseryman Ed Scanlon, in 1946. It was grafted and described in 1948, and sold thereafter. Chosen as the best of seedling NORWAY MAPLES on a Cleveland street. Small, upswept branches make an oval crown slightly more compact than ordinary seedlings are apt to; leaf dark and large.

A. platanoides Cleveland Two™
Scanlon first observed this in 1958, and introduced it in 1960. Compared to 'Cleveland' it has much superior branching habit: its branches more closely spaced along the trunk, making a very dense compact head.

A. platanoides 'Columnarbroad'
= *A. platanoides* Parkway®
Introduced in 1970 by Schmidt nursery of Boring, OR. This selection is said to be a broader and faster growing form of *A. platanoides* 'Columnare'. In addition it is tolerant of verticillium wilt disease. M. Dirr suggests it may really be *A. platanoides* 'Erectum'.

A. platanoides 'Columnare'
?= *A. platanoides* 'Pyramidalis' (cf. *A. platanoides* 'Erectum')
Raised in 1855 by Simon-Louis Frères nursery at Plantières, near Metz, France. On sale by 1878–79. In North America ≤1896. Common. Two clones at least, have been sold under this name. 1) the original oval upright form 2) the broader form with branches more widely spaced and canopy more ovate than oval, wider below the center of the head than above it. The latter has been named 'Columnarbroad' and trademarked as Parkway. 'Columnare' is a dense narrow column with erect branches.

A. platanoides 'Columnar Pyramidalis'—see *A. plat.* 'Cleveland'

A. platanoides 'Compactum'—see *A. platanoides* 'Globosum'

A. platanoides 'Crimson King' PP 735 (1947)
= *A. platanoides* 'Schwedleri Nigrum'
= *A. platanoides* 'Faassen Red Leaf' (in part)
Several red-leaved NORWAY MAPLE seedlings arose ca. 1937 in the nursery of Tips Brothers, Herck-de-Stad, Limburg, Belgium. One was taken to Barbier nursery in France, and then introduced to the U.S. in 1947–48 by Gulf Stream nursery of Wachapreague, VA. It was registered as an *A. platanoides* f. *Schwedleri* seedling. It has become very common. Attributes are: deep blood-red leaf color that persists all summer. Slightly reduced vigor, less rapid-growing than typical greenleaf specimens; less cold-hardy. Extremely similar cultivars are 'Goldsworth Purple' and 'Royal Red'; more distinctive is 'Faassen's Black'. Record: 52' × 6'4" × 51' Steilacoom, WA (1993).

A. platanoides Crimson Sentry™ PP 3258 (1972)
Originated in 1970 as a bud sport of *A. platanoides* 'Crimson King' in the nursery of A. McGill & Son, Fairview, OR. Introduced commercially in 1972.

Foliage the identical dark purple color, but held in extremely dense, compact fashion, making a slow-growing tree, initially columnar. Leaf smaller than usual. Record: 18' × 1'10" × 15¼' Aurora, OR (1993; *pl.* 1975).

A. *platanoides* Crystal®

= A. *platanoides* 'Lamis'

Introduced in the late 1980s by Bailey nursery of St. Paul, MN. The clone is a selection made in Oregon by Max Lamis. Vigorous and straight trunked; better branched than A. *platanoides* Emerald Lustre®, with a lighter-colored leaf tip.

A. *platanoides* 'Cucullatum'

CRIMPLEAF NORWAY MAPLE. Described in 1866 in France (from Latin *cucullus*, a cowl or hood). In North America ≤1893; in commerce here since ≤1907 but very rare. It is a vigorous tree of normal size but erect shape, its leaves crinkled and cupped, shallowly-lobed, nearly circular in shape, with 7–10 fanwise veins. Records: 92' × 8'0" Westonbirt, Gloucestershire, England (1982); 78' × 6'8" Chester County, PA (1980); 71' × 6'2½' Vancouver, B.C. (1994).

A. *platanoides* 'Cutleaf'—see A. *plat.* 'Dissectum' and 'Lorbergii'

A. *platanoides* 'Deborah' PP 4944 (1982)

Selected by John Mathies in 1967 as an A. *platanoides* f. *Schwedleri* seedling. Introduced in 1975–76 by Cannor nursery of Chilliwack, B.C.. New leaves bright red, later dark bronzy-green; heavy growth habit like A. *platanoides* 'Emerald Queen'; upright tree with straight trunk; yellow-orange or bronzy in fall.

A. *platanoides* 'Dissectum'

= A. *platanoides* 'Palmatifidum' (cf. A. *platanoides* 'Lorbergii')
= A. *platanoides* 'Palmati-partitum'
= A. *platanoides* 'Cutleaf' (cf. A. *platanoides* 'Lorbergii')
= A. *platanoides* 'Palmatum' K. Koch 1869, non hort. *ex* Bean

CUTLEAF NORWAY MAPLE. Described nominally in 1829, officially in 1834, in Belgium. In North

America ≤1898; in commerce here ≤1910; rare. Low, bushy, with deeply dissected, ferny leaves. Like A. *platanoides* 'Lorbergii' except bushier, and the leaves emerge bronzy, later are dark green, glossier than those of 'Lorbergii'; divided nearly to the base. The leaf tips are straight or down-pointing, the margins crinkled. See also A. *platanoides* Oregon Pride®.

A. *platanoides* 'Drummondii'

= A. *platanoides* 'Variegatum' hort. Am., non P. Miller 1752
= A. *platanoides* 'Harlequin'
= A. *platanoides* 'Silver Variegated'
= A. *platanoides* 'Argentea Variegata'

HARLEQUIN MAPLE. Introduced <1903 by Messrs. Drummond of Stirling, Scotland. Rare in North America until the 1950s. The whole disc of the leaf is bright green, with a very deep edging of white. In severe climates it is best planted in a sheltered location. See also A. *platanoides* 'Variegatum'.

A. *platanoides* Easy Street™

= A. *platanoides* 'Ezestre'
= A. *platanoides* 'Schmidtall'

Introduced in 1992–93 by Schmidt nursery of Boring, OR. Discovered as an A. *platanoides* 'Columnare' bud sport that grows faster and slightly wider, to 40' × 20' (not 35' × 15').

A. *platanoides* Emerald Lustre® PP 4837 (1982)

= A. *platanoides* 'Pond'

Introduced in 1979 by Bailey nursery of St. Paul, Minnesota. Named after Donald Pond, production manager at Bailey's Yamhill, OR facilities. Mr. Pond selected it originally. Attributes are: superior cold-hardiness; vigorous growth; better branching habit than A. *platanoides* 'Emerald Queen'; glossy foliage, the leaves somewhat red-tinged, and cupped.

A. *platanoides* Emerald Queen™

= A. *platanoides* 'McGill No. 42'

John H. McIntyre of Gresham, OR, first observed this in 1959 as a year-old seedling. Introduced in 1962–63 by A. McGill & Son nursery of Fairview, Oregon. Rapid in both height and caliper growth, making a dense rounded head. Foliage reddish-purple tinted as it emerges, becoming distinctive dark glossy-green and leathery.

A. platanoides 'Erectum'

?= *A. platanoides* 'Ascendens'
?= *A. platanoides* 'Pyramidalis' (cf. *A. plat.* 'Columnare')

MT. HOPE MAPLE. Discovered by B. Slavin in Mount Hope Cemetery of Rochester, NY. Pyramidal, with short, stout, ascending lateral branches on an erect main trunk. When described in 1931 by Slavin, the tree was 32' tall and only 9½' wide. Its leaves are darker than usual, and larger, to 10" wide. This cultivar can be described as similar to *A. platanoides* 'Columnare' yet wider-growing, with darker, larger leaves. Dating from ≤1946, the name 'Ascendens' has been commonly applied either to 'Erectum' or to a cultivar that is similar yet grows substantially larger—in 40+ years of growth up to 64' × 8'1" × 47' Seattle, WA (1992; *pl.* 1949). Its lateral branches come out at practically right angles and then sweep upward.

A. platanoides 'Ezestre'—see A. platanoides Easy Street™

A. platanoides 'Faassen Red Leaf'—see A. platanoides 'Crimson King' and 'Faassen's Black'

A. platanoides 'Faassen's Black'

= *A. platanoides* 'Faassen Red Leaf' (in part)
= *A. platanoides* 'Atropurpureum Globosum'

This originated ca. 1937 along with *A. platanoides* 'Crimson King' as one of several seedlings at Tips Brothers nursery of Herck-de-Stad, Limburg, Belgium. Propagated and distributed ca. 1946 by J.H. Faassen-Hekkens nursery of Tegelen, Holland. In the U.S. since 1954. It differs from the more common 'Crimson King', being more open, with leaves (not conspicuously wrinkled while young) held rather horizontally instead of in a drooping way. The tree also does not grow as large. In brief, 'Faassen's Black' is, despite its name, not a heartlessly dense mass of solid purple as is 'Crimson King' and its virtual twins 'Royal Red' and 'Goldsworth Purple'. 'Faassen's Black' has much more of a bronzy-brown tinge, and looks comparatively open, as if pruned. Records: 59' × 2'4" × 31' Seattle, WA (1993); 47' × 6'6" × 51' Peace Arch Provincial Park, B.C. (1994); 40' × 6'8" × 41' Mt. Vernon, WA (1993).

A. platanoides Fairview™

Introduced ≤1985 by A. McGill & Son nursery of Fairview, OR. Found in a group of *A. platanoides* 'Crimson King' seedlings. Very rapid growing, very straight, more upright habit than either *A. platanoides* 'Deborah' or f. *Schwedleri.* New growth very dark purplish-red, turning bronze, then dark green; gold in fall.

A. platanoides 'Foliis Laciniosis Crispis'—see A. plat. 'Laciniatum'

A. platanoides 'Geneva'

First listed in a 1906 catalog from Shady Hill nursery of Bedford, MA, as a new form with crimson leaves. An Ellwanger & Barry nursery catalog from 1910 says "distinct purple-leaved variety. Foliage purple in autumn." A third description says: leaf lobes shallow; purple in autumn. This cultivar apparently has been extinct commercially since the 1920s.

A. platanoides 'Globe'—see A. platanoides 'Globosum'

A. platanoides 'Globosum'

= *A. platanoides* 'Compactum'
= *A. platanoides* 'Globe'

GLOBE NORWAY MAPLE. First offered in 1873 catalog of L. Van Houtte nursery of Ghent, Belgium. In Canada ≤1896; in the U.S. nursery trade ≤1903. Common. Crown globular, growth compact. Young leaves bronzy-green. A topgrafted dense flattened globe, making a formal little lollipop tree. See also *A. platanoides* 'Almira' for a compact cultivar featuring a less offensively solid mass of foliage.

A. plat. 'Globosum Atropurpureum'—see A. plat. 'Faassen's Black'

A. platanoides 'Goldsworth Purple'

An *A. platanoides* f. *Schwedleri* seedling, of English origin <1936. Introduced in 1947–48 by W.C. Slocock's Goldsworth nursery of Woking, Surrey. In North American nurseries ≤1957–58. Leaves dull, dark purplish above, green beneath with red veins; remaining dark purple all summer. Compared to *A. platanoides* 'Crimson King' its leaves are less glossy, and not red beneath. Scarcely any nursery still uses the name 'Goldsworth Purple' in North America, but the majority of trees sold as 'Crimson King' may actually be 'Goldsworth Purple.' Record: 28' × 2'4" × 26' Lisle, IL (1986; *pl.* 1957).

A. platanoides 'Green Lace' PP 2759 (1967)

Selected as a seedling in Oregon. Introduced in 1968–69 by Schmidt nursery of Boring, OR. A cutleaf/fernleaf cultivar apparently different from the other deeply-lobed NORWAY MAPLE variants 'Dissectum', 'Laciniatum' and 'Lorbergii'. Since 'Lorbergii' is said to come largely true from seed, this may be one of its offspring. See also A. platanoides 'Oregon Pride'.

A. platanoides 'Harlequin'—see A. platanoides 'Drummondii'

A. platanoides 'Improved Columnar'—see A. platanoides 'Olmsted'

A. platanoides Jade Glen™

Introduced 1968–69 by A. McGill & Son nursery of Fairview, OR. Rapid-growing; straight-trunked; branches spreading markedly wide to form a low, broad tree. Tolerant of verticillium wilt disease.

A. platanoides 'Laciniatum'

= A. platanoides 'Laciniosum'
= A. platanoides 'Foliis Laciniosis Crispis'

EAGLE'S CLAW MAPLE. The first NORWAY MAPLE cultivar. Mentioned in John Evelyn's *Sylva* of 1670: "the *Peacock-tail Maple*, which is that sort so elegantly undulated, and crisped into variety of *curles*." Introduced to cultivation ≤1683. Offered by Ellwanger & Barry nursery of Rochester, NY, in 1867–68, but overall exceedingly rare in North America. It is a slender upright tree; its main leaf lobes cut ⅔ towards the base, the leaf tips curved downwards like claws. Records: 62' × 1'0" Abbeyleix, Ireland (1986); 46' × 6'2" Wray Castle, Cumbria, England (1987).

A. platanoides 'Laciniosum'—see A. platanoides 'Laciniatum'

A. platanoides 'Lamis'—see A. platanoides Crystal®

A. platanoides 'Lorbergii'

= A. platanoides 'Cutleaf' (cf. A. platanoides 'Dissectum')
= A. platanoides 'Palmatifidum' (cf. A. platanoides 'Dissectum')
= A. platanoides 'Palmatum' hort. *ex* Bean, non K. Koch 1869

Introduced to European cultivation in 1866. In North America ≤1897, but very rare. Named after Heer Lorberg in Berlin. A broad, short-trunked, burly tree to 40' × 9'0". Leaves big, pale green, deeply cut, the main lobes mere wings at the base; lobes ending in upturned tips.

A. platanoides Lustre®

Carlton nursery of California and Oregon, 1993–94 catalog: "our budded selection of NORWAY MAPLE, consistent in size and branching."

A. platanoides 'McGill No. 1'

Introduced ≤1962–63 by A. McGill & Son nursery of Fairview, OR. It was sparingly sold and seems to have become commercially extinct rather quickly. Like A. platanoides 'Emerald Queen' but possibly less dense.

A. platanoides 'McGill No. 42'—see A. plat. Emerald Queen™

A. platanoides Medallion™

= A. platanoides 'Medzam'

Introduced in 1994–95 by Lake County nursery of Perry, OH. Broad oval, dense habit. Red and gold fall color.

A. platanoides 'Medzam'—see A. platanoides Emerald Queen™

A. platanoides 'Miller Superform'—see A. plat. 'Superform'

A. platanoides 'Natorp'

A dwarf, and small-leaved A. platanoides f. *Schwedleri* sport raised <1958 by W.A. Natorp nursery of Cincinnati, OH. It was discontinued because of its slowness of growth.

A. platanoides 'Nigrum'—see A. platanoides 'Reitenbachii'

A. platanoides 'Oekonomienrat Stoll'—see A. plat. 'Stollii'

A. platanoides Olmsted™

= A. platanoides 'Roch'
= A. platanoides 'Rochester'
= A. platanoides 'Olmsted Columnar'
= A. platanoides 'Improved Columnar'

Obtained in Rochester, NY, by Ohio nurseryman Ed Scanlon. Scanlon first sold it in 1954. His 'Olmsted' name dates from 1959. This clone is likely A. platanoides 'Erectum' renamed. Catalog descriptions of both 'Olmsted' and 'Erectum' read very much alike, and trees received by the Seattle, WA arboretum under the two names are identical. They start life as broad columns but grow eventually too wide to qualify as "columnar" in any reasonable interpretation. Nurseries whose catalog descriptions claim 'Olmsted' is narrower than *A. platanoides* 'Columnare' are highly suspect.

A. platanoides 'Olmsted Columnar'—see A. platanoides 'Olmsted'

A. platanoides Oregon Pride®

Pacific Coast nursery of Portland 1979–80 catalog: "Our special selection of NORWAY MAPLE having deeply cut leaves resembling those of a JAPANESE LACELEAF MAPLE." W. Wandell said in 1989: "Pacific Coast's Oregon Pride® is *A. platanoides* 'Dissectum'."

A. plat. 'Palmatifidum'—see A. plat. 'Dissectum' and 'Lorbergii'

A. platanoides 'Palmatipartitum'—see A. platanoides 'Dissectum'

A. platanoides 'Palmatum'—see A. plat. 'Dissectum' and 'Lorbergii'

A. platanoides Parkway®—see A. platanoides 'Columnarbroad'

A. platanoides 'Pond'—see A. platanoides Emerald Lustre®

A. platanoides 'Princeton Gold' PP 6727 (1989)

Introduced by Princeton nursery of New Jersey. A globe-headed (40' tall × 30' wide) goldenleaf clone that doesn't revert to green, or suffer sunburn in northern climates.

A. platanoides 'Purple Heart'

Cited in *Trees* magazine in 1951, for leaves red all season. Likely *Acer platanoides* 'Crimson King', 'Faassen's Black', or 'Goldsworth Purple'.

A. platanoides 'Purpureum Reitenbachii'—see A. plat. 'Reitenbachii'

A. plat. 'Pyramidalis'—see A. plat. 'Columnare' and 'Erectum'

A. platanoides 'Reimer's Red'

Cannor nursery of Chilliwack, B.C., 1975–76 catalog: "New." No description. Since the same catalog lists *A. platanoides* 'Deborah' and 'Royal Red' it is neither of those cultivars. Probably it was obtained

from Reimer's nursery of British Columbia.

A. platanoides 'Reitenbachii'

= *A. platanoides* 'Bloodleaf'
= *A. platanoides* 'Nigrum'
= *A. platanoides* 'Purpureum Reitenbachii'
= *A. platanoides* 'Youngii'

Originated as a seedling on the manor of J. Reitenbach of Plicken, Prussia, and named by J. Caspary in honor of its discoverer. Introduced <1874 by L. Van Houtte's nursery of Ghent, Belgium. In North American commerce ≤1903. Leaves emerge reddish, next become green, although the veins remain crimson, then gradually turn red in late summer and fall. Flower clusters red. Much confused with *A. platanoides* 'Rubrum' which has green flowers, green leaves in spring and red in the fall.

A. platanoides 'Roch'—see A. platanoides 'Olmsted'

A. platanoides 'Rochester'—see A. platanoides 'Olmsted'

A. platanoides 'Royal Crimson'

Scanlon nursery of Ohio 1967–68 catalog: "a selection from 'Crimson King', without a doubt, but the foliage seems to maintain a better red color during the middle and later summer when 'Crimson King' tends to turn a dirty purple."

A. platanoides 'Royal Red(leaf)'

Discovered by Martin Holmason in 1962 as a mutant branch. Introduced in Pacific Coast nursery of Portland, OR, whose 1963–64 catalog says: "rich dark red glossy leaves throughout the growing season; good tree form." Other descriptions in catalogs suggest this may be more cold-hardy than *A. platanoides* 'Crimson King'. Some trees going under the name *A. platanoides* 'Royal Red(leaf)' look like *A. platanoides* 'Faassen's Black' while others look like *A. platanoides* 'Crimson King'.

A. platanoides 'Rubrum'

Described in 1867 in Russia. In North America ≤1932, but rare. Leaves emerge green, with normal greenish flowers, but then the leaves become progressively redder or purplish-red culminating in autumn, whilst ordinary NORWAY MAPLES usually turn yellow. Much confused with *A. platanoides* 'Reitenbachii'.

A. platanoides 'Schmidtall'—see A. platanoides Easy Street™

A. platanoides f. Schwedleri (K. Koch) Schwer.

Originated in 1864. Described in 1869. In North American commerce ≤1886. Very common. Named after Carl Heinrich Schwedler (1807–1880), garden supervisor for Prince Hohenlohe of Slawentitz, Upper Silesia, Prussia (Poland). Leaves emerge red, turn green, veined purple, during summer, then purple, orange and crimson in fall. The yellow flowers contrast handsomely with the rich red leaves in spring. It comes largely true from seed, hence more than one clone has been circulated under its name. If the usage of the cultivar name **Schwedleri** is taken to be *clonal*, only the original seedling and its vegetative offspring are entitled to the name. But as presently defined, the term cultivar can include more than one clone. Records: 88' × 8'3" Tacoma, WA (1987); 77' × 13'9" Ladner, B.C. (1994); 73' × 12'2" Chester County, PA (1980); 62' × 11'0" Grimsby, Ontario (1974); one 13'4" around at Matinecock, NY (1972).

A. platanoides 'Schwedleri Nigrum'—see A. plat. 'Crimson King'

A. platanoides 'Silver Variegated'—see A. plat. 'Drummondii'

A. platanoides 'Stollii'
= *A. platanoides* 'Oekonomienrat Stoll'

First sold in 1889 by Späth nursery of Germany. Likely named after Rudolf Stoll (1847–1913), director of a garden at Proskau, Austria. Grown in North America ≤1896; in commerce here ≤1910, yet still rare. A seedling of *A. platanoides* f. *Schwedleri*. Leaf large, roundish, to 9" wide, dark bronzy-green, leathery, with three big, shallow acute terminal lobes, often toothless. Record: 95' × 9'10" Alexandra Park, St. Leonards, Sussex, England (1990).

A. platanoides Summershade™ PP 1748 (1958)

A seedling of an open-pollinated *A. platanoides* 'Erectum'. Introduced in 1958 by Princeton nursery of New Jersey. Rapid, upright growth; leaves large, leathery, dark, highly resistant to insect injury and scorching from hot dry weather.

A. platanoides 'Superform'
= *A. platanoides* 'Miller Superform'

Introduced in 1963–64 by Milton nursery of Milton-Freewater, OR. Remarkably straight-trunked as a young tree; fast-growing to good symmetrical form; heavy dark green foliage.

A. platanoides 'Variegatum'
= *A. platanoides* 'Albo-variegatum'

Known in Europe since 1683. Possibly this was the "*striped* Norway Maple" offered in 1840–41 by Monroe nursery of Greece, NY. Be that as it may, the cultivar was also introduced to the U.S. by the Arnold Arboretum in 1925. It is rare. Leaves white variegated. Confused with *A. platanoides* 'Drummondii' (q.v.).

A. platanoides 'Walderseei'

Found in 1900 in the park of Count Waldersee in Mesendorf, Germany. First listed in the 1904 catalog of Späth nursery of Germany. Introduced to the U.S. in 1925 by the Arnold Arboretum. Very rare here. Leaf somewhat irregular, shallowly lobed. Emerging leaves gray-green with a trace of pink or brown, at maturity densely speckled with tiny white dots.

A. platanoides 'Youngii'—see A. platanoides 'Reitenbachii'

A. polymorphum—see A. palmatum

A. Pseudoplatanus L.

SYCAMORE MAPLE. GREAT MAPLE. GRAY HAREWOOD. ENGLISH HAREWOOD. SCOTTISH PLANE. From Europe, W Asia. The English name SYCAMORE derives from Greek *sykon*, a fig, and *moros*, a mulberry—i.e., the FIG-TREE with leaves like a MULBERRY TREE. The *Ficus sycomorus* of the Bible (Luke 19 : 4) is a robust tree called PHARAOH'S FIG, SYCOMORE FIG, or MULBERRY FIG. This species was introduced to North America early, possibly in 1803–1804 by C. Gore. It has become very common, and in some places is naturalized. It is an adaptable, sturdy shade tree, tolerating salt-exposure, dryness, and shade.

Leaf coarsely five-lobed, 3"–7" (11)" wide; markedly thick and dark green; fall color late and rarely other than dingy pale-golden-brown, but capable of clear yellow. Bark rarely smooth, usually flaky, grayish to beige. Records: 132' × 11'10" Lennoxlove, Lothian, Scotland (1985); 110' × 13'7" Overbrook, PA (1980); 105' × 23'11" Birnam, Perthshire, Scotland (1990); 80' × 13'11" Lyman,

WA (1992); a trunk 27'9½" around in Unterwalden, Switzerland (<1908).

A. Pseudoplatanus 'Atropurpureum'

= A. Pseudoplatanus 'Spaethii' of Dutch nurseries, non Schwerin
= A. Pseudoplatanus 'Purpureum Spaethii'

WINELEAF MAPLE. PINKLEAF MAPLE. Introduced in 1883 by Späth nursery of Germany. In North America ≤1897; in nurseries ≤1930. Common. Leaf undersides rich dark purple. See also Acer Pseudoplatanus f. purpureum.

A. Pseudoplatanus 'Brilliantissimum'

Of post-1900 British origin; described in 1905. Imported to the U.S. in 1927 by the Arnold Arboretum. Extremely rare; listed since 1980s by Greer nursery of Eugene, OR. Emerging leaves brilliant shrimp-pink, later pale yellow-green, finally dark green. Growth slow; effectively a dwarf tree with a dense, domelike head. Usually topgrafted. See also A. Pseudoplatanus 'Prinz Handjery'. Records from England: 42' × 3'9" Kew (≤1981); 38' × 3'11" East Bergholt Place, Suffolk (1971); 23' × 3'10" Brighouse, Yorkshire (1984).

A. Pseudoplatanus 'Corstorphinense'

CORSTORPHINE SYCAMORE (MAPLE). CORSTORPHINE PLANE. Originated ca. 1600 at Corstorphine, Edinburgh. Extremely rarely if ever, offered by North American nurseries. See also A. Pseudoplatanus 'Worleei'. Leaves emerge bright yellow, darken to normal green by mid-July. Records from Scotland: 85' × 14'6" Moncrieffe House, Perthshire (1982); 62' × 14'9" Dovecoate Road, Corstorphine, Edinburgh (1990).

A. Pseudoplatanus 'Erectum'

= A. Pseudoplatanus 'Pyramidalis'
= A. Pseudoplatanus 'Fastigiatum'
= A. Pseudoplatanus 'Nachtegaalplein'

Found in 1935 in the Netherlands at The Hague's Nightingale Square. First listed in Lombarts nursery catalog of 1949–50. Introduced to the U.S. in the early 1950s by Scanlon nursery of Ohio. Sold into the early 1970s, but very scarce in nurseries by the late 1980s. The original had rigidly ascendent branches. But some specimens called 'Erectum' have matured into very broad trees that no one would call erect, let alone fastigiate. Other specimens are indeed of upswept habit, and smaller than regular seedlings would be in the same number of years.

A. Pseudoplatanus f. erythrocarpum (Carr.) Pax

REDSEED SYCAMORE MAPLE. Greek erythros, red, and karpos, fruit. First offered <1864 by a French nursery. Rarely offered by North American nurseries, but trees that fit the description can be found mixed in with ordinary seedling plantings. Seed color may vary from year to year the same way fall leaf color can. A related MAPLE prized for the attractive summer redness of its seeds is Acer Heldreichii ssp. Trautvetteri.

A. Pseudoplatanus 'Euchlorum'

First sold in 1878 by Späth nursery of Germany. Very rare in North America; here ≤1897. 'Euchlorum' is from Greek eu, good, and chloros, color. The leaves are rich green and very large, deeply five-lobed, the stem yellow. Seeds also unusually large. Record: the only one known in Britain, 70' × 11'9" (1971—at East Bergholt Place, Suffolk).

A. Pseudoplatanus 'Fastigiatum'—see A. Pseudoplatanus 'Erectum'

A. Pseudoplatanus 'Leopoldii'

Originated in Belgium ca. 1860. In North American nursery trade ≤1891. More common than the similar A. Pseudoplatanus 'Simon-Louis Frères' and 'Tricolor'. Named after Leopold I, King of the Belgians (1831–65). Leaves emerge yellowish-pink, then turn green, speckled yellow and pink.

A. Pseudoplatanus Lustre®

Carlton nursery of California and Oregon 1993–94 catalog: "our budded selection" offering uniformity.

A. Pseudoplatanus 'Nachtegaalplein'—see A. Pseudo. 'Erectum'

A. Pseudoplatanus 'Nizetii'

Introduced ≤1887 by Makoy nursery of Belgium. Very rare in North America; here by 1896. Listed in 1993–94 catalog of Arborvillage nursery of Holt, MO. Leaves emerge red-brown, then turn green, variegated red to orange above; purplish beneath.

A. Pseudoplatanus 'Prinz Handjery'

Originated ca. 1860 as an A. pseudoplatanus f. purpureum seedling. First listed in the 1883 catalog of Späth nursery of Germany. In Canada ≤1897; introduced to the U.S. in 1951 by the Arnold Arboretum. Very rare. Besides topgrafting this clone, at least one nursery has sold its seedlings, observing that they "breed true." Similar to (and sometimes sold as) A.

pseudoplatanus 'Brilliantissimum'. Its emerging leaves are reddish, but it develops a wider, less dense crown, and the leaves remain yellow-dotted above, and pale purplish beneath, all summer. Record: 20' × 1'8" × 18' Victoria, B.C. (1994).

A. *Pseudoplatanus* 'Puget Pink'

Introduced in 1994–95 by Heronswood nursery of Kingston, WA. A seedling of A. *Pseudoplatanus* 'Prinz Handjery' with "brilliant shrimp-pink spring growth fading in summer to mottled pinkish-green foliage. May retain its color better in cool climates. Compact growth to 15'–20' tall." Heronswood nursery is near Puget Sound, hence the name.

A. *Pseudoplatanus* f. *purpureum* (Loud.) Rehd.

First sold commercially ca. 1828 at Bernard Saunders' nursery of Jersey, England. This *forma* name applies to any seedling whose leaf undersides are conspicuously pinkish to dark purple. In spring, the leaves emerge merely greenish-bronze. A clone of especially deep color is the 1883 A. *Pseudoplatanus* 'Atropurpureum' (q.v.). Other dark seedlings have been selected, cloned, and sold as 'Purpureum'. Sometimes the seeds are also dark reddish instead of green or pink-red. Records: 82' × 6'6" × 47' Tacoma, WA (1990); 71' × 12'9" × 59' Carnation, WA (1992).

A. *Pseudoplatanus* 'Purpureum Spaethii'—see A. *Pseudoplatanus* 'Atropurpureum'

A. *Pseudoplatanus* 'Pyramidalis'—see A. *Pseudoplatanus* 'Erectum'

A. *Pseudoplatanus* 'Simon-Louis Frères'

Introduced in Europe in 1881. In Canada ≤1896; introduced to the U.S. in 1955 by the Arnold Arboretum. Very rare. In 1993–94 catalog of Arborvillage nursery of Holt, MO. Named after the Simon-Louis Frères nursery at Plantières, near Metz, France. Emerging leaves pink, becoming variegated green and white above, green beneath.

A. *Pseudoplatanus* 'Spaethii'—see A. *Pseudo.* 'Atropurpureum'

A. *Pseudoplatanus* 'Tricolor'

Introduced in Moscow in 1864. Introduced to the U.S. by the late 1800s, and offered by a few nurseries. Very rare. Scanlon nursery of Ohio promoted it in the 1960s. Emerging leaves reddish-brown, becoming variegated green and white above, wine-colored beneath.

A. *Pseudoplatanus* f. *variegatum* (West.) Rehd.

Cultivated since 1700 in France. Introduced to the U.S. early. Rare here. A group name applicable to any SYCAMORE MAPLE seedling with its leaves white- or yellow-blotched. Records: immense old specimens in Great Britain, the tallest more than 100' and the stoutest trunks 15'3" around; 70' × 10'2" × 75' Ladner, B.C. (1994).

A. *Pseudoplatanus* 'Worley'
('Worleei')

GOLDEN SYCAMORE (MAPLE). Originated in Europe <1879. In the U.S. nursery trade ≤1891. Less rare than most color variants of SYCAMORE MAPLE. Leaves soft yellow-green at first, then rich golden, almost orange; finally fading to normal green. An improved version of A. *Pseudoplatanus* 'Corstorphinense'.

A. *pseudosieboldianum* (Pax) Kom.

KOREAN MAPLE. From S Siberia, E Manchuria, and Korea. Introduced to cultivation in 1903; E. Wilson collected seeds for the Arnold Arboretum in 1919. Extremely rarely cultivated. A slender 20' tree-like shrub related closely to A. *Sieboldianum*, A. *japonicum* and A. *palmatum*. Leaves roundish, (7) 9–11 lobed, to 5½" wide, very downy, deeply lobed. Flowers purple. Young twigs lightly hairy. Fall color brilliant orange or red. By contrast, the leaves of its Japanese cousin, "the real" A. *Sieboldianum*, have 9 lobes almost exclusively, are less deeply lobed, less conspicuously toothed, and have earlier fall color; the flowers are later, and yellowish-white rather than purple.

A. *pycnanthum* K. Koch

From central Japan, where it is rare. Japanese: *Hana-no-ki. Hana-kaede.* Introduced in 1915 by E. Wilson. Almost nonexistent in Western cultivation, with a few dating from no earlier than the 1960s in arboreta, and sold only by specialist maple nurseries (e.g., Hughes nursery of Montesano, WA). This species is the Japanese counterpart and lookalike of North America's RED MAPLE, A. *rubrum*. In general the Japanese species is smaller, its maximum recorded dimensions only 82' × 10'4". Leaves can be bronzy-red when young; to 3½" long, 2¾" wide, the stem to 3¼" long; glaucous beneath and hairless or with scattered pale hairs mostly on or near the main veins. Fall color red and yellow. Koch's 1863 name *pycnanthum* is from Greek *pyknos*, dense, and *anthos*, a flower—the flowers are dense headed. Record: 43' × 2'0" Seattle, WA (1994; *pl.* 1971).

A. rubescens Hay.
= *A. morrisonense* hort.

From China, and mountain forests of Taiwan. The specific epithet in Latin means becoming red. "*Morrisonense*" refers to Taiwan's Mt. Morrison. A comparatively cold-tender species, in the STRIPEBARK group of MAPLES. Leaf to 6" long, five-lobed (rarely three-lobed), with orange hairs beneath when very young; the stem red. It most resembles *A. capillipes*. Introduced to the U.S. in 1949 when seeds were received at the Seattle arboretum. Offered in British Columbia by 1990, being marketed as "fast, upright; red new growth and fall color." Specimens in Seattle stay green well into November, and flush very early in spring. Records: 60' × 6'0" Trewithen Gardens, Cornwall, England (1985; *pl.* 1912); 34½' × 4'2" Occidental, CA (1995).

A. rubrum L.

RED MAPLE. SCARLET MAPLE. SHOEPEG MAPLE. SWAMP MAPLE. From much of central and eastern North America, often in swampy or low-lying ground. An abundant, adaptable species, widely planted as a shade tree. Most specimens have red buds, flowers, seeds, and fall color. But the flowers can be yellow, and the fall color orange or yellow. Acidic soil gives the best fall color; fertile neutral or alkaline soil can give inferior color, but some cultivars color well in all soils. The bright red flowers of some specimens are very showy (see cv. 'Spectacular'). Leaf essentially three-lobed, 2"–6" long, nearly or as wide; the stem 1"–4" and often red. The bark is gray. Trees can be male (seedless), female or bisexual. RED MAPLES were widely planted as grafted trees in the 1970s, but proved often graft-incompatible, so more have since been cutting-grown "on their own roots." Records: 179' × 18'6" × 120' St. Claire County, MI (1984); the largest trunk was 26'0" around, at Bradford, MA (cut in 1876).

A. rubrum 'Ablaze'
Sarcoxie nursery of Sarcoxie, MO, 1974 catalog: "well-rounded head, brilliant red color, holds foliage late into fall."

A. rubrum 'Armstrong'—see A. × Freemanii 'Armstrong'

A. rubrum Autumn Blaze®—see A. × Freemanii Autumn Blaze®

A. rubrum Autumn Flame® PP 2377 (1964)
Introduced in 1964–65 by A. McGill & Son nursery of Fairview, OR. Common. Leaves smaller than average for RED MAPLE but borne in great profusion. Tree shapely, dense, becoming large and well-rounded. Among the *earliest* of RED MAPLES to color—brilliant scarlet about two weeks earlier than average. In an Alabama study, the fall color was not early, but did develop more rapidly over the entire tree, thus *appearing* to be earlier; and it did have the best color of 7 clones tested. Male.

A. rubrum 'Autumn Glory' PP 2431 (1964)
Selected by M.W. Staples of Kent, OH. Introduced in 1967–68 by the Davey Tree Expert Co. of Kent. Very rare—if produced commercially at all. Exceptional orange-red fall color; tree shape upright oval, spreading.

A. rubrum Autumn Radiance®
Pre-1990 origin. Called variously "dense and oval," or "open and rounded" in form. Consistently good orange-red fall color two weeks earlier than *A. rubrum* Red Sunset®.

A. rubrum 'Autumn Spire' PP 7803 (1992)
Raised by H.M. Pellett from seeds found near Grand Rapids, Minnesota. Introduced in 1990 after 12 years of evaluation by the University of Minnesota. Valued for cold-hardiness, neat columnar to upright-oval shape, beautiful red fall color, and showy red seedless flowers.

A. rubrum 'Bowhall'
Selected ca. 1946 by Scanlon nursery of Ohio, the original specimen in or near Cleveland; named in 1951 after the road on which it was discovered. Narrowly upright in youth, and maintaining a symmetric pyramidal form; brilliant yellow-orange to red-orange fall color. Female. This is the tree from which the similar but improved *A. rubrum* 'Scanlon' sported. Record: 49½' × 3'5" × 27½' Aurora, OR (1993; *pl.* 1966).

A. rubrum 'Columnar Walters'
Selected by Richard Walter of Maplewood, NJ. Offered ≤1958 by Princeton nursery of New Jersey (although unlisted in their catalogs). Sold by Manbeck nursery of Ohio in 1975. Rare. Rapid, attractively upright, with good fall color, and quick to drop its leaves.

A. rubrum 'Columnare'

= A. rubrum 'Pyramidale'

Introduced ≤1887 by Parsons nursery of Flushing, NY. Common. Narrow columnar with excellent fall color. Male, or predominantly so. Record: 69' × 2'11" × 21' Seattle, WA (1992; *pl.* 1949).

A. rubrum 'Curtis'

Introduced in 1949 by Mr. Vallou Curtis of Curtis nursery, Callicoon, NY. Very straight, upright-oval growth; early, attractive fall color.

A. rubrum 'Davey'—see A. rubrum Davey Red™

A. rubrum Davey Red™

= A. rubrum 'Davey'

Selected by the Davey Tree Expert company of Kent, OH. Sold sparingly since ≤1980s. Round-headed, slow, compact to 45' tall. Leaf small, thick, dark green; of outstanding yellow to dark orange-red fall color. Female. Hardier than most A. rubrum cultivars.

A. rubrum Doric™ PP 2823 (1968)

Selected ca. 1960 by Scanlon nursery of Ohio, introduced in 1964. Its columnar form inspired its name (patterned after the columns of the Parthenon). Growth slow to 30' tall. Stiff, tortuous sharp-angled fastigiate branching habit. Leaf very glossy and leathery, brilliant blood red or orange late in fall. Female.

A. rubrum 'Drake' PP 3542 (1974)

= A. rubrum 'V.J. Drake'

Named after Virgil James Drake of County Line nursery, Hartford, MI. Introduced by Schmidt nursery of Boring, OR. Tree of normal growth rate, its crown fairly natural-looking, not markedly round or pyramidal. But its fall color begins very early and goes through changes lasting a long time: distinctively turning from green to a colored border through shades of blue-violet to red and yellow.

A. rubrum var. Drummondii (H. & A. ex Nutt.) Sarg.

= A. rubrum ssp. Drummondii (H. & A. ex Nutt.) E. Murr.

SOUTHERN RED MAPLE. Discovered by Thomas Drummond (1780–1835), Scottish botanical explorer in North America in 1833–34. Named after him in 1834. The more southerly phase of the RED MAPLE population. Better-adapted to planting in the South. Leaf larger, often broader than long, more or less white and hairy beneath, thicker, usually with five deeper lobes; seeds larger, to 2" (instead of ≤1") long.

Three cultivars selected because of especially colorful seeds, are sold by Louisiana nursery of Opelousas, LA: 'Live Oak' (blood red), 'Louisiana Red' (bright red) and 'San Felipe' (outstanding). A fourth Drummondii cultivar, tested in Georgia since the late 1980s, is 'Edna Davis' featuring reliable orange-red to red fall color.

A. rubrum 'Edna Davis'—see A. rubrum ssp. Drummondii

A. rubrum Embers®

Origin unknown ≤1979–80. Much grown. May be same as A. × Freemanii 'Morgan' (q.v.). Prized for brilliant scarlet fall color, cold-hardiness, vigor and pyramidal, then rounded crown.

A. rubrum Excelsior™

Introduced 1978–79 by Handy nursery of Oregon. Little grown. Broad pyramidal shape, attained in early years of growth. Orange-red in fall.

A. rubrum Fairview Flame®

Origin unknown. Likely from the nursery of A. McGill & Son of Fairview, OR. Their 1991–92 catalog says: "bright scarlet later than A. rubrum Autumn Flame®; very vigorous; branches extremely well; average leaf size." Femrite nursery of Oregon says: "rapid vigorous upright 60' tall × 20' wide; bright scarlet midseason fall color."

A. rubrum Firedance® PP 6977 (1989)

= A. rubrum 'Landsburg'

Found by Roger B. Landsburg in the Brainerd area of northern Minnesota; introduced in 1988 by Bailey nursery. Of average size, with a good oval form and branching habit; brilliant red in fall. Exceptionally cold-hardy. Male. It may be a cultivar of A. × Freemanii.

A. rubrum 'Franksred'—see A. rubrum Red Sunset®

A. rubrum Gerling™

Selected ca. 1950 by Scanlon nursery of Ohio, and introduced in 1955–56. Named for tree expert Jacob ("Jake the magnificent") Gerling (1896–1979) of Rochester, New York. Broadly pyramidal, dense, with yellow to red fall color. Male.

A. rubrum 'Globosum'

A compact dwarf with scarlet flowers introduced in 1887 by Parsons nursery of New York. Likely commercially extinct for most or all of this century. A 1972 survey of Long Island's record-sized trees, found (at Amagansett) the largest 'Globosum' trunk only 2'8" around. See also *A. rubrum* 'Spectacular'.

A. rubrum 'Indian Summer'—see *A.* × *Freemanii* 'Morgan'

A. rubrum Karpick®

Introduced <1982 by Schichtel nursery of Orchard Park, NY. Named for Frank E. Karpick (1902–1990), city forester of Buffalo, NY. Tree fine-textured and extremely narrow; red twigs, green leaves; yellow, orange and red in fall. Male.

A. rubrum 'Landsburg'—see *A. rubrum* Firedance®

A. rubrum 'Live Oak'—see *A. rubrum* ssp. *Drummondii*

A. rubrum 'Louisiana Red'—see *A. rubrum* ssp. *Drummondii*

A. rubrum 'Morgan'—see *A.* × *Freemanii* 'Morgan'

A. rubrum Northwood® PP 5053 (1983)

Discovered by L. Snyder as a seedling near Floodwood, MN. Described in 1980. Introduced by Bailey nursery of Minnesota. Selected for cold-hardiness. Rounded-oval shape, not dense; branches ascending from the trunk at about a 45° angle. Trunk straight and sturdy. Crimson-red and orange fall color. Male. Grows poorly in alkaline soils or hot, dry prairie conditions.

A. rubrum 'October Brilliance'

Unknown <1982 origin. Little grown. M. Dirr describes it as possessing a well-shaped tight crown, 40' tall, 30' wide; delayed leaf-emergence in spring. Fall color red to pale red-orange. Male.

A. rubrum October Glory® PP 2116 (1961)

= *A. rubrum* 'PNI 0268'

Introduced in 1961–62 by Princeton nursery of New Jersey. Leaves with long red stems; stay green longer than usual into autumn, extending the seasonal display, giving dependable late-season crimson-red fall color. Tree rounded, not dense. Female.

A. rubrum Oktoberfest®

Introduced ≤1991–92 by Moller nursery of Gresham, OR. Fall color deep, bright red. Growth very strong. To 50'–60' tall. Hardy to -30°F.

A. rubrum 'Olson'

A selection from Brainerd, MN. Introduced <1990 by Bailey nursery of St. Paul, MN. Cold-hardy. Brilliant red fall color. Good branching forming an broadly oval crown.

A. rubrum 'Paul E. Tilford'—see *A. rubrum* 'Tilford'

A. rubrum 'Phipps Farm'

= *A. rubrum* 'Weston'

Weston nursery of Hopkinton, MA, introduced this (as 'Weston') ≤1973. Little grown, and perhaps extinct commercially by 1988. Named after the nursery's Phipps Farm facility. Adapted to New England. Fall color long-lasting, lovely yellow-red to superb red. Tree small, broad and rounded.

A. rubrum 'PNI 0268'—see *A. rubrum* October Glory®

A. rubrum 'Pyramidale'—see *A. rubrum* 'Columnare'

A. rubrum 'Red Skin'

Introduced in 1982 by Schichtel nursery of Orchard Park, NY. Of rounded form, with large thick leaves showing very early fall color of reddish-maroon.

A. rubrum Red Sunset®

= *A. rubrum* 'Franksred'

Originated in the late 1940s by Schmidt nursery of Boring, OR. Introduced in 1966. The most commonly planted RED MAPLE cultivar in the 1970s and '80s. The name was inspired by the song "Red Sails in the Sunset." Its fall color, at least in the north, is long-lasting and superb orange-red. The tree makes a broadly oval crown. Leaves glossy, thick, strongly three-lobed. Female.

A. rubrum Rubyfrost™

= *A. rubrum* 'Polara'

Introduced in the 1990s by Chicagoland Grows®, Inc. A 50-year old tree in Grantsburg, WI. Very cold hardy; uniform strong branching; excellent drought tolerance; good fall color.

A. rubrum 'San Felipe'—see *A. rubrum* ssp. *Drummondii*

A. rubrum Scanlon™ PP 1722 (1958)

= A. rubrum 'Bowhall' (in part)

The famous Ohio nurseryman Edward H. Scanlon (1903–1976), selected and introduced A. rubrum 'Bowhall' ca. 1951 but experienced "irregular and very unsatisfactory growth defects" with it. However, his 'Scanlon' sport from it (ca. 1954) proved superior in its distinctly stable form and reliability of fall color (brilliant orange-umber and red). Two clones, two names, and mass confusion has ensued. Apparently 'Scanlon' was sold under the 'Bowhall' name for a period prior to its official renaming, and afterwards, so when people see trees called by one name or the other now, there is no certainty as to which clone is being viewed. The two are very similar, both starting as tight columns, growing into flame-shaped densely upright specimens—'Scanlon' may be denser than 'Bowhall'. Record: 57' × 3'9" × 29' Aurora, OR (1993; pl. 1966).

A. rubrum 'Scarlet Sentinel'—see A. × Freemanii Scarlet Sentinel™

A. rubrum 'Scarsen'—see A. × Freemanii Scarlet Sentinel™

A. rubrum 'Schlesinger'

Introduced by C. Sargent of the Arnold Arboretum; the original tree found <1888 on the estate of Mr. B. Schlesinger of Brookline, MA. First marketed in Germany. Commonly planted during the 1970s and '80s. Conventional or rounded crown form is not notable. Chosen instead for its reliably early and outstanding fall color of yellow to orange to red or beet-juice red. Female.

A. rubrum Shade King™

Introduced by Handy nursery of Oregon in 1973–74. Little grown. Upright oval head, well branched in first year; 30'–50' tall, widest near top; foliage dark green. Fall color yellow to bright red. Male.

A. rubrum 'Silhouette'

Originated <1981 by W. Wandell of Urbana, IL. Little grown. Fall color red-orange. Male.

A. rubrum 'Spectacular'

An obscure cultivar. All that is known about it was written by J. Gerling (see A. rubrum 'Gerling') in 1958: "A selected form of A. rubrum 'Globosum' named 'Spectacular' develops a beautiful globular head, has pleasing gray bark and exceptional flowers larger and more attractive than those of most red maples. Tolerates sandy dry soil."

A. rubrum 'Territorial'

T. H. Belcher nursery of Boring, OR, 1991 catalog: "Leaves glossy, smaller, red in fall; rounded head."

A. rubrum '(Paul E.) Tilford'

Selected ca. 1949 by Scanlon nursery of Ohio, and named in 1951 after plant pathologist (also elected Mayor in 1967) Dr. Paul E. Tilford (d. 1986) of Wooster, OH. Common. Of rounded shape; a natural globe. But unless grown in the open it tends to develop a more pyramidal than globular shape. Fall color varies from attractive red and orange (noted in an Alabama study) to a less than handsome mixture of yellow, green, and pink-bronze. Male.

A. rubrum var. tridens —see A. rubrum var. trilobum

A. rubrum var. trilobum T. & G. ex K. Koch

= A. rubrum var. tridens Wood
= A. rubrum f. tridens (Wood) Boivin
= A. carolinianum Walt.

CAROLINA RED MAPLE. TRIDENT RED MAPLE. SMALL-FRUITED RED-MAPLE. This variant is linked to typical Acer rubrum by intermediate forms. It has a vast range (but overall is more southerly) and is itself variable. In both botany and horticulture it has been largely ignored, but selected clones referrable to it may have value if they are more drought-tolerant or in other ways worthwhile. Leaf smaller, thicker, less lobed and sometimes unlobed; glaucous and glabrous or downy white-hairy beneath. Fall color later, often golden. Flowers often yellow. Seeds smaller, yellow-brown. Bark smoother.

A. rubrum 'V. J. Drake'—see A. rubrum 'Drake'

A. rubrum 'Vans'

Introduced ≤1988 by Schichtel nursery of Orchard Park, NY. Of uniform oval habit, red fall color.

A. rubrum 'Weston'—see A. rubrum 'Phipps Farm'

A. rufinerve S. & Z.
= *A. tegmentosum* ssp. *rufinerve* (S. & Z.) E. Murr.

REDVEIN MAPLE. GREY-BUDDED SNAKEBARK MAPLE. CUCUMBER BARK MAPLE. BAT MAPLE. From Japan. Japanese: *Uri-hada-kaede*. Introduced to cultivation when sent by Siebold to Holland in 1860; independently by C.J. Maximowicz to Russia in 1862–64; offered by English nurseries by 1875, and U.S. nurseries ≤1917. Best in woodland conditions, it has not been widely grown until the 1960s. Leaf 2½"–5⅞" long—the leaf veins rusty-hairy, accounting for the name *rufinerve*, from Latin *rufus*, reddish, and *nervus*, nerve. Fall color mostly yellow, but can be orange and red. Records: 65' × 7'3" in Japan; 62' × 1'11" Seattle, WA (1990); 49' × 3'4" Seattle, WA (1990).

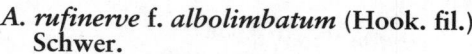

A. rufinerve f. albolimbatum (Hook. fil.) Schwer.
= *A. rufinerve* 'Hatsuyuki'

Introduced to cultivation when sent by Siebold to Holland in 1860; exhibited in England in 1869. In Canada ≤1899; imported to the U.S. by the Arnold Arboretum in 1938. Leaves variably white-variegated. Weaker, less hardy. Sold by Greer nursery of Oregon in the 1970s.

A. rufinerve 'Hatsuyuki'—see A. rufinerve f. albolimbatum

A. saccharinum L., non Wangenh. (cf. A. saccharum)
= *A. dasycarpum* Ehrh.
= *A. eriocarpum* Michx.

SILVER or SILVERLEAF MAPLE. WHITE MAPLE. WATER MAPLE. RIVER MAPLE. SOFT MAPLE. From much of central and eastern North America. The epithet *saccharinum* means sugary, from Latin *saccharum*, sugarcane. The tree's sap can be made into syrup or sugar, although this process is usually done with SUGAR MAPLE, *A. saccharum*. SILVER MAPLE is an enormous tree, of rapid growth and brittle limbs. Well-adapted to pioneer roles in the wild (it favors streambanks, floodplains, and lake edges), it grows amazingly rapidly to awkward, if not dangerously large size in crowded cities. The leaf is silvery-white beneath, 3"–6" (7½)" long and wide; stem to 6¼". Fall color is usually plain yellow with rarer orange and red splashes. Flowers appear very early in spring (or late winter). Seeds large (to nearly 3" long) and ripen in May or June. As with the closely related RED MAPLE, *A. rubrum*, it can bear male, female or mixed flowers. Records: 138' × 12'7" Pennsylvania (1893); 125' × 23'0" × 134' Oakland County, MI (1979); 115' × 24'5" × 110' Marcellon, WI (1988); 115' × 23'2" × 108' Stratford, IA (1966); 93' × 23'6" × 113' Chester County, PA (1968); 89' × 24'1" × 96' Leeds, ME (1980); 61' × 31'7" × 82' Polk County, IA (1993).

A. saccharinum 'Aureum'
GOLDENLEAF SILVER MAPLE. Introduced in 1934 by Naperville nursery of Naperville, IL. Rare. Also sold by Cole nursery of Ohio into the 1950s.

A. saccharinum 'Beebe Cutleaf Weeping'
= *A. saccharinum* 'Laciniatum Beebe'

Introduced in 1953 by Cole nursery of Painesville, OH. Uncommon. Strong upright trunk; crown weeping. The best CUTLEAF SILVER MAPLE—superior to *A. saccharinum* 'Skinneri' or 'Wieri Laciniatum'.

A. saccharinum 'Blair'
Originated in Blair, NE. Introduced <1939 by Marshall nursery of Arlington, NE. Common. Upright growth habit, short strong limbs less subject to storm breakage.

A. saccharinum 'Columnare'—see A. saccharinum 'Pyramidale'

A. saccharinum 'Crispum'
Introduced in 1875 by Ellwanger & Barry nursery of Rochester, NY. Very rare. Delicately cut and curled foliage; veins light yellow; twigs very thin.

A. saccharinum 'Fastigiatum'—see A. saccharinum 'Pyramidale'

A. saccharinum 'Golden'
Introduced ≤1947–48 by Jewell nursery of Lake City, MN. Orange-gold bark. See *A. saccharinum* 'Luteum'.

A. saccharinum 'Hance's Variegated'

Introduced in 1879 by A. Hance & Son of Red Bank, NJ. Long extinct commercially. Leaves regularly striped, splashed with creamy white throughout the growing season. Withstands sun.

A. saccharinum 'Heterophyllum'—see A. saccharinum 'Heterophyllum Laciniatum'

A. saccharinum 'Heterophyllum Laciniatum'

= A. saccharinum 'Heterophyllum'

Raised by Ellwanger & Barry nursery of Rochester, NY; introduced by them in 1880. Much grown in late 1800s and early 1900s. Subsequently rare. Luxuriant erect grower with handsomely cut asymmetrical leaves, more deeply dissected leaves than those of A. saccharinum 'Wieri Laciniatum'.

A. saccharinum f. laciniatum (Carr.) Rehd.

This serves as a group name that embraces any and all "fern-leaved" seedlings or clones, whether the trees weep or grow erect, and the leaves are deeply or slightly dissected.

A. saccharinum 'Laciniatum Beebe'—see A. saccharinum 'Beebe Cutleaf Weeping'

A. saccharinum 'Laciniatum Wieri'—see A. saccharinum 'Wieri Laciniatum'

A. saccharinum 'Lee's Red'—see A. × Freemanii 'Lee's Red'

A. saccharinum 'Lockstead'

Discovered in 1990 by N. Stewart of Stewart's Botanical Garden, Lockstead Settlement, New Brunswick. Registered in 1993. Introduced by Sheridan nursery of Ontario. Leaves small, extremely deeply lobed in threadlike fashion. Branch tips pendulous. Record: 79' × 19'8" × 39' (the original tree, ≤1993).

A. saccharinum 'Lutescens'

First sold in 1881 by Späth nursery of Germany. In Canada ≤1891; imported to the U.S. in 1927 from England by the Arnold Arboretum. Rarely grown by North American nurseries. *Hortus III* describes it: "leaves orange when young, later yellowish, especially in the sun."

A. saccharinum 'Luteum'

('Lutea')

GOLDEN SILVER MAPLE. Introduced in 1953 by Cole nursery of Painesville, Ohio. Commercially extinct.

Bark orange on young branches; fall leaf color yellow. Likely the same as Jewell nursery's *A. saccharinum* 'Golden'.

A. saccharinum 'Majesty'

Arborvillage nursery of Holt, Missouri, 1993–94 catalog: "outstanding majestic form to a local tree. Good branching habit to form a beautiful shade tree. Not a cutleaf."

A. saccharinum 'Northline'

Selected in 1970 at Morden, Manitoba. Released to nurseries in 1982. Well-adapted to very cold prairie regions. Wide branching habit. Slower growth than most cultivars. Female.

A. saccharinum 'Pendulum'

WEEPING SILVER MAPLE. Of European origin ca. 1875–1880. In North America since ≤1897 but very rare. Commercially extinct. Branches more or less pendulous. Differs from *A. saccharinum* 'Wieri Laciniatum' in that its leaf is "more 3-lobed."

A. saccharinum 'Pipal'

Introduced in 1957 by Cole nursery of Painesville, OH. Commercially extinct. Seedless. Leafs out earlier and holds its foliage later in autumn. Named for Frank J. Pipal, city forester of Omaha, NE.

A. saccharinum 'Pyramidale'

= A. saccharinum 'Fastigiatum'

= A. saccharinum 'Columnare'

First sold in 1885–86 by Späth nursery of Germany. Much grown. More than one clone might have been given this name. Descriptions vary but the gist is: upright, relatively narrow branching forming a broad column.

A. saccharinum 'Sheridan'

Introduced ≤1980 by Sheridan nursery of Ontario. "Fast growing; broadly ovate."

A. saccharinum 'Silver Queen'

Introduced in 1966 by Inter-State nursery of Hamburg, IA. Common. Cold-hardy. Fast, upright growth, with a straight central leader, stronger branching. Glossy green foliage, golden-yellow in fall. Seedless or sets few seeds.

A. saccharinum 'Skinneri'

SKINNER'S CUTLEAF SILVER MAPLE. Introduced in 1934 by Naperville nursery of Naperville, IL. Tree originally found in J.H. Skinner nursery of Topeka, KS.

Common. Branching upright to horizontal, not weeping or scarcely so. Leaves deeply dissected. Fall color yellow.

A. saccharinum var. *subtrilobatum*—see *A. saccharinum* 'Tripartitum'

A. saccharinum 'Trefoil'—see *A. saccharinum* 'Tripartitum'

A. saccharinum 'Tripartitum'
= *A. saccharinum* 'Trefoil'
= *A. saccharinum* var. *subtrilobatum* (Schwer.) Pax

Raised by Ellwanger & Barry nursery of Rochester, NY; introduced by them in 1880. Long commercially extinct. Tree vigorous, upright; leaves large, deeply three-lobed (cut nearly to the midrib).

A. saccharinum 'Turneri'

Elm City nursery of New Haven CT, 1903 catalog: "TURNER'S NEW CUTLEAF SILVER MAPLE. Originated at our nursery. Named for H.E. Turner, secretary and manager. Fernlike foliage, stem and midrib rich red." Long commercially extinct.

A. saccharinum 'Wagneri'—see *A. saccharinum* 'Wagneri Laciniatum'

A. saccharinum 'Wagneri Dissectum'—see *A. saccharinum* 'Wagneri Laciniatum'

A. saccharinum 'Wagneri Laciniatum'
= *A. saccharinum* 'Wagneri Dissectum'
= *A. saccharinum* 'Wagneri'

Introduced in 1865 by Haage & Schmidt nursery of Erfurt, Prussia. Likely "Wagneri" is a mistake for "Wager" after Sir Charles Wager (1666–1743) who in 1725 introduced SILVER MAPLE to English cultivation. Offered in 1867–68 by Ellwanger & Barry nursery of Rochester, NY. Long commercially extinct. Leaves deeply incised, narrow. A very weak grower, liable to revert to normal foliage.

A. saccharinum 'Wieri'—see *A. saccharinum* 'Wieri Laciniatum'

A. saccharinum 'Wieri Laciniatum'
= *A. saccharinum* 'Wieri'

WIER'S CUTLEAF SILVER MAPLE. Discovered by D.B. Wier (died ca. 1890s) of Lacon, IL. Sold ca. 1870 to Ellwanger & Barry nursery of Rochester, NY. Introduced in 1873 by Ellwanger & Barry. Common. Foliage abundant, deeply and elegantly cut. Tree pyramidal with weeping branches.

A. saccharinum 'Willis' Cutleaf

Introduced in 1937 by Willis nursery of Ottawa, KS. Leaves deeply shredded or dissected with abnormally slender lobes. Long commercially extinct.

A. saccharum Marsh.
= *A. saccharinum* Wangenh., non L. (cf. *A. saccharinum*)

SUGAR MAPLE. HARD MAPLE. ROCK MAPLE. From much of central and eastern North America (and subspecies into Mexico and Guatemala). A common, well known tree, important in forestry, woodworking, and horticulture, and prized for its sweet sap. Its scientific name, the Latin *saccharum*, means sugar. Its stylized leaf is Canada's national symbol. Its fall color is glowing embers, shrimp pink, or rich orange usually, sometimes merely yellow. The name HARD MAPLE contrasts it with SILVER MAPLE which is also known as SOFT MAPLE on account of the wood. The crown is markedly symmetric and the bark pale. Leaf five-lobed, 3"–6" (8") wide—to 12" in Johnnycake™. Records: 138' × 7'11" × 84' Marquette County, MI (1981; aged 342 years); 124' × 18'0" × 108' Washtenaw County, MI (1978); 106' × 19'2" Stanbridge, Québec (<1994); 93' × 22'5" × 80' Norwich, CT (1984); 78' × 21'6" × 66' Kitzmiller, MD (1977).

A. saccharum Adirondak®
= *A. saccharum* 'Adirzam'

Introduced in 1991 by Lake County nursery of Ohio. "Compact, ascending branching structure which tightly layers the leaves, increasing [the tree's] resistance to drought as compared to the species. Dense, dark green foliage retains its color late into fall. Turns golden-orange 2 weeks later than other sugar maples."

A. saccharum 'Adirzam'—see *A. saccharum* Adirondak®

A. saccharum 'Alton Odgen'

Named in 1951 by Ohio nurseryman Ed Scanlon. Named for Mr. Alton Ogden of Flint, MI. A "lyre-shaped" selection. Little distributed and long extinct commercially.

A. saccharum 'Arrowhead'

Introduced in 1979 by Schichtel nursery of Orchard Park, NY. Still in the trade but not widely grown. Upright, pyramidal head with a strong central leader and dense branching (shaped like an arrowhead). Yellow-orange to red fall color. Grows to 60' tall, 30' wide.

A. saccharum 'Bonfire' PP 3817 (1975)

Introduced in 1977–78 by Princeton nursery of New Jersey. Much grown. Broader than most SUGAR MAPLES, faster growing and more vigorous; shiny leaves that tolerate heat, resist leafhoppers, and turn a distinctive brilliant carmine-red in autumn. However, fall color in the Midwest is only yellow-orange.

A. saccharum 'Brocade'

Discovered wild at Croton Falls, NY, in 1974, when it was at least 12 years old. Propagated in 1980. Put into commerce in 1981. Registered in 1984 by the late JAPANESE MAPLE expert J.D. Vertrees of Oregon. Rare and little grown. Although of typical growth rate and crown shape, the leaves are divided deeply (⅔ to ¾ to the base), each lobe itself being narrow and three-pointed. See also A. saccharum 'Sweet Shadow'.

A. saccharum 'Caddo'
= A. barbatum 'Caddo'

CADDO SUGAR MAPLE. SOUTHWEST SUGAR MAPLE. From Oklahoma's Caddo and Canadian counties, in canyons on granitic, acidic soils. A seed-grown cultivar. Trees grown from this population show superior hardiness in Great Plains conditions, greater cold and drought tolerance, and grow well in calcareous soils. Fall color yellowish, late, unspectacular. Record: to 75' × 6'3" in the wild.

A. saccharum 'Cary' PP 2581 (1965)

Discovered ca. 1960 by John W. Ploetz at Cannoo Hills, near Millbrook, NY (now the Cary Arboretum). Named after Mary Flagler Cary (d. 1967) and introduced in 1974 by the Brooklyn Botanic Garden. Rarely grown. Tree is shorter, more compact, with denser, longer lasting foliage, and slower growing than Acer saccharum 'Newton Sentry' or 'Temple's Upright'. It also has a different habit, being narrow bell-shaped; the branches spread at about a 45° angle. The leaves are one half the size of normal (the Seattle arboretum specimen has full-sized leaves).

A. saccharum 'Coleman'

Selected ≤1950 by R.M. Nordine, propagator at the Morton Arboretum. Named ≤1958. Scarcely, if at all, offered commercially. The original specimen was broadly columnar, about 40' tall and 14' wide, on Lyn Avenue of Lake City, MN. Specimens planted in the Morton Arboretum of Lisle, IL, are broader.

A. saccharum 'Columnare'—see A. saccharum 'Newton Sentry' and 'Temple's Upright'

A. saccharum Commemoration™ PP 5079 (1983)

Selected by W. Wandell of Urbana, IL. Introduced in 1981–82 by Moller nursery of Gresham, OR. Much grown. Rapid, vigorous grower, making a densely branched canopy of heavy-textured glossy dark foliage. Resistant to leaf tatter. Fall color deep yellow-orange-red 10–14 days earlier than is usual for SUGAR MAPLE.

A. saccharum 'Davey'

Introduced ≤1990 by Davey nursery of Wooster, OH. Much grown. Rapid growth making a dense broadly oval 50' tall crown. Leaves dark; yellow-orange in fall.

A. saccharum 'Endowment Columnar' PP 4654 (1981)
= A. saccharum 'HRI 1'
= A. saccharum 'Lanco Columnar'

Introduced in 1980–81 by Siebenthaler's nursery of Dayton, OH. Much grown. Royalties help the Horticultural Research Institute Endowment fund. The clone is broadly columnar (50' tall × 15' wide), of good uniformity, with no summer scorching, excellent orange-red fall color, and no frost-cracking.

A. saccharum 'Erectum'—see A. saccharum 'Newton Sentry'

A. saccharum Fairview™

Introduced in 1975–76 by A. McGill & Son nursery of Fairview, OR. Much grown. Strong sturdy growth making a broadly oval crown. Emerald green leaves turn orange in fall. Bark much lighter colored than most.

A. saccharum 'Flax Mill Majesty' PP 5273 (1984)
= A. saccharum 'Majesty'

Introduced in 1983 by Flax Mill nursery of Cambridge, NY. Much grown. Perfectly symmetric ovoid-shaped crown, with a straight leader, abundant branches and vigorous, hardy growth. Thick, dark green leaves color markedly early to red-orange. The original specimen in Cambridge, withstood -38°F without cracking.

A. saccharum ssp. floridanum (Chapm.) Desmarais

= *A. barbatum* auct., non Michx. p.p.
= *A. floridanum* (Chapm.) Pax

SOUTHERN SUGAR MAPLE. FLORIDA MAPLE. HAMMOCK MAPLE. From the SE and SC United States, though rare in Florida. In Latin *barbatum* means bearded; from the long beard in the summit of the flower. Compared to typical SUGAR MAPLE, this is more of an understory species; it bears smaller twigs, smaller leaves (1½"–3" wide), coloring later and less brightly in fall, smaller seeds, and smoother, more whitish bark. Records: 126' × 7'5" × 57' Stevens Creek Natural Area, SC (1981); 100' × 11'7" × 64' Jasper County, GA (1989).

A. saccharum 'Flower'

Named ≤1958. An extra-narrow tree on property owned by H.C. Flower in Manchester, VT. Little circulated and long extinct commercially. Record: 48' and 36' wide at Lisle, IL (1986; *pl.* 1950).

A. saccharum 'Globosum'

Originally found in the mountains of North Carolina by W.K. LaBar, of LaBar's Rhododendron nursery near Stroudsburg, PA. Introduced ≤1942 by Kingsville nursery of Maryland. A globe, broader than tall; rich golden-red in fall. Still in the nursery trade. Nurseries usually topgraft it to produce a tree that will remain a tight rounded or oval head, 15'–25' tall, with little likelihood of growing into power-lines. Fall color is typically beautiful. Record: 38' × 2'6" × 31½' Seattle, WA (1994; *pl.* 1963).

A. saccharum 'Goldspire' PP 2917 (1969)

Introduced in 1973–74 by Princeton nursery of New Jersey. Originated as a cross between *A. saccharum* 'Newton Sentry' and 'Temple's Upright'. Compact, densely columnar or very narrow oval (40' tall × 12' wide at 35 years). Resists leaf scorch. Turns yellow or golden orange later in fall than most SUGAR MAPLES.

A. saccharum ssp. grandidentatum (Nutt. ex T. & G.) Desmarais

= *A. grandidentatum* Nutt. *ex* Torr. & Gray.

CANYON MAPLE. BIGTOOTH MAPLE. WASATCH MAPLE. WESTERN SUGAR MAPLE. From central western North America: Montana to northern Mexico. Introduced

to cultivation in 1882 when the Arnold Arboretum got seeds. In commerce ≤1905. A small tree, its 2"–5" leaves with bluntish lobes, and fall color ranging from brilliant to pastel reds and yellows. Little grown in recent decades; offered primarily by native-plant nurseries. Records: 68' × 6'8" × 44' Lost Maples State Natural Area, TX (1989); 41' × 8'3" × 51' Lincoln National Forest, NM (1981).

A. saccharum ssp. grandidentatum Rocky Mt. Glow™

= *A. grandidentatum* 'Schmidt'

Introduced ≤1990 by Schmidt nursery of Boring, OR. It was selected for its intense bright red fall color. Grown by several wholesale tree nurseries.

A. saccharum Green Mountain® PP 2339 (1964)

= *A. saccharum* 'PNI 0285'

Originated as a cross between typical *A. saccharum* and its subspecies *nigrum*. Introduced in 1964–65 by Princeton nursery of New Jersey. Common. Upright broadly oval crown; uniform vigorous growth. Leaves hairy beneath, while above they are dark, unusually thick and covered with a waxy coating, retaining full color in dry, windy summer weather. Yellow to orange and scarlet fall color.

A. saccharum 'HRI 1'—see A. saccharum 'Endowment Columnar'

A. saccharum 'Jocazam'—see A. saccharum Johnnycake™

A. saccharum Johnnycake™

= *A. saccharum* 'Jocazam'

Introduced in 1994–95 by Lake County nursery of Perry, OH. Leaves to 12" wide. Spectacular orange-red fall color. Vigorous; pyramidal habit.

A. saccharum 'Laciniatum'—see A. saccharum 'Sweet Shadow'

A. saccharum 'Lanco Columnar'—see A. sacch. 'Endowment Columnar'

A. saccharum 'Legacy' PP 4979 (1983)

Selected by W. Wandell of Urbana, IL. Introduced in 1981–82 by Moller nursery of Gresham, OR. Very vigorous dense oval habit, heavily branched. Thick, glossy leaves resist tatter. Reddish in fall, with shades of pink, orange and yellow. Performs better than many SUGAR MAPLE cultivars in drier locales and in the South. It is also exceptionally cold-hardy.

A. saccharum 'Majesty'—see A. saccharum 'Flax Mill Majesty'

A. saccharum Mountain Park™

Introduced ≤1991–92 by Moller nursery of Gresham, OR. Fall color excellent orange-red to scarlet. Branching even, not irregular. Mildew resistant.

A. saccharum 'Monumental'

Introduced in 1893 by Ellwanger & Barry nursery of Rochester, NY. Long extinct commercially. Pyramidal compact habit, the foliage of the second growth is brilliant crimson, which, contrasted with the rich green of the older foliage, produces a charming effect.

A. saccharum 'Monumentale'—see A. sacch. 'Newton Sentry' and 'Temple's Upright'

A. saccharum 'Moraine'—see A. saccharum 'Wright Brothers'

A. saccharum 'Newton Sentry'
= A. saccharum 'Columnare'
= A. saccharum 'Erectum'
= A. saccharum 'Sentry' (in part)
= A. saccharum 'Monumentale' hort., non Temple

SENTRY MAPLE. In 1954, B. Harkness proposed the name A. saccharum 'Newton Sentry' to replace F.L. Temple's name A. saccharum 'Columnare', since the latter was hopelessly confused in the nursery trade with Temple's A. saccharum 'Monumentale'. The confusion has remained, and even authoritative books and reputable nurseries continue to bungle the names and descriptions. There are two quite dissimilar cultivars, and yet mass confusion. Usually this cultivar has been sold as 'Columnare' but that name, although both oldest and most apt, has been proclaimed invalid because of a technicality. Moreover, the name 'Columnare' has also been applied to 'Temple's Upright' and to another clone ("selected from the best of those planted by Barney Slavin in Rochester, New York") sold by Scanlon nursery of Ohio in the 1960s and early '70s. The original 'Columnare' which is now properly called 'Newton Sentry' is pencil-slim, almost ludicrously skinny. It has few ascending branches, with several competing central leaders and stubby lateral branches. The leaves are dark, leathery, hairy beneath, with wavy margins. Fall color is primarily yellow and orange. The original specimen was discovered (<1871) in the yard of Claflin Grammar School of Newton, MA, and later (<1885) moved to Newton Cemetery. It was introduced commercially in 1885–86 by F.L. Temple of Shady Hill nursery of Cambridge, MA, as (here is the technical objection) A. saccharinum 'Columnare'. It is likely a cultivar of the BLACK SUGAR-MAPLE (subspecies nigrum). Records: 60' × 2'5" × 12' Spokane, WA (1988; pl. 1952); 60' × 4'2" × 17' at the Arnold Arboretum (1983); 50' × 4'2" × 14' the original specimen at Newton (1983).

A. saccharum ssp. nigrum (Michx. fil.) Desmarais
= A. nigrum Michx. fil.

BLACK SUGAR MAPLE. IOWA SUGAR MAPLE. This subspecies is darker in bark and leaf than typical SUGAR MAPLE. The leaves are less crisp-looking, being more three-lobed, droopy, and hairy beneath. Fall color is usually less spectacular. Unlike other MAPLES, often leafy stipules are at the base of the leaf stems. It tolerates alkaline soils better than typical SUGAR MAPLE, as well as more warmth and dryness, so is prized in the Midwest. Although this book indicates only three SUGAR MAPLE cultivars as BLACK MAPLES ('Greencolumn', 'Morton' and 'Slavin's Upright') there may be others (such as 'Newton Sentry'). Record: 118' × 16'6" × 127' Allegan County, MI (1986).

A. saccharum ssp. nigrum 'Greencolumn' PP 3722 (1975)
= A. nigrum 'Greencolumn'

Found in 1959 by Wm. R. Heard, as a natural seedling in Boone County, IA. Introduced commercially in 1977–78 by Schmidt nursery of Boring, OR. When found, the original specimen was estimated 75–90 years old, and stood 70' tall and 30' wide. Besides its broad columnar shape the tree had unusual alligator-like deeply furrowed bark. In cultivation it has proven tolerant of heat and dry conditions, and turns golden-orange in fall.

A. saccharum ssp. nigrum 'Morgan'
= A. nigrum 'Morgan'
Selected at the Morton Arboretum of Lisle, IL. Superb orange-red fall color. Not yet in commerce.

A. saccharum ssp. nigrum 'Slavin's Upright'
= A. nigrum 'Slavin's Upright'
= A. saccharum 'Slavin's Upright'
Selected as a 1903 seedling from a tree near Salamanca, NY. Raised in Highland Park of Rochester. Described in 1950, named in 1955, commemorating park horticulturist Bernard Henry Slavin (1873–1960). Distributed to some arboreta but scarcely ever offered commercially. Distinctly upright, with strong ascending branches, giving the whole tree a broadly columnar outline.

A. saccharum 'PNI 0285'—see A. saccharum Green Mountain®

A. saccharum 'Sandborn'
Named ≤1958. Rarely, if ever, grown commercially. Narrow columnar, 30' tall and 7' wide. On property of Mrs. E.R. Sandborn in Concord, NH.

A. saccharum 'Seneca Chief'
Introduced in 1979 by Schichtel nursery of Orchard Park, NY. Narrow, oval crown 60' tall, 30' wide; dense branching; yellow to orange fall color.

A. saccharum 'Senecaense'
= A. × senecaense Slavin
(A. saccharum × A. saccharum ssp. leucoderme)
SENECA SUGAR MAPLE. In 1919, B.H. Slavin gathered seeds of the CHALK MAPLE (A. saccharum ssp. leucoderme) from Seneca Park of Rochester, NY. None of the seedlings bred true—all resulted from cross-pollination. In 1925 nine of the hybrid trees were selected and planted in Durand Eastman Park. The name 'Senecaense' was published in 1950 and applies to any of the original nine trees; it is not a clonal name. Scanlon nursery of Ohio marketed one during the 1960s and '70s. It was described as a miniature version of ordinary SUGAR MAPLE, of a more compact crown and with smaller leaves.

A. saccharum 'Sentry'—see A. saccharum 'Newton Sentry' and 'Temple's Upright'

A. saccharum 'Skybound'
Introduced ca. 1988 by Synnestvedt nursery of Round Lake, IL. Crown tightly upright, almost oval. Fall color excellent yellow-orange.

A. saccharum 'Slavin's Upright'—see A. saccharum ssp. nigrum 'Slavin's Upright'

A. saccharum 'Summer Proof'
Origin unknown. A recent introduction, described by M. Dirr as heat-tolerant, resisting windburn, and of vigorous, spreading form.

A. saccharum 'Sweet Shadow' PP 2139 (1962)
= A. saccharum 'Laciniatum'
CUTLEAF SUGAR MAPLE. Introduced in 1961-62 by Powell Valley nursery of Gresham, OR. Still in the trade. Leaves deeply dissected in a ferny manner. Fall color exceptionally rich in the Midwest. See also A. saccharum 'Brocade'. Record: 48' × 2'9" × 35' Lynnwood, WA (1992).

A. saccharum 'Temple's Upright'
= A. saccharum 'Monumentale' of Temple, non hort.
= A. saccharum 'Columnare' (cf. A. saccharum 'Newton Sentry')
= A. saccharum 'Sentry' (cf. A. saccharum 'Newton Sentry')
Introduced in 1887–88 by F.L. Temple's Shady Hill nursery of Cambridge, MA. In 1954, B. Harkness proposed the name 'Temple's Upright' to replace Temple's 'Monumentale' which had been widely confused in the trade with Temple's 'Columnare' (that is, A. saccharum 'Newton Sentry'). Many ascending branches, one dominant central trunk; leaves yellow-green, not leathery, without wavy margins. This clone is substantially broader than 'Newton Sentry' and is not especially remarkable. Records: 85' tall at Rochester, NY (ca. 1980); 60' tall × 27' wide at the Arnold Arboretum (1976); 49' × 3'4" × 13' Hartford, CT (1988).

A. saccharum 'Wright Brothers' PP 4534 (1980)
= A. saccharum 'Moraine'
('Wright Bros.')
Introduced in 1980–81 by Siebenthaler's nursery of Dayton, OH—"the birthplace of aviation." Selected for rapid growth (about twice as fast as normal SUGAR MAPLES in trunk growth as a young tree), its uniform broad cone-shape, brilliant fall color of mottled gold,

orange, and scarlet, and its extreme cold-hardiness (hardy to -21°F). It resists frost-cracking and leaf-scorching.

A. sempervirens L.
= A. orientale auct., non L.
= A. creticum auct., non L.
= A. heterophyllum Willd.
= A. virens Th.

CRETAN MAPLE. From the NE Mediterranean region. Introduced to cultivation in 1702 when Tournefort planted one at the Jardin du Roi in Paris. Thence to England in 1752 by P. Miller. In North American cultivation ≤1964. Extremely rare; sold by Greer nursery of Oregon during the 1970s. A deciduous or partially evergreen (the epithet from Latin *semper*, always or ever, and *vivum*, alive or fresh) shrub ≤15' tall, rarely a small tree. In March it flushes chartreuse flowers, followed by the leaves. Leaf usually three-lobed, ¾"–2" long, ivy-green above; the edges untoothed or nearly so; stem ½"–⅞". Records: 40' tall at Wörlitz, Saxony (1836; *pl.* 1781); 25' × 5'5" Tregothnan, Cornwall, England (1984); 23' × 2'0" × 20¼' Seattle, WA (1994).

A. × senecaense —see A. saccharum 'Senecaense'

A. Shirasawanum Koidz.
= A. japonicum var. microphyllum Siesmayer, non Koidz.

SHIRASAWA MAPLE. From Japan. Japanese: O-itaya-meigetsu. Introduced to Western cultivation in 1876, well before 1911 when it was named after Homi Shirasawa (1868–1947). Extremely rarely cultivated—carried by maple specialist nurseries since the 1970s. Related closely to *Acer japonicum*, less closely to *Acer palmatum*, *A. Sieboldianum*, etc., this is a large shrub or small tree, with roundish leaves, 2"–5" wide, markedly shiny beneath, of 9–11 (13) lobes. The flowers are red and pale creamy-yellow. Young twigs hairless and coated with white powder. Seeds hairless, spreading at 180° angle. Fall color clear yellow, orange and red. Record: to 65' × 8'3" in Japan.

A. Shirasawanum 'Aureum'
= A. japonicum 'Aureum'
GOLDEN FULLMOON MAPLE. Introduced from Japan by Siebold to Holland ca. 1865, and by Veitch nursery of England in 1881. Thereafter Ellwanger & Barry

nursery of Rochester, NY, got it from Veitch. It has been grown a great deal more than typical *A. Shirasawanum*, and indeed was not known to belong to this species until 1981. Of bushy habit and slow stubby growth, with bright yellow foliage in spring. Best in partial shade, lest it scorch. Fall color can be gold, orange and scarlet. Record: 29' × 1'6" × 18' Tacoma, WA (1993).

A. Shirasawanum 'Junihitoye'
= A. japonicum 'Junihitoye'
(Junihitoe)
Compact; very small leaves; usually 2"–2¾", turning orange in fall. Colorful orange seeds also. To 12' tall in ten years. Offered in U.S. nurseries since the 1950s.

A. Shirasawanum 'Palmatifolium'
Origin unknown. Leaves deeply dissected in fernleaf fashion. A hardy sturdy tree to 30' tall; brilliant pale yellow to orange in fall, or yellow and gold touched with crimson. Rare. Offered by specialist maple nurseries since the 1970s.

A. Sieboldianum Miq.
SIEBOLD MAPLE. From Japan. Japanese: Itaya-meigatsu. Ko-hauchiwa-kaede. Named in 1865 after Philipp Franz Balthasar von Siebold (1796–1866). Siebold lived in Japan from 1823 to 1830, and introduced numerous Japanese plants to European cultivation. This species, however, was not one of them. It was introduced sometime between 1862 and 1864 when C.J. Maximowicz sent it to Russia. By 1879–80 it reached western Europe. C. Sargent collected seeds in Japan in 1892. Kohankie nursery of Ohio sold it in the late 1940s, but for the most part it has been sold only by maple specialist nurseries since the 1960s. It is closely related to *A. japonicum*, *A. palmatum*, *A. Shirasawanum*, and the unpleasantly named *A. pseudosieboldianum*. Leaves roundish, with (7) 9 (11) lobes; very downy when young. Fall color usually pumpkin-orange to dark red. Flowers yellowish-white, comparatively late to bloom. Records: 60' × 2'6" in Japan; 27' × 2'4" Seattle, WA (1994; *pl.* 1940).

A. spicatum Lam.
= A. montanum Ait.
MOUNTAIN MAPLE. From eastern North America, especially northwards. Called MOUNTAIN MAPLE because in the southern part of its range it is largely restricted to mountains. Although continuously offered in nurseries, and valued highly for its fall color, it is not long-lived in cultivation, being very much a

forest species. Usually a shrub. Leaf three-lobed, or weakly five-lobed, 2"–5" long. The name *spicatum* refers to its flower spikes 3"–6" long. Twigs fuzzy. The red or rose-colored seed clusters are pretty. Fall color orange, scarlet or yellow. Records: 58' × 2'9" × 31' Houghton County, MI (1982); 48' × 1'4" × 34' Leelanau County, MI (1964); 40' × 3'11" × 20' Croome, Worcestershire, England (1836; *pl.* 1830); 39' × 3'5" × 31' Baileys Harbor, WI (1987); 25' × 3'0" × 10' Great Smoky Mountains National Park, TN (≤1951).

A. striatum—see A. pensylvanicum

A. tataricum L.

TATARIAN or TARTARIAN MAPLE. TARTAR MAPLE. From SE Europe, W Asia. Introduced in 1759 to England by P. Miller. The date of its introduction to North America is unknown, but ≤1890. Usually a shrub, it can become a small tree. Its leaves (egg-shaped, unlobed usually, but three-lobed on strong shoots, 2"–4⅜" long; stem to 2¾") are scarcely what one would expect from a MAPLE, and its flowers, too, are unusual—delicately scented, creamy white, fading faintly pinkish, in May. But winged seeds show its affinities. Fall color is yellow, late and usually unspectacular. Sometimes it shows hints of flamingo-pink with green remaining in the veins. Compared to its AMUR MAPLE subspecies (with which it hybridizes), and its cultivar 'Rubrum', it is scarcely worth cultivating. Records: to 50' tall in the wild; 36' × 4'0" × 30' Madison, WI (1975); one trunk 4'10" around at Green Bay, WI (1975).

A. tataricum ssp. Ginnala (Maxim.) Wesm.
= A. Ginnala Maxim.

AMUR MAPLE. SIBERIAN MAPLE. From Turkestan, China, Manchuria, E Siberia (where the Amur Valley is), Korea, and Japan. Introduced to Russian cultivation in 1860. In 1874, the Arnold Arboretum received seeds from St. Petersburg botanic gardens. *Ginnala* is a name used by natives of Amur River Valley. Compared to typical *A. tataricum*, the AMUR MAPLE has shinier, narrower, three-lobed,

sharper leaves (1"–4½" long), and its flowers are greenish-white, then yellowish-white. The fall color is usually red. It has been much more cultivated. Left to itself, it becomes a suckering bushy tree (good for tub planting). It flushes green very early in spring. Variegated seedlings are comparatively common. Records: 49' × 9'3" Kansu, China (1925); 39' × 4'1" Skierniewice, Poland (≤1973); 33' × 3'0" × 43' Spokane, WA (1988); 24' × 5'6" × 45' Seattle, WA (1993).

A. tataricum ssp. Ginnala 'Bailey Compact'
= A. Ginnala 'Compacta'

COMPACT AMUR MAPLE. Selected and introduced ≤1975 by Bailey nursery of St. Paul, MN. Registered in 1979. Dense, compact, to 6'–8' tall. Thus a shrub, not a tree. Brilliant scarlet in fall. This cultivar is perhaps actually a selection of the subspecies *Semenowii*.

A. tataricum ssp. Ginnala 'Bergiana—see A. tataricum ssp. Ginnala 'V.N. Strain'

A. tataricum ssp. Ginnala 'Compacta'—see A. tataricum ssp. Ginnala 'Bailey Compact'

A. tataricum ssp. Ginnala 'Durand Dwarf'

A 5' tall bush, wider still. Originated as a bud mutation in Durand Eastman Park of Rochester, NY; described in July 1955.

A. tataricum ssp. Ginnala 'Embers'
= A. Ginnala 'Gordie's Select'

Selected and introduced ≤1989 by Bailey nursery of St. Paul, MN. Red seeds and outstanding scarlet fall leaf color. Likely named for Gordon Bailey.

A. tataricum ssp. Ginnala 'Flame'

Introduced ca. 1978 by the USDA Soil Conservation Service, from Missouri. A seed-propagated cultivar rather than a clone. Much grown by nurseries since its release. The claim to fame is its supposedly consistent fiery red fall color and vivid red seeds. However, the stock offered by nurseries is not uniform, with some specimens turning yellow in fall, and the growth form equally variable.

A. tataricum ssp. Ginnala 'Gordie's Select'— see A. tataricum ssp. Ginnala 'Embers'

A. tataricum ssp. Ginnala 'Mondy'—see A. tataricum ssp. Ginnala Red Rhapsody™

A. tataricum ssp. Ginnala Red Rhapsody™
= *A. tataricum* ssp. *Ginnala* 'Mondy'

Introduced ≤1991 by Monrovia nursery of California. An "improved" selection, brilliant in fall.

A. tataricum ssp. Ginnala 'Red Wing'
Introduced ≤1990 by McKay nursery of Waterloo, WI. Sold by Gurney nursery as RED WING MAPLE.

A. tataricum ssp. Ginnala 'V.N. Strain'
= *A. Ginnala* 'Bergiana'

Introduced ≤1980s by Clayton Berg's Valley nursery of Helena, MT (V N = Valley Nursery). Red seeds, brilliant red fall color, and increased hardiness. The name "strain" suggests it is seed-propagated rather than a clone. Probably if it were a clone, the best cultivar name would be 'Valley Nursery' or 'Berg'.

A. tataricum 'Hoerner'
Introduced ≤1993 by Schichtel nursery of Orchard Park, NY. A clone that has been recommended as a street tree.

A. tataricum 'Rubrum'
Regular *A. tataricum* except red fall color instead of yellowish. In commerce <1893, the year it was named officially.

A. tataricum ssp. Semenowii (Reg. & Herd.) E. Murr.
= *A. Ginnala* ssp. *Semenowii* (Reg. & Herd.) Schwer.

= *A. Ginnala* var. *Semenowii* (Reg. & Herd.) Pax

TURKESTAN SHRUB MAPLE. From Turkestan. Named in 1866 to honor the Russian scientist and traveller Peter Petrovich von Semenov-Tjan-Schansky (1827–1914). Introduced to cultivation in 1880, in Germany. To North America ≤1912; scarcely sold (under the *Semenowii* name at least) here, but present in arboreta. Closely related to subspecies *Ginnala*, but bushier (it can grow 30' tall). Leaves smaller (to 2⅜" long), less glossy, deeper lobed. Seeds bigger with wings more divergent. Fall color varies.

A. tegmentosum Maxim.
MANCHURIAN STRIPEBARK MAPLE. From Manchuria, and Korea. Introduced to cultivation by P.A. Lavallée at Segrez, France in 1877. To North America ≤1938. Rarely cultivated. A STRIPEBARK MAPLE, closely related to *A. pensylvanicum*, but having larger (to 9" wide), longer-stemmed, less hairy leaves, which flush earlier in spring and drop sooner in fall. Its twigs are also glaucous. It makes a bolder, heavier-looking tree, and, overall, a superior ornamental. Male and female flowers on separate trees. Records: to 49' tall in the wild; 46' × 3'4" × 36' Seattle, WA (1990; *pl.* 1949).

A. tegmentosum ssp. rufinerve—see A. rufinerve

A. tegmentosum 'White Tigress'
= *A.* 'White Tigress'

Introduced in 1995 by Roslyn nursery of Dix Hills, NY. "Pure chalk-white bark."

A. Trautvetteri—see A. Heldreichii ssp. Trautvetteri

A. trifidum—see A. Buergerianum

A. triflorum Kom.
THREE-FLOWERED MAPLE. ROUGH-BARKED MAPLE. From Manchuria, and Korea. Discovered in 1896 in Manchuria by V.L. Komarov. Introduced to England and the U.S. in 1923. Though considered a choice species, it has remained exceedingly rare, partly because of propagation difficulties. Related so closely to NIKKO MAPLE (*A. Maximowiczianum*) that the two taxa may well be considered one species, differing in details such as bark and pubescence. Leaflets three (rarely five), 1½"–5½" long; with a few coarse teeth or sublobes; scattered long pale hairs on both sides and on the stems and twigs. Fall color brilliant red to yellow-pink or salmon-pink. Bark finely scaly; curling in coils to give the trunk a pleasingly rugged look. In contrast, the NIKKO MAPLE is smooth-trunked, and its leaflets are untoothed, with short down. *Acer triflorum* flushes first in spring, and begins coloring a bit earlier in fall. Records: 60' tall recorded in Manchuria; 40' × 4'0" Bailey Arboretum, NY (ca. 1980); 36' tall and 60' wide at the Arnold Arboretum (1976).

A. truncatum Bge.

SHANTUNG MAPLE. PURPLEBLOW MAPLE. From N China. Shantung (Shandong) is a Province of China. Discovered in 1830. Seeds collected in NE China were sent by E. Bretschneider to Kew and the Arnold Arboretum in 1881. Scarcely offered by nurseries until the 1950s. Now being promoted as heat-tolerant and capable of giving good fall color in warmer regions. Widely planted in China, in cities there at least it adapts poorly to street conditions and suffers from insect damage and branch dieback. Closely related to and easily confused with *A. pictum*—which is a larger tree with larger leaves. Leaf five or seven-lobed, 2½"–4½" (6½") wide, usually hairless or nearly so; margins untoothed; coppery or purplish when unfolding in spring. The leaf stem has milky sap. Despite the name *truncatum* the leaf bases are not necessarily truncate. Fall color is comparatively late, usually red but can have gold, orange or yellow. Bark usually somewhat corky unlike that of the otherwise reminiscent *A. pictum* or *A. cappadocicum*. Overall the species might be likened to NORWAY MAPLE but is much smaller, and roundish, with smaller more elegant leaves. Records: 75' tall noted in the wild; 72' × 5'3" Birr Castle, County Offaly, Ireland (1986; *pl.* 1938); 56' × 7'4" × 48' Morris Arboretum, PA (1980).

A. truncatum 'Akikaze Nishiki'

= *A. truncatum* 'Shuhu Nishiki'

Origin unknown; presumably from Japan. Extremely rare. Leaves variegated creamy-white or pink, deformed, three to five-lobed, with obvious hairs beneath on the veins and on the stems. The leaves are also smaller on average, although can be 6" wide, with a stem 4⅜" long. Tree smaller; to 17' tall. It may actually be an *A. pictum* cultivar with fixed juvenile foliage.

A. truncatum 'Shuhu Nishiki'—see A. truncatum 'Akikaze Nishiki'

A. truncatum × A. platanoides 'Keithsform'—see A. truncatum × A. platanoides Norwegian Sunset™

A. truncatum × A. platanoides Norwegian Sunset™ PP 7529 (1991)

= *A. truncatum* × *A. platanoides* 'Keithsform'

Introduced in 1989 by Schmidt nursery of Boring, OR. Commonly grown since then. Yellow-orange to red fall color.

A. truncatum × A. platanoides Pacific Sunset™ PP 7433 (1991)

= *A. truncatum* × *A. platanoides* 'Warrenred'

Introduced in 1989 by Schmidt nursery of Boring, OR. Commonly grown since then. Differs from NORWAY MAPLE (*A. platanoides*) in being a smaller tree, with smaller leaves, more cordate at the base, and acute seed angles. Differs from *A. truncatum* in being larger, with larger leaves, the lobes toothed rather than entire, and the base cordate instead of usually truncate; seeds infertile. Pacific Sunset™ differs from Norwegian Sunset™ in that it colors earlier and more colorfully (yellow-orange to bright red) in fall.

A. truncatum × A. platanoides 'Warrenred'—see A. truncatum × A. platanoides Pacific Sunset™

A. Tschonoskii Maxim.

BUTTERFLY MAPLE. The origin of the name BUTTERFLY MAPLE is unknown; the Japanese name *Mine-kaede* means High Mountain Maple. From Japan, the S Kuriles, and ssp. *koreanum* E. Murr. (= var. *rubripes* Kom.) in Korea and Manchuria. Introduced to cultivation when C. Sargent sent seeds to the Arnold Arboretum in 1892. Almost never offered by nurseries. Named after Sukawa (Sugawa) T(s)chonoski (Chônosuke; 1841–1925), who was Carl Maximowicz's assistant while botanizing in Japan from 1860 to 1863. A shrub or small tree, with barely "striped" bark. Leaf 2"–4" long & wide, deeply five-lobed, rusty hairy beneath, very sharply toothed; stem often reddish. Fall color late, yellow, subdued orange or red. Record: 43' × 2'0" × 22½' Seattle, WA (1993—the year it died; *pl.* 1948).

A. velutinum Boiss. var. Van Volxemii (Mast.) Rehd.

= *A. insigne* Boiss. & Buhse var. *Van Volxemii* (Mast.) Pax

PERSIAN MAPLE. From the Caucasus. Belgian gardener Jean Van Volxem discovered this variant and sent seeds ca. 1873 to Kew, England; sent plants in 1887. In North America ≤1897; in the nursery trade here ≤1907, but has remained obscure and rare. Best compared to *A. Pseudoplatanus* (SYCAMORE MAPLE) but with large buds, larger leaves (to 12" wide, shallowly five-lobed; stem to 12" long) staying green later in fall than most MAPLES, then turning horrible brown usually, at best burnt orange. The leaf has hairs when young, but mostly these fall away except on the veins. Typical *Acer velutinum* (not cultivated) leaves stay hairy. Despite the wretched autumnal condition, the tree has a clean vigorous form and handsome summer foliage. Records: 131' × 12'4" in the wild; 88' × 8'6" Westonbirt, Gloucestershire, England (1981); 60' × 9'2" Tortworth Court, Gloucestershire, England (1972); 52' × 5'6" Sidney, B.C. (1993; *pl.* 1914).

A. velutinum 'Wolfii'

Named in Germany in 1905 after Prof. Egbert Wolf (1860–1931) of St. Petersburg. Unknown in North America. Leaves red-maroon beneath.

A. virens—see A. sempervirens

A. 'White Tigress'—see A. tegmentosum 'White Tigress'

Ægle sepiaria—see Poncirus trifoliata

ÆSculus

[HIPPOCASTANACEÆ; Horse Chestnut Family]
13–15 spp. of deciduous shrubs or trees, called HORSE CHESTNUTS or BUCKEYES. *Æsculus* is an ancient Latin name, given by the Roman naturalist Pliny to an OAK (*Quercus* sp.) with an edible seed; from Latin *esca*, food or nourishment; a reference to the ground flour from the kernels of some OAK species. The botanist Linnæus used the name *Æsculus* for the present unrelated genus, perhaps because of the large nut-like seeds. BUCKEYE and HORSE CHESTNUT leaves are borne in opposite pairs and are divided palmately into 3–11 large leaflets. In late spring or early summer the trees blossom, bearing upright panicles of attractive flowers. The fruit consists of thick, leathery husks which split in autumn to reveal shiny nuts looking like deer eyes, giving rise to the popular name BUCKEYE. Unless roasted, the nuts are poisonous. The species hybridize readily, and identification is often difficult. The "Buckeye" name is given to native American species; Old World species are called "Horse Chestnuts." Edible chestnuts are from genus *Castanea*.

Æ. arguta Buckl.
= *Æ. glabra* var. *arguta* (Buckl.) Robins.
= *Æ. glabra* var. *Sargentii* Rehd.
TEXAS BUCKEYE. WESTERN BUCKEYE. WHITE BUCKEYE.

From Texas, S Oklahoma, SE Nebraska, W Missouri and E Kansas. Introduced to cultivation in 1896 but rarely planted; thrives only in woodland settings. A shrub or small tree. The epithet *arguta* in Latin means sharply toothed, referring to the (5) 7 (11) leaflets, 2½"–6" long. Flowers pale yellow to yellow-green, in clusters 4"–8" long. Fall color cantaloupe-orange to yellow-brown. Nut husks 1"–1¾" and warty or weakly prickly. Closely related to *Æ. glabra*, but much smaller. Records: 35' × 4'8" Edwards Plateau, TX (n.d.); 33' × 1'9" Edinburgh, Scotland (1981); 32' × 3'2" × 21' Lisle, IL (1986; *pl.* 1934); 32' × 1'11" × 21' Dallas, TX (1980); 30' × 4'3" × 24' Harper, TX (1986).

Æ. × arnoldiana Sarg. 'Autumn Splendor'
= *Æ. sylvatica* 'Autumn Splendor'
[*Æ. glabra* × (*Æ. flava* × *Æ. Pavia*)]
Originated at the Minnesota Landscape Arboretum from an "*Æ. sylvatica*" nut obtained from the Morton Arboretum of Lisle, IL. But the offspring, in 1980 named 'Autumn Splendor', is thought to be a result of the parentage cited above. Since the tree maintains a dark color all summer, resists leaf-scorch, has intense maroon or brilliant red fall color, and is cold-hardy (to -25°F), it has been promoted since 1982 as a worthwhile ornamental shade tree.

Æ. austrina—see Æ. Pavia

Æ. californica (Spach) Nutt.
= *Pavia californica* (Spach) Hartweg
CALIFORNIA BUCKEYE. From California. Cultivated chiefly on the Pacific Coast. Supremely drought-adapted, it flushes early in spring, flowers, then drops its leaves and appears dead by August (or earlier). The nuts hang on and continue to ripen. Leaflets 5 (7), 2"–7" long. Flowers white or pink, in dense narrow clusters 3"–10" long. Nut husks 2"–3½" long, pear-shaped, without prickles. Bark ghostly gray-whitish, with some rusty pink. Planted in the maritime Pacific Northwest, this species flowers anytime between late May and mid-August, and its fall color is yellow, in October (in a dry summer it can go naked in September). A large shrub or small tree. Records: 60'–70' tall at Redwood City, CA (1938); 48'

× 14'6" × 78' Walnut Creek, CA (1972); 38' × 5'9" × 45' Seattle, WA (1989).

Æ. × *carnea* Hayne
= *Æ. rubicunda* Loisel.
(*Æ. Hippocastanum* × *Æ. Pavia*)

REDFLOWER HORSE CHESTNUT. RED HORSE CHESTNUT. PINK HORSE CHESTNUT. Originated ca. 1812, in Europe. Named in 1821. In North American nurseries ≤1850. Surely the most common large red-flowering tree in the temperate zone. A fertile octoploid, this hybrid reseeds readily, and its seedlings exhibit varying but essentially similar characteristics. The original seedling's flower color gave rise to the epithet *carnea*, Latin for flesh-colored. Most nurseries list the red-flowered 'Briotii' or other cultivars. Leaflets dark, 5 (7), 3"–10" long. Flowers deep pink or red, in clusters 5"–8" long. Nut husks 1½"–2" long, green with numerous pale brown freckles, minutely prickly. Trunk often with unsightly warty growths. Records: 90' × 8'10" Endsleigh, Devon, England (ca. 1978); 69' × 5'6" Seattle, WA (1988); 66' × 11'0" Sanding Park, Kent, Devon, England (ca. 1978); 64' × 7'7" Kalamazoo County, MI (1983); 62' × 7'11" Seattle, WA (1988); 46' × 9'8" × 50' Tacoma, WA (1992).

Æ. × *carnea* 'Briotii'

RUBY HORSE CHESTNUT. Dates from 1858; named after Pierre-Louis Briot (1804–1888), head gardener at Trianon Gardens of Versailles. Grown in North America since ≤1898 but rarer than typical *Æ. × carnea*—which sometimes is sold as 'Briotii'. Of compact habit; dark red flowers. Record: 92' × 8'5" Paris, France (1982; *pl.* 1862).

Æ. × *carnea* 'Fort McNair'

Introduced ≤1991–92. A selection from Fort McNair in Washington, D.C. Foliage handsome dark green until it drops. Flowers reddish-pink with yellow throats; in clusters 6"–8" long.

Æ. × *carnea* 'O'Neill Red'

Introduced ≤1979 by Monrovia nursery, California. Flowers bright red, not the flesh to scarlet of regular *Æ. × carnea*; clusters 10"–12" long. Leaves stay lustrous green, do not turn unsightly brown.

Æ. × *carnea* 'Plantierensis'
= *Æ. × plantierensis* André

NUTLESS PINK HORSE CHESTNUT. DAMASK HORSE CHESTNUT. This cultivar originated in Europe ca. 1843 as a seedling of an *Æ. Hippocastanum* that had been pollinated by *Æ. × carnea*. It was put into commerce ca.

1890 by the Simon Louis Frères nursery at Plantières, near Metz, France. Sparingly grown in North America since ≤1912. It is a sterile hexaploidal backcross hybrid. Flowers pink, producing few nuts if any.

Æ. *chinensis*—see *Æ. turbinata*

Æ. *discolor*—see *Æ. Pavia*

Æ. *flava* Soland.
= *Æ. octandra* Marsh.

YELLOW BUCKEYE. SWEET BUCKEYE. BIG BUCKEYE. From the eastern U.S. Not commonly planted, especially in the late 1980s and early '90s. Although elegant and colorful, its flowers lack the spectacular beauty of some other species, and the tree is not robust and tolerant of city life as is *Æ. Hippocastanum*. Its chief attraction is its lovely pastel to fiery fall color of yellow, salmon pink, orange, with some red; the leaf undersides are attractively pale. The name *flava*, Latin for yellow, refers to its flowers; the name *octandra* is Greek for 8 stamens. Western hunters called it BUCKEYE. Leaflets (3) 5 (7), 3"–12" long. Flowers creamy or pale yellow, in clusters 4"–7" long. Nut husks 2"–3" long, without prickles. Records: 145' × 17'10" Great Smoky Mountain National Park, TN (1984); 140' × 12'10" Bowers Creek, KY (1973).

Æ. *flava* var. *purpurascens*—see *Æ. × hybrida*

Æ. *georgiana*—see *Æ. sylvatica*

Æ. *glabra* Willd.
= *Pavia glabra* (Willd.) Spach

OHIO BUCKEYE. STINKING BUCKEYE. AMERICAN HORSE CHESTNUT. From the midwestern U.S. Commonly planted. James Brisbin, a Civil War general who loved trees passionately, said in 1888: "This tree reaches to the height of forty or fifty feet; it is one of the first trees to put forth leaves in the spring. It is only recommended for its beauty; cattle sometimes kill themselves from gorging with the nuts. As a timber tree it is a delusion and a snare, and not worth cultivating." He might have added that its fall color is especially

attractive bright red, orange or yellow. The bruised leaves and twigs stink. Leaflets 5 (7), 3"–6" long, often relatively hairless (hence the epithet *glabra*). Flowers inconspicuous, pale yellowish, in clusters 4"–8" long. Nut husks 1½"–2¼" long and prickly, unlike those of other native BUCKEYES. Records: 146' × 11'1" Liberty, KY (1973); 98' × 10'4" Crawfordsville, IN (1971); 79' × 12'5" Carlisle, PA (1978).

Æ. glabra var. *arguta*—see *Æ. arguta*

Æ. glabra var. *Sargentii*—see *Æ. arguta*

Æ. Hippocastanum L.

HORSE CHESTNUT. WHITE (HORSE) CHESTNUT. COMMON HORSE CHESTNUT. CANDLE TREE. CONKER TREE. From N Greece, Albania, and Bulgaria. A tree of magnificent stature casting dense shade, with showy white flowers in late spring. *Hippocastanum* is from Greek *hippo*, horse, and *kastanon*, chestnut (kept capitalized in the specific epithet because it is an old generic name—the vernacular name Latinized). Cultivated in W Europe since the 1500s. Introduced to North America between 1741 and 1746 when P. Collinson sent seeds to Wm. Bartram. Well known and very common; reseeding much, if not naturalized, in some locales. Leaflets (5) 7, large (to 13" × 6½") and dark. Flowers white, during April and May, in clusters 8"–12" long; can number as many as 223 per cluster; after pollination each flower turns from partly yellow to pink. Nut husks prickly, 2"–3" wide. Fall color yellow-brown, late and rarely lovely. Winter leafbuds distinctively large and varnished; sticky. Records: 134' height recorded by H. Edlin (1975); 125' × 19'2" Petworth, Sussex, England (1961); 118' × 22'0" Hurstbourne Prior's Church, Hampshire, England (1984); 108' × 11'4" Harford County, MD (1972); 92' × 12'5" Canton, CT (1988); 82' × 14'4" Greenwich, CT (1988); 83' × 14'6" Walla Walla, WA (1988); 73' × 20'8" West Brooklin,

ME (1985); 72' × 15'2" Ann Arbor, MI (1979); 71' × 15'6" Portsmouth, NH (1981).

Æ. Hippocastanum 'Aurea'

Described by Scanlon nursery of Ohio as a tree found ca. 1950, and propagated ca. 1968. Sold by Scanlon in the early 1970s. Extinct commercially. A large tree, maintaining *golden* foliage for about two months in spring, then turning green. If Scanlon's tree is indeed a new cultivar (not an old one renamed), its name, being Latin, is invalid unless it was used <1959.

Æ. Hippocastanum 'Albo-pleno'—see *Æ. Hippo.* 'Baumannii'

Æ. Hippocastanum 'Baumannii'

= *Æ. Hippocastanum* 'Flore Pleno' or 'Plena' or 'Albo-pleno'

DOUBLE HORSE CHESTNUT. NUTLESS HORSE CHESTNUT. In 1819, Constantin Auguste Napoléon Baumann (1804–1884) found a sport on an otherwise normal tree in the garden of M. Duval near Geneva. He sent grafts to his father's nursery at Bollwiller, Alsace. Sold in North America ≤1850, and commonly offered in the early 1900s. Flowers double, produce very few nuts if any; blooms several weeks later than regular *Æ. Hippocastanum*. The flowers also last longer, and the tree grows taller and narrower. Records: 105' × 12'6" Westonbirt, Gloucestershire, England (1983); 88' × 15'0" Hall Place, Kent, England (1984); 83' × 11'5" Spokane, WA (1988); 79' × 15'2" Seattle, WA (1987).

Æ. Hippocastanum 'Flore Pleno'—see *Æ. Hippocastanum* 'Baumannii'

Æ. Hippocastanum 'Plena'—see *Æ. Hippocastanum* 'Baumannii'

Æ. Hippocastanum 'Pyramidalis'

B.K. Boom says this originated in Germany ca. 1891; certainly it was introduced there by Späth nursery <1895. It may be a renaming of a clone called 'Pyramidata' by the French horticulturist A. Lavallée in 1877. Very rare in North America; here by 1896. In the 1990 catalog of Weston nursery of Massachusetts. Narrowly upright and dense but weak growth. A 1972 survey of Long Island's record-sized trees, found (at the Brooklyn Botanic Garden) the largest 'Pyramidalis' trunk only 3'5" around.

Æ. 'Homestead'

HOMESTEAD BUCKEYE. Introduced in 1990 by North Dakota State University, Brookings. Selected as a superior tree found in Brookings, ca. 110' × 11'0" × 73'. Parentage unknown but likely *Æ. glabra* × *Æ. flava*. Leaf highly resists scorching and powdery mildew. Fall color deep red with a hint of burnt orange. Flowers creamy-yellow like those of *Æ. glabra*. Usually sets no nuts.

Æ. × *hybrida* DC.
= *Æ. octandra* var. *hybrida* (DC.) Sarg.
= *Æ. octandra* var. *purpurascens* (A. Gray) Bean
= *Æ. flava* var. *purpurascens* A. Gray
(*Æ. flava* × *Æ. Pavia*)

HYBRID BUCKEYE. Named in 1813, in France. Although nurseries do not list this hybrid, it occurs occasionally, and sometimes is found in cultivation. Intermediate between its parents. Leaflets 5 (7), 4"–6" long. Flowers yellowish, reddish or (usually) mixed, in clusters 4"–6" long.

Æ. indica (Wallich *ex* Camb.) Hook.
HIMALAYAN HORSE CHESTNUT. INDIAN HORSE CHESTNUT. From the Himalayas, Nepal westward. Named in 1829; introduced to European cultivation in 1851; perhaps not established in North America until the 1950s. Very rare here and scarcely found in commerce. Compared to the common *Æ. Hippocastanum*, this species is a cold-tender, refined, glossy, connoisseur's tree, it flowers a month or so later; the leaves stay green very late into fall (mid-November in Seattle). Leaflets (5) 7 (9), 6"–12" long. Flowers whitish-pink, in clusters 5"–16" long. Nut husks 1½"–3" long, rough but not prickly. Records: to 150' × 40'0" in the wild; 70' × 8'9" Townhill Park, Hampshire, England (1985); 42' × 6'2" × 45' Los Angeles, CA (1993); 36½' × 4'4" × 26½' Victoria, B.C. (1994); 35' × 5'7" × 30' Seattle, WA (1992).

Æ. × *neglecta* Lindl.
(*Æ. sylvatica* × *Æ. flava*)
Named in 1826, in Europe. Not in commerce. See *Æ. sylvatica*.

Æ. neglecta var. *georgiana*—see *Æ. sylvatica*

Æ. × *neglecta* 'Erythroblastos'
= *Æ. neglecta* 'Roseo-variegata'
SUNRISE HORSE CHESTNUT. Found by nurseryman R. Behnsch in Silesia and introduced commercially in 1912–13 by Späth nursery of Germany. Extremely rare in North America. A precious, delicate little grafted tree. Name from Greek *erythros*, red, and *blastos*, budded. Bright shrimp-pink young leaves, then pale, chlorotic-looking green with yellow between the veins by flowering time. Fall color yellow in late September. Flowers chiefly pale yellow, with a hint of muted pink. Records: 39' × 2'2" × 21' Seattle, WA (1992); 30' × 2'9" Westonbirt, Gloucestershire, England (1982).

Æ. neglecta 'Roseo-variegata'—see *Æ.* × *neglecta* 'Erythroblastos'

Æ. octandra—see *Æ. flava*

Æ. octandra var. *hybrida*—see *Æ.* × *hybrida*

Æ. octandra var. *purpurascens*—see *Æ.* × *hybrida*

Æ. Pavia L.
= *Æ. discolor* Pursh, non hort.
= *Æ. austrina* Small
= *Æ. rubra* hort.
= *Pavia rubra* Lam.

RED BUCKEYE. RED-FLOWERING BUCKEYE. FIRE-CRACKER PLANT. FISH-POISON BUSH. SCARLET BUCKEYE. WOOLY BUCKEYE. From the southeastern U.S. Common. Best in woodland conditions. A slender shrub or small tree featuring superb garden size and excellent floral display. Named after Peter Paaw (Latinized as Petrus Pavius; 1564–1617), Dutch botanist in Leiden, Holland. Leaflets (3) 5 (7), 2"–9" long, remain green late into autumn and lack handsome fall color. Flowers showy bright red (sometimes yellow), in clusters 4"–10" long that attract hummingbirds. Nut husks 1"–2" (3") long, green beneath numerous pale brown specks. Records (reports of much larger sizes are *Æ.* × *carnea* misidentifications): to 40' tall claim both J. Loudon and C. Sargent; 39' × 4'2" Goodwood Park, Sussex, England (ca. 1978); 35' × 3'9" × 33' Georgetown, SC (1968); 21' × 1'10" × 25' Seattle, WA (1993); 20' × 1'5" × 16' Alexander, IL (1972); 17' × 2'5" × 25' Parkland, WA (1992).

Æ. Pavia 'Splendens'
= *Æ. splendens* Sarg.
Some observers claim this is the handsomest BUCKEYE. Flowers bright red, broad, in clusters to 10" long. The

leaf is pale, shiny and the leaflets broad. Overall no more handsome than the best *Æ. Pavia* seedlings. Rarely offered by nurseries, but Princeton of New Jersey has listed it since ≤1991.

Æsculus × plantierensis—see *Æ. × carnea* 'Plantierensis'

Æ. rubicunda—see *Æ. × carnea*

Æ. rubra—see *Æ. Pavia*

Æ. splendens—see *Æ. Pavia* 'Splendens'

Æ. sylvatica Bartr.
= *Æ. georgiana* Sarg.
= *Æ. neglecta* var. *georgiana* (Sarg.) Sarg.
= *Æ. neglecta* auct., non Lindl.

PAINTED BUCKEYE. GEORGIA BUCKEYE. From the southeastern U.S. The epithet *sylvatica* means of the woods. Introduced to cultivation in 1905. Very rare. Leaflets five, 4½"–6" (8") long. Flowers red and yellow, pale yellow or pink, in clusters 4"–8" long. Nut husks without prickles, 1"–2" long. Formerly referred to as *Æ. neglecta*, which is now thought to be *Æ. sylvatica × Æ. flava*. A shrub or small 30' tree; exceptionally to 60' tall. Record (identification highly suspect; likely *Æ. flava*): 144' × 13'3" Chattahoochee National Forest, Union County, GA (1970).

Æ. sylvatica 'Autumn Splendor'—see *Æ. × arnoldiana* 'Autumn Splendor'

Æ. turbinata Bl.
= *Æ. chinensis* hort., non Bge., non Diels

JAPANESE HORSE CHESTNUT. Japanese: *Tochi-no-ki*. From Japan. Introduced by Siebold to Holland ≤1862; <1880 to France; ≤1887 to North America. Grown sparingly here. Very similar to *Æ. Hippocastanum* but overall less robust and more elegant. Leaflets usually larger (to 18" × 7"), bluer beneath, and hairier. Flower clusters narrower, 6"–12" long, appearing later in spring. Nut husks smaller, to 2¼" wide, top-shaped (i.e., *turbinate*), without prickles. Fall color can be rich orange. Records: to 130' × 31'6" in Japan; 82' × 7'0" Westonbirt, Gloucestershire, England (1988); 72' × 8'8" Westonbirt, Gloucestershire, England (1988; *pl.* 1883); 65' × 6'1" × 50' Montgomery County, PA (1980); 37' × 6'4" × 34' Seattle, WA (1990).

Ailanthus

[SIMAROUBACEÆ; Quassia Family] 5 spp. of deciduous trees from East Asia. From *ailanto* (Amboinese Indonesian name for *A. moluccana* DC. or *A. integrifolia* Lamk.), meaning Heaven Tree, Sky Tree or "Reaching for the Sky," likely an allusion to its loftiness. Large trees bearing compound leaves suggestive of SUMACH (*Rhus* spp.). One species is widely grown and naturalized in North America. The only related genus in this volume is *Picrasma*.

A. altissima (Mill.) Swing.
= *A. glandulosa* Desf.
= *A. cacodendron* (Ehrh.) Schinz & Thell.
= *A. japonica* hort. *ex* Rehd.
= *Toxicodendron altissimum* Mill.

TREE OF HEAVEN. TREE OF BROOKLYN. CHINESE SUMACH. STINKING CHUN. HEAVENWOOD. PARADISE TREE. VARNISH TREE. GHETTO PALM. COPAL TREE. STINK TREE. ASHCAN TREE. From China, and a variety in Taiwan. The epithet *altissima* is the Latin superlative meaning very high or tallest, from *altus*, high. Introduced to European cultivation ca. 1750 by Pierre d'Incarville; to North America in 1784 by Wm. Hamilton. During the 1840s it was very popular here. It has long run wild in cities, spreading by reseeding and root-suckering. Roots can sucker more than 150' from the trunk. Fast-growing, its appearance is bold and tropical, with an open branching pattern of stout, lustrous, rich-colored twigs. Leaves compound, 1'–2' long (even to 6' on suckers), of 9–25 (41) leaflets. Flowers small, abundant, creamy or greenish, in June or July. Male flowers stink. Female flowers, usually on separate trees, make winged seeds, often bright orange-red in August; persisting on the trees through winter. Bark smooth, gray. Records: 102' × 8'3" Bath Botanic Garden, Avon, England (1990); 100' × 9'9" Endsleigh, Devon, England (1974); 89' × 6'11" Walla Walla, WA (1988); 82' × 17'10" Cheston-on-Wye, MD (1951); 64' × 19'10" Head of Harbor, NY (≤1992).

A. altissima f. erythrocarpa (Carr.) Rehd.

First described in 1862. Little cultivated. Seeds bright red. Name from Greek *erythros*, red, and *karpos*, fruit.

A. altissima 'Metro'

Introduced recently by W. Wandell of Urbana, IL. Male; compact crown.

A. altissima 'Pendulifolia'

Originated <1889. Imported from Europe to the U.S. in 1925 by the Arnold Arboretum. Extremely rare. Scarcely ever offered in commerce. Growth slower; leaves long, with pendulous leaflets.

A. cacodendron—see A. altissima

A. flavescens—see Toona sinensis

A. Giraldii Dode

From E Szechwan, China. Introduced ca. 1893. Described in 1907. Named after Père Giuseppe Giraldi (1848–1901), Italian missionary who collected plants in China during the 1890s. Almost certainly a minor variant of *A. altissima* rather than a separate species. Grown in U.S. botanic gardens since ≤1936. Scarcely if ever offered commercially. Records: 98' × 10'6" Paris, France (1982; *pl.* 1912); 55' × 9'8" × 75' Seattle, WA (1994; *pl.* 1972).

A. glandulosa—see A. altissima

A. japonica—see A. altissima

A. Vilmoriniana Dode

DOWNY TREE OF HEAVEN. From Szechwan and W Hupeh, China. Introduced in 1897 to France. Described in 1904. Named after French horticulturist Maurice Lévêque de Vilmorin (1849–1918). Sold during 1940s and '50s by some Ohio nurseries; likely offered also at other times and places. Very rare overall. Differs from *A. altissima* in: glossy leaflets, downy leaf-stems, occasional spines on its stems (especially on younger growth), and larger, airier flower clusters. Perhaps less cold-hardy. Recorded to 130' tall in China.

Albizia

(*Albizzia*)

[LEGUMINOSÆ; Pea Family] 100–150 spp. of mostly tropical and subtropical trees and shrubs. Related to closely genus *Acacia*. Only one species known to be hardy and lovely enough to be cultivated widely in temperate areas. Named after Filippo degli Albizzi, a Florentine nobleman, who in 1749 introduced this genus to cultivation in Tuscany from Constantinople.

A. chinensis—see A. Kalkora

A. Julibrissin Durazz.

= *A. Nemu* (Willd.) Benth.
= *Acacia Nemu* Willd.
= *Acacia Julibrissin* (Durazz.) Willd.
= *Mimosa Julibrissin* (Durazz.) Scop.

SILK TREE. JAPANESE SILK TREE. MIMOSA TREE. PERSIAN ACACIA. PINK ACACIA. PINK SIRIS. NEMU. From the Near East, Ethiopia, India, China, Taiwan, Japan, and Okinawa. Introduced to European cultivation ca. 1745 by Pierre d'Incarville and R. Bateman; to North America in 1785 by A. Michaux. A well known tree of delicate, tropical luxuriance. It thrives on much sunshine and heat. Its tiny lacy frond-like leaflets "go to sleep" by folding up at night; and drop in fall without coloring. Flowers showy pink powder puffs in summer. Seedpods flat, 3"–7" long. A rapid-growing, usually short lived tree of a natural umbrella shape. *Julibrissin* from Persian *gul-ebruschin*, meaning floss-silk (short silken threads), referring to the flowers. *Mimosa* means delicate or sensitive, from the Spanish vernacular name *Yerba mimosa*. Related to the Greek *mimos* (Latin *mimus*), mime, from its imitation of animal sensitivity: the leaflets close when touched, to mimic a wilted leaf. *Nemu* is a Japanese name. Despite its name, this SILK TREE should not be confused with the tree that feeds the silkworm— the very different WHITE MULBERRY (*Morus alba*). Records (often shrubby in the north): 60' × 6'7" × 77' Philadelphia, PA

(1969); 54' × 12'0" × 81' Webster Parish, LA (1986); 46' × 7'5" × 72' Vancouver, WA (1990); 41' × 9'8" × 60' Gilmer, TX (1971).

Albizia Julibrissin 'Charlotte'

One of two wilt-resistant cultivars introduced in 1949 by the USDA (mimosa wilt disease is caused by a fungus). From Charlotte, NC. Flowers light pink.

A. Julibrissin Flame®

A dark-flowered selection introduced ≤1990 by L.E. Cooke nursery of Visalia, CA.

A. Julibrissin 'Ernest H. Wilson'

Ernest Henry Wilson (1876–1930) sent seeds in 1918 from Korea to the Arnold Arboretum. The offspring were referred to *A. Julibrissin* var. *rosea*, and this cultivar, named only in 1968, is distinguished by its superior cold-hardiness.

A. Julibrissin var. *rosea* (Carr.) Mouill.

= *A. Julibrissin* f. *rosea* (Carr.) Rehd.
= *A. Julibrissin* 'Rosea'

HARDY SILK TREE. HARDY MIMOSA TREE. Named in France in 1870. Introduced to North America in 1918 when E. Wilson sent seeds from Korea to the Arnold Arboretum. Flowers darker pink (hence the name *rosea*) than those of typical *A. Julibrissin*; tree more cold-hardy. Grown from seeds or vegetatively.

A. Julibrissin 'Tryon'

Mimosa wilt disease was first noticed in 1930 at Tryon, NC. This wilt-resistant cultivar was introduced in 1949 by the USDA. Flowers deep pink.

A. Kalkora (Roxb.) Prain

= *A. chinensis* sensu F. Meyer, non (Osb.) Merr.

WHITE MIMOSA. From India and SW China. Described in 1814. Introduced to Western cultivation in 1818. To North America ≤1907. Grown in arboreta and botanic gardens from Washington, D.C., and southward, and on the Pacific Coast. Scarcely known in the nursery trade since the late 1950s. Its hardiness is likely similar to that of *A. Julibrissin*, but it is rare because it is less lovely. Compared to *A. Julibrissin*, it is a stronger tree, with rougher bark, only 12–16 much larger leaflets (ca. 1¼" × ⅝"), and flowers of creamy-white or yellowish. Seedpod to 6" × 1¼". *Kalkora* is a Bengal name. Records: 78' × 9'10" in China; 36' × 4'1" × 45' Los Angeles, CA (1993; *pl.* 1955).

A. Nemu—see *A. Julibrissin*

Alnus

[BETULACEÆ; Birch Family] 20–35 spp. of primarily deciduous shrubs and trees. *Alnus* is the ancient Latin name of the ALDER (not to be confused with the ELDER, genus *Sambucus*). Related to BIRCHES (genus *Betula*), but bearing seeds in distinctive miniature cones instead of in disintegrating catkin-like bodies. Characteristic of wet ground, and capable of fixing nitrogen symbiotically through root nodules. Of little glamor or color, they are planted more for reforestation and reclamation projects than for ornament. Wilson Flagg wrote over 100 years ago: "Nature seems to regard alders as plain and useful servants, not to be decked with beautiful colors or grand proportions for the admiration of the world." The elongated male flower catkins in late winter or spring often offer subtle beauty. A few species' summer foliage is glossy and makes for a handsome shade tree.

A. californica—see *A. rhombifolia*

A. communis—see *A. glutinosa*

A. cordata (Loisel.) Duby

= *A. cordifolia* Ten.

ITALIAN ALDER. NEAPOLITAN ALDER. From Italy and Corsica. Named in 1810 (Latin *cordatus*, heart-shaped, referring to the leaves). Introduced in 1815 to France; to England in 1818. In North American commerce since ≤1854. Uncommon in the trade. Catkins expand to 6½" long. Leaves glossy, 1½"–5" long, finely toothed; reminiscent of leaves of common PEAR TREES (*Pyrus communis*). Cones relatively massive, ⅝"–1¼" long. Crown spire-like. Records: 111' × 9'8" Westonbirt, Gloucestershire, England (1988); 98' × 7'6" Marble Hill Park, London, England (1990); 81' × 5'7" Seattle, WA (1993); 66' × 9'6" Canterbury Cathedral, England (1984); 59' × 16'3" × 85' Auckland, New Zealand (≤1982; *pl.* ca. 1850); 39' × 12'9" Tottenham House, Wiltshire, England (1984).

A. cordifolia—see *A. cordata*

A. crispa ssp. *sinuata*—see *A. sinuata*

A. firma S. & Z.
= *A. yasha* Matsum.

From Japan. Named in 1845 (*firma* referring to the thin but tough leaves). Introduced to Western cultivation in 1892. Exceedingly rare. Promoted since ≤1994 by Heritage Seedlings of Salem, OR. A shrub or densely branched small tree. Leaves slender and sharply pointed, 2"–4" (5¼") long, with close parallel veins of 10–18 pairs, recalling those of certain *Carpinus* (HORNBEAM trees). Winter buds unstalked, unlike those of most ALDERS. Catkins late, to 3¼" long, attractive yellow or yellow-green, unfolding with the leaves in spring. Cones oval, ⅝"–¾" long. Bark of trunk eventually comes off in large flaky plates. Records: 50' × 4'3" Hollycombe, Liphook, Hampshire, England (1984); 40' × 4'0" Kew, England (1967; *pl.* 1893); 28' × 2'4" × 27' Seattle, WA (1994; *pl.* 1968).

A. glutinosa (L.) Gaertn.
= *A. communis* Mirb.
= *A. vulgaris* Pers.

BLACK ALDER. EUROPEAN ALDER. COMMON ALDER. From Europe, N Africa, W Asia, Siberia. Introduced to North America in colonial days. Naturalized in some locales. Named *glutinosa* because of gummy or gluey young twigs and leaves. Called BLACK ALDER because of the comparatively dark bark (it isn't black). Catkins expand to 7⅝" long. Leaves broad (even roundish), shining, dark, 1½"–6¾" long. Cones ⅓"–⅝" (1") long. Very fast-growing. Records: to 115' tall in the wild; 87' × 5'6" Cumru, PA (1968); 76' × 8'9" Davenport, IA (1992); 70' × 10'11" Princeton, IL (1982); a trunk 17'6" around near Ullapool, Scotland (1986).

A. glutinosa 'Aurea'

Originated ca. 1860 in Belgium by the nurseryman D. Vervaene. In North American commerce since ≤1890. Rare. Slow, small, even shrubby, with yellowish leaves in spring, and orange bark.

A. glutinosa 'Fastigiata'—see *A. glutinosa* f. *pyramidalis*

A. glutinosa 'Imperialis'

ROYAL ALDER. Originated ca. 1853 in Belgium. In North American commerce since ≤1890. Uncommon. Slow, slender. Leaves deeply dissected. The origin of the name, meaning imperial or majestic, is unknown. Records: 56' × 3'9" Thorp Perrow, Yorkshire, England (1981); 40' × 3'2" Niagara Falls,

Ontario (1975); 39' × 5'9" Kington, Hereford & Worcestershire, England (1985); 36' × 2'4½" Spokane, WA (1992).

A. glutinosa 'Incisa'
= *A. incisa* hort.
= *A. glutinosa* 'Oxyacanthifolia'

HAWTHORN-LEAF ALDER. Originated 1800 in Germany. Very weak. A slow dense shrub or 50' tree in England. Leaf very small (usually <1" long), rounded, with broad blunt lobes, ± deeply incised, recalling those of a European HAWTHORN, *Cratægus lævigata*.

A. glutinosa 'Laciniata'

CUTLEAF ALDER. Found ca. 1750, in France. In North American commerce ≤1884. Rarer than *A. glutinosa* 'Imperialis'. Normal in tree size, but leaves cut about halfway into 6–7 lobes.

A. glutinosa 'Oxyacanthifolia'—see *A. glutinosa* 'Incisa'

A. glutinosa f. *pyramidalis* (Dipp.) Winkl.
= *A. glutinosa* 'Pyramidalis'
= *A. glutinosa* 'Fastigiata'

UPRIGHT EUROPEAN ALDER. Found ca. 1880, in Europe. In North America since ≤1896. Very rare. Narrowly upright growth. Breeds more or less true when seed-propagated, so more than one clone exists. Generally weaker and smaller than ordinary *A. glutinosa* seedlings. Record: 49' tall and 12' wide at Lisle, IL (1986; *pl.* 1948).

A. incana (L.) Moench

EUROPEAN GRAY ALDER. EUROPEAN WHITE ALDER. From Europe and the Caucasus. Alternatively, some botanists view it as a variable circumpolar species. Introduced in 1780 to English cultivation. In North American commerce ≤1915. Still in the trade. Called GRAY ALDER because of the light bark compared to that of BLACK ALDER, *A. glutinosa*. *Incana* is Latin for quite gray, hoary (referring to the downy, grayish shoots). Leaf 2"–4" long, gray-hairy. Cones ⁷⁄₁₆"–⅝" long. Records: 92' × 4'3" and 79' × 6'3" at Castle Milk, Dumfries, Scotland (1984; *pl.* 1928); 75' × 7'6" in Scandinavia (≤1968).

A. incana 'Acuminata'—see *A. incana* 'Laciniata'

A. incana 'Acutiloba'—see *A. incana* 'Laciniata'

A. incana 'Aurea'

Described in 1892 in Germany. Scarcely ever offered in North American nurseries. Twigs yellow, orange in winter. Catkins showy orange-red. Growth reduced, leaves smaller. Similar to *A. incana* 'Ramulis Coccineis' except the leaves are hairy beneath.

A. incana f. coccinea—see A. incana 'Ramulis Coccineis'

A. incana 'Incisa'—see A. incana 'Pinnata'

A. incana 'Laciniata'
= *A. incana* 'Acutiloba'
= *A. incana* 'Pinnatifida' Gren. & Godr. 1855, non Wahl. 1824
= *A. incana* 'Acuminata'

Described in 1830 in Germany. In North America ≤1896; in commerce here ≤1915. Leaves sharply, deeply incised.

A. incana 'Pendula'

WEEPING GRAY ALDER. Introduced <1896 by Van der Bom nursey of Holland. In North American commerce at least from the late 1930s into the mid-'50s. Rare. A mounded little tree. Record: 31' × 6'9" Westonbirt, Gloucestershire, England (1966).

A. incana 'Pinnata'
= *A. incana* 'Incisa'
= *A. incana* 'Pinnatifida' Wahl. 1824, non Gren. & Godr. 1855
= *A. incana* 'Pinnatifida Parvifolia'

Described in 1790 in Sweden. Scarcely grown in North America. Leaves small, deeply lobed.

A. incana 'Pinnatifida'—see A. incana 'Laciniata' and 'Pinnata'

A. incana 'Pinnatifida Parvifolia'—see A. incana 'Pinnata'

A. incana 'Ramulis Coccineis'
= *A. incana* f. *coccinea* Call.

Described in Germany in 1903. Scarcely if ever offered in North American commerce. Introduced to the U.S. in 1967 by the Arnold Arboretum. Attractive in winter with bright orange-red twigs, bright red leafbuds and catkins. The name is Latin for scarlet-twigged. Similar to *A. incana* 'Aurea' but leaves almost hairless beneath.

A. incana ssp. rugosa—see A. rugosa

A. incana ssp. rugosa var. occidentalis—see A. tenuifolia

A. incana ssp. tenuifolia—see A. tenuifolia

A. incisa—see A. glutinosa 'Incisa'

A. japonica (Th.) Steud.

JAPANESE ALDER. From E Manchuria, Korea, N Japan, Taiwan, and the Philippines. Introduced to Holland in 1866. In North America ≤1896; in commerce here ≤1930. Rare. It is only one of 10 species of *Alnus* in Japan. An elegant species with drooping, narrow, conspicuously pointed, medium-green to bluish-green leaves, 2"–7½" long, persisting into November. Cones ¾"–1" long. Bark chunky, gray with red cracks. Records: 100' × 10'4" in Japan; 73' × 4'11" Seattle, WA (1994; *pl.* 1958); 62' × 8'10" Edinburgh, Scotland (1985).

A. oregona—see A. rubra

A. rhombifolia Nutt.
= *A. californica* hort. *ex* Winkl.

WHITE ALDER. SIERRA ALDER. CALIFORNIA ALDER. From W Idaho, Washington, Oregon, California and W Nevada. Introduced to cultivation ca. 1885. Sold commonly only in California. Valued for fast growth and tolerance of wet ground. Mistletoe-prone, usually short-lived. Catkins expand to 6" long. Leaf 2"–4" (5¼") long. Cones petite, ½"–⅞" long. Named WHITE ALDER because of the pale greenish foliage. Records: to 115' tall in the wild; 105' × 11'1" Ashland, OR (1972); 99' × 14'6" Ashland, OR (1977; cut down ≤1979).

A. rubra Bong., non Marsh.
= *A. oregona* Nutt.

RED ALDER. WESTERN ALDER. OREGON ALDER. From SE Alaska to S California. Introduced to cultivation <1880. Little planted because not ornamental. Of recent importance in wetland restoration planting. Catkins expand to 7" long. Leaves 3"–7" (11") long, prominently scalloped. Cones ⅔"–1⅛" long. The epithet *rubra* is from Latin *ruber*, red; the tree's inner bark is very orange-red. The largest-growing ALDER of those in this book. Records: 136' × 4'2" Olympic National Forest, WA (1989); 104' × 20'5" Clatsop County, OR (1979).

A. rubra f. pinnatisecta (T.J. Starker) Rehd.

Discovered in 1938, 16 miles NW of Portland, OR. Similar trees were found near Mt. Adams, WA. Cultivated ≤1942. Very rarely grown as a novelty. Leaves deeply lobed in cutleaf fashion. In some cases the leaves may remain longer in fall than on typical RED ALDERS. Introduced ≤1990, 'Amazon' is a cutleaf clone referable to A. rubra f. pinnatisecta.

A. rugosa (Du Roi) Spreng.

= A. incana ssp. rugosa (DuRoi) R.T. Clausen

SPECKLED ALDER. TAG ALDER. HOARY ALDER. AMERICAN GRAY ALDER. HAZEL ALDER. From the far north and northeastern North America. Little cultivated. Closely related to A. incana, but smaller, usually a shrub. It also intergrades with the more southerly SMOOTH ALDER, A. serrulata (which by some botanists is made part of the species). Leaf 1½"–4" long. Cones 7/16"–5/8" long. The epithet rugosa from Latin rugosus, wrinkled or full of wrinkles. Records: 66' × 3'2" St. Clair County, MI (1984); 57' × 2'9" Ottawa County, MI (1972); 50' × 3'4½" Edinburgh, Scotland (1967); 50' × 2'1" Brown County, WI (1986); 19' × 3'6" Sears Island, ME (1980).

A. sinuata (Reg.) Rydb.

= A. crispa (Ait.) Pursh ssp. sinuata (Reg.) Hult.
= A. viridis ssp. sinuata (Reg.) A. & D. Löve
= A. sitchensis (Reg.) Sarg.

SITKA ALDER. SLIDE ALDER. THINLEAF ALDER. From northwestern North America and NE Asia. Introduced to cultivation in 1903. Extremely rarely grown. Shrubby. Catkins unfold with the leaves in spring, to 5" long. Leaves finely toothed; green on both surfaces, slightly shiny; essentially hairless; 2"–4" (6") long. Winter buds unstalked, unlike those of most ALDERS. Cones ½"–¾" long, on slender stems. Records: to 50' tall says W. Eliot; 37' × 2'3" × 29' Maury Island, WA (1992); 28' × 5'4" × 56' Vancouver, B.C. (1992).

A. sitchensis—see A. sinuata

A. × Spaethii Call.

HYBRID ALDER. From a natural cross in 1894 between A. japonica (which it most resembles) and the west Asian A. subcordata at Späth nursery of Germany. Used as a street-tree in Holland but virtually unheard of in North America. Here since ≤1952. The summer aspect of the tree is of exuberant health, relaxed elegance and cheerfully shiny leaves. Catkins in (late December) January expand to 8" long. Young leaves purplish except the tips of the teeth remain green; mature leaves bold, 4½"–9⅜" long. Cones to 1⅛" long; often not abundant. Breeds true by seed. Records: 88½' × 6'6½" Kew, England (1987; pl. 1937); 64' × 4'8½" Seattle, WA (1994; pl. 1952).

A. tenuifolia Nutt.

= A. incana ssp. tenuifolia (Nutt.) Breitung
= A. incana ssp. rugosa var. occidentalis (Dipp.) C.L. Hitchc.

MOUNTAIN ALDER. THINLEAF ALDER. From Alaska to New Mexico. Closely related to A. rugosa, but more treelike. Introduced to cultivation in 1880. Scarcely ever sold outside of the Rocky Mountain region. The epithet tenuifolia from Latin tenuis, thin, and folium, a leaf. The name THINLEAF ALDER has historically been applied, however (and with more accuracy), to A. sinuata. Leaves 2"–4½" (7") long, dull. Cones 3/8"–5/8" (7/8") long. Records: 71' × 7'10" Umatilla National Forest, WA (1993); 68' × 4'4" Church Canyon, NM (1976); 50' × 7'2" Wenatchee National Forest, WA (1984).

A. viridis (Chaix) DC.

EUROPEAN GREEN ALDER. From the mountains of central & southeastern Europe. Alternatively, some botanists view it as a variable circumpolar species. Introduced to cultivation in 1800 in Germany. In North American commerce ≤1930. Very rare. Usually a 10' shrub, rarely a small tree; not ornamental in either case. Catkins appear late, in May. Leaf 1"–4" long, very sharply and finely toothed. Winter buds unstalked, unlike those of most ALDERS. Cones ½"–¾" long. The epithet viridis is Latin for green. However, nothing about the species seems especially green.

A. viridis ssp. sinuata—see A. sinuata

A. vulgaris—see A. glutinosa

A. yasha—see A. firma

Amelanchier

[ROSACEÆ; Rose Family] 6–16 (25) spp., most North American. The Provençal name of the European species is amelancier for A. rotundifolia (Lam.) Dum.-Cours. Shrubs and fine-textured small trees, related to HAWTHORNS (Cratægus), CRABAPPLES (Malus), Photinia, etc. Profuse white narrow-petalled flowers in spring, are followed in early summer by edible berries which are quickly taken by birds. Fall color often bright and attractive. The trunks are slender, with tight gray bark, smooth like that of a HOLLY (*Ilex*) or BEECH (*Fagus*). In the 1980s, interest in this genus peaked, after many years of relative neglect. SERVICEBERRY or SARVIS and so on, are eastern North American names referring to a group of related shrubs and trees, which, among other things, are distinguished by flowering when the shad-fish spawn, hence SHADBUSH, SHADBLOW or SHADBERRY. Julia Rogers wrote: "We may easily trace this common name to the early American colonists who frugally fished the streams when the shad were running, and noted the charming little trees lighting up the river banks with their delicate blossoms, when all the woods around them were still asleep." Other vernacular names include JUNEBERRY (when the berries ripen), and a bookish European name, SNOWY MESPILUS, which harkens back to when the botanist Linnæus called some species *Mespilus*, whose profuse snowy white flowers shamed the sparse blossoms of the original *Mespilus* (MEDLAR tree). Botanists and nurseries have grappled with nomenclature, and confusion has prevailed over clarity. The account below is tentative, as must be, until a complete horticultural monograph on the genus is published.

A. alnifolia (Nutt.) Nutt.
= *A. florida* Lindl.

WESTERN SERVICEBERRY. PACIFIC SERVICEBERRY. SASKATOON SERVICEBERRY. Latin *Alnus*, the ALDER tree, and *folium*, a leaf, because the leaf shape recalls that of *Alnus glutinosa*. From much of northwest and north-central North America. Introduced to cultivation in 1826 by D. Douglas. Little planted, especially as a tree. Compared to most cultivated species, this has leaves of rounder outline (to 2½" × 2¼"), much coarser teeth and inferior fall color (usually plain yellow). Also its flowers are in compact clusters, later. The berries are large and several cultivars have been selected specifically for fruit-production. The two following cultivars reach sufficient size to be grown as small trees. For information on 13 others see *HortScience* September 1994, pp. 959–960. Overall the species is a suckering shrub. Records: 42' × 3'3" × 43' Beacon Rock State Park, WA (1993); 27' × 3'9" × 22' Douglas County, OR (1975).

A. alnifolia 'Altaglow'
= *A. alnifolia* 'Brooks White'

Originated <1923 in the Red Deer River Valley, Alberta. Introduced in 1960 by the Brooks, Alberta, research station. Rarely still sold. Narrow habit to 23' tall. Seldom suckers. Self-sterile. Berries creamy-white, sparse. Fall color magnificent golden, red and purple.

A. alnifolia 'Thiessen'

Selected in the wild in 1906 by Maria Loewen, and later named after her husband Issak Thiessen of Langham, Saskatchewan. Introduced commercially in 1976 by G. Krahn of Lakeshore nursery, Saskatoon, Saskatchewan. Common. To 16' tall; columnar, becoming roundish. Fruit abundant, juicy and large (to ⅔").

A. amabilis—see A. × grandiflora

A. arborea (Michx. fil.) Fern.
= *A. canadensis* Wieg., non (L.) Med.

SERVICEBERRY. JUNEBERRY. SHADBUSH. SARVICE. DOWNY SERVICEBERRY. From eastern North America. The largest species, with an attractive smooth, gray trunk. Not as pretty as *A. lævis* or its hybrids. Young leaves in spring white-hairy over green, 1½"–3" (4") long. Flower clusters more or less erect. Berries comparatively dry and insipid. Records: 76' × 10'6" × 48' near Standish, Arenac County, MI (1972); 74' × 4'11" × 34' Clarion County, PA (1983); 63' × 6'7" × 74' Barry County, MI (1984); 63' × 5'11" × 47' Cameron County, PA (1980); 60' × 9'0" × 53' Burke's Garden, VA (1986—originally called *A. lævis*); 53' × 8'11" × 55' Riverside, CT (1988).

A. arborea 'Autumn Sunset'

A recent cultivar.

A. arborea ssp. lævis—see A. lævis

A. asiatica (S. & Z.) Endl. ex Walp.

From China, Korea, and Japan. Introduced to cultivation in Holland in 1860 by Siebold. To North America ≤1881. Offered by nurseries constantly but sparingly over the decades. A shrub or small tree 25'–40' tall. Leaves white-wooly beneath while young, to 3" long, finely toothed or toothless. Flowers fragrant, in wooly clusters 1"–2½" long, blooming 2–3 weeks later than *A. arborea*. Berries purple-black, juicy, ⅜" wide. Fall color rich orange and red.

A. Botryapium—see A. canadensis and A. × Lamarckii

A. canadensis (L.) Med.
= *A. oblongifolia* (T. & G.) Roem.
= *A. Botryapium* (L. fil.) Borkh., non DC. [see *A. × Lamarckii*]

THICKET SERVICEBERRY. From eastern North America: the Atlantic Coastal Plain from Newfoundland to Georgia, mostly in swamps and lowlands. Common; widely grown. Usually a mere slender, strongly upright, multitrunked shrub <25' tall. In cultivation it can be kept in treelike form, although the roots throw up suckers. Some cultivars sold under this species' name are probably really *A. arborea* selections. The latter species has been sold as "*A. canadensis*" for decades. As with *A. arborea*, the leaves are half grown and white-felty at flowering time, 1"–2½" long, but the berries are succulent. *A. × Lamarckii* has also been sold as *A. canadensis*.

A. canadensis 'Majesty'
Introduced in 1993–94 by Handy nursery of Portland, OR. The name is unfortunately similar to *A. lævis* 'Majestic'.

A. cana. oblongifolia GLOBE SERVICEBERRY— see A. cana. 'Tailored'

A. canadensis 'Prince William' PP 6040 (1987)
Selected at Madison, WI; introduced by Tom Watson of Cambridge, WI. An 8'–12' multistem large shrub; not a tree. Berries abundant, large, resembling blueberries. Fall color a dull yellow. More formal and not as wild looking as other *A. canadensis* cultivars.

A. canadensis 'Pyramidalis'
Offered during the 1980s and '90s by Handy nursery of Oregon. Foliage glaucous, hairless at maturity; green late into fall. To 30' × 12' wide.

A. canadensis 'Silver Fountain'
Originated in Shelbyville, KY. Introduced in 1992 by Handy nursery of Portland, OR. Pendulous.

A. canadensis Spring Glory®
= *A. canadensis* 'Springtime'
= *A. canadensis* 'Sprizam'

Introduced ≤1991 by Lake County nursery of Perry, OH. To 12' tall; very compact broad columnar form. Foliage grayish green, in fall brilliant golden-amber and orange. Berries purple-black.

A. canadensis 'Springtime'—see A. canadensis Spring Glory®

A. canadensis 'Sprizam'—see A. canadensis Spring Glory®

A. canadensis 'Tailored'
= *A. oblongifolia* 'Tailored' THICKET SERVICEBERRY
= *A. oblongifolia* 'Tailored' GLOBE SERVICEBERRY
= *A. canadensis oblongifolia* GLOBE SERVICEBERRY

Ohio nurseryman Ed Scanlon found this very symmetrical globe on Long Island, NY, ca.1964 and began to grow it. Still sold in the '80s by Handy nursery of Portland, OR. Form tight, globular, 15'–20' tall. In other respects resembles typical *A. canadensis*. It can look windswept, and become broader than high. Very distinctive.

A. canadensis Tradition®
= *A. canadensis* 'Trazam'

Introduced ≤1990 by Lake County nursery of Perry, OH. To 25' tall; central leader strong, branching excellent. Foliage grayish green, in fall blazing red and orange. Berries like blueberries.

A. canadensis 'Trazam'—see A. canadensis Tradition®

A. canadensis 'White Pillar' PP 7072 (1989)
= *A. hybrida* 'White Pillar'

Selected by Peter Costich of Long Island. Introduced ≤1993 by Princeton nursery of New Jersey. Tightly columnar, dark green. Late flowering. Fall color orange-red.

A. canadensis 'White Tower'
Introduced in 1993–94 by Handy nursery of Portland, OR.

A. Cumulus®—see A. grandiflora Cumulus®

A. florida—see A. alnifolia

A. × grandiflora (Zabel) Rehd.
= *A. amabilis* hort., non Wieg.
(*A. arborea* × *A. lævis*)

APPLE SERVICEBERRY. HYBRID SERVICEBERRY. First reported in 1870. Commonly grown, yet for most of its history under different names. At present, usually only selected cultivars are sold. Intermediate between its parents, and better than either for ornamental purposes.

More floriferous than its parents, with leaves unfolding bronze or purplish; large and succulent berries. *A.* × *Lamarckii* has been confused with *A.* × *grandiflora*.

A. × *grandiflora* 'Autumn Applause'

Developed by W. Wandell of Urbana, IL. Introduced ≤1991 by McGill nursery of Fairview, OR.

A. × *grandiflora* 'Autumn Brilliance' PP 5717 (1986)

Introduced in 1986 by W. Wandell of Urbana, IL. Common. Treelike to 25' tall; heavy stems resist ice breakage. Fall color brilliant clear red-orange. Berries showy, purplish-black, sweet.

A. × *grandiflora* 'Ballerina'

Selected in Boskoop, Holland from plants sent (as *A. ovalis*—an utterly dissimilar European bush) from Hillier nursery in 1970; named and introduced in 1980 by H. J. van de Laar. Sold as a hybrid of *A. lævis*, but its exact parentage is unknown. Common in North American nurseries. A small broad tree to 20' tall. Flowers more or less pendent. Young leaves slightly bronze colored, very lightly or not at all hairy; maturing to shiny dark green. Berries as large as any in the genus (some more than ½" wide), blue-purple, very juicy, ripening later than those of *A.* × *grandiflora* 'Cole's Select'.

A. × *grandiflora* 'Cole's Select'
('Cole')

Originated by Cole nursery of Painesville, OH; introduced ≤1989. Looks more like *A. arborea* than *A. lævis*, but produces excellent berries. Fall color lovely orange-red to red.

A. × *grandiflora* Cumulus® PP 3092 (1972)

= *A. hybrida* Cumulus®
= *A. lævis* Cumulus®

Introduced by Princeton nursery of New Jersey. Commonly grown since 1979–80. To 30' tall; vigorously upright. Flowers abundant and large. Leaves thick. Fall color orange to red. Berries red, later purplish. Sickly and prone to red gall infestation, at least in Seattle.

A. × *grandiflora* 'Forest Prince'

Recent; little known.

A. × *grandiflora* 'Glenn's Upright'

RAINBOW PILLAR SERVICEBERRY. Twombly nursery of Monroe, CT, 1994 catalog: "New. Patented. 25'

fairly tight upright.".

A. × *grandiflora* 'Princess Diana' PP 6041 (1987)

Selected at Elm Grove, WI; introduced by Tom Watson of Cambridge, WI. To 25' tall, of spreading form. Flowers abundant. Foliage handsome. Berries purplish-blue, ⅜". Fall color spectacular pinkish-red, exceptionally long lasting.

A. × *grandiflora* 'Robin Hill (Pink)'

Originated <1958 at Robin Hill Arboretum, Lyndonville, NY, where Wm. A. Smith did much selecting and propagating of interesting *Amelanchier*. Common. Flowerbuds bright pink, gradually fading to white after opening. Berries small, red, juicy.

A. × *grandiflora* 'Rosea'

Offered in 1960s by Tingle nursery of Pittsville, MD. Sold as PINK SERVICEBERRY. May be same as *A.* × *grandiflora* 'Rubescens', but is not identical to 'Robin Hill (Pink)'.

A. × *grandiflora* 'Rubescens'

Raised from a seed of *A. arborea* from Seneca park of Rochester, NY. Cultivated in Durand-Eastman park, and named in 1920. Not commonly listed by nurseries. In Latin, *rubescens* means becoming red. The flower buds are purple-red, opening pale pink. The young leaves are reddish.

A. × *grandiflora* 'Strata'

Selected by the University of Wisconsin. Introduced ≤1989. Noted for its strongly horizontal branching pattern.

A. hybrida Cumulus®—see *A.* × *grandiflora* Cumulus®

A. hybrida 'Majestic'—see *A. lævis* 'Majestic'

A. hybrida 'White Pillar'—see *A. canadensis* 'White Pillar'

A. intermedia—see *A.* × *Lamarckii*

A. lævis Wieg.

= *A. arborea* ssp. *lævis* (Wieg.) S. MacKay *ex* Landry

SMOOTH-LEAVED SERVICEBERRY. ALLEGHENY SERVICEBERRY. From eastern North America. Introduced to cultivation in 1870. Common. Differs from *A. arborea* in having nearly or totally hairless leaves, strongly tinted red or coppery while young; larger flowers; berries delicious. In Latin, *lævis* means smooth; not rough, in reference to the leaves not being hairy. See also *A.* × *Lamarckii*. Records: 78' × 6'4" × 47' North Carolina (1994); 70' × 5'3" × 35' Austinville, VA (1989); 60' × 5'2" × 59' Isabella County, MI (1988); 56' × 4'10" × 62' Cass County, MI (1978); 55' × 5'11" × 65' Terre Haute, IN (1974); 36' × 7'6" × 56' Canton, NC (1989).

A. lævis Cumulus®—see *A.* × *grandiflora* Cumulus®

A. lævis Lustre®

Carlton nursery of California and Oregon, 1993–94 catalog: "our budded selection."

A. lævis 'Majestic' PP 7203 (1990)

= *A. lævis* 'Snowcloud'
= *A.* 'Snowcloud'
= *A. hybrida* 'Majestic'

Introduced by Princeton nursery of New Jersey. Exceptionally vigorous growth, to 30' tall. Form narrow, light, open and irregular, the branches spreading at a broad angle; delicate, airy and graceful. Flowers very large, wide-petalled, in large clusters. Berries showy purplish-black, sweet. Leaves dark, unaffected by leaf-spot diseases. Fall color rich scarlet or coppery orange.

A. lævis 'Prince Charles' PP 6039 (1987)

Introduced ≤1989 by Tom Watson of Cambridge, WI. Commonly grown. Vigorous, somewhat rounded habit. Flowers abundant. Fall color orange and red. Berries purplish-blue, edible. Some specimens have hairy, weakly bronze-colored young leaves, and erect flower clusters, so at best are hybrids, not purebred *A. lævis*.

A. lævis 'Snowcloud'—see *A. lævis* 'Majestic'

A. × *Lamarckii* F.-N. Schröder

= *A. Botryapium* DC., non (L. fil.) Borkh.
= *A. canadensis* auct., in part, non (L.) Med.
= *A. lævis* auct., in part, non Wieg.
= *A. intermedia* auct., non Spach
= *A.* × *grandiflora* auct., non (Zabel) Rehd.
≠ *A.* × *grandiflora* (Zabel) Rehd.

A tree of mystery and confusion. Possibly described as early as 1783. The best guess is it is a hybrid that breeds true, of North American parentage. One parent was almost certainly *A. lævis*; the other might have been *A. canadensis*. It is far more common in European cultivation than in the New World. Previously it was wrongly equated with *A.* × *grandiflora*.

In 1968 it was named after French naturalist Jean Baptiste Pierre Antoine Monet de Lamarck (1744–1829). Overall it is most similar to *A. lævis*. Leaf 1¾"–3¼" long, purplish and hairy when young. Berries sweet, juicy, ⅜".

A. oblongifolia—see *A. canadensis*

A. 'Snowcloud'—see *A. lævis* 'Snowcloud'

Amygdalus Amygdalo-persica—see *Prunus* × *persicoides*

Amygdalus communis—see *Prunus dulcis*

Amygdalus Davidiana—see *Prunus Davidiana*

Amygdalus hybrida—see *Prunus* × *persicoides*

Amygdalus Persica—see *Prunus Persica*

Andromeda arborea—see *Oxydendrum arboreum*

Annona triloba—see *Asimina triloba*

Aphananthe

[ULMACEÆ; Elm Family] 3–5 spp. from E Asia and Australia. From Greek *aphanes*, inconspicuous or obscure, and *anthe*, a flower: the tiny, inconspicuous spring flowers are "destitute of beauty." A related genus is *Celtis* (HACKBERRY).

A. aspera (Th.) Planch.

MUKU TREE. ORIENTAL ELM. From E China, Korea, Taiwan, the Ryukyus, and Japan. Introduced to Western cultivation ≤1880, the year one was planted at Berkeley, CA. Very rare; a shade tree suitable for the South and on the Pacific Coast. In Latin, *aspera* means rough or harsh, in reference to the raspy leaf surface. Leaf 1½"–4¾" long, three-veined from the base, sharply toothed; of plain yellow fall color. Fruit is a purplish-black berry, ¼"–⅓" long. The Japanese name, *Muku*, means "shaggy-haired tree." In age the trunk becomes greatly buttressed. Recorded to 131' × 18'0" in Japan.

Apollonias

[LAURACEÆ; Laurel Family] 2–3 spp. of Old World broadleaf evergreen trees, closely related to BAY LAUREL (*Laurus nobilis*). Likely named after Frederico Apollonio (*fl.* 1900), natural science professor at Catanzaro, Italy. An alternative, unlikely explanation: after the sun god Apollo or Phœbus of Greek mythology.

A. Barbujana (Cav.) Bornm.
= *A. canariensis* (Willd.) Nees
= *Laurus Barbujana* Cav.
= *L. Barbusano* Link
= *L. Barbusana* Lowe
= *L. canariensis* Willd., non Webb & Berth.

From the Canary Islands. Cultivated in England <1895. Introduced to North America ≤1970. Exceedingly rare. The scientific name is based on its vernacular. The contemporary Canarian name is *barbusano*. Leaf 3"–7" long, with translucent margin; fragrant; hair tufts in vein axils beneath. Flowers in small axillary panicles, yellowish, slightly fragrant. Fruit a dark brown berry, 7/16"–5/8" long. Bark rugged. Tree to 100' tall. Its wood is highly valued in cabinetry. A 1970 accession at the Los Angeles arboretum (48' × 4'3" × 37' in 1993) has been reseeding, and some of its offspring (commercially offered by one small nursery) have proven cold-hardy in Seattle. Additional testing is needed to determine the needs of this promising species.

A. canariensis—see *A. Barbujana*

Aralia

[ARALIACEÆ; Ginseng Family] 36–50 spp. of herbs, shrubs or small trees, often prickly. Named from the French-Canadian *aralie*, because in the late 1600s the original specimens of the genus were sent by Québec physician M. Sarrasin to the French botanist J.P. de Tournefort under that name (*i.e.*, *salsepareille* or *sarsaparilla* for *Aralia nudicaulis* L.). The following species are large suckering shrubs or small trees with stout spine-covered pithy shoots (crude-looking in winter), bold compound leaves, and large terminal clusters of small whitish flowers in summer followed by little black berries. A related genus is *Kalopanax*.

A. chinensis L.
CHINESE ANGELICA TREE. From China. Date of introduction to cultivation unknown because nearly all plants so called have turned out to be *A. elata* or *A. stipulata*. But any time between ca. 1830 and 1919 is possible. Nonetheless, the species is practically nonexistent in cultivation. It is at the Morton Arboretum of Lisle, IL. Leaves with close-matted interwoven felt of silky brown hairs beneath. Flowers greenish-white, in clusters to 16" tall. Usually a shrub.

A. chinensis var. *glabrescens*—see *A. stipulata*

A. chinensis var. *mandshurica*—see *A. elata*

A. chinensis var. *nuda*—see *A. elata* and *A. stipulata*

A. elata (Miq.) Seem.
= *A. chinensis* var. *mandshurica* (Ruprecht & Maxim.) Rehd.
= *A. chinensis* var. *nuda* Nakai, non auct.
= *A. japonica* hort., non Thumb.
= *Dimorphanthus elatus* Miq.

JAPANESE ANGELICA TREE. From Manchuria, E Siberia, Sakhalin, Korea, the S Kuriles, Japan, and the Ryukyus. Introduced in 1830. Very common. Frequently sold incorrectly as *A. chinensis* or *A. spinosa.* Flowers appear late in summer or in fall, in broad, short, spreading clusters. Leaflets with scattered hairs on both surfaces (hairless sometimes); paler beneath. Usually a stout shrub, but up to 45' × 3'6" (*elata* in Latin means tall or elevated).

A. elata 'Albo-marginata'—see *A. elata* 'Variegata'

A. elata 'Aureo-variegata'

Originated or introduced in Holland ca. 1870; botanically described in 1896. Very rare. Leaflets edged golden yellow.

A. elata 'Fastigiata'—see A. elata 'Pyramidalis'

A. elata 'Pyramidalis'

= A. elata 'Fastigiata'

Originated in England. Introduced to North American cultivation ≤1902. Grown by several nurseries in 1920s and '30s. Small leaflets; more erect in growth.

A. elata 'Variegata'

= A. elata 'Albo-marginata'

Introduced to Europe ca. 1865; botanically described in 1886. Rare. The Arnold Arboretum imported it to North America in 1953. Leaflets edged creamy white.

A. japonica—see A. elata

A. Maximowiczii—see Kalopanax septemlobus

A. spinosa L.

DEVIL'S WALKING STICK. HERCULES' CLUB. PRICKLY ASH. PRICKLY ELDER. TEAR-BLANKET. From the southeastern U. S. Uncommon in cultivation; most stock so called is really A. elata. True A. spinosa differs in being more spiny, with longer-stalked, thinner, smoother-feeling leaflets, and a tall flower cluster (to 3'–4' long). Overall it is a taller, more slender plant. Its compound leaves are, as a whole, the largest leaves borne by any native North American tree. A leaf can measure 5½' long and 4' wide. Records: 55' × 2'2" × 28' Tennessee (1994); 51' × 2'0" × 23' San Felasco Hammock State Preserve, FL (1982); 45' × 1'5" × 24' Angelina National Forest, TX (1993); 44' × 1'8" × 14' Jasper County, TX (1993); 37' × 2'8" × 15' Edenton, NC (1992); 36' × 1'7" × 30' Oakland County, MI (1979); 22' × 2'6" × 17' Milwaukee, WI (1983).

A. stipulata Franch.

= A. chinensis var. glabrescens Schneid.
= A. chinensis var. nuda auct., non Nakai

From China. Introduced ca. 1919. Basal stipular ligules long and conspicuous. Hairless or nearly so. Rare. Some stock sold as A. elata is really A. stipulata.

Araucaria

[ARAUCARIACEÆ; Monkey Puzzle Family] 15–20 spp. of very large coniferous evergreens native in the Southern Hemisphere. Mostly cold-tender. Best known may be the houseplant NORFOLK ISLAND PINE (A. heterophylla). Name from the Araucanos people of Arauco, a province of S Chile, where the earliest discovered species of the genus grows.

A. angustifolia (Bertol.) Ktze.

= A. brasiliana A. Rich.
= A. brasiliensis auct.
= A. gracilis hort.

PIRANA PINE—after Brazilian name Pino Paraná or Pinheiro do Paraná. PARANÁ PINE. CANDELABRA TREE. BRAZILIAN PINE. From mountains of S Brazil, NE Argentina, and Paraguay. Named in 1812. Latin angustus, narrow, and folium, a leaf. Introduced to cultivation in 1819 by J. Lee of Hammersmith nursery near London, England. Those trees, from Rio de Janeiro, were not cold-hardy. In 1871, specimens were exhibited at San Francisco, CA; and it was offered ≤1880 by San José nurseries. Some may be hardier than is commonly supposed. Uncommon even in California, it is mostly seen in coastal areas. When young it recalls Cunninghamia lanceolata f. glauca. Leaves rather broad despite the Latin specific name; with a glaucous bloom that can be rubbed off. Sharp and recurved, stiff, on older twigs. Forward-pointing and soft on young growth. Leaves on sterile branches 1¼"–2¼" long × ½" wide; more or less opposite. Fertile branch leaves shorter (to 1⅜" × ¼", narrowed toward each end), more densely arranged in even whorls all around twigs. Male cones 3"–5⅝" × 1¼"; female cones 5" high, 6½" wide. Seeds to 2" × ¾", edible. Records: 115' × 14'3" in the wild; 67' × 7'10" × 56' Montecito, CA (1992).

A. araucana (Mol.) K. Koch

= A. imbricata Pav.
= Pinus araucana Mol.

MONKEY PUZZLE. MONKEY PUZZLER. PUZZLE MONKEY. MONKEY TREE. MONKEY-TAIL TREE. CHILEAN PINE. CHILE PINE. From S Chile, SW Argentina. J.M. van Nassau (1604–1679) was in South America from 1637 to 1644, and either brought or one of his peers sent him) seeds which he grew into trees in the 1650s, on his estate near the Holland-Germany border. Though the Chilean chronicler Mariño de Lovera described the species in 1562–63, botanists didn't know about the tree until it was noted in 1780 by the Spaniard Don Francisco Dendariarena. In 1795 A. Menzies introduced seeds to England. In 1834 the distinctive name PUZZLE MONKEY was coined, because it would puzzle even a monkey to climb such a viciously spiny tree. [The cold-tender BUNYA-BUNYA (*A. Bidwillii*) is also sometimes called MONKEY-PUZZLE.] North American cultivation occurred ≤1861. It is common in the maritime Pacific Northwest; occasionally planted in California; very rare in the East, where winter is too cold and/or summer too hot. Its distinctive, even bizarre, appearance, makes it unforgettable. To the native people in its natural range, the tree supplied an important food: its large seeds, twice the size of almonds. They are borne only on female trees, in cones of 150–300 seeds, measuring 5"–8" in diameter, and disintegrating upon maturity. Male trees produce cucumber-shaped 5" cones which fall after releasing pollen. Bisexual trees are extremely rare, perhaps one in a 1,000. Leaves 1"–2³⁄₁₆" long × ½"–1¹⁄₁₆" wide; very thick, dark, and jaggedly sharp, overlapping like shingles (imbricate). Records: to 165' × 25'0" in Chile; 98' × 9'8" Nymans, Sussex, England (1986); 95' × 12'0" Bicton, Devon, England (1983; *pl.* 1844); 90' × 15'7" Bicton, Devon, England (1983); 87' × 11'11" Endsleigh, Devon, England (1970); 77' × 6'0" Holberg, B.C. (1995); 72' × 8'10" Bremerton, WA (1988); 69' × 9'3" Skagit City, WA (1993); 66' × 10'2" Aberdeen, WA (1993); 63' × 7'7½" Victoria, B.C. (1994); 60' × 9'9" Astoria, OR (1988).

Araucaria araucana f. *angustifolia* (Dallim.) stat. nov.

= *A. araucana* 'Angustifolia'
= *A. araucana* var. *angustifolia* Dallim.

Wm. Dallimore, in describing this variant in 1948 (Latin *angustus*, narrow, and *folium*, a leaf), said it was "often seen in cultivation." Branchlets slenderer; leaves narrower, thinner. It can be regarded as a seed-raised cultivar, but since it rarely or never has been propagated intentionally, it is best designated botanically as a forma.

A. brasiliana or *brasiliensis*—see *A. angustifolia*

A. gracilis—see *A. angustifolia*

A. imbricata—see *A. araucana*

Arbutus

[ERICACEÆ; Heath Family] 14–15 (20) spp. of broadleaf evergreen shrubs and trees. *Arbutus* is one of the ancient Latin names of *A. Unedo*. Unlike most members of the Heath Family, this genus thrives on chalky soil, and is altogether drought-tolerant. Bark usually attractively peely, colorful. Flowers urn-like, recalling those of LILY-OF-THE-VALLEY. Fruit a bumpy little berry of mealy texture, red or orange-red, borne in grape-like clusters. Hence the names STRAWBERRY TREE, and Spanish *madroño*—anglicized as MADRONA or MADRONE. They are more or less difficult to cultivate, the most adaptable species being *A. Unedo*.

A. Andrachne L.

CYPRUS STRAWBERRY TREE. GREEK STRAWBERRY TREE. EASTERN STRAWBERRY TREE. From SE Europe to SW Asia. The specific epithet from Greek *andrachne*, an ancient plant name given to the weed PURSLANE (*Portulaca oleracea*). Introduced in 1724 to England by Dr. J. Sherard. Most trees in cultivation under this name are really the hybrid *A.* × *andrachnoides*. Grown in North America since ≤1939. Although it flowers in spring, it hybridizes with the primarily fall-blooming *A. Unedo*. Bark lovely peely red to creamy beige. Leaves 2"–4" long (to 5¼" × 2¾"), weakly toothed or untoothed except on seedlings and sucker shoots. Berries ca. ½" wide, orange or orange-red. Records: to 49' × 5'5" in the wild; 27' × 6'3" Bath, Avon, England (<1908).

A. × *andrachnoides* Link
= *A. hybrida* Ker-Gawler
(*A. Andrachne* × *A. Unedo*)

HYBRID STRAWBERRY TREE. Occurs wild in Greece; also raised ca. 1800 by nurserymen Messrs. Osborn of Fulham, England. Named botanically in 1821 (from *A. Andrachne*, and Greek *-oides*, resemblance). Virtually never offered in North American commerce, yet present in botanic gardens. Grows faster to bigger size than either parent; more cold-hardy than *A. Andrachne*. Flowers in autumn or early spring; fertile; berries ⅝" but not abundant. Leaf 2"–5¼" long, sharply toothed. Young twigs with some long, gland-tipped hairs. Bark very pretty. Record: 72' × 5'3" Bodnant, Wales (1990; *pl.* 1905).

A. arizonica (Gray) Sarg.
= *A. xalapensis* H.B.K. var. *arizonica* A. Gray
= *A. xalapensis* H.B.K. ssp. *arizonica* (A. Gray) E. Murr.

ARIZONA MADRONA. From the SW United States and NW Mexico. Difficult to establish, so cultivated to a minor degree in the Southwest; otherwise limited largely to botanic gardens in the West. Leaf 1½"–3" long; slender. Flowers in May. Bark handsome peeling red. Often bushy. Record: 65' tall and multitrunked in New Mexico (1892–93); 53' × 11'11" × 52' Reilly Canyon, AZ (ca. 1988).

A. hybrida—see *A.* × *andrachnoides*

A. 'Marina'

Origin unknown; definitely a hybrid. Maybe *A.* × *andrachnoides* crossed with *A. canariensis* (not in this volume). Likely imported to San Francisco in 1917 from Europe. Subsequently propagated by pioneer nurseryman C. Abraham, in San Francisco's Marina district. Named and reintroduced to cultivation in 1984 by Saratoga Horticultural Foundation. Grown on the Pacific Coast. Difficult to grow from cuttings; grown easily by tissue culture. Twigs glandular-hairy. Leaf 3"–5¾" long, up to 2⅞" wide; toothed. Flowers carmine on sunny side, in late summer, fall, and winter. Fruit 1" wide and too abundant to make for an ideal street-tree. Record: 46½' × 8'5" × 45½' San Francisco, CA (1994; *pl.* ≤1942).

A. Menziesii Pursh

PACIFIC MADRONA. COAST MADRONA. From British Columbia to S California. Introduced to cultivation in 1827 by D. Douglas. Named after Archibald Menzies (1754–1842), who discovered it. Cultivated within its native range; scarcely successful elsewhere in North America. Leaf 3"–7" long. Flowers March through May. Berries ⅓"–½" wide, orange, then red. Bark lovely red-brown, peeling off to reveal greenish-beige. The largest member of the genus. Records: to 131' tall in the wild; 96' × 34'0" × 113' is "the Council Madrona" near Ettersburg, Humboldt County, CA (1984); Oregon's largest is 25'0" around (Rogue River, 1989).

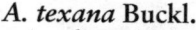

A. texana Buckl.

= *A. xalapensis* H.B.K. var. *texana* (Buckl.) A. Gray
= *A. xalapensis* H.B.K. ssp. *texana* (Buckl.) E. Murr.

TEXAS MADRONA. LADY LEGS. From the southwestern U.S. south through Mexico to Guatemala. Cultivated in the southwestern U.S. and in California since ≤1931. Attractive peely bark, pink or creamy-white when newly exposed, then reddish. Leaf 1"–3" long, hairy beneath. Flowers in hairy clusters during February-March. A shrub or small tree. Records: 36' × 5'0" × 29' Guadalupe Mountains National Park, TX (1971); 34' × 5'0" × 40' Hays County, TX (1969); 32' × 9'4" × 42' Big Bend National Park, TX (1982).

A. Unedo L.

STRAWBERRY TREE. LILY-OF-THE-VALLEY TREE. CANE-APPLE TREE. THE WINTER STRAWBERRY. KILLARNEY STRAWBERRY TREE. From Ireland, Spain, Portugal and the Mediterranean region. The name in Spain is *madroño*. This species, along with *Cornus capitata*, *Myrica rubra*, and two *Euonymus* species, is called "Strawberry Tree." The odd epithet *Unedo* is from Latin *unum edo*, meaning "I eat one" suggesting the fruit is too poor to entice human appetites. In California's nursery trade ≤1871. Common. Leaf 2"–4¼" long. Flowers October–November (rarely February–April). Despite the grittiness, the ¾"–1⁷⁄₁₆" strawberry-red fruit is edible; its apricot-colored flesh is edible raw when fully ripe in autumn, or can be dried briefly. A shrub or rarely a twisted-trunk little tree; bark brown-gray and shreddy, not strikingly handsome as on the other *Arbutus* species. Twigs when young glandular-hairy. Records: 50' tall near Parson's Green, London (≤1920); 45' × 9'2" × 50' Waikato, New Zealand (1969); 42' × 4'4" Selwood Park, Bedfordshire, England (1982); 32' × 6'0" × 34½' San Marino, CA (1993); 32' × 7'1" × 23½' Morn Park, County Cork, Ireland (ca 1835); a trunk 13'9" around in Ireland (1773).

A. Unedo 'Elfin King'

Originated in 1958 in California. A dwarf bush.

A. Unedo f. *rubra* (Ait.) Rehd.

First mentioned in 1759 by P. Miller. Named botanically in 1789. Flowers vary from rosy red (in 'Croomii') to rosy-crimson (in 'New Scarlet'). Tree generally smaller. Common, an assemblage of seedlings and clones; application of cultivar names is haphazard.

A. xalapensis var. *arizonica*—see *A. arizonica*

A. xalapensis var. *texana*—see *A. texana*

Aria Folgneri—see *Sorbus Folgneri*

Aria megalocarpa—see *Sorbus megalocarpa*

Aria Zahlbruckneri—see *Sorbus Zahlbruckneri*

Armeniaca Ansu—see *Prunus Armeniaca* var. *Ansu*

Armeniaca brigantiana—see *Prunus brigantiana*

Armeniaca dasycarpa—see *Prunus dasycarpa*

Armeniaca mandshurica—see *Prunus Armeniaca* var. *mandshurica*

Armeniaca vulgaris—see *Prunus Armeniaca*

Asimina

[ANNONACEÆ; Custard Apple Family] 8 spp. of North American small trees or shrubs. From the French *asiminier*—the old colonial name of the French in North America for the PAWPAW, from the native American *assimin*. No other genera in this book are in the ANNONACEÆ, which is essentially a tropical Family.

A. triloba (L.) Dun.
= *Annona triloba* L.

PAWPAW. PAPAW. CUSTARD APPLE. FETID SHRUB. WILD BANANA TREE. MICHIGAN BANANA. NEBRASKA BANANA. HOOSIER BANANA. HARDY BANANA. PRAIRIE BANANA. INDIAN BANANA. From much of the central and eastern U.S., and S Ontario. *Carica Papaya* is the COMMON PAPAW of Tropical America. From *papaya*, a Spanish corruption of the Carib *ababai*. A small shrubby tree. Leaves large (6"–15" long), stink like rue when crushed; yellow to cinnamon-colored in fall. Flowers inconspicuous from afar but merit close inspection—lurid purple, 2" wide (three-lobed, hence *triloba*) in March-May. Fruit usually only borne if the flowers have been cross-pollinated; edible, stubby, up to 7" long × 2½" wide, ripe in autumn. The flavor is tropical, the texture luscious and custard-like; the seeds as large as jelly beans. Among the largest fruit of any native North American plant. Records: 60' × 7'8" × 30' Newton County, MS (1986); 56' × 2'3" × 25' Pickens County, SC (1981); 47' × 2'11" × 32' S of Utica, MI (1979); 25' × 4'9" × 32' Lancaster, PA (≤1950).

Athrotaxis

[TAXODIACEÆ; Bald Cypress Family] 3 spp. of coniferous evergreens from mountainous Tasmania. The only Southern Hemisphere representatives of the Bald Cypress Family. From Greek *athroos*, crowded, and *taxis*, arrangement, alluding to the foliage. Not especially ornamental, the TASMANIAN CEDARS are curious as among the most cold-hardy of Southern Hemisphere trees. Related genera include *Cryptomeria* (JAPANESE RED CEDAR) and *Sequoiadendron* (SIERRA REDWOOD).

A. cupressoides D. Don

SMOOTH TASMANIAN CEDAR. PENCIL PINE. Named in 1839 (genus *Cupressus*, and Greek *-oides*, resemblance). Introduced to British cultivation in 1857. Date of introduction to North America not known; extremely rare here. Offered in 1994–95 by Buchholz & Buchholz nursery of Gaston, OR. A moisture-loving, slow growing tree. Bark reddish-brown, fibrous. Foliage consisting of closely held scale-like little leaves. Cones round, ⅓"–⅝", spiky. Records: to 82' tall in the wild; 46' × 6'3" × 30' Kilmacurragh, County Wicklow, Ireland (1990).

A. laxifolia Hook.

SUMMIT CEDAR. Named in 1843 (from Latin *laxi*, loose, and *folium*, a leaf). Introduced to British cultivation in 1857. Date of introduction to North America not known; exceedingly rare here and not known in commerce. Similar to *A. cupressoides* but with slightly larger cones (to ¾"), the foliage not so closely pressed, and of broader habit and better growth. It looks like a refined version of a *Cryptomeria japonica*. Records: to 59' × 8'3" Scorrier House, Cornwall, England (1990; *pl.* 1871); 33' × 4'2" Port Coquitlam, B.C. (1994; *pl.* ≤1930s).

Austrocedrus

[CUPRESSACEÆ; Cypress Family] Only one species in the genus, a coniferous evergreen. Latin *auster*, south, and *Cedrus*. Very closely related to *Calocedrus*.

A. *chilensis* (D. Don) Pichi-Ser. & Bizz.
= *Libocedrus chilensis* (D. Don) Endl.

CHILEAN INCENSE CEDAR. CHILEAN CEDAR. CHILEAN ARBORVITÆ. From mountains of S Chile and S Argentina. Introduced in 1847 to England. In California nurseries ≤1900. Rare, and limited to Pacific Coast cultivation. Foliage light green, almost inodorous when crushed. Cones $7/16$"–$5/8$" long, sparingly produced, so the tree is mostly grown by cuttings. So slow-growing that in effect it is a shrub. Records: to 80' × 20'6" in the wild; 58' tall and multitrunked at Wisley, Surrey, England (1981); 24' × 2'7½" Nelson City, New Zealand (1969; *pl.* ca. 1924); 20' tall after 46 years at Seattle, WA.

A. *chilensis* 'Viridis'

A seedling found in England. Described in 1875 in England. In California nurseries ≤1900. Extremely rare. Foliage bright green, entirely free from glaucous bands.

Azara

[FLACOURTIACEÆ; Flacourtia Family] 10–12 spp. of South American broadleaf evergreens, mostly cold-tender. Named after Félix de Azara (1742–1821), Spanish geographer and naturalist who did fieldwork in South America from 1781 to1796. Not after his brother, José Nicolás Azara (1731–1804), patron of science. Related to the deciduous East Asiatic *Idesia* and *Poliothyrsis* genera.

A. *microphylla* Hook. fil.

BOXLEAF AZARA. Chilean (Mapuche): *Chinchin*. From Chile and Argentina. Greek *micro*, very small, and *phyllon*, leaf. Introduced ca. 1861 by R. Pearce for Veitch nursery of England. Offered since ≤1895 in the California nursery trade. Common there, and rarely grown in the Pacific Northwest near the coast. Leaves ¼"–1⅛" long, dark and very shiny. Flowers inconspicuous, yellow, strongly vanilla- or chocolate-scented in late winter. Fruit a tiny one-seeded berry ¼" long, at first reddish-orange, ripening in June or July to the color of chocolate milk, yet shiny and speckled; slightly bitter vanilla-flavored. A shrubby tree of fine texture. Records: 42' tall at Tregothnan, Cornwall, England (1928); 33' × 2'2" San Francisco, CA (1995); 15' × 2'6" Seattle, WA (1990).

A. *microphylla* 'Variegata'

Introduced ca. 1916. Possibly raised by Slieve Donard nursery of Ireland. Introduced to North America ≤1966. Very rare. Leaves creamy and yellowish-variegated. Cheerfully bright. Record: 21' × 1'6" San Francisco, CA (1995; *pl.* 1966).

Belis lanceolata—see *Cunninghamia lanceolata*

Benthamia japonica—see *Cornus Kousa*

Benthamidia capitata—see *Cornus capitata*

Benthamidia florida—see *Cornus florida*

Benthamidia japonica—see *Cornus Kousa*

Benthamidia Nuttallii—see *Cornus Nuttallii*

Benzoin obtusilobum—see *Lindera obtusiloba*

Betula

[BETULACEÆ; Birch Family] 30–60 spp. known as BIRCH trees, familiar as white-barked northern denizens. Some are dark-barked, some merely bushes. Nearly all are comparatively short-lived pioneer species. Male flowers are borne in dangling caterpillar-like catkins; female flowers are absolutely inconspicuous. They are wind-pollinated and hybrids are frequent. Seeds are borne in disintegrating seed-catkins. Fall color is usually yellow. The Gaulish name, *betulla*, became the ancient Latin name *betula*. The genus most closely related to *Betula* is ALDER (*Alnus*). In most of North America, BIRCHES object to summer heat, or are subject to attack from an insect pest called bronze birch-borer (*Agrilus anxius*). In cultivation, especially in urban settings, most need much moisture to thrive.

B. alba—see *B. papyrifera*, *B. pendula*, and *B. pubescens*

B. alba laciniata gracilis pendula—see *B. pendula* 'Crispa'

B. albo-sinensis Burk.

CHINESE RED-BARKED BIRCH. From central China. Introduced to cultivation in 1901 when E. Wilson sent seeds to Veitch nursery of England. Scarcely ever grown except in the variety *septentrionalis*. Recorded to 100' × 12'0" in the wild, but it can be shrubby; bark bright orange to orange red.

B. albo-sinensis var. septentrionalis Schneid.

NORTHERN CHINESE RED-BARKED BIRCH. CHINESE PAPER BIRCH. From central China. Introduced to cultivation in 1908 when E. Wilson sent seeds to the Arnold Arboretum. In commerce ≤1957. Sold mostly by Canadian nurseries. Uncommon. Represented in cultivation both as an unnamed grafted clone, and as seedlings. Some trees distributed under this name may be intermediate with typical *B. albo-sinensis*, and others hybrids with *B. pendula*. Be that as it may, if the lovely pink cast to the bark is pronounced, gardeners are pleased. Differs from typical *B. albo-sinensis* in having matte rather than glossy leaves, averaging longer (up to 6¾" × 3⅞"), with prominent hair-tufts beneath. Bark coppery to gray-pink rather than dark reddish. It is primarily the lovely bark that arouses admiration. Describing it is difficult. Some

attempts: "dull orange-brown with pink and gray bloom" or "white with beige, to pure pink-beige." Records: 100' × 16'3" in the wild; 72' × 3'7" Westonbirt, Gloucestershire, England (1988); 50' × 2'3" Seattle, WA (1992; *pl.* 1960); 35' × 4'0" Mountlake Terrace, WA (1992).

B. alleghaniensis Britt.
= *B. lutea* Michx. fil.—misapplied
= *B. excelsa* hort., non Ait.

YELLOW BIRCH. GOLD BIRCH. CURLY BIRCH. HARD BIRCH. From eastern North America. Seldom cultivated. Related closely to SWEET BIRCH (*B. lenta*). Bark yellowish-gray, thin and peely. Leaves recall those of a CHERRY tree, 3"–6" long, clear yellow in fall. The twigs, if bruised or chewed, release a gratifying wintergreen flavor, though inferior to that of *B. lenta*. Seed-catkins stout and erect. The official tree of Québec. Records: 114' × 14'10" × 101' Mackinac County, MI (1973); 107' × 15'7" × 86' Marquette County, MI (1978); 92' × 16'1" La Patrie, Québec (<1994); 76' × 21'0" × 91' Deer Island, ME (1983).

B. × aurata Borkh.
(*B. pendula* × *B. pubescens*)

HYBRID EUROPEAN WHITE BIRCH. Nurseries don't sell this hybrid by name, but it occurs rarely. Almost always sterile, it cannot reproduce itself. It most resembles *B. pubescens* (DOWNY BIRCH). Latin *auratus* means golden—presumably the original tree described (in 1800) had a golden sheen on its bark.

B. Avalanche®
= *B.* 'Avalzam'

Introduced ≤1991 by Lake County nursery of Perry, OH. An East Asian species or hybrid, the original imported from Japan <1930 by Storrs & Harrison nursery of Painesville, OH. Great resistance to bronze birch-borer. Leaves large, thick, rich lustrous green. Bark light tan, gradually pinkish, then white. Vigorous. To 50' tall × 40' wide.

B. 'Avalzam'—see *B.* Avalanche®

B. Bhojpattra—see *B. utilis*

B. costata Trautv.
From NE Asia. Named in 1859. Introduced by Siebold to Holland ca. 1868. In North American commerce ≤1889. Extremely rare; trees so called are usually *B. davurica* or a form of *B. Ermanii*. This species is probably best suited for woodland gardens or similarly less exposed sites. In Latin, *costata* means

ribbed; from *costa*, rib, referring to the leaves, whose veins (ribs) are prominent compared to those of most other east Asiatic BIRCHES (but like those of the North American *B. alleghaniensis* and *B. lenta*). Bark thin, peely, smoothish, the color of *Prunus Maackii* (pale yellow or buff). Twigs very warty. Leaf 1¾"–3⅛" long, glossiest beneath; minutely short-hairy; with 12–14 vein pairs. Recorded to 100' tall in the wild.

B. 'Crimson Frost'

(*B. platyphylla* var. *szechuanica* × *B. pendula* 'Purpurea')

Raised in 1978. Selected in 1985. Introduced in 1989 by Evergreen nursery of Sturgeon Bay, WI. Propagated by tissue-culture. Bark white with a cinnamon hue. Leaves deep purple all summer.

B. davurica Pall.

DAHURIAN BIRCH. MANCHURIAN BIRCH. From NE China, Manchuria, Amurland, Korea, and Japan. Named in 1784. Introduced by J. Bell to England ca. 1785. To North America probably by 1883. In commerce ≤1930. Rare; generally not listed under its proper name in nurseries, but it has been distributed to arboreta and botanic gardens wrongly labeled as *B. costata* or *B. platyphylla* var. *japonica* P.I. 317211. Bark thick, spongy, shaggy, recalling that of *B. nigra* (RIVER BIRCH) but paler, softer. Can be peeled off in many thin layers. Generally gray with beige underneath, darker on old trees. Twigs warty, often with some scattered long hairs. Leaves 2"– 4⅝" × 3¼" with veins in 6–9 pairs. First species to flush in spring—in warmer zones it may leaf out too early and be damaged by late frosts. It can be of sparse, plain aspect, but the bark is interesting. Often multitrunked. Records: 98' × 8'0" Hergest Croft, Herefordshire, England (1985); 80 × 10'0" in the wild; 51' × 3'0" Seattle, WA (1994; *pl.* 1968); 37' × 4'1½" Aurora, OR (1993; *pl.* 1976).

B. Ermanii Cham.

= *B. costata* hort., non Trautv.
= *B. ulmifolia* Reg., non S. & Z., Dipp.

ERMAN'S BIRCH. GOLD BIRCH. RUSSIAN ROCK BIRCH. From much of E & NE Asia. Named in 1831. Introduced ca. 1880 to Russian cultivation; to the U.S. in 1881 when imported by the Arnold Arboretum. Rare in North America; most date from the 1940s onward. Scarcely offered by nurseries until the 1980s. Presumably named after Georg Adolph Erman (1806–1877), physicist, meteorologist, geophysicist, geographer, geologist,

paleontologist, plant collector, *and* traveler. Like the man it was named after, this species is extraordinarily variable. Bark smooth, peeling thinly; variously colored but overall grayish or white with streaks or patches of pink or dark gold. Leaf amazing in its variation, 2"–4" (5½") long × 1"–3⅜" (4") wide. Stem to 1⅛" (1¾") long. Usually ±heart-shaped. Usually markedly glossy beneath, with a "wet look." Veins in 6–9 (12) pairs. Twigs ±hairy, glandular. Buds often proportionately large. Seed-clusters stout. Ranges from dwarf trees to the largest BIRCHES of NE Asia. Selections can be made of dwarf trees with superior bark, well-suited as ornamentals for restricted places. Records: to 100' × 13'0" in the wild; 77' × 4'6" Windsor Great Park, Berkshire, England (1979); 70' × 10'5" Westonbirt, Gloucestershire, England (1988); 63' × 11'6" Grayswood Hill, Surrey, England (1966); 50' × 3'10" Seattle, WA (1994; *pl.* 1945).

B. excelsa—see B. alleghaniensis

B. fontinalis—see B. occidentalis

B. Jacquemontii—see B. utilis var. Jacquemontii

B. japonica—see B. platyphylla var. japonica

B. lenta L.

SWEET BIRCH. MAHOGANY BIRCH. BLACK BIRCH. CHERRY BIRCH. SUGAR BIRCH. SPICE BIRCH. WINTERGREEN TREE. From the eastern United States, extreme S Ontario and Québec. Little grown; its bark is too dark to suit the taste of most people, and the tree suffers in urbanized settings. In Latin *lenta* means pliant, tough but flexible. Twigs have much wintergreen oil, unlike other species except YELLOW BIRCH, *B. alleghaniensis*. Its sap is sweet. Leaf similar to that of *B. alleghaniensis*. The dark gray-brown CHERRY-like bark and wood led to the names MAHOGANY- and BLACK BIRCH. Compared to white-barked BIRCHES it is less of a pioneer species, more of a woodland tree. In the open, as generally cultivated, it is usually broad and low. Records: 117' × 8'6" Dewey Lake State Forest, KY (1979); 90' × 11'5" × 87' New Salem, MA (≤1987); 83' × 15'2" × 65' Middleton, CT (1992); 80' × 17'6" Wabash County, IL (<1882); 78' × 13'1" × 70' McKean County, PA (1981); 70' × 15'2" × 87' New Boston, NH (1961).

B. lutea—see B. alleghaniensis

B. mandshurica—see *B. platyphylla*

B. mandshurica var. *japonica*—see *B. platyphylla* var. *japonica*

B. Maximowicziana Reg.

MONARCH BIRCH. From Japan and the S Kuriles. Carl Johann Maximowicz (1827–1891) discovered this species in 1861. Introduced to Veitch nursery of England in 1888. In 1893 C. Sargent sent seeds to the Arnold Arboretum. All or nearly all MONARCH BIRCHES distributed by American nurseries during the 1940s and '50s were not true to name; instead *B. platyphylla* or other species or hybrids were being sold. By the late 1970s the real species was available commercially, although still the majority of trees so called are not true to name. The chief pretenders are big-leaved *B. Ermanii* and *B. platyphylla* var. *szechuanica*. Many nurseries list the species. Here is a true description: leaves the largest of all, to 7¾" × 5⅝"; stem to 2⅞" long; base cordate; edges finely toothed; veins in 9–12 pairs; overall, like a *Davidia* (DOVE TREE) leaf but finer-toothed, shorter-stalked, less gradually tapered. Seed-catkins 2–4 instead of solitary. Bark gray, not gleaming white. A Japanese name, *Saihada-kamba*, means RHINO-CEROS-SKIN BIRCH. Records: to 100' × 12'0" in Japan; 79' × 3'0" Windsor Great Park, Berkshire, England (1987); 65' × 6'6" Grayswood Hill, Surrey, England (1982); 62' × 6'0" Trewithen, Cornwall, England (1987); 53' × 1'10½" Seattle, WA (1993; *pl.* 1978); 41' × 3'4" Aurora, OR (1993; *pl.* 1979); a trunk 7'6" around at Wayford Manor, Dorsetshire, England (1983).

B. nigra L.

= *B. rubra* Michx. fil.

RIVER BIRCH. RED BIRCH. From the eastern U.S. Bark reddish-brown, raggedly loose and torn, becoming hard, dark gray and chunky. Leaf coarsely scalloped, shiny above, 1"–3½" (5¼") long. Valued because it endures warm climates (it is native into Florida), but still little grown compared to non-native BIRCHES. Although largely found near rivers in parts of its native range, it can grow well in ordinary cultivated conditions. Records: 120' × 9'5" Congaree Floodplain, SC (≤1978); 111' × 13'2" Lamar County, AL (1993); 95' × 13'5" Cumberland State Forest, VA (1974); 86' × 14'11" Anne Arundel County, MD (1982); 90' × 15'8" Appleton Comm., TN (1988).

B. nigra 'Cully'—see B. nigra Heritage™

B. nigra Fox Valley™

= *B. nigra* 'Little King'

Originated in the late 1970s at King nursery of Oswego, IL. Introduced ≤1991. A natural dwarf growing ca. 10' tall × 12' wide, of dense, compact habit.

B. nigra Heritage™ PP 4409 (1979)

= *B. nigra* 'Cully'

In the 1970s, nurseryman Earl Cully of Jacksonville, IL, found this clone in a St. Louis suburb. Introduced in 1979. The name Heritage underscores its being a native American selection—in a horticultural world dominated by non-native BIRCHES. The most attractive asset about this selection is its pale creamy bark (ranges from tan to creamy white to parchment white). It is also heat tolerant, fast-growing, resistant to bronze birch-borer and leaf-spot disease. In brief, the best thing so far for southerners who thirst for a whitebarked BIRCH.

B. nigra 'Little King'—see B. nigra Fox Valley™

B. nigra 'Suwanee'

Compared to typical RIVER BIRCH this cultivar has a larger and shinier leaf; salmon-white, exfoliating bark. Described in 1985 in Florida. Scarcely found in commercial production.

B. nigra Tecumseh Compact™

Discovered ca. 1985 as a seedling sport in Wisconsin. Introduced ≤1991 by Studebaker nursery of New Carlisle, OH. Grows 10'–12' tall as a large shrub or small tree; compact, with graceful, pendulous habit. Staked to make weeping specimens.

B. occidentalis Hook., non Sarg.

= *B. fontinalis* Sarg.

WATER BIRCH. SPRING BIRCH. MOUNTAIN BIRCH. From the Rocky Mountain region, broadly interpreted. Introduced to cultivation in 1874. In the Rocky Mountain nursery trade ≤1902. Planted primarily within its native range. Usually grows in clumps, rarely over 30' tall. Bark dark gray. Fall color yellow or amber, even brilliant red in the eastern Sierras. Leaf to 2½" long × 2" wide; 3–7 vein pairs. Records: to 60' tall says E. Sheldon; 55' × 4'0" × 55' Spokane,

WA (1988); 53' × 9'3" × 42' Wallowa County, OR (1973).

B. papyracea—see B. papyrifera

B. papyrifera Marsh.
= *B. papyracea* Ait.
= *B. alba* hort. (in part)

PAPER BIRCH. CANOE BIRCH. AMERICAN WHITE BIRCH. PAPERBARK BIRCH. From Alaska, Canada, and the northern U.S. The epithet *papyrifera* is Latinized from the Egyptian *papyrus*, paper (originally from Syrian *babeer*), and Latin *-fer*, from *ferre*, to bear, from the use of the bark in paper-making. Botanists divide this species into regional subspecies. It is the large growing BIRCH of the far north, and is usually but not invariably white-barked. Bark peels off in thin shreds. In texture this species is much stouter than the native GRAY BIRCH (*B. populifolia*) or non-native EUROPEAN WHITE BIRCHES (*B. pendula* and *B. pubescens*). Leaf 1½"–4½" (7"). Records: to 120' tall in British Columbia and Washington; 107' × 18'4" Cheboygan County, MI (1991); 93' × 18'1" Hartford, ME (1979).

B. papyrifera 'Chickadee'
Introduced <1989 in the Midwest. Bark exceptionally white. Form narrowly upright.

B. papyrifera 'Nam Shaw'
Siebenthaler nursery of Dayton, OH, in 1981, sold this as resistant to the bronze birch-borer. No longer available.

B. papyrifera Snowy Birch™
Introduced ≤1991 by Better Trees of St. John's, MI. Propagated by tissue culture. A synthetic multiclonal *B. papyrifera* variety originated in Michigan State University of East Lansing. Highly resists bronze birch-borer in 15+ years of testing. Cold-hardy.

B. pendula Roth.
= *B. alba* L. (in part)
= *B. verrucosa* Ehrh.

WHITE BIRCH. SILVER BIRCH. EUROPEAN WHITE BIRCH. COMMON BIRCH. WARTY BIRCH. From Europe, SW Asia, N Africa. Reported in Williamsburg, VA <1752. The commonest planted BIRCH in North America; naturalized in some locales. The epithet *pendula* from Latin *pendulus*, hanging, refers to the fine drooping twigs. Another much used name, *verrucosa*, means warty, and also refers to the twigs. Bark white, but in age the trunk becomes furrowed and gray near the ground. Leaf 1"–2½" (3") long. Records: to 120' tall says by M. Hadfield; 107' × 12'7" × 92' Leelanau County, MI (1983).

B. pendula 'Atropurpurea'—see B. pendula 'Purpurea'

B. pendula 'Aurea'—see B. pubescens 'Aurea'

B. pendula 'Crispa'
= *B. alba laciniata gracilis pendula* hort.
= *B. pendula* var. *laciniata* auct., non Wahl.
= *B. pendula* 'Gracilis' hort. (in part)
= *B. pendula* 'Laciniata' hort. (in part)
= *B. pendula* 'Dalecarlica' hort. (in part)

CUTLEAF WEEPING BIRCH. Such trees occur wild in Scandinavia, and can be named botanically *B. pendula* f. *crispa* (Reichb.) Holmb., yet for the most part, only one clone is cultivated. Extremely common. Perhaps more cold-hardy than ordinary EUROPEAN WHITE BIRCHES. Leaves more regularly but less deeply cut than *B. pendula* 'Dalecarlica'; buds pointed. Tree strongly weeping, progressively more so with age. Records: 110' × 5'9" Taymouth Castle, Perthshire, Scotland (1983); 86' × 5'7" Wenatchee, WA (1988); 73' × 10'0" Yakima, WA (1988).

B. pendula 'Dalecarlica'
= *B. alba* var. *laciniata* Wahl.

SWEDISH BIRCH. ORNÄS BIRCH. Originated in the 1700s at Sweden's Lilla Ornäs, in province Dalarno (hence the name 'Dalecarlica'). The original tree was killed by a storm in 1887. Extremely rare. Buds round, not pointed as in 'Crispa' and 'Laciniata'. Tree stiff, with only minor twigs weeping. Leaf deeply, irregularly cut. The name 'Dalecarlica' has been widely but wrongly applied to 'Crispa'.

B. pendula 'Dark Prince'
In North American commerce ≤1994. Leaves purple.

B. pendula 'Elegans Laciniata'—see B. pendula 'Gracilis'

B. pendula 'Fastigiata'
= B. pendula 'Pyramidalis'

PYRAMIDAL WHITE BIRCH. Introduced <1870 by Simon-Louis Frères nursery of France. In North American commerce since ≤1890; uncommon. Branches strictly upright, forming a narrow crown that gradually broadens with age. Records: 95' × 6'3" Alexandra Park, Hastings, Sussex, England (1983); 89' × 6'0" × 37' Redmond, WA (1990).

B. pendula 'Golden Cloud'

From Holland. Introduced ≤1988. Leaves vivid yellow (especially in spring). Growth slower, making a smaller tree than typical B. pendula.

B. pendula 'Gracilis'
= B. pendula 'Elegans Laciniata'

Cultivated since 1888 in Europe. Extremely rare because difficult to propagate. A small mop-like tree seldom more than 20' tall, without a dominant leader; twigs very thin, in clustered pony tails at branch ends. Leaf much more deeply cut than that of B. pendula 'Laciniata'. The name 'Gracilis' has been widely but wrongly applied to 'Crispa'.

B. pendula 'Gurney's Redleaf Birch'—see B. pendula 'Purpurea'

B. pendula 'Laciniata'
= B. pendula 'Gracilis' sensu Rehd. 1927, 1940

Like B. pendula 'Crispa' but a smaller tree, with leaves smaller, less incised, and buds pointed. Very rare. The tree usually called by this name is 'Crispa'.

B. pendula 'Monle'—see B. pendula Purple Rain™

B. pendula 'Obelisk'

Found wild near Arras, France by P.L.M. van der Bom; cultivated in 1956 by the Royal nursery of Alphons van der Bom at Oudenbosch, Holland. Very rare, if in North American commerce at all. Extremely fastigiate, stiffer than B. pendula 'Fastigiata'; bark gleaming white.

B. pen. 'Purple Glory'—see B. pen. 'Purple Splendor' or 'Purpurea'

B. pendula Purple Rain™
= B. pendula 'Monle'

Introduced ≤1987 by Monrovia nursery of California. An open-pollinated B. pendula 'Purpurea' seedling. In spring, difficult to distinguish from its parent. Holds its purple color better.

B. pendula 'Purple Splendor' PP 2107 (1961)
= B. pendula 'Purple Glory' (in part)

A chance seedling that was found ≤1959 by D.D. Belcher of Powell Valley nursery of Gresham, OR. Introduced ≤1965. Apparently out of commerce. Leaves purple.

B. pendula 'Purpurea'
= B. pendula 'Atropurpurea'
= B. pendula 'Purple Glory' (in part)
= B. pendula 'Real Purple'
= B. pendula 'Scarlet Glory'
= B. pendula 'Summer Glory'
= B. pendula 'Gurney's Redleaf Birch'

PURPLELEAF BIRCH. Originated ca. 1870 in France. In the North American commerce since ≤1880. Common. Leaves purple when young, fading to dark bronzy-green. Fall color orange, copper, and bronze (instead of the usual yellow of greenleaf BIRCHES). See also B. pendula 'Dark Prince', Purple Rain™ and 'Purple Splendor'. Record: 57' × 2'6" × 29' Tacoma, WA (1993).

B. pendula 'Pyramidalis'—see B. pendula 'Fastigiata'

B. pendula 'Real Purple'—see B. pendula 'Purpurea'

B. pendula 'Scarlet Glory'—see B. pendula 'Purpurea'

B. pendula 'Summer Glory'—see B. pendula 'Purpurea'

B. pendula 'Tristis'

WEEPING WHITE BIRCH. Introduced in 1867 in Holland. May be the 1866 'Elegans' of Bonamy's nursery, Toulouse, France. Uncommon in North America. However, seedlings arise which more or less fit the description. Some trees so called are really B. pendula 'Crispa' or 'Youngii'. Leaf normal. Crown of normal height, long-branched, gracefully pendulous. In Latin, tristis means sad, mournful.

B. pendula 'Youngii'

YOUNG'S WEEPING BIRCH. Introduced ≤1874 by the nursery of Maurice Young (1834–1890) of Milford, near Godalming, Surrey, England. It had been found as a chance seedling trailing on the ground. Topgrafted onto a straight seedling trunk, it makes a mop-head small weeping tree. Uncommon. Since the 1980s, some Oregon nurseries have topgrafted it onto trunks bent in and out like a slithering snake, creating a novel grotesque effect. Record: 33' × 2'6" London, England (1988); 27' × 2'6" × 27' Seattle, WA (1990).

B. platyphylla Suk.
= *B. mandshurica* (Reg.) Nakai

MANCHURIAN WHITE BIRCH. From NE Asia. Named in 1911. Rare, if in cultivation at all. It flushes very early in spring so is prone to damage from late frosts. Name from Greek *platys*, wide or broad, and *phyllon*, a leaf. Leaves shaped much like those of *B. pendula* and *B. populifolia* (i.e., broad), yet larger. Overall the tree has the bark color and foliage texture of *B. papyrifera*. Twigs hairless. Leaf usually glandular, heart-shaped like a POPLAR (*Populus*), 2"–3³⁄₁₆" long × 1¹⁄₃"–2½" wide; stem to 1¼" long; vein pairs 6–8. Records: to 65' × 8'0" in the wild; 62' × 3'4" Batsford Park, Gloucestershire, England (1987).

B. platyphylla var. *japonica* (Miq.) Hara
= *B. japonica* S. & Z., non Th.
= *B. mandshurica* var. *japonica* (Miq.) Rehd.

JAPANESE WHITE BIRCH. From mountains of Japan. In a broader concept, this variety is just a phase of the aforementioned MANCHURIAN BIRCH, and doesn't warrant nominal distinction. However, horticulturally the differences are real. Introduced to cultivation in 1887 in England. Since the 1980s, increasingly commonly cultivated in the northern States and Canada. Differs from MANCHURIAN WHITE BIRCH in growing larger, having broader-based leaves that do not flush so early in spring, and are often slightly hairy. But a midsummer examination of various specimens of the two taxa will reveal no watertight way to tell them apart solely by leaf and twig characteristics.

B. platyphylla var. *szechuanica* (Schneid.) Rehd.
= *B. szechuanica* (Schneid.) Jansson
= *B. platyphylla* ssp. *szechuanica* (Schneid.) de Jong

SZECHUAN WHITE BIRCH. From W China and Tibet. Introduced in 1908 by E. Wilson. Rarely grown compared to var. *japonica*. Some botanists regard this as a distinct species. The original introduction produced vividly white-barked trees, of extraordinarily dark bluish-green foliage, with the leaves often glandular

to a marked degree, and late to drop in autumn. The habit was broad and growth vigorous. However, when J. Rock saw many in China during the early 1920s, he found variation; the bark was of various colors. Additional study will likely vindicate botanists who think there are intermediate links with the other varieties of *B. platyphylla*. Records: 91' × 6'0" × 55' Seattle, WA (1989; *pl.* 1945); 82' × 8'0" in China.

B. platyphylla 'Whitespire'

WHITESPIRE BIRCH. A seed-propagated var. *japonica* cultivar that originated in 1956 from a single tree in the Yatsugatake mountains of Japan collected by Dr. John L. Creech, formerly a USDA plant explorer. Introduced in 1977 as "U of Wisconsin strain" by Evergreen nursery of Sturgeon Bay, WI. Named 'Whitespire' in 1983 by Ed Hasselkus of the University of Wisconsin at Madison. Very commonly grown. A narrow pyramidal white-barked BIRCH tolerant of high temperatures and resistant to the bronze birch-borer. Fine textured, glossy leaves, turning yellow in fall. Chalk-white bark. It seems the name 'Whitespire Senior' has been used since at least 1993 or 1994 to indicate a clone, perhaps the original best tree.

B. populifolia Marsh.

GRAY BIRCH. OLDFIELD BIRCH. FIRE BIRCH. WIRE BIRCH. WHITE BIRCH. From northeastern North America. Commonly planted in the early decades of this century; presently rarely offered by nurseries. A short-lived species of slender, often floppy habit. Thrives on sandy soils. Usually multitrunked and suckering from a burry base. Bark white or gray, does not peel off in thin coils. The epithet *populifolia* is from genus *Populus*, POPLAR, and Latin *folium*, a leaf. Leaf broadly triangular, shiny, 2"–3½" (5") long. Records: 80' × 3'11" Pike County, PA (1977); 77' × 6'6" Somers, CT (1987); 74' × 5'1" Annapolis, MD (1972); 60' × 7'3" near Clarksville, MD (1955).

B. populifolia 'Pendula'

WEEPING GRAY BIRCH. A study published in 1989 by F. Santamour, says many GRAY BIRCHES look pendulous, and the 'Pendula' mentioned in 1838 by the English tree expert J. Loudon was likely never widely distributed or propagated, so Santamour calls this name invalid. Valid or not, the name has scarcely been used in commerce. Detmer nursery of Tarrytown, NY, offered 'Pendula' in 1958.

B. populifolia 'Purpurea'

The Dutch tree expert B. Boom wrote that this cultivar originated in 1887 in the Netherlands. It was offered in 1892 by Ellwanger & Barry nursery of New York. A study published in 1989 by F. Santamour, says it is doubtful whether a purpleleaf GRAY BIRCH ever existed; the plant so called could well have been a hybrid between *B. populifolia* and *B. pendula* 'Purpurea'. There have long been no records of it in the nursery trade, so it can be considered extinct for all practical purposes.

B. pubescens Ehrh.

= *B. alba* L. (in part)

DOWNY BIRCH. From Europe, and far N Africa. Named in 1791. Introduced to cultivation in 1812. Commonly mixed up with *B. pendula*, and usually mistaken for it. Although it has almost never been sold under its proper name, it is found where European WHITE BIRCHES grow, and is naturalized in some locales. It can't compare ornamentally with other whitebarked species. Tolerates much wetter soil than *B. pendula*. Although the trunk is often fluted, the gray-white bark never becomes deeply chunky as in *B. pendula*. Crown fine-textured but inelegant. Fall color comparatively dismal. Leaf small, not very pointy, 1"–2½" (3") long. Twig ±prominently felty hairy, hence its names. See also *B. × aurata* and *B. turkestanica*. Records: 92' × 6'10" Ochtertyre, Tayside, Scotland (1987); 71' × 11'8" × 75' and 67' × 13'11" × 78' Aberdeen, WA (1988).

B. pubescens 'Aurea'

= *B. pubescens* 'Foliis Aureis'
= *B. pendula* 'Aurea' (in part)

In cultivation since the late 1800s or early 1900s. Extremely rare. Young leaves yellowish; twigs very downy.

B. pubescens 'Foliis Aureis'—see B. pubescens 'Aurea'

B. pubescens 'Laciniata'—see B. pubescens 'Urticifolia'

B. pubescens 'Urticifolia'

= *B. pubescens* 'Laciniata'
?= *B. pubescens* 'Quercifolia'

NETTLE-LEAF BIRCH. Found <1836 in Sweden; probably a *pendula* hybrid (i.e., referrable to *B. × aurata*).

In North American commerce ≤1891. Long commercially extinct. The name is from genus *Urtica* (nettle), and Latin *folium*, a leaf. In Europe, variants with similar deeply-toothed leaves are widely found.

B. pubescens 'Quercifolia'—see B. pubescens 'Urticifolia'

B. 'Rockimon'—see B. Rocky Mt. Splendor™

B. Rocky Mt. Splendor™ PP 6192 (1988)

= *B.* 'Rockimon'
(*B. pendula* × *B. occidentalis*)

Introduced ≤1992 by Schmidt nursery of Boring, OR. A cold-hardy broadly pyramidal tree to 45' tall × 30' wide. Fall color yellow.

B. rubra—see B. nigra

B. szechuanica—B. platyphylla var. szechuanica

B. tianschanica Rupr.

TIAN SHAN BIRCH. HEAVEN MOUNTAIN BIRCH. From central Asia and E Mongolia. Named in 1869. Introduced to North America ≤1963. Sold since 1994–95 by Heritage Seedlings nursery of Salem, OR. A shrub or small tree. Related to *B. pendula*. Twigs heavily warty, brown, hairless. Leaves ca. 1¾" × 1⅓", very glandular, can be hairy when young but become ±hairless at maturity; 5–6 vein pairs. Bark light yellow-brown or creamy-pinkish. Records: to 40' × 2'0" in the wild; 11' × 10" Seattle, WA (1994; *pl.* 1963—specimen is late to flush, of dismal health and appearance).

B. turkestanica Litvin.

TURKESTAN BIRCH. From mountain streamsides of central Asia. Named in 1914. Date of introduction to cultivation not known, but ≤1947. Very rare. Greer nursery of Oregon has been promoting it since ≤1991. Related closely to *B. pubescens* (DOWNY BIRCH) and probably should be relegated to subspecific status. Twigs less hairy, and with prominent glandular warts. Specimens in the Los Angeles arboretum are handsome. Record: 50' × 4'3" Seattle, WA (1994; *pl.* 1947).

B. ulmifolia—see B. Ermanii

B. utilis D. Don

= *B. Bhojpattra* Lindl. *ex* Wall.

HIMALAYAN BIRCH. INDIAN PAPER BIRCH. From the Himalayas and north into China. Introduced in 1849 from Sikkim to England by Sir Joseph Hooker. In North American commerce ≤1884, but almost never grown except recently in trees referred rightly or wrongly to its variety *Jacquemontii*. An extremely variable species, poorly understood. Some have stunning chalk-white bark but graceless, twiggy crowns. Some have orange-brown bark. Leaf recalls that of PAPER BIRCH, *B. papyrifera*. The epithet *utilis* in Latin means useful. Records: to 100' × 21'0" in China; 75' × 4'6" Endsleigh, Devon, England (1992); 50' × 6'3" Brook House, County Londonderry, Ireland (1976).

B. utilis var. Jacquemontii (Spach) Winkl.

= *B. Jacquemontii* Spach
= *B.* 'Jacquemontii'
= *B. utilis* ssp. *Jacquemontii* (Spach) Kit.

WHITE-BARKED HIMALAYAN BIRCH. KASHMIR BIRCH. JACQUEMONT BIRCH. From the NW Himalayas, SW and C Nepal. Introduced in 1880. Imported in 1924 from England to the U.S. by the Arnold Arboretum. Grown commonly only since the 1980s, both as a grafted but unnamed clone, and as seedlings. Named after the French naturalist Victor Jacquemont (1801–1832), in N India 1829–1832; first botanist to enter Kashmir; died of malaria. JACQUEMONT BIRCH differs from typical *B. utilis* in having only 7–10 vein pairs per leaf, instead of 10–14, but this botanic detail is not sure to be infallible, and other more meaningful distinctions may exist. The clone usually circulated has pristine white bark and good vigor. It is doubtless one of the following ten cultivars (nearly all named in Europe in the 1980s or early '90s): 'Doorenbos', 'Edinburgh', 'Grayswood Ghost', 'Hillier', 'Inverleith', 'Jermyns', 'Kashmir White', 'Sauwala White', 'Silver Shadow', 'Yunnan'. These clones are cited because some of them have made their way into North America, and others will follow. By and by we will find which are best for our needs. Record: 75' × 3'7" × 31' Seattle, WA (1988; *pl.* 1954).

B. verrucosa—see B. pendula

Bignonia Catalpa—see Catalpa bignonioides

Biota orientalis—see Thuja orientalis

Broussonetia

[MORACEÆ; Mulberry Family] 7–8 spp. of Asian trees and shrubs. Named after Pierre Auguste Marie Broussonet (1761–1807), physician and naturalist of Montpellier, France. Related genera include *Cudrania* (CHINESE SILKWORM THORN), *Ficus* (FIG), *Maclura* (OSAGE ORANGE), and *Morus* (MULBERRY).

B. papyrifera (L.) L'Hér. ex Vent.

= *Morus papyrifera* L.

PAPER MULBERRY. TAPA CLOTH TREE. From China, Taiwan, Japan, and the Ryukyus. Introduced to Europe from Japan in 1750, and initially named *Morus papyrifera* in 1753; given its present name in 1799. In North American commerce since ≤1841. Uncommon. Naturalized in some locales. The epithet *papyrifera* is Latinized from the Egyptian *papyrus*, paper (originally from Syrian *babeer*), and Latin *-fer*, from *ferre*, to bear, from the use of the bark in paper-making. In parts of Southeast Asia and the South Pacific the bark is made into a kind of paper used for umbrellas, lanterns, cords, etc. It is also pounded into a cloth called tapa. Like other MULBERRY trees (*Morus*), this is a fast-growing, tough and rugged tree; of merit in some sterile or trying places where other trees do not do well. Tolerates hot, dry conditions and has no serious pests, but is brittle and easily broken. Its appearance can be rude and coarse. Leaf large (3"–11" long), raspy, often deeply lobed, jagged and eye-catching, especially on sucker shoots. Only slight yellow fall color. Trunk pale; can be very burly. Male and female flowers borne in spring on separate trees; not showy. Females produce a round, hairy berry-like ¾"–1½" edible fruit; ripe in late summer or fall. In the cold North this is a shrub; in the South a tree. Records: 66' × 10'10" × 65' Riverside, CA (1993; *pl.* 1966); 50' × 6'0" Rochester, NY (ca. 1982); 49' × 10'3" × 68' Los Angeles, CA (1993; *pl.* 1955); 45' × 7'9" × 50' Germantown, PA (1969); 40' × 13'8" × 42' Norfolk, VA (1987); 34' × 11'6" × 45' Yorktown, VA (1989); 27' × 13'9" × 32' Quitman, TX (1973).

Butia

[PALMÆ or ARECACEÆ; Palm Family.] 8–9 (12) spp. of South American PALMS. A native south American name is *butiá*. Other PALM genera in this volume are *Ceroxylon*, *Chamærops*, *Nannorrhops*, *Sabal*, *Trachycarpus*, and *Washingtonia*.

B. australis—see B. capitata

B. capitata (Mart.) Becc.
= *B. australis* hort.
= *Cocos australis* hort., non Mart.
= *Syagrus capitata* (Mart.) Glassman

PINDO PALM. SOUTH AMERICAN JELLY PALM. HARDY BLUE COCOS PALM. From E Brazil and possibly Uruguay. Introduced to Europe in 1849; to California by 1897. Planted mostly since ≤1920s. Likely the most cold-hardy feather PALM, capable of enduring 12°F, but cannot survive prolonged freezing. If grown far north on the West Coast, it must be both sheltered from severe cold and given much summer heat. Grows slowly. Trunk short, stout. Fronds bluish, 6'– 9' long, arching, of ca. 100 leaflets on each side. Flowers striking pale yellow to pinkish-maroon. Fruit yellow, orange or red, edible, 1"–1½" long, in weighty clusters of 30–75 pounds. Ripe from August to mid-March. Cultivars have been selected for superior fruit, the pulp's consistency being similar to jelly (depending on ripeness); tasting like a pineapple-tangerine-date mix. The epithet *capitata* means headed; from Latin *caput*, head, referring to the moundlike or clustered heads of flowers and fruits. Records: 28' × 4'8" × 16' Sacramento, CA (1989); 25' × 6'3" San Marino, CA (1993).

Buxus

[BUXACEÆ; Box Family] 30–70 spp. of broadleaf evergreen shrubs and trees from both the New and Old Worlds. *Buxus* is an ancient Latin name. From Greek *pyxos*, dense or solid, referring to the hard wood or dense foliage. No other genera in this volume are in the BUXACEÆ.

B. sempervirens L.
BOX. BOXWOOD. COMMON BOX. From Europe, N Africa, SW Asia. To the U.S. sometime between 1650 and 1700. Named BOX because the wood was used for making boxes, Greek *pyxides*. A slow-growing broadleaf evergreen of dark, dense, fine foliage. Leaves very small, ½"–1¼" long, thick, narrow; borne in opposite pairs. Flowers inconspicuous yellowish-green. Wood extremely hard and heavy. Normally considered a mere shrub. It can be a tree, especially in its typical form, after the passage of decades. In the Caucasus it attains 52' in height. Even in England recorded 35' tall. In colonial times it thrived in Virginia and Tennessee. Many cultivars exist; nurseries sell primarily dwarf selections for hedging. BOX is traditionally used very successfully for topiary because it tolerates shearing, deep shade, and dryness. Long-lived. A symbol of stoicism.

Calocedrus

[CUPRESSACEÆ; Cypress Family] 2–3 spp. of coniferous evergreens. From Greek *kalos*, beautiful, and *kedros*, CEDAR. A closely related genus is *Austrocedrus*.

C. decurrens (Torr.) Florin
= *Libocedrus decurrens* Torr.

INCENSE CEDAR. From Oregon, California, the SW corner of Nevada, and N Baja California. Introduced by J. Jeffrey in 1853 to Britain. Called INCENSE CEDAR because the tree's oil has an incense-like odor. The much used name *Libocedrus* is from Greek *libos*, a drop or tear, and *kedros*, CEDAR—alluding to the resinous character of the tree, the tear-like trickling of its resin. Foliage scale-like, bright green. Cones narrow, ca. ½"–1" long and well-likened to duck bills. Bark reddish-brown and deeply furrowed. A columnar or narrowly pyramidal tree, prized for its pleasing color and neat shape. Records: 229' × 18'10" Umpqua National Forest, OR (1989); 152' × 38'6" Marble Mountains Wilderness, CA (1969).

C. decurrens 'Aureovariegata'

Described in 1896. Extremely rare. Irregular patches of golden-yellow or bright yellow sprays are mixed in with a bluish-green dominant color.

C. formosana (Florin) Florin

= *Libocedrus formosana* Florin

FORMOSAN INCENSE CEDAR. From Taiwan, where it can attain 82' × 31'0". Introduced to Western cultivation ≤1950s. Extremely rare. Cold tender; suitable only for the mildest localities where freezes are of short duration.

Camphora Camphora—see *Cinnamomum Camphora*

Caragana

[LEGUMINOSÆ; Pea Family] 50–80 spp. of deciduous shrubs or small trees, mostly from central Asia. From the Mongolian Tatar name *Caragan;* akin to the Kirghiz *Karaghan.*

C. arborescens Lam.

SIBERIAN PEA TREE or PEA SHRUB. From Siberia, Mongolia and Manchuria. Introduced in 1748 to Sweden, and 1752 to Britain. Somewhat spiny large shrub or small tree with fine foliage. Tough, utterly cold-hardy. Of ornamental value in severe continental regions. Leaf 1½"–3" long, pinnately divided into 8–14 leaflets, flushing an enchanting, very bright green early in spring. Flowers yellow, very small, mid-April into May. Seedpods 1½"–2" long. Recorded to 25' tall.

C. arborescens 'Lorbergii'

FERNLEAF PEA TREE. Originated ca. 1884 in Germany. Introduced by Heer Lorberg's nursery of Berlin. Named officially in 1906. Grown in the Midwest and prairie regions since ≤1930s. Smaller, only 7'–15' tall usually. Leaflets finely narrowed to create a ferny effect. Flowers paler, smaller. It begins as a columnar bush, but grows gaunt and sprawling with age.

C. arborescens 'Pendula'

WEEPING PEA TREE. Originated in 1854 in France. In North America ≤1896; in commerce here ≤1903. Uncommon. Topgrafted to produce a miniature weeping tree.

C. arborescens 'Sutherland'

Introduced in 1945 by Sutherland research station of Saskatchewan. Narrow columnar, to 16' tall.

C. arborescens 'Tidy'

Introduced ≤1968 by Morden research station of Manitoba. Like *C. arborescens* 'Lorbergii' but more upright, stiffer, vigorous, and seedless.

C. arborescens 'Walker'

FERNLEAF WEEPING PEA TREE. Introduced ≤1977 by Morden research station of Manitoba. A cross of *C. arborescens* 'Lorbergii' and 'Pendula' to make a fine-textured weeping plant. Named after Prof. John Walker.

Carpinus

[CARPINACEÆ; Hornbeam Family—or BETULACEÆ; Birch Family] 30–60 spp. of Northern Hemisphere deciduous trees. The ancient Latin name, from Celtic *car*, rock, and *pen*, a head—used as yokes for oxen. HORNBEAMS are trim-looking trees of small to moderate size, not well-known, colorful or dramatic, but useful for their neat foliage and troublefree, adaptable nature. The most distinctive feature is the seed cluster: each seed has a wing attached. A closely related genus is *Ostrya*, HOP HORNBEAM.

C. americana—see C. caroliniana

C. Betulus L.

EUROPEAN HORNBEAM. COMMON HORNBEAM. HORNBEECH. YOKE ELM. From Europe, SW Asia. Long cultivated in North America. Reseeding, if not naturalized in some locales. The strongest, most adaptable species. Very tolerant of pruning and shade. Called HORNBEAM because it was the tree (i.e. Old English *béam*) whose wood was as strong as horn; or because its wood was used to make yokes attached to the horns of bullocks. G.B. Emerson said in 1850 that the trunk is "marked with longitudinal, irregular ridges, resembling those on the horns of animals of the deer kind." Leaf 2"–5" long, sharply and very finely toothed; fall color poor yellow, late. On young trees the dry, brown leaves can hang on well into winter. Catkins borne in March-April. Seed wings three-pronged, 1½"–2" long. Bark smooth, gray; trunk often fluted in age. Records: 131' tall at Bialowieza National Park, Poland (≤1974); 131' × 13'6" Turkey (1992); 105' × 8'0" Wrest Park, Bedfordshire, England (1977); 98' × 12'3" Hutton-in-the-Forest, England (1979); 74' × 10'8" Auburn, WA (1992); 72' × 14'2" × 74' Greenwich, CT (1988); 61' × 13'4" Roseburg, OR (1989); 52½' × 18'9" × 105' Geneva, Switzerland (≤1967); a trunk 20'10" around at Glen Cove, NY (1972); a trunk 18'10" around at Newport, RI (1979).

C. Betulus 'Albovariegata'—see *C. Betulus* 'Variegata'

C. Betulus var. *Carpinizza* (Kit. *ex* Host) Neilr.

TRANSYLVANIAN HORNBEAM. Described in 1831. Listed in 1838 by James Booth & Sons, Flottbeck nursery of Hamburg. Extremely rare. Seed-bracts usually entire; leaves smaller, usually distinctly heart-shaped at the base, only 7–9 rather than 10–13 (15) vein pairs.

C. Betulus 'Columnaris'

Originated ca. 1885, and introduced ca. 1891 by Späth nursery of Germany. In North America ≤1897. Very rare. Strictly fastigiate and columnar, of small size. Needlessly confused with *C. Betulus* 'Fastigiata'.

C. Betulus 'Dervæsii'

= *C. Betulus* 'Pendula' (in part)
= *C. Betulus* 'Pendula Dervæsii'
= *C. Betulus* Vienna™ Weeping

WEEPING VIENNA HORNBEAM. Originally planted at the Hapsburg Palace, Vienna, Austria, by Emperor Franz Joseph in 1890, to honor the visit of the Sultan of Turkey. Ohio nurseryman Ed Scanlon saw the tree in 1959, at which time it was ca. 60' tall and wide. In 1963 Scanlon obtained scionwood, and in 1970 first sold grafted specimens, as *C. Betulus* 'Pendula'. Renamed Vienna™ Weeping Hornbeam in his 1976 catalog. See also *C. Betulus* 'Pendula'.

C. Betulus 'Erecta'—see *C. Betulus* 'Fastigiata'

C. Betulus 'Fastigiata'

= *C. Betulus* 'Pyramidalis'
= *C. Betulus* 'Erecta'

PYRAMIDAL HORNBEAM. Originated in 1876 in Germany. In North American commerce since ≤1920s. Common. Since the late 1940s it has been much more planted than any other kind of *Carpinus*. Starts as a columnar tree but rapidly becomes oval with age, then broad but still pleasingly symmetrical and looking as if it was sheared. Conventional to a fault. Records: 85' × 5'3" Colesbourne, Gloucestershire, England (1984; *pl.* 1902); 75' × 6'7" Perthshire, Scotland (1985); 72' × 7'11" Kew, England (1987) ; 65' × 8'10" Kew, England (1987; *pl.* 1894); 57' × 3'4" × 26' Seattle, WA (1988).

C. Betulus 'Frans Fontaine'

Originated as a street-tree in Eindhoven, Holland. Offered in West Coast nurseries ≤1993. Fastigiate.

C. Betulus 'Globosa'

GLOBE HORNBEAM. Originated in Europe. In North America since in 1888 when Späth nursery of Germany supplied one to the Arnold Arboretum. Extremely rare. Offered in recent years as a topgrafted, globe-headed tree by Handy nursery of Portland, OR.

C. Betulus 'Heterophylla'

= *C. Betulus* 'Quercifolia' hort. (in part), non Desf.

CUTLEAF HORNBEAM. Originated in Europe <1864; introduced by James Booth & Sons, Flottbeck nursery of Hamburg. Rare. Date of introduction to North America not known, but likely well before the late 1950s, when Scanlon nursery of Ohio began selling it (incorrectly as OAKLEAF HORNBEAM, *C. Betulus* 'Quercifolia'). Much finer-textured than typical *C. Betulus*, with narrow leaves. Best in shade or woodland settings. Exposed, dry, roadside conditions hurt it. Similar to *C. Betulus* 'Incisa' (and commonly so-sold) but some leaves more or less normal, others wholly so. *Heterophylla* means differently-, or diversely-leaved; from Greek *heteros*, different, and *phyllon*, a leaf. Record: 69' × 10'7" Jephson Garden, Leamington Spa, England (ca. 1980).

C. Betulus 'Incisa'
= *C. Betulus* 'Laciniata'

CUTLEAF HORNBEAM. First described in 1789 in England. Very rare; seldom if ever sold in North America. The name 'Incisa' has been used wrongly for the similar clone 'Heterophylla'. Leaf shorter than normal, coarsely and irregularly toothed, with only ca. 6 vein-pairs.

C. Betulus 'Laciniata'—see C. Betulus 'Incisa'

C. Betulus 'Pendula'
WEEPING HORNBEAM. Originated ca. 1850 in France. Described in 1853. In North American commerce ≤1888. Rare. Weak, mound-like, weeping. Some trees sold under the name 'Pendula' are really the clone *C. Betulus* 'Dervæsii' or Vienna™ Weeping (q.v.).

C. Betulus 'Pendula Dervæsii'—see C. Betulus 'Dervæsii'

C. Betulus 'Pinocheo'
Introduced ≤1994 by Arborvillage nursery of Holt, MO. Original specimen very narrow, strong growing, 20' tall and 5' wide.

C. Betulus 'Purpurea'
PURPLE HORNBEAM. Originated ca. 1864 in Germany. Described in 1873. In North American commerce ≤1963–64. Rare. Leaves wine-purple when young, becoming green. Records: 59' × 5'10" Kew, England (ca. 1980; *pl.* 1902); 28' tall and 34' wide Lisle, IL (1986; *pl.* 1955).

C. Betulus 'Pyramidalis'—see C. Betulus 'Fastigiata'

C. Betulus 'Quercifolia'—see C. Betulus 'Heterophyllla'

C. Betulus 'Variegata'
= *C. Betulus* 'Albovariegata'

Described in 1770. Extremely rare. Creamy-white variegated. Ohio nurseryman Ed Scanlon acquired this cultivar in 1968, but apparently sold few trees if any.

C. Betulus Vienna™ Weeping—see C. Betulus 'Dervæsii'

C. caroliniana Walt.
= *C. americana* Michx. (in part)

AMERICAN HORNBEAM. BLUE BEECH. WATER BEECH. IRONWOOD. MUSCLE TREE. From central and eastern North America, and from southern Mexico to Guatemala and Honduras. Much cultivated. Compared to *C. Betulus*, this bears brighter green leaves, 2"–4½" (5¼") long, less finely toothed, far more colorful in fall, with muted pastels of yellow, carmine-pink, rosy-purple and green. Many specimens branch very low and grow wider than tall. Its common names portray its great wood strength and BEECH-like foliage. Records: 69' × 7'11" × 56' Ulster County, NY (1982); 49' × 5'0" × 46' Newton, TX (1970); 47' × 3'7" × 34' Pulaski, IL (1987); 42' × 9'10" × 65' Stark County, OH (1982); 33' × 5'10" × 51' Portland, OR (1991); in S Mexico it reaches its largest size.

C. caroliniana 'Ascendens'
= *C. caroliniana* 'Pyramidalis'

Found in 1918 by B.H. Slavin of Rochester, NY. Branches upright, making a narrower silhouette than regular seedlings. Not in commerce but at various arboreta.

C. caroliniana 'Fastigiata'
Listed by Sherman nursery of Charles City, IA, since ≤1991–92. Possibly *C. caroliniana* 'Ascendens' renamed.

C. caroliniana 'Pyramidalis'—see C. caroliniana 'Ascendens'

C. cordata Bl.
BIGLEAF HORNBEAM. HEARTLEAF HORNBEAM. Japanese: *Sawa-shiba*. From Japan, Korea, and near Vladivostok; a variety in China. Introduced in 1879 when C. Maries sent seeds to Veitch nursery of England. In North America since 1896. Rare. Kohankie nursery of Ohio offered it in the early 1930s. The Arnold Arboretum distributed stock to nurseries in 1950. Leaf 2½"–6" long × up to 3⅜" wide, with 15–20 vein pairs; leaf base deeply cordate (Latin *cordatus*, heart-shaped). Good gold or red color in late October. Usually a large shrub, sometimes a very small tree, rarely to 50' × 6'0". Best in woodland gardens. Records: 72' tall in Anhwei, China (1925); 29' × 1'9" Kew, England (≤1985; *pl.* 1908); 19½' × 1'2½" Seattle, WA (1995; *pl.* 1969).

C. coreana Nakai
KOREAN HORNBEAM. From SW Korea. Named in 1926. In North American commerce since ≤1994.

Extremely rare. Closely related to *C. Turczaninovii* (TATARIAN HORNBEAM). Leaf ¾"–2" long, quite broad, glossy, with 10–12 vein pairs. Usually a large shrub, sometimes a small tree, to 30' tall.

C. duinensis—see *C. orientalis*

C. Fargesii—see *C. laxiflora* var. *macrostachya*

C. Henryana (H. Winkl.) W. Winkl.
= *C. Tschonoskii* var. *Henryana* H. Winkl.

HENRY HORNBEAM. From central & W China. Discovered by Augustine Henry (1857–1930), Irish doctor, botanical explorer in China, forestry professor and author. Introduced in 1907 by E. Wilson to the Arnold Arboretum. Extremely rare. Offered in 1994–95 by Heritage Seedlings nursery of Salem, OR. Leaf hairy on both sides; to 3½" × 1½" wide, with 12–16 vein pairs. Records: to 60' tall in the wild; 52' × 2'8" Wakehurst Place, Sussex, England (≤1985); 46' × 3'7" Kew, England (≤1985).

C. japonica Bl.
= *Distegocarpus Carpinus* S. & Z.

JAPANESE HORNBEAM. Japanese: *Kuma-shide*. From Japan. Introduced in 1879 to England; to North America <1890. Uncommon. Leaf dark, narrow, prominently and elegantly ribbed, 2"–5⅝" long, × ¾"–2¼" wide, with 18–25 vein pairs; leaf base can be heart-shaped, rounded, or lopsided like that of an ELM (*Ulmus*). Green and yellow in autumn. Buds large and greenish. Seed clusters distinctly tight and narrow. Tree of spreading habit. Records: to 50' × 6'3" in Japan; 35' × 2'6" Kew, England (1967; *pl.* 1895); 19' × 3'3" × 30' Seattle, WA (1994; *pl.* 1956).

C. japonica 'Ebi Odori'
= *C. japonica* 'Issai'

From Japan. Introduced in 1979 by B. Yinger. Its Japanese name means dancing shrimp, alluding to the seed clusters. Of very slow, congested growth, bearing seed clusters in great profusion even as a young plant.

C. japonica 'Issai'—see *C. japonica* 'Ebi Odori'

C. laxiflora (S. & Z.) Bl.
LOOSEFLOWER HORNBEAM. From Korea, and Japan. Introduced in 1914. Rare. Perhaps first offered commercially in the late 1950s. Leaf to 2⅞" × 1¼" with ca. 11–13 (15) vein pairs, and a pronounced drip-tip. Twigs wire-thin. Fall color can be pumpkin-orange and yellow in October, or can remain green into mid-November. Records: 55' × 17'8" in the wild; 36' × 1'10" Borde Hill, Sussex, England (ca. 1980); 26' × 3'9" × 33' Seattle, WA (1993).

C. laxiflora var. *macrostachya* Oliv.
= *C. Fargesii* Franch.

From W & C China. Introduced by A. Henry to Veitch nursery of England. In Europe this variety is more common than typical *C. laxiflora*. Whether this pattern holds in North American horticulture is not known. It has been here since ≤1897. Seed clusters larger (2⅜"–3½" rather than 2"–2¾" long). Hence Greek *macro*, large, and *stachys*, spike (seed clusters). Leaves to 4" × 2". New growth strongly tinged with pink. Records: 75' tall in Anhwei, China (1925); 36' × 3'7" Nymans, Sussex, England (ca. 1980); 26' × 7'10" Borde Hill, Sussex, England (ca. 1980; *pl.* 1932).

C. orientalis Mill.
= *C. duinensis* Scop.

ORIENTAL HORNBEAM. EASTERN HORNBEAM. From SE Europe, SW Asia. Introduced in 1739 to England by P. Miller; named in 1768. The Arnold Arboretum introduced it to North America in 1885, and distributed stock to nurseries in 1953. But it has remained extremely rare and is seen almost exclusively in botanic gardens and arboreta. Leaf 1"–2½" long × ½"–1" wide, with 11–12 (15) vein pairs. A shrub or small tree, with small leaves. Fall color late and poor, dirty green and weak yellow. Drought-tolerant. Compared to the similarly fine-textured *C. Turczaninovii*, its leaf is more finely toothed, lighter green, less hairy; and its buds have fewer scales. Records: 53' × 4'3" Kew, England (1972; *pl.* 1908); 50' × 5'9" Kew, England (1960; *pl.* 1878); 35' × 3'9" Seattle, WA (1993; *pl.* 1953).

C. Ostrya—see *Ostrya Carpinifolia* and *O. virginiana*

C. Tschonoskii Maxim.
= *C. yedoensis* Maxim.

YEDDO HORNBEAM. From NE Asia, Korea, and Japan. Introduced in 1894. Uncommon. Named after Sukawa (Sugawa) T(s)chonoski (Chônosuke; 1841–1925), who was Carl Maximowicz's assistant while botanizing in Japan during 1860–1863. Overall, much like *C. Betulus* in foliage, but hairier. Leaves to 4⅞" × 2½" (3") with (10) 12 (15) vein pairs. Can be a lovely rose-color in fall. Twigs hairy. A small tree, sometimes shrubby. Records: 69' tall in Anhwei, China (1925); 55' × 6'6" Montgomery County, PA (1980); 50' × 5'6" Kew, England (1972; *pl.* ca. 1905); 45' × 3'5½" Seattle, WA (1994; *pl.* 1953); a trunk 5'8" around at Brooklyn, NY (1972).

C. Tschonoskii var. Henryana—see C. Henryana

C. Turczaninovii Hance

TATARIAN HORNBEAM. From N China, Korea, and Japan. Named in 1869 after Nikolai Stepanovich Turczaninow (1796–1864), distinguished Russian scientist. An East Asian *C. orientalis* counterpart. Introduced in 1905 to the Arnold Arboretum. The Arnold Arboretum distributed stock to nurseries in 1953. Very rare. Leaf dark, 1¼"–2⅛" long × up to ¹⁵⁄₁₆" wide, with 9–14 vein pairs. Stipules prominent and persistent. Small tree or large shrub, with gracefully drooping branches. Fall color reddish or an unfavorable, seedy appearance—bare-looking with a few green leaves and brown seed clusters. Records: to 55' × 7'10" in the wild; 38' × 5'5" Highdown, Sussex, England (1983; *pl.* ca. 1915).

C. virginiana—see Ostrya virginiana

C. yedoensis—see C. Tschonoskii

Carya

[JUGLANDACEÆ; Walnut Family] 16–25 spp. of large deciduous trees, mostly in the New World. From *karya*, an ancient Greek name of the walnut. *Carya*, daughter of Dion, king of Laconia, was changed by Bacchus into a WALNUT TREE. The common name HICKORY is from *pawcohiccora*, a native Virginia name referring to food made by mixing pounded nuts with water. HICKORIES are stately ornamental shade trees with golden fall color. The leaves are large, compound, and handsome. But the messy nuts, and the comparative difficulty with which the trees are raised and handled in nurseries, has kept HICKORIES from becoming commonly planted. They differ in two ways from WALNUTS (*Juglans*): their twig pith is solid, not sectioned into numerous tiny chambers; their nut husks split to reveal the nuts.

C. alba—see C. ovata and C. tomentosa

C. amara—see C. cordiformis

C. austrina—see C. glabra

C. cordiformis (Wangh.) K. Koch

= *C. amara* (Michx. fil.) Nutt.
= *Hicoria amara* (Michx. fil.) Raf.
= *Hicoria cordiformis* (Marsh.) Britt.
= *Hicoria minima* (Wangh.) Britt.
= *Juglans alba minima* Marsh.

BITTERNUT HICKORY. SWAMP HICKORY. PIGNUT. From central and eastern North America—a very wide range. The epithet *cordiformis* (from Latin *cordata*, heart-shaped) means heart-shaped, perhaps referring to the nut husk. Rarely cultivated; offered very sparingly in the nursery trade since ≤1888. Very common wild in parts of the U.S., such as much of the Midwest. Buds bright sulphur-yellow, flushing later than other species. Leaflets (5) 7–9 (11). Twigs slender. Records: 171' × 12'6" West Feliciana Parish, LA (1921); 145' × 11'7" LaSalle Parish, LA (1984); 137' × 12'5" Cass County, MI (1986); 134' × 15'5" Lake Accotink, VA (≤1993).

C. glabra (Mill.) Sweet

= *C. leiodermis* Sarg.
= *C. megacarpa* Sarg.
= *C. austrina* Small
= *C. porcina* (Michx. fil.) Nutt.
= *Juglans glabra* Mill.
= *Hicoria glabra* (Mill.) Britt.

PIGNUT (HICKORY). SWEET PIGNUT. COAST PIGNUT. HOGNUT. SMOOTHBARK HICKORY. SWAMP HICKORY. BROOM HICKORY. From central and eastern North America. Rarely cultivated; offered very sparingly in the nursery trade since ≤1888. Latin *glabra* means smooth or hairless, referring to the foliage. Leaflets 5–7 (9). Nut husks thin. Records: 165' × 11'5" Baton Rouge, LA (1964); 120' × 15'½" × 102' East Baton Rouge Parish, LA (1982); 125' × 15'3" Brunswick, GA (1970); 119' × 13'1" Robbinsville, NC (1985)—wrongly called 190' tall in some reports; it was 123' tall in 1992.

C. 'Hican'

HICAN. Hybrids between any HICKORY species and the PECAN (*C. illinoinensis*). At least ten clones have been named. They are grown for nut-production, not for ornament.

C. illinoinensis (Wangh.) K. Koch

(*C. illinoensis*)
= *C. Pecan* (Marsh.) Engel. & Graebn., non (Walt.) Nutt.
= *C. olivæformis* (Michx.) Nutt.
= *Hicoria Pecan* (Marsh.) Britt.

PECAN TREE. SOFTSHELL HICKORY. From the south-central U.S., and parts of Mexico. First cultivated in northern Mexico by Spaniards in late 1600s or at any rate ≤1711. By 1772 Prince nursery sold it in New York. In 1846–47, a Louisiana slave first grafted varieties for commercial nut production. Very common and familiar. In the South it gets scab; in the North nuts may not ripen. This, the State Tree of Texas is also a hayfever culprit.
Leaflets (9) 13–15 (19), slender, curved, staying green late into fall. Nuts very well known. Tree of rapid growth and immense size. Records: 200' × 30'0" maximum recorded dimensions; 175' × 16'0" Wabash County, IL (<1875); 160'×19'7"× 95' near Mer Rouge, LA (1968); 135' × 21'4" × 145' Assumption Parish, LA (<1945); 130' × 23'10" Warren County, MS (1983).

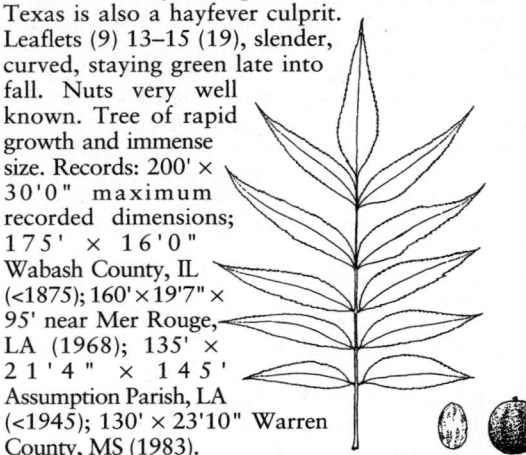

C. laciniosa (Michx. fil.) Loud.

= *C. sulcata* (Pursh) Nutt.
= *Hicoria sulcata* (Pursh) Britt.
= *Hicoria laciniosa* (Michx. fil.) Sarg.

SHELLBARK HICKORY. WESTERN SHELLBARK. THICK SHELLBARK HICKORY. BIG SHELLBARK HICKORY. BIG SHAGBARK HICKORY. BIGLEAF SHAGBARK. BOTTOMLAND HICKORY. KINGNUT. From eastern North America. The name *laciniosa* means full of flaps or folds, from the loosening plates of its ragged bark (see also *C. ovata*). Little cultivated; offered sparingly in the nursery trade since ≤1888. Leaflets (5) 7–9, large and bold. Nuts good to eat. Records: 145' × 12'7" Tea, MO (1984); 139' × 13'11" Kentucky (1994); 136' × 11'9" near New Harmony, IN (1972); 127' × 12'7" Wabash, IL (1982); 105' × 14'6" Rixeyville, VA (1986).

C. leiodermis—see C. glabra

C. megacarpa—see C. glabra

C. olivæformis—see C. illinoinensis

C. ovata (Mill.) K. Koch

= *C. alba* (L.) Nutt. *ex* Ell., non (L.) K. Koch
= *Hicoria ovata* (Mill.) Britt.

SHAGBARK HICKORY. LITTLE SHELLBARK HICKORY. EASTERN SHELLBARK. SCALYBARK HICKORY. UPLAND HICKORY. From eastern North America, and a variety in mountains of NE Mexico. The most commonly cultivated HICKORY; offered in the nursery trade since ≤1888. The epithet *ovata* refers to the egg-shaped nut husk. Leaflets 5 (7). Nuts the best of HICKORIES. Bark famous for its ragged appearance. Records: 153' × 11'0" Henry County, SC (1984); 132' × 13'5" Senoia, GA (1969); 132'×12'0"× 109' Kentucky (1994); 132'×11'6" Turkey Creek, TX (1972); 100' × 11'5" Chevy Chase, MD (1961); trunks to 15'0" around in the old-growth forests.

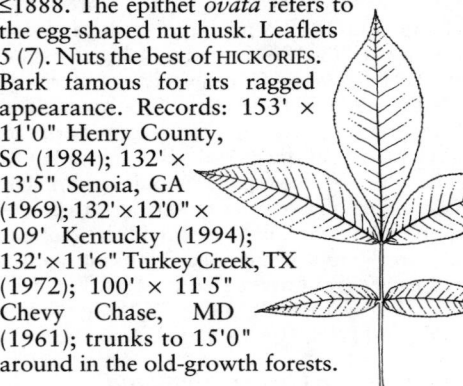

C. ovata 'Holden'

Found ca. 1966 in Hudson, Ohio, by W.A. Strong, landscape architect of Holden Arboretum. Named in 1970. Seldom if ever offered in commerce. Tree narrow, with attractive drooping habit.

C. Pecan—see C. illinoinensis

C. porcina—see C. glabra

C. sulcata—see C. laciniosa

C. tomentosa (Poir.) Nutt.

= *C. alba* (Mill.) K. Koch 1869, non *C. alba* (L.) Nutt. *ex* Ell. 1824
= *Juglans alba* L.
= *Juglans tomentosa* Poir.
= *Hicoria alba* (L.) Britt.

MOCKERNUT. WHITE HICKORY. WHITEHEART. BIGBUD HICKORY. BULLNUT HICKORY. HOGNUT. SQUARENUT. From eastern North America. Named in 1798. Rarely cultivated; offered very sparingly in the nursery trade since ≤1888. The name *tomentosa* in Latin means densely wooly with soft, matted hair—referring to the 7–9 leaflets. Nut shells thick. Bark comparatively smooth. Bud gray-white, up to 1" long. Records: 156'

× 11'8" Humphreys County, MS (1989); 125' × 13'5" Monroe County, AL (1985); 110' × 13'5" Lakeland, FL (1971).

Castanea

[FAGACEÆ; Beech Family] 12 spp. of deciduous trees or shrubs called CHESTNUTS. Ancient Latin name, from the Greek *kastana*, chestnut, after a town of that name in Thessaly. Chestnut blight is a fungal bark disease (*Cryphonectria parasitica*, earlier called *Endothia parasitica*) that arrived in New York in the late 1890s on a shipment of Japanese nursery stock that included *Castanea crenata* (JAPANESE CHESTNUT). If CHESTNUTS are planted as ornamental trees, their nuts may be a mere nuisance. Male flowers borne in strongly scented, showy slender spikes of creamy white in June or July. Female flowers inconspicuous. Isolated trees usually set few fertile nuts, which are encased in viciously spiny porcupine burs. The unrelated HORSE CHESTNUTS are genus *Æsculus*. Closely related genera include *Castanopsis* and *Chrysolepis*.

C. alnifolia—see *C. pumila*

C. americana—see *C. dentata*

C. Ashei—see *C. pumila*

C. × Blaringhemii Camus
(*C. dentata* × *C. sativa*)

CHESTNUT hybrids of many combinations have resulted both accidentally and by artifice. Of great importance in nut production, they have had only incidental use as ornamentals. By and by someone may breed a selection not for nuts but for amenity planting. The most famous hybrid in the early decades was 'Paragon', which originated ≤1880 in Germantown, PA. Often sold in U.S. nurseries at least until 1907, it was the most widely planted nut cultivar, featuring larger nuts, borne even while tree is young. Hybrids can be very difficult to distinguish and there is often dispute as to parentage. Records: 106' × 19'7" × 101' Cicero, WA (1993); 90' × 16'0" × 104' Tumwater, WA (1993).

C. Castanea—see *C. sativa*

C. chrysophylla—see *Chrysolepis chrysophylla*

C. crenata S. & Z.
= *C. japonica* Bl.

JAPANESE CHESTNUT. Japanese: *Kuri*. From Japan [and Korea]. Introduced in 1862 to the U.S. by G.R. Hall. In commerce by the 1880s. Uncommon. Leaf 3"–7" long. A small broad tree. Nuts very large (marketed often as MAMMOTH CHESTNUTS), borne freely even on young trees (6 years old), but of poor flavor. Records: 57' × 10'3" × 55' Centreville, MD (1972); 55' × 13'5" × 61' Lancaster County, PA (1978); 50' × 14'2" × 67' Cheshire, CT (1987); a trunk 15'0" around in Atera, Japan (<1909).

C. dentata (Marsh.) Borkh.
= *C. americana* Raf.

AMERICAN CHESTNUT. From eastern North America; a dominant forest species before the blight wrought havoc on it. Leaf 6"–12¼" long × 1½"–3" (4¼") wide; somewhat pendulous, thin-textured, narrow; hairy beneath only in spring; (15) 20 (29) teeth on each side. Nuts small (hazelnut-like) but sweetest of all. Records: to 140' tall says J. Illick; 100' × 53'5" Frances Cove, NC (<1939); 86' × 20'7" × 109' Carson, WA (1993).

C. heterophylla—see *C. sativa* 'Asplenifolia'

C. japonica—see *C. crenata*

C. laciniata—see *C. sativa* 'Asplenifolia'

C. mollissima Bl.

CHINESE CHESTNUT. From China and Korea (some botanists insist this species is confined to China, and that *C. crenata* grows in Japan and Korea). Introduced in 1854 by California nurseries; to the East Coast in 1903 by C. Sargent. Until the mid-1930s, very little grown. Because of blight-resistance, now more common than other kinds in much of North America. The epithet *mollissima* from Latin *mollis*, soft, and the superlative *-issima*—referring to the hairiness of the twig and leaf. Usually a low-branched, open-headed tree; rarely over 40' tall. Leaf 5"–9" long. Records: to 85' tall in China; 64' × 4'3" × 51' Seattle, WA (1988); 54' × 5'7" × 69' Seattle, WA (1988); 53' × 13'8" × 65' Bucks County, PA (1980); 47' × 10'6" × 66' Sebastopol, CA (1995); 44'

×6'1"×61' Parkland, WA (1992); 40'×10'4"×32' Lee, NH (1973).

C. pumila (L.) Mill.
= C. Ashei (Sudw.) Sudw. ex Ashe
= C. alnifolia Nutt.

ALLEGHENY CHINKAPIN (CHINQUAPIN). DWARF CHEST-NUT. From the southeastern U.S. In U.S. nurseries since ≤1841. Little cultivated. The epithet *pumila* is Latin for dwarf. The species can be a creeping waist-high shrub or a small tree. Leaf to 8½"×3¼"; veins in (7) 17 (26) pairs. Records: to 65' tall in the wild; 55'×7'1"×60' Putnam County, FL (1991); 54'×2'1"×28' Lauderdale County, MS (1986); 49'×11'4" Liberty County, FL (≤1988); 41'×8'6"×40' Daingerfield State Park, TX (1972).

C. pumila var. ozarkensis (Ashe) Tucker
From eastern Oklahoma to north-central Alabama (where it was blight-killed). Larger than typical *C. pumila*, with stouter twigs and larger leaves (to 10½"×3¾"). Record: 50'×13'1"×40' northwest of Winslow, AR (≤1960).

C. salicifolia—see C. sativa 'Asplenifolia'

C. sativa Mill.
= C. vesca Gaertn.
= C. vulgaris Lam.
= C. Castanea Karst.

EUROPEAN CHESTNUT. EURASIAN CHESTNUT. SPANISH CHESTNUT. EDIBLE CHESTNUT. SWEET CHESTNUT. ITALIAN CHESTNUT. From S Europe, N Africa, SW Asia. Introduced to North America when the Spanish brought almonds, walnuts and chest-nuts. Thomas Jefferson grafted some French scions at Monti-cello in 1773. But the first trees actually planted dated from 1803 by Eleuthère-Irénée du Pont de Nemours, owner of a Delaware gunpowder factory. Commonly grown

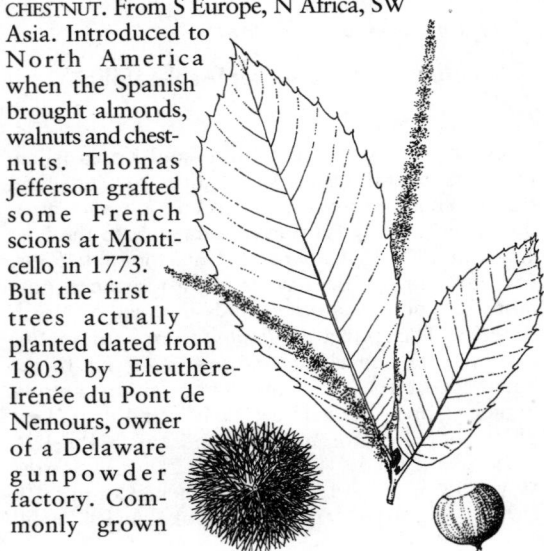

before the blight struck; still common in the blight-free portions of the West. The epithet *sativa* is Latin for sown, cultivated or planted, rather than wild. Leaf 5"–9⅜" long×2"–4¼" wide; (14) 18 (22) vein pairs. Records: 160'×38'8" Madeira (<1903); 124'×13'4" Paris (1982; *pl.* 1842); 121'×17'3" Godinton Park, Ashford, Kent, England (1983); 97'×10'10" Vancouver, B.C. (1989); 88'×20'8" Olympia, WA (1988); 77'×21'5" Vashon, WA (1992); 66'×20'9" Sherwood, OR (1975); 49'×45'1" Casillas-Ojedo-Potes, Cantabria, Spain (ca. 1980); a trunk 37'5" around at Tortworth Church, Gloucestershire, England (1983). Trunks more than 100' around used to exist in Europe, notably on Mt. Etna, Italy.

C. sativa 'Albo-marginata'—see C. sativa 'Argenteovariegata'

C. sativa 'Argenteo-marginata'—see C. sativa 'Argenteovariegata'

C. sativa 'Argenteovariegata'
= C. sativa 'Albo-marginata'
= C. sativa 'Argenteo-marginata'

SILVERLEAF CHESTNUT. Described in 1864. In North American commerce ≤1931. Very rare. Leaf varie-gated with white.

C. sativa 'Asplenifolia'
= C. sativa 'Heterophylla'
= C. heterophylla hort.
= C. laciniata hort.
= C. salicifolia hort.

Introduced in 1836 by Loddiges nursery of England. Extremely rare. In Latin, *aspleniifolius* means with leaves like the frond of the SPLEENWORT FERN. Leaves variously shaped (Greek *heteros*, different, and *phyllon*, a leaf), usually deeply cut in fern-like fash-ion, sometimes narrowly linear. Often *C. sativa* 'Laciniata' has been sold under the name 'Asplenifolia'. See also *C. sativa* 'Fountain'.

C. sativa 'Aureo-marginata'—see C. sativa 'Variegata'

C. sativa 'Aureo-variegata'—see C. sativa 'Variegata'

C. sativa 'Fountain'
Originated in 1927 by Felix Gillett nursery of Nevada City, CA. Introduced in 1931. Long commercially extinct. Leaf highly variable, no two alike, giving the tree a peculiar and striking appearance resembling a fountain. Leaves usually deeply dissected, or

extremely narrow, sometimes deformed and lop-sided. Whether this clone can be distinguished from *C. sativa* 'Asplenifolia' is not known.

C. sativa 'Heterophylla'—see C. sativa 'Asplenifolia'

C. sativa 'Laciniata'
= *C. sativa* 'Asplenifolia' (in part)
Originated ≤1838 in England. Very rare. Leaf with 20–30 narrow lobes drawn out into long thread-like points. Liable to revert to normal foliage, then switch back again. Usually short and small. Record: 98' × 11'1" Westonbirt, Gloucestershire, England (1984).

C. sativa 'Paragon'—see C. × Blaringhemii

C. sativa 'Variegata'
= *C. sativa* 'Aureo-variegata'
= *C. sativa* 'Aureo-marginata'
Described in 1755 in France. Extremely rare. Leaves variegated yellow. Since its 1755 name 'Variegata' is vague, some authorities prefer the 1870s names here cited as synonyms.

C. vesca—see C. sativa

C. vulgaris—see C. sativa

Castanopsis

[FAGACEÆ; Beech Family] 100–120 spp. of broad-leaf evergreen trees, related to both OAKS (*Quercus*) and CHESTNUTS (*Castanea*). From Greek *kastana*, a chestnut, and *-opsis*, resemblance.

C. chrysophylla—see Chrysolepis chrysophylla

C. cuspidata (Th.) Schottky
= *Quercus cuspidata* Th.
= *Lithocarpus cuspidata* (Th.) Nakai
JAPANESE CHINQUAPIN (CHINKAPIN). Japanese: *Tsubura-jii*. From Japan, China, Korea, and the Ryukyus. Introduced to Western cultivation in 1830. Rare. In North American commerce since ≤1887. Leaf 2"–4½" long, very dark green above, with an attractive silvery-bronze sheen underneath, like several *Elæagnus* species. Drooping catkins very abundant

and showy in May. Nuts acorn-like, edible, borne on long spikes. Usually a very dense shrub or small, broad tree in cultivation. Records: 150' × 29'10" in the wild; 42' × 5'0" Caerhays Castle, Cornwall, England (1984); 40' × 4'4" Trewithen Garden, Cornwall, England (1971); 28' × 10'6" × 48' Wellington, New Zealand (≤1982; *pl.* ca. 1850); a trunk 6'4" around at Oakland, CA (1994).

× Catalopsis bignonearis—see × Chitalpa tashkentensis

Catalpa

[BIGNONIACEÆ; Bignonia Family] 11–13 spp. of deciduous trees or shrubs, widely distributed. From the Muskogean name *kutuhlpa*, meaning a head with wings, from the flower shape. Heat-loving trees of rapid growth, bearing large leaves, showy summer flowers (well likened to popcorn), and slender bean-like seedpods—interesting, yet messy when they drop in winter. Fall color unremarkable yellow-green. No other genera in this volume are in the BIGNONIACEÆ.

C. bignoniodes Walt.
= *C. syringæfolia* Sims
= *C. cordifolia* Moench
= *C. Catalpa* (L.) Karst.
= *Bignonia Catalpa* L.
SOUTHERN CATALPA. COMMON CATALPA. CATALFA. CATAWBA. (INDIAN) CIGAR TREE. SMOKE-BEAN TREE. INDIAN-BEAN TREE. PENCIL-POD TREE. CANDLE TREE. CATERPILLAR TREE. WORM TREE. From SW Georgia, NW Florida, Alabama, and Mississippi. Common, although in recent decades seldom planted, because *C. speciosa* is deemed generally better. The epithet *bigno-nioides* is from genus *Bignonia*, and Greek *-oides*, resemblance — the botanist Linnæus had called the species a *Bignonia* in 1753. Caterpillars that feed on its foliage make superb fish bait. Leaf to 10½" × 8", fuzzy

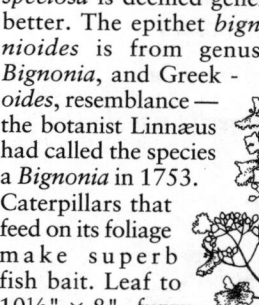

beneath, rarely lobed, malodorous when young. Flowers white, marked with two bands which begin deep yellowish then fade to red-orange; purple spotted; fragrant; in large clusters, later than those of *C. speciosa*. Seedpods as long as 16" (20"). Bark scaly. Records: 91' × 12'7" × 82' Lenawee County, MI (1981; age 187); 83' × 18'5" × 58' Water Valley, MS (1972); 52' × 32'5" × 71' Henderson County, IL (1991).

C. bignoniodes 'Aurea'

GOLDEN CATALPA. Originated in 1870 in England. Officially named in 1894. In North American commerce since ≤1888. Often offered by nurseries over the years, but overall still uncommon. It partly breeds true from seed. Tree smaller in all its parts, and leaves yellowish, sometimes becoming quite greenish by late September. Records: 42' × 3'0" Poland (≤1973); 36' × 5'9" Dulwich Park, London (1976); 30' × 7'3" Bath, England (1984); 28' × 6'1" × 51' Port Coquitlam, B.C. (1994).

C. bignoniodes 'Bungei'—see *C. bignonioides* 'Nana'

C. bignoniodes 'Nana'

= *C. bignoniodes* 'Bungei'
= *C. Bungei* hort., non C.A. Mey.
= *C. umbraculifera* Ugolini

UMBRELLA CATALPA. BROOM CATALPA. Originated in 1848 at Masson nursery in France. In North America since ≤1873. Common. A dwarf globular flowerless variant that is topgrafted to produce a miniature tree. It may be a hybrid with *C. ovata* because its young leaves often are purplish, and less hairy than typical for *C. bignonioides*. However, they are very rarely found with lobes. The real *C. Bungei* (MANCHURIAN CATALPA) is virtually never grown. Records: 17' × 7'6" × 25' and 17' × 5'2" × 31' Tacoma, WA (1990).

C. Bungei—see *C. bignonioides* 'Nana'

C. Catalpa—see *C. bignonioides*

C. cordifolia—see *C. bignonioides*

C. Duclouxii—see *C. Fargesii* f. *Duclouxii*

C. × *erubescens* Carr.

= *C. hybrida* hort. *ex* Späth
= *C. Teasiana* Dode
= *C. Teasii* Penh.
(*C. bignonioides* × *C. ovata*)

HYBRID CATALPA. Originated in 1866 in France.

Independently raised ca. 1874 from seeds of *C. ovata* in nursery of John C. Teas (1827–1907) of Bayville, IN. Common. The epithet *erubescens* is Latin for blushing, reddening. The flowers vary, but are always larger than those of *C. ovata*, are often yellowish in the bud, opening white, with the background of the lower throat frequently aging to pink, while the two stripes fade to deep reddish, with specks of orange-gold near the ends. The clusters are large and airy, and bloom longer than those of non-hybrid CATALPAS. Leaves large, broad, often lobed, purplish as they unfold, less fuzzy on their undersides than those of *C. bignonioides*. Records: 78' × 9'4" Tacoma, WA (1992); 56' × 11'3" Chilham Castle, Kent, England (1983).

C. × *erubescens* 'Adina'

= *C.* × *erubescens* 'Victoria'

Origin not known, likely European. Extremely rare. Young growth reddish; leaves downy beneath, with few lobes. Flowers with extra petals, sterile; very few seedpods. Records: 54' × 8'0" × 59' Seattle, WA (1989; now dead); 45½' × 10'6" × 65' Seattle, WA (1994).

C. × *erubescens* 'Purpurea'

PURPLE CATALPA. Origin disputed. Likely introduced <1886 by T. Meehan's nursery near Philadelphia. The most common hybrid cultivar. New growth strikingly dark purple. Flowers showy white. Leaves usually lobed.

C. × *erubescens* 'Victoria'—see *C.* × *erubescens* 'Adina'

C. Fargesii Bur.

From W China. Discovered by Père Paul Guillaume Farges (1849–1918). Introduced to cultivation ca. 1900 by E. Wilson. Introduced to North America ≤1914. Very rare. Leaf 3"–6" long, bronze when young, sometimes with one or two lobes, with fine hairs as on the young shoots. Flowers rosy-purple, peaking in mid-May. Pods 12"–18" (23½)" long. Records: to 80' × 9'5" in the wild; 62' × 3'6" Westonbirt, Gloucestershire, England (1988); 55' tall at the Arnold Arboretum (1985).

C. Fargesii f. *Duclouxii* (Dode) Gilm.

= *C. Duclouxii* Dode

From central China. Introduced in 1894 to France. Named in 1907 after Père François Ducloux (b. 1864) who collected plants in China. In North American nursery trade by 1942, when W.B. Clarke of

California offered it. Very rare. Compared to the typical form, it is hairless, and its leaves may be smaller, its pods longer, extremely slender like spaghetti: to 25½" (31") but only ≤¼" wide. Flowers in May and June, rosy-pink or rosy very light purple. Tree generally narrow, open. Records: 110' × 5'0" in the wild; 50' × 2'9" Trewithen, Cornwall, England (1985); 46' × 4'10" Bath, Avon, England (1982); 42' × 2'1" Seattle, WA (1992); 40' × 4'3" Caerhays, Cornwall, England (1984); 39' × 3'1" Sumner, WA (1993).

C. Henryi—see C. ovata

C. hybrida—see C. × erubescens

C. Kaempferi—see C. ovata

C. ovata G. Don
= C. Henryi Dode
= C. Kaempferi Sieb.

CHINESE CATALPA. JAPANESE CATALPA. From China. Introduced to Holland in 1849 by Siebold from Japan, where it had been grown for many hundreds of years. In North American commerce since ≤1874. Uncommon. In Latin ovata means egg-shaped—why the name was chosen is not known. Flowers off-whitish, not as showy as those of the two American native species. Flowers smaller than those of C. bignonioides, creamy-white with two yellow stripes that slowly darken to orange, with purplish-brown spots. Leaf dark, lightly hairy, often strongly 3–5 lobed. Seedpod to 16" long. Records: 105' × 10'9" Paris, France (1982; pl. 1852); 73' × 6'10" Sacramento, CA (1993); 72' × 8'0" Syon Park, London (1982); trunks to 12'6" around in China.

C. ovata 'Flavescens'

YELLOW CATALPA. Origin not known but it was in the Geneva botanic garden ≤1863. Introduced to cultivation in 1879; name published officially in 1914. Imported to the U.S. in 1925 by the Arnold Arboretum. Very rare. Scanlon nursery of Ohio sold it in the 1970s. Differs from typical C. ovata in having yellower, smaller, showier flowers. The leaves are the same, being finely short hairy upon both surfaces, though more obviously so above. Some leaves definitely 5-lobed. Records: 52' × 3'10" Seattle, WA (1993); 41' × 10'4" Centralia, WA (1992).

C. speciosa (Warder ex Barney) Engelm.

NORTHERN CATALPA. WESTERN CATALPA. HARDY CATALPA. From S Illinois, SW Indiana, SE Missouri, NE Arkansas, W Tennessee, and W Kentucky. Introduced to cultivation ≤1779, but not commonly grown until 1880. Hardy, with a strong upright habit, it is prized more than C. bignonioides. The epithet speciosa is from Latin speciosus: beautiful, showy. Flowers very large, although few per cluster; open as early as April 4th in Louisiana. Fall color can be bright yellow, unlike the other species. Leaf commonly 12" long. Seedpods stout, to 23" long. Bark deeply furrowed. Wood very durable. Records: to 150' tall in primeval forests; 107' × 20'2" × 85' Lansing, MI (1992); 86' × 22'0" × 84' Walla Walla, WA (1988); 70' × 19'6" × 41' Ellicott City, MD (1972).

C. syringæfolia—see C. bignonioides

C. Teasiana—see C. × erubescens

C. Teasii—see C. × erubescens

C. umbraculifera—see C. bignonioides 'Nana'

Catalpa × Chilopsis—see × Chitalpa

Cathayeia polycarpa—see Idesia polycarpa

Cedrela sinensis—see Toona sinensis

Cedrela Toona—see Toona sinensis

Cedrus

[PINACEÆ; Pine Family] 2–4 spp. of large, long-lived coniferous evergreens. Cedrus is Latinized from kedros, a name used in ancient Greece for resinous trees, chiefly JUNIPER. Cedrus needles are as sharp as pins, short and narrow, borne chiefly in dense whorls. The cones, like those of Abies, are erect and disintegrate at maturity. The bark is gray to brown, hard, and cracked into small rough scales. The trees are broad compared to most SPRUCES (Picea) and FIRS (Abies). Many trees have been called CEDAR. The term usually refers to wood qualities (fragrant, lightweight and durable) more than to outwardly visible characteristics. Most are in the CUPRESSACEÆ (Cypress Family) and do not resemble Cedrus in foliage or cones. Cedrus is a small homogenous genus limited to the Old World. While Cedrus Deodara, of the Himalayan mountains, is well differentiated, the same cannot be said of the Mediterranean species. There is solid scientific rationale for recognizing only one Mediterranean species, consisting of several subspecies. Hybrids between the ATLAS and LEBANESE CEDARS have been known since 1930 at least. A mnemonic to help distinguish the several species refers to the tips of the branches: ATLAS ascending, DEODAR drooping, and LEBANON level.

C. atlantica (Endl.) Manetti ex Carr.
= C. libani var. atlantica (Endl.) Hook.
= C. libani ssp. atlantica (Endl.) Battand. & Trab.

ATLAS CEDAR. MOUNT ATLAS CEDAR. NORTH AFRICAN CEDAR. ALGERIAN CEDAR. From the Atlas and Riff Mountains of Algeria and Morocco. Discovered in 1827. Introduced in 1839 when French gardener and dendrologist A. Sénéclauze received cones. In 1843 or 1845, Lord Somers, second Earl of Eastnor Castle, Herefordshire, England, grew seedlings from cones he had collected in the wild. In North America since ≤1850s. Common. Lush, rapidly growing and very handsome. The most variable *Cedrus*: Form varies from highly irregular, gaunt and picturesque (branches prone to breaking) to compact and formal. Some specimens mimic the broad, tabular habit so prized in the CEDAR OF LEBANON (*C. libani*). Needles olive-green to bluish-green to vivid powdery-blue, or gold in some cultivars; ½"–1¼" long, densely packed, not very sharp. Cones 2"–3¼" × 1½"–2". Records: to 164' tall, with trunks to 62'0" around in the wild; 125' × 14'7" Santa Rosa, CA (1989; now dead); 118' × 14'3" Albury Park, Sussex, England (1986); 108' × 17'3" Westonbirt, Gloucestershire, England (1982; *pl.* 1847); 107' × 14'10" Puyallup, WA (1992); 95' × 18'2" Cirencester Park, Gloucestershire, England (1989); 79' × 16'0" Seattle, WA (1987); a trunk 16'9" around in Sherwood, OR (1987).

C. atlantica 'Argentea'—see C. atlantica f. glauca

C. atlantica 'Argentea Fastigiata'
First listed in the 1956–57 catalog of Hillier nursery, England: "A narrow pyramidal gray-leaved form." This may be a mere renaming of *C. atlantica* 'Glauca Fastigiata'.

C. atlantica 'Aurea'
GOLD ATLAS CEDAR. Likely originated at Boskoop, Holland. Name published in 1900. In North American commerce since ≤1927. Uncommon. Needles golden, shorter than average. Slow growing large shrub or small tree, usually no more than 16' tall. See *C. atlantica* 'Aurea Robusta'. Records: 59' × 6'4" Ascott House, Buckinghamshire, England (1978); 58' × 4'0" Fircrest, WA (1993); 56' × 3'5" Seattle, WA (1990).

C. atlantica 'Aurea Robusta'
Originated by Ouden nursery of Boskoop, Holland, and introduced in 1932. Uncommon. This clone may be sold as *C. atlantica* 'Aurea' by some nurseries. It has much longer needles, lighter yellow, occasionally with bluish undertones if not in full sun.

C. atlantica 'Columnaris'—see C. atlantica f. fastigiata

C. atlantica 'Columnaris Erecta'—see C. atlantica f. fastigiata

C. atlantica f. fastigiata (Carr.) Rehd.
= C. atlantica 'Columnaris'
= C. atlantica 'Columnaris Erecta'

SENTINEL CEDAR. First raised ca. 1885 by the French nurseryman Lalande of Nantes. In North American commerce ≤1927. Very rare. More than one fastigiate clone has been circulated (e.g. 'Argentea Fastigiata', 'Glauca Fastigiata' and 'Granny Louise'), and seedling ATLAS CEDARS sometimes grow sufficiently narrow that they can be so designated. Form varies from near perfect pillars 70 feet tall and only 6 feet wide, to narrowly pyramidal or flame-shaped; color ranges from green to pale bluish-green. Record: 72' × 9'0" Mt. Usher, County Wicklow, Ireland (1975).

C. atlantica f. glauca Beissn.
BLUE ATLAS CEDAR. SILVER ATLAS CEDAR. Cultivated ≤1850. Name originally published in 1867 in France. Common and very popular wherever the climate permits. The most widely planted *Cedrus*. Needles markedly powdery-blue rather than greenish. Selected seedlings are grafted and sold as *C. atlantica* 'Argentea' or 'Glauca'. Records: 125' × 14'0" Brockhampton Park, Herefordshire, England (1978); 121' × 17'3" Bowood, Wiltshire, England (1984); 116' × 12'2" Olympia, WA (1993); 88' × 15'6" Redmond, WA (1992).

C. atlantica 'Glauca Fastigiata'
= C. atlantica 'Glauca Victoria'

Sold in North American nurseries since ≤1931. Apparently this cultivar name has not been officially validated. Tree markedly narrow, branches tightly upswept. Foliage powder-blue. Hillier nursery of

England in 1956–57 sold this or a similar clone as 'Argentea Fastigiata'. Record: 92' × 7'10" × 40' Everett, WA (1989).

C. atlantica 'Glauca Pendula'

BLUE WEEPING ATLAS CEDAR. Raised by nurseryman L. Paillet at Châtenay, France. Name published in 1900. In North American commerce since ≤1943. Uncommon. A selection of C. atlantica f. glauca, with absolutely dripping foliage, a curtain of limp tresses, usually broad and low unless staked. Records: 49' tall reported in Europe; 24' × 4'0" × 38' Geneva, Switzerland (≤1967; pl. ca. 1907); 16' × 4'1" × 45' Tukwila, WA (1992).

C. atlantica 'Glauca Victoria'—see C. atlantica 'Glauca Fastigiata'

C. atlantica 'Goldtip'—see C. libani 'Gold Tip'

C. atlantica 'Granny Louise'

Originated by Evans Farms nursery of Oregon City, OR. Found in their field in 1979. Named in 1986. Introduced 1988–89. Upright and very columnar. Needles short, blue, delicate.

C. atlantica 'Morocco'

Raised from seed by Wm. Goddard of Floravista Gardens, Victoria, B.C. Introduced ≤1989. Conical habit. Needles long, dark green.

C. atlantica 'Pendula'

WEEPING ATLAS CEDAR. Raised ≤1873 by Moreau, nurseryman at Fontenay aux Roses, near Paris; name published in 1875. Very rare. Nearly columnar; erect at first, then the tip nods and branches hang more or less vertically. Needles green. Hardier than C. atlantica 'Glauca Pendula'. Many seedling ATLAS CEDARS grow to be conspicuously drooping in habit, and to designate such trees the name can be used in a forma sense: C. atlantica f. pendula (Carr.) Rehd.

C. atlantica 'Rustic'

Introduced in 1962–63 by Monrovia nursery of California. Sold at least through 1979. A grafted selection of C. atlantica f. glauca, with outstanding blue color.

C. brevifolia—see C. libani ssp. brevifolia

C. Deodara (Roxb. ex Lamb.) G. Don fil.

DEODAR CEDAR. HIMALAYAN CEDAR. INDIAN CEDAR. THE DEODAR. CALIFORNIA CHRISTMAS TREE. From the Himalayas. Named in 1814. The epithet Deodara from Hindi deodar, from Sanskrit devadaru—deva, deity, and daru, wood. Hence TIMBER OF THE GODS. Introduced to cultivation sometime between 1819 and 1831. Commonly grown in North America by the 1850s. Recalling HEMLOCKS (Tsuga), DEODAR has a notably drooping habit compared to other Cedrus. Female or bisexual specimens produce squat cones (2½"–5" × 3"–4"), pale green in spring (rarely reddish-violet), then turning brown as they ripen and fall to pieces. Needles the longest in the genus, 1"–2" (3¼"), shed in late spring as new growth replaces them. Records: to 250' tall and trunks to ±50'0" around in the wild; 121' × 12'9" Minstead House, Hampshire, England (1981); 119' × 19'11" Central Otago, New Zealand (≤1982); 114' × 9'11" Seattle, WA (1988); 103' × 18'2" Bicton, Devon, England (1968; pl. ca. 1835; now dead); 101' × 17'9" Sacramento, CA (1989; pl. 1871); 88' × 18'9" Conon House, Ross, Scotland (1982).

C. Deodara 'Albospica'

('Alba Spica', 'Albospicata')
= C. Deodara 'Variegata'

Name published in 1867 in England. Rare. Said to be no longer cultivated in Europe. In 1888 catalog of J. Rock nursery of Niles, CA. Several Oregon nurseries have sold it since the 1980s. Tips of young shoots whitish, then yellowish, finally green.

C. Deodara 'Argentea'

Described in 1866 in France. Extremely rare. Fast and vigorous. Needles long, brilliant silver-gray to bluish-gray. Argentea is Latin for silvery.

C. Deodara 'Aurea'

GOLDEN DEODAR CEDAR. Described in 1866 in France. In North American nurseries since ≤1927. Common. A small tree, rarely more than 25' tall. Needles golden-yellow in spring, yellowish-green in fall, bloomed greenish-yellow in winter, especially while tree is young. See also C. Deodara 'Harvest Gold' and 'Wells' Aurea'. Records: 87' × 8'3" Vancouver, WA (1993); 55' × 9'2" Port Coquitlam, B.C. (1992).

C. Deodara 'Aurea Pendula'

Known since ≤1960s; in commerce since the 1970s. Rare. Upright with branches that hang along the main trunk. Needles yellow, becoming yellow-green in winter. The name 'Aurea Pendula' (Latin for golden weeping) is invalid unless it predates 1959.

C. Deodara 'Aurea Wells'—see C. Deodara 'Wells' Golden'

C. Deodara 'Compacta'

Introduced ≤1867 in France; reintroduced in 1917 in Holland. To North America ≤1933 by W.B. Clarke nursery of San José, CA. Very rare. Long commercially extinct. Clarke said it grew at half the normal growth rate, had very silvery foliage, and an erect leader. European descriptions of 'Compacta' call it a dwarf tree with nothing erect about it.

C. Deodara 'Cream Puff'

Raised in the 1960s from seed by Wm. Goddard of Floravista Gardens, Victoria, B.C. Introduced to U.S. commerce ≤1982–83. Semidwarf, dense. Creamy-white new growth doesn't sunscorch.

C. Deodara 'Deep Cove'

Raised in the 1960s from seed by Wm. Goddard of Floravista Gardens, Victoria, B.C. Introduced to U.S. commerce ≤1987–88. Very rare. Semidwarf. Young foliage stark white turning blue-gray, forming a dazzling contrast. Pale powder-blue color is attractive in late summer, fall and winter.

C. Deodara 'Emerald Falls'

Introduced ≤1992 by Wells nursery of Mt. Vernon, WA. Resembles and may be C. Deodara 'Repandens'.

C. Deodara 'Erecta'—see C. Deodara 'Verticillata Glauca'

C. Deodara 'Fontinalis'

Name published in 1884 in Germany. Introduced to North America in 1934 by W.B. Clarke nursery of San José, CA. Commercially extinct under this name. Especially regular, dense conical habit. Rarely grows more than 40' tall.

C. Deodara 'Gigantea'—see C. Deodara var. robusta

C. Deodara 'Gold Cone'

Raised in the 1960s from seed by Wm. Goddard of Floravista Gardens, Victoria, B.C. Introduced to U.S. commerce ≤1986–87. Very rare. Narrow pyramidal. All terminal shoots are gold and completely pendulous.

C. Deodara 'Gold Strike'

Grown <1964 by Wm. Goddard of Floravista Gar-

dens, Victoria, B.C. Broadly conical; golden. Very rare if not commercially extinct.

C. Deodara 'Harvest Gold'

Introduced in 1988–89 by Mitsch nursery of Aurora, OR. Slightly brighter gold than C. Deodara 'Aurea'. See also C. Deodara 'Wells' Golden'.

C. Deodara 'Karl Fuchs'

Introduced <1979 in Germany. Present in North America, but not grown commercially. From Pakistan or Afghanistan (named after the man who collected the seeds). Singularly attractive blue; hardy to -13°F. Needles short, in tightly appressed whorls.

C. Deodara 'Kashmir'

Raised ca. 1929 at J. Franklin Styer nursery of Concordville, PA. Survived -25°F in 1933–34. Introduced commercially in 1950. Registered in 1968. Common. Attractive bluish needles, some nearly 3" long on young specimens. A less attractive but still more cold-hardy clone is 'Shalimar'. See also C. Deodara 'Karl Fuchs'.

C. Deodara 'Kingsville'

Originated and introduced <1963 by Kingsville nursery of Maryland. Commercially extinct, at least nominally. Unusually hardy.

C. Deodara 'Klondike'

('Klondyke')

Introduced in the 1970s by Wm. Goddard of Floravista Gardens, Victoria, B.C. Introduced to U.S. commerce ≤1988–89. Rare. Dense, broadly conical tree with both needles and shoots a very unusual chartreuse-gold in winter; doesn't scorch. Doubtless the name Klondike is an allusion to the gold rich region of Canada's Yukon Territory.

C. Deodara 'Limelight'

≠ C. Deodara 'Limeglow'

Introduced in the 1970s by Wm. Goddard of Floravista Gardens, Victoria, B.C. Introduced to U.S. commerce ≤1990. Rare.

C. Deodara 'Miles High'—see C. Deodara 'Repandens'

C. Deodara 'Repandens'

= C. Deodara 'Miles High'
= C. libani 'Beacon Hill'
= C. libani 'Pendula' (in part)

Introduced ≤1930 by W.B. Clarke nursery of San José, CA. Possibly a renaming of the 1866 C.

Deodara 'Pendula'. More likely a coincidentally similar clone. Branches droop very irregularly. After being staked when young, it slowly grows tortuously upright. Recalls *Sequoiadendron giganteum* 'Pendulum'. Clone largely male; an occasional female branch possible. Sold as *C. libani* 'Pendula' in 1968–69 by Sherwood nursery of Gresham, OR. Record: 43' × 4'½" × 22' Beacon Hill Park, Victoria, B.C. (1993; *pl.* 1945).

C. Deodara var. *robusta* (Laws.) Carr.
= *C. Deodara* 'Gigantea'

Discovered in France <1850. In North American commerce ≤1927. Rare. Strong-growing, conical; branches stout, thick. Foliage very dense. Needles 2"–2⅜" (3¼") long, thick, dark green. If, as favored by some horticulturists, the name is restricted to a single clone ('Robusta') then its branching is relatively irregular, color grayish, and habit broad. Records: 72' × 7'10" Brooklands, Somersetshire, England (1982); 67' × 9'3" × 52' Beacon Hill Park, Victoria, B.C. (1993; *pl.* 1945).

C. Deodara 'Sander's Blue'

Introduced ≤1990 by Iseli nursery of Boring, OR. Resembles *C. Deodara* 'Verticillata Glauca' but is brighter blue.

C. Deodara 'Shalimar'

Seed collected in Shalimar Garden of Srinagar, Kashmir (extreme NW India). Raised from seed in 1964 at the Arnold Arboretum. Named in 1979. Uncommon. Reported to be the most cold-hardy *C. Deodara*—but see *C. Deodara* 'Karl Fuchs'. Narrow, droopy habit. Not as attractive as *C. Deodara* 'Kashmir'.

C. Deodara 'Tenuifolia'—see *C. Deodara* 'Viridis'

C. Deodara 'Variegata'—see *C. Deodara* 'Albospica'

C. Deodara 'Verticillata'

Originated at La Maulévrie arboretum of Angers, France. Name published in 1908. Not known to have been sold in North America. The name has been confused and incorrectly equated with 'Verticillata Glauca'. Branches more or less whorled. Needles green.

C. Deodara 'Verticillata Glauca'
= *C. Deodara* 'Erecta'

Raised by Thomas Cripps & Sons nursery of

Tunbridge Wells, England. Name published in 1867. In California commerce during the 1920s and '30s. Rare thereafter in North America until the late 1980s. Dense, narrowly upright bushy tree; very picturesque. Branches sparse, irregularly spaced, horizontal and drooping. Needles, long (to 3¼"), stout, lovely silvery-blue; whorled on young shoots. Mistakenly called *C. Deodara* 'Verticillata' and named HARDY DEODAR CEDAR, a name promoted by the 1923 book *Standardized Plant Names*.

C. Deodara 'Victoria'

Named <1972 by Wells nursery of Mt. Vernon, WA. Also sold in 1990 by Iseli nursery of Boring, OR. Presumably this is a selection from Victoria, B.C., in all likelihood a renaming of the specimens there that I am calling *C. Deodara* var. *robusta*. Mr. Wells (who frequently coined names for conifers he grafted) also sold a *C. atlantica* under the clonal name 'Victoria'.

C. Deodara 'Viridis'
= *C. Deodara* 'Tenuifolia'

Name published in 1850 in England. Fancher Creek nursery of Fresno, CA sold it in the 1920s and '30s. Possibly a *C. atlantica* form. Branches less drooping than on most specimens of *C. Deodara*. Needles short, thin, conspicuously vivid glossy grass-green, destitute of the usual glaucous hue.

C. Deodara 'Wells' Golden'
= *C. Deodara* 'Aurea Wells'

WELLS' GOLDEN DEODAR. Distributed in 1972 by Wells nursery of Mt. Vernon, WA. Also grown in Oregon nurseries. Uncommon. Golden yellow foliage. Broad pyramid with multiple leaders and irregular, slow growth. See also *C. Deodara* 'Aurea' and 'Harvest Gold'.

C. libani A. Rich.
= *C. libanotica* Link
= *C. libanitica* Trew *ex* Pilg.

CEDAR OF LEBANON. LEBANON CEDAR. From mountains of Turkey, Syria, Lebanon. Introduced in the 1600s to England. To France in 1734. To North America in 1746 when P. Collinson sent seeds to J. Bartram. Uncommon compared to *C. atlantica* and *C. Deodara*. The oldest of the comparatively few remaining in Lebanon is ca. 3,000 years. Most famous of all CEDARS; mentioned in the Bible. Much confused with *C. atlantica*. The LEBANON CEDAR has longer needles (¾"–1¼"), usually sharper, flushing earlier in spring and strongly contrasting their bright new green color with the dark old needles. Cones larger (2¾"–4½" × 1¾"–2½") and fewer; bark darker; twigs far less hairy. Branching usually strongly tabular whether narrow or broad. Records: 141' × 11'8" Leaton Knolls, Shropshire, England (1981); 120' × 32'6" Pains Hill, Surrey, England (1981; *pl.* <1760); 101' × 12'2" Snohomish, WA (1995); 60' × 13'6" Tacoma, WA (1990); trunks to 47'0" around in Lebanon.

C. libani var. *argentea*—see *C. libani* f. *glauca*

C. libani var. *atlantica*—see *C. atlantica*

C. libani 'Beacon Hill'—see *C. Deodara* 'Repandens'

C. libani ssp. *brevifolia* (Hook. fil.) Meikle
= *C. libani* var. *brevifolia* Hook. fil.
= *C. brevifolia* (Hook. fil.) Henry *ex* Elwes & Henry

CYPRUS CEDAR. CYPRIAN CEDAR. From Cyprus. Introduced to Europe in 1879 by Sir Samuel Baker. Named in 1880. In 1881 two were grown from seed at Kew, England. Introduced to North America in 1963, directly from Cyprus to the Arnold Arboretum. Likely it had been imported earlier via English nurseries. Sold by various nurseries since the late 1970s, usually as a grafted, unnamed clone. An open, dark-needled tree; needles not very sharp; markedly short compared to those of *C. libani*: ⅓"–⅔" (1⅛") long. The epithet *brevifolia* from Latin *brevis*, short, and *folium*, a leaf. A clone with exceptionally short needles, known since ≤1970, sold since ≤1991–92 by Iseli and Mitsch nurseries of Oregon, is 'Epsteinianum' (an illegitimate name, being in Latin form yet post-1959). Records: 82' × 4'10" Wakehurst Place, Sussex, England (1990; *pl.* ca. 1916); 72' × 6'4" Glanrhos, Powys, Wales (1988); 60' × 11'6" Cyprus (≤1908); 57' × 6'10" Portland, OR (1993; *pl.* 1971).

C. libani var. *foliis argenteis*—see *C. libani* f. *glauca*

C. libani f. *glauca* (Carr.) Beissn.
= *C. libani* var. *glauca* Knight & Perry
= *C. libani* var. *foliis argenteis* Loud.
= *C. libani* var. *argentea* Loud. *ex* Gord.

SILVER LEBANON CEDAR. Name published in 1850 in England. Blue-needled variants commonly exist wild in Turkey in the Cilician Taurus. Rare in cultivation.

C. libani 'Glauca Pendula'

Since ≤1991, nurseries on both the East Coast and Pacific Coast have sold a coarse, bluish, dwarf *C. Deodara* under this name. Some nurseries have sold *C. atlantica* 'Glauca Pendula' or *C. Deodara* 'Repandens' under this name. No authentic *C. libani* 'Glauca Pendula' exists.

C. libani 'Gold Tip'
= *C. atlantica* 'Gold Tip'

A seedling found by Fred Bergman of Raraflora nursery, Feasterville, PA. Name published in 1979. Very rare; little offered in commerce. Large irregular bush; foliage bright yellow in spring, fading to yellow and green.

C. libani 'Pendula'

Named in 1850. A dwarf; absolutely prostrate unless staked. However, in 1968–69 *C. Deodara* 'Repandens' was sold under this name by Sherwood nursery of Gresham, OR. Some nurseries sell a coarse, bluish, dwarf *C. Deodara* under this name.

C. libani 'Purdue Hardy'

Named in 1986. Very rarely in commerce, if at all. From a tree at Purdue University, Indiana, grown from a seed collected in Lebanon by E. Shaw, sown ca. 1955. Named "Hardy" because it has withstood -26°F.

C. libani ssp. *stenocoma* (Schwarz) Davis
= *C. libanitica* ssp. *stenocoma* Schwarz

Introduced in February 1902, when the Arnold Arboretum received from Walter Siehe, collector of Smyrna, ripe cones from the Cilician Taurus mountains. The name *stenocoma* (from Greek *stenos*, narrow, and *kome*, hair) was not given until 1944, based on studies in the late 1930s. North American, Dutch and German nurseries have sold a clone under this name. Properly, the supspecific name covers *any* trees from SW Turkey, as opposed to Lebanon or Syria. Such trees tend to be narrower (even columnar) and more cold-hardy, while the Lebanese trees grow broader and are less hardy. The Turkish trees are thought to have needles and cones intermediate in size between those of *C. atlantica* and typical *C. libani*. Record: 101' × 15'1" Tyler Arboretum, Media, PA (1980).

C. libanitica or *libanotica*—see *C. libani*

Celtis

[ULMACEÆ; Elm Family] 60–75 spp. of deciduous trees. *Celtis* was the Roman naturalist Pliny's name for the LOTUS, a tree with sweet berries described by Herodotus, Dioscorides, Theophrastus, and Homer. Some think they referred to this genus. An Arabic name for *Celtis australis* is *lûtus*. The modern name NETTLE TREE was given in England because *C. australis* leaves are rough and jaggedly toothed like those of nettles. In the United States the usual name is HACKBERRY, likely a corruption of HAGBERRY. *Celtis* often are rugged, handsome, deep-rooted shade trees, afflicted by few serious pests. The bark on some species is interesting. Flowers inconspicuous. Leaves often lopsided at the base, with three prominent main veins. Fall color usually plain yellow. Fruit a pea-sized, single-seeded hard berry, with sweet but scant flesh; ripe in fall. Lacking flamboyance and romantic associations, HACKBERRIES are like cinder blocks: eminently useful but stigmatized by default. Too little work has been done to test rarer species or to derive improved cultivars from the common ones. Closely related genera are *Aphananthe*, *Planera*, *Ulmus*, and *Zelkova*.

C. australis L.

EUROPEAN HACKBERRY. MEDITERRANEAN HACKBERRY. EUROPEAN NETTLE TREE. SOUTHERN NETTLE TREE. LOTE TREE. EUROPEAN HONEYBERRY. From S Europe, N Africa, SW Asia. The 1753 Linnæan epithet *australis* is from Latin *austral*, southern, given in comparison to *C. occidentalis*, western. Long cultivated in Europe; in North American commerce since ≤1900. Grown mostly in California. Drought-tolerant. Leaf sharply and coarsely toothed, 2"–6" long. Berry ⅓"–½" long, on a stem ⅝"–1" long. Records: trunks to 20'0" around in Spain says A. Henry; 131' × 14'9" Madrid, Spain (≤1988); 94' × 10'9" Sacramento, CA (1989).

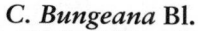

C. Bungeana Bl.

= *C. Davidiana* Carr.
= *C. sinensis* Planch., non Pers.
= *C. chinensis* Pers. *ex* Bunge

From N and W China. Named in 1852 after the eminent Russian botanist Dr. Alexander von Bunge (1803–1890) of St. Petersburg, productive author on the plants of N and NE Asia. Introduced to Western cultivation sometime between 1853 and 1882. In North America ≤1912. Offered in 1922–23 by Fruitland nursery of Augusta, GA. Extremely rare. Deserves more testing on account of its attractive, disease-free foliage. Leaf very glossy above, 1½"–3½" long. Berry ca. ¼" long, purplish-black, seed white. A small, slow-growing tree, usually at most 50' × 6'6". Records: 79' × 9'3" Kansu, China (1925); 36' × 4'0" Kew, England (1981; *pl.* 1902).

C. chinensis—see C. Bungeana

C. crassifolia—see C. occidentalis

C. Davidiana—see C. Bungeana

C. Douglasii—see C. reticulata

C. hybrida 'Magnifica'—see C. 'Magnifica'

C. lævigata Willd.

= *C. mississippiensis* Bosc
= *C. texana* Scheele
= *C. Smallii* Beadle

SUGARBERRY. TEXAS SUGARBERRY. SOUTHERN HACKBERRY. LOWLAND HACKBERRY. From the eastern U.S., mostly in the South on bottomlands. Also in NE Mexico. Named in 1811, *lævigata* in Latin meaning smooth or polished. Grown primarily in its native range. Although handsome it can also be a major weed, and short-lived. Leaf 2"–5" long, margin usually untoothed; surface hairless. Berry ¼"–⅓" long, orange-red, becoming dark purple, not wrinkled when dry. Records: 148' × 11'10" × 110' Richland County, SC (1972); 81' × 25'1" × 114' Society Hill, SC (≤1993).

C. lævigata 'All Seasons'

Introduced in 1983 by W. Wandell of Urbana, IL. Rare. Rapid growth. Free of witches' brooms. Good for the Great Plains.

C. Magnifica™ PP 2795 (1968)

= *C. hybrida* Magnifica™
= *C. occidentalis* Magnifica™
(*C. lævigata* × *C. occidentalis*)

HYBRID HACKBERRY. Introduced in 1983 by Princeton nursery of New Jersey. Faster growth than either parent; disease-resistant. Leaves large, glossy, resist leaf hopper damage. Very tolerant of cold, drought and salt. Form vase-shaped in youth, maturing to oval 50'–60' tall.

C. mississippiensis—see *C. lævigata*

C. occidentalis L.
= *C. crassifolia* Lam.
= *C. pumila* Pursh

COMMON HACKBERRY. NORTHERN HACKBERRY. SUGAR-BERRY. ONE BERRY. POMPION BERRY. HACK TREE. NETTLE TREE. UNKNOWN TREE. HOOP ASH. BEAVER-WOOD. FALSE ELM. BASTARD ELM. From much of the U.S. and extreme S Canada. Common. Often afflicted with witches' brooms. With less disease-prone *Celtis* available, there is no reason to plant seedlings of this species as ornamental trees. Bark gray, distinctively warty or pebbled. Leaf 2"–6" long. Berry ⅓"–½" long, wrinkled when dry. The 1753 Linnæan epithet *occidentalis* is Latin meaning western, given in comparison to *C. australis*, southern. Records: 134' × 11'0" Gibson County, IN (<1882); 118' × 19'7" Wayland, MI (1972); 111' × 20'2" LaPrairie, WI (1989); 85' × 17'9" × 120' West Chester, PA (1968; died in 1980).

C. occidentalis Chicagoland®
Found as a chance seedling in cultivation at South Barrington, IL. Selected in 1978 by R.G. Klehm because of its vigor, large leaves, and upright single leader. First described and sold in 1987 by Klehm nursery of Arlington Heights, IL.

C. occidentalis 'Delta'
From the south shore of Lake Manitoba. Introduced <1987.

C. occidentalis Magnifica™—see *C. Magnifica*™

C. occidentalis 'Prairie Pride' PP 3771 (1975)
Introduced in 1975 by W. Wandell of Urbana, IL. Common. Produces a well-formed, compact oval crown even at an early age. To 30'–40' tall. Leaf thick, lustrous, dark. Resistant to witches' brooms.

C. occidentalis var. *reticulata*—see *C. reticulata*

C. occidentalis 'Windy City'
Found as a chance seedling in cultivation at South Barrington, IL. Selected in 1978 by R.G. Klehm because it quickly develops an upright single leader. Foliage also attractive. First described and sold in 1985 by Klehm nursery of Arlington Heights, IL.

C. pumila—see *C. occidentalis*

C. reticulata Torr.
= *C. Douglasii* Planch.
= *C. rugulosa* Rydb.
= *C. occidentalis* var. *reticulata* (Torr.) Sarg.

NETLEAF HACKBERRY. WESTERN HACKBERRY. SUGAR-BERRY. From the western U.S., and northern and central Mexico. Named in 1828—*reticulata* means netted; from Latin *reticulum*, a little net, in reference to leaf vein network. Cultivated by the 1890s. Planted to a limited extent within its native range. Bark very hard, gray, and rough. Leaf 1"–5" long, usually thick and raspy. Berry ca. ⅓" long. Records: 74' × 11'4" × 72' Red Rock, NM (1971); 69' × 15'0" × 75' Catron County, NM (1989).

C. rugulosa—see *C. reticulata*

C. sinensis Pers., non Planch., non Hemsl.
= *C. japonica* Planch.

CHINESE HACKBERRY. CHINESE SUGARBERRY. PORTUGUESE ELM. From E China, Korea, Taiwan, and Japan. Named in 1805. In California by 1897. Grown ≤1900 by Thomas Meehan nursery of Pennsylvania. Uncommon. Hardy, long lived, thriving in all but the poorest soils, densely foliated. Leaf 2"–5½" long, dark and glossy above, paler, dull and inconspicuously hairy beneath; subtly and bluntly toothed. Berries dark orange to orange-red, ⅓" long; stalk ¼"–⅝" long. Records: to 100' tall in the wild; 75' × 10'0" × 68' Davis, CA (1994; *pl.* ca. 1920); 72' × 16'5" Japan (1994).

C. sinensis 'Pendula'
Introduced ≤1994 by Arborvillage nursery of Holt, MO. "Outstanding weeping form." *Pendula* as a cultivar name is invalid, being Latin yet post-1959.

C. Smallii—see *C. lævigata*

C. texana—see *C. lævigata*

Cephalotaxus

[CEPHALOTAXACEÆ; Plum Yew Family] 4–7 (9) spp. of coniferous evergreens called PLUM YEWS. From Greek *kephale*, a head, and *taxus*, a YEW TREE—*Taxus*-like with male flowers in clusters. Usually broad, multitrunked bushes in cultivation; with training, small trees. Grow best in shade. Needles scimitar-like, broad and curved, borne in soft-textured sprays. Fruit resembles little plums, rosy-brown when ripe in autumn; sweet, syrupy, chewy, resinous-flavored, sticky. Related to YEWS (*Taxus*) and *Torreya*. Some specimens bear exclusively male or female flowers. Many bear both kinds but a preponderance of one or the other. Most commonly cultivated in the Southeast.

C. drupacea—see *C. Harringtonia* var. *drupacea*

C. drupacea var. pedunculata—see *C. Harringtonia*

C. Fortunei Hook. fil.
(*Fortuni, Fortunii*)

CHINESE PLUM YEW. From N Burma and China, in limestone regions. Introduced in 1848–49 to Standish nursery of England by Robert Fortune (1812–1880) who reported seeing specimens 40'–60' tall. Later E. Wilson found it as large as 40' × 4'6" in the wild. Usually shrubby and multitrunked in cultivation. Grown in North America since ≤1863. Very rare; most plants sold under this name are really *C. Harringtonia*. Less hardy than *C. Harringtonia*. Needles very sharp, 1½"–5" long. Fruit to 1¼" long. Record: 42½' × 2'8" Belvedere House, County Westmeath, Ireland (1990).

C. Fortunii 'Lion's Plume'

Received from Japan in 1952 at Willowwood Arboretum of Rutgers University, Gladstone, NJ. Rare. Vigorous; needles often 6" long.

C. Harringtonia (Knight *ex* Forbes) R. Smith
= *C. pedunculata* S. & Z.
= *C. drupacea* var. *pedunculata* (S. & Z.) Miq.

From Japan. Japanese: *Inugaya*. Introduced by Siebold to Holland in 1829–30. Named in 1839, after the Earl of Harrington, England. Hence LORD HARRINGTON'S PLUM YEW. The name *C. Harringtonia* in its narrow sense applies to the nomenclatural type—a male garden clone unknown in the wild; needles 1¼"–2⅞" long, more or less horizontally spreading; male flower clusters on long (to ¾") stalks. The variable wild manifestations of the species are correctly designated *C. Harringtonia* var. *drupacea*.

C. Harringtonia var. drupacea (S. & Z.) Koidz.
= *C. drupacea* S. & Z.
= *C. sinensis* (Rehd. & Wils.) Li
= *C. Harringtonia* var. *sinensis* (Rehd. & Wils.) Rehd.
= *Podocarpus japonicus* hort. (in part)

JAPANESE PLUM YEW. COW'S TAIL PINE. From Tibet, China, Korea and Japan. Introduced by Siebold to Holland in 1829–30. Named in 1846. Common. Needles 1½"–3" long, either abruptly tipped or tapering gradually to a sharp point; sometimes forming a v-shaped parting along the twigs. Male flowers in clusters, on short stalks. Fruit to 1¼" long. A broad shrub or rarely a small tree to 40' tall. With pruning it can be kept to the form of a tree. The branches tend to elongate more each year than the terminal leader(s), even on young seedlings. Record: 25' × 7'1" × 38' Waikato, Tauranga, New Zealand (≤1982).

C. Harringtonia 'Fastigiata'
= *C. koraiana* hort. *ex* Gord.
= *Podocarpus coraianus* Sieb.
= *Podocarpus koraiana* Endl.

FASTIGIATE PLUM YEW. SPIRAL PLUM YEW. Japanese: *Chosen-maki*. Introduced by Siebold to Ghent, Belgium, in 1830. Named in 1844. To England in 1861. Common. Branches tightly ascending, recalling IRISH YEW (*Taxus baccata* 'Fastigiata'). Foliage very dark. Needles 1½"–2½" long, whorled on stout green twigs. Fruitless. More cold-hardy than most *Cephalotaxus*. Absolutely bushy, to 17' tall.

C. Harringtonia 'Fastigiata Aurea'—see *C. Harr.* 'Korean Gold'

C. Harringtonia 'Korean Gold'
= *C. Harringtonia* 'Ogon Chosen-maki'

Introduced in 1977 by B. Yinger from the Shibamichi nursery of Kawaguchi City, Japan. Like *C. Harringtonia* 'Fastigiata Aurea' (named in 1870s, needles margined yellow) but young growth at first wholly yellow, chartreuse by midsummer, green by winter.

Cephalotaxus Harringtonia 'Ogon Chosen-maki'—see *C. Harr.* 'Korean Gold'

C. Harringtonia var. *sinensis*—see *C. Harringtonia* var. *drupacea*

C. koraiana—see *C. Harringtonia* 'Fastigiata'

C. pedunculata—see *C. Harringtonia*

C. sinensis—see *C. Harringtonia* var. *drupacea*

Cerasus acida—see *Prunus Cerasus*

Cerasus avium—see *Prunus avium*

Cerasus communis—see *Prunus Cerasus*

Cerasus demissa—see *Prunus virginiana*

Cerasus emarginata—see *Prunus emarginata*

Cerasus erecta—see *Prunus emarginata*

Cerasus flore roseo pleno—see *Prunus* 'Hokusai'

Cerasus ilicifolia—see *Prunus ilicifolia*

Cerasus Lannesiana—see *Prunus Lannesiana*

Cerasus Laurocerasus—see *Prunus Laurocerasus*

Cerasus Mahaleb—see *Prunus Mahaleb*

Cerasus mollis—see *Prunus emarginata*

Cerasus nigra—see *Prunus avium*

Cerasus Padus—see *Prunus Padus*

Cerasus semperflorens pendula—see *P. Cerasus* 'Semperflorens'

Cerasus sylvestris—see *Prunus avium*

Cerasus vulgaris—see *Prunus Cerasus*

Cerasus vulgaris dupliciflora—see *Prunus Cerasus* 'Rhexii'

Cercidiphyllum

[CERCIDIPHYLLACEÆ; Katsura Family] 1–2 spp. of deciduous trees grown for shade and color. From genus *Cercis* (REDBUD) and Greek *phyllon*, a leaf. *Cercidiphyllum* is the only genus in its Family. Small male and female flowers are borne in May on separate trees; some females in bloom can be nearly as bright as blooming REDBUD trees (*Cercis* spp.). The fruit is a seed capsule shaped like a miniature banana. Unless stunted by insufficient summer moisture or extreme winter cold, KATSURA is of strong constitution. Best in part shade. Needs ample room—said to be the largest tree in China.

C. japonicum S. & Z. *ex* Hoffm. & Schultes

KATSURA TREE. From Japan. Japanese: *Katsura*. Introduced to U.S. cultivation in 1865 by T. Hogg, while he was U.S. consul in Japan. Common. A colorful, distinctive shade tree, without close visual or botanic affinity to other genera. Leaf roundish 2"–4" and unfolding attractive bronze in spring; in autumn bright yellow, orange or red, often smelling of burnt sugar, ripe apples, or wild strawberries. Tree frequently forks low and is like a titanic shrub. Records (see also var. *sinense*): 125' × 53'10" and 115' × 63'0" Japan (1994); 82' × 20'8" Philadelphia, PA (1988; *pl.* 1890); 81' × 8'0" Ft. Wayne, IN (1985); 80' × 9'11" Wethersfield, CT (1987); 70' × 19'1" Amherst, MA (1983; *pl.* 1877).

C. japonicum 'Globosum'—see C. japonicum 'Heronswood Globe'

C. japonicum 'Heronswood Globe'

= *C. japonicum* 'Globosum'

Heronswood nursery of Kingston, WA, has sold this selection since 1991 as "remarkably dense, forming a small rounded crown to 6' in eight years." Arborvillage nursery of Holt, MO, has also sold grafted specimens.

C. japonicum var. magnificum—see C. magnificum

C. japonicum 'Pendulum'

WEEPING KATSURA. Grown for more than 300 years in Japan. In North American commerce since ≤1966. Uncommon. Weeping from a top-graft to form a small mounded tree. Uncommon. See also *C. magnificum* 'Pendulum'.

C. japonicum var. *sinense* Rehd. & Wils.

CHINESE KATSURA. From W China, introduced in 1907 by E. Wilson. Sold by Kohankie nursery of Ohio in 1940s. Differs from Japanese KATSURA in being taller, usually single-trunked rather than often multitrunked; and the leaves are hairy on the veins beneath. These distinctions, of uncertain validity, are scarcely recognized horticulturally. Recorded to 130' × 55'0" in China.

C. magnificum (Nakai) Nakai

= *C. japonicum* var. *magnificum* Nakai

From mountains of Japan. Japanese: *Hiro-ha-katsura*. Introduced to Western cultivation when one was planted in Sweden in the 1880s or '90s; to France ±1900; seeds to the Seattle arboretum in 1946. Very rare in North America, but in commerce. In winter the twigs are coarser than those of regular KATSURA, with large projecting peg-like spurs bearing the buds. Has a much bolder silhouette than regular KATSURA. The leaf is broader, and often deeper blue-green. The bark is smoother. There is nothing particularly magnificent about the tree. Easily distinguished any day of the year from a regular KATSURA. Smaller. Record: 43' × 4'8" × 41' Seattle, WA (1992; *pl.* 1946).

C. magnificum 'Pendulum'

Weeping. Rarer than common KATSURA's pendulous variant, of stronger growth, greater irregularity, and ultimately taller.

Cercis

[LEGUMINOSÆ; Pea Family] 6–13 spp. of deciduous shrubs and small trees called REDBUDS. From the ancient Greek *kerkis*, a shuttle; the name given by Theophrastus to the European species (*C. Siliquastrum*), from resemblance of the pod to the weaver's implement. Prized chiefly for floral effect, which ranges from a pale purple haze to a clear, bright rosy-pink spectacle in spring before the leaves unfold. The small, pealike flowers are edible raw, a pretty addition to salads. The leaf resembles that of a LILAC (*Syringa vulgaris*). Fruit is a flattened seedpod 2"–5" long. Despite being in the Pea Family, *Cercis* lacks the ability to symbiotically produce nitrogen in the soil. They thrive in full exposure. The North Carolina State arboretum has an unexcelled collection of *Cercis*, from which much is being learned.

C. canadensis L.

COMMON REDBUD. EASTERN REDBUD. JUNEBUD TREE. REDBIRD TREE. AMERICAN JUDAS TREE. From the central and eastern U.S., southern Ontario, and parts of northern Mexico. Common in cultivation. A small, sometimes shrubby tree with heart-shaped leaves that turn yellow in autumn. Beloved for its small, numerous pink-purple flowers in spring. Leaves variable, always pointed, 2"–7" long, hairy or hairless; yellow in autumn. Oklahoma's State Tree. Records: 66' × 4'7" × 64' Wayne County, MI (1983); 47' × 8'2" × 36' Springfield, MO (1976); 44' × 10'5" × 35' Tennessee (1994); 36' × 10'0" × 27' Nashville, TN (1989); 39' × 9'0" × 42' Roanoke, VA (1991); 36' × 9'2" × 39' Charleston, MO (1968); 29' × 10'3" × 35' Manteo, NC (1993).

C. canadensis f. *alba* Rehd.

WHITEFLOWER REDBUD. First discovered <1903 in Teas' nursery of Carthage, MO (unless B.K. Boom is right in saying it originated in Austria in 1792); officially named in 1907. Uncommon until the 1980s. A clone is sold as 'Alba'; see also *C. canadensis* 'Royal'.

C. canadensis 'Flame'

≠ *C. canadensis* 'Plena'

Discovered ca. 1920 by Mr. & Mrs. A. Gratz at Fort Adams, MS. Named and introduced in 1965 by L. Gerardi nursery of O'Fallon, IL. Common. Branching is more erect than usual. Flowers open late, are large and double (with ca. 20 petals). Leaves hairy. See also *C. canadensis* 'Plena'.

C. canadensis 'Forest Pansy' PP 2556 (1965)

Originated in 1947 as a seedling at Forest nursery of McMinnville, TN. Common. Foliage purple, at least during spring and early summer. In the Southeast, summer heat makes it green by midsummer. Fall color can be a rich blend of red, green, and orange. Flowers like those of 'Rubye Atkinson' (i.e., pale petals, dark calyces).

C. canadensis var. *mexicana*—see *C. canadensis* var. *texensis*

C. canadensis var. *mexicana* Royalty™—see *C. can.* var. *texensis* Royalty™

C. canadensis 'Oklahoma'—see *C.* 'Oklahoma'

C. canadensis 'Pinkbud'
Discovered <1961 near Kansas City, MO. Extremely rare. Flowers pure, bright pink.

C. canadensis 'Pink Charm'—see *C. can.* 'Wither's Pink Charm'

C. canadensis 'Plena'
= *C. canadensis* 'Flore-pleno'
Originated <1894. Very rare. Offered by Kingsville nursery of Maryland in 1958. See also *C. canadensis* 'Flame'.

C. canadensis 'Royal'
= *C. canadensis* 'Royal White'
Originated by Mr. Royal Oakes (deceased) of Bluffs, IL, as a seedling from a native tree. First flowered in 1940. Introduced in 1950 by L. Gerardi nursery of O'Fallon, IL. Rare; recently offered by Arborvillage nursery of Holt, MO. Compared to *C. canadensis* 'Alba' it has more abundant, larger, and earlier flowers, and is more compact. The leaves are also wider-angled at the base.

C. canadensis 'Royal White'—see *C. canadensis* 'Royal'

C. canadensis 'Rubye Atkinson'
Introduced ≤1960s by Willis nursery of Ottawa, KS. Common in California commerce. Shell pink corolla, dark calyx. Leaves hairy. Withstands heat well.

C. canadensis 'Silver Cloud'
Raised from a Tennessee seedling; introduced in 1964 by Theodore R. Klein of Yellow-Dell nursery, Crestwood KY. Seldom sold; recently offered by Arborvillage nursery of Holt, MO. Leaf variegated silver-white. Flowers pink, not abundant. Tree less vigorous; best in partial shade.

C. canadensis var. *texensis* (S. Wats.) Hopkins
= *C. canadensis* ssp. *texensis* (S. Wats.) E. Murr.
= *C. occidentalis* var. *texensis* S. Wats.
= *C. texensis* (S. Wats.) Sarg.
= *C. reniformis* Engelm. *ex* S. Wats.
= *C. canadensis* var. *mexicana* (Rose) Hopkins
= *C. mexicana* Rose

TEXAS REDBUD. MEXICAN REDBUD. From the Arbuckle Mountains of southern Oklahoma to northern Mexico. Commonly grown in the Southwest. Usually shrubby. Leaves "wet look" glossy, often ruffled or undulate, thick, hairless to densely hairy, rounded and notched at apex, deeply cordate at base; short stem, usually <1" long. Records: 40' tall reported by C. Sargent; 37' × 4'9" × 41' Real County, TX (1988); 30' × 6'0" × 33' Dallas County, TX (1992).

C. canadensis var. *texensis* 'Alba'—see *C. canadensis* var. *texensis* 'Texas White'

C. canadensis var. *texensis* Royalty™
= *C. canadensis* var. *mexicana* Royalty™
Introduced <1986 by Lone Star Growers, San Antonio, TX.

C. canadensis var. *texensis* Texas Star™
Introduced <1986 by Lone Star Growers, San Antonio, TX.

C. canadensis var. *texensis* 'Texas White'
= *C. canadensis* var. *texensis* 'Alba'
= *C. reniformis* 'Alba'
= *C. reniformis* 'Texas White'
TEXAS WHITE REDBUD. Found in the late 1960s or early '70s as a seedling at Germany nursery of Fort Worth, TX. Uncommon. Many trees sold as 'Texas White' are actually a clone of *C. canadensis* f. *alba*. Vigorous; hardy. Large, pure white flowers; large shiny leaves.

C. canadensis 'Wither's Pink Charm'
= *C. canadensis* 'Pink Charm'
Discovered ca. 1943 at Mt. Solon, VA. Named after D.D. Wither. Sold since ≤1950s, first by Kingsville nursery of Maryland. Uncommon. Difficult to graft. Flowers pink. Leaves hairy.

C. chinensis Bge.
= *C. japonica* Sieb. *ex* Planch.
CHINESE REDBUD. From China. Introduced to Western cultivation in 1843 when Siebold sent it to Holland. In North American commerce since ≤1862. Common. Usually a shrub 6'–15' tall. Compared to *C. canadensis* the leaf is glossier, more elongated, thicker, with 5 veins instead of 7, a transparent thickened margin, and with poor fall coloration; the bark is smoother; the flowers larger and taste spicier. It is less hardy, too. Seedpods often very numerous and persistent.

C. chinensis 'Alba'

Flowers white. Extremely rare but available. Unless the name predates 1959 it is invalid, being Latin for white.

C. chinensis 'Arborea'

Sold in 1930s by W.B. Clarke nursery of California, and Hillier nursery of England. More treelike. Very rare. In China, E. Wilson measured specimens as large as 50' × 5'0".

C. chinensis 'Avondale'

Originated as a chance seedling in the Avondale suburb of Auckland, New Zealand. First grown by Duncan & Davies nursery of Plymouth, New Zealand. In North American commerce since ≤1985. Uncommon but available. Flowers profuse, dark pink. Habit dwarfish; not a tree.

C. chinensis 'Pink Charm'

Listed ≤1993 by Piroche Plants nursery of Pitt Meadows, B.C.

C. japonica—see C. chinensis

C. mexicana—see C. canadensis var. texensis

C. occidentalis Torr. ex Gray

CALIFORNIA REDBUD. WESTERN REDBUD. From S Oregon, California, Arizona, Nevada and Utah. Introduced to cultivation in 1886. Commonly offered for sale within its range. Almost invariably a shrub, multitrunked, broad and less than 20' tall. It can be bought as a standard. Leaf much resembles that of C. Siliquastrum, is smaller (to 5" on sappy shoots in well-watered soil) and more bluish-green, giving a metallic or jade-green look. Fall color variable. In Seattle it can have a second bloom in late summer, and stays green late into autumn, or can turn pure yellow in October. Records: 32' × 3'11" × 22' Lake County, CA (1976); 29' × 6'2" × 35' Santa Rosa, CA (1980. This tree may really be C. Siliquastrum).

C. occidentalis 'Claremont'

Introduced ≤1981 by Rancho Ana Botanic Garden of Claremont, CA. Propagated by cuttings. Rare. Flowers exceptionally abundant and with fine deep color.

C. occidentalis var. texensis—see C. canadensis var. texensis

C. 'Oklahoma'

= C. reniformis 'Oklahoma'
= C. texensis 'Oklahoma'
= C. canadensis 'Oklahoma'

Discovered in 1964 in the Arbuckle Mountains of Oklahoma. Named and released in 1965 by Otis Warren & Son nursery, Oklahoma City. Highly prized and increasingly common as propagation difficulties are overcome. Parentage disputed. Possibly C. canadensis crossed with C. canadensis var. texensis. Leaves attractively pinkish when emerging in spring; hairy beneath, very glossy above, round rather than pointed, thick. Flowers wine-red. Heat-resistant.

C. racemosa Oliv.

From China. Introduced in 1907 by E. Wilson. Introduced to North American commerce in 1940 by W.B. Clarke of California. Extremely rare in its native China; equally rare in cultivation. Leaf hairy beneath, pointed at apex, rounded at the base. Flowers pale pink, borne in 3"–5" long racemes of 10–40. Records: to 39' × 6'6" in the wild; 23' × 4'4" East Bergholt Place, Suffolk, England (1971).

C. reniformis—see C. canadensis var. texensis

C. reniformis 'Alba'—see C. canadensis var. texensis 'Texas White'

C. reniformis 'Oklahoma'—see C. 'Oklahoma'

C. reniformis 'Texas White'—see C. canadensis var. texensis 'Texas White'

C. Siliquastrum L.

JUDAS TREE. EUROPEAN REDBUD. LOVE TREE. From SW Europe to SW Asia. JUDAS TREE is literally *arbor Judæ*, a corruption of *arbor Judæa*—the tree cultivated in Jerusalem. The epithet *Siliquastrum* suggests an inferior resemblance as in poet*taster*. Because of its heart-shaped leaf it was called LOVE TREE. Grown for many centuries in Europe; very common in Rome, for example. Cultivated in California and the Pacific Coast since ≤1854. Rare in contemporary commerce. For decades some have been sold in California as C. occidentalis. Leaf round, not pointed; hairless. Flowers larger than those of most Cercis, dark rose. Much less cold-hardy than C. canadensis. Records: 65' × 4'2" Verrières-le-Buisson, France (1905; *pl.* 1822); 40' × 7'11" London, England (≤1920); 37' × 5'8" Seattle, WA (1989); 36' × 10'6" Wanganui, New Zealand (≤1982; *pl.* ca. 1865); 33' × 10'1" Geneva, Switzerland (≤1967); one 50' wide in Los Angeles, CA (1993).

Cercis Siliquastrum 'Alba'

Cultivated since the 1600s. Described officially in 1770 in England. In North American commerce since ≤1906. Rare. Flowers white.

C. Siliquastrum 'Variegatum'

Introduced ≤1875 by Barron nursery of England. Extremely rare. Leaves variegated ivory-white.

C. texensis—see *C. canadensis* var. *texensis*

C. texensis 'Oklahoma'—see *C.* 'Oklahoma'

Ceroxylon

[PALMÆ or ARECACEÆ; Palm Family] 15–20 spp. in the Andes. The National Emblem of Colombia. From Greek *keros*, wax and *xylon*, wood—that is WAX TREE, because the trunk is white and waxy. Fronds 6'–20' long with hundreds of leaflets, dark green above, silvery-white beneath. Male and female flowers mostly on separate trees. WAX PALMS set the world altitude record and height record for the Palm Family. Some grow at more than 13,000' elevation; some attain more than 200' in height. Little known; extremely rare in cultivation. Summer heat is perhaps as inimical to their growth as severe winter cold. Cool, temperate Pacific Coast regions offer the best promise for successful cultivation. The minimal data supplied below reflects the prevailing state of knowledge. Other PALM genera in this volume are *Butia*, *Chamærops*, *Nannorrhops*, *Sabal*, *Trachycarpus*, and *Washingtonia*.

C. alpinum Bonpl. *ex* DC.

= *C. andicola* HBK.

ANDEAN WAX PALM. From Colombia and Venezuela. The first species discovered, by Humboldt, in 1801, west of Bogotá. Introduced to cultivation in 1840. In California ≤1908. A young specimen is at Strybing arboretum of San Francisco, CA. Grows 100'–200'+ tall. Fronds to 20' long; trunk coated with resinous wax.

C. andicola—see *C. alpinum*

C. cerifera—see *C. ceriferum*

C. ceriferum (Karst.) Burret

= *C. cerifera* Pittier

From Venezuela. The epithet *ceriferum* from Latin *cera*, wax and *-fer*, from *ferre*, to bear, hence wax-bearing.

C. hexandrum Dugand

From Colombia, in high altitudes. Named in 1953. A young specimen is planted next to two *C. quindiuense* at Strybing arboretum of San Francisco, CA. The epithet *hexandrum* means 6 stamens; from Greek *hex*, six, and *andros*, male.

C. quindiuense (Karst.) H. Wendl.

QUINDIO WAX PALM. From Colombia, and possibly Ecuador. To 200' tall. Two young specimens grow at Strybing arboretum of San Francisco, CA. The name *quindiuense* refers to Quindio Pass of Colombia.

C. utile (Karst.) H. Wendl.

From Colombia and Ecuador, to the PALM altitude record, 13,124'–13,500' (4,000m+). The epithet *utile* is Latin meaning useful.

Chænomeles chinensis—see *Pseudocydonia sinensis*

Chamæcyparis

[CUPRESSACEÆ; Cypress Family] 6–8 spp. of coniferous evergreens bearing fine, scaly foliage. From Greek *chamai*, on the ground, hence low growing or dwarf, and *kyparissos*, CYPRESS. Differs from *Cupressus* in flattened foliage sprays, smaller cones (only 3/16"–1/2"), fewer seeds per cone scale. Some botanists judge the species not generically distinct from those of *Cupressus*. In horticulture *Chamæcyparis* are common (hundreds of diverse cultivars) and generally easily pleased and long suffering, while most species of *Cupressus* prove problem-prone. *Chamæcyparis* need adequate moisture to thrive, performing poorly where drying winds prevail; *Cupressus* often grow well in dry regions.

C. contorta torulosa—see × *Cupressocyparis Leylandii* 'Contorta'

C. formosensis Matsum.

= *Cupressus formosensis* (Matsum.) Henry

TAIWAN CYPRESS. FORMOSAN CYPRESS. From Taiwan. *C. formosensis* should not be confused with *C. obtusa* var. *formosana*. Named in 1901. Introduced in 1910 to England by Lewis Clinton-Baker. To North America in 1925 when imported from Taiwan by the Arnold Arboretum. Exceedingly rare; confined to botanic gardens and specialist collections. Ancient Taiwanese specimens are of great interest, being at once enormous and venerable. In 1818 E. Wilson reported counting 2,700 annual rings on one felled specimen. Awe inspiring, indeed. But, he pointed out, the trees were far from handsome, with thin crowns and much of the foliage usually brownish. Young specimens however, can look lush and pretty. The foliage is weakly resinous; the sprays sharp to the touch; not white-lined underneath. Cones not round, ca. $^{7}/_{16}$" long. Slow growth in cultivation. Records: to 230' × 75'6" in the wild; 65½' × 4'5" and 52½' × 7'3" Borde Hill, Sussex, England (1989).

C. Henryæ—see C. thyoides var. Henryæ

C. Lawsoniana (A. Murr.) Parl.

= *Cupressus Lawsoniana* A. Murr.

LAWSON CYPRESS. PORT ORFORD CEDAR. OREGON CEDAR. WHITE CEDAR. GINGER PINE. From SW Oregon to NW California. Introduced to cultivation in 1854 when seeds were sent from California by Wm. Murray to Charles Lawson (1794–1873), then head of Peter Lawson and Son nursery of Edinburgh, Scotland. Offered for sale in 1858–59 by Golden Gate nursery of San Francisco. Commonly grown, easily propagated, and tremendously prolific of cultivars. The following six pages include more than 50 tree-like cultivars known or supposed to have been planted in North America. Numerous dwarf cultivars, and trees grown only in Europe, are excluded. Only a tiny fraction of cultivars originated in North America. A deadly root-rot (*Phytopthora*) appeared in Oregon ca. 1950, and has resulted in a dramatic decrease of the commercial availability of the species. Many cultivars lose their distinctive attributes gradually over the years, and become difficult to identify. The various golden cultivars (17 included in this book) become merely light green in shade. Certain cultivars that are dwarfed more or less if grown via cuttings, are rendered vigorous and treelike if grafted; 'Ellwoodii' is an example. The foliage has a resinous parsley odor. Staminate flower catkins reddish-

purple in spring. Cones the size of peas, ca. ⅓". Records: 224' × 22'1" Siskiyou National Forest, OR (1989); 219' × 37'7" Siskiyou National Forest, OR (1968); trunks to 50'0" around have been reported.

C. Lawsoniana 'Albaspica'—see C. Lawsoniana f. albospica

C. Lawsoniana 'Alba Variegata'—see C. Lawsoniana f. albospica

C. Lawsoniana f. albospica (Nichols.) Beissn.

WHITE VARIEGATED LAWSON CYPRESS. Several cultivars are grouped under this name. The original English and Scottish nursery descriptions of the clones are hopelessly vague, nobody can sort the specimens seen now, and the result is utter guesswork. The only recourse is to use a general name that covers any given white-variegated tree (or shrub) encountered. The clonal names include: the original 'Albaspica' (sic) named in 1867 by R. Smith in England; the "very different" 'Albaspica' of Young's nursery <1875; the 'Alba Variegata' of Lawson's nursery <1875; the dwarf 'Albovariegata' (= 'Albopicta' or 'Albomaculata') of Veitch nursery <1881; the robust 'Argenteovariegata' of Lawson nursery ≤1862. Cultivar 'Versicolor' seems to be sufficiently distinctive, and has some yellow, so is treated separately in the present volume.

C. Lawsoniana 'Albovariegata'—see C. Lawsoniana f. albospica

C. Lawsoniana 'Allumigold'

An 'Alumii' sport found by J. Maks of Dedemsvaart, Holland. Introduced in 1966. Rare. Sold since ≤1991 by Vermeulen nursery of New Jersey. More compact than 'Alumii' and tinged golden.

C. Lawsoniana 'Alumii'
('Allumii')

SCARAB CYPRESS. Origin unknown. Introduced <1887 (attributed to R. Smith nursery of Worcester, England ca. 1870—but the name is not in Smith's 1875 catalog). One of the most common cultivars. Much confused with *C. Lawsoniana* 'Fraseri'. Narrow and flame-shaped when young, it ages to a wide bushy base topped by a narrower spire. It has upswept vertical bluish sprays of foliage and bears few cones until it is quite large. Records: 98' × 8'0" Glamis Castle, Angus, Scotland (1981); 88' × 11'3" × 24' and 73' × 13'6" × 29' Woodinville, WA (1989).

C. Lawsoniana 'Alumii Azurea'—see C. Lawsoniana 'Azurea'

C. Lawsoniana 'Argentea'

In Latin, *argentea* means silver. This name has been commonly applied to several clones with glaucous foliage. In the absence of certainty as to cultivar names, such trees can be safely designated *C. Lawsoniana* f. *glauca*.

C. Lawsoniana 'Argentea Smith'—see C. Lawsoniana 'Greycoat'

C. Lawsoniana 'Argentea Waterer'

= *C. Lawsoniana* 'Argentea' (in part)
= *C. Lawsoniana* 'Watereri' or 'Watereriana'

Raised by Anthony Waterer, nurseryman at Knap Hill, Surrey, England; sold in 1864. Sprays silvery-gray on upper side, light green beneath. Upright habit. Branches erect. Twigs short and outspread.

C. Lawsoniana 'Argenteovariegata'—see C. Laws. f. *albospica*

C. Lawsoniana 'Aurea'

Raised by A. Waterer's nursery of Knap Hill, Surrey, England; listed in the 1862 catalog. Compact if not dwarf; with scattered, pale yellow foliage. In Latin, *aurea* means gold. Full tree-sized golden LAWSON CYPRESSES sold under the name 'Aurea' are most likely to be 'Lutea' or 'Stewartii'.

C. Lawsoniana 'Aurea Spica'—see C. Lawsoniana 'Aureovariegata'

C. Lawsoniana 'Aureovariegata'

= *C. Lawsoniana* 'Aurea Spica'

Introduced <1861 by nurseryman J. Waterer of Bagshot, Surrey, England. Introduced to North American commerce ≤1878 by H. Mitchell nursery of Victoria, B.C. Regular conical or pyramidal habit. Young growth partly creamy- to bright-yellow variegated. Records: 46' × 5'4" Snohomish, WA (1995); 45' × 4'2" Tacoma, WA (1990). See also *C. Lawsoniana* 'Versicolor'.

C. Lawsoniana 'Azurea'

= *C. Lawsoniana* 'Alumii Azurea'

Origin unknown. Introduced ≤1948 (sold that year by Doty & Doerner nursery of Portland, OR). Grown by several California and Oregon nurseries since then. A sport of *C. Lawsoniana* 'Alumii' having slower growth and extremely blue foliage in large flattened sprays.

C. Lawsoniana 'Blue Jacket'

= *C. Lawsoniana* 'Milford Blue Jacket'

Originated <1892 by Young's nursery of Milford, Surrey, England. Introduced to North American commerce ≤1914 by L. Coates nursery of Morganhill, CA. Foliage dark bluish above, paler beneath. Form broadly compact conical. Stout, with spreading branches. Record: 40' × 2'6" Wisley, Surrey, England (1983).

C. Lawsoniana 'Cœrulea'

= *C. Lawsoniana* 'Glauca Cœrulea'

Raised in 1860 by A. van Leeuwen, Sr., head gardener of G.J. Alberts of Boskoop, Holland. Put into North American commerce ≤1925 by California Nursery Co. of Niles, CA. Dense pyramidal tree with lightly blue-tinged foliage in erect sprays. In Latin, *cœrulea* means blue.

C. Lawsoniana 'Columnaris'

= *C. Lawsoniana* 'Columnaris Glauca'

Raised from seed ca. 1940 by Jan Spek, nurseryman at Boskoop, Holland. Introduced to North American commerce ≤1959–60 by H.M. Eddie nursery of Vancouver, B.C. Commonly grown since then. Tree small, dense, narrow columnar; blue-gray. Young shoots tilt up to reveal paler undersides. Record: 45' × 5'2" Seattle, WA (1990; *pl.* 1952; reverting).

C. Lawsoniana 'Columnaris Glauca'—see C. Laws. 'Columnaris'

C. Lawsoniana 'Darleyensis'

= *C. Lawsoniana* 'Smithii' hort. (wrongly)
= *C. Lawsoniana* 'Smith's New Silver'

Raised by James Smith & Sons, Darley Dale nursery near Matlock, Derbyshire, England. Introduced in 1874. Columnar or narrow pyramidal; silvery-green. The name 'Darleyensis' is sometimes wrongly applied to the golden colored *C. Lawsoniana* **'Lutea Smithii'** (not known in North America).

C. Lawsoniana 'Dutch Gold'

Said to have originated in Holland <1986. Introduced by Fred Barcock of Bury St. Edmunds, Suffolk, England. In North American commerce ≤1992–93. Conical tree to 15' tall or more. Foliage soft, elegant, bright golden all year.

C. Lawsoniana 'Elegantissima'

Raised ca. 1870 by Wm. Barron & Son's Elvaston nursery of Borrowash, near Derby, England. First distributed in 1875. Young shoots canary yellow, lasting well even in winter. Conifer specialist H.

Welch says Barron's clone is no longer identifiable; the name 'Elegantissima' now is used in Britain (and North American nurseries since ≤1958) for a cultivar that Hillier nursery raised <1920: a small, broadly conical tree with pale yellow shoots and broad, flattened, fine drooping sprays, the young tips of which are variegated silvery-gray or grayish-cream; a frosted appearance of much beauty. Latin *elegans*, elegant, and the superlative *-issima*. Perhaps the younger clone should be renamed "Hillier's Elegant."

C. *Lawsoniana* 'Ellwoodii'

A juvenile form that originated ca. 1925 as a chance seedling in Swanmore Park, Bishop's Waltham, Hampshire, England. Named after G. Ellwood, the head gardener there. Described by Murray Hornibrook in 1929. Date of introduction to North American commerce not known, but by 1937 it was at Manten's nursery of British Columbia. Very common since the 1940s. A narrow oval in shape, it has exceedingly dense, prickly foliage of a bluish color, suggestive of a JUNIPER. Adult foliage is possible but rare. Bears no cones. It grows to 20' tall, or more in great age and ideal conditions. Record: 52' × 7'10" Burnaby, B.C. (1992).

C. *Lawsoniana* 'Ellwoodii Improved'

Introduced in 1960–61 by Mitsch nursery of Aurora, OR, and propagated by them since. Compared to 'Ellwoodii' it is slower, more silvery blue. The cultivar name is illegitimate, being partly Latin yet post-1959, but can be salvaged by being changed to 'Ellwood's Improved'.

C. *Laws.* 'Ellwoodii Variegated'—see C. *Laws.* 'Ellwood's White'

C. *Lawsoniana* 'Ellwood's White'

= C. *Lawsoniana* 'Ellwoodii Variegated'

Introduced in 1986–87 by Mitsch nursery of Aurora, OR. More than one variegated 'Ellwoodii' sport has been propagated, and they are usually dwarf.

C. *Lawsoniana* 'Erecta Glauca'—see C. *Laws.* 'Erecta Glaucescens'

C. *Lawsoniana* 'Erecta Glaucescens'

= C. *Lawsoniana* 'Erecta Glauca'

BLUE COLUMN CYPRESS. Originated in R. Smith's nursery of Worcester, England. Described in 1868. Columnar, slender, similar in habit to 'Erecta Viridis'

but bluish green. Introduced to North American commerce ≤1923. Uncommon. Record: 56' × 7'10" Everett, WA (1988).

C. *Lawsoniana* 'Erecta Viridis'

GREEN COLUMN CYPRESS. GREEN PYRAMID CYPRESS. Originated in 1855 at Anthony Waterer's nursery at Knap Hill, Surrey, England, as a seedling, raised from 1854 seed imported from California. The first LAWSON CYPRESS cultivar. Introduced to North American commerce ≤1878 by H. Mitchell nursery of Victoria, B.C. Very common. Tree flame shaped, from narrow to broad. Rich grass-green foliage held compactly in flat vertical sprays. Few cones made. Records: 115' × 9'4" Stourhead, Wiltshire, England (1984); 108' × 14'5" Bodnant, Gwynedd, Wales (1990); 92' × 16'6" Gliffaes Hotel, Powys, Wales (1984); 87' × 14'6" Puyallup, WA (1987); 83' × 16'6" Sumner, WA (1987); 82' × 16'0" Headfort, County Meath, Ireland (1966). See also C. *Lawsoniana* 'Green Hedger'.

C. *Lawsoniana* 'Filifera'

Origin unknown, but sold in Europe ≤1877. Grown in California nurseries ≤1927. A large often multi-trunked shrub or narrowly conical, rounded-top tree of somewhat pendulous habit rarely more than 20' tall; dense with slender drooping filiform branchlets of subdued green. *Filifera* means having threads or filaments; from Latin *filum*, thread, and *ferre*, to bear. This clone sets very few cones. Wrongly equated by some authors to 'Filiformis'—a tree with conspicuously elongated and sparingly ramified terminal twigs. Record: 46' × 3'4" Endsleigh, Devon, England (1963).

C. *Lawsoniana* 'Filiformis'

Described in 1877–78, from Europe. Extremely rare in North America. A gaunt, open tree that has long, sparse branches richly draped with elongated whip-like branchlets, often more than 2' long, with short, remote lateral divisions. Lighter green color than that of 'Filifera'. Records: 82' × 5'9" Nymans, Sussex, England (1985); 82' × 7'4" Bicton, Devon, England (1990).

C. *Lawsoniana* 'Fletcheri'

Originated as a branch sport which retained its juvenile foliage. Found on a hedge of typical C. *Lawsoniana* which had been kept closely clipped at Ottershaw nursery, near Chertsey, Surrey, England. Put into commerce in 1913 by Fletcher Brothers nursery. Officially named in 1923. In North American commerce since ≤1927; common. Broadly flame-shaped and bushy at the base, with dense feathery upswept foliage mostly semi-juvenile but sometimes bearing a few cones near the top of the tree. Color gray-green touched with bronze in winter. Records: 79' × 3'2" Wisley, Surrey, England (1990); 50' × 7'5" Royal Oak, B.C. (1989).

C. *Lawsoniana fragrans conica*—see C. *Lawsoniana* 'Wisselii'

C. *Lawsoniana* 'Fraseri'

Described in 1887. In North America ≤1898; in nurseries here since ≤1920s. Columnar, narrow at the base; foliage dull gray-green to dark dusky bluish, held like that of C. *Lawsoniana* 'Alumii' but without a skirt of billowing branches at the base. Extremely slender, dense, towering. Bears many cones. Records: 95' × 8'7" Shelton, WA (1993); 92' × 8'3" Puyallup, WA (1992). It has sometimes been regarded as the same as 'Alumii' and doubtless some nurseries have sold it under that name.

C. *Lawsoniana* f. *glauca* Beissn.

BLUE LAWSON CYPRESS. Known since the 1850s. Common. Several clones have typical growth habit but vary in their exceptionally glaucous foliage, having a bluish cast. Some of the more famous cultivars in turn have received their own names, such as 'Glauca Veitch', 'Oregon Blue', 'Spek' and 'Triomf van Boskoop'. Records: 99' × 6'10" Tacoma, WA (1988); 86' × 9'5" Olympia, WA (1988).

C. *Lawsoniana* 'Glauca Cœrulea'—see C. *Lawsoniana* 'Cœrulea'

C. *Lawsoniana* 'Glauca Spek'—see C. *Lawsoniana* 'Spek'

C. *Lawsoniana* 'Glauca Veitch'
= C. *Lawsoniana* 'Veitchii Glauca'

Likely originated as C. *Lawsoniana* f. *glauca* in Veitch nursery of England. Offered ≤1918 by Moon nursery of Pennsylvania, and was still in commerce at least into the 1980s. Name not officially published until 1937. Pyramidal form; branches and branchlets spreading, tips decurving; soft blue colored, undersides of sprays paler, the markings inconspicuous.

C. *Lawsoniana* 'Golden King'

Raised as a 'Triomf van Boskoop' seedling and introduced ≤1931 by K. Wezelenburg & Son of Hazerswoude, Holland. Sold recently in North America. An open graceful tree with drooping branch tips of a light golden yellow, deeper golden-green on the older shoots. The clone mass-produced by Monrovia nursery of California as 'Golden King' is really 'Golden Showers'.

C. *Lawsoniana* 'Golden Showers'

Introduced in 1972–73 by Mitsch nursery of Aurora, OR. Commonly grown since then. A compact small tree; bright gold, outstanding in winter; pendulous tips giving fountain-like effect. Not prone to burning in exposed sites.

C. *Lawsoniana* 'Golden Wonder'

Raised ca. 1955 by N.T. Bosman of Boskoop, Holland. Introduced in 1963 by Jan Spek of Boskoop. Sold since ≤1991 by Vermeulen nursery of New Jersey. Narrowly pyramidal, strong-growing, golden yellow.

C. *Lawsoniana* 'Gracilis'

FOUNTAIN LAWSON CYPRESS. Introduced <1866 by A. Waterer, nurseryman at Knap Hill, Woking, Surrey, England. In North America since early 1900s, but seldom offered in commerce. Apparently tends to revert to nondescript appearance in age. Extinct commercially. Tall, ascending tree; branches spreading, tips decurving; branchlets crowded, the smaller ones slightly drooping, the large ones gracefully drooping; leaves very small, dark glossy green, with bluish-bloom. Record: 83' × 6'1" Vashon, WA (1993).

C. *Lawsoniana* 'Gracilis Aurea'

Introduced in 1894 by Davis' Hillsborough nursery of County Down, Ireland. Extremely rare in North America. Bonnell nursery of Renton, WA sold it in the early 1950s, saying it had pendulous and heavy foliage, velvety golden year round.

C. *Lawsoniana* 'Green Hedger'
= C. *Lawsoniana* 'Jackman's Green'

A seedling from George Jackman & Sons, Woking nursery, at Knap Hill, Surrey, England. Introduced to North America in 1925 by the Arnold Arboretum. Rare. Recently offered by several East Coast nurseries. Regular, dense conical tree of bright green foliage, very similar to C. *Lawsoniana* 'Erecta Viridis'. Jackman's catalog says it grows 80' tall × 20' wide, and is superb for hedging. Specimens sent out by Hillier nursery of England may be incorrectly named; one such in Seattle is 33½' tall and 18' wide after 30 years; it is very dark green, bushy, with many twig tips dead.

C. *Lawsoniana* 'Greycoat'
= C. *Lawsoniana* 'Argentea' (in part)
= C. *Lawsoniana* 'Argentea Smith'

Raised in late 1860s by James Smith & Sons, Darley Dale nursery near Matlock, Derbyshire, England. Introduced in 1874–75. Sprays silvery gray on both sides. Conical-upright habit, lightly and gracefully branched; finely nodding twigs. The 1992 name 'Greycoat' was needed since 'Argentea Smith' was illegitimate.

C. *Lawsoniana* 'Hillieri'

Selected in 1910s as a seedling by Edwin Hillier (1840–1926) of Hillier nursery, England. Named and introduced in 1928. In North American commerce since ≤1944. Uncommon. Densely conical tree; small foliage in hard, often parallel upright sprays of singularly bright yellow. Cones small. Less hardy than some clones. Records: 52' × 5'9" Vancouver, B.C. (1994); 43' × 5'5" Everett, WA (1994).

C. *Lawsoniana* 'Hollandia'

('Hollandica', 'Hollandii')
Introduced ca. 1895 by Koster nursery of Boskoop, Holland. In North American commerce ≤1927. Very rare. Prized for hardiness. Very dark brilliant green. Pyramidal, robust; branches horizontal; branchlets distinctly flattened and fan-shaped; sprays on upper side on branchlets arching, partly upright, and directed forward.

C. *Lawsoniana* 'Intertexta'

Introduced ca. 1869 by Lawson and Son nursery of Edinburgh, Scotland. Very rare in North America, seldom in commerce. A slender weeping tree of dark, hard, sparse foliage. Young specimens rather tender. Records: 82' × 7'9" Fairburn, Highland, Scotland (1980); 76' × 5'10" Walcot Hall, N Shropshire, England (1963); 53' × 5'8" Vancouver, B.C. (1989).

C. *Lawsoniana* 'Jackman's Green'—see C. *Laws.* 'Green Hedger'

C. *Lawsoniana* 'Kilmacurragh'

Raised in late 1940s at the estate of the Ball-Actions of Kilmacurragh, Rathdrum, County Wicklow, Ireland. Introduced in 1951 by Hillier nursery of England. In North American commerce to a very limited extent since ≤1980. A bright green (color of INCENSE CEDAR, *Calocedrus decurrens*), very narrow small tree. Records: 41' × 3'9" Mt. Usher, County Wicklow, Ireland (1966); 36½' tall in Seattle, WA (1993; *pl.* 1952).

C. *Lawsoniana* 'Lane'

('Lanei')
= C. *Lawsoniana* 'Lanei Aurea'
Raised ca. 1938 and introduced ≤1945 by H. Lane & Son's nursery of Great Berkhamstead, Hertfordshire, England. In North American commerce since ≤1955. One of the most golden yellow LAWSON CYPRESSES. Broadly conical; slow. Sprays crowded, feathery and thin, young growth distinctly golden-yellow above, green and whitish beneath. Cones small. Similar to 'Stewartii' and 'Hillieri'. Records: 52½' × 6'6" Carae, Strathclyde, Scotland (1987); a multitrunked specimen is 34' tall (1994) at Victoria, B.C.

C. *Lawsoniana* 'Lanei Aurea'—see C. *Lawsoniana* 'Lane'

C. *Lawsoniana* 'Lutea'

Raised <1870 in nursery of G. & Wm. Rollisson, Tooting, (London), England. The earliest recorded golden LAWSON CYPRESS. In North America ≤1895; in nurseries here since ≤1925. Common. A golden yellow slender column, with narrow, drooping spire-like top. Growth slow to medium. Nurseries have applied the name 'Lutea' (Latin for yellow) to more than one yellowish cultivar. Records: 85' × 4'5" Murthly Castle, Tayside, Scotland (1983); 77' × 4'3" Dupplin Castle, Perthshire, Scotland (1970); 72' × 7'8" Brahan, Easter Ross-shire, Scotland (1989; *pl.* 1901); 67' × 5'9" Woodland, WA (1993).

C. *Lawsoniana* 'Lutescens'

Originated <1875 by L. Van Houtte, nurseryman of Ghent, Belgium. Introduced to North American commerce ≤1914 by L. Coates nursery of Morganhill, CA. Vigorous conical tree, bright golden; strikingly compact. Much like 'Lutea'.

C. *Lawsoniana* 'Lycopodioides'

Originated ca. 1890 by Van der Elst's Tottingham nursery of Dedemsvaart, Holland. Introduced in 1895–86. In North American commerce ≤1991–92. Upright small dense tree with gray-green contorted foliage. The name *lycopodioides* from genus *Lycopodium*, CLUBMOSS, and Greek *-oides*, resemblance.

C. *Lawsoniana* 'Milford Blue Jacket'—see C. *Laws.* 'Blue Jacket'

C. Lawsoniana 'Moerheimii'

Introduced ≤1934 by B. Ruys nursery of Dedemsvaart, Holland. Introduced to North American commerce ≤1955–56 by W.B. Clarke nursery of San José, CA. Clarke described it as of bushy erect habit, branch-tips yellow-variegated. Other accounts call it a vigorous conical tree to 40', with numerous fine branches bearing ascending sprays, golden when young in spring, aging to yellow-green.

C. Lawsoniana 'Monumentalis'

Raised by C. de Vos' nursery of Hazerswoude, Holland; introduced in 1873. In North America ≤1898; sold here ≤1930 by Malmo nursery of Seattle, WA; sold by Sherwood nursery of Oregon in the late 1950s. Rare. Dense slender column; to 30' or more; branches ascending closely, stout; branchlets erect, flat; leaves sky blue or azure.

C. Lawsoniana 'Oregon Blue'

Raised from seed on Arneson's nursery of Canby, OR. Propagated and introduced by Richard Bush nursery, also of Canby. Mass-produced by 1978–79. Common. Very vigorous, fast, broad conical form with outstanding silver-blue color.

C. Lawsoniana 'Pembury Blue'

Raised by Baggesen's nursery of Pembury, Kent, England; first distributed in 1961–62 by George Jackman & Sons nursery of Woking, Surrey. In North American commerce ≤1992–93. A broad, well furnished pyramid (to 25' × 8' wide) with informal sprays of dove-gray foliage; upswept form yet nodding tips. The blue color of the young growth is as pale as any.

C. Lawsoniana f. pendula (Beissn.) Beissn.

WEEPING LAWSON CYPRESS. Various clones of more or less strongly drooping habit have been grown since the 1870s. The most strongly weeping, with great limp tresses of foliage, is 'Pendula Vera' raised <1890 by nurseryman H.A. Hesse of Weener on Ems, Germany. In nurseries the trees have long been rare, but old specimens abound in the maritime Pacific Northwest. There are greenish and bluish and weakly golden-green ones, all capable of reaching 80' or more and coning profusely. Weeping cultivars of *C. nootkatensis* look similar from a distance and sometimes even in close proximity. Records: 104' × 7'2" Puyallup, WA (1992); 102' × 8'1" Endsleigh, Devon, England (1963); 92' × 5'1" Olympia, WA (1988); 85' × 11'6" Montesano, WA (1988).

C. Lawsoniana 'Pottenii'

Raised in 1900 at Cranbrook in Kent, England, in the nursery of a Mr. Potten. Introduced in 1924 by Hillier nursery; to North American commerce ≤1944–45 by W.B. Clarke nursery of San José, CA. Very rare. Dense sage-green partly juvenile foliage on a markedly slender small tree, often multitrunked. Record: 45' × 3'2" Nymans, Sussex, England (1968).

C. Lawsoniana 'Pyramidalis'

Raised <1867 by P. Smith of Bergedorf, near Hamburg, Germany. Introduced to North American commerce ≤1923. Rare. A slender column like LOMBARDY POPLAR (*Populus nigra* 'Italica'). A vague name, likely to have been used for more than one clone.

C. Lawsoniana 'Silver Queen'

Of English origin, a variation of *C. Lawsoniana* 'Lutea'; named in 1883 by A. van Geert of Ghent, Belgium. In North America ≤1895; in nurseries here ≤1928–29; still available. Uncommon. Pyramidal, regular, rather broad; branches spreading. Young sprays creamy white to silvery-gray, aging to yellowish-gray or grayish-green. Records: 92' × 9'3" Fairburn Castle, Easter Ross-shire, Scotland (1987); 77' × 3'6" Kew, England (1974); 57' × 4'11" Batsford Park, Gloucestershire, England (1963).

C. Lawsoniana 'Silver Tip'

Introduced ≤1968 by Konijn nursery of Holland. In North America since ≤1972; in commerce here since at least 1980–81 when sold by Mitsch nursery of Aurora, OR.

C. Lawsoniana 'Smithii'—see C. Lawsoniana 'Darleyensis'

C. Lawsoniana 'Smith's New Silver'—see C. Laws. 'Darleyensis'

C. Lawsoniana 'Spek'

= *C. Lawsoniana* 'Glauca Spek'

Raised in nursery of Jan Spek of Boskoop, Holland; introduced in 1942. In North American commerce since ≤1992 (unless all trees sold here as 'Spek' are really 'Columnaris'). Narrow pyramidal; strong, to 35' tall; stout-branched; foliage firm and among the most gray-blue.

C. Lawsoniana 'Stardust'

Raised ca. 1960 by L.C. Langenberg nursery of Boskoop, Holland. Introduced in 1966. In North American commerce since ≤1982. Broadly columnar and yellowish. Comparatively cold hardy.

C. *Lawsoniana* 'Stewartii'

WINTERGOLDEN CYPRESS. SUNSHINE TREE. Raised ca. 1888–1900 by D. Stewart & Son of Ferndown, Bournemouth, Dorset, England. In North American commerce ≤1914 by L. Coates nursery of California. Common. Very hardy. Medium to large conical tree; golden yellow foliage changing to yellowish-green in winter. Shoots slender, droopng. With age it grows greener and droopier. Records: 80' × 7'5" Bremerton, WA (1993); 66' × 9'0" Renton, WA (1992).

C. *Lawsoniana* 'Triomf van Boskoop'

('Triomphe de Boskoop', 'Triumph of Boskoop') Raised ca. 1890 by D. Grootendorst, nurseryman of Boskoop, Holland. Sold in North America since ≤1916. Common. A broadly columnar, open-crowned bluish tree of great vigor and superb form. One of the cultivars in the f. *glauca* group. Records: 102' × 8'2" Olympia, WA (1987; now dead); 92' × 12'0" Caledon Castle, County Tyrone, Ireland (1983).

C. *Lawsoniana* 'Veitchii Glauca'—see C. *Laws.* 'Glauca Veitch'

C. *Lawsoniana* 'Versicolor'

Raised from seed ca. 1882 by C. Jongkind Coninck, Tottenham nursery of Dedemsvaart, Holland. In North America ≤1898; sold here ≤1930 by Malmo nursery of Seattle. Uncommon. Broad conical large shrub to small tree, usually slow-growing to 15'–30' tall, with spreading branches; sprays green, spotted with creamy white or bright yellow. Many leaves near the base of the lateral growths are creamy white, and those at the apical end sulphur yellow underneath and light green on the upper side. Bears few cones.

C. *Lawsoniana* 'Watereri' or 'Watereriana'— see C. *Lawsoniana* 'Argentea Waterer'

C. *Lawsoniana* 'Westermannii'

Raised ca. 1880 by J. Jurrissen & Son, Naarden, Holland. Exhibited for the first time in 1888 at Ghent, Belgium. Introduced to North American commerce ≤1914 by L. Coates nursery of Morganhill, CA. Common. Narrowly to broadly pyramidal, moderately dense, more or less pendulous; sprays golden- or light-yellow when young; tips light yellow then yellowish-green towards the base. Greenish in winter. After decades the tree becomes less colorful, with a weak hint of old gold in spring: the top side of the youngest growth on the tree's sunny side is variegated gold, with glands showing as green; the underside wholly greenish. Cones of average size or larger. Records: 95' × 9'4" Fairburn Castle, Easter Ross, Scotland (1987); 56' × 5'3" Seattle, WA (1993).

C. *Lawsoniana* 'Winston Churchill'

A seedling of C. *Lawsoniana* 'Lutea' raised at the J. Hogger nursery of East Grinstead, Sussex, England, and introduced ca. 1945. Sold since ≤1980 by Vermeulen nursery of New Jersey. A dense narrow yellowish pyramid, much like C. *Lawsoniana* 'Stewartii'. Named after Sir Winston Churchill (1874–1965). Record: 42½' × 3'2" Wakehurst Place, Sussex, England (1988).

C. *Lawsoniana* 'Wisselii'

= C. *Lawsoniana fragrans conica* Beissn.

Raised ca. 1885 by Buetner at the forestry station at Tharandt, Germany. In 1888 named after F. van der Wissel, nurseryman of Epe, Holland. Long common in North America. Short twisted sprays of very dark bluish twigs in congested tufts borne on a slender tree with a jagged silhouette. Its reddish male flowers are prominent in spring; it makes many cones. Very strange and distinctive. Records: 85' × 12'2" Bicton, Devon, England (1990; *pl.* 1916); 82' × 8'5" Port Coquitlam, B.C. (1992); 78' × 14'1" Avondale Forest Garden, County Wicklow, Ireland (1991; *pl.* 1908).

C. *Lawsoniana* 'Yellow Transparent'

Originated as a sport of C. *Lawsoniana* 'Fletcheri' in 1955 at the H. Van 'T Hof nursery of Boskoop, Holland. In North American commerce since ≤1970–71. Like 'Fletcheri' but of slower growth, and the young foliage is light yellow-gold, turning bronzy in winter. Probably a shrub for all practical purposes.

C. *Lawsoniana* 'Youngii'

Originated <1874 by the nursery of Maurice Young (1834–1890) of Milford, near Godalming, Surrey, England. Introduced to North American commerce ≤1923. Very rare. Pyramidal; branches stout, spreading; branchlets loosely arranged, more or less twisted; sprays rather long, fernlike; leaves thick, rich glossy dark green even in winter. It has been likened to C. *obtusa* 'Filicoides' in both habit and color. Records: 85' × 6'2" Busbridge Lakes, Surrey, England (1990); 69' × 10'3" Ardross Castle, Highland, Scotland (1989).

C. *nootkatensis* (D. Don) Spach

= *Cupressus nootkatensis* D. Don
= *Thujopsis borealis* Fisch. *ex* Carr.

ALASKA (YELLOW) CEDAR. STINKING CYPRESS. NOOTKA CYPRESS. YELLOW CYPRESS. SITKA CYPRESS. From S Alaska to NW California, mostly in higher elevations. The native American word *nootka*, recorded by Captain Cook in 1778, means "go around." This

species was discovered by A. Menzies in 1793 at Nootka Sound, Vancouver Island, B.C. Introduced into Europe ca. 1850 through the St. Petersburg Botanic Garden. In North America it is grown primarily within or near its native range. Its typical wild form is comparatively dull, so cultivars comprise the vast majority of its presence in cultivation. In the wild its lifespan can surpass 3,500 years; not uncommonly 1,000 years old. Botanically it has some features suggestive of *Cupressus*, for example its failure to graft onto other *Chamæcyparis* seedlings. It is very cold-hardy. Cones the largest in the genus, up to ½" wide, but sparingly borne. Its characteristic acrid odor is pervasive. Records: 189' × 16'5" Gifford Pinchot National Forest, WA (1988); 175' × 21'0" Olympic National Park, WA (≤1955); 124' × 37'7" Olympic National Park, WA (1994).

C. nootkatensis 'Albovariegata'—see C. nootkatensis 'Variegata'

C. nootkatensis 'Argenteovariegata'—see C. nootk. 'Variegata'

C. nootkatensis 'Aurea'

Name published in 1891 in Germany. In Latin, *aurea* means gold. Normal crown habit but very bright yellow foliage and of slower growth. In contrast, *C. nootkatensis* 'Lutea' is only moderately bright yellow, with distinctly pendulous branchlets. Few nurseries list 'Aurea', many list 'Lutea', and the two cultivars in circulation have been confused. Record: 60' × 12'7" Granite Falls, WA (1995).

C. nootkatensis 'Aureovariegata'

Originated <1872 as a sport by Young's nursery of Milford, Surrey, England. Extremely rare. Similar to *C. nootkatensis* 'Variegata' but variegated bright golden yellow instead of creamy white. Most pronounced in spring and summer.

C. nootkatensis 'Glauca'

Origin unknown. Described in 1858; perhaps from Germany. Common. Like typical *C. nootkatensis* but branches notably stout, thick, often heavy, nodding; foliage distinctly blue-green; many cones.

C. nootkatensis 'Glauca Pendula'
= *C. nootkatensis* 'Pendula Glauca'

Oregon nurseries have sold this since ≤1987. The cultivar name, being in Latin yet dating from after 1959, is illegitimate. The clone itself is not especially pale or weepy.

C. nootkatensis 'Green Arrow'

Discovered by the late Gordon Bentham in B.C. Introduced to the U.S. in 1992–93 by some Oregon nurseries. "Branches drip straight down." "A living green explanation point."

C. nootkatensis 'Jubilee'

Originated ca. 1978 at Bock nursery of Canada. Name published in 1983. Very rare. A narrowly upright sport of *C. nootkatensis* 'Pendula'.

C. nootkatensis 'Laura Aurora'

A yellow-variegated sport of 'Pendula'. Introduced in 1993 by Buchholz and Buchholz nursery of Gaston, OR. Named after Laura Buchholz, daughter of the nursery owners.

C. nootkatensis 'Lutea'

YELLOW ALASKA CEDAR. Named in 1896. In Latin, *lutea* means yellow. Young growth moderately suffused yellow, with distinctly pendulous branchlets. In contrast, *C. nootkatensis* 'Aurea' has normal growth habit but is very bright yellow and of slower growth than typical *C. nootkatensis*. In commerce, 'Lutea' has been commonly offered, but in all likelihood 'Aurea' has also gone under that name. 'Lutea' has been sold in part incorrectly as cultivar 'Castlewellan Gold' of × *Cupressocyparis Leylandii*. Record: 72' × 9'6" Castlewellan, County Down, Ireland (1983).

C. nootkatensis 'Pendula'

WEEPING ALASKA CEDAR. Raised <1884 by A. van Leeuwen, nurseryman at Naarden, Holland. In North American commerce since ≤1907. Common. At least two clones in cultivation. Especially slender, gaunt and strongly weeping. Record: 74' × 8'3" Tacoma, WA (1990).

C. nootkatensis 'Pendula Argenteovariegata'
= *C. nootkatensis* 'Pendula Variegata' *sensu* Krüssmann

Introduced ≤1960 by L. Konijn nursery of Reeuwijk, Holland. Very rare. Distinctly white variegated, weeping foliage.

C. nootkatensis 'Pendula Glauca'—see C. nootk. 'Glauca Pendula'

C. nootkatensis 'Pendula Variegata'—see C. nootkatensis 'Pendula Argenteovariegata'

C. nootkatensis 'Strict Weeping'

Introduced in 1995 by Iseli nursery of Boring, OR. Habit extremely narrow and pendulous; "a living flagpole."

C. nootkatensis 'Variegata'

= C. nootkatensis 'Albovariegata'
= C. nootkatensis 'Argenteovariegata'

Originated in Europe, described in 1873. White to creamy-white variegated. In North American nurseries since ≤1930, but rare. Conifer specialist H. Welch reports the variegation is not very stable. Records: 61' × 4'2" Walcot Hall, Lydbury, North Shropshire, England (1959); 57' × 3'7" Seattle, WA (1993); 51' × 6'6" Tacoma, WA (1993).

C. nootkatensis 'Viridis'

Originated in Europe, described in 1867. Narrowly columnar, tips slightly nodding; bright green. In Latin, *viridis* means green.

C. obtusa (S. & Z.) Endl.

= *Cupressus obtusa* (S. & Z.) K. Koch
= *Retinispora obtusa* S. & Z.
= *Retinospora obtusa* hort.

HINOKI CYPRESS. From Japan and Taiwan. The old-fashioned name *Retinospora* is from Greek *retine* (resin) and *spora* (seed), the seeds of some species having spots of resin. *Hi-no-ki* is the Japanese name, meaning fire tree. Introduced to the U.S. in March 1862 by G.R. Hall. Common. Growth slow; needs ample moisture to thrive. Foliage dark green, with conspicuous white lines underneath; odor very weak. Cones ca. ⅓". Tends to grow wider than its associate *C. pisifera* (SAWARA CYPRESS). Records: to 150' × 31'6" in the wild; 87' × 8'9" Bedgebury, Kent, England (1977); 80' × 15'6" New Plymouth, New Zealand (≤1982; *pl.* ca. 1850); 80' tall at Princeton, NJ (1982); 62' × 5'0" Annapolis, MD (ca. 1980); 54' × 5'5" Delaware County, PA (1980); 53' × 4'11" Seattle, WA (1987).

C. obtusa 'Aurea'

GOLD HINOKI CYPRESS. In 1860 introduced from Japan by R. Fortune to Standish nursery of England. Common. Young growth gold, then greening. Records: 62' × 6'10" Bicton, Devon, England (1987); 53' × 7'11" Inistioge, County Kilkenny, Ireland (1966). See *C. obtusa* 'Crippsii'.

C. obtusa 'Aurea Youngi'—see C. obtusa 'Youngii'

C. obtusa var. breviramea (Maxim.) Regel

Named in 1866. In Japan it grows wild and is commonly cultivated. In North American commerce since ≤1903. Rarely offered for sale under this name; several cultivars may belong to this variety. Short branches on a tall narrow tree; foliage dense. Foliage sprays without white streaks below. Cones smaller than those of typical *C. obtusa*. The name *breviramea* from Latin *brevis*, short, and *ramulus*, a twig.

C. obtusa 'Columnaris'—see C. obtusa 'Green Diamond'

C. obtusa 'Confucius'

A sport of 'Nana Aurea' but more vigorous and of faster growth. Introduced ≤1986 by Duncan & Davies nursery of New Zealand. In North America since at least 1986. Young growth bright lemon-yellow; old growth dark yellow-gold and dark green.

C. obtusa 'Coralliformis'

= *C. obtusa* 'Tsatsumi'
= *C. obtusa* 'Torulosa'

TWISTED CYPRESS. Originated in Japan probably. In Western cultivation since ≤1903. Rare. Irregular gently twisted cordlike sprays suggesting coral; occasional small fasciated tips. Rich bright green, with a wet look. Usually a dense bush no more than 12' tall; a small tree eventually in ideal conditions. A larger, related cultivar is *C. obtusa* 'Lycopodioides'. Possibly 'Torulosa' (known in U.S. commerce since ≤1948) is not identical to 'Coralliformis'; the differences however are minor: 'Torulosa' has little cock's-comb fasciations more frequently.

C. obtusa 'Crippsii'

CRIPPS' GOLD HINOKI CYPRESS. Raised <1899 by Thomas Cripps & Sons nursery of Tunbridge Wells, Kent, England. In North American nurseries since ≤1914. Common. A broad tree with loosely spreading branches bearing dense fronds of golden foliage (bright light green in shade). Brighter and more desirable than *C. obtusa* 'Aurea', but less cold-hardy. Records: 66' × 4'3" Bagshot Park, Surrey, England (1982); 65½' × 5'4" Keir Castle, Tayside, Scotland (1985); 62' × 5'3" Tilgate, Sussex, England (1974); 51' × 6'3" Kilmacurragh, County Wicklow, Ireland (1966).

C. obtusa 'Erecta'

Raised ca. 1870 by Waterer nursery of Surrey, England. In North American commerce ≤1921. Rare. Many ascending slender branches forming a regular oval or narrowly conical tree of deep glossy green.

C. obtusa 'Fernspray Gold'

Probably a renaming of A.H. Kent's 1900 'Flicoides Aurea' or only a slightly different clone. Wrongly sold in New Zealand as 'Tetragona Aurea' until ca. 1970 when Duncan & Davies nursery named it 'Fernspray Gold'. In North American commerce since ≤1986. A 10' shrub or small tree of irregular shape with arching sprays of golden fernlike foliage.

C. obtusa 'Filicoides'

= *Retinospora filicoides* hort.

FERNSPRAY HINOKI CYPRESS. Originated in Japan. Introduced to Western cultivation when Siebold sent it to Holland ca. 1860, and Veitch to England in 1861. Uncommon in North America. The name *filicoides* means fernlike; from Latin *filix*, fern, and Greek *-oides*, resemblance. Varies from a broad bush to a narrow tree. Always slow growing, and usually gaunt and freakish in either case. Extenuated branches with densely congested short side sprays. Individual twigs fernlike. Records: 47' × 4'9" Scorrier, Cornwall, England (1959; *pl.* 1861); 40' × 6'9" Endsleigh, Devon, England (1977); 23' tall at Aurora, OR (1993; as 'Compact Filicoides').

C. obtusa var. formosana (Hay.) Rehd. ex Bail.

= *C. taiwanensis* Matsum. & Suzuk.

From Taiwan. Introduced to Western cultivation in 1910 as seed to Bayfordbury, England, by Captain Matsumura of the Imperial Japanese Navy. In North American cultivation since ≤1958. Extremely rare. Reported to thrive in the heat and humidity of parts of Texas. Visiting Taiwan in 1918, E. Wilson said these trees were much more handsome than *C. formosensis*, with shapely oval bright green crowns. Recorded to 130' × 30'0" in the wild. Differs from typical *C. obtusa* in having sharper, smaller, more flattened foliage, and smaller cones (¼"–⅖" in diameter). Possibly needs more moisture, and is less tolerant of winter cold.

C. obtusa 'Gracilis'

Originated in Japan. Introduced to Western cultivation when Siebold sent it to Holland ca. 1862. Common; more abundant than any other cultivar. Often incorrectly sold as *C. obtusa* 'Nana Gracilis'. Foliage sprays pleasingly compact, the terminal portions gracefully nodding; crown dense and dark, not especially slender. Growth slower than typical. It can reach 25'–40' tall in great age.

C. obtusa 'Gracilis Aurea'

Raised by James Veitch & Son, Coombewood, Surrey, England; name published in 1875. In North American nurseries since ≤1903. Common. Smaller and looser than *C. obtusa* 'Gracilis' with young

growth golden at first, then green. Record: 23' tall after 34 years in Seattle, WA.

C. obtusa 'Gracilis Pyramidalis'

Sold in 1968–69 by Mitsch nursery of Aurora, OR. Not in subsequent catalogs.

C. obtusa 'Graciosa'—see C. obtusa 'Loenik'

C. obtusa 'Koster Sport'

Introduced ≤1992–93 by Stanley & Sons nursery of Boring, OR, who say it looks like *C. obtusa* 'Kosteri' but grows like a large HINOKI CYPRESS. Not a dwarf. Grows about 8"–12" a year.

C. obtusa 'Loenik'

= *C. obtusa* 'Graciosa'

Originated ca. 1935 in the nursery of L. Konijn & Co. of Reeuwijk, Holland. Commonly grown in North America since 1971–72. A sport of *C. obtusa* 'Nana Gracilis' differing in the more robust and loose habit; brighter green foliage. The cultivar name 'Graciosa' (1965) being Latin yet post-1959 is illegitimate.

C. obtusa 'Lutea Nova'

= *C. obtusa* 'Nova Lutea'

Origin unknown. Uncommon, but in commerce. Young growth bright yellow or yellow-green, fading in age to ghostly pale yellow or cream; no dark green foliage. Cones extraordinarily small. To 19' tall after 32 years in Seattle, WA.

C. obtusa 'Lycopodioides'

CLUBMOSS CYPRESS. Originated in Japan. Introduced to Western cultivation in 1861. Described in 1862. Common. The name *lycopodioides* from genus *Lycopodium*, CLUBMOSS, and Greek *-oides*, resemblance. Growth very slow; usually a mere shrub. Habit open, very informal. Foliage mossy blue-green, twigs thick, congested towards ends of branches, partly fasciated. A similar but less coarsely congested, smaller cultivar is 'Coralliformis'. Records: 66' × 4'6" Leonardslee, Sussex, England (1979); 55' × 8'9" Stonefield Castle, Argyll, Scotland (1986); 54' × 5'6" Tregothnan, Cornwall, England (1985).

C. obtusa 'Magnifica'

Originated in R. Smith's nursery of Worcester, England. Described in 1874. In North America, grown at least from 1920s into the '50s, seldom since. Evidently similar to 'Gracilis' and perhaps sometimes sold incorrectly under the name 'Nana Gracilis'. Pyramidal, robust, very broad, small tree; branches horizontal; sprays deep green, broadly fan-shaped; twigs conspicuously reddish-brown.

C. obtusa 'Nova Lutea'—see C. obtusa 'Lutea Nova'

C. obtusa 'Tetragona Aurea'

Originated in Japan. Introduced to Western cultivation in 1871 by Wm. Barron & Son's Elvaston nursery of Borrowash, near Derby, England. First sold commercially in 1876. Common. Bright golden densely twisted foliage. Angular, rugged appearance, sparse branches. Growth slow; rarely a tree. Record: 56' × 3'10" Tregrehan, Cornwall, England (1987). See also C. obtusa 'Fernspray Gold'.

C. obtusa 'Torulosa'—see C. obtusa 'Coralliformis'

C. obtusa 'Tsatsumi'—see C. obtusa 'Coralliformis'

C. obtusa 'Wells' Special'

Introduced in 1977–78 by Mitsch nursery of Aurora, OR. Likely originated by Wells nursery of Mt. Vernon, WA. Similar to 'Gracilis' (i.e., the 'Nana Gracilis' of most nurseries) but stronger growing, very attractive green.

C. obtusa 'Youngii'

= C. obtusa 'Aurea Youngii'

YOUNG'S GOLD HINOKI CYPRESS. Originated <1892 by Young's nursery of Milford, near Godalming, Surrey, England. Often grown in the U.S. from ≤1917 well into the 1930s; seldom listed in catalogs since. Branchlets somewhat drooping; less golden than 'Aurea'.

C. pisifera (S. & Z.) Endl.

= Cupressus pisifera (S. & Z.) K. Koch
= Retinispora pisifera S. & Z.
= Retinospora pisifera hort.

SAWARA CYPRESS. From Japan. Introduced to Western cultivation in 1859–61. The typical form, being unremarkable and often thin, especially in age, is less commonly sold than many of its cultivars. The name pisifera from Latin pisum, pea, and ferre, to bear—alluding to the small round cones. Sawara is its Japanese name. Its ¼" cones are smaller than those of C. Lawsoniana or C. obtusa, larger than those of C. thyoides. Records: to 164' × 21'0" in Japan; 95' × 9'0" Cowdray Park, Sussex, England (1984; pl. 1870); 78' × 9'9" West Hartford, CT (1988); 60' × 8'10" Bellingham, WA (1992).

C. pisifera 'Albovariegata'—see C. pisifera 'Argenteovariegata'

C. pisifera 'Argenteovariegata'

= C. pisifera 'Albovariegata'

Originated in Japan. Introduced in 1861 by R. Fortune from Japan to England. Very rare in North America. Foliage speckled silvery-white. Tree smaller than typical C. pisifera. Record: 37' × 2'0" Bearwood, Sindlesham, Berkshire, England (1970).

C. pisifera 'Aurea'

GOLD SAWARA CYPRESS. Introduced from Japan to Holland by Siebold between 1859 and 1861. Very common in nurseries until the 1980s. New growth yellow; lighter green in summer. Growth slower than typical C. pisifera. Records: 66' × 7'8" Seattle, WA (1992). Similar to C. pisifera 'Sulphurea'.

C. pisifera 'Boulevard'

= C. pisifera 'Cyanoviridis'
= C. pisifera 'Plumosa Boulevard'
= C. pisifera 'Squarrosa Boulevard'
= Retinospora 'K. & C.'

BOULEVARD MOSS CYPRESS. A sport of C. pisifera f. squarrosa introduced ca.1934 as Retinospora 'K. & C.'—referring to Kempenger & Christiansen nursery of Newport, RI. The name 'Boulevard' was published in the 1960 catalog of Boulevard nursery, also of Newport. Common. Compared to typical squarrosa it has extremely light blue, denser foliage, and stays more compact. Best in moist soil and partial shade. Record: 29' × 3'10" Tacoma, WA (1993).

C. pisifera 'Cyanoviridis'—see C. pisifera 'Boulevard'

C. pisifera 'Dwarf Blue'—see C. pisifera 'Squarrosa Intermedia'

C. pisifera f. filifera (Sén.) Voss

= Retinospora filifera hort.

THREADBRANCH SAWARA CYPRESS. STRING SAWARA CYPRESS. Introduced in 1861 from Japan to England by R. Fortune. The name filifera means having threads or filaments; from Latin filum, thread, and ferre, to bear. Foliage more or less extraordinarily elongated, slender, cordlike and drooping. Growth varies from shrubby to treelike. Records: 82' × 7'10" Minterne House, Dorset, England (1988); 63' × 9'1" Longview, WA (1993); 59' × 8'7" Puyallup, WA (1993); 50' × 8'10" Greenwich, CT (1987).

C. pisifera 'Filifera Aurea'

GOLD THREADBRANCH SAWARA CYPRESS. Originated <1889. Similar to green *filifera* forms but foliage yellowish and growth slower. Common. Records: 41' × 3'0" Puyallup, WA (1993); 40' × 3'10" Redleaf Woods, Kent, England (1963).

C. pisifera 'Gold Dust'—see C. pisifera 'Plumosa Aurea'

C. pisifera 'Gold Spangle'

A sport of *C. pisifera* 'Filifera Aurea' that originated ≤1900 in the nursery of Koster Bros, of Boskoop, Holland; name published in 1937. Introduced to North America in 1968 by the Arnold Arboretum. Rare in commerce here. Dense small narrow pyramidal tree. Foliage very bright golden yellow, partly threadlike.

C. pisifera 'Lemon Thread'

Introduced in 1985–86 by Mitsch nursery of Aurora, OR. A fast, broadly upright, lemon yellow filiform sport of *C. pisifera* 'Squarrosa Lutea'. Both regular and threadlike foliage.

C. pisifera f. leptoclada (Endl.) Rehd. 1949 (in part)

Known since <1847. A confused name that includes or consists of *C. pisifera* 'Squarrosa Intermedia' and *C. thyoides* 'Andelyensis'.

C. pisifera f. plumosa (Carr.) Beissn.

= *Retinospora plumosa* hort.

PLUME SAWARA CYPRESS. Originated in Japan. Introduced in 1861 by J.G. Veitch to England. Common. Foliage partially juvenile, and intermediate between typical *C. pisifera* and its f. *squarrosa*. More cold hardy than many other *Chamæcyparis* cultivars. Densest, largest and most vigorous of all the SAWARA forms. Records: 115' × 8'4" Montgomery County, PA (1980); 99' × 10'0" Seattle, WA (1993); 75' × 13'1" Olympia, WA (1993).

C. pisifera 'Plumosa Argentea'

Introduced in 1861 from Japan to England by R. Fortune. Uncommon. Growth of typical *plumosa* but at first with splashes of creamy or silvery white, changing into green at maturity. Records: 57' × 5'4" Monroe, WA (1995); 55' × 4'7" Fota, County Cork, Ireland (1966); 34' × 3'1" Puyallup, WA (1993). *C. pisifera* 'Plumosa Albopicta' is a dwarf.

C. pisifera 'Plumosa Aurea'

= *C. pisifera* 'Gold Dust'

Introduced in 1861 from Japan to England by R. Fortune. Common. Like typical *plumosa* but new growth bright yellow. Records: 87' × 5'1½" Bicton, Devon, England (1968); 75' × 6'6" Tacoma, WA (1992); 70' × 9'9" Golden Grove, Carmarthenshire, S Wales (1982); 67' × 10'1" Seattle, WA (1992). Dwarf cultivars with yellowish foliage are *C. pisifera* 'Plumosa Flavescens' and 'Plumosa Lutescens'.

C. pisifera 'Plumosa Aurescens'

Originated ≤1909. Sold in North America at least during the mid-1920s into the early 1930s. Out of commerce. Like typical *plumosa* but new growth light yellow in summer, bluish green in autumn.

C. pisifera 'Plumosa Boulevard'—see C. pisifera 'Boulevard'

C. pisifera 'Plumosa Flavescens'—see C. pisifera 'Plumosa Aurea'

C. pisifera 'Plumosa Lutescens'—see C. pisifera 'Plumosa Aurea'

C. pisifera 'Plumosa Pygmæa'—see C. pisi. 'Squarrosa Intermedia'

C. pisifera 'Plumosa Sulphurea'—see C. pisi. 'Squarrosa Sulphurea'

C. pisifera 'Plumosa Vera'

= *C. pisifera* 'Plumosa Viridis'

Like typical *plumosa* but extraordinarily deep green foliage. Gone from North American commerce, or nearly so, since the 1930s.

C. pisifera 'Plumosa Viridis'—see C. pisifera 'Plumosa Vera'

C. pisifera f. squarrosa (Zucc.) Beissn. & Hochst.

= *Retinospora squarrosa* hort.

MOSS SAWARA CYPRESS. BROWN-JUNK TREE. SILVER CYPRESS. Originated in Japan. Introduced to Western cultivation in 1843 when Siebold sent it to Ghent, Begium. Very common. The name *squarrosa* from Latin means rough, referring to the recurved scaly leaves spreading outwards. Foliage juvenile, suggesting that common on JUNIPERS, being prickly, bluish-gray fluffy masses of a soft, wooly appearance. The cast off dead twig masses are its unsightly "brown junk." Partial maturation into a fertile, cone-bearing state seldom occurs. Records: 90' × 8'6" Montgomery County, PA (1980); 85' × 7'9" Bodnant, Gwynedd, Wales (1981; *pl.* 1890); 71' × 6'0" Medina, WA (1992); 61' × 12'3" Ladner, B.C. (1994); 60' × 12'6" Greenwich, CT (1988); 49' × 12'9" Everett, WA (1992).

C. *pisifera* 'Squarrosa Boulevard'—see C. *pisifera* 'Boulevard'

C. *pisifera* 'Squarrosa Intermedia'
= C. *pisifera* 'Dwarf Blue'
= C. *pisifera* 'Plumosa Pygmæa'

Known since the mid-1800s as C. *pisifera* f. *leptoclada*. Murray Hornibrook named it 'Squarrosa Intermedia' in 1923. When young, in moist rich soil, and pinched annually, this is a lovely drippy bluish dwarf, a low rounded bush with small juvenile foliage of good grayish-blue color and interesting texture. But planted in dry ground, with full exposure, and left alone, it becomes a straggly tree that looks ravished or diseased: an ungainly mix of the congested bluish juvenile foliage and long whiplike shoots of some adult foliage.

C. *pisifera* 'Squarrosa Lutea'

Originated ca. 1930 as a sport in Koster nursery of Holland; name published in 1937. In North American commerce since ≤1972–73. Uncommon. Smaller than typical *squarrosa*, with yellowish-white foliage. (Not the dwarf golden-yellow 'Squarrosa Aurea' dating from <1866.)

C. *pisifera* 'Squarrosa Sulphurea'

SULPHUR MOSS CYPRESS. Originated <1894 in Koster nursery of Holland; name published in 1937. Common in nurseries until the 1940s. Distinctly sulphur yellow spring growth, changing in winter to normal color. Shade also brings on normal color. Smaller than typical *squarrosa*. The name C. *pisifera* 'Plumosa Sulphurea' has been used for this cultivar, as well as for a dwarf properly called C. *pisifera* 'Plumosa Flavescens'.

C. *pisifera* 'Squarrosa Veitchii'
= *Retinospora Veitchii* hort.

VEITCH MOSS CYPRESS. Usually dismissed as a mere synonym of typical *squarrosa*. As more than one *squarrosa* clone exists, there is reason to believe a distinctive one was originally sold by Veitch nursery of England. U.S. nurseries have long used this name, certainly for more than one clone.

C. *pisifera* 'Sulphurea'

SULPHUR SAWARA CYPRESS. Young growth bright sulphur colored. Similar to C. *pisifera* 'Aurea' and doubtless confused with it, not to mention C. *pisifera* 'Plumosa Sulphurea' and 'Squarrosa Sulphurea'. Long out of commerce.

C. *sphæroidea*—see C. *thyoides*

C. *taiwanensis*—see C. *obtusa* var. *formosana*

C. *thyoides* (L.) B.S.P.
= C. *sphæroidea* (Spreng.) Spach
= *Cupressus thyoides* L.

ATLANTIC WHITE CEDAR. SOUTHERN WHITE CEDAR. COAST WHITE CEDAR. WHITE CYPRESS. SWAMP CEDAR. From the Atlantic Coastal Plain of the eastern U.S., Maine to Mississippi. Seldom planted. Tolerant of very wet ground such as cedar swamps. Slow and often short-lived in cultivation; not highly regarded as an ornamental. Prized for its rot-resistant, lightweight wood. The name *thyoides* means *Thuja*-like; from Greek *thya*, and *-oides*, resemblance. Cones tiny, only 3/16" wide when dry (slightly larger when fresh and moist). Record (see also its var. *Henryæ*): 60' × 10'5" near Milford, DE (1943); logs extracted from cedar swamps have measured as much as 18'6" around.

C. *thyoides* 'Andelyensis'
= C. *thyoides* 'Leptoclada'
= *Retinospora leptoclada* hort.

Raised <1850 by M. Couchois, nurseryman of Les Andelys, Normandy, France. Uncommon. A dense, tightly columnar small tree; free coning. Foliage partly adult, partly juvenile. Less hardy. Greek *leptos*, thin, and *klados*, branch or twig. Record: 72' × 8'1" Akaroa, Canterbury, New Zealand (≤1982).

C. *thyoides* 'Blue Sport'

Introduced ≤1991. Stanley & Sons nursery of Boring, OR, says "Soft blue foliage; fast growth 6"–12" per year." Buchholz and Buchholz nursery of Gaston, OR, says "A vigorous small tree nearly identical to 'Glauca Pendula'."

C. *thyoides* 'Ericoides'
= *Retinospora ericoides* hort. (in part)

Originated in 1840 in the nursery of Bergéot at Le Mans, France. Imported from Europe ca. 1857 by Fruitland nursery of Augusta, GA. Uncommon. The name *ericoides* means heathlike, from genus *Erica*, HEATH, and Greek *-oides*, resemblance. Foliage delicately soft, juvenile, gray-green in summer, plum purplish-brown in winter. Dwarf, requiring many decades to surpass 30' in height, and never reported more than 40' tall. Comparatively cold tender.

Chamæcyparis thyoides 'Foliis Variegatis'— see *C. thyoides* 'Variegata'

C. thyoides 'Glauca'
= *C. thyoides* 'Kewensis'

Described in 1847 in Europe. In Canada ≤1897; imported to U.S. in 1925 by the Arnold Arboretum. Rare. Foliage very silvery-glaucous, twigs reddish. Slow, even shrubby. Record: 20' × 1'5" Edinburgh, Scotland (1970).

C. thyoides 'Glauca Pendula'

Introduced in 1989–90 by Mitsch nursery of Aurora, OR. Fast growing small blue tree with pendulous branches; adult foliage. The cultivar name translates "blue weeping" and is illegitimate, being Latin yet post-1959. Nearly identical to *C. thyoides* 'Blue Sport'.

C. thyoides var. *Henryæ* (Li) Little
= *C. thyoides* ssp. *Henryæ* (Li) E. Murr.
= *C. Henryæ* Li

From N Florida to Mississippi. Named in 1962 after Mrs. J. Norman Henry (Mary G. Henry), of Gladwyne, PA, who had studied it since ca. 1939, and cultivated it since 1955. Perhaps grown to a limited extent by collectors, but not in general horticultural commerce. Differs from typical *C. thyoides* in having smoother bark, less flat branchlets; lighter green color; larger cones. Records: to 120' tall in the wild; 87' × 15'6" near Brewton, AL (1961).

C. thyoides 'Hopkinton'

Introduced ≤1990 by Weston nursery of Hopkinton, MA. The original, noticed in the 1950s, is now about 40' tall. Blue-gray foliage and narrow, fast-growing, open-branched habit.

C. thyoides 'Kewensis'—see *C. thyoides* 'Glauca'

C. thyoides 'Leptoclada'—see *C. thyoides* 'Andelyensis'

C. thyoides 'Variegata'
= *C. thyoides* 'Foliis Variegatis'

Introduced in 1820s by Dunganstown nursery of Ireland; not officially named until 1855. In North American commerce ≤1888. Very rare, yet still sold. Green and yellow or golden variegated. Growth

slower and more compact than typical *C. thyoides*. Record: 39' × 3'7" Milton, WA (1993).

Chamærops

[PALMÆ or ARECACEÆ; Palm Family] A genus consisting of a single, highly variable species. Name from Greek *chamai*, on the ground, hence low growing or dwarf, and *rhops*, a bush—after the comparatively shrubby habit. Other PALM genera in this volume are *Butia*, *Ceroxylon*, *Nannorrhops*, *Sabal*, *Trachycarpus*, and *Washingtonia*.

C. excelsa—see *Trachycarpus Fortunei*

C. Fortunei—see *Trachycarpus Fortunei*

C. humilis L.
= *Trachycarpus humilis* hort.

DWARF FAN PALM. MEDITERRANEAN FAN FALM. EUROPEAN FAN PALM. HAIR PALM. From the Mediterranean region; the only PALM native to Europe; the most northerly occurring PALM species. Cultivated in Italy since the 1580s. Common in California and the South; rare in coastal Oregon, Washington and British Columbia. Among the most cold-hardy PALMS, but ill suited to high rainfall or heavy soils. Of slow growth; usually multitrunked, shrubby. With good conditions and decades, a slender small tree. Male and female flowers usually on separate specimens. Flowers yellow, in spring. Fruit ½"–1¾" long, ripe in fall, yellow or brown, often stinks (rich in butyric acid, like *Ginkgo* fruit); at length odorless and edible, like a small date. Fronds 1'–3' wide, roundish, of ca. 20–30 segments; stem to 52" long, usually edged with short spines. Trunks dark brown and rough; at length gray and smooth near the very base. Records: 40' tall in Spain (ca. 1836); 30' tall at Padua, Italy (1895; *pl.* 1581); 18' × 1'7" Riverside, CA (1993).

C. Martiana—see *Trachycarpus Martianus*

C. Ritchiana—see *Nannorrhops Ritchiana*

Chionanthus

[OLEACEÆ; Olive Family] 2–4 spp. (or 100–120 by including the closely related genus *Linociera*—as favored by some botanists). Leaves opposite or subopposite. From Greek *chion*, snow, and *anthos*, a flower—referring to the light and graceful clusters of snow-white flowers. Don't confuse with the similarly-named shrub genus *Chimonanthus*, WINTERSWEET.

C. retusus Lindl. & Paxt.

CHINESE FRINGE TREE. From China, Korea, Japan, and a variety in Taiwan. Introduced to Western cultivation in 1845 by R. Fortune; in 1879 by C. Maries. In North American commerce since ≤1910; rare until ca. 1960s. The epithet *retusus* in Latin refers to blunt or rounded leaves, slightly notched at tips. Superb ornamental. Slow growing. Flowers in terminal clusters (lateral clusters in *C. virginicus*) appearing later in the year than those of *C. virginicus* (at least on the East Coast; in southern California it blooms beginning in late March). Leaves 1"–4" long, crisp, finely toothed at least when young, hairless except on the veins below; fall color (vivid yellow) may be later than that of *C. virginicus*. Records: to 80' tall in the wild; 45' × 7'0" × 30' Montgomery County, PA (1980).

C. retusus var. *serrulatus* (Hay.) Koidz.

From Taiwan. E. Wilson said all young *C. retusus* bear serrulate (finely toothed) leaves; by flowering age the margins are untoothed. H. Flint reports this variety has handsome exfoliating bark and branches lower than typical *C. retusus*. Although similar looking it differs chemically from typical *C. retusus*, and holds its leaves dry most of the winter, at least in Washington, D.C. Some nurseries may not bother with its varietal designation, and sell this tree as *C. retusus*.

C. virginicus L.

FRINGE TREE. WHITE FRINGE TREE. WHITE FRINGE. OLD MAN'S BEARD. SNOWFLOWER TREE. GRANDFATHER GRAYBEARD. GRAYBEARD TREE. POISON ASH. FLOWERING ASH. SHAVINGS. GRANCY GRAYBEARD. From the southern and eastern United States. Common in cultivation. Twigs stout, often an attractive dark

purple. Leaves thin, 3"–9½" long. Flowers dainty, white, in drooping clusters from May into July depending on year and latitude. Male and female flowers on separate trees. Male flowers more showy. Females make dark bluish indigo, thin-fleshed ¾" berries, of bitter cucumber flavor, attractively conspicuous against the yellow fall foliage. Usually a shrub. Can be grafted on *Fraxinus Ornus*. Records: 41' × 3'6" × 31' Telford Spring County Park, FL (1987); 32' × 4'5" × 35' Mt. Vernon, VA (1989).

C. virginicus 'Floyd'

Originated ca. 1945 as a chance seedling in the Sonnemann Experimental Garden of Vandalia, IL. Named ca. 1970 by J.C. McDaniel, after the late W. Floyd Sonnemann. Introduced ca. 1971–72. Very rare. Dense, upright growth. Male flowers only; no fruit set.

× Chitalpa

[BIGNONIACEÆ; Bignonia Family] A hybrid between the genera *Chilopsis* and *Catalpa*.

C. tashkentensis Elias & Wisura

= × *Catalopsis bignonearis* J. Sabuco
(*Chilopsis linearis* × *Catalpa bignonioides*)

CHITALPA. Hybridized in early 1960s at Tashkent, U.S.S.R. Introduced to North America in 1977 via the Cary Arboretum of New York; distributed generally in 1982. Commonly sold. Prized for remarkable tolerance of trying conditions, and for its attractive trumpet-shaped blooms all summer long. Best adapted in the Southwest. Leaf to 6⅝" × 1⅔", stem to ¾"; minutely downy both sides; faintly odorous when crushed; falling yellowish-green in late October. Can be kept as a shrub or trained into a tree. Growth rapid. Record: 30' × 3'4" × 32½' Los Angeles, CA (1993; *pl.* 1979).

C. tashkentensis 'Clone No. 1'—see *C. tashkent.* 'Pink Dawn'

C. tashkentensis 'Clone No. 2'—see *C. tashkent.* 'Morning Cloud'

Chitalpa tashkentensis 'Morning Cloud'
= *C. tashkentensis* 'Clone No. 2'
Flowers pale pink to white.

C. tashkentensis 'Pink Dawn'
= *C. tashkentensis* 'Clone No. 1'
Flowers deep pink, smaller. More commonly sold.

Chrysolarix amabilis—see *Pseudolarix amabilis*

Chrysolepis

[FAGACEÆ; Beech Family] 1 or 2 spp. of broadleaf evergreen trees or shrubs. From Greek *chryso-*, golden, and *lepis*, a scale. The leaf underside is golden with fine scales. Nuts small, flavorful, borne in spiny husks like those of *Castanea* (CHESTNUT). This genus was defined in 1948; some botanists regard it as not generically distinct from *Castanopsis* (genus *Castanea* and Greek *-opsis*, resemblance).

C. chrysophylla (Dougl. *ex* Hook.) Hjelm.
= *Castanopsis chrysophylla* (Dougl. *ex* Hook.) A. DC.
= *Castanea chrysophylla* Dougl. *ex* Hook.

GIANT CHINQUAPIN or CHINKAPIN. GOLDEN CHINQUA-PIN. GOLDEN CHESTNUT. From Washington into California. Introduced to cultivation in 1840s. Seldom cultivated in North America; grown sparingly by Pacific Coast nurseries that offer native trees. Leaf 2"–6" long, dark green above, the underside warm, bright sulphur-golden. Flowers in fluffy whitish spikes in June or July; heavy-smelling. In horticulture, a dense, dark, slow growing tree with high mortality as a young plant. Adapted to dry summers. Usually performs best in shade. Records: 150' × 31'6" reported by G. Sudworth (≤1908); 127' × 15'3" near Anapolis, CA (1947; now dead); 115' × 11'3" Lane County, OR (1986).

Cinnamomum

[LAURACEÆ; Laurel Family] 250 spp. of broadleaf evergreen trees and shrubs, mostly subtropical or tropical. Leaves often with three main veins. The ancient name of the CINNAMON TREE (*C. zeylandicum*), coming into Latin from Hebrew (*qinnamon*), and Phœnician, Greek (*kinnamomon*). Grown for the beautiful foliage; the flowers are inconspicuous. Related genera include *Apollonias*, *Laurus*, *Lindera*, *Neolitsea*, *Persea*, *Sassafras*, and *Umbellularia*.

C. Camphora (L.) J.S. Presl
= *Laurus camphora* L.
= *Camphora Camphora* (L.) Karst.

CAMPHOR TREE. CAMPHOR LAUREL. From China, Korea, Japan, the Ryukyus, Taiwan, and Viet Nam. Introduced to Western cultivation ≤1690 at Holland. The term "camphor" derives from the Arabic name for camphor, *kafur*. An immense tree, much valued and widely cultivated for camphor, wood, and ornament. Not cold-hardy; included in this book merely for reference to the following less lovely but frost-tolerant species.

C. chekiangense Nakai
(*chekiangensis*)
From Chekiang, China. Discovered in 1929. Named in 1939. Exceedingly rare and little known in cultivation. Camellia Forest nursery of Chapel Hill, NC, says hardy to 5°F. Leaves to 5⅜" × 1⅝".

C. glanduliferum (Wall.) Meissn.
NEPAL CAMPHOR TREE. From Nepal, E Tibet, Bhutan, China, Burma and Malay. Introduced to California ca. 1900. Very rare. Saratoga Horticultural Foundation distributed stock in 1967 to encourage its cultivation. Leaf to 6" × 3⅛"; aromatic when crushed (less so than that of *C. Camphora*; more so than that of *C. japonica*). Fruit a purple-black berry ⅓" wide. Records: to 80' tall in China; 56' × 6'9" × 56' Los Angeles, CA (1993; *pl.* 1952); 36' × 5'7" × 41' Davis, CA (1994).

C. japonicum Sieb. *ex* Nakai

= C. pedunculatum Nees

From coastal E China, Korea, Japan, the Ryukyus, and Taiwan. Named in 1836. Introduced to California ≤1900. Very rare. Leaf markedly dark, not especially glossy or fragrant, usually ca. 3½" long, to 5½" × 2⅞", stem to ⅞". Growth slow and densely shrubby; often multitrunked. Records: to 65½' × 4'1" in the wild; 34½' × 3'0" × 21½' Santa Barbara, CA (1993); 32½' tall and 39' wide (multitrunked) at Los Angeles, CA (1993).

C. pedunculatum—see C. japonicum

Citrus trifoliata—see Poncirus trifoliata

Cladrastis

[LEGUMINOSÆ; Pea Family] 4–6 spp. of deciduous trees, with alternate, compound leaves and small white flowers in large showy clusters during early summer. From Greek *klados*, a branch, and *thraustos*, brittle, referring to fragile shoots. Bark smooth, gray. Leafbuds hidden during summer by swollen base of leaf stems. Although in the Pea Family, *Cladrastis* cannot symbiotically fix nitrogen. Grown for shade and flowers; the deep yellow fall color is also handsome. The most closely related genus is *Maackia*.

C. amurensis—see Maackia amurensis

C. kentukea (Dum.-Cours.) E. Rudd

= C. lutea (Michx. fil.) K. Koch
= C. tinctoria Raf.
= Virgilia lutea Michx. fil.

YELLOWWOOD. YELLOW ASH. YELLOW LOCUST. From the southeastern U.S.; endangered in the wild. Common in cultivation. Called C. lutea until the unhappy resurrection in 1971 of a slightly older (1811, not 1813) name: *kentukea*. In Latin *luteus* means yellow. Heartwood deep yellow, soft, fine-grained, used for dyeing. Leaflets 7–11. Flowers white, fragrant, in April and May,

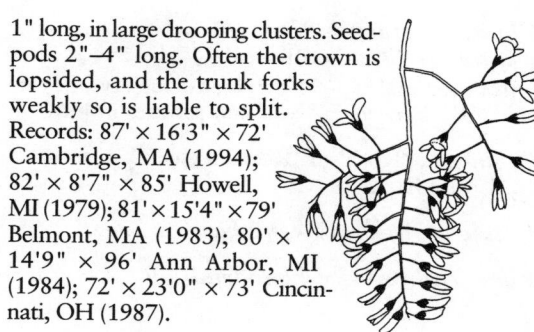

1" long, in large drooping clusters. Seedpods 2"–4" long. Often the crown is lopsided, and the trunk forks weakly so is liable to split. Records: 87' × 16'3" × 72' Cambridge, MA (1994); 82' × 8'7" × 85' Howell, MI (1979); 81' × 15'4" × 79' Belmont, MA (1983); 80' × 14'9" × 96' Ann Arbor, MI (1984); 72' × 23'0" × 73' Cincinnati, OH (1987).

C. kentukea 'Rosea'

PINK FLOWERED YELLOWWOOD. Originated at Perkins Institute for the Blind of Watertown, MA. Cultivated ≤1938 at the Arnold Arboretum. Extremely rare. Offered by Brimfield nursery of Connecticut ≤1960s, and ≤1993 by Arborvillage nursery of Holt, MO.

C. kentukea 'Sweet Shade' PP 2935 (1969)

Patented by Wm. Flemer of Princeton nursery of NJ. Very rare. Leaves and flowers especially large. Resists leafhopper insects.

C. lutea—see C. kentukea

C. platycarpa (Maxim.) Mak.

JAPANESE YELLOWWOOD. From Japan. Japanese: *Fujiki*. Introduced to Western cultivation in 1887 by H.H. Berger nursery of San Francisco, CA. The epithet *platycarpa* from Greek *platys*, wide or broad, and *karpos*, fruit, referring to the seedpod, 2" long and winged all the way around. Flowers ½" long, in airy, upright clusters to 10" long, in late June or early July (after C. kentukea blooms). Leaflets 7–15. Foliage less bold than that of C. kentukea; more bold than that of C. sinensis, and hairier than either. Records: 79' × 8'2" Japan (1994); 72' × 9'10" Kew, England (1989); 49' × 3'8" Seattle, WA (1994; *pl.* 1940).

C. sinensis Hemsl.

CHINESE YELLOW WOOD. From W China. Introduced to cultivation in 1901 by E. Wilson. Extremely rare. Few if any older than ca. 50 years known in North America. In commerce to a minor degree. Leaflets 9–17. Flowers white or blush pink, in upright clusters to 16" long. Seedpod 1½"–3" long. Remarkable for being about the last tree to flush into foliage—in Seattle during late May or the first week of June. Foliar texture and leaf size comparable to that of *Sophora japonica*. Growth slow. Habit often broad and low. Records: to 82' × 13'0" in the wild; 31' × 2'9" Seattle, WA (1994; *pl.* 1945).

Cladrastis sinensis 'China Rose'

= *C. sinensis* 'Rosa' or 'Rosea'

Introduced in 1993–94 by Handy nursery of Portland, OR. Flowers in "soft pink panicles in July."

C. sinensis 'Rosa' or 'Rosea'—see *C. sinensis* 'China Rose'

C. tinctoria—see *C. kentukea*

Clerodendron—see *Clerodendrum*

Clerodendrum

(*Clerodendron*)

[VERBENACEÆ; Verbena Family] 400–450 spp. of trees, shrubs and vines, evergreen or deciduous, mostly tropical. From Greek *kleros* (chance, lot, fortune, fate or allotment), and *dendron* (a tree) in reference to two species in Ceylon called by early botanists *arbor fortunata* and *arbor infortunata*. The following species needs training to be a small tree, and is grown for its fragrant white flowers and showy fruit.

C. trichotomum Th.

= *Volkameria japonica* hort., non Th.

HARLEQUIN GLORY BOWER. FATE TREE. PEANUT BUTTER TREE. From much of eastern Asia. Introduced to cultivation in 1843 when Siebold sent it to Holland. Introduced to North America in 1903 by J.G. Jack. Common as a large shrub; rare in tree form and size. Leaf soft and hairy, 4"–9" long. It leafs out late and opens its white flowers from July into September. Although the flowers are fragrant, the bruised leaves stink of peanut butter. Odor alone easily identifies this little tree. Turquoise berries against bright red backgrounds follow the flowers. It can be damaged by severe winter cold, but lack of summer heat also will keep it shrubby and suckering from its roots. In Portland, OR, many small trees are found. When it is a tree (to ca. 26' × 3'0") it is often low-forking and broad. Greek *tricha*, in 3's, and *tomos*, from *temnein*, to cut—referring to the division by 3's in the flower clusters, or because its branchlets are ternately divided.

Cocos australis—see *Butia capitata*

Corchorus serratus—see *Zelkova serrata*

Cordyline

[AGAVACEÆ; Agave Family] 15–20 spp. of PALM-like shrubs or trees, for the most part not frost hardy. From Greek *kordyle*, a club, bump or swelling, referring to the large, fleshy roots of some species. The common name DRACENA from Drakaina, a female dragon, because when the original "dragon-tree" is wounded, its milky juice upon drying becomes a hard gum having the same properties as the resinous substance called "dragon's blood."

C. australis (Forst. fil.) Hook. fil.

= *Dracæna australis* Forst. fil.
= *Dracæna indivisa* hort., p.p.

DRACENA PALM. GIANT DRACENA. FOUNTAIN DRACENA. CABBAGE TREE. PALM LILY. GRASS PALM. From New Zealand. Maori: *Ti Kouka*. One of New Zealand's best-known native plants. Introduced to the West in 1823. Grown extensively in California and parts of the South; rarer further north on the Pacific Coast. Latin *austral*, southern. Called CABBAGE TREE because early settlers ate the young tender heads, cabbage style. Seedlings like a tuft of grass. Then it looks like a yucca. Old specimens with swollen, corky, gray trunks and well-forked crowns. Leaves sword-like, to 3 feet long × 2½" wide. Flowers creamy white, fragrant, good as cut flowers; appearing in May, June or July in large clusters. Fruit a bluish-white berry. Tolerates swampy or wet ground as well as drought conditions. Largest member of the Agave Family. Recorded to 65½' × 69'6" in the wild; usually ≤40' × 20'0".

C. australis 'Purpurea'

= *C. australis* 'Atropurpurea'

BRONZE DRACENA. Generally seed-raised and so rather variable. Leaves more or less bronzy or purple, especially near the base. Slower growing. Uncommon.

C. indivisia (Forst. fil.) Steud.

= *Dracæna indivisia* Forst. fil.

BLUE DRACENA. MOUNTAIN CABBAGE TREE. BROADLEAF

CABBAGE TREE. Maori: *Toi*. From New Zealand. Introduced to the West ca. 1850, but most plants sold as *C. indivisia* are really *C. australis*. Authentic *C. indivisia* was introduced to North America in 1928, is extremely rare, but is in commerce. Its stem rarely branches (hence the name *indivisia*); leaves enormous and tropical looking, to 6' long and 8" wide. Flowers less showy, in drooping clusters, creamy- or greenish-white to reddish- or purplish-brown. Berries blue or purple, succulent. Smaller, rarely more than 19' tall, but recorded to 41' × 22'1". Finicky as to cultivation. Apparently ill suited to heavy clay soil, hot or cold areas, and dry conditions. Likely to succeed best in moist, cool partly shaded locations on the Pacific Coast.

Cornus

[CORNACEÆ; Dogwood Family] 40–50 spp., of mostly shrubs, showing such diversity that some botanists split the genus into several separate genera. All produce berry-like fruits. Leaves almost invariably borne in opposite pairs and have distinctively curving veins. Flowers tiny, greenish to yellow, sometimes surrounded by large, showy white or pink petaloid floral bracts of great visual appeal. *Cornus* was the ancient Latin name of CORNELIAN CHERRY, *Cornus mas*. The English name DOGWOOD derives from Old English *dagge*, a dagger, skewer, or sharp pointed object. Some say the name came about because a mange cure for dogs was made from the bark of a shrubby species. Our native FLOWERING DOGWOODS (*C. florida* and *C. Nuttallii*) are plagued by anthracnose fungal disease, caused by at least one species of *Discula*. As a result, the resistant East Asian *Cornus Kousa* has skyrocketed in popularity in recent years and there are a plethora of new cultivars and hybrids. Such a flood of new trees overwhelms the ability of nurseries and testing arboreta to evaluate the different varieties properly. Surely there are a handful of cultivars well suited to each major region of the continent, yet it will be years before the confusion subsides and the best cultivars are proven and publicized. Such a surfeit of new cultivars within a short span of years may seem unprecedented in the history of ornamental tree cultivation, but some MAGNOLIA and CRABAPPLE breeders have also proceeded with unbridled enthusiasm.

C. alternifolia L. fil.
= *Swida alternifolia* (L. fil.) Small

PAGODA DOGWOOD. BLUE (FRUITED) DOGWOOD. GREEN OSIER. PIGEONBERRY. From central and eastern North America. Common in cultivation. The alternate generic name *Swida* (*Svida*) is a Czech common name for a *Cornus*. Only this species and *C. controversa* bear their leaves alternately; all other *Cornus* bear leaves in opposite pairs. Its branches being tier-like and strongly horizontal suggest the name PAGODA DOGWOOD. Leaf 2"–6" long, to 3¼" wide, with hairs underneath; 5–6 pairs of veins; stem to 5" long. Flowers creamy white, in clusters 1½"–2½" wide, in May and June. Fruit a dark bluish-black berry ¼"–⅓", on attractive red stems, ripe in August. Fall color usually reddish-purple; can be yellow or scarlet. A shrub or small tree; grows best in partial shade. Records: 48' × 5'0" × 45' Norfolk, VA (1985); 39' × 2'1" × 27' Birmingham, MI (1992); 30' × 5'8" × 50' Old Westbury, NY (1972).

C. alternifolia 'Argentea'
= *C. alternifolia* 'Variegata'

Put into commerce ca. 1900 by F.L. Temple & Beard nursery of Massachusetts. Rare. Growth quite shrubby; to 15' tall. Leaves small and variegated. *Argentea* means silver in Latin.

C. alternifolia 'Variegata'—see *C. alternifolia* 'Argentea'

C. Aurora®—see *C. florida* × *C. Kousa* Aurora®

C. capitata Wall. *ex* Roxb.
= *Benthamidia capitata* (Wall.) Hara
= *Dendrobenthamia capitata* (Wall.) Hutch.

EVERGREEN DOGWOOD. WHITE EVERGREEN DOGWOOD. HIMALAYA STRAWBERRY TREE. BENTHAM'S CORNEL. From the Himalayas to Indochina. Introduced from Nepal to England in 1825. In California by the 1870s, and in the nursery trade there ever since. It varies considerably in hardiness but cannot tolerate regions with prolonged freezes in winter. The epithet *capitata* means headed; from Latin *caput*, head, referring to the moundlike heads of flowers and fruits. Foliage evergreen, of a peculiar shade of dull, pale green above, gray-green beneath. Some of the oldest leaves turn tawny in November, and are reluctant to drop; some turn banana-peel yellow in late spring and drop easily. Leaf drooping, 2"–5¼" long, to 2" wide, coated with minute, closely appressed hairs that give it a rough texture when touched. Flowers with four (rarely six) rounded, dark creamy or yellowish bracts in June or early July. Sometimes the bracts fade to mauvy-pink. Fruit a compound headlike cluster of reddish berries, ¾"–1½" wide, edible; ripe in fall. Shrubby, or a soft-textured small tree, often of great breadth. Records: to 80' tall in the wild; 59' × 5'6" Mount Usher, County Wicklow, Ireland (1989). Besides the following two subspecies, see *Cornus hongkongensis* for a third very closely related tree.

C. capitata ssp. angustata (Chun) Q.Y. Xiang

= *C. capitata* var. *augustata* (Chun) Fang
= *C. Kousa* var. *augustata* Chun
= *C. Kousa* var. *angustifolia* hort.
= *Dendrobenthamia augustata* (Chun) Fang

EVERGREEN KOUSA DOGWOOD. From south-central China. Introduced to North America in 1980 by T.R. Dudley of the U.S. National Arboretum. In commerce. Leaf smaller (to 3¼" × 1⅓"), dark shiny green above, pale green and hairless; pointy, more or less evergreen but capable of purplish fall color. Floral bracts white. Fruit smaller, ca. ½" wide. More cold hardy than typical *C. capitata*, but certainly less so than *C. Kousa*.

C. capitata ssp. emeiensis (Fang & Hsieh) Q.Y. Xiang

Named after Mt. Omei of Szechwan province, China. In the British Columbia nursery trade by 1993, represented as a clone called *C. omeiensis* Summer Passion™ which has liver-colored new growth.

C. capitata Mountain Moon™

Sold since the early 1990s by Piroche Plants nursery of Pitt Meadows, B.C.

C. capitata × C. Kousa—see C. 'Porlock'

C. brachypoda—see C. controversa and C. macrophylla

C. Constellation®—see C. florida × C. Kousa Constellation®

C. controversa Hemsl.

= *Swida controversa* (Hemsl.) Sojak
= *C. brachypoda* K. Koch, Miq., non C.A. Mey.
= *C. macrophylla* Koehne, non Wall.

GIANT DOGWOOD. TABLE DOGWOOD. From the Himalayas, China, Korea, Japan, Taiwan, and Viet Nam. Introduced to cultivation <1880. In North American commerce since ≤1920s; uncommon. Of *Cornus*, only this and *C. alternifolia* bear their leaves alternately instead of in opposite pairs. Leaf 3"–6½" long, to 4¼" wide, with hairs underneath; 6–9 pairs of veins; stem to 5" long. Flowers in May or early June, small, numerous in flattish creamy-white clusters 3"–7" wide. Fruit a dark purplish-black ¼" berry. Fall color variable, but usually poor (pale green and weak yellow, at best purple-red). Overall this can be regarded as a treelike version of the usually shrubby native American *C. alternifolia*. Records: to 100' tall in Taiwan; 65½' × 8'2" in China; 56' × 5'4" Westonbirt, Gloucestershire, England (ca. 1980); 52½' × 7'1" Forde Abbey, Somerset, England (1988); 47' × 4'1" × 43' Vancouver, B.C. (1992); 43' × 5'6" × 50' Philadelphia, PA (1980).

C. controversa 'Variegata'

Originated in Europe, and introduced to commerce there ≤1890. In North American commerce ≤1892. Very rare despite a great demand, because difficult to propagate. Leaves smaller (ca. 1½" long), somewhat misshapen, and edged creamy-white. Tree smaller, seldom even 10' tall. An English nickname applied because of its tiered habit, is WEDDING CAKE TREE. Record: 35' tall × 45' wide at Killarney, Ireland (the year it died, 1980; *pl.* ca. 1924).

C. coreana Wanger.

KOREAN DOGWOOD. From Korea. Introduced to the Arnold Arboretum in 1917 by E. Wilson. Extremely rare in commerce. A rugged tree, tolerant of both heat and cold, with glossy foliage and striking, deep, rugged, dark bark (like PERSIMMON, *Diospyros virginiana*). Twigs reddish-brown or purple. Leaf dark and lustrous, 2"–6" long; 3–5 vein pairs. Flowers small, creamy-white, in terminal 2"–4" wide clusters during May, June or early July. Fruit small black berries with short, pale, fine hairs; flesh green and bitter. Fall color late, plum-purple. Closely related to *C. Walteri*. Records: to 60' tall in the wild; 38' × 6'4½" × 34' Davis, CA (1995).

C. florida L.
= *Benthamidia florida* (L.) Spach
= *Cynoxylon floridum* (L.) Raf.

EASTERN DOGWOOD. FLOWERING DOGWOOD. AMERICAN BOXWOOD. From the eastern U.S., S Ontario, NE Mexico. Common, well known and much loved. Early American settlers called it BOXWOOD on account of its very hard and heavy wood. Leaf 3"–6⅛" long, to 3½" wide. Flowers bloom from late March to late May depending on latitude and year, surrounded by 4 white notched bracts. Fall color pink to spectacular electric red. Fruit a scarlet berry ½" long. Bark sepia brown or dark gray on older trunks, checkered in a manner reminiscent of alligator hide. Twigs in winter silvery-gray and tipped by button-like floral buds. Since ordinary seedlings often are sparse-blooming or ill-adapted to certain regions, many superior cultivars have been selected, more than 70 of which are included in the present volume. Records: 55' × 4'7" × 56' St. Joseph County, MI (1976); 38' × 5'7" × 39' Allen Parish, LA (1982); 31' × 7'0" × 43' Highway 431 past I-65 N, TN (1987); 25' × 8'5" × 42' Worton, MD (1990).

C. florida 'Abundance'—see C. florida 'Cloud 9'

C. florida 'Alba Plena'—see C. florida f. pluribracteata

C. florida 'American Beauty (Red)'
Origin unknown. Introduced ≤1960–61. Still in commerce. Likely a renaming of *C. florida* 'Cherokee Chief'. Floral bracts red. Berries large. Superb fall color. Vigorous.

C. florida 'Apple Blossom'
Introduced ≤1962 by Hoyt's Sons nursery of New Canaan, CT, and Wayside nursery of Ohio. Seldom if ever sold since the mid-1980s. Selected from a 30-year-old tree on a Connecticut estate. Floral bracts about the color of APPLE blossoms, i.e., pale pink fading white. Habit pyramidal.

C. florida 'Ascending'
Introduced ≤1952 by Scanlon nursery of Ohio. Long commercially extinct under this name. Strong central leader, with branches at 30° angle.

C. florida 'Autumn Gold'
In the 1993–94 catalog of Handy nursery of Portland, OR.

C. florida 'Barton (White)'
Selected in 1956 by Marvin Barton of Birmingham, AL. Introduced in 1969–70 by Tennessee Valley nursery of Winchester, TN. Seldom if ever sold since the mid-1980s. Early-blooming; upright-grower; overlapping large white bracts.

C. florida 'Bay Beauty'—see C. florida Welch Bay Beauty™

C. florida 'Belmont Pink'
Found and named ca. 1930 by Henry Hicks' nursery of Westbury, NY. Long commercially extinct. Floral bracts blush pink.

C. florida 'Big Bouquet'
Introduced in 1972 by Vermeulen nursery of New Jersey. Still in commerce. Compact habit. An especially heavy and consistent display of large, pure white floral bracts.

C. florida 'Big Giant'
Introduced ≤1969–70 by Groves nursery of Winchester, TN. Rare if not extinct commercially. Large white floral bracts.

C. florida 'Bonnie'
Discovered in Union Parish, LA, on property of Bonnie Gaddis. Selected by Dr. T.E. Pope of Louisiana State University. First propagated and sold by Robert Young nursery of Forest Hill, LA. Sold since 1982–83 by Louisiana nursery of Opelousas, LA. Blossoms on wild trees average 4½" wide, but on 'Bonnie' are 6" wide; the red berries are also showy.

C. florida 'Cherokee Brave'
Introduced ≤1994 by Phytotektor nursery of Huntland, TN. Floral bracts deep red with white bases. New growth burgundy red turning rich dark green. Of great vigor.

C. florida 'Cherokee Chief' PP 1710 (1958)
= *C. florida* 'Super Red'

Discovered by Ike Hawkersmith of Winchester, TN. First sold 1956–57. Common in commerce and very popular. Floral bracts deep rose-red. Tree with central leader and uniform branching.

C. *florida* Cherokee Daybreak™ PP 6320 (1988)

= *C. florida* Daybreak™

Originated in 1981 by Commercial nursery of Decherd, TN. Common. Bright green leaves edged creamy-white. Floral bracts white.

C. *florida* 'Cherokee Maiden'—see *C. florida* 'Ozark Spring'

C. *florida* Cherokee Princess®

= *C. florida* 'White Princess'
= *C. florida* 'Sno(w) White'

Originated by C.W. Highdon of Kentucky. Introduced in 1959–60 by Ike Hawkersmith of Winchester, TN. Common. Heavy blooming, consistent each year. Floral bracts large, white. Brilliant red fall color. Marketed as SNO-WHITE DOGWOOD by some nurseries.

C. *florida* Cherokee Sunset™ PP 6305 (1988)

= *C. florida* Sunset™

Registered in 1979 by Hubert A. Nicholson (Commercial nursery of Decherd, TN). Introduced ≤1987. Common. Leaves variegated yellow and green. Floral bracts deep pink or red.

C. *florida* 'Cloud 9' PP 2112 (1961)

= *C. florida* 'Abundance'

Found in 1951 as a chance seedling by Henry Chase, Sr., of Chase nursery, northeast of Huntsville, AL. Common and highly rated. Blooms heavily even when young. Floral bracts very large. Very good red fall color. Wide tolerance of heat and cold.

C. *florida* 'D184–11'—see *C. florida* Wonderberry®

C. *florida* 'D376–15'—see *C. florida* Red Beauty®

C. *florida* Daybreak™—see *C. florida* Cherokee Daybreak™

C. *florida* 'De Kalb Red' PP 965 (1950)

First observed in 1946, and propagated in 1947. Named for De Kalb nursery of Norristown, PA. Long commercially extinct. Semidwarf. Floral bracts deep, rich, heavy, wine-red.

C. *florida* 'Fastigiata'

= *C. florida* 'Pyramidalis'

Originated at the Arnold Arboretum in 1910. Widely distributed since 1914. Seldom grown. Long extinct commercially, perhaps because the fastigiate habit, upon propagation and growth under other conditions and climates—scarcely warrants a glance: the branches splay out to form a nondescript crown.

C. *florida* 'First Lady' PP 2916 (1969)

Introduced in 1969–70 by Boyd nursery of McMinnville, TN. Common. Leaves variegated green and yellow, changing in fall to maroon and pink. White floral bracts. Fast growth. Similar to *C. florida* 'Rainbow'.

C. *florida* 'Flore Pleno'—see *C. florida* f. *pluribracteata*

C. *florida* 'Fragrant Cloud' PP 2819 (1968)

Introduced in 1969 by Chase nursery, northeast of Huntsville, AL. Rare, but in commerce. Flowers with honeysuckle or gardenia fragrance.

C. *flor.* 'Fructi Luteo' or 'Fructo Lutea'—see *C. flor.* f. *xanthocarpa*

C. *florida* 'Gigantea'

Found and named ca. 1932 by Paul Vossberg of Westbury Rose company of Westbury, NY. From the Phipps estate, nearby (on Long Island). Long commerically extinct. Huge bracts, either 6" long (unlikely) or making floral heads 6" wide, as in *C. florida* 'Bonnie' and 'Imperial White'.

C. *florida* 'Golden Nugget'

Introduced ≤1987. Sold chiefly by mail-order nurseries such as Forest Farm of Oregon, Girard of Ohio, and Greer of Oregon. Variegated green and gold foliage similar to, but more pronounced than *C. florida* 'Holman's Gold'. White floral bracts. Red berries.

C. *florida* 'Green Glow' PP 4444 (1979)

Introduced in 1973–74 by Handy nursery of Portland, OR. A mutation of *C. florida* 'Welchii' differing in having light green blotches surrounded by darker green margins, or partly altogether dark green. Brilliant red and pink fall color. Very rapid, compact, upright growth. Floriferous; bracts white.

C. *florida* 'Hess' Select Red'

Sold since ≤1991 by Vermeulen nursery of New Jersey. Tree vigorous. Floral bracts deep red.

C. *florida* 'Hillenmeyer (White)'

Introduced in 1959–60 by Tennessee Valley nursery of Winchester, TN. Commercially extinct. Described as an excellent grower, early bloomer. Of twelve C.

florida cultivars evaluated for growth in an Oregon study, it was slowest except for 'Salicifolia'.

C. *florida* 'Hohman's Golden'
= C. *florida* 'Holman's Golden'
= C. *florida* 'Kingsville Golden'

Introduced ≤1963. Common. Henry J. Hohman (1896–1974) founder of Kingsville nursery of Maryland, is the man behind the name. Nurseries often misspell his name Holman or Hollman. Leaves gold and green variegated, in fashion similar to that of C. *florida* 'First Lady' and 'Rainbow'. Red in fall.

C. *florida* 'Imperial White' PP 4242 (1978)
Rare. Huge bracts, making floral heads 6 inches wide, as in C. *florida* 'Bonnie' and 'Gigantea'.

C. *florida* Junior Miss™
= C. *florida* 'Welch's Junior Miss'

Discovered in 1957 wild in north Mobile County, AL, by C.H. Welch of Welch Bro's nursery of Wilmar, AL. Introduced in 1968. Uncommon. Blossoms red fading to pink, with a white center and small white tips. Holds its deep pink color well even in the South; heat-tolerant. Not as cold-hardy in the North as other red-bracted cultivars. Young foliage coppery-colored.

C. *florida* 'Kingsville'—see C. *florida* 'Welchii'

C. *florida* 'Kingsville Golden'—see C. *florida* 'Hohman's Golden'

C. *florida* 'Lindley's New Double Flowering Dogwood'—see C. *florida* f. *pluribracteata*

C. *florida* 'Magnifica'
Found and named ca. 1926, introduced ≤1950 by Westbury Rose company of Westbury, NY. From the Phipps estate, nearby (on Long Island). Long commerically extinct. Huge floral bracts ca. 4" long, rounded.

C. *florida* 'Mary Ellen'—see C. *florida* f. *pluribracteata*

C. *florida* 'Moon'
Introduced ≤1937 by Howell nursery of Knoxville, TN. Long commercially extinct. Floriferous; large floral bracts.

C. *florida* 'Multibracteata'—see C. *florida* f. *pluribracteata*

C. *florida* 'Mystery' PP 2622 (1966)
Introduced ≤1965 by Chocola nursery of Winchester, TN. Very rare. Compact. Foliage dark green. Drought-tolerant. Floral bracts white with red splotches.

C. *florida* 'New Hampshire'
Introduced ≤1958 by Hetherfells nursery of Andover, MA. Long commercially extinct. Original tree a hardy, flower-producing tree in Atkinson, NH. Its flowerbuds do not blast in cold New England winters as do those on trees grown from southern sources.

C. *florida* October Glory®
= C. *florida* 'PNI 1326'

Introduced ≤1988–89 by Princeton nursery of New Jersey. Floral bracts pink. Brilliant red fall color.

C. *florida* 'Ozark Spring'
= C. *florida* 'Cherokee Maiden'

Raised from seeds collected by the former Ozark nursery of Tahlequah, OK, in the Cookson Hills region of NE Oklahoma. Named (1989) and introduced by Kansas Sate University because of superior winter-hardiness. Floral bracts white. Fall color wine-red. Well-adapted to S Kansas.

C. *florida* 'Pendula'
WEEPING DOGWOOD. Found ≤1880 in Maryland by nurseryman Thomas Meehan. In the nursery trade by 1890 and still sold. Common. Upright central shoot; no mop. Perhaps more than one weeping clone has been circulated under this name.

C. *florida* 'Pink Flame' PP 4300 (1978)
Discovered and introduced by nurseryman Mel Wills of Fairview, OR. In commerce but uncommon. A branch sport of the common clone of C. *florida* f. *rubra*, but with paler pink floral bracts and smaller, wrinkled leaves which are green in the middle, edged creamy-white and pinkish, then in late summer partly yellowish. Fall color red and pink.

C. *florida* 'Pink Sachet' PP 3993 (1976)
Introduced ≤1977–78. Uncommon. Possibly arose as a chance radiation-induced mutation of C. *florida* 'Cherokee Chief' with similar red floral bracts, but fragrance of gardenia, honeysuckle and calycanthus combined.

C. *florida* 'Plena'—see C. *florida* f. *pluribracteata*

C. florida f. pluribracteata Rehd.
= C. florida 'Alba Plena'
= C. florida 'Flore Pleno'
= C. florida 'Lindley's New Double Flowering Dogwood'
= C. florida 'Mary Ellen'
= C. florida 'Multibracteata'
= C. florida 'Plena'
= C. florida 'Welch Bay Beauty'

DOUBLE FLOWERED DOGWOOD. On several occasions DOGWOODS have been discovered in which the floral bracts number more than the typical four. The group name *pluribracteata* embraces all such specimens. One or more clone has continuously been in commerce since ca. 1915. Some are bushy, others grow to typical-size trees. The first reported originated <1914 in Orange County, NC, and featured 6–8 large bracts and many aborted smaller ones. It was propagated by Mr. J. Van Lindley of Greensboro, NC. The most recent are **'Mary Ellen'**, introduced in 1969–70 by Tennessee Valley nursery of Winchester, TN, and **'Welch Bay Beauty'** (which see). They tend to commence blooming later than normal specimens, and stay in bloom longer, but often the flowers are sparse, and on the branch undersides, so are not very showy. No fruit.

C. florida 'PNI 1326'—see C. florida October Glory®

C. florida 'Poinsett'
Sold Since 1978 by Girard nursery of Geneva Ohio. Compact, vigorous growth. Long, pointed leaves turn red in fall. Golden yellow berries in center of leaves during autumn recall the effect of a Poinsettia plant.

C. florida 'Porlock'—see C. 'Porlock'

C. florida 'President Ford'
Discovered in 1968 at Verkade nursery of Wayne, NJ. Introduced in 1976–77. Variegated foliage. Whereas other variegated C. florida cultivars (e.g., 'First Lady', 'Hohman's Golden', 'Rainbow') are all mottled similarly, they turn red in fall before or soon after frost. But 'President Ford' holds its foliage until 3 or 4 killer frosts occur, and also grows exceptionally fast and bears large leaves.

C. florida 'Pringlei'
= C. Pringlei hort.

Introduced in Texas in the 1980s. A variant of C. florida ssp. Urbiniana. Named after Cyrus Guernsey Pringle (1838–1911), who collected Mexican plants

between 1885 and 1906. Pringle discovered this variety in the Sierra Madre mountains near Monterrey. At least as originally described, the leaves differ from those of typical ssp. *Urbiniana* in having snowy-white, densely hairy undersides.

C. florida 'Pringle's Blush'
Discovered ca. 1989. Introduced by Yucca-Do nursery of Waller, TX. Floral bracts with a hint of pink.

C. florida 'Pringle's White'
Discovered in September, 1989. Introduced by Yucca-Do nursery of Waller, TX. Flowers 3" wide. Leaves distinctly ribbed, blue-green above, silver-green and hairy beneath.

C. florida 'Prosser (Red)'
Found ca. 1940 on Prosser property near Knoxville, TN. Introduced by Howell nursery of Knoxville. Commonly sold in 1950s and early '60s; nearly or wholly out of commerce since ≤ the mid-1980s. Floral bracts dark red. Very slow to bloom; a poor grower.

C. florida 'Purple Glory' PP 4627 (1981)
= C. florida 'Purple Splendor'

Originated as a chance seedling first observed in 1966 at Boyd nursery of McMinnville, TN. Introduced in 1981–82 by Boyd nursery. Uncommon. Foliage deep maroon to red-purple suffused over a light green background; holds color well all summer. Floral bracts dark pink. Small: to 15' tall.

C. florida 'Purple Splendor'—see C. florida 'Purple Glory'

C. florida 'Pyramidalis'—see C. florida 'Fastigiata'

C. florida 'Rainbow' PP 2743 (1967)
Discovered in 1964 by Armond Marzilli of Canton, OH. Introduced in 1967–68 by Schmidt nursery of Boring, OR. Common. A variegated sport that arose from stump sprouts of a regular tree that had been broken by a wayward truck. Leaves bright yellow and green turning brilliant scarlet and blue-lavender in fall. Floral bracts white.

C. florida Red Beauty®
= C. florida 'D376–15'

A controlled cross from Elwin R. Orton, Jr., of Rutgers University, NJ. Introduced in 1992.

Semi-dwarf, very dense. Blooms when still young. Floral bracts red.

C. florida 'Red Cloud'

Introduced in 1974–75 by Green Hill nursery of Winchester, TN. Rare. Floral bracts pink. Leaves have crinkled margins.

C. florida 'Red Giant'

Introduced ≤1981. Rare. Floral bracts red with white tips.

C. florida 'Redleaf'

Introduced ≤1980–81 by Byers nursery of Huntsville, AL. Red leaves and floral bracts.

C. florida 'Rich Red'

Introduced in 1960 by Weston nursery of Hopkinton, MA. Very rare. Floral bracts red.

C. florida 'Robert's Pink'

A Louisiana tree selected by S. Stokes in the early 1900s. Propagated and distributed by Robert Young nursery of Forest Hill, LA. Sold since 1982 by Louisiana nursery of Opelousas, LA. Floral bracts pink. Tree vigorous and well adapted to the Deep South.

C. florida 'Rose Valley'

Introduced in 1945 by F & F nursery of Holmdel, NJ. Floral bracts light pink. Very rare. Long extinct commercially.

C. florida 'Royal Red'

Introduced ≤1961 by Broadview nursery of Winchester TN. Uncommon. Floral bracts deep red, large. Leaves blood-red at first. Fall color bright red. Berries large, red.

C. florida f. rubra (West.) Schelle

PINK DOGWOOD. RED DOGWOOD. The first pink-bracted DOGWOOD was discovered in Virginia <1688 by the Rev. John Banister (1650–1692). Pictured in Catesby's *Natural History* of 1731—but only commercially grown beginning in the 1880s. Very common; many cultivars.

C. florida 'Salicifolia'

WILLOWLEAF DOGWOOD. Apparently originated <1950 at the Morton Arboretum of Lisle, IL. In commerce since ≤1954 but very rare. Growth bushy, slow. Leaves narrow. Name from genus *Salix*, WILLOW, and Latin *folium*, a leaf.

C. florida 'September Dog'

Registered in 1984. Discovered as a sport on a wild tree by George W. Glover of Tullahoma, TN. Flowers in September.

C. florida 'Snow Princess'

Sold since ≤1991 by Girard nursery of Geneva, OH. Very vigorous; extremely hardy. Flowers abundant, bracts extremely large. Leaves large and glossy.

C. florida 'Sno(w) White'—see C. florida 'Cherokee Princess'

C. florida 'Spring Grove' PP 8500 (1993)

Originated ca. 1947 in Spring Grove cemetery of Cincinnati, OH. Registered in 1992, when 22' tall and 32' wide. Floral bracts extremely large. Frequently bears two or three terminal floral buds.

C. florida 'Spring Song'

Introduced ≤1962 by Hoyt's Sons nursery of New Canaan, CT, and Wayside nursery of Ohio. Seldom if ever sold since the late 1960s. Selected from a 30-year-old tree on a Connecticut estate. Floral bracts "gorgeous rose-red."

C. florida 'Springtime'

Selected in 1957 at Spring Grove cemetery of Cincinnati, OH. Introduced in 1960 by E.C. Kern of Wyoming, OH. Still in commerce, but rare. Flowers borne even when tree is young; to 5" wide. Of vigorous, broad growth.

C. florida 'Stark's Giant' PP 442 (1941)

Found by Hiram H. Owens of Barbourville, KY. Introduced by Stark Bro's nursery of Missouri. The first ornamental tree to receive a plant patent. Long extinct commercially. See also C. florida 'White Giant'.

C. florida 'Sterling Silver'

Origin not known. Sold ≤1994 by Twombly nursery of Monroe, CT. "Slow. Leaves variegated dark green and clean white."

C. florida 'Stokes Pink'

Selected by Dr. J.A. Foret of Louisiana. Introduced ≤1990 by Flowerworld nursery of Loxley, AL. Tree vigorous. Floral bracts clear pink. The most reliable PINK DOGWOOD for the Deep South. Fall color red and purple.

C. florida Sunset™—see C. florida Cherokee Sunset™

C. florida 'Super Red'—see *C. florida* 'Cherokee Chief'

C. florida 'Sweetwater Red'

Originated at Sweetwater, TN. First flowered in 1940. Selected in 1954, named and introduced in 1961 by Howell nursery of Knoxville, TN. Common. Reddish young foliage. Large, red-bracted flowers. Fall color handsome red-purple. Growth fast.

C. florida 'Tingle's White'
= *C. florida* 'Tingle's Special White'

Introduced in 1959–60 by Tingle nursery of Pittsville, MD. Seldom if ever sold since 1967. Flowers abundant. Bracts white, large. Presumably named after Mr. Leamon G. Tingle, who founded the nursery in 1906, and retired in 1969.

C. florida 'Tricolor'—see *C. florida* 'Welchii'

C. florida ssp. Urbiniana (Rose) Rickett
= *C. florida* var. *Urbiniana* (Rose) Wanger.
= *C. Urbiniana* Rose

MEXICAN FLOWERING DOGWOOD. From E Mexico (Nuevo León and Veracruz). Named in 1903 after Manuel Urbina y Altamirano (1843–1906), who collected specimens in 1891. Introduced to cultivation in 1948 by F.G. Meyer. Extremely rare in commerce. Larger than typical *C. florida*, with larger leaves (to 8½" × 3¾"), retained longer into fall. Flower bracts narrow, pointy, less showy but still very elegant, giving the trees an airy, light effect. The bracts stay united, and can be blushed with pink near their tips. Names used in Mexico include: *Sochilcorona, Corona de Montezuma* and *Corona de San Pedro*. Record: 61' × 2'1" × 20' Seattle (1989; *pl.* 1952). See *C. florida* 'Pringlei', 'Pringle's Blush' and 'Pringle's White'.

C. florida 'Variegata'

Introduced ≤1891, the year B.A. Elliott nursery of Pittsburgh, PA, offered it ("striped or blotched with white"). Extremely rare. Unlikely that only one clone has been sold under the name 'Variegata'. Louisiana nursery of Opelousas, LA, has sold a white and green variegated clone under this name.

C. florida 'Weaver'

WEAVER'S WHITE DOGWOOD. Introduced in 1941 by Glen St. Mary nursery of Florida. Still in commerce. "Stronger and larger foliage, and larger and more numerous blooms." Adapted to the Deep South.

C. florida Welch Bay Beauty™
= *C. florida* 'Bay Beauty'

Found wild in Baldwin County, AL, in 1972. Introduced in 1978–79 by Welch Bro's nursery of Wilmar, AL. Flowers composed of 7 sets of whorled white bracts; blossoms up to 4½"–5½" wide; lower bracts shed before those above. Trees bloom at an early age and blooms last longer. Tree tolerates heat and drought well. A cultivar of *C. florida* f. *pluribracteata*.

C. florida 'Welchii'
= *C. florida* 'Tricolor'

TRICOLOR DOGWOOD. Selected ca. 1920 by nurseryman Mark Welch. Introduced ≤1930 by Cole nursery of Painesville, OH. Common. Leaves variegated green, creamy white and pink. Fall color rosy-purple. Often best in partial shade. Growth comparatively slow and shrubby. The late horticulturist D. Wyman wrote that the '**Kingsville**' strain is "superior." (Presumably this name refers to H. Hohman's nursery at Kingsville, Maryland.)

C. florida 'Welch's Junior Miss'—see *C. florida* Junior Miss™

C. florida 'White Cloud'

Sold by Wayside nursery of Mentor, OH, from 1946 to 1968. Still sold by nurseries. Unusually numerous flowers, even when the tree is young. Floral bracts creamy white. Foliage bronze colored.

C. florida 'White Giant'

Introduced ≤1962–63 by Broadview nursery of Winchester, TN (described by them as "One of the best and largest blooming"). Extremely rare; long extinct commercially. Possibly *C. florida* 'Stark's Giant' renamed.

C. florida 'White Princess'—see *C. florida* Cherokee Princess®

C. florida 'William's Red'

First propagated and sold by William's nursery of Forest Hill, LA. Sold in 1980s by Louisiana nursery of Opelousas, LA. Floral bracts deep rose-red.

C. florida Wonderberry®
= *C. florida* 'D184–11'

A controlled cross from Elwin R. Orton, Jr., of Rutgers University, NJ. Introduced in 1992.

Unusually vigorous. Floriferous. Leaves thick, leathery, glossy, dark. Fruit larger, nearly twice normal size.

C. florida 'World's Fair' PP 4869 (1982)

Introduced ≤1984 by Boyd nursery of McMinnville, TN. Tree hardy, drought-tolerant. Growth compact and upright. Flowers abundant even when young; floral bracts white.

C. florida f. xanthocarpa Rehd.

= C. florida var. xanthocarpa Rehd.
= C. florida 'Fructo Luteo'

YELLOW FRUITED DOGWOOD. A group name, applied in 1921 based on Saluda, NC, specimens. Other clones have originated elsewhere, such as one near Oyster Bay, NY. In commerce since ≤1931. Rare. Greek xanthos, yellow, and karpos, fruit.

C. florida × C. Kousa

= C. × rutgersensis hort.

The 6 following cultivars (the Stellar® series) were originated by Dr. Elwin R. Orton, Jr., of Rutgers University of New Jersey. Introduced in 1991–92.

C. florida × C. Kousa Aurora® PP 7205 (1990)

= C. 'Rutban'
= C. Aurora®

Erect, very vigorous; 18¾' × 18¼' in 19 years. Dense-flowered. Floral bracts white, large, overlapping. Sterile.

C. florida × C. Kousa Constellation® 7210 (1990)

= C. 'Rutcan'
= C. Constellation®

Erect, vigorous; uniformly wide from top to bottom. Estimated growth to 22' × 18'. Extremely floriferous. Airy appearance. Floral bracts don't overlap, are much longer than those of Stardust®.

C. florida × C. Kousa Galaxy® PP 7204 (1990)

= C. 'Rutdan'
= C. Galaxy®

Vigorous, upright habit. The original 17¾' × 14½' in 19 years. Floral bracts appear in a deep cup, then flatten into a wide rounded form, slightly overlapping. Sterile.

C. florida × C. Kousa Ruth Ellen® PP 7732 (1991)

= C. 'Rutlan'
= C. Ruth Ellen®

Low and spreading; broader than tall; 19' × 24'. First to bloom.

C. florida × C. Kousa Stardust® PP 7206 (1990)

= C. 'Rutfan'
= C. Stardust®

Grows 1½ times broader than tall; horizontal habit. 12' × 18' in 20 years. Floral bracts distinctly separate; not overlapping at all. Sterile.

C. florida × C. Kousa Stellar Pink® PP 7207 (1990)

= C. 'Rutgan'
= C. Stellar Pink®

Vigorous, erect; uniformly wide from top to bottom. Estimated growth to 23' × 18½'. Floral bracts rounded, overlapping, light pink and white.

C. florida × C. Nuttallii

HYBRID PACIFIC DOGWOOD. In addition to the following three cultivars, two of the same parentage grown in Europe are 'Ascona' and 'Ormonde'.

C. florida × C. Nuttallii 'Cream Cup'

Introduced ≤1991–92 by Handy nursery of Portland, OR.

C. florida × C. Nuttallii 'Eddie's White Wonder' PP 2413 (1964)

Originated in 1945 by nurseryman Henry M. Eddie (1881–1953) of Vancouver, B.C.; commercially propagated ca. 1955. Commonly sold since 1960s. Habit dense and drooping. Leaves large (to 8" × 6¼"), with superb fall color. Flowers sterile, small buttons surrounded by 4 to 6 large, rounded overlapping bracts, the whole blossom up to 4¾" wide. Flowers in late April in Seattle. Somewhat anthracnose-resistant. Record: 33' × 1'9" × 21' Lynnwood, WA (1993).

C. florida × C. Nuttallii 'Pink Blush'

Introduced ≤1991–92 by Handy nursery of Portland, OR. Growth fast and symmetrical. Flowers abundant, the bracts white with pink blush. Fall color bright red.

C. Galaxy®—see C. florida × C. Kousa Galaxy®

C. *hongkongensis* Hemsl.

= *Dendrobenthamia hongkongensis* (Hemsl.) Hutch.

HONGKONG DOGWOOD. From SE China and Viet Nam. Named in 1888. Extremely rare; in commerce since the late 1980s. Much confused with *C. capitata*, which is similar in tree form and leaf size. The main difference is technical: HONGKONG DOGWOOD has a truncate, entire calyx. Also its leaf is usually broader, thicker-textured, and slightly lustrous above; pale green rather than grayish or whitish beneath. In other words, for all practical purposes HONGKONG DOGWOOD looks like (and presumably behaves like) *C. capitata*.

C. *Kousa* (Buerg. *ex* Miq.) Hance

= *Benthamia japonica* S. & Z.
= *Benthamidia japonica* (S. & Z.) Hara
= *Dendrobenthamia japonica* (S. & Z.) Hutch.

KOUSA DOGWOOD. JAPANESE DOGWOOD. KOREAN DOGWOOD. From China, Korea, Japan, and the Ryukyus. Japanese: *Kousa*. Introduced from Japan to the U.S. by G.R. Hall in 1861–62. Very common. A superb ornamental, resistant to the anthracnose disease that disfigures the native *C. florida* and *C. Nuttallii*. Flowers appear after those of *C. florida*, the 4 bracts usually conspicuously pointy, often fading from white to pink with age. Rarely blooms a second time in late summer or fall. Leaves 1½"–4" (5¾") long, the margin often undulated. Fruit knobby, resembles a large dull raspberry (up to 1⅝" wide on stalks as long as 4") coloring lovely red from August into October, edible but nothing to celebrate. Bark flaky in patchy, attractive layers of warm beige, tan and gray. Fall color usually red and lovely. A large shrub or small tree. Poor growth in dry-summer regions unless well watered. An overwhelming flood of cultivars has appeared since 1980. Synonymy and relative merits will require years to resolve. *American Nurseryman* magazine, November 15, 1993, lists about 15 *C. Kousa* cultivars so obscure or rare that they are excluded from the present volume, which includes more than 60 cultivars. Records: 41' × 2'6" × 36' Chester County, PA (1980); 28' × 5'7" × 41' Seattle, WA (1987); 28' × 4'2" × 36' Greenwich, CT (1988).

C. *Kousa* 'Aget'

Large, long-lasting floral bracts remain to September.

C. *Kousa* 'Akabana'

Pink floral bracts. *Akabana* is Japanese for red flower, and is the name applied in Japan to all pink-flowered KOUSA DOGWOODS. The best bract color is in light shade and cooler climates. Other pink-bracted cultivars include 'Beni Fuj', 'Bush's Pink', 'Rubra' and 'Satomi'.

C. *Kousa* 'Amber'

Selected by Handy nursery of Portland, OR. Multicolored, irregular variegation on small leaves. A slow, open grower.

C. *Kousa* var. *augustata* or *angustifolia*—see C. *capitata* ssp. *angustata*

C. *Kousa* 'Autumn Rose'

Discovered by Glenda Schmoer. Introduced ≤1992 by Handy nursery of Portland, OR. Yellow to lime-green foliage in spring. Wavy leaves. Fall color pink to light red, hence the name 'Autumn Rose'. Fruit sparse.

C. *Kousa* 'Baier Lustgarten'—see C. *Kousa* 'Elizabeth Lustgarten' and 'Lustgarten Weeping'

C. *Kousa* 'Beni Fuj'

Introduced ≤1995 by Briggs and Greer nurseries of Oregon. Floral bracts deep pink. Leaf veins and stems red.

C. *Kousa* 'Big Apple'

Registered ca. 1982 by Polly (Mrs. Julian W.) Hill of Martha's Vineyard, MA. Heavy textured dark leaves. Floral bracts large. Fruit large (to 1⅓" wide). Hardy to -5°F. A large spreading tree.

C. *Kousa* 'Blue Shadow'

Registered by Polly (Mrs. Julian W.) Hill of Martha's Vineyard, MA. In commerce. Leaves very glossy, dark. Some white bracts remain at fruiting time. Excellent red fall color.

C. *Kousa* 'Bon Fire'

Introduced by Greer nursery of Oregon in 1993. Tricolored leaf (gold, light and dark green). Fall color multicolored: crimson, red and yellow.

C. Kousa 'Bush's Pink'

Chance seedling at Richard Bush's nursery of Canby, OR. Introduced by Greer nursery of Oregon in 1993. Floral bracts pink, holding their color well. Color resembles that of *C. florida* f. *rubra*.

C. Kousa 'Camden'

Found on an estate in central Maine by Mark Stavish of Eastern Plant Specialists, Georgetown, ME. Introduced ≤1991. Long flowering period (until fall). Flowers abundant, fruits abundant.

C. Kousa 'Cedarridge Scarlet'

Selected by M. Wingle of Cedar Ridge nursery, Quakertown, PA. White bracts turn red at the end of the bloom period.

C. Kousa 'China Girl'

Selected in Holland. In North American commerce ≤1990. Flowers abundant, even on young specimens. Floral bracts very large. Handsome fall color. Fruit large.

C. Kousa var. chinensis Osborn

= *C. Kousa* ssp. *chinensis* (Osborn) Q.Y. Xiang
= *C. Kousa* var. *sinensis* hort.

CHINESE KOUSA DOGWOOD. Introduced to North America in 1907, named in 1922. Sold under that name since at least 1927. Common. Experts disagree whether the name *chinensis*, based on cultivated material, is meaningful or not. Horticulturists generally deem KOUSA DOGWOODS from China more ornamental than their Japanese counterparts, but the differences (more vigorous, freer-flowering, with broader leaves) neither count for much to scientists, nor do they hold up without exception.

C. Kousa 'Doubloon'

('Dabloon')

Selected in 1970 by William Devine of Kennedyville, MD. In commerce. Tall slender tree; with extra cream-colored bracts at each flower cluster.

C. Kousa 'Dwarf Pink'

Japanese origin. Introduced to U.S. by B. Yinger of Hines nursery, Santa, Ana, CA, and Carl Hahn of Brookside Gardens of Maryland. Floral bracts narrow, light pink. Initial habit is upright. Fairly vigorous if grafted or budded; should be on own roots to maintain its dwarfness. Can grow to 8' tall and 6' wide.

C. Kousa 'Ed Mezitt'

= *C. Kousa* 'Terrace'

Selected in the early 1970s by Edmund V. Mezitt (1896–1980) of Weston nursery, Hopkinton, MA. Introduced in 1993. Floral bracts wide, overlapping. New shoots distinctly purplish in sun, the young leaves bronze colored. Mature foliage dark green in summer. Orange-red fall color.

C. Kousa 'Elizabeth Lustgarten'

= *C. Kousa* 'Baier Lustgarten' (in part)
= *C. Kousa* 'Lustgarten' (in part)
= *C. Kousa pendula* 'Elizabeth Lustgarten'

Selected by J.E. Cross of Cutchogue, NY, from a seedling at Baier Lustgarten nursery of Long Island, NY. Registered in 1977. Introduced ca. 1981. Tree upright but branches weep. At 10 years, 5½' tall × 4½' wide; at 12 years, 7' tall × 5' wide. Graceful, weeping, rounded crown. Likely a sister plant of *C. kousa* 'Lustgarten Weeping'.

C. Kousa 'Endurance'

Introduced by Weston nursery of Hopkinton, MA. Floral bracts long-lasting.

C. Kousa 'Fanfare'

Originated by Polly (Mary M.B.) Wakefield of Milton, MA. Probably named in the early 1970s. Fastigiate. Fast. Hardy to -20°F.

C. Kousa 'Gay Head'

Registered ≤1983 by P. Hill of Martha's Vineyard, MA. Floriferous; bracts vary in size, are variously curved and ruffled. Hardy to -5°F.

C. Kousa 'Gold Star'

Introduced ≤1977 by Sakata nursery of Yokohama City, Japan. Introduced to U.S. in 1978 by B. Yinger of Hines nursery, Santa Ana, CA, and Carl Hahn of Brookside Gardens of Maryland. In North American commerce by 1983. Typical except each leaf has an irregular blotch of deep butter-yellow in its center. Reversions to green shoots occur. Usually does not scorch in full sun, at least in the Northeast (in the Midwest it may do best in full shade).

C. Kousa 'Greensleeves'

Originated by Polly (Mary M.B.) Wakefield of Milton, MA. In commerce. Wavy dark leaves. Very prolific bloom. Grows fast.

C. *Kousa* 'Heart Throb'
In commerce by 1995. Floral bracts burgundy.

C. *Kousa* 'Highland'
Introduced in 1992 by Girard nursery of Geneva, OH. Precocious and very prolific bloomer. Bracts creamy-white.

C. *Kousa* 'Julian'
Originated by Polly (Mrs. Julian W.) Hill of Martha's Vineyard, MA. Named after her husband Julian W. Hill. Floral bracts curved up at tips. Fruit 1³/₁₆" wide. Excellent fall color.

C. *Kousa* 'July Jubilee'
Offered in 1991 by Mellinger's nursery of North Lima, OH.

C. *Kousa* 'Little Beauty'
From seeds collected in Korea, from wild trees. Distributed by J.C. Raulston of North Carolina in 1993. Shrubby.

C. *Kousa* 'Lustgarten'—see C. *Kousa* 'Elizabeth Lustgarten' and 'Lustgarten Weeping'

C. *Kousa* 'Lustgarten Weeping'
= C. *Kousa* 'Baier Lustgarten' (in part)
= C. *Kousa* 'Lustgarten' (in part)
Selected by J.E. Cross of Cutchogue, NY, from a seedling at Baier Lustgarten nursery of Long Island, NY. Registered in 1974. Introduced ca. 1981. So strongly weeping it is a prostrate mop unless top-grafted or staked. At 12 years, 3' tall × 10' wide.

C. *Kousa* 'Madame Butterfly'
Originated as a seedling in an Ohio nursery. Registered ca. 1982 by D.G. Leach of N Madison, OH. At time of registration the original was 20' tall, 14 years old. Rare in commerce. Extremely floriferous. Long pedicels. Floral bracts are narrow (1³/₁₆" wide) and ascend vertically about the midpoint of their length, looking like "swarms of butterflies." An imposter 'Madame Butterfly' clone with very large bracts was given to the U.S. National Arboretum by Peter Chappell of England.

C. *Kousa* 'Marble'
Introduced by Cedar Ridge nursery of Quakertown, PA. Variegated.

C. *Kousa* 'Milky Way'
Not a clone; 'Milky Way' is a group name applied to offspring of 15 C. *Kousa* var. *chinensis* seedlings sold in the 1960s by Wayside nursery of Mentor, OH. Also sold by other nurseries since then, sometimes vegetatively propagated. Very floriferous and prolific. Large bracts and fruits. Broad, bushy form. Flaking bark.

C. *Kousa* 'Moonbeam' PP 3296 (1973)
Originated by Polly (Mary M.B.) Wakefield of Milton, MA. In commerce. Vigorous; flowers 7–8" wide on long stalks. Leaves large. Hardy to -20°F.

C. *Kousa* 'Moonlight'
Originated by Polly (Mary M.B.) Wakefield of Milton, MA. Large floral bracts equal in size to those of 'Moonbeam' but not as floppy.

C. *Kousa* 'National'
Selected and introduced by Hoskins Shadow of Commercial nursery, Decherd, TN. Floriferous even as a young tree. Flowers large, with creamy-white, red-tipped bracts. Vigorous; open horizontal branching. Fruit large.

C. *Kousa* 'New Red'—see C. *Kousa* 'Satomi'

C. *Kousa pendula* 'Elizabeth Lustgarten' —see C. *Kousa* 'Elizabeth Lustgarten'

C. *Kousa* 'Pollywood'
Originated by Polly (Mrs. Julian W.) Hill of Martha's Vineyard, MA. Large, late-flowering tree. Long-lasting flowers.

C. *Kousa* 'Radiant Rose'
Origin unknown. In commerce. Large pink floral bracts. Spreading, arching habit. Red pigment in leaves, branches and fall color. May be the same as C. *Kousa* 'Satomi'

C. *Kousa* 'Repeat'
Introduced by Richard Bush's nursery of Canby, OR. Has a second or repeat bloom in late summer.

C. *Kousa* 'Repeat Bloomer'
Originated by J.G. Marano Jr., of Doylestown, PA. In commerce. Has a second or repeat bloom in late summer. Bracts large.

C. *Kousa* 'Rochester'
Introduced ≤1978 by Hoogendorn nursery of Newport, RI. Still in commerce. Large showy floral bracts. Vigorous.

C. Kousa 'Rosabella'—see *C. Kousa* 'Satomi'

C. Kousa 'Rosea'

Name applied to trees having pink floral bracts. Cultivar name invalid because Latin yet post-1959.

C. Kousa 'Rubra'

Selected ca. 1940 by Henry J. Hohman of Kingsville nursery. Never listed in the nursery's catalogs. Long commercially extinct. Floral bracts carmine-pink.

C. Kousa 'Satomi'

= *C. Kousa* 'Satomi Red'
= *C. Kousa* 'Rosabella'
= *C. Kousa* 'New Red'

Originated in Japan. Introduced to Western horticulture in the 1980s. Common. Floral bracts deep pink, long-lasting, large. Best color in light shade and cooler climates. Disease-prone.

C. Kousa 'Silver Cup'

Originated by Polly (Mary M.B.) Wakefield of Milton, MA. In commerce. White floral bracts curve upward to form an open "silver cup." Drought resistant.

C. Kousa 'Silversplash'

Introduced in 1994 by Handy nursery of Portland, OR.

C. Kousa 'Silverstar' PP 3261 (1972)

Originated by Polly (Mary M.B.) Wakefield of Milton, MA. In commerce. Upright arching vase-shaped habit. Smooth, exfoliating bark. Hardy to -20°F.

C. Kousa var. sinensis—see *C. Kousa* var. *chinensis*

C. Kousa 'Snowbird'

Originated by Polly (Mrs. Julian W.) Hill of Martha's Vineyard, MA. Sturdy, compact form. 10' tall in 25 years. Floral bracts and fruit somewhat small.

C. Kousa 'Snowboy'

Introduced ≤1977 by Sakata nursery of Yokohama City, Japan. Introduced to U.S. in 1978 by B. Yinger of Hines nursery, Santa Ana, CA, and Carl Hahn of Brookside Gardens. Leaf pale gray-green with regular white edge <¼" wide, sometimes invading to center of leaf. Occasional splashes of pink, yellow-green or paler gray-green may appear along the areas of darker gray-green. Upper surface rough sandpaper texture. Leaf tips and bases, on new shoots, often reddish. Prefers light shade; may scorch in sun. Very slow, shrubby; estimated to 8' tall.

C. Kousa 'Snowflake'

A selection of *C. Kousa* var. *chinensis*. Sold since ≤1991 by Oregon nurseries such as Forest Farm and Greer.

C. Kousa 'Southern Cross'

Introduced by Duncan & Davies nursery of New Zealand. Marketed in North America since ≤1994. Flowers borne freely. Fall color vivid red.

C. Kousa 'Speciosa'

Selected and introduced in the 1950s by J. Blaauw nursery of New Jersey. Still in commerce. A large flowering selection of *C. Kousa* var. *chinensis*. Dark green leaves curl slightly at the margins, imparting an interesting bicolor effect. Beautiful bark.

C. Kousa 'Square Dance'

Originated by Polly (Mrs. Julian W.) Hill of Martha's Vineyard, MA. Registered ca. 1982. Upright growth habit. Flowers most visible from above. Named by Pamela Harper for its overlapping bracts, which form a square pattern. Good fall color. Hardy to -5°F.

C. Kousa 'Steeple'

Originated in 1961 as a seedling raised by Polly (Mrs. Julian W.) Hill of Martha's Vineyard, MA. Registered ca. 1972. Extremely upright habit. Green glossy foliage. Good fall color.

C. Kousa 'Summer Games'

Introduced by Weston nursery of Hopkinton, MA. Variegated.

C. Kousa 'Summer Majesty'

Selected by Mitsch nursery of Aurora, OR, and named by Diane Fincham. Introduced ≤1994. Long bloom season. After 3 or 4 weeks, the white bracts acquire a pink blush for approximately another month. Possibly *Cornus florida* × *Nuttallii* 'Eddie's White Wonder' renamed.

C. Kousa 'Summer Stars' PP 3090 (1972)

Discovered as a 1964 seedling grown by P.E. Costich of Long Island, NY. Introduced in 1975 by Princeton nursery of New Jersey. Common. Precocious, heavy blooming with long retention of floral bracts. Bracts sometimes last into September. Dark green foliage changes to burgundy in fall. Drought-tolerant.

C. Kousa 'Sunsplash'

Introduced ≤1993. Bright yellow and green variegated foliage. Slow growing. Good fall color.

C. Kousa 'Temple Jewel'

Selected by Brotzman's nursery of Madison, OH. Foliage lightly variegated green, gold and pale pink. Color bold on new growth; older foliage reverts to green with a light green edge. Nowhere near as dramatic as 'Gold Star'.

C. Kousa 'Terrace'—see C. Kousa 'Ed Mezitt'

C. Kousa 'Ticknor's Choice'

Selected by horticulturist Dr. Robert L. Ticknor of Oregon. Introduced ≤1993. Floral bracts start out light green, turn white, then revert to green. Fall color orange, red and pink.

C. Kousa 'Trinity Star(s)'

Selected by Gary Handy of Handy nursery, Portland, OR. New growth mottled pink, green and white. Heavy bloomer with densely clustered flowers. Moderate growth rate. Flat topped.

C. Kousa 'Triple Crown' PP 3387 (1973)

Originated by Polly (Mary M.B.) Wakefield of Milton, MA. In commerce. Small, with dainty habit. Floriferous. Flowers often borne in clusters of three. Hardy to -20°F.

C. Kousa 'Tsukubanomine'

Introduced in 1995 by Briggs nursery of Washington, and Greer of Oregon. Flowers small but abundant, "on top of horizontal branches like butterflies."

C. Kousa 'Twinkle' PP 3386 (1973)

Originated by Polly (Mary M.B.) Wakefield of Milton, MA. In commerce. Compact, upright habit. Bracts 4–9. Fall color wine red.

C. Kousa 'Variegata'

Originated in Japan. Introduced to North America in 1862 by G. Hall, who presented it to Parsons nursery of Flushing, NY. H.H. Berger nursery of San Francisco offered it in 1892. Still in commerce in the 1990s, but now seemingly superseded by newer clones (some of which may be the original 'Variegata' renamed). Possibly several clones have been sold under this name.

C. Kousa 'Victory'

Selected by Jon Arnow of Alpine Distributors, Fairfield, CT. Similar to C. Kousa 'Madame Butterfly'. Bracts curved upward in cup form. Floriferous.

C. Kousa 'Weaver's Weeping'

Origin unknown. Sold since ≤1991 by various nurseries. Heavy flowering. Strongly weeping.

C. Kousa 'Willamette'

Introduced in 1995 by Greer nursery of Eugene, OR. In the hot summers of Oregon's Willamette Valley it holds its lush deep green color well. Flowers prolific. Fall color excellent.

C. Kousa 'Wilton'

Introduced ≤1978 by Hoogendorn nursery of Newport, RI. Floral bracts more persistent than on most KOUSA DOGWOODS.

C. Kousa 'Wolf Eyes'

Originated as a branch sport at Manor View farm of Monkton, MD. Selected in 1988. Leaf narrow, variegated: gray-green centered, white edged. Scorch-resistant. Habit compact.

C. macrophylla Koehne, non Wall.—see C. controversa

C. macrophylla Wall., non Koehne

= C. brachypoda C.A. Mey., non K. Koch, non Miq.
= Swida macrophylla (Wall.) Sojak

BIGLEAF DOGWOOD. From the Himalayas, Bhutan, China, Viet Nam, Korea, Japan, and Taiwan. Named in 1820: Greek macro, large, and phyllon, leaf. Introduced in 1827 to England. Not known in North American commerce before the 1940s; extremely rare here. A large shrub or tree. Leaves measure up to 11" × 5⅛", the stem to 1⅜"; 6–10 vein pairs. Fall color purplish. Flowers creamy white, small, in broad 4"–6" clusters during June or July. Berries blue or black, ¼". Records: to 65' × 9'5" in the wild; 40' tall at Kew, England (ca. 1987; pl. 1910); 29' tall × 43' wide at the Arnold Arboretum (1984; pl. 1951).

C. mas L.

= C. mascula L.

CORNELIAN CHERRY. LONG CHERRY TREE. MALE DOGWOOD. CHERRY DOGWOOD. From Europe, W Asia. Loudon says the name mas (Latin for male) dates from the time of Theophrastus, likely because the young plants are barren for many years after they start flowering. Called MALE DOGWOOD in contrast to C. sanguinea, the Cornus femina of old European herbals. Introduced to North America by 1655.

Common. A very distinctive species, liable to be confused only with *C. officinalis*. Shrubby unless pruned into tree shape. Slow growth, but long-lived. Very strong, long-suffering and generally troublefree. Flowers tiny but showy yellow, in late winter or early spring on the naked branches. Leaves 1"–4" long; 3–5 vein pairs. Fall color usually poor—at best a pretty, but not lovely, rosy-apricot color. Fruit a one-seeded berry, ½"–1½" long, dark red, soft and edible (plum-cranberry flavor) from mid-July through October. Fruiting cultivars exist with fruit of different colors and larger sizes. Valuable for its ability to yield fruit even in shade. A need exists for a sterile cultivar featuring upright growth and attractive fall color. Records: 45' height reported; 33' × 3'7" × 27' Edmonds, WA (1990); 30' × 7'3" × 10' Montgomery County, PA (1980); 28' × 6'4" × 37' Greenwich, CT (1988).

C. mas f. *argenteomarginata*—see *C. mas* 'Variegata'

C. mas 'Aurea'
= *C. mas* 'Foliis Aureis'

Described in 1895 in England. In North America since ≤1896. Extremely rare. Offered ≤1993 by Arborvillage nursery of Holt, MO. Leaves suffused yellow.

C. mas 'Aurea Elegantissima'
= *C. mas* 'Aureoelegantissima'
= *C. mas* 'Elegantissima'
= *C. mas* 'Foliis Aureo-variegatis'
= *C. mas* 'Tricolor'
= *C. mas* f. *aureomarginata* Schelle

Cultivated since 1772 in Germany. In North American commerce since ≤1927. Very rare. A slow growing, medium-size bush best shaded from strong sun. Leaves edged yellow, flushed violet or rose.

C. mas f. *aureomarginata*—see *C. mas* 'Aurea Elegantissima'

C. mas 'Elegantissima'—see *C. mas* 'Aurea Elegantissima'

C. mas 'Flava'
= *C. mas* 'Fructu Luteo'
= *C. mas* f. *xanthocarpa* Bean

YELLOWBERRY CORNELIAN CHERRY. Described in 1770 by Weston, in 1771 by Du Roi (as 'Fructu Cerae Coloris'). Extremely rare in North America; here ≤1923. Fruit yellow.

C. mas 'Foliis Argenteo-variegatis'—see *C. mas* 'Variegata'

C. mas 'Foliis Aureis'—see *C. mas* 'Aurea'

C. mas 'Foliis Aureo-variegatis'—see *C. mas* 'Aurea Elegantissima'

C. mas 'Fructu Luteo'—see *C. mas* 'Flava'

C. mas 'Golden Glory'
Originated by Illinois nurseryman Ralph Synnestvedt, Sr. (d. 1990). Introduced in the 1960s. The most common CORNELIAN CHERRY clone. Grows more upright. Abundant flowers.

C. mas 'Lanceolata'
= *C. mas* 'Lanceolata Albo-marginata'

Originated in France ≤1862. Extremely rare in North America. Narrow leaves, narrowly bordered white.

C. mas 'Lanceolata Albo-marginata'—see *C. mas* 'Lanceolata'

C. mas 'Macrocarpa'
Cultivated since <1877. In North America since ≤1956. Fruit large, pear-shaped.

C. mas 'Redstone'
A seed-grown cultivar released in 1991 after 44 years of evaluation by the USDA in Missouri. Superior seedling vigor. Foliage dense, glossy. Fruit production dependable. Insect and disease resistant.

C. mas 'Spring Glow'
Selected at North Carolina University State Arboretum. Named ≤1992. Flowers early, large, showy. Foliage glossy, attractive.

C. mas 'Spring Grove'
Selected at Spring Grove cemetery of Cincinnati, OH. Treelike habit, non-suckering. Leaves leathery and lustrous. The parent specimen 15½' × 1'11" × 23½' (ca. 1989).

C. mas 'Tricolor'—see *C. mas* 'Aurea Elegantissima'

C. mas 'Variegata'
= *C. mas* 'Foliis Argenteo-variegatis'
= *C. mas* f. *argenteomarginata* Schelle

Cultivated since ≤1596 in Austria. Described in 1771 by Du Roi (as 'Foliis Eleganter Variegatis'). In North American commerce since ≤1870. Rare. Leaf smaller, pale golden at first, then white on margins. Shrub or small tree. One 17½' tall and wide at Government House, Victoria, B.C. (1995).

C. mas f. *xanthocarpa*—see *C. mas* 'Flava'

C. mascula—see *C. mas*

C. 'Norman Hadden'—see *C.* 'Porlock'

C. Nuttallii Audub.
= *Benthamidia Nuttallii* (Audub.) Moldenke
= *Cynoxylon Nuttallii* (Audub.) Shafer

PACIFIC DOGWOOD. WESTERN (WHITE) DOGWOOD. From SW British Columbia through California. John James Audubon (1785–1851) first illustrated this species in his 1837 *Birds of America* and named it for its 1835 collector, the British-American botanist and ornithologist Thomas Nuttall (1786–1859)—first a printer from Liverpool, later curator of Harvard University's Botanic Garden. While individual blossoms of this species may be no more lovely than those of its close cousins *C. florida* and *C. Kousa*, the tree's great size adds grandeur the other two species lack. However, its susceptibility to anthracnose, and intolerance of watering, pruning, and similar horticultural activities, force *C. Nuttallii* to play a minor role in commerce. In its native range it grows best on well-drained slopes, with partial shade. It rarely lives more than 50 to 75 years. Leaf to 7" × 4¼", stem to 1" (larger in cv. 'Colrigo Giant'). Fall color ranges from nondescript to glowing orange-pink or brilliant crimson. Floral bracts 4–6 (rarely 8). Fruit orange or red, ripe from mid-August through early October; bitter yet eagerly sought by birds. Bark comparatively smooth. Records: 100' × 6'11" Milwaukie, OR (1944); 80' × 10'9" Seattle, WA (1990);

65' × 9'11" Olympia, WA (1988); 60' × 14'1" Clatskanie, OR (1986).

C. Nuttallii 'Boyd's Hardy'
Introduced after a 1964 freeze at Boyd nursery of McMinnville, TN. This clone was the sole survivor after a -19°F winter. Rare.

C. Nuttallii 'Colrigo Giant'
Found in 1949 by W.C. Wilson and S. Andersen, in the Columbia River Gorge a few miles west of the Bridge of the Gods on the Washington side. In commerce since 1963–64. The original tree bore flowers to 8" wide; in cultivation its progeny mostly bear flowers only 5"–7" wide. The original tree was cut ca. 1959. Leaves also extra large (to 8¾" × 5", stem to ⅜"), heavily textured. Tree vigorous. Fall color handsome.

C. Nuttallii 'Eddiei'
= *C. Nuttallii* 'Goldspot'

Found as a branch sport in 1919 near Chilliwack, B.C., by nurseryman Henry M. Eddie (1881–1953) of Vancouver, B.C. Introduced by 1923. Rare until ca. 1947. Leaves streaked and spotted gold. The clone is comparatively strong, better able to endure urban conditions than most. At its best in its second bloom during late August. Leaves red in fall. Record: 38' × 5'10" × 47' Vancouver, B.C. (1992).

C. Nuttallii 'Goldspot'—see *C. Nuttallii* 'Eddiei'

C. Nuttallii 'North Star'
In the late 1950s or early '60s, Maurice A. Atkins of Vancouver Island, Canada, subjected some *C. Nuttallii* seeds to colchicine, in hopes of inducing a variant worth naming and propagating. He succeeded, and the variant was named 'North Star' by the wife of the nurseryman who introduced the cultivar, William Goddard of Floravista Gardens, Victoria, B.C. 'North Star' is remarkable for its floral bracts: narrow, widely spaced and twisted or fluted in a pinwheel fashion. Moreover, the tree is relatively late to bloom, and defoliate, each year. Its fall color is bright red. The leaf has a notably wavy margin. Although the clone has been sold even in England, its is very rare overall, and due to its anthracnose-susceptibility, likely to remain so. It produces seeds, but they are sterile.

C. Nuttallii 'Pilgrim'

About 1959, the Saratoga Horticultural Foundation of California named this southernmost occurring specimen of *C. Nuttallii*. It grew along Highway 17 near Santa Cruz County's border. The goal had been to select a clone suitable for southern California. 'Pilgrim' never became well known or much planted.

C. Nuttallii 'Winkenwerderi'

Named after Hugo Winkenwerder (1878–1947), Dean of the University of Washington College of Forestry. The original specimen grew at the U.W. Medicinal Herb Garden, and was named ≤1946. Extinct. Accounts vary as to whether it had white variegated leaves, or merely extra large flowers.

C. officinalis S. & Z.

CHINESE CORNELIAN CHERRY. JAPANESE CORNELIAN CHERRY. KOREAN CORNELIAN CHERRY. From Japan and Korea; also possibly Chekiang, China. Introduced to Western cultivation in 1860 when Siebold sent it to the Netherlands. In North America since ≤1898. Uncommon. Closely related to the well known *C. mas*. Differs in growing larger, with larger parts. Bark is often attractive gray, flaking to reveal tan inner bark; twigs reddish, shreddy—very colorful on edges viewed when backlit by the sun. Twigs darker than those of *C. mas*. Flowers larger and often earlier than those of *C. mas*. Young flushing foliage yellowish-green rather than grayish-green. Leaf to 5⅛" long, with 5–8 vein pairs and conspicuous dirty brown hair tufts beneath. Fall color varies from pale yellow to attractive pale salmon or rich red or bright red-brown. Fruit flavor inferior to that of *C. mas*. Tree can be as shrubby, but is more ingrown, tangled and horizontal than the comparatively upright *C. mas*.

C. omeiensis Summer Passion™—see C. capitata ssp. emeiensis

C. 'Porlock'

(*C. capitata* × *C. Kousa*)
= *C. florida* 'Porlock' hort. angl.

Originated in 1958 as a self sown seedling at Underway, the garden of Norman G. Hadden (1888–1971) in West Porlock, Somerset, England. Named in 1968. Unknown in North American commerce, yet bound to be introduced because it is very popular in the UK. Alan Mitchell calls it "a big, vigorous plant laden with pink flowers all season." The floral bracts begin creamy-white but age to pink. The fruit is lovely in fall, and the foliage partially evergreen. *Cornus* 'Norman Hadden' is similar.

C. Pringlei—see C. florida 'Pringlei'

C. 'Rutban'—see C. florida × C. Kousa Aurora®

C. 'Rutcan'—see C. florida × C. Kousa Constellation®

C. 'Rutdan'—see C. florida × C. Kousa Galaxy®

C. 'Rutfan'—see C. florida × C. Kousa Stardust®

C. 'Rutgan'—see C. florida × C. Kousa Stellar Pink®

C. × rutgersensis—see C. florida × C. Kousa

C. Ruth Ellen®—see C. florida × C. Kousa Ruth Ellen®

C. 'Rutlan'—see C. florida × Kousa C. Ruth Ellen®

C. Stardust®—see C. florida × Kousa C. Stardust®

C. Stellar Pink®—see C. florida × C. Kousa Stellar Pink®

C. Urbiniana —see C. florida ssp. Urbiniana

C. Walteri Wanger.

= *Swida Walteri* (Wanger.) Sojak

From central and western China. Introduced to North America in 1907 by E. Wilson. Named in 1908. Probably first offered in commerce in 1938 by Hillier nursery of England. In the U.S. trade ≤1964–65. Extremely rare, but available commercially. A handsome small tree, with numerous 3" clusters of creamy white small flowers in early June. Leaf 2"–4½" long. Fruit a black ¼" berry. Closely related to *C. coreana*. Records: 50' × 6'0" in China; 40' × 3'3" Spetchley Park, Worcestershire, England (ca. 1990).

Corylus

[CORYLACEÆ; Hazel Family (BETULACEÆ according to some)] 10–15 spp. of deciduous hardy shrubs and small trees. Male flowers in late-winter catkins, female flowers are practically microscopic. Edible small nuts (hazels; filberts) borne in thin husks. Related to ALDERS (*Alnus*), BIRCHES (*Betula*), HORNBEAMS (*Carpinus*) and lesser-known genera. Compared to their role in nut production, HAZELS have a minor role as ornamental trees, partly because they are usually shrubby, partly because they are usually rather dull-looking. *Corylus* is an ancient Latin name, from Greek *korylos*—probably from *korys*, a helmet, after the husk on the nut. Both HAZEL and FILBERT are old English names, and are used largely interchangeably, but HAZEL is more likely to be used in reference to wild specimens, and FILBERT to cultivated ones. Frank Lamb said "a FILBERT is a HAZEL with a college education."

C. Avellana L.

EUROPEAN HAZEL. COBNUT. From Europe, W Asia, and N Africa. *Avellana* derives from Avella Vecchia, south Italy, or of Avellino, a city east of Naples, where it was much cultivated, called by the Romans *nux Avellana*. A multitrunked shrub attaining the size of a small tree, and with pruning it can be kept in tree shape. Bark smooth, gray to light brown, sometimes faintly reminiscent of CHERRY bark. Leaves 2"–4½" long, thin and softly hairy; fall color yellow. Most cultivars grown for ornament are of this species, and its hybrids (with *C. maxima*) produce the common hazelnuts of commerce. The two red- or purple-leaf cultivars attributed to *C. Avellana*, and the four listed under *C. maxima*, are confused; likely the six names refer to fewer clones, and some synonymy needs ferreting out. Records: to 60' tall in European forests; 52½' × 1'1" in woodland conditions in Seattle, WA (1994); 34' × 6'6" × 49' Vashon, WA (1993); 30' × 7'3" × 46' Victoria, B.C. (1993); 22' × 9'5" × 35' Burnett, New Zealand (1963).

C. Avellana 'Aurea'

GOLDEN HAZEL. Described in 1864 in Germany. In North American commerce since ≤1910. Rare. Leaves pale yellow-golden. Growth weak, wholly shrubby.

C. Avellana 'Contorta'

CORKSCREW HAZEL. CRAZY HAZEL. CURLY HAZEL. HARRY LAUDER'S WALKING-STICK. Originated ca. 1863 in a hedge at Frocester, Gloucestershire, England. Common in North American commerce since ≤ the late 1940s. Growth twisted, misshapen and contorted in both twig and leaf. A shy bearer of small nuts. Sir Harry Lauder (1870–1950, real surname MacLennan) was a Scottish singer who used a twisted walking stick as a prop. Record: 13' × 2'6" × 16' Tacoma, WA (1993).

C. Avellana 'Fusco Rubra'

= *C. Avellana* 'Purpurea' *sensu* Bean, non Loud.

REDLEAF HAZEL. Cultivated in the Netherlands ≤1876. First described officially in 1887. In North American commerce by 1890s yet rarely grown, because *C. maxima* 'Purpurea' has stronger, less floppy growth and equally good color.

C. Avellana 'Heterophylla'

= *C. Avellana* 'Laciniata'
= *C. Avellana* 'Quercifolia'
= *C. Avellana* 'Urticifolia'

CUTLEAF HAZEL. First described in 1825 in France. In North American commerce ≤1888, and commonly sold in the early 1900s. It has been rare for decades yet is still available. The name *heterophylla* means differently or diversely leaved (Greek *heteros*, different, and *phyllon*, a leaf). The leaf is elegantly incised and jaggedly-edged, in fernlike fashion. Some of the clonal names cited as synonyms above may actually refer to similar clones of independent origin.

C. Avellana 'Laciniata'—see *C. Avellana* 'Heterophylla'

C. Avellana 'Pendula'

WEEPING HAZEL. First described in 1867 in the Netherlands. Probably in North American commerce soon afterward. Long commercially extinct and extremely rare here.

C. Avellana 'Purple Avalon'

Origin unknown. In North American commerce since ≤1974. Rare. Leaves purplish. Growth weaker and more shrubby than typical. Not to be confused with 'Red Aveline' which is a nut-producing cultivar more than 100 years old, the nut's skin a "beautiful dark wine color."

C. Avellana 'Purpurea'—see *C. Avellana* 'Fusco Rubra'

C. Avellana 'Quercifolia'—see *C. Avellana* 'Heterophylla'

C. Avellana 'Urticifolia'—see *C. Avellana* 'Heterophylla'

C. Colurna L.

TURKISH HAZEL. CONSTANTINOPLE HAZEL. TREE HAZEL. From SE Europe and SW Asia. Cultivated since 1582 when introduced to Holland from Constantinople by Clusius. In North America since ≤1850s. Uncommon. *Colurna* derives ultimately from *Corylus*, but the details of the transformation are shadowy. A handsome, sturdy, troublefree shade tree of moderate size. Leaves 2"–6" long, shallowly lobed, toothed; deeply heart-shaped at the base; scarcely hairy; semi-glossy; bright green; stem to 2" long. Nuts small, hard, flattened, in clusters of 2–6 (15), enclosed in strangely armed husks; ripe from mid-August into October. Isolated specimens may produce only hollow nuts; for filled nuts cross-pollination is desirable. But if nut-production is the goal, other species or hybrids of *Corylus* should be planted. Bark corky. Some basal suckering may occur, and the nuts can be messy, so the tree ought be avoided where tidiness is desired. Records: 100' × 13'1" in Vienna, Austria (n.d.); 88½' × 6'3" Hergest Croft, Herefordshire, England (1985); 70' × 9'6" Syon House, London, England (1982); 70' × 5'9" Port Coquitlam, B.C. (1992); 58' × 4'6" Seattle, WA (1987); 57' × 8'1" × 60' Lisle, IL (1986; *pl.* 1922); 46' × 6'9" Montgomery County, PA (1980); a trunk 7'9" around at Brooklyn, NY (1972).

C. maxima Mill.

GIANT HAZEL or FILBERT. From S Europe. Much like *C. Avellana* but the nuts are slightly larger, in a long sock-like husk. Its leaf is the same shape but thicker, 2"–6" long. Its hybrids with *C. Avellana* are the CULTIVATED FILBERTS used for nut production. Some cultivars cited below, obviously hybrids, are sold as *maxima* clones, and so are listed here.

C. maxima 'Fortin'

Discovered ca. 1981 in Bellevue WA, at an abandoned orchard planted many years earlier by Mr. Fortin, a French immigrant. Named by M. Dolan of Burnt Ridge nursery, Onalaska, WA. In commerce in Washington and Oregon since the mid-1980s. Similar to *C. maxima* 'Rote Zeller' in having purple catkins, leaves and nut husks. Very productive. The nuts are small, pointed, in clusters of 2–8; husks purple, usually completely covering the nuts and extending ½" beyond the ends.

C. maxima 'Fortin Redleaf'—see *C. maxima* 'Red Fortin'

C. maxima 'Purpurea'

PURPLELEAF FILBERT. Cultivated since the early 1800s. Very common. Dark purple leaves and reddish nut husks. Doubtless more than one clone has been sold under this name.

C. maxima 'Red Fortin'

= *C. maxima* 'Fortin Redleaf'

Origin as per 'Fortin'. In Washington and Oregon commerce since the 1980s. Like 'Fortin' but with dark red catkins, young leaves, and nut husks. Summer foliage bronzy. Nuts borne in clusters of 1–7; small and round; the husks extend halfway the nut length.

C. maxima 'Rote Zeller'

('Rote Zellernus')

From Germany; in North American commerce since ≤1968–69. Catkins long, reddish-purple. Leaves red at first, then turn bronze-green by late summer, wholly green by autumn. Nut husks reddish, shorter than the oval nuts. Nuts borne 1–2 (3) together.

Cotinus

[ANACARDIACEÆ; Cashew Family] 2–4 spp. of deciduous shrubs or small trees. From *kotinos*, the ancient Greek name for the WILD OLIVE (*Olea europæa* var. *silvestris*). Grown for spectacular fall color, and ornamental airy plumelike seed clusters in summer. Closely related to the SUMACHS (*Rhus* spp.).

C. americanus—see *C. obovatus*

C. americanus 'Chenault's Variety'—see *C.* 'Flame'

C. americanus 'Flame'—see *C.* 'Flame'

C. Coggygria Scop.

= *Rhus Cotinus* L.

EUROPEAN SMOKE TREE. SMOKE PLANT. CLOUD TREE. VENUS SUMACH. VENETIAN SUMACH. WIG TREE. PERIWIG TREE. PURPLE FRINGE TREE. MIST TREE. JUPITER'S BEARD. From Eurasia. Cultivated in Europe since the 1590s or mid-1600s; in North American nurseries since ≤1790. Common. *Coggygria* from the Greek *kokkygea*—a modification of the name used by Theophrastus, presumably the Greek name for this plant. (Another SMOKE TREE is *Dalea spinosa* Gray, of the SW United States and adjacent Mexico.) Unless pruned into tree shape (an ongoing job), this *Cotinus* grows as a large shrub. Bees are greatly attracted to the inconspicuous blossoms in May or early June. But it isn't until after it blooms that the spent floral plumes justify the name SMOKE TREE, when they give the tree a blurry, hazy aspect with an indescribable airy, feathery charm.

Leaves 1½"–4" long, smelling of orange-peel odor when crushed, much like those of SWEETGUM (*Liquidambar*) or CHINESE PISTACHIO (*Pistacia chinensis*). The best fall color is obtained by growing it on relatively dry, sterile, sunny sites. Records: to 40' tall in the wild; 35' × 3'7" × 35' Walla Walla, WA (1993); 30' × 4'7" × 35' Spokane, WA (1988).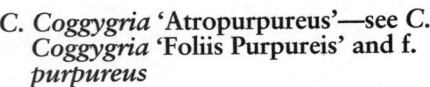

C. *Coggygria* 'Atropurpureus'—see C. *Coggygria* 'Foliis Purpureis' and f. *purpureus*

C. *Coggygria* 'Black Velvet'

Described by S. Campbell of Sebastopol, CA. Introduced ≤1994. Leaves dark purple. Flowers profuse. Good growth habit.

C. *Coggygria* 'Cooke's Purple'

Introduced ≤1992 by Greer nursery of Oregon. Attractive purple plumes.

C. *Coggygria* 'Daydream' PP 1844 (1959)

Selected at Newport nursery of Newport, MI. Rare. Leaves deep bluish-green. Plumes extra fluffy; hairs dull brown, then red-pink. Very heavy flowering. Shrubbby.

C. *Coggygria* 'Flame'—see C. 'Flame'

C. *Coggygria* 'Foliis Purpureis'

= C. *Coggygria* 'Rubrifolius'
= C. *Coggygria* 'Atropurpureus' Bean, non Burv.
Originated in 1914 in England. The original PURPLELEAF SMOKE TREE, now superseded by darker offspring. Leaves dark purplish-red at first, becoming green tinged purple. Plumes pink-red.

C. *Coggygria* 'Kromhout'—see C. *Coggygria* 'Royal Purple'

C. *Coggygria* 'Nordine (Red)'

Introduced ≤1967. Still in commerce. Named after Roy M. Nordine (1904–1989), the Morton Arboretum's propagator for 28 years. Leaves stay purplish-red all season. Plumes large, ruby-red. Fall color brilliant yellow to orange. Notably hardy.

C. *Coggygria* 'Notcutt's Variety' PP 1457 (1956)

A darker-leaved selection of C. *Coggygria* 'Foliis Purpureis' raised by Notcutt nursery of Woodbridge, Suffolk, England. Introduced to North America ≤1940. Promoted since 1956 by Wayside nursery of Mentor, OH. Leaves dark purple. Plumes purple-pink.

C. *Coggygria* 'Pink Champagne'—see C. *Coggygria* 'Pop's Pink Champagne'

C. *Coggygria* 'Pink Princess'

Listed in 1978–79 catalog of Iseli nursery of Boring, OR.

C. *Coggygria* 'Pop's Pink Champagne'

= C. *Coggygria* 'Pink Champagne'
Introduced ≤1991–92 by Evans Farms nursery of Oregon City, OR. Named in 1988 after Eldon Evans, who field-selected for consistent floriferous habit and light mauve young foliage. Plumes clear pink.

C. *Coggygria* 'Purple Supreme'

Introduced ≤1992 by Greer nursery of Oregon. Purple foliage.

C. *Coggygria* f. *purpureus* (Dupuy-Jamin) Rehd.

= C. *Coggygria* 'Atropurpureus' Burv., non Bean
First described in 1870 in France. Plumes some shade of purplish-pink or red instead of the typical pink or straw color. Leaves green. The name has been confused with purpleleaved selections.

C. *Coggygria* 'Royal Purple'

= C. *Coggygria* 'Kromhout'
Raised by Lombarts nursery and named by Kromhout nursery, both of Holland. In North America since ≤1953. Foliage darker purple than 'Notcutt's Variety'.

C. *Coggygria* 'Rubrifolius'—see *C. Coggygria* 'Foliis Purpureis'

C. *Coggygria* 'Velvet Cloak'

Originated at Newport nursery of Newport, MI. Found by Henry Kleine of Horse Shoe, NC <1962, when it was ca. 10 years old. Introduced in 1969 by Cole nursery of Painesville, OH. Foliage deep reddish-purple. Plumes fawn-colored, not purple.

C. *cotinoides*—see *C. obovatus*

C. 'Dummer Clone 2'—see *C.* 'Grace'

C. 'Flame'

= *C. americanus* 'Chenault's Variety'
= *C. americanus* 'Flame'
= *C. Coggygria* 'Flame'

Originated in Europe. Introduced to North America ≤1965. Not yet in commerce (or rarely offered). Almost certainly a hybrid. Brilliant scarlet to orange in autumn. Plumes pink.

C. 'Grace'

= *C.* 'Dummer Clone 2'

Intentional 1978 cross of *C. Coggygria* 'Velvet Cloak' with a male *C. obovatus*. One of five seedlings raised at Hillier's nursery, England. Named after Grace Dummer, hybridizer Peter Dummer's wife. Introduced ≤1984; recently in North American commerce. Vigorous; treelike. Leaf 4"–6" long, to 3" wide, light red when young, darker with age; stem red, 2" long or more. Fall color orange, red and yellow.

C. *obovatus* Raf.

= *C. americanus* Nutt.
= *C. cotinoides* (Nutt. *ex* Chapm.) Brit.
= *Rhus cotinoides* Nutt.
= *R. americana* Nutt.

AMERICAN SMOKE TREE. CHITTAMWOOD. YELLOWWOOD. From a few disjunct locales in the southeastern U.S., on rocky hills. Introduced to cultivation ≤1882. Less common than its European counterpart. Definitely treelike. Plumes far less showy, but fall color supreme: fiery scarlet and orange. Leaf less rounded (more obovate), finely downy beneath, to 7" × 5", stem to 3" long. Records: 54' × 2'6" × 29' Lewisburg, PA (1980); 49' × 4'1" × 31' Tacoma, WA (1992); 39' × 7'11" × 38' West Lafayette, IN (1984); 31' × 9'5" × 44' Willimantic, CT (1992).

Cotoneaster

[ROSACEÆ; Rose Family] 50–250 spp. of Old World evergreen or deciduous shrubs, rarely small trees. All bear small, attractive white flowers, but the majority are prized for their colorful berries and foliage. They thrive in exposed sites and lean soil. Related to *Amelanchier*, *Cratægus*, *Photinia* and other genera. From Latin *cotoneum*, a quince, and *-aster*, an inferior resemblance. Literally, quincelike. Although shrubby species are sometimes grafted as standards on HAWTHORN (*Cratægus*), CRAB APPLE (*Malus*) or MOUNTAIN ASH (*Sorbus*), there is only one species in general cultivation that often grows treelike, and even it is usually just a giant shrub.

C. *frigidus* Wall. *ex* Lindl.

HIMALAYAN (TREE) COTONEASTER. From the Himalayas, Nepal to Bhutan and SE Tibet. Introduced to England in 1824. In North America since ≤1888. Named *frigidus* because it grows in cold regions (such as the higher, cooler elevations at Gossain Than in Nepal). Despite its native haunts and its name, it is none too hardy in most of North America, and has practically been limited to the Pacific Coast nursery trade. A deciduous or semi-evergreen large shrub or small tree at most over 56' × 6'6". Leaves 2"–5" long, to 2¼" wide, dark bluish-green above, pale green with scattered, loose white hairs beneath. Flowers small, creamy white, borne in flattened 2" clusters during April, May or June. Fruit a small red berry attractive in fall and winter. Since the species is somewhat cold tender, and prone to fireblight, it is little valued. Grafting it on COMMON HAWTHORN (*Cratægus monogyna*) may serve to render it more treelike and cold-hardy. The cultivar 'Fructu Luteo' has pale yellow berries; 'Vicarii' has smaller leaves and larger brilliant red berries. Some hybrids may be better-looking, hardier, and can also be easily trained into small trees. These include: **'Cornubia'**, **'Crispii'**, **'Glabratus'**, **'John Waterer'**, and **'Rothschildianus'**. These named selections arose in England and have been grown in North America; other hybrids exist overseas but have not yet been introduced here. The difficulty of distinguishing these selections, and the lack of documentation concerning their performance, shows a need for detailed study of the group.

+ Cratægomespilus

[ROSACEÆ; Rose Family] 1 chimæra or graft-hybrid: *Cratægus monogyna* (HAWTHORN) + *Mespilus germanica* (MEDLAR). This strange tree arose when a HAWTHORN was used as a stock upon which to graft a MEDLAR. The tree can produce four kinds of growth: pure HAWTHORN, pure MEDLAR, 'Asnieresii' (see below), its "own" (i.e., typical *C. Dardarii*). Since the tree bears fruit inferior to the MEDLAR, and is no better looking than either parent, it has been grown to a very limited extent as a novelty. See also × *Cratæmespilus*. The only other graft-hybrid in this book is + *Laburnocytisus*.

C. Asnieresii—see C. Dardarii 'Asnieresii'

C. Dardarii Sim.-Louis *ex* Bellair

BRONVAUX MEDLAR. Originated <1895 in the garden of Monsieur Dardar at Bronvaux, near Metz, France. Introduced in 1902 to the U.S. by the Arnold Arboretum. Exceedingly rare. Perhaps out of commerce since the late 1940s. More MEDLAR-like than its cultivar 'Asnieresii', yet somewhat spiny. Leaves 1½"–4" long, toothless or finely toothed; unlobed to weakly lobed; short-stemmed; downy. Flowers 1½" wide, white, in clusters of 3–12; anthers 15–20. Fruit like a small medlar, ca. 1" wide.

C. Dardarii 'Asnieresii'

= *C. Asnieresii* hort.
= *C. Dardarii* 'Jules d'Asnières'

Originated in 1898 as a branch sport on the original BRONVAUX MEDLAR. Just as rare in North America as its parent. Leaves more like those of the HAWTHORN, but hairier, and less strongly and more bluntly lobed. Flowers (1" wide) and fruit (brown) also much like those of the HAWTHORN.

C. Dardarii 'Jules d'Asnières'—see C. Dardarii 'Asnieresii'

C. grandiflora—see × Cratæmespilus grandiflora

C. Smithii—see × Cratæmespilus grandiflora

Cratægus

[ROSACEÆ; Rose Family] 135–280 spp. of hardy small trees or shrubs. Eastern North America has most of the species. All produce berries called haws, and nearly all are thorny. Leaves generally small and jaggedly lobed. Flowers small, white (pink in some cultivars), primarily in May and June. Haws usually red and <1". Rugged, twisting, branches form dense heads, usually spreading rather than upright. HAWTHORNS are pioneer trees and loathe shade. Name from Greek *krataigos*, a flowering thorn, from *kratos*, strength, referring to the strong and hard wood. HAWTHORN from Old English *haga*, a hedge, and thorn: HEDGETHORN. As ornamental trees they offer seasonal beauty and often attract birds. The foliage is frequently more interesting and healthier than that of most CHERRIES (*Prunus*) or CRABAPPLES (*Malus*), two related genera. They are long suffering and endure pruning, so can be used for hedging. Many of the species are able to reproduce from seed as genetically identical individuals, a process called apomixis. Botanists used to describe nearly every variant as a separate species; despair ensued as well over 1,000 species were described (the heyday was from 1896 to 1910, when 886 new species were described). Now the trend is to recognize comparatively few species, but grant them great variability. Nonetheless, the decision as to what constitutes a species and what a mere variety is vexing, and, frankly, arbitrary. In the present volume, horticultural history is used as the primary basis—scientific examination of the genus independently done would result in a different ranking. Some taxa formerly regarded as separate species, but subsequently sunk into synonymy by botanists, are ranked at varietal status in this volume, which includes 36 species and about 60 hybrids and varieties. While far from a complete account of every species that has been grown in North America, it does contain every major ornamental species and nearly all minor ones.

C. acerifolia—see C. mollis and C. Phænopyrum

C. æstivalis (Walt.) T. & G.

MAY HAWTHORN. EASTERN MAYHAW. APPLE HAWTHORN. SOUTHERN SUMMER HAW. SHINING HAWTHORN. From moist soils on the Coastal Plain of southern North Carolina to southern Mississippi. The specific epithet, published in 1788, derives from Latin *æstiva*—of summer; because the haws ripen in summer instead of fall. Its beautiful large flowers, aromatic well-flavored red fruit, and tolerance of wet soils make it a good ornamental for moist parts of the South. Leaf unlobed, usually glossy, to 2½" long. Thorns ¾"–1⅔". Flowers ½"–¾" (1") wide, in clusters of 2–4, in February–March, before leafing; anthers 20, pink; styles and seeds 3–5. Closely related to *C. opaca*, but blooms two weeks earlier, ripens fruit earlier (6–8 weeks from blooming), and has unlobed, hairless leaves. Cultivars for fruit production include '**Big Red**', '**Big V**', '**Heavy**', and '**Lori**'. Records: 43' × 4'1" × 42' San Felasco Hammock, FL (1974); 43' × 2'6" × 19' Angelina National Forest, TX (1982).

C. altaica (Loud.) Lange

ALTAI MOUNTAIN HAWTHORN. From central Asia. Introduced to cultivation ≤1836 in England. In North America since ≤1929 but virtually never grown here except in botanic gardens; included in this volume for comparison to its close cousins *C. sanguinea* and *C. Wattiana*, with which it has been confused. Leaves to 3¼" long, much like those of *C. Wattiana*, but more deeply lobed than those of *C. sanguinea*. Flowers ill-scented, ⁹⁄₁₆"–⅝" wide; anthers 20–22, cream or palest pink; styles (3) 5; sepals short, reflexed. Haws ripens early (some in early August), soft, 5 seeded, red.

C. ambigua C.A. Mey. *ex* A. Becker

RUSSIAN HAWTHORN. From SE Russia, Turkey, and Iran. Named and introduced to cultivation in 1858. In North America since ≤1930. Rare. Promoted for its hardiness in the Great Plains and Midwest: it is adapted to extreme temperature and soil conditions. The specific epithet, published in 1858, derives from Latin and means *doubtful*. Closely related to *C. monogyna*, but usually with 2 seeds. A shrub or small tree ca. 15'–40' tall, usually as wide or wider than tall. Thorns few, to ⅝". Leaves 1"–2" long, shiny, deeply lobed. Flowers ⅝"–⅔" wide; anthers 20, purple; styles (1) 2 (3). Haws to ⁹⁄₁₆" long, first bright red, then dark red or purple-black with light dots, fleshy, succulent, edible and tasty but poisonous in "large quantity."

C. apiifolia—see *C. Marshallii* and *C. orientalis*

C. aprica Beadle

SUNNY HAWTHORN. From the SE United States; common in dry woods. Cultivated since 1876. Named in 1900, *aprica* being Latin for sunny. Seldom grown. Closely related to and often confused with *C. flava* (and its var. *lobata*). Thorns 1"–1½" long. Leaves ¾"–1½" (2") long, thick, weakly or not lobed, widest above the middle, narrowed towards the stem. Flowers ¾" wide, in clusters of 2–4 (6); anthers 10, yellow; styles 3–5. Haws green, then dull orange-red, ½" wide, 3–5 seeded, ripe in late fall; sweet and juicy. Tree small, to 24' × 2'1". Fairly ornamental.

C. arborescens—see *C. viridis*

C. Arduennæ—see *C. crus-galli*

C. Aria—see *Sorbus Aria*

C. arkansana—see *C. mollis* var. *arkansana*

C. arnoldiana—see *C. mollis* var. *arnoldiana*

C. Aronia—see *C. Azarolus*

C. 'Autumn Glory'

= *C. Oxyacantha* 'Autumn Glory'
= *C. lævigata* 'Autumn Glory'
= *C. 'Crimson Glory'*

Originated in the early 1940s as a MEXICAN HAWTHORN (*C. mexicana*) seedling, found in San Francisco's East Bay area by Edith Bewley, who planted it in her garden at Los Altos; displayed before the California Horticultural Society in October 1942; first sold as 'Crimson Glory' by nurseryman W.B. Clarke in his 1944 *Garden Aristocrats* catalog. The names refer to the haws. Common. Leaves to 2⅝" long. Flowers don't stink; ⅝"–¹¹⁄₁₆" wide; anthers (17) 20, pink, around yellow-green centers; styles 2; sepals reflexed, narrow, sharply fine-toothed. Haws large (to 1" long × ¾" wide), showy bright red, abundant, good eating; 2 big seeds. Wide-branching when grown in the open. Essentially thornless. Record: 39' × 3'3¼" × 31' San Francisco, CA (1994).

C. Azarolus L.

= *C. Aronia* (Willd.) Bosc *ex* DC.

AZAROLE (HAWTHORN). MEDITERRANEAN MEDLAR. NEAPOLITAN MEDLAR. From SE Europe, N Africa, and SW Asia (in a narrow interpretation, Crete only). Cultivated for its edible fruit for many centuries in the Mediterranean region. Introduced before the mid-1600s to northern Europe. In North American nurseries ≤1884. Very rare. Few or no thorns. Flowers ½"–¾" wide, anthers 20, purple; styles (1) 2 (3).

Leaf much like that of *C. monogyna* (COMMON HAW-THORN), 1½"–3" long, hairy on both sides. Haws ⅝"–1⅛" long, nearly as wide, yellow, orange or lustrous rich red, with some loose hairs near the end; knobby; broad; sepals villous. Seeds 1–2 (3), large. The epithet *Azarolus* is Latinized from French *azerole*, Spanish *acerola*, Arabic *az-zu' rûr*—all names for this species. Closely related to *C. monogyna* and *C. orientalis*. Records: 26' × 3'4" Antibes, France (1888); 26' × 2'8" Thorp Perrow, Bedale, Yorkshire, England (n.d.); 25' × 2'6" × 26' Seattle, WA (1992).

C. biltmoreana—see C. intricata

C. 'Blue Haw'—see C. orientalis 'Blue Hawthorn'

C. Boyntonii—see C. intricata

C. brachyacantha Sarg. & Engelm.

BLUEBERRY HAWTHORN. BLUE HAW. THE POMMETTE BLEU of west Louisiana Arcadians. From the Coastal Plain, E Texas to SW Georgia. The specific epithet *brachyacantha* was published in 1882 and means short thorns; from Greek *brachys*, short, and *akantha*, a thorn (most of its thorns are ⅓"–⅔"). Introduced to cultivation in 1900. Rare. Best suited to the South. Leaf unlobed or weakly lobed, ¾"–2" (3½") long, dark and shiny; stipules large, to 1" long. Flowers ⅓" wide; anthers 15–20; styles 3–5. Haws blue, ripe in August, ⅓"–½" long. Records: 50' tall reported by C. Sargent; 36' × 6'3" × 40' Marshall, Harrison County, TX (1973).

C. Bretschneideri—see C. pinnatifida var. major

C. brevispina—see C. Douglasii

C. californica—see C. pinnatifida var. major

C. Calpodendron (Ehrh.) Med.

= *C. tomentosa* Du Roi 1771, non L. 1753
= *C. pyrifolia* Ait.
= *C. Fontanesiana* (Spach) Steud.
= *Mespilus Calpodendron* Ehrh.

PEAR HAWTHORN. SUGAR HAWTHORN. BLACK HAW-THORN. From eastern North America. Named in the 1700s. Rare in cultivation; sold somewhat sparingly from ≤1904 into the '50s; very seldom since. The epithet *Calpodendron* is Greek for *urn-like tree*; referring to the shape of the haw. Tree often with several slender trunks, usually arching, vaselike; can be

thornless but usually has slender thorns (1"–2"). Leaves large, 2"–6½" long, copiously downy and strongly pleated as they unfold, furrowed from midrib to margin; persistently hairy beneath. Last to bloom of American species except *C. Phænopyrum* (WASHINGTON HAWTHORN). Flowers ½"–⅝" wide, ill-scented; anthers (15) 20, red fading to pink or rarely white; styles 2–5. Haws small but showy, orange-red, ellipsoid or pear-shaped, upright, sweet, succulent; 2–4 seeded; persisting well. Records: 25' tall at 35 years in the Jardin des Plantes, France (ca. 1836); 23' × 1'1" × 19' Harms Woods, Cook County, IL (1955); 22' × 2'6" × 30' Grantsville, MD (1956); 18' × 2'0" × 28' Lisle, IL (1951); 17' × 1'6" × 26' Seattle, WA (1993; *pl.* 1951). (A Portland, OR, specimen cited in *American Forests'* big tree list is really *C. punctata* f. *aurea*.)

C. Calpodendron var. gigantea Kruschke

Named in 1965; from the SE corner of Greenfield Park, Milwaukee County, WI. Not in commerce, but included here to show the range of variability this species can exhibit. Leaf to 6⅜" × 4"; flower to 15⁄16" wide; haw to ½" long.

C. Canbyi—see C. crus-galli var. Canbyi

C. × Carrierei—see C. × Lavallei

C. cerronis—see C. erythropoda

C. chlorosarca Maxim.

= *C. Schroederi* (Reg.) Koehne *ex* Späth
= *C. mandschurica* hort. *ex* Koehne

MANCHURIAN BLACK HAWTHORN. From Manchuria, Sakhalin, Korea, and Japan. Introduced to Russian cultivation in 1870; in Canada by 1896. Named in 1897. In North American commerce since ≤1930. Very rare. Hardy enough to survive on the Canadian prairie. The epithet *chlorosarca* means green fleshed; from Greek *chloros*, yellowish-green or green, and *sarx*, flesh. Tree dense, small, neatly pyramidal. Thorns short (to ⅝") or absent. Shoots dark purple-brown. Leaf 2"–4", shallowly lobed, hairy initially, becoming dark and glossy above. Flowers ⅜"–⅝" wide; anthers (15) 20, pink; styles 5. Haws round, 7⁄16"; red, then dark purple-black at maturity; flesh

green; 4–5 seeded. Likely to be confused only with
C. Douglasii (BLACK HAWTHORN).

C. chrysocarpa Ashe

= *C. coccinea* L. 1753 (in part)
= *C. Jackii* Sarg.
= *C. Piperi* Britt.
= *C. rotundifolia* Moench 1785 (in part), non
Lam. 1783

FIREBERRY HAWTHORN. ROUNDLEAF HAWTHORN. From
Newfoundland and New England to the northern
Great Lakes region; incorrectly cited in the South.
Name from Greek *chrysos*, gold, and *karpos*, fruit.
Introduced to cultivation in 1906; rarely grown.
HAWTHORN expert E. Kruschke observed: "This species and its varieties and their synonyms . . . represents probably the most confused species complex of
Cratægus, or at least equal to the confusion as shown
in such other species complexes as *C. macrosperma*
and *C. succulenta*." Shrub, rarely a 20' tree. Leaves
1"–3" long. Thorns 1"–2" long. Flowers early and
usually showy; anthers 5–10, white or pale yellow.
Haws (despite its Greek name) deep red or crimson,
(2) 3–4 seeded.

C. chrysocarpa var. *phœnicea* E.J. Palm.

= *C. rotundifolia* Moench 1785 (in part), non
Lam. 1783
= *C. coccinea* hort. (in part)

From the NE United States and SE Canada. Introduced to cultivation in 1737. Uncommon. Hairless
except for short appressed hairs sometimes found on
upper young leaf surfaces, and sometimes the flower
stems. Haws dark red, lustrous. Flowers ½"–¾" (1")
wide; anthers 5–10, yellow; styles 3–4.

C. coccinea L.

= *C. pedicellata* Sarg.

SCARLET HAWTHORN. ONTARIO HAWTHORN. From
eastern North America. The 1753 name *C. coccinea*
(Latin meaning deep red or scarlet) has been used
incorrectly for *C. chrysocarpa*, *C. intricata*, *C. Ellwangeriana*, and other taxa. Thus, some modern
botanists have stopped using the *coccinea* name, considering it is hopelessly ambiguous, but contemporary
HAWTHORN expert J.B. Phipps says it is still valid.
Nurseries once used the name widely. In 1901 C.S.
Sargent renamed this species *pedicellata* because the
flower/fruit stems (pedicels) are long and slender.
Though nurseries have not generally sold trees under
the name *C. pedicellata*, the great tree expert A.
Rehder wrote in 1938 that this was "The species
rather widely distributed in northeastern North

America that perhaps has most frequently been identified as *C. coccinea*." Leaves hairless, very sharply
toothed, 2"–4" long. Thorns 1½"–2". Flowers ½"–
⅞" wide; anthers pink or red, 5–10; styles 2–5. Haws
scarlet, ½"–⅝"; 2–5 seeded.

C. coccinea var. *macracantha*—see *C. macracantha*

C. coccinea var. *mollis*—see *C. mollis*

C. contorta—see *C. lævigata* 'Salisburifolia'

C. cordata—see *C. Phænopyrum*

C. 'Crimson Glory'—see *C. 'Autumn Glory'*

C. crus-galli L.

= *C. Arduennæ* Sarg.

COCKSPUR HAWTHORN. NEWCASTLE HAWTHORN. HOG
APPLE. PIN HAWTHORN. From eastern North America.
It was common in Newcastle, Delaware. Named in
1753. Latin *crus-galli* means "leg of a cock," *i.e.* resembling a cock's spurs—from the thorns, which can
be branched and 8" long! A very popular, much cultivated species. Several variants exist. It is difficult to
declare any one the "typical" kind. Perhaps the most
common variant has very dark foliage of a wet look
or high gloss, is armed with long thorns, branches
rigidly horizontally, and is utterly without hairiness.
Blooms tardily, in late May–early June, and stinks,
yet the profusion of flowers is lovely. Leaves 1"–4"
long, thick, wedge-shaped; amber, orange or scarlet
in autumn. Flowers (sensu stricto—see *vars.* below)
⁷⁄₁₆"–⅔"; anthers 10 (13), rose or pale yellow; styles
1–3. Haws ⅓"–⅞" wide, rather dull red, usually 2
seeded. Records: 44' × 2'9" × 45'
Bloomfield Hills, Oakland
County, MI (1961); 40' × 5'0"
× 48' Manassas, VA (1987);
27' × 6'2" × 37' near Orrville,
Wayne County, OH (1965); 26'
× 6'6" × 36' Beaver County, PA
(1978).

C. crus-galli var. *Canbyi* (Sarg.) stat. nov.

= *C. Canbyi* Sarg.

CANBY COCKSPUR HAWTHORN. From Maryland, Delaware and eastern Pennsylvania. Named in 1901 after
its discoverer William Marriott Canby (1831–1904).
Very rare in cultivation. It flushes first, blooms earlier; has shorter and fewer thorns; the leaves are less
dark, less glossy, and persist longer in fall; the haws
are larger with shiny skin and red rather than yellow

flesh, and are juicier. Flowers ½"–⅝" (¾") wide; anthers (8) 10–15 (20—reportedly) pale pink or yellow-pink; (2) styles 3–4 (5). Haws ½" long, bright red, juicy; usually 3 seeded.

C. crus-galli Crusader®

= C. crus-galli 'Cruzam'

Introduced in 1980 by Lake County nursery of Ohio. Common. A nearly or wholly thornless tree, the crown rounded. Leaves thick, glossy, orange in the fall. Haws abundant. Bark silver gray. Very disease resistant.

C. crus-galli 'Cruzam'—see C. crus-galli Crusader®

C. crus-galli 'Hooks'—see C. 'Hooks'

C. crus-galli var. horizontalis—see C. crus-galli 'Salicifolia'

C. crus-galli var. inermis Lange

THORNLESS COCKSPUR HAWTHORN. Latin *inermis* means unarmed; without thorns. Common. A relatively small tree.

C. crus-galli var. linearis—see C. crus-galli 'Salicifolia'

C. crus-galli 'Lucida'—see C. × persimilis 'MacLeod'

C. crus-galli var. prunifolia—see C. × persimilis

C. crus-galli 'Prunifolia'—see C. × persimilis 'MacLeod'

C. crus-galli var. pyracanthifolia Ait.

Found occasionally nearly throughout the range of the species, and merges into the typical form. Named in 1789 in England. In North American nursery trade ≤1891. Extremely rarely listed by nurseries. Leaf narrow (but not as slender as that of 'Salicifolia'), haws small. Flowers with 8–10 rose colored anthers, 1–2 styles.

C. crus-galli 'Salicifolia'

= C. crus-galli var. salicifolia (Med.) Ait.
= C. crus-galli var. linearis (Pers.) Ser.
= C. crus-galli var. horizontalis hort.

Cultivated in Europe <1782, when named (genus *Salix*, WILLOW, and Latin *folium*, a leaf). Scarcely known in North American horticulture. Grows horizontally, flat-topped; leaves extra-narrow (ca. 2" × ⅝"), thin. Flowers with 15–20 anthers, 3–4 styles. Not very thorny.

C. crus-galli var. splendens—see C. × persimilis 'MacLeod'

C. crus-galli var. tenax (Ashe) stat. nov.

= C. tenax Ashe
= C. Fontanesiana (Spach) Steud.—misapplied

From SE Canada and the NE United States. Originally named in 1834. Although this variety has not been listed as *tenax* by nurseries, it might have been sold as "C. crus-galli." The epithet *tenax* (Latin for holding tight, tenacious, or strong) was published in 1902. Compared to the botanically typical COCKSPUR HAWTHORN: Leaf smaller, darker, more leathery, usually narrower. Flowers bloom earlier. Anthers 20, pink. Haws smaller.

C. Douglasii Lindl.

= C. brevispina (Dougl.) Heller
= C. rivularis Nutt. ex T. & G.
= C. Suksdorfii (Sarg.) Kruschke

BLACK HAWTHORN. WESTERN BLACK HAWTHORN. BLACK THORNBERRY. From Alaska to northern New Mexico, and around Lake Superior. Discovered and introduced by David Douglas (1798–1834). Named in 1835. In North American commerce since ≤1888. Very rare; grown almost exclusively within its native range (where it can hybridize with the introduced C. monogyna). Some nurseries have sold C. macracantha under the name C. Douglasii. Bark shreddy, of unusual tan color. Thorns ⅓"–1" long. Leaves weakly lobed or practically unlobed, usually broad and dark, 1"–4" (5"), to 3" wide. Flowers ⅓"–1³⁄₁₆" wide, anthers (5) 10 (20), usually pink, sometimes light yellow; styles 2–5. Haws black, ripening early (sometimes in early July), to ½" long; flesh varies from mealy and dryish to moist, soft, greenish, and pleasingly flavored; eventually shrivels and hangs like black rasins; (3) 4 (5) seeded. Although the flowers are ornamental, the dark fruit and unspectacular fall color limit the appeal of this species. Records: 51' × 7'6" × 42' Quinault, WA (1988); 41' × 9'3" × 57' Beacon Rock State Park, WA (1993); 33' × 9'6" × 45' Sauvie Island, OR (1973).

C. Eganii—see C. macrosperma

C. elliptica—see *C. flava* var. *lobata*

C. Ellwangeriana Sarg.

= *C. pedicellata* var. *Ellwangeriana* (Sarg.) Eggl.
= *C. mollis* var. *Ellwangeriana* (Sarg.) Cowles
= *C. coccinea* auct. (in part), non L.

ELLWANGER HAWTHORN. From the NE United States; most common in western New York. Introduced to cultivation in 1900. Uncommon. Named in 1902 after nurseryman George Ellwanger (1816–1906). Most *Cratægus* experts believe ELLWANGER HAWTHORN is a variety (if not a mere synonym) of *C. pedicellata*. Botanist A. Cronquist thought it might be *C. coccinea* × *C. mollis*, an opinion seconded by the present writer. Leaves 2½"–3½". Flowers 1" wide; anthers 5–10, rose. Haws 1" long, bright crimson, very lustrous; 3–5 seeded.

C. erythropoda Ashe

= *C. cerronis* A. Nels.

CHOCOLATE HAWTHORN. CERRO HAWTHORN. From Wyoming south to Missouri, Texas, New Mexico, and Arizona. Named in 1900 (Greek *erythros*, red, and *podos*, a foot, in reference to the reddish leaf stem). In North American commerce since ≤1909. Very rare; grown almost exclusively within its native range. Thorns numerous, ¾"–2" long. Leaves 1"–3" long, very glossy, shallowly lobed, edged with fine gland-tipped teeth. Flowers ⅝"–¾" wide, anthers 5–8, pink to purple; styles usually 5. Haws deep cherry-red, then chocolate brown or mahogany, ⁵⁄₁₆". A drought tolerant shrub or small upright tree, to ca. 16' tall.

C. flava Ait.

= *C. aprica* Eggl., non Beadle

YELLOW FRUITED HAWTHORN. SUMMER HAW. HOGHAW. From S Georgia, N Florida and perhaps nearby in the SE United States, on dry sandy soil; now very rare or extinct in the wild. Introduced to cultivation in 1724 but not named until 1789. Possibly nearly extinct in cultivation. Trees called *C. flava* are nearly always really the closely related *C. aprica* or *C. flava* var. *lobata*. Thorns slender, ¾"–1¼" long. Leaves 1"–3" long. Flowers mostly solitary, ½" wide; anthers 20, red or purple; styles 4. Haws dark orange-brown, ripe in early October, dry and mealy, ½"–⅝" long, pear-shaped or ellipsoid, 4 seeded. Sparse flowers and fruit: not ornamental. Record: 30' × 3'11" × 36' Levy County, FL (1983).

C. flava var. *lobata* Lindl.

= *C. elliptica* Ait.
= *C. flava* hort., p.p., non Ait.

Origin unknown but almost certainly from the SE United States. Cultivated since 1789. Uncommon. Compared to *C. flava*, leaves more distinctly lobed. Flowers ¾" wide, in May or early June; anthers 10, purplish; styles 5. Haws greenish-yellow, stained red, ¾" long, ellipsoid or pear-shaped; pleasant flavored.

C. florentina—see *Malus florentina*

C. Fontanesiana—see *C. Calpodendron* and *C. crus-galli* var. *tenax*

C. 'Golden Giant'—see *C. mexicana*

C. grandiflora—see × *Cratæmespilus grandiflora*

C. × *grignonensis* Mouill.

(*C. mexicana* × *C. ?monogyna?*)

HYBRID MEXICAN HAWTHORN. GRIGNON HAWTHORN. EVERGREEN HAWTHORN. FRENCH HAWTHORN. A hybrid of mysterious origin. It might have been in cultivation as early as 1840. Usually authors assert that it is a *C. crus-galli* × *C. mexicana* hybrid first noticed ca. 1873 at Grignon, France [G. Krüssmann says Frankfurt, Germany]. Its name was published in 1890. It is planted widely in Holland and parts of France. In North America, apparently first marketed in a major way ≤1963 by Scanlon nursery of Ohio. It has generally been grafted at 7' on *C. monogyna* trunks. Its vigor and cold-hardiness is great. Leaves commonly ca. 2" long (on strong shoots to 3¾" × 3", with kidney-shaped stipules to 1" long). Leaves quite variably shaped, dark and glossy above, coated lightly with rough-feeling hairs; paler and notably hairy beneath. Tardily deciduous or partly evergreen. Few thorns to nearly thornless. It blooms later than many HAWTHORNS (mid-May to early June), and the flowers can fade to pink. Haws large, good to eat, to ⅞" long ⅝" wide, 1–2 seeded, red and exceptionally shiny, amazingly persistent even into the following spring, or to July.

C. 'Hooks'

= *C. crus-galli* 'Hooks'
(*C. crus-galli* × "*C. prunifolia*")

Origin unknown—maybe associated with Hooks nursery of Lake Zurich, IL. In commerce since ≤1978–79. Marketed as similar to *C. crus-galli*

(COCKSPUR HAWTHORN) but with few thorns (½"–1" long), disease-resistant foliage and smaller flowers. Foliage glossy, dense and dark. Haws red, ⅜"–⁹⁄₁₆" long, 3 seeded.

C. hupehensis Sarg.

HUPEH HAWTHORN. From W China. In W Hupeh province it was much cultivated for its edible fruit. Introduced to Western cultivation in 1907. Sold by some Ohio nurseries from the 1930s into the '50s, seldom since; rare. Leaves to 4" long, edged with glandular, incurved teeth; 3–4 lobed towards the tip. Flowers to ½" wide, numerous, hairless; anthers 20, red; styles 5. Haws dark red, to 1" wide, edible, 5 seeded. Thorns ca. ⅝" long. A small tree, ca. 16' tall.

C. intricata Lange

= C. biltmoreana Beadle
= C. Boyntonii Beadle
= C. coccinea L. (in part)

THICKET HAWTHORN. BILTMORE HAWTHORN. ALLEGHENY HAWTHORN. From eastern North America. Often offered by nurseries until after the 1960s; presently rare in commerce. Its specific epithet, published in 1895, means entangled, referring to the branches. Extremely variable. Leaves ¾"–3" long. Thorns slender, curved, 1"–2" long. Flowers ½"–¾" (1") wide; anthers 5–10, whitish, pale yellowish or pink-red. Haws ½" dull brown or red, with thin, dry flesh; (2) 3–5 seeded. Shrubby or a small tree. Records: 43' × 5'1" × 47' Oakland, MD (<1961); 23' × 7'6" × 42' Warrenton, VA (1982).

C. Jacki hort.—see C. lævigata 'Punicea'

C. Jackii Sarg.—see C. chrysocarpa

C. Korolkowii—see C. pinnatifida var. major and C. Wattiana

C. laciniata—see C. orientalis

C. lævigata (Poir.) DC.

= C. Oxyacantha auct., non L.
= C. oxyacanthoides Thuill.

ENGLISH MIDLAND HAWTHORN. ENGLISH WOODLAND HAWTHORN. From Europe. A highly variable species of great importance in horticulture. Previously the name Cratægus Oxyacantha (from Greek oxy, sharp, and akanthos, a thorn) was used to indicate both this species and the closely related C. monogyna (COMMON HAWTHORN). In North America, more specimens of C. lævigata and C. monogyna have been planted than all of the native HAWTHORNS combined. They are very common, and C. monogyna now grows wild in certain places here. In England, the name MIDLAND HAWTHORN refers to its growing mostly in the eastern counties and across the midlands, becoming rare in the north; WOODLAND HAWTHORN refers to the fact that C. lævigata most often is found in shady places on moist clay soils, usually in woods, especially in oakwoods. Compared to C. monogyna: blooms 7–14 days earlier; flowers with 2 styles instead of one, flowers borne in smaller clusters of 5–15 (not 12–20); leaves (¾"–2¼") darker, glossier, less lobed, less hairy; haws with 2 or 3 seeds rather than one. As a tree it is less stiff, less thorny, and smaller. C. lævigata is represented in North American cultivation almost exclusively by cultivars; the wild version with single white flowers is exceedingly rare. Some cultivars listed under this species are surely hybrids with C. monogyna. Such hybrids can be called C. × media. The great beauty of all these European HAWTHORNS is in their profuse flowers; for handsome foliage, fruit and fall color, North American natives are superior.

C. lævigata f. aurea (Loud.) Schneid.

= C. Oxyacantha var. xanthocarpa (Roem.) Lange
= C. Oxyacantha 'Fructu Luteo'
= C. monogyna 'Aurea'

YELLOWBERRY ENGLISH HAWTHORN. Cultivated since 1829 in Germany. Extremely rare in North America.

C. lævigata 'Autumn Glory'—see C. 'Autumn Glory'

C. lævigata 'Bicolor'

= C. lævigata 'Redrim'
= C. Oxyacantha 'Redrim'
= C. Oxyacantha 'Gumperi Bicolor'
?= C. Oxyacantha 'Pendula Rosea'
?= C. monogyna 'Roseopendula'

SINGLE DARK PINK ENGLISH HAWTHORN. Introduced <1860 by P.J. Gumpper of Stuttgart, Germany. Possibly a sport of C. lævigata 'Punicea', of identical habit, differing in floral color only. Flowers pink-red edged around a white center. Haws bright red, usually 2 seeded. Records: 31' × 4'11" × 45' Seattle, WA (1993); 30' × 5'2" × 40' Tacoma, WA (1993).

C. lævigata 'Candidoplena'

('Candida-plena')

DOUBLE WHITE ENGLISH HAWTHORN. Described in 1894 in the Netherlands. Extremely rare. Flowers double, remain pure white.

C. lævigata 'Charles X'

Origin unknown. Presumably named after the French King Charles X, the reactionary Bourbon who reigned from 1824 until deposed by the July Revolution of 1830. There is also a LILAC variety, with magenta-purple flowers, named 'Charles X' in the 1830s. This HAWTHORN was listed by U.S. nurseries from ≤1921 until at least the late 1930s. Flowers rosy-crimson, the color of those of *C. lævigata* 'Paul's Scarlet' but single, and slightly paler, with a yellow center.

C. lævigata 'Coccinea'—see C. lævigata 'Punicea'

C. lævigata Crimson Cloud™ PP 2679 (1966)

= *C. lævigata* 'Superba'

A cross of *C. lævigata* 'Charles X' and 'Paul's Scarlet'. Introduced by Princeton nursery of New Jersey. Commonly sold since the 1980s. Flowers exceptionally large, single, bright red, white star-centered. Resists leaf spot disease. Haws glossy red, oblong, single-seeded. Thornless.

C. lævigata 'Flore Plena Rosea'—see C. lævigata 'Rosea Flore Pleno'

C. lævigata 'Flore Pleno'—see C. lævigata 'Plena'

C. lævigata 'Gireoudii'

Introduced in 1899 by Späth nursery of Germany. Extremely rare in North America. A bushy, wide-branching little tree. The leaves on its lengthy summer-shoots are first dark pinkish, then variegated white, at length green.

C. lævigata 'Masekii'

DOUBLE VERY PALE PINK ENGLISH HAWTHORN. Originated by V. and K. Masek's nursery of Turnov, Czechoslovakia. Introduced in 1899 by Späth nursery of Germany. Very rare in North America. Offered in 1954 by W.B. Clarke nursery of California; and in 1966 by Wayside nursery of Mentor, OH. Record: 42' × 7'8" 47' Toppenish, WA (1993).

C. lævigata 'Mutabilis'

= *C. lævigata* 'Roseoplena'
= *C. Oxyacantha* 'Roseoplena'

DOUBLE PINK FADING TO WHITE ENGLISH HAWTHORN. Originated <1867 in the Netherlands. Extremely rare; the white is unattractive.

C. lævigata 'Paulii'—see C. lævigata 'Paul's Scarlet'

C. lævigata 'Paul's Scarlet'

= *C. Oxyacantha* 'Paul's New Double Scarlet'
= *C. Oxyacantha* 'Kermesina Plena'
= *C. Oxyacantha* 'Splendens' (cf. *C. lævigata* 'Punicea' and 'Rosea')
= *C. Oxy.* 'Coccinea Flore Pleno' (cf. *C. lævigata* 'Rosea Flore Pleno')
= *C. Oxyacantha* 'Paulii'
= *C. Oxyacantha* 'Flore Pleno Paulii'
= *C. Oxyacantha* 'Coccinea Paulii'
= *C. Oxyacantha* 'Coccinea Plena'

DOUBLE "SCARLET" ENGLISH HAWTHORN. Originated ca. 1858 as a branch sport on a double pink ['Rosea Flore Pleno'] HAWTHORN of Christopher Boyd of Cheshuntstreet, near Waltham Cross, Hertfordshire, England. Propagated by nurseryman William Paul (1822–1905). The commonest cultivar. In Seattle, this cultivar is more prone than any other HAWTHORN to defoliation from leaf spot fungus. Flowers ⅝" wide, inodorous; 37 petals, no anthers. Color not really scarlet, rather rosy crimson. Haws wider than long. Records: 41' × 6'0" × 32' Yakima, WA (1990); 37' × 7'1" × 43' Walla Walla, WA (1993).

C. lævigata 'Plena'

= *C. lævigata* 'Flore Pleno'
= *C. Oxyacantha* 'Multiplex'
= *C. Oxyacantha* 'Pleniflora'
= *C. Oxyacantha* 'Flore Pleno'
= *C. Oxyacantha* 'Albo Pleno'
= *C. monogyna* 'Albo Plena'

DOUBLE WHITE FADING TO PINK ENGLISH HAWTHORN. Originated ca. 1700 in France. Common. Seldom sold since 1960s. Latin *plena* means full or plump; having extra petals; *multiplex* means with many similar parts. Looks exactly like 'Paul's Scarlet' in habit, leaf and haws. Resists leaf spot defoliation. Flowers ½"+ wide, inodorous, white fading to pink, 29–33 petals, no anthers. Haws usually 2 seeded, sometimes 3 seeded. Record: 30' × 4'0" × 31' Tacoma, WA (1993).

C. lævigata 'Princeps Simplex'

Origin and description unknown. Sold in 1920s and '30s by Bobbink & Atkins nursery of New York. The name, translated from Latin, suggests early blooming, single flowered.

C. *lævigata* 'Punicea'

= C. *lævigata* 'Coccinea'
= C. *lævigata* 'Splendens' (see also 'Pauls's Scarlet' and 'Rosea')
= C. *Oxy.* 'Splendens' (cf. C. *lævigata* 'Pauls's Scarlet' and 'Rosea')
= C. *Oxyacantha* 'Rosa Superba'
= C. *Oxyacantha* 'Flore Puniceo'
= C. *Oxyacantha* 'Coccinea'
= C. *monogyna* 'Punicea'
= C. *rubra* 'Splendens'
= C. *Jacki* hort.

SINGLE RED ENGLISH HAWTHORN. Raised in Scotland; introduced in 1828 by Conrad Loddiges and Sons nursery. Somewhat commonly sold in North America until perhaps the 1960s. *Punicea* = scarlet. *Coccinea* = red. Tree broad and low, much like 'Bicolor' yet very unlike 'Paul's Scarlet' and 'Plena'. Pale pink buds open to flowers with dark pink-red insides and much paler backsides; 5/8" wide, anthers 20, styles 1 or 2. Haws 3/8"–7/16" long and nearly as wide, dark red; (1) 2 seeded. Confused with its sport 'Bicolor' (white center and pale red rim). Record: 32' × 4'3" × 43' Seattle, WA (1993).

C. *lævigata* 'Punicea Flore Pleno'—see C. *lævigata* 'Rosea Flore Pleno'

C. *lævigata* 'Redrim'—see C. *lævigata* 'Bicolor'

C. *lævigata* 'Rosea'

= C. *lævigata* 'Splendens' (see also 'Pauls's Scarlet' and 'Punicea')
= C. *Oxy.* 'Splendens' (cf. C. *lævigata* 'Pauls's Scarlet' and 'Punicea')
= C. *Oxyacantha* 'Flore Rubro'

SINGLE PALE PINK ENGLISH HAWTHORN. Cultivated in 1736 in Holland. Introduced to England <1790. Named officially in 1796. Rare in North America. Flowers light pink, white-centered; single. Record: a trunk 5'11" around in Leiden, Holland (1938; *pl.* 1740).

C. *lævigata* 'Rosea Flore Pleno'

= C. *lævigata* 'Flore Plena Rosea'
= C. *lævigata* 'Punicea Flore Pleno'
= C. *lævigata* 'Rubra Plena'
= C. *Oxyacantha* 'Flore Plena Rosea'
= C. *Oxyacantha* 'Rosea Plena' or 'Roseo-plena'
= C. *Oxyacantha* 'Rubra ('Rubro') Plena'
= C. *Oxy.* 'Coccinea Flore Pleno' (cf. C. *lævigata* 'Paul's Scarlet')
= C. *monogyna* 'Rubro Plena'

DOUBLE PINK (OR RED) ENGLISH HAWTHORN. Originated <1832 in Europe. The parent of 'Paul's Scarlet', differing only in flower color. Flowers carmine-pink; double. Record: 37' × 4'10" × 31' Tacoma, WA (1993).

C. *lævigata* 'Roseoplena'—see C. *lævigata* 'Mutabilis'

C. *lævigata* 'Rubra Plena'—see C. *lævigata* 'Rosea Flore Pleno'

C. *lævigata* 'Salisburifolia'

= C. *contorta* hort.
= C. *monogyna* 'Pink Corkscrew'
= C. *monogyna* 'Contorta Coccinea'

DOUBLE SCARLET CONTORTED BRANCHED ENGLISH HAWTHORN. SNAKE HAWTHORN. Origin unknown; in European commerce ≤1874. Imported to North America from Europe in 1957. In commerce here since ≤1962–63. Uncommon. Tree dwarf, to 14' tall, thornless, the branches twisted in zigzag fashion. Flowers double and similar to those of 'Paul's Scarlet'. Haws also similar. Leaves sometimes twisted as well, with few and obtuse lobes somewhat like those of a GINKGO tree. Named after an alternate generic name for *Ginkgo biloba: Salisburia* (commemorating English botanist Richard Anthony Salisbury, 1761–1829).

C. *lævi.* 'Splendens'—see C. *lævi.* 'Paul's Scarlet', 'Punicea' and 'Rosea'

C. *lævigata* 'Superba'—see C. *lævigata* Crimson Cloud™

C. × *Lavallei* Hérincq *ex* Lav.

= C. × *Carrierei* Vauv. *ex* Carr.

CARRIÈRE HAWTHORN. HYBRID COCKSPUR HAWTHORN. LAVALLÉ HAWTHORN. FRENCH HAWTHORN. Originated ca. 1870 as a seedling of a MEXICAN HAWTHORN (C. *mexicana*). Named in 1880. In North America since ≤1898; common since the 1920s. The pollen parent is unknown but widely conjectured to be C. *crusgalli*. Pierre Alphonse Martin Lavallée (1836–1884), a French horticulturist, founded the Arboretum Segrez, where this tree arose. There are two clones, both propagated by grafting on C. *monogyna*, COMMON HAWTHORN. The first is vigorous, sets few fruits, has reddish young twigs. Second is less vigorous, sets more and larger fruit, and has greenish young twigs. The second may be the clone 'Carrierei', named in 1883 after French horti-culturist Elie Abel Carrière (1818–1896). Leaves 1½"–4½" long; slender, dark green, held late into fall. Flowers ¾"–⅞"; anthers 15–20, red or yellow; styles 1–2 (3). Haws ¾" long, very showy orange-red, (1) 2–3 seeded. Thorns stout, primarily on young specimens; with age the tree lets down its guard. A superb ornamental. Records: 43' × 5'2" × 34' Seattle, WA (1988); 36' × 6'10" × 49' Seattle, WA (1993).

C. lobata—see × Cratæmespilus grandiflora

C. lucida—see C. × persimilis 'MacLeod'

C. macracantha Lodd. ex Loud.
(macrantha)
= C. succulenta var. macracantha (Lodd.) Eggl.
= C. coccinea var. macracantha (Lodd.) Dudley
= C. Douglasii hort.
= Mespilus macracantha Wenz.

LONG SPINE HAWTHORN. SPIKE HAWTHORN. From much of North America. Introduced to cultivation in 1819. Uncommon in nurseries, and very rarely offered in recent years. A shrub of dense habit, or small 15' tree. Thorns abundant, slender, somewhat curved, to 5"+ long. Leaves 1"–4" long. Flowers ⅔"–¾" wide; anthers (5) 10 (12), pale yellow or rarely pink, regular-sized (not very small as in the related C. succulenta); styles 2–3. Haws ¼"–⅛" wide, very lustrous bright crimson, usually remaining hard and dry until late in the season unlike those of C. succulenta; 2–3 seeded. Both this species and C. succulenta bear large, coral-red expanding bud scales. The fall color can be attractive.

C. macracantha var. succulenta—see C. succulenta

C. mandschurica—see C. chlorosarca

C. Marshallii Eggl.
= C. apiifolia (Marsh.) Michx. 1803, non Med. 1793
PARSLEY(LEAF) HAWTHORN. From the SE United States, in moist soil. Named in 1908 for Humphrey Marshall (1722–1801) who first described it in 1785, as Mespilus apiifolia. Very rare in cultivation. Flowers ½"–⅝" wide, early-blooming, in hairy clusters; anthers 10–20; styles and seeds (1) 2 (3). Haws bright red, ⅓" long. A handsome tree, in full bloom a dainty, glistening white. Leaves really are parsley-like, ¾"–1¾"; fall color lively tones of yellow and orange. Thorns 1"–1½". Records: 33' × 1'4" × 23' Gainesville, FL (1974); 24' × 2'1" × 20' Tyler County, TX (1993).

C. × media Bechst.
= C. × ovalis Kitaibel
(C. monogyna × C. lævigata)
HYBRID ENGLISH HAWTHORN. Named in 1797. The single white flowered form of this hybrid is not culti-vated intentionally, although is occasionally en-countered as a chance seedling. Some pink-flowered garden cultivars listed under C. lævigata are surely hybrids of this background.

C. mexicana Moc. & Sessé
= C. pubescens (H.B.K.) Steud., non C. Presl
= C. stipulacea Lodd. ex Loud.
= C. stipulosa (H.B.K.) Steud.
= Mespilus mexicana (Moc. & Sessé) DC.
= Mespilus stipulosa H.B.K.
= Mespilus pubescens H.B.K.

MEXICAN HAWTHORN. From Mexico, Guatemala, Ecuador and Peru. A Mexican name is Tejocote (Texocote). Introduced to English cultivation <1824. In California cultivation since ≤1868. Rare. In Mexico it varies from a thorny, small-fruited wild form, to nearly thornless, large-fruited cultivated trees. Attempts have been made to separate the cat-egories nominally, but the intermediacy of some specimens defies pigeon-holing. Since the thorny, small-fruited trees are not cultivated for fruit or orna-ment, the following description refers to the variants grown. Flowers open during March and April, ¾"–1" wide, in wooly-white clusters of 2–9; anthers 15–23, creamy, pink, or red; styles 2–5. Haws ¾"–1½" (2") long, golden- or orange-yellow when ripe, lightly hairy, 2–5 seeded; edible but no delicacy. Thorns few, sometimes none, to 2" long. Leaves essentially ever-green (some orange and red autumnal color), very hairy, usually unlobed, sometimes weakly lobed on suckers, coarsely toothed, 1½"–4" long; stipules modest to prominent. The only cultivar selected for ornamental planting is 'Golden Giant' sold by W.B. Clarke nursery of San José, CA, from ca. 1941 into the '50s. It has lovely extra large golden fruit, is thornless or nearly so, and quite evergreen. A small tree, rarely more than 20' × 3'0", but capable of reaching 30' tall. The cold hardiness is unknown. Two related hardy trees that look very similar are + Cratægomespilus Dardarii and × Cratæmespilus grandiflora.

C. mollis (T. & G.) Scheele
= C. coccinea var. mollis T. & G.
= C. acerifolia hort., non Moench
= C. tiliæfolia K. Koch

DOWNY HAWTHORN. SUMMER HAWTHORN. RED

HAWTHORN. TURKEY APPLE. From eastern North America. The specific epithet, published in 1840, is Latin for *soft*; referring to the hairy foliage. Common in cultivation. Variable. Can be thornless or bear numerous short thorns 1"–2" (3"). Leaves about as large as any in the genus, broad-based, 2"–6⅝". Flowers ½"–1" wide, in densely downy clusters; anthers 20, yellowish or rarely pink; styles 4–5. Haws round to pear-shaped, scarlet, to 1¼" diameter, good to eat in October. Records: 52' × 8'9" × 62' Grosse Ile, MI (1972); 35' × 8'11" × 60' West Allis, WI (1961).

C. mollis var. arkansana (Sarg.) stat. nov.
= *C. arkansana* Sarg.

From Arkansas. Introduced to cultivation in 1883. Named in 1901. Commonly cultivated. Leaves 2"–3" long. Thorns ⅓"–½" long. Flowers nearly 1" wide; anthers 20, styles 5. Leaves thick. Haws ¾"–1" long, bright crimson, very lustrous, ripening later. Fall color bright clear yellow in late October-November. C. Sargent said "unsurpassed late in autumn in the beauty of its brilliant abundant fruits long persistent on the branches."

C. mollis var. arnoldiana (Sarg.) stat. nov.
= *C. arnoldiana* Sarg.

From Connecticut and E Massachusetts. The specific epithet, published in 1901, refers to the Arnold Arboretum, where the tree was first found, growing wild on a bank near the Bussey Greenhouse. Common in cultivation. Leaves dark and shiny, 2"–3" long. Thorns 2"–3". Flowers ¾" wide, the clusters downy-hairy; anthers 10, yellow; 3–4 (5) styles. Haws bright crimson, ¾" long, ripe mid-August and dropping soon; 3–4 seeded. Branchlets zigzag. Very similar to var. *submollis*.

C. mollis var. Ellwangeriana—see C. Ellwangeriana

C. mollis 'Selection No. 1'
In the 1960s and early '70s, Ohio nurseryman Ed Scanlon sold this selection from seedling trees he had planted on a Cleveland street ca. 1955. His description: "Upsweeping branching habit; coarse gray-green leaf, slightly tomentose; fruit very showy and persistent." Specimens seen in Oregon are in no sense *C. mollis* clones, but likely represent a *C. crus-galli* or *C. punctata* variation or hybrid. Leaves broad, practically hairless, thick-textured, semi-glossy, yellow in fall, to 4" long, unlobed or can have occasional shallow shoulder lobes; 6–8 vein pairs. Thorns few, to 1½" long. Haws to ⅝" long, nearly as wide; deep red, prominently punctate; soft; sepals weakly hairy, entire or nearly so; flesh yellowish-green, juicy and good; 3–5 seeded. Fruit messy on the ground when it drops in November.

C. mollis 'Selection No. 2'
Scanlon's description (comparing it to 'Selection No. 1'): "Differs quite radically. Glossy leaf; loose, open head. Fruit showy."

C. mollis var. submollis (Sarg.) stat. nov.
= *C. submollis* Sarg.

QUÉBEC HAWTHORN. PILGRIMS' WHITETHORN. From SE Canada, NE United States. Named in 1901. Common in cultivation. Leaves 2"–3½" (5") long. Flowers in clusters of 9–17; ⅔"–⅞" wide, with a pink heart, anthers 10, creamy or yellow, styles 5. Haws ⅝"–1" wide, 3–4 (5) seeded; delicious. Thorns to 2⅛" (3") long.

C. monogyna Jacq.
= *C. Oxyacantha* var. *monogyna* Loud.

COMMON HAWTHORN. ENGLISH HAWTHORN. MAY (TREE). SINGLESEED HAWTHORN. WHITE THORN. QUICK-THORN. ONESEED HAWTHORN. From Europe, N Africa, and W Asia. Often mislabelled as *C. Oxyacantha*. It was not regarded as a separate species from *C. lævigata* until 1775. Many cultivars sold as *C. lævigata* selections are really partly or wholly offspring of *C. monogyna*. Probably the strongest and most common HAWTHORN of all. Widely naturalized in North America. Hybridizes with *C. punctata* (DOTTED HAWTHORN) and *C. Douglasii* (BLACK HAWTHORN). Leaves 1"–3" long, deeply lobed. Flowers ⅓"–½" wide, often pink tinged when they age; anthers 20, reddish; style 1 (hence the name *monogyna*). Haws ⅓"–½" long, purple to bright red. QUICK signifies *live*, and was probably applied because *live* hedges were made of HAWTHORN instead of fences of cut sprays of trees; WHITETHORN derives from the profusion of its white flowers. More thorny than *C. lævigata*. Records: 64' × 5'3" × 34' Seattle, WA (1988); 43' ×

12'7" × 48' Studley Park, Yorkshire, England (ca. 1835); 42' × 14'6" × 63' Holwood House, Kent, England (1888); 37' × 9'3" × 58' Mt. Vernon, WA (1992).

C. *monogyna* 'Albo Plena'—see *C. lævigata* 'Plena'

C. *monogyna* 'Aurea'—see *C. lævigata* f. *aurea*

C. *monogyna* 'Biflora'
= *C. monogyna* 'Præcox'

GLASTONBURY THORN. Legend has it this tree originated ca. A.D. 31 when Joseph of Arimathæa thrust his staff into the ground on Wearyall Hill, on the Isle of Avalon, later known as Glastonbury. Glastonbury is ca. 25 miles south of Bristol, England. A Cromwellian who destroyed the GLASTONBURY THORN was stabbed in one eye. The name *biflora* was published in 1770 and means flowering twice; *præcox* means early or first. This clone first blooms as early as November, but tradition enjoys reporting a Christmas bloom (which in the pre-1752 Julian calendar was in early January); its second bloom is in May. The first documentation concerning this celebrated cultivar dates from 1502. In North America it is very rare. One was planted in 1901 at Washington, D.C.; another is at the Brooklyn Botanic Garden, NY. Scanlon nursery of Ohio sold the tree in the late 1950s and early 1960s. Because of the demand by gullible buyers, some nurseries might have circulated mere seedlings or other imposters under this name. One such in the Seattle arboretum is doing well if it manages to begin blooming by late March.

C. *monogyna* 'Compacta'
= *C. monogyna* 'Globosa'
= *C. monogyna* 'Inermis Compacta'

GLOBE HAWTHORN. Introduced in 1907–08 by Späth nursery of Germany. Uncommon in North America. Scanlon nursery of Ohio began selling it in the mid-1950s. It is still in commerce. Almost invariably it is sold topgrafted, since left to its own devices it is a mere bush, without thorns or treehood. Topgrafted, it is made into a slow, compact, lollipop tree 12'–14' feet tall. Thornless (Latin *inermis* means unarmed; without thorns).

C. *monogyna* 'Contorta Coccinea'—see *C. lævigata* 'Salisburifolia'

C. *monogyna* 'Fastigiata'—see *C. monogyna* f. *stricta*

C. *monogyna* 'Filicifolia'—see *C. monogyna* 'Pteridifolia'

C. *monogyna* 'Flexuosa'
= *C. Oxyacantha* 'Tortuosa'

Originated or at any rate introduced ≤1838 by nurseryman Smith of Ayr in London. Rare in North America; here since ≤1960. Though it has single white flowers, it is confused with the double pink flowered *C. lævigata* 'Salisburifolia'. In Latin, *flexuosa* means bent alternately in opposite directions; zig-zag, alluding to the twisted branching.

C. *monogyna* 'Globosa'—see *C. monogyna* 'Compacta'

C. *monogyna* 'Inermis Compacta'—see *C. monogyna* 'Compacta'

C. *monogyna* 'Kermesina Plena'—see *C. lævigata* 'Paul's Scarlet'

C. *monogyna* 'Monumentalis'—see *C. monogyna* f. *stricta*

C. *monogyna* f. *pendula* (Loud.) Rehd.
WEEPING HAWTHORN. Originated ≤1838 in Europe. In North American commerce ≤1884. Uncommon. Branches gracefully pendulous. Record: 38' × 7'0" × 36' Bellingham, WA (1987).

C. *monogyna* 'Pink Corkscrew'—see *C. lævigata* 'Salisburifolia'

C. *monogyna* 'Præcox'—see *C. monogyna* 'Biflora'

C. *monogyna* 'Pteridifolia'
= *C. monogyna* 'Filicifolia'

FERNLEAF HAWTHORN. Originated ≤1838 in England. In North America since ≤1949; very rare. Leaves deeply lobed, wide fan-shaped and incised, lobes with dense crispate margins. Flowers white. Name from Latin *pteris*, a fern, and *folium*, a leaf.

C. *monogyna* 'Punicea'—see *C. lævigata* 'Punicea'

C. *monogyna* 'Pyramidalis'—see *C. monogyna* f. *stricta*

C. *monogyna* 'Roseopendula'—see *C. lævigata* 'Bicolor'

C. monogyna 'Rubro Plena'—see C. lævigata 'Rosea Flore Pleno'

C. monogyna f. stricta (Loud.) Zab.
= C. monogyna 'Fastigiata'
= C. monogyna 'Pyramidalis'
= C. monogyna 'Monumentalis'
= C. Oxyacantha 'Rigida'

PYRAMIDAL HAWTHORN. Originated ca. 1825 in a bed of seedlings in Messrs. Ronald's nursery, England. In North American nurseries since ≤1900. Common. More than one clone in circulation. Branching strictly upright, yet eventually splaying out in age.

C. × mordenensis Boom
(C. succulenta × C. lævigata)

Two cold-hardy HAWTHORN hybrids raised in Canada and grown primarily in northern regions. The epithet *mordenensis* refers to the agricultural research station at Morden, Manitoba.

C. × mordenensis 'Snowbird'

A 1952 seedling of C. × mordenensis 'Toba'. Introduced in 1967 by Morden research station of Manitoba. Common. Leaves dark green. Flowers double, white. Haws sparse, bright crimson, ca. ½". Hardier than 'Toba' and with better tree form, being more upright. Thornless.

C. × mordenensis 'Toba'
= C. 'Toba'

TOBA HAWTHORN. Raised in 1935 at Morden research station of Manitoba by pollinating C. succulenta with C. lævigata 'Paul's Scarlet'. Named and introduced ≤1954. Introduced commercially ≤1959. Common. In early spring it flushes green, then blooms. Leaves irregularly lobed, glossy, ca. 2⅜" long (on suckers to 4" long with 1" stipules). Flowers double, begin as gleaming white buds, opening white then fading to pink, of 25–30 petals; anthers all turned into petals; styles 2–5. Haws sparsely borne, red, shiny, ca. ½" wide; several (ca. 4) tiny seeds; flesh pink, good-eating. Thornless except a few on suckers. Trunk often twisty. Records: 24½' × 7'0" × 30' Beauport, Québec (<1994); 19½' × 2'6" × 22½' Victoria, B.C. (1994).

C. nitida (Engelm.) Sarg.
= C. viridis var. nitida Engelm. ex B. & B.
?(C. crus-galli × C. viridis)

SHINING HAWTHORN. GLOSSY HAWTHORN. Possibly a hybrid. Introduced to cultivation in 1883. Uncommon. The Latin name means shining, referring to its foliage. Trunk interestingly fluted. Leaves 1"–3½" long, slender, shiny; orange fall color. Flowers ¾" wide, many per hairless cluster; 15–20 pale yellow anthers; 2–5 styles. Haws orange-red, 2–5 seeded. Leaves lightly hairy above while young. Broad-crowned. A splendid ornamental in flowers, foliage, fruit and form. Record: 22' × 4'6" × 36' Seattle, WA (1988; *pl.* 1947).

C. odoratissima—see C. orientalis

C. opaca H. & A.

RIVERFLAT HAWTHORN. MAY HAWTHORN. MAY HAW. WESTERN MAYHAW. APPLE HAW. From the Coastal Plain of E Texas to SW Alabama; most common in Louisiana. Named in 1835. Closely related to C. æstivalis, and likely of similar value in ornamental horticulture. It blooms 2 weeks before C. æstivalis. The name *opaca* refers to the dull haws. Flowers ½"–¾" (1") wide in clusters of 3–6, in February-March, before leafing; anthers 20, reddish or rose; styles (4) 5. Leaf ± sinuately lobed, underside very hairy, 1"–2¾"; top usually matte. Haws can be solid red, but are usually yellowish, ½"–1¼". Thorns ¾"–1⅔". Records: 29' × 3'9" × 36' Jones County, MS (1989); trunks to 7'7" around cited by T.O. Warren. It can yield immensely: one tree bore 84 gallons of fruit. Cultivars for fruit include: **'Stark LA–No. 1'**, **'Super Spur'**, and **'Warren'**.

C. orientalis Bieb.
= C. laciniata Ucria—misapplied
= C. odoratissima Hornemann 1819, non (Andrews) Don 1832
= C. tanacetifolia hort., non (Poir.) Pers.
= C. apiifolia hort., non (Marsh.) Michx., non Med.

ORIENTAL HAWTHORN. SILVER HAWTHORN. BLUE HAWTHORN. From SE Europe and SW Asia. Introduced to cultivation in 1810. Very rare; offered sparingly by a few nurseries since the 1960s. On its own roots it grows too slowly for standard nursery production, so is often grafted on C. monogyna. Even then its motto could be: "What, me hurry?!" A shrub or small tree, nearly thornless. Leaves 1"–2", "frosty" bluish-gray and very hairy; very deeply lobed into slender segments, usually notably short-stemmed. Flowers ⅝"–¾" wide, opening later than those of most HAWTHORNS (in early June, along with C. crus-galli); anthers 20, purple; styles 2–5. Haws fleshy and succulent,

½"–1", brick- to coral-red or yellowish-orange, usually wider than long; seeds 2–5. A tree of superb ornamental virtues in its form, foliage and especially its lovely edible fruit. Record: 19' × 1'8½" × 20' Seattle, WA (1994; *pl.* 1945).

C. orientalis 'Blue Hawthorn'
= C. 'Blue Haw'
?= C. orientalis var. sanguinea (Schrad.) Loud.
?= C. Schraderiana Ledeb.

BLUE HAWTHORN. BLUE LEAVED HAWTHORN. SILVER HAWTHORN. More than one tree has been sold under the name BLUE HAWTHORN. Scanlon nursery of Ohio might have been the first, in the early 1960s. It seems both typical *C. orientalis* and a distinctive clone (here treated as a cultivar) were marketed under the name BLUE HAWTHORN. Although the foliage of the two trees is passably similar, their haws are very different. Both grow miserably slow on their own roots, so are grafted on *C. monogyna*. Both are small nearly thornless trees of ferny, hairy, bluish-green foliage, and large tasty haws. The clone here described as 'Blue Hawthorn' is less hairy than typical *C. orientalis*, with darker foliage, longer leaf stems and pedicels. It stays green late into fall, and bears ¾" wide, usually 4-seeded deep purple less ornamental haws (ox-blood red reports Forest Farm nursery of Williams, OR).

C. Oxyacantha—see *C. lævigata*

C. Oxyacantha 'Albo Pleno'—see *C. lævigata* 'Plena'

C. Oxyacantha 'Autumn Glory'—see *C.* 'Autumn Glory'

C. Oxyacantha 'Coccinea'—see *C. lævigata* 'Punicea'

C. Oxyacantha 'Coccinea Flore Pleno'—see *C. lævigata* 'Paul's Scarlet' and 'Rosea Flore Pleno'

C. Oxyacantha 'Coccinea Paulii'—see *C. lævigata* 'Paul's Scarlet'

C. Oxyacantha 'Coccinea Plena'—see *C. lævigata* 'Paul's Scarlet'

C. Oxy. 'Flore Plena Rosea'—see *C. lævigata* 'Rosea Flore Pleno'

C. Oxyacantha 'Flore Pleno'—see *C. lævigata* 'Plena'

C. Oxy. 'Flore Pleno Paulii'—see *C. lævigata* 'Paul's Scarlet'

C. Oxyacantha 'Flore Puniceo'—see *C. lævigata* 'Punicea'

C. Oxyacantha 'Flore Rubro'—see *C. lævigata* 'Rosea'

C. Oxyacantha 'Fructu Luteo'—see *C. lævigata* f. *aurea*

C. Oxyacantha 'Gumperi Bicolor'—see *C. lævigata* 'Bicolor'

C. Oxy. 'Kermesina Plena'—see *C. lævigata* 'Paul's Scarlet'

C. Oxyacantha var. *monogyna*—see *C. monogyna*

C. Oxyacantha 'Multiplex'—see *C. lævigata* 'Plena'

C. Oxyacantha 'Paulii'—see *C. lævigata* 'Paul's Scarlet'

C. Oxy. 'Paul's New Double Scarlet'—see *C. lævig.* 'Paul's Scarlet'

C. Oxyacantha 'Pendula Rosea'—see *C. lævigata* 'Bicolor'

C. Oxyacantha 'Pleniflora'—see *C. lævigata* 'Plena'

C. Oxyacantha 'Redrim'—see *C. lævigata* 'Bicolor'

C. Oxyacantha 'Rigida'—see *C. monogyna* f. *stricta*

C. Oxyacantha 'Rosa Superba'—see *C. lævigata* 'Punicea'

C. Oxy. 'Rosea Plena' or 'Roseo-plena'—see *C. lævi.* 'Rosea Flore Pleno'

C. Oxyacantha 'Roseoplena'—see *C. lævigata* 'Mutabilis'

C. Oxy. 'Rubra Plena' or 'Rubro Plena'—see *C. lævi.* 'Rosea Flore Pleno'

C. Oxy. 'Splendens'—see *C. lævi.* 'Paul's Scarlet', 'Punicea' and 'Rosea'

C. *Oxyacantha* 'Tortuosa'—see C. *monogyna* 'Flexuosa'

C. *Oxyacantha* var. *xanthocarpa*—see C. *lævigata* f. *aurea*

C. *oxyacanthoides*—see C. *lævigata*

C. *pedicellata*—see C. *coccinea*

C. *pedicellata* var. *Ellwangeriana*—see C. *Ellwangeriana*

C. *peregrina* Sarg.

PERSIAN HAWTHORN. Originated ≤1873, probably in SE Europe or W Asia. Named in 1913. In North American commerce ≤1926; seldom if ever offered since the 1960s. A small tree, to 30' tall. Leaves to 5" long, hairy beneath, lobed. Flowers ¾" wide, in hairy clusters. Haws ½"–1" long, dull purple. The Latin *peregrina* means of a foreign country;strange, exotic. Possibly a hybrid of C. *mollis* (DOWNY HAWTHORN) and C. *nigra* (HUNGARIAN HAWTHORN). The latter species is from SE Europe, and related to C. *monogyna* but black-fruited.

C. × *persimilis* Sarg.
= C. × *prunifolia* Pers.
= C. *crus-galli* var. *prunifolia* T. & G.
= *Mespilus prunifolia* Poir. *ex* Lam. 1797, non Marsh. 1785

PLUMLEAF HAWTHORN. BROADLEAF COCKSPUR HAWTHORN. From New York and E Ontario near Niagara Falls. Possibly a hybrid of C. *crus-galli* with C. *macracantha* or C. *succulenta*. Cultivated since the late 1700s. Common. More than one clone exists, the most prized cited below as 'MacLeod'. Branching less layered than on C. *crus-galli*, leaves broader. Twigs hairless, purple-brown. Leaves 1½"–3". Thorns few to numerous, purple, ¾"–3". Blooms earlier than C. *crus-galli*, late May or early June. Flowers ⅔"–¾" wide; styles 2–3 (4); anthers 10–20, pink or red. Haws ⅓"–⅝" long, rich red, dropping in late October or early November with the leaves; 2–3 seeded.

C. × *persimilis* 'MacLeod'
= C. *persimilis* 'Prunifolia'
= C. *crus-galli* 'Prunifolia'
= C. *crus-galli* var. *splendens* Ait. fil.
= C. *crus-galli* 'Splendens'
= C. *crus-galli* 'Lucida'
= C. *lucida* Mill.

The name 'MacLeod' (after M.M. MacLeod) was proposed in 1988 by *Cratægus* expert J.B. Phipps, to identify the *persimilis* clone most widely cultivated, known for "glowing red" or "brilliant red and orange" fall color and haws that drop comparatively early, in October. This clone has long been more common in European cultivation than here. It has been sold in North America since ≤1884, usually as C. *crus-galli* 'Splendens'. Leaves glossy, dark-green, purplish-red in fall. A small, broad tree. Record: 19½' × 4'11" Paris, France (1888).

C. *persimilis* 'Prunifolia'—see C. × *persimilis* 'MacLeod'

C. × *persistens* Sarg.

Originated when raised in 1876 at the Arnold Arboretum, from seeds sent from Paris under the name C. *lobata* (? C. *flava* var. *lobata*, or × *Cratæmespilus grandiflora*). In commerce ≤1917 into at least the mid-1950s. Uncommon. Thought to be a hybrid of C. *crus-galli* (COCKSPUR HAWTHORN). The other parent unknown. Remarkable for the persistence of its leaves. C.S. Sargent, naming it in 1913, exclaimed "it retains its leaves as green as they were in summer after those of all the other Hawthorns have fallen, and the fruit, unchanged in color and perfectly solid, remains on the branches long after Christmas,making it the most conspicuous of all the winter-fruiting plants which are hardy in New England." A low, flat tree. Thorns numerous, 1"–2" long. Flowers appear in mid-June, ¾" wide; anthers 15–20; styles 2–3. Haws ⅝" long, crimson, not lustrous; flesh yellow, mealy, of good flavor. Leaf very shiny, slightly hairy on veins above, hairless beneath; 2"–3¼" long, unlobed.

C. *Phænopyrum* (L. fil.) Med.
= C. *cordata* (Mill.) Ait.
= C. *populifolia* Walt.
= C. *acerifolia* Moench
= *Mespilus Phænopyrum* L. fil.

WASHINGTON HAWTHORN. VIRGINIA HAWTHORN. From the eastern U.S. Very common in cultivation. First named in 1781. *Phænopyrum* in Greek means having the appearance of a pear, possibly referring to the similar flowers. Nurseries still often use the name C. *cordata* (Latin for heart-shaped). Named WASHINGTON HAWTHORN because it was first commercially grown on a large scale by a Georgetown nurseryman in the late 1700s. Greatly valued and very common. Its flowers are inferior to many, but in most respects it is outstandingly ornamental. Leaves shiny,

3–7 lobed, broadly triangular, 1"–3" long, orange and scarlet in fall. Thorns 1½"–3". Flowers ½" wide, from late May into early July; anthers (18) 20, pale yellow; styles 2–5. Haws ¼"–⅜" wide, (3–) 5 seeded. Tree slender, brittle. Records: 45' × 2'3" × 25' Seattle, WA (1988); 33' × 4'6" × 39' Chattanooga National Cemetery, TN (1987); 30' × 5'2" × 32' Abingdon, VA (1989).

C. *Phænopyrum* 'Clark'

Origin unknown; in commerce <1975. Very rare. Heavy-fruiting.

C. *Phænopyrum* 'Fastigiata'

Found by B.H. Slavin in Rochester, NY. Described by A.D. Slavin in 1930–31. Cultivated to a minor extent from the 1930s into the '50s; virtually never grown since perhaps the mid-'80s.

C. *Phænopyrum* 'Manbeck'

Origin unknown but presumably associated with Manbeck nursery of Avon, OH. In commerce since ≤1986. Described as an improved selection.

C. *Phænopyrum* 'PNI 1661'—see C. *Phænopyrum* Princeton Sentry®

C. *Phænopyrum* Princeton Sentry®

= C. *Phænopyrum* 'PNI 1661'

Introduced in the 1980s by Princeton nursery of New Jersey. Very few if any thorns.

C. *pinnatifida* Bge.

From NE Asia. Named in 1833. Introduced to cultivation in 1860, in Russia. In North America since ≤1896. Much less grown than its variety *major* (treated below). Drought tolerant large shrub or small tree; few thorns, to ¾" long. Leaves conspicuously lobed (hence the name *pinnatifida*), 2"–4" long, or more on strong shoots. Flowers ⅓"–¾" wide; anthers 20, pink; styles 3–5. Haws shiny bright red, ½"–¾" long, 2–5 seeded. Resembles C. *monogyna*, but has bigger leaves of brighter green; shreddy bark; is less thorny; haws much more showy. Record: 22' × 3'9" × 32' Spokane, WA (1993).

C. *pinnatifida* var. *major* N.E. Br.

= C. *Korolkowii* Reg. *ex* Schneid. 1906, non Henry 1901
= C. *tatarica* hort.
= C. *californica* hort.
= C. *Bretschneideri* Schneid.

CHINESE BIGLEAF HAWTHORN. ASIAN HAWTHORN.

PEKING HAWTHORN. From N China, Manchuria, and Korea, where cultivated; not known wild. Introduced to cultivation in 1880. Named in 1886. In North American commerce since ≤1903. Uncommon. Thornless or nearly so. More treelike than the wild form, but still small, slow-growing. Crown heavy, leafy. Leaves less deeply lobed, shiny, larger, up to 6" long, often cupped or folded, with unusually long stems (to 2⅜"); can turn rich red or purplish in the fall. The bright red haws speckled with light dots can be 1¼" wide, sometimes pear-shaped, with a substantial pit at the base. The haws are both ornamental and edible. Their great size makes them messy when they drop.

C. *Piperi*—see C. *chrysocarpa*

C. *populifolia*—see C. *Phænopyrum*

C. *pruinosa* (H.L. Wendl.) K. Koch

= *Mespilus pruinosa* H.L. Wendl.

FROSTED HAWTHORN. WAXY FRUITED HAWTHORN. From eastern North America. The 1823 epithet *pruinosa* is Latin for *frosty*; with a glaucous bloom, referring to the haws. Uncommon in cultivation, being unspectacular. Leaves 1"–3⅜" long, rather broad; dark blue-green above, pale beneath. Thorns 1"–1½". Flowers ⅝"–1" wide, few per cluster, on long pedicels; anthers ca. 20, pink to purplish-pink or rarely creamy-white; styles 4–5. Haws to ⅝" wide; bloomy or frosted until fully ripe; the prominent, elevated calyx persists; 4–5 relatively large seeds. Frequently grows erect and strict. Records: 32' × 5'3" × 32' and 30' × 5'4" × 36' Shenandoah Co, VA (1991).

C. *pruinosa* var. *grandiflora* Kruschke

Only known in Wisconsin. Named in 1965. Not cultivated, but ought to be. "The showiest and prettiest of all native hawthorns in Wisconsin." Flowers to 1½" wide. Thorns to 3" long in one variant.

C. × *prunifolia*—see C. × *persimilis*

C. *pubescens*—see C. *mexicana*

C. *punctata* Jacq.

DOTTED HAWTHORN. FLAT TOPPED HAWTHORN. From eastern North America. Named in 1770; from Latin *punctum*—because of its dotted or spotted fruit—though it is by no means the only HAWTHORN with this characteristic. Fairly common in cultivation. Flowers ½"–¾" wide, borne in hairy clusters; anthers (15–) 20, burgundy, red, pink or yellow (rarely white); styles 2–5. Leaves 2"–4½" long, narrowed near base, broadest above the middle, unlobed, with with conspicuous straight, closely parallel veins. Thorns 1½"–3". Haws ⅝"–1" wide, dull orange-red to deep red, dotted, lightly hairy; flesh yellowish; 2–5 seeded. The haws are highly ornamental against the yellow fall foliage, but both leaves and fruit drop all too soon. Branching usually strongly horizontal. Thorns frightfully numerous and long. Records: 38' × 8'1" × 38' Canaan Valley Park, WV (1979); 39' × 4'2" × 52' Oakland County, MI (1959); 16'× 5'2" × 44' Effingham, IL (1974).

C. punctata f. aurea (Ait.) Rehd.
= C. punctata var. flava hort.
= C. punctata var. aurea Ait.
= C. punctata var. xanthocarpa (Roem.) Lav.

YELLOWBERRY DOTTED HAWTHORN. Cultivated since 1746. Rare in the North American nursery trade. Haws yellow. Records: 32' × 5'1" × 43' Chicago, IL (1955); 20' × 3'10" × 32' Seattle, WA (1992); 18' × 2'7" × 33' Hoyt Arboretum, Portland, OR (1993—long misidentified as C. Calpodendron, PEAR HAWTHORN).

C. punctata var. flava—see C. punctata f. aurea

C. punctata var. inermis—see C. punctata '(Ohio) Pioneer'

C. punctata f. intermedia Kruschke
Haws neither deep wine-red nor yellow, but intermediately colored.

C. punctata '(Ohio) Pioneer'
= C. punctata var. inermis hort.

Originated in 1962 in the nursery of Secrest Arboretum, Wooster, OH. In commerce since 1970s. Common. Tree very small, broad. Thornless. Leaves unlobed; 5–7 vein pairs; hairy beneath and (less so) above. Haws bright red, firm, ⅝"–¾" long, on hairy stems; fragrant; white fleshed, somewhat mealy, tasting sour, crisp and juicy like a 'Dolgo' crabapple; 3 big seeds. As with regular C. punctata, the leaves and fruit fall in late October and make a lovely mess.

C. punctata var. xanthocarpa—see C. punctata f. aurea

C. pyrifolia—see C. Calpodendron

C. rivularis—see C. Douglasii

C. rotundifolia—see C. chrysocarpa

C. rubra 'Splendens'—see C. lævigata 'Punicea'

C. sanguinea Pallas ex Bieb.

SIBERIAN HAWTHORN. From SE Russia through E Siberia. Named in 1784. Introduced to cultivation in 1822. In North American commerce by 1888. Extremely rare. Leaves 1½"–3½". Flowers small, in congested clusters; anthers 20; styles 3. Haws bright red, ⅓" long. Hardy enough for the Canadian prairie. Confused with its close kindred C. altaica and C. Wattiana. Record: 38' × 5'4" × 48' Seattle, WA (1993).

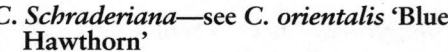

C. Schraderiana—see C. orientalis 'Blue Hawthorn'

C. Schroederi—see C. chlorosarca

C. Smithii or Smithiana—see × Cratæmespilus grandiflora

C. stipulacea—see C. mexicana

C. stipulosa—see C. mexicana

C. submollis—see C. mollis var. submollis

C. succulenta Schrad. ex Link
= C. macracantha var. succulenta (Schrad.) Rehd.
= Mespilus succulenta Schrad. ex Sweet

FLESHY HAWTHORN. SUCCULENT HAWTHORN. From the Midwest to New England and the Appalachians. Named in 1827. Uncommon in cultivation. Leaves 1½"–3¼" long, diamond-shaped. Flowers ½"–¾" wide; anthers (15) 20, reddish, pink or rarely white, very small. Haws ½"–⅝" wide, 2–3 seeded; sweet juicy flesh. Dark twigs and thorns, to 1³⁄₁₆"–2" (4"). Highly susceptible to cedar-apple rust disease. Records: 42' × 2'2" × 42' Keweenaw County, MI (1971); 36' × 4'0" × 55' Kirkwood, MO (1982); 21' × 4'3" × 30' Pipestem State Park, WV (1991).

C. succulenta var. *macracantha*—see *C. macracantha*

C. Suksdorfii—see *C. Douglasii*

C. tanacetifolia—see *C. orientalis*

C. tatarica—see *C. pinnatifida* var. *major*

C. tenax—see *C. crus-galli* var. *tenax*

C. tiliæfolia—see *C. mollis*

C. 'Toba'—see *C. × mordenensis* 'Toba'

C. tomentosa—see *C. Calpodendron*

C. Tracyi Ashe

TRACY HAWTHORN. From central Texas. Named in 1909 after Dr. C. Tracy, Texas botanist who in 1902 collected the type specimen. Extremely rare in cultivation. Promoted as a good ornamental for parts of Texas. Handsome red fall color. Pest tolerant. Related to *C. crus-galli* (COCKSPUR HAWTHORN). Flowers ⅝" wide, 7–10 per cluster; anthers 10–15, pink; styles 2–3 (4). Leaves 1"–1¾" long; hairy. Haws ca. ⅓" long, orange-red; 2–3 seeded. Thorns 1"–2⅜". Bushy, rarely to 20' tall.

C. 'Vaughn'

(*C. Phænopyrum* × *C. crus-galli*)

Originated ca. 1954 as a seedling in the New Augusta nursery of Henry Schnitzius, Indianapolis, IN. Introduced in 1968–69 by Simpson nursery of Vincennes, IN. Common. Leaf resembles that of *C. Phænopyrum* (WASHINGTON HAWTHORN), and in fall may be brilliant red. Thorns like those of *C. crus-galli* (COCKSPUR HAWTHORN), to 3" long, but not numerous. Haws like those of *C. viridis* but glossier and cherry-red, coloring early and hanging well into winter. Growth recalls *C. viridis*. Overall, little reason to believe *C. crus-galli* genes are involved in its parentage.

C. viridis L.

= *C. arborescens* Ell.

GREEN HAWTHORN. SOUTHERN HAWTHORN. TALL HAWTHORN. From the SE United States. Named in 1753 (*viridis* is Latin for green). Common in cultivation. Trunk often fluted; usually unarmed—thorns to 1½". Leaves 1"–4" long, rich orange or scarlet in autumn. Flowers ½"–¾" wide, in many-flowered clusters; anthers (10) 20, pale yellow or rarely red; styles (2) 4–5. Haws ⅛"–⅓" wide, orange-red; usually 5 seeded. Record: 40' × 5'1" × 45' Marlinton, WV (1981).

C. viridis var. *nitida*—see *C. nitida*

C. viridis 'Winter King'

Selected in 1949 at Frickton, IN. Introduced in 1955 by Simpson nursery of Vincennes, IN. Common. Similar to *C. viridis*. Flat, 2" wide flower clusters. Fruits heavily when young and retains its attractive glossy orange-red ⅜" wide haws through winter if birds don't eat them. Young bark often distinctly gray-green or silver. Leaves rust-resistant, can be lustrous red or purple and scarlet in late autumn. Leaves can be crudely lobed; lightly hairy both sides when young, albeit mostly on the veins. Little hairiness remains by autumn. Shoot leaves can be very narrow-waisted in lobing. Crown very broad. Thorns few, 1" or less.

C. Wattiana Hemsl. *ex* Lace

= *C. Korolkowii* L. Henry 1901, non Reg. *ex* Schneid. 1906

ORANGEBERRY HAWTHORN. From central Asia. Introduced to cultivation in 1888. Named in 1891. Extremely rare in North America. Sold ≤1941 by W.B. Clarke nursery of San José, CA. Bark flaky, broadly shreddy. Twigs stout, glossy; buds large. Thornless, or thorns present on sucker shoots, to ¾" long. Leaves 2"–4" long; stipules large. Flowers ½"–⅝" wide; styles 5; anthers (15) 18–20, white or pale yellow. Much defoliation from leaf spot can occur by early to mid-July. Haws yellow to orange, ½" wide, translucent and soft by August, amazingly like ripe PERSIMMON (*Diospyros virginiana*) fruits in color and texture, but without flavor, and with very hard seeds. Drops soon, by mid-September. Closely related to *C. altaica* and *C. sanguinea*. Records: 23½' × 2'3" × 22¼' Seattle, WA (1994; *pl.* 1969); 18' × 2'10" × 28½' Spokane, WA (1993).

× Cratæmespilus

[ROSACEÆ; Rose Family] Bigeneric hybrids; 2 named so far, both of natural origin. See also + *Cratægomespilus*.

C. grandiflora (Sm.) E.G. Camus
= *Cratægomespilus grandiflora* (Sm.) Bean
= *Cratægus grandiflora* (Sm.) K. Koch
= *Cratægus lobata* Bosc
= *Cratægus Smithii* Ser.
= *Cratægus Smithiana* hort.
= *Mespilus Smithii* DC.
= *Mespilus grandiflora* J. Smith
= *Pyrus Smithii* hort.
(*Cratægus lævigata* or *C. monogyna* × *Mespilus germanica*)

HAWMEDLAR. SMITH'S MEDLAR. (James Smith (1760–1840) was a British nurseryman.) A natural-occurring hybrid first noticed in France or Austria in the late 1700s. In North American commerce ≤1880. Very rare. Its winsome floral display, compared to that of the ordinary MEDLAR (*Mespilus germanica*), justified the epithet *grandiflora*. Tree very vigorous, heavy-crowned and prone to splitting; thornless, its trunk fluted; the bark flakes off in long, broad scales. Overall it bears a remarkable resemblance to MEXICAN HAWTHORN (*Cratægus mexicana*). Leaves 2"–4" long, softly felted beneath; short-stemmed; weakly lobed above the middle on shoots. Flowers in early May, white, then pinkish, 1"–1¼" wide, often semi-double. Few flowers per cluster (usually 3, often single). Petals cupped, broader than those of any HAWTHORN; anthers 20–27, pink; styles 2 (3). Fruits are like small medlars, to ¾" long, red-brown against golden-brown foliage in late October, hairy, edible, containing 1 or 2 infertile seeds. Records: 40' × 3'8" × 21' Wardour Castle, Wiltshire, England (ca. 1835; *pl.* 1805); 30' × 3'10" Vancouver, B.C. (1994).

Croton sebiferum—see *Sapiun sebiferum*

Cryptomeria

[TAXODIACEÆ; Bald Cypress Family] A genus consisting of only one species, a coniferous evergreen. From Greek *kryptos*, hidden, and *meros*, a share or part, referring to the concealed, not easily understood parts of the flowers—or to the concealing of the seeds by the cone scale bracts—or in reference to the tree's obscure relationship to the CEDAR.

C. Fortunei—see C. japonica var. sinensis

C. gracilis—see C. japonica 'Elegans'

C. japonica (L. fil.) D. Don

JAPANESE CEDAR. JAPANESE RED CEDAR. JAPANESE RED-WOOD. PEACOCK PINE (from Chinese *Kung-chio-sung*). GODDESS OF MERCY FIR (from Chinese *Kuan-yin-sha*). From China and Japan. Japanese: *Sugi*. Commonly cultivated ever since introduced to Western cultivation in the 1860s—the var. *sinense* (see below) was introduced earlier. A very important species in Japanese horticulture and forestry. More than 200 cultivars exist. It is shade tolerant, bears shearing, is long-lived and largely pest free. Cold, drying winds hurt it. Bark is a pleasing reddish-brown, fibrous and soft. Foliage is like the well known houseplant NORFOLK ISLAND PINE, but more spreading and prickly, often bronze-tinged in winter. Each awl-like needle is ¼"–½" long. Cones roundish and prickly, ½"–1". Records: to 210' × 66'0" in Japan; 121' × 14'11" Tauranga, New Zealand (≤1982; *pl.* ca. 1866); 120' × 14'3" Endsleigh, Devon, England (1970); 108' × 17'11" Monk Coniston, Lancashire, England (1983); 93' × 14'3" Tacoma, WA (1987).

C. japonica Akita strain
The offspring of seeds obtained in the mid-1980s by John Creech, are known under this name. They are believed to be superior to ordinary seedlings.

C. japonica 'Araucarioides'
Originated in Japan. Japanese: *Enko-sugi*. Introduced by Siebold to Holland in 1859. Name published in 1865; from genus *Araucaria* and Greek *-oides*, resemblance. More than one clone has been so named. Most specimens are shrubby, a few are small broad trees. Main branches rope- or snakelike with few laterals. Branchlets long (often 1'–1½'), slender, and wide apart, pendulous. Needles short, thick, curved and spreading. See also *C. japonica* 'Dacrydioides.'

C. japonica 'Benjamin Franklin'

Selected ≤1987 by Mr. B.F. Copeland on the coast of North Carolina. Salt tolerant. Remains green despite exposure to winter sun and much wind.

C. japonica 'Cristata'

= *C. japonica* 'Sekkwia Sugi'
= *C. japonica* 'Sekka Sugi'

COCK'S-COMB CRYPTOMERIA. Introduced from Yoko-hama nursery into Germany by L. Unger ca. 1900. In North American commerce since ≤1921. Uncommon. Conical and narrow; branches ascending, short, stiff; a certain percentage of branch tips and twigs tightly "glued" together to truly monstrous effect (*cristatus* in Latin means crested, plumed). The congested twigs bunches are warped and twisted. Of slow growth but a definite tree. Appealing only to lovers of freak variations. Records: 49' × 4'4" Tittenhurst Park, Ascot, Berkshire, England; 27' × 1'3" Seattle, WA (1994; *pl.* 1972).

C. japonica 'Dacrydioides'

= *C. japonica* 'Pendula'

Described in 1867. Japanese: *Sennin-sugi*. Similar to the rarer 'Araucarioides' but brownish and invariably small.

C. japonica 'Douglas'

Introduced ≤1985 by Ingleside Plantation nursery of Oak Grove, VA. Cold hardy, and does not turn brown in winter. (The Latin form 'Douglasii' is not legitimate as a cultivar name, being post-1959.)

C. japonica 'Elegans'

= *C. gracilis* hort. (in part)

PLUME CRYPTOMERIA. PLUME CEDAR. Japanese: *Yawara-sugi*. Introduced in 1854 by T. Lobb from Japan to Veitch nursery of England. In the U.S. by 1862 via G. Hall. Common; easily grown from cuttings. Much smaller than typical specimens, even bushy, often leaning at right angles, although capable of treehood. So dense that the trunk is rarely visible, unless its lower branches are removed. Very distinct in its ferny, fluffy, soft juvenile foliage which turns eye-catching purplish-brown in winter. Needles ca. 1" long. Nearly always coneless (its cones are smaller and less prickly than normal ones). Records: 82' tall reported by K. Rushforth; 70' × 13'4" Tauranga, New Zealand (≤1982); 55' × 8'2" Berkeley, CA (1989; *pl.* 1945).

C. japonica 'Elegans Aurea'

Cultivated since ≤1935 in New Zealand. In North American commerce since ≤1977–78. Some descriptions say it is a slightly smaller growing and yellowish-green 'Elegans'; but many plants called 'Elegans Aurea' are ordinary 'Elegans' except they don't turn dark in winter. Likely there has been confusion with 'Elegans Viridis'.

C. japonica 'Elegans Viridis'

Known since ≤1922 when cultivated in Holland. Grown in North America since ≤1940s. Rare. Light fresh green even in February. In Latin *viridis* means green.

C. japonica Fortunei—see C. japonica var. sinensis

C. japonica 'Kusari Sugi'—see C. japonica 'Spiraliter Falcata'

C. japonica 'Lobbii'

= *C. Lobbii* or *C. Lobbiana* hort.

Imported by Siebold or Wright from Japan to the Bogor Botanic Garden (formerly Buitenzorg), Java, Indonesia in 1825, and from there by Thomas Lobb (1820–1894) to Veitch nursery of England in 1853. Described as *Cryptomeria Lobbiana* in 1853. Commonly grown in North America. With twigs somewhat more slender than average, and densely compacted at the branch tips, this darker, tighter tree is capable of growing every bit as large as the typical *Cryptomeria*; it is also more cold-hardy, and less likely to bronze in winter.

C. japonica 'Pendula'—see C. japonica 'Dacrydioides'

C. japonica 'Sekka Sugi'—see C. japonica 'Cristata'

C. japonica 'Sekkan-Sugi'

('Sekhan Sugi')

GOLDEN CRYPTOMERIA. From Japan. Introduced to North American and European cultivation ≤1970. Rare. Foliage creamy-tipped to bright yellow-golden. Growth slow and dense. Record: 24' × 1'9" Seattle, WA (1994).

C. japonica 'Sekkwia Sugi'—see C. japonica 'Cristata'

C. japonica var. *sinensis* Sieb. *ex* S. & Z.
= *C. Fortunei* Hooibr. *ex* Otto & Dietr.
= *C. japonica Fortunei* hort.

The Chinese *Cryptomeria* population is so designated. Introduced in 1842 to England from Chusan, but all the seedlings died; reintroduced from Shanghai in 1844 by R. Fortune to the Horticultural Society of London. To the U.S. ≤1846. Golden Gate nursery of California sold it ≤1858–59. Parsons nursery of Flushing, NY, 1861 catalog had it. Overall this variant is believed to be more cold tender, so has been superseded in the nursery trade by Japanese stock. Habit more open and loose. Branches more slender and drooping; needles longer and thin; cones with fewer scales, less prickly.

C. japonica 'Spiralis'

GRANNY'S RINGLETS. Japanese: *Yore-sugi*. Introduced by Siebold to Holland ca. 1860. Described in 1870. In North American commerce since ≤1958. Branches and branchlets slender. the incurved needles so closely appressed and twisted as to simulate a spiral thread wound around them. Bright green all year. For all practical purposes a broad, dense bush. However, after many decades it can throw up a leader and grow into a tree. Maybe two forms are grown—conifer specialist H.Welch suggests the common bushy version may be from a witch's broom of the very rare treelike one. Record: 65½' × 6'11" Ochteryre, Crieff, Perthshire, Scotland (1987).

C. japonica 'Spiraliter Falcata'
= *C. japonica* 'Yore-sugi'
= *C. japonica* 'Kusari Sugi'

Originated ≤1876. Japanese: *Yore-sugi*. Like 'Spiralis' but more upright, with thinner, lighter-green needles, the branches twisting and curving. Introduced to North American commerce ≤1987. Rare.

C. japonica 'Yore-sugi'—see *C. japonica* 'Spiraliter Falcata'

C. japonica 'Yoshino'

Introduced ≤1928 by Yokohama nursery of Japan. In North American commerce since ≤1938. Common. Prized primarily for remaining green all winter.

C. Lobbiana or *Lobbii*—see *C. japonica* 'Elegans'

Cudrania

[MORACEÆ; Mulberry Family] 4–8 spp. of Old World shrubs, vines, and trees. Related very closely to *Maclura* (OSAGE ORANGE) and *Morus* (MULBERRY). From a Malayan name *cudrang* or *koederang*, a storehouse.

C. tricuspidata (Carr.) Bur. *ex* Lav.
= *Maclura tricuspidata* Carr.

CHINESE SILKWORM THORN. MANDARIN MELON BERRY. From China and Korea, usually in dry places. Introduced to France in 1862 by M. Simon. In North American cultivation ≤1870. Uncommon—probably because it is not superb as either a fruit tree or ornamental. Its great curiosity value has kept it in the specialty nursery trade. Usually a thorny shrub, rarely a root-suckering small tree. Thorns usually <⅞" long, to 1¼". Twigs can be so dark purplish as to appear almost black. Leaves 1½"–4", glossy, bright green, used in China to feed silkworms in times of scarcity of MULBERRY leaves. The leaves can be trilobed, especially on root-suckers, with the middle lobe much the smallest (hence Latin *tri*, 3, and *cuspidatus*, pointed). Fall color yellow. Male and female flowers on separate trees, appearing from May into July. Female flowers bumpy greenish pea-sized balls with pale yellow-green "antennæ," turn into orange fruits, which by November are red with a silvery sheen, looking like odd raspberries or suggesting *Cornus Kousa* fruit: ¾"–1½" wide, exuding milky sap from stem when plucked; juicy, flavored slightly like watermelon, chewier than raspberries. When dried a few days, far more flavorful, chewy, like raisins with faint cherry flavor. Most people do not esteem the fruit. A tree can bear 400 pounds of it. The trunks of very old specimens are deeply furrowed. Recorded to 59' × 6'6" in China.

Cunninghamia

[TAXODIACEÆ; Bald Cypress Family] 2–3 spp. of coniferous evergreens, suggestive of *Araucaria*. Named after Dr. James Cuninghame (d. 1709?), a surgeon with the East India Company, who found *C. lanceolata* in 1701 on Chusan Island in the East China Sea. There from 1698–1709, the doctor also discovered one of the tree's relatives, *Cryptomeria japonica*. They thrive in regions with mild winters, and require ample moisture to be at their best.

C. Konishii Hay.
= *C. lanceolata* var. *Konishii* (Hay.) Fujita

From Mount Randai, Taiwan. Discovered there by Nariaki Konishi in 1907. Introduced to the Arnold Arboretum in 1918 by E. Wilson. Extremely rare in cultivation, but in commerce to a minor degree. Probably best regarded as a mere variety or subspecies of the common *C. lanceolata*. It is no better looking. Needles shorter (to 1⅞" × ⅜"), whorled around the twigs rather than parted into two ranks. Cones smaller (⅝"–1⅛"), their scale tips are not prominently bent downward. Less cold hardy. Recorded to 164' × 25'9".

C. lanceolata (Lamb.) Hook. fil.
= *C. sinensis* R. Br. *ex* Rich.
= *Belis lanceolata* Sweet

CHINA FIR. CHINESE FIR. From China. Introduced in 1804 by W. Kerr to Kew, England, from Canton. Common. Needles broad, flat, 1"–2⅝" long, fiercely sharp. Cones squat, 1"–2" long, prickly, often growing in clusters and falling while still attached to large twigs. Tree often multitrunked or forking, suckering from the base, with reddish-brown fibrous bark. A narrow to broadly pyramidal crown of gaunt, irregular branches is topped by a rounded rather than sharply spired apex. Records: to 150' × 18'0" in the wild; 114' × 7'4" Tauranga, New Zealand (≤1982); 105' × 7'10" Bicton, Devon, England (1968); 95' × 7'0" Sacramento, CA (ca. 1983); 91' × 6'1" Vashon, WA (1993); 88½' × 9'6" Mt. Usher, County Wicklow, Ireland (1989; *pl.* 1873); 81' × 10'8" Kent, WA (1992); 60' × 11'0" × 67' Bowling Green, VA (1948; *pl.* ca. 1848).

C. lanceolata 'Chason's Gift'
Introduced ≤1993. From Johnson nursery of Willard, NC. The original specimen was 40 ' tall in 1994, when 15 years old. Grows upright from cuttings, is strikingly dense and symmetric.

C. lanceolata 'Glauca'
BLUE CHINA FIR. Name published in 1850. In North American commerce since ≤1937. Needles more or less bluish with a bloom over their dark green basic color. More than one clone in circulation, so assertions as to hardiness must be viewed with skepticism.

C. lanceolata var. Konishii—see C. Konishii

C. sinensis—see C. lanceolata

× Cupressocyparis

[CUPRESSACEÆ; Cypress Family] several bigeneric hybrids between *Cupressus* and *Chamæcyparis*. Some botanists disallow *Chamæcyparis* as a genus distinct from *Cupressus*; to them these HYBRID CYPRESSES are interspecific *Cupressus* crosses.

C. Leylandii (Dall. & Jacks.) Dall.
= *Cupressus × Leylandii* Dall. & Jacks.
(*Cupressus macrocarpa × Chamæcyparis nootkatensis*)

LEYLAND CYPRESS. Named after C.J. Leyland, a sea captain who liked trees, and grew some of the first (1888) raised *Cupressocyparis* trees at Leighton Hall, Welshpool, Wales. They were subsequently taken to Haggerston Castle, Northumberland, England. The first LEYLAND CYPRESSES in North America were grown ≤1942. For many years they were distributed primarily from one botanic garden to another, but were finally introduced commercially in the mid-1960s. Now they are common, valued for rapid growth and ease of propagation and cultivation. They are used as windbreaks, screens, hedges, and the like. Some damage can be caused by a *Phytophthora* root-rot and a canker known as *Coryneum cardinale* (= *Seiridium cardinale*), yet overall they are troublefree. There are many cultivars in Europe, but only 18 more important ones are accounted for in this volume (including some not yet known in North America). The clones can be divided into two foliage groups: plumose (sprays more like *Cupressus*) or flat-pinnate (more like *Chamæcyparis*). Cones ⅝"–¾". Records (see also *C. Leylandii* 'Haggerston Grey'): 97' × 11'5" Inverary Castle, Argyll, Scotland (1982); 80' × 6'6" Seattle, WA (1993; *pl.* 1950); 70' × 7'10" Tacoma, WA (1990); 67' × 9'11" × 57' San Francisco, CA (1995; *pl.* 1965).

C. Leylandii 'Belvoir Castle'—see *C. Leylandii* 'Robinson Gold'

C. Leylandii 'Castlewellan'
= *C. Leylandii* 'Castlewellan Gold'
= *C. Leylandii* 'Galway Gold'
= *C. Leylandii* 'Keownii'
= *C. Leylandii* 'Mellow Yellow' (in part; cf. 'Robinson Gold')
= *Cupressus macrocarpa* 'Keownii'

GOLDEN LEYLAND CYPRESS. Named after Castlewellan, Saintfield, Newcastle, County Down, Northern Ireland. Of 1962 seedling origin, after John Keown, then Head Gardener at Castlewellan, had gathered cones from a *Cupressus macrocarpa* 'Lutea' next to a *Chamæcyparis nootkatensis* 'Aurea' (or 'Lutea'). Introduced commercially ≤1970. In North American commerce ≤1978–79. Common. Foliage golden; plumose. Growth less rapid. See *Chamæcyparis nootkatensis* 'Lutea'.

C. Leylandii 'Castlewellan Gold'—see *C. Leylandii* 'Castlewellan'

C. Leylandii clone no. 1—see *C. Leylandii* 'Green Spire'

C. Leylandii clone no. 2—see *C. Leylandii* 'Haggerston Grey'

C. Leylandii clone no. 10—see *C. Leylandii* 'Naylor's Blue'

C. Leylandii clone no. 11—see *C. Leylandii* 'Leighton Green'

C. Leylandii 'Contorta'
= *C. Leylandii* 'Picturesque'
= *Cupressus macrocarpa* 'Tortuosa'
= *Cupressus macrocarpa* 'Contorta'
= *Chamæcyparis contorta torulosa* hort.

Introduced in 1972–73 by Mitsch nursery of Aurora, OR. The cultivar name is illegitimate, being Latin yet post-1959. Foliage somewhat glaucous; flat-pinnate. Stems red-brown. Few cones. The trunk, branches and sprays are conspicuously twisted.

C. Leylandii Emerald Isle™
= *C. Leylandii* 'Moncal'

Introduced in 1992 by Monrovia nursery of California. The original stock came from Britain. "Bright green flat sprays" and "dense (25' tall and 8' wide)." Likely a legitimately named clone renamed for marketing purposes.

C. Leylandii 'Galway Gold'—see *C. Leylandii* 'Castlewellan'

C. Leylandii 'Golconda'

A 1972 branch sport of *C. Leylandii* 'Haggerston Grey' from Wyboston, Bedfordshire, England. First propagated in 1974. Registered by D.F. Wyant in 1977. Foliage lemony gold, the color persistent and consistent all year. Growth rapid.

C. Leylandii 'Gold Cup'

Origin unknown. Introduced commercially ≤1980 (the year offered by Olle Olsson nursery of Monrovia, CA). Still in commerce. Foliage tips golden.

C. Leylandii 'Gold Rider'

Raised in the early 1980s from a sport on an unrecorded clone in Holland. In North America ≤1987. Still very rare here. Colored a much better yellow than the other golden cultivars; endures full sun without burning. Open, horizontal habit.

C. Leylandii 'Golden Sun'

A 1966 branch sport of *C. Leylandii* 'Haggerston Grey' from Barnham nursery, Bognor Regis, Sussex, England. Named in 1973. Golden foliage; semidwarf.

C. Leylandii 'Green Spire'
= *C. Leylandii* clone no. 1

Raised in 1888 at Haggerston Castle, Northumberland, England. Named in 1964. In North America ≤1986. Narrow columnar, dense. Foliage bright green; plumose.

C. Leylandii 'Haggerston Grey'
= *C. Leylandii* clone no. 2

An 1888 *Chamæcyparis nootkatensis* seedling at Leighton Hall, Welshpool, Wales, but sent in 1892 to Haggerston Castle, Northumberland, England. Named in 1964 (the year it was introduced to North America). Much more common than 'Leighton Green' in England, but less lovely: Branches stick out in all directions. Very rarely makes cones. The first cutting from the original tree at Haggerston Castle

Dates indicate time of year that photographs were taken.

Abies amabilis
PACIFIC SILVER FIR
3/10   Page 2
In Latin *amabilis* means
pleasing or attractive,
referring to the dark,
beautiful spire form of
this species.

Abies cephalonica
GREEK FIR
10/1   Page 3
An immense species,
combining hardiness,
drought-tolerance, and
insect resistance.

Abies grandis
GRAND FIR
11/14   Page 5
Its crushed needles smell
like tangerines.

Abies Nordmanniana
CAUCASIAN FIR
6/14   Page 7
Among the more familiar
and successful of foreign
species grown here.

Abies Pinsapo
SPANISH or
HEDGEHOG FIR
3/10   Page 8
Distinctive plump,
pointy, rigid needles.

Abies procera
NOBLE FIR
10/26   Page 9
Remarkably large
and showy cones.

Abies spectabilis
HIMALAYAN FIR
3/21   Page 10
Rare and difficult to
please in cultivation.

Abies Veitchii
VEITCH FIR
9/27   Page 10
A small tree from high
mountains of Japan; lovely
but usually short-lived.

Acacia Baileyana
COOTAMUNDRA
WATTLE
2/14   Page 11
An Australian with
"golden mimosa" flowers
cheerfully early in spring.

Acacia melanoxylon
BLACKWOOD
3/20   Page 12
More of a large shade
tree than most *Acacia*
species.

Acer campestre
ENGLISH MAPLE
9/22   Page 13
What it lacks in
flamboyant fall color is
made up by its strong,
adaptable nature.

Acer cissifolium
VINELEAF MAPLE
9/18   Page 16
An elegant and colorful
small tree from Japan.

Acer griseum
PAPERBARK MAPLE
9/7   Page 20
Besides its smooth,
peeling cinnamon bark,
it offers warm red fall
color.

Acer Heldreichii
GREEK MAPLE
10/9   Page 20
Extremely rare but of
robust constitution and
good looking.

Acer macrophyllum
BIGLEAF MAPLE
10/19   Page 22
Earth's largest MAPLE
species, with the biggest
leaves as well.

Acer Negundo
'Variegatum'
GHOST TREE or
VARIEGATED BOX ELDER
9/20   Page 24
Likely the most familiar
variegated shade tree;
grown since 1845.

Acer Opalus
ITALIAN MAPLE
11/1   Page 25
A collector's species
featuring beautiful yellow
flowers in early spring.

Acer palmatum
'Sango Kaku'
CORALBARK MAPLE
1/18   Page 26
In advanced age its fiery
winter twig color grows
subdued.

Acer platanoides
'Crimson Sentry'
'CRIMSON SENTRY'
NORWAY MAPLE
6/19   Page 41
Extremely dense, dark,
compact and tough;
sold since 1972.

Acer platanoides
'Faassen's Black'
'FAASSEN'S BLACK'
NORWAY MAPLE
7/12   Page 43
Dark all summer, large,
and not especially dense.

Acer Pseudoplatanus
f. *variegatum*
VARIEGATED
SYCAMORE MAPLE
9/8   Page 46
Excellent to brighten
a gloomy site.

Acer rubrum
RED MAPLE
10/29   Page 49
Planted by the millions
since the 1970s.

Acer rubrum
'Columnare'
COLUMNAR RED MAPLE
10/29   Page 50
A cultivar introduced
more than 100 years ago
by Parsons nursery of
Flushing, NY.

Acer rubrum 'Doric'
'DORIC' RED MAPLE
10/11   Page 50
Columnar and naturally
of reduced vigor; excellent
for tight spaces.

Acer saccharum
SUGAR MAPLE
10/12 Page 53
One of America's most
beloved and famous trees.

Acer saccharum
'Globosum'
GLOBE SUGAR MAPLE
10/29 Page 57
Promoted for planting
beneath power lines.

Acer saccharum
'Sweet Shadow'
CUTLEAF SUGAR MAPLE
10/31 Page 59
Sold since 1962. Leaves
deeply dissected in a
ferny matter.

Acer sempervirens
CRETAN MAPLE
3/27 Page 60
Extremely rare, shrubby
and subevergreen.

Acer tegmentosum
MANCHURIAN
STRIPEBARK MAPLE
11/1 Page 62
The boldest of several
STRIPEBARK MAPLE species.

Acer velutinum var.
Van Volxemii
PERSIAN MAPLE
10/16 Page 63
A rare, little known cousin
of *A. Pseudoplatanus*
(SYCAMORE MAPLE).

Æsculus californica
CALIFORNIA BUCKEYE
7/16   Page 64
Ghostly pale trunks, intense green foliage, and narrow clusters of white or pink flowers.

Æsculus × carnea
REDFLOWER HORSE CHESTNUT
5/14   Page 65
A fertile hybrid of the bushy Æ. *Pavia* and immense Æ.*Hippocastanum.*

Æsculus flava
YELLOW or SWEET BUCKEYE
5/14   Page 65
Creamy-yellow flowers are pleasant butovershadowed by glorious fall color.

Æsculus glabra
OHIO BUCKEYE
9/19   Page 65
The crushed leaves stink, but their orange or red fall color is electrifying.

Æsculus Hippocastanum 'Baumannii'
DOUBLE or NUTLESS HORSE CHESTNUT
5/6   Page 66
An excellent huge shade tree with a floral bonus and no messy nuts.

Æsculus indica
HIMALAYAN HORSE CHESTNUT
6/2   Page 67
The queen of the genus; almost unknown except on the Pacific Coast.

Albizia julibrissin
SILK TREE
9/14   Page 69
A well known tree of
delicate, tropical
luxuriance.

Alnus rhombifolia
WHITE ALDER
7/25   Page 72
Like most ALDERS, a useful
but unspectacular tree.

Araucaria angustifolia
PIRANA or
PARANÁ PINE
4/2   Page 79
A South American native
related to the well known,
bizarre MONKEY PUZZLE
(*Araucaria araucana*).

Arbutus 'Marina'
'MARINA' MADRONA
11/- [photo by R.G.
Brightman] Page 81
Sold since 1984, this
hybrid has a long
blooming season.

Arbutus 'Marina'
'MARINA' MADRONA
2/11   Page 81
Lovely red bark at the base
of the largest specimen.

Arbutus Menziesii
PACIFIC MADRONA
(MADRONE)
10/3 Page 81
This species is the largest
member of the Heath
Family (ERICACEÆ).

Arbutus Menziesii
PACIFIC MADRONA
(MADRONE)
10/4   Page 81
No tree bark is more
attractive, yet this species
is difficult in cultivation.

Asimina triloba
PAWPAW
10/23   Page 82
Hardy to cold, unlike most
of its relatives, this small
shrubby tree bears luscious
edible fruit.

Betula alleghaniensis
YELLOW BIRCH
10/11   Page 84
Also called B. *lutea*, YELLOW
BIRCH has yellowish-gray
rather than white bark.

Betula davurica
DAHURIAN BIRCH
7/-   Page 85
Shaggy bark and
tremendous cold-
hardiness.

Betula papyrifera
PAPER or CANOE BIRCH
3/15   Page 87
Birchbark canoes can be
made from this well
known species.

Betula populifolia
GRAY BIRCH
10/27   Page 89
Slender, graceful, glossy-
leaved, but with off-white
bark and a short lifespan.

Betula utilis var.
Jacquemontii
WHITE-BARKED
HIMALAYAN BIRCH
1/5   Page 91
Gleaming like arboreal
ghosts, a grove makes a
dramatic winter highlight.

Butia capitata
PINDO PALM
7/3   Page 92
From Brazil; among the
most cold-hardy of
feather-frond palms.

Calocedrus decurrens
INCENSE CEDAR
10/11   Page 92
The tree's oil has an
incense-like odor.

Calocedrus decurrens
INCENSE CEDAR
4/3   Page 92
Its red-brown, furrowed
bark goes well with its
grassy-green evergreen
foliage.

Carya ovata
SHAGBARK HICKORY
10/29   Page 98
Excellent for tough timber,
edible nuts, and golden
fall color.

Castanea sativa
EUROPEAN CHESTNUT
11/4   Page 100
Deadly chestnut blight
can kill these stately
shade and nut trees.

Catalpa bignonioides
SOUTHERN CATALPA
6/25   Page 102
Showy popcorn-like
summer flowers, large
leaves, and skinny
seedpods characterize
CATALPAS.

Cedrus atlantica
ATLAS CEDAR
12/4   Page 104
Most people prefer
powder-blue cultivars of
this North African native.

Cedrus atlantica f.
glauca
BLUE ATLAS CEDAR
6/4   Page 104
Boasting the color of
BLUE COLORADO SPRUCE,
this grows far larger.

Celtis sinensis
CHINESE HACKBERRY
3/26   Page 110
A successful shade tree in
California; worth growing
also in cooler regions.

*Cercidiphyllum
japonicum*
KATSURA TREE
10/19   Page 112
Handsome fall color is
often matched with a
peculiar sweet fragrance.

Cercis Siliquastrum
JUDAS TREE or
EUROPEAN REDBUD
4/27   Page 115
Larger flowers and
rounded leaves are unlike
those of our well known
native *Cercis canadensis*.

Chamæcyparis Lawsoniana f. *glauca (middle),* 'Erecta Viridis' *(right),* 'Stewartii' *(left)*
LAWSON CYPRESS
10/14   Page 119
The most variable of all conifers.

Chamæcyparis Lawsoniana 'Intertexta'
LAWSON CYPRESS
10/14   Page 121
A slender weeping tree of dark, hard, sparse foliage.

Chamæcyparis Lawsoniana 'Lane'
LAWSON CYPRESS
10/14   Page 121
One of 17 golden
LAWSON CYPRESS cultivars included in this volume.

Chamæcyparis nootkatensis 'Pendula'
WEEPING ALASKA CEDAR
7/9   Page 124
Several strongly pendulous clones of this species are grown.

Chamæcyparis pisifera
SAWARA CYPRESS
5/9   Page 128
Typical SAWARA CYPRESS, as shown here, is scarcely planted; its cultivars are more ornamental.

Chamæcyparis pisifera 'Boulevard'
'BOULEVARD' MOSS CYPRESS
7/31   Page 128
Semidwarf, baby-bluish, and coneless.

Chamærops humilis
DWARF or
MEDITERRANEAN
FAN PALM
4/2   Page 130
Usually a shrub, rarely a
slow-growing small tree.

Cladrastis kentukea
YELLOWWOOD
10/26   Page 133
A floriferous, broad shade
tree (known as C. *lutea*
until 1971).

Cornus capitata
EVERGREEN DOGWOOD
7/3   Page 135
The creamy flowers give
rise to attractive edible
red fruits.

Cornus controversa
GIANT or TABLE
DOGWOOD
5/14   Page 136
If its fall color or berries
were as pretty as its
flowers, this species would
not be so uncommon.

Cornus florida
'Welchii'
TRICOLOR DOGWOOD
5/3   Page 137
A FLOWERING DOGWOOD
sporting leaves of green,
white and pink.

Cornus florida ×
C. Nuttallii 'Eddie's
White Wonder'
'EDDIE'S WHITE WONDER'
DOGWOOD
4/27   Page 143
Lovely orange fall color
also adds to this small
tree's appeal.

Cornus Kousa
KOUSA DOGWOOD
9/23   Page 144
An east Asian species
recently much planted; it
resists disease better than
our natives.

Cornus Nuttallii
PACIFIC DOGWOOD
4/-   Page 150
Grand and lovely, but
touchy in cultivation
and disease prone.

Corylus Avellana
'Contorta'
CORKSCREW HAZEL or
HARRY LAUDER'S
WALKING-STICK
3/1   Page 152
A misshapen curiosity of
small size; best when seen
in winter or early spring.

Cotinus Coggygria
EUROPEAN SMOKE TREE
6/19   Page 153
Airy plumes of many
minute flowers lend a
hazy look.

Cratægus monogyna
f. *pendula*
WEEPING HAWTHORN
5/14   Page 166
Immaculate in bloom, it
lacks the glowing fall display
of many native species.

Cratægus nitida
SHINING or GLOSSY
HAWTHORN
10/18   Page 168
An excellent ornamental
small tree, largely thornless.

Cratægus orientalis
ORIENTAL HAWTHORN
10/8   Page 168
Breathtaking fruit is delicious, but tends to be borne only every other year.

× *Cratæmespilus grandiflora*
HAWMEDLAR
5/9   Page 174
A very rare hybrid, winsome in its floral display; in fall with red-brown fruit against golden-brown foliage.

Cryptomeria japonica
JAPANESE CEDAR
1/17   Page 174
Japan's most valuable timber tree is also a revered ornamental species.

Cudrania tricuspidata
CHINESE SILKWORM THORN
11/1   Page 176
Shrubby or a small thorny tree, related to OSAGE ORANGE (*Maclura*).

× *Cupressocyparis Leylandii*
LEYLAND CYPRESS
3/19   Page 177
Rapid growth to large size makes this popular.

Cupressus gigantea
TSANGPO CYPRESS
3/2   Page 182
Specimens (like this one) grown for decades in North America, are still small.

Cupressus Goveniana
var. *pigmæa*
MENDOCINO or
PYGMY CYPRESS
6/4   Page 183
Varies from knee-high to
giants nearly 200 feet tall.

Cupressus sempervirens
'Swane's Golden'
'SWANE'S GOLDEN'
ITALIAN CYPRESS
6/30   Page 185
Pure green and bluish-
green ITALIAN CYPRESSES
are more common.

Davidia involucrata
DOVE TREE
5/6   Page 187
Draped in white in spring,
this Chinese species affords
a spectacular sight.

Diospyros virginiana
COMMON PERSIMMON
8/24   Page 189
Chunky, rugged bark
is one of this tree's
distinctive attributes.

Eriobotrya deflexa
BRONZE LOQUAT
6/3   Page 193
Far more colorful and
elegant than regular LOQUAT
(*Eriobotrya japonica*).

Eriobotrya deflexa
BRONZE LOQUAT
3/21   Page 193
Sweetly fragrant, showy
flowers complement
bronzy-red young leaves.

Eriobotrya japonica
COMMON LOQUAT
4/1   Page 193
Tropical looks and edible
fruit on a surprisingly
cold-hardy tree.

Eucalyptus Bridgesiana
APPLE BOX
4/1   Page 194
A rare species, named after
M. Bridges, about whom
nothing more is known.

Eucalyptus Perriniana
(left), E. pauciflora ssp.
niphophila (right)
SPINNING GUM (left),
SNOW GUM (right)
9/18   Page 197
Two of the better known
cold-hardy species.

Eucryphia glutinosa
HARDY or DECIDUOUS
EUCRYPHIA
7/28   Page 198
A hardy South American
shrubby tree with profuse
summertime blossoms.

Fagus sylvatica
EUROPEAN BEECH
3/27   Page 202
Smooth bark on large
swollen trunks characterizes
most BEECHES.

Fraxinus americana
WHITE ASH
10/14   Page 211
A choice, noble tree for
shade, fall color, or useful
wood.

was planted in 1897 at Kyloe Wood, Northumberland, and measured in 1990: 111' × 9'10" (one is even taller: 121' × 9'7" Bicton, Devon, England; 1983; *pl.* 1916).

C. *Leylandii* 'Harlequin'

A sport of C. *Leylandii* 'Haggerston Grey' from Weston Park, Shifnal in Shropshire, England. Named in 1986, but distributed since ca. 1975. Variegated ivory-white and some creamy-white. Differs from C. *Leylandii* 'Silver Dust' in bearing plumose foliage.

C. *Leylandii* 'Hillspire'

In North American commerce ≤1990. Origin and description unknown. Likely a renaming of some other clone.

C. *Leylandii* 'Keownii'—see C. *Leylandii* 'Castlewellan'

C. *Leylandii* 'Leighton Green'

= C. *Leylandii* clone no. 11

Raised in 1911 as a MONTEREY CYPRESS seedling by Capt. J.M. Naylor, at Leighton Hall, Welshpool, Wales. First propagated in 1926, and introduced commercially in 1935. The commonest cultivar in Ireland. In North America ≤1950. Foliage flat-pinnate. Frequently makes ¾"–1" cones. The original tree, planted in 1912: 98' × 11'6" (1984).

C. *Leylandii* 'Mellow Yellow'—see C. *Leylandii* 'Castlewellan' and 'Robinson Gold'

C. *Leylandii* 'Moncal'—see C. *Leylandii* Emerald Isle™

C. *Leylandii* 'Naylor's Blue'

= C. *Leylandii* clone no. 10
= C. *Leylandii* 'New Blue'

A 1911 MONTEREY CYPRESS seedling from Leighton Hall, Welshpool, Wales. In North America ≤1964. In commerce here since ≤1978–79. Common now. Very plumose foliage, more like MONTEREY CYPRESS than is any other clone; varies from soft blue-green to deep blue-green seasonally. Rarely makes cones.

C. *Leylandii* 'New Blue'—see C. *Leylandii* 'Naylor's Blue'

C. *Leylandii* 'Picturesque'—see C. *Leylandii* 'Contorta'

C. *Leylandii* 'Robinson Gold'

= C. *Leylandii* 'Mellow Yellow' (in part; cf. 'Castlewellan')
= C. *Leylandii* 'Belvoir Castle'

Discovered ca. 1964 by Mr. G. Robinson, Head Gardener at Belvoir Castle, near Belfast, County Down, Ireland. Robinson noticed it as a seedling among some rhododendrons being cleared. He took it home. Thought to be *Cupressus macrocarpa* × *Chamæcyparis nootkatensis* 'Aurea'. In commerce since ca. 1975. In North America ≤1987. Its gold color varies but is usually brighter and more consistently yellow than 'Castlewellan'; it grows faster as well. Foliage flat pinnate.

C. *Leylandii* 'Rostrevor'

The first LEYLAND CYPRESS. Perhaps ca. 1870, this was a seedling given to the gardener at Rostrevor, County Down, Ireland. Cuttings were raised from it in 1908. The parent tree blew down before World War I. Not known in North America. Resembles 'Leighton Green' but is more vigorous and bears wider-spaced lateral sprays on the leaders. Sprays are more diamond shaped in outline and denser.

C. *Leylandii* 'Silver Dust'

= C. *Leylandii* 'Variegata'

A 1960 branch sport from 'Leighton Green' at the U.S. National Arboretum, Washington, D.C. Sent to England in 1966. In commerce since ≤1973–74. Name registered in 1976. Foliage flat-pinnate, variegated with creamy white.

C. *Leylandii* 'Skinner's Green'

= C. *Leylandii* 'Stapehill 21'

Named (in 1992) after the man who fostered this and its sibling 'Stapehill' (q.v.) as seedlings. According to K. Rushforth: more attractive than 'Stapehill', with more bluish foliage; drought tolerant. Not known in North America.

C. *Leylandii* 'Stapehill'

= C. *Leylandii* 'Stapehill 20'

About 1940, seedlings were raised in the Stapehill nursery of M. Barthélémy, at Ferndown, Wimborne, Dorset, England. They were grown from seed taken from a *Cupressus macrocarpa*. The cultivar was named in 1964, and was in North American commerce ≤1980. Rare–and perhaps just as well. K. Rushforth reports that it suffers from drought; its foliage is like that of 'Leighton Green' but in the shade the sprays become open and take on a rather moth-eaten look. Its sibling 'Skinner's Green' ('Stapehill 21') is superior.

Cupressocyparis Leylandii 'Stapehill 20'—see C. Leylandii 'Stapehill'

C. Leylandii 'Stapehill 21'—see C. Leylandii 'Skinner's Green'

C. Leylandii 'Variegata'—see C. Leylandii 'Silver Dust'

C. notabilis A.F. Mitchell
(*Cupressus arizonica* var. *glabra* × *Chamæcyparis nootkatensis*)

ALICE HOLT CYPRESS. Raised at Alice Holt Lodge, Farnham, Surrey, England, after Forestry Commission geneticists collected seed in 1956 from a SMOOTH ARIZONA CYPRESS at Leighton Hall, Welshpool, Wales. The goal had been to try raising further Leyland hybrids. But, seed was collected accidentally from a *Cupressus arizonica* var. *glabra*. The offspring was named in 1970. In North America ≤1980. Foliage in flattened sprays. An elegantly attractive bluish tree, like the seed parent in a number of ways. It does not have the super growth rate characteristic of LEYLAND CYPRESSES. Cones ½"–⅝".

C. Ovensii A.F. Mitchell
(*Cupressus lusitanica* × *Chamæcyparis nootkatensis*)

OVENS CYPRESS. Raised by Howard Ovens in his nursery at Talybont, Dyfed, Wales, from seed collected in 1961 from a *Cupressus lusitanica* at Silkwood, Westonbirt Arboretum, Gloucestershire, England. Named in 1972. It resembles the *Chamæcyparis* parent more. Flattened sprays. In North America ≤1987.

Cupressus

[CUPRESSACEÆ; Cypress Family] 13–25 spp. of coniferous evergreens. From ancient Greek *kyparissos*; in turn the Latin name for *C. sempervirens*. Some botanists refuse to allow *Chamæcyparis* status as a separate genus. But there are horticultural reasons for maintaining the distinction, as noted under the *Chamæcyparis* introduction. *Cupressus* cones are more or less marble-sized, and shiny, metallic-looking, often remaining closed for years. The culti-

vation of *Cupressus* in North America has been largely limited to California and the Southwest. Although immediately along the Pacific Coast the CYPRESS populations are usually disease-free, specimens planted in warmer, drier inland areas are plagued by cypress canker caused by *Coryneum cardinale* (= *Seiridium cardinale*). CYPRESSES are handsome ornamentals if they can evade disease and survive the winters outside their native haunts. *Cupressus* nomenclature is especially difficult with regard to the New World species: delineating species and varieties becomes nearly a matter of opinion. Identification is often hard because however well marked the trees may be in their natural population, when moved to new locales and climates they sometimes take on dramatically different appearances. Most are completely drought-tolerant and cannot abide the slightest shade. All in all, the genus is for tree lovers with ample patience.

C. arizonica Greene, non hort. (cf. C. arizonica var. glabra)
= *C. arizonica* var. *bonita* Lemm., non hort.

ARIZONA CYPRESS. ROUGH BARKED ARIZONA CYPRESS. From Arizona, New Mexico, Texas, northern Mexico; and *varieties* in S California. Discovered by E.L. Greene in E Arizona in 1880, but not cultivated except in its variety *glabra*, many cultivars of which have been selected. The epithet *bonita* is from Bonita Canyon (Spanish for *beautiful*), SE Arizona. Cones to 1". Trunk has attractive CHERRY-like bark only when young, but the branches can retain it. Practically immune to cypress canker. Records: 112' × 11'2" Big Bend National Park, TX (1982); 102' × 17'5" Coronado National Forest, AZ (≤1959); 97' × 15'1" Apache Sitgreaves National Forest, AZ (1988); 93' × 20'0" Mt. Lemmon, AZ (≤1993).

C. ariz. var. bonita—see C. arizonica and C. arizonica var. glabra

C. arizonica 'Arctic'
Introduced in 1984 by Duncan & Davies nursery of New Zealand. Slow growing upright pyramidal; branching horizontal. Foliage dark emerald green with silvery-white tips, most pronounced in the spring. Wind-hardy.

C. arizonica 'Blue Ice'
Discovered as a chance seedling in New Zealand in 1960. Introduced ≤1984 by Duncan & Davies nursery of New Zealand. In North America since ≤1985. Exceptional blue-gray color. Growth slow. Wind hardy.

C. arizonica 'Blue Pyramid'

Originated by K. Burns of Timaru, New Zealand. Introduced ≤1972. In North American commerce ≤1979. Upright pyramidal habit with closely arranged, horizontal or slightly ascending branches, densely covered with distinct, blue-tinted foliage.

C. arizonica 'Carolina Sapphire'

Raised from seed 1961. Introduced in 1982, in South Carolina. Very rapid growing when young; neater in appearance, broader and darker than 'Blue Pyramid'.

C. arizonica 'Clemson Greenspire'

Raised from seed in 1962 on Erland Nelson's Christmas tree farm at Windsor, SC. Selected in 1968. Fast growing; easily rooted; very full, lacy, bright yellow-green foliage in summer. Habit broad pyramidal. Registered in 1980 by the Department of Forestry, Clemson University, SC. Introduced in 1981.

C. arizonica 'Conica'

Origin unknown; likely in France <1937. Much like 'Pyramidalis' but less strictly erect, narrower, with slenderer branchlets and paler blue color.

C. arizonica 'Gareei'

('Garee', 'Garei')

Selected in the early 1930s by Mr. Garee of Noble nursery, Noble, OK. Introduced ≤1954–55 by Monrovia nursery of California. Hardy; drought tolerant. Branches of a distinct whipcord texture, rich silvery-blue.

C. arizonica var. glabra (Sudw.) Little

= C. arizonica ssp. glabra (Sudw.) E. Murr.
= C. arizonica hort., non Greene
= C. glabra Sudw.
= C. arizonica var. bonita hort., non Lemm.

SMOOTH ARIZONA CYPRESS. ARIZONA SMOOTH CYPRESS. From central Arizona. Discovered & introduced by Dr. Greene to the Arnold Arboretum in 1880. Commonly cultivated, usually under the name C. arizonica or C. glabra, but almost never sold as C. arizonica var. glabra. Popular throughout the South and on the West Coast. It retains its lovely peeling reddish-brown bark; foliage grayer usually, and more glandular. Practically canker-immune. Cones to 1¼" long. Variable; many cultivars. Seedlings range from sparse and ugly to attractive ultra-narrow spires of gray. Records: 83' × 12'4" Medford, OR

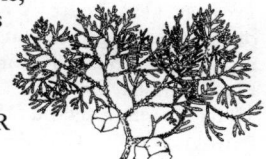

(1976); 70' × 14'2" Tonto National Forest, AZ (1984).

C. arizonica 'Golden Pyramid'

Introduced ≤1972 in New Zealand. In North American commerce ≤1992. Although described as like C. arizonica 'Blue Pyramid' but with golden-tinted foliage, at least some specimens sold in North America are really a clone of C. macrocarpa (MONTEREY CYPRESS).

C. arizonica 'Pyramidalis'

Originated in 1918. In English commerce since ≤1928. Sold in North America ≤1954–55. Common. Strictly erect habit; dense. Silvery glaucous. Cones freely. Confused with 'Conica' but broader.

C. arizonica 'Silver Smoke'

Introduced ≤1984 by Duncan & Davies nursery of New Zealand. In North America since ≤1985. Compact, conical bright silvery-gray. Slow growth, to 15' tall—almost certain to exceed this height.

C. arizonica 'Watersi(i)'

Introduced ≤1973–74 by Mitsch nursery of Oregon and Monrovia nursery of California. Extinct in commerce. Foliage gray. Habit dense and upright.

C. australis—see C. sempervirens var. indica

C. Bakeri Jeps.

= C. MacNabiana var. Bakeri (Jeps.) Jeps.
= C. Bakeri ssp. typica C.B. Wolf

MODOC CYPRESS. From old lava beds of Plumas, Shasta, Siskiyou and Modoc counties of California. Discovered in 1898 by Milo Samuel Baker (1868–1961), California botanist. Cultivated since 1930, but very rarely—primarily in botanic gardens. Lovely flaking reddish-purple bark and gray-green, glandular foliage resembling that of SMOOTH ARIZONA CYPRESS (C. arizonica var. glabra) but cones only ½"–⅝". Almost immune to canker. Record: 70' × 16'2" Plumas National Forest, CA (1963).

C. Bakeri var. Matthewsii (C.B. Wolf) stat. nov.

= C. Bakeri ssp. Matthewsii C.B. Wolf

SISKIYOU CYPRESS. From the Siskiyou Mountains of N California and SW Oregon. So similar to typical C. Bakeri that recent expert opinion has mostly disallowed the subspecific status it was given by C.B. Wolf in 1948. Yet even if it looks similar to scientists examining herbarium sheets, it may be the hardiest New

World *Cupressus*. Cultivated in 1917 at the Arnold Arboretum. Early in this century it was cultivated under the name *C. MacNabiana*. Although still in the trade it is extremely rare. Named after naturalist Oliver Vin Matthews (1892–1979) of Salem, OR, who brought it to the attention of Dr. Wolf. Foliage greener, less gray-green, less glandular than that of typical *C. Bakeri* (MODOC CYPRESS); cones larger, sometimes nearly 1" long, usually conspicuously warty. Practically immune to canker. Faster; growth coarser. Records: 129' × 10'9" Rogue River National Forest, OR (1976); one raised from seed supplied in 1942 by Matthews to the Seattle arboretum, is 53½' × 3'3½" (1994).

C. Bakeri ssp. *typica*—see *C. Bakeri*

C. cashmeriana Royle *ex* Carr.
= *C. torulosa* var. *cashmeriana* (Carr.) Kent
= *C. Corneyana* auct., non Carr.
= *C. himalaica* var. *darjeelingensis* Silba

BHUTAN WEEPING CYPRESS. KASHMIR CYPRESS. From Bhutan, Sikkim, and perhaps SE Tibet; not native in Kashmir. Discovered in 1848 by Wm. Griffith in Bhutan. Cultivated in England <1850. Named in 1867. In North America ≤1951. The stock originally imported was cold-tender; recent introductions may be hardier. In any case it should be kept in mind that this species is from areas affected by monsoons. It is supremely attractive and has long been cultivated near Buddhist temples. Foliage variable, but always slightly to strongly glaucous and pendulous. Cones ⅓"–¾" long. Records: to 164' × 31'0" in the wild; 72' × 9'9½" Ashbourne House, County Cork, Ireland (1987); 60' × 5'0" Cockington Court, Torbay, Devon, England (1984); 46' × 3'4" Berkeley, CA (1995; *pl.* 1974).

C. Chengiana S.Y. Hu
= *C. fallax* Franco (in part; cf. *C. gigantea*)

MIN CYPRESS. From W China, in the Min River region. The type specimen was collected in 1930 by Wan Chun Cheng (1904–1983), but the species was not named until 1964. Date of introduction to North America not known; put into commerce here ≤1993 by Buchholz & Buchholz nursery of Gaston, OR. Foliage green with white resin drops, PINE-scented. Crown delicate-textured, open and airy. Cones ½"–¾" (1") long. Cold-hardy to at least 20°F in China. To 131' × 20'7" in the wild; 20' tall at Berkeley, CA (1980).

C. Corneyana—see *C. cashmeriana*

C. disticha—see *Taxodium distichum*

C. disticha var. *imbricaria*—see *Taxodium ascendens*

C. disticha var. *nutans*—see *Taxodium ascendens* 'Nutans'

C. Donniana—see *C. sempervirens* var. *indica*

C. fallax—see *C. Chengiana* and *C. gigantea*

C. formosensis—see *Chamæcyparis formosensis*

C. glabra—see *C. arizonica* var. *glabra*

C. gigantea Cheng & L.K. Fu
= *C. fallax* Franco (in part; cf. *C. Chengiana*)

TSANGPO CYPRESS. From SE Tibet, in the Tsangpo River region. An endangered species. Seeds introduced to North America in 1948. Put into commerce here ≤1994–95 by Buchholz & Buchholz nursery of Gaston, OR. Specimens in Seattle and Berkeley are tightly columnar, very formal, slow, and far from being giant are the smallest of all *Cupressus* grown there. They recall IRISH JUNIPERS (*Juniperus communis* 'Hibernica'). Foliage coarse and dense, PINE-scented. Cones ⅝"–¾" long. Cold-hardy to at least 5°F in China. Records: to 147½' × 61'10" in the wild (where some are more than 1,000 years old); 18' tall at Seattle, WA (1994; *pl.* ca. 1962).

C. Goveniana Gord. *ex* Lindl.
= *C. Sargentii* var. *Goveniana* hort.

GOWEN CYPRESS. From California. Discovered near Monterey by K.T. Hartweg in 1846–47, and introduced to cultivation shortly thereafter. Named after James Robert Gowen (?–1862), Scottish horticulturist, noted developer of rhododendrons; secretary of the Horticultural Society of London at the date of this species' introduction. In North American commerce since ≤1871. Uncommon. In nature it is a small tree usually less than 33' tall. Foliage rich green or light yellowish-green; scented, says Alan Mitchell, of thyme and lemon. Cones to ⅝" long. Canker susceptible. Although trees so called had been offered by several California nurseries in the 1920s and '30s, in 1948 CYPRESS expert C. Wolf wrote: "I do not know of cultivated specimens in California except in native-plant collections." Records: 85' × 9'9" Wakehurst Place, Sussex, England (1984; *pl.* ca. 1911); 60' × 10'6" Sussex, England (1974); 50' × 7'0" Los Padres National Forest, CA (1967).

C. Goveniana var. pigmæa Lemm.
= *C. Goveniana* ssp. *pigmæa* (Lemm.) J. Bartel
= *C. pigmæa* (Lemm.) Sarg.

MENDOCINO CYPRESS. PYGMY CYPRESS. From coastal Mendocino and NW Sonoma Counties of California. Named Latin for *small* because of dwarf plants on the Mendocino White Plains—others are very large trees (to nearly 200' × 27'0"). Tree slender, with dark green, lemon-scented foliage. Bark fibrous, reddish-brown. Cones ½"–¾". Seeds often shiny jet black. Canker susceptible. Unsuited to dry interior California conditions. Record: 142' × 22'3" Mendocino County, CA (≤1993).

C. himalaica var. darjeelingensis—see C. cashmeriana

C. horizontalis—see C. sempervirens f. horizontalis

C. Lambertiana—see C. macrocarpa

C. Lawsoniana—see Chamæcyparis Lawsoniana

C. × Leylandii—see × Cupressocyparis Leylandii

C. MacNabiana A. Murr.

MACNAB CYPRESS. From California, on hot, dry hillsides. It has a wide range but is remarkably uniform. Discovered in 1853 by J. Jeffrey, introduced to cultivation in the British Isles a year later. Named in 1855, after James MacNab (1810–1878), a founder of the Edinburgh Botanical Society. Listed by U.S. nurseries since ≤1871. Some confusion in horticultural literature has resulted about the cultivation of MACNAB CYPRESS because plants of the SISKIYOU CYPRESS (*C. Bakeri* var. *Matthewsii*) were often being grown as *C. MacNabiana*. Usually a large shrub, rarely over 33' tall. Foliage dull gray-green, very glandular, often in flattened sprays like *Chamæcyparis* and *Thuja*. Cones ½"–1" long. Somewhat canker susceptible and of no particular horticultural merit because the bark is thin and fibrous, not showy; the crown shape and color are uninspiring; its hardiness and longevity is not great. (Cultivar **'Sulphurea'** was listed in the 1915–16 catalog of Fruitland nursery of Augusta, GA, as a new variety, its foliage glaucescent green with golden tips.) Records: 66' × 4'0" Bells Wood, Bayford, Hertfordshire, England (1985); 55' × 12'11" Amador County, CA (1981); 31' × 2'6" Seattle, WA (1994; *pl.* 1960).

C. MacNabiana var. Bakeri—see C. Bakeri

C. macrocarpa Hartw. ex Gord.
= *C. Lambertiana* Gord.

MONTEREY CYPRESS. From Monterey, California: a wind-swept oceanside grove at Point Lobos, another at Cypress Point, north of Carmel. In the fall of 1816, two Russians (A. von Chamisso and J.F. Eschscholtz) collected it in California. Then in the 1830s [Paxton says 1826] Dr. Fischer of St. Petersburg, supplied the Englishman A. Lambert with seeds—before the species was "officially" discovered by K.T. Hartweg in 1846. It was being tested in New York ≤1852 but was not hardy there. In Pacific Coast commerce since ≤1871. A monumental landmark tree of great character. Prominent in San Francisco's Golden Gate Park. Foliage rich, bright green, lemon-scented. Cones to 1"–1½" long (hence Greek *macro*, large, and *karpos*, fruit). Many New Zealand and Australian cultivars exist; this book lists only 12, reflecting their scarcity in North America. It performs best near the ocean and won't tolerate severe freezing. Canker easily kills it. Records (larger in cultivation than in the wild): 156½' × 15'5" Tauranga, New Zealand (≤1982; *pl.* ca. 1892); 131' × 31'0" Moreton House, Bideford, Devon, England (1986); 103' × 43'6" × 111' San Mateo County, CA (1994); 103' × 17'11" Gig Harbor, WA (1990); 100' × 32'0" × 110' Brookings, OR (≤1993); 93' × 28'5" × 83' Mendocino County, CA (1991); 78' × 22'4" Port Townsend, WA (1987).

C. macrocarpa 'Aurea Saligna'—see C. macro. 'Conybearii Aurea'

C. macrocarpa 'Contorta'—see × Cupressocyparis Leylandii 'Contorta'

C. macrocarpa 'Conybearii Aurea'
= *C. macrocarpa* 'Aurea Saligna'
= *C. macrocarpa* 'Saligna Aurea'

GOLDEN WEEPING CYPRESS. Introduced ≤1933 by Hazlewood nursery of Epping, New South Wales, Australia. Since 1936 usually called 'Saligna Aurea'. In North American commerce ≤1987.

C. macrocarpa 'Crippsii'
= *C. macrocarpa* 'Sulphurea'

Raised in the mid-1850s from imported seeds by Thomas Cripps & Sons nursery at Tunbridge Wells, Kent, England. Name published in 1874. In North American commerce to a minor extent ≤1930s. A juvenile form; tips of young branchlets creamy-yellow or silvery white; leaves spreading, sharp.

C. macrocarpa 'Donard Gold'

Slieve Donard nursery of Northern Ireland raised this in 1935. Name published in 1946. In North American commerce ≤1979–80. Foliage lime green overall, pure golden yellow at tips. Habit broad and "more shapely than usual." Branching very tight. Considered an improvement on 'Lutea'. Records: 55½' × 4'7" Occidental, CA (1995); 45' × 4'2" San Francisco, CA (1994; *pl.* 1950).

C. macrocarpa 'Fastigiata'

= C. macrocarpa 'Stricta'

Probably introduced to England by A. Lambert with the typical form in the 1830s. Columnar or narrow-pyramidal. Name published in 1850. Very rare in cultivation, either in England or North America.

C. macrocarpa 'Fine Gold'

Introduced ≤1994 by Duncan & Davies nursery of New Zealand. "Vigorous pyramidal. Foliage rich golden, closely appressed with fine slender twigs; branchlets forming a compact, sturdy tree."

C. macrocarpa 'Goldcrest'

Raised ca. 1947 by Messrs. Treseder of Truro, Cornwall, England. Much grown in Europe. Unknown in North America. Medium sized (to 40' × 10' wide) narrowly columnar dense tree. Foliage juvenile, feathery rich bright yellow.

C. macrocarpa 'Golden Pillar'

= C. macrocarpa 'Lutea Compacta'

Raised in the 1940s in Holland. Introduced to commerce in 1955. In North America since ≤1960. In commerce here ≤1992. Compact, pillarlike, yellow. Cuttings are slow to establish, but true semi-dwarf habit (to 15' × 4½' wide) develops only on its own roots—grafts grow far larger.

C. macrocarpa 'Hodginsi'—see C. macrocarpa 'Variegata'

C. macrocarpa 'Horizontalis'

= C. macrocarpa 'Lambertiana'

Originated in 1890s by G. Brunning & Sons nursery of Ripponlea, Victoria, Australia. Much grown in Australia by cuttings. Not known in North America.

C. macrocarpa 'Horizontalis Aurea'

= C. macrocarpa 'Lambertiana Aurea'

GOLDEN MONTEREY CYPRESS of Australia (see 'Lutea'). Originated probably in Victoria, Australia, in the 1890s. Only to 20' tall. Imported to North America in 1963 by the U.S. National Arboretum. In commerce here ≤1982–83. Narrow columnar. Foliage yellow.

C. macrocarpa 'Keownii'—see × Cupressocyparis Leylandii 'Castlewellan'

C. macrocarpa 'Lambertiana'—see C. macrocarpa 'Horizontalis'

C. macrocarpa 'Lambertiana Aurea'—see C. macrocarpa 'Horizontalis Aurea'

C. macrocarpa 'Lebretonii'—see C. macrocarpa 'Variegata'

C. macrocarpa 'Lutea'

GOLDEN MONTEREY CYPRESS of England (see 'Horizontalis Aurea'). Raised <1895 in Dickson's nursery of Chester, Cheshire, England. In North American commerce ≤1907. Seldom sold since 1930s. Narrow pyramidal. Bright yellow (Latin *lutea* means yellow) young growth, becoming green. Cones yellow. Often shrubby, and growth always slower than typical green seedlings. Perhaps more cold-hardy, however. Record: 108' × 15'8" Castlewellan, County Down, Ireland (1983).

C. macrocarpa 'Lutea Compacta'—see C. macro. 'Golden Pillar'

C. macrocarpa 'Saligna Aurea'—see C. macro. 'Conybearii Aurea'

C. macrocarpa 'Stricta'—see C. macrocarpa 'Fastigiata'

C. macrocarpa 'Sulphurea'—see C. macrocarpa 'Crippsii'

C. macrocarpa 'Sunshine'

In 1988–89 catalog of Mitsch nursery, Aurora, OR.

C. macro. 'Tortuosa'—see × Cupressocyparis Leylandii 'Contorta'

C. macrocarpa 'Variegata'

= C. macrocarpa 'Lebretonii'

Found in an English seedbed. Named in 1866. Very rare in cultivation. Variegated irregular creamy-white. It seems certain more than one clone has been sold as 'Variegata'. Several California nurseries from the 1880s into the 1920s sold trees said to be creamy-yellow, yellow or gold variegated. In the 1890s a clone called 'Hodginsi' was introduced by Hodgins nursery of Essendon, Victoria, Australia; it was deep green flecked with creamy variegation.

C. nootkatensis—see Chamæcyparis nootkatensis

C. obtusa—see Chamæcyparis obtusa

C. pigmæa—see C. Goveniana var. pigmæa

C. pisifera—see Chamæcyparis pisifera

C. pyramidalis—see C. sempervirens 'Stricta'

C. Royalii or Roylei—see C. sempervirens var. indica

C. Sargentii var. Goveniana—see C. Goveniana

C. sempervirens L.

ITALIAN CYPRESS. COMMON CYPRESS. MEDITERRANEAN CYPRESS. EUROPEAN CYPRESS. FUNEREAL CYPRESS. PILLAR CYPRESS. CLASSICAL CYPRESS. ROMAN CYPRESS. From S Europe, N Africa, SW Asia. Introduction to North America unknown, although in 1786 George Washington planted one at Mt. Vernon. Grown commonly in California since the 1850s. Crown more or less flame-shaped; in cultivation, dense, narrow clones are usually selected. Cones to 1⅓" long. Can live 3,000 years. Records: 164' × 6'5" Oetylos, Greece (<1910); 150' × 36'0" near Mistra, Greece (1839); 110' × 16'8" Tivoli, Italy (<1844).

C. sempervirens 'Glauca'—see C. sempervirens 'Glauca Stricta'

C. sempervirens 'Glauca Stricta'
= C. sempervirens 'Stricta Glauca'
= C. sempervirens 'Glauca'

Introduced ≤1934 in California. Common ever since. Foliage is silvery-blue; otherwise just another narrow ITALIAN CYPRESS.

C. sempervirens var. horizontalis (Mill.) Gord.
= C. horizontalis Mill.
= C. sempervirens f. horizontalis (Mill.) Voss

The wild form of the species. Rare. Scarcely ever offered in commerce. Branches more or less horizontal.

C. sempervirens var. indica Royle ex Gord.
= C. sempervirens 'Whitleyana'
= C. Roylei Carr.
= C. Royalii hort.
= C. Whitleyana Carr.
= C. Donniana hort.
= C. australis K. Koch

From the S Himalayas. Introduced to England in 1852; named in 1865; to North America ≤1922–23 by Fruitland nursery of Augusta, GA. Habit stiff, fastigiate. Cones globose.

C. sempervirens 'Pyramidalis'—see C. sempervirens 'Stricta'

C. sempervirens 'Royalii'—see C. sempervirens var. indica

C. sempervirens 'Stricta'
= C. sempervirens 'Pyramidalis'
= C. pyramidalis hort.

The oldest cultivated tree of upright habit. Not known wild. Common in cultivation. It is variable but more or less fastigiate, like a LOMBARDY POPLAR (Populus nigra 'Italica'). Records: 94' × 8'10" Sacramento, CA (1989); 82' × 8'6" Fota, County Cork, Ireland (1984; pl. 1814); 67' × 12'7" Nettlecombe Court, Williton, Somerset, England (1971); 49' × 5'8" Seattle, WA (1987; pl. 1932).

C. sempervirens 'Stricta Glauca'—see C. semper. 'Glauca Stricta'

C. sempervirens 'Stricta Variegata'—see C. semper. 'Variegata'

C. sempervirens 'Swane's Golden' PP 3839 (1976)

Originated in 1944 as a 'Stricta' seedling at Swane Brothers nursery of Sydney, New South Wales, Australia. Distributed by 1956; introduced officially in 1961. In North American commerce since ≤1977–78. Foliage golden; otherwise just another narrow ITALIAN CYPRESS. Growth slower than the green versions.

C. sempervirens 'Totem'

Introduced ≤1992 by Duncan & Davies nursery of New Zealand. A selected clone of 'Stricta' that is pleasing and dark green.

C. sempervirens 'Variegata'
= C. sempervirens 'Stricta Variegata'

Origin unknown; likely from England ca. 1848. Sold in California during the 1930s at least. Pale yellow and white intermixed on some young shoots; otherwise just another narrow ITALIAN CYPRESS.

Cupressus sempervirens 'Whitleyana'—see *C. sempervirens* var. *indica*

C. thyoides—see *Chamæcyparis thyoides*

C. torulosa var. *cashmeriana*—see *C. cashmeriana*

C. Whitleyana—see *C. sempervirens* var. *indica*

Cyclobalanopsis acuta—see *Quercus acuta*

Cyclobalanopsis glauca—see *Quercus glauca*

Cyclobalanopsis myrsinæfolia—see *Quercus myrsinæfolia*

Cydonia

[ROSACEÆ; Rose Family] Only the following species, the QUINCE TREE, grown since prehistoric times for its edible fragrant fruit. *Cydonea* was one of its ancient Latin names; from its native place Cydonia, NW Crete, now called Khania. Related to *Malus* (APPLE), *Pyrus* (PEAR), and especially *Pseudocydonia* (CHINESE QUINCE).

C. sinensis—see *Pseudocydonia sinensis*

C. oblonga Mill.
= *C. vulgaris* Pers.
= *Pyrus Cydonia* L.

COMMON QUINCE. FRUITING QUINCE TREE. GOLDEN APPLE TREE. From the Near East to central Asia. In North American commerce since 1648. A small, spreading, crooked tree. Flowers 2" wide, palest pink, in late April and May with the pale green, notably soft young foliage. Leaves 3"–7" long. Fruit on wild specimens only 1¼"–2" long; cultivars make apple or pear-sized fruit, yellow-golden, fuzzy. In Portuguese it is called *marmelo*, whence our "marmalade," which was originally made of quinces. Cultivars grown for fruit include: **'Champion'**, **'Cooke's Jumbo'**, **'Orange'** (= **'Apple'**), **'Pineapple'** and **'Smyrna'**. Records: 27' × 4'9" × 35' Tacoma, WA (1992); 23' × 5'6" × 29' Seattle, WA (1990).

C. sinensis—see *Pseudocydonia sinensis*

C. vulgaris—see *C. oblonga*

Cynoxylon floridum—see *Cornus florida*

Cytisus Adamii—see + *Laburnocytisus Adamii*

Cytisus alpinus—see *Laburnum alpinum*

Cytisus Laburnum—see *Laburnum anagyroides*

Daphniphyllum

[DAPHNIPHYLLACEÆ; Daphniphyllum Family (or EUPHORBIACEÆ, Spurge Family)] 9–25 spp. of Old World broadleaf evergreens, with foliage reminiscent of rhododendrons. From Greek *daphne* (BAY LAUREL; named after the Greek nymph and daughter of the earth goddess Gea), and *phyllon*, a leaf.

D. glaucescens—see *D. macropodum*

D. himalense ssp. *macropodum*—see *D. macropodum*

D. macropodum Miq.
= *D. glaucescens* hort., non Bl.
= *D. himalense* (Benth.) Muell.-Arg. ssp. *macropodum* (Miq.) Huang

From China, Korea, and Japan. Introduced in 1879 by C. Maries for Veitch nursery of England. In North American commerce ≤1887. Rare. Flowers inconspicuous; late April into June. Male and female sexes on separate trees. Female flowers viewed up close are like clusters of glaucous radish seeds, each topped by purple-black stigmas. Male flowers are more showy, reddish anthers. Females if fertilized produce powder-blue attractive berries. Usually a large shrub, rarely a small tree to 50' tall in the wild or ca. 25' in cultivation. Leaf 3"–8" long; its stout red petiole (to 1¾" long) is the "large foot" (Greek *makro*, large, and *podos* or *pous*, a foot). Record: 26' × 2'1½" × 15½ Seattle, WA (1994).

Davidia

[DAVIDIACEÆ; Dove Tree Family (or NYSSACEÆ or CORNACEÆ)] 1 or 2 spp. of deciduous trees. Jean Pierre Armand David (1826–1900), Basque; in China from 1862–74, discovered the tree in 1869. The most closely related genus is *Nyssa* (TUPELO).

D. involucrata Baill.

DOVE TREE. (POCKET) HANDKERCHIEF TREE. LAUNDRY TREE. KLEENEX TREE. GHOST TREE. From W China. Introduced in 1904 when E. Wilson sent seeds to Veitch nursery of England. Very rare; its var. *Vilmoriniana* (below) is usually grown. The epithet *involucrata* in Latin means provided with an involucre, a covering case. So named because each flower cluster is equipped with white leaflike bracts to 8" long, which is the glory of the tree. Hence the many English names. After the bloom is done, these bracts look like toilet paper strewn all over the ground. Leaf 3"–7⅜" long, strongly toothed; heart-shaped at the base; stem to 5¾" long. The foliage can be malodorous. Fall color varies from dull muted pastel greens, yellows and reds, to fiery orange and crimson. Fruits look like hard round underipe pears up to 1¾", borne singly or in pairs on 2"–3" stalks. Astringent flesh surrounds a hard, sharp kernel resembling a peach pit. Records: to 98½' × 15'5" in the wild; 79' × 6'6" Westonbirt, Gloucestershire, England (1988); 72' × 8'1" Villa Taranto, Pallanza, Lake Maggiore, Italy (1994); 62' × 7'6" Tregrehan, Cornwall, England (1979).

D. involucrata var. *Vilmoriniana* (Dode) Wanger.

= *D. Vilmoriniana* Dode

VILMORIN DOVE TREE. HARDY DOVE TREE. Introduced in 1897 when Père Paul Guillaume Farges sent seeds to French nurseryman Maurice Lévêque de Vilmorin (1849–1918). Much more common in cultivation than the typical kind. Leaves hairless beneath, either shiny green or pale with whitish bloom. Other reported differences may or may not bear scrutiny: The fruit may be smaller, with longer stems. The leaf may be darker. It may grow faster. It may be inferior in bloom. It may color less beautifully in fall than the hairy type. Above all, it is definitely more cold-hardy. Records: 82' × 4'3" Tilgate Park, Sussex, England (1984); 56' × 9'1" Trehane, Cornwall, England (1987); 55' × 4'8" Seattle, WA (1990); 53' × 5'4" Snohomish, WA (1990).

D. Vilmoriniana—see *D. involucrata* var. *Vilmoriniana*

Dendrobenthamia angustata—see *Cornus angustata*

Dendrobenthamia capitata—see *Cornus capitata*

Dendrobenthamia hongkongensis—see *Cornus hongkongensis*

Dendrobenthamia Kousa—see *Cornus Kousa*

Dicksonia

[CYATHEACEÆ (or DICKSONIACEÆ); Tree Fern Family]; 20–30 spp. of TREE FERNS mostly from the Southern Hemisphere. Named in 1788 after James Dickson (1738–1822), Scottish botanist, nurseryman, and naturalist. The following two species cannot be expected to grow without protection where winter cold commonly plunges below about 20°F. Exposure to sun and dryness is also anathema to them. They are of great interest, and often confused with one another. A hardier strain might be developed if more attention were paid them.

D. antarctica Labill.

WOOLY TREE FERN. MAN FERN. TASMANIAN TREE FERN. From E Australia and Tasmania. Introduced to cultivation in 1786; to England in 1824. Introduced to North America in early 1900s. Most specimens cultivated in California under the name *D. antarctica* are really *D. fibrosa*. Fronds 5'–14' long, harsh textured. In the wild, up to 50' × 12'6". Golden Gate Park in San Francisco, CA, has many fine specimens, the tallest perhaps about 23' (1995).

Dicksonia fibrosa Col.

WOOLY TREE FERN. GOLDEN TREE FERN. NEW ZEALAND TREE FERN. Maori: *Wheki Ponga, Kuripaka* or *Takote*. From New Zealand. Fronds yellowish-green, to 5' (6½') long, persisting for years as a pale brown skirt around the trunk. The hardiest TREE FERN, and one of the most commonly cultivated. Frond stems densely covered with long hairs when young. To 25' × 4'8" in the wild; very slow. Commonly seen 6'–10' tall in California.

Dimorphanthus elatus—see *Aralia elata*

Diospyros

[EBENACEÆ; Ebony Family] 200–500 spp. of mostly tropical, heat-loving, cold-tender trees. From Greek *dios*, divine, and *pyros*, wheat or grain; literally, celestial food—in allusion to the life-giving properties of the fruit. Male and female flowers borne on separate trees, but isolated female specimens can still bear fruit, which will be seedless or nearly so.

D. chinensis—see *D. Kaki*

D. japonica—see *D. Lotus*

D. Kaki L. fil.
= *D. chinensis* Bl.

KAKI PERSIMMON. JAPANESE PERSIMMON. ORIENTAL PERSIMMON. CHINESE PERSIMMON. TOMATO TREE. CHINESE FIG. From NE India, Burma, China, and Korea. Very important in Japanese cultivation. Introduced to Europe in 1789 but little known <1870. In North America since 1856; the first grafted cultivars here by 1870. Commonly available now. Prized primarily for its edible fruit, but handsome enough to be appreciated ornamentally in home landscapes. The yellowish flowers appear in late May or June, are inconspicuous and attract bees. The leaves are large (to 8⅞" × 5¼"), dark and glossy; fall color bright yellow or yellow and rosy in pastel tints. Fruit varies in size (1½"–3½") and shape, but is usually orange and by late fall the tree can look like it's loaded with a crop of tomatoes. The fruit is commercially popular in markets, being thick-skinned unlike that of *D. virginiana*. Bark pale gray and scaly. Most specimens form broad, low trees of bold, droopy texture, ca. 30' tall and wide. Records: 65' × 6'6" in the wild; 39' × 4'1" Paris, France (1982; *pl.* 1947); 27' × 2'6" × 29' Seattle, WA (1990); 26½' × 4'9" × 30½' Sebastopol, CA (1995).

D. Lotus L.
= *D. japonica* S. & Z.

DATE PLUM. ITALIAN LIGNUM-VITÆ. DATE OF TREBIZOND. BASTARD MENYNWOOD. WOOD OF LIFE. POCK WOOD. From SW Asia, N Iran, N India, China, and Korea. Cultivated in northern Europe since 1588. In North America since ≤1884. Very rare. Useful as a rootstock for fruiting cultivars of its relatives. Not sufficiently ornamental to be grown for its own appearance. Named after the Greek *lotos*, applied to many plants. Flowers inconspicuous creamy white bells with deep pink lips curled back, appearing after those of *D. Kaki* bloom, before those of *D. virginiana*. Leaves smaller (2"–6¼") than those of *D. virginiana*, and less colorful in autumn. Fruit ½"– 1" wide, yellow to orange to bloomy purplish-black, usually seedy; likened to date-flavored plums—edible but of unappealing appearance. Records: almost 100' tall in Iran; 85' × 13'1" in China; 62' × 4'4" Westonbirt, Gloucestershire, England (≤1985; *pl.* 1926); 45' × 1'7" Seattle, WA (1990); 40' × 4'5" Seattle, WA (1990; *pl.* ca. 1894); 38' × 8'2" Leiden, Holland (1938; *pl.* 1740).

D. texana Scheele

TEXAS PERSIMMON. BLACK PERSIMMON. MEXICAN PERSIMMON. Spanish: *Chapote*. From river valleys of SW Texas and NE Mexico. In the nursery trade since ≤1912. Extremely rare in cultivation. Emerging leaves fuzzy with hairs; at length thick and glossy, dark green, ¾"–1½" long; evergreen or tardily deciduous; no fall color. Flowers tiny, hanging inconspicuously in March or early April, creamy white, sweetly fragrant. Fruit ripe in August, sweet, ½"–1" wide, black, leaving an indelible black stain on everything it touches. Bark mottled pale gray and white, smooth, thin and attractively peely like that of a CRAPE MYRTLE (*Lagerstrœmia*). Cold hardy, drought tolerant. Usually shrubby or a multitrunked twiggy small tree <25' tall. Grows much faster if watered. Records: 82' tall reported by S. Spongberg; 52' × 6'0" reported by Standley; 26' × 5'7" × 31' Uvalde County, TX (1965).

D. virginiana L.

PERSIMMON. COMMON PERSIMMON. SUGAR PLUM TREE. WINTER PLUM. 'POSSUM PLUM. 'POSSUM APPLE. 'POSSUM WOOD. From the central and eastern U.S. Common and familiar as a wild fruit tree; planted sometimes for fruit or ornament. Improved fruit cultivars yield larger crops, bear when young, and are vastly superior to ordinary seedlings. Work needs to be done on selecting ornamental cultivars as well. Leaf 2"–8" long, varying from dull to slightly shiny. Fruit ⅞"–2½" wide, orange, soft, thin-skinned, tastes like eggnog; ripe in fall and winter. Bark wonderfully chunky and rugged-looking. Records: 131' × 6'9" Big Oak Tree State Park, MO (1977); 120' × 22'0" Luxora, AR (1915); 80' × 13'½" near Johnson, IN (1954); 66' × 11'4" × 85' Dardenelle, AR (1987).

Dipteronia

[ACERACEÆ; Maple Family] 2 spp. From Greek *di*, double or two; and *pteron*, a wing or feather—each seed has 2 wings, not 1 like the related genus *Acer* (MAPLE).

D. sinensis Oliv.

From central-west China. Introduced ca. 1900 by E. Wilson for Veitch nursery of England. In North America since ≤1933. Extremely rare in cultivation, but in commerce. Best in woodland gardens, where it forms an elegant, restful feature. A large shrub or small tree. Leaves 9"–24" long, compound, of 7–17 leaflets; basal leaflets can have leaflets themselves. Each leaflet is dull green, lightly hairy and coarsely toothed. Flowers tiny but in large clusters; not showy. The most ornamental quality is its red, very conspicuous winged

seeds in fall. Fall leaf color is a washed-out, even ghostly yellow. Records: to 49' tall in the wild; 37' × 3'0" Hergest Croft, Herefordshire, England (1969); 33' × 1'6½" Seattle, WA (1994; *pl.* 1970).

Distegocarpus Carpinus—see *Carpinus japonica*

Dracæna australis—see *Cordyline australis*

Dracæna indivisia—see *Cordyline australis* and *C. indivisia*

Ehretia

[EHRETIACEÆ or BORAGINACEÆ or CORDIACEÆ] 50 spp. of widely distributed shrubs and trees, primarily tropical or subtropical. Named after George Dionysius Ehret (1708–1770), German-English botanical artist. The following species are all very rarely cultivated, and are desirable primarily for their showy, fragrant flowers. Their nomenclature has often been confused.

E. acuminata R. Br.

= *E. thyrsiflora* (S. & Z.) Nakai
= *E. ovalifolia* Hassk. 1844, non Wight 1848
= *E. serrata* hort., non Roxb. 1824

TALLOW TREE. HELIOTROPE TREE. KODA. SILKY ASH. From India, China, Korea, Taiwan, the Ryukyus, Japan, the Philippines, Viet Nam, and E Australia. Named in 1810. Introduced to England between 1820 and 1827. In North American cultivation by 1911. Very rare. If, as some botanists insist, the Australian population of this far-ranging species is considered the original and narrowly-interpreted species, then the other populations must be designated either var. *obovata* (Lindl.) I.M. Johnst., or *E. ovalifolia* Hassk. The name *acuminata* (referring to the pointed leaves) means tapering into a long narrow point; from Latin *acumen*, a sharp point. Tree can be stiff-looking, suckering. Bark flaky. Leaf to 7" × 3"; stem to ¾"; glossy, short-hairy or glabrous above, paler, hairless below, or the veins with some microscopic hairs; leathery or sub-coriaceous, can be partially evergreen and has dingy yellow-green "fall color" when not; very finely toothed or apparently untoothed margins. Flowers white, PRIVET-like, fragrant, in 3"–8" terminal panicles from May to mid-July. Fruit yellow-orange, then red, finally black, hairless, ⅛" or less wide, often 4-seeded, possibly edible, certainly juicy, but can be acrid. Records: to 100' × 8'4" in Australia; 67' × 5'2" × 46' Los Angeles, CA (1993; *pl.* 1965); 25' × 6'8" × 26' Philadelphia, PA (1980).

Ehretia Anacua (Terán & Berl.) I.M. Johnst.
= *Gaza Anacua* Terán & Berl.
= *E. elliptica* DC.

ANACUA. SUGARBERRY. KNACKAWAY. KNOCKAWAY. Spanish-Mexican: *Anacua*, *Anacuita*, *Anaqua* or *Anagua*. From Texas and Mexico. Named in 1832. In commerce since ≤1912. Extremely rare in cultivation outside of Texas and Mexico. Leaf dark glaucous green, whitish beneath; raspy; tardily deciduous. Flowers fragrant, appearing from fall into spring, white or yellow, with dark centers, small, in 3" clusters. Fruit a ¼" berry, light yellow to bright orange, sweet and edible; attracts birds. Heat-loving; drought tolerant. Often a low shrub. Records: to 50' tall in the wild; 42' × 14'7" × 46' Bexar County, TX (1983); 30' × 13'6" × 54' Victoria, TX (1976).

E. Dicksonii Hance
= *E. macrophylla* hort., *sensu* auct. Japon, Hemsl., non Wall.

LARGELEAF EHRETIA. From China, Taiwan, and the Ryukyus. Named in 1862 after James Dickson—see *Dicksonia*. Introduced in 1897 by E. Wilson. Very rare; in North American commerce since ≤1940. Tree to 40' × 6'0" usually, occasionally much larger, or a mere shrub. Bark corky. Twigs stout, with scattered rough hairs when young, or hairless. Leaf large, broad, to 8" × 4¾" (sucker leaves to 13" × 7½"); stem ⅝"–2"; rough-hairy both sides, especially beneath, but variable and can be nearly hairless; thick, leathery, mildly rugose; toothed; can be glossy above; base rounded or cordate. Flowers white or slightly yellowish, fragrant, even overpoweringly so sometimes, in 2"–4" terminal panicles in summer. Fruit (greenish-yellow) yellow or orange, hairless, ½"–⅞" wide, 2-seeded. Records: 65' × 7'4" Bagatelle, Paris, France (1982; *pl.* 1897); 55' × 3'5" Birr Castle, County Offaly, Ireland (1985).

E. elliptica—see *E. Anacua*

E. macrophylla Wall., non Shiras. et al.
From the Himalayas. Nepal, Bhutan, N Assam, Burma. Named in 1824 (from Greek *macro-*, large, and *phyllon*, a leaf). A large shrub or small 20' tree. A cold-tender species, only included here to ease confusion with *E. Dicksonii*. Leaf egg-shaped, 6" × 4"; stem to ⅞"; margin irregularly toothed, base narrowed; bristly above and beneath. Flower clusters globose. Fruit to ½".

E. ovalifolia—see *E. acuminata*

E. serrata—see *E. acuminata*

E. thyrsiflora—see *E. acuminata*

Elæagnus

[ELÆAGNACEÆ; Eleagnus Family] 30–45 spp. of shrubs and small trees, evergreen or deciduous. From *elaia*, the olive, and *agnos*, Greek name for the CHASTE TREE, *Vitex Agnus-castus*. The *elaiagnos* of Theophrastus was originally applied to a WILLOW, from *helodes* (growing in marshes) and *hagnos* (pure, chaste, holy) referring to the cottony-white seed masses of the tree. Related to genus *Hippophaë* (SEA BUCKTHORN). The plants fix nitrogen symbiotically, so can thrive even on sterile soils.

E. angustifolia L.
= *E. orientalis* L.
= *E. hortensis* Bieb.
= *E. argentea* Moench, non Pursh

RUSSIAN OLIVE. OLEASTER. SILVER TREE. WILD OLIVE. BOHEMIAN OLEASTER. ZAKKOUM-OIL PLANT. JERUSALEM WILLOW. TREBIZOND GRAPE. TREBIZOND DATE. From west-central Asia. Long cultivated. Year of introduction to North America unknown. Very common. Thrives in sunny, hot, dry places and in poor soils. Wild in parts of the Rocky Mountains and Plains. Salt tolerant. A variable shrub or small tree, often spiny, with shaggy blackish bark and silvery-gray, willowy foliage (Latin *angustus*, narrow, and *folium*, a leaf). Leaves 1"–3½" long, vivid silver beneath. Flowers tiny, inconspicuous, silver-yellow, sweetly fragrant in June. Fruit silver flushed with rose, or wholly red, pea-sized to 1" long or more. OLEASTER is a Latin word, meaning WILD OLIVE TREE,

from *olea*, OLIVE TREE, and *-aster*, an inferior resemblance. Literally olivelike. The name ZAKKOUM-OIL PLANT derives from the Arabic *Zaqqûm*. As an ornamental, RUSSIAN OLIVE is refreshingly lovely in leaf, but looks twiggy and unkempt in winter. Records: 65' × 9'10" × 38' Salt Lake City, UT (1980); 58' × 10'6" × 90' Cortez, CO (1982); 57' × 8'4" × 52' Eaton County, MI (1983); 52' × 12'5" × 62' near Black Hills Speedway, SD (1991).

E. angustifolia 'Emerald Magic'

Introduced ≤1991–92 by Willoway nursery of Avon, OH. Growth upright; foliage dark silver.

E. angustifolia 'King Red'

Grown from Afghanistan seeds. Introduced by the USDA in January 1978. Common; grown from seed. Fruit burgundy-red, large (1"), sweet, mealy. Growth fast. Hardy to minus 30°–40°F.

E. argentea—see E. angustifolia

E. hortensis—see E. angustifolia

E. orientalis—see E. angustifolia

Elæocarpus

[ELÆOCARPACEÆ; Elæocarpus Family] 60–90 spp. of broadleaf evergreen trees and shrubs from the Old World tropics and substopics. From Greek *elaia*, olive, and *karpos*, fruit. No related genera are in this volume; the TILIACEÆ, Linden Family, is related.

E. sylvestris (Lour.) Poir.

= *E. decipiens* Hemsl. *ex* Forbes & Hemsl.
= *E. ellipticus* (Th.) Mak. 1904, non Smith 1809

JAPANESE BLUEBERRY TREE. From India, S China, Viet Nam, S Japan, the Ryukyus, and Taiwan. Named in 1790 (*silvestris* in Latin means wild or of the woods, not cultivated). A cutting-grown clone of this species was introduced in 1995 by Monrovia nursery of California, as one of that company's Shogun™ series of Japanese broadleaf evergreen trees. Not likely to be cold-hardy (the catalog asserts the contrary). Leaves hairless, slender, short-stemmed, to 5" ×

1⅓"; inconspicuously toothed, bronzy-red when young, dark green in summer, turning red before falling. Flowers inconspicuous, from June into August, small, yellowish-white, in slender upright clusters 2"–3" long. Fruit a bluish-black or black berry, single-seeded, ⅔"–¾" long, edible. In Japanese cultivation at least, this species makes a dense, rather formal small tree, in scale and texture like BRONZE LOQUAT (*Eriobotrya deflexa*). Recorded to 45' tall.

Embothrium

[PROTEACEÆ; Protea Family] 8 spp., all from the Southern Hemisphere. From Greek *en*, in, and *bothrion*, a small pit; the anthers are borne in cup-shaped pits.

E. coccineum J.R. & J.G. Forst.

CHILEAN FIRE TREE. FLAME TREE. Chilean (Mapuche): *Notro*. From Chile and Argentina. Introduced in 1846 by Wm. Lobb to Veitch nursery of England. In North America by 1908. Rare. Grown primarily on the Pacific Coast, and even there almost unavailable before the 1940s. A slender tall shrub or tree that grows very rapidly (one in San José, CA, grew 18' in 4 years) and blooms even when very young. It resents coddling, and should not be fertilized, as it plays a pioneer role ecologically: fast growth, short lifespan. Leaf to 7½" × 1⅕". Flowers can be yellow or white in the wild, but in cultivation are usually screaming crimson-scarlet (Latin *coccineum* means scarlet), beloved by hummingbirds. The flowers appear from April into June. When not in bloom the tree is plain at best, often a narrow, crude eyesore. (Another FIRE TREE or FLAME TREE is the cold-tender *Nuytsia*, of W Australia.) Records: 65½' × 4'4" Brodick Castle, Strathclyde, Scotland (1988); 51' × 2'9" × 19' Wauna, WA (1992); 48' × 3'2" × 19' Seattle, WA (1989; *pl.* 1955); 39' × 6'0" Mt. Usher, County Wicklow, Ireland (1989).

E. coccineum 'Eliot Hodgkin'

Sent in 1975 from Osorno, Chile, to England. Yellow flowers.

Embothrium coccineum 'Inca Flame'

Introduced by Duncan & Davies nursery of New Zealand. In North American commerce ≤1991–92. A treelike form of var. *longifolium*.

E. coccineum var. *lanceolatum* (Ruiz & Pav.) Ktze.

= *E. lanceolatum* Ruiz & Pav.

Introduced to England in 1927 by H.F. Comber. A hardier strain from the higher (ca. 5,000' elevation), drier Argentine side of the Andes, near the northern end of the species' range. Semideciduous as well as having very narrow leaves. Flowers scarlet. Favors well drained, sunny sites.

E. coccineum var. *longifolium* hort.

= *E. longifolium* hort., non Poir.

Origin obscure; introduced to British cultivation ca. 1900. Leaves long, usually evergreen. Flowers large and red. Growth robust. Less hardy.

E. coccineum 'Norquinco Valley'

A form of var. *lanceolatum* with especially abundant and vivid orange-scarlet flowers.

E. lancifolium—see *E. coccineum* var. *lanceolatum*

E. longifolium—see *E. coccineum* var. *longifolium*

Emmenopterys

[RUBIACEÆ; Madder Family] 2 spp. of deciduous trees. From Greek *emmenes*, enduring, and *pteron*, a wing or feather, as a portion of the flower enlarges into a showy, leaflike wing.

E. Henryi Oliv.

From central and SW China. Introduced by E. Wilson in 1907. Named after Augustine Henry (1857–1930), Irish doctor, botanical explorer in China, forestry professor and author. A heat-loving, cold-tender tree remarkable for being so rarely brought to bloom in cultivation. Branching bold and horizontal. It can sucker from the roots. Leaves large (to 15" × 6¾"), new growth attractively reddish fading to bronze color; stem wine-red. Flowers white, spectacular in June or July, with bracts that persist and turn pink. The first flowering in Western cultivation occured in 1971, from a tree planted in 1937 at Lake Maggiore, Italy. It first flowered in England in 1987. After 40 years of biding its time, one New Zealand specimen decided to flower in 1987. In North America it has been grown since at least the 1940s, but the first report of blossoms was in 1994, from a tree at Silver Springs, MD, grown in 1979 from seed. Records: to 100' × 13'0" in the wild; 60' tall, multitrunked at Villa Taranto, Pallanza, Lake Maggiore, Italy (1985; *pl.* 1937); 59' × 3'9" Caerhays, Cornwall, England (1984).

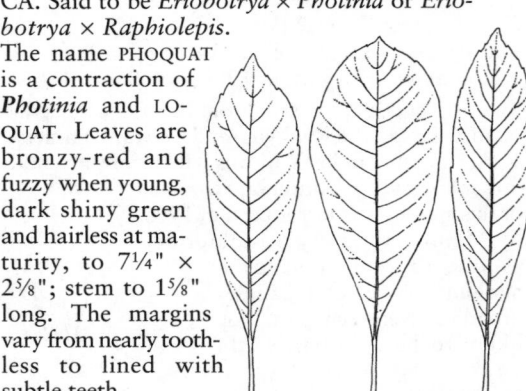

Eriobotrya

[ROSACEÆ; Rose family] 10–27 spp. of East Asian broadleaf evergreens, suitable only for areas with minimal freezing in winter. From Greek *erion*, wool, and *botrys*, a bunch of grapes, referring to the wooly, bunched fruits. Related to *Photinia* and the shrubby *Raphiolepis (Rhaphiolepis)*.

E. Coppertone™ PP 4245 (1978)

= *E. japonica* Coppertone™

PHOQUAT. Introduced by Bordier's nursery of Irvine, CA. Said to be *Eriobotrya × Photinia* or *Eriobotrya × Raphiolepis*. The name PHOQUAT is a contraction of *Photinia* and LOQUAT. Leaves are bronzy-red and fuzzy when young, dark shiny green and hairless at maturity, to 7¼" × 2⅝"; stem to 1⅝" long. The margins vary from nearly toothless to lined with subtle teeth.

E. deflexa (Hemsl.) Nakai
= *Photinia deflexa* Hemsl.

BRONZE LOQUAT. From Taiwan; perhaps introduced ca. 1918 by E. Wilson, but not widely grown until 1954. Leaves bronzy-red when young, dark green at maturity, to 9¾" × 3⅜"; stem to 1¾" long. Flowers in March-April, sweet, white and showy. A large shrub or small tree (20'–40'), often broad and rounded. Fruit yellow-green becoming orange-brown, ⅝" wide, of little consequence either ornamentally or as food. Bark smooth, gray. Much more elegantly textured and colorful than *E. japonica*, but not as cold-hardy.

E. deflexa 'Bronze Improved'
Introduced ≤1988 by Monrovia nursery of California.

E. deflexa × Raphiolepis indica PP 3349 (1973)
= *Raphiolepis* Majestic Beauty™
= *Raphiolepis* 'Montic'
(Rhaphiolepis)

Introduced in 1973 by Monrovia nursery of California. Flower clusters 10" wide, fragrant, pearly-pink, in spring. Leaves 3"–4" (6") long, dark green, sharply toothed, hairless. Shrub or a trained 15' tree. Of unproven cold-hardiness, it needs additional testing in frosty areas. Unlike Coppertone™ (above), Majestic Beauty™ certainly looks much more like a *Raphiolepis* than an *Eriobotrya*.

E. japonica (Th.) Lindl.
= *Mespilus japonica* Th.
= *Photinia japonica* (Th.) Franch. & Sav.

LOQUAT. JAPANESE MEDLAR. EVERGREEN MEDLAR. From S China and Japan. Named and introduced in 1784 to Europe; to England in 1787 by J. Banks; doubtless to the U.S. <1800. In California commerce since 1871. Common there. Leaves 6"–20½" × 5¾", leathery, firm, wrinkled, fuzzy beneath. Flowers creamy-white, fragrant, appearing anytime from August through January. Fruit edible, yellow-orange, pear shaped or apple shaped, 1"–3" long (its Japanese name *Biwa* is from the three-stringed musical instrument which the fruit resembles in shape). Bark gray and rusty colored. Many fruitful cultivars exist, such as **'Gold Nugget'** and **'MacBeth'**. It is a valuable foliage ornamental even if the flowers are often frozen so that little or no fruit ripens. Does well in containers. Tolerant of shade and dryness. A large shrub or small tree of tropical aspect; very dense. Records: 40' × 6'6½" Bay of Plenty, New Zealand (1966; *pl.* ca. 1895); 40' × 2'9" Glendurgan, Cornwall, England (1984); 39' × 3'4" Saltram House, Devon, England (1987); 29' × 3'4" Seattle, WA (1989).

E. japonica Coppertone—see E. Coppertone™

E. japonica 'Variegata'
Origin unknown. Sold ≤1895 by Sunset nursery of San Francisco, CA, and in 1900–1901 catalog of California nursery of Niles, CA. Leaves splashed creamy-white. Of low sprawling habit, perhaps to 8' tall. 'Yukige' (below) may be this cultivar renamed.

E. japonica 'Yukige'
Originally from Shibamichi nursery of Kawaguchi-shi, Saitama, Japan, where sold as *Fuiri Biwa* (VARIEGATED LOQUAT). Introduced in 1982 to the U.S. by B. Yinger, who proposed the name 'Yukige' (melting snow). Leaf often irregular and puckered, with various patterns of green, gray-green, and pure white variegations. Edges usually pure white. See *E. japonica* 'Variegata' (above).

Eriolobus florentina—see Malus florentina

Eriolobus Tschnoskii—see Malus Tschnoskii

Eucalyptus

[MYRTACEÆ; Myrtle Family] 500–600 or more spp. of broadleaf evergreens, nearly all from Australia. Known as GUM TREES, EUCALYPTS, or by many other Australian common names. The genus was named by L'Héritier in 1788, from Greek *eu*, well, and *kalyptos*, covered, referring to the calyx which first covers the flowers, then falls off like a cap or cover. EUCALYPTS range in size from sprawling shrubs called "mallees" to the tallest tree recorded in history: a *Eucalyptus regnans* that measured 435' to its broken top in 1872. California's first EUCALYPTS were planted in 1856. In the early days they were used to drain marshy land harboring malaria-carrying mosquitoes, and were grown for timber. Currently the tallest in North America are over 250' and at least one trunk measures over 52'0" around. Some species have become naturalized in California and are so common in places that they pass as natives. The trees grow tall very rapidly (so fast because they never stop; just slow down in winter); even when frozen to the ground they often resprout well. Lignotubers occur in most of the following species and enable resprouting after the tops are killed by freezing, fire, grazing or cutting. The juvenile foliage featured by many species is very decorative; it is typically powder-bluish, often rounded and stemless, whereas adult foliage tends to be greener and more willowy. Both juvenile and adult foliage is fragrant when crushed—sometimes from a distance (smells much like Vick's VapoRub®).

Most of the following species are comparatively little known in California, but have been the most promising of many tested in cold regions such as in Oregon, Washington, British Columbia and England, not to mention Kansas, Ohio and other States usually thought to be too cold for them. Their behavior in the wild, as described in Australian literature, is often dramatically different from their cultivated appearance. None of the hardy species have the showy lipstick-red flowers sported by some of their cold-tender relatives. Unless otherwise stated, all species in this account have smallish, white or creamy flowers, of no account ornamentally. EUCALYPTS are drought-tolerant, require much sun, and aside from aphids on a few, are largely pest-free in the northern hemisphere (since 1984 a beetle has pestered some California specimens). The visual and hardiness variation within a species is often confusingly great. Foliage glaucousness varies within a species the same way as it does with BLUE SPRUCES and many other trees. Frost resistance is subject to a high level of genetic variation. Gradual hardening off in autumn is more critical than how low the mercury plunges in winter. Cultural practices, such as not planting out pot-bound stock, and choosing a site with some wind protection and superb drainage, also aid a great deal.

E. Archeri Maiden & Blakely

= *E. Gunnii* ssp. *Archeri* (M. & B.) L. Johnson & D. Blaxell

ALPINE CIDER GUM. From high alti-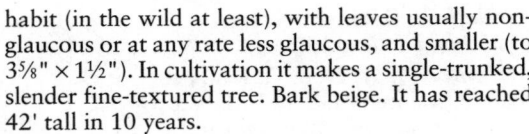
tudes (3,600'–4,600') of northern
Tasmania. William H. Archer (1820–
1874), Tasmanian architect
and expert amateur botanist,
collected the first specimen in
1848. Grown in North
America since ≤1973. Like the
well-known *E. Gunnii* (CIDER
GUM) but hardier, of poorer

habit (in the wild at least), with leaves usually non-glaucous or at any rate less glaucous, and smaller (to 3⅝" × 1½"). In cultivation it makes a single-trunked, slender fine-textured tree. Bark beige. It has reached 42' tall in 10 years.

E. Bridgesiana R.T. Bak.

= *E. Stuartiana* auct., non F. v. Muell.

APPLE BOX. From E New South Wales, E Victoria, and S Queensland. Named after M. Bridges, about whom nothing more is known. Grown in North America since ≤1939. Juvenile leaves triangular to heart-shaped, silvery-gray, pink-edged. Twigs pink. Adult leaves dull gray-green, to 8" × 1". Bark gray or light brown, scaly and not ornamental. Records: 75' × 12'0" Sacramento, CA (1989); 57' × 8'6" × 60' Santa Barbara, CA (1993).

E. cinerea F. v. Muell. ex Benth.

SILVER DOLLAR TREE. SILVER DOLLAR GUM. ARGYLE APPLE. MEALY STRINGYBARK. SPIRAL EUCALYPT. From SE New South Wales, far N Victoria. Grown in North America since ≤1931. In Latin, *cinerea* is ashy gray, referring to the foliage color. A rough-barked small tree (30'–60' tall) notable for maturing essentially in a state of permanent juvenile foliage. Such adult leaves as are made, measure up to 5" × 1". Much grown for the florist trade. Other species are also called SILVER DOLLAR GUM, in reference to the silvery-blue, roundish, 1"–2½" juvenile leaves. Not reliably cold-hardy, but comparatively common, and a fast grower, planted for fleeting beauty. Like RUSSIAN OLIVE (*Elæagnus angustifolia*), this species' pale foliage contrasts attractively with its rugged, dark trunk.

E. coccifera Hook. fil.

TASMANIAN SNOW GUM. MT. WELLINGTON PEPPERMINT. FUNNEL FRUITED GUM. From high-altitude (2,000'–4,500') Tasmania. Introduced to England in 1840. In North America since ≤1913. The epithet *coccifera* means bearing the cochineal or coccoid scale insect. This species requires cool conditions for survival, and should be given excellent drainage. Twigs of seedlings at least are conspicuously warty with red glands. Juvenile leaves to 2⅜" × 1¾"; adult leaves 1"–4" × ½"–¾"; less fragrant than most. Color varies from grayish-green to wholly dark green, usually dull but can be glossy. Bark shed in long strips, leaving a smooth white trunk, blotched or streaked gray and red. Has been likened to an evergreen *Betula pendula* (EUROPEAN WHITE BIRCH) in stature and shape. Records: to 131' tall in the wild; 92' × 5'1" Inverness-shire, Scotland (1952; *pl.* 1912); 85' × 20'6"

Powderham, Devon, England (1963; *pl.* 1840); 65' × 11'9" Kilmacurragh, County Wicklow, Ireland (1980).

E. coriacea—see E. pauciflora

E. Dalrympleana Maiden

MOUNTAIN GUM. MOUNTAIN WHITE GUM. BROAD LEAVED RIBBON GUM. BROAD LEAVED KINDLING BARK. From SE New South Wales, E Victoria, and Tasmania. Named after Richard Dalrymple Hay (1861–1943), an important forester in New South Wales. Grown in North America since ≤1930. Juvenile leaves 1⅓"–4¾" × 1³⁄₁₆"–2¾"; adult leaves 3½"–10½" × ½"–1⅜"; usually green and semi-glossy, can be dull gray-green. Twigs usually reddish. Trunk whitish and smooth; foliage willowy in heavy tresses. Records: to 197' × 20'6" in the wild; 80' × 6'6" Mt. Usher, County Wicklow, Ireland (1975).

E. Debeuzevillei—see E. pauciflora ssp. Debeuzevillei

E. delegatensis R.T. Bak.

ALPINE ASH. GUM TOPPED STRINGYBARK. WHITE TOP. WOOLLYBUTT. From far S New South Wales, E Victoria, and Tasmania. Named after its place of discovery, Delegate Mountain, New South Wales. In North America since ≤1924. One of Australia's most important commercial lumber trees; too big for ornamental use in restricted sites; certainly the largest of the cold-hardy EUCALYPTS. Not drought-hardy. Juvenile leaves 3¼"–10" × 2"–4"; adult leaves 3"–14" × ¾"–1½" (2"); green and glossy, sometimes gray-green and dull. Bark of lower trunk dark brown, fibrous; bark above shed in ribbons, leaving branches smooth and creamy. Records: to 295' × 31'0" in the wild; 125' × 29'0" × 144' Christchurch, New Zealand (≤1982); 96' × 9'9" Mt. Usher, County Wicklow, Ireland (1966; *pl.* 1905).

E. glaucescens Maiden & Blakely

TINGIRINGI GUM. TINGARINGY GUM. From SE New South Wales, NE Victoria. The first specimen was collected on Tingaringy Mountain, Victoria in 1887. The Latin epithet *glaucescens* refers to the branchlets and juvenile leaves being strikingly silvery-glaucescent. In North America since ≤1968. Juvenile leaves 1³⁄₁₆"–2¾" × 1⅛"–3¼"; adult leaves 2¾"–6" × ½"–1¼"; green or less commonly grayish-green and dull (like culinary sage leaves). Extremely variable in habit; usually a small tree in cultivation. Bark rough, stringy, beige and ugly. Records: to 164' tall in the wild; 70' tall at Rosemoor, Torrington, Devon,

England (1989); 66' × 5'6" Grey Timbers, Brimley, Devon, England (1979; *pl.* 1959); 49½' × 5'5" × 54½' San Marino, CA (1993).

E. globulus Labill.

BLUE GUM. TASMANIAN BLUE GUM. SOUTHERN BLUE GUM. THE FEVER TREE. From Tasmania and coastal Victoria. Absolutely not hardy, but it is the most common kind in California—in fact globally, even though unimportant in its homeland. The first EUCALYPT cultivated outside of Australia: in 1804 in Paris. Planted on a tremendous scale in subtropical regions for timber, pulp, and essential oil from its leaves. Its weediness, messiness and flammability in California has unfairly given the whole genus a bad name. It owes its phenomenal growth and abundance to being unpalatable to browsing animals, fast, and very adaptable. The Latin epithet *globulus*, a little button, refers to the shape of the seedpod, 1¼" wide. Records: more than 250' tall in Contra Costa County, CA (1988); 165' × 35'5" Ft. Ross, CA (1989).

E. Gregsoniana L. Johnson & D. Blaxell
= *E. pauciflora* var. *nana* Blakely

WOLGAN SNOW GUM. From SE New South Wales, on ridges near Wolgan in the Blue Mountains and the Budawang Range. Named for Jesse Gregson (1837–1919) and his son Edward Jesse Gregson (1882–1955), New South Wales residents who shared a keen interest in EUCALYPTS. Grown in North America since ≤1970. Trunk handsome whitish-gray, smooth. Twigs orange to deep blood-red. Flowers creamy. Leaf notably thick, green or somewhat glaucous, to 5" × ⅞". In the wild, grows as a mallee 7'–23' tall. For a SNOW GUM, this species is not exceptionally hardy; but it resprouts readily if winter-killed.

E. Gunnii Hook. fil.
= *E. whittinghamensis* hort.

CIDER GUM. From the central plateau of Tasmania, elevation 2,000'–4,000'. Named after Ronald Campbell Gunn (1808–1881), public officer and pre-eminent botanist in Tasmania. During spring, the bark, if damaged, exudes a sweet sap called cider by the Tasmanians (some say pioneers fermented an infusion of the leaves into a kind of cider). Cultivated in England by 1846; in North America since ≤1871.

Historically, the most commonly planted hardy EU-CALYPT. Its foliage is not so bold as many, nor its bark so pretty, but it is still handsome. It tolerates wetter soils than most species. Juvenile leaves 1"–2¾" × ¾"–2"; adult leaves 1½"–5" × ½"–1⅝"; almost invariably gray-green and dull. Bark partly scrolling off to leave the trunk smooth, pale brown to gray-green. For a very similar species, if not mere subspecies, see *E. Archeri*. Records: 121' × 12'6" Sheffield Park, Sussex, England (1984; *pl.* 1912); 110' × 11'8" Trebah, Cornwall, England (1959); 96' × 19'9" Whittinghame Castle, east of Edinburgh, Scotland (1957; *pl.* 1853); 72' × 15'3" Sidbury Manor, Devon, England (1977; *pl.* 1885); 62' × 3'8" Seattle, WA (1990); 49½' × 5'5" Los Angeles, CA (1993; *pl.* 1979).

E. Gunnii ssp. Archeri—see E. Archeri

E. Kitsoniana Maiden

GIPPSLAND MALLEE. BOG GUM. FLAT ROOT. From coastal Victoria. Named after Sir Albert Ernest Kitson (1868–1937), English geologist. Grown in North America since ≤1964. Twigs stout. Leaves predominately "intermediate" rather than juvenile or adult, the true adult ones (small and very slender) rarely seen; green, often dull, bold and coarse looking; heavy and thick; up to 6¾" × 1½". Bark smooth and grayish. A mallee, usually only 4'–20' tall in the wild. Records: to 33' tall in the wild; 29' × 5'0" × 38' Los Angeles, CA (1993; *pl.* 1965).

E. melliodora A. Cunn. ex Schauer

YELLOW BOX. HONEY BOX. YELLOW IRONBARK. From SE Queensland, New South Wales, and W Victoria. Well known in Australia; prized for timber, shade and as a honey tree (its name *melliodora* means smell of honey). Grown in North America since 1858. Extremely variable form, bark, and foliage color. Leaves are a favored food of the koala. Juvenile leaves 2"–4¼" × 1⅓"–2"; adult leaves 2"–6" × ⅓"–¾"; bright green, dull gray-green or almost blue. Flowers sometimes pink. Bark ranges from scaly brown or black to almost completely smooth; the inner bark is usually a distinctive yellow. Records: to 250' × 25'1" in the wild; some in California over 80' tall.

E. Mitchelliana Cambage

MOUNT BUFFALO GUM. WEEPING SALLY. From the Buffalo plateau of NE Victoria; its wild population endangered. Named after Sir Thomas Livingstone Mitchell (1792–1855), Surveyor-General of New South Wales and noted explorer of eastern Australia. In North America since ≤1966. Leaves markedly

slender and willowy, 3"–6" × ½"; green to pale gray-green. Bark smooth, gray or white, tinged yellowish. Usually a small weeping tree less than 40' tall. Records: to 70' tall in the wild; 50' × 2'6" Kilmun, Argyll, Scotland (1978; *pl.* 1960).

E. neglecta Maiden

OMEO GUM. OMEO ROUND LEAVED GUM. From mountains of E Victoria, first collected near Omeo in the Victorian Highlands. Named *neglecta* in reference to the possibility of it being merely a dwarf form of *E. Gunnii*. In North America since ≤1950. Twigs often square. Leaves distinctively broad, very dark bluish-green (color of collard greens) with a stout red midrib, to 6" × 5" when juvenile. Adult leaves still broad but smaller (to ca. 4" × 2"). Usually a shrubby tree 11'–33' tall. Bark shreddy-flaky, dark gray-brown, recalling that of *Cratægus monogyna* (COMMON HAWTHORN). Record: 37' × 3'5" × 21' Los Angeles, CA (1993; *pl.* 1950).

E. niphophila—see E. pauciflora ssp. niphophila

E. nova-anglica Deane & Maiden

NEW ENGLAND PEPPERMINT. BLACK PEPPERMINT. From the New England Tableland in NE New South Wales, and adjacent S Queensland. In North America ≤1950. Twigs red. Juvenile leaves vivid powder blue, to 3½" × 2⅞"; adult leaves green, very long and skinny, to 10" × 1". Bark pale brown, scaly. Records: to 65½' tall in the wild; 51' × 4'10" × 34' Los Angeles, CA (1993; *pl.* 1950).

E. parvifolia—see E. parvula

E. parvula L. Johnson & K. Hill
= *E. parvifolia* Cambage 1909, non Newberry 1895

SMALL LEAVED GUM. From highlands of extreme SE New South Wales. Discovered in 1908. In North America since ≤1927. Twigs red on sunny side. Leaves up to 4¼" × ¾", dark blue-green, highly fragrant. A small, broad tree of fine texture and dark aspect. Bark tan, sloughing off to leave a smooth grayish trunk. The 1991 name *parvula* is from Latin *parvulus*, little. Record: 44' × 8'5" × 46½' San Marino, CA (1993).

E. pauciflora Sieb. ex Spreng.
= *E. coriacea* A. Cunn. *ex* Schau.

SNOW GUM. WHITE SALLEE. GHOST GUM. CABBAGE GUM. From SE Queensland to Tasmania. Latin *paucus*, few, and *florus*, flowered—inappropriately, since this species often flowers profusely. Introduced to England in 1880; to North America well before 1914. Twigs often bright red or yellow. Juvenile leaves 1"–7" × ¾"–3¼"; adult leaves 2½"–6¼" × ½"–1¼"; green or blue-green, glossy, thick; veins parallel with the midrib unlike those of most EUCALYPTS. Bark smooth, with long pieces curling off to reveal a gray or white trunk. An open, very large shrub or small broad tree. This tree and its subspecies vary considerably in cold hardiness, but some of its forms are likely the most cold-hardy of all EUCALYPTS. Some of the subspecies are very similar and have been confused in the seed trade. Records: to 65½' tall in the wild; 62' × 3'6" Kilmun Forest Garden, Argyll, Scotland (1978; *pl.* 1952).

E. pauciflora ssp. *Debeuzevillei* (Maiden) L. Johnson & D. Blaxell

= *E. Debeuzevillei* Maiden

JOUNAMA SNOW GUM. From alpine SE New South Wales. First collected by Wilfred Alexander Watt de Beuzeville (1884–1954), a New South Wales forester, on Jounama Peak of New South Wales, in 1919. In North America since ≤1941. Leaf leathery, green, much like that of ssp. *niphophila* but perhaps darker. Bark smooth, mottled light gray and white. A short-trunked, small tree. Records: to 65½' tall in the wild; 38' × 2'9" Brimley, Devon, England (1980).

E. pauciflora var. *nana*—see *E. Gregsoniana*

E. pauciflora ssp. *niphophila* (M. & B.) L. Johnson & D. Blaxell

= *E. niphophila* Maiden & Blakely

SNOW GUM. ALPINE SNOW GUM. ALPINE GUM. From alpine SE New South Wales, NE Victoria. Greek *niphos*, snow, and *philos*, loving. In North America since ≤1940. Common. Leaves 1½"–5½" × ½"–2"; semi-glossy dark bluish-green. Trunk smooth, strikingly ghostly white to tan. Usually a short, broad tree, most noted for its bark. Records: 75' × 3'9" Kilmun, Argyll, Scotland (1978; *pl.* 1955); 41' × 5'3" Grey Timbers, Brimley, Devon, England (1979); 38' × 5'5" Berkeley, CA (1994; *pl.* 1966; now dead); 32' × 4'1" × 34' Victoria, B.C. (1995).

E. pauciflora 'Pendula'

WEEPING SALLY. From Adaminaby, New South Wales. Grown in North America since the early 1950s. Narrow, thin-crowned, with very pendulous branches like a WEEPING WILLOW. Juvenile leaves to 9½" × 4⅛"; thinner than those of the preceding subspecies.

E. Perriniana F. v. Muell. *ex* Rodw.

SPINNING GUM. ROUND LEAVED SNOW GUM. SPIN WHEEL TREE. From SE New South Wales, E Victoria, Tasmania. Named after George Samuel Perrin (1849–1900), SE Australian forester. In North America since ≤1948. Juvenile leaves curiously variable: in the loveliest form rounded and "welded" into one, of vivid glaucousness and large size (to 4⅝"), spinning around the twigs after dying and turning brown. In another variant they are more triangular, less blue—in one word: unremarkable. Adult leaves 5"–8¼" × ¾"–1½"; dull blue-green. Bark shed in coarse scrolls, leaving a smooth trunk of pale green to tan or gray. An example of a nondescript big shrub in the wild proving a worthwhile ornamental tree in cultivation. Relatively shade-tolerant. Records: 55' × 8'4" × 56' Berkeley, CA (1994); 44' × 8'0" × 49' Seattle, WA (1988).

E. Rodwayi R.T. Bak. & H.G. Sm.

SWAMP PEPPERMINT. From Tasmania, often in moist or swampy areas. Named after Leonard Rodway (1853–1936), Tasmanian surgeon-dentist with a serious interest in botany. In North America since ≤1980s, still very little known. Twigs red or purplish. Leaves dark green or dark blue-green, slender (4" × ½"), often edged red. Bark on trunk rough, fibrous, gray or tan. Recorded to 65½' tall in the wild.

E. stellulata Sieb. *ex* DC.

BLACK SALLY. MUZZLE WOOD. From E New South Wales, E Victoria. Introduced to England in 1816. In North America since ≤1908. The epithet *stellulata* means resembling small stars—in reference to the small, pointed bright yellow buds in clusters of as many as 16. Leaf dark sage-green, slender and small, exceptionally to 5⅞" × 1". Seedpods or urns are tiny, like peppercorns. Bark peely on young trees but eventually close and scaly, very dark if not black. A small to medium-sized tree. It enjoys moist soils. Records: 56' × 6'9" × 27' Berkeley, CA (1994; *pl.* 1970; cut down in 1995); 42' × 6'0" × 30' Santa Barbara, CA (1993; *pl.* 1964).

Eucalyptus Stuartiana—see *E. Bridgesiana*

E. urnigera Hook. fil.

URN GUM. URN POD GUM. URN FRUITED GUM. From SE Tasmania, at montane elevations of 1,900'–3,500'. In England since ≤1860; in North America since ≤1914. Foliage amazingly variable. Juvenile leaves ¾"–3¼" × ½"–3½"; adult leaves 2"–6" × ¾"–2"; dark green to silvery glaucous (from hardier, higher-altitude trees). Flowers white, more showy than those of the other cold-hardy species. Seedpods perfect little urns. Bark peely, smooth, pale gray or blotched greenish-yellow; often ribbed and pale brown near the base of the trunk. Usually a small tree. Records: to 147½' tall in the wild; 125' × 11'2" Avondale, County Wickow, Ireland (1966); 124' × 11'1" Mt. Usher, Co. Wicklow, Ireland (1989); 85' × 12'6" Stonefield Castle, Argyll, Scotland (1986).

E. whittinghamensis—see *E. Gunnii*

Eucommia

[EUCOMMIACEÆ; Eucommia Family] A genus of only the following species, a deciduous tree grown for shade, offering lustrous foliage and pest-free constitution. Name from Greek *eu*, good or well, and *kommi*, gum; the juice abounds in gutta-percha.

E. ulmoides Oliv.

HARDY RUBBER TREE. CHINESE THREAD TREE. STONE COTTON TREE. GUTTA PERCHA TREE. CHINESE RUKKIS TREE. From SW China; now unknown wild, but much cultivated for its medicinally valuable bark, the source of a hypertension drug. Introduced to France ca. 1896. In North America ≤1909; in commerce here since ca. 1940; extremely rare until the 1980s. The specific epithet from *Ulmus*, ELM, and Greek *-oides*, resemblance.

SILK THREAD is translated from the Chinese *Tszemien*, referring to the tree's rubber content. Gently tear a leaf, piece of the corky gray bark, or a seed, and the sap congeals into delicate rubber strands. (The name GUTTA PERCHA is more commonly applied to at least two other tropical species.) Flowers inconspicuous, in April; male and female usually on separate trees. Females make flat green winged seeds much like those of an ASH (*Fraxinus*). Leaf 3"–9½" long, dark and shiny, thin. Fall color nonexistent or pale yellow. Records: to 98' tall in China; 65' × 3'1" Paris, France (1982; *pl.* 1939); 56' × 2'10" Dublin, Ireland (1987); 55' × 6'5" Philadelphia County, PA (1980); 53' × 3'11" Seattle, WA (1990); 49' × 5'6" Kew, England (1987); 41' × 5'2" × 48' Hartford, CT (1988).

Eucryphia

[EUCRYPHIACEÆ; Eucryphia Family] 5 (6) spp. of slender, usually multitrunked summer-flowering large shrubs and trees, essentially evergreen. From Greek *eu*, good or well, and *kryphios* or *kryphia*, hidden, because the sepals form a caplike cover over the flower bud. Like so many Southern Hemisphere plants, EUCRYPHIAS are sensitive to severe cold, so are grown primarily along the Pacific Coast. Even there they are unfamiliar.

E. glutinosa (Poepp. & Endl.) Baill.
= *E. pinnatifolia* Gay

HARDY EUCRYPHIA. DECIDUOUS EUCRYPHIA. From Chile; very rare in the wild state. Named in 1839. Introduced in 1859 by R. Pearce for Veitch nursery of England. In North America since ca. 1937. In commerce here since ≤1940. Referring to the buds, the epithet *glutinosa* means sticky; from Latin *glutin*, glue, and *-osa*—gummy or gluey. Foliage deciduous to semi-evergreen or fully evergreen. Fall color yellow to orange-red or crimson. Leaves consist of 3–5 leaflets, in shape and size reminiscent of those of *Sorbus aucuparia* (COMMON MOUNTAIN ASH), except dark and shiny. Flowers are the largest of the genus (2"–2¾" wide), and the first to appear (beginning late June or early July); they are slightly almond-scented and resemble single white roses or ROSE OF SHARON (*Hypericum calycinum*), with lovely bunches of greenish-white or rarely red stamens. Highly variable from seed. Usually an 8'–20' shrub; can be trained into tree form. Prefers acidic soil. Recorded to 44' tall at Lanarth in Cornwall, England.

E. glutinosa var. plena hort.

Flowers more or less double. Seedlings occasionally exhibit this trait. Sold in North America since the 1940s. Very rare, and generally considered no improvement. *Plena* in Latin means full or plump; having extra petals. Nurseries making fine distinctions separate **'Flore Pleno'** (double) from **'Semi-pleno'** (semi-double).

E. × intermedia Bausch
(*E. glutinosa × E. lucida*)

Interesting as a cross of a hardy Chilean and a tender Tasmanian species.

E. × intermedia 'Rostrevor'

The original form of the cross. A natural garden hybrid from Rostrevor House, County Down, Ireland. First exhibited in 1936. Imported into North America in 1937; in commerce here ≤1941. Leaves glossy, scarcely-toothed above the middle, usually simple (to 2½" × 1¼"), sometimes trifoliate. Blooms fully in August, then often sporadically in September, October, November, even through January in mild winters. Flowers 1½" wide, fragrant. More free-flowering than E. glutinosa. Evergreen.

E. × nymansensis Bausch
(*E. glutinosa × E. cordifolia*)

E. × nymansensis 'Mt. Usher'

Of garden origin, at Mt. Usher, Ashford, County Wicklow, Ireland (containing the richest collection of Southern Hemisphere plants in east Ireland). *E. cordifolia* was the female parent. In North American commerce ≤1943. Leaves predominately simple. Flowers 2" wide, often double.

E. × nymansensis 'Nymansay'
= *E. × nymansensis* 'Nymans A'

NYMANS HYBRID EUCRYPHIA. The type of the cross. Sown in 1914 from seed taken of an *E. glutinosa* by Ludwig Messel of Nymans, Handcross, Sussex, England. Distributed by his son Lieutenant Messel. Imported into North America in 1937. In commerce here ≤1945. Flowers in August–September, 2"–2½" wide (larger than those of E. × intermedia), honey-scented; milk-white petals surrounding yellow, pink

or tera-cotta anthers. Leaves usually consist of 3–5 extremely dark green, shiny, sharply toothed leaflets. Foliage can turn completely brown in a severe winter, then recover to flower perfectly in summer. Growth rapid: it can reach nearly 40' in 15 years. But the tops often die in severe freezes, so it begins growing anew from lower down. Dense narrow habit. Records: 75' × 3'7" Birkhill, Fife, Tayside, Scotland (1987); 53' tall (multitrunked) at Bremerton, WA (1995); 46' × 6'3" Holmbush, Sussex, England (1987).

E. pinnatifolia—see E. glutinosa

Euodia—see Tetradium

Euonymus

(*Evonymus*)

[CELASTRACEÆ; Bittersweet Family] 170–177 spp. of shrubs, vines and trees, deciduous or evergreen. *Euonymus* is an ancient Greek name, from *eu*, good or well, and *onoma*, a name; literally of good repute: well-named—used ironically because the shrubs had the reputation of stinking, and poisoning cattle. Other *Euonymus* species than the one included here are also treelike, but are exceedingly rare in comparison. A related genus is *Maytenus*.

E. europæus L.
= *E. vulgaris* Mill.

COMMON SPINDLETREE. EUROPEAN SPINDLETREE. EUROPEAN BURNING BUSH. SKEWER WOOD. PRICK TIMBER. PRICK WOOD (used to make toothpicks and skewers). DOGWOOD (decoction of leaves used to wash dogs to free them from vermin). GATTERIDGE TREE (derived from a Saxon word signifying *a cover*—from the capsule hanging, like a cover, over the fruit). LOUSE BERRY (because the powdered leaves and berries were put on the heads of children to chase away lice). From Europe, SW Asia, and the Caucasus. Common in North America and reseeding in some locales. A truly spindly and irregularly tangled shrub-tree with an intricately twisted crown usually broader than tall. It prefers alkaline soil. Twigs dull gray-green. Flowers from late April into June, inconspicuous. Fruit a decorative seed-capsule: pink-red, bursting open in fall to reveal colorful poisonous orange seeds, contrasting with the late, bright, autumn leaf color: burnt orange or red to dark purplish. Leaves 1"–3½" long; opposite. Records: 36' × 2'9" Poland (≤1973); 35' × 4'8" Forfarshire, Scotland (ca. 1836); 27' × 2'3" × 37' Wayne County, MI (1978); 25' × 2'10" × 33' Kenosha, WI (1988); 18' × 4'0" × 31' Seattle, WA (1992).

Euonymus europæus 'Albus'
= *E. europæus* var. *leucocarpa* DC.
= *E. europæus* 'Fructo-alba'
Fruits white. Described in 1770 in England. In North American commerce since ≤1888.

E. europæus 'Aldenhamensis'
Described in 1923 by V. Gibbs of Aldenham, Hertfordshire, England. In North American commerce since ≤1950s. Very popular. Fruit large, bright pink and long stemmed.

E. europæus 'Atropurpureus'
= *E. europæus* 'Purpureus'
Arose in Germany ca. 1862. Described in 1895. In North America ≤1897; in commerce here since ≤1950s. Purple leaves. Scarlet to red fall color. Fruits dark red.

E. europæus 'Atrorubens'
= *E. europæus* 'Fructu Coccineo'
= *E. europæus* 'Fructu Atropurpureo'
Arose in Germany 1865. Described in 1903. In North America ≤1897; in commerce here since ≤1940. Fruit dark carmine-red.

E. europæus 'Aucubifolius'
('Acubæfolia')
Originated <1862. Leaves blotched yellow, many almost wholly whitish, then pinkening in fall.

E. europæus 'Fructo-alba'—see *E. europæus* 'Albus'

E. europæus 'Fructu Atropurpureo'—see *E. europæus* 'Atrorubens'

E. europæus 'Fructu Coccineo'—see *E. europæus* 'Atrorubens'

E. europæus var. *leucocarpa*—see *E. europæus* 'Albus'

E. europæus 'Purpureus'—see *E. europæus* 'Atropurpureus'

E. europæus 'Red Cap'
('Red Caps')
First observed in 1952 in a lot of seedlings at the University of Nebraska, Lincoln. Selected in 1956, introduced in 1967. Fruits more heavily than usual, and fruit of deeper red color.

E. europæus 'Red Cascade'
Originated by nurseryman Rowland Jackman of Woking, Surrey, England. Introduced to North America ≤1951. Fruit deep colored, borne abundantly even by plants in isolation.

E. europæus 'Variegatus'
Originated <1836. In North American commerce ≤1888. Several clones have been sold under this name.

E. vulgaris—see *E. europæus*

Euptelea

[EUPTELEACEÆ; Euptelea Family] 2–3 spp. of shrubs or small trees. From Greek *eu*, good or well, and genus *Ptelea*, originally ELM, now applied to the HOPTREE; referring to the seed shape. A primitive genus, related to *Cercidiphyllum* (KATSURA), *Eucommia* (HARDY RUBBER TREE), *Tetracentron* (SPUR LEAF), and *Trochodendron* (WHEEL TREE).

E. japonica—see *E. polyandra*

E. polyandra S. & Z.
= *E. japonica* hort.
JAPANESE EUPTELEA. JAPANESE TASSEL TREE. From Japan. Japanese: *Fusazakura*. Named in 1835. Introduced in 1859 by Siebold to Holland. To England in 1877. In North America ≤1897; in commerce here since ≤1937. Very rare, unspectacular, and at its best only in woodland conditions. Foliage reddish while unfolding. Each leaf is roundish, 2"–6", on an elegantly slender stem (the base of which hides the bud); the teeth are jagged and

bold, the drip tip much exaggerated, the venation prominent. Fall color red and yellow, sometimes lively, but usually pale and unmemorable, even ugly green and brown. Flowers not showy, in early April (the epithet *polyandra* means many stamens; from Greek *poly*, many, and *andros*, male). Seeds teardrop-shaped. The name TASSEL TREE refers to the clustered reddish stamens or the seeds. The tree's shiny dark brown to jet-black winter buds are fascinating up close, but most people are not sufficiently taken with the tree's appearance to get near enough to observe them. A slender large shrub or small tree, to 49' in the wild.

Evodia—see *Tetradium*

Evonymus—see *Euonymus*

Fagus

[FAGACEÆ; Beech Family] 8–10 spp. of large deciduous trees of the Northern Hemisphere, nearly all in Eurasia. Grown for shade and beautiful foliage. Flowers inconspicuous. Fruit a small edible triangular nut in a somewhat prickly bur or husk ½"–1" long. *Fagus* is the ancient Latin name for *F. sylvatica*; from Greek *phagein*, to eat; referring to the edible oily nuts. BEECHES are distinctive for their notably long and thin buds, and their smooth, pale, lovely bark, often defaced by carving. Related genera include *Castanea* (CHESTNUT), *Nothofagus* (SOUTHERN BEECH), *Quercus* (OAK), and others less familiar.

F. americana—see *F. grandifolia*

F. asiatica—see *F. orientalis*

F. castaneæfolia—see *F. grandifolia*

F. crenata Bl.
= *F. Sieboldii* (Endl.) A. DC.
= *F. sylvatica* var. *Sieboldii* (A. DC.) Maxim.
= *F. sylvatica* var. *asiatica* A. DC. (in part)

JAPANESE BEECH. Japanese: *Buna*. From Japan (and var. *multinervis* in Korea). Introduced to Western cultivation in 1888 in Germany. Extremely rare in North America. It was sold sparingly in the 1920s, and some specialty nurseries periodically offer it. It may be rare because it is a dead ringer for *F. sylvatica* (EUROPEAN BEECH) except the husks are subtly

different (more bristly, less prickly). Maybe it has better fall color—yellowish-golden in October. On a practical note, it does not grow as large. Leaf 2"–5½" long; 7–12 vein pairs. Records: to 100' × 11'10" in Japan; 76' × 4'6" Birr Castle, County Offaly, Ireland (1975); 60' × 7'9" Petworth House, Sussex, England (1983).

F. Engleriana O. Seem.
= *F. sylvatica* var. *chinensis* Franch.

CHINESE BEECH. From central China. Named after a famous German botanist, Heinrich Gustav Adolph Engler (1844–1930). Introduced by E. Wilson to the Arnold Arboretum in 1907. In North American commerce since ≤1954. Extremely rare. The trunk almost invariably divides at the very base. Crown slender, vase-shaped, with elegant light green foliage. Leaf 2"–5" long; the margins gently undulated; 10–14 vein pairs. Fall color deep yellow to golden and orange. Nut bur on a slender stalk 1½"–3" long. Records: to 75' tall in China; 55' × 14'7" × 80' Philadelphia, PA (1980).

F. ferruginea—see *F. grandifolia*

F. grandifolia Ehrh.
= *F. americana* Sweet
= *F. ferruginea* Ait.
= *F. castaneæfolia* de Vos

AMERICAN BEECH. From eastern North America, and NE Mexico. Long in cultivation, but less tolerant of urban settings than *F. sylvatica* (EUROPEAN BEECH). Also far less variable: while EUROPEAN BEECH has a multitude of ornamental cultivars, our native has none. The American has paler bark (often nearly white), and a less dense, finer silhouette. In one word it is more refined. Roots shallow and extensive, occasionally suckering. Leaf 2"–6" long, thin, sharply toothed; 9–18 vein pairs. Fall color clear yellow to gold, orange or bronzy. Nut burs ca. ¾" long. The epithet *grandifolia* is Latin from *grandis*, large, and *folium*, a leaf. Records: 161' × 13'11" × 105' Berrien County, MI (1976); 102' × 16'9" × 138' Van Buren County, MI (1983); 95' × 21'8" × 83' Delaware County, PA (1980); 85' × 15'8" × 160' White, IL (1972); 70' × 28'6" Carroll Creek, Washington County, TN (<1916).

F. macrophylla—see *F. orientalis*

F. × moesiaca (Maly) Czecz.
= *F. × taurica* Popl., p.p.
= *F. sylvatica* var. *moesiaca* (Maly) Hayek
(*F. orientalis* × *F. sylvatica*)

BALKAN BEECH. CRIMEAN BEECH. From the Balkans, eastern Central Europe and Crimea. Moesia is a region of the mid Balkan Peninsula. Like *F. sylvatica* but with narrower leaf bases, more veins per leaf, and longer, softer bristles on the nut burs. This name, indeed the very existence of this hybrid entity, is unrecognized horticulturally. For the sake of precision it is noted here, as likely including certain so-called *F. sylvatica* clones: **'Latifolia'**, **'Macrophylla'**, **'Zlatia'**; and with the largest leaves of all, **'Prince George of Crete'**.

F. orientalis Lipsky

= *F. sylvatica* var. *macrophylla* Hohen. *ex* A. DC. 1864, non Dipp. 1892
= *F. macrophylla* (Hohen.) Koidz.
= *F. sylvatica* var. *asiatica* A. DC. (in part)
= *F. asiatica* (A. DC.) Winkl.

ORIENTAL BEECH. From SE Europe to the Caspian Sea region. Named in 1864. Introduced to northern Europe between 1880 and 1904. The date of its introduction to North America is not known. Extremely rare in commerce here, but has been distributed from one botanic garden to another—at least since the 1950s and probably decades before. On a practical level, ORIENTAL BEECH is a bigleaved version of *F. sylvatica* (EUROPEAN BEECH). Leaf narrowed near base, broadest above the middle, to 8" × 4½", stem to ⅜" long; untoothed; 7–13 vein pairs. The bark may become furrowed. See also *F.* × *moesiaca*. Records: to 164' × 24'8" in the wild; 88' × 5'9" Birr Castle, County Offaly, Ireland (1985); 85' × 5'3" Battleby, Perthshire, Scotland (1991); 80' × 7'0" Edinburgh Botanic Garden, Scotland (1981); 64' × 4'2½" Seattle, WA (1994; *pl.* 1957); a trunk 8'2" around (at 1' from the ground) at Brooklyn, NY (1972).

F. Sieboldii—see *F. crenata*

F. sylvatica L.

EUROPEAN BEECH. From Europe, and east as far as the Black Sea. In North America since <1752. Common and very important as an ornamental here. An immense tree, casting deep shade. Easy to please. Leaf 2"–4"; wavy-edged, shiny; 5–10 vein pairs. When unfolding in April and early May the leaves are almost translucent, and fringed with soft silky white hairs. Fall color variable, but late and generally rusty or tarnished gold. Some leaves often cling, brown, well into winter. Nut burs ¾"–1" long, opening from mid-August into autumn. *Fagus sylvatica* is the most variable of all ornamental shade trees. Although more than 30 cultivars are

included in the next 5½ pages, still others known only in Europe are excluded. The name *sylvatica* derives from Latin *silva* and means of the woods or forest. Records: to 164' tall in the wild; 151' × 15'6" Hallyburton House, Tayside, Scotland (1986); 121' × 6'3" Seattle, WA (1992; *pl.* 1911); 105' × 21'6" × 135' near Edinburgh, Scotland (1903); 105' × 17'10" Taunton, MA (1987); 99' × 22'8" Pomfret, CT (1987); 85' × 25'0" Philadelphia, PA (1980); 80' × 26'0" Eride Park, Kent, England (1958; pollard); a trunk 31'9" around at Windsor Great Park, Berkshire, England (1864).

F. sylvatica 'Albo-marginata'—see *F. sylvatica* 'Albo-variegata'

F. sylvatica 'Albo-variegata'

= *F. sylvatica* 'Argenteo-variegata'
= *F. sylvatica* 'Albo-marginata'
= *F. sylvatica* 'Variegata'

Originated in Europe <1770, the year it was described officially. Probably introduced early into North America, but extremely rare here. Needs partial shade to be at its best. Grows about as tall as typical *F. sylvatica*, but can be gaunt and open. Leaves irregular, smaller, narrower and more pointed, often deformed; strikingly edged and streaked creamy white. Reverts easily to normal green foliage. There may be more than one clone with whitish variegated leaves. Records: 92' × 10'2" Melbury, Dorset, England (1980); 69' × 11'10" Rossdhu, Strathclyde, Scotland (1985).

F. sylvatica 'Ansorgei'

DWARF COPPER BEECH. Probably originated as an *F. sylvatica* f. *purpurea* crossed with 'Asplenifolia'. Found ca. 1884 by Carl Ansorge, of Flottbeck nursery, Hamburg, Germany. Described in 1904. It then became lost to commerce, but was found again in the 1960s. Sold in 1990–91 by Mitsch nursery of Aurora, OR. Shrubby or a small tree. Leaf narrow, crinkly, WILLOW-like, purple.

F. sylvatica 'Arcuata'—see *F. sylvatica* f. *tortuosa*

F. sylvatica 'Argenteo-variegata'—see *F. sylv.* 'Albo-variegata'

F. sylvatica var. *asiatica*—see *F. crenata* and *F. orientalis*

F. sylvatica 'Asplenifolia'

= F. sylvatica 'Salicifolia'
= F. sylvatica 'Heterophylla' (in part)
= F. sylvatica 'Incisa' (in part)

FERNLEAF BEECH. Probably originated in France. Introduced ≤1804, by Conrad Loddiges and Sons nursery of England. In Latin, *aspleniifolia* means leaves like the frond of the SPLEENWORT FERN. This is the common CUTLEAF BEECH; the rarer one in circulation (leaf less deeply cut) is treated under *F. sylvatica* f. *laciniata* (which see). Leaves narrow lanceolate, sometimes deeply pinnately lobed, variable; some are straplike to 4" × ⅕". Compared to typical EUROPEAN BEECHES, the FERNLEAF clone crown is less dark, more elegant, and slightly smaller. Records: 111' × 13'2" Busbridge Lake, Surrey, England (1990); 89' × 10'10" Walla Walla, WA (1988); 80' × 14'10" Litchfield, CT (1988); 70' × 15'0" Philadelphia, PA (1980).

F. sylvatica 'Atropunicea'—see F. sylvatica f. purpurea

F. sylvatica 'Atropurpurea'—see F. sylvatica f. purpurea

F. sylv. 'Atropurpurea Latifolia'—see F. sylv. 'Purpurea Latifolia'

F. sylv. 'Atropurpurea Macrophylla'—see F. sylv. 'Purpurea Latifolia'

F. sylvatica 'Atropurpurea Major'—see F. sylv. 'Purpurea Latifolia'

F. sylvatica 'Atropurpurea Pendula'—see F. sylv. 'Purpurea Pendula'

F. sylvatica 'Atropurpurea Rohani'—see F. sylv. 'Rohanii'

F. sylvatica 'Aurea'—see F. sylvatica 'Zlatia'

F. sylvatica 'Aurea Pendula'
('Aureopendula')

= F. sylvatica 'Pendula Aurea'

GOLDEN WEEPING BEECH. Originated as a bud sport from a WEEPING BEECH in the nursery of J.G. van der Bom, Oudenbosch, Holland; found in 1900. Extremely rare in North America. Likely not in the nursery trade here until Scanlon nursery of Ohio acquired specimens in the 1950s. Vermeulen nursery of New Jersey sold specimens ca. 1980. Leaves first bright yellow, then yellow-green. Needs part shade or it scorches; in too much shade it is greenish. A slow, narrow tree, well described as a 30' pillar of gold.

F. sylvatica 'Borneyensis'
('Bornyensis')

BORNEY WEEPING BEECH. Originated in Borney forest, near Metz, France. Introduced ca. 1870 by Simon-Louis nursery of Metz, France. In North America since at least 1895. Vermeulen nursery of New Jersey has sold specimens since ≤1980. Probably also sold as *F. sylvatica* 'Pendula'. Straight erect trunk with weeping branches. Size and rate of growth not known.

F. sylvatica 'Brocklesby'—see F. sylvatica 'Purpurea Latifolia'

F. sylvatica 'Castanæfolia'—see F. sylvatica f. laciniata

F. sylvatica var. chinensis—see F. Engleriana

F. sylvatica 'Cochleata'

= F. sylvatica 'Undulata'

SNAIL-LEAF BEECH. In the English nursery trade by 1842. In North America ≤1896. In commerce here ≤1990–91. *Cochlea* in Latin is a snail, referring to the leaves. Very slow-growing, shrubby, compact, narrow. Leaves shell-like—concave, obovate, jaggedly toothed. The leaf looks pinched lengthwise, is narrower than normal ones, its edges rolled under. A freak.

F. sylvatica 'Conglomerata'—see F. sylvatica 'Cristata'

F. sylvatica 'Contorta'—see F. sylvatica f. tortuosa

F. sylvatica 'Crispa'—see F. sylvatica 'Cristata'

F. sylvatica 'Cristata'

= F. sylvatica 'Cucullata'
= F. sylvatica 'Crispa'
= F. sylvatica 'Monstruosa'
= F. sylvatica 'Conglomerata'

COCK'S COMB BEECH. Name published in 1811, but the tree was not grown commonly before 1836. In North American commerce ≤1903. Very rare here. A gaunt, narrow, long branched, bright green tree, slow-growing but eventually tall; the Latin name means *crested* and refers to its densely clustered stemless leaves, deeply lobed and curled. Records: 88½' × 10'7" Yair House, Borders, Scotland (1984); 82' × 9'6" Wray Castle, Cumbria, England (1987); 50½' × 2'8" Vancouver, B.C. (1994; *pl.* 1978); 41' × 5'2" Wellesley, MA (1983).

F. sylvatica 'Cucullata'—see *F. sylvatica* 'Cristata'

F. sylvatica 'Cuprea'—see *F. sylvatica* f. *purpurea*

F. sylvatica 'Dawyck'
= *F. sylvatica* 'Fastigiata' (in part)
= *F. sylvatica* 'Pyramidalis' hort. (in part)

DAWYCK BEECH. COLUMNAR BEECH. Originated at Dawyck, Peeblesshire, Scotland, ca. 1800–1850. Scions were distributed in 1907; in commerce 1912–13 by Hesse nursery of Weener, Hanover. In North American nurseries since ≤1930s. Commonly sold. The clone was sterile until 1968. About 40% of its seedlings are also fastigiate. It is a columnar tree, remaining ca. 13' wide even when 50'–60' tall. In an exposed, dryish site it may quickly slow in height growth and swell to more than 20' wide. Records: 93' × 7'3" Tortworth Court, Gloucestershire, England (1980); 92' × 6'0" Arnold Arboretum, MA (1975); 87' × 8'0" the original tree at Dawyck (1982); 66' × 2'1" Seattle, WA (1993; *pl.* 1957); 62' × 4'8" Stamford, CT (1986).

F. sylvatica 'Dawyck Gold'
Raised at Rotterdam, Holland, by Dick Van Hoey Smith, from 'Dawyck' nuts produced in 1968. The pollen parent was 'Zlatia'. Tolerates full sun. Foliage gold at first, bright green in summer. In North American commerce ≤1987.

F. sylvatica 'Dawyck Purple'
= *F. sylvatica* 'Dawyck Red'

Origin same as 'Dawyck Gold'. Leaf purple. Broader and not as dense as the 'Dawyck' gold and green versions. In North American commerce ≤1987.

F. sylvatica 'Dawyck Red'—see *F. sylvatica* 'Dawyck Purple'

F. sylvatica 'Fastigiata'
= *F. sylvatica* 'Pyramidalis' (in part)

First cultivated in 1864 in Germany. The original COLUMNAR BEECH that was superseded by 'Dawyck'. Presumably no longer cultivated. It is not known whether there are specimens in North America (probably), but the name 'Fastigiata' has certainly been much used in commerce, largely if not wholly as a synonym of 'Dawyck'.

F. sylvatica 'Faux de Vesey'—see *F. sylvatica* f. *tortuosa*

F. sylvatica 'Heterophylla'—see *F. sylvatica* 'Asplenifolia' and *F. sylvatica* f. *laciniata*

F. sylvatica 'Hêtre Parasol'—see *F. sylvatica* f. *tortuosa*

F. sylvatica 'Horizontalis'—see *F. sylvatica* f. *pendula*

F. sylv. 'Incisa'—see *F. sylv.* 'Asplenifolia' and *F. sylvatica* f. *laciniata*

F. sylvatica 'Interrupta'
Raised in 1950 at Rotterdam, Holland, by Dick Van Hoey Smith, as a seedling of 'Rohanii'. Named in 1955. Offered since 1990–91 by Mitsch nursery of Aurora, OR. Leaves green and "interrupted." Described by its raiser: "After a normal petiole and leaf base the leaf stops, the main vein goes on and a second part of the leaf comes, which stops, again the main vein goes on and a third small leaflet can end the leaf."

F. sylvatica 'Interrupta Purpurea'
A purple-leaved 'Interrupta' offered since 1987–88 by Mitsch nursery of Aurora, OR. Described as a tall tree.

F. sylvatica f. laciniata (Pers.) Domin
CUTLEAF BEECH. Originated ca. 1792 as a branch sport on the Tetschen estate, Bohemia. Named officially in 1795. This group name embraces all cutleaf cultivars (e.g.: **'Asplenifolia'**, **'Castanæfolia'**, **'Heterophylla'**, **'Incisa'**, **'Laciniata'**, **'Quercifolia'** and **'Quercina'**). One cultivar ('Asplenifolia'—treated separately on the previous page) has been grown far more commonly than all the rest combined. Of the others, the least rare clone (call it 'Laciniata') has only been sparingly circulated; the remainder are practically the same as 'Laciniata', or are exceedingly rare, or have gone extinct commercially. The 'Laciniata' clone has a leaf of nearly normal size, deeply toothed about ⅓ of the distance to the middle. 'Laciniata' does not make as refined a tree as 'Asplenifolia'. Unfortunately the name *laciniata* has often been used for 'Asplenifolia'. In a technical sense this is permitted, but more precise usage is to call a clone by its clonal name, not by a general name that may refer to any of several cultivars. To review U.S. nursery catalogs from the 1800s and read that "laciniata" BEECH is offered, leaves us not knowing which clone was being sold. However it is certain that nurseries circulated more than just 'Asplenifolia'. For example, 'Quercifolia' (meaning OAKLEAF) has been called a comparative

dwarf, with smaller leaves. Records: 88½' × 16'9" Geneva, Switzerland (1967); 82' × 10'3" Capenoch, Dumfries, Scotland (1979).

F. sylvatica f. latifolia Kirchn.
= F. sylv. var. macrophylla Dipp. 1892, non Hohen. ex A. DC. 1864

BIGLEAF BEECH. Named in 1864. The name latifolia means broad-leaved; from Latin latus, broad, and folium, a leaf. Leaf much larger than typical ones, to 6" × 4" or more. Some BEECH cultivars belong either under this name, or are hybrids and are properly placed under F. × moesiaca. There is disagreement among experts. One such cultivar is 'Prince George of Crete' (sent to England in 1898 by the King of Denmark's gardener), its leaves to 7" × 5½". Other bigleaf clones have been sold as 'Latifolia' or 'Macrophylla'.

F. sylvatica 'Macrophylla'—see F. × moesiaca and F. sylvatica f. latifolia

F. sylvatica var. macrophylla—see F. orientalis and F. sylvatica f. latifolia

F. sylvatica 'Miltonensis'

MILTON WEEPING BEECH. Originated in Milton Park, Northamptonshire, England. First publicized in 1837. The original clone was less propagated than imposters, some of which are not remarkably pendulous. Be that as it may, the most commonly sold clone called 'Miltonensis' has branching that is more horizontal than that of 'Pendula' and leaves which are more rounded. In North America, it might well have been sold as 'Pendula'. Records: one ca. 70' tall in North Devon, England (1989); 66' × 20'2" × 76' Philadelphia County, PA (1980); 45' × 7'9" × 63' Milton Hall, Northamptonshire, England (1970).

F. sylvatica var. moesiaca—see F. × moesiaca

F. sylvatica 'Monstruosa'—see F. sylvatica 'Cristata'

F. sylvatica 'Nana Pendula'—see F. sylvatica f. tortuosa

F. sylvatica 'Norwegica' or 'Norwegiensis'— see F. sylvatica 'Swat Magret'

F. sylvatica 'Obelisk'—see F. sylvatica 'Rohan Obelisk'

F. sylvatica 'Pagnyensis'—see F. sylvatica f. tortuosa

F. sylvatica f. pendula (Loud.) Schelle

WEEPING BEECH. The name pendula is from Latin pendulus, hanging, referring to the fine drooping twigs. Two general categories of WEEPING BEECHES exist: mushroom and fountain. The mushroom form tends to be squat and broad, with several undulating, irregular leaders, becoming tentlike, sometimes eventually 80'–100' wide. The fountain form is narrow and can be very tall. A clone of the fountain form is 'Borneyensis'. The use of the epithet pendula in a formal sense as cited here embraces any and all WEEPING BEECH clones. On the other hand, used in a clonal sense 'Pendula' refers solely to the clone originally sold in 1836 by Loddiges nursery of England. Synonyms of the English 'Pendula' include: 'Horizontalis', 'Tabuliformis' and 'Umbraculifera'. WEEPING BEECHES of both mushroom and fountain form have long been cultivated in North America, the mushroom more common. Frank J. Scott's 1870 book reports a WEEPING BEECH was planted in 1834 at Newton, MA. Another, said to be from Belgium, was planted in 1847 by nurseryman S. Parsons at Flushing, NY. Records: 105' × 10'3" Drumlanrig Castle, Dumfries, Scotland (1984); 92' × 6'7" × 53' Portland, OR (1989); 67' × 16'0" × 76' Delaware County, PA (1980); 64' × 21'10" × 74' Cambridge, MA (1994); 50' × 10'2" × 65' Kennett Square, PA (1973); 34' tall and 88' wide at Leiden, Holland (ca. 1938; pl. 1840).

F. sylvatica 'Pendula Aurea'—see F. sylvatica 'Aurea Pendula'

F. sylvatica 'Prince George of Crete'—see F. × moesiaca and F. sylvatica f. latifolia

F. sylvatica 'Purple Fountain'

A seedling of 'Purpurea Pendula' raised in Holland. Distributed in 1975 by Grootendoorst nursery. In North American commerce ≤1983–84. Narrowly upright and forming a leader, instead of a low broad mop. Leaves less dark purple than those of its parent.

F. sylvatica f. purpurea (Ait.) Schneid.
= F. sylvatica 'Atropunicea' or 'Atropurpurea'

COPPER BEECH. PURPLE BEECH. Originated <1680 at Buch, near Zurich, Switzerland. Date of introduction into North America not known. Thomas Jefferson planted one or more at Monticello sometime between 1801 and 1809. Maybe they failed. André Parmentier introduced it <1830 near Brooklyn, NY. Common in cultivation. Comes more or less true from seed, and darker purple clones have in turn been named (e.g.:

'Riversii', 'Spaethiana', 'Swat Magret'). Paler seed-lings have been sold as COPPER BEECHES (**'Cuprea'**). They grow every bit as large as the typical green BEECHES, and are just as common in cultivation. Records: 124' × 17'3" Dorking, Surrey, England (1984); 119' × 16'0" × 81' Everett, WA (1993); 97' × 16'3" × 106' Greenwich, CT (1988); 81' × 22'5" × 104' Willimantic, CT (1988); 75' × 22'2" × 89' Wawa, PA (1979).

F. sylvatica 'Purpurea Latifolia'

= *F. sylvatica* 'Atropurpurea Latifolia'
= *F. sylvatica* 'Atropurpurea Macrophylla'
= *F. sylvatica* 'Atropurpurea Major'
= *F. sylvatica* 'Brocklesby'
= *F. sylvatica* 'Purpurea Macrophylla'

Originated <1877 in Germany. Likely a hybrid with *F. orientalis*; if so, it is technically a cultivar of *F. × moesiaca*. Not certain to be in North American com-merce. There has been confusion: possibly this clone has been sold as 'Riversii'. Both have large purple leaves (as does 'Swat Magret') but those of 'Riversii' are largest and shiniest.

F. sylvatica 'Purpurea Macrophylla'—see *F. sylvatica* 'Purpurea Latifolia'

F. sylvatica 'Purpurea Major'—see *F. sylvatica* 'Riversii'

F. sylvatica 'Purpurea Norwegiensis'—see *F. sylvatica* 'Swat Magret'

F. sylvatica 'Purpurea Pendula' ('Purpureo Pendula')

= *F. sylvatica* 'Atropurpurea Pendula'

PURPLE WEEPING BEECH. Name published in 1865 in Germany. In North American commerce ≤1903. Common. A slow-growing purple-leaved mop or mushroom, of shrub size; rarely encountered more than 5'–15' tall, but its height is primarily a result of how high it was grafted. An upright, much younger PURPLE WEEPING BEECH is 'Purple Fountain'.

F. sylvatica 'Pyramidalis'—see *F. sylvatica* 'Dawyck' and 'Fastigiata'

F. sylvatica 'Purpurea Riversii'—see *F. sylvatica* 'Riversii'

F. sylvatica 'Purpurea Spaethii'—see *F. sylvatica* 'Spaethiana'

F. sylvatica 'Purpurea Tricolor'

= *F. sylvatica* 'Roseomarginata'
= *F. sylvatica* 'Tricolor' (in part)

PURPLE TRICOLOR BEECH. ROSEPINK BEECH. Originated in 1880 in Germany. Introduced to North American commerce ≤1891. Common. Leaves purple, pink edged. The purple fades badly to bronzy-green in summer. The tree is vigorous but does not grow as large as regular GREEN, COPPER or PURPLE BEECHES. Records: one 100' tall at Balaine near Villeneuve sur Allier, France (1973); 88' × 5'3½" × 50' Port Coquitlam, B.C. (1994); 72' × 6'0" Leonards-lee, Sussex, England (1985); 48' × 5'4" × 46' Montgomery County, PA (1980); 48' × 6'4" × 35' Spo-kane, WA (1993); a trunk 8'5" around at Glen Cove, NY (1972).

F. sylvatica 'Quercifolia'—see *F. sylvatica* f. *laciniata*

F. sylvatica 'Quercina'—see *F. sylvatica* f. *laciniata*

F. sylvatica 'Quercoides'

OAKBARK BEECH. Discovered near Göttingen, Ger-many. Named in 1800 (from genus *Quercus*, OAK, and Greek *-oides*, resemblance). Extremely rare in North America. Bark rugged and grooved more like an OAK than a regular BEECH.

F. sylvatica 'Red Obelisk'—see *F. sylvatica* 'Rohan Obelisk'

F. sylvatica 'Remillyensis'—see *F. sylvatica* f. *tortuosa*

F. sylvatica 'Riversii'

= *F. sylvatica* 'Purpurea Major'
= *F. sylvatica* 'Purpurea Riversii'

RIVERS' PURPLE BEECH. Introduced <1869 by Thomas Rivers' nursery of Sawbridgeworth, Hertfordshire, England. In North American nurseries since ≤1907. The commonest PURPLE BEECH clone here. Leaves large (to 5" × 3½"), glossy, deep purple. See *F. sylvatica* 'Purpurea Latifolia'.

F. sylvatica 'Rohan Gold'

Raised at Rotterdam, Holland, by Dick Van Hoey Smith, from 'Rohanii' nuts produced in 1968. In North America since ≤1988. Leaves OAK-like as in 'Rohanii' but yellow at least in spring.

F. sylvatica 'Rohan Obelisk'

= F. sylvatica 'Obelisk'

= F. sylvatica 'Red Obelisk'

Raised at Rotterdam, Holland, by Dick Van Hoey Smith, as a seedling of 'Dawyck' pollinated by 'Rohanii'. In North American commerce ≤1987–88.

F. sylvatica 'Rohan Trompenburg'

Raised in the late 1940s or early '50s at Trompenburg Arboretum of Rotterdam, Holland, by Dick Van Hoey Smith, as a seedling of 'Rohanii' pollinated by a PURPLE BEECH. Leaves very dark purplish, longer-pointed. Also much more easily grafted, and grows better. An improvement that should eclipse the original 'Rohanii'.

F. sylvatica 'Rohanii'

= F. sylvatica 'Atropurpurea Rohani'

PURPLE OAKLEAF BEECH. PURPLE CUTLEAF BEECH. Originated on the estate of Prince Camille de Rohan at Sychrov, Bohemia, from 1888 seeds of the PURPLE BEECH clone 'Purpurea Latifolia' ('Brocklesby') pollinated by the CUTLEAF BEECH clone 'Quercifolia'. Name published in 1894. Tree put it into commerce in 1908 by V. Masek and Son nursery of Turnov. In North American nurseries since ≤1950. Common. Leaf strongly toothed, even lobed, and bronzy-purple in spring. The tree is narrower and smaller than typical BEECHES. Likely to be replaced by the recent cultivar 'Rohan Trompenburg'. Records: a trunk 6'5" around in Czechoslovakia (1985); 58' × 2'11" × 33' Seattle, WA (1993; pl. 1950).

F. sylvatica 'Roseomarginata'—see F. sylv. 'Purpurea Tricolor'

F. sylvatica 'Rotundifolia'

ROUNDLEAF BEECH. Originated <1872 near St. Johns, Woking, Surrey, England. In North America since ≤1903. Very rare. Strongly ascending branches. Small round leaves, averaging ca. 1½" × 1⅜". Growth very slow and compact, sometimes even bushy. Records: 100' × 8'9" × 60' Montgomery County, PA (1980); 79' × 9'6" Castlehill, Devon, England (1983).

F. sylvatica 'Salicifolia'—see F. sylvatica 'Asplenifolia'

F. sylvatica var. Sieboldii—see F. crenata

F. sylvatica 'Spaethiana'

('Spaethii')

= F. sylvatica 'Purpurea Spaethii'

SPAETH (OR SPÄTH) PURPLE BEECH. Introduced in 1901 by Späth nursery of Germany. In North American commerce ≤1954. Compared to the purpleleaf clone 'Riversii', this has a smaller, darker purple leaf, later to flush, and later to drop. The tree also is narrower and smaller.

F. sylvatica 'Suentelensis'—see F. sylvatica f. tortuosa

F. sylvatica 'Swat Magret'

= F. sylvatica 'Norwegica'

= F. sylvatica 'Norwegiensis'

= F. sylvatica 'Purpurea Norwegiensis'

SWAT MAGRET PURPLE BEECH. Raised in ca. 1885 by G. Frahm nursery of Elmshorn, Germany. Introduced ≤1920. In North American commerce ≤1980. Extremely rare. Leaf purple and very large, to 7⅞" long, with undulated edges; flushes early relative to other purpleleaf clones. It may be confused with 'Purpurea Latifolia'.

F. sylvatica 'Tabuliformis'—see F. sylvatica f. pendula

F. sylvatica f. tortuosa (Pépin) Hegi

PARASOL BEECH. TWISTED BEECH. Originated ca. 1825 in N France, N Germany, Denmark, and S Sweden. In North America ≤1887. Very rare. A variable assemblage, having in common more or less dwarfed habit usually at least twice as broad as tall, with twisted and partly pendulous branches. Numerous clones have been named, and nobody pretends to be able to tell them apart. They include: 'Arcuata', 'Contorta', 'Faux de Vesey', 'Hêtre Parasol', 'Nana Pendula', 'Pagnyensis', 'Remillyensis', 'Suentelensis', etc. Record: 50' × 10'2" × 65' Longwood Gardens, PA (1973); 23' × 5'0" Paris, France (1982; pl. 1852).

F. sylvatica 'Tricolor'

TRICOLOR BEECH. Originated <1870 by Simon-Louis nursery of Metz, France. Extremely rare. Needs shade. Weak; rarely grows more than 25' tall. Leaves green, edged with pink in spring, turning white in summer. The clone almost universally supplied under this name is really 'Purpurea Tricolor'.

F. sylvatica 'Umbraculifera'—see F. sylvatica f. pendula

Fagus sylvatica 'Undulata'—see *F. sylvatica* 'Cochleata'

F. sylvatica 'Variegata'—see *F. sylvatica* 'Albo-variegata'

F. sylvatica 'Zlatia'
= *F. sylvatica* 'Aurea'

GOLDEN BEECH. Discovered as a COPPER BEECH sport in a native stand of *F. × moesiaca* near Vranje in Serbia; distributed in 1890 by Späth nursery of Germany. In the North American nursery trade since ≤1954. The name 'Zlatia' is from the Serb / Croatian word for gold, *zlato*. Leaves yellow until July or August, then bright green with a golden halo of sorts. Yellow in autumn. Slower-growing than typical BEECHES. Somewhat big leaves, so probably a hybrid. Leafs-out weeks ahead of other BEECH cultivars. Records: 82' × 11'6" Hollycombe, Liphook, Hampshire, England (1984); a trunk 9'10" around at Osowa Sien, Poland (≤1973); 54' × 3'8¼" Seattle, WA (1995; *pl.* 1954).

F. × taurica—see *F. × moesiaca*

Ficus

[MORACEÆ; Mulberry Family] 700–800 spp. of mostly tropical or subtropical broadleaf evergreen shrubs, trees and vines. Only the following species, the common FIG, is deciduous, cold hardy and common in outdoors cultivation. Many houseplant *Ficus* look nothing like it. *Ficus* is an ancient Latin name, from non Indo-European sources.

F. Carica L.

COMMON FIG. EDIBLE FIG. From the E Mediterranean region and SW Asia. *Carica* is an ancient Latin name, meaning of Caria in southwest Asia Minor. Cultivated 5,000 years ago. Its role as a food producer is major. It has featured in literature and folklore. Introduced to North America <1577 by Spaniards. Common. Now bird-disseminated in parts of California.

Twigs very stout. Leaves broad, thick, hairy, palmately 3–5 lobed, 5"–13" long, with white sap. Fall color dismal, green and some yellow. The dried, canned and fresh fruit is well known in markets, but many cultivars offer variations. The trees tend to be low, broad and like giant shrubs. Bark smooth, pale gray, often very handsomely contrasting with the dark green foliage. Needs much sun and warmth to bear well. Tolerates heavy pruning and is nonchalant about most soils. Records: 80' tall in Stanislaus County, CA (<1913); 60' × 12'2" × 77' Knight's Ferry, CA (≤1921); 50' × 8'1" London, England (1748; *pl.* 1548); 31' × 5'11" × 40' Seattle, WA (1987); one planted in 1856 at Chico, CA, was more than 150' wide ≤1921; a trunk 18'0" around in Oroville, CA (≤1921; *pl.* 1853).

Firmiana

[STERCULIACEÆ; Chocolate Family] 8–10 (15) spp. of the Old World. Named after Count Karl Joseph von Firmian (1716–1782), Austrian statesman and governor of Lombardy. Nearly all members of the STERCULIACEÆ are tropical. The following species makes an odd shade tree that withstands some freezing (to ca. 0°F).

F. platanifolia—see *F. simplex*

F. simplex (L.) W.F. Wight
= *F. platanifolia* (L. fil.) Marsili
= *Sterculia platanifolia* L. fil.

CHINESE PARASOL TREE. PHŒNIX TREE. BOTTLE TREE. JAPANESE VARNISH TREE. From China, Korea, the Ryukyus, Taiwan, and Viet Nam. Introduced in 1757 from Japan to England. In North America ≤1858. Only common in parts of the Southeast; weedy in parts of the South. The name *simplex* refers to the leaves being simple; not compound. The old name *Sterculia* refers to Sterculius, a Roman god. PHŒNIX TREE is accounted for because the Chinese say that bird prefers to perch on this tree. A round-headed slender tree with a smooth greenish snakelike trunk. Leaves bold, lobed like that of the FIG (*Ficus Carica*), hairless or ± densely hairy beneath, to 15¾" long and wide, turning an ugly mix of wet cardboard color and green in late fall—or at best a good yellow color. Leafstem tough, rubbery and long. Blossoms in July or August: large clusters of lightly fragrant, creamy, star-shaped flowers ¾" wide with petal-like sepals. Seed-pods to 4"–5" long, like little parasols. The name VARNISH TREE refers to brownish fluid released by the opening seed pods. Records: 72' × 7'2½" Montpellier, France (1887); 65' tall at Little Rock, AR (ca. 1982); 58' × 6'8" Tyler, TX (1972); 45' × 5'0" Kingstree, SC (1969).

Fitzroya

[CUPRESSACEÆ; Cypress Family] Only the following species in the genus; a coniferous evergreen. Named after Captain Robert Fitzroy (1805–1865), meteorologist and commander of H.M. the *Beagle* during C. Darwin's momentous 1831–36 voyage, during which the species was discovered.

F. cupressoides (Mol.) I.M. Johnston
= *F. patagonica* Hook. fil. *ex* Lindl.

PATAGONIAN CYPRESS. ALERCE or ALERZE. *Alerce* is Spanish (from Arabic *al-arzah*, the name of *Tetraclinus articulata*, a tree of S Spain and N Africa). From S Chile and SW Argentina. The specific name from genus *Cupressus*, and Greek *-oides*, resemblance. Exploited for its valuable wood since the 16th century. Introduced in 1849 by Wm. Lobb to Veitch nursery of England. In North America ≤1871. In the wild it can live 3,400 years. Foliage scaly, consisting of bluntish, short leaves in alternating whorls of three, dark green with two bright white bands on each side. A spray in hand is reminiscent visually and in raspiness to a bluntish JUNIPER twig, but rather stout in texture and practically inodorous—a weak piney scent. Cones rounded, woody, ¼"–⅓" across. To look lovely, rich and pendulous, and to thrive in cultivation *Fitzroya* needs plentiful moisture and freedom from extreme temperatures, as well as many decades. It endures less ideal conditions stoically, but looks dreadful and grows almost imperceptibly—maybe attaining 13' in height after 34 years! Because of this, it has remained an exceedingly rare collector's item.

Records: to 164' × 37'5" in the wild; 68' × 6'6" Strone, Argyll, Scotland (1982); 58' × 7'6" Kilmacurragh, Ireland (1980).

F. patagonica—see F. cupressoides

Fokienia

[CUPRESSACEÆ; Cypress Family] Only the following species in the genus; a coniferous evergreen. Named after Fukien or Fokien (Fujian), province of SE China. Related genera include *Calocedrus* and *Chamæcyparis*.

F. Hodginsii (Dunn) Henry & Thomas
= *Cupressus Hodginsii* Dunn

From subtropical SE China, N Viet Nam, and N Laos. Discovered in 1908 in Fukien by Captain A. Hodgins of the British Merchant Service, a great collector of plants. Introduced in 1909 to England. Named in 1911. In North America ≤1927. Extremely rare, but in commerce by specialty nurseries in the Southeastern U.S. and B.C. So far only juvenile foliage (larger, that is) has been produced on cultivated specimens; it recalls that of *Thujopsis*. Cones globular, ⅔"–1" wide. Seeds used medicinally in China. Information on its size in the wild differs. Most sources allow it 40' × 3'0"; 60' is likely the usual maximum height—to 90' says Piroche Plants nursery of Pitt Meadows, B.C., and 98½' says the China Plant Red Data Book (1992). At any rate it is extremely slow in cultivation, and a 10' shrub for all practical purposes. Maybe the heat and humidity of the SE United States will prove capable of boosting it into treehood. Tolerates, and may perform better in, partial shade. Hardy to ca. 23°F.

Fortunella

[RUTACEÆ; Rue Family] 4–5 spp. of SE Asian broadleaf evergreen *Citrus* relatives, grown for the small edible fruit (eaten skin and all) and handsome foliage. The KUMQUATS (another name is KINKAN) are more or less frost-hardy unlike the commonly grown *Citrus*. Cultivated in China <1178, the genus was named in 1915 after Robert Fortune (1812–1880), Scots plant collector, who introduced the first KUMQUAT to England in 1846. KUMQUAT is from Cantonese *Kam-kwat*, meaning golden orange. They are shrubby small trees, sometimes with short thorns. A related genus is *Poncirus*, very thorny, very hardy and deciduous. Grafting *Fortunella* onto *Poncirus* increases the hardiness of the former. To grow KUMQUATS in cold-winter regions, it is necessary to site the plants in protected locations, such as under eaves, and to be braced for colder winters to reduce if not eliminate fruit yield.

Fortunella × *crassifolia* Swing.

HYBRID KUMQUAT. MEIWA or NEIWA KUMQUAT. In North American commerce since ≤1915 (the year it was named). Fruit deep orange. A variegated mutant of this is 'Centennial', named (≤1992) for the 100th anniversary of the U.S. Horticultural Research Laboratory of Orlando, FL. Thornless. Leaf to 3½" × 1½", thick (*crassifolia* in Latin means thick leaved; from *crassus*, thick, and *folium*, a leaf); the stem is unwinged. Fruit thick skinned, often seedless; to 1¾".

F. japonica (Th.) Swing.

ROUND KUMQUAT. MARUMI KUMQUAT. From Japan. First named in 1780 (as a *Citrus*). In North America ≤1890. Fruit deep orange, round, to 1¼" wide. Branches lightly thorny. Leaf to 4" × 1⅓", the stem winged. Record: 24' × 2'5" × 16' Indio, CA (1993; *pl.* ca. 1920).

F. japonica var. *margarita*—see *F. margarita*

F. margarita (Lour.) Swing.

= *F. japonica* var. *margarita* hort.

OVAL KUMQUAT. NAGAMI KUMQUAT. From SE China; known only in cultivation. First named in 1790 (as a *Citrus*). Introduced to England in 1846. The first KUMQUAT introduced to the U.S. (≤1850), and still the most common, but not the best fruit quality. Thornless or nearly so. Leaves 1½"–3" (6") long. Fruit yellow-orange, to 1¾", oblong rather than round as in *F. japonica*. Said to be the hardiest *Fortunella*. A shrub (especially if on dwarf rootstock) or small 15' tree.

Frangula Alnus—see *Rhamnus Frangula*

Frangula Purshiana—see *Rhamnus Purshiana*

Franklinia

[THEACEÆ; Tea Family] A genus of only the following species, or broadly interpreted a genus of 70 spp. Named after Benjamin Franklin (1706–1790). A shrubby deciduous tree grown for its beautiful white flowers against brilliant leaves from late July into September–October. Some of its popularity also stems from its name and unhappy fate in the wild. Related genera are *Gordonia* and *Stewartia*. In 1974, *Franklinia* pollen was applied to *Gordonia* flowers and resulted in some hybrid seedlings, but all perished.

F. alatamaha Bartr. *ex* Marsh.

= *Gordonia alatamaha* (Bartr. *ex* Marsh.) Sarg.
= *G. pubescens* L'Hérit.

FRANKLIN TREE. From the Altamaha River of SE Georgia. John Bartram discovered this "very curious shrub" in 1765, but it was rare and has not been found wild since 1803, when John Lyon saw it "near old Fort Barrington" but "not more than 6 or 8 full grown trees of it which does not spread over more than half an acre of ground." Commonly propagated by nurseries but rarely seen in landscapes because of high mortality, due to low vigor. Very susceptible to root-rot (*Phytophthora cinnamomi*), and needs well-drained soil. Nearly all cultivated specimens derive from Bartram's original tree in Philadelphia, which died ca. 1914, so the genetic base is limited regardless of how many specimens are grown from seed. Leaves 5"–10½" long, shiny, orange or scarlet in fall. Flowers fragrant, 3"–4" wide, consisting of an orange heart cupped by 5 (6) plump white petals; borne in late summer and fall. Records: 52' × 3'9" in Bartram Botanic Garden, Philadelphia, PA (≤1832); 38' × 2'8" × 28' McLean, VA (1973; died after transplanting in 1980); 37' × 6'6" × 42' Wyndmoor, PA (≤1993).

Fraxinus

[OLEACEÆ; Olive Family] 60–70 spp. of shrubs and trees, nearly all of temperate regions, known as ASH trees, from Anglo-Saxon *æsc*. Most are deciduous, bearing compound, opposite leaves. Cultivated primarily as handsome shade trees; a few smaller species bear showy white flowers. Drawbacks are that ASHES often leaf out very late in spring, and meanwhile may look stiff and graceless. They usually bear inconspicuous flowers, the sexes often on separate trees. Females can bear numerous unsightly seed clusters. The seeds are dry "keys" with wings like canoe paddles. *Fraxinus* is an ancient Latin name of *F. excelsior*, in turn from Greek *fraxis*, a fence, referring to its early use to divide property and mark boundaries. Trees known as MOUNTAIN ASHES are genus *Sorbus*, in the Rose Family. Genera related to *Fraxinus* include *Chionanthus* (FRINGETREE), *Ligustrum* (PRIVET), *Olea* (OLIVE), *Osmanthus*, *Phillyrea*, and *Syringa* (LILAC).

F. alba—see *F. americana*

F. americana L.
= *F. alba* Marsh.
= *F. biltmoreana* Beadle
= *F. juglandifolia* Lam.
= *F. excelsior* 'Juglandifolia'

WHITE ASH. AMERICAN ASH. From the eastern half of the U.S., and S Ontario. An abundant and familiar species. Important in forestry and horticulture. An airier and nobler tree than GREEN / RED ASH (*F. pennsylvanica*). Fall color often bronzy or deep purple, rarely pure yellow, usually at least a pinkish cast near the branch ends. Leaflets (5) 7–9 (13), slightly, or not toothed; usually hairless; pale beneath (hence the name WHITE ASH). Bark ash-gray, ridged in diamond furrows. Records: to 175' tall in the wild; 152' × 12'11" × 66' Union, IL (1982); 114' × 20'5" × 126' Lenawee County, MI (1976); 95' × 25'4" × 83' Palisades, NY (1983); a trunk 29'0" around in Wabash County, IN (<1882).

F. americana Autumn Applause® PP 3769 (1976)

Introduced by Wandell nursery of Urbana, IL. Common. Fall color deep purple or mahogany—some claim it to be the best fall color of all WHITE ASHES. Leaflets smaller than usual, somewhat drooping. Compact, widely rounded crown, 45' tall. Seedless.

F. americana 'Autumn Blaze'
= *F. americana* 'Blaze'

A selection made at Morden research station of Manitoba. Introduced in 1982, after 10 years of testing. The first WHITE ASH introduced because of its adaptability to the prairie region. Late to flush in spring. Form oval. Fall color purple. Few seeds produced.

F. americana Autumn Purple™
= *F. americana* 'Junginger'

Discovered at the University of Wisconsin, Madison, by Karl Junginger (1905–1991) of McKay nursery, Waterloo, WI. Introduced in 1956. Common. Rapid growth. Rounded habit. Seedless. Heavy dark green foliage, of pronounced deep purple or mahogany in fall, or mottled yellow-orange.

F. americana 'Blaze'—see *F. americana* 'Autumn Blaze'

F. americana 'Blue Mountain'

Introduced ≤1985–86 by Handy nursery of Portland, OR. Out of commerce. Perfect branching habit. Foliage deep green and glossy, deep burgundy in fall. Believed to be seedless.

F. americana 'Champaign County' PP 3762 (1975)

Introduced by Wandell nursery of Urbana, Champaign County, IL. Common. Strong, straight and vigorous. Dense crown. Develops a heavy trunk and robust branch system that nurseries appreciate. Large lustrous dark green leaves with leathery texture. The original tree at 18 years had not yet flowered—its sex was still not known in 1981. Bronze or yellowish fall color.

F. americana 'Chicago Regal'

Selected as a wild seedling in 1970 by R.G. Klehm of South Barrington, IL. Introduced to commerce in 1986. Tree vigorous; branching upright. Bark resists frost cracking. Leaf deep green in summer. Fall color regal purple with earth tones.

F. americana Cimmaron™ PP 8077 (1992)
= *F. pennsylvanica* 'Cimmzam'
= *F. Americana* 'Cimmzam'

Introduced in 1991 as a GREEN ASH. Common. Strong trunk and branch system. Thick waxy green foliage. First deep burgundy in September, then fiery brick-red in October, finally flaming orange. Seedless.

F. americana 'Elk Grove'

In 1968, R.G. Klehm of South Barrington, IL, selected this as a wild seedling from Busse Woods, Elk Grove, IL. Introduced to commerce in 1985. Tree vigorous; branching upright. Bark resists frost cracking. Leaf lustrous dark green in summer. Fall color rich royal purple. See also *F. americana* 'Royal Purple'.

F. americana 'Empire'

Introduced ≤1988 by Schichtel nursery of Orchard Park, NY. Fall color purple. Very vigorous. Dominant central leader. To 65' tall × 40' wide.

F. americana Greenspire®
= *F. americana* 'PNI 2331'

Introduced ≤1990 by Princeton nursery of New Jersey. Narrow upright habit. Fall color dark orange.

F. americana 'Hillcrest'

Listed in 1977 without description by Siebenthaler nursery of Dayton, OH. Out of commerce.

F. americana 'Junginger'—see F. americana Autumn Purple™

F. americana 'Kleinburg'

Discovered in Kleinburg, Ontario. Described in 1970. Offered by Sheridan nursery in 1973. Still in commerce until at least 1987. Rare; sold mostly in Canada. Compact upright growth to 50' tall. Dependable on heavy soils. Ideal for uniform street plantings.

F. americana 'Manitou'

Introduced in 1976 by Sheridan nursery of Oakville, Ontario. Still in commerce as of 1989. Sold primarily in Canada. Habit decidedly columnar. Grows well in heavy clay. Good purplish fall color. Probably named for the town of Manitou, southwest of Winnipeg, Manitoba.

F. americana 'Newport'—see F. pennsylvanica 'Newport'

F. americana 'PNI 2331'—see F. americana Greenspire®

F. americana 'Rosehill' PP 2678 (1966)

A chance seedling recognized as outstanding by E. Asjes, Jr., of Rosehill Gardens, Kansas City, MO. Common. Rapid, straight growth; wide angle crotching habit of lateral branches makes the tree broad. Foliage dark green; yellow, pink, or fiery bronze-red in fall. Tolerates poor, alkaline soil. Transplants well. Seedless.

F. americana 'Royal Purple'
= *F. pennsylvanica* 'Royal Purple'

In 1968, R.G. Klehm of South Barrington, IL, selected this as a wild seedling from Busse Woods, Elk Grove, IL. Introduced to commerce in 1985. Rare. Fall color royal purple, Growth shapely, upright. Bark resists frost cracking. This cultivar has also been listed under *F. pennsylvanica*, yet the fall color indicates that it belongs here. Its origin and description are suspiciously similar to those of *F. americana* 'Elk Grove'.

F. americana 'Skycole'—see F. americana Skyline®

F. americana Skyline® PP 4756 (1981)
= *F. americana* 'Skycole'

Developed and introduced by American Garden Cole of Circleville, OH. Common. Strong, upright branches. Compact oval to globular crown. Fall color orange-red. Seedless.

F. americana 'Suburban'

Introduced ≤1992 by W. Wandell of Urbana, IL.

F. americana var. texensis—see F. texensis

F. americana 'Tures'—see F. americana Windy City™

F. americana 'Waverly'

Selected near Bowmanville, Ontario. Described in 1970. Out of commerce. Compact.

F. americana Windy City™
= *F. americana* 'Tures'

Introduced ≤1994–95 by Chicagoland Grows®, Inc., of Illinois. Oval habit; strong central leader. Resists frost cracking. Burgundy fall color.

F. angustifolia Vahl

= F. rotundifolia Mill. 1768, non Lam. 1790
= F. parvifolia Lam.

NARROWLEAF ASH. From SW Europe and N Africa. Introduced to cultivation in 1800. Date of introduction to North America not known, likely ≤1870s, at the latest in the early 1900s. Very rare here except in its cultivars. Leaflets 7–13 (15); hairless or practically so, more or less narrow relative to those of most ASHES. Dating from 1804, the name *angustifolia* means narrow-leaved; from Latin *angustus*, narrow, and *folium*, a leaf. Admittedly, some specimens of *F. angustifolia* do bear leaflets that are anything but narrow. Buds brown, often in trios. Records: 100' × 7'7" Melbury Park, Dorset, England (1989); 95' × 10'4" Chiswick House, London, England (1973); 75½' × 11'1½" York, England (1989); 69' × 5'2" × 72½' Seattle, WA (1994; *pl.* 1962).

F. angustifolia 'Aurea Pendula'

= F. excelsior 'Aurea Nana' or 'Aurea Pendula'

GOLDEN WEEPING ASH. Introduced in Europe <1838. In North American commerce ≤1875. Apparently common until the turn of the century. Long commercially extinct. Twigs golden yellow. A weak grower, sprawling and shrubby. Not a tree unless topgrafted.

F. angustifolia 'Dr. Pirone'

= F. oxycarpa 'Dr. Pirone'

Named in 1961 by Scanlon nursery of Ohio, but the tree had been sold earlier as *F. excelsior* 'Pyramidalis'. One would think the two names refer to a single clone. Alas, specimens seen under each name bear out their distinctiveness. Both 'Dr. Pirone' and *F. angustifolia* 'Scanlon Pyramid' (q.v.) have been out of commerce since the late 1970s or early '80s. The easiest way to describe 'Dr. Pirone' is as similar to the well known 'Flame' and 'Raywood' cultivars in foliage, except bright green all summer and yellow in fall. 'Dr. Pirone' was originally claimed to be of tight conical form, with upsweeping branches from strong crotches. Probably it went extinct commercially because it falls over readily, and is often seedy. For as long as it endures, it is indeed a lovely tree. Twigs gray-green or olive-green. Buds brown, often in trios, blunt. Leaflets 5–7, to 2⅝" × 11/16", finely toothed. Named after Pascal (Pat) Pompey Pirone (1907–), pathologist of the New York Botanic Garden (previously at Cornell, and Rutgers, NJ).

F. angustifolia 'Flame' PP 2566 (1965)

= F. oxycarpa 'Flame'

Selected in 1961 by Scanlon nursery of Ohio; introduced in 1965. Advertised as seedless, round-headed to 35' tall, with exquisite fall color—turning from a dark glossy green to burgundy, then to a flame color. Time has shown the tree can grow a great deal larger, can be seedy, and in some years its fall color is a wan yellow-pink. For all that, it is still common. Many observers cannot believe it is different from *F. angustifolia* 'Raywood'—but it is a bit darker green in summer. For all practical purposes the two are identical and 'Raywood' is much the older name. Records: 72' × 5'6" × 48' and 61' × 5'9" × 55' Seattle, WA (1993; *pl.* 1972).

F. angustifolia var. lentiscifolia (Desf.) Henry

= F. lentiscifolia Desf. ex Bosc

Introduced to England from the Levant by the Rev. John Banister in 1710. Named officially in 1809. Very rare in North America. Leaves to 10" long, with 7–11 distantly spaced leaflets. The foliage is airy, semi-pendulous and creates a lovely billowy effect. The name *lentiscifolia* derives from *Pistacia Lentiscus*, MASTIC TREE (not in this volume) and Latin *folium*, a leaf.

F. angustifolia 'Monophylla'

= F. Veltheimii Dieck, non hort. (see F. excelsior f. diversifolia)

Cultivated since 1885 in Germany. In North America since ≤1896. Extremely rare. Inelegant. Leaf consisting of one large, jaggedly toothed leaflet (Monophylla from Greek *monos*, one, and *phyllon*, a leaf), to 4⅛" × 2⅜". Growth slow. Record: 75' × 8'0" Kensington Gardens, London, England (1978).

F. angustifolia Moraine™ PP 1768 (1958)

= F. Moraine™
= F. holotricha Moraine™

MORAINE ASH. Introduced in 1957 by Siebenthaler nursery of Dayton, OH. Common; less often grown than previously; now mostly planted in California. Buds dark brown, can be in trios instead of the normal opposite pairs of

Fraxinus. Leaflets 7–13, widely spaced, coarsely and sharply toothed, 1½"–2⅞" long, dull green above, lightly hairy near the midrib beneath. Fall color yellow. Can produce seeds. A taller, narrower, less dense clone with similar leaves is *F. angustifolia* 'Scanlon Pyramid' (q.v.).

F. angustifolia var. *oxycarpa* (M. Bieb. *ex* Willd.) stat. nov.

= *F. angustifolia* ssp. *oxycarpa* (M. Bieb. *ex* Willd.) Franco & Alf.
= *F. rotundifolia* ssp. *oxycarpa* (M. Bieb. *ex* Willd.) P.S. Green
= *F. oxycarpa* M. Bieb. *ex* Willd.

CAUCASIAN ASH. PERSIAN ASH. DESERT ASH—in Australia. From the E Mediterranean and the Caucasus. Named in 1805. Introduced to Germany ca. 1810; to England in 1815. Introduced to North America early in this century if not in 1800s. The purported differences of this ASH from typical *F. angustifolia* are trivial. Leaflets fewer, (3) 5–11 (15), hairy by midrib beneath, edged with very fine sharp teeth. The name *oxycarpa* means spiny-tipped seeds; from Greek *oxy*, sharp, and *karpos*, fruit. Prevailing botanical opinion judges the variable hairiness and leaflet number of the *oxycarpa* trees as insufficient to justify subspecific status; the seed shape is also wholly without taxonomic value. The compromise adopted in the present volume is to use varietal ranking, rather than sink the *oxycarpa* name into oblivion as a mere synonym of *angustifolia*. The name *Fraxinus oxycarpa* is firmly established in the nursery trade, and to discard it will be difficult. Horticulturally, the common clones of *oxycarpa* ('Dr. Pirone', 'Flame' and 'Raywood') are similar: their leaves are practically identical except in color, and the trees are all too prone to toppling. Records: 110' × 14'5" × 79' Eastwood Hill, New Zealand (1990; *pl.* 1880) 93' × 8'5" × 51' Tacoma, WA (1990); 70' × 10'0" × 51' Orting, WA (1992).

F. angustifolia 'Pendula'

= *F. excelsior lentiscifolia pendula* hort.
= *F. tamariscifolia pendula* Dipp.

Described in 1889 in Germany. In North American nurseries ≤1888. Extremely rare. Branches and twigs hang down in short, tight arches. See also *F. angustifolia* 'Rotundifolia Pendula'.

F. angustifolia 'Raywood'

= *F. oxycarpa* 'Wollastonii'
= *F. oxycarpa* 'Raywood'

RAYWOOD ASH. CLARET ASH. Originated ca. 1910 at Sewell nursery of Aldgate, near Adelaide, Australia.

It was bought, moved, and named 'Raywood' after Raywood Gardens of T.C. Wollaston, at Bridgewater, near Adelaide. In the British nursery trade ≤1928. Introduced to North America ≤1956. In largescale commerce here since ≤1979. Common. Leaflets (5) 7–11 (13), to 3⅜" × ¾". Fall color variable, but at its best a claret or smoky purple shade. Produces few seeds. For all practical purposes *F. angustifolia* 'Flame' is identical. Records: 71' × 11'9" × 80' Hastings, New Zealand (≤1982); 66' × 16'3" × 77' Gisborne, New Zealand (1981; *pl.* 1952); 60' × 3'1½" Seattle, WA (1994; *pl.* 1969).

F. angustifolia 'Rotundifolia Pendula'

= *F. rotundifolia* 'Pendula'
= *F. oxycarpa* 'Pendula'

Introduced to England from Germany in 1833. Not certain to be in North America. Weeping aspect. Leaflets oval rather than markedly narrow as in *F. angustifolia* 'Pendula' (which see).

F. angustifolia 'Scanlon Pyramid'

= *F. excelsior* 'Pyramidalis' (in part)

This cultivar name is new, published here for the first time because the name *F. excelsior* 'Pyramidalis' has been used for two clones, if not three. It was originally published without a description in 1877 in Paris (possibly for the tree that was described in 1889 by a German botanist as *F. angustifolia* 'Pyramidalis'— of compact growth, very sensitive to winter cold, and North African in origin). In 1958–59, Scanlon nursery of Ohio employed *F. excelsior* 'Pyramidalis' for a clone "developed by Henry Vink of Rotterdam, the Netherlands." Scanlon's clone is not an *F. excelsior*, but a variation of *F. angustifolia*. Its twig and leaf looks like that of the well known MORAINE ASH (*F. angustifolia* Moraine™). Leaflets (3) 7–9, to 4¼" × 1¼", coarsely sharp-toothed like those of 'Moraine'. It becomes a relatively taller, narrower, far less dense tree than 'Moraine'. Twigs dull olive-green. Buds brown, pointed; smaller than those of *F. excelsior*; sometimes in trios. Seeds can be produced. Foliage turns yellow and defoliates rather early for any trees in the group. This cultivar has been out of commerce since the 1970s. The name PYRAMIDAL EUROPEAN ASH has been used by nurseries for *F. angustifolia* 'Dr. Pirone' (q.v.).

F. arizonica—see *F. velutina* var. *glabra*

F. attenuata 'Tecate'—see *F. velutina* 'Tecate'

F. biltmoreana—see *F. americana*

F. bracteata—see *F. Griffithii*

F. Bungeana DC., non Hance

CHINESE DWARF ASH. CHINESE FLOWERING ASH. From N China. Named after the eminent Russian botanist Dr. Aleksandr Andreevich von Bunge (1803–1890) of St. Petersburg, productive author on the plants of N and NE Asia. Bunge discovered the tree in 1831 near Peking. Introduced in 1881 to the Arnold Arboretum. Very rare. Like a smaller, hardier *F. Ornus*. Beginning in 1963 it was promoted as a topgrafted round-headed "tailored" tree by Scanlon nursery of Ohio. Large shrub or small tree of broad habit (to 15'–20' tall); buds gray to nearly black, and large relative to the twig size. Leaflets 3–7, rich dark green, hairless; to 2" × 1". Fall color yellowish-purple to red. Flowers whitish, very fragrant.

F. californica—see *F. latifolia*

F. coriacea—see *F. velutina* var. *coriacea*

F. excelsior L.

EUROPEAN ASH. ENGLISH ASH. From Europe, SW Asia. One of the earliest European shade trees introduced to North America. Common. At present mostly planted in Canada and on the Pacific Coast. Very important in European mythology and folklore. For example—Cupid's bows were made of its wood; Yggdrasil (Igdrasil), an ASH, is the Norse Tree of Time or the World Tree. Buds sooty black, bluntish. Leaves of 9–11 (15) sharply toothed leaflets. Fall color dull yellow-green, late. The name *excelsior* from Latin *excelsus*, meaning very tall. Records: 148' × 10'6" Duncombe Park, Yorkshire, England (1956; dead since 1970); 93' × 6'8" Tacoma, WA (1990); 92' × 25'9" Tynan Abbey, County Armagh, Ireland (1976); 90' × 11'9" Wyndmoor, PA (1980); 71' × 10'11" × 74' Victoria, B.C. (1989); 61' × 14'5" Bel Air, MD (1990); 39' × 29'0" Clapton Court, Somerset, England (1988); a trunk 33'0" around at Donirey, near Clare Castle, County Galloway, Ireland (<1794).

F. excelsior 'Allgold'

A Dutch cultivar named in 1989. Much better and less seedy than *F. excelsior* 'Jaspidea'. At this writing it barely exists in North America, but presumably will replace 'Jaspidea'.

F. excelsior argenteomarginata—see *F. penn.* 'Albomarginata'

F. excelsior 'Aurea'

GOLDEN ASH. Described in 1807 in Holland. In North American commerce ≤1874–75. Very rare. Twigs golden yellow. Leaves yellow-green at first, later yellow-golden. Slow growing; small. Buds closely set. *F. excelsior* 'Jaspidea' (or the clone prevalent under that name, anyway) is often miscalled by this name.

F. excelsior 'Aurea Nana'—see *F. angustifolia* 'Aurea Pendula'

F. excelsior 'Aurea Pendula'—see *F. angustifolia* 'Aurea Pendula'

F. excelsior 'Berlin'—see *F. excelsior* 'Jaspidea'

F. excelsior f. *diversifolia* (Ait.) Lingelsh.

= *F. excelsior* var. *heterophylla* Wesm.
= *F. excelsior* var. *monophylla* (Desf.) Gren. & Godr.
= *F. excelsior* var. *simplicifolia* Pers.
= *F. Veltheimii* hort., non Dieck (see *F. angustifolia* 'Monophylla')

SINGLELEAF ASH. ONE-LEAVED ASH. Described in 1789. Grown in North America since ≤1870s. Rare. The cultivar 'Hessei' (q.v.) is its common representative in commerce. Only the terminal leaflet is developed, or sometimes there are 2 or 3 jaggedly toothed leaflets. It is a variable assemblage and breeds partly true from seed. Record: 105' × 13'2" Culreuch Castle, Stirlingshire, Scotland (1984).

F. excel. 'Diversifolia Pendula'—see *F. excel.* 'Heterophylla Pendula'

F. excelsior 'Foliis Aureis'—see *F. excelsior* 'Jaspidea'

F. excelsior 'Globosa'

= *F. excelsior* Nana' (in part)
= *F. excelsior* 'Umbraculifera' of Scanlon
= *F. excelsior* Lucerne™ of Scanlon 1976

GLOBEHEAD EUROPEAN ASH. Described in 1889. In North American commerce ≤1903. Uncommon. Scanlon nursery of Ohio began to promote it heavily in 1958–59. Nearly always topgrafted on a 7 foot standard. To 23' tall. Crown dense and quite comparable to 'Globosum' NORWAY MAPLE; in contrast *F.*

excelsior 'Rancho Roundhead' is more open, like 'Almira' NORWAY MAPLE. Foliage in late October still totally green while 'Rancho Roundhead' has some yellow. Leaves possibly larger than those of 'Rancho Roundhead'. See also *F. excelsior* 'Nana', 'Polemoniifolia' and 'Rancho Roundhead'.

F. excelsior 'Gold Cloud' PP 2286 (1963)

Introduced in 1961 by Spring Hill nursery of Tipp City, OH. Described as rapid growing, seedless; golden-yellow, lacy foliage; bright golden twigs. The German tree expert G. Krüssmann suggested it might be a renaming of *F. excelsior* 'Jaspidea'. But in 1971 nurseryman Ed Scanlon insisted it was "in no way related" to his GOLDEN DESERT ASH (i.e., 'Jaspidea').

F. excelsior 'Hessei'

HESSE SINGLELEAF ASH. Introduced in 1933–34 by Hesse nursery of Germany. In North America since 1934, but only since ca. 1978–79 has it been commonly sold. Leaves nearly always simple. Crown broad and rounded. Growth vigorous. Seedless. Named after Hermann Albrecht Hesse (1852–1937).

F. excelsior var. heterophylla—see F. excelsior f. diversifolia

F. excelsior 'Heterophylla Pendula'
= *F. excelsior* 'Diversifolia Pendula'

WEEPING SINGLELEAF ASH. Introduced in 1898 by Späth nursery of Germany. In North America by 1899. Extremely rare. A mophead.

F. excelsior 'Jaspidea'
= *F. oxycarpa* Golden Desert™
= *F. oxycarpa aurea* 'Golden Desert'
= *F. oxycarpa* 'Aurea' or 'Aureafolia'

GOLDEN ASH. STRIPED BARK ASH. Described in 1802 in France as an ASH with stems and branches bearing yellowish, longitudinal streaking. In North American commerce ≤1888. Since the early 1960s it has been sold primarily under the name *F. oxycarpa* 'Aurea'. The name 'Jaspidea' must refer to the stained quartz called jasper. Maybe more than one clone has gone under this name. Accounts vary. In 1838 the English tree authority J. Loudon said the streaks were reddish-white; the late Dutch tree expert B.K. Boom said yellow and yellowish green; the German G. Krüssmann said green. All agree the tree grows to be large, unlike *F. excelsior* 'Aurea'. Moreover the buds are not closely set on the twigs. Specimens seen by the present writer have mustard-orange, unstreaked twigs, and lovely foliage, pale yellow-green in early summer, then pale green, finally bright yellow in October. Buds black and typical for *F. excelsior*; leaflets 9–11; seeds produced. Unless the twig streaking or striping is only occasional, there must be two or more GOLDEN ASHES in circulation. Maybe the original 'Jaspidea' has been replaced by the clone that has usually been sold wrongly as an *oxycarpa* cultivar (GOLDEN DESERT ASH). See also *F. excelsior* 'Gold Cloud'. [There are yellow-leaved ASHES which were described long ago in Europe, but have played a minor role, if any, in North American commerce: 'Foliis Aureis' (a.k.a. 'Berlin') and 'Transonii'.] Records: 79' × 8'0" Hergest Croft, Herefordshire, England (1985); 69' × 10'10" Highnam Court, Gloucestershire, England (1988); 88' × 10'0" × 64' New Zealand (≤1982).

F. excelsior 'Juglandifolia'—see F. americana

F. excelsior 'Kimberly (Blue)'
= *F. quadrangulata* 'Western Blue'
= *F. quadrangulata* 'Kimberly Blue'
= *F. pennsylvanica* 'Kimberly Blue'

In commerce under the name 'Kimberly Blue' since ≤1954. Very common. Origin not known. Possibly from Kimberly nursery of Kimberly, ID. Another assertion is it was grown from seeds collected a from a superior, mature tree in the Morton Arboretum of Lisle, IL. Similar to, and possibly the same as *F. excelsior* 'Rancho Roundhead'. Hardy. Small, compact, very symmetrical roundheaded or oval tree with beautiful blue-green shading of leaves. Seedless. Record: 52' × 5'10" × 50½' Davis, CA (1994).

F. excelsior lentiscifolia pendula—see F. angustifolia 'Pendula'

F. excelsior Lucerne™—see F. excelsior 'Globosa'

F. excelsior 'Monophylla'—see F. excelsior f. diversifolia

F. excelsior 'Nana'

GLOBE ASH. Originated in France ca. 1805. Rare. Leaves 4"–6" long, of mostly 11 distantly-spaced leaflets. Authorities tend to equate this and *F. excelsior* 'Globosa', but it is likely the two trees are only similar clones. The name 'Nana' has been used for the very different *F. excelsior* 'Polemoniifolia' as well. It is likely that 'Polemoniifolia' has small leaves, 'Nana' medium leaves, and 'Globosa' large leaves. All three cultivars are compact and need to be topgrafted to be trees. Nana is Latin for dwarf.

F. excelsior 'Pendula'

WEEPING ASH. Originated <1725 in a field owned by the vicar of Gamlingay, near Wimpole in Cambridgeshire, England. In North American commerce since ≤1840s. Less commonly sold in the 1900s than in the 1800s. It weeps from whatever height it is grafted. A low, mop-like tree. Seeds abundant. Records: 72' × 6'4" London, England (1989); 42½' × 8'6" Goatchers, Washington, Sussex, England (1989); 38' × 5'5" × 32' Everett, WA (1993); 32' × 5'2" × 35' Victoria, B.C. (1989); 23' × 8'4½" × 57' Wellington, New Zealand (1969; pl. ≤1850).

F. excelsior 'Pendula Wentworth'
('Pendula Wentworthi')

Cultivated <1877 in France. Trunk and terminal branch always erect, with distictly pendulous side branches. Much rarer than regular 'Pendula'. Record: 64' × 5'3" Kew, England (1969).

F. excelsior 'Polemoniifolia'
= F. excelsior 'Nana' (in part)

Named ≤1816. Leaves 1³⁄₁₆"–3¼" long, of 11–15 very crowded leaflets. See F. excelsior 'Globosa' and 'Nana'. The formidable name 'Polemoniifolia' derives from genus Polemonium (JACOB'S LADDER), and Latin folium, a leaf.

F. excelsior 'Pyramidalis'—see F. angustifolia 'Scanlon Pyramid'

F. excelsior 'Rancho (Roundhead)'
= F. quadrangulata 'Globosum' of Scanlon

Introduced in 1959–60 by Scanlon nursery of Ohio. Very rare; out of commerce. Needlessly confused with F. excelsior 'Globosa'. In contrast, 'Rancho Roundhead' is not topgrafted, grows larger (to 30'+), and is less dense. It could pass for F. excelsior 'Kimberly Blue' (and the two may be the same). The crown is indeed roundish.

F. excelsior var. simplicifolia—see F. excelsior f. diversifolia

F. excelsior 'Transoni'—see F. excelsior 'Jaspidea'

F. excelsior 'Umbraculifera'—see F. excelsior 'Globosa'

F. excelsior 'Westhof's Glorie'

Introduced ca. 1947 by J.C. & P.C. van 't Westeinde at 's-Heer-Arendskerke, Holland. In North America ≤1958; in commerce here ≤1968–69. Uncommon. More common in Canada than the U.S. Selected for good street-tree qualities: very straight-trunked, upright-branched and nearly seedless. A very handsome specimen in the Seattle arboretum since 1970 is lush, with smaller leaves than normal, 9 (11) leaflets totally hairless and dark green. A specimen so labeled at VanDusen Gardens of Vancouver, B.C., is a RED ASH (F. pennsylvanica): leaflets (5) 7–9; some leaves on strong shoots with the lowermost pair of leaflets subtended by another pair of tiny leaflets. So, at least two very dissimilar clones have gone under the same name.

F. Griffithii C.B. Clarke
= F. bracteata Hemsl.

From NE India, Upper Burma, parts of China and south into Java. Named in 1882 after British botanist William Griffith (1819–1845). Introduced to Western cultivation in 1901 when E. Wilson sent seeds to Veitch nursery of England. Extremely rare in North America. Offered in 1942 by W.B. Clarke nursery of San José, CA. Leaflets 5–11, leathery, 1"–3" (5") long, untoothed, hairless, deep green, very glossy, held until late fall. Twigs square. Flowers fragrant and greenish-white in large airy clusters. To 60' tall in the wild. Probably cannot stand severe cold winters.

F. holotricha Koehne
= F. Pallisiæ Wilmott

BALKAN ASH. From SE Europe. Introduced to cultivation in 1870. Named in 1906 from cultivated specimens in Späth's nursery of Berlin. In North America since ≤1935, but extremely rare and presumably unimportant horticulturally. Very like F. angustifolia except twigs and foliage densely downy (holotricha means all-hairy; from Greek holo, whole or entire, and trichos, hair). Leaflets 9–13, to 1½" long, grayish hairy on both sides when young.

F. holotricha Moraine™—see F. angustifolia Moraine™

F. juglandifolia—see F. americana

F. lanceolata—see F. pennsylvanica var. lanceolata

F. lanuginosa—see F. Sieboldiana

F. *latifolia* Benth.

= *F. oregona* Nutt.
= *F. californica* hort.
= *F. pennsylvanica* ssp. *oregona* (Nutt.) G.N. Mill.

OREGON ASH. From (possibly SW British Columbia) W Washington to central California; often in low, wet soils. Named in 1844. Introduced to cultivation in 1870. Very rare. Buds tawny. Leaflets usually 7, stalkless or nearly so. Main leafstalk and leaflet undersides sparsely, evenly coated with long pale hairs; leaflet margins clumsily toothed or more often toothless; leaflets broad and not elegantly pointed—they appear rather dull and unrefined compared to many ASH leaves (*latifolia* means broad-leaved; from Latin *latus*, broad, and *folium*, a leaf). Fall color yellow, in October. Bark thin, scaly, and can be flaked off with one's fingers. Records: to 150' tall according to D. Peattie; 111' × 5'10" × 39' Tacoma, WA (1990); 59' × 21'11" × 45' Sauvie Island, OR (1975).

F. *lentiscifolia*—see *F. angustifolia* 'Lentiscifolia'

F. *longicuspis* var. *Sieboldiana*—see *F. Sieboldiana*

F. *malacophylla* Hemsl.

From S Yunnan, China, in limestone mountains. Introduced to Western cultivation ≤1940s. Extremely rare. Sold ≤1991 by San Marcos Growers nursery of Santa Barbara, CA. Additional testing is needed to evaluate its cold-hardiness; it certainly has ornamental merit and can withstand heat and dryness. Tardily deciduous (by May or June in southern California) or partly evergreen. Leaflets firm-textured, wrinkled, varying from dark glossy green to dull green, (5) 9–19, curly, to 5" × 1½", stalkless, untoothed; veins sunken above; inconspicuously hairy near midrib and on veins, especially in lower portion of leaflet; main leafstem narrowly winged, persistently hairy. Flowers small, white, in June-July. Seeds ⅝" long. Trees in Santa Barbara are broad and low, with open crowns. Bark smooth when young, becoming lovely, flaking, pale gray outside, cream and green within. The name *malacophylla* is from Greek *malacos*, soft

to the touch, and *phyllon*, a leaf. A cultivar called 'Queen Mary' was in California <1979 but no more is known about it. Records: ca. 50' tall at the Los Angeles arboretum; 33½' × 3'3" × 36' Santa Barbara, CA (1993; *pl.* 1948).

F. *mandshurica* Rupr.

MANCHURIAN ASH. From NE Asia and Japan. Named in 1857. Introduced to England from St. Petersburg in 1882. To North America ≤1896. In commerce here ≤1930. Very rare; least so in the Midwest. Very cold-hardy, but in some regions susceptible to frost-damage due to early spring new growth. Leaf crisp, sharp, and boldly elegant, to 2' long; often with a bronzy cast. Leaflets (7) 9–11 (15), very long and narrow (to 8½" × 2¾"), finely sharply toothed, with pronounced drip tips, and almost no hairs (prominent rusty hair tufts at nodes). Fall color red or yellow. Bark rough. Buds reminiscent of those of *F. excelsior*. Records: to 100' × 20'7" in the wild; E. Wilson said this ASH was, after *Populus Maximowiczii*, the largest tree in Korea.

F. *mandshurica* 'Mancana'

Selected in 1969 at Morden research station of Manitoba. The original tree had been raised from a seed collected in Manchuria in 1926. The name 'Mancana' was published in 1982 (contraction of *Man*churian *Can*ada?). Subsequently grown by several major wholesale nurseries. This clone offers guaranteed hardiness, seedlessness and yellow fall color. Crown densely oval. Tree easily transplanted; tolerates drought as well as excess moisture; no serious disease problems.

F. *Mariesii*—see *F. Sieboldiana*

F. *Moraine*™—see *F. angustifolia* *Moraine*™

F. *nigra* Marsh.

= *F. sambucifolia* Lam.

BLACK ASH. SWAMP ASH. BASKET ASH. BROWN ASH. HOOP ASH. WATER ASH. From NE North America. Rarely cultivated. It grows in swamps and muddy river banks, and not only tolerates boggy soils, but needs moisture to perform acceptably. Usually short lived. Fall color early, poor yellow or rusty brown. Habit slender. Bark in age becomes scaly. Basket makers have long valued the tough wood. Leaflets 5–13, finely toothed, stalkless. The epithet *nigra* refers to its dark buds, twigs, foliage and heartwood. Records: 155' × 8'3" Adrian, MI (1984); 87' × 15'3" Bath, OH (1969); a trunk 17'4" around at Sparkhill, NY (1944).

F. nigra 'Columnar' PP 3754 (1975)

Patented by Ashur L. Cordes of Henning, MN. Not distributed commercially.

F. nigra 'Fallgold'

Selected in 1969 at Morden research station of Manitoba, from seedlings of a native stand near Portage la Prairie, Manitoba. Introduced in 1975. In commerce. Very hardy; seedless; branching upright. Foliage disease-free, its bright golden yellow fall color retained longer than most trees of this species.

F. oregona—see F. latifolia

F. Ornus L.

= *Ornus europæa* Pers.

MANNA ASH. FLOWERING ASH. From S Europe, SW Asia. Cultivated in northern Europe by the early 1700s; in North American commerce since ≤1840. Uncommon here. Thrives in dry sites. *Ornus* is one of the ancient Latin names for *F. Ornus*. Flowers showy, creamy white (a form in Hungary has violet flowers), from April into July depending on the tree, the locale and the year. Seed clusters unsightly, so seedless selections are often grafted. Fall color usually subdued; ranges from murky burgundy to vibrant pink-orange. Leaflets (5) 7 (9), dark green, shallowly toothed, broad. Bark smooth and gray like a BEECH (*Fagus*). Buds usually gray. Records: 85' × 8'1" Kensington Gardens, London, England (1990); 75½' × 10'10" Haremere Hall, Kent, England (1987); 69' × 7'0" Puyallup, WA (1992); 53' × 9'6" Seattle, WA (1988; dead since 1992).

F. Ornus 'Arie Peters'

A Dutch selection from Italian seeds raised by T. van Eeten, named after nurseryman Arie Peters of Opheusden, Holland. Described in 1981. In North America ≤1987. Extremely rare; perhaps not commercially available here. Broad oval crown. Leaves 7"–9⅜" long. Flowers equally distributed over the tree in May-June with some blooming later and lasting into September. Not seedless.

F. Ornus 'Emerald Elegance'

Originally selected by Scanlon nursery of Ohio. Named and introduced ≤1992–93 by Handy nursery of Portland, OR. Seedless. Fall color yellow.

F. Ornus 'Victoria'

Origin not known. Selected in Victoria, B.C., probably by the late W.H. Warren in the 1960s or perhaps early '70s. A topgrafted densely oval small tree. Leaflets 7, large, dark. Buds large, gray. Seedless. Remains green late into fall. Planted on streets in Victoria, and at VanDusen Gardens, Vancouver, B.C. Well worth additional propagation.

F. oxycarpa—see F. angustifolia var. oxycarpa

F. oxycarpa 'Aurea' or 'Aureafolia'—see F. excelsior 'Jaspidea'

F. oxycarpa aurea 'Golden Desert'—see F. excelsior 'Jaspidea'

F. oxycarpa 'Dr. Pirone'—see F. angustifolia 'Dr. Pirone'

F. oxycarpa 'Flame'—see F. angustifolia 'Flame'

F. oxycarpa 'Golden Desert'—see F. excelsior 'Jaspidea'

F. oxycarpa 'Pendula'—see F. angustifolia 'Rotundifolia Pendula'

F. oxycarpa 'Raywood'—see F. angustifolia 'Raywood'

F. oxycarpa 'Wollastonii'—see F. angustifolia 'Raywood'

F. Pallisiæ—see F. holotricha

F. parvifolia—see F. angustifolia

F. Paxiana Lingelesh.

PAX FLOWERING ASH. From the Himalayas and W China. Introduced to Western cultivation in 1901, by E. Wilson for Veitch nursery of England. Named in 1907, after Ferdinand Albin Pax (1858–1942), a German botanist. Extremely rare. Sold in 1951–52 by W.B. Clarke nursery of San José, CA. A large shrub or small tree. Foliage resembles that of certain ELDERS (*Sambucus cerulea* or *S. Ebulus*). Leaflets 7–9 (11), to 7⅛" × 2½". Buds at twig ends are comparatively enormous, ca. ⅝" long and wide. Flowers creamy white, in large, showy terminal clusters during May or June. Growth slow. Fall color early and poor gold. Records: to 70' tall in the wild.

F. pennsylvanica Marsh.

= F. pubescens Lam.

GREEN ASH. RED ASH. From central and eastern N
America. Very common. GREEN ASH (for synonymy
see F. pennsylvanica var. lanceolata) is considered
the hairless-twigged phase of the species, RED ASH
the hairy-twigged population. Intermediates occur.
GREEN ASH is favored in horticulture. The broadest
species concept of F. pennsylvanica encompasses F.
latifolia (OREGON ASH) and F. velutina (VELVET ASH)
as well. Leaflets (5) 7–9; fall color almost invariably
yellow. The name RED ASH refers
to a reddish tinge in
the inner bark. Most of
the 32 cultivars listed below are comparatively
young. The oldest
and most com-
mon is 'Marshall
Seedless'. Seedling
specimens tend to
grow taller than
grafted trees. Records:
145' × 15'5" × 70'
Estill County, KY
(1976); 131' × 20'2" × 121' Cass County,
MI (1981).

F. pennsylvanica Aerial™ PP 7120 (1990)

= F. pennsylvanica 'Lednaw'

Patented by W. Wandell. Sold by Lake County nursery of Perry, OH, as an improved sport of F.
pennsylvanica 'Summit'. Seedless. Crown narrow
upright, growing to 45' × 12' instead of 60' × 40'.

F. pennsylvanica 'Albomarginata'

= F. pennsylvanica 'Argentea Marginata'
= F. pennsylvanica 'Variegata'
= F. excelsior argenteomarginata hort.

Originated ≤1865 in Germany. In English nurseries
≤1875. Very rare in North America. A narrow-
crowned RED ASH; leaflets with very irregular white
margins; coarse-looking; 7 leaflets edged with crude
bluntish teeth.

F. penn. 'Argentea Marginata'—see F. penn. 'Albomarginata'

F. pennsylvanica 'Aucubæfolia'

Described in Germany in 1864. Leaflets splashed and
dotted with gold. Extremely rare. The name refers to
the familiar shrub Aucuba japonica, grown primarily
in a gold-variegated cultivar.

F. pennsylvanica 'Bailey'—see F. pennsylvanica 'Newport'

F. pennsylvanica 'Bergeson' PP 4904 (1982)

Selected from seed collected in northern Minnesota
by Melvin or Paul L. Bergeson of Bergeson nursery,
Fertile, MN. Introduced commercially in 1981.
Common. Fast growth; straight-trunked. Bark has
soft bronze tinge. Leaves long and slender with a
definite shine. Seedless. Yellow in fall. Exceptional
cold-hardiness.

F. pennsylvanica 'Cardan'

Named and released in 1979 by the USDA Soil Conservation Service. Intended as a windbreak tree for
the northern Great Plains. A seed-propagated cultivar: the third open-pollinated generation that originated from a single-tree seed collection made by
Ernest George in 1954 in Montana. 'Cardan' has not
been common; nurseries sell their own selected seedless cultivars, especially the patented ones.

F. pennsylvanica 'Cimmzam'—see F. americana Cimmaron™

F. pennsylvanica Dakota Centennial™

= F. pennsylvanica 'Wahpeton'

Selected in 1986 (presumably in the town of
Wahpeton, ND) by Dale E. Herman. Introduced by
North Dakota State University of Fargo. Common.
Fast-growing. Desirable scaffold branches with a
strong central leader and lateral branches more open
than on a typical ASH. Globe shaped crown. Seedless.
Glossy dark foliage, yellow in fall. The name refers
to North Dakota's admittance as the 39th State in
1889.

F. pennsylvanica 'Emerald' PP 3088 (1972)

A seedling of Nebraska origin. Introduced in 1971 by
Marshall nursery of Arlington, NE. Common.
A seedless RED ASH. Leaflets broad, hairy beneath;
yellow in fall, remaining two or three weeks longer
than those of regular RED or GREEN ASHES. Bark HACK-
BERRY-like (rough, corky). Overall much like 'Marshall Seedless' but with more apical dominance—not
at all roundheaded.

F. pennsylvanica 'Fan-West'—see F. velutina Fan West™

F. pennsylvanica 'Goldie'

Introduced ≤1988 by Schichtel nursery of Orchard
Park, NY. A GREEN ASH with leaves green in spring,

deep shades of yellow through July and August. Rounded form 40' × 30' wide.

F. pennsylvanica 'Harlequin'

Discovered in 1987 as a branch sport in Québec. Registered in 1993. Leaves variegated green to gray-green with irregular white margins.

F. pennsylvanica 'Honeyshade' PP 3385 (1973)

Originated in 1945 at Rockford nursery, but only named and introduced in 1973, by Klehm nursery of Arlington Heights, IL. Rare. A seedless GREEN ASH. Foliage "extremely" glossy. Fast growth. Branching habit horizontal.

F. pennsylvanica 'Jewell'

Introduced ≤1975–76 by Jewell nursery of Lake City, MN. Still sold by Jewell through 1992. Well-branched crown. Leaves dark, shiny. Seeds few.

F. pennsylvanica 'Johnson'—see *F. pennsylvanica* Leprechaun™

F. pennsylvanica 'Kankakee'

Introduced ≤1992 by Kankakee nursery of Aroma Park, IL.

F. pennsylvanica 'Kimberly Blue'—see *F. excel.* 'Kimberly (Blue)'

F. pennsylvanica 'Kindred'

Selected by Ben Gilbertson of Kindred, ND. Introduced 1979–80 by Cross nursery of Lakeview, MN. Common. Extremely hardy. Dark green foliage. Seedless. Transplants easily; grows symmetrically. Upright spreading.

F. pennsylvanica 'King Richard'

Selected in 1970 by R.G. Klehm of South Barrington, IL. Introduced to commerce in 1985. Rare. Growth uniform, upright. Foliage glossy, deep green. Seedless.

F. pennsylvanica var. *lanceolata* (Bork.) Sarg.

= *F. lanceolata* Borkh.
= *F. viridis* Michx. fil., non Bosc
= *F. pennsylvanica* var. *subintegrima* (Vahl) Fern.

GREEN ASH. Very common. Less hairy and said to be hardier than RED ASH. This variety is one extreme of a continuum of varying hairiness within the species.

F. pennsylvanica 'Lednaw'—see *F. pennsylvanica* Aerial™

F. pennsylvanica 'Leeds'—see *F. pennsylvanica* Prairie Dome™

F. pennsylvanica Leprechaun™

= *F. pennsylvanica* 'Johnson'

Introduced ≤1994 by Wayne Johnson nursery of Menomonee Falls, WI. A chance seedling found ca. 1983 by M. Yanny at Johnson nursery. A compact, dwarf form sold topgrafted. Leaves of half size.

F. pennsylvanica 'Mahle'

Introduced ≤1988 by Bailey nursery of St. Paul, MN. Original tree in K.A. Mahle's yard in Woodbury, MN. Branches exceptionally well as a young tree, forming a broad oval head at maturity. Good foliage. Seedless.

F. pennsylvanica 'Marshall (Seedless)'

= *F. pennsylvanica* 'Sterile' of Siebenthaler nursery

George A. Marshall, of Marshall nursery, Arlington, NE, obtained this tree from the Porter-Walton nursery of Salt Lake City, sometime after 1946. Cole nursery of Painesville, OH, purchased specimens from Marshall and first used the name 'Marshall Seedless' in 1955. By far the most commonly planted GREEN ASH cultivar. Possibly more than one clone. Dark, shiny green disease-resistant foliage, yellow in fall. Tree durable, tolerant, drought resistant. Seedless. Visually, it is just a regular male GREEN ASH.

F. pennsylvanica 'Newport'

= *F. pennsylvanica* 'Bailey'
= *F. americana* 'Newport'

Introduced in 1979–80 by Bailey nursery of St. Paul, MN. Common. Straight trunked, of good habit. Seedless. Leaves glossier than most, sharply toothed. Very hardy.

F. pennsylvanica 'Niobrara'

Introduced in 1957 by Cole nursery of Painesville, OH. Extinct commercially. Pyramidal with much the same form as PIN OAK (*Quercus palustris*). Produces seeds.

F. pennsylvanica ssp. *oregona*—see *F. latifolia*

F. pennsylvanica 'Patmore' PP 4684 (1981)

Selected in 1967 from seedlings growing in the town of Vegreville, Alberta, by Richard H. Patmore (deceased) of Patmore nursery, Brandon, Manitoba. Introduced in 1976. Common. Extremely hardy. Seedless. Foliage shiny. Erect trunk; evenly branched crown. Looks much like *F. pennsylvanica* 'Marshall Seedless'.

F. pennsylvanica Prairie Dome™
= F. pennsylvanica 'Leeds'

Selected in 1986 (likely in the town of Leeds, ND) by D.E. Herman. Introduced by North Dakota State University of Fargo. Compact, very densely distinctly oval, aging to globular. Seedless.

F. pennsylvanica Prairie Spire™
= F. pennsylvanica 'Rugby'

Selected in 1986 (presumably in the city of Rugby, ND) by Dale E. Herman. Introduced by North Dakota State University of Fargo. In commerce. Compact columnar form becoming narrowly pyramidal to elliptical. Seedless. Bright golden yellow in fall.

F. pennsylvanica 'Robinhood'
('Robin Hood')

Selected in 1970 by R.G. Klehm of South Barrington, IL. Introduced to commerce in 1985. Very rare. Growth uniform, upright. Foliage vibrant green. Seedless.

F. pennsylvanica 'Royal Purple'—see F. americana 'Royal Purple'

F. pennsylvanica 'Rugby'—see F. pennsylvanica Prairie Spire™

F. pennsylvanica 'Select'

Introduced ≤1991 by Manbeck nursery of New Knoxville, OH. A sport selected from F. pennsylvanica 'Marshall Seedless'. Straight trunk and broad ascending habit. Fall color orange to rust.

F. pennsylvanica Sherwood Glen™

Selected by R.G. Klehm of South Barrington, IL. Introduced to commerce in 1984. Very rare. Leaves thick, dark green. Habit uniform and upright.

F. pennsylvanica Skyward™
= F. pennsylvanica 'Wandell'

Introduced in 1988 by Willet N. Wandell of Urbana, IL. Uncommon. Narrow crown. Heavy and dense foliage, deep bronze-red in fall. Leaves thick. Bark rough.

F. pennsylvanica 'Sterile'—see F. penn. 'Marshall (Seedless)'

F. pennsylvanica var. subintegerrima—see F. penn. var. lanceolata

F. pennsylvanica 'Summer Green'

Introduced ≤1987–88 by McKay nursery of Waterloo, WI.

F. pennsylvanica 'Summit'

First noted and selected for propagation in 1948 by Frank L. Seifert. Introduced in 1957 by Summit nursery of Stillwater, MN. Very common. Fast; upright to pyramidal with a strong central leader; medium green leaves pointed and narrow. Claimed to be the first GREEN ASH to turn yellow in fall—or at any rate coloring before 'Marshall Seedless'. In Seattle there is no difference in timing or shading of color: watered trees stay green later. Very hardy. Broad-crowned compared to 'Marshall Seedless', with narrower leaflets which are less sharply toothed; shaggier bark; much darker buds; and a more prominent, larger terminal leaflet. It can produce some seeds but needs stress to do so.

F. pennsylvanica var. texensis—see F. texensis

F. pennsylvanica 'Tornado'

Introduced ≤1974 by Smith nursery of Charles City, IA. Extremely rare, or extinct commercially. Strong, straight; hardy. Makes seeds.

F. pennsylvanica Urbanite® PP 6215 (1988)

Introduced in 1987 by Wandell nursery of Urbana, IL. Common. Dense, broadly pyramidal. Seedless. Leaves heavy, lustrous, bronzy in fall. Bark heavily furrowed even at an early age.

F. pennsylvanica 'Variegata'—see F. penn. 'Albomarginata'

F. pennsylvanica ssp. velutina—see F. velutina

F. pennsylvanica 'Vinton'

Introduced ≤1960 by Linn County nursery of Center Point, IA. Commercially extinct. Seedless. Likely named after the town of Vinton, IA.

F. pennsylvanica 'Wahpeton'—see F. penn. Dakota Centennial™

F. pennsylvanica 'Wandell'—see F. pennsylvanica Skyward™

F. pennsylvanica 'Wasky' PP 7036 (1989)

Patented by Willet N. Wandell of Urbana, IL

F. pennsylvanica 'Wheeler'
Introduced ≤1988 by Schichtel nursery of Orchard Park, NY. A compact, rounded globe crown 25' tall and wide.

F. pistaciæfolia—see F. velutina

F. pubescens—see F. pennsylvanica

F. quadrangulata Michx.
BLUE ASH. WINGED ASH. From the central U.S. and extreme S Ontario. Uncommon in cultivation; difficult to propagate. There has been exasperating commercial confusion with F. excelsior 'Kimberly Blue'. Most trees sold as BLUE ASH are F. excelsior. Some attempts have been made to select an authentic F. quadrangulata of superior ornamental merit. Even if any clones have been named, none have become commercially important. Bark rough and scaly, even shaggy. Twigs at least of vigorous young shoots usually square in cross-section, and always with prominent lines or slight wings. Leaflets (5) 7–9 (11), sharply toothed. Fall color yellow, ranging from pale and dull to clear and bright. The inner bark yields a blue dye. Tolerates lime soils. Records: 150' × 8'6" Montgomery County, PA (1980); 104' × 13'1" Brownsville, IN (<1982); 90' × 14'8" Danville, KY (1982); 60' × 16'7" × 74' Paris, KY (1985).

F. quadrangulata 'Globosum'—see F. excel. 'Rancho (Roundhead)'

F. quadrangulata 'Kimberly Blue'—see F. excel. 'Kimberly (Blue)'

F. quadrangulata 'Western Blue'—see F. excel. 'Kimberly (Blue)'

F. rotundifolia—see F. angustifolia

F. rotundifolia ssp. oxycarpa—see F. angustifolia var. oxycarpa

F. rotundifolia 'Pendula'—see F. angustifolia 'Rotundifolia Pendula'

F. sambucifolia—see F. nigra

F. serratifolia—see F. Spaethiana

F. Sieboldiana Bl.
= F. Mariesii Hook. fil.
= F. lanuginosa Koidz.
= F. longicuspis var. Sieboldiana (Bl.) Lingelsh.
JAPANESE FLOWERING ASH. CHINESE FLOWERING ASH. From Japan, Korea and China. Named in 1850, after Philipp Franz von Siebold (1796–1866). Introduced to Western cultivation ≤1878. Rare. A large shrub or small tree, of neat, clean aspect. In effect, a dainty, refined and dwarf version of F. Ornus. Flowers showy, white (or tinged lavender), in airy, delicate clusters during May or June. Seeds can be attractive purplish in summer. Bark smooth, gray. Leaves to 8" long, leaflets 3–5 (7), inconspicuously bluntly toothed, the nodes purplish; lowermost pair of leaflets notably small. Largest leaflets 4¼" × 1¾". Buds gray to nearly black, large compared to the very slender twigs. Needs sun to thrive; poor in shade. Records: to 50' × 7'0" in Japan; 28' × 1'5½" Seattle, WA (1994; pl. 1959).

F. Spaethiana Lingelsh.
= F. serratifolia hort. (in part); non Michx.
SPÄTH'S ASH. From Japan. Japanese: Shioji. Introduced to Western cultivation in 1873. Named in 1907 after Späth (Spaeth) nursery of Germany. Extremely rare. Offered in 1964–65 by Scanlon nursery of Ohio. Foliage bold. Leaves to 18" long, leaflets (5) 7–9, thick, hard, the teeth sharp and curled upwards. Largest leaflets 9" × 2¾". Bark rough. Records: to 50' tall in Japan; 36' × 4'0" Kew, England (1969; pl. 1896).

F. tamariscifolia pendula—see F. angustifolia 'Pendula'

F. texensis (Gray) Sarg.
= F. americana var. texensis Gray
= F. americana ssp. texensis (Gray) G.N. Mill.
= F. pennsylvanica var. texensis hort.
TEXAS ASH. From S Oklahoma and Texas. Discovered in 1852. Rarely cultivated but available in Texas. Resembles AMERICAN ASH. Leaflets 5 (9), thick, large, rounded. Fall color yellow, gold and red. Cold hardy, drought tolerant. The cultivar **'Autumn Carnival'** was introduced ≤1992 by Aldridge nursery of Von Ormy, TX. Records: 80' × 6'6" Kew, England (1984; pl. 1901); 66' × 4'6" Lost Maples State Natural Area, TX (1989); trunks to 9'5" around in the wild.

F. Uhdei (Wenz.) Lingelsh.
SHAMEL ASH. EVERGREEN ASH. MEXICAN ASH. From Mexico. Named after Carl A. Uhde, who collected Mexican plants in the mid-1800s. Introduced to California in 1938 by Dr. Archibald (Archie) Dixon Shamel (1878–1956), plant physiologist of Riverside, CA. Originally from the seed of a selected tree located above Tepic, Nayarit, Mexico. Raised by Armstrong

nursery of Ontario, CA, the resulting trees were distributed around the state to test the species' adaptability. Since ≤1946 other nurseries have sold it. With adequate irrigation, the trees grow amazingly fast and bear lovely, large, deep green leaves. In Mexico, it is commonly called *Fresno* and the wood is used for furniture, house construction, etc.—it is likely the most generally used of any timber grown in its region. Hardiness varies, but usually serious damage occurs at 15°F. Other drawbacks are brittle limbs, weedy seedlings and invasive roots. Leaflets 5–9, toothed irregularly; hairy at base of midrib on left and right side; narrow, pointy, shiny, to 6¼" long. Evergreen in mild winters, but this feature is variable with different cultivars; it can have beautiful yellow and orange fall color. Records: 167' × 23'0" Uruapan, Mexico (1982); 82' × 8'6" × 47' Santa Barbara, CA (1993; *pl.* 1947) 80' × 13'4" × 60' Sacramento, CA (1994).

F. Uhdei 'Hagen'

Introduced ≤1951 by Hagen nursery of San Marino, CA. Extremely rare. Long commercially extinct.

F. Uhdei Majestic Beauty™ PP 2860 (1969)
= *F. Uhdei* 'Monus'

Introduced in 1966–67 by Monrovia nursery of California. Still in commerce. Exceptionally large (to 16" long), glossy dark leaves. More reliably evergreen. Vigorous; strong branching habit. Round-headed. Seedless. Specimens at the Los Angeles arboretum look utterly like ordinary *F. Uhdei* seedlings.

F. Uhdei 'Monus'—see F. Uhdei Majestic Beauty™

F. Uhdei 'Orange County'

Introduced ≤1988 by Orange County nursery of Norwalk, CA. A budded selection offering uniformity. Vigorous. Green until mid-December.

F. Uhdei 'Sexton'

Introduced ca. 1970 by Paul Gaines nursery of San Dimas, CA. Extremely rare. Commercially extinct. Possibly named after botanist Don K. Sexton. Compact rounded crown. Large leaflets.

F. Uhdei 'Tecate'—see F. velutina 'Tecate'

F. Uhdei 'Tomlinson' PP 2567 (1965)

Introduced in 1965 by Tomlinson Select nursery of California. Still in commerce. Thick leathery dark green foliage. Leaflets 3–9, high-gloss; youngest ones bronzy or purplish; margins wavy, sharply and coarsely toothed. White hairs along the midrib beneath. Although described as slower growing and smaller than typical *F. Uhdei*, one planted in 1967 in Los Angeles, measured 79' × 8'10" × 43½' in 1993. Said to never flower. Possibly a hybrid.

F. Veltheimii—see F. angust. 'Monophylla' and F. excelsior f. diversifolia

F. velutina Torr.
= *F. pistaciæfolia* Torr.
= *F. pennsylvanica* ssp. *velutina* (Torr.) G.N. Mill.

VELVET ASH. ARIZONA ASH. DESERT ASH. From the SW United States and N Mexico. Cultivated since ≤1897. Common. Botanists argue whether to use only the name *velutina*, or to name the variations within this species. An extreme yet reasonable opinion is that everything called *F. velutina* (VELVET ASH) or *F. latifolia* (OREGON ASH) is just a phase within a continental-wide *F. pennsylvanica* (GREEN / RED ASH). The course adopted for the present book assumes it is a matter of interpretation, and horticultural tradition can therefore be maintained, using varietal distinctions where they have practical significance. VELVET ASH is of great value as a shade tree able to endure the alkaline soils and dry conditions of the Southwest. Its bright green foliage turns yellow in fall. Since it is highly variable, descriptions of it must be general. Leaflets single or 3–5 (9), more or less velvety hairy beneath; above either dull and hairy or bright green and glossy; usually less than 4" long. For the most part it is a small tree. Records: 85' × 6'2" × 78' Presidio County, TX (1976); 81' × 14'0" × 86' Modesto, CA (1991); 73' × 11'6" × 61' Grant County, NM (1981).

F. velutina Berrinda®

Introduced ≤1992–93 by L.E. Cooke nursery of Visalia, CA. It tolerates more cold than typical *F. velutina*.

F. velutina var. coriacea (S. Wats.) Rehd.
= *F. coriacea* S. Wats.

MONTEBELLO ASH. LEATHERLEAF ASH. From Baja California, New Mexico, Arizona and Texas. Commonly cultivated in southern California. Leaves leathery, rough, scarcely hairy. Leaflets (3) 5 (7), shortly stalked.

F. velutina Fan-Tex® PP 2412 (1964)
= F. velutina 'Rio Grande'

Selected by Eddie Fanick of San Antonio, TX. It may actually be a form of F. Uhdei. Introduced ≤1962–63 by Aldridge nursery of Von Ormy, TX. Very common. Seedless. Fast; to 60' or more. Large dark leaves to 12" long, of 7–9 leaflets 4"–6" long. Leafs out early, holds foliage late: golden yellow in fall. Uniform symmetric top growth. Tolerates heat and drought well. Borer resistant. Bark nearly white. As early as 1914, nurseries called certain trees RIO GRANDE ASHES, so as a vernacular that name may apply to any number of seedlings, yet in a modern clonal sense it refers primarily to Fan-Tex®.

F. velutina Fan West™
= F. pennsylvanica 'Fan-West'

Found by Eddie Fanick of San Antonio, TX, as a natural seedling on the banks of the Guadalupe River. Introduced in 1976–77 by L.E. Cooke nursery of California. Still common in nurseries. Described as a seedless Texas GREEN ASH crossed with an VELVET ASH (and overall more closely resembling a GREEN ASH). Leaves light olive green. Good branch structure. Very hardy.

F. velutina var. glabra (Thornb.) Rehd.
= F. arizonica hort.

Cultivated since 1916. Common. Leaflets glossy, scarcely hairy; bright yellow in fall. The most common cultivar is 'Modesto'.

F. velutina 'Modesto'
= F. velutina var. glabra 'Modesto'

MODESTO ASH. Introduced <1940. All stock traces back to an individual tree of unknown origin in a city park of Modesto, CA. The most common of all velutina variants. Grown up and down the Pacific Coast and in the Southwest. Small, delicate lacy leaves, 3–7 shiny dark green hairless leaflets, on a 45' round-headed seedless tree; bright yellow in fall. Tolerates alkalinity. Fast growing but does not grow awkwardly large. Bark shaggy.

F. velutina 'Orange County'

Introduced ≤1988 by Orange County nursery of Norwalk, CA. A budded selection offering a straight, well-trunked tree. Vigorous.

F. velutina 'Pendula'

WEEPING ARIZONA ASH. Introduced ≤1940 by W.B. Clarke nursery of San José, CA. Long extinct commercially. Branches pendulous.

F. velutina 'Rio Grande'—see F. velutina Fan-Tex®

F. velutina 'Stribling'

Seedless. No additional description known, but the tree has been in commerce. Likely associated with Stribling nursery of Merced, CA.

F. velutina 'Sunbelt'

Introduced ≤1991–92 by L.E. Cooke nursery of Visalia, CA. Dense, uniform oval crown.

F. velutina 'Tecate'
= F. Uhdei 'Tecate'
= F. attenuata 'Tecate'

Originally found as a 25' tree in Baja California (Tecate is on the California / Baja California border, east of Tijuana). Name registered in 1951. Not known to have been in commerce. Leaflets usually 5, untoothed, the tips drawn out or attenuate. Probably a selection of F. velutina var. coriacea, but perhaps of var. Toumeyi (Britt.) Rehd., the latter synonymous with F. attenuata M.E. Jones.

F. velutina var. Toumeyi—see F. velutina 'Tecate'

F. velutina 'Von Ormy'
('Von Ormi')

Introduced ≤1985–86 by Aldridge nursery of Von Ormy, TX. Rather narrow-leaved. Seedless. Vigorous.

Fraxinus viridis—see F. pennsylvanica var. lanceolata

Gaza Anacua—see Ehretia Anacua

Ginkgo

[GINKGOACEÆ; Ginkgo Family] Only the following species in the genus, a common and celebrated deciduous tree. The Dutch botanist Kaempfer transliterated the Chinese name *Yin Hsing* (Silver Apricot, applied on account of the silvery sheen on the orange fruit) to *Ginkgo*. Earth's most primitive extant broadleaved tree: fossils more than 65 million years old are identical to today's trees. Cultivated for shade, glorious yellow fall color. Widely adapted to varying conditions, troublefree, but stunted by dryness. *Ginkgo* is not closely related to any other trees.

G. biloba L.
= *Salisburia adiantifolia* Sm.

GINKGO. MAIDENHAIR TREE. GOLDEN FOSSIL TREE. STINK BOMB TREE. From SE China. Possibly introduced to Utrecht, Holland ca. 1727–1730; certainly nurseryman James Gordon at Mile End, England had seedlings in 1754. First planted in North America by William Hamilton in 1784 near Philadelphia. The synonym *Salisburia*, much used in the 1800s, was applied in 1796 because its author regarded *Ginkgo* as "equally uncouth and barbarous." The epithet *biloba* and English name MAIDENHAIR TREE refer to the unique fan-shaped leaf. The tree usually bears male and female flowers on separate individuals. A *Ginkgo* can be 45 years old or more before flowering: since it can live more than 1,000 years it need not rush into reproduction. Indeed its youthful appearance is gangling, remarkable primarily for the pure yellow fall color and curious leaf; but in advanced age the bearing grows majestic. Male flowers are dangling catkins in April or May; female flowers are inconspicuous greenish affairs. Female trees can set fruit without pollination. Fruit orange with a silver bloom, soft, putrid, ripe in fall, enclosing an edible triangular nut, of chewy texture. Males flush, and defoliate, ca. 2–4 weeks earlier than females, and often grown taller. Bark pale ashy gray. *Ginkgo* extracts are valuable medicinally. Records: to 200' × 47'0" in China and Korea; 157' × 25'3" in Japan (1994); 128' × 13'10" Longwood Gardens, Kennett Square, PA (1987); 106' × 22'4" Tyler Arboretum, Media, PA (1980); trunks more than 17'0" around are also in CT, IL, MD and NY.

G. biloba Autumn Gold™
Selected in 1951 and introduced in 1955 by Saratoga Horticultural Foundation of California—their first cultivar of the species to be distributed to nurseries. Common. Male. Oval upright crown. The original specimen from the corner of El Abra Way and Lincoln Avenue, San José, CA.

G. biloba var. epiphylla Mak.
= *G. biloba* 'Ohazuki' ('Ohazaki', 'Ohatsuki', 'Okazuki')

Long known in Japan, and named there in the 1950s. In European commerce since ≤1968. Introduced to North America ≤1986 but extremely rare. A mere curiosity with its fruit stalks broad, winglike. Japanese *Ohatsuki-icho* is vernacular for it.

G. biloba 'Fairmount'
Introduced in 1962 by Saratoga Horticultural Foundation of California. Still being sold in West Coast nurseries. Propagated from a male grafted tree planted in 1876 during the Centennial Exposition in Philadelphia, at the site of the Horticultural Hall in Fairmount Park. Dense, upright pyramidal crown. Branches upswept, but tree not fastigiate. Fall color can be inferior. In 1975 the original specimen measured 55' × 7'10" × 20' wide.

G. biloba f. fastigiata (Henry) Rehd.
= *G. biloba* 'Sentry'

SENTRY GINKGO. First cultivated ≤1888; described in 1896 in a clonal sense. The name usage adopted here is in a group sense, to embrace any strongly columnar or narrowly pyramidal specimens, be they chance seedlings or named cultivars. 'Mayfield' and 'Princeton Sentry' are the main cultivars. Record: 135' × 9'2" × 30' Barnes Arboretum, Merion, PA (1980).

G. biloba 'Golden Girl'
Introduced ≤1994 by Arborvillage nursery of Holt, MO. "Outstanding local female specimen turns butter gold each fall."

G. biloba 'Kew'
A tree from Kew gardens of England, planted in 1762. In no way special, but sold for its historic associations.

G. biloba 'Laciniata'
= *G. biloba* 'Macrophylla Laciniata'

CUTLEAF GINKGO. LARGELEAF GINKGO. Raised in 1840 by the botanist Reynier of Avignon, France; put into commerce by A. Sénéclauze's nursery. Described in

1854. Not known in North American commerce. Fast. Leaves large, 7"–12" wide, with several deep notches.

G. biloba 'Lakeview'

Named in 1955 after Lakeview Cemetery of Cleveland, by Scanlon nursery of Ohio. Sold from the late 1950s into the mid-'60s. Male. Broadly pyramidal.

G. biloba 'Liberty Splendor'

Introduced ≤1994 by Arborvillage nursery of Holt, MO. "Outstanding local female specimen that has strong central leader and beautiful wide pyramidal form. Will rival any Greenspire® Linden or Bradford Pear for form."

G. biloba 'Macrophylla Laciniata'—see G. biloba 'Laciniata'

G. biloba 'Magyar'

Introduced ≤1991 by Princeton nursery of New Jersey. A uniform, upright male.

G. biloba 'Mayfield'

Selected ca. 1948 by Scanlon nursery of Ohio. Sold in the 1950s and still sparingly available. A *fastigiata* clone. Male. Very narrow, strictly fastigiate like LOMBARDY POPLAR (*Populus nigra* 'Italica').

G. biloba 'Ohazuki'—see G. biloba var. epiphylla

G. biloba 'Palo Alto'

Introduced in 1955 by Scanlon nursery of Ohio. Sold into the mid-'60s. A broad male. In Spanish, *palo alto* means tall timber.

G. biloba 'Pendula'

WEEPING GINKGO. Originated in 1855. Named in 1862 by Charles van Geert of Ghent, Belgium. In North American commerce ≤1960. Rare. A small umbrella-shaped tree with weakly pendulous branches. Usually topgrafted.

G. biloba 'PNI 2720'—see G. biloba Princeton Sentry®

G. biloba 'Princeton Gold' PP 2675 (1966)

Selected by Princeton nursery of New Jersey. Male with a strong central leader and perfect regularity of branching habit. Never advertised by Princeton, it was discontinued because of propagation difficulties. Some arboreta have specimens.

G. biloba Princeton Sentry® PP 2726 (1967)
= G. biloba 'PNI 2720'

The original was planted in 1940 in the Roosevelt boulevard of Philadelphia. Introduced in 1972–73 by Princeton nursery of New Jersey. Common. A *fastigiata* clone. Male.

G. biloba 'Santa Cruz'
= G. biloba 'Umbrella'
= G. biloba 'Umbraculifera'

Introduced in 1951 by Scanlon nursery of Ohio. Also offered in 1960–61 by W.B. Clarke nursery of San José, CA. Both received propagating stock from Saratoga Horticultural Foundation of California. Now out of commerce. The original tree was in Santa Cruz, CA. Low, spreading umbrella form. Good shape to plant underneath power lines, but unfortunately it is female, so drops messy fruit.

G. biloba 'Saratoga'

Introduced in 1975 by the Saratoga Horticultural Foundation of California. Common in Pacific Coast commerce. Dense, compact habit with ascending branches, and a distinct central leader. Bushy, slow growth. Male.

G. biloba 'Sentry'—see G. biloba f. fastigiata

G. biloba Shangri-La® PP 5221 (1984)

Selected by W. Wandell of Urbana, IL. Uncommon. Male. Compact, dense and full. Growth rapid. Bright yellow in fall.

G. biloba 'Sinclair'

Selected by Princeton nursery of New Jersey; never advertised because of propagation difficulties. Offered in 1977 by Siebenthaler nursery of Dayton, OH. Commercially extinct. Male; well-branched.

G. biloba 'Sterile'

Siebenthaler nursery of Dayton, OH, used this name for male grafted trees. It can scarcely qualify as a valid cultivar name.

G. biloba 'Tubeleaf'
= G. biloba 'Tubiformis' ('Tubiforme')

Introduced (as 'Tubiformis') ≤1991–92 by Mitsch nursery of Aurora, OR. Weird. Shoot leaves laciniate; spur leaves ± with connate lobes forming a broad funnel. Unless the Latin cultivar name 'Tubiformis' was published <1959, it must be de-Latinized—although not necessarily as done above.

Ginkgo biloba 'Tubiformis'—see *G. biloba* 'Tubeleaf'

G. biloba 'Umbraculifera'—see *G. biloba* 'Santa Cruz'

G. biloba 'Umbrella'—see *G. biloba* 'Santa Cruz'

G. biloba 'Variegata'

This name has been applied to more than one clone. One originated as a seedling at A. Leroy's Angiers nursery, and was described in 1854 in France. Another was introduced from Japan to the U.S. ca. 1861 by G.R. Hall. More than one California nursery sold 'Variegata' in the 1880s and '90s. Very rare, but still in commerce. Both clones bear variegated leaves, streaked creamy-yellow to yellow, some wholly yellow. At least one is female.

G. biloba 'Woodstock'

Introduced ≤1994 by Chicagoland Grows®, Inc. Male. Strong central leader, excellent branching, uniformly oval crown.

Gleditschia—see *Gleditsia*

Gleditsia

(*Gleditschia*)

[LEGUMINOSÆ; Pea Family] 10–14 spp. of thorny deciduous trees in the temperate Northern Hemisphere. Grown for shade and delicately beautiful foliage. Leaves pinnately compound. Flowers not showy; small, in greenish clusters during May or June. Fruit usually a large, flat many-seeded pod. Fall color yellow. The name is the simplified and Latinized name from that of Linnaeus' close friend Johann Gottlieb Gleditsch (1714–1786), professor of botany and director of botanic gardens at Berlin. Although leguminous, *Gleditsia* lacks the ability to fix nitrogen symbiotically, unlike LOCUSTS in the genus *Robinia*.

G. aquatica 'Elegantissima'—see *G. triacanthos* 'Elegantissima'

G. horrida—see *G. japonica*, *G. triacanthos*, and *G. sinensis*

G. japonica Miq.
= *G. horrida* (Th.) Mak. 1803, non Salisb. 1797, non Willd. 1806

JAPANESE HONEY LOCUST. From Japan and China. Might have been introduced to Western cultivation as early as 1800, but no later than 1854, the year a California nursery offered it. Very rare. Compared to *G. triacanthos*: fewer and weaker spines (to 4"); fewer leaflets (16–24) with comparatively few subdivided; smaller pods (8"–12"), and does not grow as large. Overall there is no practical difference between the two species except size; the Japanese species is less cold hardy. Flower clusters 2⅜"–5¾" long. Records: to 80' × 6'3" in the wild; 43' × 3'3" Kew, England (1976; *pl.* 1873); 30' × 1'8¼" Seattle, WA (1994; *pl.* 1941).

G. japonica var. *koraiensis* Nakai
= *G. koraiensis* hort.

KOREAN HONEY LOCUST. Extremely rare. Little known. Likely more cold hardy, and with larger flowers, leaves and pods than the Japanese type.

G. koraiensis—see *G. japonica* var. *koraiensis*

G. sinensis Lam.
= *G. horrida* Willd. 1806, non Mak. 1803, non Salisb. 1797

CHINESE HONEY LOCUST. SOAP BEAN TREE. From China. Introduced, says E.Wilson, by D'Incarville to Paris, in the mid-1700s. Named in 1786. In North America ≤1811. In commerce here by 1823. Rare. Thorns ferociously abundant, stout, sharp, and much branched. Flower clusters to 7" long. Leaflets 8–14 (18), larger (to 3⅜" × 1½") and bolder-looking than those of *G. triacanthos*, sometimes persistently green when the American natives are yellow or bare, but eventually turning lovely rich yellow. In China the 5"–11" pods are used as a soap substitute for washing hair and fine clothing. Drought-tolerant. Invaluable as a conversation piece, but dangerously armed. Records: to 85' × 13'0" in the wild; 56' × 5'6" Nymans, Sussex, England (1983); 41' × 3'0" Seattle, WA (1994; *pl.* 1945).

G. sinensis 'Inermis'—see *G. triacanthos* 'Elegantissima'

G. triacanthos L.
= *G. horrida* Salisb. 1797, non Willd. 1806, non Mak. 1803

HONEY LOCUST. COMMON HONEY LOCUST. HONEY SHUCKS LOCUST. SWEET BEAN TREE. THORNY LOCUST.

THORNY ACACIA. SWEET LOCUST. From the central and eastern U.S., and extreme S Ontario. Very common in cultivation. Overplanted in the 1970s. Valued for light airy shade and tiny leaflets making minimal mess. Needs hot summers to thrive. The name from Greek *tri*, three, and *akantha*, a thorn. It is thorny to an amazing degree: up to 1' long and branched. Leaf with 14–36 leaflets. Virtually all of the following 36 cultivars are thornless (see f. *inermis*) and set few pods. Pods 8"–24" long, usually contorted, with sweet edible pulp. Records (including thornless specimens): to 150' tall in the wild; 130' × 12'4" × 106' Washtenaw County, MI (1976); 129' × 18'0" Posey County, IN (<1875); 115' × 17'0" ×124' Wayne County, MI (1972); 92' × 18'9" × 112' near Queenstown, MD (1945); 90' × 19'5" × 88' Greencastle, PA (1991).

G. *triacanthos* 'Arrowhead'—see G. *triacanthos* Skyline®

G. *triacanthos* 'Aurea'—see G. *triacanthos* 'Sunburst'

G. *triacanthos* 'Beatrice'

Original tree in Beatrice, NE. Introduced ≤1955 by Inter-State nursery of Hamburg, IA. Nearly or wholly out of commerce since ca. 1980. Shaped very much like the AMERICAN ELM (*Ulmus americana*), widespread at the top. Thornless; usually podless.

G. *triacanthos* 'Bujotii'
= G. *triacanthos* 'Pendula'
= G. *triacanthos* 'Bujoti Pendula'
= G. *triacanthos* 'Excelsa Pendula'

WEEPING HONEY LOCUST. Described in 1845 in France. Named for M. Bujot (Buyot), of Chiary, near Château-Thiery (Aisne) nurseryman who discovered it. Sold in North America from ≤1880s into the early 1900s. Extremely rare. Thornless. Foliage exceedingly graceful, drooping. Leaflets smaller, quite narrow. An immense specimen, ca. 110' × 16'0" at Saint-Gaudens National Historic Site, Cornish, NH. Some writers insist 'Bujoti' leaflets are at least partly mottled white—a confusion with G. *triacanthos* 'Foliis Variegatis'.

G. *triacanthos* 'Bujoti Pendula'—see G. *triacanthos* 'Bujoti'

G. *triacanthos* 'Christie' or 'Christie's Halka'—see G. *triac.* Halka™

G. *triacanthos* 'Columnaris'

Described in Germany in 1913, from a beautiful old columnar form in a park in Belgium. Introduced to North America in 1966 by the Arnold Arboretum. G. Krüssmann says it is identical to 'Elegantissima', but F. Santamour disagrees.

G. *triacanthos* 'Compacta'—see G. *triacanthos* 'Elegantissima'

G. *triacanthos* 'Continental' PP 1752 (1958)

Introduced ≤1973 by Princeton nursery of New Jersey. Still in commerce. Vigorous, with a narrow crown of stout branches. Thornless; virtually podless. Leaves exceptionally large, finely cut.

G. *triacanthos* 'Cottage Green'

Introduced ≤1978 by Cottage Gardens nursery of Lansing, MI. Thornless. Podless.

G. *triacanthos* 'Elegantissima'
= G. *triacanthos* 'Compacta'
= G. *sinensis* 'Inermis'
= G. *aquatica* 'Elegantissima'

GLOBE HONEY LOCUST. BUSHY HONEY LOCUST. Raised by nurseryman Charles Breton of Orléans, ca. 1880. Described in France in 1905. In North American commerce ≤1891. Sold by some Ohio nurseries from the 1930s into the '50s. Very rare. Dense, bushy, forming a tight vase shaped crown; very slow. Thornless; smaller leaflets. Elegantissima means very elegant or most elegant; from Latin *elegans*, elegant, and the superlative *-issima*. Nurseries have propagated it variously on its own roots, ground-budded and topgrafted. Records: 40' tall at Stanford, CA (1938; *pl.* 1920); a very old, multitrunked specimen 32' tall × 39' wide in Seattle (1992). See also G. *triacanthos* 'Columnaris'.

G. *triacanthos* 'Emerald Kascade'

Introduced ≤1992 by Duncan & Davies nursery of New Zealand. Weeping; needs training to grow over 16' tall. Thornless. Podless.

G. *triacanthos* 'Emerald Lace' PP 3260 (1972)

A seedling selected in 1970 by John H. McIntyre at Fairview, OR. Introduced in 1973–74 by A. McGill & Son nursery of Fairview, OR. Out of commerce since ≤ mid-1980s. Thornless. Rapid, strong growth. Unusual foliage: dark; while young of twisted, ruffled appearance, produced at an acute angle to the stem; branch angle less than 90°.

G. *triacanthos* 'Excelsa Pendula'—see G. *triacanthos* 'Bujotii'

G. *triacanthos* Fairview™

Introduced in 1975–76 by A. McGill & Son nursery of Fairview, OR. Still in commerce. Thornless. Growth rapid, strong. Like G. *triacanthos* 'Moraine' but much stronger.

G. *triacanthos* 'Foliis Variegatis'

Cultivated in Silesia (SW Poland) <1864. Leaflets white-mottled. Slow growing, thornless. Likely this clone was distributed partly or wholly as G. *triacanthos* 'Bujotii' or under one of the synonyms cited under that cultivar. But its origin, proper name, and present availability are unknown. Record: 44' × 2'1½" Vancouver, B.C. (1994).

G. *triacanthos* 'Golden'—see G. *triacanthos* Sunburst®

G. *triacanthos* 'Golden Halo'—see G. *triacanthos* Sunburst®

G. *triacanthos* 'Goldenwest'—see G. *triacanthos* Sunburst®

G. *triacanthos* Green Arbor®

Introduced in 1971 by Handy nursery of Portland, OR. Out of commerce since ≤ mid-1980s. Thornless. Rapid; habit rather open early in life, becoming dense eventually; foliage lush and dense, unlike any other HONEY LOCUST; 50'–60' tall; thornless.

G. *triacanthos* 'Green Glory' PP 2786 (1968)

Developed and offered in 1964 by Ralph Synnestvedt & Associates, Burr Oak nursery of Glenview, IL. Still in commerce. Very rapid, thornless, podless. Notably dense, dark foliage. A straight trunk with a central leader. Symmetrical broad pyramidal head. Retains color later in fall than other HONEY LOCUSTS.

G. *triacanthos* 'Green Sentinel'

Introduced ≤1991 by L.E. Cooke nursery of Visalia, CA. Distinctly pyramidal, with a sturdy trunk. Podless.

G. *triacanthos* Halka™ PP 3096 (1972)

= G. *triacanthos* 'Christie'
= G. *triacanthos* 'Christie's Halka'

A chance seedling discovered and patented by Chester J. Halka of Englishtown, NJ. Introduced in 1976–77 by Schmidt nursery of Boring, OR. Very common. Thornless. Vigorous; may be fastest growing of all HONEY LOCUSTS. Thick heavy trunk developed at an early age; upright growing with a rounded head; lateral branches more horizontal than pendulous.

G. *triacanthos* 'Impcole'—see G. *triacanthos* Imperial®

G. *triacanthos* Imperial® PP 1605 (1957)

= G. *triacanthos* 'Impcole'

Introduced in 1956 by Cole nursery of Painesville, OH. Very common. Thornless. Graceful globular or rounded crown, with refined, dainty bright foliage. Strong, spreading, yet compact, reportedly grows only 35' tall. But one planted in 1956 in Seattle: 52' × 3'1½" × 44½' (1994).

G. *triacanthos* f. *inermis* (L.) Zab.

THORNLESS HONEY LOCUST. Described in 1763. Prince nursery of Flushing, NY, had it for sale by 1827. Virtually all cultivars in commerce are more or less thornless. *Inermis* in Latin means unarmed; without thorns. About 20% of the seedlings breed true, so it is easy to raise them. They grow just as large as the thorny trees. Most also set fewer pods than the wild thorny specimens.

G. *triacanthos* 'Inermis Aurea'—see G. *triacanthos* Sunburst®

G. *triacanthos* 'Lake's No. 1'

Introduced in 1974 by Shenandoah nursery, Shenandoah, IA. Very rare; out of commerce. Small (to 30' tall), spreading. Thornless.

G. *triacanthos* 'Lake's No. 2'—see G. *triacanthos* 'Royal Green'

G. *triacanthos* 'Majestic' PP 1534 (1956)

Introduced in 1957 by Cole nursery of Painesville, OH. Scarcely in commerce since the mid-'80s. Strong, exceptionally graceful tree of spreading growth habit, entirely thornless; light pod crop.

G. triacanthos 'Marando Weeping' PP 6913 (1989)

Patented by Vincent Marando of Bayside, NY. Propagation rights assigned to Speer and Sons nursery of Woodburn, OR.

G. triacanthos 'Maxwell'

Originated in the yard of Earl Maxwell, Lincoln, NE. Introduced in 1957 by Plumfield nursery of Fremont, NE. Extinct commercially. "Nice" growth habit, thornless, podless.

G. triacanthos 'Moraine' PP 836 (1949)

Introduced in 1949 by Siebenthaler nursery of Dayton, Ohio. Very common. The first heavily promoted, mass-produced THORNLESS HONEYLOCUST. Podless. Large vigorous tree with vase-like, broad spreading crown.

G. triacanthos 'Nana'

Possibly originated <1838 in England. Extremely rare in North America. A compact shrub or small tree with short, broad, intensely dark green leaflets. Thornless. Podless. (*Nana* is Latin for dwarf.) Records: 79' × 5'6" Kew, England (1981); 25' × 2'1½" × 12' Sidney, B.C. (1994; *pl.* 1914).

G. triacanthos 'Park'

Introduced ≤1958 by Marshall nursery of Arlington, NE. Long commercially extinct. Thornless, podless.

G. triacanthos 'Paul Bunyan'

Introduced ≤1977 by Ilgenfritz nursery of Monroe, MI. Extinct commercially. A tall growing, free branching, thornless tree.

G. triacanthos 'Pendula'—see G. triacanthos 'Bujotii'

G. triacanthos Perfection™ PP 6709 (1989)
= G. triacanthos 'Wandell'

Introduced ≤1989 by Wandell nursery of Urbana, IL. Fast growth. Well balanced crown. Thornless.

G. triacanthos 'Pin Cushion' PP 2680 (1966)

Introduced in 1968–69 by A. McGill & Son nursery of Fairview, OR. Commercially extinct. Unusual dark green foliage formed in clusters spaced at intervals along the branches. Thornless, podless.

G. triacanthos 'PNI 2835'—see G. triacanthos Shademaster®

G. triacanthos 'Prairie Sky'

Originated ca. 1980 at Maple Creek, Saskatchewan. Named and introduced by Roseberry Gardens of Thunder Bay, Ontario. Very upright, symmetrical. Primarily of value for its cold hardiness.

G. triacanthos 'Royal Green'
= G. triacanthos 'Lake's No. 2'

A chance seedling, introduced in 1970 by Shenandoah nursery of Shenandoah, IA. Trunk straight and sturdy. Crown compact and upright. Thornless.

G. triacanthos Rubylace® PP 2038 (1961)

Introduced in 1964 by Princeton nursery of New Jersey. Still in commerce. Thornless, podless. Bright ruby red young growth turning somber bronzy green. Smaller than typical HONEY LOCUSTS.

G. triacanthos 'Seiler'
('Sieler')

Introduced in 1949 by Linn County nursery of Center Point, IA; sold by them until at least 1958. Out of commerce. Large, widespreading tree, almost completely podless.

G. triacanthos Shademaster® PP 1515 (1956)
= G. triacanthos 'PNI 2835'

Introduced in 1956 by Princeton nursery of New Jersey. Common. Rapid; vigorous. Straight strong trunk, ascending branches, symmetric top. Thornless; probably podless. Heavy dark foliage held longer in fall than that of most cultivars. Resists drought. Disease free. Canker resistant.

G. triacanthos 'Skycole'—see G. triacanthos Skyline®

G. triacanthos Skyline® PP 1619 (1957)
= G. triacanthos 'Skycole'
= G. triacanthos 'Arrowhead'

Introduced in 1957 by Cole nursery of Painesville, OH. Common. Distinctive pyramidal form; strong central leader, sturdy trunk; crown upright and initially narrow, pointed—eventually rounded to flat-topped. Emerging leaflets have reddish-bronze cast then change to notably dark leathery foliage; large, closely spaced leaflets.

G. triacanthos 'Stephens'

Found on the farm of Dan V. Stephens, northwest of Arlington, NE. Introduced ≤1939 by Marshall nursery of Arlington. Thornless, straight growing and symmetrical. Long extinct commercially.

Gleditsia triacanthos 'Summergold'

Introduced in 1971 by Handy nursery of Portland, OR. Extinct commercially. Open, elegant, lacy appearance; foliage bright golden when young, turning to yellow green; 40–50' tall. May be *G. triacanthos* Sunburst® renamed.

G. triacanthos Summer Lace®

Introduced in the early 1980s. Common. Very strong grower. New foliage is light green turning rich dark green at maturity. Grows taller than most cultivars.

G. triacanthos Sunburst® PP 1313 (1954)

= *G. triacanthos* 'Suncole' (the official cultivar name)
= *G. triacanthos* 'Goldenwest'
= *G. triacanthos* 'Golden'
= *G. triacanthos* 'Golden Halo'
= *G. triacanthos* 'Sunsplash'
= *G. triacanthos* 'Aurea'
= *G. triacanthos* 'Inermis Aurea'

Discovered as a seedling in 1947, patented and introduced in 1954–55 by Cole Nursery of Painesville, OH. Very common. Bright golden young foliage; green by late summer except the youngest tips still pale. Thornless; podless. Irregular habit of winding branches. Canker susceptible. Records: 54' × 5'8" × 63' Walla Walla, WA (1993); 48' × 5'11" × 45' La Crosse, WI (1986).

G. triacanthos 'Suncole'—see *G. triacanthos* Sunburst®

G. triacanthos 'Sunsplash'—see *G. triacanthos* Sunburst®

G. triacanthos True Shade®

Introduced in 1973 by Pacific Coast nursery of Portland, OR. In commerce. Strong; striking dark shiny bark and lush, light green foliage. Growth fast, making a heavy trunk even when young.

G. triacanthos 'Wandell'—see *G. triacanthos* Perfection™

G. vestita Chun & How *ex* B.G. Li

From Hunan, China, where it is an endangered species. Named in 1982 (meaning *clothed* in Latin). Introduced ≤1994–95 by Piroche Plants nursery of Pitt Meadows, B.C. Leaflets 10–16 (18), to 2½" × 1" and sparsely hairy on both surfaces. Pods 6"–13" long, densely golden hairy.

Glyptostrobus

[TAXODIACEÆ; Bald Cypress Family] A genus of only the following species, a deciduous conifer. From Greek *glyptos*, engraved, carved, or cut in, and *strobilos*, a cone, referring to "the median slit in the margin of the scales" or to "the spirally arranged cone-scales." Related closely to *Taxodium* (BALD CYPRESS), differing in having trimorphic rather than dimorphic leaves; the cones and seeds also differ.

G. heterophyllus—see *G. pensilis*

G. lineatus—see *G. pensilis* and *Taxodium ascendens* 'Nutans'

G. pensilis (Staunt.) K. Koch

= *G. lineatus* auct., non (Poir.) Druce
= *G. sinensis* Henry *ex* Loder
= *G. heterophyllus* (Brongn.) Endl.
= *Taxodium heterophyllum* Brongn.
= *Taxodium distichum pendulum* hort., non Carr. 1867

CHINESE SWAMP CYPRESS. CHINESE WATER PINE. CHINESE BALD CYPRESS. CANTON WATER PINE. From swampy lowlands of coastal SE China. Introduced to England in 1804 by Wm. Kerr. Date of introduction to North America not known, but in the 1800s; most presently known here date from the 1980s. A problem with tracking its history is the gross confusion between it and *Taxodium ascendens* 'Nutans'. In China it varies from a 15' shrub to a substantial tree. Rare in the wild; planted along rice field borders. Bark soft, reddish, papery-flaky, thick and spongy. Cones egg-shaped, ¾" or slightly longer, can be closed with finger pressure; fragile. Spectacular brilliant crimson November color. Young twigs remain pale green. To thrive it must have a very damp, warm site, and freedom from severe winter freezes. Records: to 128' × 21'6" in the wild; 41½' × 2'2½" × 14' Davis, CA (1994; *pl.* 1983); 40' × 2'4½" Dunloe Castle, County Kerry, Ireland (1987).

G. sinensis—see *G. pensilis*

Gordonia

[THEACEÆ; Tea Family] 30–70 spp. of evergreen shrubs and trees; nearly all native in subtropical eastern Asia. Named after a well-known nurseryman, James Gordon (1728–1791), of Mile End, London. In 1758 John Ellis said of him "He has more knowledge in vegetation than all the gardeners and writers on gardening in England put together." Curiously, the genus almost was named for Alexander Garden (1730–1791), M.D., from Scotland, who settled at Charlestown, SC. Dr. Garden desired to have the LOBLOLLY BAY named after himself, but his letter arrived a month too late—so another genus (not in this volume) was named *Gardenia* after him. Genera related to *Gordonia* include *Franklinia* and *Stewartia*.

G. Alatamaha—see *Franklinia Alatamaha*

G. Lasianthus (L.) Ellis

LOBLOLLY BAY. HOLLY BAY. BLACK LAUREL. SUMMER CAMELLIA. From eastern North Carolina to S Mississippi on the coastal plain, in shallow swamps, moist ground and low rich bottomlands. Loblolly refers to the moist depressions in which the tree often grows. Cultivated in northern nurseries since ≤1840s. Uncommon. Cannot endure severe cold. *Lasianthus* is a 1735 generic name, meaning hairy-flowered: from Greek *lasios*, hairy, and *andros*, a male, alluding to the hairy stamens. Leaves 4"–6" long, shiny. Flowers 2"–3" wide, white, long stemmed, July–September. Bark reddish. Often shrubby, but in ideal conditions it is a tall narrow tree, handsome in foliage and flower. Records: to 100' tall in the wild; 94' × 13'7" × 52' Hugh's Island, Ocala National Forest, FL (1985).

Guilandina dioica—see *Gymnocladus dioica*

Gymnocladus

[LEGUMINOSÆ; Pea Family] 2–5 spp. of deciduous trees, all from east Asia except the one treated below. Name from Greek *gymnos*, naked, and *klados*, a branch, referring to its many months of starkly deciduous nature—or to the soft young wood, devoid of buds (which are inconspicuous). Or because the foliage is mostly at the *ends* of the branches. Although leguminous, *Gymnocladus* lacks the ability to symbiotically fix nitrogen. The most closely related genus is *Gleditsia* (HONEY LOCUST).

G. canadensis —see G. dioica

G. dioica (L.) K. Koch
(*dioicus*)
= G. canadensis Lam.
= *Guilandina dioica* L.

KENTUCKY COFFEETREE. KENTUCKY MAHOGANY. COFFEE NUT TREE. (K)NICKER TREE. STUMP TREE. LUCK BEAN. CHICOT (French-Canadian for "dead tree"). From the central and eastern U.S. and extreme S Ontario. Bold textured in winter, changing when in leaf to a fine-medium effect. Leaves pink-bronze when unfolding; doubly pinnate-compound, very large (to 6' long), of often 100 or more leaflets. Flowers greenish-white in May–June. Fall color yellow. Pods huge (6"–10" long) and leach a caustic substance that damages car paint finish; male trees are good street trees. The roasted seeds were used in pioneer times as a coffee substitute. Records: 135' tall at Winterthur Gardens, DE (ca. 1982); 122' × 11'11" × 72' Sumner, WI (1986); 112' × 14'1" × 109' Hartford, MI (1986); 82' × 15'6" × 75' east of Madison, OH (1973); 78' × 17'8" × 84' West Liberty, KY (1985).

G. dioica 'Espresso'
From 2011 Regis Drive, Davis, CA, where it was selected as one of the best of an entire street planted with specimens in the early 1960s. Introduced in 1993 by Schmidt nursery of Boring, OR. Podless.

Halesia

[STYRACACEÆ; Storax Family] 4–5 spp. of deciduous shrubs and trees, all in the SE United States except one in China. Grown for their lovely white flowers in spring. The fruit is a dry, brown, silvery-winged seed—hence the name SILVERBELL. Named after Stephen Hales (1677–1761), English clergyman, scientist and inventor, author of *Vegetable Staticks*. A 1976 revision of *Halesia* has left many people shaking their heads. Related genera include *Pterostyrax* and *Styrax*.

H. carolina L.
= *H. tetraptera* Ellis
= *Mohrodendron carolinum* Britt.

SILVERBELL TREE. SNOWDROP TREE. OPOSSUM WOOD. CALICO WOOD. TISS WOOD. BELL TREE. TISSUEWOOD. WILD OLIVE. RATTLE BOX. From the southeastern U.S. Common in cultivation. A large shrub or small tree. Leaves thin, dull, finely toothed, variably hairy, 2"–5" long. Fall color yellow. Flowers ½"–¾" long. Seeds ¾"–1½" long, four-winged (the name *tetraptera* means four-winged; Greek *tetr*, four, and *pteron*, a wing or feather).

H. carolina var. *monticola* Rehd.
= *H. monticola* (Rehd.) Sarg.

MOUNTAIN SILVERBELL. From mountains of Tennessee and North Carolina. Introduced to cultivation ca. 1897 by H.P. Kelsey. Named in 1913. Larger leaves, flowers and seeds, shaggier bark, and above all definite treehood. Leaves as in the type but bigger: 5"–9" (11") long. Flowers ⅝"–1" long, can be pink ('Rosea'). Seeds 1½"–2¼" long. Records: to 100' tall; 95' × 10'1" Philadelphia County, PA (1980); 86' × 13'6" Great Smoky Mountains National Park, TN (1987).

H. carolina 'Silver Splash'
A sport selected in 1992 at Tyler Arboretum, Media, PA. Leaves randomly variegated silver-white and yellow.

H. diptera Ellis
TWO WING SILVERBELL. From the southeastern U.S. Named in 1761. Uncommon in cultivation. In reference to the seed, the name *diptera* means two-winged; Greek *di*, double or two, and *pteron*, a wing or feather. Leaves to 8" × 5½" (larger on suckers). Blooms 2–3 weeks later than its relatives, very free-flowering. A small tree, usually less than 30' tall. Records: 66' × 5'6" Asheville, NC (1982); 42' × 9'6" Cincinnati, OH (1989).

H. diptera var. *magniflora* Godfrey
(*magnifica* hort.)

From W Florida. Cultivated since ≤1929. Named in 1958. Very rare but prized and becoming more available as its virtues are heralded. Flowers twice as large (¾"–1³⁄₁₆") as typical and more showy.

H. hispida—see *Pterostyrax hispida*

H. monticola—see *H. carolina* var. *monticola*

H. tetraptera—see *H. carolina*

Hamamelis persica—see *Parrotia persica*

Hemiptelea

[ULMACEÆ; Elm Family] Only the following species in the genus. From Greek *hemi*, half, and genus *Ptelea*, an ancient Greek name of the ELM, now applied to the HOPTREE—referring to the shape of the seed wing. A related genus is *Zelkova*.

H. Davidii (Hance) Planch.
= *Zelkova Davidii* (Hance) Hemsl.
= *Planera Davidii* Hance

From NE and central China, E Mongolia, Manchuria, and Korea. Named in 1868, after J.P.A. David (see genus *Davidia*, DOVE TREE). Introduced to cultivation in 1899; to North America in 1904 when the Arnold Arboretum obtained seeds from Korea. Extremely rare here. A scrubby small tree, branches usually thorny. Used for hedging in N China. Thorns to 5" long on young specimens. Leaves small, like those of SIBERIAN ELM (*Ulmus pumila*). Flowers tiny, inconspicuous. Fall color pinkish-maroon. Cold hardy, pest free, but homely. Record: 48' × 6'4" × 41' Amherst, MA (1986).

Hesperopeuce Mertensiana—see *Tsuga Mertensiana*

Hicoria spp.—see *Carya* spp.

Hippophaë

[ELÆAGNACEÆ; Eleagnus Family] 2–7 spp. of Eurasian shrubs or trees with deciduous silvery WIL-LOW-like foliage, inconspicuous spring flowers, and ornamental juicy berries. *Hippophaës* is the ancient Greek name of a spiny plant. Related to RUSSIAN OL-IVE (*Elæagnus*). Capable of fixing nitrogen symbioti-cally, so thrives on poor soils. Flower sexes borne on separate trees; inconspicuous, in April or May.

H. rhamnoides L.

SEA BUCKTHORN. SALLOW THORN. WILLOW THORN. From Eurasia. Long cultivated. Uncommon. Named from *Rhamnus* (BUCKTHORNS), and Greek *-oides*, re-semblance. Very often shrubby in the wild; in culti-vation easily trained to a 30' tree. Males grow larger; females are prettier. Leaves ¾"–3½" long, very slen-der, dark green and speckled silvery above; silvery beneath; tardily deciduous. Buds coppery. Orange berries from late July into autumn and winter (edible but perhaps slightly poisonous in quan-tity; vitamin-rich and possibly valuable as anticancer agents). Can root sucker. Very cold hardy. Record: 33' × 3'7" Wisley, Surrey, England (1983).

H. rhamnoides var. *procera* Rehd.

From W China. Named in 1915. Introduced to cultiva-tion in 1923. Extremely rare. Grows to 59' × 4'6" (Latin *procera* means tall); less hardy. Leaves hairier, also.

H. rhamnoides ssp. *salicifolia*—see *H. salicifolia*

H. rhamnoides ssp. *yunnanensis* Rousi
= *H. sinensis* (Rousi) Y.S. Lian & X.L. Chen

From SE Tibet and W China. Introduced to North America ≤1948. Extremely rare. Bark plated, shreddy. Spines ¼"–½" long. Twig hairs rust colored. Leaves dark green above with inconspicuous silver dots; silvery underneath; to 3¾" × ¾" (including the short stem). Record: 33' × 3'6" Seattle (1994; *pl.* 1948).

H. salicifolia D. Don
= *H. rhamnoides* ssp. *salicifolia* (D. Don) Servett.

From the Himalayas. Named in 1825, from Latin *Salix*, WILLOW, and *folium*, a leaf. Introduced in 1822. Very rare. Compared to *H. rhamnoides*: more tree-like, less cold hardy, less fruitful, less spiny. Leaves

more sage-green than silvery-grayish, 1½"–4" long. Fruit yellow, not very ornamental. Graceful pendu-lous branches. Deeply furrowed bark. Recorded to 50' × 5'0".

H. sinensis—see *H. rhamnoides* ssp. *yunnanensis*

Hovenia

[RHAMNACEÆ; Buckthorn Family] 1–2 (5) spp. of deciduous trees from east Asia. Named after David ten Hoven (1724–1787), senator of Amsterdam, pa-tron of botany. Related genera include *Rhamnus* and *Ziziphus*.

H. acerba—see *H. dulcis*

H. dulcis Th.
= *H. acerba* Lindl.

JAPANESE RAISIN TREE. HONEY TREE. From China, Korea, and Japan. Named in 1781 (*dulcis* means sweet in Latin). Introduced to England in 1812. In North America ≤1862. In commerce here since ≤1880. Uncommon. A shade tree bearing peculiar edible fruit. Leaves with three main veins from the base; to 8¾" × 6", stem to 3½"; pale yellow fall color. Flowers tiny, fragrant; white, yellowish-white or greenish-white, in late June to late July; much liked by bees. Fruit a 3-seeded black, shiny dry capsule, borne on a contorted fleshy peduncle which is the sweet, edible part. Color russet to ruby red, pulp yellowish-green, chewy, rasin flavored. Ripe in October. A heat-loving tree of poor performance in cool-summer regions. Records: to 115' × 13'0" in the wild; 88' × 8'10" × 52' Morris Arboretum, PA (1988; *pl.* 1880).

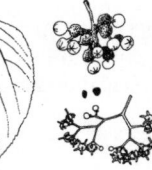

Idesia

[FLACOURTIACEÆ; Flacourtia Family] Only the following species in the genus. Named after Eberhard Ysbrant Ides (b. 1660), a Dutch statesman and traveller who visited China in the 1690s. A deciduous tree prized for its large handsome leaves and showy berries. Related genera are *Azara* and *Poliothyrsis*.

I. *polycarpa* Maxim.

= *Polycarpa Maximowiczii* Linden *ex* Carr.
= *Cathayeia polycarpa* (Maxim.) Ohwi

THE WONDER TREE. From China, Korea, Japan, the Ryukyus, and Taiwan. Discovered in 1860, and shortly thereafter introduced to Western cultivation. In North American commerce ≤1888. Rare. The name *polycarpa* is Greek for *many-fruited*, from the numerous and many-seeded berries. Flowers greenish, from April into June, not showy, yet sweetly fragrant; sexes borne on separate trees; W. Hazlewood says the top spur of the main trunk is long in the male, and short in the female. Leaves bold, heart-shaped, dark above, pale beneath, to 13" × 10" with a red stem to 8¼" long. Fall color wan yellow; not vibrant or especially lovely. Berries in 10" clusters, yellow, orange, brick red or brownish. If not taken by squirrels or birds, they can remain all winter, still firm, orange and ornamental into late March. Crushed, the seedy berries are malodorous like *Clerodendrum* leaves. Records: 65' × 3'7" Stourhead, Wiltshire, England (1987); 49'×4'11" Bute Bark, Cardiff, Wales (1990); 45' × 2'9" × 47' Vancouver, B.C. (1994); 39' × 7'6" × 50' Tauranga, New Zealand (≤1982).

Ilex

[AQUIFOLIACEÆ or ILICINEÆ; Holly Family] 400–800 spp. of evergreen (rarely deciduous) shrubs or trees. Widely distributed in both hemispheres. Several species are very familiar for thorny evergreen leaves and bright red berries, highly prized as Christmas decorations. Named *Ilex* from the resemblance of the leaves to the *Ilex* of Virgil: the HOLM OAK (*Quercus Ilex*). The English name HOLLY is from Old English *holegn*, later *holme*. In no group of trees is there less clarity between shrubbiness and treehood; the present account attempts to exclude HOLLIES that never attain treehood. The following 20 pages contain fewer than 400 entries; for rarer species and cultivars (not to mention shrubs), see publications by the Holly Society of America. All cultivars are to be considered female (berry-bearing) unless the text states "sex unknown" or "male." Some females ("self-fertile" or "bisexual") can bear fruit even without being pollinated by males. On nearly all HOLLIES the flowers are inconspicuous, greenish, yellowish or white (rarely lavender to red). The berries are inedible, where not poisonous.

I. 'Adonis'

(*I.* 'Nellie R. Stevens' × *I. latifolia*)

A 1962 cross made at the U.S. National Arboretum, Washington, D.C. Named and introduced in 1991. Leaf to 4⅝" × 2⅜", dark and glossy, edged with 9–13 bluntish spines on each side. A male; its female counterpart is *I.* 'Venus'.

I. × *altaclerensis* (hort. *ex* Loud.) Dallim.

(*altaclarensis*)
= *I. Aquifolium* var. *altaclarensis* hort. *ex* Loud.
(*I. Aquifolium* × *I. Perado*)

HIGHCLERE HOLLY. HYBRID ENGLISH HOLLY. From Europe. The name derives from Alta Clera, the medieval Latin name for Highclere, in north Hampshire, England, where this hybrid was first raised in the early 1800s. HIGHCLERE HOLLIES can be likened to robust ENGLISH HOLLIES (*I. Aquifolium*), sporting variously larger leaves and/or berries, and often growing more vigorously. Some are as cold-hardy as nearly any ENGLISH HOLLIES. They have been cultivated enough that backcrossing has occurred, so some cultivars defy our efforts to classify them as regular ENGLISH HOLLIES or hybrids. Sometimes a cultivar can look absolutely like a typical ENGLISH HOLLY except for comparatively gigantic berries. For record sizes, see the cultivars 'Camelliæfolia', 'Hendersonii', 'Hodginsii' and 'Wilsonii'.

I. × altaclerensis 'Atkinsoni'

Introduced in the early 1900s by Fisher, Son & Sibray nursery of Handsworth, Sheffield, England, and named after their managing director William Atkinson. Tree vigorous but sparse. Twigs green. Leaves broad (to 5¼" × 3½"), glossy black-green (darkest of all), corrugated, with prominent venation (looks like polished leather) and small, forward-pointing spines. Male.

I. × altaclerensis 'Atrovirens Variegata'

Origin not known. Seldom grown. Likely another clone renamed. Twigs reddish-purple. Leaves evenly spiny in one plane; margin dark green; a feathered, golden blotch mixed with pale green in the center; colors bright and effective; conspicuous. Male.

I. × altaclerensis 'Balearica'

= I. Aquifolium var. balearica hort., non (Desf.) Loes.
= I. Aquifolium 'Balearica'
= I. Aquifolium 'Balearica Platyphylla'
= I. Aquifolium 'Green Plane'
= I. Perado var. balearica hort.
= I. balearica hort.

Originated in England in the mid-1800s. Reportedly from the Balearic Islands. This clone is the female counterpart of I. × altaclerensis 'Maderensis'. Twigs green or olive-green. Leaves broad, to 5⅜" × 2¾"; thick, flat; bright green. Most leaves spineless; a few with erratically placed spines—rarely with short spines fairly well represented along the edges. Berries large. Some trees so named are really I. × altaclerensis 'Belgica'.

I. × altaclerensis 'Belgica'

= I. Perado hort., non Ait.
= I. belgica hort.
= I. Aquifolium 'Belgica'

In commerce since ≤1874 as DUTCH HOLLY. Strong growing. Twigs stout, green to yellow-green. Leaves of average I. Aquifolium size but somewhat narrow (to 4" × 1¾"), glossy; usually spineless or armed with few spines. Berries large, orange-red, profuse.

I. × altaclerensis 'Camelliæfolia'

('Camelliifolia')
= I. Aquifolium 'Camelliæfolia'
= I. Aquifolium 'Heterophylla Major'
= I. Aquifolium 'Magnifica'
= I. Aquifolium 'Laurifolium Longifolium'

Introduced ≤1865 in France. Common. The name derives from genus Camellia, and Latin folium, a leaf. Leaves a joy to behold because of their unexcelled glossiness; large, dark green, and elongated (to 5¼" × 2¼"), reddish-purple when young, mainly spineless; stems purplish. Twigs purple. Berries large, bright red. Growth vigorous. Records: 71' tall at Essex, England (≤1967); 62' × 2'9" Tacoma, WA (1992); 50' × 4'4" Seattle, WA (1990). See also I. Aquifolium 'Ciliata Major'.

I. × altaclerensis 'Colburn'

= I. laurifolia 'Colburn'

Introduced <1958 by Beadle of North Carolina. Obscure and rare. Similar to 'Camelliæfolia' but more spinose and divaricate.

I. × altaclerensis 'Donningtonensis'—see I. Aqui. 'Donningtonensis'

I. × altaclerensis 'Dr. Huckleberry'—see I. Aqui. 'Dr. Huckleberry'

I. × altaclerensis 'Eldridge'

Introduced ca. 1900 by J.M. Batchelor of Long Island, NY. Rare. Named after the Mrs. Roswell Eldridge estate of Great Neck, Long Island. Leaves large (to 5" × 2½"), flat and relatively dull like those of I. × altaclerensis 'Hendersonii' but not as dark; slightly spinier, and twigs wholly green.

I. × altaclerensis 'Fisheri'—see I. Aquifolium 'Fisheri'

I. × altaclerensis 'Foxii'—see I. Aquifolium 'Foxii'

I. × altaclerensis 'Golden King'

= I. Aquifolium 'Golden King' (in part)

A sport of I. × altaclerensis 'Hendersonii' that originated <1876 at the Bangholm nursery of the Lawson Company, Edinburgh, Scotland. Distributed in 1898. Leaves broad (to 4" × 2⅝"), boldly edged rich yellow; few spines or small, appressed teeth. Record: 30' × 4'2" Vashon, WA (1992).

I. × altaclerensis 'Hendersonii'

= I. Aquifolium 'Hendersonii'
= I. Hendersonii hort.

Raised in the early 1800s by Edward Hodgins, nurseryman of Dunganstown, Ireland. Mr. Henderson was a friend of the man [Mr. John Shepherd—curator of Liverpool botanic garden] who supplied propagating material to the Handsworth nursery of Fisher and Holmes. Vigorous. Leaves dark, comparatively dull, scarcely spiny, to 5⅜" × 2½". Twigs green with a faint purplish flush. Berries large but not very bright or abundant. A male counterpart is 'Hodginsii'. Record: 66' × 3'3" Westonbirt, Gloucestershire, England (1979).

I. × altaclerensis 'Hendersonia Aurea'—see I. × altac. 'Lawsoniana'

I. × altaclerensis 'Hodginsii'
= I. × altaclerensis 'Shepherdii' (in part)
= I. Aquifolium 'Hodginsii'
= I. Hodginsii hort.

Raised ca. 1810 by Edward Hodgins, nurseryman of Dunganstown, County Wicklow, Ireland. Vigorous. Male, and occasionally a female. Twigs purple. Leaves large, broad, glossy dark black-green; often spineless. Resembles I. × altaclerensis 'Shepherdii' but darker; very like 'Nobilis' but less spiny. Some trees sold under the name 'Hodginsii' are really the much more common I. × altaclerensis 'Hendersonii'. Record: 72' × 5'3" Ballamoor, Isle of Man (1978).

I. × altaclerensis 'J.C. van Tol'—see I. Aquifolium 'J.C. van Tol'

I. × altaclerensis 'James G. Esson'
= I. Aquifolium 'Essen' (sic)

Selected and named in 1949 when 12' tall, at the New York Botanical Garden. An I. × altaclerensis seedling named after James G. Esson, superintendent of the Mrs. Roswell Eldridge estate, Great Neck, Long Island, NY. Vigorous. Berries abundant, large (⁷⁄₁₆" long), shiny red, in clusters. Leaves smaller (to 4½" × 2"), glossier and richer green than those of I. × altaclerensis 'Eldridge' and can have 4–6 well-developed spines along each side. Twigs purplish. Record: 37' × 2'1" Seattle, WA (1994; pl. 1950).

I. × altaclerensis 'Laurifolia'—see I. Aquifolium 'Laurifolia'

I. × altaclerensis 'Lawsoniana'
= I. × altaclerensis 'Hendersonia Aurea'
= I. Aquifolium 'Lawsoniana'
= I. Lawsoniana hort.

Originated as an I. × altaclerensis 'Hendersonii' sport ca. 1850 at Hodgins' nursery of Cloughjordan, County Tipperary, Ireland. Widely distributed by Lawson nursery of Edinburgh, Scotland. Leaves splashed creamy-yellow in the center; marginal portions two shades of green. Not as fruitful or vigorous as its parent; prone to reverting to pure green growth.

I. × altaclerensis 'Maderensis'
= I. maderensis hort., non Lam.
= I. Aquifolium 'Maderensis'
= I. Perado (platyphylla) 'Maderensis'
= I. platyphylla 'Maderensis'

MADEIRA HOLLY. Cultivated since <1854. Leaf flat, regularly spined, to 4⅓" × 2¾". Twigs green. Much like I. × altaclerensis 'Balearica' but male. Ilex Perado is also called MADEIRA HOLLY.

I. × altaclerensis 'Marnockii'
= I. Aquifolium 'Marnockii'

Originated ≤1875 as a chance seedling at Fisher, Son & Sibray nursery of Handsworth, Sheffield, England. Twigs purplish above. Leaves almost as large as those of I. × altaclerensis 'Camelliæfolia' but less dense and ornamental. Leaf shape acute, with a peculiar twist about the middle. Margins usually thick, usually spineless, but can be spiny. Berries profuse but not very large.

I. × altaclerensis 'Moorei'

Introduced between 1930 and 1947 by Fisher, Son & Sibray nursery of Handsworth, Sheffield, England. Twigs green tinged purplish. Leaves broad (to 5" × 3"), polished dark green, tough, prominently veined; strongly spiny (reminiscent of those of I. × altaclerensis 'Wilsonii'). Male.

I. × altaclerensis 'Mundyi'
= I. Aquifolium 'Mundyi'
= I. Mundyi hort.

Introduced in 1898 by Fisher, Son & Sibray nursery of Handsworth, Sheffield, England. Named after Mr. Mundy of Shipley Hall, Derby. Twigs green. Leaves thick, dullish green, oval or roundish oval, regularly slender-spined; the prominently veined upper surface looks ribbed. Male.

I. × altaclerensis 'N.F. Barnes'
= I. Aquifolium 'N.F. Barnes'

Origin not known. Introduced <1958. Rare. Habit bushy. Twigs purple. Leaves gracefully long; well spined; under normal altaclerensis size (to 3⅝" long); thick, dark and shiny.

I. × *altaclerensis* 'Nigrescens'

= *I. Aquifolium* 'Nigrescens'
= *I. Balearica* 'Nigrescens'
= *I. platyphylla* 'Nigrescens'

Origin not known; introduced ca. 1845. Accounts vary as to its sex. A male and a female have gone under this name. Most sources say the twigs are purple or purplish-green; HOLLY expert S. Andrews says green. Maybe the original male has green twigs, and the female 'Nigrescens' dark twigs? Leaves very dark; not undulate; ovate to broad elliptic to 4" × 2½". Spineless or with some small spines.

I. × *altaclerensis* 'Nobilis'

= *I. Aquifolium* 'Nobilis'
= *I. nobilis* hort.

Sold in England since ≤1870s. Rare. A disputed cultivar, similar or identical to *I. × altaclerensis* 'Hodginsii'. Twigs purple. Male.

I. × *altaclerensis* 'Nobilis Picta'

= *I. Aquifolium* 'Picta' (golden blotched)

Sold in England since ≤1870s. Rare. A creamy-gold blotched male sport of *I. × altaclerensis* 'Hodginsii'. Some trees so labeled are really *I. × altaclerensis* 'Lawsoniana'.

I. × *altaclerensis* 'Post Office'—see *I. Aquifolium* 'Post Office'

I. × *altaclerensis* 'Purple Shaft'

An *I. × altaclerensis* 'Balearica' sport discovered in the early 1960s in Hillier's nursery of England. Named in 1965. Tree gaunt when young. Twigs dark purplish. Leaves not especially big (to 3½" × 2"); spineless or nearly so; berries large, abundant.

I. × *altaclerensis* 'Shepherdii'

= *I. Aquifolium* 'Shepherdii'
= *I. Shepherdii* hort.

Edward Hodgins, nurseryman of Dunganstown, Ireland, sent *I. × altaclerensis* 'Hodginsii' to John Shepherd, curator of Liverpool botanic garden, who in turn sent it to Fisher and Holmes of Handsworth nursery, Sheffield, England, and they distributed it as 'Shepherdii'. However, Knap Hill nursery sold something quite different as 'Shepherdii', similar to *I. × altaclerensis* 'Maderensis' but with longer spines. Some U.S. nurseries from the 1930s into the late '50s, listed both 'Hodginsii' and 'Shepherdii'. What then is the proper name of the non-'Hodginsii' clone sold as 'Shepherdii'? It is vigorous. Twigs green. Leaves bright glossy green, flat, mostly spined. Male.

I. × *altaclerensis* 'T.H. Everett'

Of U.S. origin. Named <1982 after the horticulturist Thomas H. Everett. A male pollinator.

I. × *altaclerensis* 'W.J. Bean'

= *I. Aquifolium* 'W.J. Bean'

Introduced in the 1920s by Fisher, Son & Sibray nursery of Handsworth, Sheffield, England. Named after horticulturist William Jackson Bean (1863–1947). Compact habit. Twigs green. Leaves dark, larger than average leaves of *I. Aquifolium*; few, very bold spines. Berries very large, bright red, long persistent.

I. × *altaclerensis* 'Whittingtonensis'—see *I. Aqui.* 'Whittingtonensis'

I. × *altaclerensis* 'Wilsonii'

= *I. Aquifolium* 'Wilsonii'
= *I. Wilsonii* hort., non Loes.

Originated in the early 1890s as a chance seedling at Fisher, Son & Sibray nursery of Handsworth, Sheffield, England. The most common *altaclerensis* clone in North America. Crown compact. Twigs green. Leaves large (to 5½" × 3½") and broad, very spiny with numerous even spines, usually in the same plane and pointing upward, deep glossy green with prominent paler venation. Berries very large. Record: 55' × 11'0" × 65' Bay of Plenty, New Zealand (1972).

I. *Aquifolium* L.

ENGLISH HOLLY. EUROPEAN HOLLY. HOLM. HULVER. From Europe, N Africa, SW Asia. *Aquifolium* is the ancient Latin name; from *acus*, a needle, and *folium*, a leaf. Leaves dark, lustrous, very spiny. Flowers appear on the second-year twigs in spring. More ornamental but less cold hardy than AMERICAN HOLLY (*I. opaca*). ENGLISH HOLLIES and their hybrids are supremely hardy, beautiful and naturalized in the maritime Pacific Northwest (where it has been grown since ≤1869). Some are grown successfully on the East Coast, but overall their role is minor there: the northeast is too cold, the southeast too hot and dry. Much more variation is known in *I. Aquifolium* than in any other HOLLY. Indeed few trees of any kind have sported such a diversity of cultivars. Many of the cultivar descriptions following are from the 1874–76 work of Thomas Moore. Alas, some cultivars with perfectly valid Old World names were renamed by Brownell nursery of Oregon; the resulting confusion is a plague. Surely some of the following 150 or so cultivars are really hybrids referrable to *I. × altaclerensis*. Records (see also *I. Aquifolium* 'Laurifolia'): 95' × 3'7" Ashburnham Park, Sussex, England

(1983); 85' × 10'5" Finlaystone, Strathclyde, Scotland (1988); 33' × 11'8" × 39' Coupeville, WA (1991); the Roman naturalist Pliny cited one trunk 35'0" around.

I. Aquifolium 'Albomarginata'—see I. Aqui. 'Argentea Marginata'

I. Aquifolium 'Albo-marginata Pendula'— see I. Aquifolium 'Argentea Marginata Pendula'

I. Aquifolium 'Alcicornis'

Cultivated since ≤1874. The name means elk-horned; from Latin *alces*, elk, and *cornis*, horned. Leaves bright green, 3½" × 1¾" with prominent stiff spines. Twigs greenish. Free-growing in form. Male.

I. Aquifolium var. altaclerensis—see I. × altaclerensis

I. Aquifolium 'Amber'

Raised ca. 1950 by Hillier nursery of England. Introduced in 1964. Twigs green. Leaves nearly spineless. Berries large, bronze-yellow.

I. Aquifolium 'Angustifolia'

= *I. Aquifolium* 'Littleleaf'
= *I. Aquifolium* 'Petit(e)'
= *I. Aquifolium* 'Serrata' (in part; cf. *I. Aquifolium* 'Crassifolia')
= *I. Aquifolium* 'Myrtifolia Stricta'
= *I. Aquifolium* 'Pernettyæfolia'

Cultivated since ≤1838. Clones of both sexes go under this name. Brownell Holly Farms of Milwaukie, OR, sold the male as **'Petit'** and the female as **'Petite'**. Growth slow and bushy yet forming a small tree. Foliage shiny blackish-green. Leaves small (1½" × ½"), very narrow (Latin *angustus*, narrow, and *folium*, a leaf), with weak, narrow, regular spines on each side, and a pronounced long apex. Berries small. Twigs purple. Similar to *I. Aquifolium* 'Myrtifolia' and 'Serratifolia'. See also 'Barnes', 'Ciliata', 'Echo', 'Lillibet', 'Lilliput', 'Lineata', and 'Microphylla'.

I. Aquifolium 'Angustifolia Albo Marginata'
= *I. Aquifolium* 'Angustifolia Variegata'

Cultivated since ≤1874. Twigs purple. Leaf mottled green; edged creamy white. Sex not known.

I. Aquifolium 'Angustifolia Aurea Maculata'

Cultivated since ≤1878. Extremely rare. Gold blotched. Male.

I. Aquifolium 'Angustifolia Variegata'—see I. Aquifolium 'Angustifolia Albo Marginata'

I. Aquifolium 'Angustimarginata Aurea'

Cultivated since ≤1874. Very rare. Twigs dark purple. Leaves 2" long, narrow, strongly spiny, dark mottled green with a narrow deep yellow margin. Male.

I. Aquifolium 'Apricot Glow'

Introduced ≤1965 by John Wieman holly nursery of Portland, OR. A seedling from *I. Aquifolium* 'Yellow Beam'. Named for its berry color. Leaves big, spiny. Berries to ⅝" wide.

I. Aquifolium 'Argentea Elegantissima'—see I. Aquifolium 'Argentea Marginata Elegantissima'

I. Aquifolium 'Argentea Handsworthensis'— see I. Aquifolium 'Handsworth New Silver'

I. Aquifolium 'Argentea Latifolia'—see I. Aquifolium 'Silver Queen'

I. Aquifolium 'Argentea Marginata'
= *I. Aquifolium* 'Silvary'
= *I. Aquifolium* 'Albomarginata'
= *I. Aquifolium* 'Argenteovariegata'
= *I. Aquifolium* 'Silver Beauty'
= *I. Aquifolium* 'Silver Edge'
= *I. Aquifolium* 'Silver Broadleaf'
= *I. Aquifolium* 'Silver Leaf'
= *I. Aquifolium* 'Silver Princess'
= *I. Aquifolium* 'Silver Variegated'
= *I. Aquifolium* 'Teufel's Silver Variegated'
= *I. Aquifolium* 'Latifolia Argenteo Marginata'

BROAD LEAVED SILVER HOLLY. Commonly cultivated as "Striped Holly" by 1691. The most commonly grown variegated HOLLY. Young growth pink. Twigs green. Leaves dark green, edged creamy white. Brownell Holly Farms of Milwaukie, OR, coined the 'Silvary' name in 1935: i.e. *silver* varie*gated*. More than one subtly different clone exists, but HOLLY documentation is presently insufficient for distinguishing them. Records: 56' × 6'1" Tayside, Scotland (1986); 55' × 6'10" Tillamook, OR (1994); 39' × 4'4" Everett, WA(1993).

I. *Aquifolium* 'Argentea Marginata Elegantissima'

= I. *Aquifolium* 'Argentea Elegantissima'
= I. *Aquifolium* 'Elegantissima'

Cultivated since <1863. Twigs green. Leaves 2"–2½" long, dark green mottled gray, broadly edged creamy-white. Spines bold, regularly developed, divaricate because of the wavy surface of the leaf. Male.

I. *Aquifolium* 'Argentea Marginata Erecta'

= I. *Aquifolium* 'Silver Charm'
= I. *Aquifolium* 'Upright Silver-Striped'

Introduced in the 1800s to Knap Hill nursery of Surrey, England by Mr. R. Godfrey. Leaves flat, 2" long, with a very regular marginal series of strongly developed spines. Center mottled green; broad creamy white margin. The name 'Silver Charm' was used ≤1964 by Brownell Holly Farms of Milwaukie, OR.

I. *Aquifolium* 'Argentea Marginata Pendula'

= I. *Aquifolium* 'Albo-marginata Pendula'
= I. *Aquifolium* 'Pendula Argenteomarginata'
= I. *Aquifolium* 'Argentea Pendula'
= I. *Aquifolium* 'Pendula Argentea'
= I. *Aquifolium* 'Pendula Variegata'
= I. *Aquifolium* 'Argentea-marginata Pendula'
= I. *Aquifolium* 'Silver Weeping'
= I. *Aquifolium* 'Perry's Weeping'

PERRY'S SILVER WEEPING HOLLY. Originated ≤1858 by Perry's nursery of England. Compact mushroom or mound-shaped, strongly weeping. Twigs purple. Leaves white-edged. Not free-fruiting. Record: 13' × 2'11" × 18' Vashon, WA (1992).

I. *Aquifolium* 'Argentea Medio-picta'

= I. *Aquifolium* 'Silver Milkboy'
= I. *Aquifolium* 'Silver Milkmaid'
= I. *Aquifolium* 'Silver Star'
= I. *Aquifolium* 'Argentea Variegata' (in part)
= I. *Aquifolium* 'Medio Picta' (Milkmaid)
= I. *maderensis* 'Medio Picta' (Milkmaid)

Cultivated since ≤1820. Twigs green. Leaves spiny, variegated green and silvery. Both sexes available: 'Silver Milkmaid' & 'Silver Milkboy'. Brownell Holly Farms of Milwaukie, OR, coined the **'Silver Star'** name <1964 for "a female bud-sport, leaf bold and very well armored." Maurice Young's nursery of Surrey, England, in 1874 listed a **'Weeping Milkmaid'** as "a new and distinct variety; good weeping habit, having a creamy-colored blotch in the center of the leaf."

I. *Aqui.* 'Argentea Pendula'—see I. *Aqui.* 'Argentea Marginata Pendula'

I. *Aquifolium* 'Argentea Regina'—see I. *Aquifolium* 'Silver Queen'

I. *Aqui.* 'Argentea Variegata'—see I. *Aqui.* 'Argentea Medio-picta'

I. *Aqui.* 'Argenteovariegata'—see I. *Aqui.* 'Argentea Marginata'

I. *Aquifolium* 'Aurantiaca'

= I. *Aquifolium* 'Moonlight' (cf. I. *Aquifolium* 'Flavescens')

Grown since ≤1874. Leaves typical but flushed golden bronze. In Latin, *aurantiacus* means orange colored. Similar to or identical to 'Flavescens' the MOONLIGHT HOLLY.

I. *Aquifolium* 'Aurea Marginata'

('Aureo-marginata')

Cultivated since ≤1750. A group name. Twigs usually green. Leaves dark green, edged yellow or gold. Similar but less spiny clones have been called **'Heterophylla Aurea Marginata'**. Record: 26' × 4'10" Ferndale, WA (1991).

I. *Aqui.* 'Aurea Marginata Latifolia'—see I. *Aqui.* 'Golden Queen'

I. *Aquifolium* 'Aurea Marginata Ovata'—see I. *Aqui.* 'Ovata Aurea'

I. *Aqui.* 'Aurea Marginata Rotundifolia'—see I. *Aqui.* 'Rubricaulis Aurea'

I. *Aquifolium* 'Aurea Medio Picta'

This is a group name that includes cultivars with gold-blotched leaves: I. *Aquifolium* 'Golden Butterfly', 'Golden Milkboy', 'Golden Milkmaid', 'Harlequin', 'Painted Lady', etc.

I. *Aquifolium* 'Aurea Picta Latifolia'—see I. *Aqui.* 'Golden Milkboy'

I. *Aquifolium* 'Aurea Regina'—see I. *Aquifolium* 'Golden Queen'

I. *Aqui.* 'Aureo Marginata Angustifolia'—see I. *Aqui.* 'Aurifodina'

I. *Aquifolium* 'Aurifodina'

= I. *Aquifolium* 'Muricata'
= I. *Aquifolium* 'Bicolor'
= I. *Aquifolium* 'Goldmine'
= I. *Aquifolium* 'Marginata Bicolor'
= I. *Aquifolium* 'Aureo Marginata Angustifolia'

SMUDGE HOLLY. Upright or pyramidal habit, dense. Twigs usually green and purple. Leaves slender, usually 1¾" (to 3½") long; dark green, flushed or marbled dull yellow-green, the edge unevenly marked tawny orange-yellow, sometimes extending over half the leaf. Spines few, scattered. The variegation assumes a distinctive tawny hue in winter. Very fruitful. A male counterpart is 'Laurifolia Aurea'.

I. Aquifolium f. bacciflava (West.) Rehd.
= I. Aquifolium 'Xanthocarpa'
= I. Aquifolium 'Fructu Luteo'
= I. Aquifolium 'Chrysocarpa'
= I. Aquifolium 'Yellow Berried'
= I. Aquifolium 'Flava'
= I. Aquifolium 'Yellow Beam'
= I. Aquifolium 'Yellow Fruit'
= I. Aquifolium 'Berigold'

YELLOWBERRY ENGLISH HOLLY. Cultivated since ≤1657. As employed here the name is used in a group rather than a clonal sense. Latin *bacca*, berry, and *flavus*, yellow. Some of the names listed above are synonymous, others represent distinct cultivars; but without special study they are impossible to sort. Record: 38' × 3'8" Tacoma, WA (1990).

I. Aquifolium baccis flavis—see I. opaca f. xanthocarpa

I. Aquifolium 'Bailey's Pride'
Introduced in 1965 by Monrovia nursery of California. Tall. Leaves attractively glossy, dark and spiny. Berries rich red, abundant.

I. Aquifolium 'Balearica'—see I. × altaclerensis 'Balearica'

I. Aquifolium 'Balearica Platyphylla'—see I. × altac. 'Balearica'

I. Aquifolium 'Balkans'
('Balkan')

A clone grown at the Missouri Botanic Garden from Yugoslavian seeds collected in 1934. In commerce since ≤1964. Prized for cold hardiness. Leaves smooth, glossy and dark. Berries abundant.

I. Aquifolium 'Balkans Male'
= I. Aquifolium 'Marshall Tito'
As 'Balkans' but male.

I. Aquifolium 'Barnes'
Introduced <1958. Very rare. A globular male sport of I. Aquifolium 'Angustifolia', serving as an excellent pollinator. Leaves small, quadrangular, with 5–7 sharp, divaricate spines.

I. Aquifolium 'Beacon'
Selected in a "French-English" HOLLY orchard; sold since ≤1945 by John Wieman holly nursery of Portland, OR. Twigs green. A heavy, consistent bearer of extra-large, distinctly bright orange-red berries in large quantities.

I. Aquifolium 'Beadle's Spiny Leaf'
Sold since ≤1956 by Ten Oaks nursery of Clarksville, MD. Leaves deep green, very spiny. Berries bright red.

I. Aquifolium 'Beautyspra'
Selected as an Oregon seedling ca. 1930 by John Wieman holly nursery of Portland, OR. A hardy seedling, with cherry-red berries and pronounced spiny, crinkled leaves, somewhat smaller than average. Early-bearing, early-ripening. Recommended for landscaping and orcharding.

I. Aquifolium 'Belgica'—see I. × altaclerensis 'Belgica'

I. Aquifolium 'Berigold'—see I. Aquifolium f. bacciflava

I. Aquifolium 'Bicolor'—see I. Aquifolium 'Aurifodina'

I. Aquifolium 'Big Bull'
Selected in 1935 by Teufel nursery of Portland, OR. Male; selected because it is an excellent pollinator. Twigs green. Leaves scarcely spiny, very shiny. Very hardy and vigorous.

I. Aquifolium "Bisex"
This designation, used by several HOLLY nurseries in the 1950s, refers apparently to hermaphrodite selections, or at any rate to cultivars that set berries without needing to be pollinated.

I. Aquifolium 'Blue Stem'
Sold since ≤1959–60 by Monrovia nursery of California. Especially neat with compact foliage and abundant berries.

I. Aquifolium 'Bonanza'
Introduced ≤1964 by Brownell Holly Farms of Milwaukie, OR. Leaves closely grouped, rich green,

well-spined and wavy; deeply channeled along the midrib; triangular in shape. Abundant fruit borne in clusters.

I. Aquifolium 'Boulder Creek'

Introduced ≤1957 by Leonard Coates nursery of San José, CA. Marketed by Monrovia nursery of California since ≤1965–66. Heavy-stemmed, upright. Leaves bold and large, glossy black-green. Berries abundant, brilliant red.

I. Aquifolium 'Bronze and Clouded Gold'

Imported from overseas and named ≤1964 by Brownell Holly Farms of Milwaukie, OR. Nearly identical to I. Aquifolium 'Flavescens'. Leaf perhaps narrower and more spiny.

I. Aquifolium 'Brownell Special'—see I. Aquifolium 'Special'

I. Aquifolium 'Butler'

Sold since ≤1956 by Ten Oaks nursery of Clarksville, MD. Very hardy. Leaves dark. Berries bright red.

I. Aquifolium 'Calamistrata'—see I. Aquifolium 'Crispa'

I. Aquifolium 'Camelliæfolia'—see I. × altaclerensis 'Camelliæfolia'

I. Aquifolium 'Canary Island'—see I. Perado ssp. platyphylla

I. Aquifolium 'Captain Bonneville'

Introduced ≤1964 by Brownell Holly Farms of Milwaukie, OR. Found near Bonneville Dam of Washington. Broad leaves. Male.

I. Aquifolium 'Captain Royal'—see I. Aquifolium "Dutch type"

I. Aquifolium var. centrochinensis—see I. ciliospinosa

I. Aquifolium 'Chambers'

Introduced ≤1948 by W.B. Clarke nursery of San José, CA. Symmetrical and compact. Twigs purplish. Leaf of average size, prickly, somewhat thick and rubbery. Berries profuse, well-placed.

I. Aquifolium 'Chief'

Sold since ≤1966 by John Wieman holly nursery of Portland, OR. Hardy. Abundant flowers. Male.

I. Aquifolium var. chinensis—see I. corallina

I. Aquifolium 'Chrysocarpa'—see I. Aquifolium f. bacciflava

I. Aquifolium 'Ciliata'

('Ciliatum')
= I. Aquifolium 'Ciliatum Minus'

Introduced <1826. In the group of small-leaved cultivars typified by 'Angustifolia'. Both male and female clones have gone under this name. Small; of neat narrow pyramidal habit. Twigs purple. Leaves ovate or lanceolate, shining, 1½"–2" × ½"–¾"; margined with weak, long, regularly placed spines, forming a kind of fringe to the edge.

I. Aquifolium 'Ciliata Major'

Introduced <1852. Common. Vigorous. Twigs purplish. Leaves dark glossy, purplish when unfolding in spring, becoming bronzy-green by winter; ovate or ovate-oblong, flat, ciliate-margined with crowded, long, broad-based, curved spines held in plane; basal leaf portion usually entire; apex more or less prolonged. Many bright red berries. I. × altaclerensis 'Camelliæfolia' may be the same genetically but not visually, being propagated from less spiny growth higher on the tree, while 'Ciliata Major' is propagated from the spiny apron or skirt near the tree base. If this is true, the status of the two as separate cultivars is still valid, since they are readily distinguished, but 'Ciliata Major' must be reclassified as an altaclerensis.

I. Aquifolium 'Ciliatum Minus'—see I. Aquifolium 'Ciliata'

I. Aquifolium 'Coleman'

Selected for cold hardiness after it was unhurt after a severe 1955 freeze in Washington State. Berries also ripen early: by October 17.

I. Aquifolium 'Contorta'—see I. Aquifolium 'Crispa'

I. Aqui. 'Contorta Aureopicta'—see I. Aqui. 'Crispa Aurea Picta'

I. Aquifolium 'Coronation'

Grown <1970 for the commercial HOLLY bough trade in Oregon. Berries ripe by October 17 at Corvallis, OR.

I. Aquifolium 'Covergirl'

Originated in Portland, OR. Sold since ≤1964 by John Wieman holly nursery of Portland. Very compact: dense, broad, mound-shaped and dwarf. Leaves unusually small, 1½" × ¾".

I. Aquifolium 'Crassifolia'

= I. Aquifolium 'Serrata' (in part; cf. I. Aquifolium 'Angustifolia')

LEATHERLEAF HOLLY. SAW LEAVED HOLLY. Grown since the mid-1700s. Rare. Twigs purplish-green. Leaves viciously spiny, thick, narrow and often curved, 1½" × ¾". Shrubby. Male.

I. Aquifolium 'Crinkle Green'

Sold by John Wieman holly nursery of Portland, OR. Low and globular growth, for easy harvest in HOLLY orchards.

I. Aquifolium 'Crinkle Variegated'

Selected ≤1945 as an I. Aquifolium 'Argenteo Mediopicta' sport by John Wieman holly nursery of Portland, OR. Low and globular growth, for easy harvest in HOLLY orchards. Leaf silver variegated.

I. Aquifolium 'Crispa'

= I. Aquifolium 'Calamistrata'
= I. Aquifolium 'Contorta'
= I. Aquifolium 'Screwleaf'
= I. Aquifolium 'Marginata' (in part)
= I. Aquifolium 'Tortuosa' (in part; cf. 'Recurva')

SCREWLEAF HOLLY. CALAMITY HOLLY. Cultivated since <1838; said to be a sport of I. Aquifolium 'Ferox'. Sometimes confused with I. Aquifolium 'Recurva'. A freak. Twigs purple. Leaves thick, often blunt-ended, twisted spirally and rolled under, rugose, spineless or with 1–3 spines; more variable than other cultivars. A sterile male. Growth slow and shrubby, but can become eventually a 46' tall tree. Record: 30' × 2'4" Ladner, B.C. (1994).

I. Aquifolium 'Crispa Aurea'—see I. Aquifolium 'Crispa Aurea Picta'

I. Aqui. 'Crispa Aurea Maculata'—see I. Aqui. 'Crispa Aurea Picta'

I. Aquifolium 'Crispa Aurea Picta'

= I. Aquifolium 'Contorta Aureopicta'
= I. Aquifolium 'Marginata Aureopicta'
= I. Aquifolium 'Crispa Aurea Maculata'
= I. Aquifolium 'Tortuosa Aurea Picta'
= I. Aquifolium 'Crispa Aureo-picta'
= I. Aquifolium 'Crispa Aurea'
= I. Aquifolium 'Crispa Variegata'
= I. Aquifolium 'Crispa Picta'
= I. Aquifolium 'Variegated Screwleaf'

GOLD-BLOTCHED SCREW HOLLY. Originated <1854 as a sport of 'Ferox Aurea'. Twigs purple. Leaves twisted, leathery, with a thick margin; glossy, puckered on the surface, almost shapeless from the twisting and irregular development of the spines, when present. Deep green and pale green, blotched gold and creamy. Male.

I. Aquifolium 'Crispa Aureo-picta'—see I. Aqui. 'Crispa Aurea Picta'

I. Aquifolium 'Crispa Picta'—see I. Aquifolium 'Crispa Aurea Picta'

I. Aquifolium 'Crispa Variegata'—see I. Aqui. 'Crispa Aurea Picta'

I. Aquifolium 'Deluxe'

= I. Aquifolium 'Teufel's Deluxe'

Selected ca. 1935 by Teufel nursery of Portland, OR. Commonly sold since ≤1958. Rank, hardy. Twigs green. Leaves exceptionally large (to 4⅝" × 2½") and dark. Early-ripening large berries. Excellent for orchards and landscaping. May be an I. × altaclerensis cultivar.

I. Aquifolium 'Donningtonensis'

= I. × altaclerensis 'Donningtonensis'

Cultivated in England since ≤1874. Free, pyramidal growth. Twigs very dark purple. Leaves variable in size (often 2" × ¾") and form, stout textured, purplish green (contrasting with bright green cultivars), with a purple streak along the midrib beneath. Generally lanceolate, often turned curved sickle-like; frequently with a small lateral and often falcate lobe at the base. Spineless or with several strong, quite divaricate spines. Male. See also I. Aquifolium 'Smithiana'.

I. Aquifolium 'Dr. Huckleberry'

= I. × altaclerensis 'Dr. Huckleberry'

Selected in 1946 at Brighton, OR. Rapid growing, early cropping. Well balanced. Twigs purplish. Leaves medium to large, wavy, scarcely spiny, and hold their color well under adversity. Berries exceptionally bright red, oval, ripening very early: by October 5th.

I. Aquifolium 'Dude'

A gold-edged sport discovered ca. 1935 in Gresham, OR. Introduced by John Wieman holly nursery of Portland, OR. A male, normally producing much pollen.

I. Aquifolium "Dutch type"
= I. Aquifolium 'Hollandica'

A group name applied since ≤1930s in California and the Pacific Northwest to ENGLISH and HIGHCLERE HOLLIES differing from the cultivars commonly grown for the Christmas trade. Leaves flat, glossy, dark, usually spineless. Berries usually larger, more uniformly round, abundant, early to ripen, firm to handle. Cultivars so called include: I. × altaclerensis 'Belgica' and 'Camelliæfolia', I. Aquifolium 'Post Office' and 'Pyramidalis'. Brownell Holly Farms of Milwaukie, OR, selected some DUTCH cultivars ≤1964, and named the best three: 'Captain Royal' (male), 'Firelight' and 'Royal Red'.

I. Aquifolium 'Early Cluster'

Selected in 1932 by John Wieman nursery of Portland, OR. Cold-hardy. Berry clusters extremely heavy, borne even on young trees.

I. Aquifolium 'Early Commercial'

Introduced in 1965–66 by Monrovia nursery of California. Berries abundant even at an early age.

I. Aquifolium 'Earlygold'

Originated ca. 1944 by Teufel nursery of Portland, OR. A golden-variegated sport of I. Aquifolium 'Zero'. Leaves similar in color to those of I. Aquifolium 'Lilygold', but retained 3 years. Berries early-ripening, firm, bright scarlet.

I. Aquifolium Ebony Magic™—see I. Ebony Magic™

I. Aquifolium 'Echinata'—see I. Aquifolium 'Ferox'

I. Aqui. 'Echinata Argentea Marginata'—see I. Aqui. 'Ferox Argentea'

I. Aquifolium 'Echinata Aurea'—see I. Aquifolium 'Ferox Aurea'

I. Aquifolium 'Echo'

Introduced ≤1963 by Brownell Holly Farms of Milwaukie, OR. Small, wavy-leaved fruiting mutation of I. Aquifolium 'Angustifolia'.

I. Aqui. 'Elegans Aurea Marginata'—see I. Aqui. 'Golden Queen'

I. Aquifolium 'Elegantissima'—see I. Aquifolium 'Argentea Marginata Elegantissima'

I. Aquifolium 'Escort'

Introduced ≤1935 by Brownell Holly Farms of Milwaukie, OR. A dependable pollinator for commercial plantations.

I. Aquifolium 'Essen'—see I. × altaclerensis 'James G. Esson'

I. Aquifolium 'Evangeline'—see I. Aquifolium 'Hazel'

I. Aquifolium 'Father Charles'

Introduced ≤1958 by Holly Hedge nursery of Centreville, MD. It may be a spiny version of I. Aquifolium 'Laurifolia', or a synonym of I. × altaclerensis 'Camelliæfolia'.

I. Aquifolium 'Favorite'

Sold since ≤1966 by John Wieman holly nursery of Portland, OR. Leaves medium spiny, flat, with slight crinkles. Berries medium to large, bright red, borne early, ripening early. Produces sprays of unusual quality, excellent for arrangements.

I. Aquifolium "Femina"

All this name indicates is female, or berrybearing. "Mascula" is the male equivalent.

I. Aquifolium 'Ferox'
= I. Aquifolium 'Echinata'
= I. Aquifolium 'Hedgehog'

HEDGEHOG HOLLY. GREEN PORCUPINE HOLLY. Known since ≤1635. Allied to 'Crispa'. Leaves convex and ferociously bristling with numerous short spines. Ferox in Latin means defiant or fierce. Twigs purple. A sterile male. Less common than its variegated version 'Ferox Argentea'. Record: 27' × 2'10" Longview, WA (1993).

I. Aquifolium 'Ferox Argentea'
= I. Aquifolium 'Ferox Variegata'
= I. Aquifolium 'Ferox Argentea Marginata'
= I. Aquifolium 'Echinata Argentea Marginata'

SILVER HEDGEHOG HOLLY. SILVER-STRIPED HEDGEHOG HOLLY. SILVER-VARIEGATED HEDGEHOG HOLLY. VARIEGATED PORCUPINE HOLLY. SILVER STRIPED PORCUPINE HOLLY. Known in England by 1662. Compared to 'Ferox': slower growing; leaves edged creamy white. Also a sterile male. Records: 34' × 3'10" Walcot Park, Shropshire, England (1975); 26' × 3'0" Mount Vernon, WA (1995).

I. Aqui. 'Ferox Argentea Marginata'—see *I. Aqui.* 'Ferox Argentea'

I. Aquifolium 'Ferox Aurea'
= *I. Aquifolium* 'Echinata Aurea'
= *I. Aquifolium* 'Golden Porcupine'

GOLD HEDGEHOG HOLLY. GOLD-BLOTCHED HEDGEHOG HOLLY. Cultivated since ≤1760. Leaves with a central blotch of deep gold or yellow-green. Sterile male. Rare compared to 'Ferox Argentea'.

I. Aquifolium 'Ferox Variegata'—see *I. Aquifolium* 'Ferox Argentea'

I. Aquifolium 'Fertilis'
Introduced <1958 by Monrovia nursery of California. Grows well in southern California in cool, moist sites. Leaves vivid bright green. Sets a light crop of seedless berries even without pollination. Probably other nurseries have used the name 'Fertilis'.

I. Aquifolium 'Firecracker'
Introduced ≤1935 by Brownell Holly Farms of Milwaukie, OR. Said to be low and bushy; but specimens seen by the present writer are like typical *I. Aquifolium* in habit, albeit slow like *I. Aquifolium* 'Pyramidalis'. Twigs purplish flushed. Leaves spiny. An early and abundant producer of crimson berries in clusters.

I. Aquifolium 'Firelight'—see *I. Aquifolium* "Dutch type"

I. Aquifolium 'Fisheri'
= *I. × altaclerensis* 'Fisheri'

Raised by Fisher, Son & Sibray nursery of Handsworth, Sheffield, England. Bold, free-growing, handsome. Twigs usually green, sometimes purple. Leaves variable, very dark; thick; margin thick, somewhat spiny with strong, very divaricated spines. Male.

I. Aquifolium 'Flava'—see *I. Aquifolium* f. *bacciflava*

I. Aquifolium 'Flavescens'
= *I. Aquifolium* 'Lutescens'
= *I. Aquifolium* 'Moonlight' (cf. *I. Aquifolium* 'Aurantiaca')

MOONLIGHT HOLLY. Cultivated since ≤1854. Growth slow and compact, rarely more than 15' tall. Young leaves pure yellow, remaining yellowish-flushed in age, the yellow variable in extent and position. Leaves otherwise thick, strongly waved, armed with prominent spines. Berries few to many—likely because more than one clone is called 'Flavescens'. 'Aurantiaca' is very similar but flushed golden bronze. Brownell Holly Farms of Milwaukie, OR, sold a male MOONLIGHT HOLLY as 'Phantom Gold', and a female variant ('Aurantiaca' renamed?) as 'Bronze and Clouded Gold'.

I. Aquifolium 'Foxii'
= *I. × altaclerensis* 'Foxii'

Introduced <1863. Twigs purple. Leaves small (≤2½" long), very glossy, dark, spiny. Male; an excellent pollinator. Brownell Holly Farms of Milwaukie, OR, sold a female under the name 'Foxii'.

I. Aquifolium "French-English group"
Originally selected and propagated by P.H. Peyran of Hollycroft Gardens, Gig Harbor, WA, from French stock. Twigs dark blue or purplish. Leaves durable, thick, leathery. Rapid growers but late in bearing, and late ripening: October 30.

I. Aquifolium 'Fructu Aurantiaca'
('Fructu Aurantiaco')
= *I. Aquifolium* 'Orange Gem'

ORANGEBERRY HOLLY. Introduced <1863 in England. Berries deep orange, sometimes flushed scarlet. The name 'Orange Gem' was coined by Brownell Holly Farms of Milwaukie, OR.

I. Aquifolium 'Fructu Luteo'—see *I. Aquifolium* f. *bacciflava*

I. Aquifolium 'Globe'
= *I. Aquifolium* 'Wieman's Globe'

Selected ca. 1930 as an Oregon seedling by John Wieman holly nursery of Portland, OR. A compact globe-shaped tree. Berries carmine. Winter hardy in the East.

I. Aquifolium Gold Coast™ PP 5143 (1983)
= *I. Aquifolium* 'Monvila'

Introduced in 1984 by Monrovia nursery of California. Small, many branched evergreen shrub to 8' tall. Leaves small, dark green, edged bright golden-yellow. Male.

I. Aquifolium 'Golden Beau'
Introduced ≤1963 by Teufel nursery of Portland, OR. Bright golden variegated. Male.

I. Aquifolium 'Golden Beauty'
Originated <1935 by W.B. Clarke nursery of San José, CA. Variegated with very pronounced bright gold. Unusually vigorous growth.

I. *Aquifolium* 'Golden Butterfly'

Named and introduced <1964 by Brownell Holly Farms of Milwaukie, OR. Like 'Golden Milkmaid' but smaller: "little pixie with slender pointed leaves gaily splashed with gold; fruits freely."

I. *Aquifolium* 'Golden Gate'

Sold ≤1963 by Brownell Holly Farms of Milwaukie, OR. Like *I. Aquifolium* 'Ovata Aurea' except female.

I. *Aquifolium* 'Golden King'—see *I.* × *altaclerensis* 'Golden King' and *I. Aquifolium* 'Golden Queen'

I. *Aquifolium* 'Golden Milkboy'

= *I. Aquifolium* 'Aurea Picta Latifolia'

Similar to 'Golden Milkmaid' but with larger leaves, and male.

I. *Aquifolium* 'Golden Milkmaid'

Cultivated since ≤1750. Leaves flat, spiny with a large splash of gold in the center. Some similar gold-blotched cultivars are: 'Golden Butterfly' and 'Harlequin' (both female), and 'Golden Milkboy' (male). The name *I. Aquifolium* 'Aurea Medio Picta' can be used in a group sense to include any and all such cultivars.

I. *Aquifolium* 'Golden Porcupine'—see *I. Aquifolium* 'Ferox Aurea'

I. *Aquifolium* 'Golden Queen'

= *I. Aquifolium* 'Golden King' (in part)
= *I. Aquifolium* 'Regina Aurea'
= *I. Aquifolium* 'Aurea Regina'
= *I. Aquifolium* 'Elegans Aurea Marginata'
= *I. Aquifolium* 'Aurea Marginata Latifolia'

QUEEN HOLLY. Cultivated since <1867. Common. Twigs green. Leaves broad, spiny, mottled dark and pale green with gray shading and a broad yellow-gold edge. Male. As befits its sex, often called 'Golden King' in U.S. commerce. On the other hand, the *I.* × *altaclerensis* 'Golden King' is female. And 'Silver Queen' is male. Logic yields to custom in these matters, and the result sends rational beings screaming.

I. *Aquifolium* 'Goldmine'—see *I. Aquifolium* 'Aurifodina'

I. *Aquifolium* 'Grandis Argentea Marginata'— see *I. Aquifolium* 'Handsworth New Silver'

I. *Aquifolium* 'Green Knight'

Named and introduced <1950 by Brownell Holly Farms of Milwaukie, OR. "Dark ornamental stately male." Leaves broad, not especially spiny. Young twigs partly purple. May be an *Ilex* × *altaclerensis*.

I. *Aquifolium* 'Green Maid'

Named and introduced <1940 by Brownell Holly Farms of Milwaukie, OR. Hardy, vigorous, graceful, dense. Twigs green. Leaves large. Berries well dispersed, large, early-ripening.

I. *Aquifolium* 'Green Pillar'

Named and introduced in 1971 by Hillier nursery of England. Splendidly narrow and attractive.

I. *Aquifolium* 'Green Plane'—see *I.* × *altaclerensis* 'Balearica'

I. *Aquifolium* 'Green Shadow'

Named and introduced <1964 by Brownell Holly Farms of Milwaukie, OR. Leaf normal but centered light green, enclosed by a strong dark green band. The opposite of *I. Aquifolium* 'Misty Green'.

I. *Aquifolium* 'Handsworthensis'
('Handsworth')

Introduced <1863 by Fisher, Son & Sibray nursery of Handsworth, Sheffield, England. Twigs green or brownish. Leaves ovate, small (ca. 1¾" × ¾") with regular forward-pointing spines, margins slightly undulate. Growth compact, symmetric and conical. Male.

I. *Aquifolium* 'Handsworth New Silver'

= *I. Aquifolium* 'Argentea Handsworthensis'
= *I. Aquifolium* 'Grandis Argentea Marginata'
= *I. Aquifolium* 'Silver Plane'
= *I. Aquifolium* 'Handsworth Silver'

Introduced <1850 by Fisher, Son & Sibray nursery of Handsworth, Sheffield, England. Stout, vigorous growth. Twigs purple. Leaves very dark, mottled with green and grayish green, broadly edged clear white; well armed with large spines mostly in the plane. Free fruiting. An otherwise similar male cultivar called 'Silverboy' was sold by Brownell Holly Farms of Milwaukie, OR.

I. *Aqui.* 'Handsworth Silver'—see *I. Aqui.* 'Handsworth New Silver'

I. *Aquifolium* 'Harlequin'

Named and introduced <1958 by Brownell Holly Farms of Milwaukie, OR. Similar to *I. Aquifolium*

'Golden Milkmaid' but not as tall and graceful. Twigs purple. Habit dense. Leaves waved and spiny, edged dark green, the center pale green and bright gold.

I. *Aquifolium* 'Hastata'
= *I. Aquifolium* 'Latispina Minor'

Introduced <1863 by Fisher, Son & Sibray nursery of Handsworth, Sheffield, England. A dwarf; at best a slow-growing little tree 8'–10' tall. Twigs purple. Leaves small (ca. 1¼" × ½"), narrow (shaped like those of sheep sorrel, *Rumex Acetosella*), stiff, the basal part disproportionately spiny. Male.

I. *Aquifolium* 'Hazel'
= *I. Aquifolium* 'Evangeline'

Originated on the Whitney estate of Woods Hole, MA. Named <1970 by J. K. Lilly, III, of Massachusetts. Compact, conical habit. Leaves dense and spiny. Berries abundant, red. Cold hardy.

I. *Aquifolium* 'Hedgehog'—see *I. Aquifolium* 'Ferox'

I. *Aquifolium* 'Hendersonii'—see *I. × altaclerensis* 'Hendersonii'

I. *Aquifolium* f. *heterophylla* (Ait.) Loes.

Described officially in 1789. A group name including variants (seedlings or cultivars) with both spineless and spiny leaves, but predominately sparsely spiny or spineless. The two clones most commonly provided under this name by nurseries include 'Laurifolia' (vigorous large male) and 'Pyramidalis' (fruitful small female).

I. *Aquifolium* 'Heterophylla Aurea Marginata'—see *I. Aquifolium* 'Aurea Marginata'

I. *Aquifolium* 'Heterophylla Major'—see *I. × altac.* 'Camelliæfolia'

I. *Aquifolium* 'Hodginsii'—see *I. × altaclerensis* 'Hodginsii'

I. *Aquifolium* 'Hollandica'—see *I. Aquifolium* "Dutch type"

I. *Aquifolium* 'Ingramii'
= *I. Aquifolium* 'Polka Dot'

Introduced <1875 by Fisher, Son & Sibray nursery of Handsworth, Sheffield, England. Twigs purple. Leaves small (1¼" × ½"), pink or white when unfolding, the middle becoming dark olive-green; somewhat mottled and rugose; margins remain freckled grayish-white; evenly edged with plane spines. Male.

I. *Aquifolium* 'Integrifolia'
?= *I. Aquifolium* 'Integrifolium Latifolium' (in part)
= *I. Aquifolium* 'Rotundifolium' (in part)

Origin not known, likely from England ≤1874. Twigs purple. Leaves spineless, thick, dark, to 2" × 1"; with a slight twist. Like *I. Aquifolium* 'Scotica' but leaf not so rounded or twisted. Some nurseries have sold *I. Aquifolium* 'Pyramidalis' (or similar clones) as 'Integrifolia'.

I. *Aquifolium* 'Integrifolium Latifolium'—see *I. Aqui.* 'Integrifolia'

I. *Aquifolium* 'Ivory'

Sold ≤1966 by John Wieman holly nursery of Portland, OR. Leaf soft green, with wide and varying margin of pale ivory. Berries red.

I. *Aquifolium* 'J.C. van Tol'
('Jan C. van Tol')
= *I. × altaclerensis* 'J.C. van Tol'
= *I. Aquifolium* 'Van Tol'
= *I. Aquifolium* 'Lævigata Polycarpa'
= *I. Aquifolium* 'Polycarpa'

Originated in Holland ca. 1895–1900; introduced in 1904. Common. Leaves dark, high-gloss, sparsely toothed, slightly bullate. Berries large, bright glossy red, abundant. Self fertile. Possibly a hybrid with *Ilex cornuta* (CHINESE HOLLY).

I. *Aquifolium* 'Lævigata Polycarpa'—see *I. Aquifolium* 'J.C. van Tol'

I. *Aquifolium* 'Latifolia Argenteo Marginata'—see *I. Aquifolium* 'Argentea Marginata'

I. *Aquifolium* 'Latispina'
= *I. Aquifolium* 'Trapeziformis'

Introduced <1854. Free-growing; fine pyramidal habit. Twigs dark purple. Leaves usually with 2–3 broad spines, commonly deflexed like the tip, occasionally hooked backwards with a rounded shoulder. Glossy, very deep green; leathery; edges thickened. Entire leaf sometimes slightly twisted. Male. Similar to *I. Aquifolium* 'Monstrosa'.

I. *Aquifolium* 'Latispina Major'—see *I. Aquifolium* 'Monstrosa'

I. Aquifolium 'Latispina Minor'—see *I. Aquifolium* 'Hastata'

I. Aquifolium 'Laurifolia'
= *I.* × *altaclerensis* 'Laurifolia'

SMOOTH LEAVED HOLLY. Grown since <1743 in France. Common. Erect, tall habit. Twigs dark purple. Leaves dark, very glossy, smooth, flat or slightly undulated, slender, mostly spineless. Male. Records: 65½' × 4'4" Clumber Park, Nottinghamshire, England (1979); 59' × 8'5" Dillington House, Somerset, England (1988); 58' × 4'4" Seattle, WA (1987).

I. Aquifolium 'Laurifolia Aurea'
= *I. Aquifolium* 'Mistigold'

Cultivated since <1883. As described by Brownell Holly Farms of Milwaukie, OR: A male counterpart of *I. Aquifolium* 'Aurifodina'—almost identical in leaf shape except an impish twist to each sharp spine. Brighter gold edge, too. Twigs purplish or reddish-brown.

I. Aqui. 'Laurifolium Longifolium'—see *I.* × *altac.* 'Camelliæfolia'

I. Aquifolium 'Lawsoniana'—see *I.* × *altaclerensis* 'Lawsoniana'

I. Aquifolium 'Lewis'
Named <1970 by S.H. McLean of Baltimore, MD. Upright habit. Leaves dark, spines divaricate. Berries abundant, large, deep red.

I. Aquifolium 'Lillibet'
Introduced ≤1964 by Brownell Holly Farms of Milwaukie, OR: an *I. Aquifolium* 'Angustifolia' sport with somewhat broader leaves and low, spreading habit. Fruitful.

I. Aquifolium 'Lilliput'
As *I. Aquifolium* 'Lillibet' except male. Almost certainly a mere renaming of *I. Aquifolium* 'Myrtifolia'.

I. Aquifolium 'Lilygold'
('Lily Gold')

Introduced <1953 by Teufel nursery of Portland, OR. Leaves edged bright gold turning pink or red in winter. Bushy.

I. Aquifolium 'Little Bull'
= *I. Aquifolium* 'Teufel's Little Bull'

Introduced ≤1963 by Teufel nursery of Portland, OR.

An *I. Aquifolium* 'Angustifolia' mutation with glossy, spiny leaves ca. three times as large as those of normal 'Angustifolia'. Habit compact and dwarf but upright. Good pollinator.

I. Aquifolium 'Littleleaf'—see *I. Aquifolium* 'Angustifolia'

I. Aquifolium 'Longspra'
Sold since ≤1925 by John Wieman holly nursery of Portland, OR. Very hardy. Rapid growing orchard-type tree. Branches long and spreading.

I. Aquifolium 'Louise'
Introduced by Teufel nursery of Portland, OR. A seedling of 'Teufel's Hybrid' selected in 1948. Vigorous. Hardy to 0°F. Leaves very glossy, dark, held for 3 years; less spiny than those of typical *I. Aquifolium*. Berries large, scarlet.

I. Aquifolium 'Lutescens'—see *I. Aquifolium* 'Flavescens'

I. Aquifolium 'Madame Briot'

Described in 1866 in France. Maybe related to Pierre-Louis Briot (1804–1888) of *Æsculus* × *carnea* 'Briottii'. Twigs greenish flushed dark purple. Leaves average to large sized, narrow-ovate, strongly spiny, gold-edged, center mottled gold and light green. Berries plentiful.

I. Aquifolium 'Maderensis'—see *I.* × *altaclerensis* 'Maderensis'

I. Aquifolium 'Magnifica'—see *I.* × *altaclerensis* 'Camelliæfolia'

I. Aquifolium 'Malmborg'
Sold <1958 by Clarendon nursery of Pinehurst, NC, and by Audubon Holly Gardens of Audubon, PA. Named after HOLLY enthusiast Gustaf E. Malmborg of Elizabethtown, PA. Leaves well spined. Berries heavily borne.

I. Aquifolium 'Marginata'
A name applied since <1838 to various clones (such as 'Crispa') with colorful or thickened leaf edges.

I. Aqui. 'Marginata Aureopicta'—see *I. Aqui.* 'Crispa Aureo Picta'

I. Aquifolium 'Marginata Bicolor'—see *I. Aquifolium* 'Aurifodina'

I. Aquifolium 'Marnockii'—see *I. × altaclerensis* 'Marnockii'

I. Aquifolium 'Marshall Tito'—see *I. Aquifolium* 'Balkans Male'

I. Aquifolium "Mascula"

All this name indicates is maleness, no berrybearing. The female equivalent is "Femina".

I. Aqui. 'Medio Picta' (Milkmaid)—see *I. Aqui.* 'Argentea Medio-picta'

I. Aquifolium 'Mistigold'—see *I. Aquifolium* 'Laurifolia Aurea'

I. Aquifolium 'Misty Green'

Introduced <1964 by Brownell Holly Farms of Milwaukie, OR. Leaves with 2 tones of green; centers dark green, edged with a broad, marginal band of a paler shade.

I. Aquifolium 'Monstrosa'

= *I. Aquifolium* 'Latispina Major'
= *I. monstrosa* hort.

Introduced ≤1854 by Fisher, Son & Sibray nursery of Handsworth, Sheffield, England. Dense growth. Twigs green. Leaves broad, with huge broad-based spines mostly erect, but the tip spine downward. Male. Related to *I. Aquifolium* 'Latispina'.

I. Aquifolium 'Monler'—see *I. Aquifolium* Sparkler™

I. Aquifolium 'Monvila'—see *I. Aquifolium* Gold Coast™

I. Aqui. 'Moonlight'—see *I. Aqui.* 'Flavescens' and 'Aurantiaca'

I. Aquifolium 'Mundyi'—see *I. × altaclerensis* 'Mundyi'

I. Aquifolium 'Muricata'—see *I. Aquifolium* 'Aurifodina'

I. Aquifolium 'Myrtifolia'

Introduced <1830. Small-leaved and neat. Twigs both green and purplish. Leaves usually 1¼"–1½" × ½"–⅝"; ovate-lanceolate; margin spineless or with 1–2 spines, or moderately spiny. Similar to *I. Aquifolium* 'Angustifolia' yet with broader spines. Male (some American authors say female). Apparently sold as 'Lilliput' by Brownell Holly Farms of Milwaukie, OR.

I. Aquifolium 'Myrtifolia Aurea'—see *I. Aqui.* 'Myrtifolia Aurea Maculata' and 'Myrtifolia Aurea Marginata'

I. Aquifolium 'Myrtifolia Aurea Maculata'

= *I. Aquifolium* 'Myrtifolia Aurea' (in part)

Originated in England <1874. Dwarf and dense, 5' tall. Twigs green. Leaves small (to 2⅜" × 1¼"), narrow, spiny, gold-blotched. Male.

I. Aquifolium 'Myrtifolia Aurea Marginata'

= *I. Aquifolium* 'Myrtifolia Aurea' (in part)

Originated in England ≤1863. Dwarf and dense, 5'–13' tall. Twigs purplish. Leaves small (to 2½" × 1"), narrow, spiny, gold-edged. Male.

I. Aquifolium 'Myrtifolia Stricta'—see *I. Aquifolium* 'Angustifolia'

I. Aquifolium 'N.F. Barnes'—see *I. × altaclerensis* 'N.F. Barnes'

I. Aquifolium 'New Brunswick'

Sold ≤1956 by Ten Oaks nursery of Clarksville, MD. Leaf dark, large. Male.

I. Aquifolium 'Nigrescens'—see *I. × altaclerensis* 'Nigrescens'

I. Aquifolium 'Nobilis'—see *I. × altaclerensis* 'Nobilis'

I. Aquifolium 'Orange Gem'—see *I. Aquifolium* 'Fructu Aurantiaca'

I. Aquifolium 'Oregon Favorite'

Introduced ≤1958 by Teufel nursery of Portland, OR. One in the Seattle arboretum is an ordinary-looking female, with its berries perhaps slightly larger than average.

I. Aquifolium 'Oregon Majesty'

Introduced ≤1963 by Brownell Holly Farms of Milwaukie, OR. Described only as a female "beyond compare."

I. Aquifolium 'Oregon Select'

A chance Oregon seedling selected and named in 1947. Tree matures and bears fruit early. Twigs green. Leaves shiny, generally spiny. Berries bright red, early ripening. Sprays well balanced, good for commercial cutting.

I. Aquifolium 'Ovata'

Cultivated since ≤1854. Slow growth to 10' or more. Twigs purple. Leaves small (to 2" × 1⅛") deep opaque green (like I. × altaclerensis 'Hodginsii'), very thick. Regular, scarcely spiny teeth, the sinuses between them unusually even, regular, and pronounced. Male.

I. Aquifolium 'Ovata Aurea'

= I. Aquifolium 'Aurea Marginata Ovata'
= I. Aquifolium 'Ovata Aurea Marginata'

Cultivated since ≤1874. Leaves smaller than average, roundish-ovate, mottled dark green and some gray with a broad edge of yellow-gold. Twigs purple. Male. (A similar female is I. Aquifolium 'Golden Gate'.)

I. Aquifolium 'Ovata Aurea Marginata'—see I. Aqui. 'Ovata Aurea'

I. Aquifolium 'Painted Lady'

Introduced ≤1963 by Brownell Holly Farms of Milwaukie, OR. In the 'Aurea Medio Picta' group; gaudy in fall but in spring the gold discolorations fade away.

I. Aqui. 'Path-o-Gold'—see I. Aqui. 'Pyramidalis Aurea Marginata'

I. Aquifolium 'Pendula'

WEEPING HOLLY. Described in 1842. A dense mophead mound without a leader; usually <10' tall. Must be topgrafted to be a tree. Twigs purple. Leaves dark, spiny.

I. Aqui. 'Pendula Argentea'—see I. Aqui. 'Argentea Marginata Pendula'

I. Aquifolium 'Pendula Argenteomarginata'—see I. Aquifolium 'Argentea Marginata Pendula'

I. Aqui. 'Pendula Variegata'—see I. Aqui. 'Argentea Marginata Pendula'

I. Aquifolium 'Pernettyæfolia'—see I. Aquifolium 'Angustifolia'

I. Aqui. 'Perry's Weeping'—see I. Aqui. 'Argentea Marginata Pendula'

I. Aquifolium 'Petit(e)'—see I. Aquifolium 'Angustifolia'

I. Aquifolium 'Phantom Gold'—see I. Aquifolium 'Flavescens'

I. Aquifolium 'Picta' (golden blotched)—see I. × altac. 'Nobilis Picta'

I. Aquifolium 'Pilkington'

A seedling selected ca. 1900. Named by Herman F. Bleeg of Oregon. Likely associated with nurseryman J.B. Pilkington of Portland, OR. Once planted widely as one of the best green-stemmed "Bleeg" types for commercial bough cutting. Similar to I. Aquifolium 'Dr. Huckleberry'. Leaves thick, black-green, wavy, spiny, shiny. Rapid growing, early cropping. Berries large, early ripening, bright Chinese red, oval.

I. Aquifolium 'Pinto'

An I. Aquifolium 'Early Cluster' mutation discovered in 1935 by John Wieman holly nursery of Portland, OR. Leaves very glossy, splashed with gold in the center. Consistent bearer of round, red berries which remain long on cut branches indoors. Winter hardy. Recommended for landscaping and orcharding.

I. Aquifolium 'Platyphylla Pallida'

Sold <1950 by nurseries in Pennsylvania and North Carolina. Leaves broad, deep green, sparsely spined. Either an I. Perado variant or a cultivar of I. × altaclerensis.

I. Aquifolium 'Polka Dot'—see I. Aquifolium 'Ingramii'

I. Aquifolium 'Polycarpa'—see I. Aquifolium 'J.C. van Tol'

I. Aquifolium 'Post Office'

= I. × altaclarensis 'Post Office'

Introduced ≤1964 by Brownell Holly Farms of Milwaukie, OR. Of historic interest. From a tree planted in 1874 at the pioneer post office in downtown Portland, OR. Likely a "Dutch type." Twigs green. Leaves essentially spineless.

I. Aquifolium 'Princess Pat'

Introduced ≤1963 by Brownell Holly Farms of Milwaukie, OR. A natural conical form of exceptional symmetry, it can develop a sheared appearance. Twigs green.

I. Aquifolium 'Pyramidalis'

('Pyramid')

= I. Aquifolium 'Pyramidalis Compacta'

Originated in Holland ca. 1885. Common. A gaunt cultivar of I. Aquifolium f. heterophylla. Twigs green. Leaves scarcely spiny. Berries abundant and very early to redden. Growth slow, ≤20' tall in 45 years. During the 1940s an I. × altaclarensis clone was sold as 'Pyramidalis' but had purple pendant twigs, and large, darker leaves. Some nurseries also incorrectly sold 'Pyramidalis' or a similar clone as I. Aquifolium 'Integrifolia'.

I. Aquifolium 'Pyramidalis Aurea Marginata'

= I. Aquifolium 'Path-o-Gold'

In the 'Aurea Marginata' group. Leaves long, slender, sharply pointed, nearly flat with occasional spines within the leaf plane. Each leaf boldly edged brightest gold. Winter resistant.

I. Aquifolium 'Pyramidalis Compacta'—see I. Aqui. 'Pyramidalis'

I. Aquifolium 'Recurva'

= I. Aquifolium 'Serratifolia Compacta'

= I. Aquifolium 'Tortuosa' (in part; cf. 'Crispa')

Grown since <1789. Dwarf and dense, to 15'. Twigs dull olive, flushed purplish. Leaves small (ca. 1½"), very spiny, dark; the apex often recurved and twisted. Male.

I. Aquifolium 'Rederly'

Originated ca. 1903 south of Portland, OR. Introduced ≤1935 by Brownell Holly Farms of Milwaukie, OR. The first named HOLLY of that nursery. Compact and tall. Twigs olive-green and slender. Leaves small, glossy dark green. Berries big, in heavy clusters, coloring red early—but not the earliest of all by any means. One study showed earlier cultivars include 'Dr. Huckleberry' (Oct 5) 'Teufel's Hybrid' (Oct 7) 'Bleeg' (Oct 11), and eight additional taxa before 'Rederly' (Oct 21).

I. Aquifolium 'Regina Aurea'—see I. Aquifolium 'Golden Queen'

I. Aquifolium 'Ricker'

Originated in eastern North America. Cultivated since ≤1964. Five specimens dating from that year in the Seattle arboretum are ordinary looking, perhaps with rather straight long limbs.

I. Aquifolium 'Riddle'

Sold ≤1964 by Tingle nursery of Pittsville, MD. Leaves large. Sex not known.

I. Aquifolium 'Robinson'

Origin not known; cultivated <1970. Leaves glossy, deep green, narrow (3" × 1"), with margins undulated, divided into numerous very fierce, divaricate spines often ½" long. Male.

I. Aquifolium 'Rotundifolium'—see I. Aquifolium 'Integrifolia'

I. Aquifolium 'Royal Red'—see I. Aquifolium "Dutch type"

I. Aquifolium 'Rubricaulis Aurea'

= I. Aquifolium 'Aurea Marginata Rotundifolia'

Cultivated since ≤1867. Slow growth; a small tree. Twigs red-brown (hence the Latin name rubricaulis). Leaves broad, gold-edged, spines red-tipped. Berries bright scarlet. Record: 25' × 2'9" Mount Vernon, WA (1995).

I. Aquifolium 'San Gabriel'

Introduced <1979 in California. Large shrub or pyramidal small tree. Twigs purple. Leaves shiny, dark, with prominent spines. Self-fertile. Berries medium sized.

I. Aquifolium 'Scotch Gold'

Introduced ≤1964 by Brownell Holly Farms of Milwaukie, OR. In the 'Aurea Marginata' group. Leaves broad, gold-edged. Male.

I. Aquifolium 'Scotica'

Cultivated since <1838. Twigs purple. Leaves smaller than average (2" × 1"), shiny, thick, broad, deep green, spineless. The apex can be sharp but is usually rounded. Sometimes a faint cup-like depression below the apex.

I. Aquifolium 'Scotica Aurea'

Origin not known, <1900. Dwarfish. Leaves with a broad gold edge.

I. Aquifolium 'Scotica Aureopicta'

Originated ≤1850 in England. Confused with 'Scotica Aurea' but blotched rather than edged with gold.

I. Aquifolium 'Screwleaf'—see *I. Aquifolium* 'Crispa'

I. Aquifolium 'Serrata'—see *I. Aqui.* 'Angustifolia' and 'Crassifolia'

I. Aquifolium 'Serratifolia'

Origin not known but <1838. Resembles 'Myrtifolia' but has more decidedly divaricate spines and tends to recurve at the apex. Habit pyramidal. Twigs green or purplish. Leaves lanceolate, <1½" × ½"; glossy dark green, stiff; midrib convexly curved and the leaf edges are brought up to form a channel. Numerous regular, stout spines are moderately divaricate. Male. Obscure if not extinct variations sold in England in the 1870s include: 'Serratifolia Aurea Maculata' and 'Serratifolia Alba Marginata'.

I. Aquifolium 'Serratifolia Compacta'—see *I. × altac.* 'Recurva'

I. Aquifolium 'Shepherdii'—see *I. × altaclerensis* 'Shepherdii'

I. Aquifolium 'Shortspra'

Selected as a seedling ca. 1932 by John Wieman holly nursery of Portland, OR. Habit compact. Twigs green. Berries orange-red. Extremely hardy.

I. Aquifolium 'Sickler'

Sold since ≤1966 by John Wieman holly nursery of Portland, OR. Named after L.E. Sickler of Oregon. Leaves dark, glossy. Berries bright red.

I. Aquifolium 'Silvary'—see *I. Aquifolium* 'Argentea Marginata'

I. Aquifolium 'Silver Beauty'—see *I. Aqui.* 'Argentea Marginata'

I. Aquifolium 'Silverboy'—see *I. Aqui.* 'Handsworth New Silver'

I. Aquifolium 'Silver Broadleaf'—see *I. Aqui.* 'Argentea Marginata'

I. Aqui. 'Silver Charm'—see *I. Aqui.* 'Argentea Marginata Erecta'

I. Aquifolium 'Silver Edge'—see *I. Aquifolium* 'Argentea Marginata'

I. Aquifolium 'Silver King'—see *I. Aquifolium* 'Silver Queen'

I. Aquifolium 'Silver Leaf'—see *I. Aquifolium* 'Argentea Marginata'

I. Aquifolium 'Silver Milkboy'—see *I. Aqui.* 'Argentea Medio-picta'

I. Aquifolium 'Silver Milkmaid'—see *I. Aqui.* 'Argentea Medio-picta'

I. Aquifolium 'Silver Plane'—see *I. Aqui.* 'Handsworth New Silver'

I. Aquifolium 'Silver Princess'—see *I. Aqui.* 'Argentea Marginata'

I. Aquifolium 'Silver Queen'

= *I. Aquifolium* 'Argentea Latifolia'
= *I. Aquifolium* 'Argentea Regina'
= *I. Aquifolium* 'Silver King' in the U.S.

Originated <1863. Growth rather slow and pyramidal. Twigs blackish purple or reddish brown. Leaves shrimp-pink when young, becoming dark green marbled gray and bordered creamy white. Male, though a female in the 'Argentea Marginata' group was sold as 'Silver Queen' by Brownell Holly Farms of Milwaukie, OR.

I. Aquifolium 'Silver Star'—see *I. Aquifolium* 'Argentea Medio-picta'

I. Aquifolium 'Silver Variegated'—see *I. Aqui.* 'Argentea Marginata'

I. Aqui. 'Silver Weeping'—see *I. Aqui.* 'Argentea Marginata Pendula'

I. Aquifolium 'Smithiana'

('Smithii')

Originated ≤1874. Habit dense. The green counterpart of 'Donningtonensis'. Twigs green or tinged reddish-purple. Leaves narrow, 2"–2½" × ¾"–1"; glossy, bright green, thin. Spines absent or distant, irregular, and weakish. Male.

I. Aquifolium Sparkler™

= *I. Aquifolium* 'Monler'

Introduced ≤1964 by Monrovia nursery of California. Exceptionally robust. Leaves shiny, dark. Berries prolific, glistening red, borne at an early age.

I. Aquifolium 'Special'

= *I. Aquifolium* 'Brownell Special'

Introduced ≤1940 by Brownell Holly Farms of Milwaukie, OR. Named after Ambrose Brownell or his nursery. Fast; thrifty. Leaves large, deep green, well-spined. Berries very large, opalescent red, generously produced. 'Teufel's Special' sold in the mid-1960s may be identical.

I. Aquifolium 'Squire'

Selected from a shipment of seedlings from Pennsylvania in 1925, growing on the former G.G. Whitney estate in Woods Hole, MA. Propagated by Wilfred Wheeler of MA, and others. Male.

I. Aquifolium 'St. George'

Described as a "brother" to 'Squire'. Leaves glossy, green, oblong.

I. Aquifolium 'Sunnybrooke'

Introduced ≤1963 by Brownell Holly Farms of Milwaukie, OR. "The ultimate in divarication." Male. Female counterpart is 'Sunnyside'.

I. Aquifolium 'Sunnyside'

Introduced ≤1963 by Brownell Holly Farms of Milwaukie, OR. Like 'Sunnybrooke' but female and leaves slightly smaller. "The most prickly in all Hollydom." Yet a large specimen in Strybing Arboretum of San Francisco is not more prickly than some others.

I. Aquifolium 'Teufel'

Introduced ≤1954. Habit especially neat. Berries abundant.

I. Aquifolium 'Teufel's Deluxe'—see I. Aquifolium 'Deluxe'

I. Aquifolium 'Teufel's Hybrid'

Selected <1940 by Gustav Teufel of Teufel nursery of Portland, OR. Twigs green. Leaves exceptionally glossy. Berries borne consistently even on a young tree, early-ripening, bright red.

I. Aquifolium 'Teufel's Little Bull'—see I. Aquifolium 'Little Bull'

I. Aqui. 'Teufel's Silver Variegated'—see I. Aqui. 'Argentea Marginata'

I. Aquifolium 'Teufel's Special'—see I. Aquifolium 'Special'

I. Aquifolium 'Teufel's Weeping'—see I. Aquifolium 'Teufel's Zero'

I. Aquifolium 'Teufel's Zero'

= I. Aquifolium 'Teufel's Weeping'
= I. Aquifolium 'Zero'

Introduced ≤1958. Narrow upright habit, the branches long, thin and graceful, with a slight weeping effect. Leaves very dark, average size or smaller. Twigs purplish. Berries bright red, early ripening and persistent. Vigorous; cold-hardy. Likely the name zero suggests the tree made it unhurt through a 0°F winter.

I. Aquifolium 'Thornton'

From a tree found in 1962, believed to be about 30 years old, on a farm 7 miles north of Warwick, MD. Leaves glossy, dark year round. Hardy.

I. Aquifolium 'Tortuosa'—see I. Aquifolium 'Crispa' and 'Recurva'

I. Aqui. 'Tortuosa Aurea Picta'—see I. Aqui. 'Crispa Aurea Picta'

I. Aquifolium 'Trapeziformis'—see I. Aquifolium 'Latispina'

I. Aqui. 'Upright Silver-Striped'—see I. Aqui. 'Argentea Marginata Erecta'

I. Aquifolium 'Van Tol'—see I. Aquifolium 'J.C. van Tol'

I. Aqui. 'Variegated Screwleaf'—see I. Aqui. 'Crispa Aurea Picta'

I. Aquifolium 'Varigold'

Introduced ≤1963 by Brownell Holly Farms of Milwaukie, OR: "Our name. Best of all the gold-margined hollies of the traditional English type to come to our attention. Leaves waved, spined and strongly edged with bold gold. Dependable fruiting." Doubtless some other cultivar renamed.

I. Aquifolium 'Vera Kent'

Sold ≤1958 by Holly Hedge nursery of Centreville, MD, and Wilmat Holly Company of Gladwyne, PA. Origin, characteristics and sex not known.

I. Aquifolium 'W.J. Bean'—see I. × altaclerensis 'W.J. Bean'

I. Aquifolium 'Whitesail'

Sold since ≤1966 by John Wieman holly nursery of Portland, OR. A seedling of I. Aquifolium 'Handsworth New Silver'. Leaves unusually long, silver-variegated, with a wider "more spectacular" white edge.

I. Aquifolium 'Whittingtonensis'
= I. × altaclerensis 'Whittingtonensis'

Introduced <1874 by Fisher, Son & Sibray nursery of Handsworth, Sheffield, England. Twigs purple. Leaves shiny dark green, narrow, thinnish, 2½" × ⅝" or to 3" × 1"; spines numerous, stiff, divaricate. Confused with the much darker 'Donningtonensis'. Male.

I. Aquifolium 'Wieman's Globe'—see I. Aquifolium 'Globe'

I. Aquifolium 'Wilsonii'—see I. × altaclerensis 'Wilsonii'

I. Aquifolium 'Winter King'

Introduced ≤1955 by Brownell Holly Farms of Milwaukie, OR. Of "maximum hardiness." Male.

I. Aquifolium 'Winter Queen'

Introduced ≤1955 by Brownell Holly Farms of Milwaukie, OR. Of "maximum hardiness." Female. Twigs green, flushed purple. Leaves large, with few, but very large, spines. Berries very large, to nearly ½" long. Probably an I. × altaclerensis clone renamed.

I. Aquifolium 'Xanthocarpa'—see I. Aquifolium f. bacciflava

I. Aquifolium 'Yellow Beam'—see I. Aquifolium f. bacciflava

I. Aquifolium 'Yellow Berried'—see I. Aquifolium f. bacciflava

I. Aquifolium 'Yellow Fruit'—see I. Aquifolium f. bacciflava

I. Aquifolium 'Yohn'

Sold ≤1958 by Millcreek nursery of Newark, DE, and Wilmat Holly Company of Gladwyne, PA. Origin and characteristics not known.

I. Aquifolium 'Yuleglow'

Commercially grown in Oregon <1970. Berries ripen October 18th at Corvallis, OR.

I. Aquifolium 'Zero'—see I. Aquifolium 'Teufel's Zero'

I. × aquipernyi Gable ex W.B. Clarke
(I. Aquifolium × I. Pernyi)

This name, used since ≤1948, is not yet scientifically validated. In practice it is used as a group name to include cultivars that may have differing parentage, yet look more or less alike. Nurseries have sold male ("Mascula") and female ("Femina") specimens, as well as named cultivars. The following are the most prominent, but at least 6 other cultivars exist.

I. × aquipernyi 'Aquipern'
= I. × aquipernyi 'Gable'
= I. × aquipernyi 'Gable's Male'

The first form of the hybrid, raised in 1933 by Joseph B. Gable (1886–1972) of Stewartstown, PA. Distributed ≤1949. Male.

I. × aquipernyi 'Brilliant'—see I. 'Brilliant'

I. × aquipernyi Dragon Lady™ PP 4996 (1983)

Originated by Mrs. F. Leighton (Kathleen) Meserve of Long Island, NY. Introduced ≤1981.

I. × aquipernyi 'Gable' or 'Gable's Male'—see I. × aquipernyi 'Aquipern'

I. × aquipernyi 'San José'

Origin not known, possibly in California. Some say this is a cross of I. ciliospinosa and I. Henryi. In commerce since ≤1966. Commonly sold since ca. 1980. A shrub, in ideal conditions and after decades possibly a very small tree to 15' tall. Reminiscent of I. Pernyi 'Veitchii' yet far weaker. Leaves to 2" × 1⅜", with 2–4 spines on each side. Berries longer (⅜"–⁷⁄₁₆") than wide and distinctly stalked. Blooms very early in spring, as does I. 'Brilliant'. Very unlike the rare tree Ilex × Koehneana 'San José' except in name, yet much confused with it.

I. × attenuata Ashe
= I. Topeli hort.
= I. × attenuata 'Topeli'
(I. Cassine × I. opaca)

TOPEL HOLLY. Found wild in Florida; named in 1924; cultivated since 1931. Commonly planted since the 1950s. Every year it seems more cultivars sold as I. opaca selections are found in actuality to be hybrids. Leaves spiny or spineless, elegantly narrow (2¼" × ¾"), to wide (4¾" × 1¼"), with an attenuated base.

Berries ¼"–⅜". A large shrub or small tree, varying from spindly to pleasingly plump. Record: 32' × 1'8" Seattle, WA (1994; *pl.* 1944).

I. × *attenuata* 'Alagold'

Discovered in 1965 as a seedling of *I.* × *attenuata* 'Fosteri no. 2' at Webb nursery of Huntsville, AL. Introduced in 1979. Leaf to 1½" × ½", mostly spineless. Berries yellow, ¼".

I. × *attenuata* 'Attakapa'

As described in the 1992–93 catalog of Louisiana nursery of Opelousas, LA: a tall, upright cone-shaped tree. Berries red.

I. × *attenuata* 'Aurantiaca'

Origin not known. Berries large, orange, profuse.

I. × *attenuata* 'Big John'

As described in the 1992–93 catalog of Louisiana nursery of Opelousas, LA: habit pyramidal. Leaves dark and glossy. Male.

I. × *attenuata* 'Blazer'

Discovered in 1965 as a seedling of *I.* × *attenuata* 'Fosteri no. 2' at Webb nursery of Huntsville, AL. Introduced in 1980. Leaves 1¾" × 1", spineless. Berries bright red and abundant. Slow.

I. × *attenuata* 'Eagleson'

Introduced <1990 by Eagleson nursery of Port Arthur, TX. Very fast to 15' tall. Berries abundant.

I. × *attenuata* 'East Palatka'

= *I. opaca* 'East Palatka'

Propagated since ≤1926. Very popular. Named after East Palatka, FL. Leaves small (to 2" × 1"), nearly spineless, pale green, often yellowish. Berries abundant, large.

I. × *attenuata* 'Fosteri'

= *I. opaca* 'Fosteri'
= *I. Fosterii* hort.

Five natural seedling HOLLY hybrids (*I. Cassine* var. *angustifolia* × *I. opaca*) were selected by E.E. Foster of Bessemer, AL. Introduced ≤1953. The clones 'Fosteri no. 1' and 'Fosteri no. 5' were like an inferior *I. opaca*, and discarded in favor of 'Fosteri no. 2' (an overplanted female) and 'Fosteri no. 3' (also female) and 'Fosteri no. 4' (a male sold as a pollinator). The name *I.* × *attenuata* 'Fosteri' has continued to be used generally for any clone number a given nursery happens to sell. The females bear abundant berries. Leaves small, narrow, dark and glossy, spiny. FOSTER HOLLIES can grow 20'–30' (50') tall.

I. × *attenuata* 'Gato'

As described in the 1992–93 catalog of Louisiana nursery of Opelousas, LA: Leaves bright green. Berries bright red.

I. × *attenuata* 'Hume'

= *I. opaca* 'Hume'

Originated by Dr. Hardrada Harold Hume (1875–1965), founder of Glen St. Mary nursery of Florida. Propagated since 1909. Sold commonly in the 1940s and '50s. Vigorous, yet bushy. Leaves light green, wholly or nearly spineless. Berries abundant, large.

I. × *attenuata* 'Hume no. 2'

= *I. opaca* 'Hume no. 2'

Propagated since 1909. Leaves flat, thin, sparsely if at all spined, glossy, to 3½" long. Berries abundant, dark red. To 35' tall.

I. × *attenuata* 'Lake City'

= *I. opaca* 'Lake City'

Selected by H. Hume of Lake City, FL. Introduced ≤1933. Common. Leaves light green, spines short. Berries large, abundant, orange-red. Vigorous. Open-branched.

I. × *attenuata* 'Rosalind Sarver'

= *I. opaca* 'Rosalind Sarver'
= *I. opaca* 'Mrs. Sarver'

Introduced by Sarver nursery of San Marcos, CA. Promoted heavily ≤1958 by Monrovia nursery of California. Leaves light green. Self-fertile. Berries bright red. Similar to *I.* × *attenuata* 'East Palatka'.

I. × *attenuata* 'Savannah'

= *I. opaca* 'Savannah'

Found by W.H. Robertson, Parks Commissioner of Savannah, GA. Introduced <1953. Still in commerce. Well adapted to clay and high humidity. Leaf light green, sparsely spined, to 4" × 1½". Very fruitful; one of the heaviest bearers. Grows 20'–30' tall in upright columnar form.

I. × *attenuata* 'Topeli'—see I. × *attenuata*

I. *balearica*—see I. × *altaclerensis* 'Balearica'

I. *balearica* 'Nigrescens'—see I. × *altaclerensis* 'Nigrescens'

I. belgica—see *I.* × *altaclerensis* 'Belgica'

I. bioritensis Hay.

= *I. ficoidea* hort. U.S., non Hemsl.

BIORITSU HOLLY. From SW China, Burma, and Taiwan. First collected at Bioritsu, Taiwan. Introduced to cultivation in 1900. Named in 1911. In North American commerce ≤1939. Rare. Leaf to 2½" × 1¼", each side with 2–4 spines, the stem ≤⅛". Berries ⅓"–⁷⁄₁₆" long. Usually shrubby, but capable of becoming a 30' tree. Closely related to if not identical to *I. Pernyi* 'Veitchii'. In 1990 T.R. Dudley (d. 1994) published an article insisting *I. Pernyi* 'Veitchii' was a mere synonym of BIORITSU HOLLY. But S. Andrews, another HOLLY expert, disagrees. The present writer considers the jury still out.

I. 'Brilliant'

= *I.* × *aquipernyi* 'Brilliant'
= *I. Pernyi* 'Brilliant'
(*I. ciliospinosa* × *I. Pernyi*)

Originated in 1935 by nurseryman W.B. Clarke of California. Parentage also has been cited as *I. Aquifolium* 'Golden Beauty' × *I. Pernyi* or *I. ciliospinosa* × *I. Henryi*. In any case, the clone most resembles *I. ciliospinosa*. Named 'Brilliant' ≤1947. In the East Coast nursery trade by ≤1954. A large shrub or small slender tree. Leaves less dull than those of *I. ciliospinosa*, lighter green, less hairy, with prominent short spines; to 2⅜" × 1". Self-fertile; berries ⅜" wide on stalks <¼". Record: 21' tall in Seattle, WA (1994; *pl.* 1950).

I. Buergeri Miq.

From E China, and Japan. Named in 1866, after Heinrich Buerger (1804–1858), German botanical explorer and collector in the Orient. Introduced to North America ≤1960. Extremely rare. A shrub to 20' usually; rarely a 50' tree. Tolerant of frost, but needs heat to thrive. Seattle specimens (all male) planted in 1964 are still spindly shrubs. Twigs and leaf stems minutely hairy. Leaves bright green, untoothed or minutely serrulate, with drawn out yet blunt drip-tips; to 3½" × 1⅜"—reminiscent of *I. integra* foliage. The young spring growth looks like smoked salmon with a glaze. Flowers yellowish-green, fragrant, in April-May. Berries to ¼" wide.

I. Burfordii—see *I. cornuta* 'Burfordii'

I. canariensis—see *I. Perado*

I. caroliniana—see *I. vomitoria*

I. Cassine L. 1753, non Walt. 1788

= *I. Dahoon* Walt.

DAHOON. HENDERSON WOOD. From the coastal SE United States, central Mexico, W Cuba, NE Puerto Rico, and the Bahamas. Alfred Rehder explained: "*Cassine* or *cassena* is the name in the language of the Timucua Indians for an exhilarating beverage prepared from the leaves of *I. vomitoria*, which had been confused with this species. The name seems to have been borrowed from the Muscogee word *ássi*, leaves, modified by a prefix." The DAHOON is a slender small tree prized for its berries, bright red or occasionally yellow or orange, ¼"–⅓" wide. It tolerates wet, acidic soil. Leaf narrowed toward the base, broad above the middle, spineless but can be weakly toothed near the tip, 1½"–4" long, to 1⅔" wide. Flowers appear April–June. Records: 72' × 2'10" Osceola National Forest, FL (1975); 40' × 4'7" Ft. Pierce, FL (1992).

I. Cassine var. *angustifolia* Ait.

NARROWLEAF DAHOON. Named in 1789. Much grown, mostly in Alabama and Georgia, since ≤1933. Leaves extremely slender, 2"–3" long. The term *angustifolia* means narrow-leaved; from Latin *angustus*, narrow, and *folium*, a leaf.

I. Cassine 'Baldwin'

Introduced <1976. Upright conical. Red berries.

I. Cassine 'Bryanii'

Discovered in 1938 in Myrtle Beach, SC. Named after Mr. J.B. Bryan of that locality. Berries yellow.

I. Cassine 'Glencassine'

Selected and propagated <1947 by H.H. Hume of Glen St. Mary nursery, Florida. Leaf to 4" × 1⅔", bright green and glossy. Twigs dark. Dense and well foliated.

I. Cassine f. *Lowei* S. Blake

YELLOWBERRY DAHOON. Named in 1924 after George D. Lowe (b. ca. 1878), who reported more than 1,000 yellow-berried specimens were growing near Baxley, GA. A form of *I. Cassine* var. *myrtifolia*. Other yellow-berried specimens were reported earlier (in 1902) near Camille, also in south Georgia. In commerce ≤1934.

I. Cassine var. *myrtifolia* (Walt.) Sarg.

= *I. Cassine* ssp. *myrtifolia* (Walt.) E. Murr.
= *I. myrtifolia* Walt.

MYRTLELEAF HOLLY. MYRTLE DAHOON. Named in

1788. In commerce by ≤1934. Common. Leaf usually ½"–1½" long, to ¼" wide. Similar to *I. Cassine* var. *angustifolia* but with still smaller leaves. Record: 46' × 5'7" near Lawtey, FL (1972).

I. Cassine 'Uncle Herb'

= *I. myrtifolia* 'Uncle Herb'
= *I. myrtifolia* 'Steed's'

A form of *I. Cassine* var. *myrtifolia*. Originated ca. 1970 at Steed's nursery of Candor, NC. Named in 1990 after Herbert Steed. Leaves glossy, dark, curved, to 1½" × ⅓".

I. 'CB 10' × I. latifolia—see I. 'Mary Nell'

I. centrochinensis—see I. ciliospinosa and I. corallina

I. chinensis—see I. purpurea

I. ciliospinosa Loes.

= *I. centrochinensis* hort. U.S. (in part), non S.Y. Hu 1949
= *I. Aquifolium* var. *centrochinensis* hort.
= *I. Fargesii* hort., non Franch.

From W China. Introduced in 1908 by E. Wilson. Named in 1911. In North American commerce since ≤1938. Uncommon. A huge shrub or slender, arching 30' tree. Related to *I. dipyrena* but in habit and leaf size looks more like the hybrid *I.* 'Brilliant'. Leaf narrow, to 2½" × ⅞", matte, finely toothed with up to 6 minute spines per side. Berries ⁵⁄₁₆" wide, on very short stalks, in clusters of 2–4.

I. corallina Franch.

= *I. Aquifolium* var. *chinensis* hort., non Loes.
= *I. centrochinensis* hort. U.K. (in part), non S.Y. Hu 1949

From W & SW China. Named in 1886. Introduced ca. 1900 by E. Wilson for Veitch nursery of England. In North American commerce by ≤1948. Very rare. Shrub or small tree to 39' tall. Leaf to 6" × 2", spiny- to bluntly-toothed, glossy. Berries ⅛"–⅕" wide, nearly stalkless, red, in small clusters.

I. cornuta Lindl. & Paxt.

CHINESE HOLLY. HORNED HOLLY. From E China and Korea. Introduced by R. Fortune in 1846. Named in 1850. In North America since ≤1900. Common. Leaves highly distinctive, trapezoid-like or quadrangular, thick, 1½"–4" long, with 3–5 enormous spines. Bisexual as a rule. Berries ⅓"–½" on 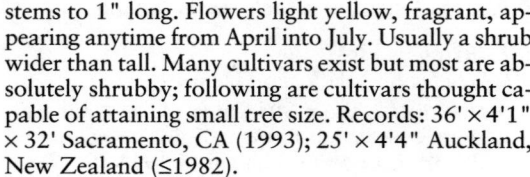 stems to 1" long. Flowers light yellow, fragrant, appearing anytime from April into July. Usually a shrub wider than tall. Many cultivars exist but most are absolutely shrubby; following are cultivars thought capable of attaining small tree size. Records: 36' × 4'1" × 32' Sacramento, CA (1993); 25' × 4'4" Auckland, New Zealand (≤1982).

I. cornuta 'Avery Island'—see I. cornuta 'Jungle Gardens'

I. cornuta 'Burfordii'

= *I. Burfordii* hort.

BURFORD HOLLY. About 1895, the curator of the National Botanic Gardens of Washington, D.C., sent to Thomas William Burford (1851–1920), head gardener of Atlanta's Westview Cemetery, an unusual CHINESE HOLLY seedling which had only one spine. In 1931, Mr. S.R. Howell, nurseryman of Knoxville, TN, visited the cemetery and admired the tree. It was in commerce by 1933, and has been extensively propagated since. Compared to regular *I. cornuta* it is less spiny, darker, its branches more drooping, its growth faster. As Ambrose Brownell said succinctly, it is "*cornuta* minus the horns." Very fruitful. Can grow 25' tall. Dwarf and other cultivars have sported from it (e.g.: 'Carissa').

I. cornuta 'Cajun Gold'

GOLDTIP BURFORD HOLLY. Introduced ≤1960. Gold-tinted foliage.

I. cornuta 'Cornuta #2'—see I. cornuta 'National'

I. cornuta 'D'Or'

Originally found in Columbus, Georgia, by Mrs. Carl Singletary. Introduced ≤1959 by Callaway Gardens. Berries large, yellow (*d'or* is French for golden), later to ripen. Leaves spineless or nearly so.

I. cornuta 'Dr. Kassab'—see I. 'Doctor Kassab'

I. cornuta "Femina"

This merely signifies a female.

I. cornuta 'Hume'

Originated by S.H. McLean's nursery of Towson, MD. An *I. cornuta* 'Burfordii' seedling that first flowered in 1952. Leaves flat, dark, thick, to 2⅜" × 1¼", quadrangular, 5 small spines. Twigs purple.

I. cornuta 'Jungle Gardens'

Originated ca. 1920 by Jungle Gardens nursery of

Avery Island, LA. Foliage typical. Berries abundant, light yellow. A male known as **'Avery Island'** has been confused with this cultivar.

I. cornuta 'Kingsville Special #1'

Originated <1958, by Kingsville nursery of Kingsville, MD. A strong-growing shrub. Leaves large, leathery, almost spineless.

I. cornuta 'Lehigh Valley'

Introduced <1970. From Luther K. Ziegler of Lehigh Valley nursery. Cold hardy. Berries very abundant.

I. cornuta "Mascula"

This merely signifies a male.

I. cornuta 'National'

= *I. cornuta* 'Cornuta #2'

Introduced <1918 by Glen St. Mary nursery of Florida, who obtained it from the U.S. National Botanic Garden, Washington, D.C. Fruitful. Leaves spineless. Like *I. cornuta* 'Burfordii' but of more compact, upright growth, and smaller berries.

I. cornuta 'Nellie R. Stevens'—see I. 'Nellie R. Stevens'

I. cornuta 'O' Spring'

Introduced <1976. Variegated light green, yellow and cream. Male.

I. cornuta 'Shangri-La'

In 1939 Jackson M. Batchelor of North Carolina, crossed a large-berried bigleaf CHINESE HOLLY with a handsome small-leaved male. 'Shangri-La' was selected and named in 1947. Treelike to 20' or more in ten years. Berries to ¾".

I. cornuta 'Shiu-ying'

A 'Burfordii' seedling named in 1958 by S.H. McLean of Towson, MD. Slow, small, compact tree. Leaves glossy, dark, quadrangular. Brilliant scarlet-red fruit in bunches of 7–8 on elongated stems. Its name is associated with the botanist Dr. Shiu-ying Hu. *Shiu* in Chinese means elegant, and *ying* flower or plant.

I. cornuta 'Sunrise'

= *I. cornuta* 'Variegated Burford'

Introduced by Tom Dodd nursery of Semmes, AL. Leaves yellow-edged near the apex, sometimes wholly yellow. Identical otherwise to *I. cornuta* 'Burfordii'.

I. cornuta 'Variegated Burford'—see I. cornuta 'Sunrise'

I. cornuta 'Willowleaf' PP 2290 (1963)

Originated at Cartwright nursery of Collierville, TN. Dense lateral branching creates a broad growth habit. Leaves lustrous, dark, long, narrow, with a slight twist. Blood red berries produced readily. Large 15' shrub or small tree.

I. crenata Th. ex J.A. Murr.

= *I. Fortunei* hort. *ex* Miq., non Lindl.

JAPANESE HOLLY. BOX-LEAVED HOLLY. From Japan, Korea, the S Kuriles, S Sakhalin, Taiwan, the Philippines; disjunctly in Fukien (Fujian) China, and the Himalayas. Named in 1784. Introduced in 1860 by Siebold to Holland. A variable species; hundreds of cultivars are detailed in a 1992 USDA checklist. Generally a bush, rarely a small tree. Common. More like BOXWOOD (*Buxus sempervirens*) than like other HOLLIES. Leaves ½"–1½" (2"), dark green, bluntly toothed (hence the name *crenata*). Flowers in May or June. Berries black, solitary, ¼"–⅓", short stalked. Record: 22' × 1'0" Seattle, WA (1993; *pl.* 1950); 18' × 1'6" × 19' Tacoma, WA (1992).

I. Dahoon—see I. Cassine

I. dipyrena Wall.

HIMALAYAN HOLLY. From the E Himalayas, Upper Burma and W China. Named in 1820. Introduced in 1840. Not known in North American cultivation until ≤1944; nearly all here date from after 1957. Very rare. Twigs green or purplish. Leaves 2"–5" long, to 1¾" wide, usually rather dull, with fine spines; stem purplish. Young growth often purplish. Flowers pale green. Berries ⅓"–⁷⁄₁₆" long; usually containing 2 seeds (*di-pyrena* means 2 seeded—most *Ilex* bear more than 2 seeds). Somewhat tender, but tolerates frost and occasional severe freezes. Records: 56' × 4'11" Leonardslee, Sussex, England (1987); 54' × 5'8" Linton Park, Kent, England (1984); 26' tall Seattle, WA (1993; *pl.* 1959); in the wild, trunks measure as large as 16'0" around.

I. 'Doctor Kassab'

(*I. cornuta* × *I. Pernyi*)
= *I. cornuta* 'Dr. Kassab'

Named in 1965 after its originator, Dr. Joseph Kassab (1908–1991) of Wallingford, PA. Compact narrow conical to columnar 20' tall. Leaves spiny, ≤1⅔" long. Berries bright red.

I. Ebony Magic™ PP 5004 (1983)
= I. Aquifolium Ebony Magic™

Introduced by Willoway nursery of Avon, OH. Vigorous pyramid to 20' tall. Twigs bluish-black. Leaves dark, glossy. Male and female clones sold. Berries deep orange-red, ½". Likely an I. × Meserveæ hybrid.

I. 'Edward J. Stevens'—see I. 'Nellie R. Stevens'

I. 'Emily Bruner'
(I. cornuta 'Burford' × I. latifolia)

Discovered in 1960 by Mrs. A.C. (Emily) Bruner of Knoxville, TN. A 'Burford' seedling from a chance I. latifolia pollinization. 'Emily Bruner' was the best female of several that arose; the best male was named Ilex 'James Swan'—at whose Swan Bakery the cross had occurred. Introduced ≤1967–68. A vigorous large shrub or small tree 12'–20' tall. Leaves ca. 4"–5" long, dark to medium green, glossy, coarsely toothed but not spiny. Berries ⁵⁄₁₆" long, abundant, in large clusters.

I. Fargesii—see I. ciliospinosa

I. ficoidea—see I. bioritensis

I. Fortunei—see I. crenata

I. Fosterii—see I. × attenuata 'Fosteri'

I. Hendersonii—see I. × atlaclerensis 'Hendersonii'

I. Hodginsii—see I. × atlaclerensis 'Hodginsii'

I. 'Hollowell'
(I. cornuta × I. Aquifolium)

Introduced ≤1964. Rare. Named for Eugene A. Hollowell (1900–1977) of Port Republic, MD. Intensely dark, very glossy leaves, untoothed or with some scattered spines mostly near the apex; to 3¾" × 2". A definite tree, to 20' tall or more. Male. Of the same parentage are Ilex 'Edward J. Stevens' (male) and Ilex 'Nellie R. Stevens' (female).

I. integra Th. ex J.A. Murr.
= Othera japonica Th.
= Ilex Othera Spreng.

MOCHI TREE. From China, Japan, the Ryukyus, and Korea. Named in 1784, from Latin integer, whole or entire, not lobed or toothed; referring to the spineless, blunt tipped leaves. Mochi is a Japanese name. Introduced in 1864 by C.J. Maximowicz to St. Petersburg. In North America since ≤1896. Common. A shrub or small, usually multitrunked tree, at most 40' tall in cultivation. Although Korean strains are hardier, the commonly grown stock has proved cold-tender, especially when young, and thrives only in the Southeast and Pacific Coast. Leaves 1½"–4" long, bright green to dark green, blunt and utterly untoothed. Flowers yellowish-green, in February–April. Berries usually large and pale red, ⅓"–¾" long, short-stemmed. Some specimens makes deep red berries, and in Korea a yellow-berried variant is known. Overall, the tree is most notable for its lovely foliage, and males tend to be superior ornamentals. Record: 82' × 20'7" Sohuksan, Korea (1985).

I. integra 'Green Shadow'
Introduced <1983 by Brookside Gardens of Maryland. Variegated creamy-white, some pink on new growth.

I. 'James Swan'—see I. 'Emily Bruner'

I. × Koehneana Loes.
(I. Aquifolium × I. latifolia)

First reported in Florence, Italy; introduced ≤1890s. Named in 1919, after Bernhard Adalbert Emil Koehne (1848–1918) a prominent German botanist and dendrologist. An excellent hybrid combining surprising cold-hardiness with bold leaves. Leaves 4"–7" long, armed on each side with 8–17 small spiny teeth. Information is spotty on the cultivars, since they are rare and little known. As they multiply and are planted, identification will be problematic.

I. × Koehneana 'Agena'
Named in 1991 by the U.S. National Arboretum, Washington, D.C. Originally received in 1962 from Duncan & Davies nursery of New Zealand. Leaf to 5¾" × 2½", each side edged with up to 12 short spiny teeth. Berries to ⅝" long. Extremely vigorous; more so than the other 6 Koehneana clones in the arboretum.

I. × Koehneana 'Ajax'
Named in 1991 by the U.S. National Arboretum, Washington, D.C. The clone had originally been received in 1960 as "Ilex Perado" from Hillier nursery of England. Leaf to 5" × 3", each side edged with 9–17 short spiny teeth. Growth vigorous and rapid. Male.

I. × Koehneana 'Chestnut Leaf'
Raised in France. Very rare in North America. Teeth up to 14 per side. Both male and female clones are called by this name.

I. × *Koehneana* 'Chieftain'

Named in 1967 by S.H. McClean of Towson, MD. Leaves light green, flat, with 8–10 short spines per side. Male; flowers profuse.

I. × *Koehneana* 'Dangerfield'—see I. × *Koehneana* 'Wirt L. Winn'

I. × *Koehneana* 'Hohman'

Introduced <1991.

I. × *Koehneana* 'Jade'

Named in 1967 by the U.S. National Arboretum, Washington, D.C. Leaves very dark green. Male.

I. × *Koehneana* 'Lassie'

Registered in 1970 by S.H. McClean of Towson, MD.

I. × *Koehneana* 'Ruby'

Named in 1967 by the U.S. National Arboretum, Washington, D.C. Leaves very dark green, margins wavy.

I. × *Koehneana* 'San José'

= I. 'San José (Hybrid)'

Introduced in 1955–56 by W.B. Clarke nursery of San José, CA, at which time it was stated to be *I. atlaclerensis* 'Wilsonii' × *I. sikkimensis*. Although a bold tree, it has been much confused with the spindly bush *Ilex* × *aquipernyi* 'San José'. Leaves gigantic (to 7⅛" × 3¼") with as many as 14 short teeth per side. Self-fertile. Berries to 7/16" long on stalks equally long. Twigs and leaf stems hairy. Habit bolt upright, sparse with long branching at first, eventually dense in age, to 35' tall or more. Berries still red and showy into mid-August.

I. × *Koehneana* 'Wirt L. Winn'

= I. × *Koehneana* 'Dangerfield'
= I. 'Wirt L. Winn'

Introduced ≤1965. Registered in 1966 by Wendell Winn. Developed in Winn's nursery of Norfolk, VA. Dark CHESTNUT-like leaves to 5¼" × 2½", armed by up to 11 short spiny teeth per side. Berries slightly longer than broad (to ⅜"), orange-red, in dense clusters near shoot ends.

I. *latifolia* Th. *ex* J.A. Murr.

= I. *Tarajo* hort. ex Goepp.

TARAJO (HOLLY). LUSTERLEAF HOLLY. MAGNOLIA LEAF HOLLY. From E China, and Japan. Named in 1784, from Latin *latus*, broad, and *folium*, a leaf. Introduced by Siebold to Holland between 1829 and 1840. In North American commerce since 1897. Uncommon. Remarkable for its large, dark, usually glossy leaves, recalling EVERGREEN MAGNOLIA (*Magnolia grandiflora*). Although tolerant of some freezing, it needs summer heat to luxuriate. Leaf to 9¾" × 3⅞", can be wholly untoothed, but is usually toothed but never jaggedly spiny except on suckers. Flowers from March to June, greenish or yellow, not whitish like those of most *Ilex*. Berries salmon-pink, ⅓", short-stemmed in dense clusters. In less than ideal conditions it is a stiff shrub of yellowish cast. Few in North America are more than 40' tall. Record: 65' × 6'2" Anhwei, China (1925).

I. *latifolia* 'Lustgarten'

Developed ca. 1950 by Baier Lustgarten nursery of Long Island, NY. Described by that firm as "the hardiest of all *Ilex*." Upright with deep green foliage and elegant appearance."

I. *laurifolia* 'Colburn'—see I. × *atlaclerensis* 'Colburn'

I. *Lawsoniana*—see I. × *atlaclerensis* 'Lawsoniana'

I. *maderensis*—see I. × *altaclerensis* 'Maderensis' and I. *Perado*

I. *maderensis* 'Medio Picta' (Milkmaid)—see I. *Aquifolium* 'Argentea Medio-picta'

I. 'Mary Nell'

= I. 'CB 10' × I. *latifolia*
(I. 'Red Delight' × I. *latifolia*)

Originated in 1962, and named in 1981 by Tom Dodd nursery of Semmes, AL. Named after Mary Nell McDaniel, wife of Dr. J.C. McDaniel (1912–1982) of the University of Illinois, Urbana. Leaves extremely glossy, to 4" × 1¾", margins with many spines. Berries in clusters, long remaining red and showy, to ⅜" wide.

I. × *Meserveæ* S.Y. Hu
(*I. Aquifolium* × *I. rugosa*)

BLUE HOLLY. Raised by Mrs. F. Leighton (Kathleen) Meserve of Long Island, NY. Named in 1970. A series of dark-twigged, dark-foliaged, hardy shrubs, the largest, **Blue Stallion®** or 'Mesan' PP 4804 (1982) is the most vigorous, to 16' × 12' wide.

I. monstrosa—see *I. Aquifolium* 'Monstrosa'

I. Mundyi—see *I.* × *altaclerensis* 'Mundyi'

I. myrtifolia—see *I. Cassine* var. *myrtifolia*

I. myrtifolia 'Steed's'—see *I. Cassine* 'Uncle Herb'

I. myrtifolia 'Uncle Herb'—see *I. Cassine* 'Uncle Herb'

I. 'Nellie R. Stevens'
(*I. Aquifolium* × *I. cornuta*)
= *I. cornuta* 'Nellie R. Stevens'

Discovered at the home of Eunice P. Highley in Oxford, MD. Propagated in 1952. In commerce since ≤1955. Named for Nellie R. Stevens, its original owner, an aunt of Mrs. Highley. Very popular. A small tree, 20'–40' tall. Durable; drought resistant; hardier than *I. cornuta*. Leaves often attractively puckered; to 3⅜" × 1⅝", with several big spines. Berries to ½" long, bright orange-red, borne at an early age. (Males of the same parentage are 'Edward J. Stevens' and 'Hollowell'.)

I. nobilis—see *I.* × *altaclerensis* 'Nobilis'

I. Oldhamii—see *I. purpurea*

I. opaca Ait.

AMERICAN HOLLY. WHITE HOLLY. From the eastern and southern U.S., mostly along the coast. The heyday of AMERICAN HOLLY culture was from the 1940s into the '60s. The name *opaca* means opaque or dull, referring to the leaf surface as contrasted to that of ENGLISH HOLLY (*I. Aquifolium*). Leaf 1½"–5¾", spiny. Flowers appear on new growth in May or June. Berries ¼"–½". Wherever *I. Aquifolium* thrives, it is preferred to *I. opaca*. But *I. opaca* is lovely in its own right and far more cold-hardy. Still, the existence of more than 1,000 cultivar names is preposterous, as few are really distinctive. In the following pages only 79 are allowed, and even that is perhaps

too liberal. Some of those included will surely be found to be of hybrid origin and will later be reclassified as *I.* × *attenuata* cultivars. For details on hundreds of others, consult the 1973 **International Checklist of Cultivated Ilex, Part 1,** *Ilex opaca.* All clones are female unless the text states "male." Records: 100' × 5'8" West Feliciana Parish, LA (<1921); 99' × 8'2" Congaree Swamp, SC (1978); 74' × 9'11" Chambers County, AL (1987); 72' × 11'1" Pamlico County, NC (1951); 53' × 13'4" × 61' near Hardin, TX (<1961).

I. opaca 'Arden'

Discovered in 1922 at Arden, DE, by G. Nearing. Introduced in 1926 by Arden nursery. Common. Easily propagated. Of good growing habit (develops a central leader as a young plant), handsome appearance and wonderful fruiting qualities. Berries elongated.

I. opaca 'Beverly'—see *I. opaca* 'Bountiful'

I. opaca 'Big Mack'

Introduced <1968. Berries very large and abundant.

I. opaca 'Big Red'

Selected and introduced in 1937 from southern New Jersey, by E. Dilatush of Robbinsville, NJ. Leaves dark. Berries large, profuse.

I. opaca 'Bittersweet'

Introduced in 1942 by E. Dilatush of Robbinsville, NJ. Dilatush got it from Dr. P.W. Zimmerman at Yonkers, NY, who in turn obtained it from Massachusetts. Berries turn almost overnight from green to orange in late October, and then turn red in December.

I. opaca 'Bladen Maiden'

Originated <1959 on an old estate in Bladen County, NC. Selected and named by YELLOWBERRY HOLLY expert Jesse D. Rankin (1911–1987) of Salisbury, NC. Berries very large, saffron-yellow (see *I. opaca* f. *xanthocarpa*).

I. opaca 'Bountiful'
= *I. opaca* 'Beverly'

Original tree in Beverly, NJ. Introduced in 1942 by E. Dilatush of Robbinsville, NJ. Habit compact and formal. Leaves dark green, spiny. Heavy bearer. Hardy in the north.

I. opaca 'Boyce Thompson'—see *I. opaca* f. *xanthocarpa*

I. opaca 'Bradshaw'

A seedling of *I. opaca* 'Delia Bradley' selected and introduced ca. 1935 by H. Hohman of Kingsville nursery, Maryland. Leaf large, very dark, well-spined. Heavy fruiter. Berries a good red, usually in clusters.

I. opaca 'Brilliantissima'—see I. opaca 'George E. Hart'

I. opaca 'Brown no. 9'—see I. opaca 'Jersey Knight'

I. opaca 'Calloway'—see I. opaca f. xanthocarpa

I. opaca 'Canary'

Introduced ca. 1938–39 from North Carolina by E. Dilatush of Robbinsville, NJ. Perhaps the most common yellowberry cultivar (see *I. opaca* f. *xanthocarpa*).

I. opaca 'Cardinal'

Selected in Massachusetts by E. Dilatush of Robbinsville, NJ. Introduced ≤1936. Dilatush said: "absolutely my most valuable holly." Compact and slow. Foliage ordinary. Very heavy bearer. Hardy in the north.

I. opaca 'Carrie'—see I. opaca f. xanthocarpa

I. opaca 'Cecil Yellow'—see I. opaca f. xanthocarpa

I. opaca 'Cheerful'

Selected and named ca. 1928 by H. Hohman of Kingsville nursery in Maryland. Leaf dark above, lighter beneath, with whitish-green teeth. Berries large, cherry-red.

I. opaca 'Clark'

Selected ca. 1930 by Miss E.C. White of Whitesbog, NJ. Leaf shiny, deeply toothed. Excellent for hedges. Berries very bright red.

I. opaca 'Croonenburg'

Discovered on the estate of Aristides Croonenberg (a farmer, born in Belgium in 1848), near Norfolk, VA. Introduced in 1934. Leaf to 3¾" × 2½" with 7–9 spines; very dark green, not the usual yellowish tint. Growth slow and columnar. Bisexual.

I. opaca 'Cumberland'

Selected in 1939 by C. Wolf of Millville, NJ. Named in 1949. Foliage very glossy. Berries bright red, large, prolific.

I. opaca 'Dan Fenton'

Originated as a 1961 seedling of *I. opaca* 'Maurice River'. From Rutgers University of New Jersey. Named after HOLLY enthusiast Daniel G. Fenton of Millville, NJ. Introduced in 1988. Leaves exceptionally glossy, unusually dark. Vigor high. Tree dense.

I. opaca 'David'

Introduced in 1950 by C. Wolf of Millville, NJ. Tree dense. Leaves dark, small. A good male pollinator.

I. opaca 'Delia Bradley'

Selected ca. 1928 at Lorely, MD. Introduced ca. 1930 by Kingsville nursery of Maryland. Dense upright pyramidal. Fruits even when young. Hardy north. Leaf nearly flat, medium-size. Berries dark glossy red, abundant.

I. opaca 'East Palatka'—see I. × attenuata 'East Palatka'

I. opaca 'Eleanor'

Selected ca. 1939 in Cumberland County, NJ, by C. Wolf of Millville, NJ. Named and introduced in 1944. Leaf thick, convex, dark. Berries abundant, round.

I. opaca 'Emily'

Found <1947 at West Barnstable, Cape Cod, MA, by W. Wheeler and J.M. Batchelor. Named after Wheeler's wife. Berries huge, to ½" wide. Leaves smaller than those of many cultivars, and inclined to curve (as though *I. cornuta* genes had a role).

I. opaca 'Fallaw'—see I. opaca f. xanthocarpa

I. opaca 'Farage'

('Forage')

Distributed <1947 by Miss E.C. White of Whitesbog, NJ. The name is a contraction of "left garage" because the original tree at New Lisbon, NJ, was moved to the left of the garage on the White property. Leaves nearly 2 times as long as wide, deep green, glossy, nicely toothed. Berries bright red, shiny, abundant. Tree strong, broadly spreading.

I. opaca "Femina"

This merely signifies a female.

I. opaca 'Fosteri'—see I. × attenuata 'Fosteri'

I. opaca 'Frierson Golden'—see *I. opaca* 'Golden Fleece'

I. opaca 'Fruitland (Nursery)'—see *I. opaca* f. *xanthocarpa*

I. opaca 'Galleon Gold'—see *I. opaca* f. *xanthocarpa*

I. opaca 'George E. Hart'
= *I. opaca* 'Brilliantissima'
= *I. opaca* 'Pyramidalis'
Selected ca. 1945 in New York. Introduced by George E. Hart nursery of Malvern, NY. Very dense pyramidal. Leaf small, dark, abundantly spined. Profuse clustered brilliant red berries.

I. opaca 'Golden Fleece'
= *I. opaca* 'Frierson Golden'
Found in South Carolina <1940. Named in 1948 by Brownell Holly Farms of Milwaukie, OR. The synonym refers to Dr. William C. Frierson of Westminster, NC. Exceedingly tender, susceptible to sunburn. A parallel of *Ilex Aquifolium* 'Flavescens'. A yellowberry cultivar has also been sold as 'Golden Fleece'.

I. opaca 'Goldie'—see *I. opaca* f. *xanthocarpa*

I. opaca 'Greenleaf'
= *I. opaca* 'Peace'
Introduced ≤1969 by Monrovia nursery of California. Fast growing. Leaves bright green, spiny. Berries bright red. Neither 'Greenleaf' or 'Peace' was sanctioned in the 1973 International *Ilex opaca* checklist. It may be an *I. × attenuata* cultivar.

I. opaca 'Hampton'
Selected at Hampton, VA. Introduced ≤1942 by Kingsville nursery of Maryland. One received that year by the Seattle arboretum is healthy, and the biggest of all two dozen *I. opaca* trees in the collection (38' × 2'5" in 1994). Leaf medium, prominently spined, crinkled. Very attractive texture.

I. opaca 'Happy New Year'—see *I. opaca* 'Old Leather Leaf'

I. opaca 'Hedgeholly'
Selected near Porterwood, WV. Introduced ≤1947 by Bosley nursery of Mentor, OH. Habit dense and broad, useful for hedging. Good berry display.

I. opaca 'Helen Mitchell'—see *I. opaca* f. *xanthocarpa*

I. opaca 'Hookstra(w)'—see *I. opaca* 'Old Heavy Berry'

I. opaca 'Howard'
Originally found on the Howard farm near MacClenny, FL, and named by Dr. H.H. Hume of Florida. Introduced ≤1933. One of the most common cultivars. Vigorous, compact. Leaves glossy, sparsely spined. Berries abundant, bright red. Somewhat tender in Pennsylvania. Possibly a *Cassine* hybrid (i.e., *Ilex × attenuata*).

I. opaca 'Hume'—see *I. × attenuata* 'Hume'

I. opaca 'Hume No. 2'—see *I. × attenuata* 'Hume No. 2'

I. opaca 'Jersey Delight'
An intentional 1958 *opaca* hybrid ('Old Heavy Berry' × 'Isaiah') produced at Rutgers University of New Jersey. Introduced in 1989. Dense, symmetrical, with very reflective foliage. A male.

I. opaca 'Jersey Knight'
= *I. opaca* 'Brown no. 9'
= *I. opaca* 'Judge Brown no. 9'
Selected in 1945 at the home of Judge Thomas Brown of Locust, NJ. Named in 1965. Introduced by Rutgers University of NJ. Common. Leaves dark. Winter hardy. Male.

I. opaca 'Jersey Princess'
Released in 1976 for the U.S. Bicentennial by the Holly Society of America and Rutgers University of NJ. Leaf very glossy, dark. A good cropper. Berries vivid red.

I. opaca 'Johnson'
Found in 1934–35 near Sunnyburn, PA (on the Johnson farm) by J.B. Gable. Introduced ≤1940. Leaves and berries large. Very hardy.

I. opaca 'Joyce'
Selected <1940 in New Jersey by Miss E.C. White. Introduced ≤1942. Leaves dark, evenly toothed and glossy. Growth rapid. Berries very brilliant red.

I. opaca 'Judge Brown'
Selected ca. 1945 at the home of Judge Thomas Brown of Locust, NJ. Introduced in 1947. Leaf dark green, glossy. Berries scarlet, large, egg-shaped, shiny.

I. opaca 'Judge Brown no. 9'—see *I. opaca* 'Jersey Knight'

I. opaca 'King Christmas'—see *I. opaca* 'Old Leather Leaf'

I. opaca 'Knight'
Selected ca. 1930 at Silver Spring, MD, by Dr. A. Quaintance, who gave it to Dr. Paul Knight at the University of Maryland, who gave it to Ten Oaks nursery of Clarksville, MD, who introduced it ≤1950. Their description: "Perfect pyramid straight as a Tulip Tree. Leaf well-toothed. Berries deep red, hang all winter."

I. opaca 'Lacquerberry'
Introduced ≤1990s. Berries very large and glossy.

I. opaca 'Lady Alice'
A New Jersey selection by C. Wolf of Millville, NJ. Introduced ≤1950. Leaf thick, large, dark and glossy. Twigs slender. Vigorous growth. Berries red, large.

I. opaca 'Lake City'—see *I. × attenuata* 'Lake City'

I. opaca 'Leatherleaf'—see *I. opaca* 'Old Leather Leaf'

I. opaca 'Longwood Gardens'—see *I. opaca* f. *xanthocarpa*

I. opaca 'Mae'
From New Jersey. Selected <1940 by Miss E.C. White of Whitesbog, NJ. Introduced ≤1947. Narrow columnar. Branches slender. Berries only average in size but plentiful.

I. opaca 'Manatico'—see *I. opaca* 'Menatico'

I. opaca 'Manig'
From New Jersey. Selected <1940 by Miss E.C. White of Whitesbog, NJ. Introduced ≤1942. Leaf dark, glossy, with large spines. Leaves closely spaced. Berries bright red, abundant, unusually big.

I. opaca 'Maple Swamp'
('Swamp Maple')
Introduced ≤1948–49 by Tingle nursery of Pittsville, MD. Growth compact. Berries bright red.

I. opaca 'Marion'
('Merion')
Selected in 1935–36 by H. Hume in Marion County,

FL. Introduced ≤1947. Leaf twisted, pale green unlike the *I. opaca* usual color. Berries golden-yellow (see *I. opaca* f. *xanthocarpa*).

I. opaca 'Maryland'—see *I. opaca* f. *xanthocarpa*

I. opaca "Mascula"
This merely signifies a male.

I. opaca 'Maurice River'
Selected in 1939 from Maurice River, Cumberland County, NJ, by C. Wolf of Millville, NJ. Introduced ≤1949. Leaf dark, stiff, curved, glossy. Berries bright red, globose.

I. opaca 'Maxwell Point'
Originally Discovered at Maxwell Point, MD, by nurseryman H.J. Hohman. Introduced ≤1947. Fast growth to a large, dense tree. Leaves dark, large, very spiny. Berries profuse.

I. opaca 'Menatico'
('Manatico')
Selected <1939 in Salem County, NJ, by C. Wolf of Millville, NJ. Introduced ≤1949. Leaves closely spaced, stiff and well colored. Berries very abundant, bright red.

I. opaca 'Merion'—see *I. opaca* 'Marion'

I. opaca 'Merry Christmas'
Found by E. Dilatush ca. 1940 near Bayville, NJ. The best HOLLY he knew. Very common in cultivation. Rapid, compact, fruitful and hardy. Foliage excellent; leaves dark, thick and glossy.

I. opaca 'Miss Helen'
Selected by S.H. McClean in 1936 south of Baltimore, MD. Introduced ≤1947. Named after Mrs. Stewart (Helen) McClean (1904–1989) of Towson, MD. Conical, dense. Berries early-ripening, abundant, big. Very adaptable; dependable in colder regions.

I. opaca 'Morgan Gold'—see *I. opaca* f. *xanthocarpa*

I. opaca 'Morris Arboretum'—see *I. opaca* f. *xanthocarpa*

I. opaca 'Mrs. Santa'
A Georgia seedling selected ca. 1924 at Guyancourt nursery of Guyancourt, DE. Introduced ca. 1933.

Leaves medium-sized, curved, glossy. Berries bright red, spectacularly large. A good grower; superb for hedging.

I. opaca 'Mrs. Sarver'—see *I.* × *attenuata* 'Rosalind Sarver'

I. opaca 'Old Heavy Berry'
= *I. opaca* 'Hookstra(w)'
Selected ca. 1923 by E. Dilatush and D. Leach, on the Hookstra estate of Burlington, NJ. Named by residents of Burlington, NJ. Introduced ≤1937. One of the most common cultivars. Very highly regarded. Vigorous; heavy bearer. Leaf large, bright green and exceptionally glossy; concave. Notably hardy.

I. opaca 'Old Leather Leaf'
= *I. opaca* 'Leatherleaf'
= *I. opaca* 'Happy New Year'
= *I. opaca* 'King Christmas'
Selected in 1929 by E. Dilatush. Introduced in 1947. Leaf large, heavily textured. Bushy, broad, very leafy, of slow growth. Male.

I. opaca 'Osa'
Selected by Miss E.C. White of Whitesbog, NJ. Introduced ≤1947. Leaves stiff, glossy, curved, with many short spines. Fruit abundant.

I. opaca 'Peace'—see *I. opaca* 'Greenleaf'

I. opaca 'Princeton Gold'—see *I. opaca* f. xanthocarpa

I. opaca 'Pyramidalis'—see *I. opaca* 'George E. Hart'

I. opaca 'Red Velvet'
Selected in 1953 by C. Wolf of Millville, NJ. Introduced ≤1956. Leaves deep green, fairly glossy. Berries bright red.

I. opaca 'Richards'
Introduced in 1949 by the USDA. From Harmony Hall of Maryland. Leaves very large, dark, glossy. Berries big. Vigorous.

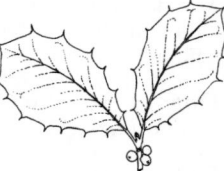

I. opaca 'Rosalind Sarver'—see *I.* × *attenuata* 'Rosalind Sarver'

I. opaca 'Saint Mary'—see *I. opaca* 'St. Mary'

I. opaca 'Saint Stephen'—see *I. opaca* 'St. Stephen'

I. opaca 'Satyr Hill'
From S.H. McLean's nursery of Satyr Hill Road, Baltimore, MD. Introduced ≤1960. The original tree was 30' tall, compact and pyramidal, with large red berries.

I. opaca 'Savannah'—see *I.* × *attenuata* 'Savannah'

I. opaca 'Skookum'
Introduced ≤1947 by Kingsville nursery of Maryland. Tree broad, dense, with lush foliage. Leaf concave, rich dark olive green, spiny.

I. opaca 'Slim Jane'
A selection by C. Wolf of Millville, NJ. Named in 1949. Leaf thick, narrow, dark, glossy. Berries abundant, very large, orange-red. (The male counterpart is 'Slim Jim'.)

I. opaca 'Splendorberry'
Introduced in 1958. Originated by E.E. Walters of Neptune, NJ. Strong, straight growing. Berries big, deep red.

I. opaca 'St. Mary'
('Saint Mary')
Selected by W. Wheeler from the island of St. Mary in Osterville Bay, MA. Introduced ≤1947. Dense, compact, even dwarf. Leaf bright green, small, twisted at the apex, sharply toothed. Berries abundant, medium-sized, bright red, produced singly, borne when tree is young. Very hardy.

I. opaca 'St. Stephen'
('Saint Stephen')
Selected ca. 1928 and introduced <1948 by Kingsville nursery of Maryland. It was described as "a sister seedling of *I. opaca* 'Delia Bradley' and a heavy fruiter."

I. opaca 'Steward's Cream Crown'—see *I. op.* 'Steward's Silver Crown'

I. opaca 'Steward's Silver Crown' PP 4367 (1979)
= *I. opaca* 'Steward's Cream Crown'
Originated as a bud mutation first observed in 1957. Named after T. Linwood Steward, Jr. Average red berries. Leaves silver variegated.

I. opaca f. *subintegra* Weatherby

SPINELESS AMERICAN-HOLLY. Named in 1921, for leaves that are "nearly entire or spineless." Nurseries have rarely employed the name. A clone circulated under this name has glossy rather small leaves, with few spines, is vigorous, open-branched and female. Males have also been sold.

I. opaca 'Swamp Maple'—see *I. opaca* 'Maple Swamp'

I. opaca 'Taber no. 3'

Introduced ≤1933 by Glen St. Mary nursery of Florida. Self-fertile. Common. Narrowly pyramidal, even fastigiate. Leaf bright green, evenly toothed. Berries bright red, profuse, usually persist one year.

I. opaca 'Toner'

Selected ≤1942 near Toner Hall at St. Elizabeth's Hospital, Washington, D.C. Introduced <1951. Good form. Fine foliage. Leaf medium-size, of a pleasing green. Berries bright red.

I. opaca 'Trisco'

Introduced ≤1945 by Kingsville nursery of Maryland. Vigorously upright, becoming broad. Attractive foliage and berries.

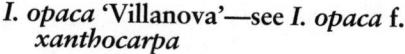

I. opaca 'Villanova'—see *I. opaca* f. *xanthocarpa*

I. opaca 'West Virginia'

Introduced ≤1986. Developed by O.M. Neal at the University of West Virginia. Fast growing.

I. opaca 'William Hawkins'

Named after its discoverer. In commerce ≤1990s. Male. Leaves slender, long, with prominent spines. Dense and shrubby.

I. opaca 'Wyetta'

Originated in southern New Jersey, Named in 1964. Fast, dense, compact large pyramid. Leaves shiny, strongly spined, dark. Berries prolific, large, shiny red.

I. opaca f. *xanthocarpa* Rehd.

= *I. Aquifolium baccis flavis* Walter

YELLOWBERRY AMERICAN HOLLY. First named in 1788. Cultivated since 1811 in England, since <1900 in the U.S. More than 40 clones have been named, such as: 'Bladen Maiden', 'Boyce Thompson', 'Calloway', 'Canary', 'Carrie', 'Cecil Yellow', 'Fallaw, 'Fruitland (Nursery)', 'Galleon Gold', 'Goldie', 'Helen Mitchell', 'Longwood Gardens', 'Marion', 'Maryland', 'Morgan Gold', 'Morris Arboretum', 'Princeton Gold', 'Villanova', 'Yellow Virginia Giant'.

I. opaca 'Yellow Fruit'—see *I. opaca* f. *xanthocarpa*

I. opaca 'Yellow Virginia Giant'—see *I. opaca* f. *xanthocarpa*

I. Othera—see *I. integra*

I. pedunculosa Miq.

LONGSTALK HOLLY. From China, Japan, and Taiwan. Named in 1866. Introduced by C. Sargent in 1892 or 1893. Common. Leaf 1"–3" (4¾") long, thin, wavy and wholly untoothed. Flowers in June. Berries ¼", on slender stalks as long as 2³⁄₁₆". Usually a large floppy shrub; can be a multitrunked small tree to 30' tall. Its amazingly soft, PEAR-like foliage is sometimes tinted purplish.

I. pedunculosa 'Vleck'

Introduced ≤1994 by Beaver Creek nursery of Poplar Grove, IL. Notably hardy.

I. Perado Ait.

= *I. maderensis* Lam.
= *I. Perado* var. *maderensis* (Lam.) Loes.
= *I. canariensis* Poir.

MADEIRA HOLLY— See also *I. × altaclerensis* 'Maderensis'. From Madeira. Introduced by J. Gordon to England in 1760. Named in 1789. In North American commerce ≤1925. Rare, largely because it is cold-tender. A large shrub or 50' tree. Leaf 2"–4" long. Berries ca. ⅜". Crossed with ENGLISH HOLLY (*I. Aquifolium*) this yields the HIGHCLERE HOLLIES (*I. × altaclerensis*). Indeed, sometimes HIGHCLERE cultivars (such as 'Belgica') have been sold as *I. Perado*.

I. Perado var. *balearica*—see *I. × altaclerensis* 'Balearica'

I. Perado var. *maderensis*—see *I. Perado*

I. Perado 'Maderensis'—see *I. × altaclerensis* 'Maderensis'

I. Perado ssp. *platyph[ylla* (Webb & Berth.) Tutin

= *I. Perado* var. *platyphylla* (Webb & Berth.) Loes.
= *I. platyphylla* Webb & Berth.
= *I. Aquifolium* 'Canary Island'

CANARY ISLAND HOLLY. From the Canary Islands. Introduced to England in 1842. Hardier than typical *I. Perado*. Leaves to 6" × 3" or even 8" × 4½", short-toothed. The name from Greek *platys*, wide or broad, and *phyllon*, a leaf.

I. Pernyi Franch.

PERNY HOLLY. From central and W China. Discovered in 1858 by Abbé Paul Hubert Perny (1818–1907), a French missionary, the first botanical explorer of Kweichow province. Named in 1883. Introduced by E. Wilson for Veitch nursery of England in 1900. In North America since ≤1912; in commerce here since ≤1935. Common. Usually a gawky bush, virtually never a tree. Leaves ¾"–1½" long, to ¾" wide, with 2–3 spines on each side; stemless. Flowers pale yellow, in April or May. Berry ¼"–⅓" wide and nearly stalkless. Record: 36' × 1'5" Pollok House, Strathclyde, Scotland (1986).

I. Pernyi 'Brilliant'—see *I.* 'Brilliant'

I. Pernyi 'Veitchii'
= *I. Pernyii* var. *Veitchii* (Veitch) Rehd.
= *I. Veitchii* Veitch

Introduced to England with the original *I. Pernyi* in 1900. A male clone named in 1912 after Veitch nursery. In North American commerce ≤1938. Rarer and much larger than typical *I. Pernyi*. Leaves short-stemmed, very glossy (wet look) and "quarter-sized" (to 2⅜" × 1¼") whereas typical *Pernyi* has "dime-sized" leaves of average gloss. Also more treelike. One in Seattle is 30' tall, 22' wide (1992; *pl.* 1945). Some nurseries have sold *I. × aquipernyi* under this name, and indeed 'Veitchii' resembles it far more than it does typical *I. Pernyi*. See also *I. bioritsensis*.

I. platyphylla—see *I. Perado* ssp. *platyphylla*

I. platyphylla 'Maderensis'—see *I. × atlaclerensis* 'Maderensis'

I. platyphylla 'Nigrescens'—see *I. × atlaclerensis* 'Nigrescens'

I. purpurea Haask.
= *I. chinensis* Hu 1949, non Sims
= *I. Oldhamii* Miq.

KASHI HOLLY. From China and Japan. Named in 1844. The epithet *purpurea* likely referring to its lilac-lavender flowers. Introduced to cultivation ≤1900. Extremely rare, being difficult to propagate by cuttings. Leaves narrow, to 5¾" × 2", toothed inconspicuously, not the least bit spiny; very glossy, thin and LAUREL-like. Berries glossy red, to ⅜" long. Crown airy, branches slender; twigs dark. Records: to 50' tall in the wild; 48' × 2'3" Seattle, WA (1994; *pl.* 1941).

I. 'San José (Hybrid)'—see *I. × Koehneana* 'San José'

I. 'September Gem'
(*I. ciliospinosa* × *I. aquipernyi*)

Hybridized in 1957 at the U.S. National Arboretum, Washington, D.C. Released in 1978. At 20 years, the original specimen was only 7' tall and wide. Much slower than most *I. × aquipernyi* specimens, it can become a small tree in ideal conditions, at least in the maritime Pacific Northwest. Leaves to 4¼" × ¾" (usually <2" × ½"), 3 spines per side. Berries ⁷⁄₁₆" wide, red by early September.

I. Shepherdii—see *I. × atlaclerensis* 'Shepherdii'

I. Tarajo—see *I. latifolia*

I. Topeli—see *I. × attenuata*

I. Veitchii—see *I. Pernyi* 'Veitchii'

I. 'Venus'
(*I.* 'Nellie R. Stevens' × *I. latifolia*)

A 1962 cross made at the U.S. National Arboretum, Washington, D.C. Named in 1991. Leaf to 5⅛" × 2½", dark and glossy, edged with 11–13 (19) short blunt spines on each side. Berries to ⁷⁄₁₆" long in tight masses. Its male counterpart is *I.* 'Adonis'.

I. vomitoria Ait.
= *I. Cassine* Walt. 1788, non L. 1753
= *I. caroliniana* Loes. 1891, non Mill. 1768

YAUPON. CASSENA YAUPON. CHRISTMAS BERRY. CASSENA. CASSINA. EMETIC HOLLY. From the southeastern U.S. Coastal Plain. Some native Americans cultivated this tree and used the "Black Drink" ceremonially. The epithet *vomitoria* means causing vomiting: the stimulating brew is emetic if drunk to excess. (See *I. Cassine* for the name CASSENA.) Leaves ½"–1¼" (2"), bluntish and weakly toothed. Flowers in April. Berries ¼" wide, translucent scarlet.

A very adaptable and valuable ornamental. Tolerates sun or shade and poor drainage; drought resistant. Its only drawback is sensitivity to severe cold. Bark pale gray and attractive. Usually multitrunked and often small, it barely qualifies as a tree. Record: 45' × 4'1" Devers, TX (1972).

I. vomitoria 'City of Houston'—see *I. vomitoria* 'Pride of Houston'

I. vomitoria 'Dare County'—see *I. vomitoria* 'Virginia Dare'

I. vomitoria 'Folsom Weeping'
Introduced ca. 1960. A weeping cultivar. Berries red. A small tree.

I. vomitoria 'Gold Top'
Introduced by Woodlanders nursery of Aiken, SC. New growth golden.

I. vomitoria 'Gray's Greenleaf'
An upright spreading small tree. Red berries.

I. vomitoria 'Gray's Weeping'
Introduced <1980. Similar to 'Folsom Weeping'.

I. vomitoria 'Jewel'
Introduced <1976. A cutting-grown female.

I. vomitoria 'Lynn Lowrey'
Named after a plant collector of Conroe, TX. Sold by Tom Dodd nursery of Semmes, AL. Leaf exceptionally big.

I. vomitoria 'Nobilis'
Discovered in the 1930s by Mr. Garee of Noble nursery, Noble, OK. Still in commerce by 1957, but very rare. The one tree in perfect condition among several thousand common YAUPONS badly injured or killed by an unusually severe freeze. Cutting-grown. Leaves slightly thinner in texture and larger than average. Grows fast and is compact.

I. vomitoria f. *pendula* Foret & Solym.
WEEPING YAUPON. Found by Price Magee of Folsom nursery in an area of ca. 80 acres southeast of Folsom, LA. Named in 1960. Common To 30' tall in the wild, of both sexes. In cultivation most 'Folsom Weeping' are no more than 12' tall. A similar weeping cultivar is 'Gray's Weeping'.

I. vomitoria 'Poole's Best'
Introduced <1980. Strong; compact. Fruit abundant.

I. vomitoria 'Pride of Houston'
= *I. vomitoria* 'City of Houston'
Introduced ≤1954–55. Common. Leaves small. A medium-sized shrub. Berries eyecatching red, abundant.

I. vomitoria 'Pyramidalis'
Sold ≤1943 by Greenbrier Farms of Norfolk, VA.

I. vomitoria 'Royal'
Sold (in 1979–80) by Grandview nursery of Youngsville, LA: "a selected seedling."

I. vomitoria 'Saratoga Gold'
Sold by Tom Dodd nursery of Semmes, AL. Berries yellow. Large shrub or very small tree.

I. vomitoria 'Shadow's Female'
Introduced <1980. Large shrub or small tree. Leaves large, dark. Berries red. Hardier than most—surviving -10°F.

I. vomitoria 'Virginia Dare'
= *I. vomitoria* 'Dare County'
Found <1982 by Mr. Barton of Manns Harbor, Dare County, NC. Orange berries.

I. vomitoria 'Wiggins Yellow'
Introduced <1976. Berries yellow.

I. vomitoria 'Will Fleming'
= *I. vomitoria* 'Will's Yaupon'
From Houston, TX. Introduced ≤1992 by Mr. Fleming. Fastigiate. Male.

I. vomitoria 'Will's Yaupon'—see *I. vomitoria* 'Will Fleming'

I. vomitoria 'Yawkeyii'
Found on the South Island Plantation of Thomas A. Yawkey (1903–1976), Georgetown County, SC. Cuttings taken in 1939. Named in 1945. Berries yellow.

I. Wilsonii—see *I.* × *atlaclerensis* 'Wilsonii'

I. 'Wirt L. Winn'—see *I.* × *Koehneana* 'Wirt L. Winn'

Illicium

[ILLICIACEÆ; (allied to MAGNOLIACEÆ) Illicium Family] ca. 40 spp. of broadleaf evergreen shrubs or trees, of warm-temperate or subtropical regions, mostly in SE Asia. Name from Latin *illicio* or *illicere* (to attract, entice, or allure) referring to the pleasant anise-like fragrance. Since these plants are barely cold-hardy and at best grow slowly into small trees, they scarcely deserve inclusion in this book. The following species is not as often grown as the native American *Illicium* species, but is featured because, being foreign, it is less often documented and more likely to arouse wonder. *Illicium* is the only genus in its Family. The most closely related genus is *Magnolia*.

I. anisatum L.

= *I. religiosum* S. & Z.

JAPANESE STAR ANISE. JAPANESE ANISE TREE. ANISEED TREE From S Korea, Japan, the Ryukyus, and Taiwan. Attributions to China result from confusion. Introduced by Siebold to Holland, then probably sent to England ca. 1790. To North America by the 1850s or before, since one was exhibited in December 1851 at the Pennsylvania Horticultural Society as a plant "*new*, and recently introduced." In commerce here since ≤1887. The epithet *anisatum* is from Latin *anisum*, anise, and *-atum*, provided with. It is an incense plant. Leaves glossy green, 2"–4¼" long, sweetly scented when crushed. Flowers from March into May, creamy-white or pale yellow and not remarkably showy. Fruit a star-like cluster of seed capsules. Poisonous—a related species (*I. verum* Hook. fil.) provides the edible star anise). A shrub or small tree to 30' tall; valued for its handsome foliage and perfume. In the maritime Pacific Northwest it performs best as a woodland garden tree. In the Southeast it is less hardy and vigorous than the native American species.

I. anisatum 'Pink Star'

Selected at North Carolina State University Arboretum. New shoots crimson. Flowerbuds distinctly pink.

Ioxylon pomiferum—see *Maclura pomifera*

Juglans

[JUGLANDACEÆ; Walnut Family] 15–20 spp. of deciduous trees (with a few evergreen or shrubby). *Juglans* is contracted from one of the ancient Latin names of *J. regia*; from *Jovis* (of Jupiter) and *glans* (an acorn or nut); the nut of Jupiter. WALNUT from Old English *wealh*, Welshman or foreign, and *hnutu*, nut (the nut from Gaul or Rome as opposed to the native HAZEL). Historically these trees have been grown more for their edible nuts and choice timber than for ornament and shade. But enough of them grace country dwellings, urban park landscapes and front yards that they must be included in a book on landscape trees. Their flowers, tiny, greenish and borne in spikes, are wholly unappealing. The leaves are pinnately compound and often handsome. Fall color is usually a plain yellow at best. A baneful influence known as alleopathy is associated with some species, whereby chemicals released by the trees suppress the growth of most other vegetation. The nuts, although edible and usually delicious, are a mere nuisance when the tree is considered from an ornamental viewpoint. As a whole, *Juglans* are remarkably free from diseases and insect ravages; caterpillars, mistletoe and other minor blemishes do assault some, however. The presence of aged WALNUT trees is noble, and their shade refreshing. The most closely related genus is *Carya* (HICKORY and PECAN).

J. ailantifolia Carr.

= *J. Sieboldiana* Maxim., non Göpp.

= *J. mandshurica* ssp. *Sieboldiana* (Maxim.) Kit.

= *J. cordiformis* Dode var. *ailantifolia* (Carr.) Rehd.

= *J. japonica* hort. (in part)

JAPANESE WALNUT. Japanese: *Kurume. Onigurumi.* From Japan and Sakhalin. Introduced to Europe ≤1852. In North America ≤1860. Common. Named *ailanthifolia* in 1878 (from *Ailanthus*, TREE OF HEAVEN, and *folium*, a leaf). Leaflets (9) 11–17 (21). Husks vary from about 1¼"–1½" wide and roundish, to about 2" long by 1½" wide, felty sticky. Nuts 1¼"–1⅝" long, smoothish or weakly bumpy and pocked. The variable nuts ripen early. The nut flavor, the bark and branching recalls BUTTERNUT (*J. cinerea*), yet the foliage is bolder—some leaves to 3' long. It tends to have smooth bark, the trunk often forks very low into several major sections; the crown grows broader than high. Records: 111' × 9'4" Bois de Boulogne, Paris, France (1982; *pl.* 1852); 75' × 7'5"

× 65½' Sillery, Québec (<1994); 66' × 5'0" × 63' Lisle, IL (1986; *pl.* 1956); 59' × 9'6" × 77' Olympia, WA (1993); 49' × 15'9" × 72' Ferndale, WA (1992); 36' × 37'8" × 95' Waikato, New Zealand (≤1982; *pl.* ca. 1890).

J. *ailantifolia* var. *cordiformis* (Maxim.) Rehd.
= *J. cordiformis* Maxim., non Wangh.
= *J. Allardiana* Dode
= *J. coarctata* Dode
= *J. Lavallei* Dode

HEARTNUT. FLAT WALNUT. Japanese: *Himegurumi*. Introduced in 1862 to Russia; to North America shortly thereafter. Less common than typical JAPANESE WALNUT. Habit and leaflets the same. Nuts 1¼"–1½" long, ±heart-shaped and sharp-pointed, borne in long, dangling clusters; easily cracked. Nut expert L. Geraldi of Illinois said HEARTNUTS were his favorite flavor. Records: 37' × 6'4" × 64' Puyallup, WA (1992); 35' × 10'2" × 65' Paris, WI (1987).

J. *Allardiana*—see J. *ailantifolia* var. *cordiformis*

J. × *Bixbyi* Rehd.
= *J. Sargentii* Sudw.
(*J. cinerea* × *J. ailantifolia*)

This cross was first observed in Indiana ca. 1903, and described in 1919 by nut enthusiast Willard G. Bixby (b. ca. 1869) of Long Island, NY. When BUTTERNUT (*J. cinerea*) is hybridized with HEARTNUT (*J. ailantifolia* var. *cordiformis*), the offspring are called BUART NUTS. Some such seedlings are sold as rootstocks. Overall it is a rare tree known only by nut growers.

J. *californica* S. Wats.

SOUTHERN CALIFORNIA WALNUT. From coastal southern California. Named in 1875. Introduced to cultivation in 1889. Extremely rare. Much confused with *J. Hindsii* (NORTHERN CALIFORNIA BLACK WALNUT). Leaflets (9) 11–15 (19). Husks (⅝") ¾"–1" (1¼"). Nuts ½"–¹⁵⁄₁₆" wide, usually moderately grooved. A small tree, rarely to 30' tall, usually multistemmed. The reported record specimen is suspect in its

gargantuan size—almost certainly a hybrid or another species: 116' × 20'1" near Chico, CA (1972).

J. *californica* var. *Hindsii*—see J. *Hindsii*

J. *cathayensis* Dode
= *J. collapsa* Dode
= *J. Draconis* Dode
= *J. formosana* Hay.

CATHAY WALNUT. CHINESE BUTTERNUT. CHINESE WALNUT. From W and central China, and Taiwan. Introduced between 1899 and 1903. Named in 1909. (Cathay is an old name for China.) Very rare in North America. Leaflets (9) 11–19, the largest 10" long. Husks 1⅞"–2¾" long, felty sticky. Nuts 1¾"–2⅜" long by 1⅝" wide, very jagged and spiny, very much like butternuts. Some recent European references place this species in synonymy under *J. mandshurica*. Its flower spikes are much longer, and nuts too jagged, however; it must be allowed at least varietal status. It grows with immense vigor, bears tropical-looking foliage (leaves to 4¼' long), yet its nuts are a pain, being messy and not the best to eat. Records: 92' tall in Anhwei, China (1925); 76' × 17'8" × 83' Issaquah, WA (1993); 69' × 10'6" × 105' Auburn, WA (1993).

J. *cinerea* L.

BUTTERNUT. WHITE WALNUT. OILNUT. From eastern North America. *Cinerea* refers to ashy gray, the bark's color. Leaflets (9) 11–15 (17). Husks 1½"–3⅜" long, felty sticky. Nuts 1⅜"–2½" long, very deeply grooved and jagged. Compared to its associate the BLACK WALNUT (*J. nigra*), this is a weaker, shorter-lived species, less valued. For all that, it is still well known and common. The trunk is often short, the bark always gray and much less fissured than that of BLACK WALNUT. Its nuts really do taste buttery, and are first to ripen of the North American *Juglans*. As a dye source, this tree yields fawn, gray, and black. BUTTERNUT is particularly stunted in compact, poor, dry soils. In recent years a canker has spread rapidly and killed many specimens. Hybrids with HEARTNUT (see *J. × Bixbyi*) are known as BUART NUTS, and offer superior disease resistance, vigorous growth, and their nuts are easier to crack. Records: to 125' tall in the wild; 102' × 20'8" × 90' Portland, OR (1973;

died in 1984); 96' × 14'11" × 139' Lexington, MI (1985); 80' × 19'10" × 76' Chester, CT (1988); 80' × 18'6" × 104' Eugene, OR (1987).

J. coarctata—see *J. ailantifolia* var. *cordiformis*

J. cordiformis—see *J. ailantifolia* var. *cordiformis*

J. collapsa—see *J. cathayensis*

J. cordiformis var. *ailantifolia*—see *J. ailanthifolia*

J. Draconis—see *J. cathayensis*

J. elæaopyren—see *J. major*

J. formosana—see *J. cathayensis*

J. fraxinifolia—see *Pterocarya fraxinifolia*

J. Hindsii (Jeps. *ex* R.E. Smith) Rehd.
= *J. californica* var. *Hindsii* Jeps.

NORTHERN CALIFORNIA BLACK WALNUT. From central California. Richard Brinsley Hinds (1812–1847), British surgeon of the Royal Navy, interested in plant geography, discovered this species in 1837 on the Sacramento River. Introduced to cultivation in 1878. Rare. Not officially named until 1908. Leaflets (9) 11–19 (23). Husks (1¼") 1½"–1¾" (2") wide, smooth, semi-glossy, light yellow-green. Nuts (⅞") 1"–1⅛" (1½") wide, very smooth and faintly grooved if at all. The foliage is handsome bluish-green, the nut husks bright green in fall. Highly drought resistant. Record: 115' × 24'2" × 106' Napa, CA (1986).

J. Hindsii × J. nigra
ROYAL HYBRID WALNUT. An intentional cross made in 1879 by L. Burbank of Santa Rosa, CA. Offspring fast-growing and productive. Since the 1920s, scarcely ever sold except by nut nurseries. The cross occurs spontaneously in California, where the eastern U.S. *J. nigra* has been much planted. Leaflets (11) 17–19 (23), more slender and less hairy than those of *J. nigra*. Husks 1½"–2" (2¼") wide. Nuts (¾") 1"–1¼" (1⅞") wide, weakly to moderately grooved. Records: 118' × 17'6" × 137' Santa Rosa, CA (≤1950); 88' × 13'0" × 79' Tacoma, WA (1990); 84' × 13'1" × 85' Seattle, WA (1988).

J. Hindsii × J. regia
PARADOX HYBRID WALNUT. An intentional cross made in 1878 by L. Burbank of Santa Rosa, CA. Named in 1893. Rare (only common in parts of California's Central Valley). Leaflets (7) 11–15. Nuts ⅞"–1⅜" wide, often squarish, thick-shelled, weakly grooved; of inferior quality and lightly borne. Records: a trunk 19'0" around near Yuba, CA (<1939); one 100' wide, its trunk 14'0" around at Whittier, CA (1969; *pl.* 1907); 73' × 12'9" × 75' Puyallup, WA (1993).

J. × intermedia Carr.
(*J. regia* × *J. nigra*)
HYBRID WALNUT. Named in 1863 in France. Most similar to *J. regia*, but normally with 11 leaflets. Rare. Seedlings from *J. regia* which resulted from pollination by *J. nigra* usually show great vigor, but the nuts are no improvement, being thick-shelled and small-meated. Records: 115' × 17'1" × 118' Geneva, Switzerland (≤1967); 98' × 12'3" Hergest Croft, Herefordshire, England (1985); 89' × 18'8" × 111' near Corvallis, OR (1989); 84' × 13'2" Vancouver, WA (1990).

J. × intermedia 'Vilmoreana'
= *J. intermedia Vilmoreana* Carr.
= *J. intermedia* var. *Vilmoreana* (Carr.) Schneid.
Originated at Verrières le Buisson (near Paris), home of the famous Vilmorin-Andrieux nursery firm founded in 1746. The VILMORIN HYBRID WALNUT was planted in 1816; it was named in 1863; in 1905 it measured 92' × 10'2". This clone sets few nuts, which have the shape of those of *J. regia*, and the deep furrows of *J. nigra*. It was being sold as grafted specimens in North America ≤1892, but is extremely rare. The only specimen seen by this writer dates from 1914 in Sidney, B.C., and has 11–13 (15) markedly narrow leaflets, subtly toothed, to 6¾" × 1⁹⁄₁₆", fragrant when crushed. No nuts seen.

J. japonica—see *J. ailanthifolia*

J. Lavallei—see *J. ailantifolia* var. *cordiformis*

J. major (Torr. *ex* Sitsgr.) Heller
= *J. rupestris* var. *major* Torr. *ex* Sitsgr.
= *J. microcarpa* var. *major* (Torr. *ex* Sitsgr.) Benson
= *J. elæaopyren* Dode
= *J. neomexicana* Dode
= *J. Torreyi* Dode

ARIZONA BLACK WALNUT. From southwestern North America. Its name *major*, given in 1853, refers to it being larger than its cousin *J. microcarpa*. Introduced to cultivation ca. 1894. Very rare. Leaflets 9–15 (25). Husks (1") 1¼"–1½" (2⅛") wide, semi-smooth, dull or glossy green. Nuts (¾") 1"–1⅜" wide, medium to deeply rough-grooved. Overall, a smaller version of *J. nigra* that retains its green foliage later into autumn. Records: 85' × 18'9" × 95' Mimbres Valley, NM (1987); 60' × 9'10" × 117' near Winkleman, AZ (1962).

J. mandshurica Maxim.

MANCHURIAN WALNUT. From N China, Manchuria, and the Russian Far East. Named in 1856. Introduced in 1859 by C.J. Maximowicz to St. Petersburg. In North America ≤1879, but not much promoted until ca. 1937, when its cold-hardiness made it look promising for the northern prairie region. Leaflets (9) 11–19. Husks 1¾"–2¼" long, felty sticky. Nuts 1½"–2⅛" long, deeply pocked, moderately rough. Some sources say the nuts can be round, and scarcely over an inch wide. The first *Juglans* to flush in spring. Very closely related to *J. ailanthifolia*. Records: 85' tall at Rochester, NY (ca. 1980); 72' × 12'2" × 105' Bear Creek, OR (1989).

J. mandshurica var. stenocarpa Maxim.

= *J. stenoptera* Maxim.

Named in 1859. (Greek *stenos*, narrow, and *karpos*, fruit). Extremely rare and little known. Introduced to western Europe ≤1903. Twigs nearly hairless, leaves huge (terminal leaflet to 7"–10" long); nut cylindric-oblong. It has been described as nearly intermediate between *J. mandshurica* and *J. cathayana*.

J. mandshurica ssp. Sieboldiana—see J. ailanthifolia

J. microcarpa Berl.

= *J. rupestris* Engelm. *ex* Torr.

TEXAS BLACK WALNUT. LITTLE WALNUT. RIVER WALNUT. From southwestern North America. Named in 1850. (Greek *mikros*, small, and *karpos*, fruit.) Very rare in cultivation. Leaflets 11–25. Husks ¾"–1¼" wide, smooth, unpocked. Nuts ⅝"–⅞" wide, moderately grooved. The petite foliage and nuts render this a serviceable ornamental, in a class of its own among *Juglans*. Can be shrubby. Records: 59' × 10'6" × 96' Camal County, TX (1972); 50' × 13'4" × 80' Denton County, TX (1980).

J. microcarpa var. major—see J. major

J. neomexicana—see J. major

J. nigra L.

BLACK WALNUT. EASTERN BLACK WALNUT. COMMON BLACK WALNUT. AMERICAN BLACK WALNUT. From the eastern U.S. and far S Ontario. Owes its name *nigra* (black) to its dark bark and nuts. An important, widely distributed, much cultivated species, noble and long-lived. The wood is of supreme value. Stains from the husks are infamous; the nuts are difficult to crack, yet taste delectable. Numerous cultivars exist that feature improved nuts. Leaflets 13–27, powerfully aromatic. Husks 1½"–2¾" wide, usually dull and rough. Nuts 1⅛"–1¾" wide, usually very rough and deeply grooved, sometimes sharply jagged, usually very dark. Records: to 165' × 28'3" in the virgin forests of bygone times; 130' × 23'2" × 140' Sauvie Island, OR (1991).

J. nigra 'Deming Purple'

Origin not known. Exceedingly rare. Leaves purple.

J. nigra 'Laciniata'

CUTLEAF or FERNLEAF BLACK WALNUT. In 1926 about 30 cut-leaved BLACK WALNUT trees were found at Milton State nursery of Milton, PA. Mr. J. Hershey of Nut Tree nursery, Downingtown, PA, obtained one, propagated and sold it in 1937. The Arnold Arboretum obtained scionwood and distributed grafts in 1954 to nurseries. Difficult to propagate, it has remained very rare. Like CUTLEAF SUMACH (*Rhus typhina* 'Dissecta') its leaves are bipinnate, elegantly shredded.

J. regia L.

= *J. sinensis* (DC.) Dode

PERSIAN WALNUT. COMMON WALNUT. ENGLISH WALNUT. EUROPEAN WALNUT. CIRCASSIAN WALNUT. ROYAL WALNUT. MADEIRA NUT. From much of Asia, and likely the Balkans. The epithet *regia* from Latin *regius*, of or belonging to a king, royal—probably referring to the value accorded the nuts—*nux regia*. Likely introduced to North America in colonial days; certainly ≤1825. A major economic crop in California. Common. Leaflets (5) 7–9 (13), blunt and wide, untoothed. Husks 1½"–3½" wide, smooth and glossy, splitting partly when ripe (unlike those of other *Juglans*). The familiar store and market walnut, some so thin-shelled that finger pressure can crack them. Catkins in April-May look like green caterpillars 2"–5" long. Bark pale gray and relatively smooth—ASPEN-like when young. Records: to 120' × 28'0" in the wild; 105' × 12'1" and 88' × 20'8" Boxted Hall, Suffolk, England (1990); 87' × 17'8" Pilton, Northamptonshire, England (1964); 76' × 16'6" St. Michaels, MD (1972); 76' × 12'5" Fall City, WA (1992); 68' × 26'11" × 105' Manutuke, New Zealand (≤1982; *pl.* ca. 1837).

Juglans regia 'Carpathian'

CARPATHIAN WALNUT. From the Carpathian Mountains of Poland, introduced by the Rev. Paul C. Crath in 1934. The term CARPATHIAN WALNUT is now applied generally to all cold-hardy *J. regia* in North America, whether from Crath or other sources. Such trees are common. They are vigorous, of slender growth, often with brownish twigs; hardy, one of the last trees to leaf out in spring.

J. regia 'Filicifolia'—see *J. regia* 'Laciniata'

J. regia 'Laciniata'

= *J. regia* 'Filicifolia'

CUTLEAF WALNUT. Originated in the early 1800s in England. Described in 1830. In North American commerce ≤1892–93. Very rare. Weak, with an open crown. Leaves finely dissected and ferny. Nuts of fair size and first quality, borne abundantly. Record: 59' × 6'1" Linton Park, Kent, England (1985).

J. regia 'Manregian'

MANREGIAN WALNUT. This name referred originally the *"Man*churian *regia* strain" introduced by F. Meyer in 1906; but it turned out such trees really came from western China. Introduced and named in 1954 by Moses Adams of Salem, OR. Known only to nut specialists. Resembles plain *J. regia* but is more hardy. Better than 'Carpathian' but less cold-hardy. The nuts are large.

J. regia 'Pendula'

WEEPING WALNUT. Discovered in Waterloo, Belgium, ca. 1850; distributed by A. Gothier of Fontenay aux Roses, France. Described in 1853. In North American commerce ≤1892–93. Extremely rare. Like a WEEPING WILLOW in habit. Nuts of medium size, good.

J. rupestris—see *J. microcarpa*

J. rupestris var. *major*—see *J. major*

J. Sargentii—see *J.* × *Bixbyi*

J. Sieboldiana—see *J. ailanthifolia*

J. sinensis—see *J. regia*

J. stenoptera—see *J. mandshurica* var. *stenocarpa*

J. Torreyi—see *J. major*

Juniperus

[CUPRESSACEÆ; Cypress Family] 45–60 spp. of coniferous evergreen shrubs and trees. *Juniperus* is an ancient Latin name. These have been called the camels of the tree world, thriving in dry, hot regions. They cannot get too much sun, and suffer in shade. On some species the foliage is wholly sharp and needle-like ("acicular" or "awl-like"). On some it is largely scalelike, resembling that of *Cupressus*, or a mixture of prickly juvenile foliage and scaly adult foliage. Juvenile foliage is more apt to be retained on pruned portions, or specimens growing in "lean" soils or colder climates. Although many JUNIPERS are mere groundcovers, enough are treelike, at least with age, that they require 20 pages in this book. The numerous cultivars are difficult to sort. Many lose their distinctive attributes as they age; documentation has always lagged far behind nursery naming. The fruit is a berry in everyday speech, called a "cone" by academics. JUNIPERS can be bisexual like most trees, or male or female. It is of great value to know the sex in order to identify cultivars.

J. barbadensis—see *J. virginiana* var. *silicicola*

J. californica Carr.

CALIFORNIA JUNIPER. SWEET-BERRIED JUNIPER. DESERT WHITE CEDAR. From arid parts of California, extreme S Nevada, W Arizona, and NW Mexico. Introduced to cultivation in 1853 when Wm. Lobb sent it to Veitch nursery of England. In North American cultivation since ≤1918; extremely rarely grown. Much like *J. occidentalis* (WESTERN JUNIPER) but smaller, with a deeply folded trunk. It also requires less water than *J. occidentalis* or *J. osteosperma*. Indeed, it needs excellent drainage to do well at all. Berries reddish-brown beneath a whitish bloom (rather than bluish-black as in *J. occidentalis*), ⅜"–¾" long, 1–2 (3) seeded. Usually shrubby. Most writers cite 40' as its maximum height; Ouden says 46'. The overall record: 33' × 7'10" × 40' Colusa County, CA (1976).

J. californica 'Glauca'

Introduced ≤1929 in California; sold into the mid-1930s at least; long commercially extinct. A pyramidal tree of medium size. Young juvenile foliage beautiful silvery bluish-green.

J. californica f. Lutheyana Howell & Twisselmann

A columnar form from Kern County, CA. Named in 1968 for Robert and Carol Luthey, its discoverers. To 16' tall in the wild. Not known in commerce.

J. californica ssp. osteosperma—see J. osteosperma

J. californica var. utahensis—see J. osteosperma

J. canadensis—see J. communis

J. chinensis L. (cf. J. chinensis var. dioica)
(J. sinensis)
= J. Reevesiana hort. ex Endl.
= J. chinensis 'Reevesi' or 'Reevesiana'
= J. chinensis 'Foemina Reevesi'

CHINESE JUNIPER. From China, Mongolia, Japan, Taiwan etc. Introduced <1767 from China to Uppsala, Sweden. Then from Canton to England in 1804 by Wm. Kerr via the East India Company. Ouden says a previous introduction was <1767. Date of introduction to North America not known, but it has long been very common here. Most of its variations are resistant to cedar-apple rust disease, unlike the native J. virginiana (EASTERN RED CEDAR). The taxonomy and nomenclature of J. chinensis is controversial and badly muddled. In 1947 P.J. van Melle addressed the problems in his book Review of Juniperus chinensis et al. No one has studied J. chinensis so thoroughly. Subsequent writers vary in their reaction to van Melle's proposals; the most common response has been a sense of hesitancy, doing next to nothing, waiting to see if someone else will wholeheartedly embrace the name changes proposed. The present writer uses a middle approach to the treelike forms of J. chinensis, keeping van Melle's proposed new species at a varietal level—for those who wish to recognize them at all. Van Melle declared that the originally-described J. chinensis was one thing, while the subsequent introductions of its significantly different relatives were not differentiated under this name. As a result, too many dissimilar variants were called J. chinensis. In particular, the sphærica variety (species, says van

Melle) has often superseded the original concept of J. chinensis. The original J. chinensis is cultivated almost exclusively in its female forms (discussed under J. chinensis 'Fœmina'). It is a slow, often rather short-lived pyramidal tree. The foliage is relatively weakly scented. It is less hardy than some of its varieties such as sphærica and especially pyramidalis. Male and female flowers are borne on separate trees. The main leader of the tree is not vertical; it leans, forming a flattish plume. The adult shoots nod at the tips. In adolescence, the adult foliage usually occurs only in the outer, younger parts of the tree. Juvenile leaves are predominantly in trios on vigorous twigs, but in opposite pairs on weak shoots. Berries vary widely, with 2–8 seeds. Records (of whatever people call J. chinensis): to 80' tall in the wild; 68' × 8'9" Bedgebury, Kent, England (1983); 60' × 3'3" Spokane, WA (1988); 50' × 9'10" Mamhead Park, Devon, England (1962); 40' × 17'0" Peking, China (<1915).

J. chinensis 'Albovariegata'—see J. chinensis var. pyramidalis 'Variegata' and J. chinensis var. torulosa 'Variegata'

J. chinensis 'Argenteovariegata'—see J. chinensis var. pyramidalis 'Variegata'

J. chinensis 'Aurea'

GOLDEN CHINESE JUNIPER. YOUNG'S GOLDEN JUNIPER. A male branch sport from ca. 1855 at Maurice Young's nursery, Milford, Godalming, Surrey, England. Described in 1863; distributed in 1872. In North American commerce ≤1890. Uncommon. Foliage primarily adult, golden-tinged. At its brightest in spring when the male flowers and young foliage coincide. Van Melle says this is a clone of the original conception of J. chinensis. Growth slow. Record: 49' × 3'4" Golden Grove, Dyfed, Wales (1982).

J. chinensis 'Aureo-variegata'—see J. chinensis var. torulosa 'Variegata'

J. chinensis 'Bleak House'—see J. chinensis var. pyramidalis

J. chinensis 'Blue Alps'
= J. squamata 'Blue Alps'

Discovered in 1968 by H.J. Welch in an Austrian garden. Named in 1981. In North American commerce ≤1987. Spectacular silvery-blue. Large shrub or upright small, open tree.

J. chinensis 'Blue Point'

TEARDROP JUNIPER. Originated <1963 somewhere in the U.S. Common. A large teardrop of very dense pale blue gray foliage. Foliage mostly juvenile on young specimens, mostly adult at maturity. Female, or bisexual—at any rate it can bear fruit.

J. chinensis 'Chugai'—see J. chinensis 'Olympia'

J. chinensis columnaris 'Blue Pyramid'—see J. chin. 'Columnaris'

J. chinensis 'Columnaris'

= *J. sphærica* var. *pseudo-mas* van Melle
= *J. chinensis* 'Pyramidalis' (in part; cf. *J. chinensis* var. *pyramidalis*)
= *J. chinensis* 'Columnaris Viridis'
= *J. chinensis* 'Mas' and 'Mascula' (in part)
= *J. chinensis columnaris* 'Blue Pyramid'

GREEN COLUMNAR CHINESE JUNIPER. Van Melle says this variant was originally introduced by R. Fortune to England in 1845. However, the clone in common circulation is a selection raised from seeds collected by F. Meyer in 1905, at Hupeh, China; sent to Chico, CA. In commerce <1926. Common. Foliage all or nearly all juvenile (until the tree is decades old), softly prickly; overall color grayish green. A narrowly pyramidal to columnar 20'–50' tree with a single undivided trunk, the foliage thicker near the base. Each tree bears both flower sexes, but is usually predominately male. The name 'Mas' has been applied to more than one clone. Although very different in appearance, 'Columnaris' has been confused in name with *J. chinensis* var. *pyramidalis*. It is less easily distinguished from *J. chinensis* var. *neaboriensis*. Records: 44' tall at Lytchett Heath, Poole, Dorset, England (1967); 40' × 2'10½" × 13' Lisle, IL (1986; *pl.* 1939); 30½' × 10½' wide at Los Angeles, CA (1993; *pl.* 1968).

J. chinensis 'Columnaris Glauca'

= *J. sphærica* var. *pseudo-mas* f. *columnaris* (USDA) van Melle
= *J. chinensis* var. *pyramidalis* f. *glauca* Slavin
= *J. chinensis* 'Pyramidalis Glauca'

BLUE COLUMNAR CHINESE JUNIPER. CHINESE BLUE COLUMN JUNIPER. Originated as the preceding. Common. Compared to the preceding, all the foliage is juvenile; the tree is narrowly columnar; slower; the overall color is bluish-gray.

J. chinensis 'Columnaris Hetzii'—see J. chin. 'Hetzii Columnaris'

J. chinensis 'Columnaris Viridis'—see J. chinensis 'Columnaris'

J. chinensis 'Corymbosa'—see J. chinensis 'Oblonga'

J. chinensis 'Corymbosa Glauca'—see J. chinensis 'Robusta Green'

J. chin. 'Corymbosa Variegata'—see J. chin. var. torulosa 'Variegata'

J. chinensis 'Corymbosa Viridis'—see J. chinensis var. torulosa

J. chinensis 'Densa Glauca'

Origin not known. In the nursery trade from at least 1927 until 1987. Solid deep blue juvenile foliage. Possibly a denser, more glaucous variant of the ubiquitous SPINY GREEK JUNIPER (*J. chinensis* var. *pyramidalis*). Or it may simply be the common *pyramidalis* clone.

J. chinensis 'Denserecta' Spartan™—see J. scopulorum Spartan™

J. chinensis var. dioica (van Melle) stat. nov.

= *J. sphærica* var. *dioica* van Melle
= *J. chinensis* sensu Beissn. 1897, non L.
= *J. chinensis* auct. (in part), and U.S. hort. (in part), non L.
= *J. chinensis fœmina* Beissn. 1901

Date of introduction not known, but ≤1890s. A columnar to broad pyramidal tree. It varies much in the retention of its juvenility. Juvenile leaves not markedly short or widely spread, nor markedly rigid and prickly (as they are in var. *neoboriensis*). Berries usually distinctly bilobed.

J. chinensis 'Excelsa'—see J. chinensis var. pyramidalis

J. chinensis 'Fairview'—see J. chinensis 'Hetzii Columnaris'

J. chinensis 'Fiore Special'

Introduced ≤1991 by Fiore nursery of Prairieview, IL. Blue-green, pyramidal. Resists cedar-apple rust disease.

J. chinensis fœmina—see J. chinensis var. dioica

J. chinensis 'Fœmina'

('Femina')
= *J. fœmina* hort.

This name (meaning female) has given rise to confusion. It has been used a great deal since ≤1850. In a broad sense it can refer to any female (or bisexual) CHINESE JUNIPER. In a narrow taxonomic sense its proper (i.e. first or original) application may be limited to the female of typical *J. chinensis* (a.k.a. 'Reevesii': John Reeves (1774–1856), an employee of the East India Company, was keen on Chinese natural history during 1812–1831). In practice, the name has also partly been used as a synonym for the clone 'Oblonga' (a.k.a. 'Sylvestris'). Since 'Oblonga' is not easily (if at all) distinguished, the result is that 'Fœmina' ends up referring to a female of typical *J. chinensis*. Such trees are generally shorter and broader than male specimens, and are more common. The foliage is mostly adult, dense, and rich green, the tips nodding. Short shoots here and there bear juvenile foliage (prickly, bluish needles in trios). After a more or less prolonged adolescence, many berries are borne.

J. chinensis 'Foemina Reevesi'—see J. chinensis

J. chinensis Fortunei—see J. chinensis var. Sheppardii

J. chinensis 'Helle'—see J. scopulorum Spartan™

J. chinensis 'Hetzii Columnaris'

= *J. chinensis* 'Columnaris Hetzii'
= *J. chinensis* 'Hetzii Fastigiata'
= *J. chinensis* 'Fairview'
= *J. scopulorum* 'Fairview'
≠ *J. chinensis* 'Hetzii' (a bush)

GREEN COLUMN JUNIPER. Originated during the early 1930s as a seedling in the F.C. Hetz & Sons' Fairview Evergreen nursery of Fairview, PA. Strong growing, broad-based dense columnar to narrow pyramidal tree, 15'–30' tall; mostly juvenile, sharp needles; bright bluish-green. Large silver berries. Especially resistant to cedar-apple rust disease. Very common. Record: 25' × 1'7" × 10' Los Angeles, CA (1993; *pl.* 1968).

J. chinensis 'Hetzii Fastigiata'—see J. chinensis 'Hetzii Columnaris'

J. chinensis 'Hibernica'—see J. communis 'Hibernica'

J. chinensis 'Idylwild'—see J. virginiana 'Idyllwild'

J. chinensis 'Iowa'

Dr. T.J. Maney of the Iowa State College introduced this (and 'Story', plus the bushy 'Maney' and 'Ames') from seedlings raised by Dr. V. Stoutemeyer, from Japanese seeds sown about 1934. In commerce since the 1950s. Uncommon. Dense, irregularly upright. Dark green. Berries inconspicuous. Record: 25½' × 16½' wide at Los Angeles, CA (1993; *pl.* 1968).

J. chinensis 'Japonica Oblonga'—see J. chinensis 'Oblonga'

J. chin. 'Japonica Variegata'—see J. chin. var. torulosa 'Variegata'

J. chinensis 'Kaizuka'—see J. chinensis var. torulosa

J. chin. 'Kaizuka Variegata'—see J. chin. var. torulosa 'Variegata'

J. chinensis var. Keteleeri Beissn.

= *J. Keteleeri* hort.
= *J. virginiana* 'Keteleeri'
= *J. sphærica* var. *Keteleeri* (hort.) van Melle

The first mention of the *Keteleeri* name is in 1846. The tree was probably raised by Joseph Baptiste Keteleer (1813–1903), a French nurseryman born in Belgium, for whom the coniferous genus *Keteleeria* was named. This variety was officially described in 1910. It was commonly sold in North America in the 1920s and '30s, but was going out of favor by the 1950s. A remarkably vigorous narrowly pyramidal tree, with showy large (⅓"–½" and more) berries, having an attractive blue bloom. Foliage bright to dull or dark green, primarily adult. Only female specimens are cultivated, but they represent more than one clone. Record: 40' × 4'8" Seattle, WA (1988; *pl.* 1944).

J. chinensis 'Mas' or 'Mascula'—see J. chinensis 'Columnaris'

J. chinensis mascula Carr.—see J. chinensis var. sphærica

J. chinensis 'Mission Spire'

= *J. virginiana* 'Mission Spire'

Origin not known. Sold ≤1966–67 by Hess nursery

of New Jersey. Vigorous, upright. Foliage glossy bluish-green with a distinctive lilac-mauve cast in winter. From Mission Gardens of Techny, IL. Probably similar to *J. chinensis* 'Iowa'.

J. chinensis 'Mountbatten'

Originated as a seedling at Sheridan nursery of Ontario. Name officially published in 1948, in honor of Lord Mountbatten when he visited Toronto in 1948 to open the Canadian National Exhibition. Common. Dense, narrow pyramidal tree 10'–20' tall, similar to IRISH JUNIPER (*J. communis* 'Hibernica'). Foliage mostly juvenile and gray; green in adult stage. Female. Bark flaky.

J. chinensis var. *neaboriensis* (Veitch) Beissn.

≠ *J. neaboriensis* Laws. ex Gord. (i.e., *J. Oxycedrus* ssp. *macrocarpa*)
= *J. neaboriensis* Veitch
= *J. sphærica* var. *neaboriensis* (Veitch) van Melle

Likely introduced from China to France by A. David. Named (meaning "of New Borneo") in 1881. During the 1920s and '30s it was commonly listed by East Coast nurseries. Since ca. 1960, the tree has rarely been listed in nurseries, probably because of the influence of writers claiming it a synonym, plus popular agreement with van Melle's assertion that it has little landscape value. According to van Melle it always bears its flower sexes on separate individuals. Its juvenile foliage is markedly prickly and rigid. The juvenile leaves are often short and widely spaced. It forms a dense green to grayish narrow pyramid 10'–16' tall. Berries are conspicuously notched; seeds usually 2–4.

J. chinensis 'Obelisk'

Raised from seed from Japan about 1930 by F.J. Grootendoorst & Sons nursery of Boskoop, Holland. Introduced in 1946. In North American commerce ≤1948. Uncommon. A slender 10'–20' tall column. Often leaning when old. Foliage dense, prickly, juvenile, of a distinct glaucous-white or steel-blue appearance. Needles 7/16"–5/8" long. Female.

J. chinensis 'Oblonga'

≠ *J. communis* var. *oblonga* (Bieb.) Parl.
= *J. chinensis* 'Corymbosa'
= *J. chinensis* 'Sylvestris'
= *J. chinensis* 'Japonica Oblonga'
= *J. japonica* 'Corymbosa'
= *J. japonica* 'Sylvestris'
= *J. oblonga* (in part)

Introduced <1927; first sold in New Jersey, Massachusetts and other northeastern states. Sold as 'Sylvestris' in the South and West. Common. Originally thought to be a dwarf, it becomes a small tree ca. 20' tall. It may be a clone but according to van Melle is virtually indistinguishable from female seedlings of typical *J. chinensis*. Foliage both silvery (juvenile) and bright green (adult). Broadly pyramidal, gently and pleasingly irregular; usually <25' tall. Female. See also *J. chinensis* 'Fœmina'.

J. chinensis 'Olympia'

= *J. chinensis* 'Chugai'

Raised from seed from Japan about 1930 by F.J. Grootendoorst & Sons nursery of Boskoop, Holland. Distributed in 1956. In North American commerce during the 1960s. Rare. A slender column, bearing both types of foliage. Female.

J. chinensis 'Ontario Green'

Sold in the 1980s by Connon nursery of Ontario. Very rare. Strong growing, upright, similar to *J. chinensis* 'Mountbatten' but less prone to red spider attacks. Dark green.

J. chinensis var. *pendula* Franch.

= *J. sphærica* var. *pendula* (Franch.) van Melle

WEEPING CHINESE JUNIPER. Original introduction not known, but likely ca. 1882 by A. David from the south of Shenai, W China, into France. Named in 1884. (Previous to 1884 the epithet *pendula* was often used to refer to the shrub PFITZER JUNIPER.) In North American commerce ≤1903. Very rare (deservedly so says van Melle). Pyramidal, markedly pendulous; often sparsely branched. Juvenile foliage dull grayish-green, adult foliage green. Flower sexes on separate trees; a male clone is most commonly cultivated. Record: 30' × 1'1" Kew, England (1969).

J. chinensis var. *pyramidalis* (Carr) Beissn.

= *J. excelsa* 'Stricta' (in part)
= *J. densa glauca* hort. U.S. (in part; cf. *J. chinensis* 'Densa Glauca')
= *J. chinensis* 'Pyramidalis' (in part; cf. *J. chinensis* 'Columnaris')
= *J. chinensis* 'Bleak House'
= *J. chinensis* 'Stricta'
= *J. chinensis* 'Excelsa'
= *J. Sheppardii* var. *pyramidalis* (Carr.) van Melle
= *J. stricta* hort.

SPINY GREEK JUNIPER. Introduced by Siebold to Ghent, Belgium, in 1843. Long commonly planted in North America; not recently in favor, yet still in commerce. Very hardy. Inextricably confused with the comparatively tender and rare authentic GRECIAN JUNIPER

(*J. excelsa*). Broadly columnar to conical, very dense. Foliage mostly juvenile, harshly prickly, grayish- to bluish-green or silvery-gray. Needles ⅛"–½" long, in trios. Male flowers predominate. For all practical purposes this is a stiff, prickly shrub, but with great age loses its lower foliage and becomes a small tree. At least two clones exist: 'Pyramidalis' is more harshly prickly and can bear some adult foliage; 'Stricta' is softer and wholly juvenile. Records: 32' × 3'3" Arlington, WA (1995); 26' × 3'2" Tacoma, WA (1993).

J. chinensis 'Pyramidalis Glauca'—see *J. chin.* 'Columnaris Glauca'

J. chinensis pyramidalis f. *glauca*—see *J. chin.* 'Columnaris Glauca'

J. chinensis var. *pyramidalis* 'Variegata'
= *J. Sheppardii* var. *pyramidalis* f. *variegata* (Carr.) van Melle
= *J. excelsa* 'Stricta Variegata'
= *J. excelsa* 'Variegata'
= *J. chinensis* 'Albovariegata' (in part)
= *J. chinensis* 'Argenteovariegata'
= *J. chinensis* 'Stricta Variegata'
= *J. chinensis* 'Variegata'

Introduced ca. 1860 by R. Fortune to England. In North American commerce ≤1887. Common until recently. A female clone, creamy-white variegated. Juvenility less consistently persistent than that of the common clones of var. *pyramidalis*. Often thought to be a dwarf, and indeed is usually a shrub. But some become trees 30' tall, bearing much more adult foliage and many berries.

J. chinensis recurva—see *J. recurva*

J. chinensis 'Reevesi' or 'Reevesiana'—see *J. chinensis*

J. chinensis 'Robusta Green'
?= *J. chinensis* 'Corymbosa Glauca'
?= *J. chinensis* 'Torulosa Glauca'

Origin not known. Introduced ≤1957. Common. Either there is a blue-green original 'Robusta' and an unmitigated green 'Robusta Green', or the name 'Robusta Green' is singularly inapt. Or perhaps some other pure green cultivar has been sold incorrectly as 'Robusta Green'. Most plants sold as 'Robusta Green' are not , as claimed by nurseries, "rich" or "brilliant" or "intense" green. They are dull gray-green. The habit is broad, informal and rugged. It could be likened to a grayish HOLLYWOOD JUNIPER (*J.*

chinensis var. *torulosa*). Berries freely borne, some male flowers also. It grows slowly to 12'–18' tall.

J. chinensis var. *Sheppardii* (Veitch) Hornibrook
= *J. Sheppardii* (Veitch) van Melle
= *J. chinensis Fortunei* hort. U.S. (in part)
= *J. Fortunei* C. de Vos, non van Houtte *ex* Gord.
= *J. Fortunei glauca* C. de Vos
= *J. sphærica Sheppardii* Veitch
= *J. sphærica glauca* Fortune *ex* Gord.

Introduced ≤1825 to England. Common, although not known to most nurseries or horticulturists as *Sheppardii*. Usually multitrunked. The juvenile habit is regularly pyramidal, the adult habit irregularly so, with some irregular branching, sometimes tortuous. Mature specimens often producing long, slender ultimate twigs. Male and female flowers either on the same or on separate individuals. Adult foliage usally grayish to gray, can be green but not bright green. Terminal shoots of adult twigs nodding. Van Melle, who makes this a species, places under it the var. *torulosa* and var. *pyramidalis*. Recorded to 18' tall.

J. chinensis 'Skyrocket'—see *J. scopulorum* 'Skyrocket'

J. chinensis 'Spartan'—see *J. scopulorum* Spartan™

J. chinensis 'Spearmint'—see *J. scopulorum* 'Spearmint'

J. chinensis var. *sphærica* (Lindl.) stat. nov
= *J. chinensis mascula* Carr.
= *J. Fortunei* hort. *ex* Carr.
= *J. sphærica* Lindl.

Introduced in 1845 from Shanghai by R. Fortune to Standish & Noble nursery of England. Habit narrowly pyramidal to columnar. Adult foliage green. The adult terminal shoots do not nod; there are no long, slender ultimate twigs. The flowers are for the most part obviously of both sexes on each tree, although young specimens bear mostly male flowers. In some cultivars the sexes are exclusively male or female. Van Melle, who makes this a species rather than a variety, places under it: var. *pseudo-mas*, var. *dioica*, var. *neaboriensis*, var. *pendula*, and var. *Keteleeri*.

J. chinensis 'Spiralis'—see *J. chinensis* var. *torulosa*

J. chinensis 'Steel Blue'—see J. scopulorum 'Steel Blue'

J. chinensis 'Story'

Dr. T.J. Maney of the Iowa State College introduced this (and 'Iowa', plus the bushy 'Maney' and 'Ames') from seedlings raised by Dr. V. Stoutemeyer, from Japanese seeds sown about 1934. Introduced in 1947. Rare. Male. A symmetrical, slender large shrub or small tree. Foliage adult, dark green.

J. chinensis 'Stricta'—see J. chinensis var. pyramidalis

J. chin. 'Stricta Variegata'—see J. chin. var. pyramidalis 'Variegata'

J. chinensis 'Sylvestris'—see J. chinensis 'Oblonga'

J. chinensis var. torulosa (Eastwood) Bailey

= J. Sheppardii var. torulosa (Eastwood) van Melle
= J. chinensis 'Kaizuka'
= J. chinensis 'Spiralis'
= J. chinensis 'Viridifolia' or 'Viridis'
= J. chinensis 'Corymbosa Viridis'

HOLLYWOOD JUNIPER. TWISTED JUNIPER. Introduced from Japan to California, probably in the 1880s. Edward C. Gill's nursery of Oakland, CA, in 1890 listed "the form of *Juniperus chinensis* with twisted branchlets." Not known widely until after 1920. Very popular since the 1950s. Its hardiness not great: most specimens are on the West Coast and in the South. Branching irregular, twisted, with dense tufts of swirling foliage. Foliage primarily adult, bright green, but sometimes overlaid with a gray bloom (as in *J. chinensis* 'Robusta Green'). Male and female flowers on separate specimens; a brilliant green female clone is most common. Berries ⅓". A unique and unforgettable tree. Records: 95' × 11'9" north of San José, CA (<1967); 45' × 5'11" × 37' Berkeley, CA (1989); 27' × 4'0" × 21' Tacoma, WA (1993).

J. chinensis 'Torulosa Glauca'—see J. chinensis 'Robusta Green'

J. chinensis var. torulosa 'Variegata'

= J. chinensis 'Torulosa Variegata'
= J. chinensis 'Variegated Kaizuka' or 'Kaizuka Variegata'
= J. chinensis 'Aureo-variegata'
= J. chinensis 'Japonica Variegata'
= J. chinensis 'Albovariegata' (in part)
= J. chinensis 'Corymbosa Variegata'

VARIEGATED HOLLYWOOD JUNIPER. This name is here used to include more than one clone. CHINESE JUNIPER expert van Melle recognized two variegated HOLLYWOOD JUNIPERS (*aureo-variegata* and *albonotha*). In U.S. commerce since ≤1938. Uncommon. Compared to common HOLLYWOOD JUNIPER the variegated versions are slower growing and smaller (the clone 'Japonica Variegata' is especially bushy), besides being creamy-yellow variegated. The twisted habit is also less striking. Record: 28' × 4'7" × 24' Burlington, WA (1993).

J. chinensis 'Variegata'—see J. chin. var. pyramidalis 'Variegata'

J. chin. 'Variegated Kaizuka'—see J. chin. var. torulosa 'Variegata'

J. chinensis 'Viridifolia' or 'Viridis'—see J. chinensis var. torulosa

J. chinensis 'Wintergreen'

Origin not known, <1957. Common. A 12'–20' dense-branching, deep gray-green, pyramidal tree.

J. communis L.

= J. canadensis hort.

COMMON JUNIPER. ENGLISH JUNIPER. DWARF JUNIPER. GROUND CEDAR. From much of the Northern Hemisphere; no other conifer species is so widely distributed. Commonly sold in prior decades; rare since 1980. Gin (genévrette) is made from from barley, rye or other grains, and this JUNIPER's berries. Needles wholly in trios, ¼"–¾" long, the upper side with a single broad white band. Male and female flowers on separate specimens. Berries black or bluish, ¼"–½" with 2–3 seeds. Usually a groundcover shrub. Rarely a small tree. Records: 55' tall at Idd, SE Norway (1979); 46' × 8'10" Neplo, Poland (≤1973); 26½' × 3'0" × 8¼' Victoria, B.C. (1995); 20' × 7'1" near Karrineholm, Sweden (1992); 20' × 4'1" England (ca. 1835); 18' × 1'5" Glen Haven, MI (1973).

J. communis 'Ashfordii'

Origin not known, ≤1920s. May be connected with Ashford Park nursery of Atlanta, GA. Common from the 1930s into the early '60s. May be commercially extinct. Columnar and much like the well known IRISH JUNIPER (*J. communis* 'Hibernica'). 'Ashfordii' is denser, healthier, longer-lived and larger.

J. communis var. caucasica—see J. communis var. oblonga

J. communis 'Cracovia'

POLISH JUNIPER. Found at Cracow, in Poland. Introduced to England ≤1820. In North American commerce ≤1917. Scarcely sold since the late 1950s. Descriptions vary widely—from a dense columnar 8' shrub to a robust, loosely pyramidal small 15' tree. Branchlet tips nodding. Needles dull yellow-green, to 7/16" × 1/16". Intermediate between the typical *J. communis* and its forma *suecica* (SWEDISH JUNIPER).

J. communis 'Excelsa Pyramidalis'—see J. communis 'Pyramidalis'

J. communis 'Fastigiata'—see J. communis 'Hibernica' and J. communis f. suecica

J. communis 'Gold Cone'

Introduced ≤1980 by Kordes nursery of Bilsen, Germany. In North American commerce ≤1988. Like 'Hibernica' but golden-yellow.

J. communis 'Hibernica'

= *J. communis* 'Fastigiata' (in part)
= *J. communis* 'Stricta'
= *J. communis* 'Hibernica Stricta'
= *J. chinensis* 'Hibernica'
= *J. hibernica* Lodd.
= *J. fastigiata* hort.

IRISH JUNIPER. Introduced in 1836 in England. Not necessarily of Irish origin (in Latin, *Hibernia* is Ireland). Common. Much confused with SWEDISH JUNIPER (*J. communis* f. *suecica*). A tight, very narrow columnar large 8' shrub or small tree, to 18' (30') tall. Needles shorter, less pointed than in typical *J. communis*. Somewhat cold-tender; easily damaged by sun and wind scald, or bent over by heavy snow. Foliage effect bluish-green. Needles green, or bronzy in winter, mostly 1/4"–1/3" long. Record: 30' × 2'2" × 12' Bryant, WA (1995).

J. communis 'Hibernica Pyramidalis'—see J. comm. 'Pyramidalis'

J. communis 'Hibernica Stricta'—see J. communis 'Hibernica'

J. communis 'Hibernica Suecica'—see J. communis f. suecica

J. communis var. oblonga (Bieb.) Parl.

= *J. oblonga* Bieb.
= *J. communis* f. *oblonga* (Bieb.) Boom
= *J. communis* 'Oblonga'
= *J. communis* var. *caucasica* Endl.

CAUCASIAN JUNIPER. From Armenia and the E Caucasus. Cultivated ≤1826 in Paris. A shrub 4'–7' tall, with oblong berries. Included here only to help guard against confusion with the following:

J. communis 'Oblonga Pendula'

A confused entity. This name was used in 1838 for a specimen at Kew, England, that resembled var. *oblonga* "except," wrote J. Loudon, "the habit of the main branches is fastigiate, and the points of the shoots pendulous. A very graceful 5' high plant." F.J. Scott in 1870 said this variety was from Japan, was introduced ca.1855, was a warm light green color, and grew 20' tall. The English conifer expert G. Gordon said in 1875 that *J. taxifolia* H. & A. (and its synonym *J. oblonga pendula* Loud.) was a quite hardy pendulous bush 10' tall from Loo-Choo and N China. The Standish & Noble nursery of Bagshot, England, 1852 catalog, reports that R. Fortune saw 50' examples of this JUNIPER in China. Subsequent writers have continued to provide conflicting accounts. The common denominator is weepiness. This variety, or at least its name, has been in North American commerce since ≤1888, but to a limited extent. Whether it is an honest tree at all, or a mere synonym of *J. formosana*, requires more study. At the very least the name signifies a pendulous shrub capable of growing 10' tall, with needles 1/2"–3/4" long.

J. communis 'Pyramidalis'

= *J. communis* 'Hibernica Pyramidalis'
= *J. communis* 'Excelsa Pyramidalis'

Introduced in 1908 by Hesse nursery of Germany. Differs from *J. communis* 'Hibernica' in having a broader crown and needles not so distinctly glaucous.

J. communis 'Stricta'—see J. communis 'Hibernica'

J. communis f. suecica (Mill.) Beissn.

= *J. communis* 'Fastigiata' (in part)
= *J. communis* 'Hibernica Suecica'
= *J. suecica* Mill.

SWEDISH JUNIPER. Described in 1768 in England (in Latin, *Suecia* is Sweden). Wild in Scandinavia and E Russia. Several similar clones are in cultivation, all with upright habit and nodding twig tips. Overall its color is bluish, while the much confused IRISH JUNIPER

(*J. communis* 'Hibernica') is greenish. SWEDISH JUNIPER is also hardier. G. Gordon wrote in 1875: "In the forest of Fontainbleau, in France, this variety has attained the height of 50 feet, and produced most excellent timber."

J. Coxii—see *J. recurva* var. *Coxii*

J. densa glauca—see *J. chinensis* var. *pyramidalis*

J. Deppeana Steud.
= *J. pachyphlæa* Torr.

ALLIGATOR JUNIPER. CHECKER(BARK) JUNIPER. THICKBARK JUNIPER. MOUNTAIN CEDAR. WESTERN JUNIPER. From the Southwest U.S., and Mexico. In a narrow view, the typical version is scarcely known in cultivation if at all; var. *pachyphlæa* (meaning thick-barked) the ALLIGATOR or SWEET-FRUITED JUNIPER (limited to western New Mexico) is. It differs in minor details and is seen in cultivation as a slow-growing small tree, its foliage wholly juvenile, intensely blue-white, each ¼" needle with an exuded resin droplet. Named after Ferdinand Deppe (1794–1861), German botanist. Introduced to cultivation ≤1873. Very rare. Foliage not as stout or aromatic as that of *J. occidentalis* (WESTERN JUNIPER) or *J. scopulorum* (ROCKY MOUNTAIN JUNIPER). The ghostly silver foliage renders young specimens lovely and unmistakable; the chunky bark is the chief feature of aged ones. For optimal growth it needs heat and full sunlight. Male and female flowers are on separate trees. Berries ⅓"–⅝" or even ¾" with (1) 2–4 (5) seeds. The following five cultivars are all extremely rare and more information about them is needed; see also *J. occidentalis* 'Glenmore Blue Sierra'. Records: 71' × 19'11" Coronado National Forest, NM (<1945); 57' × 29'7" Tonto National Forest, AZ (1962).

J. Deppeana 'Davis Mountain Weeping'
Sold ≤1993 by Buchholz & Buchholz nursery of Gaston, OR. Needs training to become a tree.

J. Deppeana 'McFetters'
Discovered in the mountains of Arizona. Introduced ≤1982 by the Catalina Heights nursery of Ralph McFetters, at Tucson, AZ. Foliage exceptionally pale blue.

J. Deppeana 'Mt. Santos'
In circulation among conifer specialists. Irregular conical form. Silvery-blue color.

J. Deppeana 'Ohmy Blue'
Sold ≤1993 by Buchholz & Buchholz nursery of Gaston, OR.

J. Deppeana 'Silver'
In commerce <1975. A very glaucous selection.

J. drupacea Labill.
SYRIAN JUNIPER. From arid lands of S Greece, Turkey, Lebanon and W Syria. Possibly introduced to England as early as 1820, but it was definitely in French cultivation before it became generally distributed in 1853–54 by T. Kotschy. In North American commerce ≤1888. Extremely rare. Considered by many the finest of all JUNIPER trees. A light green, columnar male, is grown easily from cuttings. Not markedly cold-hardy. Needles wholly in threes, to ½"–⅞" × ⅛" (widest needles of all JUNIPERS); stiff, spiny. Berries brown or bluish with a glaucous bloom, ¾"–1⅛", edible, with 3 united seeds. Records: 141' × 11'6" Turkey (1993); 69' × 7'0" Batsford Park, Gloucestershire, England (1986).

J. excelsa Bieb.
GRECIAN JUNIPER. From SE Europe to SW Asia. Introduced to cultivation when J. Tournefort brought one from the Levant to Paris in 1702; it was 62' tall with 15' of clear trunk by 1835. In North American cultivation ≤1888, but extremely rare. Most plants so called are really *J. chinensis* var. *pyramidalis*. Male and female flowers borne on the same tree. Berries ⅓"–½", dark purplish-brown, glaucous; 3–6 (9) seeded. Narrow conical form, with slender twigs bearing exceedingly fine, mostly adult foliage. Records: to 100' × 22'4" in the wild; 52½' × 5'10" Adhurst St. Mary, Hampshire, England (1985).

J. excelsa 'Stricta'—see *J. chinensis* var. *pyramidalis*

J. excel. 'Stricta Variegata'—see *J. chin.* var. *pyramidalis* 'Variegata'

J. excelsa 'Variegata'—see *J. chinensis* var. *pyramidalis* 'Variegata'

J. Fargesii—see *J. squamata* var. *Fargesii*

J. fastigiata—see *J. communis* 'Hibernica'

J. fœmina—see *J. chinensis* 'Fœmina'

J. formosana Hay.

= *J. communis* 'Oblonga Pendula' (in part)

FORMOSAN JUNIPER. TAIWAN JUNIPER. PRICKLY CYPRESS. From Tibet, S China, and Taiwan. Introduced in 1844 by R. Fortune to England. In North America since ≤1912. Extremely rare. Much confused with *J. rigida* and *J. communis* 'Oblonga Pendula'. The name PRICKLY CYPRESS is said to be a translation from the Chinese *Tze Poh*. A bush or small tree, often multitrunked. Reminiscent of *J. rigida* (NEEDLE or TEMPLE JUNIPER). Branchlets drooping. Needles ½"–1" (1¼") long, wholly in trios, spreading, spiny-pointed, with two broad whitish bands. Berries shining reddish or orange-brown, ¼"–⅜" and 3-seeded. At least some specimens are cold-tender. Recorded to 50' tall in the wild; writers claiming 75'–80' are confusing it with *J. squamata* var. *Fargesii*.

J. Fortunei—see *J. chin.* var. *Sheppardii* and *J. chin.* var. *sphærica*

J. Fortunei glauca—see *J. chinensis* var. *Sheppardii*

J. hibernica—see *J. communis* 'Hibernica '

J. japonica 'Corymbosa'—see *J. chinensis* 'Oblonga'

J. japonica 'Sylvestris'—see *J. chinensis* 'Oblonga'

J. Keteleeri—see *J. chinensis* var. *Keteleeri*

J. Lemeeana—see *J. squamata* var. *Fargesii*

J. Libretoni glauca—see *J. virginiana* 'Lebretoni'

J. Libretonia—see *J. virginiana* 'Lebretoni'

J. lucayana—see *J. virginiana* var. *silicicola*

J. macrocarpa—see *J. Oxycedrus* ssp. *macrocarpa*

J. morrisonicola—see *J. squamata*

J. neaboriensis—see *J. chinensis* var. *neaboriensis* and *J. Oxycedrus* ssp. *macrocarpa*

J. oblonga—see *J. chinensis* 'Oblonga' and *J. communis* var. *oblonga*

J. occidentalis Hook. fil.

WESTERN JUNIPER. SIERRA JUNIPER. WESTERN REDCEDAR. From central WA to southern CA. Introduced to cultivation ca. 1840. Rare. Foliage among the most fragrant and resin-coated of all JUNIPERS. Berries ¼"–⅓", bluish black with a bloom; (1) 2–3 seeded. Some judge this species the handsomest of all California JUNIPERS. Record: the BENNETT JUNIPER, ca. 4,000 years old, due west of Sonora Pass in the Stanislaus National Forest, CA: 86' × 40'0" × 58' (1983). In 1954 the same tree was said to be 87' × 42'9" × 51'.

J. occidentalis 'Callahan Blue'

Recently introduced. Very rare. Likely named after Frank Callahan of Gold Hill, OR; sawmill operator, seed collector, and nominator of many record-size trees.

J. occidentalis 'Glauca'

= *J. occidentalis* 'Sierra Silver'

SIERRA SILVER JUNIPER. Introduced ≤1943 by W.B. Clarke nursery of San José, CA. Still sold by Monrovia nursery of California at least until 1966. Habit slim and conical; foliage notably attractive, bluish.

J. occidentalis 'Glenmore Blue Sierra'

Introduced <1957 by R.E. More of Buffalo Creek, CO. Very glaucous. Likely misattributed to *J. occidentalis*, because the berries, bark and glaucousness are all characteristic of *J. Deppeana* var. *pachyphlœa*. Glenmore is 7,000' elevation, with temperature plunges to minus 35–50°.

J. occidentalis 'Robinsonii'

= *J. scopulorum* 'Robinsonii'

Found ca. 1935 by William Robinson of Gilliam County, OR. Described in 1945. Extremely rare. Nearly five times taller than wide, extremely dense, deeper green than usual.

J. occidentalis 'Sierra Silver'—see *J. occidentalis* 'Glauca'

J. osteosperma (Torr.) Little

= *J. utahensis* (Engelm.) Lemm.
= *J. californica* var. *utahensis* Engelm.
= *J. californica* ssp. *osteosperma* (Torr.) E. Murr.

UTAH JUNIPER. BIGBERRY JUNIPER. From the arid western U.S., chiefly in Great Basin mountains: E Idaho to W New Mexico and CA. Introduced ca. 1900 by J. Purpus to Darmstadt, Germany. Exceedingly rare in cultivation. Its name means bone-seed (Greek *osteon*, bone, and *sperma*, seed). A distinctive pagoda-shaped tree. Branch ends downswept while upswept on *J. californica*. It can be hard to tell from ONESEED JUNIPER (*J. monosperma*, a fat bush—but to 29' × 14'0" × 28' in New Mexico 1981), however each specimen bears both male and female flowers, it is more often single-trunked, and the juvenile foliage stays blue longer. Foliage usually not glandular. Berries reddish-brown, glaucous, ¼"–⅜" (¾"), 1 (2) seeded. Records: 50' × 19'4" × 53' Lake Powell, UT (1975); 30' × 22'9" × 26' Duchesne County UT (1991).

J. osteosperma 'Glenmore'

Introduced <1957 by R.E. More of Buffalo Creek, CO. Extremely rare; extinct commercially. Slender and symmetrical.

J. Oxycedrus L.

PRICKLY JUNIPER. SHARP CEDAR (a literal translation of the pre-Linnæan name of Greek *oxy*, sharp, and *Cedrus*—the original *J. Oxycedrus* bears relatively less prickly needles). From S Europe, the Caucasus and Iraq. Cultivated since 1739; usually judged not worth growing as an ornamental. Exceedingly rare. A loose sprawling shrub or compact small tree of open, drooping habit. Needles wholly in trios, ½"–¾" (1") long, the upper side with two attractive whitish bands separated by a narrow green midrib. Male and female flowers are on separate trees. Berries ⅜"–½" wide, ripening glossy reddish-brown, occasionally glaucous when young; seeds (1) 2–3 (4). Records: to 46' × 10'0" in the wild; 27' × 1'6" Bedgebury, Kent, England (1967); 23' tall in Seattle, WA (1994; *pl.* 1962).

J. Oxycedrus ssp. macrocarpa (Sibth. & Sm.) Ball

= *J. macrocarpa* Sibth. & Sm.
= *J. neaboriensis* Laws. *ex* Gord.

PLUM JUNIPER. LARGE BERRIED JUNIPER. From S Europe to Iraq, in maritime areas. Probably should not be considered a subspecies. Essentially it is a big-berried variant of typical *J. Oxycedrus*. Named in 1813 (Greek *macro*, large, and *karpos*, fruit). Known in cultivation since ca. 1600 in Austria. A prostrate shrub or upright small tree. Needles as in typical *J. Oxycedrus* but average longer (¾"–1⅛"). Berries ½"–⅝", glaucous blue at first, then dull purplish brown; edible. Usually 3-seeded. Record: 30' tall at

Borde Hill, Sussex, England (1958).

J. pachyphlæa—see J. Deppeana

J. Pingii Cheng ex Ferré

From China. A species named in 1940; of controversial affinity and status. In North American commerce since ≤1993–94. Graceful, weeping. Closely related to *J. squamata* var. *Fargesii*.

J. recurva Buch.-Ham. ex D. Don

= *J. chinensis recurva* hort.

HIMALAYAN (WEEPING) JUNIPER. DROOPING JUNIPER. SACRED JUNIPER. From the E Himalayas, N Burma, Tibet, and W Yunnan. Introduced to cultivation probably ca. 1817 by Loddiges nursery of England. Grown in France by ca. 1822. Named in 1825. Little grown in North America. Kohankie nursery of Painesville, OH, sold it during the 1930s and '40s. A shrub or small tree closely related to, if not a mere variant of, *J. squamata*. Needles wholly in trios, ⅛"–⅓". Male and female flowers borne on the same or on separate individuals. Berries ⅓"–⅜" long, dark purplish brown or black, 1-seeded. Records: 62' × 4'1" Birr Castle, County Offaly, Ireland (1986); 52½' × 7'6" Mount Usher, County Wicklow, Ireland (1989).

J. recurva var. Coxii (A.B. Jacks.) Melv.

= *J. Coxii* A.B. Jacks.

COX'S WEEPING JUNIPER. COFFIN JUNIPER. From N Burma to Yunnan and E Tibet—never found below 10,000 feet elevation. Introduced in 1920 by Euan Hillhouse Methven Cox (1893–1977) and R.J. Farrer. Named in 1932. In North American commerce ≤1951. Extremely rare. A narrow, pendulous tree. Compared to typical *J. recurva*: branchlets longer, more pendulous; needles lax, more widely spaced, ¼"–½" long and proportionately wider, bright green; berries similar. As for growth rate, COX'S JUNIPER would seem to grow faster, and is less commonly multitrunked. The assertion that coffins were made of wood from this variety (COFFIN JUNIPER) may be erroneous, based on confusion with *Taiwania* trees. The same goes for the reports of dimensions to 100' × 30'0". Records: 48' × 6'9" Castlewellan, County Down, Ireland (1982); 46' × 5'0" Exbury, Hampshire, England (1987).

J. recurva var. squamata—see J. squamata

J. Reevesiana—see J. chinensis

J. rigida S. & Z.

NEEDLE JUNIPER. TEMPLE JUNIPER. From NE China, Korea, and Japan. Latin for stiff or rigid. Introduced in 1861 by J.G. Veitch to England. In North American nurseries ≤1915. Uncommon. Cold-hardy. Very attractive with softly pendulous twigs. Needles wholly in trios; ½"–¾" (1") long, sharp. Male and female flowers are on separate trees. Berries ¼"–⅜" brownish-black, slightly glaucous, 2–3 seeded. Usually a broad, irregular shrub. Records: to 56' tall in the wild; 50 × 5'6" Hawkhurst, Kent, England (1984); 49' × 5'6" Tong's Wood, Kent, England (1984); 32½ × 2'7" Victoria, B.C. (1995).

J. rigida 'Pendula'

Introduced <1990. Uncommon. Strong apical dominance with downswept branches. Branchlets hang straight. Its cultivar name is illegitimate, being Latin yet post-1959.

J. scopulorum Sarg.

= *J. virginiana* var. *scopulorum* (Sarg.) Lemm.
= *J. virginiana* ssp. *scopulorum* (Sarg.) E. Murr.
ROCKY MOUNTAIN JUNIPER. ROCKY MOUNTAIN RED-CEDAR. COLORADO JUNIPER. COLORADO REDCEDAR. From much of western North America. The name *scopulorum* derives from Latin *scopulus*, a cliff or rock, in reference to the tree's habitat. Introduced to cultivation in 1836. Common. Closely related to and hybridizes with EASTERN REDCEDAR (*J. virginiana*). Best in a continental climate; wet climates tend to stunt it. Some of the many cultivars following are surely *J. virginiana* clones or hybrids. *Scopulorum* usually bears coarser, more aromatic foliage than *virginiana*, and its berries need two years to ripen. Records: to 78' tall in British Columbia; 70' × 8'1" Saanich Peninsula, B.C. (1994); 64' × 9'8" × 28' Anacortes, WA (1988); 40' × 20'7" × 21' the 1,500 year-old JARDINE JUNIPER of Cache National Forest, UT (1989); in 1945 the same tree was measured 45' × 26'8" (at its very base).

J. scopulorum 'Admiral'

Introduced ca. 1956 by by Mount Arbor nursery of Shenandoah, IA. Still in commerce. Broadly conical-pyramidal form. Foliage gray-green, adult. Female. Record: 21½' × 10½' wide at Los Angeles, CA (1993; *pl.* 1982).

J. scopulorum 'Alba'

Introduced <1958 by Kansas nursery of Salina, KS. Commercially extinct. Pyramidal. Foliage bright frosty blue.

J. scopulorum 'Albino'

Introduced <1928 by D. Hill nursery of Dundee, IL. Sold by that nursery at least into the late '30s. Long extinct commercially. Of medium height.

J. scopulorum 'Argentea'—see *J. scopulorum* 'Hill's Silver'

J. scopulorum 'Big Blue'

Introduced ≤1950 by Plumfield nursery of Fremont, NE. Long extinct commercially. To 15'–22' tall. Much juvenile foliage. Blue-green, not so pale as many cultivars, not very blue.

J. scopulorum 'Blue Arrow'

= *J. virginiana* 'Blue Arrow'
Originated <1980. From T. Tesselaar of Pine Grove nursery, Niagara-on-the-Lake, Ontario. Introduced in 1987. Narrow, strictly erect tree with the habit of *J. scopulorum* 'Skyrocket' but more compact, the branches better clothed. Foliage somewhat coarse, deep blue.

J. scopulorum 'Blue Heaven'

(*J. scopulorum* 'Blue Haven')
Introduced <1945 by Plumfield nursery of Fremont, NE. Common. Neat pyramidal tree 15'–20' tall, compact while young, becoming open or loose; strikingly bright blue-gray year-round. Female.

J. scopulorum 'Blue Moon'

Introduced ≤1931 by D. Hill nursery of Dundee, IL. Still in commerce in the early 1980s. Foliage mostly adult, silvery blue, fine and delicate. Broadly pyramidal form to ca. 15' tall. Female.

J. scopulorum 'Blue Pillar'

Introduced in 1958 by Girard nursery of Geneva, OH. Dense columnar habit. Foliage among the tightest of all, prickly, bright silvery-blue. Of exemplary performance in Seattle, WA—one planted in 1962 is 16' tall × 4' wide (1994).

J. scopulorum 'Blue Pyramid'

Selected by A.B. Thomsen of Skalborg, Denmark. Introduced <1988. Very hardy. Not as blue as *J. scopulorum* 'Blue Heaven' but of the same shape, and more compact. The only *J. scopulorum* cultivar known to do well in the Danish coastal climate.

J. scopulorum 'Blue Queen'
Introduced ≤1958 by Monrovia nursery of California.

J. scopulorum 'Chandler Blue'
= *J. scopulorum* 'Chandler Silver'
= *J. scopulorum* 'Chandleri'

Origin not known. Possibly selected in the Black Hills. D. Wyman said it was likely selected by Chandler nursery of Prairie Village, KS. Maybe it originated with Chandler Landscape & Floral Company of Kansas City, MO. In commerce <1936. By 1946 it was one of the best known of the pyramidal blue forms. Still sold as late as the 1960s. Compact bluish-silver, to 25' tall.

J. scopulorum 'Chandleri'—see *J. scopulorum* 'Chandler Blue'

J. scopulorum 'Chandler Silver'—see *J. scopulorum* 'Chandler Blue'

J. scopulorum 'Colorado Green'—see *J. scopulorum* 'Cologreen'

J. scopulorum 'Cologreen'
= *J. scopulorum* 'Colorado Green'

Selected in the wild in 1935 by Marshall nursery of Arlington, NE. Introduced ≤1945. Very common. Bright green; symmetric, compact narrow columnar form, 12'–20' tall. Foliage adult, with a few scattered gray juvenile tufts. Berries borne.

J. scopulorum 'Columnar Sneed'
= *J. scopulorum* 'Sneed's Columnar'
= *J. scopulorum* 'Sneed(ii)'

Found by the Sneed nursery of Oklahoma City. Introduced ≤1956–57. Uncommon, especially since the mid–sixties. Columnar. Branching coarse, open. Foliage compact. Color called variously gray-blue, gray-green or green-blue. Both juvenile and adult foliage are present. Color descriptions based on young specimens would reflect the preponderance of bluish young foliage. Also, other cultivars (called vaguely 'Column' or 'Columnaris') might have been confused with 'Columnar Sneed'.

J. scopulorum 'Commando'
Introduced ≤1956 by Mount Arbor nursery of Shenandoah, IA. Very rare; long commercially extinct. Narrowly pyramidal, dark green.

J. scopulorum 'Crawford'
Origin not known. In commerce <1965. Very rare. Possibly named after Harold S. Crawford (1907–1990) of Willis nursery, Ottawa, KS. A broadly pyramidal, gray-blue tree.

J. scopulorum 'Cupressifolia Erecta'
= *J. scopulorum* 'Greenspire'
?= *J. scopulorum* 'Cupressifolia Green'

Origin not known. Sold since 1966–67 by Monrovia nursery of California. The cultivar name being Latin, is invalid if it was applied after 1959. The name 'Greenspire' was coined ≤1968, but has not been employed much. Possibly a 'Greenspire' exists that is not identical to 'Cupressifolia Erecta'. Monrovia's description of 'Cupressifolia Erecta': "Tall, upright, dense. Foliage rich green, needlelike, with undertones of silvery blue." Monrovia's clone may be a renaming of 'Cupressifolia Green', which, says the D. Hill nursery catalog of 1939–40, was "Introduced by one of the Holland nurseries. Grown from D. Hill seedlings supplied many years ago."

J. scopulorum 'Cupressifolia Glauca'
?= *J. scopulorum* 'Cupressifolia Blue'

Selected in 1932 by F.C. Hetz & Sons' Fairview Evergreen nursery of Fairview, PA. Very rare and commercially extinct. Densely pyramidal; twigs somewhat pendulous, thin, silvery.

J. scopulorum 'Dewdrop'
= *J. scopulorum* 'Kenyoni'

Selected from the wild by Kenyon, nurseryman of Dover, OK. Introduced ≤1945. Uncommon. Its form resembles a giant drop of dew. Very compact, almost looking sheared. Foliage both juvenile and adult; silver-blue. To 13' tall, perhaps more. Growth slow.

J. scopulorum 'Emerald (Green)'
Origin not known. Probably selected by R.E. More of Buffalo Creek, CO. Introduced ≤1942. Rare; likely commercially extinct. Compact bright green pyramid, to 18' or more. Male.

J. scopulorum 'Erecta Glauca'
Origin not known. Sold since 1956–57 by Monrovia nursery of California. Uncommon, especially since ca. 1980. Neat pyramidal or loosely columnar habit, splaying in age. Foliage silvery-blue, of feathery texture.

J. scopulorum 'Fairview'—see *J. chinensis* 'Hetzii Columnaris'

J. scopulorum 'Fulgens'

Introduced ≤1950 by Plumfield nursery of Fremont, NE. Very rare. Foliage silvery (*fulgens* in Latin means to shine or glisten). Narrow pyramid 15'–20' tall. Berries one-seeded.

J. scopulorum 'Funalis'

Origin not known, ≤1945. Very rare. Branches slender. Bluish-green.

J. scopulorum 'Glauca'

Probably a general name for bluish seedlings or cultivars. This name appears in a few nursery catalogs from 1948 to ca. 1960.

J. scopulorum 'Gracilis'

Introduced ≤1950 by Plumfield nursery of Fremont, NE. Very rare. Foliage fine, silvery blue. Compact, straight upright to 17' tall. Female; some berries one-seeded. May be a *J. virginiana* cultivar.

J. scopulorum 'Gray Gleam' PP 848 (1949)

Selected as a chance seedling in 1944 by Scott Wilmore of Wilmore nursery, Wheatridge, CO. Common. Very bright silvery-gray, nearly all juvenile foliage. Symmetric, very dense column slowly grows to 15'–20' tall. Male.

J. scopulorum Green Ice™

= *J. scopulorum* 'Monwade'

Introduced ≤1989 by Monrovia nursery of California. Broadly pyramidal; medium sized (to 15' × 10' wide); branching is tight. Icy-green new tip growth is erect, with gray-green older growth.

J. scopulorum 'Greenspire'—see J. scop. 'Cupressifolia Erecta'

J. scopulorum 'Grizzly Bear'

Origin not known. Uncommon. Likely it originated with Chandler Landscape & Floral Company of Kansas City, MO. That nursery was selling it ≤1950. One received that year by Seattle's arboretum is an upright thing in ill health, bearing juvenile foliage, in pairs and trios. J. Searles describes 'Grizzly Bear' as an extremely hardy, broadly rounded shrub, new foliage gray and old green, producing a two-toned effect.

J. scopulorum 'Hall'—see J. scopulorum 'Hall's Sport'

J. scopulorum 'Hall's Sport'

= *J. scopulorum* 'Hall'

Selected as a seedling by Marshall nursery of Arlington, NE. Introduced ≤1945. Rare. Foliage mostly juvenile. Stiffly upright and compact. Slow-growing.

J. scopulorum 'Hill's Silver'

= *J. scopulorum* 'Argentea'
= *J. scopulorum* 'Hillii'

Selected <1922 from the Black Hills of South Dakota. Introduced <1926 by D. Hill nursery of Dundee, IL. Common until the 1960s. A silvery-blue compact narrow column; to 22' tall.

J. scopulorum 'Hill Weeping'—see J. scopulorum 'Pendula'

J. scopulorum 'Hillii'—see J. scopulorum 'Hill's Silver'

J. scopulorum 'Kansas Silver'

Introduced <1958 by Kansas nursery of Salina, KS. Commercially extinct. Fast growing, pyramidal, silvery blue.

J. scopulorum 'Kenyoni'—see J. scopulorum 'Dewdrop'

J. scopulorum 'March Frost'

Origin not known, <1983. Rare. Vigorous. Upright. Blue-green.

J. scopulorum 'Marshall'

Found ca. 1935 by G.A. Marshall at a cemetery in Columbus, NE. Commercially extinct. Rather loosely pyramidal, silvery-blue tree.

J. scopulorum 'Medora'

Selected in the Badlands near Medora, ND. Introduced <1942. Has stayed in the trade and is among the most widely grown cultivars. Narrow, nearly columnar form, very dense; slow to 12' tall. Foliage soft bluish-green; both adult and juvenile.

J. scopulorum 'Moffetii'

Selected in the Rocky Mountains in 1937 by Lloyd A. Moffet (1887–1963) of Plumfield nursery, Fremont, NE. Common. Densely pyramidal; strong, to 20' tall. Foliage heavy, silvery-green, both juvenile and adult. Exceptionally hardy.

J. scopulorum 'Montana Green'
= J. scopulorum 'Montana No. 1'
Introduced <1953 by Plumfield nursery of Fremont, NE. Rare. Very slow. Small or medium sized; densely conical. Foliage dark green. The name 'Montana' was used in a general sense as early as 1941, for trees raised in nurseries from seeds obtained in Montana.

J. scopulorum 'Montana No. 1'—see J. scopulorum 'Montana Green'

J. scopulorum 'Monwade'—see J. scopulorum Green Ice™

J. scopulorum 'Moonglow'
Origin not known; if not a ca. 1969 renaming of 'Moonlight', at least some specimens of the latter have probably been sold as 'Moonglow'. Very common. Fast-growing 12'–20' tall, broadly columnar or pyramidal; not exceptionally dense. Foliage mostly adult, pale silvery blue-gray. Both male and (more often) female specimens have been sold as 'Moonglow'.

J. scopulorum 'Moonlight'
Selected <1928 by D. Hill nursery of Dundee, IL. Common until the late 1960s (when the name 'Moonglow' began circulating). Loose, open pyramid, 8'–12' tall. Foliage all adult; very light blue. Male.

J. scopulorum 'Mounteneer'
('Mountaineer')
Introduced in 1960–61 by Monrovia nursery of California. Extinct commercially. Dark green, pyramidal form.

J. scopulorum 'North Star'
= J. virginiana 'North Star'
Selected <1928 by D. Hill nursery of Dundee, IL. Still sold in Canada as of 1987. Foliage adult, fine, light shiny-green. Shapely, conical and compact; to 12' tall.

J. scopulorum 'Pathfinder'
Selected ≤1937 by L.A. Moffet of the Plumfield nursery, Fremont, NE. Common. Broad, open pyramidal form, regular in outline, to 15–20' tall. Foliage in rather flat sprays, bluish-gray even in winter.

J. scopulorum 'Pendula'
WEEPING ROCKY MOUNTAIN JUNIPER. Origin not known. Almost certainly several clones have been called by this name. The name 'Pendula' was in use ≤1933. In 1934, Plant Patent 89 was awarded to Carl Burton Fox for a "weeping scopulorum juniper." L. Kumlien in 1936 wrote that J. scopulorum 'Hill Weeping' was found in north Montana, and featured long, graceful drooping branches; but that the "Weeping Colorado Juniper" was even more weeping, with branchlets somewhat longer and finer-foliaged. A specimen labeled 'Pendula' planted in Spokane, WA, in 1938 is a glaucous, gaunt tree with ascending branches drooping their sprays. W.B. Clarke nursery of San José, CA obtained 'Pendula' ca. 1950 from the Boyce Thompson Arboretum, and was selling it by the late 1950s. Clarke's clone was upright after initial staking, with pendulous, thin, silvery branchlets. Trees labeled 'Perpendens' or 'Rependens' or 'Tolleson's Weeping' are also pendulous.

J. scopulorum 'Perpendens'—see J. scopulorum 'Pendula'

J. scopulorum 'Pillaris'—see J. scopulorum 'Skyrocket'

J. scopulorum 'Platinum' PP 1070 (1952)
Selected by Willis nursery of Ottawa, KS. Seldom sold since ca. 1970. Dense broad-based pyramid, to 17' tall. Foliage bright silvery-blue all year. Female.

J. scop. 'Pyramidalis Viridifolia Hillii'—see J. scop. 'Viridifolia'

J. scopulorum 'Rependens'—see J. scopulorum 'Pendula'

J. scopulorum 'Robinsonii'—see J. occidentalis 'Robinsonii'

J. scopulorum 'Silver Beauty'
Selected ≤1932 by D. Hill nursery of Dundee, IL. Commercially extinct since the 1960s. Pyramidal to 30' tall. Foliage greenish silver, more silvery at the tips of the branchlets.

J. scopulorum 'Silver Column'
Selected <1933 near Smithers, B.C., by Dr. M.B. Davis of the Dominion Arboretum in Ottawa. Named ≤1945. Perhaps not in commerce—at most sparingly so, and since the 1980s. Narrow, compact column. Foliage silvery, juvenile. Hardy and very drought-resistant.

J. scopulorum 'Silver Cord'

Introduced <1953 by Plumfield nursery of Fremont, NE. Very rare; almost commercially extinct. The straightest-stemmed JUNIPER of any grown by that nursery. A compact, very narrow tree. Foliage bluish-silver.

J. scopulorum 'Silver Glow'

Selected <1928 by D. Hill nursery of Dundee, IL. Perhaps extinct in commerce since the late 1960s. A very narrow little tree after the fashion of *J. scopulorum* 'Skyrocket'. Foliage vibrant silver-gray.

J. scopulorum 'Silver Queen'

Selected <1936 by D. Hill nursery of Dundee, IL. Likely never common. Extinct commercially. Very narrow pyramidal form, very glaucous. Foliage of both types.

J. scopulorum 'Skyrocket'

= *J. scopulorum* 'Pillaris'
= *J. chinensis* 'Skyrocket'
= *J. virginiana* 'Skyrocket'

SKYROCKET JUNIPER. Propagated but unnamed in the former Schuel nursery of South Bend, IN, in 1949 (1939?). Not common until after 1972. Grows to 25' tall or more. Very narrow, silvery. Male. Some specimens, either because of the way they were propagated, or because of the growing conditions, are not remarkably slender.

J. scopulorum 'Sneed's Columnar'—see J. scop. 'Columnar Sneed'

J. scopulorum 'Sneed(ii)'—see J. scopulorum 'Columnar Sneed'

J. scopulorum 'Sparkling Skyrocket'

= *J. virginiana* 'Sparkling Skyrocket'
= *J. virginiana* 'Sparkle'

Introduced in 1982 by Vermeulen nursery of New Jersey. Like *J. scopulorum* 'Skyrocket' but creamy-white variegated; broader.

J. scopulorum Spartan™

= *J. chinensis* 'Helle'
= *J. chinensis* 'Spartan'
= *J. chinensis* 'Denserecta' Spartan™

Introduced in 1961–62 by Monrovia nursery of California. Common. Fast, dense, compact narrow pyramid; to 20' tall. Foliage rich green. Berries blue, small, easily squished, single-seeded. Clearly *J. scopulorum* (or *J. virginiana*) despite being sold as *J. chinensis*.

J. scopulorum 'Spearmint'

= *J. chinensis* 'Spearmint'
= *J. virginiana* 'Spearmint'

Origin not known; possibly from Hines nursery of Santa Ana, CA. Introduced ≤1980. Common. Densely columnar, to 15' × 4' wide. Foliage bright green, both juvenile and adult. Berries one-seeded.

J. scopulorum 'Springbank'

Originated by John Parry of London, Ontario. Parry gave it to S. Park of London and to Bulk nursery of Boskoop, Holland, who introduced it in 1965. In North American commerce ≤1969. A graceful, narrow small tree, to 12' tall. Foliage intense blue.

J. scopulorum 'Springtime'

Selected by Mount Arbor nursery of Shenandoah, IA; introduced in 1956. Very rare. Dark green, pyramidal.

J. scopulorum 'Staver'

?= *J. virginiana* 'Stover' *sensu* M. Dirr 1990

Origin not known. Likely it originated with Chandler Landscape & Floral Company of Kansas City, MO. That nursery was selling it ≤1950. Rare. Foliage gray-green. Compact to open, pyramidal; growth rapid to 23' tall or more. Male.

J. scopulorum 'Steel Blue'

≠ *J. chinensis* 'Steel Blue'

Origin not known; in California commerce <1957. Rare. One planted in 1970 at Los Angeles, CA, is 20' × 12' wide (1993), male, and very blue. (G. Krüssmann describes *J. chinensis* 'Steel Blue' as flat-growing, blue-green, hardly disseminated, and dating from ≤1977.)

J. scopulorum 'Sterling Silver'

Origin not known. Described by M. Dirr in 1990 as a compact pyramid with interesting twisting tight silver blue foliage.

J. scopulorum 'Stikine Spire'

A tree under this name was received in 1977 at the University of British Columbia. Likely found near the Stikine River of NW British Columbia. Not known to be in commerce.

J. scopulorum 'Sutherland'

Selected by W.G. Sutherland of Boulder, CO. Introduced in 1925. Common. Foliage bright green or silver-green. Very bushy yet upright. Female.

J. scopulorum 'Tolleson's Blue Weeping'

Origin not known. In commerce (as 'Tolleson Weeping') since ≤1945. Very common only since ca. 1973. A tree with beautiful pendulous bluish foliage. See also *J. scopulorum* 'Pendula'. Record: 26' × 2'10" × 26' Los Angeles, CA (1993; *pl.* 1969 as *J. scopulorum* f. *rependens*).

J. scopulorum 'Tolleson's Green Weeping'

Origin not known. In commerce ≤1979. Less common than its blue associate.

J. scopulorum 'Victory'

Introduced <1936 by D. Hill nursery of Dundee, IL. Commercially extinct. Attributes not known.

J. scopulorum 'Viridifolia'

= *J. scopulorum* 'Pyramidalis Viridifolia Hillii'

Introduced <1923 by D. Hill nursery of Dundee, IL. Now extinct commercially, it was sold at least into the late 1950s by several nurseries. Very narrow; ascending branches. Foliage bright green. Some growers have equated the name 'Viridifolia' with *J. scopulorum* 'Cologreen'.

J. scopulorum 'Welchii'

Introduced <1940 by Plumfield nursery of Fremont, NE. Common. Narrow pyramidal to columnar form; dense, to 15'–30' tall. Foliage silvery green; young growth more silvery. Female.

J. scopulorum 'Wichita Blue'

Origin not known. In commerce ≤1979. Common. Broadly pyramidal, very irregular loose habit; 15'–30' tall. Foliage vivid blue-gray. Male.

J. Sheppardii—see J. chinensis var. Sheppardii

J. Sheppardii var. pyramidalis—see J. chinensis var. pyramidalis

J. Sheppardii var. pyramidalis f. variegata—see J. chinensis var. pyramidalis 'Variegata'

J. Sheppardii var. torulosa—see J. chinensis var. torulosa

J. silicicola—see J. virginiana var. silicicola

J. sinensis—see J. chinensis

J. sphærica—see J. chinensis var. sphærica

J. sphærica var. dioica—see J. chinensis var. dioica

J. sphærica glauca—see J. chinensis var. Sheppardii

J. sphærica var. Keteleeri—see J. chinensis var. Keteleeri

J. sphærica var. neaboriensis—see J. chinensis var. neaboriensis

J. sphærica var. pendula—see J. chinensis var. pendula

J. sphærica var. pseudo-mas—see J. chinensis 'Columnaris'

J. sphærica var. pseudo-mas f. columnaris—see J. chinensis 'Columnaris Glauca'

J. sphærica Sheppardii—see J. chinensis var. Sheppardii

J. squamata Buch.-Ham. ex Lamb.

= *J. morrisonicola* Hay.

= *J. recurva* var. *squamata* (Buch.-Ham. *ex* Lamb.) Parl.

FLAKY JUNIPER. From Afghanistan, N India, Bhutan, N Burma, Tibet, Nepal, China, and Taiwan. Introduced to England in 1824 (as *J. recurva* var. *squamata*) and named that year. In North American commerce ≤1873–74. Very rare. This species and *J. recurva* merge bafflingly; some say *J. squamata* should include *J. recurva* as a synonym. Or, in the narrowest sense, *J. squamata* is an alpine shrub, prostrate or 5' tall. E. Wilson reported it "ascending to higher altitudes than any other woody plant except an *Ephedra*." Needles bluish-green, wholly in trios, ⅛"–½" long, in age persisting on the twigs as dry brown scales (hence the name *squamata*—scaly in Latin). Berries inconspicuous, ¼"–⅓", black, 1-seeded. It is almost exclusively shrubby in cultivation. Records: to 50' × 10'0" in the wild; 14' × 5" Westonbirt, England (1966).

J. squamata 'Blue Alps'—see J. chinensis 'Blue Alps'

J. squamata var. Fargesii (Kom.) Rehd. & Wils.

= *J. Lemeeana* Lévl. & Blin

= *J. Fargesii* Kom.

FARGES' WEEPING JUNIPER. From W China, Tibet. Introduced by E. Wilson to the Arnold Arboretum in 1907–08. Named in 1914 after Père Paul Guillaume Farges (1844–1912). Compared to typical *J. squamata*, this is consistently treelike; its foliage droops handsomely; the needles are yellowish-green, longer, narrower, ¼"–½", the upper side with narrow gray bands; berries to ¼" long, smaller and less lustrous. Records: to 90' × 22'0" in the wild; 38' × 5'0" Seattle, WA (1993; *pl.* 1937).

J. squamata 'Meyeri'

MEYER JUNIPER. FISHBACK or FISHTAIL JUNIPER. Introduced in 1914. Described in 1922. Very common. Named after Frank Nicholas Meyer (1875–1918), Dutchman who collected plants for the USDA beginning in 1905. A female clone, usually a shrub, at most making a broad, 30' tall shrubby tree. The Chinese call it FISHTAIL JUNIPER. Needles like those of typical *J. squamata* but to ½" long, very glaucous, bluish with very broad white bands on upper side, and (most of all) very densely congested. Berries to ¼", change from reddish-brown to shining black. Record: 29' × 5'6" × 39' Tacoma, WA (1993).

J. stricta—see J. chinensis var. pyramidalis

J. suecica—see J. communis f. suecica

J. utahensis—see J. osteosperma

J. venusta—see J. virginiana 'Venusta'

J. virginiana L.

EASTERN REDCEDAR. PENCIL CEDAR. RED JUNIPER. From the eastern half of the U.S., and S Ontario and Québec. Common in cultivation. The southern population of broad, loosely branched trees is considered typical; the northern narrow, dense ones are var. *creba*. Most cultivars are from var. *creba*. Many hybrids with its close cousin *J. scopulorum* (ROCKY MOUNTAIN JUNIPER) occur from the Dakotas to Oklahoma. The two species are similar, but the eastern tree has finer, less aromatic foliage, and berries that ripen in one year instead of two. Juvenile foliage borne mostly in opposite pairs. Berries 1–3 seeded. Cedar-apple rust disease causes 1"–2" fruiting bodies, orange in spring. CHINESE JUNIPER (*J. chinensis*) resists this disease, but is susceptible to juniper twig blight (*Phomopsis* fungal disease) which *J. virginiana* resists. On many specimens the foliage turns dull brown in winter, leading to the selection of cultivars without such an unsightly habit. Records: to 120' tall in the South; 81' × 12'11" Jasper County, TX (1972); 80' × 12'3" E Feliciana Parish, LA

(1984); 71' × 17'2" Grant Parish, LA (1987); 55' × 17'7" × 68' Coffee County, GA (1989).

J. virginiana 'Alba-variegata'—see J. virginiana 'Variegata'

J. virginiana 'Albospica'

= *J. virginiana* 'Albovariegata' (in part; cf. *J. virginiana* 'Variegata')
= *J. virginiana* 'Argentea'

WHITE-TIP REDCEDAR. Described in 1887 in Europe. Extremely rare. Many of the youngest growths tipped white or creamy-white. Confused with *J. virginiana* 'Triomphe d'Angers' and 'Variegata'.

J. virginiana 'Albovariegata'—see J. virg. 'Albospica' and J. virg. 'Variegata'

J. virginiana 'Argentea'—see J. virginiana 'Albospica'

J. virginiana 'Aureo-variegata'

Cultivated <1850 in England. In North American commerce ≤1910. Extremely rare. Many of the young tips variegated yellow

J. virginiana 'Baker's Blue'

Origin not known. Twombly nursery of Monroe, CT, 1994 catalog: "Upright. Definite bluish cast.".

J. virginiana 'Blue Arrow'—see J. scopulorum 'Blue Arrow'

J. virginiana 'Blue Mountain'

Sold ≤1967 by Sheridan nursery of Ontario. Compact, vigorous to 15' tall. Foliage medium blue.

J. virginiana 'Burkii'

BURK REDCEDAR. In commerce since ≤1905. Possibly originated by Bobbink & Atkins nursery of East Rutherford, NJ. Named officially in 1932. Common. Dense, broadly pyramidal, 15'–30' tall. Foliage coarse-textured, light bluish-silver or "steel blue," plum-purplish in winter. Both adult and juvenile foliage. Male. May be a *J. scopulorum* cultivar or hybrid.

J. virginiana 'Canaertii'
('Cannarti')

CANAERT REDCEDAR. Named after Frédéric Canaert d'Hamale (1804–1888), horticulturist of Mechelen, Belgium. Described in 1868. Common. At first a compact pyramid; eventually more open and irregular with stout spreading branches. Foliage distinctive dark rich grass-green, largely adult, not purplish in winter. Berries many, with attractive bluish bloom. To 15'–40' tall usually, but one 62' × 2'7" at Dalków, Poland (≤1973).

J. virginiana 'Chamberlaynii'

= *J. virginiana* 'Pendula' (in part)

Originated ≤1850. Extremely rare in North America and not known in commerce here; better known in Europe. Confused with *J. virginiana* 'Pendula Nana' by Hillier nursery of England. Vigorous tree, tall, bearing long and slender primary branches and mostly glaucous, pendulous juvenile foliage. Female.

J. virginiana 'Cinerascens'

Cultivated in France <1855 but may be extinct there. In North America ≤1896. Extremely rare. Open, conical, vigorous. Young foliage ashy-gray to silver white (in Latin, *cinerascens* means becoming gray).

J. virginiana 'Corcorcor'—see J. virginiana Emerald Sentinel™

J. virginiana var. creba Fern. & Grisc.

NORTHERN REDCEDAR. The epithet *creba* means frequent in Latin. This variety represents the slender type, found in the Northeast, as opposed to the broader type found in the South. Most cultivars are of this variety.

J. virginiana 'Cupressifolia'

Introduced ≤1929. Named officially in 1932 by E.L. Kammerer of the Morton Arboretum, Lisle, IL. Rare. Pyramidal, rather loose, with CYPRESS-like, soft yellow-green foliage. The 'Cupressifolia' of L. Kumlien (1946) and nurseries is *J. virginiana* 'Hillspire' (q.v.).

J. virginiana 'DeForest Green'

Origin not known, likely from Kansas. Sold ≤1957. Commercially extinct. Pyramidal, similar to *J. virginiana* 'Canaertii' but deeper green, faster growing, and more cold-hardy.

J. virginiana 'Dundee'—see J. virginiana 'Hillii'

J. virginiana 'Elegantissima'

GOLDTIP REDCEDAR. GOLDTIP JUNIPER. LEE'S GOLDEN JUNIPER. Described in 1882. Common once; presently very rare in commerce. Bushy, pyramidal, usually not over 20' tall. Foliage both adult and juvenile; tips of twigs golden yellow. Bronzy in winter. Record: 26' × 1'3" Bedgebury, Kent, England (1969).

J. virginiana Emerald Sentinel™ PP 5041 (1983)

= *J. virginiana* 'Corcorcor'

Introduced in 1980 by Conard-Pyle nursery of West Grove, PA. Columnar, 25'–30' tall, emerald green all year. Sturdy. Rapid.

J. virginiana 'Fastigiata'

Raised and introduced in 1933–34 by Hesse nursery of Germany. In North American commerce by the late 1930s when sold by Siebenthaler nursery of Dayton, OH. Very rare. Narrow, columnar; sprays very thin, bluish-green.

J. virginiana 'Filifera'

Introduced <1923 by D. Hill nursery of Dundee, IL. Extremely rare but still in commerce. Broadly pyramidal. Long, much divided branches of bluish-gray slender threadlike twigs (from Latin *filum*, thread, and *ferre*, to bear). Male.

J. virginiana f. glauca (Carr.) Beissn.

SILVER REDCEDAR. Originally described in 1850. Common. Seed-grown and selected for color; some clones have been grafted. A common one is a female that tends to start life as a dense column of very pale silver, but grows vigorously into an irregular tree. Record: 50' × 6'6" Endsleigh, Devon, England (1963).

J. virginiana 'Goldspire'

From Lincoln nursery of Grand Rapids, MI; introduced in 1981. Erect, conical tree. Foliage markedly golden yellow.

J. virginiana 'Grey Rock'

Introduced in 1960 by Sheridan nursery of Ontario. Out of commerce by 1982. Broadly upright to 15' tall. Foliage gray-green. Very hardy.

J. virginiana 'Henryi'

Origin not known. Sold <1958 by Willis nursery of Ottawa, KS. Almost commercially extinct. Dense upright dark green pyramid.

J. virginiana 'Hillii'

= *J. virginiana* 'Dundee'
= *J. virginiana* 'Pyramidiformis Dundee'
= *J. virginiana* 'Pyramidiformis Hillii'
≠ *J. virginiana* 'Pyramidalis Hillii'

HILL'S DUNDEE JUNIPER. Selected ca. 1913 by David Hill (1847–1929) of Dundee, IL. Common. Dense and columnar, growing slowly to 15'–20'. Foliage soft, juvenile, pale bluish green or gray green in spring and summer, purplish-plum in fall and winter. Male. Among the hardiest of uprights.

J. virginiana 'Hillspire'
= J. virginiana 'Cupressifolia' of Kumlien (1946) and nurseries, non E.L. Kammerer (1932)

HILLSPIRE JUNIPER. Raised ca. 1925 by D. Hill nursery of Dundee, IL, and inadvertently named 'Cupressifolia' so another name ('Hillspire') had to be chosen. Common. A symmetrical, formal column or compact pyramid, 15'–30' tall. Foliage adult, dark green even in winter. Male.

J. virginiana 'Idyllwild'
= J. chinensis 'Idylwild' (sic)

Origin not known. Introduced ≤1978–79. A broad-based informal pyramid. Foliage dark green. Rapid growing, to 20' × 7' wide.

J. virginiana 'Keteleeri'—see J. chinensis var. Keteleeri

J. virginiana 'Lebretoni'
= J. Libretonia hort.
= J. Libretoni glauca hort.

Origin not known. Introduced ≤1925 in California (as J. Libretonia). Rare. Compact pyramid with ascending branches; to 15' tall. Foliage intensely glaucous. Some, perhaps most of the trees sold under this name are actually ALLIGATOR JUNIPER (J. Deppeana var. pachyphlæa).

J. virginiana 'Manhattan Blue'
Introduced <1958 by Robert Scott of Manhattan, KS. Common. Compact broad pyramid; to 15–20' tall. Foliage bluish-green; both adult and juvenile. Female. Record: 31' × 2'5" × 16' Los Angeles, CA (1993; pl. 1968).

J. virginiana 'Mission Spire'—see J. chinensis 'Mission Spire'

J. virginiana 'Nevin's Blue'
Introduced <1957 and sold by more than one Kansas nursery. Attributes not known. Commercially extinct.

J. virginiana 'North Star'—see J. scopulorum 'North Star'

J. virginiana 'Nova'
Introduced ca. 1950 by D. Hill nursery of Dundee,

IL, as HILL'S NEW JUNIPER. Uncommon. Loosely upright pyramid. Foliage gray-green to rich medium green, purplish in winter. To 20' tall. Very hardy.

J. virginiana 'Pendula'
WEEPING REDCEDAR. Various clones have been called 'Pendula'. Between ca. 1850 and 1900 three forms were known in Britain. 1) Spreading, numerous short branches and pendulous branchlets clothed with adult foliage only; male; 2) the female clone 'Chamberlaynii' (q.v.) 3) the female clone 'Pendula Viridis' (q.v.). The handsomest is the third, the only one generally cultivated now. Conifer specialist R. Fincham says the prostrate male clone 'Reptans' also is sold as 'Pendula'. Various North American nurseries have listed 'Pendula' over the decades, but in no manifestation can it be called common. Another pendulous clone is 'Smithii' (q.v.). Until all the JUNIPER cultivars of weeping habit are collected and studied, they will remain confusing.

J. virginiana 'Pendula Viridis'
= J. virginiana 'Pendula' (in part)

Described 1862. In North American commerce ≤1870. Like a WEEPING WILLOW. Elongated pendulous branchlets. Foliage all adult, bright light green. Female. (P. van Melle says the plant originally called by this name is a shrub, J. × media 'Arbuscula'.)

J. virginiana 'Platte River'
Origin not known. Likely refers to the river in Nebraska or Missouri. Sold as early as 1902 by D.M. Andrews of Boulder, CO. Andrews described it as very compact, symmetrical and strongly purplish-tinged in winter. Another description, from the 1926 catalog of D. Hill nursery of Dundee, IL: "Pyramidal; dark green to bluish. A hardy northern strain seed-grown by us for many years." R.E. More said in 1957 that its hardiness in Colorado suggests it has some J. scopulorum genes. Given the above information, 'Platte River' seems best treated as a name not for a clone, but for a hardy western strain or hybrid of J. virginiana.

J. virginiana 'PNI 3570'—see J. virg. Princeton Sentry®

J. virginiana Princeton Sentry®
= J. virginiana 'PNI 3570'

Introduced ≤1988–89 by Princeton nursery of New Jersey. Compact, narrow, bluish-green, 25'–30' tall; purple-green in winter.

J. virginiana 'Pseudocupressus'

Cultivated since ≤1929. Described officially in 1932 (from Greek *pseudes*, false, and genus *Cupressus*). Uncommon. Narrow column; branches hug the trunk closely. Foliage juvenile, the upper side light green, underside bluish-green; color of the new growth quite pronounced pale gray-green. To 20'–40' tall.

J. virginiana 'Pyramidalis'

This name was published in France in 1867, and its application has been variously interpreted. It can be considered in a collective sense, indicating generally any very slender specimen. In a narrow sense it may refer to an unusually fastigiate and densely formal columnar clone, bearing mostly adult, bright green foliage (which sounds like 'Pyramidalis Hillii'). Nurseries over the years have doubtless provided different clones under this name. Since ca. 1970 the name has very seldom been used.

J. virginiana 'Pyramidalis Hillii'

≠ *J. virginiana* 'Pyramidiformis Hillii'—see *J. virginiana* 'Hillii'

HILL PYRAMIDAL JUNIPER. Introduced ≤1927 by nurseryman David Hill (1847–1929) of Dundee, IL. Long extinct commercially at least under this name—likely sold as 'Pyramidalis'. Foliage rich dark green, adult predominating. Very rapid grower.

J. virginiana 'Pyramidiformis Dundee'—see J. virginiana 'Hillii'

J. virginiana 'Pyramidiformis Hillii'—see J. virginiana 'Hillii'

J. virginiana 'Schottii'

SCHOTT REDCEDAR. Known in British cultivation as early as 1855. Common. Narrow pyramid or column, like *J. virginiana* 'Canaertii' but lighter green to slightly yellowish green, with more ascending branch tips, and a more rounded top; foliage adult. Although generally small and dense, it has reached 80' in height at Angers, France (1973).

J. virginiana var. or ssp. scopulorum—see J. scopulorum

J. virginiana 'Sherwoodii'

A 1935 seedling at the Sherwood nursery of Portland, OR. Rare. Conical, narrow, dark green, similar to *J. virginiana* 'Canaertii' but the tips of the shoots creamy in spring, solid bright green in summer, very dark plum-colored in winter.

J. virginiana var. silicicola (Small) Silba

= *J. virginiana* ssp. *silicicola* (Small) E. Murr.
= *J. silicicola* (Small) Bailey
= *J. barbadensis* hort., non L.
= *J. lucayana* hort., non Britt.

SOUTHERN REDCEDAR. SAND CEDAR. COAST JUNIPER. From SE Texas to North Carolina, chiefly along the coast. Its Latin name means growing in sand. Differs from typical *J. virginiana* in having more slender twigs, larger male cones, smaller berries (<¼"). From an ornamental view, it is very lovely and semi-pendulous, yet less cold-hardy, so has been planted almost exclusively within its native range. Records: 80' × 16'1" Archer, FL (1988); 49' × 28'1" × 62' DeLand, FL (1993).

J. virginiana 'Skyrocket'—see J. scopulorum 'Skyrocket'

J. virginiana 'Smithii'

= *J. virginiana* Smithii pendula hort. *ex* Beissn.

May be from the Richard Smith nursery of England. Officially named in 1891. In North American commerce ≤1921. Uncommon, especially since the 1960s. Ouden says this is a synonym of 'Pendula Viridis'. P. van Melle says the name is a synonym of the shrub *J. × media* 'Arbuscula'. U.S. nurseries selling it in the 1920s described it as a small compact pyramidal tree; the branches sparingly ramified and pendulous; foliage light grass-green, even in winter.

J. virginiana Smithii pendula—see J. virginiana 'Smithii'

J. virginiana 'Sparkle'—see J. scopulorum 'Sparkling Skyrocket'

J. virg. 'Sparkling Skyrocket'—see J. scop. 'Sparkling Skyrocket'

J. virginiana 'Spearmint'—see J. scopulorum 'Spearmint'

J. virginiana 'Stover'—see J. scopulorum 'Staver'

J. virginiana 'Towsoni'

Discovered as a seedling. Introduced ≤1930 by Towson nursery of Maryland. Long extinct commercially. Compact; upright to 30'–40' tall. Foliage gray-green with a touch of silver-blue in summer; purple-blue in fall.

J. virginiana 'Triomphe d'Angers'

Described in 1874 in Europe. Presumably from Angers, France. Extremely rare. Slow, conical, scanty but dense growth; branches and branchlets thin, creamy-white blotched and speckled over dark bluish-green. Rather tender. Resembles *J. virginiana* 'Albospica'.

J. virginiana 'Variegata'

= *J. virginiana* 'Albovariegata' (in part; cf. *J. virginiana* 'Albospica')
= *J. virginiana* 'Alba-variegata'
= *J. virginiana* 'Variegata Alba'

Named in 1851 by Lawson nursery of Edinburgh, Scotland. Extremely rare. White variegated.

J. virginiana 'Variegata Alba'—see *J. virginiana* 'Variegata'

J. virginiana 'Venusta'

= *J. venusta* hort. (in part)

Introduced in 1882 by Ellwanger & Barry nursery of Rochester, NY. In Latin, *venusta* means beautiful. Narrowly columnar, to 25' or more. Foliage mostly adult, dark green—on young plants light silvery or bluish-green. Rapid growing. Confused with *J. chinensis* var. *pyramidalis* (a.k.a. *J. excelsa* 'Stricta').

J. virginiana 'Vinespire'

Introduced in 1967 by the Horticultural Research Institute of Vineland, Ontario. Very rare, if in commerce at all. Narrowly columnar; to 16' tall.

Kalopanax

[ARALIACEÆ; Ginseng Family] 1 or 2 spp. of deciduous trees from E Asia. From Greek *kalos*, beautiful or handsome, and *Panax* (GINSENG), a related herbaceous genus—from *pan*, all, and *akos*, a remedy. The only related genus in this volume is *Aralia*.

K. pictus—see *K. septemlobus*

K. pictus f. *Maximowiczii*—see *K. septemlobus* f. *Maximowiczii*

K. ricinifolium—see *K. septemlobus*

K. septemlobus (Th. *ex* J.A. Murr.) Koidz.

= *K. pictus* Nakai
= *K. ricinifolium* (S. & Z.) Miq.
= *Acanthopanax septemlobus* (Th. *ex* J.A. Murr.) Koidz. *ex* Rehd.
= *Acanthopanax ricinifolius* (S. & Z.) Seem.
= *Acer septemlobum* Th. *ex* J.A. Murr.

PRICKLY CASTOR-OIL TREE. From E Siberia, Korea, Japan, China, Manchuria, the S Kuriles, Sakhalin, and the Ryukyus. Introduced to Western cultivation ca. 1865 by C.J. Maximowicz. In North American commerce <1892. Rare. The specific epithet refers to the leaf and means seven lobes in Latin. Leaf SYCAMORE-like, large (to 14" wide, the stem to 15¼" long); fall color unspectacular dull yellowish or reddish in October. The leaf resembles that of the castor bean (*Ricinus communis*), while the trunk and branches are prickly with short stout spines, hence the English name. Flowers creamy-white, minute yet abundant and conspicuous in late July and August. Berries tiny, reddish-black, green inside, on whitish stalks; overall vaguely like those of ELDER (*Sambucus*). Bark brown, deeply furrowed. A large shade tree performing best in moist soil, it is bold and unconventional, with something of a primitive aura. Records: to 100' × 20'0" in the wild says E. Wilson; 72' × 5'4" Warren House, Surrey, England (1988); 68' × 10'3" Emmetts, Ide Hill, Kent, England (1984); 57' × 7'0" Arnold Arboretum, MA (ca. 1980); 50' × 5'9" Seattle, WA (1993; *pl.* 1948); 40' × 9'3" × 58' Philadelphia, PA (1980).

K. septemlobus f. *Maximowiczii* (van Houtte) H. Ohashi

= *K. pictus* f. *Maximowiczii* (van Houtte) Hara
= *K. pictus* var. *Maximowiczii* (van Houtte) Hand.-Mazz.
= *Acanthopanax ricinifolius* var. *Maximowiczii* (van Houtte) Schneid.
= *Aralia Maximowiczii* van Houtte

Named and introduced to cultivation in 1874. As rare as the typical form. Named after Carl Johann Maximowicz (1827–1891), Russian who botanized in Japan 1860–1863. Leaves deeply lobed, can be divided more than halfway to the base.

Keteleeria

[PINACEÆ; Pine Family] 2–3 spp. (or 4–10 if one makes fine distinctions) of coniferous evergreens. Named after Joseph Baptiste Keteleer (1813–1903), French nurseryman born in Belgium. Suited to drier, warmer regions than most *Abies* (FIR), the genus to which it is most closely related. In especially hot climates (such as California's Central Valley), *Keteleeria* needs irrigation to perform well. Young specimens at least are sensitive to freezing winters.

K. calcarea—see *K. Davidiana*

K. chien-peii—see *K. Davidiana*

K. cyclolepis—see *K. Fortunei*

K. Davidiana (Bertr.) Beissn.
= *K. calcarea* Cheng & Fu
= *K. Chien-peii* Flous
= *K. dopiana* Flous
= *K. hainanensis* Chun & Tsiang
= *K. pubescens* Cheng & Fu
= *K. Roulletii* (A. Cheval.) Flous
From China, S Viet Nam, S Laos, and Taiwan. Discovered in 1869 by J.P.A. David (see genus *Davidia*, DOVE TREE). Introduced to Western cultivation in 1888–89. To North America ≤1923; in commerce here ≤1925. Extremely rare. Needles 1"–3⅛" long, ⅛" or more wide, sharp on youngsters—old plants can bear blunt, notched needles. Cones erect, reddish, soon green, and at maturity pale chestnut-brown, (2") 4"–8" long. Twigs usually densely covered with yellowish-gray hairs. Bark pale, soft and corky. Although stiff-looking when young, aged specimens become progressively less formal and rival the relaxed elegance characteristic of HEMLOCKS (*Tsuga*). Records: to 164' tall in the wild says K. Rushforth; to 131' × 19'8" in the wild says E. Wilson; 70' × 10'0" × 57½' and 64' × 5'1" × 42' San Marino, CA (1993; *pl.* <1943); 47' × 4'0" Berkeley, CA (1989; *pl.* 1935).

K. dopiana—see *K. Davidiana*

K. Fortunei (A. Murr.) Carr.
= *K. cyclolepis* Flous
= *K. oblonga* Cheng & L.K. Fu

From coastal, subtropical S China. Robert Fortune (1812–1880) introduced this to England in 1844. Rarer than *K. Davidiana*; probably less cold-hardy. Twigs smooth, or hairy at first. Needles (½")1"–1⅜" (1½") long. Cones are purple when young (not green), 2⅜"–7" (10⅞") long. Recorded to 100' × 15'5" in the wild.

K. hainanensis—see *K. Davidiana*

K. oblonga—see *K. Fortunei*

K. pubescens—see *K. Davidiana*

K. Roulletii—see *K. Davidiana*

Koelreuteria

[SAPINDACEÆ; Soapberry Family] 3 (4) spp. of small deciduous trees with compound leaves; native in Asia; heat-loving and sun-needing. Named after Joseph Gottlieb Kölreuter (1733–1806), German professor of natural history at Karlsruhe, "the father of hybridizing plants." The GOLDEN RAIN TREES are prized for their bright yellow flowers and attractive bladder-like "Chinese lantern" seedpods. All three of the following species have reseeded readily, if not weedily, in certain parts of the United States. Related genera include *Sapindus* (SOAPBERRY) and *Xanthoceras* (YELLOW-HORN).

K. bipinnata Franch.
= *K. integrifolia* Merrill
CHINESE LANTERN TREE. CHINESE FLAME TREE. EVERGREEN GOLDEN RAIN TREE. SOUTHERN GOLDEN RAIN TREE. BOUGAINVILLEA TREE. RED RAINTREE. From China. Named in 1886. Introduced to Western cultivation in 1888. In North America ≤1897; in commerce here ≤1905. Uncommon. Compared to the common GOLDEN RAIN TREE (*K. paniculata*), this is a larger, much faster, more delicate and luxurious-looking, less cold-hardy species, tolerating ca. 15° or even 0°F. The flowers are not as showy (but still very worthwhile), the seedpods far more attractive—though surpassed by those of the more tender *K. elegans* (with which it is often confused). Leaves

very unlike those of *K. paniculata*, being fully bipinnate (like KENTUCKY COFFEE TREE, *Gymnocladus*), with as many as 50 leaflets. Leaflets lightly hairy, to 5½" × 2½"; varying from inconspicuously toothed to untoothed, few or none of them lobed (and only weakly so). Fall color late and yellowish. Flower clusters to 2½' long from late August into early October. Seedpods longer (to 2") and wider (to 1⅜") as well as more colorful than those of *K. paniculata*, the portions broad and not so triangular as in *K. paniculata*. Seeds later to ripen. Records: to 82' tall in the wild; 60' × 7'1" × 59½' Santa Barbara, CA (1993).

K. elegans (Seem.) A.C. Sm.

From Fiji. Cold tender.

K. elegans ssp. *formosana* (Hay.) F.G. Meyer

= *K. formosana* Hay.
= *K. Henryi* Dümmer

FLAMEGOLD. FORMOSAN GOLDEN RAIN TREE. CHINESE FLAME TREE. CHINESE LANTERN TREE. From Taiwan. Introduced to North America ≤1916. In commerce since ≤1927 in Florida. Extremely rare except in the Deep South. Most if not all stock grown in North America is definitely cold tender; reports to the contrary must be viewed with skepticism. It warrants inclusion in this volume only because it is so often mixed up with *K. bipinnata*. Flowers yellow, borne in upright clusters in September-October. Leaf large and doubly compound like that of *K. bipinnata*, but glossier, with as many as 60 leaflets, finely toothed, nearly or wholly hairless, to 4¼" × 1¼". The great attraction is its conspicuous rose-red to coral-red seedpods (to 1½"), at their prime in late October and early November. Growth rapid. Crown less heavy than that of *K. bipinnata*; more elegant. Records: 58' × 5'1" × 48½' Los Angeles, CA (1993; *pl.* 1965); 35' × 5'3" Davis, CA (1992; *pl.* ca. 1958).

K. formosana—see *K. elegans* ssp. *formosana*

K. Henryi—see *K. elegans* ssp. *formosana*

K. integrifolia—see *K. bipinnata*

K. japonica—see *K. paniculata*

K. paniculata Laxm.

= *K. japonica* Sieb.

GOLDEN RAIN TREE. SHOWER TREE. PRIDE OF INDIA. VARNISH TREE. GATE TREE. CHINA TREE. From China and Korea. Introduced from N China to St. Petersburg ca. 1750 by Pierre d'Incarville; to England in 1763. Named in 1772. In North America by 1790. Common. The name GOLDEN RAIN refers to its yellow flowers (the similarly named GOLDENCHAIN tree is genus *Laburnum*). PRIDE OF INDIA is a name shared with *Melia Azedarach* (CHINABERRY) and *Lagerstœmia speciosa* (not in this volume). VARNISH TREE is also applied to *Ailanthus altissima* (TREE OF HEAVEN), *Rhus Potaninii* and *R. verniciflua*. GATE TREE alludes to many specimens planted at entryways in certain Midwestern locales. In China this species is *Luan*, the tree planted on the graves of scholars—nonetheless the name CHINESE SCHOLAR TREE is given to *Sophora japonica*. By any name, *K. paniculata* is a distinctive small tree of irregular growth, its trunk usually crooked or leaning. Leaves compound, 6"–18" long; leaflets 7–17, toothed (and often divided themselves), shrimp-pink to bronze in spring, dark green in summer; fall color varies from negligible to bright yellow. Flowers in large, loose clusters, variably from July into early October. Seedpods light green when young, pale pink-brown at maturity, 1½"–2" long, less handsome than those of *K. bipinnata* and *K. elegans*. Often short-lived. Records: to 80' tall in the wild; 65' × 9'0" Washington, D.C. (ca. 1980); 62' × 5'0" Sandford Park, Cheltenham, Gloucestershire, England (1989); 55' × 4'2" Tacoma, WA (1990); 46' × 5'9" Boston, MA (1974); 40' × 6'0" Salt Lake City, UT (1991); a trunk 8'2" around on Long Island, NY (1972).

K. paniculata var. *apiculata* (Rehd. & Wils.) Rehd.

Introduced in the early 1900s by E. Wilson, but subsequently found to be synonymous with the typical kind.

Koelreuteria paniculata 'Fastigiata'

Originally raised from seeds sent in 1888 from Shanghai to England. Officially described in 1929. Introduced to North America ≤1937. In commerce here ≤1957. Very rare. Stiffly upright and narrow. Flowers sparse. Record: 49' × 2'0" Exbury House, Beaulieu, Hampshire, England (1987).

K. paniculata September Gold™

Discovered ca. 1960 as a 25-year-old specimen at the University of Indiana at Bloomington. Introduced commercially in 1967 by Scanlon nursery of Ohio. Rare. Flowers from late August well into September. Panicle much larger and more densely branched than normal. Very floriferous.

+ Laburnocytisus

[LEGUMINOSÆ; Pea Family] A bigeneric graft-hybrid or chimæra between *Laburnum* and *Cytisus*. The only other graft-hybrids in this book are +*Cratægomespilus Dardarii* (BRONVAUX MEDLAR), another singular production from 19th-century France; and (perhaps) the CRABAPPLE *Malus* 'Kelsey'.

L. Adamii (Poit.) Schneid.
= *Laburnum Adamii* (Poit.) Kirchn.
= *Cytisus Adamii* Poit.

CHIMÆRIC GOLDENCHAIN. ADAM'S LABURNUM. PURPLE LABURNUM. PINK LABURNUM. Monsieur Jean Louis Adam (1777–1830), at his nursery of Vitry, near Paris, in 1825 grafted a DWARF PURPLE BROOM bush (*Cytisus purpureus*) onto a GOLDENCHAIN tree (*Laburnum anagyroides*), thereby accidentally producing a freak. The resulting tree, while primarily like regular GOLDENCHAIN, bears some foliage and flowers of the *Cytisus*, and some of intermediate character. Blooming in mid-May, it is an arresting novelty of part yellow and part rosy-purple. The rest of the year it is ugly, or at best plain. Introduced to North America in the 1800s, it is still very rare. Records: 33' × 5'0" × 35' Burnaby, B.C. (1992); 26' × 6'0" Tarbat, Highland, Scotland (1983).

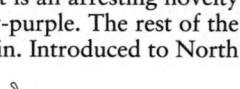

Laburnum

[LEGUMINOSÆ; Pea Family] 2–3 spp. of deciduous large shrubs or small trees, featuring showy yellow pealike flowers in dangling chains like those of *Wisteria* vines, giving rise to the name GOLDENCHAIN. In virtually every European language *Laburnum* is called GOLDEN RAIN, a name preferred in America for *Koelreuteria*. *Laburnum* is the ancient Latin name. Leaves trifoliate and clover-like, folding up at night; devoid of fall color worth a second glance. Bark soft and greenish-brown. Branches stiff and brittle. Wood very dark and heavy. Seedpods narrow, unsightly. Poisonous.

L. Adamii—see + *Laburnocytisus Adamii*

L. alpinum (Mill.) Bercht. & Presl
= *Cytisus alpinus* Mill.

ALPINE GOLDENCHAIN. SCOTCH LABURNUM. From S and C Europe. Not native in Scotland, but commonly planted there in the 18th and early 19th centuries. In North America ≤1874. Uncommon. Larger, more cold-hardy, and blooms later in spring than *L. anagyroides*. Leaves, pods and twigs essentially hairless. Flowers in late May or early June; the chains tight and slender, 10"–16" long. Records: 52½' × 3'2" Brooklands, Somerset, England (1982); 40' × 6'3" × 48' Scotland (ca. 1830); 36' × 6'9" × 23' Hoquiam, WA (1992); 30' × 6'0" × 26' Seattle, WA (1988); a trunk 13'1" around at Megginch Castle, Perthshire, Scotland (1986).

L. alpinum 'Pendulum'

WEEPING ALPINE GOLDENCHAIN. Described in 1838 in England. In North American commerce primarily since 1958. Uncommon. Absolutely weeping in mophead fashion, its height depends on how high it is grafted. For all practical purposes it is bush-sized, less than 12' tall. Less floriferous than typical specimens.

L. anagyroides Med.
= *L. vulgare* Bercht. & Presl
= *Cytisus Laburnum* L.

GOLDENCHAIN. COMMON LABURNUM. BEAN TREFOIL TREE. GOLDENRAIN TREE. FRENCH ASH. BEAN TREE. PEA TREE. From C and S Europe. In North American commerce ≤1790. Common. In recent decades its place in nurseries has been taken by its hybrid *L.* × *Watereri*. The specific epithet *anagyroides* derives from genus *Anagyris* (shrubs), and Greek *-oides*, resemblance. Flowers from mid-April into mid-May (early June), in chains ca. 6"–12" long. Seedpods unsightly dull brown, 2"–3" long. Cultivars exist but have been extinct in general commerce for decades. Records: 56' × 16'0" × 36' Leiden, Holland (1937; *pl.* 1601); 26' × 5'3" × 25' Tacoma, WA (1990).

L. Vossii—see *L.* × *Watereri* and *L.* × *Watereri* 'Vossii'

L. Vossii 'Columnaris'—see *L.* × *Watereri* 'Columnaris'

L. vulgare—see *L. anagyroides*

L. × *Watereri* (Kirchn.) Dipp.
= *L. Vossii* hort. (in part)
(*L. anagyroides* × *L. alpinum*)
HYBRID GOLDENCHAIN. HYBRID LABUR-NUM. Known since ca. 1840. Named in 1864. Common in North American commerce since the 1940s. Flower chains 12"–16" long or more. Seedpods few. Records: 34' × 4'7" Seattle, WA (1990); 29' × 5'11" Tacoma, WA (1992).

L. × *Watereri* 'Columnaris'
= *L. Vossii* 'Columnaris'

Origin unknown. As described in the 1987–88 catalog of Belcher nursery of Boring, OR: Narrow, upright form; flower chains somewhat short but very thick. Being post-1959, yet Latin, 'Columnaris' is invalid as a cultivar name.

L. × *Watereri* 'Longest and Latest'
Obscure; likely a mere English nursery name for *L. alpinum*. In North America since the <1962 but not known in commerce here. Said to bear 15" flower chains in June.

L. × *Watereri* 'Parksii'
('Parkesii')
Advertised for sale in 1842 by John Damper Parks (1792–1866), nurseryman of Dartford, Kent, England. Believed to have been superseded by 'Vossii' (below) which has longer flower chains.

L. × *Watereri* 'Vossii'
= *L. Vossii* hort. (in part)
VOSS'S LABURNUM. Described in 1875 by Cornelis de Vos (1806–1895), of Hazerswoude, near Boskoop, Holland. Flower chains exceptionally long, to 18"–24". Although virtually all contemporary nursery listings indicate 'Vossii', there is good reason to believe many specimens so called are another clone, as the flower chains are not nearly long enough.

Lagerstrœmia

[LYTHRACEÆ; Loosestrife Family] 30–55 spp. of mostly tropical shrubs and trees from SE Asia and Australia; popularly known as CRAPEMYRTLES. Named after Magnus von Lagerström (1696–1759) of Gothenburg; Swedish merchant, director of the East India Company, and friend of Linnaeus. The flower petals are ruffled and crinkled crape-like; the glossy leaves and smooth pale trunk recall the original MYRTLE (*Myrtus communis;* not in this volume). A good account of the CRAPEMYRTLES is The *Lagerstrœmia* Handbook / Checklist; A Guide to Crapemyrtle Cultivars, published in 1978 by the American Association of Botanical Gardens and Arboreta.

L. Fauriei Koehne
COPPERBARK CRAPEMYRTLE. JAPANESE CRAPEMYRTLE. From Yakushima Island of S Japan; very rare in the wild. Named after Père Urbain Faurie (1847–1915), French missionary in Japan, Taiwan and Korea. Introduced in 1956 by J.L. Creech of the USDA. Although the flowers are relatively small and only known in white, the tree offers major advantages. Its bark is lovely peely brown or reddish. Leaves bright green, to 5⅞" × 2½", lightly hairy on the veins of the lower surface, resisting powdery mildew. As a result it has been used much in hybridizing, yet has very rarely been in commerce in its purebred state. As cold-hardy as *L. indica*. Record: 44' tall multitrunked specimen at Los Angeles, CA (1993; *pl.* 1958).

L. Fauriei 'Fantasy'
Selected at North Carolina State University Arboretum. Bark red; excellent white flowers, and tree form.

L. Fauriei 'Townhouse'
A seedling of 'Fantasy' from North Carolina State University. It grows in a student townhouse garden in the campus arboretum. Its bark is the darkest observed.

L. indica L.
CRAPEMYRTLE. CRÊPEMYRTLE. LADIES' STREAMER (a corruption of *Lagerstrœmia*). FLOWER OF THE SOUTH. LILAC OF THE SOUTH. From China, Korea, adjacent Far

East Asia; widely naturalized in India and elsewhere. Introduced to Europe in 1747; named in 1759. Michaux's nursery at Charleston, WV, had it sometime between 1787 and 1796. Common. Typically a large shrub, it can easily be trained into tree form. The pale brown, peely bark is ample reason to promote heavy trunks. Most attention is lavished on the gorgeous flowers. In the wild the flowers are rose- or carmine-red. In cultivation they show wonderful variability: white, light pink, dark rose, red, lavender or dark purple. They appear in great terminal clusters 6"–20" long, from June into October. The flowering periods often cited in the following cultivar descriptions are from Byers nursery of Huntsville (now Meridianville), AL, and are intended to show relative blooming sequence. Leaf 1"–3¼" long, often attractively red-tinged when young; glossy and only microscopically hairy; fall color a good gold and rosy red. CRAPEMYRTLE needs sun and relishes heat. Certain clones endure considerable freezing once they become established. Still it is primarily associated with the South and California. Powdery mildew is a serious problem in many locales. Cultivars abound, and can be obtained in dwarf sizes as well. Hybrids are tending to replace many purebred selections. The following account has 33 *L. indica* cultivars, followed by 16 hybrids. Many others exist. Most cultivars with names of native American tribes were introduced by the USDA. Records: 60' × 6'1" Wolfsnare Plantation, VA (n.d.); 58' × 9'8" × 50' Huger, SC (1960); 41' × 5'10" × 38' Roganville, TX (1970); 34' × 2'5" × 22' Princess Anne, MD (1990); 33' × 7'1" × 35' Augusta, GA (1972); 32' × 1'5" × 19' Seattle, WA (1990).

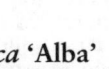

L. indica 'Alba'
= *L. indica* 'White'

WHITE CRAPEMYRTLE. Cultivated since 1816. The first cultivar. In North American commerce ≤1825. Common. Flowers white.

L. indica 'Basham's Party Pink'—see hybrid section

L. indica 'Byers' Hardy Lavender'—see *L. ind.* 'Hardy Lavender'

L. indica 'Byers' Red Standard'—see *L. ind.* 'Byers' Standard Red'

L. indica 'Byers' Standard Red'
= *L. indica* 'Byers' Red Standard'

Introduced in 1955 by Byers nursery of Huntsville, AL. Flowers soft red in mid-July. Fall color orange. Tall growing.

L. indica 'Byers' Wonderful White'
Introduced by Byers nursery of Huntsville, AL. Flowers clear white in late June in very large clusters. Fall color yellow. Very cold hardy.

L. indica 'Carmine'—see *L. indica* 'Crimson'

L. indica 'Carolina Beauty'
Selected ca. 1940 by Dailys nursery of South Carolina. Common. Flowers deep bright red in mid-July. Leaves dark green, of poor mildew resistance. Fall color orange.

L. indica 'Catawba'
A 1960 cross of 'Light Lavender' and 'Dwarf Purple' introduced in 1967 by the USDA. Flowers dark purple in mid-July. Leaves dark green; highly mildew-tolerant. Fall color brilliant red-orange. Small, but can grow 20' tall.

L. indica 'Cherokee'
A 1960 hybrid of 'Low Flame' and a "hardy red," introduced in 1970 by the USDA. Flowers brilliant clear red ("the truest red of any crapemyrtle" says D. Egolf). Leaves mildew-tolerant. Small, but will grow at least 12' tall.

L. indica 'Conestoga'
A 1960 cross of 'Alba' and 'Low Flame' introduced in 1967 by the USDA. Flowers lavender, in early July. Leaves dark green. Fall color yellow. Small, but can grow 18' tall.

L. indica 'Country Red'
= *L. indica* 'Durant Red'
= *L. indica* 'Pure Red' of Monrovia nursery 1960

Originated in 1952 and introduced in 1956 by Durant nursery of Durant, OK. Flowers blood red; opening 3 weeks later than most cultivars. Leaves mildew-resistant. One of the hardiest.

L. indica 'Crimson'
= *L. indica* 'Carmine'
= *L. indica* 'New Crimson'

Introduced ≤1872. Commercially extinct. Flowers bright deep crimson in profuse large clusters.

L. indica 'Durant Red'—see *L. indica* 'Country Red'

L. indica 'Glendora White'

A chance seedling discovered in a city park of Glendora, CA, in 1957. Named and introduced in 1959 by Monrovia nursery of California. Flowers large, snowy white or with a faint pink tint, ruffled in dense clusters. Leaves almost free of mildew. Interesting bark and branching pattern.

L. indica 'Gray's Red'
= L. indica 'Rubra Grayi'

Originated <1926 by D. Gray of Elverta, CA. Still common in the nursery trade. Flowers brilliant rich red.

L. indica 'Hardy Lavender'
= L. indica 'Byers' Hardy Lavender'

Introduced in 1960 by Byers nursery of Huntsville, AL. Flowers medium lavender in late July. Leaves dark green. Fall color red. Small, 12'–20' tall.

L. indica 'Kellogg's Purple'

Introduced in 1955–56 by Monrovia nursery of California. Uncommon. Flowers intense purple.

L. indica 'Lavender'—see L. indica 'Purpurea'

L. indica 'Lilac'—see L. indica 'Purpurea'

L. indica 'Magenta'—see L. indica 'Rubra'

L. indica 'Near East'
= L. indica 'Shell Pink'

Introduced from E Asia ca. 1870, yet lost commercially ca. 1890; found surviving in Louisiana in the early 1930s; reintroduced to commerce in 1938–39 (as "a new flesh pink variety with large, profuse flowers") by Overlook nursery of Crichton, AL. The name 'Near East' dates from 1952–53. Still sold. Flowers very pale pink, in mid-July. Leaves light green, of moderate mildew resistance. Fall color yellow to orange. Shrubby. Among the least cold-hardy.

L. indica 'New Crimson'—see L. indica 'Crimson'

L. indica 'Orchid'

A chance seedling selected in 1947, named in 1948, introduced in 1949 by Aldridge nursery of Von Ormy, TX. Flowers light orchid with a touch of white. Leaves deep green.

L. indica 'Pendula'—see L. indica 'Weeping Pink'

L. indica 'Peppermint'—see L. indica 'Peppermint Lace'

L. indica 'Peppermint Lace' PP 3169 (1972)
= L. indica 'Peppermint'

An Otto Spring hybrid seedling; named and introduced in 1972 by Monrovia nursery of California. Flowers deep rose-pink edged in white. Small but not invariably shrubby.

L. indica 'Pink'

PINK CRAPEMYRTLE. An old cultivar. The 1978 *Lagerstrœmia* checklist does not recognize 'Pink' as a clone, considering it, perhaps, a mere common name for any pink selection a nursery happens to sell. Nonetheless a clone circulates commercially under the name 'Pink': Flowers pink in mid-July. Leaves of moderate mildew resistance. Fall color yellow-orange. Less hardy than most cultivars.

L. indica 'Potomac'

A 1962 selection introduced in 1967 by the USDA. Very common. Flowers clear medium-pink in late June. Leaves dark green. Fall color orange. Excellent tree form.

L. indica 'Powhatan'

A 1960 cross of 'Dwarf Purple' and 'Light Lavender' introduced in 1967 by the USDA. Flowers light lavender in late July. Leaves glossy green. Fall color yellow-orange. Small, but can grow 20' tall.

L. indica 'Prostrata'—see L. indica 'Weeping Pink'

L. indica 'Pure Red'—see L. indica 'Country Red'

L. indica 'Purple'—see L. indica 'Purpurea'

L. indica 'Purpurea'
= L. indica 'Purple'
= L. indica 'Lavender'
= L. indica 'Lilac'
= L. indica 'Violacea'

Cultivated since 1822. Common. Flowers light purple, in mid-July. Leaves dark green, of moderate mildew resistance. Fall color orange. Less hardy than most cultivars.

L. indica 'Purity'

Origin unknown. Sold by more than one nursery in California ≤1962–63. Still in the trade as of 1980 but may be commercially extinct now. Flowers pure white.

L. indica 'Red'—see *L. indica* 'Rubra'

L. indica 'Red Star'—see *L. indica* 'Watermelon Red'

L. indica 'Regal Red'

A chance seedling selected in the late 1960s, and introduced in 1972 by Byers nursery of Huntsville, AL. Flowers dark red in mid-July. Leaves dark green. Fall color red-orange. To 16' tall, growing broad.

L. indica 'Rose'—see *L. indica* 'Rosea'

L. indica 'Rosea'

= *L. indica* 'Rose'

PINK CRAPEMYRTLE. Cultivated since 1825. Common. Flowers very deep rose. How this differs from 'Pink' is not known, but nobody pretends there is only one pink-flowered clone.

L. indica 'Rosea Pendula'—see *L. indica* 'Weeping Pink'

L. indica 'Rubis'—see *L. indica* 'Rubra'

L. indica 'Rubra'

?= *L. indica* 'Scarlet' (in part)
= *L. indica* 'Magenta'
= *L. indica* 'Red'
= *L. indica* 'Rubis'

RED CRAPEMYRTLE. Cultivated since ≤1874. Common. Flowers dark rosy red.

L. indica 'Rubra Grayi'—see *L. indica* 'Gray's Red'

L. indica 'Scarlet'

Sold by U.S. nurseries ≤1880, until at least the 1920s. Flowers scarlet. Probably sold partly as 'Rubra'.

L. indica 'Seminole'

A 1960 cross of 'Low Flame' and a "hardy pink," introduced in 1970 by the USDA. Common. Flowers clear medium pink in mid-July. Fall color yellow. Small, but can grow 15' tall.

L. indica 'Shell Pink'—see *L. indica* 'Near East'

L. indica 'Snow White'

Origin unknown. In commerce ≤1949. Flowers white, in numerous small clusters. Leaves light green. (A dwarf shrub of this name has been sold since 1960 by Select nursery of Brea, CA.)

L. indica 'Special Red'

Introduced ≤1976 by Aldridge nursery of Von Ormy, TX. Flowers dark red. Not as vigorous as 'Watermelon Red'.

L. indica Twilight™

A chance seedling selected in 1957; named and introduced in1958 by Texas nursery of Sherman, TX. Flowers dark purple, in heavy clusters. Vigorous.

L. indica 'Violacea'—see *L. indica* 'Purpurea'

L. indica 'Watermelon Pink'—see *L. indica* 'Watermelon Red'

L. indica 'Watermelon Red'

= *L. indica* 'Watermelon Pink'
= *L. indica* 'Red Star'

Introduced ≤1922–23 by T.V. Munson nursery of Denison, TX. Very common, but more than one clone has been sold under the name. Flowers dark pinkish-red as the name suggests.

L. indica 'Weeping Pink'

= *L. indica* 'Pendula'
= *L. indica* 'Prostrata'
= *L. indica* 'Rosea Pendula'

Introduced in 1930 by Griffing nursery of Beaumont, TX. Rare. Flowers pink. Habit weeping.

L. indica 'Weeping White'

A chance seedling selected in 1956 by J.B. Fitzpatrick of Sherman, TX. Introduced in 1978. Rare. Flowers white. Branches pendulous.

L. indica 'White'—see *L. indica* 'Alba'

L. indica 'William Toovey'—see *L. indica* 'Wm. Toovey'

L. indica 'Wm. Toovey'

= *L. indica* 'William Toovey'

Introduced ≤1927 by Howell nursery of Knoxville, TN. Very common. More than one clone has gone under this name. Flowers pink-red in mid-July. Fall color red-orange. Usually ca. 12' tall.

L. Limii Merrill

From Fukien, China. Discovered in 1922; named in 1925 (after the president of Amoy University, Dr. Lim Boom Keng, who strongly promoted botany in Fukien). This species, related to *L. subcostata* (not in this volume), is exceedingly rare and little known. Sold in 1994–95 by Piroche Plants nursery of Pitt

Meadows, B.C. Leaves dull and very downy when young, to 5⅜" × 2⅛". Flowers pink to "soft purple," in clusters 7" long. A shrub or small tree.

Lagerstrœmia hybrids

In 1962, Donald Egolf at the U.S. National Arboretum began hybridizing CRAPEMYRTLES. Well over 100,000 seedlings were raised, and only the best named. All have been given Indian names. They include purebred *L. indica* crosses (described above), and interspecific crosses involving *L. Fauriei* (listed below). Advantages of hybrids include resistance to powdery mildew, more attractive bark, and often superior fall color and hardiness. All of the following except 'Basham's Party Pink' and 'Tinsley' were developed by the U.S. National Arboretum.

Lagerstrœmia 'Apalachee'

L. indica "Azuka Dwarf Hybrid" × *L. Fauriei*

Selected in 1976, introduced in 1987. Flowers light lavender-purple. Fall color dull orange to russet to dark red.

Lagerstrœmia 'Basham's Party Pink'

L. indica × *L. Fauriei*

The first natural hybrid; a chance seedling selected in 1963, named 1965 by B.M. Basham of Conroe, TX. Introduced in 1965. In 1973 the original was 35' tall and wide. Flowers lavender-pink. Leaves mildew-resistant. Fall color orange-red to yellow.

Lagerstrœmia 'Biloxi'

(*L. indica* 'Dwarf Red' × *L. Fauriei*) × (*L. indica* 'Low Flame' × *L. Fauriei*)

Selected in 1977, introduced in 1987. Flowers pale pink, in July; recurrent. Leaves mildew-resistant. Fall color dark yellow-orange to orange red to dark red. Tall growing. Very hardy.

Lagerstrœmia 'Chotaw'

(*L. indica* 'Pink Lace' × *L. Fauriei*) × *L. indica* 'Potomac'

Selected in 1970, introduced in 1990. Flowers clear bright pink. Fall color bronze-maroon. Tall growing.

Lagerstrœmia 'Comanche'

L. indica "Dark Red" × (*L. indica* × *L. Fauriei*)

Selected in 1973, introduced in 1986–87. Flowers coral pink in early July. Leaves dark green. Fall color dark orange-red to dark purple. Very hardy.

Lagerstrœmia 'Lipan'

(*L. indica* 'Pink Lace' × *L. Fauriei*) × [(*L. indica* 'Rubra' × *L. indica* 'Carolina Beauty') × *L.* 'Basham Party Pink']

Selected in 1975, introduced in 1986–87. Flowers medium lavender in mid-July. Leaves dark green. Fall color light orange to russet to dull red. Bark very attractive.

Lagerstrœmia 'Miami'

(*L. indica* 'Pink Lace' × *L. Fauriei*) × [*L. indica* Firebird™ × (*L. indica* × *L. Fauriei*)]

Selected in 1976, introduced in 1987. Flowers dark coral pink in mid-June; recurrent. Leaves dark green. Fall color orange to dark russet. Tall growing.

Lagerstrœmia 'Muskogee'

L. indica 'Near East' × *L. Fauriei*

Hybridized in 1964, selected in 1969, introduced in 1976. Flowers light lavender in mid-June. Leaves glossy dark green. Fall color red-orange. Tall growing. (The parentage cited also as *L. indica* 'Pink Lace' × *L. Fauriei*.)

Lagerstrœmia 'Natchez'

L. indica 'Near East' × *L. Fauriei*

Hybridized in 1964, selected in 1969, introduced in 1976. The most common hybrid. Flowers white in mid-June. Leaves dark green. Fall color red-orange to burgundy. Tall growing. Very hardy. Bark very attractive dark cinnamon. (The parentage cited also as *L. indica* 'Pink Lace' × *L. Fauriei*.)

Lagerstrœmia 'Osage'

(*L. indica* 'Dwarf Red' × *L. Fauriei*) × (*L. indica* 'Pink Lace' × *L. Fauriei*)

Selected in 1976, introduced in 1986–87. Flowers clear pink in July. Leaves lustrous green. Fall color red.

Lagerstrœmia 'Sioux'

[*L. indica* 'Tiny Fire' × (*L. indica* × *L. Fauriei*)] × [(*L. indica* 'Pink Lace' × *L. Fauriei*) × *L. indica* 'Catawba']

Selected in 1979, introduced in 1986–87. Flowers dark pink in late July. Leaves dark green. Fall color light maroon to bright red. Very hardy.

Lagerstrœmia 'Tinsley'

L. indica × *L. Fauriei*

A chance seedling at the residence of C.D. Tinsley of Houston, TX. Selected ca. 1965, and named in 1969 by B.M. Basham of Conroe, TX. Introduced in 1970.

Rare. Flowers lavender. Leaves mildew-resistant. Vigorous.

Lagerstrœmia 'Tuscarora'
L. 'Basham Party Pink' × L. indica 'Cherokee'

Hybridized in 1967, selected in 1971, introduced in 1979–80. Common. Flowers dark coral-pink in late June or early July. Leaves dark lustrous green. Fall color red-orange. Tall growing. Very hardy.

Lagerstrœmia 'Tuskegee'
L. indica 'Dallas Red' × L. 'Basham Party Pink'

Hybridized in 1968, named in 1981, introduced in 1986. Flowers dark pink to near red. Fall color orange-red. Tall growing.

Lagerstrœmia 'Wichita'
(L. indica 'Pink Lace' × L. Fauriei) × [L. indica Firebird™ × (L. indica × L. Fauriei)]

Hybridized in 1972, selected in 1975, introduced in 1987. Flowers light magenta to lavender in early July; recurrent. Leaves lush dark green. Fall color russet to mahogany. Tall growing. Very hardy.

Lagerstrœmia 'Yuma'
(L. indica 'Pink Lace' × L. Fauriei) × [(L. indica × L. subcostata) × (L. indica "Hardy Light Pink" × L. indica 'Rubra')]

Hybridized in 1972, selected in 1976, introduced in 1986–87. Flowers medium lavender in early July. Leaves dark green. Fall color dull yellow-orange to russet to light mahogany. Very hardy.

Larix

[PINACEÆ; Pine Family] 9–15 spp. of deciduous conifers, all from the temperate northern hemisphere. Larix is the ancient Latin name. LARCH (derived from the Latin) and TAMARACK (of native American origin) are the most prevalent English names. The spring flush of tender LARCH greenery on the erstwhile dead-looking twigs of winter is most refreshing. The golden fall color is glorious as a finale each year. The only genus apt to be confused with Larix is Pseudolarix (GOLDEN LARCH). Other deciduous coniferous genera are Ginkgo (MAIDENHAIR TREE), Glyptostrobus (CHINESE BALD CYPRESS), Metasequoia (DAWN REDWOOD) and Taxodium (BALD CYPRESS).

L. amabilis—see Pseudolarix amabilis

L. americana—see L. laricina

L. dahurica—see L. Gmelini

L. dahurica var. Principis-Rupprechtii—see L. Gmelini var. Principis-Rupprechtii

L. decidua Mill.
= L. europæa DC. ex Lamb. & DC.

EUROPEAN LARCH. COMMON LARCH. From the Alps of Europe. Can live more than 2,000 years. Long common in cultivation. It was originally called Pinus decidua (the DECIDUOUS PINE) when many genera were lumped loosely as variations within Pinus. Needles ¾"–1¼" (2⅜") long. Cones ¾"–2⅛" long, persisting on the twigs. Records: to 180' × 28'0" in the wild; 151' × 9'9" Glenlee Park, southwest Scotland (1979); 109' × 7'1" Spokane, WA (1988); 102' × 19'4" Monzie Castle, Perthshire, Scotland (1985; pl. 1738); 95' × 10'10" Spokane, WA (1988); 86' × 13'9" Northfield, VT (1980).

L. decidua 'Julian's Weeping'—see L. Kaempferi 'Pendula'

L. europæa—see L. decidua

L. decidua f. pendula (Laws.) R.E. Fries
WEEPING EUROPEAN LARCH. Various clones and selected seedlings of more or less pendulous habit have been sold as L. decidua 'Pendula' since the 1800s, yet the mass-produced clone sold in recent years is L. Kaempferi 'Pendula' (q.v.). The present author has seen no recently marketed specimens of authentic weeping L. decidua and regards it as extremely rare.

L. decidua ssp. polonica (Racib.) Domin
= L. polonica Racib.
= L. sudetica Domin
= L. decidua var. polonica (Racib.) Ostenf. & Syr.-Lars.

POLISH LARCH. SUDETAN LARCH. From NW Ukraine, SE Poland, N Czechoslovakia. Nearly extinct. Described in 1890. Introduced to cultivation in 1910. In North America ≤1925. Extremely rare; found exclusively in arboreta, botanic gardens and the like. Overall, intermediate between EUROPEAN LARCH (L.

decidua) and SIBERIAN LARCH (*L. sibirica*). Cones ⅝"–1" long, the scales relatively few, rounded, concave. Foresters observe growth differences between SUDETAN and POLISH LARCHES, but botanical distinctions between these two populations are not definable, hence they are lumped under one name. Records: 115' × 9'10" Trebaczew, Poland (≤1973); 108' × 8'11" Ashburnham Park, Sussex, England (1983); 87' × 5'3" Bedgebury, Kent, England (1982; *pl*. 1926); 79' × 3'9" Wind River Arboretum, WA (1988).

L. decidua 'Pyramidalis'

Originated in 1908 by Ellwanger & Barry nursery of Rochester, NY; given that year to the Rochester Parks Department, who described it in 1932. Ascending branches, some almost erect. Not to be confused with the 1868 *L. decidua* 'Fastigiata'. Not known to be in commerce.

L. decidua ssp. sibirica—see L. sibirica

L. deci. 'Varied Directions'—see L. × eurolepis 'Varied Directions'

L. × eurolepis Henry

= *L.* × *marschlinsii* Coaz 1917, non hort.
= *L.* × *hybrida* auct., non Schröd.
= *L.* × *Henryana* Rehder
(*L. Kaempferi* × *L. decidua*)

DUNKELD LARCH. HYBRID LARCH. First raised from seeds of JAPANESE LARCHES (*L. Kaempferi*) sown in 1901, planted in the park in the Castle of Marschlins, in the Swiss Canton of Graubünden. Independently raised ca. 1904 at Dunkeld in Perthshire, Scotland. The cross has subsequently occurred frequently. Such hybrids are usually of faster, more luxuriant growth than either parent. In North America ≤1907; in commerce here ≤1916. Rarely offered by name, but specimens which were raised and distributed as either EUROPEAN or JAPANESE LARCHES can be found in parks and collections. The 1919 name *eurolepis* is a contraction of the then-current names *Larix europæa* and *Larix leptolepis*. In 1982, some botanists disinterred and championed the 1917 name *Larix marschlinsii*—but there is uncertainty as to its correctness, so until the matter is settled, banish it to synonymy, "from whence it's sprung, unwept, unhonored, and unsung." Records: 132' × 8'3" Strone House, Cairndow, Argyll, Scotland (1985); 92' × 10'3" Munches, Kirkcudbrightshire, Scotland (1985); 80' × 7'7" Philadelphia, PA (1980); 69' × 9'3" Tacoma, WA (1993).

L. × eurolepis 'Varied Directions'

= *L. decidua* 'Varied Directions'

Discovered by S. Waxman of the University of Connecticut. Named and introduced ca. 1980. Uncommon in commerce. Of vigorous spreading habit. Branches go in various directions but eventually arch down and cover the ground. Twigs thick, golden-tan. Cones often fused into pairs; cone scales slightly recurved at their tips.

L. europæa—see L. decidua

L. europæa var. dahurica—see L. Gmelini

L. europæa ssp. sibirica—see L. sibirica

L. Gmelini (Rupr.) Rupr. ex Kuzen.

= *L. dahurica* (Laws.) Turcz. *ex* Trautv.
= *L. europæa* var. *dahurica* (Laws.) Loud.

DAHURIAN LARCH. From the vast plains of E Siberia, and (its varieties) elsewhere in NE Asia. The conifer expert G. Gordon wrote of this species in 1875 (*The Pinetum*, p. 169): "A small tree, dwarfing down by climate to a stunted bush, or irregular-growing little tree, only a few feet high, with twisted, half-pendulous branches. . . found in Northern Siberia, on the bleak mountains of Dahuria, and in the arctic regions of Siberia, a mere little sprawling shrub, amongst the last vestiges of arborescent vegetation in those places, also in cold mountainous places, from the Ural Mountains to the Pacific Ocean." Introduced to Britain in 1827. The specific name *L. Gmelini* was published in 1845, probably after Johann Georg Gmelin (1709–1755), botanist in Siberia; maybe after his nephew Samuel Gottlieb Gmelin (1744–1774), who also explored Asia; Alan Mitchell says after Johann Friedrich Gmelin (1748–1804), a German naturalist. In North America ≤1912; in commerce here ≤1931. Able to withstand no end of severe freezing, drought and heat. Variable, little known, and generally unimportant to horticulture. Some of its races may be useful in the colder regions of Canada. It flushes early and in many places can be hurt by late spring frosts. Needles ⅝"– 1⅝" long. Cones ⁷⁄₁₆"–1³⁄₁₆" long. Records: to 180' tall says Ouden; 82' × 4'0" Kyloe Wood, Northumberland, England (1977); 68' × 3'6" Hergest Croft, Herefordshire, England (1978); 55' × 6'11" Achamore, Strathclyde, Scotland (1986); 50' × 2'10" Hales Corners, WI (1979).

L. Gmelini var. olgensis (Henry) Ostenf. & Syr.-Lars.

= *L. olgensis* Henry

OLGA BAY LARCH. From the Olga Bay region NE of Vladivostok, Russia. Extremely rare, but in commerce. Gaunt, not thrifty. Twigs beige, densely hairy. Needles to ca. 1" long (to 3" on those of young vigorous shoots).

L. Gmelini var. Principis-Rupprechtii (Mayr) Pilg.
= L. Gmelini ssp. Principis-Rupprechtii (Mayr) E. Murr.
= L. dahurica var. Principis-Rupprechtii (Mayr) Rehd. & Wils.
= L. Principis-Rupprechtii Mayr

PRINCE RUPRECHT'S LARCH. From NE China, Manchuria and NW Korea. Introduced from Korea in 1903 by Dr. Mayr, who named it in 1906. In North America ≤1909; in commerce here ≤1931. Extremely rare. The most vigorous form of L. Gmelini. Cones larger, 1"–1¾" long, with numerous scales. Recorded to 100' × 6'6" in the wild.

L. Griffithiana (Lindl. & Gord.) Carr.
= L. Griffithii Hook. fil. & Thoms.

HIMALAYAN LARCH. SIKKIM LARCH. From the Himalayas, in E Nepal, Sikkim, Bhutan, Tibet, and the Burma-Yunnan border. Discovered in 1837 by William Griffith (1810–1845), British botanist and physician who studied plants in India. Introduced by J. Hooker from Nepal to England in 1848. Named in 1855. It has been a miserable flop in cultivation. Exceedingly rare; tender. Twigs hairy. Needles 1"–1⅝" long. Cones the largest in the genus: (2") 2¾"–3⅛" (4⅓") long; their bracts protruding. Records: 71' × 6'3" Coldrenick, Cornwall, England (1970; pl. ca. 1848); 58' × 7'9" Strete Ralegh, Devon, England (1972; pl. 1848).

L. × Henryana—see L. × eurolepis

L. × hybrida—see L. × eurolepis

L. Kaempferi (Lamb.) Carr.
= L. leptolepis (S. & Z.) Sieb. ex G. Gord.

JAPANESE LARCH. From Japan. Japanese: Kara-matsu. Introduced to Western cultivation in 1861 by J.G. Veitch. Named after Engelbert Kaempfer (1651–1716), German physician for the Dutch East India Company, and botanist. (Some old books apply the name Larix Kaempferi to GOLDEN LARCH, Pseudolarix amabilis.) In North American nurseries ≤1887. The much used synonym leptolepis is from Greek leptos, slender, and lepis, a scale, referring to the cone's fine, slender scales. Common. Differs from

EUROPEAN LARCH (L. decidua) in having glaucous pinkish rather than yellowish or tan twigs, wider needles of a bluish cast, and squat cones with scale tips recurved. Fall color often golden rather than merely yellow. Needles ½"–1¾" long. Cones ½"–1⅝" long. Records: 131' × 9'9½" Blair Atholl, Perthshire, Scotland (1987; pl. 1886); 108' × 10'6" Dunkeld, Perthshire, Scotland (1988; pl. 1885); 103' × 10'4" Hanover, NH (1978); 103' × 4'11" McKean County, PA (1980); 83' × 9'9" West Chester, PA (1980); trunks to 12'6" around in Japan.

L. Kaempferi 'Blue Rabbit'
Found ca. 1960 by Konijn nursery of Holland. In North American commerce ≤1993–94. Habit narrow, foliage strikingly blue.

L. Kaempferi 'Diana'
('Diane')
Found by G.D. Bohlje in 1974 near Westerstede, Oldenburg, Germany. Introduced in 1983; in North American commerce ≤1993. Branches and needles twisted. Less vigorous.

L. Kaempferi 'Pendula'
= L. decidua 'Julian's Weeping'

WEEPING JAPANESE LARCH. Raised by Hesse nursery of Germany. Name published in 1896–97. Described by Hillier nursery of England as a tall elegant tree with long weeping branches. The clone common in North American commerce since ca. 1986 is a topgrafted little tree, almost universally sold as L. decidua 'Pendula'.

L. laricina (Du Roi) K. Koch
= L. americana Michx.

TAMARACK. EASTERN LARCH. AMERICAN LARCH. HACKMATACK. BLACK LARCH. From across N America in the far north. Tolerant of boggy soils. The epithet laricina means LARCH-like; this species was originally considered a PINE—i.e., Pinus laricina recalled the European Pinus Larix (now Larix decidua). Although TAMARACK is valued for its very durable, strong and heavy wood, the tree has played a inconsequential role in ornamental horticulture; foreign species are superior, especially as regards fall color. Crown often candelabrum shaped. Needles bluish, ¾"–1⅝" long. Cones small, ⅓"–¾" long. Records: 125' × 7'8" Minnesota (<1890); 109' × 8'2" Benzie County, MI (1983); 108' × 11'4" Phoenix, MD (1990); 95' × 9'8" Jay, ME (1966); 92' × 11'11" Wells, ME (1983); 62' × 12'1" × 75' Coventry, CT (1986).

L. leptolepis—see *L. Kaempferi*

L. Lyallii Parl.

SUBALPINE LARCH. ALPINE LARCH. MOUNTAIN LARCH. TIMBERLINE LARCH. WOOLY LARCH. From high mountains, S Alaska to SE British Columbia, SW Alberta, N Idaho, Washington, and W Montana. David Lyall (1817–1895), Scots surgeon and naturalist, discovered it in 1860 while working on the International Boundary Survey. Named in 1863; introduced to cultivation ≤1899. A delightful heartwarming tree in its native setting, it has never succeeded in cultivation and remains extremely rare. Twigs stout, pink, densely white wooly. Needles to 1½" long, of horsetail texture. Cones 2" long with very dark scale bracts, the slender protruding spine tips fragile and easily broken. Records: 101' × 22'1" × 84' Wenatchee National Forest, WA (1990; now dead); 95' × 20'9" × 77' Wenatchee National Forest, WA (1986).

L. × marschlinsii—see *L. × eurolepis*

L. occidentalis Nutt.

WESTERN LARCH. WEST AMERICAN LARCH. WESTERN TAMARACK. MONTANA LARCH. From parts of British Columbia, Alberta, Idaho, Montana, Washington, and Oregon. Discovered by Lewis and Clark in 1806. Introduced to cultivation in 1881. Rare, but in commerce and somewhat successful in cultivation. Needles grass-green, 1"–2¾". Cones 1"–2" long, with conspicuous protruding bracts. The largest LARCH. Characteristically slender, tall-growing and short-branched. In 1898 C. Sargent wrote of it: "The most remarkable fact, perhaps, about this tree is the smallness of leaf surface in comparison with height and thickness of stem, and there is certainly no other instance among the trees of the northern hemisphere where such massive trunks support such small short branches and sparse foliage." Records: to 250' tall says C. Sargent; 192' × 14'3" Umatilla National Forest, WA (1989); 177' × 24'5" near Kootenai National Forest, MT (1972); D. Douglas found trunks 30'0" around in 1827.

L. olgensis—see *L. Gmelini* var. *olgensis*

L. polonica—see *L. decidua* ssp. *polonica*

L. Principis-Rupprechtii—see *L. Gmelini* var. *Principis-Rupprechtii*

L. russica—see *L. sibirica*

L. sibirica (Münchh.) Ledeb.
= *L. russica* (Endl.) Sab. *ex* Trautv.
= *L. sukaczevii* Dylis
= *L. europæa* ssp. *sibirica* (Münchh.) Domin
= *L. decidua* ssp. *sibirica* (Ledeb.) Domin

SIBERIAN LARCH. RUSSIAN LARCH. From NE (European) Russia, W Siberia, N Mongolia. Named in 1770. Introduced to Scotland in 1806 by Duke John of Atholl, from seeds procured from Archangel (N Russia). J. Loudon says "Introduced to England by Messrs. Loddiges [nurserymen], to whom the seed was sent by Prof. Pallas, about the end of the 1700s." Be that as it may, it has performed poorly in the British Isles and is rare there. In North America since ≤1896; an introduction was made in 1912 from St. Petersburg via F. Meyer, who reported it was "an excellent lumber tree requiring only a very short season to mature, 10 weeks of summer being apparently sufficient to complete the whole process of coming into leaf and shedding again. Great value as an ornamental in cool, uncongenial climes—one of the tallest trees in St. Petersburg." Off and on it has been offered in nurseries, but has never proved a popular or very successful species. Performs well in Montana and the adjacent provinces of Canada. Of supreme cold-hardiness, it has been ranked as a "Zone 1" tree. Needles (1³⁄₁₆"–2" long) flush early in spring, so are liable to late frost injury. Cones 1"–1⅔" long. Records: to 147' × 18'5" in the wild says M. Vidakovic; 57' × 3'2" Lisle, IL (1986; *pl.* 1955).

L. sibirica 'Conica'

Introduced ≤1990 by Iseli nursery of Boring, OR. An upright narrow spirelike tree. Branches nearly horizontal, swept up at the tips. Needles light green. The cultivar name is illegitimate, being Latin yet post-1959.

L. sudetica—see *L. decidua* ssp. *polonica*

L. sukaczevii—see *L. sibirica*

Laurocerasus caroliniana—see *Prunus caroliniana*

Laurocerasus lusitanica—see *Prunus lusitanica*

Laurocerasus officinalis—see *Prunus Laurocerasus*

Laurus

[LAURACEÆ; Laurel Family] 2 spp. of Old World broadleaf evergreen trees. *Laurus* is one of the ancient Latin names, in turn from some non Indo-European source. Related genera include *Apollonias*, *Cinnamomum* (CAMPHOR TREE), *Lindera*, *Neolitsea*, *Persea*, *Sassafras* and *Umbellularia*.

L. albida—see *Sassafras albidum*

L. Barbujana or **L. Barbusano**—see *Apollonias Barbujana*

L. Borbonia—see *Persea Borbonia*

L. Camphora—see *Cinnamomum Camphora*

L. canariensis—see *Apollonias Barbujana*

L. glauca—see *Neolitsea sericea*

L. nobilis L.

BAY LAUREL. APOLLO'S LAUREL. ROMAN LAUREL. GRECIAN LAUREL. POET'S LAUREL. SWEET LAUREL. ROYAL BAY. SWEET BAY. From the Mediterranean region. Date of introduction to North America unknown, but J. Bartram had it for sale in 1792. In California commerce ≤1858. Common. The Latin word *nobilis* means excellent, famous or renowned; noble. This tree is rich in culinary, historical and literary memories. Leaves dark, 1½"–7¼", the margin translucent and often conspicuously crimped or crisped; sweetly fragrant when crushed. Flowers very small and not very noticeable, whitish-yellow, from March to May; the two sexes usually on separate individuals. Males have showier flowers. Females produce shiny blackish berries ca. ⅝" long. In the north it may be a mere shrub, kept small by freezing winter. In more moderate regions it makes a dense, dark tree of neat aspect. It is often used clipped in formal garden design, and used as a tub plant. Records: to 70' tall in Spain and Italy; 69' × 3'0" Margam Park, near Port Talbot, W Glamorgan, Wales (1985); 62' × 3'4" Sacramento, CA (1989); 60' × 14'6" × 50' Nelson City, New Zealand (1973).

L. nobilis 'Saratoga'—see *L.* 'Saratoga'

L. nobilis 'Sunspot'

Introduced from a Japanese nursery to the U.S. in 1982 by B. Yinger and Brookside Gardens of Maryland. Rare. Leaf green, heavily and irregularly mottled pale yellow with smaller blotches of gray-green.

L. 'Saratoga'

= *L. nobilis* 'Saratoga'
(*L. nobilis* × *L. azorica*) × *L. azorica*

Bred in the 1950s by Frank J. Serpa of Fremont, CA. Introduced in 1986 by Saratgoa Horticultural Foundation of California. Of more natural tree form. Leaves less dark, but larger and rounder than those of *L. nobilis*. Resists psyllid attacks. Young shoots and leaf stems reddish. A male clone.

L. regia—see *Umbellularia californica*

L. Sassafras—see *Sassafras albidum*

Libocedrus chilensis—see *Austrocedrus chilensis*

Libocedrus decurrens—see *Calocedrus decurrens*

Libocedrus formosana—see *Calocedrus formosana*

Ligustrina pekinensis—see *Syringa pekinensis*

Ligustrina reticulatum—see *Syringa reticulata*

Ligustrum

[OLEACEÆ; Olive Family] 50 spp. of deciduous or (mostly) evergreen shrubs and small trees. Called PRIVETS. *Ligustrum* is the ancient Latin name of *Ligustrum vulgare*. As a whole, PRIVETS are used as hedging shrubs. They feature creamy-white flowers and black inedible berries. Many kinds are in cultivation but few achieve tree size. Certain larger shrubs are occasionally trained into tree form, notably **L. japonicum** Th. (JAPANESE or WAXLEAF PRIVET) and **L. sinense** Lour. (CHINESE or AMUR RIVER SOUTH PRIVET). Both of these species have been recorded more than 40' tall the Southeast, where they have gone wild. Genera related to *Ligustrum* include *Chionanthus*

(FRINGETREE), *Fraxinus* (ASH), *Olea* (OLIVE), *Osmanthus*, *Phillyrea*, and *Syringa* (LILAC).

L. lucidum Ait. fil.

= *L. macrophyllum* hort.

TREE PRIVET. GLOSSY PRIVET. SHINING PRIVET. CHINESE PRIVET. WHITE WAX TREE. WOA TREE. From China and Korea. Introduced to England in 1794 by J. Banks. Named in 1810. The name *lucidum* in Latin means shining. In North America ≤1847. Common. More than 20 cultivars have been listed, but some are only shrubby, some are synonymous, some are really *L. japonicum* clones, and some are so obscure that their characteristics are wholly unknown. A few of the more important ones are included below. The tree is beautiful. Drawbacks include a propensity to sucker from its base, to get hurt if not killed by severe freezing, to break badly under snow loads; allergenic flowers, messy berries, and weedy seedlings. Leaves dark, glossy, 3"–6" long, borne in opposite pairs. Flowers showy in late summer, creamy-white, fragrant from a distance; covering the tree. In China the tree is used as the chief producer of white or insect wax—a large scale insect (called Pe-La) is encouraged to "make itself at home" in the tree, and the wax it secretes in turn is widely employed for candle-making, polishing, and in medicine. Records: 95' × 10'10" Mexico (1982; *pl.* ca. 1862); 73' × 8'1" × 69' Sacramento, CA (1989); 48' × 16'0" × 70' Waikato, New Zealand (1970; *pl.* ≤1860); 44' × 4'2" Seattle, WA (1993).

L. lucidum 'Aureum'

In commerce ≤1933. Very rare. Leaves golden and partly green. Record: 36' × 3'3" × 40' Bournemouth Park, England (1986).

L. lucidum 'Excelsum Superbum'

SILVERLEAF PRIVET. Introduced ≤1906–1907 by Fruitland nursery of Augusta, GA. Rare. Leaf edged and speckled silver and gold.

L. lucidum 'Recurvifolium'

CRINKLELEAF PRIVET. Introduced ≤1931. Common. Leaves dark, with curved margins. Good for hedging as it endures shearing well.

L. lucidum 'Variegatum'

This name, in use since at least 1874, has been applied to more than one clone. One nursery describes it as "white-edged" and another as "gold and green variegated."

L. macrophyllum—see L. lucidum

Lindera

[LAURACEÆ; Laurel family] 80–100 (150) spp. of shrubs and trees, deciduous or evergreen, most of them tender. Named after Swedish botanist Johann Linder (1676–1723). Related genera include *Cinnamomum* (CAMPHOR TREE), *Laurus*, *Neolitsea*, *Persea*, *Sassafras* and *Umbellularia*.

L. cercidifolia—see L. obtusiloba

L. obtusiloba Bl.

= *L. cercidifolia* Hemsl., non hort.
= *L. triloba* hort., non (S. & Z.) Bl.
= *Benzoin obtusilobum* (Bl.) Ktze.

JAPANESE SPICEBUSH. From China, Japan, and Korea. Introduced in 1880 by C. Maries to England. Extremely rare in North America. Best in woodland conditions free of severely cold winters. A large shrub or small 30' tree (at most 50' tall). It is, and looks like, a relative of the *Sassafras* tree. Buds large and roundish. Foliage has the same textural quality and color as a lush REDBUD (*Cercis canadensis*). Leaves vary from unlobed to one- or tri-lobed, 3"–7" long; brilliant bronzy-red when young; yellow in fall; spicily fragrant when crushed (smells like *Calycanthus* shrubs). Tiny yellow flowers in early March are studded along the slender bare branches. Females make single-seeded, thin-fleshed acrid berries ⅓" long, first green, next red, then deep wine-red, finally shining black in October, borne in clusters near the twigs and obscured by the leaves. Since the handsome horizontally layered foliage and springtime flowers are the most attractive features, and females grow smaller, males might well be preferred where trees are desired. Records: 20' × 1'8¼" × 34½' and 16' × 1'10" × 38' Seattle, WA (1994; *pl.* 1961).

L. triloba—see L. obtusiloba

Liquidambar

[HAMAMELIDACEÆ; Witch Hazel Family (some botanists say ALTINGIACEÆ)] 4 spp. of large deciduous trees, known as SWEET GUMS. A mongrel name from Latin *liquidus*, fluid or liquid, and Arabic *'anbar* (amber); in allusion to the fragrant terebinthine juice or gum known as liquid storax which exudes from the bark of *L. orientalis*. This storax has been burned as an incense; other products from the trees are used in perfumery. The leaves, shaped starfish- or MAPLE-like, smell sweet when crushed. Flowers inconspicuous, in late spring. The fruit is a dry spiky seedball on a long stalk. A related genus is *Parrotia* (PERSIAN IRONWOOD), and its hybrid × *Sycoparrotia*.

L. acerifolia—see *L. formosana*

L. formosana Hance
= *L. acerifolia* Maxim.

FORMOSAN SWEETGUM. CHINESE SWEETGUM. From China, Indo-China, and Taiwan. Introduced to the United States from Taiwan <1881; to England in 1884. Rare. A strong tree of broad, heavy aspect, and irregular shape. Twigs hairy when young; never corky. Leaves 3–5 lobed, finely toothed, red-green or pale coppery-pink as they unfold; to 8½" wide; stipules often conspicuous and persistent. In the north it is late to flush, and the flowers appear with the young leaves. Fall color varies from purple to blood-red, chestnut-brown, orange or yellow in the north, to yellow or beige in late December in southern California (where the tree can be nearly ever-green). Seedballs resemble burdock burs 1½" wide. Records: to 130' × 15'0" in the wild; 85' × 7'9" Savannah, GA (1975); 66' × 6'4" Sacramento, CA (1989).

L. formosana 'Afterglow'
Originated by Saratoga Horticultural Foundation of California. Named and introduced <1958. Rare. New growth purplish; fall color rosy-red. Leaves three-lobed, essentially hairless.

L. formosana var. *monticola* Rehd. & Wils.
Originally described from specimens collected in 1907 by E. Wilson in E Szechwan and W Hupeh, China. In Latin *monticola* means inhabiting mountains. Branches and leaves less hairy or hairless; leaves three-lobed. More cold-hardy. Not a watertight distinction. Botanically, var. *monticola* has been abandoned as meaningless. If the name is applied consistently to hardier stock it still has horticultural value. The ideal course is to select cold-hardy clones of attractive fall color, and assign them cultivar names.

L. imberbe—see *L. orientalis*

L. orientalis Mill.
= *L. imberbe* Ait.

TURKISH SWEETGUM. ORIENTAL SWEETGUM. From a tiny area in Turkey, essentially; also from Rhodes. Introduced to French cultivation ca. 1750; to England in 1759. Imported from England to the U.S. in 1937 by the Arnold Arboretum. Exceedingly few in North America date <1956. Very rare. One of the BALM OF GILEADS. It varies from a large shrub to an ample shade tree with a dense bushy crown. The leaves are the smallest (3"–6") and most deeply lobed in the genus, and suggest those of some ENGLISH MAPLES (*Acer campestre*). They are also relatively weakly scented. Fall color is often late (in November or December), and varies from muted yellow or dull brown to bright red or gold. Compared to *L. Styraciflua* it is a smaller, weepier, more suckery tree. Bark very chunky and dark. Records: 100' tall at L'Arboretum de Balaine, N of Moulins, France (1967); 48' × 10'1" × 49½' Santa Barbara, CA (1993; *pl.* 1960); 37' × 5'9" × 34½' Aurora, OR (1993; *pl.* 1968).

L. Styraciflua L.
SWEETGUM. RED GUM. STARLEAF GUM. GUM TREE. ALLIGATOR TREE. OPOSSUM TREE. BILSTED. From the southern and eastern U.S. and parts of central America (as far south as Nicaragua). In 1651 the Spaniard F. Hernandez published an account of this tree's liquid amber. The tree's gum has been used for wounds, in medicine, as incense, and for chewing. *Styraciflua* is capitalized because it is an old generic name (from Greek *storax*, a gum, and *fluo*, to flow—storax

flowing). Storax is an exuded aromatic balsam, originally from *Styrax officinalis*, but now obtained from *Liquidambar orientalis*. Aside from the spiky woody seedballs (½"–1½" wide), this is a superb urban shade tree, symmetric in youth, becoming tall and irregular. Leaf retention and fall color varies greatly from sub-evergreen to brilliant autumnal color. Some specimens hold "fall color" well into February or even March. Leaves 4"–8" wide. The twigs can be heavily corky-ridged, hence the name ALLIGATOR TREE, as P. Henderson explained in 1881: "this is the tree whose rough, triangular branches, are sold in the streets of New York as the Alligator Plant. These pieces of stick are sold by the thousands every season, to unsophisticated city men, with about as much chance of growing as their fence pickets." Records: 200' × 21'6" near Florence, SC (1944); 164' × 17'0" Lower Wabash Valley, IN (<1875); 136' × 23'2" Craven County, NC (1986); trunks to 22'0 around in Mexico.

L. *Styraciflua* 'Aurea'—see *L. Styraciflua* 'Variegata'

L. *Styraciflua* 'Aureum'—see *L. Styraciflua* 'Variegata'

L. *Styraciflua* 'Aurora'

Introduced in 1977–78 by the Royal nursery of Alphons van Der Bom, Oudenbosch, Holland. In North American commerce ≤1991. Rare. Foliage bright yellow variegated. Fall color described by Skylark nursery of California as "technicolor sequence of yellow, orange, red and purple."

L. *Styraciflua* Burgundy™

Originated by Saratoga Horticultural Foundation of California. Introduced commercially in 1962. Common. Leaves burgundy colored in November or December and can remain on the tree, fully colored, into January. Habit narrow.

L. *Styraciflua* 'Corky'

Originated <1965 by Kingsville nursery of Maryland. Named in 1984. Officially described in 1991. Branches extremely corky. Fall color excellent rosy-red. Strongly upright, narrowly pyramidal.

L. *Styraciflua* Festival™

Discovered in the yard of Paul Lee of Saratoga, CA. Named by Saratoga Horticultural Foundation of California. Introduced to commerce in 1964. Common. Tall, narrow crowned. Fall color golden touched with shades of apricot or peach and red.

L. *Styraciflua* 'Fremont' PP 5183 (1984)

Patented by Frank J. Serpa of Fremont, CA. Characteristics not known. Not known in commerce.

L. *Styraciflua* 'Goduzam'—see *L. Styraciflua* 'Variegata'

L. *Styraciflua* 'Gold Dust'—see *L. Styraciflua* 'Variegata'

L. *Styraciflua* 'Golden'—see *L. Styraciflua* 'Variegata'

L. *Styraciflua* 'Golden Treasure'

Raised in Australia. Introduced in 1974 by Duncan & Davies nursery of New Zealand. In North America ≤1976. Rare. Leaves gold-edged, in autumn changing to cream or pale yellow and then white; the dark green portion turns burgundy and the lighter green becomes orange and pink. Tree slow growing. Twigs corky.

L. *Styraciflua* 'Gum Ball'

Discovered by H.B. Stubblefield of McMinnville, TN. Introduced in 1965 by Forest nursery of McMinnville. Shrubby; not a tree unless topgrafted to make a lollipop-head dwarf. Fruitless. Leaves remain green late into fall or early winter.

L. *Styraciflua* 'Kia'

Selected in Canberra, Australia (*kia* is an aboriginal word meaning spear). Described in 1968. In North American commerce ≤1990. Rare. A tall, narrow spirelike tree with autumn color of rich orange turning crimson, then purple.

L. *Styraciflua* 'Lane Roberts'

Raised by Hillier nursery of England. Introduced ≤1971. Fall color reliable crimson-red. Twigs smooth.

L. *Styraciflua* 'Midwest Sunset'

Developed by Warren & Son nursery of Oklahoma City, OK, and introduced in the mid-1960s. Selected for good fall color, but it proved inferior in tests in Texas and Illinois. Commercially extinct.

L. *Styraciflua* 'Moonbeam'

Introduced in 1976 by Duncan & Davies nursery of New Zealand. In North American commerce ≤1991. Rare. Summer foliage blushed with pale yellow. Red, yellow and purple in fall.

L. Styraciflua 'Moraine' PP 4601 (1980)

Introduced ≤1982 by Siebenthaler nursery of Dayton, OH. Uncommon. Hardy to -21°F (or even -35°F). Outstanding red fall color. Twigs not corky. Rapid.

L. Styraciflua 'Obtusiloba'—see L. Styraciflua 'Rotundiloba'

L. Styraciflua Palo Alto™

Selected in 1954 (as a street-tree on the 300 block of Bryant Street, Palo Alto, CA) by Saratoga Horticultural Foundation of California. Introduced commercially in 1956. Common. Fall color consistent brilliant orange-red, sometimes with clear yellow.

L. Styraciflua 'Plattsburg'

Introduced ≤1993 by Arborvillage nursery of Holt, MO: "a local specimen [Plattsburg is north of Kansas City, MO] with heavy rough cork-like bark."

L. Styraciflua 'Rotundiloba'

= L. Styraciflua 'Obtusiloba' sensu M. Dirr 1983

Discovered ca. 1930 near Cameron, NC, by Mr. R.E. Wicker of Pinehurst, NC. Propagated ≤1942. Scarcely sold until the late 1980s. Original specimen is at Chapel Hill, NC, and 90' tall (1991). Leaf lobes rounded rather than pointed. Fall color late, yellow, crimson, burgundy and purple. Fruitless. May not be hardy far north because of its late dormancy.

L. Styraciflua 'Variegata'

= L. Styraciflua 'Aurea' or 'Aureum'
= L. Styraciflua 'Golden'
= L. Styraciflua Gold Dust®
= L. Styraciflua 'Goduzam'

GOLDEN SWEETGUM. Described in 1880. In North America ≤1914. Common. Most specimens encountered date from 1940 onward. Some leaves one half to three quarters gold; some speckled with gold. In fall the gold turns pink and the green turns red.

L. Styraciflua 'Worplesdon'

Introduced ≤1967 by George Jackman & Sons, Woking nursery of Surrey, England. Named after the firm's new nursery (Worplesdon is between Guildford and Woking). In North American commerce <1990. Uncommon. Rich purple, orange and yellow autumn tints and beautiful finger-like leaf lobing. Twigs not corky.

Liriodendron

[MAGNOLIACEÆ; Magnolia Family] 2 spp. of majestic trees grown for shade. Known as TULIP TREES or YELLOW POPLARS. From Greek *leirion*, a LILY, and *dendron*, a tree. The truncate leaf is unique. Although the green and orange flowers of early summer are interesting up close, they are not very conspicuous. Nor are the seedcones ornamental. But as stately shade trees with pleasing foliage, the trees excel. Most closely related to *Magnolia*. Certain *Magnolia* species and hybrids are also called TULIP TREES.

L. chinense (Hemsl.) Sarg.

= L. Tulipifera var. chinense Hemsl. (and var. sinensis Diels)

CHINESE TULIPTREE. From China, and N Viet Nam. Discovered in 1875. Introduced in 1901 by E. Wilson for Veitch nursery of England. Introduced to North America shortly thereafter. In commerce here ≤1930. Very rare. Not as cold-hardy, large, or dense as its American relative. Leaves orange to brown as they unfold in spring. At maturity very pale beneath, wholly hairless, and quite narrow-waisted. Bark smooth, very pale. Records: 87' × 7'3" Wakehurst Place, Sussex, England (1984); 85' × 7'2" Fota Island, County Cork, Ireland (1987; *pl.* 1936); 78' × 8'10" Borde Hill, Sussex, England (1987).

L. chinense × L. Tulipifera

HYBRID TULIP TREE. Raised by the U.S. National Arboretum. Sold in the 1990s by Camellia Forest Nursey of Chapel Hill, NC.

L. Tulipifera L.

TULIP TREE. TULIP POPLAR. YELLOW POPLAR. WHITEWOOD. SADDLE(LEAF) TREE. From the eastern U.S. and extreme S Ontario. The epithet *Tulipifera* applied in 1753 derived from Miller's old generic name *Tulipifera Liriodendron*—tulip-bearing; from tulip, and Latin *-fer*, from *ferre*, to yield or bear. A common and familiar towering tree with a pillar-like trunk. Called YELLOW POPLAR because it has yellowish foliage leafing out in March, yellow-golden color in November, leaves that flutter in the wind, and lightweight and whitish wood like that of POP-LARS (*Populus* spp.). It can live 600 years. Records: 200' × 23'8" × 136' Cass County, MI (1983); 198' × 28'8½" near Asheville, NC (ca. 1930); 146' × 31'2" × 125' Bedford, VA (1986); 120' × 38'0" Indiana (1875).

L. Tulipifera 'Ardis'

Named in 1970 to honor Mrs. W. Floyd Sonnemann of Vandalia, IL, who, with her husband, first selected the tree in 1957. Extremely rare. Dwarf; "the original seedling and those budded from it are handsome miniatures of the species with ¼ to ⅓ the normal leaf size and tree height."

L. Tulipifera 'Arnold'—see L. Tulipifera 'Fastigiatum'

L. Tulipifera 'Aureo-maculatum'—see L. Tulip. 'Aureo-pictum'

L. Tulipifera 'Aureo-marginatum'

= *L. Tulipifera* Majestic Beauty™
= *L. Tulipifera* var. *panache* hort.
= *L. Tulipifera* 'Variegata'
= *L. Tulipifera* 'Luteo-marginatum'
= *L. Tulipifera* 'Foliis Luteo-marginatis'

Originated ca. 1865 in Germany. In North American commerce ≤1891. Uncommon. Most specimens date from 1986 or later, after Monrovia nursery of California began mass-producing it. Leaf variegated: gold-edged (turning greenish-yellow by late summer), green-centered. Tree somewhat slower growing, and its leaf smaller than typical. Records: 80' × 9'6" × 65' Port Coquitlam, B.C. (1992); 78' × 7'0" Royal Crescent, Bath, England (1988).

L. Tulipifera 'Aureo-pictum'

= *L. Tulipifera* 'Aureo-maculatum'
= *L. Tulipifera* 'Medio-pictum'
= *L. Tulipifera* 'Foliis Aureo-pictis'
= *L. Tulipifera* 'Foliis Aurea Maculata'
= *L. Tulipifera* 'Foliis Medio-pictis'

In European commerce ≤1875. Exceedingly rare. Center of leaf yellow blotched.

L. Tulipifera var. chinense—see L. chinense

L. Tulipifera 'Contortum'—see L. Tulipifera 'Crispum'

L. Tulipifera 'Crispum'

= *L. Tulipifera* 'Contortum'

Originally named in 1869 in Germany. To North America in 1895 after the Arnold Arboretum imported stock from Europe; reimported in 1949. Extremely rare. Leaves somewhat contorted, broader than long, the margins undulate.

L. Tulipifera 'Fastigiatum'

= *L. Tulipifera* 'Arnold'
= *L. Tulipifera* 'Pyramidalis' (or 'Pyramidale')

Originated in Europe. First mentioned (as 'Pyramidalis') in 1877 by the French horticulturist P.A. Lavallée. To North America ≤1888; in commerce here ≤1927. Common. Records: 78' × 5'0" Arduaine, West Highlands, Scotland (1992); 72' × 3'9" Wakehurst Place, Sussex, England (1974).

L. Tulipifera 'Foliis Aurea Maculata'—see L. Tulip. 'Aureo-pictum'

L. Tulipifera 'Foliis Aureo-pictis'—see L. Tulipifera 'Aureo-pictum'

L. Tulip. 'Foliis Luteo-marginatis'—see L. Tulip. 'Aureo-marginatum'

L. Tulipifera 'Foliis Medio-pictis'—see L. Tulipifera 'Aureo-pictum'

L. Tulipifera f. integrifolium Kirchn.

Known in Europe <1821. In North American commerce ≤1888. Extremely rare. Leaves unlobed. Records: 65' × 7'6" Kew, England (1967); 23½' × 2'7" × 25½' a topgrafted tree at Victoria, B.C. (1994).

L. Tulip. 'Luteo-marginatum'—see L. Tulip. 'Aureo-marginatum'

L. Tulipifera Majestic Beauty™—see L. Tulip. 'Aureo-marginatum'

L. Tulipifera 'Medio-pictum'—see L. Tulipifera 'Aureo-pictum'

L. Tulipifera var. panache—see L. Tulipifera 'Aureo-marginatum'

L. Tulip. 'Pyramidalis' or 'Pyramidale'—see L. Tulip. 'Fastigiatum'

L. Tulipifera var. sinensis—see L. chinense

Liriodendron Tulipifera 'Tortuosum'

Described in 1965 by D. Wyman of the Arnold Arboretum: "peculiar with contorted twigs." Origin unknown. Not known in commerce.

L. Tulipifera 'Variegata'—see *L. Tulipifera* 'Aureo-marginatum'

Lithocarpus

[FAGACEÆ; Beech Family] 100–300 spp. of broadleaf evergreen trees and shrubs, nearly all from E Asia. From Greek *lithos*, stone, and *karpos*, fruit, alluding to the hard shell of the acorn of the species first described (*L. javensis*). A genus much like *Quercus* (OAK) but with the catkins upright instead of dangling. As a whole they are not especially cold-hardy, and are best on the Pacific Coast and in shaded, cooler locales of the Southeast.

L. cuspidata—see Castanopsis cuspidata

L. densiflorus (H. & A.) Rehd.
= *Quercus densiflora* H. & A.

TANBARK OAK. TAN OAK. From SW Oregon and California. Introduced to cultivation in 1865. In California commerce since the 1920s. Rarely grown. Its bark was used to tan leather. Foliage of a dusty green cast. Leaves to 8" × 3⅛", dark green above, gray-blue beneath, leathery, shaped like those of CHESTNUT trees (*Castanea* spp.), with many parallel veins and shallow teeth; very hairy when unfolding. Flowers borne in strong-smelling creamy-white 2"–4" spikes in July; not especially ornamental, and certainly messy. Acorns large (1"–1½"), with burry cups. Valuable for ironclad constitution and useful for dry Pacific Coast sites. Its dwarf and cutleaf forms are more appreciated than the robust typical tree as garden subjects. Records: 208' × 14'0" Monterey County, CA (1914); 100' × 28'8" × 76' Kneeland, CA (1969); 92' × 22'6" × 84' Six Rivers National Forest, CA (1991).

L. densiflorus f. attenuato-dentatus J. Tucker, Sundahl & D.O. Hall

CUTLEAF TANOAK. More than one was discovered in 1962 in Yuba County, CA. Named in 1969. Extremely rare. Leaves deeply lobed in fernlike fashion. It can be raised from cuttings, and since probably only one clone is being circulated, perhaps a cultivar name is in order to replace the unwieldy formal name. Record: 40' × 2'10" × 25' Seattle, WA (1993; *pl.* 1972).

L. edulis (Mak.) Nakai
= *Pasania edulis* Mak.
= *Quercus edulis* Mak.
= *Quercus lævigata* hort. (in part), non Bl. (cf. *Quercus acuta*)

From Japan, and the Ryukyus. Introduced to Western cultivation ≤1842. Extremely rare; offered ≤1992 by Yucca-Do nursery of Waller, TX. The epithet *edulis* is Latin for edible, referring to the ¾" acorns, which are borne on spikes of 3–7. Leaf slender, untoothed, shiny bright light green above (not as glossy as that of *L. Henryi*), pale bronzy-green and minutely hairy beneath; to 8¼" × 2⅞", stem to 1" long. Although recorded to 65' × 9'6" in the wild, it is usually a large shrub or elegant small tree in cultivation.

L. Henryi (Seem.) Rehd. & Wils.

From C China. Introduced in 1901 by E. Wilson to England. Extremely rare; offered ≤1993 by Woodlanders nursery of Aiken, SC. Presumably named after Augustine Henry (1857–1930). The foliage looks like something we'd expect on a house plant. Leaf glossy, slender LAUREL-like, to 13" × 2⅞". Records: to 65½' × 9'10" in the wild; 52' × 3'3" Caerhays Castle, Cornwall, England (1975).

Litsea sericea—see *Neolitsea sericea*

Maackia

[LEGUMINOSÆ; Pea Family] 6–8 (12) spp. of deciduous trees. Named to commemorate Richard Karlovich Maack (1825–1886), a Siberian explorer, teacher, and naturalist. *Maackia* has interesting summer flowers, but dreadful fall color, like the related *Robinia* (LOCUST). Leaves pinnately compound. The most closely related genus is *Cladrastis* (YELLOWWOOD).

M. amurensis Rupr. & Maxim.
= *Cladrastis amurensis* (Rupr. & Maxim.) K. Koch
MANCHURIAN MAACKIA. From Manchuria, Korea, Ussuri, the Kuriles, and Japan. Named in 1856. Introduced to Western cultivation in 1864. In North American commerce ≤1907. Uncommon. Leaflets 7–9 (13), broad, untoothed, essentially hairless. Poor fall color of green, yellow and brown (if not bare) in late October, when *M. chinensis* is still green. Flowers dull whitish, in summer in upright narrow 4"–8" clusters. Seedpods 1¼"–3¾" long. Ornamentally inferior in flowers and foliage to *Cladrastis* (YELLOWWOOD). Varies from a 5' shrub to an 82' tree. Record: 36' × 2'8" Seattle, WA (1994; *pl.* 1940).

M. amurensis var. Buergeri (Maxim.) Schneid.
JAPANESE MAACKIA. From Japan and Korea. Introduced to cultivation in 1892. In North America ≤1893; in commerce here ≤1939. Extremely rare. Named after Heinrich Buerger (1804–1858), of Germany and Holland. Differs from the typical form in that leaflets are hairy beneath. Flowers white, spotted green, in congested, squat clusters from late June into early August. Record: 49' × 7'10" × 56' Seattle, WA (1989; *pl.* 1940).

M. chinensis Takeda
= *M. hupehensis* Takeda
CHINESE MAACKIA. From China. Introduced in 1908 by E. Wilson. Although North American nurseries have almost never listed this species, they have often sold it wrongly as *M. amurensis*. CHINESE MAACKIA is the superior ornamental, being less coarse, with more slender twigs and finer foliage (same texture as *Robinia* and *Sophora*). Leaf 5"–11" long; leaflets 9–17. When unfolding from

the buds in April or early May they are densely silvery with hairs; in autumn they remain green after *M. amurensis* is bare. Flowers white, borne in 6"–8" spikelike clusters in (late June) July-August. Seedpods 1"–2" (3⅝") long. Bark *Laburnum*-like. Records: to 75' × 7'0" in the wild; 40' × 5'8½" × 50' Seattle, WA (1994; *pl.* 1940).

M. hupehensis—see M. chinensis

Machilus Thunbergii—see *Persea Thunbergii*

Machilus yunnanensis—see *Persea yunnanensis*

Maclura

[MORACEÆ; Mulberry Family] Only the following species in the genus. [Some botanists stretch the number by including genus *Chlorophora* of ca. 5 spp.]. Named after William Maclure (1763–1840), distinguished geologist. Related genera include *Broussonetia* (PAPER MULBERRY), *Cudrania* (CHINESE SILKWORM THORN), *Ficus* (FIG), and *Morus* (MULBERRY).

M. aurantiaca—see M. pomifera

M. pomifera (Raf.) Schneid.
= *M. aurantiaca* Nutt.
= *Toxylon pomiferum* Raf. *ex* Sarg.
(*Ioxylon*)
OSAGE ORANGE. HEDGE APPLE. HEDGE TREE. BOW WOOD. BOWDOCK. BOWDARK. From NE Texas, SE Oklahoma, and SW Arkansas. The wood was used to make archery bows. Widely naturalized beyond its original native land. Common. First cultivated ≤1810 in St. Louis, MO. It was widely planted as a living hedge after 1848, but was gradually replaced by barbed wire ca. 1875. The name *pomifera* is Latin for fruit-bearing—*pomum*, fruit, and *ferre*, to bear—in allusion to the weird brain-like fruits, 3"–6" wide, to 19 ounces. They mature from pale green to yellowish in October, are inedible, contain milky juice, and repel cockroaches. Foliage brilliant green, yellow in fall. Leaves 1½"–9" long,

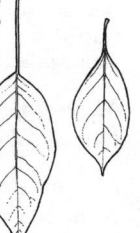

glossy. Twigs very spiny. Male and female flowers on separate trees in May or early June. Male flowers are dull yellowish small balls on stalks, hidden in the leaf axils. Female flowers like green golf balls with over 350 thread-like styles ⅞" long, radiating out like tentacles on a sea anemone. Bark tawny, furrowed and raggedly attractive. A yellow dye is obtained from the wood. Hardy under adverse conditions, and good looking, *Maclura* is worthy of more extensive planting, but people are rightly desirous of thornless and fruitless cultivars. Records: 100' × 17'9" Kennedyville, MD (1990); 68' × 24'3" × 100' Essex County, VA (1987); 64' × 25'0" × 96' Patrick Henry Estate, Brookneal, Charlotte County, VA (≤1993).

Maclura pomifera 'Altamont'
Selected by J.C. McDaniel of Urbana, IL. Named ≤1979. Male. Thornless. Branching more upright than usual.

M. pomifera 'Bois D'Arc Supreme'
Originated <1980. Under evaluation at Kansas State University.

M. pomifera 'Chetopa'
A thornless male released in 1973 by Kansas State University. Named for an Osage Indian chief.

M. pomifera 'Double O'
Origin and attributes unknown.

M. pomifera 'Fan D'Arc'
Introduced <1980 by Aldridge nursery of Von Ormy, TX. Nearly thornless. Totally fruitless. Large, dark leaves.

M. pomifera f. *inermis* (André) stat. nov.
= *M. pomifera* var. *inermis* (André) Schneid.
THORNLESS OSAGE ORANGE. Described in 1896. In Latin, *inermis* means unarmed; without thorns. Most OSAGE ORANGE cultivars fall under this general name. For more than 20 years various clones have been tested at Kansas State University. It has been found that so called thornless trees are often only mature states of the typical tree, and as soon as they are propagated their youthful growth is spiny.

M. pomifera 'Park'
Originated <1980 by Willis nursery of Ottawa, KS.

M. pomifera 'Pawkuska'
A thornless male released in 1973 by Kansas State University. Named after an Osage Indian chief.

M. pomifera 'White Shield'
Discovered near Hammond, OK. Introduced ≤1993 by Sunshine nursery of Clinton, OK. Named after a Cheyenne Indian chief. Thornless, fruitless.

M. pomifera 'Wichita'
Selected in 1978 from a wild specimen on the Glen Goering farm south of Wichita, KS. Under evaluation at Kansas State University; as of 1991 it was the least spiny cultivar known there.

M. tricuspidata—see *Cudrania tricuspidata*

Magnolia

[MAGNOLIACEÆ; Magnolia Family] 80–125 spp. of deciduous or evergreen trees and shrubs. Named after Pierre Magnol (1638–1715), French professor of botany at Montpelier. MAGNOLIAS are planted primarily because of their glorious flowers; a few species are valued quite as much for their foliage; one (*M. acuminata*) serves as shade tree. They are woodland trees for the most part, and hate dry or sterile soil. Dull fall color is a drawback of most. The flowerbuds on many species are large and silky, attractive all winter. The North American natives all bloom in early summer after the leaves expand; many Asian species bloom in early spring on naked twigs, creating the most excitement. Since MAGNOLIA flowers often do not have strongly differentiated petals and sepals, the term "tepal" serves to include both. The fruit, often attractive in autumn, is a coblike seedcone, more or less elongated and red, opening to dangle plump orange seeds. In recent years horticultural emphasis has switched from the species to hybrids. Unwieldy masses of rarer MAGNOLIAS exist— more than 400 kinds of MAGNOLIA are sold by Louisiana nursery of Opelousas, LA. As customary, the present volume (with 241) includes only the major kinds and a selection of obscure ones. Some shrub species are included because of their role in hybridization. Most MAGNOLIAS are mentioned in *The World of Magnolias* book by D.J. Callaway (1994). Updated news is in the twice-yearly journal *Magnolia*, published by the Magnolia Society. Related genera include *Liriodendron* (TULIP TREE), *Manglietia*, and *Michelia*.

M. '14 Karat'

Origin unknown. Introduced ≤1995 (year listed by Fairweather Gardens nursery, Greenwich, NJ): "Flowers porcelain-white, unusually thick-petaled.

M. acuminata (L.) L.

= *M. Candollii* (DC.) Link
= *M. rustica* hort. (in part)

CUCUMBER TREE. MOUNTAIN MAGNOLIA. INDIAN-BIT-TER. From the eastern U.S., and extreme S Ontario; the most widely distributed North American MAGNO-LIA. Commonly cultivated. Often planted as a shade tree because of its great size. Flowers 2"–4" long, in-conspicuous yellowish-green, appearing with foliage of similar color from late April into early June. Leaves to 13" × 7½". The specific epithet *acuminata* (sharply pointed) was given in comparison to the less pointy leaves of *M. virginiana* (SWEETBAY). Its fall color can be better than any other MAGNOLIA, gleaming gold, standing out in a genus known for sub-par autum-nal coloration. The unripe seedcones resemble small cucumbers and actually might have been pickled by pioneers, hence the name CUCUMBER TREE. At matu-rity the seedcones are colorful red, 2"–4" long. The name INDIAN-BITTER was explained by F. Michaux in 1802, and paraphrased by D.J. Brown in 1832: "Most of the inhabitants of the country bordering on the Alleghanies gather the cones of this tree about midsummer, when they are half ripe, and steep them in whiskey: a glass or two of this liquor, which is extremely bitter, they habitually take in the morning, as a preser-vative against autumnal fevers." A rugged, straight-trunked, large tree; its bark brown and furrowed. Records: 125' × 18'4" Great Smoky Mountains National Park, TN (1946); 120' × 11'3" Warren County, PA (1980); 94' × 20'3" North Can-ton, OH (1979); 75' × 24'5" × 83' Waukon, IA (1985); 65' × 13'8" × 108' Henry, IL (1980).

M. acuminata var. or ssp. cordata—see M. acum. var. subcordata

M. acuminata 'Golden Glow'

Propagated in 1957 from a tree growing wild in Sevier County, TN. Very rare—but Duncan & Davies nursery of New Zealand has begun mass-production. Flowers bright yellow.

M. acuminata var. subcordata (Spach) Dandy

= *M. acuminata* ssp. *cordata* (Michx.) E. Murr.
= *M. acuminata* var. *cordata* (Michx.) Sarg.
= *M. cordata* Michx.

YELLOW CUCUMBER TREE. Rare in the wild. Cultivated since ca. 1800. Uncommon. Tree smaller than the typical kind, with smaller leaves, less furrowed bark, less cold-hardy, and especially distinct, delightfully bright canary yellow flowers which may appear not only in spring but also from late July into September. In cultivation it is usually represented as a grafted clone, of bushy small tree size. Records: 102' × 12'1" × 63' Longwood Gardens, Kennett Square, PA (≤1993; *pl.* ca. 1800); 89' × 12'9" × 90' Virginia Beach, VA (1993).

M. acuminata var. subcordata 'Miss Honeybee'

Originated as a chance seedling. Introduced <1972 by J. Merrill nursery of Painesville, OH. Rare, but in commerce. Flowers larger than typical, and opening widely, bright yellow, with twisted petals.

M. acuminata var. subcordata 'Yellow Bird'—see M. 'Yellow Bird'

M. 'Alba Superba'—see M. × Soulangiana 'Alba Superba'

M. 'Alexandrina'—see M. × Soulangiana 'Alexandrina'

M. 'Amabilis'—see M. × Soulangiana 'Amabilis'

M. 'André Leroy'—see M. × Soulangiana 'André Leroy'

M. 'Ann'

(*M. Kobus* var. *stellata* × *M. liliiflora* 'Nigra')
Originated in 1955 as an intentional cross at the U.S. National Arboretum. Named in 1965, along with 7 similar hybrids which became collectively known as "the Girls" (referring to the cultivar names) or "the Kosar-DeVos hybrids" (referring to the scientists in-volved). They were bred in an effort to secure floral displays late enough to avoid injury from spring frosts. The eight cultivars are more or less shrubby; 'Ann', 'Betty' (especially), 'Ricki' and 'Susan' are the most treelike. All have late, dull fall color. 'Ann' has been in commerce since ≤1976; it blooms first, has smaller but more profuse flowers, which are tulip-shaped, sweet scented, the 6–9 tepals stained purple.

M. 'Apollo'
(*M. liliiflora* 'Nigra' × *M. Campbellii* var. *mollicomata* 'Lanarth')

Bred by F.M. Jury of New Zealand. In North American commerce ≤1992. Sister seedling of *M.* 'Iolanthe'. Buds deep rose-pink, opening to bowl-shaped flowers, 9" wide, rosy-red shading to light purple at the base, of rich and fruity fragrance. Blooms when young. To at least 20' tall.

M. Ashei—see M. macrophylla var. Ashei

M. 'Athene'
(*M. Soulangiana* 'Lennei Alba' × *M.* 'Mark Jury')

Bred by F.M. Jury of New Zealand. In North American commerce ≤1992. Flowers cup and saucer fashioned, 8"–10" wide, rosy-purple and white, richly fragrant. Blooms when young. To at least 25' tall. A clone of the same parentage is *M.* 'Milky Way'.

M. 'Atlas'
(*M.* 'Mark Jury' × *M. Soulangiana* 'Lennei')

Bred by F.M. Jury of New Zealand. In North American commerce ≤1992. Flowers 14" wide, lilac-pink. Blooms when young. To at least 20' tall.

M. auriculata—see M. Fraseri

M. australis—see M. virginiana var. australis

M. 'Betty'
(*M. Kobus* var. *stellata* f. *rosea* × *M. liliiflora* 'Nigra')

Originated in 1956 as an intentional cross at the U.S. National Arboretum. Named in 1965, along with 7 similar hybrids which became collectively known as "the Girls" (referring to the cultivar names) or "the Kosar-DeVos hybrids" (referring to the scientists involved). They were bred in an effort to secure floral displays late enough to avoid injury from spring frosts. The eight cultivars are more or less shrubby; 'Ann', 'Betty' (especially), 'Ricki' and 'Susan' are the most treelike. All have late, dull fall color. 'Betty' has been in commerce since ≤1978; it is common, definitely one of the best of the 8. Flowers to 8" wide, the 12–19 tepals reddish-purple with darker purple at the base, white inside. More treelike; readily forms a single trunk and grows to 20' tall.

M. biloba—see M. officinalis f. biloba

M. × brooklynensis Kalmb.
(*M. acuminata* × *M. liliiflora*)

BROOKLYN MAGNOLIA. Originated as an intentional cross at the Brooklyn Botanic Garden. Named accordingly in 1972. The following cultivars are important.

M. × brooklynensis 'Evamaria' PP 2820 (1968)

Originated in 1954 at the Brooklyn Botanic Garden. Extremely rare. Named after its breeder, Evamaria Sperber. Flowers appear in May and June, upright, 4" wide, rosy-purple, with some hints of green and yellow. Fertile, vigorous and cold-hardy.

M. × brooklynensis 'Hattie Carthan'
= *M.* 'Hattie Carthan'
(*M. brooklynensis* 'Evamaria' × *M. brooklynensis* #209)

Originated as an intentional cross in 1968 at the Brooklyn Botanic Garden. Introduced in 1984. Named after Hattie Carthan (1901–1984), who founded the Magnolia Tree Earth Center in Brooklyn in 1973. Flowers light yellow with magenta-rose veins extending from the base halfway up the center of the tepals.

M. × brooklynensis 'Woodsman'
= *M.* 'Woodsman'

Bred by J.C. McDaniel of Urbana, IL. Registered in 1974. Introduced ≤1975. Uncommon. Leaves glossy. Flowers multicolored—greenish-yellow, pink and purple; larger, darker and more attractive than those of 'Evamaria'. A large shrub or small tree. Very cold-hardy.

M. 'Brozzonii'—see M. × Soulangiana 'Brozzonii'

M. 'Butterflies' PP 7456 (1991)
(*M. acuminata* 'Fertile Myrtle' × *M. denudata* 'Sawada's Cream')

Bred by P. Savage of Bloomfield Hills, MI. Introduced ≤1988. Flowers dark yellow, appearing before the leaves.

M. 'Caerhays Belle'
(*M. Sargentiana* var. *robusta* × *M. Sprengeri* 'Diva')

Bred in 1951 at Caerhays Castle, Cornwall, England. First flowered in 1965. In North America <1972; first flowered here in 1977. Rare, but being mass-produced by Duncan & Davies nursery of New

Zealand. Young specimens exhibit strong apical dominance, and have withstood subzero winters without injury. Flowers appear in February-March; ca. 12" wide, freely borne, nodding, clear pink, of 12 broad tepals. Seedcones very ornamental.

M. Campbellii Hook. fil. & Thoms.

CAMPBELL MAGNOLIA. PINK TULIPTREE. PINK MAGNOLIA. From the Himalayas in N India, Nepal, Bhutan, Tibet, and SW China. Named in 1855 after Dr. Archibald Campbell, (1805–1874), British Political Resident in Darjeeling, India. Introduced to cultivation in 1865 or 1868 when plants were sent to England from the Calcutta Botanic Gardens. One bloomed in Ireland in 1885, perhaps the first in Europe. This species calls forth praise approaching veneration. To grow a *Magnolia Campbellii*, wait for many years, then invite your friends to see its amazing flowers, was a sort of pinnacle MAGNOLIA lovers dreamt of for decades. The species has also been rightly judged a straggly, tender prima donna, impractically slow to bloom, and really no better than some new hybrids (a good "poor man's *Campbellii*" is *M. Sprengeri*). In North America it has been successful primarily on the Pacific Coast, and even there is rare. One obtained in 1924 from Stuart Low nursery of London, England, and planted in San Francisco first flowered in 1940, possibly for the first time in the U.S. It has been in North American commerce since 1937. From seedling to blooming age requires ca. 15–46 years. Grafted trees bloom much sooner. Flowers appear very early in spring (usually February-March; rarely into early May) on naked twigs; almost crimson, ca. 10" wide, among the finest in the genus because of their inner whorl of erect tepals. Leaves 6"–14" long. Records: to 150' × 20'0" in the wild; 88½' × 7'1" Leonardslee, Sussex, England (1988); 85' × 7'9" Nymans, Sussex, England (1985); 75' × 9'0" Wakehurst Place, Sussex, England (1984); 69' × 13'0" Belgrove, County Cork, Ireland (1978); 64' × 3'4½" Seattle, WA (1994; *pl.* 1952); 60' × 6'1" San Francisco, CA (1992); 58½' × 15'10" × 73' Stratford, New Zealand (≤1982; *pl.* ca. 1918).

M. Campbellii f. alba hort.

= *M. Campbellii* var. *alba* Treseder

WHITE CAMPBELL MAGNOLIA. The form most common in the wild. First planted in 1926 by J.C. Williams at Caerhays Castle, Cornwall, England. In San Francisco, one was raised ca. 1934 from seeds imported from G. Ghose nursery of Darjeeling, India; it was planted in Strybing Arboretum, has flowers 8" wide, of 12 tepals. Grafts of it were sold (as 'Alba') ≤1955–56. Other clones are *M. Campbellii* var. *mollicomata* 'Maharanee', *M. Campbellii* var. *mollicomata* 'Strybing White', and *M. Campbellii* 'Stark White' (q.v.). Whiteflowered *M. Campbellii* seem to grow more strongly and are often less tender than the typical kind. A specimen at Chyverton, England, has borne flowers up to 17" wide. Record: 79' × 5'2" Borde Hill, Sussex, England (1987; *pl.* 1925).

M. Campbellii 'Charles Raffill'

= *M.* 'Charles Raffill'

(*M. Campbellii* × *M. Campbellii* var. *mollicomata*)
Originated as an intentional cross made in 1946 by Charles Percival Raffill (1876–1951) of Kew, England. First flowered in 1959. In North America ≤1965; in commerce here ≤1988. Very rare, but it has been offered recently by Duncan & Davies nursery of New Zealand. Flowers deep rose-pink in bud, opening 6"–10" wide, rosy-purple outside, white inside flushed pinkish-purple. Blooms when comparatively young. Record: 62' × 6'4" Trengwainton, Cornwall, England (1987).

M. Campbellii 'Darjeeling'

The original clone is in the Lloyd Botanic Garden of Darjeeling, India. Named 'Darjeeling' in 1967. Flowers darkest rose; relatively late in spring. Extremely rare in North America.

M. Campbellii 'Eric Walther'

(*M. Campbellii* × *M. Campbellii* var. *mollicomata*)
V. Reiter, Jr., of San Francisco, obtained this clone, unnamed, from a B.C. nursery ca. 1949. Strybing Arboretum of San Francisco obtained its specimen from Reiter in 1965, and named it after Eric Walther (1893–1959), a California horticulturist. Extremely rare. It blooms later than most. Flowers 8"–10" wide. It was described as narrowly erect, but an old specimen in Reiter's garden is broad.

M. Campbellii 'Hendrick's Park'

From Hendrick's Park of Eugene, OR. Named and introduced in 1971 by Gossler Farms nursery of Springfield, OR. Flowers 11"–12" wide, deep rich pink to rose. Remarkable for surviving subzero winters.

M. Campbellii 'Lanarth'—see **M. Camp. var. mollicomata 'Lanarth'**

M. Campbellii 'Late Pink'

Strybing Arboretum of San Francisco named this ≤1958. Flower size, shape and color normal, but consistently 2 weeks later than most to bloom in spring. In commerce ≤1976. Record: 48' × 6'7½" × 56' the original specimen in Strybing Arboretum (1995).

M. Campbellii var. mollicomata (W.W. Sm.) F. King.-Ward

= *M. Campbellii* ssp. *mollicomata* (W.W. Sm.) Johnstone
= *M. mollicomata* W.W. Sm.

CHINESE CAMPBELL MAGNOLIA. DOWNY CAMPBELL MAGNOLIA. Discovered in 1914 by G. Forrest; introduced to English cultivation that year. In North American commerce since ≤1951. Much more tractable to cultivation than typical CAMPBELL MAGNOLIA. This variety tends to bloom when younger (9–12 years old from seed, 6–8 from graft), grows faster, is hardier, is more likely to be multitrunked; flowers usually paler, never cup-shaped, open a week or two later in spring. A complaint is the flowers lack the clarity and richness of specimens of typical CAMPBELL MAGNOLIA, tending instead to be "muddy purplish." The name *mollicomata* (Latin meaning bearing soft hairs) refers to its hairy flower stalks. Seedcones to 10" long, 2½" wide. Records: to 80' tall in the wild; 56' × 10'2" Trewithen, Cornwall, England (1987).

M. Campbellii var. mollicomata 'Lanarth'

= *M. Campbellii* 'Lanarth'

PURPLE LANARTH MAGNOLIA. Raised at Lanarth, Cornwall, England, from seed collected in Yunnan, China, by G. Forrest in 1924. First flowered in 1947. In North American commerce ≤1981; only made readily available since ≤1992 because of Duncan & Davies nursery of New Zealand. Flowers cyclamen-purple, with even darker stamens; very large (9"–12" wide). Leaves broad, oblong, thick, quite blunt, like those of *M. Sargentiana* var. *robusta* in this respect. Tree vigorous and erect, the original ca. 70' tall in 1978.

M. Campbellii var. mollicomata 'Maharaja(h)'

Raised and named by D. Todd Gresham, who obtained the original seedling from W.B. Clarke nursery of San José, CA in the spring of 1954. It was named and described in 1963. Extremely rare. Flowers to 11" wide (even 15" says 1976–77 catalog of Little Lake nursery of Auburn, CA). Tepals white, except pure, medium-fuchsia purple at the base. Gresham exclaimed: "No muddy magenta shading, but a pure and very exciting color, new to me in magnolias."

M. Campbellii var. mollicomata 'Maharanee'

Raised by D. Todd Gresham of Santa Cruz, CA; named in 1964. Very rare. Flowers delicate white, perfectly symmetric, 8"–10" wide, with texture of smooth kidskin.

M. Campbellii var. mollicomata 'Strybing White'

Named ≤1958 after a specimen in Strybing Arboretum of San Francisco. Flowers ivory white, 12" wide, not cup and saucer shaped—the saucer droops. Leaves large. In commerce ≤1976. A prime candidate to be confused with the Strybing clone called *M. Campbellii* 'Alba'.

M. Campbellii 'Stark's White'

Originated as a G. Ghose nursery seedling offered by W.B. Clarke nursery of San José, CA. In 1938, when 1' high, it was sold to John H. Stark, M.D. (d. 1975), of Oakland, CA. First flowered in 1949. Named in 1962 by V. Reiter, Jr. No longer in commerce. Flowers comparable in size and shape to the Strybing Arboretum clone called *M. Campbellii* 'Alba' but of a better form.

M. Candollii—see **M. acuminata**

M. 'Charles Coates'

(*M. Sieboldii* × *M. tripetala*)

Selected from seedlings found ca. 1946 by C.F. Coates, propagator at Kew, England. Named in 1958 when it first flowered. In North America ≤1966; in commerce here ≤1976. Very rare. A large shrub or small tree (to 18' tall in 25 years). Leaves more like those of *M. tripetala*, yet smaller (to 10" × 5"). Flowers more like those of *M. Sieboldii*, but erect rather than nodding. Flowers very fragrant, cup-shaped, 4" wide, creamy white with reddish stamens; in (April) May-June.

M. 'Charles Raffill'—see **M. Campbellii 'Charles Raffill'**

M. 'Chyverton'

?(*M. Dawsoniana* × *M. Sprengeri*)
= *M. Dawsoniana* 'Chyverton'
= *M. Dawsoniana* 'Chyverton Red'

A seedling of *M. Dawsoniana*, raised at Caerhays Castle, Cornwall, England, and planted in 1944 at Chyverton, Truro, Cornwall. First bloomed in 1967. In North American commerce ≤1976. Extremely rare. Highly regarded. Flower color quite variable from year to year, bright crimson outside (fading to carmine pink), white inside; crimson anthers and styles. Tepals narrow. Record: 44' × 3'1" Vancouver, B.C. (1994; *pl.* 1986).

M. citriodora—see *M. denudata*

M. compressa—see *Michelia compressa*

M. conspicua—see *M. denudata*

M. cordata—see *M. acuminata* var. *subcordata*

M. cylindrica Wils.

ANHWEI MAGNOLIA. From China, provinces of S Anhwei (Anhui) to N Fukien (Fujian). Discovered in 1925, named in 1927, its original description saying "this very distinct new species is well distinguished by its thin, narrow, prominently reticulated leaves, by its slender petioles, and by its cylindric fruits." Cultivated since 1936. In North American commerce ≤1940. Rare. Flowers pure white or (usually) pink-tinged at the base, ca. 4" tall, of 9 tepals (the outermost 3 tiny and sepal-like), appearing on naked twigs. Leaves dark green above, glaucous beneath, with minute pubescence; to 8" × 3⅞" (larger on sucker shoots). Seedcones to 4" × 1½". An elegant-textured large shrub or broad small tree. Most specimens cultivated as *M. cylindrica*, although hardy and pleasing, may really be a hybrid with *M. denudata* (YULAN). The plant(s) usually grown as *M. cylindrica* may also be *M. amœna* (not in this volume) Records: 37' tall at Livonia, MI (1972; *pl.* 1937); 30' × 1'7" × 23½' Seattle, WA (1994; *pl.* 1949); trunks to 3'0" around in the wild.

M. 'Dark Shadow'

= *M.* × *Gresham* 'Dark Shadow'

Raised by D. Todd Gresham of Santa Cruz, CA. Parentage unknown. Named ≤1989 by Magnolia nursery of Chunchula, AL. Flowers 4"–5" wide, deep red-purple outside, off-white inside; stamens showy dark red. Tree compact, oval, 25'–30' tall.

M. Dawsoniana Rehd. & Wils.

DAWSON MAGNOLIA. From W China, rare in the wild. Introduced in 1908–1909 by E. Wilson. Named after Jackson Thornton Dawson (1841–1916), a North American horticulturist, for 43 years at the Arnold Arboretum, and one of its superintendents. First flowered in cultivation ca. 1932 in Ireland. In North American commerce ≤1948. Several in California bloomed in 1960. Rare. Flowers, appearing in March and April on naked twigs, are sideways-facing, 10" wide, white lightly suffused with purple—a pale purple or rosy pink effect overall. Darker flowered variants exist. Related closely to *M. Sargentiana*, but hardier, smaller in twig, leaf and flower. Better for small gardens. Leaves to 6" × 3", hairless or nearly so. Records: 70' × 5'9" Birr Castle, County Offaly, Ireland (1985; *pl.* 1946); 75½' × 3'1½" Seattle, WA (1994; *pl.* 1951); 61' × 4'5" Seattle, WA (1990; *pl.* 1953).

M. Dawsoniana 'Chyverton'—see *M.* 'Chyverton'

M. Dawsoniana 'Chyverton Red'—see *M.* 'Chyverton'

M. 'Deep Purple Dream'—see *M.* × *Soulang.* 'Deep Purple Dream'

M. Delavayi Franch.

CHINESE EVERGREEN MAGNOLIA. From SW China. French Jesuit, Abbé Pierre Jean Marie Delavay (1834–1895), a missionary, discovered it in 1886. It was named after him in 1889. In 1899 E. Wilson sent seeds to England. In North America ≤1927; in commerce here ≤1947. Extremely rare. Successful only along the Pacific Coast. Like a *M. grandiflora* without the gloss and sparkle; just foliage of gross luxuriance. The leaves, reported E. Wilson, are "larger than those of any other evergreen tree that can be grown in cool-temperate lands." They measure 8"–15" × 5"–8", dull bluish-green. Flowers creamy, 7"–10" wide, appearing sporadically in summer. Seedcones to 6" × 2¼". Often a giant shrub with more than one trunk. Records: 59' × 5'4" Caerhays Castle, Cornwall, England (1984); 50' × 4'0" Thorn House, Wembury, Devon, England (1977); 43' tall × 39' wide multitrunked at Berkeley, CA (1993; *pl.* 1959).

M. denudata Desr.

= *M. heptapeta* (Buc'hoz) Dandy
= *M. conspicua* Salisb.
= *M. Yulan* Desf.
= *M. citriodora* hort.

YULAN. YULAN MAGNOLIA. CHINESE WHITE MAGNOLIA. CHANDELIER MAGNOLIA. WHITE YULAN. LILY TREE. From E China; no longer wild, but cultivated there since ca. 600 A.D. Introduced to the West in 1789 when J. Banks imported it to England. In North American commerce ≤1854. Uncommon. Mostly grafted, or (with pains) cutting-grown, so most specimens are a clone. The Latin *denudata* means bare or naked of leaves when blooming— the 3"–7" leaves emerge after its 4"–7" wide ivory-white flowers bloom (March to May). Records: to 80' tall in China; to 59' tall in Japan; 56' × 6'0" × 38' Tyler Arboretum, Media, PA (1980); 43' × 8'9" × 44' Old Greenwich, CT (1987); 40' × 8'6" × 39' Woodland, WA (1990).

M. *denudata* var. *elongata*—see M. *Sprengeri* var. *elongata*

M. *denudata* 'Forrest's Pink'—see M. 'Forrest's Pink'

M. *denudata* 'Purple Eye'—see M. 'Purple Eye'

M. *denudata* var. *purpurascens*—see M. *Sprengeri*

M. *discolor*—see M. *liliiflora*

M. *diva*—see M. *Sprengeri*

M. 'Elisa Odenwald'
('Elsie Odenwald')
= *M. × Gresham* 'Elisa Odenwald'
(*M. Soulangiana* 'Lennei Alba' × *M. Veitchii*)
Raised ≤1964 by D. Todd Gresham of Santa Cruz, CA. Named in 1984 by Louisiana nursery of Opelousas, LA. Flowers late, to 12" wide, creamy white outside, touched pink-purple at the base; pure white inside; fragrant. Tree of upright, flaring multi-trunked habit.

M. 'Elizabeth' PP 4145 (1977)
(*M. acuminata* × *M. denudata*)
Bred in 1956 by Evamaria Sperber of the Brooklyn Botanic Garden. Named, registered and patented in 1977; named after Elizabeth Scholtz (Van Brunt), then Director of the Garden. Introduced with considerable fanfare in 1980. Only commonly advertised since 1986. Flowers yellow, to 7" wide, from late March into May (early July). Sterile. Two clones have

circulated under the name 'Elizabeth', and the incorrect clone may be the more common. In the maritime Pacific Northwest, what passes for 'Elizabeth' is a flop: the peculiarly luminous yellow of the opening flower rapidly deteriorates into a cold, creamy or greenish white; it is also subject to *Botrytis* infestation that stains the petals dirty brown. The comparatively new *M.* 'Butterflies' (q.v.) is likely to be better. A third clone of the same parentage is *M.* 'Ivory Chalice'.

M. *elliptilimba*—see M. *Zenii*

M. *elongata*—see M. *Sprengeri* var. *elongata*

M. 'Elsie Odenwald'—see M. 'Elisa Odenwald'

M. *exoniensis*—see M. *grandiflora* 'Exmouth'

M. *foetida*—see M. *grandiflora*

M. *Fordiana*—see *Manglietia Fordiana*

M. 'Forrest's Pink'
= *M. denudata* 'Forrest's Pink'
Originally planted in 1925; selected <1976 by Treseders' nursery of Truro, Cornwall, England. Named after the plant collector George Forrest (1873–1932). In North American commerce ≤1986. Very rare. Intermediate between *M. Sprengeri* and *M. denudata*. Flowers appear on naked twigs, are soft raspberry-pink, of light fruity fragrance.

M. *Fraseri* Walt.
= *M. auriculata* Bartr.
FRASER MAGNOLIA. INDIAN PHYSIC. EAR-LEAVED UMBRELLA TREE. From mountain valleys of the SE United States. Closely related to *M. macrophylla*. Named after John Fraser (1750–1811), the Scots collector of plants who introduced this species to England in 1786. In North American commerce since the 1800s, but never commonly sold. Leaves like gigantic arrowheads 8"–15" (24") long, hairless, with two prominent "earlike" lobes near the base. The October fall color is a heartwarming pumpkin-pie color to dark brick-red or caramel brown. Flowers yellow-tinted, 6"–10" (12") wide; late April into early June. Records: 110' × 9'5" × 59' Great Smoky Mountains National Park, TN (1993); and a different tree in the same park 107' × 9'8" × 55' (1988).

M. 'Freeman'
(*M. virginiana* × *M. grandiflora*)
An intentional hybrid bred in 1930–31 by Oliver M. Freeman of the U.S. National Arboretum. Freeman

raised many seedlings. They were variable. None of the offspring were hardier than *M. grandiflora*; the flowers were intermediate in size. They look more like *M. grandiflora* than *M. virginiana*. The clone 'Freeman' was named and released in 1962 because of its comparatively narrow if not columnar habit, cold-hardiness, and free-flowering nature. Leaves to 10¼" × 4½"; with faint brownish felt beneath. Flowers creamy-white, slightly fragrant, ca. 5" wide, not floppy. Practically sterile. Some arboreta, and perhaps nurseries, have mistakenly used the name 'Freeman' to refer to any of the National Arboretum seedlings or their second-generation offspring. As a result some collections have round-headed trees labeled 'Freeman', producing seedcones and even seeds. Authentic 'Freeman' has been very rare in commerce. A second clone of the same parentage but floppy habit and narrower leaves is *Magnolia* 'Maryland' (q.v.). Records: the original specimen in 1970 was 40' tall × 16' wide; 32' × 1'10" × 17' Seattle, WA (1994; *pl.* 1959).

M. 'Full Eclipse'
= *M. × Gresham* 'Full Eclipse'
Raised by D. Todd Gresham of Santa Cruz, CA. Named and in commerce ≤1990. Parentage unknown. Flowers early, red-purple outside, the tips curling back to reveal white insides. Tree columnar; to 30' tall in 10 years.

M. 'Galaxy'
(*M. liliiflora* 'Nigra' × *M. Sprengeri* 'Diva')
A hybrid made in 1963 at the U.S. National Arboretum; a sister seedling of *Magnolia* 'Spectrum' (see also *M.* 'Northwest'). First flowered in 1972; named and released in 1980. Common in commerce. Flowers to 10" wide, light purple, in late April. Vigorous upright pyramidal tree to 20'–40' tall. Very cold hardy. Combines the clean, rose-pink but ephemeral *M. Sprengeri* 'Diva' flowers with the reddish-purple, long-season *M. liliiflora* 'Nigra' ones; fragrance unlike that of either parent, quite sweet and recalls cotton candy.

M. gallissoniensis—see M. grandiflora 'Gallissonnière'

M. 'George Henry Kern' PP 820 (1949)
= *M. stellata* 'George Henry Kern'
= *M. × Soulangiana* 'George Henry Kern'
(*M. Kobus* var. *stellata* × *M. liliiflora*)
Raised by Wyoming nursery of Cincinnati, OH. Rare. It has mistakenly been attributed as a hybrid

of *M. Kobus* var. *stellata* and *M. Soulangiana*. Named after G. Kern (killed in France on V.E. Day 1945). Flowers of 8–10 tepals, lilac-red outside, white inside. Blooming season lengthy. Much like "the Girls" hybrids (i.e., 'Ann', 'Betty', 'Ricki', and 'Susan').

M. glauca—see M. virginiana

M. glauca var. major—see M. × Thompsoniana

M. glauca var. Thompsoniana—see M. × Thompsoniana

M. globosa var. sinensis—see M. sinensis

M. × Gossleri—see M. 'Marjory Gossler'

M. grandiflora L.
= *M. fœtida* (L.) Sarg.
EVERGREEN MAGNOLIA. SOUTHERN MAGNOLIA. GREAT FLOWERED MAGNOLIA. (GREAT) LAUREL MAGNOLIA. LOBLOLLY MAGNOLIA. BULL BAY. BIG LAUREL. From the SE United States. Very common, familiar and much planted throughout the world where the climate permits. A broadleaf evergreen (in the cold north it can be deciduous). Leaves thick like leather or plastic, 4"–10" (14½") long, glossy above; beneath variable from nearly hairless to coated with gray to rich brown fuzz. The epithet *grandiflora* means large-flowered (Latin *grandis*, large, and *floris*, flower). Flowers white, varying in size a great deal, even on the same tree from year to year, typically 6"–10" wide (to 16" in 'Celestial'); from late April to July with fewer into October (often more prolonged in cultivation than in the wild). Seedcones vary from pale beige to brilliant red; 2"–5" long. Including synonyms, ca. 175 cultivar names exist. The present volume contains 51—the important few and a selection of the legion minor ones. For details on rarer ones, consult the Magnolia Society's publications, or *The World of Magnolias* by D.J. Callaway (1994). A solidly built timber tree as well as a peerless ornamental. Records: 147' × 12'0" West Feliciana Parish, LA (<1921); 140' × 13'4" × 64' Tangipahoa Parish, LA (1985); 122' × 20'3" × 63' Smith County, MS (1986); 86' × 20'3" × 96' Bladen County, NC (1978); 72' × 21'10" × 71' Biloxi, MS (1967).

M. grandiflora 'Angustifolia'

Named in France ≤1817. Not important in North America. Leaves to 8" × 2", wavy; slightly fuzzy beneath. The name means narrow-leaved; from Latin *angustus*, narrow, and *folium*, a leaf.

M. grandiflora 'Bergen's Bronze'

Sold ≤1983 by Bergen nursery of Brea, CA.

M. grandiflora 'Blackwell'

= *M. grandiflora* 'H.D. Blackwell'

Introduced ca. 1986 by Louisiana nursery of Opelousas, LA. Leaves very glossy, undulating, very fuzzy beneath. Blooms when young.

M. grandiflora Blanchard™

= *M. grandiflora* 'D.D. Blanchard'

Discovered in the early 1960s in the yard of Decatur D. Blanchard (1904–1973) of Wallace, NC. Propagated by Robbins nursery of Willard, NC; in large-scale production only since 1980. Leaves very dark glossy green above, intense with copper fuzz beneath. Flowers typical. Compact pyramidal habit.

M. grandiflora Bracken's Brown Beauty® PP 5520 (1985)

Discovered in 1968 by Ray Bracken in his nursery at Easley, SC. Rare but recently heavily promoted. Very dense narrowly pyramidal shape—amazingly compact. Leaf attractively brown-fuzzy, 5" × 2". Flowers prolific; half of normal size, 5"–6" wide.

M. grandiflora 'Bronze Beauty'

Selected ≤1961 at the University of Florida, Gainesville. Rare. Leaf elliptic, to 9¾" × 4"; dull green and fuzzless beneath. Unfolding leaves are a well-marked dark bronze for 2–3 weeks.

M. grandiflora 'Cairo'

From 2808 Washington Street, Cairo, IL. Named in 1966 by J.C. McDaniel. Leaves thinner and more flexible than typical, very highly polished above, moderately gray-brown fuzzy beneath. Flowers more acute-tipped than is usual, of average size or slightly larger. Overall, 'Cairo' offers a cleaner, less heavy-looking specimen. Be that as it may, it has remained extremely rare. Cold-hardy to 0°F.

M. grandiflora 'Celestial'

Named in 1963 by D. Todd Gresham of Santa Cruz, CA. A broad tree, extremely rare. Leaf large, shiny, moderately fuzzy. Flowers shamelessly large, to 16" wide; blooms profusely over a long period.

M. grandiflora 'Charles Dickens'

Originated (planted ca. 1862) on the property of Charles Dickens, in Franklin County, TN. Selected and named <1965. Leaf 5" × 4" and rusty-fuzzy beneath. Flowers 8"–10" wide. Seedcones profuse, vivid red, very large (to 4½" wide), very conspicuous and ornamental from mid-September until November. The tree is a fertile tetraploid and has partly been distributed commercially as seedlings, because it has been so difficult via vegetative propagation. 'Charles Dickens' may be a hybrid, its parentage *M. grandiflora* × *M. macrophylla* or *M. Ashei*. Some seedlings of 'Charles Dickens' in the Seattle arboretum bear leaves as large as 10⅝" × 4⅞", not very fuzzy beneath, and produce few seedcones.

M. grandiflora 'Claudia Wannamaker'

Named after Mrs. A.J. Wannamaker (1908–1992), who bought the original as an 18" tall seedling in 1945. Introduced by Shady Grove nursery of Orangeburg, SC. In large-scale production since the late 1960s. Leaf small, 4"–7" × 2"–3", brown-fuzzy beneath. Flowers small, 3"–4" wide from May until September; blooms profusely at an early age. A medium-broad pyramidal tree.

M. grandiflora 'D.D. Blanchard'—see M. grandiflora Blanchard™

M. grandiflora 'Edith Bogue'

A seedling bought from a Florida nursery, and planted in 1917 by Edith A. Bogue (b. 1872) in Montclair, NJ. Registered in 1961. In commerce since ≤1970s. "The greatest proven hardiness of any commercially available cultivar in the Delaware Valley." Leaves narrower than normal; foliage dense. The original specimen 60' tall and 35' wide in 1983.

M. grandiflora 'Exmouth'

= *M. grandiflora* 'Lanceolata'
= *M. grandiflora* 'Exoniensis'
= *M. grandiflora* 'Oxoniensis'
= *M. grandiflora* 'Stricta'
= *M. exoniensis* Loud.

Introduced from the Carolinas to England in 1734 by Sir J. Colliton at Exmouth. Originally selected because of its cold hardiness. In North American commerce ≤1888; still sold. Leaves narrow, slightly rusty-fuzzy beneath. Habit erect, comparatively narrow and sharp pointed. Blooms early and freely. Flower large, slightly contracted, often with another row of smaller tepals in the middle, giving a fuller or double appearance. Possibly the clone has some genes of *M. virginiana* var. *australis*.

M. grandiflora 'Exoniensis'—see *M. grandiflora* 'Exmouth'

M. grandiflora 'Fairhope I'

Introduced <1988 by Magnolia nursery of Chunchula, AL. Leaves large, nearly round, blunt-tipped, wavy; little fuzz. Foliage dense. Crown rounded. Named after Fairhope, AL, which (like Chunchula) is near Mobile.

M. grandiflora 'Fairhope II'

Introduced <1988 by Magnolia nursery of Chunchula, AL. Leaves narrow lance-shaped, slightly rippled; brown fuzzy beneath. New growth silver-tinted.

M. grandiflora 'Ferruginea'

Introduced <1817. Still in commerce, but rare. The name means rust-colored in Latin. Leaves densely rusty-red fuzzy beneath. Free flowering. Habit compact, becoming rounded in age.

M. grandiflora 'Gallissonnière'

= *M. galissoniensis* hort.

Introduced in the 1740s to France by Roland-Michel Baron de la Gallissonnière (1693–1756), the governor of Canada. Propagated since 1856 because of its proven cold-hardiness. Named in 1869. In North American commerce ≤1888. Rare. Leaves gray or reddish-brown fuzzy beneath. Flowers medium sized to very large.

M. grandiflora 'Gloriosa'

Introduced ≤1856 in France; in North American commerce ≤1860. Common until perhaps the 1950s. Leaves to 14" long and proportionately broad; bronze-fuzzy beneath. Blooms when young. Flowers to 12"–15" wide.

M. grandiflora 'Goliath'

Origin unknown, likely from a nursery in Angers, France. Named <1910 at Charles Smith & Son's Caledonia nursery, Guernsey, founded in 1850, a famous nursery at the time. In North American commerce ≤1940s. Leaves oval, broad and rounded, thinly fuzzy to hairless. Flowers large (8"–12" wide); blooms while young. Growth compact. Record: 26' × 4'4" × 23½' Seattle, WA (1992).

M. grandiflora 'Harold Poole'

Discovered in 1972 as a seedling by nurseryman Harold Poole, Sr., of Forest Hill, LA. Registered in 1983. First bloomed in 1987; flowers 6"–8" wide.

Leaves narrow, strap-like, averaging 8" × 1½". Habit compact and shrublike.

M. grandiflora 'H.D. Blackwell'—see *M. grandiflora* 'Blackwell'

M. grandiflora 'Hasse'

Introduced <1983 by Shady Grove nursery of Orangeburg, SC. Leaves small, dark and glossy.

M. grandiflora 'Lakeside'

Introduced <1988 by Magnolia nursery of Chunchula, AL. Leaf large, curvy. Growth very fast. Easily raised from cuttings.

M. grandiflora 'Lanceolata'—see *M. grandiflora* 'Exmouth'

M. grandiflora 'Little Gem'

Selected in 1952 by Steed's nursery of Candor, NC. Little sold until 1978. Subsequently very common. Flowers (to 8¾" wide) and leaves (to 7½" × 2½") smaller than usual. Habit compact and narrowly upright; to 20' tall and 10' wide in 20 years. Needs summer heat to thrive; poor in cool-summer regions due to fungal susceptibility which makes the twig tips die back.

M. grandiflora 'Mainstreet'

Introduced ca. 1986 by Cedar Lane nursery of Madison, GA. A fastigiate columnar tree.

M. grandiflora Majestic Beauty™ PP 2250 (1963)

= *M. grandiflora* 'Monlia'

Originated by John and Mary Wallner. Introduced by Monrovia nursery of California. As common or more so than any other clone. Leaves light-green, broad, like paddles, with little fuzz beneath; like those of the RUBBER PLANT houseplant *Ficus elastica*. Tree branches readily break from wet snow loads. Flowers gigantic, 12" wide.

M. grandiflora 'Margaret Davis'

Introduced <1983 by Shady Grove nursery of Orangeburg, SC. Flowers 8"–12" wide. Leaves persist two years; narrow; dark green above, brown fuzzy beneath. Habit broad, flame-shaped.

M. grandiflora 'Margarita'

Originated ca. 1937. Introduced in 1958 by Saratoga Horticultural Foundation of California. Relatively dwarfish, after 20 years only 18' tall × 20' wide. Leaves glossy. Blooms the first year from grafts.

M. grandiflora 'Monland'—see *M.* Timeless Beauty™

M. grandiflora 'Monlia'—see *M. grandiflora* Majestic Beauty™

M. grandiflora 'Nannetensis'

Introduced ca. 1865 by the Delaunay nursery of Angers, France. The name from Namnetes, the ancient Roman name for Nantes, France. In North American commerce ≤1888. Very rare. Flowers very large, double, and abundant.

M. grandiflora 'North Star'

Selected at North, SC. Introduced ≤1993 by Woodlanders nursery of Aiken, SC. Tight pyramidal habit.

M. grandiflora 'Overton'

Introduced <1988 by Robbins nursery of Willard, NC. A rugged lookalike of *M. grandiflora* 'St. Mary'.

M. grandiflora 'Oxoniensis'—see *M. grandiflora* 'Exmouth'

M. grandiflora 'Pioneer'

A tree selected in Oregon City, OR. In North American commerce <1965. Similar to *M. grandiflora* 'Victoria' in cold-hardiness and general appearance but shrubbier, blooms a month earlier, and leaves have less fuzz beneath.

M. grandiflora 'Poconos'

Found in the Pocono Mountains, PA. Selected and registered by Bruce Keyser. Introduced in 1994–95. At least as hardy as 'Edith Bogue'. Leaves glossy, medium green, with very light fuzz.

M. grandiflora 'Precoce du Grand Jardin' — see *M. grand.* 'Præcox'

M. grandiflora 'Precoce du Mans'—see *M. grandiflora* 'Præcox'

M. grandiflora 'Præcox'

Introduced ≤1817 by the Cels nursery of Montrouge, France. Early- and long-flowering. More than one clone might have been called 'Præcox' (Latin for early). In the 1888 nursery catalog of John Rock, San José, CA, two French clones are listed: *M. grandiflora* 'Precoce du Grand Jardin' (flowers early, of medium size); *M. grandiflora* 'Precoce du Mans' (flowers early, double). See also *M. grandiflora* 'Præcox Fastigiata'.

M. grandiflora 'Præcox Fastigiata'

A seedling from a tree in Clifton Park, Baltimore, MD; or a 'Præcox' seedling. Introduced ≤1957 by Kingsville nursery of Maryland. Tree narrowly upright, flowering from mid-June into autumn frosts.

M. grandiflora 'Queen Mary'—see *M. grandiflora* 'St. Mary'

M. grandiflora 'Rotundifolia'

Known ≤1817 in France and England. Loudon in 1838 said of this: "Leaves roundish. Not a very distinct or handsome variety, and not a free flowerer." P. Riedel adds "very dark green roundish leaves, nearly blunt." In North American commerce ≤1943. Rare; extinct commercially. The name has been used in a general rather than a clonal sense, and in that spirit *M. grandiflora* 'Charles Dickens' has been referred to as a cultivar of it.

M. grandiflora 'Ruff'

Named after the owner, Wallace Ruff, of Eugene, OR. Introduced in 1973 by Gossler Farms nursery of Springfield, OR. Leaves deep green above, with brick-red fuzz beneath.

M. grandiflora Russet™ PP 2617 (1966)

Introduced in 1952 by Saratoga Horticultural Foundation of California. Rare until 1967; subsequently very common. Leaf small (to 6½" × 2¾"), unusually heavily coated with thick brown fuzz. Flowers 6"–8" wide, with extra tepals. Habit narrow, with erect branching. The original was 23' tall, 10' wide in 1966.

M. grandiflora 'St. George'

Introduced ≤1967 in England. In North American commerce ≤1981. Very rare. Very cold-hardy. Seldom needs more than 3 years to bloom. Flowers with 22–25 tepals. Leaves dark with fuzz beneath.

M. grandiflora 'St. Mary'
= *M. grandiflora* 'Queen Mary'

Originated ca. 1905 when Glen St. Mary nursery of Glen St. Mary, FL, bought it (as a year-old seedling) from Joseph Vestal & Son nursery of Little Rock, AR. Propagated since 1910. Named in 1940. The most common cultivar in the United States for many years. It has a bushy crown yet is no dwarf: the original was 55' × 5'6" (1961). Leaf 6"–10" long, to 4" wide, dark and glossy above, of average rusty-red fuzz beneath; edge undulated. Flowers abundant, cupped, 5" wide; blooms young.

M. grandiflora Samuel Sommer™ PP 2015 (1961)

Selected in 1952 by the Saratoga Horticultural Foundation of California. First bloomed in 1953. The first cultivar of *M. grandiflora* to get a patent. Introduced to the general public in February 1961. Very common. Robust, upright, densely clothed. Branches ascend sharply. Leaves broad, leathery, cupped, glossy dark green above, rusty-brown fuzzy beneath; to 10½" × 5¼". Flowers 10"–14" wide. Seedcones often abundant and handsome. Named after Samuel C. Sommer, President of the Board of Trustees of the Saratoga Horticultural Foundation.

M. grandiflora 'San Marino' PP 2830 (1968)

Selected in 1951 in San Marino, CA. Introduced in 1970 by Saratoga Horticultural Foundation of California. Rare. Leaves scarcely fuzzy beneath. Habit compact. Growth slow. Flowers small (4" wide).

M. grandiflora 'Satin Leaf'

Original tree near Tallahassee, FL. Introduced <1950 by Southern States nursery of MacClenny, FL. Leaves large, with deep red-brown fuzz beneath. Flowers large.

M. grandiflora 'Semme's Select'—see *M. grand.* 'Symmes' Select'

M. grandiflora 'Shady Grove'

Several cultivars have been originated in recent decades by Shady Grove nursery of Orangeburg, SC. Provisional names include: "Shady Grove No. 4" (horizontal branches; broad, open appearance) and "Shady Grove No. 6" (a well defined, tapering, flag-pole leader; vigorous).

M. grandiflora 'Silver Tip'

Registered ca. 1980 by Louisiana nursery of Opelousas, LA. Leaves "huge," with thick silvery-gray fuzz beneath, glossy green above.

M. grandiflora 'Smith Fogle'—see *M. grandiflora* 'Smitty'

M. grandiflora 'Smitty'

= *M. grandiflora* 'Smith Fogle'

Introduced <1988 by Shady Grove nursery of Orangeburg, SC. Named for M. Smith Fogle of the nursery. Like *M. grandiflora* 'Margaret Davis' but with broader leaves, very brown beneath. Flowers 8"–11" wide. Tree robust, densely oval, coarse-textured.

M. grandiflora 'Spring Hill'

Introduced <1988 by Magnolia nursery of Chunchula, AL. Foliage exceptionally elegant. Leaves very glossy deep green above, fuzzy beneath; elliptic with pointed tips. Not subject to leaf blotch. Flowers pure white. Columnar to pyramidal habit.

M. grandiflora 'Stalwart'

Originated ca. 1937. Introduced in 1958 by Saratoga Horticultural Foundation of California. Flowers freely produced, even when tree is young. Tree vigorous with a dense narrow crown. The original specimen was 49' tall and 26' wide after 35 years.

M. grandiflora 'Stricta'—see *M. grandiflora* 'Exmouth'

M. grandiflora 'Suede'

Origin unknown, named <1975. Extremely rare. Leaf with very thick brown fuzz beneath, recalling that of *M. grandiflora* 'Russet' yet larger (to 6⅝" × 4⅛").

M. grandiflora 'Sunset'

Found as a seedling in the woods by Glen St. Mary nursery of Florida. Extremely rare. The original was 8' tall by 1961. Leaf variegated light yellow, to 8½" × 3¾".

M. grandiflora 'Symmes' Select'

('Semme's Select')

Discovered in 1966 by John Symmes (1923–1973) of Cedar Lane nursery of Madison, GA. Sold largely by Wayside nursery. It was a seedling from a tree at Westview Cemetery of Atlanta, GA. Leaves rich dark green above, brown fuzzy beneath. Flowers of typical size, abundant, even when the tree is young. Compact.

M. grandiflora Timeless Beauty™—see *M.* Timeless Beauty™

M. grandiflora 'Victoria'

Origin unknown. In commerce by the 1920s. By the late 1930s it was being sold from Georgia to England. Common. One conjecture is that the name was given to an Exbury form imported from England by Layritz nursery of Victoria, B.C.; this form was cold-hardy, floriferous, and had handsome fuzz on the leaves. However 'Victoria' might have been named in England first, and imported to North America under its own name. In any case, likely more than one clone has been sold as 'Victoria'. A description in the 1937–38 catalog of Fruitland nursery, Augusta, GA: "Differs from *M. grandiflora* 'Gloriosa' only in shape of leaves, which are long and narrow and without the bronze color underneath." It is not as hardy or as fast as *M. grandiflora* 'Edith Bogue'. The common clone of contemporary commerce has pointy leaves, shiny above, rusty-red fuzzy beneath, with conspicuous red stipules. Flowers average to large (8"–12" wide), markedly fragrant. Growth bushy, but not dwarf; it resists snow breakage well. Records: 37' × 4'3" × 31' Seattle, WA (1993); 27' × 4'5½" × 34' Aurora, OR (1993; *pl.* 1967).

M. grandiflora 'Workman'

Introduced <1981 by Louisiana nursery of Opelousas, LA. Very compact and shrubby (to 20' tall × 15' wide in 25 years). Flowers small, 4½"–5" wide; from April into November. Leaves small, ca. 6" × 3".

M. × *Gresham* 'Dark Shadow'—see *M.* 'Dark Shadow'

M. × *Gresham* 'Elisa Odenwald'—see *M.* 'Elisa Odenwald'

M. × *Gresham* 'Full Eclipse'—see *M.* 'Full Eclipse'

M. × *Gresham* 'Heaven Scent'—see *M.* 'Heaven Scent'

M. × *Gresham* 'Joe McDaniel'—see *M.* 'Joe McDaniel'

M. × *Gresham* 'Jon Jon'—see *M.* 'Jon Jon'

M. × *Gresham* 'Manchu Fan'—see *M.* 'Manchu Fan'

M. × *Gresham* 'Moondance'—see *M.* 'Moondance'

M. × *Gresham* 'Peppermint Stick'—see *M.* 'Peppermint Stick'

M. × *Gresham* 'Pink Goblet'—see *M.* 'Pink Goblet'

M. × *Gresham* 'Raspberry Ice'—see *M.* 'Raspberry Ice'

M. × *Gresham* 'Royal Crown'—see *M.* 'Royal Crown'

M. × *Gresham* 'Royal Flush'—see *M.* 'Royal Flush'

M. × *Gresham* 'Sangreal'—see *M.* 'Sangreal'

M. × *Gresham* 'Sayonara'—see *M.* 'Sayonara'

M. × *Gresham* 'Spring Rite'—see *M.* 'Spring Rite'

M. × *Gresham* 'Todd Gresham'—see *M.* 'Todd Gresham'

M. Halleana or *Halliana*—see *M. Kobus* var. *stellata*

M. 'Hattie Carthan'—see *M. brooklynensis* 'Hattie Carthan'

M. 'Heaven Scent'

= *M.* × *Gresham* 'Heaven Scent'
(*M. Veitchii* × *M. liliiflora* 'Nigra')

Raised in 1955, and named by D. Todd Gresham of Santa Cruz, CA. In commerce since the 1980s. Flowers lavender-pink at the base fading to white at the tips; 9 narrow tepals 5" long; strongly fragrant.

M. heptapeta—see *M. denudata*

M. × *highdownensis*—see *M. Wilsonii*

M. hypoleuca S. & Z.

= *M. obovata* Th., non Ait. *ex* Link, non Willd.

JAPANESE SILVERLEAF MAGNOLIA. WHITELEAF MAGNOLIA. Japanese: *Ho-no-ki*. From Japan and the Kuriles. Very closely related to *M. officinalis*. Named in 1794. Introduced in 1818 to Leiden, Holland; in 1854 to San Francsico; in 1865 to the eastern U.S. Common. Closely related to UMBRELLA TREE (*M. tripetala*), but without the floppy foliage and foul floral odor (a hybrid between these two species is *M.* 'Silver Parasol'). Leaves 8"–18" long, rounded rather than narrowly tapered near the base; vivid silver beneath (Greek *hypo*, beneath, and *leucon*, white). Flowers powerfully and deliciously fragrant, white with prominent crimson stamens; looking like 8" wide water lilies from May into July. Seedcones 5"–8" long, slender, scarlet. Fall color in October can be purplish, dull brown, to tawny gold with green. Whether the color is of

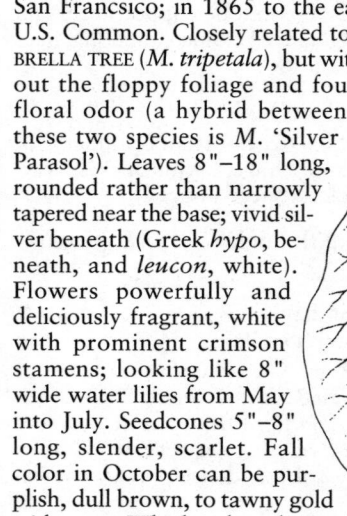

wet cardboard or a strong brown, there is a powerful contrast with the shocking white leaf undersides, seen as the fallen leaves form a mosaic on the ground. In early November the fallen leaves of some are chalky white. Records: to 105' × 29'2" in the wild; 66' × 3'0" Weasenham Hall, Norfolk, England (1991; *pl.* ca. 1960); 64' × 4'7" and 46' × 8'5" Tacoma, WA (1992).

M. *hypoleuca* 'Silver Parasol'—see M. 'Silver Parasol'

M. *insignis*—see *Manglietia insignis*

M. 'Iolanthe'
(*M. × Soulangiana* 'Lennei' × *M.* 'Mark Jury')
Raised in New Zealand in 1966; first flowered in 1970; introduced in 1974; in North American commerce <1981. Flowers in (late January) April–May, large (10"–11" wide), cup-shaped, rosy-pink, creamy-white inside, nodding and floppy (suggestive of those of *M. Sargentiana* var. *robusta*); borne even at an early age. A vigorous small tree.

M. 'Ivory Chalice'
(*M. acuminata* × *M. denudata*)
A intentional hybrid raised by D. Leach of North Madison, OH; registered in 1985. Flowers 6" wide, creamy-white to yellowish-green, borne over a long period. Hardy to -22°F. Two cultivars of the same parentage are *M.* 'Butterflies' and *M.* 'Elizabeth'.

M. 'Jersey Belle'
(*M. sinensis* × *M. Wilsonii*)
Originated as a chance hybrid in 1970 at the château de la Fosse in France. Raised in Jersey. Described in 1981; named in 1983. Extremely rare in North America. Overall habit, and leaf shape closer to that of *M. Wilsonii*. Flowers 5"–6" (8") wide, of 9 tepals. Leaf ca. 9" × 5½".

M. 'Joe McDaniel'
= *M. × Gresham* 'Joe McDaniel'
(*M. Veitchii* × *M. Soulangiana* 'Rustica Rubra')
Raised by D. Todd Gresham of Santa Cruz, CA. Named in 1984 by Louisiana nursery of Opelousas, LA. A tall, robust tree. Tulip-shaped dark red-violet buds open to bowl-shaped flowers. Named after horticulturist Joseph C. McDaniel (1912–1982), of Urbana, IL.

M. 'Jon Jon'
= *M. × Gresham* 'Jon Jon'
Raised by D. Todd Gresham of Santa Cruz, CA.

Parentage unknown. Named ≤1989 by Magnolia nursery of Chuncula, AL. Flowers very fragrant, late, 10"–12" wide, white tinted with rose at the base. A small rounded tree, to 20' tall.

M. × *kewensis* Pearce (nom. nud.)
= *M. salicifolia* 'Kewensis'
(*M. Kobus* var. *Kobus* × *M. salicifolia*)
Originally described in 1957 based on a vigorous specimen that arose ca. 1938 at Kew, England. It bears pure white 6" wide flowers. In 1976, S. Spongberg wrote that the tree called *M. × kewensis* is merely a variation of *M. salicifolia*, so he renamed it *M. salicifolia* 'Kewensis'. Whether or not the original Kew tree is a hybrid, other specimens of the same parentage clearly exist; the cultivar 'Wada's Memory' is the best example. No such hybrid clone has become common in commerce (least rare is 'Wada's Memory'). The hybrids differ from *M. salicifolia* by a combination of characteristics. They are more apt to be vigorous and large; the leaves are not so bluish beneath, and are often larger; the leafbuds are hairy. In details, such hybrids resemble *M. salicifolia* more than *M. Kobus*. Alas, if STAR MAGNOLIA is considered a mere variety of KOBUS MAGNOLIA (as in the present volume), the name *M. × kewensis* must be submerged into synonymy under the name *M. × Proctoriana*, which originally designated only hybrids between *M. salicifolia* and STAR MAGNOLIA (*M. Kobus* var. *stellata*). If the STAR MAGNOLIA is maintained as a separate species, the name *M. × kewensis* remains valid.

M. × *kewensis* 'Slavin's Snowy'—see M. × *Proctoriana* 'Slavin's Snowy'

M. × *kewensis* 'Wada's Memory'—see M. × *Proctoriana* 'Wada's Memory'

M. *Kobus* DC.
= *M. præcocissima* Koidz.
= *M. Thurberi* Parsons *ex* W. Robinson
KOBUS MAGNOLIA. NORTHERN JAPANESE MAGNOLIA. Japanese: *Kobushi*. From Japan. The Japanese name means "fist" because the flower buds are distinctively pointed, grayish, hairy and shaped like a fist. Flowers ca. 4" wide, petals 6–9, snow-white or faintly flushed pink-purple near the base; appearing on naked twigs (mostly in

April). Named in 1817. Introduced to the U.S. in 1862 by G.R. Hall. Parsons nursery of Flushing, NY, had it by 1870. It is the hardiest Asian MAGNOLIA, and is common. Much used as a rootstock. Records: 72' × 9'2" Portland, OR (1989); 58' × 5'7" × 59' Avondale, WA (1992).

M. Kobus var. borealis Sarg.

HOKKAIDO MAGNOLIA. From central and N Japan and S Korea. Introduced to the eastern U.S. in 1876 by W.S. Clark; it first flowered in Brookline, MA, in 1899. Named in 1908. An ill-defined variety, supposedly hardier, larger and more vigorous. Leaves to 8" × 4"; flowers to 5" wide. C. Ingram wrote in 1957: "plants so called are merely extra vigorous examples of the type. Out of a large batch of seedlings one will often obtain specimens that might, with justification, be allocated to either one or the other of these supposed forms, while others again will be intermediate between the two." R. Brightman says var. borealis exhibits superior wind resistance and its definite tree-like habit is elegantly proportionate with its leaves and flowers, making it a better ornamental. It makes sense that trees from northern Japan will be hardier, but whether they deserve varietal distinction is doubtful. Another option is to call such trees by the cultivar name 'Borealis'. In Latin, borealis means of or from the north.

M. Kobus var. Lœbneri (Kache) Spong.

= M. × Lœbneri Kache
(M. Kobus var. Kobus × M. Kobus var. stellata)

LÖBNER MAGNOLIA. Originally described after a deliberate cross was made <1910 by German horticulturist Max Löbner (1870–1947) of Dresden. The first offspring flowered in 1917. The name was published in 1920. Original seedlings were sold in 1923. By the late 1950s several U.S. nurseries listed M. × Lœbneri—a name which came to be used in a group sense, referring to any seedlings or clones of the same parentage (KOBUS × STAR). Most specimens look more like KOBUS than STAR MAGNOLIAS. Flowers 4"–6" (8") wide, white or pink; tepals 11–15 (30). Recorded to 45' tall.

M. Kobus var. Lœbneri 'Ballerina'

= M. × Lœbneri 'Ballerina'
= M. stellata 'Ballerina'
(M. Kobus var. Lœbneri 'Spring Snow' × M. Kobus var. stellata 'Waterlily')

An intentional 1960 cross by J.C. McDaniel of Urbana, IL; introduced in 1969. Common since 1976. Tepals to 30 or more, flushed pale pink at the base. More fragrant than 'Spring Snow'. Tree smaller than the common M. Kobus var. Lœbneri 'Merrill', as well as later-blooming.

M. Kobus var. Lœbneri 'Champaign'

= M. × Lœbneri 'Champaign'

Selected by J.C. McDaniel of Urbana, IL. In commerce ≤1994–95. Uniform, upright oval crown. Flowers tinted pink.

M. Kobus var. Lœbneri 'Donna'

= M. × Lœbneri 'Donna'

Selected by H. Heineman of Scituate, MA. In commerce ≤1990. Very hardy. Flowers 8" wide.

M. Kobus var. Lœbneri 'Leonard Messel'

= M. × Lœbneri 'Leonard Messel'
= M. × Soulangiana 'Leonard Messel'

Raised ca. 1950 at Nymans, Handcross, Sussex, England (home of Lieutenant Colonel Leonard Charles Rudolf Messel, 1873–1953). A chance cross of M. Kobus and M. stellata f. rosea. In North America ≤1963. In commerce here ≤1976. Common. Purplish buds open to light pink flowers 4½"–5" wide, with ca. 12 drooping lilac-pink tepals. Not as fragrant as many M. Kobus variants, but overall best of the pink STAR MAGNOLIAS.

M. Kobus var. Lœbneri 'Merrill'

= M. × Lœbneri 'Merrill'
= M. × Lœbneri 'Dr. Merrill'
= M. stellata 'Dr. Merrill'

IMPROVED STAR MAGNOLIA. A deliberate cross from the Arnold Arboretum, sown in 1939; first flowered in 1944; named in 1952 after Elmer Drew Merrill Ph.D. (1876–1956), botanist, Arnold Arboretum director. In commerce ≤1958. Common. A robust small tree. Flowers large, white (flushed pink at first), early; ca. 15 tepals. Record: 29' × 3'2" Aurora, OR (1992).

M. Kobus var. Lœbneri 'Neil McEacharn'

= M. × Lœbneri 'Neil McEacharn'

Raised at Windsor Great Park, England, from M. Kobus var. stellata f. rosea seed obtained ca. 1951 from Villa Taranto, Pallanza, Italy. Named in 1962 for the founder of that famous Italian garden, Neil Boyd McEacharn (1885–1964). In North American commerce ≤1981. Rare. Flowers small, profuse, white or flushed pale pink. Vigorous.

M. Kobus var. Lœbneri 'Snowdrift'
= M. × Lœbneri 'Snowdrift'

Hillier nursery of England adopted this name ≤1969 for a clone descended from one of the original seedlings from the 1910 cross in Germany. In North American commerce ≤1981. Rare. Larger flowers than M. Kobus var. stellata with about 12 broad tepals; leaves also a little larger.

M. Kobus var. Lœbneri 'Spring Joy'—see M. 'Spring Joy'

M. Kobus var. Lœbneri 'Spring Snow'
= M. × Lœbneri 'Spring Snow'
= M. × Lœbneri 'Illinois (No. 1)'
= M. stellata 'Spring Snow'

Planted in 1931; discovered many years later by J.C. McDaniel in the President's garden at Urbana, IL. Introduced to commerce ca. 1970. Flowers exceptionally fragrant, pure white, of ca. 15–20 tepals, 3"–4" long.

M. Kobus var. Lœbneri 'Star Bright'
= M. × Lœbneri 'Star Bright'
= M. stellata 'Star Bright'

Introduced ≤1965 in England; in North American commerce <1974 by Tom Dodd nursery of Semmes, AL. Flowers white, tepals many, narrow; slightly fragrant. A vigorous small tree.

M. Kobus var. Lœbneri 'Willowwood'
= M. × Lœbneri 'Willowwood'
= M. 'Willowwood'

Named after the arboretum of that name in Gladstone, NJ. A chance garden cross from ca. 1941—a seedling of M. Kobus var. stellata f. rosea. Introduced ≤1953. Rare. Flowers to 7" wide, of 11–14 tepals.

M. Kobus var. stellata (S. & Z.) Blackb.
= M. stellata (S. & Z.) Maxim.
= M. tomentosa Th.
= M. Halleana Robinson

STAR MAGNOLIA. STARRY MAGNOLIA. From central Honshu, Japan. G.R. Hall brought it to the U.S. in 1862; to Britain ca. 1877–78. Very common. Flowers chalk-white, starlike, with 9–20 (60) narrow straplike tepals, completely covering the branches like a mantle of snow very early in spring. Frost often blights them in less than ideal locales. Leaves 2"–5" long. A dense twiggy shrub; rarely a small tree with a bushy crown. More treelike if grafted on typical M. Kobus than if grown vegetatively. Records: 36' × 3'0" × 30' Cambridge, MA (1994); 30' × 3'1" × 29' Lewisburg, PA (1980).

M. Kobus var. stellata 'Centennial'
= M. stellata 'Centennial'

Originated in 1943 as a M. Kobus var. stellata f. rosea seedling at the Arnold Arboretum. Flowers large (to 5¼" wide), showy, with wide tepals slightly tinged pink. Vigorous, to 15'–18' tall. Named in the arboretum's centennial year, 1972. Offered commercially ≤1975–76. Common.

M. Kobus var. stellata 'Dawn'
= M. stellata 'Dawn'

Discovered in 1974 in the garden of Mrs. Charles McAfee of Bethesda, MD. Propagated and named by H.C. Hopkins of Bethesda. Extremely rare. Pale pink in the bud, opening white banded with pink on the outside. Numerous (to 50+) narrow tepals.

M. Kobus var. stellata 'Halliana'
= M. stellata 'Halliana'
(Halleana)

The "typical" stellata form introduced to the U.S. by George R. Hall in 1862.

M. Kobus var. stellata 'Jane Platt'
= M. stellata 'Jane Platt'
= M. stellata 'Rosea Jane Platt'

Named and introduced ≤1980 by Gossler Farms nursery of Springfield, OR. Named after Jane Kerr (Mrs. John W.S.) Platt (1908–1989), an accomplished and beloved gardener of Portland, OR. Flowers not the darkest pink, but the most fade-resistant; tepals 20–30 (60).

M. Kobus var. stellata 'Keiskei'
= M. stellata var. Keiskei Mak.
= M. stellata 'Kikuzaki'

Named after Keisuke Ito (1803–1901), a Japanese plant collector. Described in Japan in 1912. In North American commerce ≤1986. Extremely rare. Shrubby, with smaller (2"), pink flowers; 20–30 tepals. Borne in profusion even on two-year old plants.

M. Kobus var. stellata 'King Rose'
= M. stellata 'King Rose'

Originated in New Zealand. In North American commerce ≤1985. Rosy-pink buds open white tinged at the base with delicate blush pink. Tepals many. Blooms early. Very bushy and small.

M. *Kobus* var. *stellata* f. *rosea* (Veitch) stat. nov.
= M. *stellata* f. *rosea* (Veitch) Schelle
= M. *stellata* 'Rosea' (in part)
= M. *stellata* 'Pink'

PINK STAR MAGNOLIA. Introduced to North American cultivation when the Domoto Brothers nursery of Oakland, CA imported it from Japan sometime after 1885. Veitch nursery of England independently imported it from Japan, and exhibited it in England in 1893. Very common. Pink buds largely fade white in opening. The name has been used for more than one clone, as seedlings sometimes come up pink. Indeed, the majority of named STAR MAGNOLIA clones have pink in their flowers, at least partly, and probably were raised from the original 'Rosea' clone. The course adopted in this volume is to give *rosea* status as a botanical forma name, since cultivar names in woody plants usually indicate particular clones. The clone most commonly encountered in commerce as 'Rosea' can still be sold by that cultivar name, even though the botanical formula exists as a convenient group designation. Alternatively, one could use the name 'Rosea' with the understanding that it may refer to any of several similar clones or seedlings. Records: 28' × 2'5" × 25' Seattle, WA (1992); 22' × 5'1" × 28' Puyallup, WA (1993).

M. *Kobus* var. *stellata* 'Royal Star'
= M. *stellata* 'Royal Star'

A 'Waterlily' seedling raised in 1947 on Long Island; introduced in 1959–60 by John Vermeulen nursery of New Jersey. Very common. Pale pink buds open to white, much larger flowers than usual (to 6" wide; to 30 tepals), opening a week or so later than typical STAR MAGNOLIAS. A shrublike tree. Very cold-hardy. Some nurseries have sold 'Waterlily' under this name.

M. *Kobus* var. *stellata* 'Rubra'
= M. *stellata* 'Rubra'

RED STAR MAGNOLIA. Imported ca. 1925 from K. Wada nursery of Japan. Extremely rare until after 1945, still uncommon, being difficult to propagate and of shrubby, spreading, slow growth. Buds dark purple-pink, opening to pink which lasts even to when the flowers are spent and shedding. Tepals ca. 15.

M. *Kobus* var. *stellata* 'Waterlily'
= M. *stellata* 'Waterlily'

Beginning in the 1920s, possibly 4 clones have been circulated under this name. It is, or they are, common. Usually credited to ≤1939 and Greenbrier Farms

nursery of Norfolk, VA. They are characterized by pink buds opening later than usual, to highly-scented white flowers with numerous tepals: (11) 14–18 (36), comparatively short and less floppy—giving a waterlily look. Strong, erect growth.

M. *Kobus* 'Wada's Memory'—see M. × *Proctoriana* 'Wada's Memory'

M. 'Legacy'
(M. *denudata* × M. *Sprengeri* 'Diva')

A intentional hybrid raised by D. Leach of North Madison, OH; registered in 1991. Flowers 9" wide, rich dark pink at the base, lighter towards the tips; white inside. Very vigorous.

M. *Lenneana*—see M. × *Soulangiana* 'Lennei'

M. *Lennei*—see M. × *Soulangiana* 'Lennei'

M. *Lennei* var. *speciosa*—see M. × *Soulangiana* 'Speciosa'

M. *liliiflora* Desr.
(*liliflora*)
= M. *quinquepeta* (Buc'holz) Dandy
= M. *purpurea* Curtis
= M. *discolor* Vent.

LILY MAGNOLIA. PURPLE LILY MAGNOLIA. From China, but widely cultivated in Japan. Introduced in 1790 to England; named in 1792; to North America ≤1811. Common. Much used in hybridization. A shrub or rarely a very small tree (34' × 5'6" × 40' Philadelphia, PA, 1980). Despite its diminutive size, closely related to the giant CUCUMBER TREE (M. *acuminata*). Flowers slender and purplish, appearing with the leaves in mid- to late spring and early summer. A clone known as 'Nigra' since <1884 has larger, especially dark purple flowers, and has often been sold as if it were a cultivar of M. × *Soulangiana*.

M. × *Lœbneri*—see M. *Kobus* var. *Lœbneri*

M. × *Lœbneri* 'Ballerina'—see M. *Kobus* var. *Lœbneri* 'Ballerina'

M. × *Lœbneri* 'Champaign'—see M. *Kobus* var. *Lœbneri* 'Champaign'

M. × *Lœbneri* 'Donna'—see M. *Kobus* var. *Lœbneri* 'Donna'

M. × *Lœbneri* 'Dr. Merrill'—see M. *Kobus* var. *Lœbneri* 'Merrill'

M. × *Loebneri* 'Illinois (No. 1)'—see *M. Kobus* var. *Loebneri* 'Spring Snow'

M. × *Loebneri* 'Leonard Messel'—see *M. K.* var. *Loebneri* 'Leonard Messel'

M. × *Loebneri* 'Merrill'—see *M. Kobus* var. *Loebneri* 'Merrill'

M. × *Loebneri* 'Neil McEacharn'—see *M. K.* var. *Loebneri* 'Neil McEacharn'

M. × *Loebneri* 'Snowdrift'—see *M. Kobus* var. *Loebneri* 'Snowdrift'

M. × *Loebneri* 'Spring Joy'—see *M.* 'Spring Joy'

M. × *Loebneri* 'Spring Snow'—see *M. Kobus* var. *Loebneri* 'Spring Snow'

M. × *Loebneri* 'Star Bright'—see *M. Kobus* var. *Loebneri* 'Star Bright'

M. × *Loebneri* 'Willowwood'—see *M. Kobus* var. *Loebneri* 'Willowwood'

M. macrophylla Michx.
= *M. Michauxi* hort.

BIGLEAF MAGNOLIA. LARGE-LEAVED MAGNOLIA. GREAT-LEAVED MAGNOLIA. ELEPHANT EAR. SILVER LEAF. BIG BLOOM. From the SE United States; rare in the wild. Discovered by A. Michaux in 1795. First cultivated when one was planted ca. 1800 by Matthias Kinn at Germantown, PA. Common. A gargantuan leaf (to 3½' long) that supplies a tropical motif, sets this species apart. (Greek *macro*, large, and *phyllon*, leaf.) Grown more for foliage than flowers. No other noncompound tree leaves are larger outside of the tropics (except maybe those of a stooled *Paulownia*). Leaves silvery beneath; the very base with little lobes. Flowers marvelous, 8"–20" wide, immaculate white except usually dark red-purple at tepal base; sweetly perfumed, from (April) May into early July, difficult to see, being borne high amongst the great leaves. It needs a sheltered position or else wind ruins the foliage, rendering the tree bedraggled and crude. Records: 105' × 5'6" D. Boone National Forest, KY (1989); 68' × 7'7" × 57' Gaston, MD (1990); 42' × 8'8" × 43' Centreville, MD (1990).

M. macrophylla var. *Ashei* (Weatherby) D. Johnson
= *M. Ashei* Weatherby
= *M. macrophylla* ssp. *Ashei* (Weatherby) Spong.

ASHE MAGNOLIA. DWARF BIGLEAF MAGNOLIA. SANDHILL MAGNOLIA. COW CUCUMBER. From NW Florida, SE Alabama, and perhaps SE Texas; very rare in the wild. Named in 1926, after its discoverer, William Willard Ashe (1872–1932) of the U.S. Forest Service. Extremely rare in cultivation until the 1990s. Very similar to BIGLEAF MAGNOLIA (*M. macrophylla*), but a precocious bloomer with smaller leaves and flowers. Much better suited to urban residential landscape needs than its enormous, clumsy peer. Leaf to 19" × 9". Flowers 5"–12" wide, sometimes doubled. Record: 52' × 4'7" × 37' Henry Foundation, Gladwyne, PA (≤1993).

M. macrophylla 'Holy Grail'
Bought as a seedling in 1956 by D. Todd Gresham of Santa Cruz, CA. First bloomed in 1962. Named and introduced ca. 1963. Extremely rare. Flowers shaped like a chalice. Tepals to 8" × 5" with their bases electric blue-violet.

M. macrophylla 'Whopper'
Selected by J.C. McDaniel of Urbana, IL. Registered in 1974. Very rare. Giant flowers (to 18" wide) and leaves.

M. major—see *M.* × *Thompsoniana*

M. 'Manchu Fan'
= *M.* × *Gresham* 'Manchu Fan'
(*M. Soulangiana* 'Lennei Alba' × *M. Veitchii*)
Raised by D. Todd Gresham of Santa Cruz, CA. Named ≤1979. In North American commerce ≤1986. Very rare. Large, goblet-shaped, creamy-white flowers faintly purplish-stained at the base.

M. 'Marillyn'
(*M. liliiflora* 'Nigra' × *M. Kobus*)
Originated in 1954 as an intentional cross at the Brooklyn Botanic Garden. Introduced in 1989. Flowers bright purple, 5" long. Sterile. Leaves to 7" × 4". Superior cold-hardiness. A large shrub, the original 15' tall in 1989.

M. 'Marjory Gossler'
('Marj Gossler')
(*M. denudata* × *M. Sargentiana* var. *robusta*)
= *M.* × *Gossleri* hort.
Bred by P. Savage of Bloomfield Hills, MI. Introduced to North American commerce ≤1986 by Gossler Farms nursery of Springfield, OR; named after one of the nursery's owners. Reddish-pink buds open to pink-flushed flowers 10"–12" wide.

M. 'Mark Jury'

(*M. Campbellii* var. *mollicomata* 'Lanarth' × *M. Sargentiana* var. *robusta*)

A chance hybrid raised by Felix M. Jury of New Zealand. Named ≤1978. Introduced to North American commerce ≤1986. Flowers 10"–11" wide, pure light pink, blushed rose and tinged lavender-purple on the margins. A tall, narrow tree.

M. 'Maryland'

(*M. virginiana* × *M. grandiflora*)

An intentional hybrid bred in 1930–31 by O.M. Freeman of the U.S. National Arboretum. Freeman raised many seedlings. They were variable. None of the offspring were hardier than *M. grandiflora*; the flowers were intermediate in size. They look more like *M. grandiflora* than *M. virginiana*. The clone 'Maryland' was named in 1967 because of its superior performance and acceptance in England, and its ease of propagation by cuttings. Leaves to 12¼" × 4⅝"; with faint brownish felt beneath. Flowers white, slightly fragrant, floppy, borne over many months. The crown is broad and branches whippy and slender. Eventually the twigs become hairless (those of its less common sibling *M. 'Freeman'* remain hairy). A shrublike small tree.

M. Michauxi—see M. macrophylla

M. 'Milky Way'

(*M. Soulangiana* 'Lennei Alba' × *M.* 'Mark Jury')

Bred by F.M. Jury of New Zealand. In North American commerce ≤1993. Flowers white, tinged pink at the base. Blooms when young. To 20' tall. A clone of the same parentage is *M.* 'Athene'.

M. mollicomata—see M. Campbellii var. mollicomata

M. 'Monland'—see M. Timeless Beauty™

M. 'Moondance'

= *M. × Gresham* 'Moondance'

Raised by D. Todd Gresham of Santa Cruz, CA. In North American commerce ≤1992. Flowers early, pure white or blushed pink at the base, to nearly 12" wide. A vigorous tree.

M. Nicholsoniana—see M. sinensis and M. Wilsonii

M. 'Niemetzii'—see M. × Soulangiana 'Niemetzii'

M. 'Nimbus'

(*M. hypoleuca* × *M. virginiana*)

Bred in 1956. Selected in 1974. Introduced in 1980 by the U.S. National Arboretum. Uncommon. Flowers in May, creamy white, ca. 6" wide, of lemon-like fragrance; sterile. Named nimbus because its flowers are like white clouds. Leaves to 12" long, whitish-blue and hairy beneath; partially evergreen. Very vigorous small 30'–40' tree.

M. 'Norbertii'—see M. × Soulangiana 'Norbertii'

M. 'Northwest'

= *M. × Soulangiana* 'Northwest'

(*M. liliiflora* 'Nigra' × *M. Sprengeri* 'Diva')

Introduced ≤1989 by Hazel Dell Gardens of Canby, OR. Very rare. Of the same parentage as *M.* 'Galaxy' and 'Spectrum'.

M. obovata—see M. hypoleuca

M. officinalis Rehd. & Wils.

MEDICINAL MAGNOLIA. SPICE MAGNOLIA. ASIAN UMBRELLA MAGNOLIA. From central and W China, and naturalized if not native in Korea. Its bark and flowerbuds are used in Chinese traditional medicine, hence the epithet *officinalis*. Discovered in 1885 by A. Henry. Introduced to the West in 1900 when E. Wilson sent seeds to England. Closely related to *M. hypoleuca*. Extremely rare in North America: specimens so labeled in collections are often *M. hypoleuca*. Leaves invariably narrowly tapered (as in *M. tripetala*) at the base, the underside of average glaucousness rather than boasting the vivid chalky paleness seen on many specimens of *M. hypoleuca*. Also the leaves are smaller on average (the largest 21" × 10½"; stem to 1¾") than those of *M. hypoleuca*, and have more prominent midribs; the twigs are slenderer and tawny or pale brown, hairy—instead of stout, glaucous and purplish. The leafstalks and twigs release less fragrance when crushed or scratched. Flowers 5"–8" wide, creamy-white, in May-June, with tepals narrower and less showy than those of *M. hypoleuca*. Seedcones to 5" long, very broad. Records: to 70' tall in the wild; 56' × 4'3" Birr Castle, County Offaly, Ireland (1985); 52' × 4'6" Borde Hill, Sussex, England (1974).

M. officinalis f. biloba (Rehd. & Wils.) stat. nov.

= *M. officinalis* var. *biloba* Rehd. & Wils.

= *M. biloba* Rehd. & Wils.

Introduced in 1936 from the Lushan Botanic Garden.

Less rare than typical *M. officinalis*. Leaves conspicuously bilobate or notched instead of acute at the apex. Record: 39' × 3'8" × 25½' San Francisco, CA (1994; *pl.* ca. 1959).

M. 'Orchid'

= *M. stellata* 'Orchid'
(*M. Kobus* var. *stellata* × *M. liliiflora*)
Originated as a chance seedling at Hillenmeyer nursery of Lexington, KY. Named ≤1961. Very rare. Six rather uniform red-purple petals, and 3 tiny sepals. More cold-hardy than either parent, but very shrubby.

M. Oyama—see M. Sieboldii

M. parviflora—see M. Sieboldii

M. parviflora var. Wilsonii—see M. Wilsonii

M. 'Paul Cook'

(*M. Soulangiana* 'Lennei' seedling × *M. Sprengeri* 'Diva')
Bred by Dr. F. Galyon of Knoxville, TN; registered in 1975. In commerce ≤1991. Flowers 10"–12" wide, light to rich pink outside, pure white inside. Fertile. Vigorous. Cold-hardy.

M. 'Peppermint Stick'

= *M.* × *Gresham* 'Peppermint Stick'
(*M. liliiflora* × *M. Veitchii*)
Raised in 1955 by D. Todd Gresham of Santa Cruz, CA. Named ≤1962. Introduced to North American commerce ≤1986. Narrow buds open to large flowers, white marked purple—much like *M.* × *Veitchii* but more freely produced. Other clones of the same parentage are *M.* 'Raspberry Ice' and *M.* 'Royal Crown'.

M. 'Pickard's Ruby'

= *M.* 'Ruby'
A hybrid derived from *M.* × *Soulangiana* 'Picture'. Raised in Kent, England by A.A. Pickard; registered ca. 1980. Introduced to North American commerce ≤1994 by Duncan & Davies nursery of New Zealand. Flowers rich ruby-red, large (to 11" wide), of pleasant fragrance. Blooms when young. Nearly fastigiate.

M. 'Pickard's Sundew'

= *M.* × *Soulangiana* 'Sundew'
= *M.* 'Sundew'
A seedling of *M.* × *Soulangiana* 'Picture', named in 1968 by A.A. Pickard of Kent, England. In North American commerce ≤1986. Flowers goblet-shaped, 10" wide, white with pink flush and purplish stripe, in April–May. Fast and vigorous; to 30' tall in 10 years.

M. 'Picture'—see M. × Soulangiana 'Picture'

M. 'Pink Goblet'

= *M.* × *Gresham* 'Pink Goblet'
(*M. Veitchii* × *M. Soulangiana* 'Rustica Rubra')
Raised by D. Todd Gresham of Santa Cruz, CA. Named and introduced to commerce ≤1989. Flowers goblet-shaped, 10"–11" wide, rich pink, late April into May. Vigorous.

M. 'Porcelain Dove'

(*M. globosa* × *M. virginiana* var. *australis*)
Bred in 1965 by D. Todd Gresham of Santa Cruz, CA. Named in 1986. Introduced to commerce ≤1993 by Fairweather Gardens nursery of Greenwich, NJ. Flowers porcelain-white. Leaves much like those of *M. virginiana* (SWEET BAY).

M. præcocissima—see M. Kobus

M. 'Pristine'

(*M. Kobus* var. *stellata* 'Waterlily' × *M. denudata*)
Bred in 1968 by J.C. McDaniel of Urbana, IL. Introduced to commerce <1980. Flowers the same pristine ivory-white color of *M. denudata* with twice the number of tepals. Growth habit intermediate. Hardy to -15°F.

M. × Proctoriana Rehd.

(*M. salicifolia* × *M. Kobus* var. *stellata*)—the former interpretation
(*M. salicifolia* × *M. Kobus*)—the present interpretation
Originated as a chance *M. salicifolia* seedling in 1928 at the Arnold Arboretum. Named in 1939, after T.E. Proctor of Massachusetts, in whose garden the seed had been collected. The name *M.* × *Proctoriana* used to refer exclusively to crosses between *M. salicifolia* and STAR MAGNOLIAS. Now (at least for those who regard STAR MAGNOLIA as a mere variety of KOBUS MAGNOLIA) it must also include specimens formerly designated by the name *M.* × *kewensis* (i.e., *M. salicifolia* × KOBUS MAGNOLIA). A third scenario, proposed in 1976 by Dr. S. Spongberg, says all such so called hybrid trees are mere variations of *M. salicifolia*. A slender tree of dense bushy habit, to 40'–50' tall or more. Flowers 3"–4" wide, white, appearing on naked twigs.

M. × *Proctoriana* 'Slavin's Snowy'

= M. *salicifolia* 'Slavin's Snowy'
= M. × *kewensis* 'Slavin's Snowy'
= M. *Slavinii* Harkn.

A chance seedling (M. *Kobus* var. *stellata* × M. *salicifolia*) from Rochester, NY; first flowered in 1917. Named in 1954 after horticulturist Bernard Henry Slavin (1873–1960). In commerce ≤1958. Rare. Flowers white, pink flushed near the base, 3"–5" wide. A small tree to 40' tall with a dense bushy crown.

M. × *Proctoriana* 'Wada's Memory'

= M. × *kewensis* 'Wada's Memory'
= M. 'Wada's Memory'
= M. *Kobus* 'Wada's Memory'
= M. *salicifolia* 'Wada's Memory'
(M. *Kobus* var. *Kobus* × M. *salicifolia*)

In March 1940 this tree was one of several seed-raised plants that the Seattle arboretum bought (as KOBUS MAGNOLIA) from Koichiro Wada (1911–1981) of Hakoneya nursery, Numazu-shi (later of Yokohama), Japan. The flowers proved unusually large (to 7" wide) and showy, so the clone was propagated from 1952 onward. It is rare but in commerce. The name 'Wada's Memory' was chosen by Wada himself in 1957, and was published in spring of 1959. In 1992 the original seedling measured 42' × 4'4" × 31'; a cutting-grown specimen near the original is 47' tall (1993).

M. 'Purple Eye'

= M. *denudata* 'Purple Eye'

Originated in England <1950. In North America ≤1966; rare; in commerce here ≤1986. Flowers white with a purple blush at the base of the tepals, looking like a purple eye. Blooms from February to May depending on latitude. Less hardy than M. *denudata* (YULAN), it may be a clone of M. × *Soulangiana*.

M. 'Purple Prince'

(M. *liliiflora* 'Darkest Purple' × M. *Soulangiana* 'Lennei')

Bred by Dr. F. Galyon of Knoxville, TN; registered in 1976. Flowers deep purple, globular, 10" wide. A large shrub or small tree.

M. *purpurea*—see M. *liliiflora*

M. *quinquepeta*—see M. *liliiflora*

M. 'Raspberry Ice'

= M. × *Gresham* 'Raspberry Ice'
(M. *liliiflora* × M. *Veitchii*)

Raised in 1955 by D. Todd Gresham of Santa Cruz, CA. Named ≤1962. Flowers 9" wide and like those of M. 'Royal Crown' but a week later and colored a softer purple; Louisiana nursery says "luminous lavender-pink." Shrubby.

M. 'Ricki'

(M. *liliiflora* 'Nigra' × M. *Kobus* var. *stellata*)

Originated in 1955 as an intentional cross at the U.S. National Arboretum. Named in 1965, along with 7 similar hybrids which became known collectively as "the Girls" (referring to the cultivar names) or "the Kosar-DeVos hybrids" (referring to the scientists involved). They were bred in an effort to secure floral displays late enough to avoid injury from spring frosts. The eight cultivars are more or less shrubby; 'Ann', 'Betty' (especially), 'Ricki' and 'Susan' are the most treelike. All have late, dull fall color. 'Ricki' has been in commerce since ≤1978; it is common. Buds long pointed and upright red purple, opening in late April to 4"–6" wide cup shaped flowers, of 10–15 rather narrow tepals, pink to deep red-purple at the base outside; white inside. Sterile. Of strict habit.

M. 'Royal Crown'

= M. × *Gresham* 'Royal Crown'
(M. *liliiflora* × M. *Veitchii*)

Raised in 1955 by D. Todd Gresham of Santa Cruz, CA. Named ≤1962. Flowers crownlike, 10"–12" wide, of 9–12 erect tepals (the outermost reflexed); deep purplish-pink in the bud, opening paler (dark red-violet outside, white inside). Blooms when young. A small tree. Other clones of the same parentage are M. 'Peppermint Stick' and M. 'Raspberry Ice'.

M. 'Royal Flush'

= M. × *Gresham* 'Royal Flush'
(M. *Soulangiana* 'Lennei Alba' × M. *Veitchii*)

Raised in 1955 by D. Todd Gresham of Santa Cruz, CA. Named ≤1962. Flowers to 12" wide, white with a "royal purple flush" at the base. Blooms in February-March, or later in the north.

M. 'Ruby'—see M. 'Pickard's Ruby'

M. *rustica*—see M. *acuminata* and M. × *Soulangiana* 'Rustica Rubra'

M. salicifolia (S. & Z.) Maxim.

ANISE MAGNOLIA. WILLOWLEAF MAGNOLIA. Japanese: *Tamu-shiba*. From Japan. Named in 1872. The name *salicifolia* means willow-leaved; from genus *Salix*, WILLOW, and Latin *folium*, a leaf. Introduced to the West when C. Sargent and J.H.Veitch collected seeds in the fall of 1892. Uncommon in cultivation. Related to *M. Kobus* but flowers earlier in spring, blooms at a younger age, is more fragrant, has larger sepals, nearly or wholly hairless leafbuds, and is a tidier, narrower tree of finer texture. Flowers white except sometimes tinted pink at the base, appearing in April on naked twigs; sepals promi-

nent. Leaves to 6½" × 2½" (3"), pale beneath, often attractively bronzy when young. Twigs smell lemony; leaves smell of anise. Typically a slender, upright tree. Records: 60' × 3'5" Nymans, Sussex, England (1983); 50' × 3'½" Seattle, WA (1993; *pl.* 1949); 40' × 5'0" × 42' Delaware County, PA (1980).

M. salicifolia 'Else Frye'

In 1947 the Seattle arboretum received this tree from Else M. Frye (1884–1962) of Seattle. Mrs. Frye originally obtained it from the W.B. Clarke nursery of San José, CA. The clone is almost fastigiate, with many clear-white spicily fragrant flowers ca. 6" wide—almost half again as large as normal; the thick tepals open wide to reveal the crimson stamens. Propagated ≤1957, and named thereafter; in commerce ≤1972–73. Extremely rare. Difficult to propagate; very similar to 'Iufer' (below). The original tree: 34' × 2'2" (1994).

M. salicifolia 'Iufer'

Named after Ernest J. Iufer (1896–1980) of Iufer Landscape Company, Salem, OR. This clone originally was sent from England to Seattle, then Mr. Iufer obtained it. In commerce ≤1980. Very rare (difficult to propagate). Exceptionally choice, with large (to 7" wide) white flowers, blooming even when young. Very similar to 'Else Frye' (above).

M. salicifolia 'Kewensis'—see M. × kewensis

M. salicifolia 'Kochanakee'

Origin unknown. In commerce ≤1986. Flowers large. Growth vigorous. Similar to *M. salicifolia* 'W.B. Clarke'.

M. salicifolia 'Miss Jack'

Originated as a seedling from the University of British Columbia. Introduced commercially ≤1980. Uncommon. The fastest and largest growing *M. salicifolia*. Exceptional flowering ability. Flowers tinted pink at the base. Leaves broad. It may be a hybrid with *M. Kobus*.

M. salic. 'Slavin's Snowy'—see M. × Proctoriana 'Slavin's Snowy'

M. salicifolia 'W.B. Clarke'

Introduced and named after W.B. Clarke nursery of San José, CA. In commerce ≤1965–66. Rare. Flowers abundant, larger than those of *M. salicifolia* 'Miss Jack', and foliage heavier.

M. salic. 'Wada's Memory'—see M. × Proctoriana 'Wada's Memory'

M. 'Sangreal'

= *M.* × *Gresham* 'Sangreal' (*M. liliiflora* × *M. Veitchii*) Raised by D. Todd Gresham of Santa Cruz, CA. Named ≤1992. Flowers cup-shaped, red-purple, large (8" wide), early. Vigorous.

M. Sargentiana Rehd. & Wils.

SARGENT MAGNOLIA. From W China. Introduced in 1908 by E. Wilson. Named in 1913 after Charles Sprague Sargent (1841–1927), American tree expert and first director of the Arnold Arboretum. Exceedingly rare in its typical form, especially in North America; var. *robusta* (below) is the usual representative, being more desirable. Leaves to 4"–8" long. Flowers rosy-pink, to 8" wide, in March and April on naked twigs. Seedcones to 5" long. Records: to 80' × 10'0" Yin-Kou, China (1903); 60' × 4'9" Caerhays Castle, Cornwall, England (1975; *pl.* 1921).

M. Sargentiana var. robusta Rehd. & Wils.

Discovered and introduced by E. Wilson in 1908. In commerce ≤1948. Rare; limited practically to Pacific Coast cultivation. Differs from typical SARGENT MAGNOLIA in bearing longer leaves (to 8½"), and larger, plumper flowers (8"–13" wide) appearing when plant is younger. Seedcones to 10" long. First flowered in San Francisco in 1953; in Seattle in 1959. It is variable but always sensational. The University of British Columbia has one with leaves bilobate like those commonly seen on *M. officinalis* f. *biloba*. Cultivars offer nearly white to rosy-purple forms of var. *robusta*. Records: 70' × 4'0" Seattle, WA (1994; *pl.* 1953); 48' × 7'1" Seattle, WA (1990).

M. *Sargentiana* var. *robusta* 'Blood Moon'

From Strybing Arboretum of San Francisco. Named <1975. Very rare. Flowers darker.

M. 'Satellite'—see *M. virginiana* 'Satellite'

M. 'Sayonara'

= *M.* × *Gresham* 'Sayonara'
(*M. Soulangiana* 'Lennei Alba' × *M. Veitchii*)

Raised in 1955, and named by D. Todd Gresham of Santa Cruz, CA. In commerce ≤1986. Uncommon. Flowers large and globular, 7"–12" wide, ivory-white, flushed pink at the base; in March. A bushy small tree.

M. *Schiedeana* Schlecht.

From Mexico, Veracruz to Tepic and Sinaloa. Christian Julius Wilhelm Schiede (1798–1836), M.D. and botanist, discovered it in 1829. Named in 1864. Introduced to cultivation in 1931. Extremely rare. In commerce ≤1981. A broadleaf evergreen, cold-tender and suitable only for parts of Texas and the Pacific Coast. Habit of cultivated specimens narrow, somewhat scrawny. Not superior to *M. grandiflora* as an ornamental, it does offer novelty and exotic appeal. Still, "rarity is good; excellence is best." Leaves 6"–7" long, ca. 3" wide; stem to 1¼" long. Flowers 5"–8" wide, creamy-white, consisting of 3 sepals and 6 petals 2"–3" long. Seedcones 3¼" long. Records: 82' × 5'3" in the wild; 42½' × 2'10½" San Marino, CA (1993). See *M. tamaulipana* for the Seattle stock grown under this name.

M. 'Serene'

(*M. lilliflora* × *M.* 'Mark Jury')

Bred in the 1970s by F.M. Jury of New Zealand. In North American commerce ≤1991–92. Flowers deep rose, large, bowl-shaped. Blooms when young. Small upright tree of strong growth to 16' tall.

M. *Sieboldii* K. Koch

= *M. Oyama* Kort
= *M. parviflora* S. & Z. 1845, non Bl. 1825

OYAMA MAGNOLIA. Japanese: *Oyama-renge*. From Japan, Manchuria, and Korea; and disjunctly in SE China. Introduced to Germany ca. 1850. Introduced by T. Hogg to the U.S. from Japan ca. 1865. In commerce here ≤1887. Common. Named after Philipp Franz Balthasar von Siebold (1796–1866). Siebold lived in Japan from 1823 to 1830, and introduced numerous Japanese plants to European cultivation. The Japanese name *oyama* refers to a mountain, and *renge* means lotus blossom. A coarse-textured shrub or very small, broad, bushy tree. Leaves 4"–6" (8¼") long, broadly rounded or abruptly short-pointed at the apex. Egglike buds open to white flowers, often cupped, with deep red or pale hearts, 3"–4" wide, nodding or horizontal, appearing with the young leaves, from late April to mid-August. Several cultivars with extra petals exist. Records: to 33' tall in the wild; 12' tall × 24' wide Caerhays Castle, Cornwall, England (1926; *pl.* 1912).

M. *Sieboldii* ssp. *sinensis*—see *M. sinensis*

M. 'Silver Parasol'

= *M. hypoleuca* 'Silver Parasol'
(*M. hypoleuca* × *M. tripetala*)

Obtained as a chance hybrid in 1927 at the Arnold Arboretum. Described in 1976. Flowers and leaves more like those of *M. tripetala*, but the silvery bark and large seedcones are like those of *M. hypoleuca*. The name 'Silver Parasol' refers to the "silvery gray bark and the parasol-like arrangement of the large leaves." Leaf 12"–16" long, 5"–8" wide, slightly grayish beneath. Flowers in late May or early June, 8"–10" wide, sweetly fragrant, of 9 (12) tepals. The original tree 49' × 4'7" × 45' (1981).

M. *sinensis* (Rehd. & Wils.) Stapf

= *M. Nicholsoniana* hort. *ex* Millais, non Rehd. & Wils.
= *M. Sieboldii* ssp. *sinensis* (Rehd. & Wils.) Spong.
= *M. globosa* var. *sinensis* Rehd. & Wils.

CHINESE OYAMA MAGNOLIA. From W China. Introduced to cultivation in 1908 by E. Wilson. Named in 1913. Uncommon; most specimens in North America were sold after 1948. Related very closely to *M. Sieboldii*, but absolutely shrubby, with a broader leaf (to 8⅓" × 7"), wooly beneath, and more droopy, larger, less cupped flowers (3"–5½" wide) and seedcones (3"). Blooms from May into July. With training it can become a 20' tree.

M. *sinensis* × *M. Wilsonii*—see *M.* 'Jersey Belle'

M. *Slavinii*—see *M.* × *Proctoriana* 'Slavin's Snowy'

M. × *Soulangiana* Paris Linn. *ex* Soul.-Bod.

(*Soulangeana*)
(*M. denudata* × *M. liliiflora*)

SAUCER MAGNOLIA. COMMON MAGNOLIA. TULIPTREE. LIILY TREE. Chevalier Etienne Soulange-Bodin, was a retired French cavalry officer at Fromont on the Seine, near Paris; and director of the Royal Institute of Horticulture. He immortalized his name by raising seedlings of this cross ca. 1820. In 1819, Soulange exclaimed: "To gardens I cheerfully devote the remainder of my life. I shall not retrace the sad picture of the past. The Germans have encamped in my garden. I have encamped in the gardens of the Germans. It had doubtless been better for both parties to have stayed at home and planted their cabbages." Soulange's hybrid first flowered in 1826. Forms of the same parentage likely arose in Japan well before they did in France. From YULAN was inherited tree size and whitish floral color; from LILY MAGNOLIA, shrubby habit and purplish floral color. SAUCER MAGNOLIAS have been in North America since ca.1830; in commerce here since 1832. They have become by far the most common deciduous MAGNOLIAS in cultivation. A great many cultivars exist, often difficult to distinguish. The 25 cited below are more or less common unless otherwise noted. In March and April the naked branches burst their silky buds, giving rise to lovely flowers white inside and usually striped purple and white outside. Some cultivars are nearly pure white, others deep burgundy. Even after the trees assume full summer foliage, flowers often appear sporadically. Leaves 3"–6" long. Records: 51' × 14'0" × 63' Towson, MD (1972); 34' × 10'0" × 61' Greenwich, CT (1987); 30' × 10'4" × 54' Philadelphia Zoo, PA (1980).

M. × *Soulangiana* 'Alba'

WHITE SAUCER MAGNOLIA. Other than being a general name for any white or nearly white-flowered SAUCER MAGNOLIA seedlings or cultivars, this name has been used to refer to 'Alba Superba' and 'Amabilis'. Some authors have tried to limit the compass of the name to a single clone. This is folly because there is no way a single clone can be identified as the original 'Alba' or distinguished from offspring of similar appearance. Much better to render it botanically M. × *Soulangiana* f. *alba* and thereby clearly allow it to serve as the group name for white SAUCER MAGNOLIAS.

M. × *Soulangiana* 'Alba Superba'
= M. 'Alba Superba'

Introduced ≤1835 by the Cels nursery of Montrouge, France. Flowers large, somewhat light pink or purplish near the base at first, becoming nearly white when fully opened. More than one clone has been so sold. Some writers describe 'Alba Superba' as pure white; others say it is identical to 'Amabilis'.

M. × *Soulangiana* 'Alexandrina'
= M. 'Alexandrina'

Possibly raised, and certainly distributed ≤1831 by the Cels nursery of Montrouge, France. Flowers dark purplish-pink; white inside. Blooms midseason. Leaves larger. Several cultivars so called; a clone with its flowers white, stained purple at the base, is properly 'Alexandrina Alba'. Record: 27' × 3'8" × 33' Tacoma, WA (1993).

M. × *Soulangiana* 'Amabilis'
= M. 'Amabilis'

Introduced ≤1865 by Baumann nursery of Bollwiller, Alsace, France. The name *amabilis* in Latin means pleasing or attractive. Flowers similar to 'Alba Superba' but growth slower, weaker. Less common. Certainly some mixing of stock has occurred and as a result 'Alba Superba' has been sold as 'Amabilis' (and vice versa).

M. × *Soulangiana* 'André Leroy'
= M. 'André Leroy'

Introduced <1892 by André Leroy (1801–1875), nurseryman of Angers, France. Relatively rare in North America; most specimens have been sold since 1955. Flowers large, cup-shaped, wholly dark rose to orchid-purple outside; white inside; deliciously fragrant; late.

M. × *Soulangiana* 'Brozzonii'
= M. 'Brozzonii'

Likely named after Camillo Brozzoni of Italy. Introduced ≤1873 by A. Leroy, nurseryman of Angers, France. Tall, narrow buds open to large flowers (to 10" wide), white overall but faintly shaded with light purple at the base; late. Leaves bold, to 10" long. Growth strongly upright. Similar to M. × *Soulangiana* 'Picture' but flowers less purple. Record: 35' × 3'6" × 38' Seattle, WA (1993; *pl.* 1947).

M. × *Soulangiana* 'Burgundy'

Introduced in 1943 by W.B. Clarke nursery of San José, CA. Uncommon. Flowers large, well rounded like large tulips, wine-purple about halfway up on outside of petals, then pinker; white inside; early.

M. × *Soulangiana* 'Coates'

Originated as a seedling of 'Rustica Rubra' from Leonard Coates nursery of San José, CA. Introduced ≤1973 by Gossler Farms nursery of Springfield, OR. Very rare. Compared to 'Rustica Rubra' the color is much lighter and softer. Quick growing but shrubby.

M. × *Soulangiana* 'Deep Purple Dream'

= *M.* 'Deep Purple Dream'

Originated as a seedling of *M.* × *Soulangiana* 'Lennei' from Tom Dodd nursery of Semmes, AL. Very rare. Flowers notably dark red-purple, late. A strong growing small tree.

M. × *Soul.* 'George Henry Kern'—see *M.* 'George Henry Kern'

M. × *Soulangiana* 'Grace McDade'

Introduced (as 'Large White') in 1945 by Semmes nursery of Semmes, AL. Named ca. 1951 by Clint McDade of Semmes nursery. Uncommon. Flowers very large (to 9" or even 11" wide), almost double regular size; white, pink-tinted at base. Fast grower but shrubby. Since some authors use this name to refer to a pink or rosy-flowered clone, it appears more than one clone circulates as 'Grace McDade'.

M. × *Soulangiana* 'Lennei'

= *M. Lennei* hort.
= *M. Lenneana* hort.

LENNÉ MAGNOLIA. Originated <1850 by Giuseppe Manetti, of Monza, Italy. Named after Peter Joseph Lenné (1789–1866), German botanist. Introduced in 1853 by nurseryman A. Topf of Erfurt, Prussia. In North American commerce ≤1900. Flowers very large, goblet shaped; tepals thick, overlapping, deep purple outside, creamy-white inside; relatively late to bloom. Leaves broad, to 11" × 6⅜", less hairy beneath. Twigs stout. Shrubby, sprawling, open, flattish; normally at most 25' tall; to 40' with training and decades in a good climate. A similar but tree-like cultivar is 'Rustica Rubra'. Fruitful; sometimes its seedlings have been sold under the name.

M. × *Soulangiana* 'Lennei Alba'

Originated ca. 1905 by K.O. Froebel of Zurich, Switzerland. Introduced in 1930–31 by W. Keessen, Jr., of Aalsmeer, Holland. In North American commerce ≤1955. Uncommon. Flowers large, goblet-shaped, pure ivory-white, without a trace of pink. Earlier than those of 'Lennei' but still relatively late. Growth habit similar to that of 'Lennei'. Domoto in 1961 wrote that the plant sold since 1955 as 'Lennei Alba' by W.B. Clarke nursery of San José, CA, is a seedling from that nursery, rather than the European clone itself. The Clarke clone flowers are much smaller, creamy, with a slight basal mark, and bloom about two weeks after *M. denudata*. A specimen of 'Lennei Alba' from Hillier's nursery in England, growing since 1948 in the Seattle arboretum, often bears leaves with a lobe near the apex, and its flowers are small also. Perhaps the original 'Lennei Alba' is very rare in North America.

M. × *Soul.* 'Leonard Messel'—see *M. Kobus* var. *Lœbneri* 'Leonard M.'

M. × *Soulangiana* 'Lilliputian'

('Liliputian')

Introduced ≤1946 by Semmes nursery of Semmes, AL. Uncommon. A miniature SAUCER MAGNOLIA, in both habit and bloom. Late flowering. Flowers small, white flushed purple at base. A charming shrub, either multistemmed or single-trunked.

M. × *Soulangiana* 'Lombardy Rose'

Introduced ≤1946 by Semmes nursery of Semmes, AL. Uncommon. A 'Lennei' seedling but faster and freer blooming. Flowers large (ca. 8" wide), the lower portions dark rose, upper white; white inside.

M. × *Soulangiana* 'Niemetzii'

= *M.* 'Niemetzii'

Introduced in 1907 by W.F. Niemetz (*fl.* 1898–1922) of Temesvar, Romania. Extremely rare. Fastigiate. Flowers purplish, recalling those of 'Rustica Rubra' and 'Lennei'.

M. × *Soulangiana* 'Nigra'—see *M. liliiflora*

M. × *Soulangiana* 'Norbertii'

= *M.* 'Norbertii'
('Norbertiana')

Introduced ≤1835 by the Cels nursery of Montrouge, France. Previously common but practically out of commerce now. Flowers white, heavily stained purple at base; one of the latest to bloom. Slow growing; erect habit.

M. × *Soulangiana* 'Northwest'—see *M.* 'Northwest'

M. × *Soulangiana* 'Pelton'—see *M.* × *Soulangiana* 'Verbanica'

M. × *Soulangiana* 'Picture'
= *M.* × *Soulangiana* 'Wada's Picture'
= *M.* 'Picture'
Discovered in a garden of Kaga Castle, in Kanazawa, Ishikawa Prefecture, Japan. Introduced to cultivation ≤1925 by nurseryman K. Wada. In the U.S. since ≤1963. In commerce here <1975. Red-purple buds open to amazingly large flowers (10"–14" wide), soft pink outside, white inside, tepals thick and fleshy; scented of violets. Blooms well when young; blooms profusely when mature. Strong, narrowly upright. Leaves large and rounded like those of 'Lennei'. Similar to *M.* × *Soulangiana* 'Brozzonii' but flowers not as pale.

M. × *Soulangiana* 'Pink Superba'
Introduced ≤1953 by Semmes nursery, Semmes, AL. Rare. Identical to 'Alba Superba' in habit and growth but flowers deep pink.

M. × *Soulangiana* 'Purpliana'
('Purpleana')
Introduced ≤1944–45 by Overlook nursery of Crichton, AL. Rare. Flowers very large, bright clear reddish-purple; 9 tepals; blooms late in the season. Leaf slightly smaller than most hybrids. Vigorous; erect but not large. Some stock of it has been sold wrongly as *M.* × *Soulangiana* 'Burgundy'.

M. × *Soulangiana* 'Rosea'
Named in 1915. Very rare. Flowers fragrant; large, white with carmine-rose center.

M. × *Soulangiana* 'Rustica Rubra'
= *M. rustica* hort. (in part)
A 'Lennei' seedling introduced ≤1880s by C. Wezelenburg of the Hazerswoude nursery, Holland. In North American commerce ≤1893. Like 'Lennei' but flowers more rosy-red, smaller; early-blooming; leaves hairier. Treelike and vigorous, broad-crowned. Record: 28' × 4'11" × 33' Seattle, WA (1993).

M. × *Soulangiana* 'San José'
Introduced ≤1940 by W.B. Clarke nursery of San José, CA. Clarke said in 1940: "by far the earliest *Magnolia* we know of, commencing to bloom here in early January, a month ahead of any others. In spite of this it has a long blooming season." Flowers very large (tepals to 5" long), white, lightly flushed pink. To 25' tall and wide.

M. × *Soulangiana* 'Speciosa'
= *M. Lennei* var. *speciosa* hort.
= *M.* 'Speciosa'
STRIPED SAUCER MAGNOLIA. Introduced ≤1825 by the Cels nursery of Montrouge, France. Flowers large, white, flushed slight purplish at base; late to bloom (with 'Brozzonii'). Leaves smaller than normal. Notably upright, tall and fast.

M. × *Soulangiana* 'Sundew'—see M. 'Pickard's Sundew'

M. × *Soulangiana* 'Susan'—see M. 'Susan'

M. × *Soulangiana* 'Triumphans'
= *M.* 'Triumphans'
('Triumphant')
Introduced ≤1854 in Germany. Extremely rare. Flowers early, large, rose-purple outside, white within. Similar to but not as desirable as 'Rustica Rubra'.

M. × *Soulangiana* 'Verbanica'
= *M.* × *Soulangiana* 'Pelton'
Possibly originated at Lake Maggiore, or Pallanza, Italy. Introduced <1873 by André Leroy, nurseryman of Angers, France. Buds long, slender and pointed. Flowers evenly light purplish-pink outside, white inside; later-blooming than most. Tepals to 4⅜" × 2⅜".

M. × *Soulangiana* 'Wada's Picture'—see M. × Soul. 'Picture'

M. 'Speciosa'—see M. × *Soulangiana* 'Speciosa'

M. 'Spectrum'
(*M. liliiflora* 'Nigra' × *M. Sprengeri* 'Diva')
A hybrid bred in 1963 at the U.S. National Arboretum; a sister seedling of *Magnolia* 'Galaxy' (see also *M.* 'Northwest'). First flowered in 1973; named and released in 1984. Common in commerce. Compared to 'Galaxy' it has less fragrant, darker, larger (10"–12" wide) flowers with narrower tepals, narrower and hairier leaves, a broader habit, and is less cold-hardy, being well suited to hot climates.

M. *Sprengeri* Pamp.
= *M. denudata* var. *purpurascens* Rehd. & Wils. (in part)
= *M. Sprengeri* var. *diva* Stapf *ex* Johnstone
= *M. diva* Stapf *ex* Millais
SPRENGER MAGNOLIA. Discovered ca. 1885 by A. Henry. From central & W China. Introduced in 1900

by E. Wilson. Named in 1915, after Carl Ludwig Sprenger (1846–1917), German nurseryman. Rare. Flowers appearing in March and April on naked twigs; 6"–8" wide, carmine pink to deep red, erect with the inner segments spreading to expose the central column. Flowers at an earlier age than *M. Campbellii*, but the flowers are delicate and susceptible to wind-injury. Leaves to 10" × 6". Seed-cones to 6" long. Records: to 60' tall in the wild; 44' × 4'2" × 36' Aurora, OR (1993; *pl.* 1966).

M. *Sprengeri* 'Diva'

GODDESS MAGNOLIA. Veitch nursery of England grew 8 *M. Sprengeri* from 1900 E. Wilson seeds. One went to Caerhays Castle, Cornwall, and bloomed ≤1919. It boasted 8"–10" flowers of a fine shade of rosy-pink, and more cup-shaped. It was named 'Diva'. In North American commerce ≤1955. Both at Caerhays and in Washington, D.C., there are 'Diva' specimens which are near examples of *M.* × *Soulangiana* 'Lennei Alba', so 'Diva' seedlings are often hybrids. Even when they are not, they should be referred to as 'Diva' seedlings (or as *M. Sprengeri*), because the name 'Diva' is clonal and should refer exclusively to vegetatively-propagated stock from the original specimen. Leaves to 6⅝" long. Seedcones to 9" long, often profuse and showy. Hardy to -20°F. Records: 68' × 4'0" Borde Hill, Sussex, England (1975); 59' × 5'5" Trewithen Garden, Cornwall, England (1971); 56' × 6'6" Caerhays Castle, Cornwall, England (1975; *pl.* 1912); 53' × 3'0" × 33' Seattle, WA (1992; *pl.* 1952).

M. *Sprengeri* var. *elongata* (Rehd. & Wils.) Johnstone

= *M. denudata* var. *elongata* Rehd. & Wils.
= *M. elongata* Millais

WHITE SPRENGER MAGNOLIA. Introduced in 1900–1901 by E. Wilson. In North American commerce ≤1948–49. Extremely rare because less desirable; yet more cold-hardy. Flowers smaller, to 4" wide, pure- or creamy-white, sometimes rosy at the base. Leaves relatively narrow (at least twice as long as wide), nearly hairless. A small tree, to 30' tall, perhaps eventually to 50' × 6'0".

M. 'Spring Joy'

= *M.* × *Lœbneri* 'Spring Joy'
= *M. Kobus* var. *Lœbneri* 'Spring Joy'
(*M. Kobus* var. *stellata* 'Royal Star' × *M. Proctoriana* 'Wada's Memory')

Bred by J.C. McDaniel of Urbana, IL. In North American commerce ≤1981. Very rare. Flowers pure white; to 6" wide. Vigorous.

M. 'Spring Rite'

= *M.* × *Gresham* 'Spring Rite'
(*M. Soulangiana* 'Lennei Alba' × *M. Veitchii*)

Raised by D. Todd Gresham of Santa Cruz, CA. Named ≤1962. Introduced ≤1991 by Gossler Farms nursery of Springfield, OR. Flowers large (12" wide), bowl-shaped, white with very faint rosy-pink staining. Blooms when young.

M. 'Star Wars'

(*M. Campbellii* × *M. liliiflora*)

Bred in the 1970s by O. Blumhardt of New Zealand. Named ≤1982. In North American commerce ≤1991. Flowers rich pink-purple, star-shaped, 10"–12" wide. Very free-flowering over an extended season. Fertile. The original was 25' tall at 10 years.

M. stellata—see *M. Kobus* var. *stellata*

M. stellata 'Ballerina'—see *M. Kobus* var. *Lœbneri* 'Ballerina'

M. stellata 'Centennial'—see *M. Kobus* var. *stellata* 'Centennial'

M. stellata 'Dawn'—see *M. Kobus* var. *stellata* 'Dawn'

M. stellata 'Dr. Merrill'—see *M. Kobus* var. *Lœbneri* 'Merrill'

M. stellata 'George Henry Kern'—see *M.* 'George Henry Kern'

M. stellata 'Halliana'—see *M. Kobus* var. *stellata* 'Halliana'

M. stellata 'Jane Platt'—see *M. Kobus* var. *stellata* 'Jane Platt'

M. stellata var. *Keiskei* or 'Kikuzaki'—see *M. Kobus* var. *stellata* 'Keiskei'

M. stellata 'King Rose'—see *M. Kobus* var. *stellata* 'King Rose'

M. stellata 'Orchid'—see *M.* 'Orchid'

M. stellata 'Pink'—see *M. Kobus* var. *stellata* f. *rosea*

M. stellata f. *rosea* or 'Rosea'—see *M. Kobus* var. *stellata* f. *rosea*

M. stellata 'Rosea Jane Platt'—see *M. Kobus* var. *stellata* 'Jane Platt'

M. stellata 'Royal Star'—see *M. Kobus* var. *stellata* 'Royal Star'

M. stellata 'Rubra'—see *M. Kobus* var. *stellata* 'Royal Star'

M. stellata 'Spring Snow'—see *M. Kobus* var. *Lœbneri* 'Spring Snow'

M. stellata 'Star Bright'—see *M. Kobus* var. *Lœbneri* 'Star Bright'

M. stellata 'Waterlily'—see *M. Kobus* var. *stellata* 'Waterlily'

M. 'Sundew'—see *M.* 'Pickard's Sundew'

M. 'Susan'
(*M. liliiflora* 'Nigra' × *M. Kobus* var. *stellata* f. *rosea*)
= *M.* × *Soulangiana* 'Susan'
Originated in 1956 as an intentional cross at the U.S. National Arboretum. Named in 1965, along with 7 similar hybrids which became collectively known as "the Girls" (referring to the cultivar names) or "the Kosar-DeVos hybrids" (referring to the scientists involved). They were bred in an effort to secure floral displays late enough to avoid injury from spring frosts. The eight cultivars are more or less shrubby; 'Ann', 'Betty' (especially), 'Ricki' and 'Susan' are the most treelike. All have late, dull fall color. 'Susan' has been in commerce since ≤1978; it is common. A very large bush, or can be trained to tree form. Habit narrow. Long slender erect red purple buds, open to 4"–6" wide, reddish-purple upright flowers of 6 slightly twisted tepals, with magenta stamens; in April. Vigorous; hardy.

M. tamaulipana Vazquez
= *M. Schiedeana* hort. (in part), non Schlecht. 1864
From Tamaulipas, NE Mexico, where it is endemic. Introduced as seeds (thought to be of *M. Schiedeana*) collected by F.G. Meyer and D.J. Rogers in 1948 at 4,500' elevation. In commerce ≤1950. Exceedingly rare. It was not separated from *M. Schiedeana* and made a new species until 1990, although <1970 the MAGNOLIA expert J.E. Dandy believed it deserved such status. An evergreen, with flowers that smell like those of *M. hypoleuca*. Flowers creamy white, 3" tall, 6" wide, composed of 9 very thick tepals (measuring to 4½" × 2¾"). In the wild it flowers from May into July; in Seattle, where an original introduction first flowered in 1971, it often blooms in winter as well as summer, but rarely sets seedcones (described to 3½" × 1¾"). Flowerstems and leaves with whitish or palest-brown fuzz, the leaves at length hairless, to 9½" × 4"; stem to 1⅞" long. Overall, *M. tamaulipana* (as with *M. Schiedeana*), is no more ornamental than its commonly culti-vated evergreen cousin *M. grandi-flora.* Recorded to 100' × 5'3" in the wild. A specimen collected in 1990 was named 'Bronze Sentinel' in 1992: its young leaves are purple-bronze.

M. × *Thompsoniana* Cels *ex* St.-Hilaire
= *M. glauca* var. *Thompsoniana* Loud.
= *M. glauca* var. *major* Sims
= *M. major* (Sims) Schneid.
(*M. virginiana* × *M. tripetala*)
The first MAGNOLIA hybrid known (at least to the West). Archibald Thompson (1753–1832), a London nurseryman, raised this in 1808, as a *M. virginiana* seedling. Probably Thompson acquired the seed from John Lyon, a collector in North America. Introduced to cultivation in 1817. Described officially in 1820. Prince nursery of Flushing, NY, had it by 1829. Rare in North America. Less hardy than either parent, and very ungainly. A shrubby, brittle, multistemmed small tree. Flowers lightbulb-shaped, to 6" wide, very sweet, from (April) early May into September; ster-ile. Leaf to 10" × 5", glaucous beneath; sometimes partially evergreen. Records: 40' tall, multitrunked, in Belgium (1975); 24' × 1'11" × 20' Seattle, WA (1992); a trunk 4'8" around at Flushing, NY (1972).

M. × *Thompsoniana* 'Urbana'
An intentional 1960 cross made by J.C. McDaniel of Urbana, IL. Registered in 1969; in commerce ≤1976. Hardier than the original clone, and flowers superior in size and quality. Sterile. Leaves larger and darker. A multitrunked, arching shrub. Blooms mostly in June. More difficult to propagate and less common.

M. Thurberi—see *M. Kobus*

M. Timeless Beauty™ PP 6178 (1988)
= *M.* 'Monland'
= *M. grandiflora* 'Monland'
= *M. grandiflora* Timeless Beauty™

First propagated in 1969 by Robert Eiland of Charmwood nursery, Millbrook, AL. Named and propagated in a big way when Monrovia nursery of California got it in the 1980s. 'Monland' is an acronym of Monrovia and Eiland. Said to be a wild *M. grandiflora* × *M. virginiana* hybrid. Undistinguished foliage, but excitingly large (10"–12" wide) flowers that bloom well into fall unlike typical *M. grandiflora* growing in the Deep South.

M. 'Todd Gresham'
= *M.* × *Gresham* 'Todd Gresham'
(*M. Soulangiana* 'Rustica Rubra' × *M. Veitchii*)

Named in 1984 after one of the foremost MAGNOLIA breeders, Drury Todd Gresham (1909–1969), of Santa Cruz, CA. Flowers 10" wide, deep purple outside, white inside with some purple. Vigorous, fast.

M. tomentosa—see *M. Kobus* var. *stellata*

M. tripetala (L.) L.
= *M. Umbrella* Desr.

UMBRELLA TREE. UMBRELLA MAGNOLIA. ELKWOOD. From the eastern U.S. Common. The 1753 name *tripetala*, Latin for 3 petals, is believed to have been given in reference to the three sepals which are longer than the 6 or 9 petals ("*trisepala*" would have been more accurate). The name UMBRELLA TREE refers to the large leaves whorled around the stems. The name ELKWOOD originated in the mountains of Virginia, probably from the resemblance which the points of the shoots bear to the horns of the elk. Leaves to 1'–2' (3') long. Flowers in (late April) May-June, 5"–8" (10") wide, of attractive white narrow tepals, but smelling vile. Tree usually multi-trunked and broad. In 1870 F.J. Scott summed it beautifully: "A species that always seems to be in doubt whether to be a shrub or a tree." Records: 85' × 7'6" Pennsylvania (ca. 1980); 64' × 2'8" Seattle, WA (1989; *pl.* 1940); 55' × 10'6" Bucks County, PA (1980).

M. 'Triumphans'—see *M.* × *Soulangiana* 'Triumphans'

M. Umbrella—see *M. tripetala*

M. × *Veitchii* auct., *emend.* Bean
(*M. Campbellii* × *M. denudata*)

VEITCH MAGNOLIA. The first intentional MAGNOLIA hybrid. Bred in 1907 by nurseryman Peter C.M. Veitch (1850–1929) of England. Six seedlings resulted. In 1970 the one chosen for vegetative propagation was given the cultivar name 'Peter Veitch'. First flowered in 1917. Named in 1921. In North American commerce ≤1938–39. Rare. Flowers notably erect, pink, 6" wide, appearing on naked twigs, mostly in April. Leaves to 15" × 7". Records: 95' × 6'9" Caerhays Castle, Cornwall, England (1984; *pl.* 1921); 56' × 9'0" Trewidden, Cornwall, England (1979); 48' × 6'2" × 51' Seattle, WA (1990).

M. × *Veitchii* 'Columbia'
Introduced in 1995 by Monrovia nursery of California. Said to be from the U.S. National Arboretum, to have creamy-white, purple-based flowers, and to grow 35' tall and 20' wide.

M. × *Veitchii* 'Isca'
WHITE VEITCH MAGNOLIA. The best white-flowered seedling of four raised. Named and introduced ≤1950. Actually the flowers are only partly white, with some pink. Extremely rare in North America. California's renowned nurseryman W.B. Clarke said he never saw hybrid vigor better exemplified.

M. virginiana (L.) L.
= *M. glauca* L.

SWEET BAY (MAGNOLIA). SILVER BAY. WHITE LAUREL. BEAVER TREE. SWAMP LAUREL. SWAMP SASSAFRAS. WHITE BAY. SWAMP BAY. From the eastern U.S. According to J. Loudon (1838): called BEAVERWOOD "because the root is eaten as a great dainty by the beavers, and these animals are caught by means of it." and Michaux says they prefer it to any other wood for constructing their dams on account of the softness of the wood. Common. Can be evergreen, semi-evergreen or deciduous. Evergreen specimens are by far superior ornamentals. Leaf sparkling dark green above, ghostly pale beneath; to 8" × 3". Flowers small (2"–4" wide), white, lemony or rose-scented, from May into July (September). Varies from a suckering shrub to a tree with a strong tendency to fork. Records: 95' × 11'0" ×47' Gainesville, FL (1963); 92' × 14'5" × 52' Union County, AR (1991); 91' × 13'1" × 46' Leon County, FL (1971); 45' × 16'0" × 55' Germantown, PA (1980).

M. virginiana var. australis Sarg.
= M. australis (Sarg.) Ashe

SOUTHERN SWEETBAY. EVERGREEN SWEETBAY. Named in 1919; in Latin, australis means of or from the south. Overall more abundant in the wild. Flowers self-incompatible. Fragrance stronger, more lemon-like. Leaves often evergreen. Often a large tree.

M. virginiana 'Havener'
Selected in 1970 by J.C. McDaniel of Urbana, IL, from a plant in Mount Pulaski, a little community of central Illinois. Introduced <1975. Very rare. Flowers exceptionally large (to 4½" wide), with more tepals, sometimes 20 (8 in typical M. virginiana). It breeds rather true from seed. A stocky plant.

M. virginiana 'Henry Hicks'
Originated as a tree given by Long Island nurseryman Henry Hicks (1870–1954) to Swarthmore College, PA. Named ≤1967. Holds its foliage all year, even in the north. It may be a clone of M. virginiana var. australis. Must be grafted; difficult from cuttings.

M. virginiana 'Mayer'
Named ≤1966. Very rare. A seed-reproducing, pre-cocious, free-blooming, shrubby form. From Prof. Robert W. Mayer's plant in Champaign, IL. Cuttings readily root.

M. virginiana 'Milton'
Planted ca. 1955 in Milton, MA. Named in 1981 by the Arnold Arboretum. Hardy to -10°F. Evergreen; leaves to 6" × 1½". Blooms in July and August. Despite its self-fertile flowers, it may be a clone of M. virginiana var. australis.

M. virginiana 'Satellite'
= M. 'Satellite'

Raised at the U.S. National Arboretum in the 1970s from Tennessee seeds of M. virginiana var. australis. Introduced to commerce ≤1986. Rather shrubby. Flowers creamy white and quite flat at full bloom. The usual lemony M. virginiana fragrance.

M. virginiana 'Willowleaf Bay'
A selected seedling raised ca. 1982 by Tom Dodd nursery of Semmes, AL. Introduced ≤1992 by Ridgecrest nursery of Wynne, AR. Leaves noticeably narrower than those of most specimens of M. virginiana var. australis, and clustered densely at the ends of the branches.

M. 'Vulcan'
(M. liliiflora 'Nigra' × M. Campbellii var.
    mollicomata 'Lanarth')

Bred by F.M. Jury of New Zealand. Introduced in 1990. In North American commerce ≤1992. Mass-produced by Duncan & Davies nursery of New Zealand. Flowers ca. 10" wide, brilliant ruby red, of 8–10 tepals. Blooms when young. Foliage like that of 'Lanarth'. To at least 20' tall.

M. 'Wada's Memory'—see M. × Proctoriana 'Wada's Memory'

M. × Watsonii—see M. × Wieseneri

M. × Wieseneri Carr.
= M. × Watsonii Hook. fil.
(M. hypoleuca × M. Sieboldii)

Possibly introduced to the U.S. ca. 1880 from Japan (as M. parviflora). Certainly introduced from Japan to the West when exhibited by M. Wiesener in 1889 at Paris. Named after him in 1890; in 1891 named after William Watson (1858–1925) of England. In North American commerce ≤1896. Rare; difficult to propagate; expensive. Flowers erect, ivory white, 4"–8" wide, with a large clump of dark stamens; powerfully scented (some say of pineapple), appearing from late April into early October; mainly in June and July. Sterile. Leaf to 10" × 5". Habit ungainly. A large shrub or small tree with odd long whippy shoots. If you seek a light and airy effect, steer clear of this MAGNOLIA. If you value heady fragrance, it is will stifle all competition. Records: 27' × 2'5" × 23' Centralia, WA (1993); 24' × 3'7" × 29' Seattle, WA (1993).

M. 'Willowwood'—see M. Kobus var. Lœbneri 'Willowwood'

M. Wilsonii (Fin. & Gagnep.) Rehd.
= M. parviflora var. Wilsonii Fin. & Gagnep.
= M. Nicholsoniana Rehd. & Wils., non hort.
= M. × highdownensis Dandy

WILSON MAGNOLIA. From W China. Discovered by the great plantsman Ernest Henry Wilson (1876–1930) in 1904; introduced in 1908. Named in 1913.

In North American commerce ≤1942. Rare. Closely related to *M. Sieboldii* and *M. sinensis*, yet with elongated leaves. Flowers hang upside-down, 3"–5" wide; from late April into early June. Leaf to 10½" × 5"; dull green above, softly hairy and pale beneath. Wilson said, at least in the wild it is a "quite common bush or thin tree to 25' tall." Cultivated specimens exist more than 30' tall and wide, but are almost invariably multitrunked. Best planted high, as on a bank, where people can gaze up at the flowers.

Magnolia Wilsonii 'Bovee'

Named after Bovee's nursery of Portland, OR. In commerce ≤1984–85. Rare. Described by Gossler Farms nursery of Springfield, OR: "Flowers 6" wide, with pure porcelain-white tepals of excellent substance. Seedcones large, very decorative. Grows best in semi-shade. Hardy tree to 25' tall." Leaves smallish, narrow and pointy.

M. 'Woodsman'—see M. × brooklynensis 'Woodsman'

M. 'Yellow Bird'

= *M. acuminata* var. *subcordata* 'Yellow Bird'
(*M. brooklynensis* 'Evamaria' × *M. acuminata*)

Originated in 1967 as an intentional cross at the Brooklyn Botanic Garden. Introduced in 1981. Uncommon. Flowers deep yellow, appearing with the leaves, smaller but more intense than those of *M. × brooklynensis* 'Evamaria', and 1–2 weeks later. A fertile tetraploid.

M. 'Yellow Lantern'

(*M. acuminata* var. *subcordata* × *M. Soulangiana* 'Alexandrina')

Bred by P. Savage of Bloomfield Hills, MI. Registered in 1985. Flowers tulip-shaped, clear lemon-yellow. Very hardy. Vigorous, upright with a single trunk.

M. Yulan—see M. denudata

M. Zenii Cheng

= *M. elliptilimba* Law & Gao

ZEN MAGNOLIA. From Hunan and Kiangsu (Jiangsu), China; extremely rare and endangered in the wild. Named in 1933, after W.C. Zen, an educator. In North America since 1980; first bloomed here in 1988; in commerce ≤1992. Closely related to *M. denudata* and *M. cylindrica* but less ornamental than either. Flowers in March and April, appearing on naked twigs, to 5" wide, of 9 white tepals, flushed rosy-purple; fragrant. Leaf to 6¼" × 3". A small tree, recorded to 36' × 3'0" in the wild.

Mallotus

[EUPHORBIACEÆ; Spurge Family] 140 spp. of mostly tropical and subtropical trees and shrubs. From Greek *mallotos*, fleecy, wooly, in turn from *mallos*, a lock of wool; alluding to the usual wooly fruit. A related genus is *Sapium*.

M. japonicus (Th.) Muell.-Arg.

= *Croton japonicum* Th.
= *Rottlera japonica* (Th.) Spreng.

From Japan, central China, Taiwan, the Ryukyus, and Korea. Introduced to cultivation in 1866. Exceedingly rare and mostly restricted to botanic gardens and arboreta. Barely tolerates freezing; suitable for the mildest regions only. A large shrub or small tree with handsome foliage. Leaves reddish (like Poinsettia "blossoms") while unfolding; to 10" × 6"; sometimes lobed. Fall color yellowish-green. Male and female flowers on separate trees; males yellowish, females red; in May, June, July, or as late as September. Bark vaguely like that of a STRIPEBARK MAPLE. Records: to 50' tall in the wild; 41' × 4'8" × 39' Los Angeles, CA (1993; *pl.* 1964).

× Malosorbus florentina—see Malus florentina

Malus

[ROSACEÆ; Rose Family] 25–35 (50) spp. of deciduous trees and shrubs. *Malus* is the ancient Latin name of the APPLE TREE; from Greek *malon* or *melon*, and Latin *malum*, an apple. The name CRABAPPLE may derive from *scrubba*, modern "scrub," as the European *Malus sylvestris* is a wild bushy species bearing unappetizing fruit. ORCHARD APPLE trees, lovely though they be, are grown primarily for fruit rather than ornament, and therefore their practically innumerable cultivars are not included in this book. Some general information about them is supplied (see *Malus × domestica*). 415 CRABAPPLES (and APPLES) are included, largely restricted to cultivars grown for ornament. There are fully as many unlisted cultivars named and grown primarily for their edible fruit. A few edible cultivars of wide fame are included—'Dolgo' is an example. Sometimes the same name is applied to an edible variety (whether a CRABAPPLE or an ORCHARD APPLE) and to a purely ornamental variety. This confusing situation arises when nurseries or breeders are unaware of the other variety's existence—'Cardinal' is an example.

CRABAPPLES bloom in spring, mostly March through May, bearing flowers which vary a great deal in color, size, fragrance and visual appeal. It is common for the flowerbuds to be red, opening to pink or white flowers. Typically each flower has 5 petals; semi-double or doubled flowers bear extra petals. Occasionally some trees produce a few flowers again in September. The fruit ripens between July and November. It varies from about ¼" to more than 2¾" long or wide. Whether or not the calyx (leftover sepals) is retained at the bottom of the fruit, or drops away, is a detail that helps make identifications precise. All *Malus* fruits are edible, but often they are too small, sour or otherwise poor to entice human consumption. CRABAPPLES have been grown for food and ornament for hundreds of years, and their number is legion. During the 1980s they rose to unprecedented heights of popularity. Father John L. Fiala (1924–1990) of Falconskeape, near Medina, Ohio, had been grafting by age 12, and made important LILAC and CRABAPPLE hybrids. Between 1981 and 1983 he registered 24 *Malus* cultivars, most of them introduced to commerce by Klehm or Lake County nurseries; the present volume includes 42 Fiala CRABAPPLES (he named 120!), including some not yet introduced commercially. Fiala's book **Flowering Crabapples; the genus *Malus***, was published in 1994.

Four major diseases scourge *Malus*, and vary from region to region in intensity. The writer lives in a region where scab (fungus) thrives, doing terrible harm, but powdery mildew (fungus) is minor, and there is no trouble to speak of from cedar apple rust (fungus), and fireblight (bacterium). Some plant pathologists, including L.P. Nichols of Pennsylvania State University, and T. Green of the Morton Arboretum, Lisle, IL, have advocated abandoning the use of disease-prone species and cultivars. Since some of the old fashioned CRABAPPLES bear exquisite flowers, putting to shame many disease-free selections, many people still prefer to spray their trees or to endure disease so long as they still are compensated with a sensational spring fête for two or three weeks. Similarly, although CRABAPPLES tend to need cold winters to perform best, some Californians take pains to grow miserable-looking (to the northerner) specimens of *Malus*, because the flowers are so heartening. Two problems occur with dismissing a cultivar as disease-prone. First of all, misidentification is frequent, and can result in innocent cultivars being branded guilty. Second, specimens of some cultivars may be disease-prone while other specimens of (nominally) the same cultivar are disease-free. This may be due to the development of mutant strains, to rootstock effects, or to virus-free propagation. *Malus* 'Robinson' is this way in Seattle—most are hideous and not worth growing; some are endurable. Moreover, diseases vary in strength from year to year. In brief, the variables are many, and those who try to rank cultivars as troublefree, so-so, and disease-ridden, should exercise restraint. The remarks tendered below regarding disease resistance are of necessity general. What works in Michigan may not work in Alabama or Oregon. The International Ornamental Crabapple Society, based in the Morton Arboretum of Lisle, IL, is conducting ongoing disease evaluations and doing other worthy work.

M. **AA No. 328**—see *M.* **'Red Barron'**

M. **AA No. 6639**—see *M.* **'Blanche Ames'**

M. **AA No. 19039**—see *M.* **'Henrietta Crosby'**

M. acerba—see *M. sylvestris*

M. **'Adams'**
= *M. Adamsi* hort.
Originated as a chance seedling ca. 1947 at the West Springfield, MA, residence of Walter Adams, former president of Adams nursery of Westfield, MA. Introduced <1952. Very common. Tree to 20' tall and

wide, broadly rounded, sparse and very open, or eventually dense. Red buds open to pink flowers, 1½" wide. Leaves tinged reddish in spring, turning green; orange-red in fall. Fruit glossy carmine-red to dark red, (½") ⅝" (¾") long, with small calyx scars; abundant, persistent. Pulp crisp, blood-red. An annual bearer. Good disease resistance.

M. *Adamsi*—see M. 'Adams'

M. 'Adirondack'

Selected in 1974 from 500 open-pollinated *M. Halliana* seedlings inoculated with blight. Grown for 13 years and found free of infection. Developed by D.R. Egolf of the U.S. National Arboretum. Released in 1987. Propagated by several major wholesale nurseries. Compact, strongly upright habit. Red buds open to waxy-white 1¾"–2¼" wide flowers, with traces of carmine, and heavily-textured petals. Leaf dark green, hairy at first, becoming hairless; sharply toothed. Fruit ⅝" long; stem to 1⅛" long; yellow-pink mostly blushed with red, becoming brilliant orange-red and enduring until December. Good disease resistance.

M. × *adstringens* Zab. *ex* Rehd.

= *Pyrus* × *adstringens* hort.
(*M. domestica* × *M. baccata*)

CULTIVATED CRABAPPLE. A clumsy group name, dating from 1903, little used recently, but in past decades used, rightly or wrongly, for numerous clones, including 'Almey', 'Hopa' and 'Transcendent'. The difficulty is in differentiating offspring of this parentage (*M. domestica* × *M. baccata*) from those of the *M.* × *robusta* group (*M. prunifolia* × *M. baccata*). A. Rehder wrote that the former usually have hairier leaves, shorter flower and fruit stems, and larger, often depressed fruits with a more impressed calyx. Complicating the matter, specimens of *M.* × *robusta* have been crossed with *M.* × *domestica*, so where do their offspring fit nominally? The *adstringens* name, thus, can be applied with certainty to few clones, mostly those bearing fruit large enough to be cultivated economically, but too small to be termed regular apples.

M. 'Alamata'—see M. 'Almata'

M. 'Albright'

(*M. baccata* × a ROSYBLOOM CRABAPPLE)

Originally raised by Mr. W.O. Albright in 1948. A chance seedling introduced and named in 1964 by the Beaverlodge, Alberta, research station. Uncommon.

Pink buds open to 2" wide pink flowers. Fruit dark purple-red, with red pulp; 1¼" long, persistent. Fair disease resistance.

M. *aldenhamensis*—see M. × *purpurea* 'Aldenhamensis'

M. 'Almata'

('Beautiful Arcade' APPLE × M. 'Fluke 38' CRABAPPLE) × M. 'Redflesh'
('Alamata')

Selected in 1941 and introduced in 1942 by N. Hansen of South Dakota. Uncommon. Similar to *M. Sieversii* 'Niedzwetzkyana'. Red buds open to very large clear pink flowers, often semi-double; stem very wooly. Leaves reddish at first, ultimately gray-green. Fruit 2½"; wine-red inside and out; very tasty. Growth fast; vigorous to 22' tall. Poor disease resistance.

M. 'Almey'

= M. 'MR 452' (i.e., "Morden Rosybloom No. 452")
= M. 'Sunglory'

Named in 1945, at Morden research station of Manitoba. After John Robert Almey (1895–1988), horticulturist of the Canadian Pacific Railway, Winnipeg. In 1963 this ROSYBLOOM CRABAPPLE was selected as Canada's centennial tree for 1967. A famous and widely planted clone, 'Almey' is so disease-prone that fewer are planted each year. Compared to the ubiquitous and similar *Malus* 'Hopa', it is smaller and more open (but varies according to rootstock and age from vigorously upright to almost weeping). Its flowers are darker red, larger (1¾"–2⅝" wide), with distinct white petal bases, on long flowerstems (to 1⅜" long), in clusters of 5–8 instead of 4–5. Leaves purplish when very young but very quickly green; sharply toothed, albeit indistinctly so. The fruit are fewer, harder, ribbed, orange covered with carmine or crimson, ⅞" long, persisting instead of dropping when ripe; the calyx almost always drops away; the pulp is yellow-golden, firm, and foul-tasting. Record: 20' × 2'8" × 31' Lynnwood, WA (1993).

M. 'Amaszam'—see M. American Masterpiece™

M. 'Amberina' PP 6942 (1989)

= M. × *Zumi* 'Amberina'
(M. Christmas Holly™ × M. 'Kirk')

Bred by the late Father J.L. Fiala of Falconskeape, near Medina, OH. Registered in 1981. Introduced by Klehm nursery of South Barrington, IL. Since Christmas Holly™ itself is a *Zumi* seedling, there is justification for citing 'Amberina' as a *Zumi* cultivar. 'Amberina' is a strongly upright small tree. Deep red buds open to creamy-white flowers. Fruit brilliant orange-red; abundant. Fall leaf color bright gold. Disease resistant.

M. 'American Beauty' PP 2821 (1968)
(*M.* Hartwigii 'Katherine' × *M.* 'Almey')

First flowered in 1962; selected in 1963; introduced in 1970 by Princeton nursery of New Jersey. Common. Flowers double, clear red, 2" wide, almost sterile. Leaves bronzy-red when young, then bronzy-green, at length tinted yellow-green; some leaves lobed; teeth blunt. Can be shrubby, or a small tree 15'–20' tall. Fruit dark red, ½" wide, the calyx falling reluctantly; stem downy, 1½" long; pulp harsh flavored, red. Two other cultivars of the same parentage are *M.* 'Pink Perfection' and *M.* 'Snowcloud'.

M. American Masterpiece™
= *M.* 'Amaszam'

Introduced ≤1990 by Lake County nursery of Perry, OH. Grown by several major wholesale nurseries. Flowers brilliant red from the first tight buds to petal fall. Foliage maroon. Fruit pumpkin-orange. Pyramidal habit, to 25' tall and 20' wide.

M. American Spirit™
= *M.* 'Amerspirzam'
= *M.* 'Milton Baron #4'

Bred by Dr. Milton Baron of East Lansing, MI. Introduced in 1989 by Lake County nursery of Perry, OH. Dark red buds open to red flowers, fading pink. Leaves reddish-purple. Fruit dark red, glossy, ⅓"–½" long; calyx drops. Habit rounded, to 18' tall and wide.

M. 'Amerspirzam'—see M. American Spirit™

M. 'Ames White'
From Iowa State College, at Ames. Introduced <1977. Rare. Flowers pink to white. Fruit yellow. Excellent disease-resistance.

M. 'Amisk'
= *M.* × *purpurea* 'Amisk'

An open-pollinated seedling of *M. Sieversii* 'Niedzwetzkyana'. Raised in 1920 by I. Preston of Ottawa's Dominion agricultural experiment station. One of the original ROSYBLOOM CRABAPPLES. Selected in 1930 and named for Amisk Lake of NE Saskatchewan. Very rare. Carmine buds open to pink

2" wide flowers. Fruit red and yellow, 1⅜" long. An alternate-year bearer. Poor disease resistance.

M. 'Anaros'
Originated <1940 by Dr. S.Wheeler of Rosthern, Saskatchewan. An open-pollinated seedling of the Russian APPLE 'Antonovka'. Rare; sold by Dropmore nursery of Manitoba during the 1950s and '60s. Still in other Canadian nurseries as of 1987. A leafy, healthy tree of dwarf habit bearing broad leaves resembling those of an ORCHARD APPLE (*M.* × *domestica*), though not very hairy. Flowers heavily textured, to 2½" wide, also resembling those of *M.* × *domestica*. Fruit yellow and red, 1⅜"–1½" wide or long; calyx bumpy and persistent; stem to 1½" long; the crop mostly fallen to the ground by late July.

M. 'Angel Choir'
(*M. baccata* 'Plena Alba' × *M. Zumi*) × (*M. Zumi* × *M.* 'Van Eseltine')

Bred by the late Father J.L. Fiala of Falconskeape, near Medina, OH. *M.* 'Bridal Crown' is a sibling. Selected in 1962. Registered ≤1983. Small, upright, 12' tall, finely branched tree. Pale pink buds open to white, double flowers. Fruit deep red, ⅜". Highly disease-resistant.

M. angustifolia (Ait.) Michx.
= *M. coronaria* var. *angustifolia* (Ait.) Fiala
= *Pyrus angustifolia* Ait.

SOUTHERN (WILD) CRABAPPLE. NARROWLEAF CRABAPPLE. From the eastern U.S., mostly in the South. Half-evergreen in mild areas. Previously much planted; in recent years scarcely in commerce. Flowers fragrant, violet-scented, 1" wide, with pink veins against white background. Blooms relatively late in spring (from late March to mid-May, according to latitude). Leaves thick, shiny, slender, lightly hairy to hairless. The name *angustifolia* means narrow-leaved; from Latin *angustus*, narrow, and *folium*, a leaf. Shoot leaves lobed and more hairy. Fruit ¾"–1", greenish. Poor disease resistance. Records: 46' × 4'6" × 34' Williamsburg, VA (1976); 44' × 8'0" × 50' Chestertown, MD (1990); 35½' × 6'6" × 48½' Swannanoa, NC (1981).

M. angustifolia 'Flore Pleno'—see M. ioensis 'Plena' and M. 'Prince Georges'

M. angustifolia 'Plena'—see *M.* 'Prince Georges'

M. angustifolia 'Roseo-plena'—see *M.* 'Prince Georges'

M. Anne E®
= *M.* 'Manbeck Weeper'

Introduced <1990 by Manbeck nursery of New Knoxville, OH. Uncommon. Broad, weeping habit, to 11' tall and 15' wide in ca. 14 years. Pink buds open to prolific white flowers. Fruit ⅜", bright red, persisting on the tree after leaf drop. Good yellow fall color. Scab and blight resistant.

M. 'Api'—see M. 'Lady'

M. 'Arctic Dawn'
Originated in 1941 when Morden research station of Manitoba gave Beaverlodge station of Alberta a *M. Sieversii* 'Niedzwetzkyana' seedling. Possibly the pollen parent was *M. baccata*. Beaverlodge named and introduced 'Arctic Dawn' in 1952 (along with *M.* 'Snowcap'). Rare; sold by Dropmore nursery of Manitoba from 1959 until 1968. Valued for its extreme hardiness, but not ornamental enough for milder regions. Semi-weeping habit. Pink buds open to white and pink flowers, ¾" wide. Fruit purplish-red, <½". Fair disease resistance.

M. 'Arctic Red'
A seedling of *M.* 'Osman' raised in 1928 by Mr. J.A. Wallace of Beaverlodge, Alberta. Registered ≤1972. In commerce ≤1975–76. Extremely hardy; produces fruit in northern Alberta.

M. × *arnoldiana* (Rehd.) Sarg. *ex* Dunbar
= *M. floribunda* var. *arnoldiana* Rehd.
= *Pyrus* × *arnoldiana* (Rehd.) Bean
(*M. floribunda* × *M. baccata*)

Originated in 1883 at the Arnold Arboretum. Named in 1908. Common and long popular, but weak and disease-prone, so going extinct commercially. Like a larger-flowered, larger-fruited, but smaller-sized *Malus floribunda*. Bushy, 6'–10' (28') tall, compact and graceful; with somewhat zigzag twigs. Buds bright red, shaped like snowdrop flowers, held on wirelike flowerstems up to 2"–3" long. Flowers in clusters of 4–6, shell-pink, aging almost white; to 1⅞" wide; sometimes semi-double. Fruit ½"–⅝" long, yellow, butterscotch blushed, large-scarred, on stems to 2½" long. When profuse and glossy the fruit is lovely.

M. 'Arrow'
An open-pollinated seedling of *M. Sieversii* 'Niedzwetzkyana'. Raised in 1920 by I. Preston of Ottawa's Dominion agricultural experiment station. One of the original ROSYBLOOM CRABAPPLES. Selected in 1930 and named for Arrow Lake of S British Columbia. Extremely rare. Deep purplish-red buds open (later than most ROSYBLOOM cultivars) to purplish-pink flowers, 1⅓"–1½" wide. Fruit dull purplish-red, 1"–1⅓", persisting until late winter. Poor disease resistance.

M. *asiatica*—see M. *prunifolia*

M. 'Athabasca'
An open-pollinated seedling of *M. Sieversii* 'Niedzwetzkyana'. Raised in 1921 by I. Preston of Ottawa's Dominion agricultural experiment station. One of the original ROSYBLOOM CRABAPPLES. Selected in 1933 and named for Athabasca Lake of NW Saskatchewan and NE Alberta. Extremely rare; at least one Ontario nursery sold it ca. 1940. Purplish-red buds open early in the ROSYBLOOM season to pale flowers of purplish-pink with white claws; 1¾"–2" wide. Fruit yellowish-orange to red, 1³⁄₁₆"–1½", useful for jelly, and attractive before they fall. An alternate-year bearer.

M. *atropurpurea*—see M. × *Eleyi*

M. × *atrosanguinea* (Späth) Schneid.
= *Pyrus floribunda atrosanguinea* Späth
= *Pyrus atrosanguinea* Späth
= *Malus floribunda* var. *atrosanguinea* Bean
= *M. Halliana atrosanguinea* hort.
(?*M. Halliana* × *M. Sieboldii*)

CARMINE CRABAPPLE. RED JAPANESE CRABAPPLE. Originated <1889 at the Arnold Arboretum. In the nursery trade by 1898. Common. Like a pinkflowered *M.* × *floribunda* but smaller (usually low and mushroom-shaped, rarely to 20'), with an airier, less dense crown; its leaves larger, darker, glossier, less hairy, more frequently lobed, coarser toothed, and bearing prominent stipules. Blood-red buds (in Latin, *atrosanguinea* means deep blood red) open to pink flowers that do not fade to white; 1³⁄₁₆" wide. Fruits usually few, ¼"–⁷⁄₁₆" long, and of absolutely no ornamental value; yellow, or yellowish with a red blush—sometimes wholly red. B.O. Case nursery of Vancouver, WA, sold it as 'Ming Shing' which means "Stars of Heaven."

M. 'Autumn Delight'

Selected in the Royal Botanic Garden of Hamilton, Ontario. Introduced ≤1990 by Connon nursery of Ontario. Pink buds open to white flowers. Tree of pendulous habit; in full bloom it looks like a white mound. Fruit small, colorful starting in August and remaining until late fall: yellow-orange to brilliant orange-scarlet.

M. 'Autumn Glory'

(*M. Zumi* × *M. Zumi* 'Woosteri')

Bred by the late Father J.L. Fiala of Falconskeape, near Medina, OH. Registered in 1984. Tree vigorous, somewhat upright, to 12' tall. Deep bright red buds open to blush white flowers, finally pure white. Leaves deep green, heavy-textured. Fruit glossy, bright orange-red, ¼" across, slightly oval, beginning to color in late August, persisting until birds eat them in December-January. High disease-resistance.

M. 'Autumn Gold'

Selected in the Royal Botanic Garden of Hamilton, Ontario. Introduced ≤1990 by Connon nursery of Ontario. Similar to *M.* 'Autumn Delight' in flower and appearance but the fruit is yellow turning to yellow-orange in fall.

M. 'Autumn Treasure'

(*M.* 'Wintergold' × *M.* 'Red Swan')

Bred by the late Father J.L. Fiala of Falconskeape, near Medina, OH. Named in 1975; registered in 1987. Not yet in commerce. Red buds open to white flowers. Fruit gold, coloring early; showy, ¼". Tree small, refined, 10' tall and wide, pendulous.

M. baccata (L.) Borkh.

= *Pyrus baccata* L.

SIBERIAN CRABAPPLE. From much of Asia. Introduced to Western cultivation in 1784 when sent to Kew, England by John Græfer. Common. Although the well-established book name SIBERIAN CRABAPPLE is applied to this species, in practice the name has been used at least as often for hybrids of *M. baccata*. In Latin, *baccata* means berry-bearing. Flowers white, 1"–1½" wide. Fruit usually pea-sized (⅓"–⅝"), yellowish or yellow-brown or red, usually longer than wide, the calyx wholly dropping off leaving a smooth scar. Records: to 50' tall in the wild; 41' × 9'9" × 42' Ste Foy, Québec (<1994); 41' × 6'3" × 47' Seattle, WA (1992); 38' × 8'0" × 50' Baltimore, MD (1972); 33' × 7'4" × 45½' Medford, WI (1989).

M. baccata 'Andrew Tures'

Introduced <1992 by Matt Tures' Sons nursery of Huntley, Il. Origin and attributes not known.

M. baccata 'Aspiration'

A seedling raised in 1946 at the Seattle arboretum. From New York Botanical Garden seed of *M. baccata* var. *himalaica*. Named ca. 1957, for its aspiring branches of fastigiate habit. Extremely rare; not in commerce. Flowers like those of *M. baccata* 'Columnaris', which is to say, early in the season—although it flushes a bit later than 'Columnaris'; pure white, 1¾" wide. Calyx and flowerstems hairy, not nearly hairless as 'Columnaris'. Fruit differs in being pear- or rosehip-shaped, not round, and twice as large (1³⁄₁₆" long), but has the same yellow and red coloration when seen in mid-September, and the same slender 1⅜" stem. In November the fruit can become dark red. The tree has all the shape and scab of 'Columnaris' and looks nothing like its reputed parent the healthy, scabfree, round-berried var. *himalaica*. Fall color yellow and early. The original specimen 42' × 4'6" × 37' (1992).

M. baccata 'Columnaris'

= *M. baccata* 'Pyramidalis'

COLUMNAR SIBERIAN CRABAPPLE. Received in 1927 as grafts (under another name) from Kew, England, by the Arnold Arboretum. Named and introduced in 1940 by the Arnold Arboretum. Common. A. Rehder thought it much like a columnar form of *M. baccata* 'Jackii'. Although narrowly upright when young, it splays out in age. Creamy-white buds open to early, pure white flowers 1½"–1⅔" wide. Fruit sometimes sparse; round; yellow or yellow with a red cheek, pea size (some larger than ½"), pitted where the calyx was. Scab-prone. Leaves hairless.

M. baccata var. ellipsoidea—see M. baccata var. himalaica

M. baccata 'Gracilis'

DWARF SIBERIAN CRABAPPLE. WEEPING SIBERIAN CRABAPPLE. A specimen that fits this description was obtained (as *Pyrus Malus pendula*) in 1903 by the Dominion Arboretum of Ottawa from the Arnold Arboretum. Nonetheless, the usual account of the origin of 'Gracilis' is: it was introduced in 1910 via seeds sent from Wm. Purdom in Shensi, China, to Veitch nursery of England; in 1913 a specimen was sent to the Arnold Arboretum, and grew into a tree which occasioned the cultivar being named in 1920. It has been rare in commerce. It breeds largely true when raised from seed. Shrubby, slow, graceful, semi-pendulous—at most to 30' tall. Numerous thin long branches and slender twigs. Leaf narrow, small, sharply toothed. Rose-pink buds open to small, fragrant, white flowers 1⅓"–1⅔" wide, with star-like petals. Fruit ⅓"–⁷⁄₁₆" long, yellow, red or brownish-red.

M. baccata var. *himalaica* (Maxim.) Schneid.
= *M. baccata* var. *ellipsoidea* Yü

HIMALAYAN CRABAPPLE. From Kashmir to Bhutan. Named in 1873. Possibly introduced to cultivation ca. 1919. Certainly seeds were collected by J. Rock and distributed in 1933. This variety is poorly understood and needs research. It has remained very rare but has circulated among botanic gardens and arboreta. Descriptions of it vary; the following is based on Seattle specimens. They bloom later than most *M. baccata* cultivars, and have very hairy flowerstems and calyces suggesting it is certainly a distinctive *M. baccata* variety. They are scab-free, dense, healthy, and possess astonishing vigor. Fruit profuse; pure red, becoming gooey by late October or in November; ⅜" to ½" long and wide; stems to 2⅛" long. (Some writers say *M. baccata* var. *himalaica* fruit is yellow with a red cheek.) Record: 38' × 5'0" × 41' Seattle, WA (1991).

M. baccata 'Jackii'

JACK CRABAPPLE. In 1905, John George Jack (1861–1949), Canadian professor of dendrology, sent scions from Seoul to the Arnold Arboretum. This cultivar was named after him in 1915. Common. Vigorous; upright, broadly rounded, to 30'–40' tall. Likely a good street-tree. Large, milk-white or slightly pink buds open to pure white 1½" wide flowers (larger than most forms of SIBERIAN CRABAPPLES). A cloud of solid white in bloom. Leaves barely toothed, dark above, strikingly paler below. Fruit firm, to ⅝" long, shiny, dark red-purple, with tiny scars; stem to 2⅜" long. Disease resistance fair.

M. baccata 'Lady Northcliffe'—see *M.* 'Lady Northcliffe'

M. baccata 'Manchu'

Originated in Brookings, SD, after N. Hansen grew seeds of *M. baccata* var. *mandschurica* from Harbin, Manchuria, collected in 1924. Introduced ca. 1960. Both the clone and its open-pollinated seedlings are called 'Manchu' and the primary use is seedlings grown for rootstocks.

M. baccata var. *mandshurica* (Maxim.) Schneid.
= *M. mandshurica* (Maxim.) Kom.
= *M. cerasifera* Spach, non Zab.
= *Pyrus baccata* var. *mandshurica* Maxim.

MANCHURIAN CRABAPPLE. From Manchuria, N China, Ussuri, Korea, Sakhalin, S Kuriles, Japan. The northernmost CRABAPPLE says A. den Boer. Introduced to England <1825. Introduced in 1882 to the Arnold Arboretum. Uncommon. Despite the name, this tree is widely distributed in NE Asia, and varies from a bush to nearly 100' tall. In the north at least, it vies with *M.* × *micromalus* to be the first CRABAPPLE to flower in spring, with pure white, notably fragrant flowers 1½" wide; sepals hairy, unlike those of typical *M. baccata*. Leaves broad, sharp-toothed and hairier than most *M. baccata* forms. Goes bare early in fall. Fruit usually red, sometimes yellow, ripens early; to ⅝" on a 1" stem. A broadly rounded, sturdy tree. Fair disease resistance. Records: to 98' tall says the *Flora of the U.S.S.R.*; to 65' × 7'6" in the wild says E. Wilson; 49' × 7'10" Benenden, Kent, England (1991; *pl.* 1920); 38' × 4'2" × 41' Seattle, WA (1992).

M. baccata 'Pyramidalis'—see *M. baccata* 'Columnaris'

M. baccata 'Rosthern'

Origin not known but probably Canadian. Rosthern is a city north of Saskatoon, Saskatchewan. In commerce ≤1975. Extremely rare. A tree of pyramidal shape, bearing red fruit.

M. baccata 'Walters'

Selected in Maplewood, NJ, and named after Richard Walters, formerly city arborist there. Introduced ≤1985–86 by Princeton nursery of New Jersey. Uncommon. Pink buds open to pure white flowers. Fruit small, yellow or red. To 30' tall; scab and fireblight resistant. Said to be splendid for use as a street-tree. Very hardy.

M. 'Barbara Ann'

An Arnold Arboretum 1946 seedling of *M.* 'Dorothea' (presumably pollinated by a *M.* × *purpurea* variant). First flowered in 1957; named in 1964 by horticulturist Donald Wyman, after his younger daughter. Introduced by the Arnold Arboretum in 1966. Rare. Flowers semi-double (12–15 petals), purple-pink, then fading, 1½"–2" wide. Fruit purple or purplish-red <½". Leaves reddish during entire growth period. Poor disease resistance.

M. 'Baskatong'

(*M.* 'Simcoe' × *M.* 'Meach')

Raised by Ottawa's Dominion agricultural experiment station. Introduced <1948. Named for Baskatong Lake, 90 miles north of Ottawa. Uncommon. Grows to 30' tall and wide, spreading much like *M.* × *floribunda*. Leaves deep purple, changing to dark bronzy-green all summer, reddish in fall. Buds attractive, highly colored maroon-red; flowers in clusters of 3–6, spinel-red fading to light purplish-red, the petals with white claws; 1¾" wide. Fruit dark reddish-purple with russet marks, 1", edible. Fair to good disease resistance.

M. 'Beauty'

Originated by N. Hansen of South Dakota, from *Malus* × *robusta* seeds obtained from the St. Petersburg Botanic Gardens in 1919. Selected ca. 1925, introduced ca. 1929. Uncommon. Tree fastigiate when young. Flowers like those of *M.* × *domestica* (ORCHARD APPLE) pure white, 1¾"–2" wide, fragrant, from ivory or pink-tinged buds; sepals remarkably long. The *M.* × *domestica* influence shows in the broad leaves, white hairs, and short flowerstems—usually <1" long, rarely to 1⅜" long. Fruit abundant, pinkish red to brilliant red, quarter-dollar sized (to 1½" wide), flattened, with a large brown pit where the calyx was; handsome, earning its cultivar name, though harshly disappointing to taste. Ripe and falling from mid-September to early November. An alternate-year bearer. Vigorous. Record: 38' × 3'2" Seattle, WA (1993; *pl.* 1952). Fair disease resistance.

M. 'Bechtel'—see M. *ioensis* 'Bechtel'

M. 'Beverly'

Parentage not known except one parent was likely *M.* × *floribunda*. Introduced ca. 1940 by Clavey Ravinia nursery (of Illinois?). Named after Beverly Clavey. Common. To 25' tall, upright spreading, becoming rounded. Dark red buds open to clear white flowers, to 1⅜' wide (like those of *Prunus cerasifera*), on long, slender slightly hairy stems. Leaves small, fine textured. Fruit profuse, showy, bright red, roundish, ½"–⅝" (¾"); calyx usually drops, leaving small scars. Disease resistance varies but is generally good. There are excellent scabfree specimens with much bright red fruit, while others are gawky, disgustingly scabby, with plain red fruit.

M. B.F. 6—see M. 'Jubilee'

M. *bhutanica*—see M. *toringoides*

M. 'Big Red'

Introduced ≤1990 by Weston nursery of Hopkinton, MA.

M. 'Big River'

An open-pollinated *M. baccata* seedling, the pollen parent likely *M.* 'Hopa'. Introduced decades ago by P.H. Wright of Moose Range, Saskatchewan. Extremely rare; still in commerce. Foliage reddish-purple. Flowers deep rose-pink to purplish-red, 1¾" wide. Fruit bright red, ⅓". Extremely hardy.

M. 'Birdland'

Originated by Johnson nursery of Menomonee Falls, WI. Named <1983. Named because birds love the fruit. Pink buds open to white flowers 1½" wide. Fruit glossy yellow with orange-red blush, ca. ¼"–½" long; calyx drops. Tree broadly rounded, to 30' tall and wide.

M. 'Blanche Ames'

= *M.* AA No. 6639

Selected in 1939 at the Arnold Arboretum. Named in 1955 after botanical artist Blanche Ames, wife of the Harvard botanist and orchidologist Oakes Ames. Introduced in 1947. Very rare. Claimed to be an open-pollinated seedling of *M. spectabilis* 'Riversii'. It doesn't in the least take after that distinctive tree. Its leaves and buds are similar to those of *M.* × *Hartwigii* 'Katherine' but the fruits, flowers and tree habits differ. Buds half pink. Flowers white; small, to 1½" wide; double, with 13–19 (23) narrow petals; delicately pretty. An enchanting sight, the tree partly weeps, its branches slender and light enough to sway gently in the breeze. Alas, by early May the tree is ugly with scab. Can be fecund or practically fruitless. Fruit pea-sized, to ½"; yellow mostly covered with red, conspicuously shiny; either elliptic or wider than long; with very large scars (usually with a protruding tip) where the calyx was; slender nearly hairless stems to 2¼" long, reddish if exposed to sun. Seeds 3 or fewer, usually aborted. Record: 30' × 6'3" × 41' Seattle, WA (1992; *pl.* 1950).

M. 'Bob White'

= M. × Zumi 'Bob White'

A chance seedling from Massachusetts <1876. Introduced to cultivation by the Arnold Arboretum. Common. Valued for persistent fruit. A broad, dense tree, its crown full, with little scab, but not pretty—just plain. Suited for street-tree use. Bark scaly like that of FLOWERING DOGWOOD (*Cornus florida*). Pink buds open to small but profuse, white flowers, 1"–1¼" wide; stems hairy. Leaves dark above, downy beneath, with sharp teeth. Some small lobes on sucker leaves. Fruit ⅓"–⅝"; pale yellow or yellowish-brown; lightly hairy; with large calyx scars; on hairy stems to 1⅜" long; long persistent, providing February food for quail, hence the name 'Bob White'. An alternate-year bearer.

M. Brandywine®

= M. 'Branzam'

(M. 'Almey' × M. coronaria 'Klehm's Improved Bechtel')

Originated by Simpson nursery of Vincennes, IN. Named and introduced <1979 by Lake County nursery of Perry, OH. Uncommon. Tree to 25' tall and 20' wide, vase-shaped, then rounded; rapid growing. Flowers double, fragrant, deep rose. Leaves large, green with a distinct burgundy overcast; fall color attractive deep purple or reddish-brown. Fruit yellow-green (some with a pink or orange blush), to 1½" wide, stem to 1⅜" long; drops in October. Disease resistance fair.

M. 'Branson'—see M. × Soulardii 'Wynema'

M. 'Branzam'—see M. Brandywine®

M. brevipes (Rehd.) Rehd.

= M. floribunda var. brevipes Rehd.

= Pyrus brevipes (Rehd.) L.H. Bailey

NIPPON CRABAPPLE. Origin not known, possibly from Japan (Nippon is a name for Japan). Introduced in 1883. Named in 1920. In commerce ≤1930. Little known, extremely rare. Like the well-known M. × floribunda but denser growing; stiff-branched, usually a shrub. Leaf 2"–3" long; never the least bit lobed; quite like those of M. × floribunda but with closer, sharper teeth. Pink buds open to white flowers 1³⁄₁₆" wide. Fruit red or yellow-crimson, ½"–⅝" wide, upright or nearly upright, on thin, short (Latin *brevis*, short, and *pes*, foot, referring to the stem)

purple stems, which are ¼"–⁷⁄₁₆" (⅝") long; sepals mostly deciduous. Poor disease resistance.

M. 'Bridal Bouquet'

Introduced ≤1990 by Princeton nursery of New Jersey. To 18'–20' tall. Flowers very large, double, white. Very few fruit.

M. 'Bridal Crown'

(M. baccata 'Plena Alba' × M. Zumi) × (M. Zumi × M. 'Van Eseltine')

Bred by the late Father J.L. Fiala of Falconskeape, near Medina, OH. M. 'Angel Choir' is a sibling. Registered ≤1983. Not yet in commerce. Tree upright, very finely branched, 11'–12' tall. Pure white buds open to profuse, double, white flowers resembling a bridal corsage. Fruit reddish, to ca. ½".

M. 'Brier'

= M. 'Brier's Sweet'

From Burgess Buel Brier (b. 1817) of Baraboo, WI. An edible CRABAPPLE described in 1870 as a cross of a SIBERIAN CRABAPPLE with 'Bailey' APPLE. Commercially extinct or nearly so; disease-prone. Fruit pale yellow, washed with a lively red, striped carmine. Tree vigorous and hardy.

M. 'Brier's Sweet'—see M. 'Brier'

M. 'Burgandy'

('Burgundy')

= M. Simpson 4-17

(M. 'Van Eseltine' × M. 'Almey')

Introduced ≤1979 by Simpson nursery of Vincennes, IN. Uncommon. Foliage rich red during the growing season. Flowers dark red, abundant, of grapelike fragrance. Fruit maroon. Tree slender, vase-shaped.

M. 'Burton'

= M. Burtoni hort.

= M. 'Burton's Yellow-fruited'

Chance seedling of ca. 1937 from Burton's nursery of Casstown, OH. Extremely rare. Pink buds open to white flowers. Fruit yellow, 1⅞". Excellent disease-resistance.

M. Burtoni—see M. 'Burton'

M. 'Burton's Yellow-fruited'—see M. 'Burton'

M. 'Butterball'

Raised at the Seattle arboretum from M. × Zumi 'Calocarpa' seeds received in 1946; named in 1956.

Extremely rare; better known in Europe than in North America. Rosy buds open to white flowers in early May, 1¾₆"–1½" wide. Fruit ¾"–1½" wide, yellow-orange; calyx stays or drops. A small, broad-crowned tree.

M. 'Butterfly'
(*M.* 'Dorothea' × *M. floribunda*)

Bred by the late Father J.L. Fiala of Falconskeape, near Medina, OH. Registered ≤1983. A small tree, to 8'–10' tall. Bright pink buds open to light pink flowers. Fruit bright red, ca. ⅜".

M. 'Callaway'
= *M.* 'Ida Cason'

Selected by Fred Galle at Callaway Gardens, 85 miles S of Atlanta, GA (named after Ida Cason Callaway). It had been obtained in 1954 from a northern nursery as "*M. prunifolia*" but later was identified as a *M. Sieboldii* hybrid. Named 'Callaway' in 1964. Common in commerce. Well adapted to the Southeast and widely planted there. Light pink buds open to large white flowers, 1"–1½" wide. Fruit bright red, ¾"–1¼"—useful for jelly and canning. Leaves bright green and large. Tree 15'–25' tall, rounded. Fair disease resistance. Sutherland nursery of McMinnville, TN, has sold seedlings of it.

M. calocarpa—see M. × Zumi 'Calocarpa'

M. Camelot®
= *M.* 'Camzam'

Introduced in 1991 by Lake County nursery of Perry, OH. Common. Dwarf, rounded, compact, slowly to 10' tall and 8' wide. Dark red-purple buds open to white, fragrant flowers 1½" wide, with some pink on the petal backs and edges. Leaves burgundy when young, then dark green, thick, leathery, sharply toothed; they could pass for those of a FLOWERING CHERRY. Fruit ⅜"–⅝" long, red, turning soft and rich burgundy in early autumn; calyx drops; pulp tasty.

M. 'Cameron'
(*M.* 'Arrow' × *M.* Hartwigii 'Katherine' or *M.* 'Dorothea')

Originated in 1956 in Ottawa. Named in 1970 for Mr. D.F. Cameron, ornamental plant breeder who raised it (as well as *M.* 'Maybride'). Introduced in 1973. Very rare. Leaf shiny bronze in spring, dark green in summer. Flowers double, bright purplish-red outside with a clear pink center, 1¾" wide. Fruit lustrous purple ⅝"; abundant. Tree vigorous, oval, with moderately wide-angled branches.

M. 'Camille'
= *M. floribunda* 'Camille'

Selected from among a group of *M.* × *moerlandsii* 'Profusion' trees imported from Europe by W.H. Perron nursery of Ville de Laval, Québec. Suspected of hybrid origin. Reddish leaves, large pink flowers, delicious red fruit to 2⅜" wide, ripe in September. Introduced by Perron; registered in 1983.

M. 'Camzam'—see M. Camelot®

M. 'Canary'

A chance seedling introduced ≤1990 by Simpson nursery of Vincennes, IN. Uncommon. Medium-sized, vigorous; slender branches, spreading with age; crown somewhat open. Leaves frequently deeply lobed, with persistent hairs on both sides. Red buds open to abundant small, white, flowers, 1⅛" wide, with overlapping petals. Fruit canary-yellow to orange-yellow, ¼"–⁷⁄₁₆" wide, on stems ≤¾" long. Disease-resistant.

M. Candied Apple®—see M. 'Weeping Candied Apple'

M. 'Candymint' PP 6606 (1989)
= *M. Sargentii* 'Candymint'

A *Malus Sargentii* seedling introduced by Simpson nursery of Vincennes, IN. Common. A small tree of picturesque, horizontal, very low, vigorous growth. Twigs dark purple. Leaves purplish and white-hairy when young, then dark green; thick and bold; very sharply toothed, with some strong lobes. Some leaves as large as 4½" × 4". Carmine buds open to flowers with pink petals edged red; effective over a long period. Fruit dark purple. Disease prone in Seattle, but described as resistant in the Midwest.

M. Canterbury™
= *M.* 'Canterzam'

Introduced in 1993 by Lake County nursery of Perry, OH. Uncommon. A rounded compact dwarf to 10' tall and 15' wide. Deep pink buds open to light pink flowers. Leaves dark wine-green. Fruit ¼" bright red.

M. 'Canterzam'—see M. Canterbury™

M. 'Cardinal'—see M. 'Princeton Cardinal'

M. 'Cardinal's Robe(s)'
(*M.* 'Liset' × *M.* 'Amberina')

Bred by the late Father J.L. Fiala of Falconskeape, near Medina, OH. Named in 1970 (after James Cardinal Hickey of Washington, D.C.), registered in

1987. Not yet in commerce. Habit rounded, to 15'. Leaves dark reddish-green. Bright orange-red buds open to bright red flowers. Fruit bright red, to ½". Bark unique, like that of a CHERRY TREE.

M. 'Cascole'—see M. White Cascade®

M. 'Cashmere'—see M. × sublobata

M. 'Centennial'
(M. 'Dolgo' × M. 'Wealthy')
From Excelsior, MN. An intentional cross, 1931; selected in 1940; introduced in 1957. Uncommon; grown primarily for its edible fruit. The name refers to the centennial of Minnesota's admission as the 32nd state in 1858. Pink buds open to white flowers. Fruit egg-shaped, red-striped over yellow-orange, 1¾"–2" wide; stem long and slender; calyx persists; ripe and delicious from late August through early September. Large, thin leaves with sharp teeth. Good disease resistance.

M. Centurion®
= M. 'Centzam'
= M. Simpson 11-57
(M. Zumi 'Calocarpa' × M. 'Almey')
Developed by Simpson nursery of Vincennes, IN. Named in 1978 by Lake County nursery of Perry, OH. Introduced in 1979. Common. Narrow upright columnar form, growing rapidly to 30' tall and 15' wide, gradually widening to a broad vaselike or rounded crown. Red buds open to dark pink flowers, 1½"–2" wide. Fruit cherry-red, becoming glossy, showy for 2 months or more, ½"–⅝" long, faintly ribbed, with small calyx scars; pulp amber-colored. Leaves purple when young, aging to glossy bronzy-green in summer. Good fall color. Good disease resistance.

M. 'Centzam'—see M. Centurion®

M. cerasifera—see M. baccata var. mandshurica and M. × robusta

M. cerasifera atropurpurea—see M. × Eleyi

M. 'Charlottæ'—see M. coronaria 'Charlottæ'

M. 'Cheal's Crimson'—see M. prunifolia 'Cheal's Crimson'

M. 'Cheal's Golden Gem'
= M. 'Golden Gem'
= M. prunifolia 'Golden Gem'

Introduced <1919 by J. Cheal & Sons nursery of Sussex, England. Very rare in North America. Pink buds open to white flowers, 1⅕" or more wide. Fruit yellow, ½"–1", freely borne, ripe in September. Upright 25' tall tree. Excellent disease resistance, except fireblight.

M. 'Cheal's Weeping'
('Cheel's Weeping')
= M. 'Cheal's Scarlet Weeping'
Introduced ca. 1950 by J. Cheal & Sons nursery of Sussex, England. Uncommon in North America; sold mostly in Canada. Habit weeping. Flowers light (lilac-) red. Fruit few, dark red, ¾". Susceptible to scab.

M. 'Chestnut'
= M. Minnesota 240
Raised at Excelsior, MN, as an open-pollinated 'Malinda' APPLE seedling. Selected in 1921, introduced commercially in 1946. Common. Grown primarily for its edible fruit. Red buds open to white flowers. Fruit orangish to bronze-red colored, 2" wide, chestnut-like flavored. Tree small but vigorous, and productive.

M. 'Chilko'
An open-pollinated seedling of M. Sieversii 'Niedzwetzkyana'. Raised in 1920 by I. Preston of Ottawa's Dominion agricultural experiment station. One of the original ROSYBLOOM CRABAPPLES. Selected in 1930 and named for Chilko Lake of SW British Columbia. Seldom grown; virtually out of commerce since the late 1950s. Tree broad-crowned. Flowers to 1¾"–2" wide, purplish-red, fading to purple-pink. Fruit 1½"–2" long, bright crimson with shiny skin, edible—much like those of M. 'Dolgo' but with purplish pulp. An alternate-year bearer. Leaves purplish at first.

M. 'Crimson Weeper'—see M. 'Echtermeyer'

M. 'Chrishozam'—see M. Christmas Holly™

M. Christmas Holly™
= M. 'Chrishozam'
Raised by the late Father J.L. Fiala of Falconskeape, near Medina, OH. A seedling of M. Zumi. Registered ≤1983. Common. Upright to wide spreading, dense, small to medium sized, 10'–15' tall. Bright red buds open to white flowers 1½"–1⅝" wide. Fruit HOLLY-like, very bright red, ⅜" long, persistent; fruitful each year. Leaves dark green, yellow late in fall. Good disease resistance.

M. Cinderella®
= *M.* 'Cinzam'

Introduced in 1991 by Lake County nursery of Perry, OH. Uncommon. A genetic dwarf. Upright habit to 8' tall and 5' wide (taller if topgrafted). Tiny red buds open to white flowers. Leaf wine-colored and frosty-looking at first, becoming green; deeply lobed. Fruit golden, ¼"; held into late autumn.

M. 'Cinzam'—see M. Cinderella®

M. 'Colonel Lee'

Mr. Guy Lee brought this in the early 1920s from his mother's home in Chestnut Hill, MA, to the Bay State nursery of Framingham, MA. Named by the nursery; sold by them into the 1940s; commercially extinct. Carmine buds open to abundant 2⅜" wide, rosy-pink flowers, fading to dull pink. Branching upright.

M. communis—see M. × domestica

M. 'Copper King'
(*M.* 'Satin Cloud' × *M.* 'Shinto Shrine')

Bred by the late Father J.L. Fiala of Falconskeape, near Medina, OH. Named in1977, registered in 1987. Not yet in commerce. Habit round, to 10'–12' tall and wide. White buds open to large spicily-fragrant white flowers. Fruit ½", reddish-copper. Fall leaf color yellow to orange.

M. Coralburst™ PP 2983 (1970)
= *M.* 'Coralcole'
('Coral Burst')

Raised ca. 1954 as a seedling of *Malus* 'Van Eseltine' (Fiala says of *M. Sieboldii*) at Gardenview Horticultural Park of Strongsville, OH. Introduced in 1968 by Cole nursery of Painesville, OH. Common. A rounded, slow-growing bushy dwarf, often top-grafted at 2½'–3½'. Coral-pink buds open to single or semi-double rose-pink flowers, ½" wide. Leaves small, dull dark grayish-green, very hairy, sharply toothed, <2" × ⅞". Fruit sparse, tiny and dull, to ⁷⁄₁₆" wide, yellow-green with brown speckles; stem hairy, to 1¹⁄₁₆" long. Record: 14' × 1'7" × 16½' Spokane, WA (1993; *pl.* 1971). Good disease resistance.

M. 'Coral Cascade' PP 7142 (1990)

Originated <1967. Introduced in 1989 by Gardenview Horticultural Park of Strongsville, OH. Uncommon, if not rare. Deep coral-red buds open to blush white flowers. Fruit pinkish coral-orange, ½" long, colors in September and darkens with frost; persists until January. Tree to 15' tall, of graceful arching

habit, weeping with age. Leaves deep green. Excellent disease resistance.

M. 'Coralcole'—see M. Coralburst™

M. coronaria (L.) Mill.
= *M. glabrata* Rehd. BILTMORE or ALABAMA CRABAPPLE.
= *M. glaucescens* Rehd. DUNBAR CRABAPPLE.
= *M. lancifolia* Rehd. ALLEGHENY CRABAPPLE.
= *Pyrus coronaria* L.

AMERICAN CRABAPPLE. GARLAND CRABAPPLE. WILD SWEET CRABAPPLE. From the Midwest and eastern U.S., and S Ontario. Cultivated in Pennsylvania since ca. 1750. Common. In Latin *coronarius* means suitable for a wreath or crown; wreathed or garlanded. Pink buds open to white flowers 1½"–2" wide, sweetly fragrant. Leaves hairless. Fruit green or yellow-green, hard and waxy, ¾"–1⅝" wide. Records: 57' × 3'0" Beaver County, PA (1985); 57' × 2'6" Seattle, WA (1990; *pl.* 1946); 37' × 5'10" Hampstead, VA (1976). Poor disease resistance. Related to the PRAIRIE CRABAPPLE (*M. ioensis*), and SOUTHERN CRABAPPLE (*M. angustifolia*); hybridizes with ORCHARD APPLE (see *M.* × *heterophylla*).

M. coronaria 'Big O'

A seed-grown cultivar—minimal variation observed in offspring. Seed collected by the USDA Soil Conservation Service in Floyd County, GA. Introduced in 1992. Resists cedar-apple rust.

M. coronaria 'Charlottæ'
= *M. coronaria* 'Flore Pleno' (in part)
= *M.* 'Charlottæ'
= *Pyrus Charlottæ* hort.

CHARLOTTE CRABAPPLE. A cultivar of *M. coronaria* var. *dasycalyx*. Discovered ca. 1902 in a pasture near Waukegan, IL. Named for Charlotte, wife of its introducer, Edward P. DeWolf. Introduced by the Arnold Arboretum. Common previously; superseded now by *M. coronaria* 'Klehm's Improved Bechtel'. Flowers 2"–2½" wide, pale pink; 12–20 petals; blooming when leaves are fully open, not before as does *M. ioensis* 'Plena'. Fruit 1⅕"–1½" (1⅔") wide, stem to 1½" long and conspicuously swollen as it joins the fruit. Fall color yellow to vivid red and orange. Poor to fair disease resistance.

M. coronaria var. dasycalyx Rehd.

GREAT LAKES CRABAPPLE. From the SW part of the Great Lakes region, S Ontario to probably NE Illinois; common in Ohio and N Indiana. Named in

1920. Almost never listed by name in nurseries, yet two of its cultivars have been widely sold: 'Charlottæ' and 'Klehm's Improved Bechtel'. Distinguished from typical *M. coronaria* by having fuzz on the flower-stem and sepals (*dasycalyx* is from Greek, meaning very hairy sepals). This variety has been suggested as possibly a hybrid with *M. ioensis*.

M. coronaria 'Elk River'—see *M. ioensis* 'Elk River'

M. coronaria 'Flore Pleno'—see *M. coronaria* 'Charlottæ'

M. coronaria 'Fluke'—see *M. × Soulardii* 'Fluke'

M. coronaria var. *ioensis*—see *M. ioensis*

M. coronaria 'Klehm's Improved Bechtel'
= *M. ioensis* 'Klehm's Bechtel'
= *M. ioensis* 'Klehm's Improved Bechtel'
= *M. ioensis* 'Klehmi'
= *M. ioensis* 'Klehm's No. 8'
John Klehm founded Klehm nursery in northern Illinois in 1852. By 1990, the company had 3 locales, and was owned by Roy, Carl and Arnold Klehm. This clone was selected by Clyde Klehm in a Chicago park. It is a cultivar of *M. coronaria* var. *dasycalyx*. In commerce ≤1953. Very common. A tree of great value for sweet-scented, lovely flowers, and rich orange fall color. It fruits regularly. It is so much better than the original BECHTEL CRABAPPLE (*M. ioensis* 'Plena') that some nurseries stopped selling the original, and instead offer Klehm's under the old name. Klehm's is far more disease-resistant. Flowers 1⅝"–2⅛" (2½") wide, of ca. 18 (26) petals; short, broad downy sepals. Record: 25' × 2'8" × 27' Seattle, WA (1993).

M. coronaria 'Margaret'
= *M.* 'Margaret'
Introduced <1973. Selected by R.A. Fenicchia of the Rochester, NY, park system. Extremely rare. Flowers double, pink, in CHERRY-like clusters. Fruit greenish.

M. coronaria 'Mercer'—see *M. × Soulardii* 'Fluke'

M. coronaria 'Nieuwlandiana'
Raised in 1928 by B.H. Slavin in Rochester, New York; introduced in 1931. Rare. Named after the Rev. Julius Arthur Nieuwland (1878–1936). Nieuwland was a professor of botany and chemistry at Notre Dame University, and the founding editor of *The American Midland Naturalist* journal. Flowers double, with 12–19 (27) petals; pink, fragrant, 2½" wide, very open rather than cupped and heavy. Fewer petals than *M. coronaria* 'Charlottæ'. Opens earlier in the season than similar cultivars. Essentially hairless. Leaves weakly hairy, very wide, somewhat lobed; turning yellow in fall. Fruit like slightly flattened green golfballs 1"–2" wide, on stems at most over 3" long.

M. coronaria var. *platycarpa*—see *M. × heterophylla*

M. coronaria 'Plena'—see *M. ioensis* 'Plena'

M. coronaria 'Thoms'
= *M. coronaria* Thomsi hort.
= *M. Thomsi* hort.
In 1920, Louis Thoms, an employee of Siebenthaler nursery of Dayton, Ohio, discovered this on his farm near Franklin, OH. Introduced in 1927. Extremely rare; not in commerce. Flowers pink, 1⅔" wide. Fruit greenish-yellow, 1" wide.

M. coronaria Thomsi—see *M. coronaria* 'Thoms'

M. 'Cotton Candy'
An open-pollinated *M.* 'Van Eseltine' seedling. Introduced <1979 by Gardenview Horticultural Park of Strongsville, OH. Very rare. Upright, somewhat rounded, slow growing to 10' tall. Deep pink buds open to semi-double, pink flowers. Fruit deep yellow, ½"; browns soon and falls. Leaves dark green, heavy. Fair disease resistance.

M. 'Cowichan'
An open-pollinated seedling of *M. Sieversii* 'Niedzwetzkyana'. Raised in 1920 by I. Preston of Ottawa's Dominion agricultural experiment station. One of the original ROSYBLOOM CRABAPPLES. Selected in 1928 (Preston's favorite of the 33 ROSYBLOOMS she raised) and named in 1930 for Cowichan Lake of Vancouver Island, B.C. Uncommon. Pale red buds open to pink flowers which fade to pale pink or nearly white—the lightest color of Preston's ROSYBLOOMS; 1¾" wide, profuse. Fruit 1½" wide; bright crimson to reddish-purple with some pale yellow or ivory; pulp pink; good for jelly. Good fall leaf color. Tree vigorous, to 30' tall; habit spreading. Poor disease resistance.

M. cratægifolia—see *M. florentina*

M. 'Crimson Brilliant' PP 939 (1950)

A ROSYBLOOM CRABAPPLE that appeared ca. 1939 as a *Malus × Eleyi* seedling from A. den Boer of Des Moines, IA. Introduced by Wayside nursery in 1952. Previously common; now commercially extinct or nearly so. Small tree. Flowers 1½" wide, semi-double (5–10 petals), carmine with a white center star. Fruit ¾" wide, dark purplish red with russet marks. Purplish-green foliage. Poor disease resistance.

M. 'Crimson Sunset' PP 2801 (1968)

Introduced by Princeton nursery of New Jersey. Commercially extinct.

M. 'Dainty'
= *M.* Kerr #63-1

A ROSYBLOOM seedling originated ca. 1959 and selected in 1963 by W. Les Kerr in Saskatchewan. Registered in 1969. Uncommon. Flowers rosy-red, ca. 1½" wide. Fruit brownish, ¼"–½" wide; calyx stays or drops. Young leaves bronzy-red; at maturity dark green; narrow. A dense, somewhat pendulous, slenderly-branched broad tree, to 26' tall and 36' wide. Scab-susceptible.

M. 'Dakota Beauty' PP 648 (1944)

A chance *M. Sieversii* 'Niedzwetzkyana' seedling discovered by C.A. Hansen in 1938 at Brookings, SD. Introduced commercially in 1940. Flowers ornamental, large, mostly double, pinkish-red. Fruit ½"–1" wide, dark red; pulp juicy, red. Tree hardy, bushy.

M. 'Dakota Pink Eye'
= *M.* 'Pink Eye'
= *M.* 'Will's Pink Eye'
= *M.* 'Diamond Jubilee'

Introduced in 1943 by Will nursery of Bismarck, ND. Renamed 'Diamond Jubilee' in 1956 to honor Will's 75th anniversary. Very rare. Said to be a variation of *M. baccata*. Pinkish-red buds open to white flowers with pink streaks radiating from the center. Fruit (reports D. Wyman in 1955) not particularly outstanding, red, 1", can be used for jelly. Hinsdale nursery of Illinois says the fruit is golden. It would seem the fruit's shady side and blush side vary much in color.

M. 'Dartmouth'

From New Hampshire <1883; derived partly from 'Red Astrachan' APPLE. Very rare; little grown in North America (offered by a B.C. nursery in 1948); better known in Europe. Flowers 1⅓" wide, white. Fruit brilliant deep crimson over yellow, bloomy,

1⅔"–2" wide; of high quality for jelly. An alternate-year bearer. Tree semi-weeping, open-branched.

M. *dasyphylla* Borkh. 'Plena'
= *M. pumila* 'Plena'
= *M. pumila* 'Translucens'
= *M. spectabilis* 'Alba Plena'
= *M. spectabilis* f. *albi-plena* Schelle
= *M. sylvestris* 'Flore Plena'
= *M. sylvestris* 'Plena'

DOUBLEFLOWERED DANUBE CRABAPPLE. The DANUBE CRABAPPLE is wild in E Europe's Danube River basin and N Balkan region. Its cultivar 'Plena' (with double flowers), has been grown in Europe since <1770 when it was first described officially. It is still little known, however. In North America since ≤1896, it has remained consistently rare, with few nurseries offering it. In the 1980s it became rarer than ever, and may be extinct commercially in the 1990s. Pinkish buds open to white flowers, double (13–15 petals), to 1½" wide, in very dense clusters completely covering the tree. Ugly with scab soon after. Leaves are thick, broad, very downy and veiny (*dasyphyllus* is from Greek, meaning very hairy-leaved). Tree slow growing, of middling health. Fruit sparse, ripe in early September, edible but not good apples, yellow and red, to 1¾" wide, on a stout stem.

M. 'Dauphin'
= *M.* 'Red Dauphin'
= *M.* 'Dauphin Rosybloom'

An open-pollinated seedling of *M. Sieversii* 'Niedzwetzkyana'. Raised in 1920 by I. Preston of Ottawa's Dominion agricultural experiment station. One of the original ROSYBLOOM CRABAPPLES. Selected in 1930 and named for Dauphin Lake of Manitoba. Very rare; seldom in commerce since ca. 1960. Flowers attractive bright reddish. Fruit bright red, to nearly 1½", hangs well. Foliage bronze in summer, red in fall.

M. 'Dauphin Rosybloom'—see M. 'Dauphin'

M. 'David'

Received by A. den Boer of Des Moines, IA, from the Morton Arboretum in 1940 as buds of "*M. Halliana* var. *spontanea*" but Den Boer believed he had been sent buds from a rootstock. In 1957 the selection was named after a grandson of Den Boer's. Light pink buds open to white flowers, 1½" wide. Fruit ⅜"–⅝" wide, shiny scarlet, with large scars, and crisp yellow pulp; persistent. A compact rounded tree to 12'. Leaves green. Good disease resistance.

M. × *Dawsoniana* Rehd.

= *Pyrus* × *Dawsoniana* (Rehd.) L.H. Bailey
(*M. fusca* × *M. domestica*)

HYBRID PACIFIC CRABAPPLE. Named in 1907 after bring raised in 1881 at the Arnold Arboretum from Oregon seeds. In commerce ≤1921. Very rare in cultivation. Common wild in Oregon's Willamette Valley, and occasional in Washington and southern British Columbia. Jackson Thornton Dawson (1841–1916) was a horticulturist who worked at the Arnold Arboretum for 43 years, and was one of its superintendents. Pink buds open to white flowers, 1"–1½" wide. Fruit yellow to yellow and red, 1"–2" long; edible. Fall leaf color can be excellent. Records: 80' × 4'5" × 45' Seattle, WA (1993); 46' × 5'3½" × 46' Seattle, WA (1992). Fair to excellent disease resistance.

M. den Boer Seedling 54-1—see M. 'Guiding Star'

M. × denBoerii—see M. 'Evelyn'

M. 'Diamond Jubilee'—see M. 'Dakota Pink Eye'

M. diversifolia—see M. fusca

M. 'Dolga Pink'

Tankard nursery of Exmore, VA, 1980 catalog: "We named this one! Vigorous. Flowers similar to those of M. 'Hopa'; larger fruits."

M. 'Dolgo'

= M. 'Snow-White Crab'

A *Malus* × *robusta* seedling imported from Russia in 1897 by N. Hansen of South Dakota. Introduced in 1917. Very common. Although originally named 'Dolga' (meaning "long" in Russian), nurseries were miscalling it 'Dolgo' ≤1926 and the corruption stuck. Slightly pink buds open to early, pure white, abundant, fragrant flowers, 1½"–2" wide. Fruit oval, yellow and deep red, 1¼" long, delicious for eating in late July and August; usually drops by mid-September. An alternate-year bearer. Leafy, healthy, vigorous and large. Fair disease resistance. Records: 37' × 2'10" × 35' Seattle, WA (1992; *pl.* 1952); 25' × 7'8½" × 44' Alma, Québec (<1994).

M. × *domestica* Borkh. 1803, non Poir.

= *M. pumila* auct. p.p., non Mill.
= *M. communis* Poir. (in part)
= *M. sylvestris* var. *domestica* (Borkh.) Mansf.
= *M. Malus* Britt.
= *Pyrus Malus* L. (in part)
= *Pyrus pumila* K. Koch, non J. Neumann *ex* Tausch

ORCHARD APPLE. APPLE TREE. COMMON APPLE. CULTIVATED APPLE. EDIBLE APPLE. From Eurasia, of ancient hybrid origin. To North America <1600. William Blaxton's 'Yellowing Sweeting' (renamed 'Sweet Rhode Island Greening') is probably the first named apple to originate in the U.S. (ca. 1650). APPLE trees were running wild in North America before Johnny Appleseed and they are very widespread, familiar and need no lengthy description here. Certain APPLE cultivars bear fruit no larger than certain ornamental CRABAPPLES; there is no firm line to distinguish APPLE and CRABAPPLE varieties. Records: 70' × 11'9" × 45' Burke's Garden, VA (1986); 55' × 10'2 × 52' Norwalk, CT (1987); 44' × 15'3" × 49' Bedford, NH (1993); 43' × 7'1" × 95' Aquasco, MD (1990); 40' × 14'7" × 89' Lyman, ME (1968).

M. 'Donald Wyman'

A chance seedling that arose <1950 at the Arnold Arboretum. Named in 1970, after Donald Wyman (1904–1993), the arboretum horticulturist from 1936 to 1970. Very common. Carmine buds open to white flowers 1¾" wide, appearing quite like those of *M. baccata*. Essentially hairless parts. A great crop of ½" long red fruit persists well. Although some fruit is a bit big for typical *M. baccata*, the cultivar in most respects fits the description; the leaves are broader, and bluntly toothed. Good disease resistance; very little scab.

M. 'Dorothea'

A chance seedling that arose at the Arnold Arboretum. It first flowered in 1943. Named after Donald Wyman's older daughter. Introduced in 1948. Very common previously, now seldom sold. Parentage claimed to be M. Halliana 'Parkmanii' × M. arnoldiana. Very like *Malus* × *Scheideckeri*. Deep carmine buds open to 1⅘"–2" wide, double, pink flowers, with 10–16 (19) petals; sepals deep red, scarcely hairy; stems hairy. Leaves narrow, finely and sharply toothed. Fruit sparse, hairy, green becoming yellow, sometimes with a pink blush; ½"–⅝" wide; calyx stays or drops; stem to 2¹⁄₁₆" long. Poor disease resistance; scabby. A small tree, 12'–15' (25') tall and as wide or wider, of open habit. Record: 17' × 3'4" × 27' Tacoma, WA (1993).

M. 'Dorothy Rowe'

A 1955 seedling of *M. spectabilis* 'Riversii'; first flowered in 1962. In 1964 named after D.S. Rowe of Cincinnati, OH. Very rare; not in commerce. Flowers white to creamy-white, single to semi-double, with many yellow anthers. Fruit glossy, bright red, 1".

M. 'Doubloons' PP 7216 (1990)

M. 'Spring Song' × (*M.* 'Dorothea' × *M.* 'Wintergold')

Bred by the late Father J.L. Fiala of Falconskeape, near Medina, OH. Named in 1968, registered in 1987, introduced in 1988 by Schmidt nursery of Boring, OR. A refined, rounded 11' tall and wide tree, bushy at first. Bright red buds open relatively late in spring to white, double (10–15 petals) flowers, 1¼"–1½" wide. Fruit ⁷⁄₁₆"–⅝"; roundish; yellow-gold turning deeper gold or beige, or yellow with butterscotch blush; calyx drops. Twigs purple. Leaves dark, heavy-textured, like those 'Red Delicious' APPLE, but strong shoots bear some lobed leaves.

M. 'Dr. van Fleet'

Origin not known. Introduced ≤1939. Commercially extinct for decades. Apparently more than one clone was sold under this name. D. Wyman reported in 1943 that specimens purchased by several sources were actually *M.* × *purpurea*. Nurseryman Paul Wohlert said it appears to be a type of APPLE, but dilatory in production of flowers and fruit. Probably named after Dr. Walter Van Fleet (1857–1922) of the USDA, "A plantsman with wide and varied interests."

M. 'Echter Meyer'—see *M.* 'Echtermeyer'

M. 'Echtermeyer'

('Echtermayer')
= *M.* 'Oekonomierat Echtermeyer'
= *M.* 'Echter Meyer'
= *M.* 'Hugo Echtermeyer'
= *M.* × *purpurea* 'Pendula'
= *M.* *sylvestris* 'Niedzwetzkyana Pendula'
= *M.* × *gloriosa* 'Oekonomierat Echtermeyer'
= *M.* 'Pink Weeper'
= *M.* 'Crimson Weeper'
= *M.* 'Russel's Crimson Weeper'

WEEPING PURPLE CRABAPPLE. Introduced in 1914 by Späth nursery of Germany. Origin disputed. Most likely *M.* *Sieversii* 'Niedzwetzkyana' × *M.* 'Exzellenz Thiel'. This many-named ROSYBLOOM CRABAPPLE has been, and is, very common. But it is scabby and it is finally giving way to newer healthier cultivars. Flowers purplish-red fading to washed-out pink. Habit more weepy than *M.* 'Red Jade'. Leaves purplish in spring, dark green by late summer. Fruit ¾"–1¼" long, purplish-red, oblong, sparse to abundant; calyx stays; flavor ok. Records: 24' × 1'10" × 19' Walla Walla, WA (1993); 12' × 2'11¼" × 24' Spokane, WA (1992).

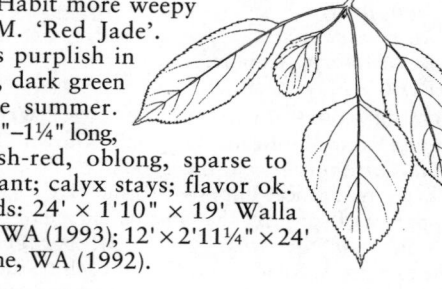

M. 'Edna Mullins'

= *M.* 'White Weeper'

A chance seedling of a "Japanese Flowering Crabapple." Selected in the late 1940s, and named 'White Weeper' at Weston nursery of Hopkinton, MA. Renamed 'Edna Mullins' in 1973 (after the nursery's recptionist since 1951). Sold by several large wholesale nurseries. From catalog descriptions it appears similar to *M.* 'Blanche Ames'.

M. 'Egret'

(*M.* 'Van Eseltine' × *M.* 'Serenade') × (*M.* *Zumi* #768 × *M.* 'Red Jade')

Bred by the late Father J.L. Fiala of Falconskeape, near Medina, OH. Registered ≤1983; in commerce. Very small 6' tall tree with fine, long, weeping branches. Deep pink buds open to pinkish-white semi-double to double flowers. Leaves long, narrow, heavily-textured. Fruit round, red, to ⅜". "The only known weeper to make double flowers."

M. 'E.H. Wilson'

Named after Ernest Henry Wilson (1876–1930), world-famous plantsman. Introduced <1931 by William Sim nursery of Cliftondale, MA. Extremely rare; no longer in commerce. Carmine to rose-pink buds open to white flowers, 1¾"–1⅞" wide. Fruit orange and red to red, 1"–1³⁄₁₆". Poor disease resistance.

M. 'Eleanor Adams'

Introduced ≤1991 by Jewell nursery of Lake City, MN. Very rare. Origin and description not known.

M. × *Eleyi* (Bean) Hesse

= *M.* 'Jay Darling'
= *M.* × *purpurea* 'Eleyi'
= *M. sylvestris* 'Eleyi'
= *M. floribunda atropurpurea* hort. (cf. *M.* × *purpurea*)
= *M. cerasifera atropurpurea* hort.
= *M. atropurpurea* hort.
= *Pyrus × Eleyi* Bean

ELEY CRABAPPLE. JAY DARLING CRABAPPLE. Very common. History confusing. Originally known ≤1904 as *Malus atropurpurea* at the Croux & Fils nursery of Châtenay, France. Imported to the U.S. <1915. An apparent offspring of the same parentage (reportedly *M. Sieversii* 'Niedzwetzkyana' × *M. spectabilis*—yet the experts A. Rehder and G. Van Eseltine thought it doubtful *M. spectabilis* was involved) arose independently, sometime between 1900 and 1914 in East Bergholt Place, Suffolk, England, and was named for the owner, Charles Eley (1872–1960). This latter tree was described officially in 1920 as *M.* × *Eleyi*, and soon after was introduced commercially by Notcutt nursery of England. The Arnold Arboretum introduced *M.* × *Eleyi* to the U.S. in 1921. The French strain was named *Malus* 'Jay Darling' in 1943 by Arie den Boer, after an Iowan of that name (1876–1962; conservationist, cartoonist, first president of Des Moines Men's Garden Club). Donald Wyman reported in 1955 that it was chiefly sold as *M. pumila Niedzwetzkyana*! A famous and widely planted ROSYBLOOM CRABAPPLE by any name. Dark red-purple buds open to red flowers 1¼"–1¾" wide, on thin stems to 2⅜" long. Fruit deep purple, bewilderingly variable in size and shape; always ½"–1"+ long or wide, and usually retaining the calyx. Most fruits in the U.S. are wider than long and short-stemmed, but on the Pacific Coast the egg-shaped ones with longer stems (to 2⅜"+) predominate. Disease-prone, often looks terrible except when in bloom. An alternate-year bearer. The trunk is characteristically short and burly, with sprouts of reddish leaves. Additional planting is now discouraged. Record: 31' × 5'7" × 45' Longview, WA (1993).

M. 'Elise Rathke'

('Eva Rathke', 'Elisa Rathke', 'Elsie Rathke')
= *M. pumila* 'Pendula'
= *Pyrus Malus* 'Pendula'

A weeping version of an ordinary ORCHARD APPLE, originated ca. 1874 by L.A. Doering (Döring) of Elbing, Germany. Introduced ca. 1885 by nurseryman F. Rathke of Praust (near Danzig), Poland. Officially described in 1884. Introduced to the U.S. by the Arnold Arboretum in 1896. Uncommon; no longer in commerce. Red buds open to pinkish-white flowers, 1¾" wide. Fruit to 2¾", green with a purplish-red cheek; of fair eating quality. More than one clone must go under the name, because some descriptions refer to purplish leaves, others to yellow fruit. The clone is usually topgrafted.

M. 'Ellen Gerhart'

(*M. Zumi* 'Calocarpa' × *M.* 'Van Eseltine')
= *M.* Simpson 14-13

Bred and introduced by Simpson nursery of Vincennes, IN. Named for an employee who helped with the original 1953–54 crosses and resultant seedlings. First flowered in 1958. Uncommon. Habit very broad, almost weeping. Flowers pale pink, single or semi-double. Foliage green; fall color attractive. Fruit ½"–⅝", glossy bright red, persistent; somewhat flattened, with distinctive conelike prominent calyx scar of rusty or golden color. Disease resistance poor.

M. 'Ellwangeriana'

= *M. floribunda Ellwangeriana* hort.

Closely related to, if not a hybrid of *M.* × *floribunda*. Likely named after nurseryman George Ellwanger (1816–1906), but it is unlisted in available catalogs of the old Ellwanger & Barry nursery of Rochester, NY. In commerce ≤1941. Extremely rare; no longer in commerce. Pink buds open to white flowers. Fruit ½"–⅝"; bright red. An alternate-year bearer. Fair disease resistance.

M. 'Elsie Rathke'—see *M.* 'Elise Rathke'

M. 'Erie'

An open-pollinated seedling of *M. Sieversii* 'Niedzwetzkyana'. Raised in 1920 by I. Preston of Ottawa's Dominion agricultural experiment station. One of the original ROSYBLOOM CRABAPPLES. Selected in 1930 and named for Lake Erie. Little known; extremely rare. Purplish-red buds open to rosy-pink to lavender flowers, with pale lavender claws, 1⅔"–2" wide. Fruit dark red to orange, 1"; an alternate-year bearer.

M. 'Eva Rathke'—see *M.* 'Elise Rathke'

M. 'Evelyn'

= *M. ioensis* 'Purpurea'
= *M. ioensis* 'Red Leaf'
= *M. ioensis* 'Seedling Red No. 1'
= *M.* × *denBoerii* Krüss. (*M. ioensis* × ?*M. purpurea*)

A chance *M. ioensis* seedling of Arie den Boer of Des Moines, IA. Selected in 1939. Named in 1953 (after the wife of Arie's son John), but had been introduced previously as *M. ioensis* 'Seedling Red No. 1'. Uncommon. Flowers gorgeous bright rose, suggesting *M. Sieversii* 'Niedzwetzkyana' affinity, with short stems (<1"), and a very white wooly calyx tube; sweet smelling, 1"–1¾" wide; appearing before those of purebred *M. ioensis* trees. Leaves blunt, light reddish-purple at first, greening in maturity, very hairy; fall color superb orange. Tree can be gawky, to 35' tall. Fruit 1"–1⅜" wide, of little or no beauty: hard, lightly white-hairy, yellow-green, red-blushed, with numerous pale brown minute specks; calyx persists. Stem to 1⅛" long. Pulp white, juicy, amazingly sour and puckery—useful for jelly. Fruit drops in October.

M. 'Evereste'

Introduced ≤1980 in Europe. Extremely rare in North America but in commerce here ≤1987, and very promising. Red buds open to white flowers, 2" wide. Leaves dark green, heavy like those of *M. × domestica* (ORCHARD APPLE). Fruit profuse, cherry size (less than 1" wide); yellow becoming orange or red; calyx stays and becomes fleshy, or drops away, leaving a pit; flavor acceptable. Tree small and conical.

M. Excalibur™

= *M.* 'Excazam'

Introduced in 1991 by Lake County nursery of Perry, OH. Uncommon. A dwarf tree to 10' tall and 8' wide with upright dense habit; branches heavily spurred. Flowers white. Leaf green, deeply lobed. Fruit ¼", light gold in fall.

M. 'Excazam'—see M. Excalibur™

M. 'Exzellenz Thiel'

= *M. Thiel* hort.
= *M. floribunda* 'Excellence Thiel'
= *M. × Scheideckeri* 'Excellenz Thiel'
= *M. × gloriosa* 'Excellence Thiel'
(?= *M. floribunda × M. prunifolia* 'Pendula')

THIEL CRABAPPLE. Introduced in 1909 by Späth nursery of Germany. Introduced to the U.S. by the Arnold Arboretum in 1912. Comparatively seldom grown in North America. Red buds open to soft rose flowers which fade to white, 1¾" wide, sometimes semi-double. Fruit ½"–¾"; yellow, red-cheeked, angular; calyx drops. An alternate-year bearer. A dainty, small weeping tree, often topgrafted.

M. 'Ferrill's Crimson'

Introduced <1953 by Ferrill's nursery of Salem, OR. A ROSYBLOOM CRABAPPLE much grown in the 1960s by Oregon nurseries; since then extinct commercially. Flowers darkest red, like those of *Malus* 'Royalty', 'Profusion' and 'Liset' but later, fewer, larger, with more prominent bright white centers. Leaves wide, dark, and sharply toothed. Trees gaunt, sparse. Bark pale, peeling off in thin, large flakes. By late August the foliage is tinged dingy brown, rusty looking; it resembles *M.* 'Irene' strongly. Fruit few, ⅝"–¾" (1¼") long, narrow, very dark red, bloomy, not noticeable, stems to 1⁹⁄₁₆" long, the latter less hairy than those of *M.* 'Purple Wave'. Fruit falls in late September; fair to good flavor.

M. 'Fiore's Improved'—see M. ioensis 'Fiore's Improved'

M. 'Firedance'

(*M. Zumi* 'Woosteri' × *M.* 'Red Jade') × *M.* 'Molten Lava'

Bred by the late Father J.L. Fiala of Falconskeape, near Medina, OH. Registered ≤1983. Not yet in commerce. A graceful weeping 5' dwarf tree, heavily-branched. Red buds open to white flowers. Fruit bright red.

M. 'Flame'

= *M.* Minnesota 635

A chance seedling from the Minnesota Fruit Breeding Farm, selected in 1920, introduced in 1934. Common. Pink buds open to white flowers 1½" wide. Fruit to ¾"–⅘" long, deep red on sunny side, yellowish on shaded side; hairy; calyx persistent; pulp well flavored; stem to ⅝" long, hairy. Tree to 25' tall. Poor disease resistance; scabby.

M. flexilis hort.

Eastern and midwestern U.S. nurseries sold this from at least 1888 until 1940. Today nobody seems to know whether it is a distinct cultivar or the name is just synonymous with another *Malus*. Flowers "delicate rose-pink," followed by "clusters of beautiful small scarlet fruit." Sounds like *M. Halliana*. J.L. Fiala says it is similar to *M. baccata* 'Gracilis' but larger. It is not in commerce but can be seen in some botanic gardens and arboreta.

M. 'Florence'

= *M.* 'Stark Florence'

Originated ca. 1886 at the Minnesota Fruit Breeding Farm. Introduced ≤1903 by Stark nursery of Louisiana, MO. Almost extinct commercially. Pink buds open to white flowers 1½" wide. Fruit yellow-white with a pinkish-red blush, 1½–2". Grown for its handsome fruit, excellent for jelly.

M. florentina (Zucc.) Schneid.

= *M. cratægifolia* (Savi) Koehne
= × *Malosorbus florentina* (Zucc.) Browicz
= *Pyrus cratægifolia* Savi
= *Pyrus florentina* (Zucc.) O. Targ.-Tozz.
= *Eriolobus florentina* (Zucc.) Stapf
= *Cratægus florentina* Zucc.

HAWTHORN-LEAF CRABAPPLE (also applied to *M. transitoria*). ITALIAN CRABAPPLE. BALKAN CRABAPPLE. From Italy, the Balkan Peninsula, and north Turkey. Some have said this is a hybrid: *Malus sylvestris* × *Sorbus torminalis*. Named in 1809. Introduced to cultivation in Germany in 1853; to North America ca. 1897. Extremely rare; sold by Kohankie nursery of Ohio in the late 1930s and the '40s. Not as hardy as most CRABAPPLES. Later to bloom than most CRABAPPLES (in May). While most are in bloom, this still has erect densely fuzzy buds tipped by white sepals that sparkle against neatly scalloped little leaves, giving an attractive silvery aspect. In full bloom it looks like a HAWTHORN (*Cratægus*). Pale pink buds open to white flowers, ⅝"–1⅜" wide. By late August and early September, the trees give a HAWTHORN aspect—profuse pea-size fruit against small, jaggedly-lobed leaves (to 4" long). Fruit lightly hairy; has a strong red side facing the sun, otherwise is green—very sun-responsive; the calyx drops away leaving a hole. Scab-free, very healthy and fruitful. Adequate to pleasant fall color in October. Fruit turns brown, soft and rotten in late October, is totally gone by early November. The best of the five specimens in Seattle is full of lipstick-red fruit and quite lovely in October. A tree at Aurora, OR, can remain green into mid-November. CRABAPPLE expert L. Nichols found this species' disease resistance poor, especially as regards fireblight. Record: 23' × 1'8" Seattle, WA (1994; *pl.* 1972).

M. × floribunda Sieb. ex van Houtte

= *M. pulcherrima* (Asch. & Graebn.) K.R. Boynt.
= *Pyrus floribunda* Sieb. *ex* Kirchn., non Lindl.
= *Pyrus pulcherrima* Asch. & Graebn.

JAPANESE CRABAPPLE. SHOWY CRABAPPLE. From Japan; not known wild. Three different suggested parentages are *M. baccata* × *M. Sieboldii* (Zabel); *M. baccata* × *M. micromalus* (Wenzig); *M. prunifolia* × *M. Sieboldii* (Schneider). The name *floribunda* means producing abundant flowers; from Latin *flori*-, a flower, and *abundus*, to over-flow, to abound in. Introduced to Holland <1856 by Siebold. Sent to the U.S. in 1862. Very common and familiar. Tree rounded or wider than tall. Red buds open to profuse pink flowers which fade to white, 1"–1½" wide. Fruit ¼"–½" wide or long, yellowish with a reddish blush; usually not showy or abundant. Good disease resistance. Records: 39' × 5'9" Horsham Park, Sussex, England (1982); 33' × 4'8" × 44' Seattle, WA (1993); 28' × 6'1" × 53' Hartford, CT (1988).

M. floribunda var. *arnoldiana*—see *M. × arnoldiana*

M. floribunda atropurpurea—see *M. × Eleyi* and *M. × purpurea*

M. floribunda var. *atrosanguinea*—see *M. × atrosanguinea*

M. floribunda var. *brevipes*—see *M. brevipes*

M. floribunda 'Camille'—see *M.* 'Camille'

M. floribunda Ellwangeriana—see *M.* 'Ellwangeriana'

M. floribunda 'Excellence Thiel'—see *M.* 'Exzellenz Thiel'

M. floribunda 'Flore Pleno'—see *M. Halliana* 'Parkmanii'

M. floribunda 'Hillieri'—see *M. × Scheideckeri* 'Hillieri'

M. floribunda 'Lemoinei'—see *M. × purpurea* 'Lemoinei'

M. floribunda purpurea—see *M. × purpurea*

M. × floribunda 'Rosea'

Introduced ≤1991 by Millane nursery of Connecticut. Said to differ from typical *M. × floribunda* in being more compact, with pinker flowers.

M. × *floribunda* 'Snowbank'
= *M.* 'Snowbank'
= *M.* × *Zumi* 'Snowbank'

Introduced <1928 by Wohlert nursery of Narberth, PA. Very rare; commercially extinct for decades. Raised from an open-pollinated *M.* × *floribunda*. Pink buds open to white flowers, 1³⁄₁₆" wide. Fruit yellow, ⁷⁄₁₆". An alternate-year bearer. Apparently this clone has been associated with nurseryman Harlan Page Kelsey (1872–1959) of Salem, MA. But it should not be confused with *Malus* 'Kelsey'.

M. *floribunda* var. *spontanea*—see M. *Halliana* var. *spontanea*

M. Fox Fire™
= *M.* 'Fozam'

Introduced ≤1990 by Lake County nursery of Perry, OH. Tree 15' tall and at least as wide; broad and spreading. Bark dark charcoal-gray. Leaves dark green. Pink buds open to snow white flowers. Fruit ½", fiery red with a gold beak.

M. 'Fozam'—see M. Fox Fire™

M. 'Franz Lipp'
Originated (or introduced) ca. 1960 by Matt Tures' Sons nursery of Huntley, IL. Named after a Chicago landscape architect. Still in commerce. Attributes not known.

M. 'Frau Luise Dittmann'—see M. *spectabilis*

M. 'Freeman'
= *M. Freemanii* hort.

Presumably originated by (or at any rate named after) Oliver M. Freeman at the U.S. National Arboretum. Introduced ≤1993–94 by Arborvillage nursery of Holt, MO: "large-growing; striking purple foliage."

M. *fusca* (Raf.) Schneid.
= *M. rivularis* (Dougl. *ex* Hook.) Roem.
= *M. diversifolia* (Bong.) Roem.
= *Pyrus diversifolia* Bong.
= *Pyrus fusca* Raf.

OREGON CRABAPPLE. PACIFIC CRABAPPLE. WESTERN CRABAPPLE. From S Alaska to N California. More closely related to the SIBERIAN CRABAPPLE (*M. baccata*) than to the other North American *Malus* species. Named in 1830 (Latin *fuscus*, dusky or brownish). Introduced to England between 1831 and 1836 by D. Douglas; introduced to the Arnold Arboretum in 1882. In commerce ≤1931. Extremely rare. The trees are pretty in bloom, like an ORCHARD APPLE, but bear smaller flowers (¾"–⅞" wide, with white-downy parts), and ornamentally boring fruit (small, yellowish-brown), and their sometimes blazing orange and scarlet fall color is erratic from tree to tree and year to year. Someone should propagate a clone that demonstrates consistently superior fall color. Remarkably slender in twig and branch. Leaves vary from unlobed to obviously lobed. Fruit usually ≤½" long (den Boer: some trees make round or nearly round fruit), bloomy yellow-brown; pulp crisp, juicy and sour to the highest degree. Hard at first, soon the fruit turns soft and brown. Records: 79' × 5'5" × 47' Nisqually Wildlife Refuge, WA (1988); 45' × 5'11½" × 63½' Seattle, WA (1995); 42' × 8'7" × 43' Vancouver Island, B.C. (1991). *M.* × *Dawsoniana* is the hybrid of *M. fusca* with ORCHARD APPLE.

M. 'Garnet' (cf. M. 'Gemstone')
A seedling of *M.* 'Yellow Siberian' raised in Valley River, Manitoba, by nurseryman W.J. Boughen. Introduced in 1930. Still sold by Boughen at least into the 1940s. Now extremely rare. Grown for fruit rather than ornament. Fruit to 2", dark red (hence the name "garnet"); holds late on tree; prolific. Tree very cold-hardy.

M. 'Garry'
= *M.* 'MR 455' (i.e., "Morden Rosybloom No. 455")

A ROSYBLOOM CRABAPPLE raised at Morden research station of Manitoba. First flowered in 1935. Named after 1945. Introduced commercially 1962. Rare; scarcely ever sold since 1974. Tree sturdy of trunk, graceful of branching, upright, to 20' or more. Maroon buds open to deep rose-red flowers, 1½"–1⅝" wide, sepals remarkably long. Leaves broad, reddish and hairy only when unfolding, maturing essentially hairless, dark green, with red veins. Fruit dark purple, bloomy, finally cherry-red, roundish, ⅝"–⅞"; calyx persists prominently; pulp yellowish, stained pink, of poor flavor; stems to 1¾" long, dark purple. Overall the tree is a poor substitute for *M.* 'Hopa' in that it has less lively flowers, lacks the clean willowy leaves and splendid fruit, and is an alternate bearer.

M. 'Gemstone'
= M. 'Garnet' (in part)
(M. Zumi 'Wooseri' × M. Zumi Christmas Holly™)

Bred by the late Father J.L. Fiala of Falconskeape, near Medina, OH. Registered ≤1983—it should not have been granted rights to the name 'Garnet' and was later renamed 'Gemstone'. Not yet in commerce. A small tree, to 8' tall. Deep carmine-red buds open to blush white flowers. Leaves very narrow, dark green. Fruit very glossy, deep garnet red, ¼", long firm and persisting.

M. 'Geneva'

An open-pollinated seedling of M. Sieversii 'Niedzwetzkyana'. Raised in 1920 by I. Preston of Ottawa's Dominion agricultural experiment station. One of the original ROSYBLOOM CRABAPPLES. Selected in 1930 and named for Geneva Lake of Ontario. Selected ca. 1928. Introduced commercially in 1930. Rare. Still sparingly sold. Pink buds open to white flowers. Fruit red, ornamental, of fair eating quality; 2". Tree hardy but of poor disease resistance. (Malus 'Van Eseltine' was originally introduced under this name in 1941.)

M. 'Gibbs' Golden Gage'
= M. 'Golden Gage'

A chance seedling from the garden of the Hon. Vicary Gibbs (1853–1932) at Aldenham, Hertfordshire, England. Introduced in 1923; introduced to North America in 1925. Very rare. Pink buds open to white flowers. Fruit yellow, 1' thick, waxy, almost translucent, abundant, persistent all winter. Excellent disease resistance.

M. glabrata—see M. coronaria

M. 'Gladwyne'
(M. angustifolia × M. ioensis 'Plena')

An intentional cross made in 1939 by Mrs. Norman J. Henry of Gladwyne, PA. Not introduced commercially, or has been to a minor degree. Flowers double, sweetly fragrant. See Malus 'Prince Georges' for a clone of the same parentage.

M. glaucescens—see M. coronaria

M. 'Glen Mills'—see M. × Zumi Winter Gem™

M. × gloriosa Lemoine
= M. hybrida var. gloriosa Lemoine
(M. Sieversii 'Niedzwetzkyana' × M. Scheideckeri)

Introduced in 1931 by Lemoine nursery of Nancy, France. In 1936 the Arnold Arboretum introduced it to North America. Uncommon; no longer in commerce. Flowers 1⅔" wide, light purple-red; few. Foliage bronze-red. Fruit ca. 1¼" wide, bright red.

M. × gloriosa 'Excellence Thiel'—see M. 'Exzellenz Thiel'

M. × gloriosa 'Oekonomierat Echtermeyer'— see M. 'Echtermeyer'

M. 'Goi Toi'—see M. Halliana 'Parkmanii'

M. 'Golden Beauty'—see M. 'Yellow Siberian'

M. 'Golden Dream'
(M. 'Wintergold' × M. Zumi 'Wooseri')

Bred by the late Father J.L. Fiala of Falconskeape, near Medina, OH. Named in 1960; registered in 1987. Not yet in commerce. Habit rounded, 12' tall and wide. Red buds open to white flowers. Fruit bright yellow-gold, round, ¼"–⁷⁄₁₆".

M. 'Golden Gage'—see M. 'Gibbs' Golden Gage'

M. 'Golden Galaxy'
(M. Centurion® × M. 'Gypsy Gold')

Bred by the late Father J.L. Fiala of Falconskeape, near Medina, OH. Named in 1974; registered in 1987. Not yet in commerce. An upright fan-shaped tree to 16'. Pale pink buds open to white flowers. Fruit bright gold, ½".

M. 'Golden Gem'—see M. 'Cheal's Golden Gem'

M. 'Golden Hornet'
= M. × Zumi 'Golden Hornet'

Originated <1949 at Waterer, Son and Crisp nursery of England. Probably a M. × Zumi 'Calocarpa' seedling. Introduced to North America in 1955 by the Arnold Arboretum. Uncommon. Pink buds open to white 1½" flowers in the manner of the M. × robusta group. R.A. de J. Hart finds it the best pollinator for ORCHARD APPLES. Foliage healthy, little or no scab. Fruit the most showy of all: roundish, abundant, yellow, then gold, large (⅝"–1" long, on 1" stems); calyx usually drops away, sometimes stays. An outstanding small tree for winter ornament. Grows to 25' tall.

M. 'Goldfinch'

Parentage not known; likely a *M. baccata* seedling. Raised ca. 1920 from a seed found under an Arnold Arboretum tree by Mrs. Horatio Gates Lloyd of Haverford, PA. Introduced ca. 1953 by Swarthmore College of Pennsylvania. Extremely rare; no longer in commerce. Named for its ⁷⁄₁₆" yellow fruit. Flowers 1⅓" wide, white. Poor disease resistance.

M. 'Goldilocks'

(*M.* 'Tetragold' × *M.* 'Coral Cascade')

Bred by the late Father J.L. Fiala of Falconskeape, near Medina, OH. Named in 1976, registered in 1987. Not yet in commerce. A refined semi-weeper 15' tall and wide. Red buds open to white flowers. Fruit ¼"–⁷⁄₁₆"; golden-copper.

M. 'Gorgeous'

Raised <1925 by H.R. Wright of Avondale, Auckland, New Zealand. Reportedly *M. Sieboldii* × *M. Halliana*. Such parentage seems highly unlikely; more likely the tree is a *M. prunifolia*. In North America ≤1925. Very rare. Rose-pink buds open to white or pale pink-blushed flowers, 1"–1¼" wide. Fruit profuse, bright crimson red, with orange-red undersides, shiny, ¾"–1⅛" long; stems ⅝"–1³⁄₁₆" long; calyx persists; pulp yellow, delicious. Highly ornamental. A small if not dwarf tree, rarely more than 12'–15' tall. Leaf PLUM-like, to 4⅞" × 2⅜", hairless. This cultivar has partly been distributed as *Malus* 'Striped Beauty'.

M. 'Guiding Star'

= *M.* den Boer Seedling 54-1

Discovered by A. den Boer of Des Moines, IA; introduced by Wayside nursery in 1963. Uncommon. Tree quite narrow, conical. Rose-pink buds open to pure white flowers, fragrant, double (14–18 petals), 2"–2¼" wide. Fruit ⅝", yellow with a red blush. Fair disease resistance.

M. Guinevere® PP 7773 (1992)

= *M.* 'Guinzam'

Introduced in 1991 by Lake County nursery of Perry, OH. Grown by several major nurseries. A rounded genetic dwarf 10' tall and wide. Flowers mauve and white. Extremely dark "midnight green" foliage has a distinctive "deep wine frost." Fruit ¼"–½", bright red and persistent in fall.

M. 'Guinzan'—see M. Guinevere®

M. 'Gwendolyn'

A *Malus* × *floribunda* seedling raised in 1936 by A. den Boer of Des Moines, IA. Introduced in 1944. Very rare. Named after Mrs. Keith (Gwendolyn) Tobin of Des Moines, IA—where the tree was. Flowers 1½" wide, pink. Fruit red, 1", profuse. Disease resistant.

M. Halliana Koehne

= *Pyrus Halliana* hort. *ex* Sarg.

HALL CRABAPPLE. Not known in the wild, but originated in China. Cultivated and called *Kaido* or *Hanakaido* in Japan. Dr. George Rogers Hall (1820–1899) introduced it and many other Japanese plants to the U.S. in 1861–62. Very rare in cultivation here. E. Wilson called this species the PINK PEARL OF THE ORIENT. Shrubby and small, of remarkable beauty, yet comparatively cold-tender. Leaves dark, narrow, hairless. Carmine buds open to bright shell pink flowers, 1"–1½" wide; petals pink and narrow; styles 3–5, of average length—not sticking out; not obviously hairy at base; flowerstems red, hairless, to 1⅝" (2⅛") long. Young growth tinted red. The one drawback is its fruit: neither abundant nor showy, just roundish, hard, late-ripening yellow-red or purplish pea-sized things about ⅓" wide. Stays leafy and green late, into November; fall color red and burgundy. Record: In March 1925, J. Rock reported seeing one 29½' tall in W Szechuan, bearing rich pink flowers 1³⁄₁₆"–1⅔" wide, with 3 styles.

M. Halliana atrosanguinea—see M. × atrosanguinea

M. Halliana 'Parkmanii'

= *M. floribunda* 'Flore Pleno'
= *M. Parkmanii* hort.
= *Pyrus Parkmanii* hort.

PARKMAN CRABAPPLE. Not known in the wild in Japan; called *Yae-kaido*. Introduced from Japan to the U.S. in 1861. Very common until the 1980s. Named after historian Francis Parkman (1823–1893). Except for bearing mixed single and semi-double flowers, much like typical *M. Halliana*. Shrubby or a small tree; slow-growing. Flowers semi-double (5–16 petals), clear deep pink, 1¼"–1¾" wide, on very long (to 2³⁄₁₆"), blood-red, wire-like stems. Leaves dark, leathery, narrow, glossy, hairless, with short, winged reddish stems. Fruit sparse, to ⁵⁄₁₆" wide, red, dark purple on sunny side, green on shady side, on long slender stems. Still green and leafy into November. B.O. Case nursery of Vancouver, WA, sold it as 'Goi Toi' which means "The tears of the dragon." Fair to good disease resistance; some mislabeled specimens in CRABAPPLE disease trials have given it a bad rap. Record: 22' × 2'2" × 26' Seattle, WA (1993).

M. *Halliana* var. *spontanea* (Mak.) Koidz.

= M. *spontanea* (Mak.) Mak.
= M. *floribunda* var. *spontanea* Mak.

Wild on Mt. Kirishima in Kyushu, Japan. Introduced to North America in 1919 by the Arnold Arboretum. Exceedingly rare. Pink buds open to white flowers, smaller (1³⁄₁₆" wide) than those of typical M. *Halliana*, the calyx and stem less deeply colored, the stem shorter. Blooms in mid-May rather than mid-April as does typical M. *Halliana*. Leaves only 1³⁄₁₆"–1²⁄₃" long. Fruit red, shiny, profuse. An alternate-year bearer. Habit vase-shaped and wider than tall, very dwarf and twiggy.

M. Hamlet®

= M. 'Hamzam'

Introduced in 1991 by Lake County nursery of Perry, OH. A rounded dwarf to 10' tall and wide. Deep scarlet buds open to rosy pink, fragrant flowers. Leaf green with a wine-red overcast. Fruit ¼"–½", bright red in fall.

M. 'Hamzam'—see M. Hamlet®

M. 'Hansen's Red Leaf Crab'—see M. 'Hopa'

M. 'Hargozam'—see M. Harvest Gold®

M. × *Hartwigii* Koehne

= *Pyrus* × *Hartwigii* hort.
(M. *baccata* × M. *Halliana*)

Originated in Germany, <1906. Possibly named after August Karl Julius Hartwig (1823–1913), German horticulturist. G. Krüssmann says it was introduced in 1906 by Karl Gustav Hartwig of Lübeck, Germany, but the precise origin is not known. Extremely rare in North America. Pink buds open to white, early, scab-prone flowers; single or semi-double, 5–15 petals; 1½" (2" says Hillier) wide, in clusters of as many as 8. Flowerstems hairless, to 1⅝" long; calyx tube lightly hairy on the outside and clearly so inside. Fruit sparse, red or purplish-red, ½"–⅗" wide, with a large scar where the calyx was. Trees vigorous. Poor disease resistance. Record: 35' × 3'0" × 27½' Seattle, WA (1994; *pl.* 1955).

M. × *Hartwigii* 'Katherine'

= M. 'Katherine'

A chance seedling found ca. 1928 by B.H. Slavin, in Durand-Eastman Park of Rochester, NY. Named (for his daughter-in-law Katherine Clark Slavin) and distributed in 1943 by the Arnold Arboretum. Common. Profuse pink buds open to light pink flowers, fading to white; large (to 2⅛" wide), double (20–26 petals), with narrow petals. Compared to M. 'Blanche Ames' it has earlier, larger, fewer flowers with more petals. Leaves narrow, hairless, finely and sharply toothed. Few fruit set: ⅓" wide, yellow, sometimes with a tawny reddish blush, hard and somewhat shiny, faintly ribbed, with a big calyx scar, on stems to 1⅝" long. An alternate-year bearer. A small, weak, dense tree, rarely more than 12' tall. Somewhat scabby. Records: 24' × 1'7" × 24' Puyallup, WA (1993); 21½' × 1'10" × 24' Seattle, WA (1994; *pl.* 1948).

M. Harvest Gold®

= M. 'Hargozam'

Introduced ≤1984 by Lake County nursery of Perry, OH. Common. A vigorous upright tree to 20' tall and 15' wide, of excellent street-tree form. Salt tolerant. Pink buds open to white flowers. Leaf dark green, often lobed. Fruit ⅜"–⁷⁄₁₆"; greenish-yellow to golden-yellow and persisting until mid-December. Excellent disease resistance except for scab.

M. 'Helen'

A *Malus* × *Eleyi* seedling raised ca. 1939 by A. den Boer of Des Moines, IA. Named in 1951. Very rare; commercially extinct. Flowers 1½"–2" wide, purple. Leaf narrow, of a peculiarly bright red color. Shrubby, with horizontal twigs. Fruit ½"–¾" wide, purple-red.

M. 'Henningi'

Originated <1975 at Enterprise nursery of Wrightsville, PA. Introduced in the 1980s by Schmidt nursery of Boring, OR. Tree upright spreading 25' tall and wide. Leaves shiny, green. Flowers white. Fruit orange-red, ⅝". High disease resistance.

M. 'Henrietta Crosby'

= M. AA No. 19039
(M. *arnoldiana* × M. *Sieversii* 'Niedzwetzkyana')

Originated as an Arnold Arboretum intentional cross in 1939; introduced in 1947. Named in 1955 for Mrs. S.V.R. Crosby (b. 1872) of Manchester, MA, long a member of the Arnold Arboretum Visiting Committee. Uncommon; may be commercially extinct. A ROSYBLOOM CRABAPPLE. Flowers deep magenta, fading to pink; look like those of *M. × Eleyi* but the petals are a bit darker. The leaves are narrower, less hairy; leaf teeth sharp. Fruit profuse, roundish but usually longer, ≤1⅛"; dark red, bloomy; calyx nippled; skin with indented dots; pulp bright pink, harsh tasting. A dwarf tree.

M. 'Henry F. DuPont'

Raised at the Arnold Arboretum. Exact parentage variously reported as 1) from an open-pollinated seedling of the hybrid *M. arnoldiana × M. Eleyi*; 2) raised as a 1946 seedling of *M.* 'Henrietta Crosby'. Named in 1955 for Henry F. DuPont (1880–1969) of Winterthur, DE, long a member of the Arnold Arboretum Visiting Committee. Introduced in 1956. Rare; primarily in botanic gardens and arboreta. A ROSYBLOOM CRABAPPLE. Flowers first reddish-purple, then pink, fading to nearly lavender; large (1⅔" wide); profuse. Some flowers have more than 5 petals. Young leaves red, soon turn green. Since the leaves are green, the abundant deep red, bloomy fruits show up well in mid-September. Fruit ½"–⅝" long, waxy, bright if rubbed — like those of *M.* 'Vanguard' but warped. Disease resistance poor to fair. Record: 27½' × 1'9" × 29½' Seattle, WA (1994; *pl.* 1956).

M. 'Henry Kohankie'

Said to have originated from seed of *Malus Sieboldii* received from Japan between 1933 and 1938. Almost certainly a *Malus × robusta*. Raised at Henry Kohankie & Son nursery of Painesville, OH. Named after Henry J. Kohankie (1887–1979). Registered in 1965. Uncommon. Pink buds open to white flowers 1⅓"–1⅞" (in the manner of the *Malus × robusta* group). Fruit edible, late ripening (*i.e.*, late October) carmine-red and green-yellow, shiny, 'Dolgo'-like, to 1½" long on 1¼" long hairy stems; calyx persists. Tree rounded, 20' tall and wide. Good to excellent disease resistance.

M. × *heterophylla* Spach

= *M. × platycarpa* Rehd.
= *M. coronaria* var. *platycarpa* (Rehd.) Fiala
= *Pyrus × platycarpa* (Rehd.) L.H. Bailey
= *Pyrus heterophylla* Steud., non Reg. & Schmalh.
(*M. coronaria × M. domestica*)

GEORGIA CRABAPPLE. This cross occurs in the wild in eastern North America. It differs from *M. × Soulardii* (*M. ioensis × M. domestica*) chiefly in bearing broader, less hairy leaves and having only slightly hairy flowerstems. The SOUTHERN CRABAPPLE (*M. angustifolia*) tends to bloom too late to easily cross with the ORCHARD APPLE, so rarely produces hybrids. All hybrids of the eastern American native CRABAPPLES and ORCHARD APPLES result in offspring more closely resembling the native species. The 1834 name *heterophylla* is very obscure, and the 1913 *platycarpa* name has been commonly used instead. *Heterophylla* means differently or diversely leaved; from Greek *heteros*, different, and *phyllon*, a leaf. *Platycarpa* is from Greek *platys*, wide or broad, and *karpos*, fruit. These hybrids are almost never offered commercially, especially since the 1940s. Naturally they are variable. The trees can be somewhat thorny. The fruit is usually 1¼"–2⅜" wide. Records: a specimen planted in 1950 in Seattle was 41' × 2'5" in 1994; its pink buds open to very large pink flowers; its fruit are yellow-green with a red blush, waxy, hard, and smell like quinces, to 1¾" wide; stems 1½"–2" long. The leaves are unlobed, and edged with fine, sharp teeth. A tree south of Newark, DE, was 26' × 3'7" (1942).

M. × *heterophylla* 'Hoopesii'

= *M. × platycarpa* 'Hoopesii'

HOOPES' CRABAPPLE. Originated <1876 in a nursery in West Chester, PA. Long commercially extinct. Fruit to 2" wide. Leaves weakly lobed, if at all.

M. × *heterophylla* 'Mathews'

('Matthews'; 'Mathew')
= *M. Matthewi* hort.

Although this tree might have originated with C. Downing <1873, in the 1890s it was named after and popularized by Benton A. Mathews (b. 1840) of Knoxville, IA. Still in commerce but very rare. Flowers pinkish-white, fragrant, 2¼" wide. Leaves very large, APPLE-like, smooth. Fruit yellow-green, 2"–2½" wide, good for jelly. It is an alternate-year bearer. Other trees, including a clone with showy lemon-yellow fruit, have been distributed wrongly under the name 'Mathews'. *M.* 'Kentucky Mammoth' may be a synonym of the real 'Mathews'.

M. 'Hillieri'—see *M. × Scheideckeri* 'Hillieri'

M. Holiday Gold™

= *M.* 'Hozam'

Introduced in 1995 by Lake County nursery of Perry, OH. Pink buds open to pure white, fragrant flowers.

Fruit bright gold. Habit rounded, to 18' tall and 12' wide.

M. 'Hopa'

= M. × *adstringens* of some authors
= M. 'Hansen's Red Leaf Crab'
= M. '(Pink) Sunburst'
= M. 'Starburst' (in part)
(M. *baccata* × M. *Sieversii* 'Niedzwetzkyana')

HOPA CRABAPPLE. From Niels Hansen of South Dakota. Not an intentional cross. Introduced in 1920. *Hopa* means beautiful in the Sioux language. A hardy, extremely popular ROSYBLOOM CRABAPPLE, but disease-prone. Flowers large (1⅝"–1¾" wide), bright purplish-pink; petals spread widely, fade to rosy color; parts hairy; stem to 1⅛" (2") long but usually ¾" or less; sepals ⅜" long, more or less reflexed. Leaves like those of M. *Sieversii* 'Niedzwetzkyana', with teeth blunt except on shoots. Fruit roundish, ¾"–1⅛" long, like tomatoes in their yellow-pink to orange-red color and shape; calyx usually drops but can persist and turn into fleshy bumps. Pulp mealier than that of M. 'Almey' and pinkish, of bearable flavor; good for jelly. By November the fruit are dropped. Fruit stems usually <¾"; to ⅞". Record: 35' × 4'7" × 47' Tacoma, WA (1992).

M. 'Hopa Cutleaf'

Introduced ≤1979 by Baier Lustgarten nursery of Long Island, NY. "A lovely new variety with extremely attractive cut leaves."

M. 'Hozam'—see M. Holiday Gold™

M. 'Huber'—see M. Royal Fountain™

M. 'Hugo Echtermeyer'—see M. 'Echtermeyer'

M. hupehensis (Pamp.) Rehd.

= M. *theifera* Rehd.
= *Pyrus hupehensis* Pamp.
= *Pyrus theifera* (Rehd.) L.H. Bailey

TEA CRABAPPLE. HUPEH CRABAPPLE. From China, Assam, Bhutan. Introduced in 1900 by E. Wilson for Veitch nursery of England; introduced to the U.S. in 1907 by the Arnold Arboretum. Common. Named in 1910, referring to Hupeh province; the synonym *theifera* is from the genus *Thea*, tea, and Latin *ferre*, to bear. E. Wilson reported "in central China, where it is a feature of the thickets and margins of woods on the mountains, the peasants collect and dry the leaves and from them prepare a palatable beverage which they call red tea." Very closely related to M. *Halliana*, less closely to M. *baccata*. Flowers large (2" wide), CHERRY-like, with broad white petals; parts essentially hairless. Flowerstems to 2⅛" long. Blooms relatively late, in mid-May. Fruits shiny, abundant, longstemmed, yellow-red to murky or pleasing red, ⅜"–⅝" long or wide. Foliage healthy and attractive. Leaves reddish when young, becoming shiny, large, wide and spoonlike in shape (or narrowly tapered and not spoonlike—leaf size and shape varies considerably). In general, *Malus hupehensis* is a superior ornamental, especially strong in its dark, glossy leaf character and elongated branching habit. The trunks fork low and branches spread wide—excellent for espaliering. Can be a large shrub. Appearance greatly enhanced by careful pruning. Fair to excellent disease resistance. Records: 56'×7'6" Bodnant, Gwynedd, Wales (1989); 36'×2'10"×36' Seattle, WA (1992); 24'×4'3"×40' Seattle, WA (1992).

M. hupehensis 'Cardinal'—see M. 'Princeton Cardinal'

M. hupehensis 'Cornell'

Name registered in 1988 by Pardon W. Cornell of North Dartmouth, MA. Tree vase-shaped. Disease-resistant. Light pink buds open to pinkish-white, fragrant flowers. Fruit ⁷⁄₁₆", yellowish becoming red.

M. hupehensis f. rosea Rehd.

= M. *theifera* 'Rosea'

ROSE TEA CRABAPPLE. Originated with the original M. *hupehensis* introduction of 1900 to England. Named in 1915. In North American commerce ≤1931. Rare. Apparently this is a natural seedling variant. In China the specimens seen by E. Wilson were described as blooming the color of M. *Halliana* but in a greater profusion. This would be wonderfully beautiful. In 1943, D. Wyman reported that trees called by this name in North America were not true to name, and that the real thing might not exist here at all. In England a clone circulates under the name 'Rosea' and bears pale pink flowers.

M. hupehensis 'Wayne Douglas'

= M. 'Wayne Douglas'

Selected by Polly Hill of Martha's Vineyard, MA, from seeds sown in 1959. Registered in 1977. In commerce. Spreading, gnarled, twisted branches from a short, massive trunk—very picturesque. Fruit slightly larger than that of typical *M. hupehensis.*

M. 'Hyslop'

Origin North American, but the details are lost; it was old and common by 1869. Still in commerce. Grown primarily for its edible fruit. Pink buds open to white flowers. Fruit very brilliant dark red or purplish, thickly bloomed; roundish, 1½". Ripens late in the season. An alternate-year bearer, sometimes annual. Leaves large. Tree very cold-hardy. Often severely hurt by fireblight.

M. *hybrida* var. *gloriosa*—see M. × *gloriosa*

M. 'Ida Cason'—see M. 'Callaway'

M. 'Indian Magic'
= *M.* Simpson 11-63
(*M. Zumi* 'Calocarpa' × *M.* 'Almey')

A seedling raised ca. 1955 at Simpson nursery of Vincennes, IN. First flowered in 1958. Introduced for trial ca. 1969; named in 1975 for an Arabian horse owned by Robert Simpson. Common. Tree broadly rounded, too low and wide for street-tree usage. Red buds open to showy rose-pink flowers 1½" wide. Fruit abundant, ⅝" long, with small calyx scars; glossy red changing to golden-orange, then brown; persisting August through November. Leaf purplish when young, becoming dark green, coarsely toothed, often lobed on shoots. Poor to fair disease resistance.

M. 'Indian Summer'
(*M. Zumi* × *M.* 'Almey')
= *M.* Simpson 11-58

A seedling raised ca. 1955 at Simpson nursery of Vincennes, IN. Sister seedling of *M.* 'Centurion'. Common. Tree to 18' tall and 20' wide; of low, wide, open form. Maroon-red buds open to rose-red flowers. Leaf purplish when young; teeth blunt. Fruit bright red, ½"–¾" long, with small calyx scars; yellow-pink pulp; persistent. Fall leaf color good. Good to excellent disease resistance.

M. 'Inglis'—see M. White Angel®

M. *ioensis* (Wood) Britt.
= *Pyrus ioensis* (Wood) L.H. Bailey
= *M. coronaria* var. *ioensis* Wood

PRAIRIE CRABAPPLE. IOWA CRABAPPLE. WESTERN CRABAPPLE. Named after Iowa, where it was first distinguished in 1860 as a variety (of *M. coronaria*). Seldom grown except in its cultivars. Pink buds open to white, fragrant flowers. Similar to *Malus coronaria*

but with narrower, less lobed, fuzzy leaves, and smaller fruit. Fruit like abundant dull green golfballs. Poor disease resistance. Records: 46' × 3'0" × 48' Oakland County, MI (1991); 27' × 4'6" × 32' Lisle, IL (<1961).

M. *ioensis* Blanco™
= *Pyrus ioensis texana* Blanco™

Introduced <1986 by Lone Star Growers nursery of San Antonio, TX. Flowers ½" wide, white to pink in late spring. Leaves dark green; yellow in fall. Fruit small, greenish-yellow. Tree rounded, to 25' tall. Tolerates alkaline soil.

M. *ioensis* 'Boone Park'

In August 1940, Clyde Heard and A. den Boer of Des Moines, IA, found this tree in the municipal park of Boone, (near Des Moines) IA. In commerce ca. 1955. Extremely rare. Leaf narrower than typical. Rose-red to deep rose-pink buds open to light rose-pink flowers 1⅔" wide. Teeth at base of petal are large and irregular. Fruit dull green to dull yellow-green, 1³⁄₁₆".

M. *ioensis* 'Elk River'
= *M. coronaria* (var. *dasycalyx*) 'Elk River'

A chance seedling found by A.W. Keays in Elk River, MN. It was used by N. Hansen for breeding in South Dakota <1917, and was sold itself ≤1930. Very rare. Three of its hybrid offspring include *Malus* 'Kola', 'Redflesh' and 'Red Tip'. Flowers pink and ornamental. Fruit 1³⁄₁₆" wide, useful for jelly. Tree small, to 10' (18') tall. Very cold-hardy.

M. *ioensis* 'Fimbriata'

FRINGE PETAL CRABAPPLE. Originated by B.H. Slavin, in Rochester, NY; first described and named in 1931. Extremely rare; in botanic gardens and arboreta. Flowers double, deep pink, cupped into heavy bowls; 2" wide if flattened; fragrant; 25–34 petals. Petals fimbriate near the claw. Leaves hairy, relatively narrow, very downy. Fruitless most years, it can make a few green, dotted fruits to 1⅜" wide, sparsely hairy; stem stout, downy, to 1⅜" long. Tree to 25' tall. Differs from BECHTEL CRABAPPLE (*M. ioensis* 'Plena') in having fimbriate petals, a narrower habit with more ascending branches, and in bearing spiny spurs.

M. *ioensis* 'Fiore's Improved'
= *M.* 'Fiore's Improved'

A seedling from Charles Fiore nursery of Prairie View, IL. Introduced <1964. Very rare; commercially extinct. Flowers twice as big as usual *M. ioensis*, occasionally semi-double. Fruit ⅓ larger. Bark very smooth.

M. ioensis 'Flore Plena Nova'—see *M. ioensis* 'Plena Nova'

M. ioensis 'Klehmi'—see *M. coronaria* 'Klehm's Improved Bechtel'

M. ioensis 'Klehm's Bechtel'—see *M. coronaria* 'Klehm's Improved Bechtel'

M. ioensis 'Klehm's Improved Bechtel'—see *M. coronaria* 'Klehm's Improved Bechtel'

M. ioensis 'Klehm's No. 8'—see *M. coronaria* 'Klehm's Improved Bechtel'

M. ioensis 'Nevis'
= *M.* 'Nevis'

An open-pollinated *M. ioensis* seedling from Nevis, MN. Introduced in 1930 by N. Hansen of South Dakota. Extremely rare; no longer in commerce. Dwarf; to 6' tall; suitable for ornamental use except scabby. Flowers pink. Fruit dark green, waxy, 1"–1½" wide.

M. ioensis 'Nova'—see *M. ioensis* 'Plena Nova'

M. ioensis 'Plena'
= *M. coronaria* 'Plena'
= *M.* 'Bechtel'
= *M. angustifolia* 'Flore Pleno' (cf. *M.* 'Prince Georges')
= *Pyrus angustifolia* 'Flore Pleno'

BECHTEL CRABAPPLE. Discovered in an old fence row about 1840. Cultivated since 1888. Named for E.A. Bechtel of Staunton, IL. Until perhaps the 1970s it was the most-planted American CRABAPPLE. Its disease-susceptibility, plus the ascension of better clones such as 'Klehm's Improved Bechtel' are spelling its commercial extinction. A small tree, with scaly bark, blooming late in the season—late May. Flowers (have a delicious sweet violet fragrance), 2"–2½" wide; fully double (20–33 petals); sepals slender. Fruit few or none, 1¼" wide, green. Record: 29' × 2'11" × 27' Tacoma, WA (1993)

M. ioensis 'Plena Nova'
= *M. ioensis* 'Nova'
= *M. ioensis* 'Flore Plena Nova'
= *M.* 'Plena Nova'

In 1928 the Morton Arboretum of Lisle, IL, received "*Malus ioensis flore plena nova*" from Augustine nursery of Normal, IL. Very rare; in commerce as late as 1969 at least. Likely a *M. ioensis* 'Plena' sport, to which it is similar except in bearing darker pink flowers. Flowers 1¾"–2" wide; petals 18–35. As with 'Plena' the fruit are very few, greenish-yellow, 1¼".

M. ioensis 'Prairie Rose'
= *M.* 'Prairie Rose'

Open-pollinated *M. ioensis* seedling, (pollen-parent presumed to be *M. ioensis* 'Plena') raised and named by the University of Illinois at Urbana, and introduced in 1956 by Simpson nursery of Vincennes, IL. Uncommon. Similar to *M. ioensis* 'Plena' but deeper pink, not fading as much, slightly fewer petals (17–25); utterly fruitless; habit more upright; better disease-resistance.

M. ioensis 'Prince Georges'—see *M.* 'Prince Georges'

M. ioensis 'Purpurea'—see *M.* 'Evelyn'

M. ioensis 'Red Leaf'—see *M.* 'Evelyn'

M. ioensis 'Seedling Red No. 1'—see *M.* 'Evelyn'

M. 'Irene'

A *Malus* × *Eleyi* seedling raised ca. 1939 by A. den Boer of Des Moines, IA. Introduced in 1951. Uncommon. A low, broad and dark ROSYBLOOM CRABAPPLE. The September foliage and fruit is similar to that of *M.* 'Ferrill's Crimson', except that the sparse oblong fruit is wider and persists longer; to 1⅓" long, 1" wide, on stems to 1" long. Tastes delicious. 'Irene' is also a dwarfish tree compared to 'Ferrill's Crimson' and blooms earlier, its petals are wider, and the flowers average 4 instead of 3 styles. Poor disease resistance. Record: 14' × 1'11" × 27' Seattle, WA (1994; *pl.* 1962).

M. Ivanhoe™
= *M.* 'Ivazam'

Named in 1991 by Lake County nursery of Perry, OH. Still not introduced to commerce as of 1995. Small, to 10' tall, of rounded form. Flowers scarlet. Leaves burgundy, frosted with hairs.

M. 'Ivazam'—see *M.* Ivanhoe™

M. 'Jay Darling'—see *M.* × *Eleyi*

M. 'Jay Darling Red Seedling #3'—see *M.* 'Purple Wave'

M. 'Joy Morton'—see *M.* Morning Sun™

M. 'Jewelberry'

= *M.* Simpson 7-62

In 1954 Dr. D.F. Dayton of the University of Illinois, Urbana, sent this clone to Simpson nursery of Vincennes, IN. Simpson tested it, introduced it, and it has become common in the 1980s and '90s. T. Green in 1991 said its parentage was *M. floribunda* × *M. purpurea*. The present writer disagrees and thinks it more likely to be in the *M.* × *Zumi* group. A dense shrub or dwarf tree ca. 8' tall and 12' wide, finer-textured than *M. Sargentii*. Very small red buds open to pale pink and white flowers, which fade to white. Leaves often deeply lobed. Fruit glossy bright red, ½", with ugly brown scars visible when lifted up; stems short, usually <1" but up to 1½" long. Fair to good disease resistance.

M. 'Jewelcole'—see *M.* Red Jewel™

M. 'Joan'

= *M.* × *robusta* 'Joan'

Discovered in 1918 by John Dunbar (1859–1927) Assistant Superintendent of Rochester Parks system, NY. Dunbar had come to the U.S. from Scotland in 1887. This cultivar was named for his granddaughter. Extremely rare. Commercially extinct. It should not be confused with the 'Joan' ORCHARD APPLE (dating from a 1906 cross, selected in 1918; introduced in 1932). Indeed, 'Joan' bears flowers like an ORCHARD APPLE, though maybe a bit less hairy than most; the petals are widely spaced. Fruit excellent, like mini 'Gravenstein' APPLES. Ready to eat by mid-October. Exquisitely pretty when polished, like a jewel, and the flavor as fine as any APPLE. To 1¾" wide; yellow largely striped and washed red; calyx persistent; stems to 1⅝" 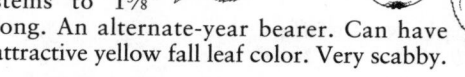 long. An alternate-year bearer. Can have attractive yellow fall leaf color. Very scabby.

M. 'John Downie'

Found in 1875 by nurseryman Edward Holmes of Whittingdon nursery, Lichfield, Staffordshire, England. Mr. John Downie was a friend of Holmes, and also a nurseryman; he lived near Edinburgh. Available since 1885; introduced by the Arnold Arboretum to the U.S. in 1927. Uncommon; grown nearly exclusively for its edible fruit. Pink buds open to large white flowers. Fruit exceptionally ornamental as well as delicious, 1¼" long, orange-yellow blushed with scarlet. An alternate-year bearer. Record: 33' × 4'3" Westonbirt, Gloucestershire, England (1986).

M. 'Jubilee'

= *M.* B.F. 6

A seedling of *Malus* 'Hopa' introduced by Brooks research station of Alberta in 1937 (as B.F. #6). Named 'Jubilee' in 1955. Very rare; probably extinct commercially since the late 1970s. Extremely cold-hardy, but poor disease resistance.

M. *Kaido*—see *M.* × *magdeburgensis* and *M.* × *micromalus*

M. *kansuensis* (Batal.) Schneid.

= *Pyrus kansuensis* Batal.

KANSU CRABAPPLE. From NW China. Named in 1893. Introduced in 1904 to England and in 1911 to the Arnold Arboretum. Extremely rare; practically only at botanic gardens and arboreta. Flowers creamy or pure white, ⅝" wide—like those of *Prunus cerasifera* (CHERRY PLUM); some are double; stems lightly hairy. Leaves vary from quite hairy beneath to hairless; sharply serrate. Leaves on vigorous shoots can be lobed, especially in their upper halves. Can have good fall color. Little scab; yet an unattractive tawny cast. Fruit ½" long, whitish with prominent brown speckles, then yellow or red, finally soft and brown; ends pitted where the calyx was; stems ≤1⅛" long. A small, often shrubby tree. Record: 26' × 3'3" St. Clere House, Kent, England (1986).

M. 'Katherine'—see *M.* × *Hartwigii* 'Katherine'

M. 'Kelsey'

KELSEY CRABAPPLE. First flowered in 1966. Introduced in 1969–70 by the Morden research station of Manitoba. Common. Manitoba's official Centennial tree. Named for Henry Kelsey (1667–1724), the first European to cross Hudson's Bay and see Manitoba (ca. 1690–1692). A ROSYBLOOM CRABAPPLE. Flowers profuse, purplish-red, 1"–2" wide, semi-double, of 10–16 petals. Leaves first reddish, then bronzy, finally green with red veins. Fruit described variously as purple, purplish-red, or bright dark red. Trees at the Yakima, WA, arboretum, bear two kinds and are clearly of a chimæric nature. Perhaps other 'Kelsey' specimens also make two kinds of fruits. The first kind are like blueberries, being small (⅜"–⅝"), dark purple, and bloomed; the calyx stays, very prominently sitting atop the ribbed end of the fruit. The second kind of fruit is larger and more colorful:

¾"–1"; orange-red like that of *M.* 'Hopa', bloomy; calyx stays; flesh mealy. Very cold-hardy. Grows 15'–20' tall, of low-branching, compact, upright-rounded habit.

M. 'Kentucky Mammoth'—see *M.* × *heterophylla* 'Mathews'

M. 'Kerr'
= *M.* 'Morden 352'
(*M.* 'Dolgo' × *M.* 'Haralson')
Named for W. Les Kerr, who originated this cultivar in 1938. Described in 1944; introduced in 1952 by Morden research station of Manitoba. Uncommon. Grown for its edible fruit—oval, dark purple-red, twice the size of those borne by *M.* 'Dolgo'.

M. Kerr #63-1—see *M.* 'Dainty'

M. 'Kibele'
= *M.* Morton Arboretum 447-59
Originated as a chance seedling <1949 on the south edge of Springfield, OH. Later moved to the back yard of Mr. and Mrs. R.R. Kibele, for whom it was named. Introduced by Clarice Hickox of Springfield. Rare. Dark red buds open to rose-pink flowers. Leaves purplish-red at first, becoming reddish-green; some lobing. Fruit ⅜"–½" wide, dark burgundy red; calyx drops; pulp red; stem to 1¼" long. A rounded compact shrubby tree 8' tall, wider. Fair to poor disease resistance.

M. 'Kinarzam'—see *M.* King Arthur™

M. King Arthur™
= *M.* 'Kinarzam'
Introduced in 1991 by Lake County nursery of Perry, OH. Uncommon. Soft pastel pink buds open to white flowers. Dark green leaves. Fruit ¼"–½", bright red in fall. Tree to 12' tall and 10' wide, of rounded upright habit—the most vigorous of the Lake County dwarf CRABAPPLES.

M. 'Kingsmere'
An open-pollinated seedling of *M. Sieversii* 'Niedzwetzkyana'. Raised in 1920 by I. Preston of Ottawa's Dominion agricultural experiment station. One of the original ROSYBLOOM CRABAPPLES. Selected in 1930 and named for Lake Kingsmere of Ontario. Rare. Commercially extinct. A small tree; the habit like ORCHARD APPLE (*M.* × *domestica*). Deep carmine buds open to purple-pink 2⅛" wide flowers. Fruit 1³⁄₁₆", crimson over purplish-brown, greenish-brown on the shady side; edible, excellent for jelly.

M. 'Kirk'
(*M. Zumi* #243 × *M. Zumi* #768)
Bred by the late Father J.L. Fiala of Falconskeape, near Medina, OH. Named in 1980. Registered ≤1983. In commerce. Red buds open to white flowers. Fruit rich red, abundant, ⅞". Tree rounded upright, to 15' tall.

M. 'Kola'
(*M. ioensis* 'Elk River' × 'Duchess' or 'Oldenburg' Russian APPLE)
From N. Hansen of Brookings, SD. Introduced in 1922. Extremely rare but not extinct commercially. *Kola* means friend in the Sioux language. Flowers 1⅞"–2¼" wide, palest pink, fragrant. Among the earliest of the *M. coronaria* clan to bloom. Leaves broad and large, to 4½" × 4"; stem to 1¾" long; weakly lobed; lightly hairy beneath at first, most hairs falling away, making leaves practically hairless by fall. Looks much like *M. coronaria*. Fruit profuse, 2⅜" wide (Den Boer says they can be more than 2½" wide), yellow-green, waxy, with quince-like fragrance. Fascinating. A tetraploid. Record: 31½' × 2'8" × 25' Salem, OR (1993).

M. 'Lady'
= *M.* 'Api'
CHRISTMAS APPLE. Grown in France for ca. 400 years. In North American commerce during the 1800s, scarcely thereafter. Samuel J. Rich nursery of Oregon promoted it into the 1960s as a dual ornamental-edible variety. Scab-susceptible but still in commerce among fruit fanciers. Tree somewhat dwarfish, to ca. 20' tall. Branches erect, slender, dense. Leaves rather narrow; not large. Fruit 1⅔"–2" wide, beautiful clear pale yellow with a deep red blush; hangs well; excellent crisp flesh and flavor; late-season (September–January). The fruit was much used for Christmas decorations.

M. 'Lady Northcliffe'
= *M. baccata* 'Lady Northcliffe'
Raised at Aldenham, Hertfordshire, England. Uncertain parentage but likely a *M. baccata* (G. Chadbund says it is an upright-growing form of *M.* × *floribunda*). Imported to the U.S. by the Morton Arboretum in 1929. Extremely rare; no longer in commerce. A small, rounded, dense tree with profuse flowers. Rose-red buds open to pale pink flowers, fading white, 1"+ wide. Fruit yellow and red or honey-colored, ⁹⁄₁₆" long; calyx drops. Fair disease resistance.

M. Lancelot® PP 8056 (1992)
= *M.* 'Lanzam'

Introduced in 1991 by Lake County nursery of Perry, OH. Uncommon. Red buds open slowly to white flowers 1"–1¼" wide. Crisp green leaves, downy when young. Fruit lasts until the New Year, ¼"–½" long; yellow-green to gold; calyx drops. Tree dwarf, slowly reaching 10' tall and 8' wide; branching erect and foliage dense.

M. lancifolia—see M. coronaria

M. 'Lanzam'—see M. Lancelot®

M. Lemoinei—see M. × purpurea 'Lemoinei'

M. 'Leprechaun'
M. Zumi Christmas Holly™ × *M.* 'Kirk'

Bred by the late Father J.L. Fiala of Falconskeape, near Medina, OH. Registered ≤1983. In commerce. A small 8' tall tree. Red buds open to white flowers with a red reverse. Leaves heavy-textured. Fruit abundant, bright red; ⅛"–¼"; round; firm into December.

M. 'Leslie'
= *M.* 'Valley City #3'

A ROSYBLOOM CRABAPPLE seedling raised at Northwest nursery of Valley City, ND. The seed had been supplied from Morden research station of Manitoba. Named in 1945, after W.R. Leslie, superintendent of the Morden station. Extremely rare; out of commerce. Apt to be confused with the equally rare and little known (possibly identical) *M.* 'Leslie Copperleaf' (sold ≤1967). Flowers deep purple-red. Fruit dark red ⁷⁄₁₆"–⅝". Disease resistance poor.

M. 'Lewis Dittman'—see M. spectabilis

M. 'Linda'
Raised as a *Malus* × *arnoldiana* descendent by A. den Boer of Des Moines, IA. Named in 1958 after his granddaughter Linda E. den Boer. Extremely rare. Rose-red to carmine buds open to pale-pink 1¾" wide flowers. Fruit bright to dark crimson 1³⁄₁₆". There is also a 'Linda' ORCHARD APPLE.

M. 'Liset'—see M. × moerlandsii 'Liset'

M. 'Little Troll'
(*M.* 'Molten Lava' × *M.* 'Leprechaun')

Bred by the late Father J.L. Fiala of Falconskeape, near Medina, OH. Named in 1975, registered in 1987. Not yet in commerce. A 15' tall, very refined graceful weeper. Brilliant red buds open to white flowers. Fruit bright orange-red, ¼".

M. 'Lizette'—see M. × moerlandsii 'Liset'

M. 'Louisa'
Polly Hill of Martha's Vineyard, MA, selected this from a seedling in 1962 and named after her daughter, Louisa Spotswood, of Washington, D.C. Related to *M. baccata*. Introduced in the 1980s by Schmidt nursery of Boring, OR. Red buds open to pink flowers 1¼"–1½" wide; petals widely spaced; stems slender and reddish. Fruit ⅜"–½" long; lopsided; yellow with an orange-red blush; with a small calyx scar. Tree dwarf, to 15' tall and wide, with thin, strongly weeping branches that sprawl along the ground. Leaves rarely lobed. Resists scab; rust-susceptible (at least in Seattle, WA).

M. 'Lullaby'
(*M. Zumi* 'Wooster' × *M.* 'Red Jade')

Bred by the late Father J.L. Fiala of Falconskeape, near Medina, OH. Named in 1980. Registered ≤1983. In commerce. "Essentially a smaller, finer form of *Malus* 'Red Jade'. Far more disease resistant." A low, weeping 6' tall tree. Red buds open to large white flowers. Leaves narrow, deep green. Fruit smaller than that of 'Red Jade'.

M. 'Luwick'
(*M. Zumi* #768 × *M. purpurea* 'Lemoinei') × [(*M.* 'Echtermeyer' × *M. Zumi* #243) × *M. Zumi* #1023]

Bred by the late Father J.L. Fiala of Falconskeape, near Medina, OH. Named in 1978 (after his mother). Registered ≤1983. In commerce. A graceful weeping 5' tree. Deep pink buds open to pale blush-pink flowers. Leaves narrow, deep green. Fruit sparse, rich red, ca. ¼".

M. 'Lynn Lowrey'
(*M. angustifolia* × *M. Eleyi*)

Bred at Houston Natural History Museum. Registered in 1976. Introduced by Herbert K. Kurand of Raleigh, NC. Extremely rare. Named after a plant collector of Conroe, TX. Suited for the Gulf Coastal Plain, adapted to lowland soil, low-chill requirement.

M. Madonna® PP 6672 (1989)
= *M.* 'Mazam'

Bred by the late Father J.L. Fiala of Falconskeape, near Medina, OH. Named in 1979. Introduced in 1987 by Lake County nursery of Perry, OH. Common.

Pink buds open to large (2½"–3" wide), double, white, fragrant, flowers, opening early, long-lasting. Young leaves bronze. Fruit ½"; golden-yellow with red blush; has a huge calyx scar, with a central point. A compact upright tree to 18' tall and 10' wide. Scabby.

M. × *magdeburgensis* Hartw.

= *M. Kaido* Dipp. 1893, non (Sieb. *ex* Wenz.) Pardé 1906
= *Pyrus* × *magdeburgensis* hort.
(*M. domestica* × *M. spectabilis*)

MAGDEBURG APPLE. Originated in Germany, possibly as early as 1850; originally described in 1893. Magdeberg is ca. 75 miles west of Berlin. Very rare in North America, perhaps least so in the 1950s; now commercially extinct. Purplish-red buds open to pink flowers, 1¾"–2⅛" wide, double with (5) 10–15 petals. Much *M.* × *domestica* (ORCHARD APPLE) influence in the flowers, tree form, and foliage, also *M. spectabilis* influence, though rather downy. Leaves downy, with coarse teeth. Fruit few, to 1⅝" wide, 1¼" long, like a mini APPLE, yellow with a reddish blush, a hairy ⅞" stem, flavor acceptable. Record: 27' × 2'0" × 28½' Seattle, WA (1994; *pl.* 1952).

M. 'Magenta'

A seed-grown ROSYBLOOM CRABAPPLE cultivar—the offspring breed about 80% true. Introduced ≤1992 by the USDA Soil Conservation Service. Highly resists cedar-apple rust and fireblight; moderately resists scab. Fruit dark red, ½".

M. 'Makamik'

MAKAMIK CRABAPPLE. An open-pollinated seedling of *M. Sieversii* 'Niedzwetzkyana'. Raised in 1921 by I. Preston of Ottawa's Dominion agricultural experiment station. Selected in 1930 and named for Lake Makamik in western Québec. The most common of all 33 of Preston's ROSYBLOOM CRABAPPPLE series. Dark red buds open to profuse, pleasing, purplish-red flowers, fading to a lighter tint, 1⅞" wide. Young leaves not very dark red. Tree shapely, vigorous, large, healthy and fruitful. It may be too big for average front yards, and the fruit too messy. Fruit (to 1⅛") usually longer than wide, conspicuously narrowed to its end, where the swollen, persistent calyx remains. Its color is bloomy red; lenticels of sharp, irregular shapes are numerous and conspicuous. Flavor ok. Record: 34' × 3'3" × 34½' Seattle, WA (1994; *pl.* 1962).

M. *Malus*—see *M.* × *domestica*

M. 'Manbeck Weeper'—see *M.* Anne E®

M. *mandshurica*—see *M. baccata* var. *mandshurica*

M. 'Margaret'—see *M. coronaria* 'Margaret'

M. 'Maria'

(*M. purpurea* 'Lemoinei' × *M.* 'Red Jade') × (*M.* 'Liset' × *M.* 'Red Jade')

Bred by the late Father J.L. Fiala of Falconskeape, near Medina, OH. Named in 1978 (after the Virgin Mary). Registered ≤1983. In commerce. A graceful weeping 12' tall tree. Deep orange-red buds open to bright red flowers, fading pale red. Leaves very bright red when young, then bronzy, becoming green and heavily textured. Fruit ½"; deep red, shiny; very abundant.

M. 'Marshall Oyama'

Origin obscure; imported to the U.S. by Boyce Thompson Arboretum in 1930. Rare. Nearly extinct commercially. Narrowly upright fastigiate habit while young, splaying with age. Red buds open to pinkish-white flowers, 1⅓"–1⅝" wide. Fruit often 1½" or more wide, carmine or crimson over a yellow background.

M. 'Martha'

Originated by P.M. Gideon of Excelsior, MN. Described in 1879. Commercially extinct. Grown for its edible fruit. Fruit bright red, clear yellowish on shady side, 1¾" wide. Very cold-hardy.

M. 'Martha-Dolgo'

(*M.* 'Martha' × *M.* 'Dolgo')

Introduced commercially ≤1943. Extremely rare. Grown for its edible fruit. Blooms a few days later than *M.* 'Dolgo'; flowers larger, more attractive; fruits twice as big.

M. 'Mary Currelly'

Originated in Welcome, Ontario, by W.T. Macoun. Selected about 1951. Macoun presented it to C.T. Currelly, curator of the Royal Ontario Museum, who named it after his wife. Introduced in 1954. Extremely rare; not in commerce. Flowers large (2⅜" wide), mauve-pink. Fruit ¾"–1" wide, round, rosy-pink to red, fine for jelly. An alternate-year bearer.

M. 'Mary Potter'

(*M. Sargentii* 'Rosea' × *M. atrosanguinea*)

Originated at the Arnold Arboretum in 1939. Since it was "a daughter of *M. Sargentii*" it was named (in 1955) for a daughter (Mrs. Nathaniel Bowditch Potter) of Charles Sargent. Introduced in 1947. Common. A triploid that tends to breed true from seed. Pink-red buds open to fragrant white flowers, 1" wide; the calyx, stems, and sepals hairless. Fruit abundant, red, bloomed, ⅜"–½", roundish; calyx drops. Tree broad, low, semi pendulous, with a very pretty branching habit. Notably flaky bark. Some leaves deeply lobed. Record: 20¾' × 3'3½" × 27½' Seattle, WA (1994; *pl.* 1956). Fair to good disease resistance.

M. 'Mathews'—see M. × *heterophylla* 'Mathews'

M. *Matthewi*—see M. × *heterophylla* 'Mathews'

M. 'Matt Tures'

Introduced in the 1990s by Chicagoland Grows®, Inc. Named after Matt Tures, Illinois nurseryman. Said to be a seedling of *M. Sargentii*. Dense, wide habit. Dark rose to rose-magenta buds open to pink flowers. Foliage red-tinted. Fruit few or none. Disease resistance excellent.

M. 'Maybride'

(*M.* 'Dorothea' × *M.* 'Makamik')

Bred in 1956 by the Ottawa agricultural research station. Introduced ≤1970. Uncommon. Pink buds open to pure white flowers, double and semi-double (17–18 petals) 2" wide. Fruit ¾"; greenish overlaid dull red on the sunny side. Branches wide spreading.

M. 'Maysong'

(*M.* 'Silver Moon' × an unnamed octoploid *Malus* seedling)

Bred by the late Father J.L. Fiala of Falconskeape, near Medina, OH. Named in 1975, registered in 1987. Tree very upright and narrow, spreading to vase-shaped in age; to 20' tall. Pinkish-white buds open to large white flowers. Fruit red, ½".

M. 'Mazam'—see M. Madonna®

M. 'Meach'

(*M. Sieversii* 'Niedzwetzkyana' × *M. Sieboldii*)

An open-pollinated seedling of *M. Sieversii* 'Niedzwetzkyana'. Raised in 1920 by I. Preston of Ottawa's Dominion agricultural experiment station. One of the original ROSYBLOOM CRABAPPLES. Selected in 1930 and named for Meach Lake of Québec. Extremely rare. Extinct commercially. Flowers purplish-red, 2" wide. Fruit bright canary-yellow, round, showy; ⅞"–1".

M. × *micromalus* Mak.

= *M. spectabilis* var. *Kaido* Sieb. *ex* Wenz.

= *M. Kaido* (Sieb. *ex* Wenz.) Pardé 1906, non Dipp. 1893

= *Pyrus spectabilis* var. *Kaido* (Sieb. *ex* Wenz.) Kirchn.

= *Pyrus Ringo* var. *Kaido* Sieb. *ex* Wenz.

= *Pyrus Kaido* (Sieb. *ex* Wenz.) Mouillef.

= *Pyrus micromalus* (Mak.) L.H. Bailey

KAIDO CRABAPPLE. MIDGET CRABAPPLE. Known only in cultivation; probably a *M. spectabilis* hybrid (with *M. baccata* or *M. floribunda*). Introduced from Japan to Europe ca. 1845 via Siebold, who named it in 1856. Common in North America, but becoming extinct commercially. According to T. Makino, it was formerly called *Kaido* in Japan, a name now applied to *M. Halliana* and probably also to *M. × floribunda*. The singularly inapt 1908 name *micromalus* means midget *Malus*, from Greek *mikros*, small, and *Malus*. Dark carmine buds open to palest pink flowers 1½"–2" wide; early—one of the first to bloom. Flowerstems and calyx tube lightly hairy. Tree leafy, with long, slender dark leaves. Bark pale grayish, smooth. Fruit abundant, roundish, ribbed, ½"–⅞" wide, first green, eventually yellow, red-blushed, turning butterscotch brown as it rots—similar to that of *M. × Scheideckeri*; the calyx usually drops. Some writers incorrectly call the fruit an unqualified red. At most it is reddish-brown on the sunny side. Although the fruit is not showy, in bloom and vigor the tree excells. Poor to fair disease resistance. Record: 37' × 3'1" × 38' Seattle, WA (1993).

M. 'Midnight'

A seedling of *Malus* 'Beauty' raised by P.H. Wright of Moose Range, Saskatchewan. Introduced in 1953. Extremely rare and commercially extinct. A purpleleaf CRABAPPLE. Hardy to -55°F. Carmine buds open to pink flowers 1⅓" wide.

M. 'Millet'

Introduced ≤1952 by Will nursery of Bismarck, ND. Extremely rare; commercially extinct. A *Malus* 'Hopa' seedling with "rather large fruit and good flavor, as well as all the beauty of 'Hopa'."

M. 'Milton Baron #2'—see M. Sugar Tyme®

M. 'Milton Baron #4'—see M. American Spirit™

M. 'Ming Shing'—see M. × atrosanguinea

M. Minnesota 240—see M. 'Chestnut'

M. Minnesota 635—see M. 'Flame'

M. × moerlandsii Doorenbos
(*M. Sieboldii* × *M. purpurea* 'Lemoinei')

Raised <1938 by S.G.A. Doorenbos in Holland. Likely a connection with the Ir. Ch. P. Moerlands of Grave, Holland, cited in some Netherlands Dendrology Society yearbooks. If so, the name could be written *Moerlandsii*.

M. × moerlandsii #8—see M. × moerlandsii 'Liset'

M. × moerlandsii 'Liset'
= M. 'Liset' or 'Lizette'
= M. 'Success'
= M. × moerlandsii #8

A ROSYBLOOM CRABAPPLE raised <1938 by S.G.A. Doorenbos, director of parks in the city of the Hague, Holland. Named *Malus* 'Success' in 1951, and renamed *M.* 'Liset' in 1952, after Doorenbos' oldest granddaughter. In North American commerce since the 1960s. Common. Flowers similar to those of *M. × moerlandsii* 'Profusion' but fuller (less space between the petals), less hairy parts, longer stems—to 1⅞". Tree much smaller growing; beginning upright and sometimes nearly columnar, it broadens in age. Foliage very dark purplish in early summer, army-green by late August. Leaves numerous, large, especially wide, giving the tree a bulky look. Fruit profuse, ½" (–1") very deep purplish red, at first thinly bloomed, with a conspicuous pale pit or "eye" where the calyx was. By November, the fruit is hideously dark, shiny, not pretty. Varies from comparatively disease-free to severely scabby. Likely both misnamed stock and regional differences account for this variance. Record: 27' × 3'7" × 35' Seattle, WA (1993).

M. × moerlandsii 'Profusion'
= M. 'Profusion'

A ROSYBLOOM CRABAPPLE in North American commerce ≤1958. Common. The name refers to the numerous flowers relative to those of *M. × purpurea*. The fruit, too, can be profuse. Deep red buds open to violet-red flowers, fading to violet-pink, ≤1½" wide. A rich spectacle in full April bloom, then paler in May. Leaves reddish-purple when young, then, if not destroyed by scab, becoming bronzy-greenish, finally green changing to amber in October; midrib and stem remain purplish. Some sucker leaves are lobed at the middle. Spur leaves subtly toothed, almost untoothed except at the apex. Fruit deep red or purple with a few pale speckles near the stem, ⅜"–½" wide, calyx scar usually small; stem to 1¼" long. Despite being called shrubby or small, it can grow large: 35' × 3'6" × 40' Seattle, WA (1992; *pl.* 1958). Despite its reputation for good disease-resistance, it is hideously scabby in the maritime Pacific Northwest.

M. 'Mollie Anne'
(*M.* 'Dorothea' × *M. Zumi*) × (*M.* 'Shinto Shrine' × *M.* 'Lullaby')

Bred by the late Father J.L. Fiala of Falconskeape, near Medina, OH. Named in 1978, after Mollie Anne Fiala Pesata, a sister of the hybridizer. Registered ≤1983. In commerce. A tetraploid, induced through colchicine treatment. Semi-weeping; very fine branches; to 12' tall and 10' wide. Deep red buds open to finely-petalled, feathery, white flowers. Leaves heavily-textured, deep green. Fruit described in conflicting fashion—as ½" buff-gold, or ¼" deep red.

M. Molten Lava®
= M. 'Molazam'
(*M.* 'Red Jade' × *M. Zumi* 'Calocarpa') × (*M. Zumi* Christmas Holly™ × *M.* 'Red Jade')

Bred by the late Father J.L. Fiala of Falconskeape, near Medina, OH. Named in 1980, registered ≤1983. Introduced by Lake County nursery of Perry, OH. Common. A medium-size, broad weeper, 12' tall and 15' wide. Sometimes topgrafted. Red-pink buds open to white, 1½" wide flowers. Fruit profuse, shiny orange-red, with small calyx scars, like those of *M. baccata* in size and shape: ½" long. At first partly hidden by the leaves, the fruit persists. Fall foliage bright yellow. Distinctive yellowish bark in winter. Scarcely scabby.

Fraxinus angustifolia
'Flame'
'FLAME' ASH
10/16   Page 213
Refined foliage of
burgundy hue in autumn.

Fraxinus excelsior
'Globosa'
GLOBEHEAD EUROPEAN ASH
10/27 [photo by R.G. Brightman]
Page 215
Squat and bushy, yet grafted high
on a straight trunk to make a
formal small tree.

Fraxinus excelsior
'Jaspidea'
GOLDEN ASH
9/29   Page 216
Pale yellow-green in spring,
and bright yellow in fall, it
is pale green during
summer.

Fraxinus Ornus
MANNA or
FLOWERING ASH
5/14   Page 219
Attractive blossoms, a
smooth BEECH-like trunk,
and admirable toughness.

Fraxinus Uhdei
SHAMEL or
EVERGREEN ASH
7/31   Page 223
A Mexican native noted
for rapid growth to
towering size.

Fraxinus velutina
'Modesto'
'MODESTO' ASH
7/30   Page 225
Bright green, elegant foliage
that turns yellow in fall.

Ginkgo biloba
GINKGO or
MAIDENHAIR TREE
10/26 Page 226
Unique in its "fossil"
ancestry, this celebrated
Chinese tree is reliably
golden in autumn.

Gleditsia sinensis
CHINESE HONEY
LOCUST
11/5 Page 228
Fiercely thorny, with larger
leaves than our native
Gleditisa triacanthos.

Gleditsia triacanthos
'Elegantissima'
GLOBE or BUSHY
HONEY LOCUST
11/8 Page 229
A shrubby, thornless,
podless cultivar.

Gleditsia triacanthos
Sunburst®
SUNBURST® HONEY
LOCUST
5/14 Page 232
Screaming lemon-yellow
in early summer. Thornless,
podless.

*Glyptostrobus
pensilis*
CHINESE SWAMP
CYPRESS
7/29 Page 232
A REDWOOD relative that
loves heat and ample
moisture.

Ilex Aquifolium
ENGLISH HOLLY
1/5 Page 239
Far prettier yet not as
hardy as AMERICAN HOLLY
(*Ilex opaca*).

Ilex Aquifolium
'Amber'
'AMBER' ENGLISH HOLLY
10/25   Page 240
One of hundreds of
cultivars. Sold since 1964.

Ilex Aquifolium
'Flavescens'
MOONLIGHT HOLLY
3/1   Page 246
Shrubby and aptly named.

Juglans Hindsii
NORTHERN CALIFORNIA
BLACK WALNUT
7/31   Page 272
Lesser known than other WALNUTS,
this species has bluish-green leaves
and smooth-shelled nuts in bright
green husks.

Juniperus Deppeana
ALLIGATOR or
CHECKERBARK JUNIPER
3/26   Page 282
Ghostly silver foliage
renders young specimens
lovely and unmistakable;
chunky bark is the chief
feature of aged ones.

Juniperus scopulorum
'Tolleson's Blue
Weeping'
'TOLLESON'S BLUE
WEEPING' JUNIPER
3/30   Page 290
Limp tresses of soft blue
on a small tree.

Juniperus squamata
var. *Fargesii*
FARGES' WEEPING
JUNIPER
3/8   Page 290
Subtly weeping branch tips
lend a droopy aspect to
this Chinese tree.

Juniperus squamata
'Meyeri'
MEYER JUNIPER
9/10   Page 291
Irregular form, prickly
metallic blue foliage, and
small size.

Keteleeria Davidiana
4/2   Page 296
Huntington Gardens of
California has North
America's largest specimen
of this extremely rare east
Asian conifer.

Lagerstrœmia Fauriei
COPPERBARK or JAPANESE
CRAPEMYRTLE
3/30   Page 299
Its small white flowers are
not as choice as its lovely
peeling bark.

Larix decidua
EUROPEAN LARCH
9/16   Page 304
LARCHES and TAMARACKS
are deciduous conifers;
they often feature rich
gold fall color.

Ligustrum lucidum
GLOSSY, CHINESE, or
TREE PRIVET
7/22   Page 309
Most PRIVETS are hedging
shrubs. This tree has
strong-smelling flowers
succeeded by small blue-
black berries.

*Liriodendron
Tulipifera*
TULIP TREE or YELLOW
POPLAR
11/9   Page 312
One of America's largest
and most unusual hard-
wood forest species.

Maackia amurensis var.
Buergeri
JAPANESE MAACKIA
10/21   Page 315
Little known to Western
horticulture; less ornamental
than the related YELLOWWOODS
(*Cladrastis* spp.).

Maclura pomifera
OSAGE ORANGE
8/30   Page 315
Thornless, fruitless
cultivars will encourage
the additional planting of
this valuable tree.

Magnolia acuminata
CUCUMBER TREE
11/1   Page 317
Magnolia species are not
known for showy fall
color; this one can supply
gleaming gold.

Magnolia Campbellii
'Stark's White'
'STARK'S WHITE'
CAMPBELL MAGNOLIA
2/11   Page 320
Fragrant pure white
flowers, some 10 inches
wide.

Magnolia grandiflora
EVERGREEN or
SOUTHERN MAGNOLIA
1/17   Page 323
One of the world's most
popular and widely
planted trees.

Magnolia Kobus var.
Lœbneri 'Leonard
Messel'
'LEONARD MESSEL'
MAGNOLIA
3/19   Page 330
Pink flowers of dainty
proportions in early spring
on a small tree.

Magnolia macrophylla
BIGLEAF MAGNOLIA
7/4   Page 333
Elephantine leaves and
flowers lend a splendid
tropical air.

Magnolia tamaulipana
TAMAULIPAS MAGNOLIA
7/15   Page 343
From Mexico, a broadleaf
evergreen with sweet,
sporadic summer flowers.

Magnolia tripetala
UMBRELLA TREE
6/6   Page 344
Attractive, slender, vile-
smelling flowers surrounded
by substantial leaves.

Magnolia virginiana
SWEET BAY
3/23   Page 344
A charming small tree, best
in its evergreen cultivars.

Mallotus japonicus
7/1   Page 346
In the Spurge Family
(EUPHORBIACEÆ), this
extremely rare east Asian
is an intriguing foliage
specimen.

Malus × atrosanguinea
CARMINE CRABAPPLE
3/31   Page 350
Now commercially obsolete,
an old-fashioned disease-
prone CRABAPPLE.

Malus 'Dolgo'
'DOLGO' CRABAPPLE
3/26   Page 360
Pure white flowers and large, red, edible fruit.

Malus × *floribunda*
JAPANESE or SHOWY CRABAPPLE
3/22   Page 364
Perhaps the most profuse blooming of all CRABAPPLES.

Malus 'Garry'
'GARRY' CRABAPPLE
3/31   Page 365
A "rosybloom" CRABAPPLE from Canada.

Malus 'Henry F. DuPont'
'HENRY F. DUPONT' CRABAPPLE
4/8   Page 369
Mr. DuPont (1880–1969) helped the Arnold Arboretum, and this tree was named for him in 1955.

Malus hupehensis
TEA or HUPEH CRABAPPLE
4/8   Page 370
Its tiered, broadly extended branching and CHERRY-like blossoms lend this Chinese native an aristocratic poise.

Malus ioensis 'Plena'
BECHTEL CRABAPPLE
5/3   Page 372
Deliciously sweet fragrance, yet on a very disease-prone tree.

Malus × *moerlandsii*
'Profusion'
'PROFUSION' CRABAPPLE
4/8   Page 378
Profuse violet-red flowers
yield to murky bronzy-
greenish foliage all
summer.

Malus 'Professor
Sprenger'
'PROFESSOR SPRENGER'
CRABAPPLE
11/1   Page 383
Its average flowers go
unnoticed, but the fruit
display is heartwarming.

Malus × *purpurea*
'Lemoinei'
LEMOINE CRABAPPLE
3/27   Page 385
Dazzling red spring flowers
help us overlook its disease-
infected summer months.

Malus × *Scheideckeri*
SCHEIDECKER
CRABAPPLE
3/31   Page 391
Excellent flowers and fruit
displays, but diseases limit
its usage.

Malus 'Sundog'
'SUNDOG' CRABAPPLE
9/14   Page 398
Gorgeous red fruit, and
large palest-pink flowers
in spring.

Maytenus boaria
MAYTEN TREE
5/30   Page 405
Aptly likened to an evergreen
WEEPING WILLOW, this South
American native varies in
droopiness.

Mespilus germanica
MEDLAR
1/5   Page 407
A crooked little tree prized, above all, for its weird little fruits.

Metasequoia glyptostroboides
DAWN or CHINESE REDWOOD
11/9   Page 408
Grown in the Western World since 1948, this rediscovered "fossil tree" is very popular.

Morus alba
WHITE or SILKWORM MULBERRY
11/8   Page 409
The leaves of this tree, ultimately, may wind up as silk.

Nothofagus obliqua
ROBLE SOUTHERN-BEECH
3/1   Page 415
A very rare, rugged OAK relative from Chile and Argentina.

Nyssa sinensis
CHINESE TUPELO
10/25   Page 416
Water-loving, this species offers lush, bold foliage with superb fall color.

Nyssa sylvatica
TUPELO, BLACK, or SOUR GUM
11/5   Page 416
Well known, an ideal ornamental shade tree with glossy foliage, usually red in fall.

Ostrya carpinifolia
EUROPEAN
HOP-HORNBEAM
3/1   Page 419
Aside from dismal fall
color, this species has
much to recommend it.

Ostrya virginiana
AMERICAN
HOP-HORNBEAM
7/28   Page 419
Anything but glamorous,
it is troublefree and offers
subtle beauty of form
and foliage.

Oxydendrum arboreum
SORREL TREE or
SOURWOOD
11/2   Page 419
One of the most colorful,
elegant and ornamental of
all North American natives.

Parrotia persica
PERSIAN IRONWOOD
or WITCH-HAZEL
11/5   Page 420
A hard-wooded, often
shrubby and irregular
little tree.

Photinia Davidsoniæ
5/31   Page 424
Large, lovely orange-red
berries, and great size, set
this extremely rare species
apart.

Photinia serratifolia
CHINESE PHOTINIA
5/9   Page 425
Now superseded commer-
cially by REDTIP (Photinia ×
Fraseri), its flashy hybrid.

Picea Abies
NORWAY SPRUCE
10/16   Page 426
By far the most commonly
cultivated foreign SPRUCE;
many cultivars exist.

Picea Abies 'Cupressina'
CYPRESS NORWAY SPRUCE
3/1   Page 426
An elegantly tapering, slender
variant, all too rare.

Picea Breweriana
SISKIYOU or WEEPING
SPRUCE
10/14   Page 429
Blue-green needles borne
in hanging curtains.

Picea glauca 'Conica'
DWARF ALBERTA
WHITE SPRUCE
8/28   Page 430
A pure bright green natural
dwarf that looks sheared.

Picea likiangensis var.
purpurea
PURPLECONE SPRUCE
7/12   Page 432
A Chinese species with
attractive cones.

Picea Omorika 'Nana'
DWARF SERBIAN SPRUCE
10/16   Page 433
Usually a dense broad
shrub, it can be a tight
pyramidal tree.

Picea orientalis
ORIENTAL or
CAUCASIAN SPRUCE
1/4   Page 434
Neat, dark, glossy and
tough; overall better than
NORWAY SPRUCE
(*Picea Abies*).

Picea sitchensis
SITKA SPRUCE
10/-   Page 437
The largest SPRUCE species;
with broad branching and
very prickly needles.

Pinus attenuata
KNOBCONE PINE
12/31   Page 440
From Oregon and
California; its rock-hard,
curved cones are highly
distinctive.

Pinus Coulteri
BIGCONE PINE
2/-   Page 443
Producer of the world's
heaviest pine cones. A bold
and striking giant.

Pinus Coulteri
BIGCONE PINE
4/3   Page 443
The cones can weigh from
5 to 8 pounds.

Pinus densiflora
JAPANESE RED PINE
11/8   Page 443
Winding red trunks bear
tabular whorls of light
foliage.

Pinus densiflora
'Umbraculifera'
TANYOSHO or JAPANESE
UMBRELLA PINE
7/3   Page 444
Dense, small, and
mushroom-shaped.

Pinus halepensis
ALEPPO or
JERUSALEM PINE
4/1   Page 446
A Mediterranean native,
of open habit; planted
mostly in California and
the Southwest.

Pinus Lambertiana
SUGAR PINE
10/18   Page 448
The largest PINE species,
with the longest cones.
From Oregon to Mexico.

Pinus nigra
AUSTRIAN BLACK PINE
12/4   Page 450
No foreign PINE is more
common in North
American cultivation.

Pinus Pinaster
CLUSTER PINE
10/8   Page 453
Excellent character, as well
as soil-binding value.

Pinus Pinea
ITALIAN STONE PINE
4/2   Page 453
A distinctive symbol of
Mediterranean landscapes;
the PINE OF ROME.

Pinus ponderosa
PONDEROSA or
WESTERN YELLOW PINE
3/15   Page 454
The West's most common
PINE, widely distributed
and cultivated.

Pinus radiata
MONTEREY PINE
9/18   Page 454
Famous as a rapid growing
forestry species.

Pinus Sabiniana
FOOTHILL, GRAY, or
DIGGER PINE
4/12   Page 456
A California native with
thin foliage against dark
trunks.

Pinus Strobus
EASTERN WHITE PINE
7/20   Page 456
Beloved as an ornamental,
valued for its lumber.

Pinus Strobus f. *nana*
DWARF EASTERN
WHITE PINE
3/1   Page 457
Intended as bushes, some
"dwarf" specimens
reassert their treehood.

Pinus sylvestris
'Watereri'
WATERER SCOTS PINE
12/30   Page 459
A broad, small, rounded
cultivar.

Pinus Torreyana
TORREY or SOLEDAD
PINE
2/14   Page 460
Rare and often stunted in
the wild, this booms in
cultivation.

Pistacia atlantica
MT. ATLAS PISTACHIO or
MASTICH
5/30   Page 461
Less colorful than *Pistacia chinensis*, this species is very
rare as an ornamental.

Pistacia chinensis
CHINESE PISTACHIO
11/9   Page 461
Grown for fine foliage, not
for its small berrylike fruit.

Platanus × acerifolia
HYBRID PLANETREE
or SYCAMORE
12/4   Page 462
Quintessential as the
cosmopolitan urban street
and park shade tree.

Platanus racemosa
CALIFORNIA SYCAMORE
4/4   Page 465
Handsome and hardy yet
highly prone to fungal
disease.

Populus alba
'Pyramidalis'
PYRAMIDAL or BOLLE
WHITE POPLAR
10/29   Page 468
Sculptural smoky-gray
trunks form a symmetric
crown, narrow at first,
eventually goblet shaped.

Populus balsamifera
ssp. *trichocarpa*
BLACK COTTONWOOD or
WESTERN BALSAM POPLAR
10/10   Page 470
Enormous; strongly aromatic
in spring; golden in fall.

Populus × canadensis
'Serotina'
HYBRID BLACK POPLAR or
ITALIAN BLACK POPLAR
4/29   Page 472
A male clone grown more for
wood in the past, than as an
ornamental presently.

Populus koreana
KOREAN POPLAR
3/23   Page 477
Bright apple-green early
spring flush is fragrant and
uplifting.

Populus lasiocarpa
CHINESE NECKLACE
POPLAR
8/31   Page 477
A coarse-textured tree,
difficult to place tactfully
in designs.

Populus nigra
BLACK POPLAR
3/8   Page 478
Almost never planted in this,
its typical form; cultivars
alone are favored.

Populus nigra
'Afghanica'
GHOST POPLAR
4/6   Page 478
A slender, pale-barked
female clone.

M. 'Molazam'—see *M.* Molten Lava®

M. 'Montreal Beauty'

One of the first, if not the first, ornamental cultivars to originate in Canada. Introduced <1833 in Québec by R. Cleghorn, near Montreal. In the U.S. since <1835 when Prince nursery of Flushing, NY, sold it. Very rare; since the early 1900s it has been better known in England than in North America. A large shrub or small tree. Pink buds open to scented white flowers, 2" wide. Fruit yellowish-green, mostly covered with a red blush; 1½"–2" long; good for jelly.

M. 'Morden 352'—see *M.* 'Kerr'

M. Morning Sun™
= *M.* 'Joy Morton'

A seedling of *M.* × *Zumi* 'Calocarpa', from the Morton Arboretum of Lisle, IL. Introduced ≤1993 by Chicagoland Grows®, Inc. Rare. Red buds open to pink flowers, fading white, to 1⅞" wide. Fruit orange, to ⅝" long; calyx drops; stem to 2" long; pulp hard, foul-flavored. Leaves recall those of *Malus baccata*, never lobed and scarcely hairy even when young. Tree vigorous, broad. Rust-susceptible in Seattle, WA.

M. Morton Arboretum 447-59—see *M.* 'Kibele'

M. 'Mount Arbor Special'

A *Malus* 'Hopa' seedling from ca. 1937. The pollen-parent was likely *M.* 'Red Silver'. Introduced in 1939 by Mount Arbor nursery of Shenandoah, IA (founded in 1875). Very rare; no longer in commerce. Carmine buds open to reddish-pink 1" flowers, fading to dull pink. Fruit reddish-purple, russet-dotted, ¾"; not persistent. Foliage "brilliant reddish-purple." Excellent disease resistance.

M. 'MR 450'
(i.e., "Morden Rosybloom No. 450")
≠ *M.* 'Oakes'

Raised at Morden research station of Manitoba. Described and distributed in the 1940s. Extremely rare; commercially extinct. Tree broad spreading, vigorous, with strong rounded crotches. Flowers large, of radiant, lively, scarcely fading red; long petals of medium width. Fruit bright scarlet-red, to 1" long; pulp rich bright red, sharp-flavored; clings well into mid-October.

M. 'MR 451'—see *M.* 'Pink Beauty'

M. 'MR 452'—see *M.* 'Almey'

M. 'MR 453'—see *M.* 'Sundog'

M. 'MR 454'
?= *M.* 'Spring Glory'
(i.e., "Morden Rosybloom No. 454")

Raised at Morden research station of Manitoba. Described and distributed in the 1940s. Rare; no longer in commerce. Tree narrowly columnar, suggesting the outline of a many POPLARS. It is the deepest of Morden's 8 ROSYBLOOM CRABAPPLE selections in its purplish-red leaf color, and the darkest in bark color. Twigs thin and willowy. Deep red buds open (late) to small rosy flowers which fade to pink. Fruit dark red with waxy bloom, round; 1³⁄₁₆"; calyx drops; pulp deep red, acid; clings tightly into mid-October.

M. 'MR 455'—see *M.* 'Garry'

M. 'MR 456'
(i.e., "Morden Rosybloom No. 456")

Raised at Morden research station of Manitoba. Described and distributed in the 1940s. Exceedingly rare; no longer sold. A broad shrub rather than a tree; the numerous branches remarkably limber and pliable; young shoots may be looped without breakage. Some branches are drooping. The bush is tough. Red buds open to rosy flowers, fading to pink. Fruit red, small, dropping in mid-October.

M. 'MR 457'—see *M.* 'Selkirk'

M. 'Naragansett'

Bred (one parent was *M.* 'Wintergold') by D.R. Egolf of the U.S. National Arboretum. Selected in 1979. Released in 1986, after 10 years of observation showed it to be disease-free. Common. Carmine buds open to pink-tinged or snow-white flowers, 1³⁄₁₆"–1⅔" wide. Fruit glossy bright cherry-red, with light orange underside, ¾", brilliant until December. A small, 15' tall tree with a broad crown and wide crotch angles.

M. 'Nertchinsk'

Seedlings bearing this name were introduced in 1924 by N. Hansen of South Dakota. From Nertchinsk, eastern Siberia, near the headwaters of the Amur River. Extremely rare; long commercially extinct. One planted in 1950 in Seattle bears nondescript white flowers, is probably a pure *M. baccata*, and if not, is certainly a hybrid. Fruit to ⁷⁄₁₆" wide, sparse to moderately produced, yellow blushed pink; the calyx drops leaving a conspicuous scar; stem to 1⅜" long. Scabby.

M. 'Neville Copeman'

A *Malus* × *Eleyi* seedling raised by T.N.S. Copeman of Roydon Hall, Diss, Norfolk, England. Introduced in 1954 by Nottcutt nursery of Woodbridge, Suffolk, England. Seldom grown and little known in North America. Resembles *M.* × *Eleyi* in its reddish flowers and purplish foliage but is stronger, with more showy fruit, orange-red to glossy carmine. Poor disease resistance.

M. 'Nevis'—see *M. ioensis* 'Nevis'

M. *Niedzwetzkyana*—see *M. Sieversii* 'Niedzwetzkyana'

M. 'Nipissing'

An open-pollinated seedling of *M. Sieversii* 'Niedzwetzkyana'. Raised in 1920 by I. Preston of Ottawa's Dominion agricultural experiment station. One of the original ROSYBLOOM CRABAPPLES. Selected in 1930 and named for Nipissing Lake of SE Central Ontario. Very rare; still in commerce. Carmine-red buds open to deep pink flowers fading to pale lavender, 1½"–1⅔" wide. Fruit mostly dark red with orange-yellow, the shady side bronze-green; 1⅓". An alternate-year bearer. Leaves purplish red turning green. Poor disease resistance.

M. 'North Dakota Peace Garden'

Jewell nursery of Lake City, MN, has listed this ≤1980 without a description.

M. 'Oakes'

≠ *M.* 'MR 450'

An open-pollinated seedling from *Malus* 'Scugog' seeds that originated <1950 at the Morden research station of Manitoba. Selected and introduced by William Oakes of Glenelm nursery of Miami, Manitoba. Extremely rare; not in commerce. Flowers light purplish-red. Fruit dark red; 1⅝". Leaves purplish. Valued for cold-hardiness above all. Poor disease resistance.

M. 'Oekonomierat Echtermeyer'—see *M.* 'Echtermeyer'

M. 'Ormiston Roy'

Parentage not known. William Ormiston Roy (1874–1959), landscape architect, horticulturist and traveler, of Montreal, found this <1933 in Des Moines, IA. Named and introduced in 1954 by A. den Boer of Des Moines, IA. Common. Rose-red buds open to pale pink flowers, fading to pure white; 1½" wide; resembling those of *M.* × *floribunda*. Fruit shiny, green, yellow, then orange-yellow with a reddish blush; reddish after frost; ½"; abundant and persistent into winter. Leaf sharp-toothed, like that of *M. hupehensis*. Tree vigorous, wide, to 20' tall and 25' wide or more. Fair to good disease resistance.

M. 'Osman'

(*M. baccata* × *M.* 'Osimoe'/'Hibernal' Russian APPLE)

Bred <1904 by W. Saunders of Ottawa; named in 1911. Sold from 1958 to 1976 by Dropmore nursery of Manitoba. Valued for the prairie provinces because of its cold-hardiness and edible fruit. Flowers like an ORCHARD APPLE: pink buds open to white, 2"–2¼" wide, but calyx tube is hairless. Fruit good eating, and showy (looking like red plums from a distance); reddish, oval, 1" (1½") wide; calyx persists; stem to 1⅛" long, lightly hairy; dropped by mid-September. Little scab, but fireblight-prone.

M. 'Pagoda'

(*M.* 'Red Swan' × *M.* 'Autumn Glory')

Bred by the late Father J.L. Fiala of Falconskeape, near Medina, OH. Named in 1970, registered in 1987. Not yet in commerce. A rounded, weeping tree, to 12' tall and wide. Bright carmine buds open to white flowers. Fruit brilliant orange-red, 7/16".

M. 'Park Centre'

Introduced ≤1985 by Willoway nursery of Avon, OH. Uncommon. Flowers light pink. Foliage glossy green. Fruit yellow-golden, dropping in fall with the foliage. Tree vigorous, narrowly upright to vase-shaped, 20'–25' tall. Disease resistant.

M. *Parkmanii*—see *M. Halliana* 'Parkmanii'

M. 'Parrsi'—see *M.* Pink Princess™

M. 'Patricia'

A seedling of *Malus* 'Hopa' raised by Arie den Boer of Des Moines, IA. Selected in 1939, introduced in 1953, named after the wife of den Boer's son Henry. Rare. Deep purplish-red buds open to purple flowers, 2" wide, the petal claws white. Fruit juicy, tasty, dark red, 1¾"– 2" wide. Growth compact, sturdy. Poor disease resistance.

M. 'Peachblow'

Origin not known, but in U.S. commerce <1930. Extremely rare; long commercially extinct. Related to *M.* × *floribunda*. Habit more upright. Dark pink buds open to white flowers, 1³⁄₁₆" wide. Fruit ⁷⁄₁₆", red, coloring early.

M. 'Pillar of Fire'—see M. 'Strathmore'

M. 'Pink Beauty'
= M. 'MR 451' (i.e., "Morden Rosybloom No. 451")

Raised <1945 at Morden research station of Manitoba. One of 1,700 second generation ROSYBLOOM CRABAPPLE seedlings raised in an effort to obviate the undesirable magenta floral tint so prevalent in the original ROSYBLOOM series. Named and introduced commercially ≤1957–58 by Simpson nursery of Vincennes, IN. Extremely rare; extinct commercially. Flowers glowing rich rose, almost magenta-free; remaining bright. Leaf bluntish-toothed, reddish when young, maturing bluish-green, the fall color pretty like that of the yellow-orange of pencils. Fruit ¾"–¹⁵⁄₁₆" wide, dark red, prominently pale-speckled; calyx persists; pulp red; stem slender, to 1¼" long. Record: 24' × 4'9" × 46' Seattle, WA (1992; pl. 1948).

M. 'Pink Cascade'

A ROSYBLOOM CRABAPPLE seedling selected in 1946 by W.L. Kerr of Sutherland, Saskatchewan. Named and introduced in 1969 by Inter-State nursery of Hamburg, IA. Very rare. Branches hang down, making a narrow tree, 14' tall and 7' wide, at length about 16' tall and wide. Flowers light pink. Leaf big (like that of M. 'Sundog'). Fruit sparse, bright red, to ½"–¾" long; calyx drops.

M. 'Pink Dawn'

Introduced during the 1980s by Willoway nursery of Avon, OH. Uncommon. Broad, upright habit to 18' tall. Foliage green. Flowers pink. Fruit burgundy purple, dropping in fall with the foliage.

M. 'Pink Eye'—see M. 'Dakota Pink Eye'

M. 'Pink Perfection' PP 2912 (1969)
(M. Hartwigii 'Katherine' × M. 'Almey')

First flowered in 1960. Introduced in 1969–70 by Princeton nursery of New Jersey. Common. Grows to 15'–20' tall; sturdy, oval to rounded, at length very broad. Deep carmine-red buds open to clear pink, 2"–2³⁄₈" wide flowers, double (15–20 petals). Leaves thick, green, narrow, sharply toothed, conspicuously pointed. Fruit bloomy yellow-orange, sometimes with a pink blush on the sunny side, ½"–¾" wide; calyx stays or drops; stem often much-swollen, downy like the fruit itself. Two other cultivars of the same parentage are M. 'American Beauty' and M. 'Snowcloud'. Poor disease resistance.

M. Pink Princess™
= M. 'Parrsi'

A Malus Sargentii seedling introduced ≤1988 by Schmidt nursery of Boring, OR. Uncommon. Purple buds open to pink flowers. Fruit bloomed purple, ¼"–⁷⁄₁₆" wide; calyx drops; pulp red. Leaves purplish when young, then dark green; yellow in fall; lobed on shoots; coated on both sides with short inconspicuous white hairs. Tree low and spreading broadly; pendulous in part; to 8' tall and 12' wide.

M. 'Pink Satin'

Introduced in the 1980s by Simpson nursery of Vincennes, IN. Rare. Dark reddish-purple buds open to clear pink flowers, profuse on long plumes; 1³⁄₈" wide; the calyx tube and stem with white hairs. Leaves medium to dark green, heavy like those of an ORCHARD APPLE; some on the strong shoots lobed. Fruit ³⁄₈"–1¹⁄₁₆" wide, showy red, with crisp yellow pulp; a pit where the calyx was; persistent. Tree vigorous, upright rounded; gaunt when young.

M. 'Pink Spires'

A ROSYBLOOM CRABAPPLE seedling selected by W.L. Kerr of Sutherland, Saskatchewan. Introduced ≤1966. Common. Dark lavender buds open to pink flowers; early. Leaves purple-red in spring, turning to bronzy-green in summer, spectacular red-orange in fall. Fruit purplish-red, ½", persistent. Very cold-hardy and adapted to the Great Plains. To 26' tall; symmetrical and narrowly upright. Poor to fair disease resistance.

M. 'Pink Star'

A bud sport of Malus 'Hopa' introduced ≤1991 by Waynesboro nursery of Virginia. Very rare. Flowers soft pink, star-shaped. Leaves emerge bronze and mature to green. Disease resistance far superior to that of its parent. Tree first upright, spreading with age; to 20'–25' tall.

M. 'Pink Sunburst'—see M. 'Hopa'

M. 'Pink Weeper'—see M. 'Echtermeyer'

M. 'Pioneer Scarlet'

A ROSYBLOOM seedling of unknown parentage introduced <1954 by A.L. Young of Bonnie Brook Farms of Brooks, Alberta. Extremely rare. Commercially extinct. Flowers light rose, 2⅜" wide. Leaves broad, oval, downy when young; greenish; stem reddish and hairy. Very cold-hardy.

M. 'Pixie'

Originated by A. den Boer of Des Moines, IA. Introduced in 1948. Exceedingly rare. Commercially extinct. Flowers pink. Fruit red. Tree tiny and semi-pendulous.

M. × platycarpa—see M. × heterophylla

M. × platycarpa 'Hoopesi'—see M. × heterophylla 'Hoopesi'

M. 'Plena Nova'—see M. ioensis 'Plena Nova'

M. 'Prairie Maid'

= M. Simpson 8-29
(M. Zumi 'Calocarpa' × M. 'Van Eseltine')

Introduced ≤1988 by Simpson nursery of Vincennes, IN. Rare. Reddish-purple buds open to profuse flowers 1"–1½" wide, deep pink fading to whitish. Fruit ½" wide, orange-red; calyx drops. Leaves rusty-coppery when young, with silver hairs; lobed strongly on shoots. Tree compact, forks low, broadly rounded, medium sized. Proven disease-resistant at the Morton Arboretum.

M. 'Prairie Rose'—see M. ioensis 'Prairie Rose'

M. 'Prairifire'

[(M. Zumi 'Calocarpa' × M. Sieversii 'Niedzwetzkyana') × M. atrosanguinea] × M. 'Liset'

Introduced in 1982 by Dr. Daniel F. Dayton of the University of Illinois, Urbana. Common. Crimson buds open to dark purplish-red flowers, not fading, 1⅝" wide. Leaves mostly unlobed; sharply toothed, deep red-purple when young, maturing dark tawny green, orange in fall. Fruit ⅜"–½" long, shiny purplish-red; pulp red; calyx drops, leaving prominent scars; stem slender, to 1⅓" long. Tree low, dense, broadly rounded, to 20' tall and wide. Winter bark dark red and CHERRY-like with numerous prominent lenticels. Good disease resistance; not scab immune, but suffers very little.

M. Prattii (Hemsl.) Schneid.

= Pyrus Prattii Hemsl.

From central and W China. Likely only a variant of M. yunnanensis. Named in 1895 for its 1888 or 1889 discoverer, the English naturalist Antwerp E. Pratt (fl. 1880s to 1910s), who arrived in China in 1887 as a private, amateur plant collector. Introduced in 1904 by E. Wilson for Veitch nursery of England. Introduced in 1909 to North America; extremely rare here. Almost never offered commercially. Very tardy to bloom, among the last Malus of all. Flowers ¾" wide, in many-flowered clusters. Foliage texture overall like that of a LINDEN (Tilia) or DOVE TREE (Davidia). Leaves to 6¼" × 4⅜"; stem to 1¹⁵⁄₁₆" long; broad, downy beneath; fall color dreadful yellow-green. Fruit ornamentally nil, brown-speckled, greenish with a red blush, eventually yellow-brown, finally soft and red-brown; persistent calyx; grainy pulp; ⅜"–1¹⁄₁₆" wide; hairy stems. Scabless. Record: 40' × 3'3" Seattle, WA (1993; pl. 1957).

M. 'Prince Georges'

= M. angustifolia 'Flore Pleno' (cf. M. ioensis 'Plena')
= M. angustifolia 'Roseo-plena'
= M. angustifolia 'Plena'
= M. ioensis 'Prince Georges'
(M. ioensis 'Plena' × M. angustifolia)

Originated in 1919 when seed from the Arnold Arboretum was raised at Glenn Dale, MD. In 1930, scions of the offspring were sent to the Arnold Arboretum. The clone was commercially circulated ≤1927 as a double-flowered M. angustifolia before it was renamed in 1943 'Prince Georges' (after the county in Maryland where it was raised). Once common, presently almost never sold. Flowers bloom late in May, fragrant, pink, 2" wide; very double, with (10–16) 25–41 (50–61) petals. Leaves exceptionally narrow, sharply toothed, lightly hairy below, glossy above, remaining green very late, as M. angustifolia often does, finally displaying great fall color in November. Fruit rarely borne, green, ⅞" wide; stem 1¾"– 2⅜" long. Branching structure very horizontal. Scab not bad. Record: 19' × 1'9" × 23' Lynnwood, WA (1993). A clone of the same parentage is M. 'Gladwyne'.

M. 'Princeton Cardinal' PP 7147 (1990)

≠ M. 'Cardinal' PP 2035 (1961)—an edible
    CRABAPPLE cultivar
= M. hupehensis 'Cardinal'

Introduced by Princeton nursery of New Jersey. Common. Although the name M. hupehensis 'Cardinal' has been used, the clone's parentage is cited as having nothing to do with M. hupehensis: M. 'Strawberry Parfait' × M. 'Crimson Cloud'. The clone cannot be called simply Malus 'Cardinal' because that name was used for a different cultivar 29 years previously. The only accurate way out of the mess seems to be to erect a new name, Malus 'Princeton Cardinal' (or something else unique and appropriate). Flowers bright red. Foliage glossy red all summer. Fruit small and deep red. Tree broad-headed, 15' tall. Good disease resistance.

M. 'Professor Sprenger'

Raised <1950 by S.G.A. Doorenbos of the Hague, Holland. Named after A.M. Sprenger, director of the horticultural experiment garden at Wageningen, Holland. Introduced to commerce ≤1958; in North America only common since the 1970s. Said to be a M. × Zumi clone, leaves and flowers scarcely different yet with larger orange-red fruit. Red buds open to white flowers. Fruit orange-red, ⅝"–¾" long—about the size and shape of those of Malus 'Hopa'. Leaves dark green. To 45' tall and 35' wide reports J. Sabuco. Trunk reddish while young. Disease resistance good to excellent; can be ugly with scab.

M. 'Profusion'—see M. × moerlandsii 'Profusion'

M. prunifolia (Willd.) Borkh.

= M. asiatica Nakai
= Pyrus prunifolia Willd.

PLUMLEAF CRABAPPLE. PLUM-LEAVED APPLE. PEAR-LEAF CRABAPPLE. INU CRABAPPLE. Highly variable; probably a hybrid. From Asia; although unknown in a wild state there, it is reported naturalized in parts of eastern North America. Introduced in 1758 to England by P. Miller. To the U.S. <1831. Uncommon. Pink or red buds open to white flowers flushed with pink, 1½" wide, with long and hairless sepals. Fruit red, yellow or orange, less than an inch to 1½" long, the calyx staying. Considered as an ornamental, M. prunifolia is ordinary in flower and leaf, but notable for its large, colorful, persistent fruits. Record: 39' × 5'7½" × 46' Salem, OR (1993).

M. prunifolia 'Cheal's Crimson'

= M. prunifolia 'Fructu Coccinea'
= M. 'Cheal's Crimson'

Introduced ≤1896 by J. Cheal & Sons nursery of Sussex, England. In North American commerce since the 1950s; rare. Pink buds open to white flowers 1"–1⅝" wide—with hairless parts and looking like those of purebred M. baccata. Foliage and fruit like that of Malus 'Golden Hornet' but less hairy. Leaves like M. baccata but huge. Fruit plentiful, first yellow-orange, becoming wholly red, bloomy, speckled, like a smallish 'Dolgo' fruit but less elliptic, more approximating roundness (¾"–1" wide); calyx stays or sometimes drops. Good eating. Tree to 40' tall and 30' wide. Scabby.

M. prunifolia 'Fastigiata'—see M. prunif. var. Rinki 'Fastigiata'

M. prunifolia 'Fructu Coccinea'—see M. prunif. 'Cheal's Crimson'

M. prunifolia 'Golden Gem'—see M. 'Cheal's Golden Gem'

M. prunifolia 'Pendula'

Named in 1874. In Canada by 1896. In 1926 the Arnold Arboretum got scions from Kew, England. In North American commerce ≤1931. Extremely rare. Fruit orange, ¾" long. Branches pendulous.

M. prunifolia var. Rinki (Koidz.) Rehd.

= M. Ringo Sieb. ex Dipp.
= Pyrus Ringo (Sieb.) Wenz.

CHINESE APPLE. CHINESE PEAR-LEAF CRABAPPLE. RINGO. Introduced ca. 1850 by Siebold from Japan to Holland. Named in 1856. More common than typical M. prunifolia in North America. Called Rinki or Ringo in Japan; the name To-ringo means CHINESE APPLE. This variety is the Chinese and Japanese counterpart of the West's ORCHARD APPLE (M. × domestica) but the fruit is smaller, not impressed at its base, with a raised fleshy calyx. Fruit greenish-yellow or pure yellow to red. Flowers as in the common ORCHARD APPLE but with longer and slenderer stems. The leaves are more sharply toothed and usually less hairy, but leaf shape and hairiness vary. Compared to typical M. prunifolia, the var. Rinki is hairier, has somewhat shorter flowerstems, and ±pinkish, larger flowers (to 2"), and larger (to 2⅜" long) fruits. Ornamentally, it is no better in bloom than an ORCHARD APPLE, but its fruit can be lovely, and persistent. The fall leaf color can be beautiful. But the tree is an alternate bearer, and scabby.

M. prunifolia var. Rinki 'Fastigiata'
= M. prunifolia 'Fastigiata'

UPRIGHT PLUMLEAF CRABAPPLE. Raised in 1908 at the Arnold Arboretum from seeds extracted from fruits bought in a Peking street market by F. Meyer. Named in 1926, when 18' tall and 6' wide. In commerce ≤1943. Very rare. Tree more or less fastigiate at least when young; spreading in age. Flowers 1⅝" wide. Fruit depressed globose or sometimes slightly pear-shaped, nearly 1" wide, dark purple-red (the 1993 Lake County nursery catalog says "yellow and red"), the stem stout and ≤⅔" long.

M. prunifolia 'Veitch's Scarlet'—see M. 'Veitch's Scarlet'

M. pulcherrima—see M. × floribunda

M. pumila—see M. × domestica and M. sylvestris

M. pumila var. Niedzwetzkyana—see M. Sieversii 'Niedzwetzkyana'

M. pumila 'Pendula'—see M. 'Elise Rathke'

M. pumila 'Plena'—see M. dasyphylla 'Plena'

M. pumila 'Translucens'—see M. dasyphylla 'Plena'

M. Purdue U. 15-56—see M. 'Ralph Shay'

M. 'Purple Prince' PP 8478 (1993)
(M. 'Bluebeard' × M. 'Liset') × M. 'Gemstone'

Bred by the late Father J.L. Fiala of Falconskeape, near Medina, OH. Named in 1970, registered in 1987. Introduced in 1991–92 by Schmidt nursery of Boring, OR. Blood-red buds open to profuse magenta flowers, fading to pink, 1¼"–1½" wide. Leaves purple and hairy when young, then deep purple-green, finally bronzy-green; to 5" × 3¼"; can be strongly lobed as on Malus × moerlandsii 'Profusion'. Fruit ⅜"–⅝" wide, purple with a fine blue cast; pulp red; a pit where the calyx was. Young bark purple, in age like that of a CHERRY TREE. Tree vigorous; to 20' tall and wide; rounded.

M. 'Purple Wave'
= M. 'Jay Darling Red Seedling #3'

A chance Malus × Eleyi seedling raised by A. den Boer of Des Moines, IA. Selected ca. 1939; named in 1951 and introduced in 1953 by Inter-State nursery of Hamburg, IA. Uncommon. Flowers dark red-purple, 1½"–1⅔" wide; petals white-based, sometimes 6–7. Flowerstem, calyx, and sepals all hairy. Leaves very dark purplish-green and broad like those of M. 'Ferrill's Crimson' and 'Irene', with exceedingly fine, sharp teeth; with persistent white hairs, especially beneath. By leaf alone it cannot be distinguished from those two cultivars, but its fruit is smaller, and perhaps more abundant: to ¾" long, dark purple, bloomy; pulp blood-red, good to eat; calyx persists; stem hairy, to 1⅜" long. Tree shrubby and small, to 16' tall; broad growth (like M. 'Irene'), with a "wave-like effect."

M. × purpurea (Barbier) Rehd.
= M. floribunda atropurpurea (cf. M. × Eleyi)
= M. floribunda purpurea Barbier
= Pyrus purpurea (Barbier) Woolley

(M. Sieversii 'Niedzwetzkyana' × M. atrosanguinea)

PURPLE CRABAPPLE. Originated ca. 1900 by Barbier nursery of France; introduced in 1910. Now virtually extinct in commerce, the PURPLE CRABAPPLE was widely sold throughout most of this century. Disease problems, scanty blooms, and better cultivars have rendered it an old-fashioned eyesore. Flowers magenta, 1"–1⅜" (1¾) wide, sometimes limited to the top of the tree; early in the season. Fruit are like dark, hard red-purple cherries, about ¾"–1", with prominent persistent calyces. Leaves sharply toothed, dark purple when young, aging to green. Record: 41' × 4'10" × 42' Seattle, WA (1987).

M. × purpurea 'Aldenhamensis'
= M. aldenhamensis hort.
= Pyrus aldenhamensis hort.

ALDENHAM CRABAPPLE. Originated as a chance seedling ca. 1912 in the garden of the Hon. Vicary Gibbs (1853–1932) at Aldenham, Hertfordshire, England. Introduced to the Arnold Arboretum in 1923. Previously much grown in North America, ALDENHAM CRABAPPLE has lost favor, and since the 1980s has rarely been sold. Unlike typical PURPLE CRABAPPLE, it is dwarfish, 10'–12' (20') tall, the flowers (1⅔"–2") appear 2 weeks later and are semi-double (5–11 petals); it often blooms again in fall. Leaf teeth closely appressed, sharply toothed. Fruit abundant, ⅝"–1⅛" wide, dark red-purple beoming lovely cherry-red, ribbed at the ends, speckled with tiny whitish freckles; hefty stems to 2¾" long; persistent calyces. Flavor plain.

M. × purpurea 'Amisk'—see M. 'Amisk'

M. × purpurea 'Eleyi'—see M. × Eleyi

M. × *purpurea* 'Lemoinei'

= M. *floribunda* 'Lemoinei'

= M. *Lemoinei* hort.

= *Pyrus Lemoinei* hort.

LEMOINE CRABAPPLE. Introduced in 1922 by Lemoine nursery in Nancy, France. In 1925 introduced to the U.S. by the Arnold Arboretum. Very commonly sold during the 1950s; almost commercially extinct now. More than one clone has travelled under the name 'Lemoinei' so until the matter is clarified, the following description is tailored loosely enough to fit all of the variable specimens the writer has seen. Compared to typical PURPLE CRABAPPLE, 'Lemoinei' is more robust, often with a handsome trunk. It is slow to form flowerbuds (at age 10–12 years), and scabby right from the start, yet (for the little it's worth) less scabby than typical PURPLE CRABAPPLE. Flowers larger (1¾"–2⅛" wide) but usually fewer, sometimes semi-double, of superior redness—supremely showy, a beautiful, pure sight. Leaves often lobed, and strongly so; often very glossy. Fruit purple-red or red, roundish but can be either wider than long or longer than wide, ½"–1", the calyx stays or drops, the pulp is pinkish like that of M. 'Hopa', or reddish. Stems to 1³⁄₁₆" and lightly hairy.

M. × *purpurea* 'Pendula'—see M. 'Echtermeyer'

M. 'Pygmy'

Raised by W.K. Kerr of Saskatchewan. Introduced <1968. In Canadian commerce <1989. A very twiggy, dense dwarf tree forming a 13' globe of a formal, sheared look. Foliage dark purplish-green. Flowers deep purplish-red.

M. 'Radiant'

A seedling of *Malus* 'Hopa' selected ca. 1940 at the University of Minnesota; named and introduced in 1957–58. Common. Its name refers to the luminous color of the deep red buds opening to pinkish-red flowers. Similar to M. × *moerlandsii* 'Profusion' but blooms earlier, with not as dark an effect. Praised to a substantial degree elsewhere, in the maritime Pacific Northwest it is wretchedly unhealthy and fruitless, or bears a few attractive fruits, but too few and set against too ugly a foliar backdrop. Leaf reddish-purple when young, maturing green; sharp-toothed. Fruits pea-sized, persisting well,

mimicking *Rosa canina* hips excellently: bright red on the sunny side, yellow-pink on the shady side, to ⅞" long; harsh-tasting yellow pulp; stem to 1½" long. Record: 29' × 2'11" × 29' Seattle, WA (1993; *pl.* 1957).

M. 'Rainbow'

Since ≤1958 some U.S. nurseries have sold trees consisting of four or five cultivars budded on one *Malus* rootstock. The result is a deservedly rare freak; ditto its nickname "5-N-1 Crabapple." From nursery to nursery there may be different combinations. One set is: M. 'Almey', M. 'Dolgo', M. × *Eleyi*, M. 'Hopa', and M. × *purpurea* 'Aldenhamensis'.

M. 'Ralph Shay'

= M. Purdue U. 15-56

(M. 'Wolf River' APPLE × M. *Zumi* 'Calocarpa')

Introduced ≤1976 by Simpson nursery of Vincennes, IN. Common. Named after Dr. Junior Ralph Shay (1918–1980), Purdue University fruit breeder and plant physiologist. Flowers white. Fruit 1¼" wide, calyx ±stays; brilliant red by October and retaining its color later than most other CRABAPPLES; never drops. Delicious crisp yellow pulp. Tree to 15' tall, vigorous, sturdily branched. Leaf unusually dark green, lobed on shoots. Normally healthy, it can be scabby in the maritime Pacific Northwest.

M. 'Rebirzam'—see M. Redbird™

M. 'Red Barron'

('Red Baron')

= M. AA No. 328

Originated from an Arnold Arboretum tree. Introduced ≤1984 by Simpson nursery of Vincennes, IN. Common. Very dark red buds open to dark solid pink flowers, 1½"–1⅞" (2") wide. Leaves bronzy-red, fading quickly to bronzy-green with purplish venation; bluntish teeth; lightly hairy. Fruit dark to bright red, to ⅝" long; ribbed; calyx drops leaving a small to medium pit-scar; stem red, weakly hairy, 1⅓" long. Pulp pink or red, harsh-flavored. Habit compact and narrowly columnar to 18' tall and 8' wide. Fair disease resistance. (A 'Red Baron' ORCHARD APPLE was raised in Minnesota as a 'Golden Delicious' hybrid in 1926, selected in 1940, and named and introduced in 1969.)

M. Redbird™

= M. 'Rebirzam'

M. *Zumi* 'Woosteri' × (M. *Zumi* Christmas Holly™ × M. *Zumi* #678)

Bred by the late Father J.L. Fiala of Falconskeape, near Medina, OH. Named in 1974, registered ≤1983. In commerce. An upright-rounded, small 10'–15' tall tree. Brilliant red buds open to white flowers. Fruit bright red, 3/8"–5/8", profuse, very early maturing, beginning to color in August.

M. 'Red Dauphin'—see M. 'Dauphin'

M. 'Redfield'
(M. 'Wolf River' APPLE × M. Sieversii 'Niedzwetzkyana')

A ROSYBLOOM CRABAPPLE bred in 1924 at the research station, Geneva, NY. Introduced for trial in 1938. Rare. Commercially extinct. Flowers rosy-red, 1 5/8" wide, amazingly similar to those of M. Sieversii 'Niedzwetzkyana' and scarcely different—'Redfield' has a white-wooly calyx and narrower petals. 'Redfield' leaves are rounded at the base rather than narrowed, as well as being broader, healthier and a bit hairier. Fruit giant, up to 3¾" wide, as large as an ORCHARD APPLE; red skin; a white core surrounded by red pulp. Plenty are borne, but they are are marred visually by a bloomy coating, and the leaves being so dark and dull result in the tree not being ornamental in fruit. Fruit ripe from mid-August, into early October, fallen by November. Edible, but primarily a novelty to use in pie baking. Tree like an ORCHARD APPLE in habit and looks.

M. 'Redflesh'
(M. Sieversii 'Niedzwetzkyana' × M. ioensis 'Elk River')

A ROSYBLOOM CRABAPPLE bred by N. Hansen in South Dakota, introduced in 1928. Rare, but still in commerce. Grown primarily for its edible fruit. Flowers purplish-red to light rose, 1¾" wide. Leaves purple-tinted when young, becoming bronzy-green. Fruit resembles 'Red Delicious' apples, 2" long, ripe in September-October, rosy-red inside and out, or greenish-brown on the shady side. An alternate-year bearer. Malus 'Red Tip' is a Hansen hybrid of the reverse parentage.

M. 'Redford'
(M. 'Wolf River' APPLE × M. Sieversii 'Niedzwetzkyana')

A ROSYBLOOM CRABAPPLE bred in 1921 at the research station, Geneva, NY. Introduced for trial in 1938. Same parentage as M. 'Redfield' and similar but with larger, paler pink flowers. Inferior; discarded. Offered by some nurseries in the 1950s, however. Now extremely rare. An alternate-year bearer.

M. 'Red Jade' PP 1497 (1956)

Originated in 1935 as an open-pollinated Malus 'Exzellenz Thiel' seedling. Introduced in 1953 by the Brooklyn Botanic Garden. Common. Buds ivory, tinted with faded lipstick-pink tinge, opening white, 1"–2" wide, fragrant, like those of M. baccata. Each flower like an ORCHARD APPLE blossom yet the parts and leaves are only a little hairy. Fruit 5/8" long, first yellow-green with a pink blush, turning orange-red and then bright red; persistent—classic M. baccata type, as are the leaves. Poor to fair disease resistance; when disease-free, the foliage is glossy, vibrant green. Tree a weeper, to 15' tall. Not a vulgar mop like Malus 'Echtermeyer', 'Red Jade' grows broader. Record: 14' × 2'8" × 28½' Seattle, WA (1993; pl. 1953).

M. Red Jewel™ PP 3267 (1972)
= M. 'Jewelcole'

Introduced by Cole nursery of Circleville, OH. Registered ≤1975. Common. Pink buds open to pure white flowers, small, 1" wide or less. Fruit brilliant red 3/8"–½"; persists and looks like HOLLY berries; stem to 1¼" long. Flushes early, the bright green spring leaves contrasting prettily with the still persisting red fruit. Stays green late, into November—at least while a young specimen. Looks like a M. Sieboldii offspring; it may be a M. × Zumi offspring, with harder, longer-lasting fruit. Leaf persistently hairy on both sides, sometimes lobed. Habit upright pyramidal to 18' tall and 12' wide, with horizontal branching. Fair to excellent disease resistance.

M. 'Red Peacock' PP 7022 (1989)
M. 'Molten Lava' × (M. 'Luwick' × M. Zumi #243)

Bred by the late Father J.L. Fiala of Falconskeape, near Medina, OH. Named in 1969. Introduced ≤1989 by Klehm nursery of Illinois. Tree small, semi-weeping, to 12' tall and 14' wide. Bright red buds open to soft pink or white, ruffled flowers. Fruit shiny orange-red, ½"; persistent. Dark green foliage.

M. 'Red River'

(*M.* 'Dolgo' CRABAPPLE × *M.* 'Delicious' APPLE)

Bred by A.F. Yeager of Fargo, ND. Selected in 1934. Introduced ca. 1937. Very rare, commercially extinct. Flowers pink, 2" wide. Fruit bright red, late-season, 1⅝"–2" long; edible and of high quality.

M. 'Red Rock'

Introduced <1992 by Matt Tures' Sons nursery of Huntley, IL. Origin and attributes not known.

M. 'Red Ruby'—see M. 'Royal Ruby'

M. 'Red Siberian'

= *M.* × *robusta* 'Red Siberian'

Originated in France. Described in 1803. In North American commerce since <1831 when Prince nursery of Flushing, NY, sold it. Fruit decidedly ornamental, borne in clusters, red, ¾"–1" diameter; calyx stays or drops. **'Large Red Siberian'** is a vigorous, hardy tree, alternate-bearing, with larger fruit (to 1½"). Both of these, doubtless representing various clones, were formerly commonly grown for their edible fruit, but are now commercially extinct. A variation on the theme is *Malus* 'Yellow Siberian' (q.v.).

M. 'Red Silver'

(*M. baccata* × *M. Sieversii* 'Niedzwetzkyana')

A ROSYBLOOM CRABAPPLE bred in 1928 by C.A. Hansen of South Dakota. Widely grown since the mid-1940s. Still common in nurseries. Flowers deep red to china-rose, 1¼"–1½" wide; petals narrow. Foliage reddish-bronze with silvery white hairs in spring, becoming dingy-colored bronzy-green in summer. Leaf sharp-toothed; lobed on suckers. Fruit dark purplish-red, ¾" long, calyx usually stays and can become fleshy; stem to 1" long or more; too dark to be showy, not pleasant for eating raw, the fruit can be used to make jelly. Tree can be an alternate bearer. Tree to 30' tall and 15' wide, with willowy branch tips tending to droop. Fireblight prone.

M. 'Red Snow'—see M. 'Red Swan'

M. 'Red Splendor'

Selected in 1948 by Melvin Bergeson of Fertile, MN; descended from a *Malus* 'Red Silver' seedling. Common. A small, rounded 30' tree of open and graceful habit. Deep ruby buds open to light pink flowers 1⅘"–2" wide, keeping their color well and contrasting with the purplish young leaves. Leaves age to dark bronzy-green, and can change to attractive fall color.

Fruit shiny bright red, ½"–⅝" long; calyx drops; persistent. Good disease resistance.

M. 'Red Star'

(*M.* 'Dorothea' × *M. Halliana* 'Parkmanii')

Introduced ≤1981 by Weston nursery of Hopkinton, MA. Tree of upright, wide habit. Flowers double, red with a white center. Fruit red, small.

M. 'Red Swan' PP 6974 (1989)

= *M.* 'Red Snow' (in part)

M. 'Molten Lava' × (*M.* 'Red Jade' × *M. purpurea* 'Lemoinei')

Bred by the late Father J.L. Fiala of Falconskeape, near Medina, OH. Named ('Red Snow') in 1967, registered ≤1983. Introduced by Klehm nursery of Illinois. A finely branched weeper, to 10' tall. Deep orange-red buds open to light pink bell-shaped 1½" wide flowers that turn creamy-white. It looks like a WEEPING CHERRY TREE in bloom. Leaves fine, narrow, ca. 2½" long, heavy-textured; attractive gold in fall. Fruit bright red, elliptical, ¼"–½" thick. Matures in early September and lasts until December or January.

M. 'Red Tip'

= *M.* × *Soulardii* 'Red Tip'

(*M. ioensis* 'Elk River' × *M. Sieversii* 'Niedzwetzkyana')

A ROSYBLOOM CRABAPPLE introduced in 1919 by N. Hansen of Brookings, SD. Rare; commercially extinct. Carmine buds open to pink flowers 1⅝"–1¾" wide; late. Young leaves red-tipped; fall color orange. Fruit 1⅝"–2" wide, yellow-green, red-blushed. CRABAPPLE expert A. den Boer doubted 'Niedzwetzkyana' was involved in the parentage, the German expert G. Krüssmann suggested 'Red Tip' might have originated as an *M.* × *heterophylla* (*M. coronaria* × *M. domestica*); and nurseryman Paul Wohlert opined "likely *M. ioensis* × *M. Eleyi*." The present writer has not studied a 'Red Tip' specimen, but trusts in Hansen's careful documentation. *Malus* 'Redflesh' is a Hansen hybrid of the reverse parentage.

M. 'Renée'

Bred by Dr. C.D. Schwartze (1902–1988), of the Washington State University at Puyallup. Named for his eldest granddaughter, R. Scheyer. Introduced in 1973. Extremely rare; scarcely in commerce. Crimson buds open to dark pink flowers. Leaves reddish-bronze, then dark green; very sharply toothed. Fruit profuse, purple, to ¾"; roundish; pulp sour; calyx drops. To 18' tall, of roundish, irregular habit. Blooms early, with *M.* 'Dolgo' and *M.* × *micromalus*.

M. 'Rescue'

= *M.* Scott 1

An open-pollinated 'Blushed Calville' APPLE seedling from Scott, Saskatchewan, at the Dominion research station. Introduced to commerce in 1933. Common; primarily grown for its edible fruit. Pink buds open to white flowers, 1" wide. Fruit to 1½" wide, greenish-yellow, largely washed and striped red; pulp yellowish-white, firm, sweet, subacid, pleasant; ripe in late August. Tree medium tall, rounded; healthy; very hardy. Resists fireblight.

M. Ringo—see *M. prunifolia* var. *Rinki*

M. Ringo f. *sublobata*—see *M.* × *sublobata*

M. rivularis—see *M. fusca*

M. 'Robinson'

Selected and named <1970 by C.M. Hobbs nursery of Indianapolis, IN. Named after James Robinson, on whose land the tree was found. Introduced in the 1980s. Common. Tree vigorous, to 25' tall or more. Hyped as the fastest-growing CRABAPPLE. Crimson buds open to deep pink flowers. Leaves dark purple when young, becoming bronzy dark green with red veins, thinly coated beneath with white hairs; some shoot leaves remarkably large and lobed; edged with fine, sharp teeth; fall color can be handsome. Fruit dark red, at first bloomed, becoming quite glossy, ⅜"–⅝"; has an orange pit where the calyx was; stem to 1⅞" long; pulp red, flavor ok. Excellent disease resistance, except often scabby in the maritime Pacific Northwest.

M. × *robusta* (Carr.) Rehd.

= *Pyrus* × *robusta* hort.
= *Pyrus microcarpa* var. *robusta* Carr.
= *Pyrus baccata cerasifera* Regel
= *Malus cerasifera* Zab., non Spach
(*M. baccata* × *M. prunifolia*)

CHERRY CRABAPPLE. ORCHARD CRABAPPLE. The Latin name refers to the solid strength and vigor of this hybrid, first raised ≤1815 in Europe. Numerous clones including *Malus* 'Red Siberian' and 'Yellow Siberian' may be placed under the *robusta* banner. Purebred SIBERIAN CRABAPPLE (*M. baccata*) was economically little valued because of its tiny fruits. So it was crossed with *M. prunifolia* to produce larger-fruited offspring, which were then cultivated as SIBERIAN CRABAPPLES. Bafflingly similar offspring can result from *M. baccata* × *M. domestica*, for which the name *M.* × *adstringens* has been used. Since many *robusta* cultivars exist, the following description is necessarily almost uselessly general: Pink buds open to white flowers, 1½"–2¾" wide, on trees looking like ORCHARD APPLES (*M.* × *domestica*) but slenderer; leaves comparatively thin and scantily hairy; fruit like miniature apples, yellow, red-blushed, or wholly red, ¾"–1¾". The calyx sometimes drops, sometimes is retained as a swollen bumpy tip; stems ¼"– 2". For the greater part of this century certain North American nurseries offered trees under the *robusta* name, but now, although the trees are common in the landscape, the usage of the ambiguous name has plummeted, and good riddance. Old specimens of the trees can be enormous, 40' or 50' tall and wide, and when laden with colorful fruit in late summer or fall, are breathtakingly lovely.

M. × *robusta* 'Erecta'

= *M.* × *robusta* 'Fastigiata'

COLUMN CHERRY CRABAPPLE. Raised at the Arnold Arboretum from seeds sent in 1904 by C. Sargent from Peking. Named officially in 1926. In commerce ≤1934. Rare. Pink buds open to single and semi-double white flowers 1⅝" wide. Leaves finely sharp-toothed. Fruit yellowish with a dark crimson cheek, or usually all red; roundish, ¾"–1"; the calyx reluctant to drop; pulp white, bearably flavored; stem short, ca. ½" long. Tree recorded to 40' tall and 25' wide.

M. × *robusta* 'Fastigiata'—see *M.* × *robusta* 'Erecta'

M. × *robusta* 'Joan'—see *M.* 'Joan'

M. × *robusta* 'Persicifolia'

PEACHLEAF CRABAPPLE. In 1910, Wm. Purdom collected seeds in N China. One such seedling, raised by Veitch nursery of England, was sent to the Arnold Arboretum in 1913, and grew into such a distinctive specimen that it was individually named in 1920. In commerce ≤1934. Very rare. It tends to have a multitrunked, shrubby habit of a tight cone shape. Pink buds open to white flowers 1⅝" wide. Leaves dark green, to 4" × 1⅛"; stem to 1¼" long; finely sharp-toothed—hence narrow and PEACH-like; can have rich golden-red fall color. Fruit profuse, attractive, persists well, showy red like those of *Malus* 'Hopa', to nearly ⅞" long, with white, poor-flavored pulp, yet good for jelly-making. Fair to good disease resistance.

M. × *robusta* 'Red Siberian'—see M. 'Red Siberian'

M. *Rockii*—see M. *sikkimensis* 'Rockii'

M. 'Rosseau'

An open-pollinated seedling of M. *Sieversii* 'Niedzwetzkyana'. Raised in 1920 by I. Preston of Ottawa's Dominion agricultural experiment station. One of the original ROSYBLOOM CRABAPPLES. Selected in 1930 and named for Rosseau Lake of southern Ontario. Very rare; out of commerce. Maroon-red buds open to rose-red flowers 1⅝"–1¾" wide; petal claws white. Foliage bronzy-green in spring, bright red in fall. Fruit annual, bright red, 1", hangs until late fall. Tree rounded, dense, to 40' tall.

M. "Rosybloom"

The name ROSYBLOOM CRABAPPLE is applied generally to dozens of trees, either intentional hybrids or open-pollinated seedlings or descendents of M. *Sieversii* 'Niedzwetzkyana', which retain more or less the purplish to rosy floral color, and usually feature reddish young leaves as well. The first trees so called were 33 raised in 1920–21 and named by Isabella Preston of Ottawa's Dominion agricultural experiment station; the term ROSYBLOOM was coined by W.T. Macoun, also of the station. Later on, W.R. Leslie of the Morden, Manitoba, raised 1,700 ROSYBLOOM seedlings and selected eight of the best for introduction. Leslie's selections originally were given numbered names such as M. 'MR 452'—meaning Morden Rosybloom No. 452. Most of the eight were renamed such as M. 'Almey'. Still other breeders and nurseries added to the ROSYBLOOM group, and not a year goes by without Mother Nature producing another somewhere. The present volume has more than 50 trees which may be called ROSYBLOOM cultivars.

M. Round Table™ series

Produced by Jim (James W.) Zampini of Lake County nursery, Perry, OH. In the early 1970s, Zampini began to select superior dwarfs from seedlings of M. *baccata*, M. *Sargentii,* and M. *Sieboldii.* These cultivars include: Camelot® ('Camzam'), Canterbury™ ('Canterzam'), Cinderella® ('Cinzam'), Excalibur™ ('Excazam'), Guinevere® ('Guinzam'), Hamlet® ('Hamzam'), Ivanhoe™ ('Ivazam'), King Arthur™ ('Kinarzam'), Lancelot® ('Lanzam'), Sir Galahad™ ('Sirgazam').

M. 'Royal Beauty'

Origin unknown, ≤1980. Common. Flowers reddish-purple. Fruit cherry-red, round, ¼"–⁷⁄₁₆". Leaves reddish-purple when young, becoming dark green, purplish beneath. A small weeping tree with slender, hanging reddish-purple stems.

M. Royal Fountain™
= M. 'Huber'

Discovered as chance seedling by Huber's nursery of Middletown, DE. Introduced in 1992–93 by Schmidt nursery of Boring, OR. Flowers rose-red to deep pink. Fruit ⅜"; deep red. Foliage purplish-bronze most of the season. Good scab and mildew resistance. Moderately fast to 10' tall, a graceful weeper that serves as a substitute for the disease-prone *Malus* 'Echtermeyer'.

M. 'Royal Ruby' PP 3052 (1971)
= M. 'Red Ruby'
(M. 'Van Eseltine' × M. 'Almey')

Bred ca. 1955 by Simpson nursery of Vincennes, IN. Introduced in 1969 by Cole nursery of Ohio. Common. Tree form upright, narrow, sub-fastigiate, to 15' tall and 12' wide. Deep maroon buds open to reddish-pink flowers as in the ROSYBLOOM group; double (15–25 petals); to 2½" (3") wide. Blooms late. Calyx lightly hairy, sepals erect, flowerstem hairless, to 2" long. Fruit pear-shaped or oblong-deformed, bloomed-red, sparse, ca. ½"–¾" long; calyx can stay. Leaves dark green, glossy, sharp toothed. Foliage prone to an unhealthy, yellowish cast. Poor disease resistance.

M. Royal Scepter™
= M. 'Royscezam'

A seedling of *Malus* Madonna® introduced ≤1992 by Lake County nursery of Perry, OH. Buds large, dark red, opening intermittently to fragrant double white and mauve flowers. Foliage wine-red. Fruit orange-red. Habit upright, to 18' tall and 10' wide.

M. 'Royal Splendor' (original)
(M. 'Serenade' × M. 'Amberina')—in registration documents
(M. 'Red Swan' × M. 'Autumn Glory')—in Fiala's book

Bred by the late Father J.L. Fiala of Falconskeape, near Medina, OH. Named in 1976, registered in 1987. Not yet in commerce. A graceful semi-weeper, to 10' tall and 14' wide. Carmine-red buds open to white flowers. Fruit ½"; bright orange with a red cheek.

M. 'Royal Splendor' (invalid)

A chance *Malus* 'Royalty' seedling registered in 1993 by Paul G. Olsen of Roseberry Gardens, Thunder Bay, Ontario. Flowers bright pink with a white eye. Fruit ½"; purple. Leaves purple, glossy.

M. 'Royalty'

A ROSYBLOOM seedling, the pollen parent possibly *Malus* 'Rudolph'. Selected in 1958 by W.L. Kerr of Sutherland, Saskatchewan; named and introduced in 1962. Common. Flowers purple, large, almost like the leaf color, amazingly dark. Leaves purple, thin, hairless, shiny, sharp-toothed. Fruit bloomy, blueberry-sized (½"–⅝"), too dark purple to be showy; calyx stays. The darkest foliage of all CRABAPPLES, passing for a PURPLELEAF PLUM. Poor disease resistance: fireblight gets it; at best, weak scab resistence; can be sparse-crowned and ugly. Green root suckers an eyesore. Record: 27' × 3'4" × 40' Ferndale, WA (1993).

M. 'Royscezam'—see M. Royal Scepter™

M. 'Ruby Luster'

A ROSYBLOOM offspring introduced ≤1991 by Zelenka nursery of Grand Haven, MI. Scarlet red flowers. Leaves lobed on shoots. Fruit sparse, dull red-brown, silver-specked, 1"–1¼"; pulp crisp, blood-red, acceptably flavored or even delightful; calyx stays. Bark can be CHERRY-like. Scab resistant.

M. 'Rudolph'

A *Malus Sieversii* 'Niedzwetzkyana' seedling or a 2nd generation ROSYBLOOM CRABAPPLE introduced in 1954 by Dr. F.L. Skinner of Dropmore, Manitoba. Its dark ruby-red buds reminded Skinner of Rudolph the red-nosed reindeer. Common. Flowers deep rosy-red, 1¾"–2" wide; sometimes semi-double. Fruit orange-yellow, ¾" long, persistent. Foliage glossy, bronzy-brown becoming dark green. Tree vigorous.

M. 'Russel's Crimson Weeper'—see M. 'Echtermeyer'

M. 'Ruth Ann'

= *M.* Simpson 4-28

A seedling raised at Simpson nursery of Vincennes, IN. Tested in the 1970s. Rare, but still sold. Named for an employee who assists with office duties as well as nursery operations. Flowers semi-double, rose-red. Leaf green. Fruit ½"; dull maroon. Habit vase-shaped. Good disease resistance.

M. *Sargentii* Rehd.

= *Pyrus Sargentii* (Rehd.) Bean
= *M. Toringo* var. *Sargentii* hort.

SARGENT CRABAPPLE. PIGMY CRABAPPLE. Named for Charles Sprague Sargent (1841–1927), who in September 1892 introduced it to the U.S. from a brackish marsh near Mororan, Hokkaido, Japan. Not known as a wild species in Japan. Named in 1903. In the *Flora of Japan*, this name is placed as a synonym under *M. Sieboldii*, and probably at most should be ranked as a variety of that species. Long widely planted in North America, and deservedly popular. It does not hybridize readily but breeds largely true when raised from its own seed. Palest pink buds open to pure white flowers, 1" wide, the roundish petals cupped around a heart of gold anthers; very fragrant; calyx tube pretty red on the sunny side. Fruits red, pea-sized (⅓"), numerous, attractive against the yellow leaves in October, turning soft early but hanging well; sweet flavored like rosehips. Leaves dark green, lobed on strong shoots, hairy above and beneath. A scabfree shrub or bushy, broad little tree; some are topgrafted at 6'. Record: 15' × 1'11" × 31' Seattle, WA (1993).

M. *Sargentii* 'Candymint'—see M. 'Candymint'

M. *Sargentii* 'Lustgarten Strain'

Introduced ≤1979 by Baier Lustgarten nursery of Long Island, NY. "We have what believe to be the finest DWARF SARGENT CRABAPPLE—very contorted with lower branches trailing the ground."

M. *Sargentii* 'Pink'

Introduced ≤1991 by Manbeck nursery of New Knoxville, OH. Red buds open to pink flowers. New growth reddish.

M. *Sargentii* 'Rancho Ruby'

Found in 1963 and introduced ≤1974–75 by Scanlon nursery of Ohio. Still sold in 1980s by Handy nursery of Portland, OR. Sold topgrafted on a 7' standard, to make a tree with a rounded crown ca. 15'–20' tall. Flowers outstanding ruby-red, double. Fruit small, yellowish.

M. Sargentii 'Rosea'

PINKBUD SARGENT CRABAPPLE. Sent to the Arnold Arboretum in 1921 as a two-year-old seedling from Rochester, NY. Named in 1943 and introduced by the Arnold Arboretum. Rare. Dark pink buds open to white flowers, slightly larger than those of typical *M. Sargentii* (1⅓"–1½"). Fruit slightly larger. Tree larger growing. Less disease-resistant.

M. Sargentii 'Roselow'

('Roseglow' *sensu* Dirr 1990)

A seed-grown cultivar—minimal variation observed in offspring. From the Rose Lake Plant Materials Center of East Lansing, MI, of the USDA Soil Conservation Service. Introduced ≤1978. Rare. Flowers fragrant, white. Fruit dark red ¼". A dense tree to 8' tall and 10' wide.

M. Sargentii 'Tina'

Introduced ≤1974 by Wm. McReynolds of Hook's nursery of Lake Zurich, IL, and named after his granddaughter. Common. Dwarfer than typical *M. Sargentii*, growing only 4'–5' tall. Topgrafted sometimes. Excellent disease resistance.

M. 'Satin Cloud' PP 6956 (1989)

(*M.* Coralburst™ × tetraploid *M. Zumi*) × (tetraploid *M.* 'Dorothea' seedling × tetraploid *M. Zumi*)

Bred by the late Father J.L. Fiala of Falconskeape, near Medina, OH. Named in 1970, registered ≤1983. Introduced by Klehm nursery of Illinois. An octoploid resulting from colchicine treatment of a seedling from the above cross. A small, very upright rounded 10' tall tree. Branches very fine, with very short internodes. Pale pink buds open to pure white, cinnamon-scented flowers. Leaves heavily textured, deep green; in fall deep orange, reddish-mauve, and yellow. Fruit ca. ⅜"; amber yellow.

M. × Scheideckeri Späth ex Zab.

= *Pyrus Scheideckeri* (Späth *ex* Zab.) Wittm.
= *Pyrus spectabilis floribunda Scheideckeri* Späth
(*M. floribunda* × *M. prunifolia*)

SCHEIDECKER CRABAPPLE. Originated by J.P. Scheidecker's nursery of Munich, Germany. First announced in print in 1887. Common. Pale red buds open to pale pink flowers, fading white, semi-double, 9–14 (20) petals; 1⅜"–1¾" wide, on downy stems; calyx wooly; five styles. Flowers like those of *Malus* 'Blanche Ames' except hairier, with shorter stems. Leaves long, slender, sharply toothed, hairy on both sides, especially beneath. Fruit often scarce, yellow-green, at length becoming orange-yellow (orange-juice color), roundish, slightly ribbed, ½"–¾", at most ⅞" wide; usually dropping the calyx; on a lightly hairy stem to 1⅞" long. Flavor bland. Tree small and bushy; slow. B.O. Case nursery of Vancouver, WA, sold it as 'Wah Me' which means "The Modest Maiden." Fair to poor disease resistance. Record: 21' × 3'2" × 24' Seattle, WA (1992; *pl.* 1944).

M. × Scheideckeri 'Excellenz Thiel'—see M. 'Exzellenz Thiel'

M. × Scheideckeri 'Hillieri'

('Hillier')
= *M. floribunda* 'Hillieri'
= *M.* 'Hillieri'

An offspring of *M.* × *Scheideckeri*. Selected out of a shipment of plants brought from Holland by Hillier nursery of England. In 1928, the year it was named, it was introduced to the U.S. by the Morton Arboretum. In commerce here ≤1942. Uncommon. Differs from *M.* × *Scheideckeri* in having less doubled flowers, and greater vigor. Deep red buds open to pink flowers which fade nearly white, single or semi-double (5–10 petals), to 1½" wide; in clusters of 5–8; calyx tube and stems hairy. Fruit ⁷⁄₁₆"–¾" wide, yellow to orange. Record: 29' × 4'0" × 35' Edmonds, WA (1993).

M. 'Schmidtcutleaf'—see M. transitoria Golden Raindrops™

M. Scott 1—see M. 'Rescue'

M. 'Scugog'

An open-pollinated seedling of *M. Sieversii* 'Niedzwetzkyana'. Raised in 1920 by I. Preston of Ottawa's Dominion agricultural experiment station. One of the original ROSYBLOOM CRABAPPLES. Selected in 1928 and named in 1930 for Scugog Lake of SE Ontario. Very rare; extinct commercially. Dark purplish-red buds open to 1¾"–2" flowers of purplish-red (quickly fading), the petals with white claws. Fruit to 1¾" wide, brownish-purple; pulp red; edible in early September; good for jelly. An alternate-year bearer. Foliage bronzy-green. Fireblight prone.

M. 'Sea Foam' (of J. Fiala, M. Dirr 1990)

(*M.* 'Red Jade' × *M. baccata*) × (*M. Zumi* #243 × *M. baccata* 'Jackii')

Bred by the late Father J.L. Fiala of Falconskeape, near Medina, OH. Registered ≤1983. Not in Fiala's 1994 CRABAPPLE book and not yet in commerce (unless renamed). Strongly weeping, very low, 5' tall or less. Deep red buds open to pure white flowers. Fruit bright red, ⅜"–½".

M. 'Seafoam' (of den Boer)

An open-pollinated (*M. Sieboldii* was possibly the pollen parent) *Malus* 'Echtermeyer' seedling selected ca. 1939–40 by A. den Boer of Des Moines, IA. Named in 1952. Very rare; out of commerce. Branches semi-pendulous. Rose-pink to carmine buds open to white flowers, with a trace of pink to flushed with deeper pink, 1⅓"–2" wide. Leaf deeply lobed, green. Fruit yellow; ½"–⅝".

M. 'Selkirk'

= *M.* 'MR 457' (i.e., "Morden Rosybloom No. 457")

Raised at Morden research station of Manitoba. One of 1,700 second generation ROSYBLOOM CRABAPPLE seedlings raised in an effort to obviate the undesirable magenta floral tint so prevalent in the original ROSY-BLOOM series. First flowered in 1939; widely tested and even sold in nurseries (as 'MR 457') before being named 'Selkirk' in 1962. Common since then, marketed as an improved *Malus* 'Hopa'. Named after a town in Manitoba named Selkirk, itself named after Lord Thomas Douglas Selkirk (1771–1820) who encouraged the migration of displaced Scottish farmers into the Red River Valley of Manitoba. Tree upright vase-shaped, spreading in age, rounded, to 25' tall and wide. Flowers 1½"–2⅜" wide, deep purplish-pink, with rounded petals; stamens long and prominent. Leaves glossy, reddish-green changing to dark greenish-bronze, then dark green; leaf teeth blunt or barely sharp. Fruit very glossy, ¾"–1" wide, with a prominent calyx scar; ribbed; bright cherry-red, early, abundant, extremely attractive; pulp pink or red, plain to good-tasting; stem to 2¹⁄₁₆" long. Tree scabby but highly valued where this disease is not a severe problem.

M. 'Sensation'

(*M.* 'Serenade' × *M.* 'Amberina')

Bred by the late Father J.L. Fiala of Falconskeape, near Medina, OH. Named in 1976. Introduced <1990. A graceful semi-weeper to 12' tall and wide. Carmine-red buds open to white flowers. Leaves dark green. Fruit bright orange with a red cheek, ½" wide; persistent.

M. 'Sentinel'

= *M.* Simpson 12-77

Introduced by Simpson nursery of Vincennes, IN.

Named in 1978. Common. It certainly has *M. baccata* in its background. Narrowly upright to 20' tall and 12' wide. Likely a good street-tree. Red buds open to white flowers, tinged pale pink. Leaves dark green. Fruit showy, dark red, ½" long, persistent; pulp yellow; stem short, to 1¹⁄₁₆" long. Tree suffers only a little from scab.

M. 'Serenade' PP 6957 (1989)

(*M. toringoides* × *M. Zumi*) × (*M. Zumi* 'Golden Candles' × *M. Zumi* #768)

Bred by the late Father J.L. Fiala of Falconskeape, near Medina, OH. Named in 1968, registered ≤1983. Introduced by Klehm nursery of Illinois. A semi-weeping tree, to 12' tall and wide. Deep pink buds open to pale blush-white flowers. Leaves heavily textured. Fruit abundant, ½" long, pale yellow with a deep orange-gold blush that becomes burnt orange or deep burnt golden-orange after frost.

M. Serenity™

= *M.* 'Serzam'

Introduced in 1995 by Lake County nursery of Perry, OH. Flowers abundant, brilliant white. Fruit gold, blushed bright red, coloring early. Tree of rounded habit, to 30' tall and 25' wide.

M. 'Serzam'—see M. Serenity™

M. 'Shakers' Gold'

Discovered at Shaker Heights, OH, by H. Ross of Strongsville, OH. Named ≤1980 by the late Father J.L. Fiala of Falconskeape, near Medina, OH. In commerce. Tree upright and spreading with age, to 16' tall. Soft pink buds open to white flowers, 1⅝" wide. Fruit ¾", light yellow, after frost deepening to yellow with a red blush, touched with reddish; persisting firm through January. Fair disease resistance.

M. 'Shakespeare'

Introduced ≤1957–58 by Scanlon nursery of Ohio. Commercially extinct or nearly so. A "tailored" or topgrafted variation of *M.* × *atrosanguinea* that retains its pink without fading. A small tree. Leaves lobed on shoots; edged with sharp teeth; persistently hairy beneath. Fruit yellow, red-blushed, about ⅓" long, with a cavity; stem lightly downy, to 1¼" long.

M. 'Shawnee'

Introduced <1991 by Manbeck nursery of New Knoxville, OH. Red buds open to pink flowers. Fruit small, red, persistent. A tree of dense, rounded habit, 25' tall and wide. Fall foliage color yellow.

M. 'Sherwood Park'

(*M. baccata* × *M.* 'Almey')

Registered in 1985. Selected by Thomas H. Machin of Sherwood Park, Alberta. Not known to have been introduced commercially. Flowers bright pink. Leaves small, dark, shiny green. A small, spreading tree.

M. "Siberian"

Most trees called SIBERIAN CRABAPPLES are *M. baccata*, and *M.* × *robusta* cultivars such as 'Red Siberian', 'Yellow Siberian' etc.

M. Sieboldii (Reg.) Rehd.

= *M. Toringo* Sieb. 1856, non Nakai 1916
= *Pyrus Toringo* Sieb. *ex* Miq.
= *Pyrus Sieboldii* Reg.

TORINGO CRABAPPLE. (In Japanese, *to-ringo* is applied to *M. prunifolia* var. *Rinki*, while *M. Sieboldii* is known as *zumi*.) From Japan. Introduced to Holland ca. 1845 by Philipp Franz Balthasar von Siebold (1796–1866). Named *M. Toringo* in 1856. Renamed *M. Sieboldii* in 1915 by A. Rehder because Siebold's use of the name "was a mistake." In March 1979, D. Wijnands argued that mistake or not, the older name *Toringo* is valid according to the rule of priority. The present writer, following the example of several prominent horticultural books published recently, conserves the familiar *Sieboldii* name. This species was previously much sold; presently it is extremely rare in commerce. In the narrow sense, SIEBOLD CRABAPPLE is a shrub or bushy little tree with yellow fruit, while larger-growing, more variable forms of the species are designated var. *arborescens*. But in a practical sense, the intergrading plant sizes, and fruit colors, argue for using only one name—to cover shrubs or trees, with fruit variously yellow, orange or red. In fact it may not be going too far to also include *M. Sargentii* under the epithet *M. Sieboldii*. Red or reddish-pink buds open to profuse white or slightly pink flowers with downy stems and sepals. Leaves characteristically lobed on strong shoots (sometimes almost like those of the AMUR MAPLE, *Acer tataricum* ssp. *Ginnala*), persistently hairy on both sides; usually of a tawny cast. Fruit usually yellow-orange (the color of orange juice); roundish, ¼"–⅓" (⁷⁄₁₆"), calyx drops; stems to 1" or more, hairy.

M. Sieboldii var. arborescens Rehd.

= *M. Toringo* Nakai 1916, non Sieb. 1856

From Korea and Japan. Introduced in 1892 from seeds collected in Japan by C. Sargent. Named in 1915. This, nature's typical version of *M. Sieboldii*, differs from the narrowly-conceived nomenclaturally typical *M. Sieboldii* in the following respects. The tree grows larger; flowers larger, less pink in the bud; leaves less lobed, less hairy; fruit larger (to ⁷⁄₁₆"), variable in color and shape. Although much grown in the 1920s, it has become commercially extinct. Record: 34' × 4'1" × 38' Seattle, WA (1992).

M. Sieboldii 'Fuji'

In 1942 the U.S. National Arboretum received a seedling from Glenn Dale, MD. It grew into a distinctive tree, so was selected in 1961 and named in 1968. The original specimen was 28' tall and 46' wide when 40 years old. Rare; in commerce. Deep carmine-pink or purplish-red buds open comparatively late to PEAR-like flowers, greenish-white with traces of purplish-red, 1½" wide, semi-double (10–15 petals); calyx and stems scarcely hairy. Leaves narrow, hairy on both sides, often lobed, sharply toothed. Fruit yellow-orange, ⅜"–¹¹⁄₁₆" wide; stem hairy, to 1½" long. Tree scabfree.

M. Sieboldii 'Wooster(i)'—see M. × Zumi 'Wooster(i)'

M. Sieboldii var. Zumi—see M. × Zumi

M. Sieversii (Ldb.) M. Roem. 'Niedzwetzkyana'

= *M. pumila* var. *Niedzwetzkyana* (Dieck) Schneid.
= *M. Niedzwetzkyana* Dieck
= *Pyrus Niedzwetzkyana* (Dieck) Hemsl.

REDVEIN CRABAPPLE. TURKESTAN APPLE. RUSSIAN PURPLE CRABAPPLE. From Turkestan, SW Siberia. The ancestral parent of virtually all the ROSYBLOOM and PURPLE-LEAF CRABAPPLES. Johann Sievers, born in Hanover (possibly in 1731), died by suicide in St. Petersburg in 1795, was a pharmacist, botanist, and explorer. While he travelled in S Siberia and Mongolia during the 1790s, he discovered this Central Asian species, which was named after him in 1830. In 1891, the purplish-pigmented clone of the species was named after Julian Niedziecki (1845–1918), Austrian geologist and traveller who was plant-collecting in Turkestan ca. 1880. *M. Niedzwetzkyana* was described, its name published, and introduced to cultivation by Dr. Dieck of Zoeschen, Germany, based on a cultivated specimen grown from seeds of a tree found in the Ili District of Central Asia. To call 'Niedzwetzkyana' a species therefore (as has been done), stretches credibility. It is a cultivar—of what species is the only question; some say *M. Sieversii* is itself not a distinctly valid species, just a mere version of another species.

In any case the tree is the original ROSYBLOOM type, and has been planted a great deal, although is nearly commercially extinct now. It is very similar to *Malus* 'Redfield' but not as hairy, and the leaves are narrower. 'Niedzwetzkyana' tends to be scabby beyond telling, yet leafy withal, of a tired bronze-yellow cast. Fruit few, large, frequently 2" or more (to 2¾"+), dull deep purple. Blooms similar to those of *Malus* 'Hopa' except are narrower in petal, with a less bounteous display, on shorter flowerstems; also the flowers are 1½"–1¾" rather than 2" wide. Record: 28' × 4'5" × 47' Woodland, WA (1993).

M. sikkimensis (Wenz.) Koehne *ex* Schneid.
= *Pyrus sikkimensis* (Wenz.) Hook. fil.

SIKKIM CRABAPPLE. From the Himalayas in E Nepal, Sikkim, Bhutan, Assam, SE Tibet, and NW Yunnan, China. Introduced in 1849 by Sir J. Hooker to Kew, England. To the U.S. possibly by 1895. Always extremely rare. D. Hill nursery of Dundee, IL, and W.B. Clarke nursery of San José, CA, offered it in 1940. It is not especially handsome and may be an alternate bearer, yet its disease-resistance may prove useful in breeding. Clearly related to *M. baccata*, but way too hairy for most forms of that species. Tree vase-shaped, fastigiate below, then flopping out above; usually remaining small (≤26' tall). The trunk and limbs are beset with conspicuous, coarse bluntish thornlike spurs. Leaves darkest green imaginable, narrow, very hairy, never lobed. Pink buds open to white flowers, 1" wide. Fruit dull bloomy green-brown, with a whisper of red; longstemed, teardrop-shaped, ⅝" long, red and scarred where the calyx drops off; of no ornamental value. Tree healthy and scabfree, profuse in foliage. D. Wyman in 1943 reported *M. sikkimensis* as one of very few CRABAPPLES known to breed largely true from seed. Seeds sent from the New York Botanical Garden in 1947 to the Seattle arboretum, apparently produced a hybrid. But both typical *M. sikkimensis* and the 'Rockii' strain (below) need critical study, because there is unreconcilable variation in written descriptions and cultivated specimens.

M. sikkimensis 'Rockii'
= *M. Rockii* Rehd.

ROCK CRABAPPLE. HIMALAYAN CRABAPPLE. From W China. Joseph Francis Charles Rock (1884–1962), Austrian linguist, and USDA plant collector, discov-

ered this CRABAPPLE in 1922. It was named in 1933. Scarce and little known in cultivation. Grows larger than typical SIKKIM CRABAPPLE. Floral parts lightly hairy. Fruit profuse, first pale green, lightly hairy, teardrop-shaped, with a pit where the calyx was, red on its sunny side by early October; much of the crop goes soft and red-brown by mid- or late-October, at which time it tastes just like applesauce—robins love feasting on it. Scarcely any scab.

M. 'Silver Drift'

Introduced ≤1987 by Simpson nursery of Vincennes, IN. Origin not known but certainly has some genes of *M. baccata*. Flowers like those of *M. baccata*. Resembles *Malus* 'Snowdrift' except ½" long red fruits with good color into December. Leaves large, like those of *Malus* 'Dolgo', never lobed. Tree vigorous.

M. 'Silver Moon'
= *M.* Simpson 1

First bloomed in 1950. Introduced in 1968–69 by Simpson nursery of Vincennes, IN. Sold by several major wholesale tree nurseries since the mid-1980s. Resembles *M. baccata* var. *himalaica*. A vigorous, compact columnar tree of medium size, 20' tall and 15' wide—good street-tree form. Pale pink buds open very late (one of the last), to snow-white flowers on terminal shoots, after the tree is in full leaf. Leaf sharply toothed. Fruit ½" wide, reddish or dark red-purple; yellow pulp; medium-size calyx scars; not showy, but persistent. Good disease resistance.

M. silvestris—see M. sylvestris

M. 'Simcoe'

An open-pollinated seedling of *M. Sieversii* 'Niedzwetzkyana'. Raised in 1920 by I. Preston of Ottawa's Dominion agricultural experiment station. One of the original ROSYBLOOM CRABAPPLES. Selected in 1930 and named for Simcoe Lake, 40 miles north of Toronto. (John Graves Simcoe (1752–1806) was the first Lieutenant-Governor of Upper Canada.) Seldom grown by nurseries, and commercially extinct, 'Simcoe' remains in a few collections. D. Wyman proposed discarding it in 1955. Tree small but strong-growing. Dark red buds open to light purplish-pink flowers, 1¾"–2" wide, fading much. Copper-tinted young foliage. Fruit 1"; carmine and orange, or bright purplish-red. An alternate-year bearer.

M. Simpson 1—see *M.* 'Silver Moon'

M. Simpson 4-17—see *M.* 'Burgandy'

M. Simpson 4-28—see *M.* 'Ruth Ann'

M. Simpson 4-53—see *M.* 'Yellow Jewell'

M. Simpson 6-15—see *M.* 'White Candle'

M. Simpson 7-62—see *M.* 'Jewelberry'

M. Simpson 8-29—see *M.* 'Prairie Maid'

M. Simpson 11-57—see *M.* 'Centurion'

M. Simpson 11-58—see *M.* 'Indian Summer'

M. Simpson 11-63—see *M.* 'Indian Magic'

M. Simpson 12-77—see *M.* 'Sentinel'

M. Simpson 14-13—see *M.* 'Ellen Gerhart'

M. 'Sinai Fire' PP 7492 (1991)
(*M.* 'Red Swan' × *M.* 'Amberina')

Bred by the late Father J.L. Fiala of Falconskeape, near Medina, OH. Named in 1974, registered in 1987. Introduced 1991–92 by Schmidt nursery of Boring, OR. An upright semi-weeping tree to 15' tall and wide. Ivory-pink or red buds open to white flowers 1¼"–1⅝" wide. Fruit ½"–⅝" long or wide, orange-red to red; calyx drops. The long, high-gloss, tapered leaves recall JAPANESE PLUM leaves (but are not obovate). Branching horizontal or inclined to droop. Minimal scab.

M. sinensis—see *Pseudocydonia sinensis*

M. Sir Galahad™
= *M.* 'Sirgazam'

Introduced in 1993 by Lake County nursery of Perry, OH. A rounded dwarf to 10' tall and 8' wide. Soft pastel pink buds open to white flowers. Leaf dark lustrous green, thick, leathery. Fruit ½"; gold slowly turning red in winter.

M. 'Sirgazam'—see *M.* Sir Galahad™

M. 'Sissipuk'

An open-pollinated seedling of *M. Sieversii* 'Niedzwetzkyana'. Raised in 1920 by I. Preston of Ottawa's Dominion agricultural experiment station. One of the original ROSYBLOOM CRABAPPLES. Selected in 1930 and named for Sissipuk Lake of British Columbia. Very rare; probably commercially extinct.

Deep carmine-red buds in clusters of 6–7 open (later than those of most ROSYBLOOM cultivars) to deep pink flowers, fading fast to pale pink, 1"–1½" wide, the well-spaced narrow petals with prominent basal white spots. Leaves bronzy when young, with blunt or sharp teeth. Tree can be nearly dead-looking from scab in bloom time, but by mid-September sport a full, green, handsome leafy crown. Fruit very dark purple-red, like that of a PURPLELEAF PLUM, wider than long, ¾"–1¼" on a ⅞"–1⅜" stem; calyx drops. Pulp red, not well flavored. An alternate-year bearer.

M. 'Snowbank'—see *M.* × *floribunda* 'Snowbank'

M. 'Snowcap'

Originated in Ottawa, as an "*M. baccata sibirica*"; sent in 1941 to Beaverlodge research station of Alberta. Named and introduced (along with *Malus* 'Arctic Dawn') by Beaverlodge in 1952. Very rare; still in commerce. Known primarily for supreme cold-hardiness—to -60°F. Pink-tinged buds open to white flowers 2⅜" wide. Fruit bright red, ½" long; persistent.

M. 'Snowcloud' PP 2913 (1969)
('Snow Cloud')
(*M.* Hartwigii 'Katherine' × *M.* 'Almey')

First flowered in 1963; selected in 1964, introduced in 1970 by Princeton nursery of New Jersey. Common. Deep pink buds open to masses of pure white flowers 2"–3" wide; 13–15 petals; hairy stems and calyx tube. Leaves narrow, dark green, with sharp teeth; lightly hairy while young. Twig bark exfoliates. Fruit sparse, yellow with a pink blush, ½" wide, a pit where the calyx was; stem 1¼" long, swollen. Tree vigorous, upright when young, broadening in age. Scabby and scale-infested to a hideous degree. Two other cultivars of the same parentage are *M.* 'American Beauty' and *M.* 'Pink Perfection'.

M. 'Snowdrift'

A chance seedling, almost certainly a *M. baccata* selection; H. Flint says a *M.* × *Zumi* hybrid. First observed in 1955; named and introduced in 1965 by Cole nursery of Painesville, OH. Common. A straight-trunked, strong grower 15'–25' tall; compact, rounded; of good street-tree form. Also used as a commercial pollenizer. Pink-red buds open to white flowers, fragrant, cupped, 1¼"–1¾" wide; petals broad; stem to 2¼" long. Leaves glossy, with fine, sharp teeth; very pest resistant. Fruit abundant, persistent, glossy orange-red, ⅜"–⁷⁄₁₆" wide; pulp red; calyx drops; stem long and slender. Nearly disease free.

M. 'Snow Magic' PP 4815 (1982)

Registered in 1979. Suspected *M.* 'Snowdrift' × *M.* 'Gorgeous'; selected and introduced by Willoway nursery of Avon, OH. Sold by several major wholesale tree nurseries since the mid-1980s. Broadly upright to 20' tall; compact. Young bark cherry-orange. Pink buds open to white flowers. Leaf green. Fruit dark red, ⅜" thick, remains till midwinter. Good disease-resistance.

M. 'Snow-White Crab'—see M. 'Dolgo'

M. × Soulardii (L.H. Bailey) Britt.

= *Pyrus Soulardii* L.H. Bailey
(*M. ioensis* × *M. domestica*)

Named in 1891 for James Gaston Soulard (1798–1878) of Galena, IL, who introduced it to cultivation in 1868. The original specimen was a chance seedling that arose after 1844 on a farm ca. 12 miles from St. Louis, MO. This SOULARD CRABAPPLE has understandably been confused with the SOULARD APPLE raised at Galena by Mr. Soulard. The fruit on Soulard's original specimen is yellowish-green, red blushed, to 2¼" wide. However, the epithet *Malus* × *Soulardii* can be applied to any *M. ioensis* × *M. domestica* crosses. Apparently no *Soulardii* selections are still in commerce. See *M.* × *heterophylla* for the cross *M. coronaria* × *M. domestica*. Record: 26' × 2'3" × 35' Philadelphia, PA (1969).

M. × Soulardii 'Fluke'

= *M.* × *Soulardii* 'Mercer'
= *M. coronaria* 'Mercer'
= *M. coronaria* 'Fluke'

Discovered ca. 1892 near Sherrard, Mercer County, IL, by N.K. Fluke of Davenport, IA. Fruit to 2⅝" wide, weighing 3 ounces. Apparently extinct commercially since the 1920s.

M. × Soulardii 'Giant'

Discovered in 1911 near Sherrard, Mercer County, IL. Introduced in 1917 by N. Hansen of South Dakota. Long extinct commercially. Fruit to 3" wide, weighing 4 ounces.

M. × Soulardii 'Mercer'—see M. × Soulardii 'Fluke'

M. × Soulardii 'Red Tip'—see M. 'Red Tip'

M. × Soulardii 'Wild Red'

= *M.* 'Wild Red'

Originated (or introduced) ca. 1907 by Linn County nursery of Iowa. Sold by some nurseries in Iowa at least into the 1940s. Now commercially extinct. Fruit usually <2" wide, dull green and red; lovely when polished.

M. × Soulardii 'Wynema'

= *M.* 'Wynema'
= *M.* 'Branson'

Discovered ca. 1920 by Abner Branson, near Oskaloosa, IA. Named for an Indian youth of that region. Very rare; commercially extinct. A dwarf tree. Flowers pink, flushed rose. Leaf often lobed. Fruit 2" wide, yellow-green, cheek dark red to brownish, sometimes almost entirely covered with red. An alternate-year bearer.

M. 'Sparkler'

A seedling of *Malus* 'Hopa' from the University of Minnesota. It looks like *M. baccata* was the pollen parent. First flowered in 1945; selected in 1947, introduced commercially in 1969. Common in the Midwest. Flowers 2" wide, rose-pink. Fruit dark red, ¼"–⅝" long; calyx drops. Leaves reddish when young, then dark green. Tree large, broad, branching semi-pendulous; to 15' tall and 24' wide. Scab-susceptible.

M. spectabilis (Ait.) Borkh.

= *Pyrus spectabilis* Ait.
= *M.* 'Frau Luise Dittmann'
= *M.* 'Lewis Dittman'
= *M. spectabilis* 'Flore Pleno'
= *M. spectabilis* 'Plena'
= *M. spectabilis* 'Rosea Fl. Plena'

CHINESE CRABAPPLE. CHINESE FLOWERING (CRAB)APPLE. CHINESE DOUBLE FLOWERING CRABAPPLE. SHOWY CHINESE CRABAPPLE. TAI TANG CRABAPPLE. Not known in the wild; long cultivated in N China—maybe the oldest ornamental CRABAPPLE cultivar of all. Cultivated in the West by 1780, when England's Dr. John Fothergill grew the typical variety with semi-double flowers. A single-flowered variant was grown by 1825. David Hosack's Elgin Botanic garden (New York City) catalog of 1811 is the first New World evidence of cultivation. Much offered in North American nurseries in the 1800s and earlier 1900s, but since the 1970s, increasingly discarded in favor of superior alternative cultivars. The epithet *spectabilis* is Latin for remarkable or showy. Red buds open to soft pink, large fragrant flowers, 1³⁄₁₆"–2⅛" wide, double (13–16 petals), in scantily-produced clusters against a sea of foliage. Trees unappealing, scabby and gawky, often nearly fruitless. Foliage sparse, conspicuously lustrous. Leaves narrow, highly glossy above, pale lettuce-green and hairy on veins beneath; often with a yellowish tint. Fruit in mid-September is yellow, red-blushed, roundish, ¾" long or sometimes larger (to ⅞" or rarely even 1 ³⁄₁₆"), calyx persistent; stem thickened markedly. An alternate-year bearer. Tardily deciduous. Records: 36' × 6'11" Cambridge, England (≤1982); 33' × 2'6" Seattle, WA (1992; *pl.* 1952).

M. spectabilis 'Alba Plena' or f. albi-plena— see M. dasyphylla 'Plena'

M. spectabilis 'Flore Pleno'—see M. spectabilis

M. spectabilis 'Grandiflora'

In 1918, W.B. Clarke nursery of San José, CA, listed a pink, double-flowered CRABAPPLE as "Large Flesh Pink." Clarke renamed it in 1929 *M. spectabilis* 'Grandiflora'. Said to bloom 10–14 days before "typical" *M. spectabilis* and to have larger flowers. Commercially extinct (at least by this name) since the 1940s.

M. spectabilis var. Kaido—see M. × micromalus

M. spectabilis 'Plena'—see M. spectabilis

M. spectabilis 'Riversii'

= *M. spectabilis* 'Rosea Plena'

RIVERS' CRABAPPLE. Raised <1864 in the nursery of Thomas Rivers (1798–1877), Sawbridgeworth, Hertfordshire, England. Name first published in 1872. Introduced to North America <1883 by Parson's nursery of Flushing, NY. Flowers more double (to 21 petals) than typical *M. spectabilis*, pinker, larger—often 2" and up to 2⅜" wide. Leaves wider. Fruit larger, perhaps greener. Very rare; half-a-dozen other cultivars have been sold under its name.

M. spectabilis 'Rosea Fl. Plena'—see M. spectabilis

M. spectabilis 'Rosea Plena'—see M. spectabilis 'Riversii'

M. spectabilis 'Van Eseltinei'—see M. 'Van Eseltine'

M. spontanea—see M. Halliana var. spontanea

M. 'Spring Glory'—see M. 'MR 454'

M. 'Spring Snow' PP 2667 (1966)

Discovered by A.J. Porter in 1963 as a 25-year old tree in Parkside, Saskatchewan. Introduced in 1965–66 by Inter-State nursery of Hamburg, IA. Common. Thought to be a seedling of *Malus* 'Dolgo'. Flowers single, fragrant, produced in masses of pure white; nearly sterile. Leaves rich bright green. Fruit ¾"–⅞" long; yellow with reddish blush; calyx usually drops; pulp tart and good. Scab susceptible. Record: 25' × 3'8" × 29' Yakima, WA (1994; *pl.* ca. 1975).

M. 'Spring Song' PP 6958 (1989)

(*M.* 'My Bonnie' × *M. Zumi*) × (*M.* 'Dorothea' × *M.* 'Wintergold')

Bred by the late Father J.L. Fiala of Falconskeape, near Medina, OH. Named in 1979, registered ≤1983. Introduced by Klehm nursery of S. Barrington, IL. An upright, compact, vase-shaped tree 10' tall and 7' wide. Deep pink buds open to baby-pink flowers, fading white, 2" wide. Leaf of very good texture. Fruit yellow-amber, ½".

M. 'Springtime' (of Fiala; see below)

(*M. atrosanguinea* × *M.* 'Echtermeyer')

Bred ≤1962 by the late Father J.L. Fiala of Falconskeape, near Medina, OH. Exceedingly rare; not yet in commerce. Tree small, fountain-shaped 8' tall and 10' wide, with long slender branches. Flowers lavender-orchid, 1"–1⅕" wide. Leaf reddish-bronze. Fruit dull red-purple, ½". Scabby. Useful for hybridizers only.

M. 'Springtime' (registered name; see above)

Originated in 1957 as a chance seedling in Rockwood, Ontario. Described in 1971. Introduced in 1973 by Sheridan nursery. Extremely rare; out of commerce. Similar to *M.* 'Dorothea' but foliage paler green, shoots have more prominent lenticels, flowers initially deeper pink, fruits more golden and closer to those of *M. baccata* in form.

M. 'Starburst'—see M. 'Hopa' (≤1987, J.L. Fiala used this name for his not yet introduced hybrid M. 'Van Eseltine' × M. 'Maria')

M. 'Stark Florence'—see M. 'Florence'

M. 'Strathmore'

= *M.* 'Pillar of Fire'

A ROSYBLOOM CRABAPPLE seedling raised <1949 at Morden research station of Manitoba. Previously commonly sold; still in commerce but increasingly being superseded because of disease susceptibility. Scab makes it painful to behold. Still, the tree is beautifully shaped and textured—displaying one of the most distinctive, impressive silhouettes of all, a joy to behold in contrast to the meager plainness and suckering madness so common in the genus. The trunk is pleasingly spiraled and twisted, the crown narrowly conical. Fall leaf color often striking red and scarlet. Flowers pink, 1¾"–2" wide. Fruit scarce; soft in mid-September, colored deep red and bright, not bloomed, about 1" long at most, irregularly oval, on a hairless stem 1¼" long. Pulp the color of pink lemonade. Record: 36½' tall at Seattle, WA (1994; *pl.* 1958).

M. 'Strawberry Parfait' PP 4632 (1981)

(*M. hupehensis* × *M. atrosanguinea*)

Introduced in 1982 by Princeton nursery of New Jersey. Common. A little tree, reportedly eventually to 25' tall; vase shaped, spreading. Flowers fragrant, pink with rose margins. Leaves reddish-purple when young, sparsely hairy; mature leaves thick, glossy, dark green, very finely sharp-toothed. Fruit often sparse, ½"–¾" wide, yellow with red blush or glossy orange-red, with a large, shallow calyx scar.

M. 'Striped Beauty'

Introduced in 1930 by the USDA (as BPI 88577) from Wright nursery of New Zealand. Very rare. Pink buds open to white flowers, ¾"–1" wide. Fruit a choice edible, yellow and red; 1". Some trees distributed under this name may be another introduction (BPI 64333; *Malus* 'Gorgeous').

M. × *sublobata* (Dipp.) Rehd.

= *Pyrus* × *sublobata* hort.
= *M. Ringo* f. *sublobata* Dipp.
= *M.* 'Cashmere'

(*M. Sieboldii* × *M. prunifolia* var. *Rinki*).

YELLOW AUTUMN CRABAPPLE. ZABEL CRABAPPLE. CASHMERE CRABAPPLE. First named in 1878 by H. Zabel; L. Dippel's name dates from 1893. Introduced to New World cultivation when C. Sargent raised it at the Arnold Arboretum from seeds he'd brought from Japan in 1892. This cross independently arose <1916 at Aldenham House, England, and that clone (indistinguishable) was named 'Cashmere'. Although various Midwest nurseries offered it during the 1930s–1940s, it thereafter declined in commerce, although is still found in many collections. A tree of ruggedly handsome appearance. Related to ORCHARD APPLE (*M.* × *domestica*), to judge by its foliage, but the *M. Sieboldii* clan is suggested by its bark being more finely flaky (reminiscent of that of *M. ioensis*), and the leaves lobed at their middles on strong shoots. Red buds open to profuse white flowers 1½" wide. Fruit yellow or yellow-orange, round, ribbed, ½"–¾"; calyx stays or drops; stem thin, hairy, pink, <1" long. The fruit makes a very good show. Record: 32' × 2'5½" × 39' Seattle, WA (1994; *pl.* 1953).

M. 'Success'—see M. × *moerlandsii* 'Liset'

M. Sugar Tyme® PP 7062 (1989)

('Sugartime')
= *M.* 'Sutyzam'
= *M.* 'Milton Baron #2'

A creation of Dr. Milton Baron of East Lansing, MI. Named Sugar Tyme® ≤1983. Common. Tree vigorous, upright-spreading to oval (18' tall and 15' wide); good street-tree form. Pale pink buds open to snowy white flowers, 1" wide. Leaf crisp green, slender, hairy, sharply toothed. Fruit at first bloomy green with a red blush, becoming rich red ¼"–½" (⅝"); persistent mid-September through January; large calyx scars; yellow pulp; slender red 1" stem. Good disease resistance.

M. 'Sunburst'—see M. 'Hopa'

M. 'Sundog'

= *M.* 'MR 453' (i.e., "Morden Rosybloom No. 453")

A ROSYBLOOM CRABAPPLE raised at Morden research station of Manitoba. A *Malus Sieversii* 'Niedzwetzkyana' seedling selected in 1939, named and introduced in 1947. Previously common—now out of commerce. Named for the prairie "winter rainbows" often popularly termed sundogs. Tree begins life with columnar habit but ends up widely vase-shaped. Red buds open to huge, profuse, palest pink flowers. Young leaves red. Quite sumptuous in full bloom. By mid-June the glossiness of the fruit, utterly without bloom, is striking. In September the tree has copious, gorgeous fruit, to 1⁵⁄₁₆" long, deep scarlet-red, shiny, contrasting well with the dark green leafy crown; stem to 2⅛". Leaves to 5" × 3". One flaw is the leaves can turn yellowish on the edges from some disorder; another drawback is that the fruit falls in October. Still, while in bloom, and until the fruit-fall, it is superb.

M. 'Sunglory'—see *M.* 'Almey'

M. 'Sunset'
M. 'Liset' × (*M. purpurea* 'Lemoinei' × *M.*
'Wintergold')
Bred by the late Father J.L. Fiala of Falconskeape,
near Medina, OH. Named in 1979, registered ≤1983.
Not in commerce. A small, upright tree, 10' tall and
wide. Orange-red buds open to bright red to mauve
flowers. Leaf reddish. Fruit deep claret red, ½".

M. 'Sutyzam'—see *M.* Sugar Tyme®

M. Sweet Perfume™
= *M.* 'Swezam'
Introduced ≤1983 by Lake County nursery of Perry,
OH. A tree to 18' tall and 12' wide, of rounded habit.
Pink buds open to white flowers, the most fragrant
of any CRABAPPLES grown by Lake County nursery.
Leaf dark green. Fruit bright gold.

M. 'Swezam'—see *M.* Sweet Perfume™

M. *sylvestris* (L.) Mill.
(*silvestris*)
= *Pyrus sylvestris* Gray
= *Pyrus Malus* var. *sylvestris* L.
= *M. acerba* Mérat
= *M. pumila* hort. (in part)
EUROPEAN WILD CRABAPPLE. EUROPEAN WILD APPLE.
From Europe and SW Asia. The Latin *silvestris* means
wild; not cultivated. And this species has indeed, in
its purebred state, rarely been cultivated since 1768
in England. Hybrids involving it exist in Europe, and
possibly some are in North America, as here it has
been used to a minor extent as a rootstock. Ornamental cultivars attributed to it, notably the so-called
'Plena', are not purebred. The unalloyed species is remarkable for its thorniness and lack of hairiness.
Except for a few hairs on its young, unfolding spring
growth, it is essentially glossy and hairless. Pink or
white buds open to white flowers ≤1½" wide. The
fruit is yellowish-green, rarely slightly reddish, to
1⅓", sour—the original "crab apple." Although usually a scrawny little tree, in 1974 one was recorded
78' tall in Poland's Bialowieza National Park.

**M. *sylvestris* var. *domestica*—see *M.* ×
*domestica***

M. *sylvestris* 'Eleyi'—see *M.* × *Eleyi*

M. *sylvestris* 'Flore Plena'—see *M. dasyphylla*
'Plena'

M. *sylvestris* 'Niedzwetzkyana Pendula'—see
M. 'Echtermeyer'

M. *sylvestris* 'Plena'—see *M. dasyphylla*
'Plena'

M. 'Tanner'
('Tanner's Variety')
Originated <1931 by J.A. Tanner, of Palo, IA. Rare
or at best uncommon. Tree dwarf if not shrubby.
May be a *M. baccata* clone, but more likely a hybrid.
Precocious. Deep pink buds open to pearly or
creamy-white flowers 1⅝"-2" wide; fragrant. Leaf
green, narrow. Fruit ⅝" long, orange-red or red,
persistent; calyx drops. An alternate-year bearer.
Disease-prone.

M. *theifera*—see *M. hupehensis*

M. *theifera* 'Rosea'—see *M. hupehensis* f.
rosea

M. *Thiel*—see *M.* 'Exzellenz Thiel'

M. *Thomsi*—see *M. coronaria* 'Thoms'

M. 'Thunderchild'
Introduced <1973 by P.H. Wright of Saskatoon,
Saskatchewan. Common. Tree to 20' tall; compact,
upright-spreading to rounded. Flowers deep red to
delicate rose, blooming while the new foliage is green,
then the foliage turns dark red-purple in summer.
Fruit sparse, ½"-⅝" dark red, persists well.

M. 'Timiskaming'
An open-pollinated seedling of *M. Sieversii*
'Niedzwetzkyana'. Raised in 1920 by I. Preston of
Ottawa's Dominion agricultural experiment station.
One of the original ROSYBLOOM CRABAPPLES. Selected
in 1930 and named for Timiskaming Lake of SW
Québec. Extremely rare; commercially extinct. Deep
carmine to deep maroon-red buds open to rosy-red
flowers with a white center, fade to purplish-pink,
1¾"-2" wide. Fruit dark purplish-red, ¾"-1⁵⁄₁₆". An
alternate-year bearer.

M. 'Tomiko'
(*M.* 'Meach' × *M. Eleyi*)
An open-pollinated seedling of *M. Sieversii*
'Niedzwetzkyana'. Raised in 1920 by I. Preston
of Ottawa's Dominion agricultural experiment
station. One of the original ROSYBLOOM CRABAPPLES.
Introduced <1953. Named for Tomiko Lake in the
Nipissing area of Ontario. Extremely rare; almost

commercially extinct. Dark maroon buds open to 1¾"–2" wide flowers, crimson, fading to pale lavender-pink. Foliage rich red to purplish—perhaps the best purple foliage of any Canadian ROSYBLOOM CRABAPPLE. An annual bearer.

M. 'Tops-In-Bloom'

Origin not known. Introduced <1990. Flowers rose, 1½" wide. Fruit described variously as orange-red or purple; urn-shaped, ca. ½" wide; calyx persists. Young leaves bronzy, at maturity dark green. Tree upright, rounded, 25' tall.

M. Toringo—see M. Sieboldii and M. Sieboldii var. arborescens

M. Toringo var. Sargentii—see M. Sargentii

M. toringoides (Rehd.) Hughes

= *M. bhutanica* (W.W. Smith) J.B. Phipps
= *M. transitoria* var. *toringoides* Rehd.
= *Pyrus toringoides* (Rehd.) Osborn

CUTLEAF CRABAPPLE. From W China—as E. Wilson reports: "the mountain fastnesses of the Chino-Thibetan borderland." Introduced in 1904 by E. Wilson for Veitch nursery of England. To the Arnold Arboretum in 1907–1908. Rare. Its 1915 specific name means Toringo (see *M. Sieboldii*), and Greek -*oides*, resemblance. The 1911 *bhutanica* epithet was resurrected in 1994 as the first validly published name, and for those who wish to be technically correct, it must replace the familiar *toringoides* name. Flowers late in the season, ≤1" wide, white, with very downy parts, resembling those of *M. fusca*. Shoot leaves strongly lobed. Attractively rugged, OAK-like habit of growth, not at all dense. Foliage can be dingy appearing—looking thirsty. Fruit profuse, ⅝" long. In June the fruit is waxy with a bloom; in mid-September, yellow-green, red-cheeked, pear shaped, often markedly narrowed to the stem. Fruit is at the peak of its showy red color in late October and early November; in spite of its abundance, the sight is not heartwarming. An alternate-year bearer. Scab moderate to bad. Records: 79' tall in Kansu, China (1925–26); 31' × 2'7" × 30' Seattle, WA (1992; *pl.* 1948).

M. toringoides 'Macrocarpa'

Raised <1933 by Major F.C. Stern, Goring-by-the-Sea, Sussex, England. Grown from seeds obtained from the Arnold Arboretum. Imported to U.S. by the Arnold Arboretum in 1933; introduced to commerce in 1939. Extremely rare; commercially extinct. The name from Greek *macro*, large, and *karpos*, fruit. Fruit profuse, to 1⅛" long and almost as wide, red-cheeked, with deep clear pits. They drop quickly, beginning in September, before those of typical *M. toringoides*. Flavor almost good; when partly rotted their flavor is hauntingly like that of PERSIMMONS (*Diospyros virginiana*). They make a mess under the tree like the fruit of *Sorbus domestica*. Record: 28' × 2'10" × 30½' Seattle, WA (1994; *pl.* 1960).

M. 'Trail'
(*M.* 'Northern Queen' × *M.* 'Rideau')

A Wm. Saunders 1904 cross at Ottawa's Central experiment farm. Selected and named 1913; introduced in the 1920s. Still in commerce. Grown primarily for its edible fruit. Pink buds open to white flowers, 1⅝" wide. Fruit 1⅝"; orange-red, of good dessert quality. Tree hardy and productive.

M. 'Transcendent'

Unknown history. Still in the nursery trade, it was grown as early as 1844 when Wm. Prince's Flushing, NY, nursery catalog listed it. One of the very best eating CRABAPPLES; widely planted. Tree robust and broad, to 25' tall or more. Young parts downy at first. Pink buds open to white flowers, 1⅝" wide. Fruit to 1¾", red-striped on a golden-yellow background, or nearly all reddish; ripe late August through mid-September. Pulp dark yellow, hard, delicious. Much like *Malus* 'Joan'.

M. transitoria (Batal.) Schneid.

= *Pyrus transitoria* Batal.

TIBETAN CRABAPPLE. HAWTHORN-LEAF CRABAPPLE. From NW China. Named in 1893. Introduced in 1911 by Wm. Purdom from Kansu to the Arnold Arboretum. Dropmore nursery of Manitoba sold it beginning in 1937. Few nurseries have listed it in North America, and whether it was sold true-to-name is uncertain. What is transitory about it is unknown. It is extremely rare. This species can barely be justified as separate from *M. toringoides*. It is a smaller more slender version; its leaves are usually smaller, more lobed, hairier; fruits smaller, rounded, yellow (bright red—claims D. Wyman; J. Rock says yellow and red). Brilliant butter yellow autumnal foliage. Record: 23' × 6'2" Kansu, China (1925–26).

M. transitoria Golden Raindrops™

= *M.* 'Schmidtcutleaf'

Introduced in 1991–92 by Schmidt nursery of Boring, OR. A highly distinctive and promising little tree; but how it differs from typical *M. transitoria* is unspecified. Healthy foliage like *Acer tataricum* ssp. *Ginnala*, that is: red shoots bearing glossy, lobed leaves. Fruit profuse, clear golden-yellow, ⅜" wide. Probably too bushy for street-tree usage, said to grow to 18' tall and 13' wide.

M. transitoria var. toringoides—see M. toringoides

M. Tschonoskii (Maxim.) Schneid.
= *Eriolobus Tschonoskii* (Maxim.) Rehd.
= *Pyrus Tschonoskii* Maxim.

LARGELEAF CRABAPPLE. PILLAR CRABAPPLE. From Japan, where it is called *O-urajiro-no-ki* or *Zumi-no-ki*. Introduced by C. Sargent to the Arnold Arboretum in 1892. Uncommon. Named in 1873 after Sukawa (Sugawa) T(s)chonoski (Chônosuke; 1841–1925), who was Carl Maximowicz's assistant while botanizing in Japan from 1860 to 1863. A species with ho-hum flowers and worthless fruit, but of strong constitution, attractive narrow form and flaming fall color—burgundy to orange. Pink buds open to white flowers, 1¼" wide. Fruit usually sparse and not showy, to 1¼"; yellow-green or brownish, hard and sour. Resists scab, but severely susceptible to fireblight. Branching upright; good street-tree form. Can grow very tall. Records: 59' × 3'0" Westonbirt, Gloucestershire, England (1981); to 52' × 6'6" in the wild; 46' × 5'0" Knaphill nursery, Surrey, England (1988).

M. 'Tures(i)'
Named after Matt Tures' Sons nursery of Huntley, IL. Uncommon. The 1979–80 catalog of Hinsdale nursery of Illinois says: "Pink buds open to white flowers. Fruit yellow. Branching irregular." Disease-prone.

M. 'Valley City'
Northwest nursery of Valley City, ND, introduced ≤1951 at least five cultivars (as 'Valley City #1', 'Valley City #2', etc.). Some nurseries abbreviated the names (e.g., *Malus* 'VC–4'). They are very rare, and either commercially extinct or have been renamed. Finch Arboretum of Spokane, WA, has (all) five of the cultivars.

M. 'Valley City #3'—see M. 'Leslie'

M. 'Van Eseltine'
= *M. spectabilis* 'Van Eseltinei'
= *Pyrus Van Eseltinei* hort.
(*M. spectabilis* 'Plena' × *M. arnoldiana*)

Glen Parker van Eseltine (1888–1938), bred this in 1930 at Geneva, NY. Introduced in 1938 as *Malus* 'Geneva'; renamed 'Van Eseltine' in 1943. Common. Tree begins as notably narrow, but flares out with age. Large bright mahogany-red buds open to very large rose and white flowers, 2"–2⅜" wide, double, 13–20 petals; calyx very broad; stem 1½" long. Leaves glossy light green, slender, finely sharp-toothed, hairless; stems red. Fruit sparse, small, pear-shaped, yellow or with a red blush or entirely pale red; ¾" wide with huge calyx scars. Fair disease resistance. Record: 27' × 4'6" × 39' Puyallup, WA (1993).

M. 'Vanguard'
A seedling of *Malus* 'Hopa' from the University of Minnesota, selected in 1940. Named and introduced in 1963. Common, but becoming less so yearly. A ROSYBLOOM CRABAPPLE, flushing relatively early. Flowers rosy-red, 1⅜"–2" wide. Leaves reddish while young, very big, very lightly hairy. Fruit to ⅞" long, beautiful bright red; calyx drops; stem to 1½" long; flavor poor. Tree semi-dwarf, vase-shaped in youth, slowly growing to 20' tall and wide. Poor disease resistance.

M. 'VC–1' through 'VC–5'—see M. 'Valley City'

M. 'Veitch's Scarlet'
= *M. prunifolia* 'Veitch's Scarlet'
(*M.* 'King of the Pippins' or 'Red Pippins' APPLE × 'Red Siberian' CRABAPPLE)

Raised <1905 by Veitch nursery of England. Popular in England, and grown in Australia, but little grown in North America, being largely limited to Canadian cultivation. Pink buds open to white flowers, 1⅓" wide. Fruit egg-shaped, scarlet, crimson on the sunny side, 1¾" wide; good eating. A small 20' tall tree.

M. 'Velvetcole'—see M. Velvet Pillar™

M. Velvet Pillar™ PP 4758 (1981)
= *M.* 'Velvetcole'

A ROSYBLOOM CRABAPPLE introduced in 1981 by Cole nursery of Painesville, OH. Common. Flowers ca.

1½" wide; petals close together; calyx tube dark, hairless; stems barely hairy, 1¼" long. Leaves purplish when young, sharply toothed. Fruit sparse, reddish, ½". Narrowly upright, slow, small, to 20' tall and 12' wide. Very scab-prone.

M. Victorian (Crab)™
= M. 'Viczam'

Introduced ≤1994 by Lake County nursery of Perry, OH. Of rounded form, 12' tall and 15' wide. Mauve buds open to double, white flowers. Fruit red.

M. 'Viczam'—see M. Victorian Crab™

M. 'Volcano'
(M. Zumi #243 × M. Zumi 'Woosteri')

Bred by the late Father J.L. Fiala of Falconskeape, near Medina, OH. Named in 1961, registered ≤1983. In commerce. Of upright growth, to 18' tall. Red buds open to blushed white flowers. Leaf heavily textured. Fruit fiery orange-red, ⅜"–½"; especially liked by birds.

M. 'Wabiskaw'

An open-pollinated seedling of M. Sieversii 'Niedzwetzkyana'. Raised in 1920 by I. Preston of Ottawa's Dominion agricultural experiment station. One of the original ROSYBLOOM CRABAPPLES. Selected in 1930 and named for Wabiskaw Lake of Alberta. Rare; commercially extinct. Vigorous upright habit. Branches tend to break badly from ice. Deep rose-red buds open to single and semi-double flowers, purplish-red with pale purplish centers, 1¾" wide. Fruit few, slightly angular, carmine-red with yellow or brown on the shaded side, 1¼". Fall leaf color orange-red. Disease resistance poor.

M. 'Wah Me'—see M. × Scheideckeri

M. 'Wayne Douglas'—see M. hupehensis 'Wayne Douglas'

M. Weeping Candied Apple® PP 4038 (1977)
= M. Candied Apple®
= M. 'Weepcanzam'

Introduced ≤1978 by Lake County nursery of Perry, OH. Common. A 10'–15' tall tree branching broadly horizontally to pendulously, with an irregular pattern. Red buds open to pink flowers, 1" wide. Leaves heavy-textured, purplish when young, then dark green with an overcast of red; hairy; sharp-toothed. Fruit bright cherry-red, ⅜"–⅜" wide, with a calyx pit,

stem to 1⅝" long; pulp harshly astringent; persistent until February or March. Nearly disease free.

M. 'Weepcanzam'—see M. Weeping Candied Apple®

M. White Angel®
= M. 'Inglis'

Originated ca. 1947 as a chance seedling. Presumably a M. Sieboldii descendant. Selected ca. 1955 by Louis Beno of Youngstown, OH. Registered in 1960. Introduced in 1962 by Inglis nursery. Common. Tree strongly upright, first vase shaped, becoming too wide (to 20' tall and wide) for street-tree usage. Pink buds open to profuse white flowers, 1¾" wide, fragrant. Weakly hairy parts, long flowerstems. Fruit profuse, looking like wild hazelnuts in size and shape, complete with the huge brown basal scar; ½"–⅝" (¾") wide, red, and pitted; pulp yellow. Attractive glossy foliage. Overall, a good healthy tree. Fair to good disease resistance except hurt by cedar-apple rust.

M. 'White Candle'
= M. Simpson 6-15
(M. 'Van Eseltine' × M. 'Almey')

Originated by Simpson nursery of Vincennes, IN. First flowered in 1959. Introduced in 1969–70 by Inter-State nursery of Hamburg, IA. Common. Red buds open to light pink or nearly white flowers, to 2½"–3" wide, semi-double. Leaf green, bluntly toothed. Fruit sparse, red, ⅝"–⅞" wide; calyx drops; stem to 1⅝" long. Foliage dark green, persisting until late in fall. Habit compact; sturdy stiffly upright, with spur type branches; to 15' tall and 3' wide, in time to 20' tall and 8' wide.

M. White Cascade® PP 3644 (1974)
= M. 'Cascole'

Registered and introduced in 1974 by Cole nursery of Painesville, OH. A seedling from an open-pollinated M. × Zumi. Common. Red buds open to white flowers. Leaves hairy, narrow, sharply toothed. Fruit abundant, first green with a beige blush, finally yellowish to russet, ⅜"–½" long; calyx drops; stem long and slender. Tree to 15' tall and wide, weeping. Good disease resistance.

M. 'White Weeper'—see M. 'Edna Mullins'

M. 'Whitney'

Originated <1869 by nurseryman Alexis Randolph Whitney (b. 1824) of Franklin Grove, IL. Common; grown primarily for its edible fruit. To 2¼" wide, clear waxen yellow, almost wholly striped with lively dark red. Ripe August–early September. Fireblight prone. In form and leaf the tree looks much like an ORCHARD APPLE (*M. × domestica*).

M. 'Wickson' PP 724 (1947)
(*M.* 'Yellow Newton' APPLE × *M.* 'Spitzenburg' CRABAPPLE)
Bred by Albert F. Etter of Ettersburg, CA. Introduced commercially in 1944. Still in commerce; grown for its edible fruit. Fruit 1⅝"–2" wide, brilliant red, juicy, oblong.

M. 'Wies'
Origin not known. In a 1980 study of disease resistance, it ranked excellent. Very rare; not in commerce. Flowers pink. Leaves purplish. Fruit very dark red to purple (maybe too dark to be attractive), ½"–⅝". Tree upright.

M. 'Wild Red'—see M. × *Soulardii* 'Wild Red'

M. 'William Sim'
Introduced <1931 by nurseryman William Sim of Cliftondale, MA. Extremely rare; long commercially extinct. Ivory-pink buds open to white flowers, like a late-season *M. baccata*. Scantily hairy, profuse, to 2¾" wide (reminiscent of those of *Poncirus trifoliata*). Flowerstems and sepals green but the calyx tube is deep blood red. Fruit red, shiny, oval, ¾"–1⅜" long; recalling that of *Malus* 'Dolgo'. Likely a *M. × robusta* cultivar. Tree large-growing. Little scab.

M. 'Will's Pink Eye'—see M. 'Dakota Pink Eye'

M. Winter Gem™—see M. × *Zumi* Winter Gem™

M. 'Wintergold'
('Winter Gold')
Originated in Holland, sometime between 1939 and 1946. In North American commerce since ≤1970s. Previously more commonly sold than it is now. Pink buds open relatively late in spring to white flowers, 1"–1½" wide, on hairless slender stems to 1½" long. Young growth lightly hairy. Leaves can be remarkably deeply lobed; edged with sharp teeth. Fruit shiny, greenish-yellow to clear-yellow, or with an orange, beige or pink blush; ⅓"–½" wide; calyx persistent or (usually) drops. Tree upright-rounded, to 30' tall and 20' wide. Poor to fair disease resistance.

M. 'Woven Gold'
M. 'Wintergold' × (*M.* 'White Cascade' × *M.* 'Peter Pan')
Bred by the late Father J.L. Fiala of Falconskeape, near Medina, OH. Named in 1965, registered in 1987. Not yet in commerce. A semi-weeper to 12' tall and wide. Carmine-red buds open to white flowers. Fruit ⁷⁄₁₆"; bright yellow-gold; calyx persists.

M. 'Wynema'—see M. × *Soulardii* 'Wynema'

M. 'Yellow Jewel'
= *M.* Simpson 4-53
Originated by Simpson nursery of Vincennes, IN. Uncommon. Deep pink buds open to pink-white. Fruit bright yellow; ⅜" wide. Tree slow-growing, compact, to 8' tall.

M. 'Yellow Siberian'
= *M.* 'Golden Beauty'
Originated <1826. In the U.S. since <1831 when Prince nursery of Flushing, NY, sold it. Once grown for its edible, decorative fruit. Later used as a rootstock. Commercially extinct. Fruit similar to that of 'Red Siberian' but bigger, and clear golden-yellow.

M. 'Young America'
Originated ca. 1900, but unknown until 1925 when distributed by the Fruit Testing Association of Geneva, NY. Still sold to a minor degree for its red, edible 2" fruit. Poor disease resistance.

M. *yunnanensis* (Franch.) Schneid.
= *Pyrus yunnanensis* Franch.
YUNNAN CRABAPPLE. From W China. Named in 1890. Seeds were introduced by E. Wilson to the Arnold Arboretum in 1909. The typical version is not cultivated except in botanic gardens and arboreta; the following variety has been in commerce.

M. *yunnanensis* var. *Veitchii* (Veitch) Rehd.
= *Pyrus Veitchii* hort.
VEITCH CRABAPPLE. From central China. Introduced in 1901 by E. Wilson to Veitch nursery of England. Sent to the Arnold Arboretum the same year, or at any rate ≤1907. In North American commerce ≤1934. Rare. VEITCH CRABAPPLE as originally described differs from YUNNAN CRABAPPLE in being comparatively tall and erectly branched, with leaves distinctly heart-shaped at the base, less hairy, more lobed, with brighter red fruit. But there are intermediate forms, which may justify combining not only typical *M. yunnanensis* and var. *Veitchii*, but *M.*

Prattii as well. In horticulture, only var. *Veitchii* has been at all prominent. The stock usually sold is fastigiate in youth, becoming vase-shaped and ultimately broad; at most over 40' tall and wide. The fall color can be a superb orange and scarlet. In flower and fruit it is not showy, yet can have fair to high disease-resistance. In this performance it recalls its big-fruited relative *M. Tschonoskii*, which is denser, of a richer green summer leaf color, and more sparing in fruit-production. Late to bloom; only *M. Prattii* is later. Greenish-white buds open to white *Sorbus*-like flowers in dense, flattened clusters (of as many as 15–20). Each flower is ¾" wide, with white anthers which turn carrot-orange; the sepals are rigidly curled back; the white, then orange, petals are far-flung, displaying the stamens prominently. Leaves large (to 7⅛" × 4¼"; stem to 2½" long), scabfree, but off-color. Fruit plentiful, dull, slightly hairy, first greenish-pink, then red on the sunny side, pale-brown dotted, round, ½"–⅝" wide; pulp grainy. Even if the fruit is abundant it is ornamentally nil. The fall leaf color is the highlight. Record: 29' × 3'7" × 37½' Seattle, WA (1994; *pl.* 1949).

M. 'Zumarang'

= *M.* × *Zumi* 'Rang'
('Zumirang' *sensu* Dirr 1990)

Introduced in the 1980s by Willoway nursery of Avon, OH. Uncommon. Flowers white. Leaf green. Fruit wine red, ⅜"; persisting until midwinter. Habit upright, broadly pyramidal to rounded. Bark CHERRY-like.

M. × Zumi (Matsum.) Rehd.

= *M. Sieboldii* var. *Zumi* (Matsum.) Asami
= *M. Sieboldii* sensu Fiala 1994
= *Pyrus Zumi* Matsum.
(*M. baccata* var. *mandshurica* × *M. Sieboldii*)

ZUMI CRABAPPLE. From Japan (rare) where it is called *O-zumi*. In 1892 C. Sargent introduced it from Hondo to the Arnold Arboretum. Named in 1899. Common since <1930. Sometimes ZUMI CRABAPPLE is considered a mere variant of *M. Sieboldii* instead of a hybrid. Whether it is a *Sieboldii* variant or a variable hybrid, some authors act as if it is a clone, and limit their description too narrowly to that of the type specimen. Much confusion has occurred with ZUMI, its seedlings, and its cultivar 'Calocarpa'. As a result, a variety of trees have been marketed as ZUMI CRABAPPLE. The description following serves as a realistic conservative

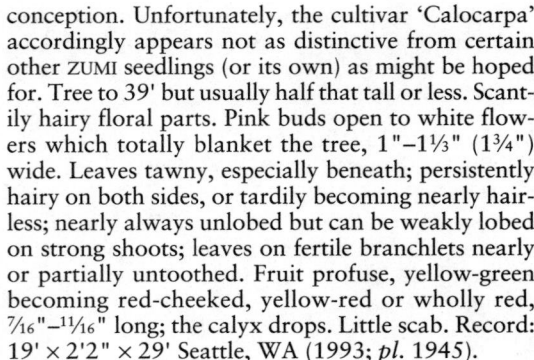

conception. Unfortunately, the cultivar 'Calocarpa' accordingly appears not as distinctive from certain other ZUMI seedlings (or its own) as might be hoped for. Tree to 39' but usually half that tall or less. Scantily hairy floral parts. Pink buds open to white flowers which totally blanket the tree, 1"–1⅓" (1¾") wide. Leaves tawny, especially beneath; persistently hairy on both sides, or tardily becoming nearly hairless; nearly always unlobed but can be weakly lobed on strong shoots; leaves on fertile branchlets nearly or partially untoothed. Fruit profuse, yellow-green becoming red-cheeked, yellow-red or wholly red, ⁷⁄₁₆"–¹¹⁄₁₆" long; the calyx drops. Little scab. Record: 19' × 2'2" × 29' Seattle, WA (1993; *pl.* 1945).

M. × Zumi 'Amberina'—see M. 'Amberina'

M. × Zumi 'Bob White'—see M. 'Bob White'

M. × Zumi 'Calocarpa'

= *M. calocarpa* hort.
= *M. Zumi* var. *calocarpa* (Rehd.) Rehd.

REDBUD CRABAPPLE. From Japan. Raised at the Arnold Arboretum in 1890 from Japanese seeds supplied by W.S. Bigelow. Introduced to cultivation in 1905. Named officially in 1915. Common. A markedly dense small tree, its branches spreading to form a crown ultimately wider than tall. Flowers similar to ZUMI (described variously as smaller or larger depending on one's idea of ZUMI itself). Leaves easily found lobed and obviously toothed. The reason for this clone's popularity, and its main attraction is the exceptionally profuse, bright red, showy, persistent fruit (*calocarpa* from Greek *kalos*, beautiful, and *karpos*, fruit.), to ½" wide on a stem to 1⅝" long. Severely hurt by fireblight, but resists scab well. As with typical ZUMI CRABAPPLE, this cultivar has been partly seed-propagated, and accordingly a variety of specimens are so labeled.

M. × Zumi 'Glen Mills'—see M. × Zumi Winter Gem™

M. × Zumi 'Golden Hornet'—see M. 'Golden Hornet'

M. × Zumi 'Rang'—see M. 'Zumarang'

M. × Zumi 'Schichtel's'

Introduced ≤1988 by Schichtel's nursery of Orchard Park, NY. An "improved var. with more compact habit." To 14' tall and 12' wide.

M. × *Zumi* 'Snowbank'—see *M.* × *floribunda* 'Snowbank'

M. × *Zumi* Winter Gem™
= *M.* × *Zumi* 'Glen Mills'
= *M.* 'Glen Mills'

Discovered by Pete Overdevest of Glen Mills, PA. Introduced ≤1988 by Glen Mills nursery. Uncommon. Ivory-pink buds open to white flowers, 1⅝"–1¾" wide (absolutely like those of *M. baccata*); calyx turns red and drops away. Fruit ⅜"–7⁄16" long, red, with a small smooth scar where the calyx was; stem long and slender (to 1⅞"). Leaves dark, broad. Vigorous; upright; may work as a street tree. Minimal scab.

M. × *Zumi* 'Wooster(i)'
= *M. Sieboldii* 'Wooster'

Raised in 1949 and named by the late Father J.L. Fiala of Falconskeape, near Medina, OH. Fiala used this clone a great deal in his hybridizing work. Tree broadly ovate. Bark tannish-coral. Salmon-coral buds open to fragrant white flowers. Fruit ½", dark orange-red, abundant. Disease free.

M. 'Zumirang'—see *M.* 'Zumarang'

Manglietia

[MAGNOLIACEÆ; Magnolia Family] 25 spp. of broadleaf evergreen trees. The name derives from a Malay or Javanese name for one of the species. Related closely to *Magnolia*, which differs in technical floral details (*i.e.*, 2 rather than 4–6 ovules per carpel). Another closely related genus is *Michelia*. The following two *Manglietia* species probably can grow wherever evergreen forms of SWEETBAY (*Magnolia virginiana*) are hardy. Too little is known about them for definitive guidance or to state unequivocally that one is hardier or more ornamental than the other. *Magnolia*-lovers and rare plant connoisseurs are evaluating them.

M. Fordiana Oliv.
= *Magnolia Fordiana* (Oliv.) Hu

From Hong Kong, Viet Nam and SE China; extremely rare in the wild. Named in 1891 after Charles Ford (1844–1927), British botanist and plant collector in S China. Introduced to Western cultivation

≤1934. Most if not all specimens date no earlier than 1981. In North American commerce ≤1987. Exceedingly rare. It might be likened to the SWEETBAY (*Magnolia virginiana*), but with stiffer foliage. Leaves bronzy when young; at maturity to 9" × 2¾", dark green above, ghostly pale beneath. Flowers from (April) May into July, 4" wide; consisting of thick petals, waxy white with a pink tinge; anthers many, pink to brilliant red. Bark smooth and gray. Records: to 98½' × 15'6" in the wild; 24' tall at Berkeley, CA (1993; *pl.* 1981).

M. insignis (Wall.) Bl.
= *Magnolia insignis* Wall.

From the central Himalayas, Burma, Tibet, W China, and N Viet Nam. Named in 1824 (meaning distinguished or remarkable in Latin). Introduced to Western cultivation ca. 1912 by G. Forrest. In North American commerce ≤1976–77. Extremely rare. Leaves evergreen to semi-evergreen, to 8¼" (11¾") × 2⅜" (3⅛"), dark glossy green above, paler beneath. Flowers in May or June; fragrant, 3"–5" wide; pure white, creamy-white, pale or deep pink, or suffused purple. Seedcone 3"–4" long, bright purple at first. Records: to 120' tall in the wild; 66' × 10'2" Caerhays Castle, Cornwall, England (1985; *pl.* 1928).

Maytenus

[CELASTRACEÆ; Bittersweet Family] 200–255 spp. of mostly tropical and subtropical trees and shrubs. From *maitén*, the native Chilean (Mapuche) name of the species first described. A related genus is *Euonymus*.

M. boaria Mol.
= *M. chilensis* DC.

MAYTEN TREE. CHILEAN MAYTEN. MAITEN TREE. From Chile and Argentina. Named in 1782. The specific epithet means of cattle, which are very fond of eating the leaves. The common name is Chilean; the Araucarian name is *Huripo*. Introduced to England in 1822 or 1829. In North America

≤1878. Common only in parts of California; it tends to perform best in northern California (and is weedy in some locales there). Hardiness varies according to the source of seeds (or cuttings). Like an evergreen WEEPING WILLOW, with elegant and sparkling foliage sprays. However, some specimens are much weepier than others. Some are airy-crowned, others densely leafy. Leaves 1"–2½" long. Flowers greenish-yellow, tiny and inconspicuous in March and April. The young fruit turns a rusty green and splits in late November, showing a small seed of brilliant Dutch vermilion or a deeper blood red; the old seeds are black. Seeds rice-like in size. Tolerates, but dislikes, very dry conditions. Records: to 100' × 10'6" in the wild; 63' × 9'11" × 60' Christchurch, New Zealand (1970); to 40'–50' tall and wide in California and Ireland.

Maytenus boaria Greenshowers™

A seedling from the arboretum at Davis, CA. Introduced ≤1978 (officially in 1982) by Saratoga Horticultural Foundation of California. Strongly pendulous.

M. chilensis—see *M. boaria*

Melia

[MELIACEÆ; Mahogany Family] 3–5 spp. of deciduous or subevergreen trees from the Old World tropics and subtropics. *Melia* is an ancient Greek name for *Fraxinus Ornus*, MANNA ASH—from the similar leaves. The only related genus in this volume is *Toona*.

M. australis—see *M. Azedarach*

M. Azedarach L.

= *M. australis* Sweet
= *M. japonica* G. Don
= *M. sempervirens* Swartz

CHINABERRY. BEAD TREE. PRIDE OF INDIA. FALSE SYCAMORE. HOLY TREE. ARBOR SANCTA. HILL MARGOSA TREE. CHINA TREE. PERSIAN LILAC. PARADISE TREE. PRIDE OF CHINA. PATERNOSTER TREE. SYRIAN BEAD-TREE. WHITE CEDAR. From N India to central China, the Ryukyus, Taiwan, and represented in Australia by a variety. The specific name *Azedarach* derives from Persian *azad-dirakht*, free or noble tree—possibly because of its cathartic, emetic uses. Cultivated in England since the late 1500s. André Michaux's nursery at Charleston, SC, had it sometime between 1787 and 1796. One was raised in 1789 in North Carolina. Now it is considered "a worthless weed" in much of the southern U.S. The reasons for its earlier wide dispersal are several. The tree has glossy, handsome dark foliage, consisting of large doubly-compound leaves divided into many sharply-toothed leaflets. It bears sweetly fragrant lilac (or pink) flowers in April, May or June. It tolerates heat, cold (to 0°F) and drought. It grows rapidly. The foliage stays green late into fall. On the debit side, its creamy-white to yellow, translucent, ½"–¾" berries are poisonous, its fallen seeds slippery like roller bearings (can be used to make necklaces and rosaries), and it can reseed weedily and be short-lived. On the whole, *Melia* is frowned upon. One has survived the Seattle winters for about 25 years, and evidently in cooler climates it is not so weedy or undesirable. Records: to 147½' tall in Australia; 82' × 10'2" × 73' near Brantley, AL (1968); 78' × 15'0" × 60' near Luverne, AL (1970); 75' × 18'6" × 96' Hawaii (1967).

M. Azedarach var. *umbraculiformis* Berckmans

= *M. Azedarach* 'Umbraculiformis'

TEXAS UMBRELLA-TREE. Originated <1860 in Texas. Common. Grown from seed and cuttings. Crown broad and dense. Record: 35' × 8'0" × 42' Hemet, CA (1993).

M. Azedarach 'Umbraculiformis Aurea'

Introduced ≤1922–23 by Fruitland nursery of Augusta, GA. Long commercially extinct. Leaves golden.

M. japonica—see *M. Azedarach*

M. sempervirens—see *M. Azedarach*

Meliosma

[SABIACEÆ; Sabia Family] 20–25 (60) spp. of mostly tropical or subtropical forest trees from SE Asia and the New World. Mostly broadleaf evergreens, a few deciduous. Genus named in 1823, from Greek *meli*, honey, and *osme*, odor or perfume; in allusion to the fragrant flowers. No other genera in this volume are in the SABIACEÆ.

M. Veitchiorum Hemsl.

From W and central China, in moist woods. Discovered and introduced in 1901 by E.Wilson for Veitch nursery of England. Named in 1906. Exceedingly rare; an exotic curiosity. A deciduous tree, with ascending and very slightly spreading brittle branches forming a loose pyramidal head. Leaves pinnately compound, of 9–11 (13) leaflets, the largest to 8½" long, untoothed or sparsely and coarsely toothed; handsome dark gold in October, the stalks remaining red. Flowers honey-scented, yellow or greenish-yellow or creamy-white, in 1'–2' long and wide drooping clusters during May. Isolated trees can set viable seeds. Fruit a bluish-bloomed black berry ripe in August or September, ⅓"–¾" long and wide, soapy when squished. Bark soft, corky, and rough. Records: to 65½' × 8'2" in China; 56' × 4'3" Nymans, Sussex, England (1985); 39' × 4'11" County Kildare, Ireland (1989); 36½' × 1'7" Seattle, WA (1993; *pl.* 1963).

Mespilus

[ROSACEÆ; Rose Family] A genus of only 2 species, the following a coarse shrub or small tree primarily known for its odd edible fruit. *Mespilus* is one of the ancient Latin names. From Greek *mesos*, half, and *pilos*, a ball—in allusion to the fruit shape. Closely related genera are *Cotoneaster* and *Cratægus*

(HAWTHORN). For MEDLAR-HAWTHORN hybrids, see + *Cratægomespilus* and × *Cratæmespilus*.

M. germanica L.
= *Pyrus germanica* (L.) Hook. fil.

MEDLAR TREE. HOSEDOUP. OPEN-ARSE. From SE Europe to central Asia, in woods. Introduced to North America ≤1735. Large-fruited cultivars have been grown in Europe since ≤1623, and in North America ≤1841. Such fruit can be 2½" wide. The wild form of MEDLAR has stout spines and 1" fruit. The fruit can be picked in October and allowed to ripen indoors, or can be eaten fresh off the tree from late October into December. It is brown, top-shaped, rock hard when unripe, then when ripe becomes soft, mushy, and yields delicious applesauce if squeezed (the taste reminds children of playdough). One of the best known cultivars is 'Nottingham' (of superb flavor, but small size, on a more erect tree). Leaves 3"–7" long, to 2¾" wide; subtly toothed or essentially untoothed; hairy on both sides; very short-stemmed. Overall the leaves much recall those of QUINCE (*Cydonia oblonga*). Fall color late, a mosaic of green, orange, red and purple. Flowers pinkish or (usually) white, 1"–1¾" wide, in May or early June; borne among the luxuriant leaves one here and one there rather than in clusters; not especially ornamental. Records: 59' × 3'11" Townhill Park, Hampshire, England (1985); 30' × 6'3" Claremont, Surrey, England (1986); 12' × 2'5" × 27' Seattle, WA (1993; *pl.* 1957).

Mespilus grandiflora—see × *Cratæmespilus grandiflora*

Mespilus japonica—see *Eriobotrya japonica*

Mespilus mexicana—see *Cratægus mexicana*

Mespilus prunifolia—see *Cratægus persimilis*

Mespilus pubescens—see *Cratægus mexicana*

Mespilus Smithii—see × *Cratæmespilus grandiflora*

Mespilus stipulosa—see *Cratægus mexicana*

Metasequoia

[TAXODIACEÆ; Bald Cypress Family] A genus of only the following species, a deciduous conifer of widespread fame, now common. Derived from Greek *meta*, changed, and genus *Sequoia* (REDWOOD), to which it is related. Another close cousin is BALD CYPRESS (*Taxodium*). *Metasequoia* is more cold-hardy and elegant than the evergreen REDWOODS. Too commonly, planters forget it is a REDWOOD that needs room to grow enormous.

M. glyptostroboides Hu & Cheng

DAWN REDWOOD. CHINESE REDWOOD. DECIDUOUS REDWOOD. From West-central China in mountainous E Szechwan, SW Hupeh, NW Hunan. Discovered in 1941, described in 1944, introduced in 1948—in January of that year the Arnold Arboretum got seeds and distributed them. The epithet *glyptostroboides* from genus *Glyptostrobus* (which see), and Greek -*oides*, resemblance. Named DAWN REDWOOD in 1948 by Dr. Ralph W. Chaney, Berkeley paleobotanist, in reference to early fossil records. The needles taste like carrot greens. Fall color varies but is usually pleasing yellows, gold, apricot, bronzy, and reds. Cones ¾"–1" long, on slender 2" stems. In 1971, male catkins (nearly 1' long) were noted at San Rafael, CA. Records: to 200' × 34'6" in the wild; 104' × 9'6" Williamsburg, VA (1981); 98' × 11'3" Willowwood, NJ (1987); 94' × 12'3" Winterthur, DE (1987); 79' × 12'10" Bailey Arboretum, NY (1981).

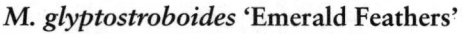

M. glyptostroboides 'Emerald Feathers'

Selected for its ease of vegetative propagation. Named ≤1971–72. Grown primarily in Europe.

M. glyptostroboides 'National'

Chosen out of 200 U.S. National Arboretum seedlings in 1958; in commerce ≤1963. Common. A compact, very narrow regular spire.

M. glyptostroboides 'Sheridan Spire'

Originated in 1960 as a sport in a row of cuttings at Sheridan nursery of Ontario. First sold in 1976. Common. Narrow, compact. Fine textured. Bright green; fall color handsome orange-brown.

Michelia

[MAGNOLIACEÆ; Magnolia Family] 40–80 spp. of SE Asian broadleaf evergreen trees. Named after Pier Antonio Micheli (1679–1737), botanist at Florence. A little known genus, 29 species were named in the 1980s. Differs from *Magnolia* in having axillary rather than terminal flowers. A third related genus is *Manglietia*.

M. compressa (Maxim.) Sarg.

= *Magnolia compressa* Maxim.

From China, S Japan, the Ryukyus, the Philippines, and Taiwan (the most widely distributed species in the genus). Named in 1872—*compressa* in Latin means dense or pressed together, referring to the seeds. In the California nursery trade since 1887. Subsequently planted in the Southeast, and Pacific Northwestern U.S. Rare. Grown mostly for foliage. Leaves dark above, very pale beneath, 3"–4¾" long, with rusty hairs when young, then hairless; faintly aromatic when crushed. Flowers deliciously fragrant but not especially showy, from (February) March to June, white (or creamy-yellow) with a purplish center, 1"–2" wide. Records: to 65½' × 6'3" in the wild; 32½' × 2'7" × 23½' Seattle, WA (1994; *pl.* 1954).

M. × Foggii Savage (nom. subnud.)

(*M. Doltsopa* × *M. Figo*)

Bred <1973 by P.J. Savage, Jr. First bloomed in 1978. Named in 1981 for John (Jack) Fogg, Jr., (1899–1982), botanist, founder of the Magnolia Society. Fertile. In commerce; cultivars 'Jack Fogg' and 'Picotee' are sold. Since neither parent is absolutely cold-tender, this hybrid may prove frost-resistant.

M. fulgens Dandy

From China. Named in 1930 (meaning shining or glistening in Latin). Introduced to North American commerce in 1993 by Piroche Plants of Pitt Meadows, B.C. To 75' tall in the wild. Hardy to 0°F.

M. Maudiæ Dunn

From China. Named in 1908, after a woman named Maud. Introduced to North American commerce in 1993 by Piroche Plants of Pitt Meadows, B.C. Leaf 2½"–7" long, white-bloomed beneath. Flowers pure white, fragrant. To 60' tall in the wild. Hardy to 10°F.

M. platypetala Hand.-Mazz.

From Hunan, China. Named in 1921 (*platypetala* from Greek *platys*, wide or broad, and *petalon*, a leaf—in modern usage a petal). Introduced to North American commerce in 1993 by Piroche Plants of Pitt Meadows, B.C. Leaf slender, untoothed, glaucous beneath; to 8½" × 2¼". Flowers white. To 60' tall in the wild. Hardy to 0°F.

M. Wilsonii Finet & Gagnep.

From China. Named in 1906, after the great plantsman Ernest Henry Wilson (1876–1930). Introduced to North American commerce in 1993 by Piroche Plants of Pitt Meadows, B.C. Foliage gray-green. Flowers soft yellow, in April and May. To 60' tall in the wild. Possibly identical to *M. sinensis* Hemsl. & Wils., also named in 1906. Hardy to 10°F.

Micromeles alnifolia—see *Sorbus alnifolia*

Micromeles Folgneri—see *Sorbus Folgneri*

Mimosa Julibrissin—see *Albizia Julibrissin*

Mohrodendron carolinum—see *Halesia carolina*

Morella californica—see *Myrica californica*

Morus

[MORACEÆ; Mulberry Family] 7–12 spp. of deciduous shrubs or trees. *Morus* is one of the ancient Latin names, also used for BLACKBERRIES (genus *Rubus*). Above, all these species have been valued for silk production and their edible blackberry-like fruit (delectable but eaten mostly by birds and children because it doesn't lend itself to market production). Regarding ornamental usage of the trees, the berries are considered a liability on account of their messiness and staining ability. For PAPER MULBERRY see genus *Broussonetia*. Related genera include *Cudrania* (CHINESE SILKWORM THORN), *Ficus* (FIG), and *Maclura* (OSAGE ORANGE). For all its economic importance, *Morus* is a poorly understood genus, and a thorough study of it would be welcome.

M. acidosa—see *M. australis*

M. alba L.

WHITE MULBERRY. SILKWORM MULBERRY. From China (likely also adjacent Asia). Introduced to Chinese cultivation ca. 2,800 B.C., for silk-production. Introduced to Mexico ca. 1522 for silk-production. Some cultivars have been selected for superior berries. Its use as an ornamental tree is relatively recent. Leaves cheerful bright green, 3"–8¾" long, to 6⅜" wide, thin, faintly hairy, often deeply lobed. Fall color usually pure yellow, sometimes a mixture of green, yellow, golden and brown. Flowers inconspicuous, greenish-white, in April–June. Individual trees usually predominantly male or female. Berries at maturity vary from white, to pink, dark red or purplish-black; sweet and edible, like little blackberries (⅓") ½"–1" (2¾" in cv. 'Tehama'). Several so other "species" of *Morus*, might easily be mere subspecies of *M. alba*: *M. australis*, *M. bombycis*, and *M. cathayana*. Records: to 100' tall on the Japanese Bonin Islands; 82' × 16'1" × 93' Lenawee County, MI (1976); 55' × 23'0" × 81' Leavenworth, KS (1982); 61' × 22'5" × 80' Holt County, MO (1982).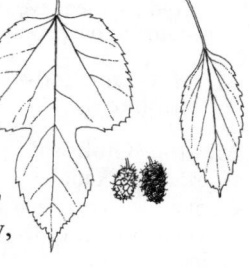

M. alba 'Acerifolia'—see *M. alba* 'Stribling'

M. alba 'Arizona'—see *M. alba* 'Arizona Fruitless'

M. alba 'Arizona Fruitless'

= *M. alba* 'Arizona'

Introduced ≤1954 by Del Rancho Fortuna nursery of California. Sold at least until about 1960. "A selected strain of *Morus alba* 'Kingnan'." Its "upright branches form a goblet head. Vigorous. Leaves smaller and less glabrous than regular 'Kingnan'."

M. alba 'Chaparral'

FRUITLESS WEEPING MULBERRY. Origin not known. W. Wandell says it was discovered by the University of New Mexico at Las Cruces. In commerce since ≤1966–67. A possible earlier name is *M. alba* 'Roeding's Weeping', advertised ≤1952 by the California Nursery Company of Niles. (George Christian Roeding, 1868–1928, was associated with Fancher Creek nursery of Fresno, CA.) Until Scanlon nursery of Ohio began selling 'Chaparral' in 1974–75, it was known only in the Southwest and California. It has become common and outsells the identical but fruitful *M. alba* 'Pendula'.

M. alba 'Champaign'

Introduced by J.C. McDaniel of Urbana, IL. Registered ≤1974. Extremely rare; not in commerce. Doubtless the name refers to Champaign, IL. A vigorous, upright male that is more cold-hardy than other FRUITLESS MULBERRIES. Leaves mostly unlobed.

M. alba 'Contorta'—see *M. bombycis* 'Unryu'

M. alba 'Cutleaf Fruitless'—see *M. alba* 'Stribling'

M. alba Fan-San® PP 2681 (1966)

Patented by Eddie Fanick of San Antonio, TX. Introduced ≤1967–68 by L.E. Cooke nursery of Visalia, CA. Sold by them ever since. Fast. Fruitless. Leaves large, glossy, dark, and deeply cut.

M. alba 'Fruitless'—see *M. alba* 'Kingan' and 'Stribling'

M. alba 'Globosa'

?= *M. alba* 'Nana'

GLOBE-HEADED MULBERRY. Introduced in 1917 by Meehan nursery of Dresher, PA. Long commercially extinct. Outline similar to the GLOBE CATALPA (*Catalpa bignonioides* 'Umbraculifera'). Topgrafted on a 5'–7' standard. Bushy, compact crown useful for formal effect.

M. alba 'Holicong Weeping'

Found as a seedling at Coles nursery of Pennsylvania. Named ≤1989. Very rare, if in commerce at all. Leaves invariably lobed.

M. alba 'Illinois Everbearing'—see *M.* 'Illinois Everbearing'

M. alba 'Kingan'

= *M. alba* 'Fruitless' (in part)

Introduced in 1932 by Porter-Walton nursery of Salt Lake City, UT. The original description: "Kingman (Fruitless) 30' tall. A good strong growing dense shade tree, but without fruit, thus avoiding the staining of walks under the tree. Extremely rapid in growth and one of the best shade or street trees for southern Utah, Nevada, and other hot, dry, arid climates." The spelling has been 'Kingan' or 'Kingnan' beginning with a 1942 catalog of W.B. Clarke nursery of San José, CA, and in six other nursery's

catalogs examined by the present writer. The tree has become common, especially in California; it grows fast even in heat, dryness and alkalinity.

M. alba var. *latifolia*—see *M. alba* var. *multicaulis*

M. alba 'Macrophylla'

= *M. macrophylla* Moretti
= *M. latifolia* hort.
= *M. hispanica* hort.

Cultivated since ≤1815 in France. Named officially in 1829 (Greek *macro*, large, and *phyllon*, a leaf). In English nurseries by 1836. In North American commerce as early as 1841–42 (if sold as ITALIAN WHITE MULBERRY). Very rare; commercially extinct. Leaf unlobed, to 9" × 6", smooth, glossy, succulent. Fruit white, succulent.

M. alba 'Maple Leaf'—see *M. alba* 'Stribling'

M. alba 'Morettiana'

MORETTI MULBERRY. DANDOLO MULBERRY. Named after Giuseppe Moretti (1782–1853), botany professor at the University of Pavia, Italy. He first publicized this variety in 1815. In North American commerce ≤1870. Still grown in early 1900s; subsequently extinct in commerce (or renamed). It was for silk-culture, not ornament. Compared to *M. alba* var. *multicaulis* it is less hardy and less productive. Leaves large, thin, glossy, unlobed. Berries black.

M. alba var. *multicaulis* (Perrottet) Loud.

= *M. alba* var. *latifolia* Bur.
= *M. multicaulis* Perrottet
= *M. sinensis* hort.

SILKWORM MULBERRY. ITALIAN MULBERRY. Cultivated ≤1821 in France, after Perrottett, "agricultural botanist and traveller of the marine and colonies of France" introduced it from Manila, the Philippines, where it was grown as an ornamental. Named officially in 1824 (Latin *multi*, many, and *caulis*, a stem). In North American nurseries ≤1826. It was the plant of "mulberry mania" which swept the country between then and ca. 1844. During that time everyone and his brother tried to get rich producing silk. Commercially extinct or nearly so since ca. 1930. Leaves seldom or never prominently lobed, dull, thin and large, to 16" × 12". Berries long, black. More of a large shrub suckering from the roots than a tree; it can be trained into a tree. More cold-tender than ordinary WHITE MULBERRY trees, it may be actually a variant of *M. australis*.

M. alba 'Nana'—see *M. alba* 'Globosa'

M. alba 'Pendula'

= *M. alba* var. *tatarica* 'Pendula'

WEEPING MULBERRY. Originated ca. 1883 with nurseryman John C. Teas (1827–1907) of Carthage, MO. In commerce ≤1890 both in Europe and North America. Described officially in 1892. Very common. Absolutely pendulous, it must be topgrafted, and makes a dense mound. Leaves glossy, usually lobed, to 8" × 6". Berries abundant, ripe between late June and early October, black, small. A swell little tree for children to hide under and eat the fruit. P.J. van Melle hated WEEPING MULBERRY: "its branches grow downward, like cows' tails, with no more grace and a good deal less use. And there it stands, for years on end, in Beauty's way,—growing thicker and uglier with age until someone comes along with sense enough to chop it down." Record: 16' × 3'11" × 17' Milwaukee, WI (1983).

M. alba 'Roeding's Weeping'—see *M. alba* 'Chaparral'

M. alba 'Stribling'

= *M. alba* 'Maple Leaf'
= *M. alba* 'Cutleaf Fruitless'
= *M. alba* 'Stribling's Fruitless'
= *M. alba* 'Fruitless' (in part)
= *M. alba* 'Acerifolia'
= *M. alba* 'Striblingi'

Advertised ≤1952 by the California Nursery Company of Niles. Doubtless named after Stribling nursery of Merced, CA. Common. Leaves recall those of a FIG TREE (*Ficus Carica*); dark; larger and more deeply lobed than on *M. alba* 'Kingan'.

M. alba 'Striblingi' or 'Stribling's Fruitless'— see *M. alba* 'Stribling'

M. alba var. *stylosa*—see *M. australis*

M. alba var. *tatarica* (Pall.) Ser.

= *M. tatarica* Pall.

RUSSIAN MULBERRY. TATARIAN MULBERRY. Introduced in 1784 by A. Michaux to Loddiges' nursery of England. Brought to North America ca. 1875 by Russian Mennonites. Named the same year. In North American commerce <1900. Common. Leaves and berries are relatively small. Very cold-hardy, drought-tolerant, and content with poor ground. Often planted to attract birds.

M. alba var. *tatarica* 'Pendula'—see *M. alba* 'Pendula'

M. alba 'Urbana'

Introduced by J.C. McDaniel of Urbana, IL. Registered ≤1974. Similar to *M. alba* 'Pendula' except fruitless. Presumably differs somehow from *M. alba* 'Chaparral'.

M. australis Poir.

= *M. acidosa* Griff.
= *M. alba* var. *stylosa* (Ser.) Bur.
= *M. stylosa* Ser.
= *M. indica* Roxb., non L.

AINO MULBERRY. JAPANESE MULBERRY. KOREAN MULBERRY. From China, Korea, Japan, the Ryukyus, and Taiwan. Named in 1796 (from Latin *austral*, southern). In North American commerce ≤1884. Rare. A shrub or small tree. Leaves dull green, to 6" long; sharply toothed, variously lobed; not used to feed silkworms. Berries dark red to shining black. For all practical purposes, identical to *M. alba*, except less hardy. Record: 30' × 2'4" × 50' Lisle, IL (1986; *pl.* 1940).

M. australis 'Unryu'—see *M. bombycis* 'Unryu'

M. bombycis Koidz.

= *M. Kagayamæ* Koidz.

From Japan, Sakhalin, the S Kuriles, and Korea. The name *bombycis* is from Greek *bombyx*, silkworm — the leaves of this tree being fed to silkworms. A species closely related to or synonymous with *M. alba*. Recorded to 49' × 10'4".

M. bombycis 'Unryu'

('Unruyu', 'Urryu')
= *M. alba* 'Contorta'
= *M. australis* 'Unryu'
= *M. latifolia* 'Spirata'

CONTORTED (CHINESE) MULBERRY. Introduced from Japan to Western cultivation ≤1981. Rapidly becoming common. *Unryu* likely means twisted in Japanese, as the vernacular for *Salix Matsudana* 'Tortuosa' is *Unryu Yanagi*. The name 'Spirata' is invalid as a cultivar name unless it was in use <1959. A broad shrubby tree with zig-zag branches. Leaf to 10" × 8¼"; stem to 2¼" long; unlobed but not flat; semi-glossy above. Spring catkins up to 1¾" long, inconspicuous. Berries few, small.

M. hispanica—see M. alba 'Macrophylla'

M. 'Illinois Everbearing'
(M. alba × M. rubra)
= M. alba 'Illinois Everbearing'

A hybrid that looks more like M. alba than M. rubra. It originated in Illinois, was discovered in 1947 and introduced commercially in 1958. Uncommon; grown nearly exclusively for its abundant, flavorful, nearly seedless black berries produced late June through late September, on a vigorous small tree. Leaves to ca. 6" × 4"; unlobed, thin, resembling those of M. alba. Hardy to -25°F.

M. indica—see M. australis

M. Kagayamæ—see M. bombycis

M. latifolia—see M. alba 'Macrophylla'

M. latifolia 'Spirata'—see M. bombycis 'Unryu'

M. macrophylla—see M. alba 'Macrophylla'

M. multicaulis—see M. alba var. multicaulis

M. nigra L.
= M. persica hort.

BLACK MULBERRY. COMMON MULBERRY. PERSIAN MULBERRY. From central Asia, widely cultivated in SW Asia and S Europe. In North American commerce ≤1771. Rare; primarily on the Pacific Coast; it can tolerate 0°F (cv. 'Wellington' even -20°F). Flushes later than M. alba. Leaves 3"–5" (9") long, roundish overall, rarely lobed, deeply heart-shaped at the base, dark and glossy above, thinly coated with rough hairs (at least while young), fuzzy beneath; held later into autumn than those of either M. alba or M. rubra. Berries set even without pollination; short-stalked, large, plump, juicy, delicious, dark purplish-black, ripe from late June until October. Usually a rugged-looking little tree with a burry trunk and broad crown. More shade tolerant than M. alba. Records: to 82' tall says G. Hegi; 52' ×

5'8" London, England (1987); 35' × 6'4" × 60' London, England (≤1920); 29' × 10'0" Wye, Kent, England (1988); 28' × 6'6½" × 28' Davis, CA (1992). A Morus alba at Westminster, MD, has been claimed the "national champion" M. nigra since ≤1955.

M. nigra 'Black Beauty' PP 4913 (1982)
Armstrong nursery of Ontario, CA, sells a dwarf under this name.

M. papyrifera—see Broussonetia papyrifera

M. persica—see M. nigra

M. platanifolia hort.
In eastern North American commerce since at least the early 1970s. Rare. Probably a renaming of M. alba 'Kingan' or 'Stribling' or the like. Leaves glossy, large, lobed. Fruitless. Said to be from France. The name platanifolia derives from genus Platanus (PLANETREE or SYCAMORE), and Latin folium, a leaf.

M. rubra L.
RED MULBERRY. PURPLE MULBERRY. AMERICAN MULBERRY. From the eastern half of the U.S., and extreme S Ontario. Common wild where native, and selected cultivars have long been grown for fruit ('Johnson' from Ohio <1845, 'Hicks' arose in Georgia ca. 1850, 'Stubbs' dates from about 1875, etc.). Not grown as an ornamental tree. It hates climates unlike that of its accustomed range. Leaves large (to 10"), lobed or unlobed, raspy above, more or less downy beneath. Berries dark red to purple, very large, 1"–1½" (2½") long, delicious in July. Bark dark reddish-brown. Records: one 93' tall in Illinois (1983); 72' × 19'2" × 99' Berrien County, MI (1988); 63' × 21'8" × 78' Edmond, OK (≤1993).

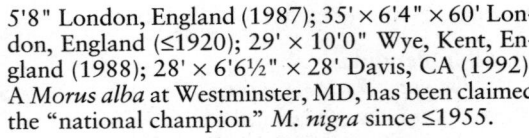

M. sinensis—see M. alba var. multicaulis

M. stylosa—see M. australis

M. tatarica—see M. alba var. tatarica

Myrica

[MYRICACEÆ; Wax Myrtle Family] 35–50 spp. of evergreen or deciduous shrubs or trees. From *myrike*, the Greek (ultimately Semitic) name for the TAMARISK (*Tamarix*) or some other fragrant shrub. Some botanists divide the genus into *Morella* and *Myrica*. A less disruptive alternative is to stretch the definition of *Myrica* to include the closely related SWEETFERN shrub (*Comptonia*). Besides the following species, others of smaller size occur in eastern North America, the largest and most widely distributed being *M. cerifera* (SOUTHERN WAX MYRTLE). The berries yield wax useful for candle making. *Myrica* thrives on sandy, barren soils, and can fix nitrogen symbiotically. Easy to grow, but not showy. All of the cold-hardy species are either utterly bushy or must be pruned into treehood.

M. californica Cham. & Schlecht.
= *Morella californica* (Cham. & Schlecht.) Wilbur

PACIFIC WAX MYRTLE. PACIFIC BAYBERRY. From coastal California, Oregon and SW Washington. Named in 1835. Introduced to cultivation in 1848, but very rare until the 1970s. Leaves WILLOW-like, evergreen, 2"–5¾" long, weakly scented to quite scentless. Flowers inconspicuous, in April and May. Fruit a dry little purplish berry, lightly wax-covered, tightly clustered on the twigs. Tolerates many soils and exposures; highly adaptable. Usually a very large shrub; easily trained to a small tree. Records: 38' × 4'4" × 34' Siuslaw National Forest, OR (1972); 29½' × 3'1" × 25¼' Seattle, WA (1994).

Nannorrhops

[PALMÆ or ARECACEÆ; Palm Family] 1–4 spp. of shrubby PALMS. From Greek *nannos*, dwarf, and *rhops*, a bush; in allusion to the dwarf, bushy habit. Other PALM genera in this volume are *Butia*, *Ceroxylon*, *Chamærops*, *Sabal*, *Trachycarpus*, and *Washingtonia*.

N. Ritchiana (Griff.) Aitch.
= *Chamærops Ritchiana* Griff.
(*Ritchieana*)

MAZARI PALM. From low, arid, cold mountains of Afghanistan, S Iran, Pakistan, and NW India; to 5,000' elevation. Named in 1844 after David Ritchie (1809–1866), surgeon of the Bombay Medical Service, and plant collector in India and adjacent countries. *Mazari* is a vernacular name. First introduced in 1866; reintroduced several times, apparently first successfully so in 1935. In commerce here ≤1939. Specimens first flowered in North America in 1944. Extremely rare; testing is needed to determine its cold-hardiness and size. It may prove less stunted in cultivation than in the wild. Usually of clumping, shrub habit, much branched; rarely 20'–25' tall in tree-form. Very useful to people in its native habitat: its young delicate fronds are eaten; it is used as a fuel; its wool is good tinder and it can be made into rope. Fronds 1'–2' (4½') long and wide, beautifully pale glaucous blue, of (7) 20–30 (40) divisions; the stem 12"–18" long, unarmed, wooly. Flowers small, white or creamy-white.

Negundo aceroides—see *Acer Negundo*

Negundo fraxinifolium—see *Acer Negundo*

Neolitsea

[LAURACEÆ; Laurel Family] 60–80 spp. of East Asian broadleaf evergreen trees and shrubs. The name derives from *neo*, new, and genus *Litsea*. Male and female flowers are borne on separate individuals; fruit a berry. Related genera include *Apollonias*, *Cinnamomum* (CAMPHOR TREE), *Laurus* (BAY LAUREL), *Lindera*, *Persea*, *Sassafras*, and *Umbellularia*.

Neolitsea sericea (Bl.) Koidz.

= *N. glauca* (Sieb.) Koidz.
= *N. latifolia* Koidz., non S. Moore
= *Laurus glauca* Sieb.
= *Litsea sericea* Bl.

From E China, Korea, Japan, and Taiwan. Named in 1825. Date of introduction to cultivation not known (<1950). Exceedingly rare in North America until the late 1980s and the '90s. Performs well in those climates where its kindred broadleaf-evergreen species can grow. Above all, valued for foliage. In May the emerging young leaves contrast strikingly with the old mature ones, being fully felted or silky (*sericea* means silky in Latin). Mature leaves aromatic when crushed, 3-veined from near the base, toothless, to 7⅛" × 2¾". They are matte green above; the silky hairs more or less fall off, in some cases remaining as a ghostly pale silky sheen on the undersides. Flowers yellow, small and inconspicuous in September or October. Females produce berries, first green, at length glossy red, to ⅝" long. Records: to 40' tall in the wild; 25' tall in Seattle, WA (1995; *pl.* 1968).

Nothofagus

[FAGACEÆ; Oak Family] 20–40 spp. of Southern Hemisphere trees related to BEECHES (*Fagus*), all but 7 evergreen. From Greek *nothos*, false or spurious, and genus *Fagus*, the BEECH. (Note that the prefix was not meant to be *Noto-*, southern.) They prefer cool, moist conditions, and are ill-suited to (if at all enduring) severe-winter regions. The seven species following are so varied that it is difficult to generalize about them. None, however, are flashy; their demeanor varies from prim to ragged. Since their flowers and fruits are minute and usually go unseen, their form and foliage is what we value—and, frankly, "an acquired taste" is necessary to love them. The common names cited for the Chilean species represent Araucarian, Mapuche and English spellings of the same basic names.

N. alpina—see N. procera

N. antarctica (Forst. fil.) Oerst.

ANTARCTIC (SOUTHERN-) BEECH. ÑIRRE. GUINDO. From Argentina, Chile, and Tierra del Fuego. It grows as close to the Antarctic as any tree. Named in 1787. Introduced to Britain in 1830. In North America ≤1912. Not sold by nurseries until the early 1950s. Still rare. Probably the hardiest *Nothofagus*. It also tolerates blasting wind and salty air. A shrub or small tree. Valued for its rugged, twisted branching and petite foliage. The Chilean name ÑIRRE means *fox*. Leaves small and crinkly, of beeswax or faint cinnamon fragrance when rubbed, ½"–1⅜" (1¾") long, dark green, shiny on both surfaces, minutely toothed; few veins. Flowers tiny and inconspicuous, in April or May. Fall color usually dismal, but optimists describe the best as "yellow" or "rusty red." The young bark has CHERRY-like lenticels. Records: to 115' tall in the wild; 85' × 7'3" Arduaine, Strathclyde, Scotland (1986); 59' × 3'6" Sheffield Park, Sussex, England (1986); 55' × 4'9" Seattle, WA (1994; *pl.* 1951); 48' × 5'9" Abbeyleix, County Laois, Ireland (1985).

N. antarctica 'Puget Pillar'

Named in 1990, from a tree grown since 1951 in the Seattle arboretum. Reportedly of tighter, more upswept habit than usual. Propagated by softwood cuttings.

N. betuloides (Mirb.) Bl.

OVAL-LEAVED SOUTHERN-BEECH. From Chile, Argentina, and Tierra del Fuego. Named in 1827. Introduced to Britain in 1830. In North America ≤1924. Extremely rare. The specific epithet derives from genus *Betula*, BIRCH, and Greek *-oides*, resemblance. The hardiest evergreen *Nothofagus*. Overall, much like *N. Dombeyi*. Leaves ½"–1⅛" long. Records: to 100' × 22'0" in the wild; 85' × 8'9" Mt. Usher, County Wickow, Ireland (1966); 59' × 8'0" Powerscourt, County Wickow, Ireland (1990); 59' × 9'6" Hafordunos, Gwynedd, Wales (1984; *pl.* 1847).

N. Cliffortioides—see N. Solanderi var. Cliffortioides

N. Dombeyi (Mirb.) Bl.

DOMBEY (SOUTHERN-) BEECH. COIGÜE. COIHUE. From Chile and W Argentina. Named in 1827 after Joseph Dombey (1742–1794), French surgeon and botanist. Introduced to North America ≤1912. *Coihue* in Araucanian means "place alongside the water." Can live 700 years. A majestic and elegant evergreen, the largest Chilean native tree. Leaves intense dark shiny green, surprisingly petite for such a huge tree (½"–1⅜"). Records: to 165' × 40'0" in the wild; 118' × 7'9" Muncaster Castle, Cumbria, England (1984); 115' × 13'8" Mt. Usher, County Wicklow, Ireland (1989); 88' × 4'3" Seattle, WA (1994; *pl.* 1949).

N. fusca (Hook. fil.) Oerst.

RED (SOUTHERN-) BEECH. NEW ZEALAND RED BEECH. Maori: *Tawhai Raunui*. From New Zealand. The Latin epithet *fusca* means dark brown or somber, referring to the foliage and wood. Introduced to cultivation ca. 1876–1880. Introduced to San Francisco <1915. Extremely rare in North America. Evergreen, but with red and copper tones in autumn and winter. Leaves 1"–1½", bluntly toothed. Although an immense tree in the wild, it is usually slow growing and sparse in cultivation. Records: to 140' × 37'8" in the wild; 94' × 9'9" Nymans, Sussex, England (1985).

N. nervosa—see *N. procera*

N. obliqua (Mirb.) Bl.

ROBLE (SOUTHERN-BEECH). ROBLE PELLÍN. COYAN. HUALLE. From Chile and W Argentina. Named in 1827. ROBLE PELLÍN means heart of OAK. Possibly introduced to cultivation in 1849 by Wm. Lobb, but certainly in 1902 by H.J. Elwes. In North America ≤1912; in commerce here by the 1950s. Very rare. In advanced age it makes an airy, impressively large shade tree. Yet until it reaches imposing size, it is the least handsome *Nothofagus*, devoid of beauty except sometimes in autumn. Leaves dull above, pale below, 1½"–3½" long; raggedly, coarsely toothed; stems shortly hairy (sometimes the leaf surfaces and twigs also). Some leaves are larger and paler, usually hairless; others smaller, darker, shinier and hairy; 7–10 vein pairs. Fall color late, in Chile chrome-yellow to orange; in the United Kingdom it can be brilliant yellow or pale orange, often with much crimson; in Seattle it varies from sulking, dirty, yellow-green to apricot-orange. Records: to 160' × 41'3" in the wild; 118' × 8'0" near Horsham, Sussex, England (1985); 75' × 10'9" Berkshire, England (1975; *pl.* 1905); 69' × 5'2" Seattle, WA (1994; *pl.* 1956); 68' × 8'2" San Francisco, CA (1989).

N. procera (Poepp. & Endl.) Oerst.

= *N. nervosa* (Phil.) Dim. & Mil.
?= *N. alpina* (Poepp. & Endl.) Oerst.

RAOUL. RAUOL. RAULÍ. From Chile and W Argentina.

The name RAULÍ is from Araucanian. Named *procera* (Latin for tall) in 1838. Introduced to cultivation ≤1909. The first successful introduction might have been a few years later. Almost none in North America date before 1960. Leaves to 4¾" long, recalling those of a HORNBEAM (*Carpinus*), with ca. 15–20 pairs of veins. Fall color late and lovely: brilliant scarlet to rich tangerine or yellow. Records: 105' × 10'11" Mt. Usher, County Wicklow, Ireland (1989); 98½' × 13'6" Brodick Castle, Arran, Scotland (1988).

N. Solanderi (Hook. fil.) Oerst.
(*Solandri*)

BLACK BEECH. Maori: *Tawhai Rauriki*. From New Zealand. Named after Daniel Carl Solander (1736–1782), botanist on Captain Cook's first voyage. Joseph Banks and Solander discovered this species in Queen Charlotte Sound in 1769. Introduced to San Francisco <1915. Very rare. Tree airy, slender, with petite, dark leaves; recalls *Azara microphylla* in foliage texture and the arrangement of its leaves in neat rows. Leaves ¼"–¾" long, HOLLY-green above, sage-green beneath. Flowers crimson, tiny, in April. Branches spreading; not at all pendulous. Best in sheltered or woodland settings; it hates dryness, wind, or soggy soils. Slow growing. Records: trunks to 15'8" around in New Zealand; 84' × 6'3" Wakehurst Place, Sussex, England (1984); 52' × 2'10½" San Francisco, CA (1993).

N. Solanderi var. *Cliffortioides* (Hook. fil.) Poole

= *N. Cliffortioides* (Hook. fil.) Oerst

MOUNTAIN BEECH. Named in 1844 (it resembles genus *Cliffortia*, an African genus in the Rose Family). Introduced to San Francisco <1915. Very rare; in commerce by the 1950s. Differs from typical *N. Solanderi* in having smaller, thicker, pointier leaves, buckled with their edges rolled under. It flushes a bit later in spring and is possibly hardier; usually it grows smaller. But many intermediate trees exist. Records: 92' × 7'6" Nymans, Sussex, England (1985); 77½' × 9'5" Woodside, CA (1994); 39' × 2'6" San Francisco, CA (1993).

Nyssa

[NYSSACEÆ; Tupelo Family] 5–10 spp. of deciduous trees grown for handsome foliage, the flowers going unnoticed; female trees produce small, sour berries. Named after *Nyssa* or *Nysa*, a mythological Greek water nymph who raised the infant Bacchus. The species first described grows in wet and swampy ground. Related genera are *Cornus* (DOGWOOD) and *Davidia* (DOVE TREE).

N. aquatica L.
= *N. uniflora* Wangh.
= *N. tomentosa* Michx.

WATER TUPELO. SWAMP TUPELO. COTTON GUM. WATER GUM. WILD OLIVE. From the southeastern United States, in swamps (hence the name *aquatica*). Rarely cultivated. Leaves sometimes lobed or boldly toothed; whitish beneath; to 12" × 4"; stem to 3¼" long, red. Fall color dull yellow. Berries to 1" long, dark purple. Records: 124' × 20'11" Congaree Swamp, SC (<1978); 110' × 18'1" near Camden, SC (<1956); 105' × 28'0" Southhampton County, VA (1991); 105' × 27'1" Kinder, LA (1970).

N. biflora—see N. sylvatica

N. multiflora—see N. sylvatica

N. sinensis Oliv.
CHINESE TUPELO. From China and Viet Nam. Discovered in 1888 by A. Henry. Introduced in 1902 by E. Wilson for Veitch nursery of England. Most trees in cultivation date from after 1980. Needs very moist sites to thrive. Prized for its handsome purplish-brown young leaves, grayish-silky beneath. Leaves large (to 10½" × 3⅜") presenting a lush, bold effect. Fall color yellow or red, often gorgeous. Fruit a bluish berry ⅜"–⅝" long, borne 2–3 together on a stem to 2" long. A large shrub or small tree. Recorded to 88½' tall in Anhwei Province (1925); trunks to 6'3" around in the wild.

N. sylvatica Marsh.
= *N. biflora* Walt.
= *N. villosa* Michx.
= *N. multiflora* Wangh.

TUPELO. BLACK GUM. TUPELO GUM. SOUR GUM. BEE GUM. UPLAND YELLOW-GUM. SNAG TREE. UMBRELLA TREE. SWAMP HORNBEAM. BLACK TUPELO. BEETLE BUNG. PEPPERIDGE. HORNPIPE. From the eastern U.S., far S Ontario, and parts of Mexico. Common in cultivation. One of the richest honey-producing trees in the world. The branches are often crowded. Leaves glossy, to 7¼" × 3¼"; among the best for exciting yellow-apricot to flaming scarlet or bright crimson fall color. Berries ½"–¾" long, borne singly or in pairs or trios, dark blue, sour, edible but thin-fleshed; ripe between November and January. Bark handsomely chunky. Tolerates but does not require wet soil. Records: 141' × 16'2" × 93' Louisiana (1994); 139' × 15'1" near Easterly, TX (1971); 130' × 15'9" Brooksville, MS (1965); 117' × 16'7" Harrison County, TX (1969); 102' × 19'10" Suffolk County, VA (1988); 92' × 27'0" Glen Arm, MD (1990).

N. sylvatica 'Dirr'
A specimen noted near Athens, GA, by horticulturist Dr. Michael A. Dirr. Leaves remarkably large, leathery, with brilliant red fall color. Named at North Carolina State University Arboretum.

N. sylvatica 'Miss Scarlet'
Introduced ≤1993–94 by Arborvillage nursery of Holt, MO: "An outstanding local plant selected for brilliant red fall color. Very ornamental blue fruit."

N. tomentosa—see N. aquatica

N. uniflora—see N. aquatica

N. villosa—see N. sylvatica

Olea

[OLEACEÆ; Olive Family] 20 spp. of broadleaf evergreen shrubs and trees, all from the Old World. *Olea* is the ancient Latin name of the OLIVE TREE; akin to Greek *elaia*, the OLIVE. For the RUSSIAN OLIVE see *Elæagnus*. Related genera include: *Chionanthus* (FRINGE TREE), *Fraxinus* (ASH), *Ligustrum* (PRIVET), *Osmanthus*, *Phillyrea*, and *Syringa* (LILAC).

O. europæa L.
COMMON OLIVE. From SW Asia. A world famous tree, the long renowned emblem of peace. Introduced to cultivation ca. 3,600 B.C. In the wild it is thorny, the leaves are smaller, and fruit usually ≤⅝" long.

Cultivars can be thornless, with fruit 1½" long. Spaniards brought it to North America <1577. At the turn of the century fruiting cultivars such as 'Manzanillo' and 'Mission' were popular; they are still in the nurseries over 90 years later, but in addition there are new, often patented clones, some of which are fruitless, ornamental selections. The tree is now wild, being bird disseminated in parts of California. Needs dryness to thrive. It can withstand freezing winters where the temperature doesn't plunge below about 10°–0°F. It does poorly in wet-summer regions. The tree will live and serve as an ornamental well beyond its ideal zone as a commercial fruit-producer. As ornamentals, OLIVE TREES offer a long life (1,500 years), drought tolerance, gnarled trunks with handsome cavities and folds, and dusty-looking gray-green foliage. The fruit, although prized for oil, is amazingly messy, and the roots sometimes sucker. Leaves narrow, leathery, very dark green above and whitish beneath; to 3" × ¾"; borne in opposite pairs; venation indistinct. Flowers yellowish-white, not showy, in the summer. Records: to 98½' tall says Hylander; trunks to 23'6" around in Spain; 58' × 11'9½" × 55' Cornwall Park, Auckland, New Zealand (1971; *pl.* ca. 1861); 51' × 9'7" × 37½' Davis, CA (1994); 50' × 11'6" × 34½' Sacramento, CA (1989; *pl.* 1870); 39' × 29'6" Jerusalem, Israel (1892).

O. europæa Majestic Beauty™ PP 5649 (1986)
= *O. europæa* 'Monher'

Introduced in 1985 by Monrovia nursery of California. Fruitless. Crown open, refined. Foliage light green. Leaves long and narrow.

O. europæa 'Manzanillo'
('Manzanilla')

The dominant fruiting cultivar. Also widely planted for landscape use. Roundheaded, small, with choice, broad fruit.

O. europæa 'Mission'

A very old cultivar. It has proved fully hardy in Seattle. Fruit smaller than that of 'Manzanillo'.

O. europæa 'Monher'—see O. europæa Majestic Beauty™

O. europæa 'Skylark Dwarf'

Introduced ≤1987–88. Presumably named after Skylark nursery of Santa Rosa, CA. To 10'–15' tall, of neat habit with small leaves and only a light fruit crop.

O. europæa 'Swan Hill' PP 3197 (1972)

Discovered in 1960 by H.T. Hartmann of Davis, CA, near Swan Hill, Victoria, Australia. Named ≤1967. Widely planted in Arizona and Nevada, to a lesser degree in California. Hardy to 15°F. Yields little airborne pollen, so is good for planting where allergies are a problem. Grows much like 'Manzanillo' but is fruitless. Leaves narrow. Resists verticillium wilt disease if grown from cuttings, not if grown form grafts.

Olea ilicifolia—see Osmanthus heterophyllus

Oreodaphne californica—see Umbellularia californica

Ornus europæa—see Fraxinus Ornus

Osmanthus

[OLEACEÆ; Olive Family] 15–30 spp. of broadleaf evergreen shrubs and trees. From Greek *osme*, fragrance or odor, and *anthos*, a flower; the flowers are fragrant. Most are from the Old World (A denizen of bottomlands and swamps of the Deep South is *O. americanus*, DEVILWOOD). Foliage more or less HOLLY-like. As with HOLLIES (*Ilex* spp.) the leaves are most spiny on young specimens or sheared plants; unlike HOLLIES, the leaves are opposite, not alternate. Male and female flowers borne on separate plants, tiny, often inconspicuous, but sweetly fragrant. Fruit a bluish berry. Generally best in partial shade. Related genera include: *Chionanthus* (FRINGE TREE), *Fraxinus* (ASH), *Ligustrum* (PRIVET), *Olea* (OLIVE), *Phillyrea*, and *Syringa* (LILAC).

O. Aquifolium—see O. heterophyllus

O. armatus Diels

CHINESE OSMANTHUS. From W China. Introduced in 1902 by E. Wilson for Veitch nursery of England. In North American nursery trade ≤1928. Rare. A stout shrub or small tree, slow growing and broad. Leaves to 7¼" × 2¾", with up to 7–10 spiny teeth per side. In advanced age the plant makes smaller, less spiny leaves. Hardy to about 0°F. Flowers in October or November, creamy-white. Berries ¾" long. Needs shade to thrive; hates sun. Recorded to 30' tall; usually matures at half that height.

Osmanthus Forrestii—see O. yunnanensis

O. × Fortunei Carr.
= O. ilicifolius var. latifolius hort.
(O. heterophyllus × O. fragrans)

HYBRID OSMANTHUS. HARDY TEA-OLIVE. Introduced in 1856 by Siebold to Holland; named after Robert Fortune (1812–1880), who introduced it to England in 1862. In North American commerce ≤1927. Common—much rarer in nurseries since the 1980s than it was previously. Less cold hardy than O. heterophyllus. Leaves to 3¾" long, each side edged with up to 12 spiny teeth. Flowers smell like apricots when they bloom in October and November. The clone of common cultivation is male. Records: 28' × 11'9" Tauranga, New Zealand (1969; pl. ca. 1875); 24' × 5'6" × 24' Seattle, WA (1992); 22' × 10'0" × 35' St. Heliers, New Zealand (1971).

O. × Fortunei 'Equinox'
Originated in Japan. Introduced to Western cultivation in 1982 by B. Yinger. Leaves variegated creamy-white—on young growth often chartreuse.

O. × Fortunei 'San José'
= O. 'San José'
(O. heterophyllus × O. fragrans 'Aurantiacus')

Raised in 1934 by W.B. Clarke nursery of San José, CA. Introduced ≤1941. Uncommon. Compared to typical O. × Fortunei, flowers larger, creamy-yellow; shrubbier, less cold-hardy. Leaves to 4¾" × 2" with 8–13 spiny teeth per side. Growth fast.

O. heterophyllus (G. Don) P.S. Green
= O. Aquifolium Sieb.
= O. ilicifolius (Hassk.) hort. ex Carr.
= Olea ilicifolia Hassk.

COMMON OSMANTHUS. HOLLY OLIVE. CHINESE HOLLY. FALSE HOLLY. SWEET HOLLY. HOLLY-LEAF TEA-OLIVE. From Japan, the Ryukyus, and Taiwan. Introduced in 1843 by Siebold to Holland. Reintroduced in 1856 by T. Lobb for Veitch nursery of England. Long common in North America. The name from Greek heteros, different, and phyllon, a leaf; referring to its variability, especially in the leaf margins. Usually a very large shrub; with training and decades, a small tree. Tolerates clipping and shade. Leaves 1½"–2½" (4½") long, usually

prickly (as many as 5 spines per side), but variable as the name indicates. Flowers tiny, white and inconspicuous in fall, but sweetly fragrant. Berries ripen in June (borne only on female specimens). (A purpleleaf and several old variegated cultivars exist, but are wholly shrubby. During the 1970s and early '80s, five cultivars, most featuring variegated foliage, were introduced from Japan. None are thought likely to become trees: 'Akebono', 'Goshiki', 'Kembu', 'Ogon' and 'Sasaba'.) Records: 22' × 3'1" × 27' Seattle, WA (1993; pl. 1953); 18' × 3'11" × 33' Tacoma, WA (1993).

O. heterophyllus 'Gulftide'
Discovered at Glenn Dale, MD, in 1952 by an employee of Gulf Stream nursery of Wachapreague, VA. Introduced to commerce ≤1960. Common. Compared to typical O. heterophyllus, more upright and of narrower growth habit, with a fairly narrow crown. Possibly more hardy. Except for juvenile foliage, the leaves are mostly spineless. More than one clone may be in circulation; the description given here is for the original.

O. ilicifolius—see O. heterophyllus

O. ilicifolius var. latifolius—see O. × Fortunei

O. 'San José'—see O. × Fortunei 'San José'

O. yunnanensis (Franch.) P.S. Green
= O. Forrestii Rehd.

From NW Yunnan and Szechuan, China. Introduced by G. Forrest in 1923. In North American commerce since the 1950s. Very rare. Leaves to 9½" × 2½" with up to 54 spiny teeth per side. Young growth in May is bronzy, fringed with pink teeth. Flowers (late January) February-March. Not as cold-hardy as the other Osmanthus in this volume. Rapid growing. Records: to 45' tall in the wild; 42½' × 4'6" East Bergholt Place, Suffolk, England (1972).

Ostrya

[CARPINACEÆ or BETULACEÆ; Hornbeam or Birch Family] 8–10 spp. of deciduous trees known as HOP HORNBEAMS. Ostrya is Latinized from the Greek name, ostrys. The name HOP HORNBEAM refers to the hoplike (whitish, papery bladders) seed clusters borne by trees related to HORNBEAMS (*Carpinus*). *Ostrya* bark is shreddy, with thin, brownish scales—not taut, gray and muscular-looking like that of *Carpinus*. The trees are anything but glamorous, but are troublefree and offer subtle beauty of form and foliage.

O. carpinifolia Scop.

= *O. vulgaris* Willd.
= *Carpinus Ostrya* L. (in part)

EUROPEAN HOP-HORNBEAM. From S Europe, SW Asia, and the Caucasus. Introduced to cultivation ≤1724. Extremely rare in North America. Latin *Carpinus*, HORNBEAM tree, and *folium*, a leaf. A vigorous tree, featuring usually an upright candelabra shape. Lack of handsome fall color is the main shortcoming: late, yellow-gold and green. Male catkins borne in April, to 5" long. Leaves sharply toothed, to 5¼" × 2⅜". Seed clusters 1"–2" long. Records: to 80' tall in the wild; 72' × 5'9" Killerton, Devon, England (1983); 66' × 4'4" Seattle, WA (1990; *pl.* 1957); 50' × 15'8" Langley Park, near Norwich, England (<1908); 43' × 10'4" Bulstrode Park, Buckinghamshire, England (1983).

O. Knowltonii Cov.

WESTERN HOP-HORNBEAM. From the SW United States. Named in 1894 after Frank Hall Knowlton (1860–1926), U.S. botanist, journal editor, and discoverer of this species in 1889. Cultivated since 1914. Exceedingly rare; of no special merit. A shrubby little tree, with short, broad, fuzzy leaves that feel like peach fuzz when caressed.

O. virginiana (Mill.) K. Koch

= *O. virginica* Willd.
= *Carpinus Ostrya* L. (in part)
= *Carpinus virginiana* Mill.

AMERICAN HOP-HORNBEAM. EASTERN (U.S.) HOP-HORNBEAM. BEETLEWOOD. STONEWOOD. LEVERWOOD. IRONWOOD. HARDTACK. DEER WOOD. From central and eastern North America (and a variety in Central America, extending south to Honduras). The only *Ostrya* at all commonly planted in North America. Leaf to 6¼" × 2¾", golden yellow in fall, coloring better and earlier than *O. carpinifolia*. Seed clusters 1½"–2½" long. Records: 76' × 6'4" × 35' Dempseytown, PA (1972); 74' × 9'7" × 111' Grand Traverse County, MI (≤1993); 70' × 9'6" × 57' near Winthrop, ME (1954).

O. vulgaris—see *O. carpinifolia*

Oxydendrum

(*Oxydendron*)

[ERICACEÆ; Heath Family] Only the following species in the genus. From Greek *oxys,* acid or sour, and *dendron,* a tree; alluding to the leaves' sour taste. A related genus is *Arbutus* (MADRONA).

O. arboreum (L.) DC.

= *Andromeda arborea* L.

SORREL TREE. SOURWOOD. SORRELWOOD. LILY-OF-THE-VALLEY TREE. TITI. From the eastern U.S. Originally called *Andromeda arborea*—the tree Andromeda, as the other species in that genus are mere shrubs. Common in cultivation. Leaves PEACH-like, to 9" × 3½", lustrous, of dependably brilliant scarlet red fall color (sometimes polished-copper, orange, or yellow). Flowers waxy-white, urnlike, tiny, on long slender spikes drooping in clusters in summer. A narrow-crowned tree of supreme elegance and ornamental value. Best in acidic soils. It hates dryness. Records: 118' × 6'5" near Robbinsville, NC (1972); 100' × 6'2" Morrisville, PA (1980); 96' × 8'5" Tennessee (1994); 80' × 7'7" Great Smoky Mountains National Park, TN (1961).

O. arboreum 'Chameleon'

A chance seedling selected by P. Hill of Massachusetts in 1990, when it was 32 years old. Very variable fall color. In commerce.

Padus Laurocerasus—see *Prunus Laurocerasus*

Padus lusitanica—see *Prunus lusitanica*

Padus Maackii—see *Prunus Maackii*

Padus racemosa—see *Prunus Padus*

Padus serotina—see *Prunus serotina*

Padus virginiana—see *Prunus virginiana*

Parrotia

[HAMAMELIDACEÆ; Witch Hazel Family] Only the following species in the genus, grown for fall color, peely bark, and its pleasingly irregular branching. Named after F.W. Parrot (1792–1841), German naturalist, traveller, professor of Medicine at Dospat. For related genera see *Liquidambar* (SWEETGUM) and × *Sycoparrotia* (*Parrotia* × *Sycopsis*).

P. persica (DC.) C.A. Mey.
= *Hamamelis persica* DC.

PERSIAN IRONWOOD. PERSIAN WITCH-HAZEL. From N Iran (Persia), and the Caucasus. Introduced to cultivation in 1840, from St. Petersburg to England. Since the 1950s it has been increasingly planted in North America. Usually a gigantic shrub with picturesque wide branching, not of tree form unless pruned. (In 1972, Ohio nurseryman Ed Scanlon reported a seedling of columnar habit, 16' tall × 4' wide.) Bark handsome and mottled, peeling like a LACEBARK ELM (*Ulmus parvifolia*). Leaves lopsided, shortstemmed, to 7" long, wavy, shiny, with varying but always exciting fall color. Flowers tiny red tassels in (late January) February–March. Records: to 80' tall in the wild; an 8-trunked tree 60' tall × 75' wide at the Arnold Arboretum, MA (*pl.* 1881); 60' × 3'2" Tacoma, WA (1990); 59' × 6'3" × 49' Geneva, Switzerland (≤1967); 46' × 4'1" Abbotsbury, Dorset, England (1986); 46' × 4'11" Portland, OR (1989); a trunk 8'8" around (at 6" from the ground) Flushing, NY (1972).

P. persica 'Biltmore'
Introduced ≤1994 by Earth Shade nursery of Warne, NC.

P. persica 'Pendula'
Selected in 1934 at Kew, England. Although the Arnold Arboretum imported stock from England in 1966, most specimens in North America date from 1986 or after. A compact mound of arching, somewhat pendulous branches, scarcely able to surpass 10' tall.

P. persica 'Select'
Introduced ≤1993–94 by Buchholz & Buchholz nursery of Gaston, OR. Young leaves lime-green with a purple edge.

P. persica 'Vanessa'
Origin not known. Sold in 1995 by Twombly nursery of Monroe, CT. "Columnar. Showy red-burgundy leaf tips thru early summer."

Pasania edulis*—see *Lithocarpus edulis

Paulownia

[SCROPHULARIACEÆ; Figwort Family] 6–7 spp. from China and SE Asia. Named in 1835 when Anna Paulowna (1795–1865) was 40 years old; hereditary princess of Holland, daughter of Czar Paul I of Russia. Stout, pioneer trees valued as ornamentals, and useful as fast-growing soil-binders; they withstand drought and a certain mount of alkali. Overall they recall genus *Catalpa*, but can be distinguished any day of the year. The bark is smooth and gray. In March, April, or early May, before the leaves emerge, spectacular terminal clusters of trumpet-shaped flowers appear. (Tasting as good as they smell, the flowers create a delightful sensation added to a salad.) The leaves are late to flush, immense, dull green, generally more or less fuzzy, and drop without fall color; often they are heart-shaped at the base, and bear three broad lobes. The flowerbuds are prominent, light brown, felty-hairy. The seed pods are at first apple-green and sticky, ripen brown and look pecan-like, split in half and release hundreds of winged seeds. In colder regions the flowerbuds often are killed in winter, whereupon the trees must be enjoyed for their ample foliage alone. No other genera in this volume are in the SCROPHULARIACEÆ.

P. Duclouxii—see *P. Fortunei*

P. Fargesii—see *P. tomentosa* 'Lilacina'

P. Fargesii 'Lilacina'—see *P. tomentosa* 'Lilacina'

P. Fortunei (Seem.) Hemsl.
= *P. Duclouxii* Dode

From S & SE China, Viet Nam, and Taiwan. Named in 1867, after Robert Fortune (1812–1880), who first collected it. Introduced to North America in 1914 by F. Meyer. Extremely rare. Flowers appear before those of *P. tomentosa*, are larger (to 4" long × 3¼" wide); most of the inside is creamy white with numerous purple speckles, but the outer portions are of a lavender background; the throat has yellow raised ridges like those of *P. tomentosa* 'Lilacina'. Seedpods elongated and woody, 2"–3⅛" × ⅝". Seeds the largest in the genus. Records: to 90' × 22'0" in the wild; 79' × 18'6" Anhwei, China (1925); 50' × 3'4" Seattle, WA (1995; *pl.* 1940).

P. imperialis—see *P. tomentosa*

P. lilacina—see *P. tomentosa* 'Lilacina'

P. tomentosa (Th.) S. & Z. *ex* Steud.
= *P. imperialis* S. & Z.

EMPRESS TREE. ROYAL PAULOWNIA. BLUE CATALPA. PURPLE CATALPA. FOXGLOVE TREE. PRINCESS TREE. COTTON TREE. From China and Korea. First described in 1784–85 (*tomentosa* is Latin for "having soft, matted hair"). Siebold shipped this species (with numerous other plants) to Holland in January 1829 —it arrived in 1830. To England and France by 1834; P. Henderson says 1840 to the U.S.; Prince nursery of Flushing, NY, sold it here ≤1844–45. In California by 1856. A very common, distinctive and well known tree. Now wild in parts of the U.S. It can grow 20' in one year. Leaves huge, soft, wooly, shaped like those of the sunflower plant. Flowers fragrant, big (1½"–2¾" long, to 2" wide); they have been likened to those of the tropical *Jacaranda* trees; they are pale violet- to sky-blue, with stripes of pale creamy-yellow and purple dots. The 1"–1½" seedpods can have 2,000 seeds. Shade intolerant (but casts dense shade itself). In Japan, called *Kiri*, and its wood is highly prized—when alive it is soft, but when dry is hard, durable, very easily worked; used for *geta* (clogs). Records: 105' × 20'3" × 70' Philadelphia County, PA (1969); 79' × 15'9" Geneva, Switzerland (≤1967); 75' × 20'7" Baltimore, MD (1972); 71' × 15'5" Portland, OR (1993); 66' × 17'4" Greenwich, CT (1987); 64' × 21'8" × 67' Evansville, IN (1989).

P. tomentosa 'Alba'
Cultivated since 1905. Extremely rare. Flowers white.

P. tomentosa 'Lilacina'
= *P. lilacina* Sprague
= *P. Fargesii* hort. 1929, non Franch. 1896
= *P. Fargesii* 'Lilacina'

Sometime between 1893 and 1897 (probably in 1896) P.G. Farges sent seeds of what would come to be named *P. tomentosa* 'Lilacina' to Vilmorin nursery of France. The tree raised flowered in 1905, and in 1938 was named *P. lilacina* (a compound word from the English "Lilac" and the Latin suffix *-ina*, like). Well before it was named, 'Lilacina' had been circulated as "*P. Fargesii*." 'Lilacina' differs from typical *P. tomentosa* in its paler, larger flowers (to 3⅜" × 2⅝"), spotless within; flowering a bit later; and less lobed leaves. It is also hardier and more robust. It breeds more or less true from seeds. In 1993, Roy Lancaster suggested it may be a cross of *P. Fargesii* and *P. tomentosa*. To call it a cultivar may be as unsatisfactory as to rank it a species; maybe the best category is at the rank of a botanical variety of *P. tomentosa*. More study is needed. Its date of introduction to North America, and comparative abundance is unknown. Almost certainly some nurseries have sold it simply as *P. tomentosa*. In Seattle it has been grown since at least 1948, and is routinely superior to typical *P. tomentosa*. One planted in 1951: 68' × 7'0" × 52' (1988).

P. tomentosa 'Somaclonal Snowstorm'
Originated ca. 1984 at the University of Massachusetts, Amherst, as a tissue-culture-induced variant. It grew slower and had some leaves flecked and blotched with white and light green or yellow-green. Named ≤1987, and introduced—only to prove a dud: an inconstant variation that usually looks absolutely typical.

Pavia californica—see *Æsculus californica*

Pavia glabra—see *Æsculus glabra*

Pavia rubra—see *Æsculus Pavia*

Persea

[LAURACEÆ; Laurel Family] More than 150 spp. of broadleaf evergreen trees and shrubs. The best known species is hopelessly cold tender—the AVOCADO TREE (*P. americana* Mill.). *Persea* is an ancient Greek name of Theophrastus referring to some Egyptian fruit-bearing tree (perhaps what we call ASSYRIAN PLUM, *Cordia Myxa*). Related genera include *Apollonias, Cinnamomum* (CAMPHOR TREE), *Laurus* (BAY LAUREL), *Lindera, Neolitsea, Sassafras,* and *Umbellularia* (OREGON MYRTLE). The 1957 union of the 1831 genus *Machilus* and *Persea* is controversial; some botanists maintain *Machilus* as a separate genus of 35–100 spp.

P. Borbonia (L.) Spreng.
= *P. carolinensis* (Catesb.) Nees
= *P. littoralis* Small
= *Laurus Borbonia* L.
REDBAY. SHORE BAY. From the SE United States. Named in 1753 (*Borbonia* is an old generic name for *Persea*). Rarely cultivated. Leaves 2"–5" long, dark and shiny above, pale beneath; appearing practically hairless (unless magnified); aromatic when crushed; orange-crimson in late winter / spring. Flowers tiny, creamy-white, from April into July. Fruit a shiny, bluish-black berry ½" long, borne on an attractive red stem. REDBAY is less common and widespread than its var. *pubescens* (below). Records: 77' × 12'8" × 52' Florida (1994); 58' × 13'8" × 68' Randolph County, GA (1971).

P. Borbonia var. pubescens (Pursh) Little
= *P. Borbonia* ssp. *pubescens* (Pursh) E. Murr.
= *P. palustris* (Raf.) Sarg.
= *P. pubescens* (Pursh) Sarg.
SWAMP BAY. SWAMP REDBAY. Named in 1814. Differs from typical *P. Borbonia*: leaves average slightly larger (to 7" long), are coated beneath with brownish fuzz (like the twigs); flowers slightly larger, bark thinner; grows primarily in very wet sites. Most contemporary botanists consider it a distinct species. It also grows in the Bahamas. Records: 83' × 13'5" Pettigrew State Park, NC (1991); 50' × 6'3" Cheasapeake, VA (1986).

P. carolinensis—see *P. Borbonia*

P. littoralis—see *P. Borbonia*

P. palustris—see *P. Borbonia* var. *pubescens*

P. pubescens—see *P. Borbonia* var. *pubescens*

P. Thunbergii (S. & Z.) Kosterm.
= *Machilus Thunbergii* S. & Z.
From China, S Korea, Japan, the Ryukyus, and Taiwan. Named in 1846 after Carl Peter Thunberg (1743–1828), Swedish physician, and pupil of Linnæus. The alternate generic name *Machilus* derives from the Moluccan name *makilo*. Date of introduction to Western cultivation not known. Extremely rare. Leaves weakly scented; shiny dark green above, beautifully pale gray-green beneath; hairless; untoothed; to 6" × 2¾"; stem to 1¼". Flowers in March–May, tiny, greenish, in upright clusters. Fruit blackish-purple, ⅜" wide. A dense, small tree in cultivation. Recorded to 100' × 19'8" in the wild.

P. yunnanensis (Lecomte) Kosterm.
= *Machilus yunnanensis* Lecomte
From W China, specifically Yunnan Province. Exceedingly rare. A Seattle specimen, raised in 1938 is 34' tall, with three trunks 6"–8" thick (1994). Its seedlings have been sold by local nurseries since 1989. Leaves 3"–6" long, no more than 1¼" wide, quite WILLOW-like; dark above, pale beneath, smelling faintly citrus-like when crushed. An elegant foliage tree, the flowers and fruit brown and wholly inconspicuous.

Persica Davidiana—see *Prunus Davidiana*

Persica vulgaris—see *Prunus Persica*

Phellodendron

[RUTACEÆ; Rue Family] 3–10 spp. of deciduous trees, so similar to one another that they might well be considered one variable species. Leaves opposite, compound, the stalks hiding the leafbuds. Grown as imposing shade trees. Flowers inconspicuous, yellowish-green, in broad clusters in summer, succeeded by black berries ⅓"–½" wide, of resinous odor. Male and female flowers on separate trees. From Greek *phellos*, cork, and *dendron*, a tree; in allusion to the thick corky bark. The original CORK TREE is *Quercus Suber*. Though the name is similar to *Philodendron*, they are not related to the well-known houseplants. Some other genera in the RUTACEÆ include

Fortunella (KUMQUAT), *Poncirus* (HARDY ORANGE), *Ptelea* (HOP TREE), *Tetradium*, and *Zanthoxylum*.

P. amurense Rupr.

AMUR CORK TREE. From N China, Manchuria, Korea, Ussuri, Amur, and Japan. Introduced to cultivation in 1856 in Russia. In North America ≤1874. Common. A flattish-topped or at any rate round-headed, broad tree. Bark thick and corky. Leaves of (5) 11 (15) leaflets. Flowers in June. Of rapid growth as long as there is ample moisture and good soil. Not a good street tree, being uneven, irregular, gaunt, and dropping fruit that stains sidewalks. Cold-tolerant and heat-loving; needs a continental climate to be at its best. Where happy, it reseeds weedily. Records: 78' × 12'2" Belgium (1985); 75' × 14'5" × 84' Amherst, MA (1986); 55' × 13'7" × 70' Bryn Mawr, PA (1980); a trunk 18'0" around in Montgomery County, PA (<1970).

P. amurense Macho®

Introduced in 1985 by W. Wandell of Urbana, IL. Common. Fruitless. Broad, upright habit.

P. amurense 'PNI 4551'—see P. amurense Shademaster®

P. amurense var. sachalinense Fr. Schmidt

= *P. sachalinense* (Fr. Schmidt) Sarg.

SAKHALIN PHELLODENDRON. From W China, Sakhalin, Korea, and N Japan. Raised at the Arnold Arboretum in 1877 from seeds sent from Japan by Dr. W.S. Clark. A tree given by Clark and planted in 1877 at the Massachusetts Agricultural College, is still alive. In North American commerce ≤1910. Uncommon; probably often sold as "*P. amurense*." Bark far less corky than that of *P. amurense*. It can reseed, and in other ways act exactly like *P. amurense*. Leaflets 7–11; fall color soft, glowing yellow. Recorded to 80' × 9'6" in the wild.

P. amurense Shademaster®

= *P. amurense* 'PNI 4551'

Introduced <1990 by Princeton nursery of New Jersey. Uncommon. Fruitless.

P. chinense Schneid.

CHINESE PHELLODENDRON. From China. Introduced by E. Wilson in 1907 to the Arnold Arboretum. In North American commerce ≤1918. Uncommon. Bark not corky. Leaflets wooly beneath. Record: 36' × 5'4" × 39' Philadelphia, PA (1980).

P. chinense var. glabriusculum Schneid.

Far less hairy than typical *P. chinense*. Very rare. Sold from (at least) 1928 until 1938 by H.P. Kelsey nursery of Salem, MA.

P. sachalinense—see P. amurense var. sachalinense

Phillyrea

[OLEACEÆ; Olive Family] 2–4 spp. of broadleaf evergreen shrubs or small trees, all from the Mediterranean region. The ancient Greek name. Perhaps from *phyllon*, a leaf; literally, a leafy plant—the flowers being inconspicuous—or, says J. Loudon, from *Philyra*, the mother of Chiron, who was changed into a tree. Related genera include: *Chionanthus* (FRINGE TREE), *Fraxinus* (ASH), *Ligustrum* (PRIVET), *Olea* (OLIVE), *Osmanthus*, and *Syringa* (LILAC).

P. latifolia L.

= *P. media* L.

MOCK PRIVET. JASMINE BOX. SHARPBERRY TREE. From the Mediterranean region. Introduced to cultivation in 1594 in Holland. Named in 1753 (Latin *latus*, broad, and *folium*, a leaf). In North American commerce ≤1909. Rare; primarily on the Pacific Coast. Prized for its compact habit, glistening foliage and troublefree disposition. If it sported large flowers or showy fruits, people would stampede for it. Leaves very glossy, to 2" × 1⅜" but usually ≤1½" long. Flowers from March into June, tiny, greenish- or creamy-white. Berries deep purplish or slate black, dull and inconspicuous, ¼"–⅓" wide, with one large seed; bitter. It might be likened to an improved *Ilex crenata* (JAPANESE HOLLY). Very slow and shrubby for many years; eventually of tree size. Records: 46' × 5'6" Nelson, New Zealand (1973; *pl.* ca. 1872); 42' × 6'10" and 29' × 7'2" Paris, France (1982; *pl.* 1880); 28½' × 2'0" Seattle, WA (1994; *pl.* 1956); 27½' tall (multitrunked) × 32½' wide Santa Barbara, CA (1993); 26' × 5'3" Westonbirt, Gloucestershire, England (1989).

P. media—see P. latifolia

Photinia

[ROSACEÆ; Rose Family] 40–60 spp. of shrubs or trees, evergreen or deciduous; mostly in E Asia and Mexico. Flowers small, white, in clusters which give rise to colorful berries. From Greek *photeinos*, shining or bright, alluding to lustrous leaves of some species. Related genera include: *Amelanchier* (SERVICEBERRY), *Cotoneaster*, *Cratægus* (HAWTHORN), *Sorbus* (MOUNTAIN ASH).

P. Beauverdiana Schneid.

From West-central China, Viet Nam, and Taiwan. Introduced in 1900 by E. Wilson for Veitch nursery of England. Named after Gustave Beauverd (1867–1942), botanist and artist. In North American commerce ≤1940 (offered that year by W.B. Clarke nursery of San José, CA). Extremely rare. A bushy small slender tree, often multitrunked. Prized above all for its fall color, often scarlet, although the deep red berries are also handsome. Trained as a tree it can form a broad, pendulous crown. Leaves hairless, finely and sharply toothed, to 5" × 2¾"; stem to ⅝" long. Berries scarlet, ¼" wide. Record: 36' × 3'3" Swansea, Wales (1981).

P. Beauverdiana var. notabilis (Schneid.) Rehd. & Wils.

Introduced in 1908 by E. Wilson from W Hupeh, China. Larger in all its parts. Leaves to 7⅜" × 3¼", with scattered, loose white hairs beneath. Flowers to ⁹⁄₁₆" wide, in clusters to 4" wide which gracefully and lightly mantle the tree in May. Berries orange-red, ⅓" long. Leaves late to assume fall color (in November). A small tree of arching branches bearing slender twigs and thin, parchment-like leaves. Records: 37' × 1'11" Seattle (1993; *pl.* 1960); 33' × 2'3" Kew, England (1981; *pl.* 1909).

P. Davidiana (Decne.) Cardot

= *Stranvæsia Davidiana* Decne.

From China, Viet Nam, and a *var.* in Taiwan. Until the 1980s this was known as *Stranvæsia Davidiana*—a genus named after the Hon. William Thomas Horner Fox-Strangways (1795–1865), the 4th Earl of Ilchester, and a botanist. The specific epithet honors Jean Pierre Armand David (1826–1900), a Basque who discovered this species in 1869. Introduced in 1907 by E. Wilson. An evergreen shrub usually; a slender small tree if pruned into one. Leaves to 6" × 1½". Berries bright red, ¼"–⅜" wide, borne in abundance and persisting all winter.

P. Davidsoniae Rehd. & Wils.

From W Hupeh, China. Introduced in 1900 by E. Wilson for Veitch nursery of England. Wilson wrote: "One of the handsomest evergreen trees in central China. Named for Mrs. Henry Davidson of the Friend Foreign Mission, Chengtu, Szechuan, as a mark of esteem and in grateful remembrance of services rendered after my serious accident in the autumn of 1910." Exceedingly rare in North America. Perhaps not in commerce until 1993, when offered by Piroche Plants nursery of Pitt Meadows, B.C. Closely related to *P. serratifolia*, but with larger flowers (in June) and berries (⁵⁄₁₆" wide, orange-red), and smaller leaves (to 6¼" × 1¾"; stem to 1¼" long). Grows larger than any other cultivated *Photinia*. Records: 84' tall at Eastwood Hill Arboretum, New Zealand (1990; *pl.* 1928); 75½' × 7'8" × 52' San Francisco, CA (1994; *pl.* 1950); 65½' × 6'6" Anhwei, China (1925); 55½' × 4'9" × 45½' Berkeley, CA (1994).

P. deflexa—see Eriobotrya deflexa

P. × Fraseri Dress

(*Frazeri*)

= *P. glabra Fraseri* hort.

(*P. serratifolia* × *P. glabra*)

HYBRID PHOTINIA. FRASER PHOTINIA. RED-TIP. Named officially in 1961. Extremely common. An evergreen, usually planted as a shrub, often used for hedges, it can become treelike if left alone, or encouraged. Valued for its bright red young leaves in spring. Leaves finely toothed; to 6¾" × 3".

P. × Fraseri 'Birmingham'

Originated in 1940. Selected by Oliver (Ollie) W. Fraser (1887–1978) of Fraser nursery of Birmingham, AL, from a bed of *P. serratifolia* seedlings. First sold in 1955 by Tom Dodd nursery of Semmes, AL. This is the first clone and the most common. Record: 26' × 3'6" × 30' Seattle, WA (1994; *pl.* 1959).

P. × Fraseri Indian Princess™ PP 5237 (1984)

= *P. × Fraseri* 'Monstock'

Introduced in 1985 by Monrovia nursery of California. A sport discovered in their nursery. Slow, dense, dwarf. Orange-coppery new growth. Leaf half of typical size.

P. × Fraseri 'Monstock'—see P. × Fraseri Indian Princess™

P. × *Fraseri* 'Red Robin'
= *P. glabra* 'Red Robin'

Raised at Robinson's nursery of Masterton, New Zealand. In North American commerce ≤1979–80. Compact habit. Brilliant red young growth.

P. × *Fraseri* 'Robusta'
= *P. glabra* 'Robusta'

Introduced <1952 by Hazlewood's nursery of Sydney, Australia. In North America ≤1966; in commerce here ≤1992. Young growth of brilliant tones of salmon, copper or scarlet, but not retaining the color as long as 'Red Robin'. Growth hardy and vigorous.

P. glabra *Fraseri*—see P. × *Fraseri*

P. glabra 'Red Robin'—see P. × *Fraseri* 'Red Robin'

P. glabra 'Robusta'—see P. × *Fraseri* 'Robusta'

P. *japonica*—see *Eriobotrya japonica*

P. *serratifolia* (Desf.) Kalkman
= *P. serrulata* Lindl.

CHINESE PHOTINIA. CHINESE TOYON. From central and E China, Taiwan, and the Philippines. Named from Latin *serrula*, a small saw (referring to the teeth edging the leaves). Introduced in 1804, likely by Wm. Kerr. In North American commerce ≤1874. Common; recently superseded in commerce by its hybrids (brighter red, mildew-free). Leaves evergreen, polished, to 8¾" × 3½"; when emerging in spring rosy-chocolate or bronze colored, and very pretty, but not stunning like the *P.* × *Fraseri* clan. Flowers white, in clusters 6" wide during (March) April and May. Berries ¼" wide, red. Records: 49' × 7'1" × 50' Akaroa, New Zealand (1970); 48' × 4'1" × 36' Seattle, WA (1993); 36' × 8'0" Bath, Avon, England (1988).

P. *serratifolia* 'Nova'
= *P. serrulata* 'Nova'

Raised from seeds imported from China ca. 1926. Introduced in 1934 by W.B. Clarke nursery of San José, CA. Common. Spring foliage intense copper instead of bronze. Unlike regular California *P. serratifolia* stock, it sets berries, in clusters up to 10"–12" wide. Also less mildew-prone and somewhat smaller-growing.

P. *serratifolia* 'Nova Lineata'
= *P. serrulata* 'Nova Lineata'
?= *P. serrulata* 'Aculeata'

Introduced in 1943 by W.B. Clarke nursery of San José, CA. Rare. Leaves with a narrow, irregular white stripe along the midrib. Monrovia nursery's 1954–55 catalog says: variegated with large spots of amber-yellow and shades of green.

P. *serrulata*—see P. *serratifolia*

P. *serrulata* 'Aculeata'—see P. *serratifolia* 'Nova Lineata'

P. *serrulata* 'Nova'—see P. *serratifolia* 'Nova'

P. *serrulata* 'Nova Lineata'—see P. *serratifolia* 'Nova Lineata'

Picea

[PINACEÆ; Pine Family] 34–37 spp. of tall, narrow, coniferous evergreens, in cool temperate regions of the Northern Hemisphere. *Picea* is an ancient Latin name for a pitch-producing PINE, from *pix* or *picis* (pitch). The common name SPRUCE, of Anglo-Saxon origin, first referred exclusively to the European species *P. Abies* (NORWAY SPRUCE). Most have needles ¼"–1" long, usually squarish, but flat in a few species. Older twigs are rough with tiny pegs or warts. The bark is thin, flaky and scaly. The dangling cones are mostly 2"–4" long, composed of delicate, thin scales. The ripe cones fall intact (rather than disintegrating as in *Abies*—the FIRS). SPRUCES do best in cool or cold regions with ample moisture; summer heat and dryness stunt them. Even in ideal climates, shade, aphids and the loss of vigor attendant with age can cause them to look thin and ugly. While in their prime they are valued for their spirelike, neat form, and fine evergreen foliage.

P. *Abies* (L.) Karst.
= *P. excelsa* (Lam. & DC.) Link
= *P. vulgaris* Link
= *Pinus Abies* L. 1753, non Du Roi 1771
= *Abies excelsa* Lam. & DC.
= *Abies Picea* Mill. 1768, non Bluff & Fingerh. 1825

NORWAY SPRUCE. NORWEGIAN SPRUCE. COMMON SPRUCE. FINNISH SPRUCE. SPRUCE FIR. From Europe, east to the Urals. Extremely common in cultivation, well known, parent of hundreds of cultivars, mostly dwarf. One of the darkest, most somber of all trees. Stately and tough. Needles ⅓"–¾" (1⅛") long, wholly dark green. Cones larger than those of most species, 4"–9" long. NORWAY SPRUCE seedlings are often used as a rootstock for rare Chinese and Japanese SPRUCES, many of which perform better this way than on their own roots. Records: 226' × 11'6" Carpathian mountains (<1897); 156' × 14'2" Studley Royal, Ripon, North Yorkshire, England (1956; *pl.* ca. 1750; died <1966); 143' × 19'7½" in the Grisons (<1906); 124' × 10'7" Bloomfield Hills, MI (1983); 124' × 10'0" Finksburg, MD (1990); 120' × 15'0" × 66' New York (1994); 116' × 13'10" Brooklyn Township, PA (1991); 108' × 15'5" Durham, NH (1976); 95' × 13'4" Easton, CT (1987); 94' × 14'2" St. Joseph, PA (1989); 75' × 14'4" Chenequa, WI (1990).

P. *Abies* 'Acrocona'

Originated near Uppsala, Sweden. Named in 1890 (meaning *apex-tufted* since many cones have tufts of short, hard needles at their apex. Bears both ordinary cones and long monstrous ones atop the branchlet ends. The clone commonly circulated bears cones freely even when young; moreover it is of reduced size, sometimes remaining a large shrub.

P. *Abies* 'Aurea'

GOLDEN NORWAY SPRUCE. Known since 1838 in England. Name published in 1855. Common. Doubtless more than one clone has circulated as 'Aurea'. Young needles bright yellow, aging to soft yellow-green. Less vigorous than ordinary seedlings. Can scorch in full sun. A related cultivar is 'Finedonensis'. Records: 108' × 6'0" Westonbirt, Gloucestershire, England (1980); 64' × 6'2" Vancouver, B.C. (1994).

P. *Abies* Cold-Pruf™

Under this name are sold exceptionally cold-hardy seedlings. Introduced in 1992 by Forgene Inc. of Wisconsin.

P. *Abies* f. *columnaris* (Jacques) Rehd.

COLUMNAR NORWAY SPRUCE. From Switzerland and parts of Germany and Scandinavia. Described in 1853 in France. Rarely listed by North American nurseries. It was offered at the turn of the century, and is still sold in the 1980s. Crown narrowly columnar. Branches very short, horizontal or somewhat inclined downward, densely set.

P. *Abies* 'Cranstonii'

Raised ca. 1840 by John Cranston's nursery of Hereford, England. Described in 1850. A cultivar of *P. Abies* f. *virgata*. Nurseries have sold both 'Cranstonii' and the common 'Virgata' clone under the latter name, and it is not known which of the two is commoner. They are similar freaks, caricatures more apt to raise eyebrows than elicit murmurs of approval. Stark they stand, sparingly branched, the branches long and thick, snakelike, with very few branchlets. Needles ¾"–1⅕" long, whorled, often somewhat undulate. 'Cranstonii' is more gaunt than 'Virgata', may grow larger, and has flatter needles, possibly slightly longer.

P. *Abies* 'Cruenta'

('Crusita')

Originated in Europe <1978. Sold ≤1993 by some Oregon nurseries. Slow, upright; a little tree. Young growth bright red-purple, soon fading to green.

P. *Abies* 'Cupressina'

CYPRESS NORWAY SPRUCE. Discovered ca. 1904 by Dr. Thomas in Tambach, Thuringia, Germany. Named in 1907. In North America since 1910; commonly sold only since the 1980s, replacing the less desirable *P. Abies* 'Pyramidata'. A dense broad column with tightly ascending branches. Needles shorter and cones smaller than typical. Compared to 'Pyramidata' it is denser, ultimately rounded at its apex and overall of a narrow oval shape. Record: 48' × 3'8" Lisle, IL (1986; *pl.* 1928).

P. *Abies* 'Elegantissima'

Raised by C. de Vos of Hazerswoude, near Boskoop, Holland. Named <1867. In North American commerce ≤1903. Foliage golden-yellow in spring, changing to green in autumn. Specimens sold since ca. 1990 by conifer specialist nurseries may be a different clone than the original. The clone presently sold is vigorous, with creamy new growth (at least on the top side of needles); aspect very droopy. By November the foliage looks a bit bleached, with cream-tinged needles which appear flattened on the upper side of the twigs.

P. Abies 'Fastigiata'—see P. Abies 'Pyramidata'

P. Abies 'Finedonensis'

Found as a seedling at Finedon Hall, Northamptonshire, England. Named in 1862. Extremely rare in North America, but in commerce. Young needles light yellow or yellowish-white, then bronzy, eventually green. Can be sun-scalded. Of reduced vigor but ordinary pyramidal habit; branches and branchlets nearly horizontal.

P. Abies 'Frohburg'

A seedling of P. Abies 'Inversa' from A. Haller nursery of Aarburg, Switzerland. Named in 1973. Habit vigorous, upright, and strongly pendulous. The 1993–94 catalog of Buchholz & Buchholz nursery of Gaston, OR: "An improved 'Pendula'. Less wild-looking. Needles thinner, shorter, more appressed."

P. Abies 'Hillside Upright'

Originated as a witches' broom found at Hillside Gardens of Lehighton, PA, Named ≤1970. Rare. Semi-dwarf, densely conical, irregularly-branched. Needles very dark green.

P. Abies 'Inversa'

('Inverta')

A cultivar of P. Abies f. pendula. Introduced ca. 1855–58 by Richard Smith of St. John's nursery, Worcester, England. A very pendulous small tree, both branches and twigs hanging down the stem. Very dense. In North America since ≤1870, but not as common as the shrubby weeper 'Reflexa', which is usually prostrate unless staked. Records: 52' × 4'3" × 27' Puyallup, WA (1992); 50' × 6'0" × 17' Philadelphia, PA (1980).

P. Abies 'Mucronata'

= P. mucronata hort.

SHARPLEAF SPRUCE. Found in 1835 by M. Briot, of Trianon Garden, Versailles, France. Described officially by J. Loudon in 1841 (Latin *mucro*, a sharp point, and *-atus*, provided with). Common since the 1950s. Broadly conical, semi-dwarf, 15'–30' tall. Inelegant, dark, and compact. Vigorous and hardy. Thick blue-green needles on curved branches; numerous large orange-brown buds in winter.

P. Abies ssp. obovata (Leded.) Hultén

= P. Abies var. obovata (Ledeb.) Fellm.
= P. obovata Ledeb.

SIBERIAN SPRUCE. From N Europe to NE China. Often considered a separate species, but it intergrades with P. Abies. Introduced to France in 1852. Very rare in North America. Twigs thin and hairy. Needles duller-colored, sharper, short (⅓"–¾" long). Cones 2⅜"–4" long, with scales wide and rounded (hence the name *obovata*) rather than narrowed and notched as in typical P. Abies. Slow growing, small and homely in cultivation. Of no value usually and seldom grown. Records: to 164' tall in the wild says *Flora Europæa*; to 115' × 6'2" in China; 65½' tall at the Arnold Arboretum (1982; *pl.* 1901); 62' × 5'0" Dawyck, Peeblesshire, England (1974; *pl.* 1910).

P. Abies f. pendula (Booth *ex* Laws.) N. Sylvén

WEEPING NORWAY SPRUCE. Cultivated since ≤1836 in Europe. A collective name for any more or less pendulous P. Abies cultivar or seedling, ranging from prostrate groundcovers to trees more than 130' tall. The most common weeping cultivar is 'Reflexa' (not a tree). Others are 'Frohburg', 'Inversa' and 'Wale's Drooping'.

P. Abies 'Pyramidata'

('Pyramidalis')

= P. Abies 'Fastigiata'

PYRAMIDAL NORWAY SPRUCE. Of French origin. Described in 1853. Common, but sold much less often now than in the past. Vigorous, almost fastigiate, like LOMBARDY POPLAR. Similar to 'Cupressina' but larger, less dense, and sharply spired at the apex rather than relatively rounded. Records: 82' × 7'4" Geneva, Switzerland (1985); 48' × 2'11" × 15' Lisle, IL (1986; *pl.* 1928).

P. Abies f. viminalis (Alstr.) Lindman

LONGBRANCHED NORWAY SPRUCE. Described in 1777 from the neighborhood of Stockholm, Sweden. Very rare in North America, but in commerce. Tree broadly pyramidal, full-sized. Main branches almost horizontal, in well-spaced whorls; secondary branchlets long, slender, pendulous. Records: 65' × 6'9" Zelazowa Wola, Poland (≤1973); 51' × 3'11" Lisle, IL (1986; *pl.* 1934).

P. Abies f. virgata (Jacques) Rehd.

SNAKEBRANCH SPRUCE. RAT-TAIL SPRUCE. Named in 1853 in France (Latin *virga*, a rod, in reference to the wand-shaped, slender and straight shoots). Common. An occasional variant in the wild, thus with a botanical name. Grown in cultivation mostly by grafted clones 'Cranstonii' and 'Virgata'. More than one clone has been distributed under the name 'Virgata'. Sparingly branched, the branches long and thick, snakelike, with very few branchlets. Needles ¾"–1⅓" long, whorled, often somewhat undulate. 'Cranstonii' is more gaunt than 'Virgata', may grow larger, and has flatter needles, possibly slightly longer. When in doubt of clonal identity the only recourse is to designate such trees as *P. Abies* f. *virgata*. In such spirit are cited these records: 73' × 5'0" Seattle, WA (1992); 52' × 6'0" × 45' Lisle, IL (1986; *pl.* 1926).

P. Abies 'Wale's Drooping'
= *P. Abies* 'Wale's Weeping'

A cultivar of *P. Abies* f. *pendula*. Named after William Wale of Dorchester, MA. Cultivated <1870 and still in commerce as late as 1905, but long extinct at least nominally. Attributes not known; apparently not a mere synonym of 'Inversa'.

P. Abies 'Wale's Weeping'—see *P. Abies* 'Wale's Drooping'

P. ajanensis—see *P. jezoensis*

P. alba—see *P. glauca*

P. Alcockiana or Alcoquiana—see *P. bicolor*

P. ascendens—see *P. brachytyla*

P. asperata Mast.

DRAGON SPRUCE. CHINESE SPRUCE. From W China. Introduced when E. Wilson sent seeds to the Arnold Arboretum in 1910. In commerce since the 1920s. Extremely rare. Needles very sharp and stout (*aspera* is Latin for rough), ½"–¾" (1⅛") long, glossy dark green to dull gray-green or even powder-bluish. Cones 3"–5" (6") long. Buds large, often with loose scales at the tips. Twigs hairy or hairless. Records: 147½' tall in Tibet (1926); 75' × 6'4" Rochester, NY (≤1980); 70' × 4'4" Seattle, WA (1990; *pl.* 1947). The variation within this species is poorly understood. A study is needed to compare the 5 following so called varieties (conifer specialist J. Silba accepts none of them even at a varietal level), resolving both their botanical placement and horticultural value. None offers ornamental value that cannot be easily beat by other SPRUCES. They are vigorous, yet graceless, coarse, often gaunt, of unremarkable color, and abominably prickly.

P. asperata var. aurantiaca (Mast.) Boom
= *P. aurantiaca* Mast.

ORANGE-TWIG DRAGON SPRUCE. CHETO SAN SPRUCE. From W Szechuan, where it is endangered. Introduced in 1908. Exceedingly rare and little known. Twigs yellow, changing to orange (*aurantiacus* means orange-yellow). Specimens raised from seeds of the original importation to the Arnold Arboretum have varied in details. For example, though originally described as having hairless twigs, some have hairy twigs. The needles tend to be greener, shorter (mostly ⅓"–¾") and less stout than most *asperata* specimens.

P. asperata var. heterolepis (Rehd. & Wils.) Cheng *ex* Chen
= *P. heterolepis* Rehd. & Wils.

REDTWIG DRAGON SPRUCE. Introduced in 1910. Exceedingly rare and little known. Likely unworthy of varietal distinction. Twigs bright reddish or yellow-brown, hairless. Bud-scales loose, reflexed. Needles bluish-green. Cones 3½"–5½" long; the lower scales deeply bilobed. Greek *heteros*, other, and *lepis*, peel, husk, or scale. Record: 76' × 5'4" Cos Cob, CT (1987).

P. asperata var. notabilis Rehd. & Wils.

Introduced in 1910. Very rare. In commerce in the 1920s, and still in the '80s and '90s. Differs from typical *P. asperata* chiefly in the shape of the cone scales —narrowed towards the apex. Needles a trifle longer, cones likewise. Recorded to 100' × 10'0" in China.

P. asperata var. ponderosa Rehd. & Wils.

Introduced in 1910. Very rare. In commerce in the 1920s. Differs from typical *P. asperata* in having thicker bark and larger cones, 4¾"–6½" (7") long. In Latin, *ponderosa* means ponderous; heavy.

P. asperata 'Reflexa'—see *P. asperata* var. *retroflexa*

P. asperata var. retroflexa (Mast.) Boom
= *P. retroflexa* Mast.
= *P. asperata* 'Reflexa'

TAPO SHAN SPRUCE. Introduced in 1911. Rare. In commerce in the 1920s, the '50s, and still in the '80s and

'90s. Differs from typical *P. asperata* in having grayer and very flaky bark. Cones 4"–5" long. Needles long and stout, often very glaucous. Twigs hairy. Buds big. Name from Latin *retro*, back or backward, and *flexus*, bent. Recorded to 150' × 13'0" in China.

P. aurantiaca—see *P. asperata* var. *aurantiaca*

P. Balfouriana—see *P. likiangensis* var. *Balfouriana*

P. bicolor (Maxim.) Mayr

= *P. Alcockiana* (Veitch *ex* Lindl.) Carr.
= *Pinus Alcoquiana* (Veitch *ex* Lindl.) Parl.
= *Abies Alcoquiana* Veitch *ex* Lindl.—(in part—*P. jezoensis*, too)

ALCOCK SPRUCE. Japanese: *Ira-momi. Matsu-hada.* From mountains of Honshu, Japan. Introduced in 1861 by J.G. Veitch, who named it *Alcoquiana* after his companion on the expedition, Sir Rutherford Alcock (1809–1897), British Minister at Tokyo. Uncommon in North America; here since ca. 1870; still in commerce. Needles ⅜"–¾" long, dark green above, bluish beneath (hence *bicolor*). Cones 2"–4¾" long. Records: to 115' tall in the wild; 85' × 5'6" Tayside, Scotland (1983); 71' × 9'8" Wellesley, MA (1984).

P. brachytyla (Franch.) Pritz.

= *P. Sargentiana* Rehd. & Wils.
= *P. ascendens* Patschke

SARGENT SPRUCE. From W China. Introduced in 1901 by E. Wilson for Veitch nursery of England. Extremely rare in North America; promoted since the 1980s by Buchholz & Buchholz nursery of Gaston, OR. The name *brachytyla* from Greek *brachys*, short, and *tylos*, a lump or knob (referring to the twigs). The English name commemorates Charles Sprague Sargent (1841–1927), great American tree expert. A superb ornamental with neat foliage on a broad-crowned tree. Twigs slender, pale. Needles flat, ⅜"–⅝", glossy grass-green above, vivid powder-blue beneath, the contrast lovely. Cones 2½"–5" long. Records: to 131' × 13'0" in the wild; 105' × 6'9" Stourhead, Wiltshire, England (1984); 85' × 8'3" Wakehurst Place, Sussex, England (1984; *pl.* 1914).

P. brachytyla var. *complanata* (Mast.) Cheng *ex* Hu

= *P. complanata* Mast.

From Tibet and W China. Introduced in 1903 by E. Wilson for Veitch nursery of England. Extremely rare in North America. Needles slightly longer (to 1"), sharper. Cones larger (to 6") brown or purplish-brown when young instead of greenish, purple-tinged. Likely unworthy of botanical distinction. The colorful immature cones are lovely. In Latin, *complanata* means flattened out as in a plane—likely in reference to the needles.

P. Breweriana S. Wats.

(*Brewerana*)

SISKIYOU SPRUCE. WEEPING SPRUCE. BREWER SPRUCE. From the Siskiyou Mountains of SW Oregon and NW California; the rarest of 7 native American SPRUCE species. Discovered in 1863 near Mt. Shasta by William Henry Brewer (1828–1910), botany professor at Yale University. Introduced to cultivation in 1891 (the year R. Douglas nursery of Waukegan, IL, had seedlings). Uncommon. Foliage more or less pendulous. Needles flat, bluish-green, to 1⅜" long, not prickly. Twigs hairy. Bark flaky. Cones 2½"–5½" long. Of slow to moderate growth. Easily stunted by shade or dryness; in a mild climate of sufficient humidity it can be luxurious. Prized for its pendulous sprays, of an attractive dusty or gray cast from a distance. Recorded to 200' × 19'0" in the wild; so far at most 66' × 6'6" in cultivation.

P. Breweriana 'Mt. Magic'

Named ≤1980s by Wells nursery of Mt. Vernon, WA. A grafted clone that looks utterly ordinary to the present writer.

P. canadensis—see *P. glauca*

P. complanata—see *P. brachytyla* var. *complanata*

P. Engelmannii (Parry) Engelm.

= *P. glauca* ssp. *Engelmannii* (Parry) T.M.C. Taylor

ENGELMANN SPRUCE. ENGELMANN BLUE SPRUCE. ROCKY MOUNTAIN WHITE SPRUCE. From the Cascades and Rockies throughout western North America. Closely related to and hybridizes with WHITE SPRUCE (*P. glauca*). Discovered in 1862 on Pike's Peak by C. Parry, who sent seeds to the Arnold Arboretum in 1863. Named after George Engelmann (1809–1884), German-American physician and botanist of St.

Louis, MO. Common in cultivation but much over-shadowed by the more robust and variable *P. pungens* (COLORADO SPRUCE). Twigs finely hairy. Needles slender, pliable, usually gray-green, often curved, ½"–1⅛" long. Cones 1½"–3" long. Records: 238' × 25'6" Whatcom County, WA (1970); 213' × 19'1" Alpine Lakes Wilderness, WA (1987); 179' × 24'2" Payette Lake, ID (1968); 129' × 24'10" Squamish Forest District, B.C. (1992).

P. Engelmannii f. *glauca* (R. Smith) Beissn.

Named ≤1874 in England. Common. Needles decidedly bluish rather than greenish. The counterpart of BLUE COLORADO SPRUCE (*P. pungens* f. *glauca*).

P. Engelmannii 'Vanderwolf's Blue Pyramid'

Introduced in 1969 by Vermeulen nursery of New Jersey. It had been sold as *P. Engelmannii* 'Glauca' until 1971.

P. excelsa—see *P. Abies*

P. glauca (Moench) Voss

= *P. canadensis* (Mill.) B.S.P., non (Michx.) Link
= *P. alba* (Ait.) Link

WHITE SPRUCE. CANADIAN SPRUCE. SKUNK SPRUCE. CAT SPRUCE. SINGLE SPRUCE. From a vast range: Alaska through Canada and the far northern U.S. Common in cultivation. Needles ⅓"–¾" long, slender, scarcely prickly, usually glaucous, hence the names *glauca* and WHITE. The crushed needles smell bad to some people. Cones 1"–2½" long. Records (see also var. *albertiana*): 128' × 9'8" Koochiching County, MN (1975); 103' × 10'11" Luce County, MI (1975); 89' × 11'8" Elmwood, WI (1986).

P. glauca var. *albertiana* (S. Br.) Sarg.

ALBERTA WHITE SPRUCE. WESTERN WHITE SPRUCE. From the Rockies in SW Canada (chiefly Alberta), Montana, Wyoming. Cultivated since 1904; common although sometimes sold simply as "*P. glauca.*" An ill-defined variety, not allowed at all by some botanists. The most important distinction is that it grows larger; bark flakier; needles longer (to 1³⁄₁₆"), twigs often hairy. Cones are often described as short and broad, but can be larger (to 2¾"). Records: to 184' × 12'6" in Alberta; 170' × 7'4" Conroy Creek, B.C. (1985)

P. glauca 'Aurea'

Named in 1866. Rare. Needles golden-yellow on upper side.

P. glauca 'Cærulea'

('Cœrulea')
= *P. glauca* 'Glauca'

Named in 1866 (Latin for sky- or heavenly-blue). First brought into notice by Mr. Plumbly, in the collection of conifers of Charles Dimsdale, at Essenden, near Hatfield, in Hertfordshire, England. Rare since the 1920s. Habit very compact. Needles short, densely crowded, distinctly silvery, gray-blue.

P. glauca 'Conica'

DWARF ALBERTA (WHITE) SPRUCE. Discovered in 1904 in Alberta (hence it is a cultivar of var. *albertiana*). Very common. Bushy and dwarf, dense, conical, and pure bright green, suggesting a giant moss plant. Formal and tidy, it looks trimmed. Can grow about 15' tall after many decades. Over the years many named mutations have been propagated, most of them miniature; golden and glaucous ones may grow about as large as the ordinary clone.

P. glauca var. *densata* Bailey

BLACK HILLS SPRUCE. From the Black Hills of SW South Dakota. South Dakota's State Tree. (The Black Hills were so named because a dark-needled *Pinus ponderosa* makes them appear black from a distance.) This SPRUCE, cultivated since the 1920s, and very variable, is variable. Color varies from green to the same blue as many *Picea pungens* (COLORADO SPRUCE) forms. Usually symmetrical, compact and bushy, but not necessarily much different from certain other *P. glauca* trees. Records from the wild: 93' × 7'5" and 89' × 8'1" South Dakota (1989).

P. glauca 'Dent'

Named ≤1985 in Oregon. Listed in 1993–84 catalog of Buchholz & Buchholz nursery, Gaston, OR: "Lush creamy-white variegation. Semi-dwarf."

P. glauca ssp. *Engelmannii*—see *P. Engelmannii*

P. glauca 'Fastigiata'

Raised ca. 1865 by A. Sénéclauze, nurseryman at Bourg Argental, France. Exceedingly rare. Narrow pyramidal; branches erect. Needles widely set, short.

P. glauca 'Ft. Ann'

('Fort Ann')

Named ≤1983 in Oregon. Elongated very sparse branches; irregular habit; large

P. glauca 'Glauca'—see *P. glauca* 'Cærulea'

P. glauca 'Gloriosa'

Origin and attributes not known. Sold ≤1931 by Kohankie nursery of Painesville, OH. Extremely rare and long commercially extinct.

P. glauca 'Pendula'

WEEPING WHITE SPRUCE. Discovered <1867 at Versailles, France. Long present in North America, but exceedingly rare until ca. 1992 when Iseli nursery of Boring, OR began promoting it. Branches very pendulous. Looks like a wet rag, grows slowly to 30' tall or more and needs no staking.

P. Glehnii (Fr. Schmidt) Mast.

SAKHALIN SPRUCE. SAGHALIN SPRUCE. Japanese: *Aka-ezo-matsu. Shinko-matsu*. From N Japan and S Sakhalin. Discovered in 1861 by Peter van Glehn (1837–1876; Russian botanist and plant explorer) and F. Schmidt. Introduced in 1877 by C. Maries to Veitch nursery of England. Introduced as seeds to the Arnold Arboretum in 1894. Uncommon. Foliage flushes early in spring. Twigs somewhat hairy, pale reddish; needles short (¼"–⅝" long), sharp and bright green. Cones 1½"–3½" long. Bark notably flaky. Slender branches and shoots. Although vigorous when young, it slows in age, and is not one of the more ornamental species. Records: to 130' × 15'6" in the wild; 85' × 5'2" Murthly Castle, Perthshire, Scotland (1981; *pl.* 1897); 57' × 7'0" Headfort, County Meath, Ireland (1966; *pl.* 1912).

P. heterolepis—see P. asperata var. heterolepis

P. hondoensis—see P. jezoensis var. hondoensis

P. 'Hy-blu'—see P. Spartan Spruce®

P. jezoensis (S. & Z.) Carr.

= *P. ajanensis* (Lindl. & Gord.) Fisch. *ex* Trautv. & Mey.

YEDDO SPRUCE. YEZO SPRUCE. JEZZO SPRUCE. From Manchuria, Korea, Kamchatka, the S Kuriles, Sakhalin, and N Japan—*i.e.* Hokkaido, formerly known as Yezo. Introduced to England in 1861 by J.G. Veitch; to Holland the same year by Siebold; and to the U.S. in March 1862 by G.R. Hall. Uncommon. Needles flat, dark glossy green above, dull blue beneath, ½"–¾" long. Cones 1½"–3¼" long. Records: to 230' × 20'0" in the wild; 49' × 5'2" Seattle, WA (1990).

P. jezoensis var. hondoensis (Mayr) Rehd.

= *P. hondoensis* Mayr
= *Abies Alcoquiana* Veitch *ex* Lindl. (in part—*P. bicolor*, too)

HONDO SPRUCE. Japanese: *To-hi*. From central Japan. Introduced to England in 1861 by J.G. Veitch. Uncommon; generally considered superior. Twigs darker. Needles shorter (⅜"–⅝"). duller above yet brighter white beneath. Cones slightly smaller (2"–2¾"). Growth flushes later, thus more frost-tolerant. Records: 118' × 8'10" Endsleigh, Devon, England (1990); 90' × 11'0" Benmore, Argyll, Scotland (1983; *pl.* 1880); 50' × 3'8" Bremerton, WA (1988).

P. koraiensis—see P. Koyamai

P. kosteriana—see P. pungens 'Koster'

P. Koyamai Shiras.

= *P. Moramomi* hort.
(*Koyamae*)

KOYAMA SPRUCE. Japanese: *Yatsugatake-to-hi*. From Mt. Yatsu of Honshu, Japan, where it is very rare; N Korea, and continental NE Asia. Discovered in 1911 by Mitsuo Koyama (1885–1935). Introduced in 1914 to the Arnold Arboretum by E. Wilson. Uncommon; of little appeal. Has the same nondescript appearance as a green *P. pungens* (COLORADO SPRUCE). Buds very pitchy. Needles ⅓"–¾" long, bluntish, bluish-green, upswept on pinkish-orange, hairy twigs. Cones 1½"–4½" long. Records: to 82' tall in the wild; 70' × 4'3" Stanage Park, Powys, Wales (1978; *pl.* 1920); 66' × 5'9" Bedgebury, Kent, England (1981; *pl.* 1928); 57' tall at the Arnold Arboretum (1982); 50' × 3'5" Seattle, WA (1994; *pl.* 1960). (J. Silba and K. Rushforth say most trees labelled *P. Koyamai* are KOREAN SPRUCE, *P. koraiensis* Nakai; others say *P. koraiensis* itself is not specifically distinct from *P. Koyamai*.)

P. likiangensis (Franch.) Pritz.

LIKIANG SPRUCE. From SE Tibet and W China (including Likiang Province). Discovered in 1884. Introduced in 1904 by E. Wilson for Veitch nursery of England. Until ca. 1990 this was virtually never sold in the U.S., and it is a poorly understood, variable species. John Silba says most specimens called *P. likiangensis* are really the variety *Forrestii* (which see). Twigs beige, usually hairy. Needles ⅓"–¾" long, dark green above, bluish beneath. Buds pitchy. Cones 2"–5" long. Records: to 130' × 10'0" in the wild; 88½' × 7'10" Powerscourt, County Wicklow, Ireland (1989).

P. *likiangensis* var. *Balfouriana* (Rehd. & Wils.) E.H. Hillier

= *P. Balfouriana* Rehd. & Wils.

Very like *P. likiangensis* var. *purpurea*: needles ⅓"–⅝" long, not as pale beneath, blunter. Cones 2"–3½" long. Twigs hairy. Likely named after John Hutton Balfour (1808–1884), Scots botanist.

P. *likiangensis* var. *Forrestii* Silba

= *P. yunnanensis* hort. *ex* Wils.

Collected by George Forrest (1873–1932) in the Likiang range, where specimens reached 150' tall. Prized for attractive gray-bluish foliage contrasting with bright pink male catkins and purplish-red young cones. Differs from typical *P. likiangensis* in its purplish-brown and deeply fissured bark (instead of pale gray and shallowly fissured); thick, pale tan twigs (instead of thin, whitish-brown ones); needles silvery-blue-gray to blue-green and nearly quadrangular (rather than dark green and somewhat flat); cones to 3⅛" long (rather than 4½"); and is likely more cold hardy.

P. *likiangensis* var. *montigena* (Mast.) Cheng *ex* Chen

= *P. montigena* Mast.

NORTHERN LIKIANG SPRUCE. CANDELABRA SPRUCE. From W China. Discovered by E. Wilson in 1903. Seeds sent to the Arnold Arboretum in 1910–11. Uncommon. The epithet *montigena* means mountain-begot; from Latin *mons*, mountain, and *geno*, born or produced. Descriptions of this variety differ. Surely dissimilar trees go under the name. Most specimens so called are, for all practical purposes, *P. asperata* (DRAGON SPRUCE). Needles ⅓"–⅝" long. Cones 2¾"–5⅛" long. Twigs on clones in contemporary commerce are hairless, and thereby do not conform to the original description. Records: to 100' × 13'0" in the wild; 70' × 4'7" Seattle, WA (1994; *pl.* 1949); 40' tall at the Arnold Arboretum (1982).

P. *likiangensis* var. *purpurea* (Mast.) Dall. & Jacks.

= *P. purpurea* Mast.

PURPLECONE SPRUCE. From W China and E Tibet. Introduced in 1910 by E. Wilson to the Arnold Arboretum. Uncommon. Needles ⅓"–⅝" long, dark green above, pale gray-green beneath. Twigs hairy. Cones 1¼"–2¼" (3") long, purple when young. Apex of tree notably narrow with ascending branches. Records: to 118' tall in the wild; 85' × 5'0" Westonbirt, Gloucestershite, England (1988; *pl.* 1931); 72' × 6'0" Eastnor Castle, Herefordshire, England (1984). Many experts believe this should rank as a separate species, and if so, the variety *Balfouriana* ought to be placed in subordination to it.

P. *mariana* (Mill.) B.S.P.

= *P. nigra* (Ait.) Link

BLACK SPRUCE. DOUBLE SPRUCE. SWAMP SPRUCE. GUM SPRUCE. BOG SPRUCE. LASH-HORN. From Alaska, Canada, and the northeastern U.S. Uncommon in cultivation. The specific name *mariana* was originally used by botanist P. Miller as synonymous with North America; this species is not native in Maryland. The young shoots are boiled for SPRUCE beer. Needles very short, ¼"–⅝" (¾"), usually bluish-green but can be pure green. Cones notably small, ½"–1⅞" long, unusually persistent. The smallest SPRUCE; of convenient garden size. Records: to 100' × 12'6" in the wild; 83' × 5'0" Superior National Forest, MN (1972); 78' × 5'2" Taylor County, WI (1989); 74' × 7'2" Rhinefield Drive, Hampshire, England (1961; *pl.* 1861); 62' × 6'9" Caerhays Castle, Cornwall, England (1971).

P. *mariana* 'Aurea'

Introduced in 1891 by Hesse nursery of Germany. Extremely rare. Needles wholly shining golden.

P. *mariana* 'Aureovariegata'

Introduced <1909 by Hesse nursery of Germany. Very rare. Needle tips yellow-gold, at least on young foliage. Lovely; looks from a distance like a yellow-tipped BLUE COLORADO SPRUCE.

P. *mariana* 'Doumetii'

Originally planted ca. 1835 at Château de Balaine (15 k north of Moulins, France); described in 1855. In North America ≤1897; rare, but in commerce. A dwarf tree of dense, broad habit. Needles very thin and sharp. Grows to ca. 20' tall.

P. *mariana* 'Fastigiata'

This was E. Carrière's 1867 name for a dwarf with slender needles. Trees sold in the 1980s as "*P. nigra* 'Fastigiata'—COLUMNAR BLACK SPRUCE" are really a *P. Abies* cultivar (such as 'Cupressina').

P. *mariana* 'Fast Wells'—see *P. mariana* 'Wellspire'

P. *mariana* 'Wellspire'

Introduced <1991 by Wells nursery of Mt. Vernon, WA. Called COLUMNAR BLACK HILLS SPRUCE, *Picea mariana* Fast Wells. The actual identity of this clone is anyone's guess, the nursery evidently confusing three species: *P. Abies, P. glauca* and *P. mariana*. Likely a *P. Abies* cultivar mislabeled.

P. Maximowiczii Reg. ex Mast.

= P. obovata var. japonica (Maxim.) Beissn.

JAPANESE BUSH SPRUCE. Japanese: Hime-bara-momi. From Japan's Mt. Yatsu and Mt. Senjo, Shinano Province (rare). Discovered in 1861 by Tschonoski, a Japanese collector who assisted Carl Johann Maximowicz (1827–1891). Introduced by them to St. Petersburg Botanic Garden; also by Siebold to Holland in 1865. In North America since ≤1895. Very rare. In mid-May its bright mossy-green young foliage contrasts beautifully with its dark old interior. Tree bushy, congested, broad, and slow. Needles rigid, very sharp, well-spaced, ⅜"–⅞" long, dark shiny green. Cones 1¼"–3½" long. Records: to 150' × 15'0" in the wild; 50' × 4'9" × 40' Philadelphia, PA (1980); 40' × 2'7½" × 20' Lisle, IL (1986; pl. 1953); 22½' × 2'0" × 21½' Seattle, WA (1994; pl. 1950).

P. Menziesii—see P. sitchensis

P. Meyeri Rehd. & Wils.

MEYER BLUE SPRUCE. CHINESE BLUE SPRUCE. MEYER SPRUCE. From N China to Inner Mongolia. Found February 25, 1908 in a temple garden by Frank Nicholas Meyer (1875–1918); USDA agricultural explorer. Introduced in 1908. Extremely rare; most trees so called are P. asperata (DRAGON SPRUCE). Whether the authentic species is in commerce or not, at least the name P. Meyeri has been attached to SPRUCES sold in the 1980s and '90s. The real thing is characterized by hairy twigs, curved, non-pungent quadrangular needles ⅓"–¾" long, and cones (2¼"–2¾" long) with rounded or truncate scales.

P. Meyeri × P. pungens

Specimens seen since ≤1992 in nurseries bearing this ascribed parentage are P. asperata (DRAGON SPRUCE).

P. montigena—see P. likiangensis var. montigena

P. Moramomi—see P. Koyamai

P. Morinda—see P. Smithiana

P. morrisonicola Hayata

MT. MORRISON SPRUCE. From Taiwan. Discovered in 1900 on Mt. Morrison. Introduced in 1918 by E. Wilson. Exceedingly rare; in commerce since ≤1993 as a grafted plant, but one clone sold as P. morrisonicola is some other species (with ½" needles, green above, blue beneath, twigs hairy). Twigs slender, very pale, hairless. Needles slender, not densely borne, wholly dark green, ¼"–¾" long. Buds scarcely or not resinous. Cones 1½"–3¾" long. Picea Wilsonii is somewhat similar. Records: to 164' × 20'0" in the wild; 59' × 4'1" Birr Castle, County Offaly, Ireland (1988; pl. 1929); 31' × 3'0" San Francisco, CA (1994; raised from seed in 1958); 20' tall in Seattle, WA (1994; raised from seed in 1958).

P. mucronata—see P. Abies 'Mucronata'

P. nigra—see P. mariana

P. obovata—see P. Abies ssp. obovata

P. obovata var. japonica—see P. Maximowiczii

P. Omorika (Panc.) Purk.

SERBIAN SPRUCE. SERVIAN SPRUCE. Omorika is the Balkan vernacular for SPRUCE. From the limestone mountains of the upper Drina River Valley in Yugoslavia (SW Serbia). Discovered in 1872; described from twigs and cones in 1875 by J. Pancic, naturalist of Belgrade, then seen by him in 1877, and subsequently introduced to cultivation via Messrs. Froebel of Zurich, who received seeds from Pancic. In 1881 the Arnold Arboretum received seeds. In North American commerce since ≤1900. Common, and among the finest ornamentals. It tolerates polluted air better than most SPRUCES. Distinctively droopy, often very narrow, and always graceful. Twigs hairy. Needles flat, scarcely spiny, ⅓"–1" long, dark green above, blue beneath. Cones 1¼"–2½" long, dark, egg-shaped. Records: to 164' tall says M. Vidakovic; 108' × 6'9" Murthly Castle, Perthshire, Scotland (1983; pl. 1897); 61' × 5'4" Lake Stevens, WA (1992).

P. Omorika 'Berliner's Weeper'

Originated <1979 by Ben Berliner of Long Island, NY. In large-scale commerce since ≤1991–92. Habit narrowly upright with branches strongly pendulous.

P. Omorika 'Nana'

DWARF SERBIAN SPRUCE. Originated ca. 1930 as a witches' broom in the nursery of Goudkade Bro's, Boskoop, Holland. In North American commerce since ≤1958. Common. Usually a dense dwarf shrub as broad or broader than high; it can become a tight pyramidal tree with upswept twigs showing the needles' whitish undersides. Record: 24' tall and 12½' wide Sidney, B.C. (1994; pl. ca. 1962).

P. Omorika 'Pendula'

WEEPING SERBIAN SPRUCE. Named in 1920 in Germany. In North American commerce since ≤1941. Uncommon. This name is used for more than one clone of markedly pendulous habit, from semi-dwarf to full-sized specimens.

P. orientalis (L.) Link

ORIENTAL SPRUCE. CAUCASIAN SPRUCE. EASTERN SPRUCE. From the Caucasus and Asia Minor—*i.e.*, the original "Orient." Introduced to Western European cultivation in the 1820s. Common. It tolerates dry climates better than does *P. Abies* (NORWAY SPRUCE). Habit richly elegant and neat. Twigs hairy. Needles dark green, glossy, ¼"–½" long. Cones 2"–4" long. Among the best SPRUCES for general cultivation; along with *P. Omorika* (SERBIAN SPRUCE). Records: to 210' × 20'6" in the wild; to 164' × 18'0" in Turkey; 131' × 10'1" Camperdown Park, Tayside, Scotland (1985); 96' × 8'10" Lima, PA (1980); 92' × 12'11" Cortachy Castle, Angus, Scotland (1981; *pl.* 1873); 85' × 9'7" Seattle, WA (1993).

P. orientalis 'Atrovirens'

Originated in Holland. Named in 1911. Extremely rare. In North American commerce ≤1989–90. Exceptionally rich, dark green.

P. orientalis 'Aurea'

GOLD ORIENTAL SPRUCE. Raised by P. Smith, nurseryman of Bergedorf, near Hamburg, Germany. Named in 1873. Two or more clones bear this name. Very rare in North America; in commerce. Young shoots creamy- or golden-yellow all year. Records: 60' tall at Vernon Holme, Kent, England (≤1975); 44' × 3'8" Lisle, IL (1986; *pl.* 1926).

P. orientalis 'Aureo-spicata'

Described in 1906–1907. Uncommon. Usually wrongly equated with 'Aurea'. Young growth ivory-yellow in May, green by July.

P. orientalis 'Compacta Aurea'—see P. orientalis 'Skylands'

P. orientalis 'Early Gold'

A mutation of *P. orientalis* 'Aurea' introduced ≤1968 by L. Konijn nursery of Reeuwijk, Holland. In North American commerce since ≤1980. Rare. Described by Vermeulen nursery as a semi-dwarf, broad spreading tree. Young foliage in spring gold, almost lemon yellow, turning green in summer. Its spring growth flushes two weeks before that of 'Aureo-spicata', hence its name.

P. orientalis 'Gowdy'

Origin not known. Introduced ≤1958 by Kingsville nursery of Maryland. Uncommon. Habit extremely upright; very narrow pyramidal; foliage rich green.

P. orientalis 'Gracilis'

COLUMNAR ORIENTAL SPRUCE. Originated and distributed ≤1903 by van Geert or A. Kort, nurserymen of Belgium. In North American commerce since ≤1917. Uncommon. A dense, slow-growing tree 20' tall, branches regularly spreading; twigs crowded, short and thin. Needles ca. ¼" long, shining light green.

P. orientalis 'Green Knight'

A grafted clone sold by Wells nursery of Mt. Vernon, WA. Looks normal to the present writer.

P. orientalis 'Skylands'

= *P. orientalis* 'Compacta Aurea'

Introduced ≤1979 by Skylands Botanical Garden of Ringwood State Park, NJ. Very rare in commerce until ca. 1992. Upper side of needles golden year-round on young shoots (especially on the tips).

P. Parryana—see P. pungens

P. polita (S. & Z.) Carr.

= *P. Torano* (Sieb.) Koehne

TIGERTAIL SPRUCE. Japanese: *Hari-momi. Bara-momi.* From Japan. Introduced to England in 1861 by J.G. Veitch; to North America in 1862 by G.R. Hall. Uncommon. The Latin name *polita* (polished or adorned) probably refers to the lustrous smoothness of the needles and buds. The vernacular is said to refer to the habit of very old trees having shoots curved in the shape of a tiger's tail. Needles dark, sharpest of all, like nails—rigid, stout and fiercely sharp, ½"–1" long. Cones 2"–5" long. Habit usually gaunt, stiff-branched and wholly graceless, but the tree is fascinating (the same way a shark might be). Records: to 150' × 12'6" in the wild; 95' × 10'5" Endsleigh, Devon, England (1990; *pl.* ca. 1900); 80' × 5'10" and 70' × 6'10" Witherthur, DE (1987).

P. pungens Engelm.
= *P. Parryana* Sarg.

COLORADO SPRUCE. From the Rocky Mountains, S Idaho to New Mexico. Discovered in 1862. Introduced to cultivation that year. Color varies from drab olive-green to bright silvery-bluish—the latter cultivated to surfeit (see *P. pungens* f. *glauca*). Twigs and needles (¾"–1¼") relatively stout. The name *pungens* means piercing (of the point of the needles). A stiff, usually narrow tree. Cones 2"–4" long, delicately crisped. Records: 148' × 13'11" Rio Blanco County, CO (1982); 126' × 15'11" Gunnison National Forest, CO (1964; now dead); 122' × 15'6" Ashley National Forest, UT (1980).

P. pungens f. *argentea* Beissn.
A collective name (Latin for silvery) dating from 1887 for cultivars with silvery-colored needles. In a practical sense this seldom-used name is a synonym of *P. pungens* f. *glauca*.

P. pungens 'Aurea'
= *P. pungens* 'Lutea'

Raised by W.F. Niemetz, nurseryman of Temesvar, Romania. Named in 1905. In North American commerce since ≤1927. Rare. New growth gold, changing to blue-green.

P. pungens 'Baby Blueyes' PP 5457 (1985)
Discovered in 1972 as a seedling at Verl Holden's nursery of Silverton, OR. A BLUE SPRUCE differing from most cultivars in developing terminal leader dominance early on grafted specimens. Growth slow; habit dense and symmetrical. D & M nursery of Portland, OR, says it grows slower than *P. pungens* 'Hoopsii' and faster than *P. pungens* 'R. H. Montgomery' (a dwarf); color like *P. pungens* 'Moerheimii'.

P. pungens 'Bakeri'
Originated in a batch of seedlings in Massachusetts. Propagated and introduced ≤1927 by Ellery Baker, then manager of Hiti nursery of Pomfret, CT. Common. Needles longer and bluer than most.

P. pungens 'Blue Totem'
Origin not known. In commerce ≤1992. Quite upright and narrow, not so prettily blue as many cultivars, however.

P. pungens 'Coplen'
(?= 'Copeland', 'Coplane')

Introduced ≤1958 by Kingsville nursery of Maryland. Long commercially extinct unless renamed. Very light blue.

P. pungens 'Egyptian Pyramid'
Introduced ≤1980 by Vermeulen nursery of New Jersey. Dwarf, dense, broadly pyramidal; blue.

P. pungens 'Eisler Fastigiate'—see *P. pungens* 'Iseli Fastigiate'

P. pungens 'Elegantissima'
Named ≤1985 (the cultivar name, post-1959 yet Latin, is illegitimate). Weak, bushy, sickly colored, exceedingly rare. New growth white.

P. pungens 'Endtz'
('Endts', 'Endtzii')

Introduced ca. 1925 by L.J. Endtz, a nurseryman of Boskoop, Holland. In North America since ≤1960; rare. Dense pyramidal tree with horizontal branches, small, spur-like upright twigs. Young needles bright blue, contrasting with rich green old ones.

P. pungens 'Fastigiata'
In Canadian commerce ≤1987. Listed in the 1993–94 catalog of Buchholz & Buchholz nursery, Gaston, OR. The cultivar name, post-1959 yet Latin, is illegitimate.

P. pungens 'Fat Albert'
Selected by Jean Iseli <1965. Introduced ≤1978. Common. Semi-dwarf; densely compact broad pyramid; 10'–15' tall. Forms a leader naturally, needing no staking. Named after the cartoon character made famous by Bill Cosby.

P. pungens 'Foxtail'
= *P. pungens* 'Iseli Foxtail'

Selected by Jean Iseli ca. 1965. Introduced ≤1978 by Iseli nursery of Boring, OR. Common. A crude, broad, asymmetrical bluish column. Exceedingly prickly terminal shoots often irregularly pointed. Reported the best BLUE SPRUCE cultivar for the Southeast.

P. pungens f. *glauca* (Reg.) Beissn.
COLORADO BLUE SPRUCE. BLUE COLORADO SPRUCE. BLUE SPRUCE. SILVER SPRUCE. First raised from a cutting in 1877 at Knap Hill nursery of Surrey, England. Named in 1883. Very common. BLUE SPRUCES far outnumber the olive-green ones because nurseries

select blue seedlings in deference to the public demand. Virtually all *P. pungens* cultivars are in this category. If it wasn't for their lovely color and great hardihood, the BLUE SPRUCES would offer nothing remarkable by way of ornament.

P. pungens 'Glauca Pendula'

Named in 1891. Introduced in 1895 by Koster nursery of Boskoop, Holland. Rare. A giant shrub, wider than tall, without a leader; slow. Has been equated erroneously with *P. pungens* 'Koster'.

P. pungens 'Green Spire'

= *P. pungens* 'Iseli Green Spire'

Selected in 1972 by Iseli nursery of Boring, OR. Dense, broad pyramidal form. Foliage green.

P. pungens 'Henry B. Fowler'

Noticed in the early 1960s and introduced <1990 by Weston nursery of Hopkinton, MA. A BLUE SPRUCE. Tree unusually dense. Needles extremely sharp.

P. pungens 'Hill'

Introduced ≤1976 by D. Hill nursery of Dundee, IL. Needles brighter blue than those of 'Koster'. Very rapid growth; very straight leader.

P. pungens 'Hoopsii'

Selected at the old Hoops nursery of Germany. Introduced ≤1955 by Grootendorst nursery of Holland. Common. Among the bluest of BLUE SPRUCE cultivars. Difficult to propagate and to form into a good tree. Dense conical form.

P. pungens 'Hoto'

Introduced in 1972 at Boskoop, Holland. In North American commerce <1986. Sold mainly in Canada. Fast growing to 60' tall; conical, dense. Bright bluish-gray.

P. pungens 'Ice Blue'

Introduced ≤1993 by Lake County nursery of Perry, OH. To 40' tall. Bright silvery-blue all year. A grafted selection with compact, dense pyramidal form.

P. pungens 'Iseli Fastigiate'

?= *P. pungens* 'Eisler Fastigiate'

Originated ca. 1963 by Jean Iseli (1934–1986). Introduced in ≤1978 by Iseli nursery of Boring, OR. Common. A semi-dwarf, columnar BLUE SPRUCE.

P. pungens 'Iseli Foxtail'—see P. pungens 'Foxtail'

P. pungens 'Iseli Green Spire'—see P. pungens 'Green Spire'

P. pungens 'Iseli Snowkiss'—see P. pungens 'Snowkiss'

P. pungens 'Koster'

= *P. Kosteriana* hort.

Distributed <1885 by Arie Koster, nurseryman of Boskoop, Holland. Koster's stock was not grafted from a singled selected glaucous clone, but consisted of mixed grafts of a population of glaucous forms grown from seeds. Then C.B. van Nes & Son (Blaauw & Co.) nursery selected 10 plants of Koster's stock, uniform in shape and similar in color, named it wrongly *P. pungens glauca compacta* 'Koster' in 1908, and renamed it *P. pungens glauca compacta* in 1913. This form has become common in commerce and its correct name is 'Koster'. In practice over the decades, the buyer might receive anything under the name KOSTER BLUE SPRUCE. For example, in 1921, Bobbink & Atkins nursery of New Jersey, offered *P. pungens* 'Glauca', 'Kosteri', 'Kosteri Compacta', and 'Kosteri Pendula'. Book and catalog descriptions of 'Koster' vary; the only common denominator is blue foliage.

P. pungens 'Lutea'—see P. pungens 'Aurea'

P. pungens 'Mission Bay'

Originated in 1973 by R. Jack of Silver Falls, OR. Registered in 1981 by F.J. Crowe of San Diego, CA. Normal habit. Foliage steel-blue all year.

P. pungens 'Mission Blue'

Introduced <1980 by Mission Gardens of Techny, IL. Uncommon. Pyramidal, compact and very symmetrical; to 40' tall. Foliage intense bright blue.

P. pungens 'Moerheim(ii)'

Raised by B. Ruys Royal Moerheim nursery of Dedemsvaart, Holland. Introduced in 1912. In North American commerce since ≤1921. Common. Needles bright blue, 1"–1⅓" long. Habit dense, pyramidal. Often called slender or narrow, but at least some trees distributed under this name are broad.

P. pungens 'Morden (Blue)'

Introduced in 1944 by Morden research station of Manitoba. Likely out of commerce since the 1960s. Foliage blue. Densely conical tree with compound overlapping branches.

P. pungens 'Pendula'

Origin not known. In North American commerce ≤1915. Extremely rare until Iseli nursery of Boring, OR began mass-producing it ca. 1978. Likely identical to 'Glauca Pendula'. Habit pendulous. Iseli says stake it when young or else use it as a groundcover. See also *P. pungens* 'Rowe Weeping' and 'Shilo Weeping' and 'Teton'.

P. pungens 'Rowe Weeping'

Named after Stanley M. Rowe of Cincinnati, OH. Propagated ca. 1990 by conifer specialist R.L. Fincham. The original specimen was about 30' tall and 5' wide, weeping.

P. pungens 'Royal Knight'

Originated as a 1955 seedling from *P. pungens* 'Koster' or 'Moerheim'. Raised by J.C. Bakker nursery of St. Catherines, Ontario. Named and introduced in 1983 by Vermeulen nursery of New Jersey. Uniform compact pyramidal habit. Develops a straight well-filled outline without pruning or staking. Slightly darker blue than 'Koster'.

P. pungens 'Shilo Weeping'

Propagated in the early 1980s from a Shilo Inn motel in Portland, OR. Introduced ≤1992 by Iseli nursery of Boring, OR. This, unlike *P. pungens* 'Pendula', has an upright leader; its side branches hang down in dense blue curtains. See also *P. pungens* 'Rowe Weeping'.

P. pungens 'Snowkiss'

= *P. pungens* 'Iseli Snowkiss'

Selected <1965 by Jean Iseli of Boring, OR. Introduced ≤1981. Rare. Color of *P. pungens* 'Hoopsii' but the needles recall those of 'Moerheim'. Young twigs pale pink.

P. pungens 'Spek(ii)'

Originated ca. 1925 by Jan Spek nursery of Boskoop, Holland. In North American commerce ≤1937. Rare. Strong, open pyramidal form. Needles reflexed, widely spaced, very glaucous.

P. pungens 'Spring Ghost'

Introduced ≤1994–95 by Buchholz & Buchholz nursery of Gaston, OR. "Creamy-white spring growth, lost in June to blue."

P. pungens 'Sunshine'

Origin not known. In commerce ≤1990. New growth flushes lemon-yellow, ages to medium-blue and yellowish. A full sized tree.

P. pungens 'Teton'

Thirteen peculiar trees, varying from prostrate to upright and weeping, were discovered in west-central Wyoming in the 1990s. Names given in 1993 to clones include: 'Teton Beauty', 'Teton Big Goose', 'Teton EM', 'Teton Long Neck', 'Teton Serpent', and 'Teton Tower'.

P. pungens 'Thomsen'

Found by Martin Thomsen in a private garden at Lancaster, PA. Introduced ca. 1928 by Thomsen nursery of Mansfield, PA (since 1934 Thomsen's Planteskole at Skalborg, Denmark). Common. Like *P. pungens* 'Hoopsii' in being intensely pale blue, but needles are twice as thick.

P. pungens 'Tiffin'

Registered and introduced in 1976 by K.V. Tiffin of Midhurst, Ontario. Rare. Sold in the 1980s and '90s by Sheridan nursery of Ontario. Very uniform habit, compact; slow. Foliage bright blue.

P. pungens 'Walnut Glen'

Origin not known. Introduced ≤1982. Rare. Needles powder-blue, with creamy or golden-yellow variegation in spring. The young specimens burn if exposed to sun. Habit compact.

P. purpurea—see P. likiangensis var. purpurea

P. retroflexa—see P. asperata var. retroflexa

P. rubens Sarg.

= *P. rubra* (Du Roi) Link, non A. Dietr.

RED SPRUCE. YELLOW SPRUCE. HE BALSAM. From northeastern North America, south along mountains into North Carolina. Valuable for timber. Rarely cultivated, being barely handsome (thinly furnished) and less tolerant of urban life than many other SPRUCES. Needles wholly green, ⅓"–¾" long. Cones reddish-brown, 1"–2½" long. The name HE-BALSAM compares it to SHE-BALSAM (*Abies Fraseri*). Records: to 162' × 15'0" in the wild; 123' × 14'1" Great Smoky Mountains National Park, NC (1986).

P. rubra—see P. rubens

P. Sargentiana—see P. brachytyla

P. sitchensis (Bong.) Carr.

= *P. Menziesii* Carr.

SITKA SPRUCE. WESTERN SPRUCE. TIDELAND SPRUCE. COASTAL SPRUCE. ALASKA SPRUCE. SILVER SPRUCE. AIRPLANE SPRUCE. From S Alaska to NW California, in moist coastal lowlands. Named after Sitka (now Baranof) Island, SE Alaska; it is the State Tree of Alaska. Introduced to cultivation in 1831 by D. Douglas. Uncommon. Foliage recalls that of *P. jezoensis* (YEDDO SPRUCE), but the needles (glossy dark green above, powder-blue beneath) are sharper and longer (½"–1¼"). Cones 2"–4" long. The largest SPRUCE, of supreme value for lumber (originally airplanes were made of its wood). Crown notably broad. Grows too large for routine ornamental purposes, and is often buggy. It really needs temperate rainforest conditions to thrive. Records: 314' × 31'5" Carmanah Valley, B.C. (1992); 305' × 21'11" Queets Valley, WA (1988); 237' × 48'8" near Hoh River, WA (1973); 206' × 56'1" Seaside, OR (1988); 191' × 58'11" Quinault Lake, WA (1988); trunks to 81'6" around in the primeval forest.

Picea Smithiana (Wall.) Boiss.
= *P. Morinda* (Loud.) Link

WEST HIMALAYAN SPRUCE. MORINDA SPRUCE. WEEPING SPRUCE. INDIAN SPRUCE. From the western and central Himalayas, Afghanistan to Nepal, and SW Tibet. Introduced in 1818 by Dr. George Goven (*fl.* 1820s–1830s) of Cupar, Scotland, who had received cones from his son, which he presented to the Earl of Hopetoun in West Lothian, Scotland. Named in 1832, some say after Sir James Edward Smith (1759–1828), British botanist, 1st President of the Linnean Society. But it appears to really commemorate *Mr. Smith*, the Hopetoun *gardener* who first raised the tree. Early on, the name was also spelled *Smythiana* by Lawson nurseries. G. Gordon reports *Morinda* is from the Himalayas, meaning nectar, or honey of flowers, on account of the resinous drops or tears found on the young cones and other parts of the tree, resembling honey. The species is not among the very cold-hardy ones, and although eastern U.S. nurseries sold it earlier, probably the oldest and certainly the largest specimens in North America date from California, where it has been grown since ≤1893, and in commerce since ≤1925. Tree of droopy habit. Cones very large, 4"–7⅞" long. Needles longest of all, ¾"–2¼". Records: 230' × 24'0" in the wild; 128' × 11'4" Cuffnels, Lyndhurst, Hampshire, England (1980; *pl.* 1856); 115' × 14'11" Taymouth Castle, Scotland (1990); 80' × 18'4" Bicton, Devon, England (1957; *pl.* 1842; now dead); 58' × 6'9" Sacramento, CA (1989).

P. Spartan Spruce®
= *P.* 'Hy-blu'
(*P. glauca* × *P. pungens*)
Hybridized in 1967 at Michigan State University. Introduced in 1991 by Better Trees, Inc., of St. Johns, MI. Seed-propagated.

P. Torano—see P. polita

P. vulgaris—see P. Abies

P. Watsoniana—see P. Wilsonii

P. Wilsonii Mast.
= *P. Watsoniana* Mast.

WILSON SPRUCE. From central and W China. Introduced in 1901 by Ernest Henry Wilson (1876–1930) for Veitch nursery of England. In North America since ≤1912. Rare. Twigs strikingly pale ashy-gray or whitish, usually hairless (rarely weakly hairy); not as rough with pegs as most SPRUCES. Needles ⅓"–1" long, wholly dark green and shining. Buds dark, shiny, chestnut-brown, weakly resinous. Cones 1½"–3¼" long. The extremely rare and less hardy *Picea morrisonicola* is similar, but its twigs are never hairy. Records: to 180' tall in SW Kansu, China says S–C. Lee; to 177' tall in SW Kansu, China (1926) says J. Rock; 69' × 5'6" Birr Castle, County Offaly, Ireland (1988; *pl.* 1916); 50' tall at Arnold Arboretum (1982; *pl.* 1912); 39½' × 1'10" Seattle, WA (1994; *pl.* 1957).

P. yunnanensis—see P. likiangensis var. Forrestii

Picrasma

[SIMAROUBACEÆ; Quassia Family] 6–8 spp. From Greek *pikrasmos*, bitterness, alluding to the bark and leaves. The only related genus in this volume is *Ailanthus* (TREE OF HEAVEN).

P. ailanthoides—see P. quassioides

P. quassioides (D. Don) Bennett
= *P. ailanthoides* Planch.
= *Simaba quassioides* D. Don
From the Himalayas through China to Korea, Taiwan, and Japan. Introduced to cultivation in 1890.

Exceedingly rare in North America. The 1825 epithet *quassioides* from genus *Quassia*, and Greek *-oides*, resemblance. (The genus *Quassia* itself was named after a slave named Qassi or Quassi who first discovered the use of its bark as a febrifuge.) Usually a large shrub or multitrunked tree less than 30' tall. Leaves compound, of 7–17 leaflets. Flowers tiny, greenish or yellow, in April–May. Fruit a dry berry, green, red, then black. Fall color can be rich orange and scarlet. Records: to 65½' tall in the wild; 28' × 5'6" Kew, England (1981).

Pinus

[PINACEÆ; Pine Family] 90–110 spp. of coniferous evergreens. The ancient Latin *Pinus* was a tree producing pitch. In turn from Greek *pinos*, a word used by Theophrastus for a PINE tree. PINES are adaptable, widely distributed, and well known, with distinctive needles and woody cones. Two broad classes exist. The WHITE or SOFT PINES bear usually 5 often bluish-green needles per bundle; the ripe cones usually drop quickly. The RED, BLACK, PITCH or HARD PINES bear usually 2 or 3 pure green or yellow-green needles per bundle; the ripe cones sometimes persist for years; the wood is heavier. The present volume's 60 species are as follows: 20 five-needled, 17 three-needled, 22 two-needled, and 1 one-needled (*P. monophylla*). Compared to most coniferous genera, PINES are far more variable, more economically important, and more revered for their appearance both in the wild and in cultivation. Supremely drought tolerant for the most part, the one thing they cannot abide is shade. A serious disease, white pine blister rust, is caused by the fungus *Cronartium ribicola*.

P. Abies—see Picea Abies

P. albicaulis Engelm.
= *P. flexilis* var. *albicaulis* (Engelm.) Engelm.
WHITEBARK PINE. NORTHERN NUT PINE. ALPINE WHITE-BARK PINE. From high mountains of western North America, often dwarfed by the harsh timberline climate. Discovered either by T. Drummond in 1826 or J. Frémont in 1842. Introduced to cultivation in 1852 by J. Jeffrey. Named in 1863 (Latin *albi*, white, and *caulis*, a stem). Very rarely cultivated, and almost never worthwhile, being difficult to establish, slow growing and nondescript. Some dwarf cultivars exist. Possibly most trees sold as *P. albicaulis* are the similar and closely related *P. flexilis* (LIMBER PINE). Needles 5 per bundle, 1⅓"–3¼" long. Cones 1⅓"–3½" long, dark chocolate or purple, not opening, but disintegrating after ripe. Aged specimens in the wild often have handsome pale bark. Records: 90' × 12'3" Alpine Lakes Wilderness, WA (1993); 85' × 18'2" Grand Teton National Park, WY (1944); 69' × 27'7" Sawtooth National Recreation Area, ID (1980).

P. albicaulis 'Algonquin Pillar'
Introduced ≤1987 by Hortico nursery of Waterdown, Ontario.

P. Apacheca—see P. Engelmannii

P. araucana—see Araucaria araucana

P. aristata Engelm. *ex* Parry & Engelm.
= *P. Balfouriana* var. *aristata* (Engelm.) Engelm.
BRISTLECONE PINE. FOXTAIL PINE. HICKORY PINE. PRICKLE-CONE PINE. COLORADO BRISTLECONE PINE. ROCKY MOUNTAIN BRISTLECONE PINE. EASTERN BRISTLECONE PINE. From high, arid mountains in W Colorado, N New Mexico and N Arizona. Discovered and introduced to cultivation in 1861 by C. Parry of the Arnold Arboretum. Common. See also *P. longæva*. Remarkably densely foliated, dark, and slow-growing, of bushy habit. Needles (1,2,3,4) 5 per bundle, 1"–2" long, bearing conspicuous drops of whitish resin. Cones 1½"–3½" (4½") long, with fragile, short needlelike bristles. *Aristata* means awned, referring to the long and delicate cone prickles or bristles. Records: 76' × 11'0" Carson National Forest, NM (1985); 72' × 11'6" Colfax County, NM (1986); 24' × 12'8" Colorado (1990).

P. aristata var. longæva—see P. longæva

P. aristata 'Sherwood Compact'
Originated <1983. An absolute dwarf, growing like the DWARF ALBERTA WHITE SPRUCE (*Picea glauca* 'Conica'). Needles with inconspicuous white pitch droplets (it may be a *P. longæva* cultivar). Some Oregon conifer nurseries branch-graft it onto *P. Strobus* to make it treelike—essentially a toy tree, exceedingly rare and an expensive novelty for those to buy who have more dollars than sense.

P. arizonica—see *P. ponderosa* var. *arizonica*

P. Armandii Franch., non Wils.

CHINESE WHITE PINE. (PÈRE) DAVID'S PINE. ARMAND PINE. From NE India, N Burma, SE Tibet, west-central China, E Taiwan, Korea, and S Japan. Discovered in 1873 by the Jesuit Basque, Jean Pierre Armand David (1826–1900). Introduced in 1895 when P. Farges sent seeds to Vilmorin nursery of France; A. Henry sent seeds to England 1897. In North America ≤1905; extremely rare here. Resists blister rust, but often has poor color and slow growth —seemingly diverting too much of its energy to cone production. HIMALAYAN WHITE PINE (*P. Wallichiana*) is superior. Needles (4) 5 per bundle, 3½"–6" long. Cones 4"–8" long, massive and pitchy— the best thing about this species. Records: to 120' × 20'0" in Taiwan; 85' × 10'2" Fota, County Cork, Ireland (1987); 63' × 3'3" Seattle, WA (1993; *pl.* 1939).

P. Armandii 'Pendula'

Introduced ≤1994 by Girard nursery of Geneva, OH. "Long pendant branches." Being Latin yet post-1959, the cultivar name is invalid.

P. attenuata Lemm.

= *P. tuberculata* Gord. 1849, non D. Don 1836
KNOBCONE PINE. From SW Oregon, W California, and N Baja California. Introduced by K. Hartweg into England in 1847. Rarely cultivated, especially outside California. In Seattle at least it is a lushly foliated tree of booming vigor and handsome form, its green far more lively than that of *P. nigra*. In botanical Latin, *attenuata* means gradually drawn out, tapered or narrowed to a point—suggested by the long tapering cones and by the slender crown. Needles (2) 3 per bundle, 3"–7½" long. Cones 4"–6" long, curved, rock hard and knobby, in conspicuous whorls, long persisting unopened. The tree can "swallow" its cones into its branches. Record: 117' × 11'3" Shasta County, CA (1976).

P. × attenuradiata Stockw. & Righ.

(*P. attenuata* × *P. radiata*)
The first hybrid produced at the Institute of Forest Genetics / Eddy Arboretum of Placerville, CA. Pollen of *P. radiata* was applied in 1927 to *P. attenuata*. The hybrid seedling sprouted in 1929 and was 65' tall at 21 years, nearly 80' tall by 1967. The goal was to combine KNOBCONE PINE's tolerance of cold and poor site conditions, with MONTEREY PINE's exceptionally rapid wood-producing quality. The cross is also found occurring naturally. The hybrid was named in 1946, and has been planted in botanic gardens since ≤1950; in commerce since ≤1982; very rare—mostly offered in California. Needles 2–3 per bundle, 2½"–7" long. Cones 3"–4" long, with smaller prickles than those of *P. attenuata* and stouter overall, with swollen scales.

P. australis—see *P. palustris*

P. austriaca—see *P. nigra*

P. Ayacahuite Ehrenb. *ex* Schlecht.

MEXICAN WHITE PINE. From mountain slopes of SE Mexico, S Guatemala, N El Salvador, W Honduras. Discovered by C.G. Ehrenberg in 1836; named in 1838 (*Ayacahuite* or *acalocote* is a vernacular name); introduced from Guatemala by K. Hartweg to England in 1840. Extremely rare in cultivation. Some specimens are cold-tender, others hardy. See also the very similar *P. strobiformis*. Needles 5 per bundle, 4"–6" (8") long, often exceedingly thin and pendulous. Cones 6"–12" (18") long. Records: to 160' × 18'0" in the wild; 85' × 11'6" Bodnant, Gwynedd, Wales (1990; *pl.* 1902); 66' × 7'7" San Francisco, CA (1989; *pl.* 1950); 61' × 10'0" Chester County, PA (1980). (The hybrid *P. Strobus* × *P. Ayacahuite* was introduced in 1993–94 by Buchholz & Buchholz nursery of Gaston, OR.)

P. Ayacahuite var. *brachyptera*—see *P. strobiformis*

P. Ayacahuite var. *reflexa*—see *P. strobiformis*

P. Ayacahuite var. *strobiformis*—see *P. strobiformis*

P. Balfouriana (Jeff.) Grev. & Balf. *ex* A. Murr.

FOXTAIL PINE. From northern and central California mountains. Discovered and introduced to cultivation in 1852 by J. Jeffrey. Named for John Hutton Balfour (1808–1884), botany professor at the Royal Botanic Garden, Edinburgh, and chairman of the committee that sent J. Jeffrey to California. Practically never cultivated—the oldest cultivated specimens known in California date from 1935. Very slow growing. Closely related to *P. aristata* and *P. longæva* (BRISTLE-CONE PINES). Needles (4) 5 per bundle, 1"–1½" long, densely set on twigs, giving rise to the name FOXTAIL PINE. Cones 2½"–5" long. Records: to 100' tall; 76' × 26'4" Trinity National Forest, CA (1982).

P. Balfouriana var. *aristata*—see *P. aristata*

P. Balfouriana 'Horseshoe Pillar'

Discovered in 1987 in Horseshoe meadow, Inyo County, CA. Not propagated until ca. 1989, named in 1991; not yet in commerce. Likely to remain exceedingly rare unless a big conifer nursery decides to mass-produce it. Habit narrowly pyramidal.

P. Banksiana Lamb.

= *P. divaricata* (Ait.) Dum.-Cours.

JACK PINE. HUDSON BAY PINE. GRAY PINE. (NORTHERN) SCRUB PINE. HORNCONE PINE. PRINCESS PINE. LABRADOR PINE. From much of Canada, and the Great Lakes region to New England. Named after Joseph Banks (1743–1820), botanist, for 42 years president of the Royal Society, a great patron of learning. Common in cultivation. In 1933, G.P. Brett said "The great advantage of *Pinus Banksiana* is the fact that it grows well anywhere except in water, even where hardly any soil exists." Usually crooked, always slender and of sickly hue, often looking anemic or starving, it should not be planted where any better species can thrive. Its cones, often gray or ashy colored, may account for the name GRAY PINE. Needles 2 per bundle, ¾"–1¾" long, yellowish-green. Cones 1"–3" long, persistent, bent, strongly curved, often dented. Records: to 100' × 9'6" in the virgin forests; 97' × 5'9½" Highland, WI (1985); 96' × 5'3" Ontario (1979); 68' × 7'8½" Marquette County, MI (1993; age ca. 140); 60' × 7'8" Wadena County, MN (1976); 51' × 7'10" Kakabeka Falls, Ontario (1976).

P. Banksiana 'Schoodic'

Originated by A.J. Fordham of the Arnold Arboretum; raised from seeds gathered on Shoodic Peninsula of Maine. Selected in 1974. In commerce ≤1986–87. A mat unless topgrafted.

P. Banksiana 'Uncle Fogy'

Found in Richfield, MN. Named in 1970. In commerce. Prostrate unless topgrafted.

P. brutia Ten.

= *P. halepensis* var. *brutia* (Ten.) Henry
= *P. halepensis* ssp. *brutia* (Ten.) Holmboe.
= *P. pyrenaica* auct. (in part)

BRUTIAN PINE. CALABRIAN PINE—also used for *P. nigra* ssp. *Laricio*. CALABRIAN CLUSTER-PINE. PYRENEAN PINE. TURKISH PINE. From the Ægean region, Cyprus, Turkey and the Near East. Named in 1811. Originally described as being found in Calabria Province (ancient Brutium) in Italy, but unclear whether it was native or introduced there. Introduced to English cultivation in 1834 by A. Lambert. Introduced from Yugoslavia to North America in 1963 by the Arnold Arboretum. In commerce here ≤1967–68. Mostly grown in California and the Southwest; less popular than its *eldarica* variant. Some botanists assert that the only constant difference between *P. brutia* and *P. halepensis* (ALEPPO PINE) is that *P. halepensis* has pendulous cones on stalks ⅜"–¾" long. Be that as it may in the Old World, at least the *brutia* stock grown in the U.S. tends to be relatively cold-hardy, slow, densely branched with close, heavy limbs, and densely foliaged with stout needles, building in age into a rounded crown like that of *P. Pinea* (ITALIAN STONE PINE). Needles 2 per bundle, (3") 4"–7" (8") long, stout. Cones 2"–4⅜" long, borne stalkless or nearly so, at right angles to branchlets. Vigorous. Crown often irregular. Records: to 80' tall in the wild; 66' × 5'8" and 49' × 6'10" Davis, CA (1993).

P. brutia Christmas Blue™

= *P. eldarica* Christmas Blue™

Introduced ≤1986 by Monrovia nursery of California. Seed-grown, from a tree of "more symmetrical pyramidal shape and blue-green color."

P. brutia var. *eldarica* (Medw.) Magini & Tulstr.

= *P. brutia* ssp. *eldarica* (Medw.) Nahal.
= *P. eldarica* Medw.
= *P. halepensis* var. *eldarica* Fitsch.
= *P. halepensis* var. *mondell* hort.

EILAR PINE. AFGHAN PINE. PAKISTANIAN PINE. MONDELL PINE. From a semi-desert environment of the Republic of Georgia, Mt. Eilar Ugi, or Eller Oukhi. Named in 1902, when it was described as from "central Transcaucasia near the Eldar desert, in the Eilaroougi cliffs on the right bank of the river Jora." Widely cultivated in Iran, Afghanistan, and Pakistan. First introduced to North America in 1913, apparently to no effect. Seeds from three locales of Afghanistan's Herat region were distributed by the USDA in 1960. Widely cultivated in California and the Southwest since the late 1970s. Fast growth even in blistering heat, poor soil, etc. Differs from typical *P. brutia* in its straighter, less dense crown (foliage and cone characteristics practically indistinguishable). Needles 2 (3) per bundle, 2⅝"–6" (8½") long. Cones 2"–4½" long, stalkless, at right angles to the branchlets or slightly tilted backwards. Trunk straight, like that of *P. nigra*; bark deeply rugged. Records: to 55' tall in the wild; 49' × 6'7" Davis, CA (1993).

P. brutia var. *Pityusa* (Stev.) Silba

= *P. brutia* ssp. *Pityusa* (Stev.) E. Murr.
= *P. halepensis* var. *Pityusa* (Stev.) Gord.
= *P. Pityusa* Stev.
(*Pithyusa*)

BLACK SEA PINE. From the Black Sea region. Discovered near Pezundan (Pitsunda), the ancient Pityus (Pithyum), on the eastern coast of the Black Sea; named *Pityusa* in 1838 (*pithys* in Greek means PINE). Called by some botanists a mere *P. brutia* synonym, and it may be, in a technical sense. But almost never cultivated because typical *P. brutia* and its var. *eldarica* are vastly superior. *Pityusa* specimens at Davis Arboretum, CA, right near the preceding taxa, are bent and inferior. Needles 2 per bundle, 4"–7" long (claimed in some books to be ≤2"). Cones 2⅜"–4" long. Recorded to 100' tall in the wild.

P. Bungeana Zucc. *ex* Endl.

LACEBARK PINE. From mountains of N China. Dr. Aleksandr Andreevich von Bunge (1803–1890) of St. Petersburg, productive author on the plants of N and NE Asia, was a Russian botanist who collected the type specimen in a temple garden near Peking in 1831. Introduced from China to Britain by R. Fortune in 1846. In North America ≤1879. Rare. An airy, not dense tree, with widely spaced needles. In cultivation, commonly more or less bushy, with several trunks. Slow-growing whether wild or cultivated, but worth waiting for—ultimately it has milk-white bark. "White bark, like white hair, takes time." Since few trees are wild anyway, and our cultivated stock may be limited to the progeny of one or very few specimens, part of the slowness may be blamed on self-pollinated offspring that is too inbred. Even young trees can have handsomely mottled, albeit not white bark. Needles 3 (5) per bundle, 2"–5½" long. Cones 1½"–3" long. Seeds edible. Records: to 120' × 21'0" in China; 65' × 16'0" (around 11 trunks) Brookline, MA (<1988); 62' × 5'5" Philadelphia, PA (1988).

P. Cembra L.

SWISS STONE PINE. AROLLA PINE. RUSSIAN CEDAR. *Cembra* is the Italian name for *Pinus Cembra*. From the Alps of Central Europe, into central Asia in the Carpathians. Introduced to cultivation in 1746 by the Duke of Argyll; in North America ≤1856. Common. Resists blister rust. Slow growing, dense and tidy of crown. Perfect size for small urban lots. Needles 5 per bundle, 2"–3½" (5") long. Cones 2"–3½" long, purple-blue, never opening.The seeds are sold in Europe for food and for oil. Records: to 130' × 22'0" in the wild; 118' × 8'9" Castle Milk, Dumfries, Scotland (1983); 90' × 11'0" Taymouth Castle, Perthshire, Scotland (1970); 59' × 6'10" Cazenovia, NY (1957; *pl.* 1856); 40' × 4'7" Delaware County, PA (1980).

P. Cembra 'Chalet'

Introduced in 1972 by Vermeulen nursery of New Jersey. A dense rounded column of soft bluish green.

P. Cembra 'Columnaris'—see *P. Cembra* 'Stricta'

P. Cembra 'Glauca'

Described in 1866. Exceedingly rare. Needles silvery-white. Growth slow. See also *P. Cembra* 'Silver Sheen'.

P. Cembra 'Silver Sheen'

Introduced in 1968 by Vermeulen nursery of New Jersey. Listed as *P. Cembra* 'Glauca' until 1971. Tall, slender, pyramidal form. Silver-blue foliage.

P. Cembra 'Stricta'

= *P. Cembra* 'Columnaris' (in part)

Originated in France ca. 1850. Named in 1855. Extremely rare; in U.S. commerce ≤1980. Tightly columnar. Record: 30' tall and 7½' wide at Philadelphia, PA (1946; *pl.* 1910).

P. Cembra 'Thume'

Origin not known. Twombly nursery of Monroe, CT, 1994 catalog: "Blue dense column to 30' tall."

P. cembroides Zucc. *ex* K. Bayer

MEXICAN PIÑON. NUT PINE. MEXICAN STONE PINE. THREE-NEEDLE PINYON. Spanish: *Pino Piñonero*. From Mexico mainly, and the extreme SW United States. Introduced ca. 1829 to Germany. Named in 1832; from *Pinus Cembra* (SWISS STONE PINE), and Greek - *oides*, resemblance. Very rarely cultivated in North America. Needles (2) 3 (4,5) per bundle, 1"–2" (2¾") long. Cones 1"–2½" long. Other PIÑONS in this volume are *P. edulis* and *P. monophylla*. Record: 66' × 9'3" Big Bend National Park, TX (1982).

P. cembroides var. *edulis*—see *P. edulis*

P. cembroides var. *monophylla*—see *P. monophylla*

P. chilghoza—see *P. Gerardiana*

P. contorta Dougl. *ex* Loud.

= *P. inops* Bong. 1833, non Soland. 1789

SHORE PINE. SCRUB PINE. BEACH PINE. COAST PINE. BIRD'S-EYE PINE. SCREW PINE. PRICKLY PINE. KNOTTY PINE. From much of western North America; a larger altitudinal distribution than any other *Pinus*. Introduced to cultivation in 1831 by D. Douglas. Commonly cultivated in the West. The epithet *contorta* refers to the young shoots often being twisted. Needles 2 per bundle, 1"–3" (4") long. Cones ¾"–2½" long, persistent, prickly. Tree size and density varies according to races as noted below. Bark deep and rugged on the typical version. Foliage brighter green than some of the species which might be considered peers: *P. Banksiana* (JACK PINE), *P. Mugo* (MUGO PINE), and *P. uncinata* (MOUNTAIN PINE). Records of the typical version: 123' × 8'2" Shelton, WA (1993); 101' × 11'6" Bryant, WA (1992).

P. contorta var. *latifolia* Engelm. *ex* S. Wats.

= *P. contorta* ssp. *latifolia* (Engelm. *ex* S. Wats.) Critchfield

LODGEPOLE PINE. TAMARACK PINE. ROCKY MOUNTAIN LODGEPOLE PINE. From S Canada to S Colorado, mostly in the Rocky Mountains. Introduced by J. Jeffrey to Scotland in 1853. Rare in cultivation. Growth usually tall and slender. Bark thin. Needles long. Cones heavy, often asymmetric; persistent but not opening until fire or great age induce them to. The name LODGEPOLE PINE refers to Indian usage of slender trees for building lodges (not tepees). Records: to 200' tall says A. Henry and Wm. Dallimore; 135' × 11'5" Valley County, ID (1980); 125' × 12'4" Chiloquin, OR (1983); 43' × 13'1" Olympic National Park, WA (1980).

P. contorta var. *Murrayana* (Grev. & Balf.) Engelm. *ex* S. Wats.

= *P. Murrayana* Grev. & Balf.

= *P. contorta* ssp. *Murrayana* (Grev. & Balf.) Critchfield

SIERRA LODGEPOLE PINE. From SW Oregon to N Baja California. Introduced to cultivation in 1853. Rare. Named after Andrew Murray (1812–1878), Scots botanist and conifer specialist. Trunk massive.

Needles thick. Cones lightweight, symmetric, opening at maturity, falling in a few years. Records: 118' × 19'1" Stanislaus National Forest, CA (1985); 114' × 19'11" San Bernardino National Forest, CA (1975); 106' × 20'2" Stanislaus National Forest, CA (1987); 91' × 21'2" Stanislaus National Forest, near Sonora, CA (1967).

P. Coulteri D. Don

BIGCONE PINE. COULTER PINE. From SW California and N Baja California. Named after Thomas Coulter (1793–1843), the Irish botanist and physician who discovered it in 1832. Introduced to cultivation the same year by D. Douglas. Uncommon; grown almost exclusively along the Pacific Coast. A bold and striking giant. Needles 3 per bundle, 6"–14" long. Cones the most massive of any PINE, 8"–14" (20") long, weighing to 5–7 (8) pounds, yellowish, fiercely clawed; seeds large, edible. Records: 144' × 17'0" Angeles National Forest, CA (<1951); 139' × 16'11" San Diego County, CA (1986; now dead); 116' × 17'3" North Otago, New Zealand (≤1982); 70' × 14'2" Victoria, B.C. (1995).

P. densiflora S. & Z.

= *P. Massoniana* hort. *ex* Mast.

JAPANESE RED PINE. Japanese: *Aka-matsu* (red pine). *Me-matsu* (female pine—because of abundant little cones). From NE China, E Korea, and Japan. Has been regarded as the commonest tree in Japan. Introduced in 1852 by Siebold to Holland. In North America ≤1862. Common in cultivation. Remarkably reddish in trunk and limb, much like SCOTS PINE (*P. sylvestris*). Habit usually irregular, often multi-trunked. Needles 2 per bundle, 3"–5" long. Cones 1¼"–3" long, sometimes dozens per cluster (*densiflora* means densely flowered). Records: to 164' × 20'6" in the wild; 75' × 4'3" Leonardslee, Sussex, England (1984); 71' × 4'11" Seattle, WA (1993); 66' × 8'6" Nuneham Court, Oxfordshire, England (1978; now dead); 43' × 7'6" × 43' Seattle, WA (1987); a trunk 9'10" around on Long Island, NY (1972).

P. densiflora 'Aurea'

= *P. densiflora* 'Ogon-aka-matsu'

Introduced to the U.S. in 1862 by G.R. Hall. Described in 1890 by H. Mayr. Extremely rare. Patches of needles light golden yellow amongst those of normal color.

P. densiflora 'Heavy Bud'
= *P. densiflora* 'Large Bud'

Introduced ≤1972 by Vermeulen nursery of New Jersey. Called an "IMPROVED TANYOSHO PINE; bright green needles; large red buds."

P. densiflora 'Jano-me'—see P. densiflora 'Oculus-draconis'

P. densiflora 'Large Bud'—see P. densiflora 'Heavy Bud'

P. densiflora 'Oculus-draconis'
= *P. densiflora* 'Jano-me'

DRAGON EYE PINE. In North American commerce ≤1887. Described in 1890. Uncommon. Growth less vigorous. Needles banded yellow. Paler yellow than *P. Thunbergii* 'Oculus-draconis'.

P. densiflora 'Ogon-aka-matsu'—see P. densiflora 'Aurea'

P. densiflora 'Pendula'
= *P. densiflora* 'Shidare-aka-matsu'

WEEPING JAPANESE RED PINE. Described in 1890. In North America since <1916. Uncommon. Dwarfish. Pendulous or prostrate. Must be topgrafted or staked to be treelike.

P. densiflora 'Shidare-aka-matsu'—see P. densiflora 'Pendula'

P. densiflora 'Sunburst'

Originated ca. 1974 as a seedling from a witches' broom at the Morton Arboretum, Lisle, IL. Named ≤1989, when 10' tall and 12' wide, with bright yellow, extra long needles radiating around each terminal bud.

P. densiflora 'Tagyo-sho'—see P. densiflora 'Umbraculifera'

P. densiflora 'Tanyo-sho'—see P. densiflora 'Umbraculifera'

P. densiflora 'Umbraculifera'
= *P. densiflora* 'Tanyo-sho'
= *P. densiflora* 'Tagyo-sho'

TANYOSHO PINE. (JAPANESE) UMBRELLA PINE. JAPANESE TABLE PINE. Described in 1890 by H. Mayr. Name from Latin *umbraculum*, umbrella, and *ferre*, to bear. Common. More than one clone exists, and the vigor and size is also affected by the rootstock. A mushroom-shaped tree usually treated as a dwarf shrub.

Slow growing. Cones smaller than typical. Records: 32' × 8'4" × 35' Tacoma, WA (1988); 28' × 9'0" × 35' Westport, CT (1988).

P. divaricata—see P. Banksiana

P. echinata Mill.
= *P. mitis* Michx.

SHORTLEAF PINE. SOUTHERN YELLOW PINE. SHORTSTRAW PINE. ARKANSAS PINE. COMMON YELLOW PINE. ROSEMARY PINE. LONG-TAG PINE. From the eastern U.S., especially in the South. *Echinata* means spiny or prickly, describing the cones. Not commonly grown for ornament, being serviceable rather than choice. Cold tolerant but needs heat to thrive. Needles 2 (3) per bundle, 2¼"–5" long, fine and flexible, short compared to those of certain other Southern PINES. Twigs pink and hairless. Cones 1½"–2½" long. Can sprout from the stump. Records: 146' × 10'7" Morganton, NC (1954); 138' × 11'0" Myrtle, MS (1980); 127' × 13'10" near Sandy Creek, TX (1967).

P. edulis Engelm.
= *P. monophylla* var. *edulis* (Engelm.) M.E. Jones
= *P. cembroides* var. *edulis* (Engelm.) Voss

PIÑON (PINYON). NUT PINE. TWO-NEEDLE PIÑON. COLORADO PIÑON. ROCKY MOUNTAIN PIÑON. From the southern Rocky Mountain region, scarcely into Mexico. Introduced by K. Hartweg into England in 1847. In U.S. commerce ≤1888. Uncommon in cultivation, usually remaining compact and bushy—one was only 10' tall after 48 years at the Arnold Arboretum. At least ten species are called PIÑON. This is the common U.S. one; most are Mexican. They are characterized by slow, bushy growth and small cones containing large seeds valued for food (pine nuts). For nut production, plant several specimens to cross-pollinate. Other PIÑONS in this volume are *P. cembroides* and *P. monophylla*. Needles (1) 2 (3) per bundle, (¾") 1"–1½" (2⅜") long; stiff. Cones 1½"–2¾" long. Seeds to ¾" long. Records: to 75' tall at most; 69' × 17'9" Cuba, NM (1982).

P. eldarica—see P. brutia var. eldarica

P. eldarica 'Christmas Blue'—see P. brutia 'Christmas Blue'

P. Engelmannii Carr.
= *P. latifolia* Sarg.
= *P. Apacheca* Lemm.
= *P. macrophylla* Engelm. 1848, non Lindl. 1839

APACHE PINE. ARIZONA LONGLEAF PINE. From mountains of extreme SW New Mexico and SE Arizona, and (mostly) N Mexico. Named in 1854 after George Engelmann (1809–1884), distinguished German-American physician and botanist of St. Louis, MO. Exceedingly rare in cultivation. Offered in 1993 by Piroche Plants nursery of Pitt Meadows, B.C. Closely related to *P. ponderosa*. Luxuriant long and graceful needles, 3–4 (5) per bundle, 9"–13" (16") long. Cones 4"–7" long. Record: 98' × 10'2" Coronado National Forest, AZ (1983).

P. excelsa—see *P. Wallichiana*

P. flexilis James

LIMBER PINE. ROCKY MOUNTAIN WHITE PINE. SQUIRREL PINE. From the Rocky Mountains, S Canada to (inconsequentially *into*) Mexico. Discovered in 1820 by Dr. Edward James. Introduced to England in 1851 by J. Jeffrey. Cultivated in the U.S. since ≤1861. Common. Very cold-hardy. Branches long, amazingly limber, hence the name *flexilis*. Foliage dense, dark bluish-green. Needles (3,4) 5 (6) per bundle, 2"–3½" long. Cones 3"–5" long, thick-scaled; seeds wingless. Practically identical to *P. strobiformis* (SOUTHWESTERN WHITE PINE). Records: to 85' tall at most; 80' × 7'11" Delaware County, PA (1980); 67' × 19'0" San Isabel National Forest, CO (ca. 1948); 58' × 22'11" Uinta National Forest, UT (≤1990); 43' × 29'5" N Fork Little Willow Canyon, UT (1972); 39' × 29'3" × 37' Twin Peaks Wilderness Area, UT (1987). The following 14 cultivars, if studied and their origins carefully traced, would surely be reduced, with several names being mere synonyms.

P. flexilis var. *albicaulis*—see *P. albicaulis*

P. flexilis 'Cesarini Blue'

Origin unknown; doubtless associated with conifer enthusiast Joe Cesarini of Maryland. Sold since ≤1993 by Buchholz & Buchholz nursery of Gaston, OR. Needles bluish.

P. flexilis 'Extra Blue'

Origin unknown. Sold since ≤1985 by Iseli nursery of Boring, OR. Needles very bluish.

P. flexilis 'Fastigiata Glauca Vanderwolf'—see *P. flexilis* 'Vanderwolf's Pyramid'

P. flexilis 'Firmament'

A 1982 renaming of the clone sold in Germany as 'Glauca'. Needles bluish.

P. flexilis 'Glauca'

BLUE LIMBER PINE. Origin unknown. Sold since <1979 by Phyto Ecology nursery of Ridgely, MD. Needles bluish. Likely various clones have been marketed under this name. 'Glauca' is invalid as a cultivar name, being Latin, unless it was in use <1959. At least one clone sold in Europe as 'Glauca' has been renamed 'Firmament'.

P. flexilis 'Glauca Pendula'

= *P. flexilis* 'Pendula Glauca'
= *P. flexilis* 'Pendula'

WEEPING LIMBER PINE. Originated as early as 1941. Introduced ≤1970 by Vermeulen nursery of New Jersey. Habit prostrate. Very vigorous. Needles long, bluish. 'Glauca Pendula' is invalid as a cultivar name, being Latin, unless it was in use <1959.

P. flexilis 'Glenmore'

= *P. flexilis* 'Glenmore Silver'
?= *P. flexilis* 'Glenmore Pyramid'

Found in 1944 by R.E. More of Glenmore Arboretum, Buffalo Creek, CO, and distributed in 1949 by Wilmore nursery of Wheatridge, CO. Needles long (to 4½"), bright green and silvery instead of olive-green and gray. Tree habit open, growing large. Record: 63' × 4'3½" Seattle, WA (1994; *pl.* 1951).

P. flexilis 'Glenmore Dwarf'

Found by R.E. More of Glenmore Arboretum, Buffalo Creek, CO, and distributed ≤1955. Extremely rare. Needles of average length and color, but tree less vigorous, more compact, and with shorter annual shoots. Record: 15½' × 2'0" × 14' Seattle, WA (1994; *pl.* ca. 1960).

P. flexilis 'Glenmore Pyramid'—see *P. flexilis* 'Glenmore'

P. flexilis 'Glenmore Silver'—see *P. flexilis* 'Glenmore'

P. flexilis 'Millcreek'

Origin not known. Twombly nursery of Monroe, CT, 1995 catalog: "excellent blue; full pyramidal habit."

P. flexilis 'Pendula'—see *P. flexilis* 'Glauca Pendula'

P. flexilis 'Pendula Glauca'—see *P. flexilis* 'Glauca Pendula'

P. flexilis 'Pyramidalis'
Origin and attributes unknown. Offered ≤1958 by Brimfield Garden nursery of Wethersfield, CT, and Trautman nursery of Franksville, WI.

P. flexilis var. reflexa—see *P. strobiformis*

P. flexilis 'Riverbend'
Listed since ≤1993 by Wells nursery of Mt. Vernon, WA. "Grown at our Riverbend Farm here in Skagit Valley."

P. flexilis 'Scratch Gravel'
Found in 1963 by nurseryman C. Berg of Helena, MT, at Scratch Gravel, Silver City Road, Lewis & Clark County, MT. Original specimen believed to be 50–150 years old. Registered in 1970. Dense, upright, symmetrical, robust.

P. flexilis 'Silver'
Introduced ≤1976–77 by D. Hill nursery of Dundee, IL. A grafted, silver-blue clone.

P. flexilis 'Temple'
= *P. flexilis* 'Tiny Temple'
Introduced in 1972 by Vermeulen nursery of New Jersey. "Short needles (≤2¾") and branching habit create somewhat of an oriental temple effect, especially if pruned moderately annually."

P. flexilis 'Tiny Temple'—see *P. flexilis* 'Temple'

P. flexilis 'Vanderwolf's Pyramid'
= *P. flexilis* 'Fastigiata Glauca Venderwolf'
Introduced in 1972 by Vermeulen nursery of New Jersey. Likely named after the nursery's general supervisor, Rein W. Vanderwolf. Common. "Shorter branchlets closely spaced make a compact tall pyramid of silver and dark green." Tree vigorous.

P. funebris—see *P. tabulæformis*

P. Gerardiana Wall. ex D. Don
= *P. chilghoza* Elphinstone
NEPAL NUT PINE. CHILG(H)OZA PINE. From the Himalayas: in NE Afghanistan, NW Pakistan, Kashmir, N India, SW Tibet. It was discovered by Captain Patrick Gerard (1795–1838) of the Bengal Native Infantry, one of the earliest explorers of the northwest Himalaya. Seedlings were raised in Britain shortly before 1838. In North America ≤1863. Extremely rare, but in commerce. Closely related to *P. Bungeana* (LACEBARK PINE), but has larger cones; longer edible seeds; and is usually single-trunked. Needles 3 per bundle, 2"–4" long. Cones (4") 6"–10" long; seeds to 1" long. Records: to 85' × 12'0" in the wild; 49' × 3'11" Cambridge Botanic Garden, England (1989; *pl.* ca. 1900).

P. Greggii Engelm. ex Parl.
From mountains of E Mexico. Named after Josiah Gregg (1806–1850), trader, writer, and botanical explorer, who discovered it in 1847. In cultivation ca. 1905. Exceedingly rare. Of interest as a Mexican PINE more cold-hardy than even some Californian species. Needles bright yellow-green, delicate, 3 per bundle, 3"–5" (6") long; held for only two years, giving the tree a sparse look. Young twigs often glaucous. Cones 1½"–4" (6") long, curving back on the branches, in clusters; spineless; often warped like those of *P. Banksiana* (JACK PINE). Records: to 100' tall in the wild; 54' × 5'10" Fota, County Cork, Ireland (1966; *pl.* 1911); 39' × 3'7" Seattle, WA (1994; *pl.* 1960); 35' × 4'½" Davis, CA (1992; *pl.* 1965).

P. Griffithii—see *P. Wallichiana*

P. halepensis Mill.
=*P. maritima* (Ait.) Lamb. 1803, non Poir. 1804, non (Ait.) Ait. fil. 1813
ALEPPO PINE. JERUSALEM PINE. From the Mediterranean region; the most widespread PINE there. The name refers to the ancient city Aleppo, or Halep (NW Syria near the Turkish border). Called JERUSALEM PINE because it is the most common naturally occurring and planted conifer in Israel. Introduced to cultivation in 1683 by Bishop Compton of London. In California since ≤1859. Common there and in the Southwest. A large tree with an open rather than dense mass of foliage. Very closely related to *P. brutia*, but with stalked, backward-pointing, smaller, narrower cones, and usually much shorter, softer needles. Also less cold-hardy than *P. brutia*. Needles 2 (3) per bundle, 2½"–5¼" long, slender. Cones 2"–4¾" long, backward turned and long persisting on the branches. Records: 144' × 9'9" Redlands, CA (1993); 94' × 8'10" Sacramento, CA (1989); 87' × 10'5" Santa Barbara, CA (1993); 94' × 11'9½" Davis, CA (1993).

P. halepensis var. brutia—see *P. brutia*

P. halepensis var. eldarica—see *P. brutia* var. eldarica

P. halepensis var. *mondell*—see *P. brutia* var. *eldarica*

P. halepensis var. *Pityusa*—see *P. brutia* var. *Pityusa*

P. Hartwegii Lindl.
= *P. Montezumæ* var. *Hartwegii* (Lindl.) Engelm. *ex* Shaw
= *P. rudis* Endl.

From high mountains of Mexico, S Guatemala, and Honduras, and from the highest peak in NW El Salvador. On the high, snow-capped mountain peaks of Mexico (to 12,000' elevation), this species is the only PINE to grow at timberline. Discovered in December 1836 or shortly thereafter by Karl Theodor Hartweg (1812–1871); introduced by him in 1839 to the Horticultural Society of London, but none date from then. Not cultivated in North America outside of arboreta or specialty collections, but much grown in England. Closely related to, but hardier than *P. Montezumæ*. Needles (3,4) 5 per bundle, (2½") 4"–6" (7") long. Cones 2"–6½" long, dark. Records: to 120' tall in the wild; 92' × 6'9" Bolderwood, New Forest, Hampshire, England (1979); 70' × 7'3" Coolhurst, Sussex, England (1976).

P. Heldreichii Christ
= *P.* × *nigradermis* Fuk. & Vid.

HELDREICH PINE. Named after Greek botanist Theodor von Heldreich (1822–1902). From Albania, Greece, and Yugoslavia. Introduced into Britain in 1844. Named in 1863. Exceedingly rare in North America. Nursery references to this tree may safely be assumed to be mistakes for *P. leucodermis*. Some arboretum specimens are similarly mislabeled. Needles 2 per bundle, 2⅜"–4¼" long. Cones 2"– 3⅛" long. Recorded to 115' tall in the wild. Probably actually a hybrid of *P. nigra* and *P. leucodermis*.

P. Heldreichii 'Aureo-spicata'—see *P. leucodermis* 'Aureo-spicata'

P. Heldreichii var. *leucodermis*—see *P. leucodermis*

P. himekomatsu—see *P. parviflora*

P. hwantungensis—see *P. kwangtungensis*

P. inops—see *P. contorta* and *P. virginiana*

P. insignis—see *P. radiata*

P. Jeffreyi Grev. & Balf. *ex* A. Murr.
= *P. ponderosa* var. *Jeffreyi* (Balf. *ex* A. Murr.) Vasey

JEFFREY PINE. From SW Oregon, California, a bit of Nevada, and N Baja California. John Jeffrey (1826–1854?) was first a gardener at Edinburgh, then a plant collector who introduced this PINE in 1852. His last letter was sent in August 1853 from Yuma, AZ. His fate remains unknown. JEFFREY PINE is related closely to PONDEROSA PINE, but is stouter, darker, and less commonly cultivated. Its bark odor is described variously as the odor of violets, pineapple, honey, orange or vanilla—instead of turpentine-like as in PONDEROSA PINE. A tree of brute strength, massive size and noble bearing. Needles 3 per bundle, 5"–13" long. Cones 5"–12" (15") long, rather light considering their size and bulky appearance. Records: to 300' × 37'8" near Yosemite, CA (1891); 197' × 25'7" Stanislaus National Forest, CA (1984).

P. 'Kellogg Hybrid Pine'
(*P. nigra* × *P. densiflora*)

Hybridized at Michigan State University's Kellogg Experimental Forest. Introduced in 1991 by Better Trees, Inc., of St. Johns, MI. A seed-propagated cultivar.

P. koraiensis S. & Z.

KOREAN PINE. KOREAN WHITE PINE. KOREAN NUT PINE. MANCHURIAN WHITE PINE. From E Korea, Manchuria, the Russian Far East, and Japan. Introduced ca. 1859 by Siebold to Holland; in 1861 J.G. Veitch to England (M. Vidakovic says 1846 to Europe). In North America ≤1870. Uncommon. Needles 5 per bundle, 2½"–5" long, prettily blue-green. Cones 3½"–6" long, heavy, not liberating the large edible seeds. Habit usually very long-branched and broad. Records: to 150' × 15'6" in the wild; 72' × 8'0" St. Paul d'Abbotsford, Québec (<1994); 72' × 5'2" Crarae, Strathclyde, Scotland (1987); 65½' × 5'6" Fota, County Cork, Ireland (1987); 60' × 4'6" Sidbury Manor, Devon, England (1977); 59' × 2'2" Wind River, WA (1990); 33' × 4'8" Tacoma, WA (1990); a trunk 5'4" around on Long Island, NY (1972).

P. koraiensis 'Glauca'

Introduced ≤1936 by Tingle nursery of Pittsville, MD. Needles "more bluish." Long extinct commercially. Might have been another species misnamed. See *P. koraiensis* 'Silveray'.

P. koraiensis 'Morris Blue'

At the Morris Arboretum, near Philadelphia, PA, specimens cannot be distinguished from *P. koraiensis* 'Silveray'. In commerce ≤1992.

P. koraiensis 'Silveray'

Discovered in 1977 in Germany. Named and introduced in 1978. In North American commerce. Very blue needles. In Europe at least, sometimes sold as 'Glauca'.

P. kwangtungensis Chun ex Tsiang

≠ *P. hwangshanensis* Hsia *ex* Tsoong
= *P. Wangii* Hu & Cheng var. *kwangtungensis* (Chun *ex* Tsiang) Silba
?= *P. hwantungensis* hort.

KWANGTUNG PINE. GUANGDON(G) PINE. From SE China. Named in 1938. Extremely rare; in commerce sparingly since the late 1980s. Habit recalls that of *P. Cembra* (SWISS STONE PINE). Foliage similar to that of *P. parviflora* 'Glauca' (JAPANESE WHITE PINE) but stouter, with needles longer, stiffer, pointier and thicker. Needles 5 per bundle, 1½"–3" (5") long. Twigs glaucous, hairless or extremely minutely pubescent. Cones 1½"–4" (6⅝") long. Bark rough. Records: to 100' × 15'8" in the wild; 35' × 2'8½" Seattle, WA (1993; *pl.* 1940).

P. Lambertiana Dougl. ex Taylor & Philips

SUGAR PINE. GIGANTIC PINE. BIG PINE. From SW Oregon to N Baja California. Introduced to cultivation in 1827 by D. Douglas. Named after Aylmer Bourke Lambert (1761–1842), British botanist, scientific patron, author of the first major book in English relating to conifers: *The Genus Pinus*, 1803. Very rarely cultivated. This tree rubs elbows with REDWOODS and has been styled the King of PINES. In 1894 J. Muir wrote: "the noblest pine yet discovered, surpassing all others not merely in size but also in kingly beauty and majesty." Alas, it is highly susceptible to blister rust—although some of its populations resist the disease. Needles 5 per bundle, 3"–4½" long. Cones the longest of all PINES, (7") 10"–30" long, containing large edible seeds. Can live more than 600 years. Its wounded trunk releases sugar. Records: to 300' × 63'0" in the forest primeval say T. Howell, A.S. Fuller, and E. Sheldon; 270' × 29'0" Yosemite National Park, CA (1991); 245' × 57'9" Oregon (1826); 232' × 36'10" California (1994); 216' × 32'0" N Fork Stanislaus River, CA (1972). Record specimens cultivated outside the native range include 121' × 12'10" New Zealand (≤1982); 95' × 9'11" Shropshire, England (1984); 78' × 9'1" Seattle, WA (1988), 70' × 9'2" Bryn Mawr, PA (≤1966).

P. Laricio var. austriaca—see P. nigra

P. Laricio var. calabrica—see P. nigra var. corsicana

P. Laricio var. caramanica—see P. nigra var. Pallasiana

P. Laricio var. Pallasiana—see P. nigra var. Pallasiana

P. Laricio var. Poiretiana—see P. nigra var. corsicana

P. latifolia—see P. Engelmannii

P. leucodermis Ant.

= *P. Heldreichii* var. *leucodermis* (Ant.) Markgraf *ex* Fitsch.
= *P. Heldreichii* ssp. *leucodermis* (Ant.) E. Murr.

BOSNIAN PINE. BOSNIAN REDCONE PINE. HERZEGOVINIAN PINE. SNAKESKIN PINE. GRAYBARK PINE. Also called BALKAN PINE, a name usually applied to *P. Peuce*. From mountains in Yugoslavia, N Greece, Bulgaria, Bosnia-Herzegovinia, Montenegro, Macedonia, Albania, and S Italy. Discovered by J.K. Maly in 1864; named, and introduced to Vienna the same year. In North America ≤1912, but exceedingly rare until ca. 1976; now commonly cultivated. Confused with *P. Heldreichii*. A dark, bolt upright medium-sized tree. Young trunks and the branches retain smooth light gray bark (*leucodermis* means white skin, from Greek *leukos* and *derma*) for a long time; the shoots upon losing their needles are similar to snakeskin due to closely spaced leaf cushions. Needles 2 per bundle, 2⅜"–3½" (4¼") long. Needles at the tips of the shoots in brush-like tufts. Cones 2"–4" long, dark purple-red when young. Records: 100' × 18'8" in the wild; 85' × 7'0" Stratfield Saye, Hampshire, England (1986); 65½' × 8'3" Tyninghame, East Lothian, Scotland (1984); 45' × 3'1½" Seattle, WA (1994; *pl.* 1949).

P. leucodermis 'Aureospicata'
= *P. Heldreichii* 'Aureospicata'
Introduced in 1952–53 by Hesse nursery of Germany. In North American commerce ≤1976. Very rare. Needles yellow-tipped. Growth slow.

P. leucodermis 'Satellit'
Raised on the estate of Max von Gimborn, Doorn, Holland, and introduced to commerce ≤1970 by Fa. L. Konijn & Son, Tempelhof nursery, Reeuwijk, near Boskoop. Extremely rare in North American commerce. Habit dense, erect, with very dark foliage.

P. longæva D.K. Bailey
= *P. aristata* var. *longæva* (D.K. Bailey) Little
= *P. aristata* ssp. *longæva* (D.K. Bailey) E. Murr.
INTERMOUNTAIN BRISTLECONE PINE. GREAT BASIN BRISTLECONE PINE. WESTERN BRISTLECONE PINE. ANCIENT PINE. From central Utah, S Nevada, and E California's White Mountains. Named in 1970 (previously regarded as a variant of *P. aristata*, BRISTLECONE PINE). Needles (3,4) 5 per bundle, 1"–1¼" long. Cones 2⅜"–4" long. One aged 4,600 years is called "Methuselah." The oldest are more than 4,900 years. Exceedingly rare in cultivation. Essentially a curiosity piece for collectors. It needs alkaline soil to get established, is finicky and slow. The oldest cultivated specimens known in California date from 1936. Records: to 50' tall; 47' × 39'4" White Mountains, CA (1972; "The Patriarch").

P. longifolia—see *P. Roxburghii*

P. macrophylla—see *P. Engelmannii*

P. maritima—see *P. halepensis*, *P. nigra* var. *corsicana* and *P. Pinaster*

P. Massoniana—see *P. densiflora* and *P. Thunbergii*

P. 'Mercury'
(*P. Wallichiana* × *P. parviflora*)
Described in 1962, based on a specimen near a statue of Mercury at the Morris Arboretum, near Philadelphia, PA. In largescale North American commerce

≤1993. Needles 2¼"–6¼" long. Cones 3½"–6" long, persistent; made even on young grafted specimens.

P. mitis—see *P. echinata*

P. mongolica—see *P. tabulæformis*

P. monophylla Torr. & Frém.
= *P. cembroides* var. *monophylla* (Torr. & Frém.) Voss
SINGLE-NEEDLE PIÑON. SINGLE-LEAF PIÑON. ONELEAF PINE. NUT PINE. From SE Idaho to N Baja California. Introduced in 1848 by K. Hartweg to Britain. Cultivated in North America since ≤1859; very rare. Needles unique among *Pinus*, only 1 (2) per bundle, ¾"–2⅛" long, usually a pretty bluish color. Cones 1½"–3½" long. Other PIÑONS in this volume are *P. cembroides* and *P. edulis*. Records: 55' × 7'0" Cassia County, ID (1973); 53' × 11'7" north of Reno, NV (1979); 45' × 13'8" Inyo County, CA (1991); 43' × 12'10" Yosemite National Park, CA (1971).

P. monophylla var. *edulis*—see *P. edulis*

P. monophylla 'Elegance'
Introduced ≤1993–94 by Stanley & Sons nursery of Boring, OR. "Selected here. 8' tall × 2' wide in 15 years. Looks like a tall vase that closes back at the top."

P. monophylla 'Stanley's Pyramid'
Introduced ≤1993–94 by Stanley & Sons nursery of Boring, OR. "Selected here. 8' tall × 2½' wide in 15 years. Uprite. Needles blue."

P. montana—see *P. Mugo*

P. montana var. *rostrata*—see *P. uncinata*

P. montana var. *uncinata*—see *P. uncinata*

P. Montezumæ Lamb.
MONTEZUMA PINE. ROUGH-BARKED (or ROUGH-BRANCHED) MEXICAN PINE. From Mexico, S Guatemala. Named in 1832 after Montezuma II (1480?–1520), the last Aztec Emperor, penultimate ruler, brought to ruin by Cortés. Introduced to England by K. Hartweg in 1839. Cultivated in the U.S. since ≤1863. Very rare; practically limited to California. A stout, bold, exuberant species, with long branches of luxurious foliage. More cold-hardy than *P. patula* (JELECOTE PINE) but so variable that only certain trees endure much freezing. See also the close ally *P. Hartwegii*. Needles (3,4) 5 (6,7,8) per bundle, 6"–

12" (18") long, varying in droopiness and thickness as well as length. Though a 5-needle pine, it does not in the least look like the WHITE PINES. Cones (2½") 4½"–6" (14") long, quite like those of *P. Jeffreyi.* Bark deep and chunky (the name ROUGH-BRANCHED MEXICAN PINE is likely a corruption of ROUGH-BARKED MEXICAN PINE). Records: 141' × 7'3" Mexico (1982); 88½' × 15'8" Endsleigh, Devon, England (1987); 49' × 4'6" Seattle, WA (1993; *pl.* 1965).

P. Montezumæ var. *Hartwegii—see P. Hartwegii*

P. monticola Dougl. *ex* D. Don

WESTERN WHITE PINE. IDAHO WHITE PINE. CALIFORNIA WHITE PINE. MOUNTAIN WHITE PINE. SOFT PINE. SILVER PINE. FINGERCONE PINE. From B.C. to W Montana and S California. Introduced in 1831 by D. Douglas. In Latin *monticola* means inhabiting mountains. Rarely cultivated. Its dark silvery-black trunk is straight and slender, bearing close whorls of dark, dense bluish-green branches. Closely related to *P. Strobus* (EASTERN WHITE PINE), but denser, narrower, with stiffer foliage, hairier twigs and larger cones. Needles 5 per bundle, 2½"–5½" long. Cones 5"–15" (18") long, shaped like giant bananas. Records: to 290' tall ≤1897; 239' × 20'7" near Medford, OR (1972); 214' × 21'5" Clearwater National Forest, ID (1981); 207' × 26'5" Bovill, ID (1944); 151' × 32'10" El Dorado National Forest, CA (1991).

P. Mughus—see P. Mugo

P. Mugo Turra
= *P. Mughus* Scop.
= *P. montana* Mill.

MUGO or MUGHO PINE. DWARF MOUNTAIN PINE. SWISS MOUNTAIN PINE. KNEE PINE. From mountains in parts of Europe. Named in 1764, *Mugo* being an old Tyrolese name. In Latin, the 1768 name *montana* means of the mountains. Needles 2 per bundle, 1"–2" long. Cones ¾"–1½" long. Shrubby more often than not. As L. Kumlien said, "short and stout and round about." Many cultivars exist. Record: 24' × 3'11" × 42' Seattle, WA (1992). Its treelike cousin is *P. uncinata* (MOUNTAIN PINE).

P. Mugo var. *rostrata—see P. uncinata*

P. Mugo ssp. *uncinata—see P. uncinata*

P. muricata D. Don
= *P. remorata* Mason

BISHOP PINE. PRICKLECONE PINE. From coastal California and N Baja California. Its specific epithet means muricate (from Latin *murex*, a mollusk yielding a purple dye and armed with sharp points or prickles, and *-atus*, provided with) or rough with hard sharp spines (referring to the cone). Discovered by T. Coulter in 1832 near San Luis Obispo; called OBISPO PINE, then translated to BISHOP PINE. Introduced to cultivation in 1846 by K. Hartweg. In California commerce since ≤1871. Rarely grown elsewhere. Excellent tolerance of seaside conditions. An irregular, limby tree with conspicuous prickly cones. Needles 2 per bundle, 3½"–7" long. Cones 2"–4" long, always persistent; usually strongly lopsided, and usually prickly. Records: 126' × 8'8" Hanmer Forest, North Canterbury, New Zealand (1970); 121' × 12'2" Mendocino County, CA (1976); 112' × 14'4" Mendocino County, CA (1986).

P. muricata var. *borealis* Axelrod

NORTHERN BISHOP PINE. SONOMA BISHOP PINE. While BISHOP PINES from Mexico and S California have smooth, gray bark, long slender branches, and coarse, sparse green needles—those from N California (*borealis* means of the north) have very rough rusty bark, short branches, fine, dense blue-green needles. At the Eddy Arboretum "we have been completely unable to cross *P. muricata* blue northerly with green southerly races."

P. Murrayana—see P. contorta var. *Murrayana*

P. nepalensis—see P. Wallichiana

P. nigra Arn.
= *P. austriaca* Hoess
= *P. nigricans* Host
= *P. Laricio* var. *austriaca* (Hoess) Loud.

AUSTRIAN BLACK PINE. EUROPEAN BLACK PINE. COMMON BLACK PINE. From E Austria, NE Italy, Yugoslavia, W Romania, Albania, Bulgaria, N Greece. Named in 1785. Cultivated in Holland between 1750–1780; to Britain 1835 by Lawson nursery of Edinburgh; in North America thereafter. Extremely common; comes up wild in places. Dark, massive and rugged, indomitable. Devoid of romance or elegance,

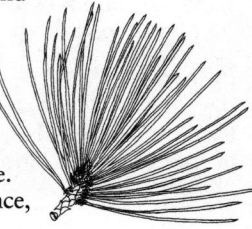

and often awkward, AUSTRIAN PINE is, like dirt, necessary. Its varietal peers cited below are not as dreary. Needles 2 per bundle, 3"–5½" long; long-persistent unlike its allies with two-year retention only. Cones 2"–4" long, borne singly or in groups of up to 6 in a whorl. Records: to 150' × 21'0" in the wild; 138' × 10'9" Dawyck, Peebles, Scotland (1984; *pl.* 1840); 93' × 10'0" New York (1994); 90' × 11'3" Seattle, WA (1993); 85' × 14'11" Keir Castle, Tayside, Scotland (1985; *pl.* 1851); 76' × 12'3" Walla Walla, WA (1988).

P. nigra 'Arnold Sentinel'

Raised in 1970 at the Arnold Arboretum from seeds collected in western Turkey. Tightly upright; the original clone in 1987 was 16' tall and 4' wide. A cultivar of *P. nigra* var. *Pallasiana*.

P. nigra var. *calabrica*—see *P. nigra* var. *corsicana*

P. nigra var. *caramanica*—see *P. nigra* var. *Pallasiana*

P. nigra var. *corsicana* (Loud.) Hyl.

= *P. nigra* ssp. *Laricio* (Poir.) Maire
= *P. nigra* var. *Poiretiana* (Ant.) Aschers & Graebn.
= *P. nigra* var. *calabrica* (Loud.) Schneid.
= *P. nigra* var. *corsica* hort.
= *P. nigra* var. *maritima* (Ait. fil.) Melv.
= *P. maritima* (Ait.) Ait. fil. 1813—misapplied; see *P. halepensis*
= *P. Laricio* var. *Poiretiana* Ant.
= *P. Laricio* var. *calabrica* Loud.

CORSICAN (BLACK) PINE. CALABRIAN PINE. From Calabria (i.e., S Italy), Sicily, Corsica. Possibly Algeria. Introduced from Corsica to England in 1759 by P. Miller (*Laricio* is the common name in southern Europe, and is an ancient name for LARCH). Named in 1804. Its alternative name commemorates Jean Louis Marie Poiret (1755–1834). In North American commerce since ≤1888. Rare. Compared to typical *P. nigra*, a tall, light-crowned tree with slender branches and pale bark. Needles 2 per bundle, 4"–6¾" long. Cones 2"–3½" (4") long. Records: to 180' × 23'0" in the wild; 150' × 13'1" Adhurst St. Mary, Hampshire, England (1985); 122' × 5'1" Vancouver, B.C. (1992); 114' × 10'9" Tacoma, WA (1989); 70' × 15'6" Llanfacreth, Merioneth, Wales (1968).

P. nigra var. *corsica*—see *P. nigra* var. *corsicana*

P. nigra 'Helena'

= *P. nigra* 'Variegated'

Discovered at Stanley & Sons nursery of Boring, OR, soon after the 1980 eruption of Mt. St. Helens, WA. Introduced to commerce ≤1992–93. Needles dark green and yellow variegated. Of spreading habit. 8"–16" growth yearly.

P. nigra var. *maritima*—see *P. nigra* var. *corsicana*

P. nigra 'Monstrosa'

Under this name a dwarf was described in 1867 in France. But an entirely different clone was described in 1933 based on a specimen then 34' tall and 12' wide in Rochester, NY. The latter version, though it be as monstrous as anything, has no right to usurp the name of the dwarf. But it has. Habit columnar, with few branches in widely separated whorls; twigs irregular, short, thick, contorted. Needles shining dark green, stiff, ca. 6" long.

P. nigra 'Nishiki'

Discovered by Stanley & Sons nursery of Boring, OR. Introduced ≤1993–94. "Double banding of orange on regular green leaves."

P. nigra var. *Pallasiana* (D. Don) Schn.

= *P. nigra* ssp. *Pallasiana* (D. Don) Holmboe
= *P. nigra* var. *caramanica* (Loud.) Rehd.
= *P. Laricio* var. *caramanica* Loud.
= *P. Laricio* var. *Pallasiana* (D. Don) Endl.
= *P. taurica* hort.

CRIMEAN (BLACK) PINE. TURKISH BLACK PINE. TAURIAN PINE. TARTARIAN PINE. From S Greece, SW Cyprus, W Turkey, Crimea, W Syria. Named after Peter Simon Pallas (1741–1811) who introduced seeds of this PINE to Britain ≤1790. Its alternative name *caramanica* means coming from Karaman (Turkey). Often fastigiate or globose in the wild. The trunk tends to fork candelabrum fashion, making a broad-crowned tree. Its numerous branches limit its value as timber but make it interesting in the landscape. Needles 2 per bundle, 4"–7" long, twisted. Cones 2¼"–4¼" long. Records: to 147½' tall says the *Flora of the U.S.S.R.*; 134½' × 14'1" Beaufort Castle, Highland, Scotland (1985); 111' × 17'6" Kingston Lacy nursery, Wimborne, Dorset, England (1983); 91' × 4'8" Wind River, WA (1988); 82' × 29'9" Turkey (1991); 72' × 12'2" Mt. Vernon, WA (1988).

P. nigra var. *Poiretiana*—see *P. nigra* var. *corsicana*

P. nigra 'Variegated'—see *P. nigra* 'Helena'

P. nigricans—see *P. nigra*

P. × nigradermis—see *P. Heldreichii*

P. palustris Mill.
= *P. australis* Michx. fil.

LONGLEAF PINE. SOUTHERN YELLOW PINE. SOUTHERN PINE. LONGSTRAW PINE. HILL PINE. HEART PINE. HARD PINE. PITCH PINE. SOUTHERN PITCH PINE. GEORGIA PINE. From SE Virginia to SE Texas. Important for timber. The inapt Latin name of 1768, *palustris*, means of swamps or marshes. Seldom cultivated for ornament, especially outside of its native range. Growth initially very slow, for 5–12 years looking like a clump of grass before growing upward. Its branches used to be shipped to northern cities because of their handsome foliage. Needles 3 (4,5) per bundle, 8"–18" (24") long. Cones 6"–10" long. Records: to 150' × 12'7" in the wild; 134' × 9'4" near Hemphill, TX (1972); 125' × 10'5" Angelina National Forest, TX (1977; now dead).

P. parviflora S. & Z.
= *P. pentaphylla* Mayr
= *P. himekomatsu* Miyabe & Kudo

JAPANESE WHITE PINE. From Japan (and an island or two off S Korea). Introduced to France in 1846. To England in 1861 by J.G. Veitch. The name *parviflora* (Latin *parvus*, small, and *floris*, a flower) means small-flowered. Wild specimens have very slender 3½" long needles and grow as "normal" WHITE PINES. Such trees are rarely seen in North America. The commonly cultivated form of this species is a compact, baby-bluish sort, rightly or wrongly often called 'Glauca' (which see), with needles ≤2¼" long. Needles 5 per bundle. Cones 1½"–4" long. Sometimes the tree is grafted on *P. Thunbergii* (JAPANESE BLACK PINE) which stunts and slows it. Numerous dwarf cultivars exist. Records: 98½' × 11'6" Japan (1994); 82' × 7'0" Stourhead, Wiltshire, England (1984); 59' × 2'11" Wind River, WA (1988); 56' × 8'6" Boconnoc, Cornwall, England (1983).

P. parviflora 'Baldwin'
From J.W. Spingarn of Baldwin, NY. Introduced ≤1976. Called "a superior blue-green."

P. parviflora 'Brevifolia'
= *P. parviflora* 'Glauca Brevifolia'
= *P. parviflora* 'Ha-tsumari-goyo'

Named in 1890. In North America ≤1965. In commerce here ≤1980. Very rare. The name *brevifolia*

from Latin *brevis*, short, and *folium*, a leaf. A small narrow tree. Branches sparse, ascending. Needles only ¾"–1⅕" long.

P. parviflora 'Early Cones'
= *P. parviflora* 'Glauca Early Cones'

Introduced ≤1991 by Vermeulen nursery of New Jersey. "Good blue-green foliage. Loaded with large cones."

P. parviflora 'Emperor'
Introduced in 1979 by Vermeulen nursery of New Jersey. Compactly branched and beautifully dressed with whorls of medium length slightly twisted emerald-green needles.

P. parviflora 'Gimborn's Ideal'
Raised on the estate of Max von Gimborn (1874–1964), of Doorn, Holland, and introduced to commerce ≤1960 by L. Konijn & Son, Tempelhof nursery, Reeuwijk, near Boskoop, Holland. In North American commerce ≤1980. Uncommon. A dense large shrub or small tree with fastigiate branching, to 25' tall. Needles fine, glaucous-green.

P. parviflora 'Gimborn's Pyramid'
Origin exactly as the preceding. In North American commerce ≤1980. Rare. Compact, broad and slow-growing, to 10' tall; branches densely borne; branchlets erect. Needles very glaucous, especially in spring and early summer.

P. parviflora 'Glauca'
= *P. parviflora* 'Silver'

Cultivated in the West since ≤1909 (the year described). Common, much more so than either the wild version or any other cultivar. Often sold merely as "*P. parviflora*." Needles usually ≤2" long, twisted to reveal their blue sides prettily. A toy of a tree, with profuse dark cones. Records: to 65½' tall says Ouden; 43' × 4'3" Puyallup, WA (1992); 33' × 8'3" × 37' Tacoma, WA (1989).

P. parviflora 'Glauca Brevifolia'—see *P. parviflora* 'Brevifolia'

P. parviflora 'Glauca Early Cones'—see *P. parviflora* 'Early Cones'

P. parviflora 'Ha-tsumari-goyo'—see *P. parviflora* 'Brevifolia'

P. parviflora 'Ja-no-me-goyo'—see *P. parviflora* 'Oculus-draconis'

P. parviflora 'Oculus-draconis'
= P. parviflora 'Ja-no-me-goyo'
= P. parviflora 'Ogon Janome'

GOLDEN DRAGON-EYE PINE. In North American commerce ≤1976. Rare. Bluish-tipped needles banded bright yellow while young, aging to green. Slow, remaining small.

P. parviflora 'Ogon Janome'—see P. parviflora 'Oculus-draconis'

P. parviflora 'Silver'—see P. parviflora 'Glauca'

P. parviflora 'Tempelhof'
Raised on the estate of Max von Gimborn, Doorn, Holland, and introduced to commerce ≤1965 by Fa. L. Konijn & Son, Tempelhof nursery, Reeuwijk, near Boskoop, Holland. In North American commerce ≤1979–80. Uncommon. Like 'Glauca' but grows faster, and possibly is bluer.

P. parviflora 'Venus'
Raised on the estate of Max von Gimborn, Doorn, Holland, and introduced to commerce ≤1965 by Fa. L. Konijn & Son, Tempelhof nursery, Reeuwijk, near Boskoop, Holland. Sold in North America since ≤1993 by Buchholz & Buchholz nursery of Gaston, OR. Slow and compact but not a dwarf. Needles light blue, much shorter than those of 'Glauca' and much compressed against the twigs.

P. patula Schiede & Deppe ex Schlecht. & Cham.
JELECOTE PINE. MEXICAN WEEPING PINE. MEXICAN YELLOW PINE. MEXICAN PINE. From mountains of E Mexico. Discovered in 1828; introduced to England soon after. The epithet patula is Latin for spreading out open and broad; not dense—likely referring to the branching pattern. Habit slender, graceful, weeping and very attractive. Trunk reddish. Long cultivated in California, but scarcely elsewhere in North America. Severe winter cold browns the shiny grass-green needles somewhat or kills the tree. If someone could raise a more cold-hardy clone, wealth would result. A much hardier very close cousin is P. Greggii. Needles 3 (4,5) per bundle, 4"–12" long, strongly weeping, very slender and shining. Cones 2½"–4¾" long. Records: 139' × 11'3" Waiotapu Forest, New Zealand (≤1982; pl.

ca. 1890); 134' × 6'6" Mexico (1982); 86' × 9'2" Santa Rosa, CA (1989).

P. pentaphylla—see P. parviflora

P. Peuce Griseb.
(P. Peuke)

MACEDONIAN (WHITE) PINE. MACEDONIAN STONE PINE. GREEK STONE PINE. YUGOSLAV PINE. BALKAN PINE. From the Balkan Mountains of Yugoslavia, Albania, Bulgaria and Greece. Discovered in 1839; named in 1844 (Peuce, in Latin, is an adopted Greek name of a PINE or a pitch-bearing tree). Introduced to cultivation in 1864 in Germany. In North America ≤1894. Uncommon. An adaptable, handsome tree of formal bearing. Highly resists blister rust that kills P. Strobus, P. Lambertiana, P. monticola, etc. In great age it resembles P. Strobus. Needles 5 per bundle, 3"–4½" long. Cones 3"–7" long. Records: to 130' tall in the wild; 105' × 13'7" Stourhead, Wiltshire, England (1984; pl. ca. 1864); 67' × 3'11" Seattle, WA (1990; pl. 1947)

P. Pinaster Soland.
= P. maritima Poir. 1904, non Lamb. 1803, non (Ait.) Ait. fil. 1813

CLUSTER PINE. SEASIDE PINE. MEDITERRANEAN PINE. BOURNEMOUTH PINE. LANDES' PINE. BORDEAUX PINE. MARITIME PINE. PINASTER (PINE). DILL-SEED TREE. TREE OF GOLD. From SW Europe, NW Africa. Thrives on sand. Planted extensively for seaside erosion-control, for timber and for naval stores production. Pinaster is Latin for a wild PINE. From pin, and aster, wild, not cultivated—as was P. Pinea (ITALIAN STONE PINE). Cultivated <1596 in England. In California commerce since ≤1858. More or less common on the Pacific Coast; rare elsewhere in North America. Remarkable in age for its long, often leaning, red, bare trunk of deeply plated bark, surmounted by a romantically irregular and luxurious crown of branches bearing long, thick needles, and large cones. Needles 2 (3) per bundle, 5"–10" long. Cones 4"–10" long, often in star-like whorls or clusters (up to 61). Records: to 120' × 18'6" in the wild; 114 × 10'4" Garnons, Herefordshire, England (1969); 102' × 15'8" New Zealand (≤1982); 96' × 17'9½" Waimate North, Northland, New Zealand (1970); 88' × 10'9" Allen, WA (1989); 85' × 15'0" Sheffield Park, Sussex, England (1968; pl. ca. 1800).

P. Pinea L.
ITALIAN STONE PINE. MEDITERRANEAN STONE PINE. THE PINE OF ROME. UMBRELLA PINE. PARASOL PINE. From the Mediterranean region, but not N Africa. Introduced

<1548 to Britain. In the U.S. since ≤1818. In California commerce since ≤1871. Common on the Pacific Coast; rare elsewhere in North America, being hurt by severe cold (especially when a seedling). The name STONE PINE comes from its very hard seed shells; SWISS STONE PINE (*P. Cembra*) is wholly dissimilar. *Pinea* is the classical Latin name for pine nuts. Characteristic of many Mediterranean landscapes, this is a mushroom or umbrella-shaped tree beloved for its picturesque appearance. Its distinctive broad habit ranks among the world's elite of memorable tree shapes. Alas, it is prone to falling over or breaking. Needles 2 (3) per bundle, 3"–5" (8") long. Cones 3¼"–6" long, massive and nearly globular; seeds large (¾"–⅞"), sooty black, hard-shelled and edible. Records: 120' × 21'4" Rome, Italy (<1844; "the Colonna Pine"); 95' × 16'1" Sacramento, CA (1989; *pl.* 1870); 95' × 11'4" San Marino, CA (1978); 72' × 17'3" New Zealand (≤1982); 60' × 14'2" Santa Barbara, CA (<1974); 52' × 8'8" × 135' Rotorua, New Zealand (1972); 50' × 8'5" Seattle, WA (1992).

P. Pityusa—see *P. brutia* var. *Pityusa*

P. ponderosa Dougl. *ex* Laws.

PONDEROSA PINE. (WESTERN) YELLOW PINE. BULL PINE. BLACKJACK PINE. SIERRA BROWNBARK PINE. WESTERN RED PINE. HEAVY PINE. BIG PINE. From much of the western half of North America. Discovered and introduced in 1826 by D. Douglas. Very common in cultivation. The most far-ranging and best known of western North American PINES. Name from Latin for ponderous or heavy, referring to the wood. The State Tree of Montana. Of excellent constitution, a grand landscape tree. Needles (2) 3 per bundle, 5"–11¼" long. Cones 3"–6" (8") long, light for their size, prickly. Some populations seem genetically predisposed to produce multiple-stemmed or forking tops. Records: to 300' × 47'0" in pioneer times say J.G. Lemmon, E. Sheldon and A.S. Fuller; 262' × 18'2" Shasta-Trinity National Forest, CA (1966); 236' × 22'2" Sierra National Forest, CA (1974); 223' × 23'11" Plumas, CA (1974); 174' × 28'4" La Pine, near Bend, OR (1993).

P. ponderosa var. *arizonica* (Engelm.) Shaw

= *P. ponderosa* ssp. *arizonica* (Engelm.) E. Murr.
= *P. arizonica* Engelm.

ARIZONA PINE. From mountains of SE Arizona, extreme SW New Mexico, and (mostly) NW Mexico. Rarely cultivated. Offered in 1993 by Piroche Plants nursery of Pitt Meadows, B.C. Needles 3–5 per bundle, 5"–10" long, markedly slender. Cones 2"–3½" long, less prickly than typical ones. Records: to

120' × 14'2" in the wild; 118' × 12'2" Pima County, AZ (1993); 104' × 11'4" Coronado National Forest, AZ (1977).

P. ponderosa var. *Jeffreyi*—see *P. Jeffreyi*

P. ponderosa 'Pendula'

Described in 1934, when the 1913 original was 65' tall in Rochester, NY. Long extinct in commerce. Very slender; branches few, more or less pendulous. Needles drooping, 8"–11" long.

P. ponderosa var. *scopulorum* Engelm.

= *P. ponderosa* ssp. *scopulorum* (Engelm.) Weber
= *P. scopulorum* (Engelm.) Lemm.

ROCKY MOUNTAIN (PONDEROSA or YELLOW) PINE. BLACK HILLS PONDEROSA PINE. INTERIOR PONDEROSA PINE. From E Montana to north Mexico in the Rocky Mountains. South Dakota's Black Hills were so named because this dark-needled PONDEROSA PINE there makes them appear black from a distance. The Latin name *scopulorum* derives from *scopulus*, a cliff or rock, in reference to the tree's habitat. Very rarely cultivated outside of its native range. Needles usually 3 per bundle, 3"–6" long. Cones to 3" long. Records: 128½' × 15'7" Santa Fe National Forest, NM (1981); 120' × 16'8" Yauapai County, AZ (1985).

P. ponderosa 'Twodot Columnar'

Found by nurseryman C. Berg of Helena, MT, in Twodot, MT, in 1964, when it was likely 20–30 years old. Habit markedly narrow, with upright branching.

P. pungens Lamb. *ex* Michx. fil.

TABLE MOUNTAIN PINE. HICKORY PINE. POVERTY PINE. PRICKLY PINE. BUR PINE. From the eastern U.S., mainly in the Appalachian region on dry, gravelly ridges; common on Table Mountain, NC. Rare in cultivation. The epithet *pungens* means piercing; sharp pointed, referring to the peculiar, stout, hooked cone spines. A crab of a PINE, of irregular crown and picturesque habit. Needles 2 (3) per bundle, 1½"–3" long. Cones 1¼"–4" long, cruelly prickly, tenaciously persistent and ornamental. Records: 97' × 7'3" west of Covington, VA (1981); 94' × 8'1" Stokes County, NC (1987); 76' × 7'7" Dahlonega, GA (1969); trunks to 9'6" around have been noted.

P. pyrenaica—see *P. brutia*

P. radiata D. Don

= *P. insignis* Dougl. *ex* Loud.

MONTEREY PINE. INSIGNIS PINE. RADIATA PINE. From a few isolated groves of California's central coast, and

Cedros and Guadalupe Islands, Mexico—the latter insular trees also considered by some rather a variation of *P. muricata* (BISHOP PINE). Spaniards in California grew this species before Western botanists knew it or grew it overseas. A cone was sent by Lapeyrouse from Monterey to Paris, France in 1787, and 12 seedlings were raised. D. Douglas rediscovered the species in 1831–32, then sent seeds to England. Its 1836 name *radiata* is Latin either referring to the radiate or rayed lines on the cone scales, or (from *radiatus*) means glittering. Its 1838 name *insignis* means remarkable—from the rich green foliage, etc. M. Vidakovic says "the most widely cultivated of all pines." World famous for rapidity of growth; propagated by seeds, cuttings and grafts. Introduced to New Zealand in 1870. In North America, mostly cultivated only on the Pacific Coast. Needles (2) 3 (4) per bundle, 2½"–5" (7") long, shiny grass-green. Cones 3"–7" long, lopsided, glossy, staying unopened on the tree indefinitely. Can grow 9' in one year! Its Achilles' heel is susceptibility to browning or killing in severe winter cold. Though foresters love it, landscapers can find MONTEREY PINE'S unbridled growth more than they bargained for. Records: 211½' × 10'8" New Zealand (1980; *pl.* 1927); 165' × 13'7" near Napa, CA (1954); 164' × 27'6" South Canterbury, New Zealand (≤1982); 125' × 22'0" Aptos, CA (1968); 85' × 29'0" Hamwood, County Meath, Ireland (1968).

P. radiata 'Aurea'

Raised <1910 in New Zealand. Extremely rare in North America. Many of its young needles largely yellow. Most attractive in winter. Records: 77' × 11'8" near Timarau, New Zealand (≤1982); 42' × 5'0" San Francisco, CA (1994; *pl.* 1968).

P. radiata 'Marshwood'

Originally found in Taringatura State Forest, New Zealand, in 1981. Not yet in North American commerce. Foliage golden.

P. radiata Majestic Beauty™

Introduced ≤1979–80 by Monrovia nursery of California. "Cutting grown, perfectly shaped broad cone with strong branching."

P. reflexa—see *P. strobiformis*

P. remorata—see *P. muricata*

P. resinosa Ait.

RED PINE. NORWAY PINE. From the Great Lakes region to beyond Maine. Named NORWAY PINE because its timber was likened to that of NORWAY SPRUCE (*Picea Abies*), not (as often asserted) after a small village in Maine where this tree was once abundant. RED PINE is well explained by its bark. Common in cultivation. Needles 2 (3) per bundle, 4"–7" long, notably brittle and of a peculiar soft yellow-green color. Cones 1"–2½" long. Records: 154' × 10'3" Watersmeet, MI (1985—the same tree was 124' × 10'4" in 1993); 135' × 8'7" Highland, WI (1984); 90' × 12'4" Lyndeboro, NH (1972); trunks to 15'6" around existed once.

P. resinosa 'Aurea'

Origin unknown. In commerce ≤1972. Extremely rare. Needles yellowish-green. Cultivar name invalid, being Latin yet post-1959.

P. rigida Mill.

PITCH PINE. NORTHERN PITCH PINE. TORCH PINE. SAP PINE. From the eastern U.S., but not far south; and extreme S Ontario and Québec. Named *rigida* because of its rigid or stiff cones scales. Somewhat commonly cultivated. Though utterly graceless, it is tough as nails. Its abundant presence suggested the name "PINE barrens" for great areas of Cape Cod, Long Island, and New Jersey. Only this and *P. canariensis* (not in this volume) have trunks often besprouted with needle tufts. Bark excessively rough, deeply cleft, and very dark. Can tolerate salt spray. The stumps sprout, unlike most PINES, but do not grow back into trees. D. Browne in 1832 wrote "On mountains and gravelly lands, the wood is compact, heavy and surcharged with resin, whence is derived the name PITCH PINE. In swamps, on the contrary, it is light, soft, and composed almost wholly of sap; it is then called SAP PINE." Needles 3 per bundle, 2"–5½" long, yellow-green. Cones 1¼"–4" long, persistent and prickly. Records: 101' × 11'5" Poland, ME (1979); 88' × 9'11" Hiddenite, NC (1967); 70' × 12'2" Lyndeboro, NH (1975).

P. rigida 'Sherman Eddy'

Discovered in the 1930s by Boston landscape architect Sherman Eddy in the Pocono Mountains, PA. Sold ≤1979 by Weston nursery of Hopkinton, MA. Grows slowly, 4"–6" yearly to eventually ca. 15' tall.

P. rigida var. *serotina*—see *P. serotina*

P. Roxburghii Sarg.
= *P. longifolia* Roxb. *ex* Lamb., non Salisb.

CHIR PINE. EMODI PINE (both native names). From the Himalayas: NW Pakistan, N India, Nepal, Sikkim, Bhutan, in subtropical, monsoon regions. Presumably named after William Roxburgh (1751–1815). Introduced to Western cultivation in 1801. Barely cold-hardy; primarily grown in California (there since ≤1897). Some specimens may prove hardier, especially if grafted. Needles (2) 3 per bundle, 8"–16" long, pendulous, slender. Cones 4"–8" long, with big edible seeds. Records: to 180' × 35'0" in the wild; 102' × 12'8" Sacramento, CA (1989).

P. rudis—see P. Hartwegii

P. Sabiniana Dougl. *ex* D. Don

FOOTHILL PINE. GRAY(NEEDLE) PINE. GHOST PINE. DIGGER PINE. Essentially from bone-dry foothills and mountains surrounding the Central Valley of California. Named after Joseph Sabine (1770–1837), secretary of the Horticultural Society of London, patron of David Douglas, attorney, naturalist. Introduced to England in 1832 by D. Douglas. In California commerce ≤1858; little grown even there. Very distinctive; a ghostly tree with blackish bark. Sparsely foliated, grayish and weepy, this PINE is often multi-trunked candelabrum fashion, with squat, dark, conspicuous and very persistent cones. Needles 3 per bundle, 7"–14" long, drooping. Cones 5"–11" long, massive, heavily clawed. Many California Indians, derogatorily designated Diggers by white settlers, ate its large seeds. Records: 161' × 15'6" Redding, CA (1986); 160' × 16'7" × 80' near Coalinga, Fresno County, CA (1972); 114' × 18'6" Bar 71 Ranch, CA (1990); 76' × 16'0" × 85' Red Bluff, CA (1984).

P. × Schwerinii Fitsch.
(*P. Strobus* × *P. Wallichiana*)

Described in 1930 from a tree planted in 1905 (as *P. Strobus*) on the estate of Graf Fritz Kurt Alexander von Schwerin (1856–1934) at Wendisch-Wilmersdorf, near Berlin. Named in 1930. In North American commerce since ≤1962. Extremely rare. It inherits blister rust resistance from *P. Wallichiana*. Needles 5 per bundle, 3½"–5½" (7⅝") long. Cones 3"–6" (7½") long.

P. scopulorum—see P. ponderosa var. scopulorum

P. serotina Michx.
= *P. rigida* ssp. *serotina* (Michx.) Clausen
= *P. rigida* var. *serotina* (Michx.) Loud. *ex* Hoopes

POND PINE. MARSH PINE. POCOSIN PINE. From S New Jersey to central Alabama on the Coastal Plain, often in wet soils—as D. Browne in 1832 wrote: "on the borders of ponds, and in swamps where the soil is black and miry." The epithet *serotina* is Latin for late-coming (because its cones don't open for many years). D. Peattie explains "Pocosin, in the language of the Delaware Indians and other Algonquin tongues, means a small but deep pond or bog." Almost never cultivated for ornament. Very closely related to PITCH PINE (*P. rigida*). Needles 3 (4) per bundle, 5"–9" (11") long. Cones 2"–3" long, prickly. Records: 120' × 8'0" Patterson, GA (1989); 94' × 9'7" Scotland County, NC (1977); 89' × 10'9" Thomas County, GA (1992).

P. sinensis—see P. tabulæformis

P. strobiformis Engelm.
= *P. reflexa* (Engelm.) Engelm.
= *P. flexilis* var. *reflexa* Engelm.
= *P. Ayacahuite* ssp. *strobiformis* (Engelm.) E. Murr.
= *P. Ayacahuite* var. *reflexa* (Engelm.) Voss
= *P. Ayacahuite* var. *brachyptera* Shaw

SOUTHWESTERN WHITE PINE. BORDER WHITE PINE. MEXICAN WHITE PINE. SOUTHERN LIMBER PINE. From extreme SE Arizona, SW New Mexico, and (mostly) northern Mexico. Discovered by Dr. Wislizenus in Mexico in 1846. Named in 1848, *strobiformis* meaning with the form of *P. Strobus*. Cultivated ≤1937. Commonly available from nurseries only since the 1980s. Resists blister rust. Differs from LIMBER PINE (*P. flexilis*) in details only—no stomata on the needle backs, and cones larger, the apices of the scales narrowed and not as truncate. Needles (2,3,4) 5 per bundle, 2"–4" long. Cones 5"–10" (18") long. Records: 111' × 15'5" Lincoln National Forest, NM (1974). See also *P. Ayacahuite*.

P. Strobus L.

EASTERN WHITE PINE. NORTHERN WHITE PINE. WEYMOUTH PINE. PUMPKIN PINE. SOFT PINE. From the central and eastern U.S., SE Canada; and the disjunct var. *chiapensis* Martínez, in Chiapas and Oaxaca, Mexico, as well as W Guatemala and SW British Honduras. The name *Strobus* was taken by the botanist Linnæus from the Roman naturalist Pliny, who applied it to a tree of Carmania (a province of ancient Persia), used for fumigating or incense. Called

WEYMOUTH PINE in England since 1730. SOFT PINE and PUMPKIN PINE refer to its light, firm wood, smoothly cut in any direction. Once of supreme economic importance to the lumber industry, WHITE PINE has subsequently become very common in cultivation. It is lovely, soft-looking, and gracious. The State Tree of both Maine and Michigan; the Provincial Tree of Ontario. Needles 5 per bundle, 3"–5½" long. Cones 4"–8" (10") long, slender and pitchy. Records: to 270' × 37'6" in the forest primeval; 201' × 15'6" Marquette County, MI (1984); 177' × 12'5" Allegheny National Forest, PA (1980); 160' × 18'8" Douglas County, WI (1983); 148' × 17'7" Haliburton County, Ontario (1975); 147' × 18'2" Blanchard, ME (1972); 125' × 19'9" Keneenaw County, MI (1983); 79' × 20'0" Monterey, MA (1978).

P. Strobus 'Alba'

Originated ≤1825. Described in 1838 in England. Rare. Needles shorter than typical, when young quite whitish. Bark much paler. See also 'Nivea'.

P. Strobus 'Bennett Clump Leaf'

Named by or after Wm. Bennett of Christiansburg, VA. In commerce ≤1983. Extremely rare. The bundles of 5 needles welded into one big needle (or *looking* as one, anyway). Fast growing.

P. Strobus 'Bennett Contorted'

Originated at Blacksburg, VA. Noted in 1966, when ca. 10 years old, by Wm. M. Bennett of Christiansburg, VA. Registered in 1967. In commerce. A contorted, shrubby small tree. Staking not needed.

P. Strobus 'Bergman Variegated'

Named after Fred Bergman of Raraflora nursery, Feasterville, PA. Introduced ≤1982. Needles banded yellow.

P. Strobus 'Blue Mist'

Introduced in 1979 by Vermeulen nursery of New Jersey. "Blue tinted soft foliage; compact habit."

P. Strobus 'Contorta'

CONTORTED WHITE PINE. From Seneca Park, Rochester, NY. First propagated ≤1921. Named in 1931. In 1934 the original specimen was 16' tall and 9' wide. Extremely rare. Confused with 'Torulosa'. Trunk contorted; branches slightly ascending, twisted; branchlets contorted; needles densely set, 2"–3" long. Cones 1½"–2½" long.

P. Strobus 'Crazy (Form)'

Introduced in 1977 by Vermeulen nursery of New Jersey. "New growth is twisted and contorted; growth rate slow."

P. Strobus 'David'

Raised ca. 1964 as a seedling from a witches' broom in Granby, CT. After 25 years, 15' tall and 11½' wide.

P. Strobus 'Fastigiata'

= P. Strobus 'Pyramidalis'

UPRIGHT WHITE PINE. Described in 1884. Cultivated since 1897 at the Arnold Arboretum. Common. See also 'Lenore'. Records: 120' × 7'1" × 32' Lenox, MA (1993); 77' × 7'4" × 39' Delaware County, PA (1980).

P. Strobus 'Glauca'

Described in 1893 in Germany. Needles bluish-green. Extremely rare.

P. Strobus 'Hillside Winter Gold'

= P. Strobus 'Winter Gold'

From Hillside Gardens of Lehighton, PA. Introduced ≤1980. Uncommon. Green in summer (or with needles only weakly tipped yellowish), yellow in winter. Can be gaunt.

P. Strobus 'Lenore'

Originated as a seedling ca. 1952 from Washington Crossing, NJ, State nursery. Registered ca. 1971. In commerce since ≤1980. Very rare. Distinctly columnar habit, 20' tall and 6' wide. Narrower than P. Strobus 'Fastigiata'.

P. Strobus f. nana (Hornibrook) Welch

Dwarf, bushy cultivars under this name since <1850 have been known in some cases to eventually shoot their bolts and become small trees. Likewise with some specimens called 'Radiata' and 'Umbraculifera'. Such trees tend to be compact and broad, with cones to 3" and needles only to 2¾" long.

P. Strobus 'Nivea'

SNOW PINE. Named in 1850 in England. In North American commerce ≤1903. Long commercially extinct or hopelessly confused with 'Alba'. Some specimens so labeled in collections are not even P. Strobus cultivars.

P. Strobus 'Pendula'

WEEPING WHITE PINE. Described in 1866. Probably the best known weeping conifer; common. Semi-dwarf. Branches horizontal and floppy with the branchlets pendulous. Record: 27' × 3'10" × 24' Puyallup, WA (1992).

P. *Strobus* 'Pyramidalis'—see *P. Strobus* 'Fastigiata'

P. *Strobus* 'Radiata'—see *P. Strobus* f. *nana*

P. *Strobus* 'Torulosa'

('Tortuosa', 'Tortuosoe')

TWISTED WHITE PINE. CONTORTED WHITE PINE. Introduced ≤1977. Common. Not the same as 'Contorta' (which see). Conspicuously twisted needles and to a lesser degree the branches. Looks diseased. Cultivar name invalid, being Latin yet post-1959.

P. *Strobus* 'U Conn'

('Unconn', 'Uconn')

Originated as a seedling from a witches' broom in CT. Named by the University of Connecticut. Introduced in 1979. In commerce since ≤1987. After 15 years, the original was 10½' tall and 7' wide—grafted specimens grow faster. Needles bright green, 2" long.

P. *Strobus* 'Umbraculifera'—see *P. Strobus* f. *nana*

P. *Strobus* 'White Mountain'

Discovered ca. 1972 as a seedling. Introduced by Weston nursery of Hopkinton, MA. Brilliant silvery-blue needles. Vigorous.

P. *Strobus* 'Winter Gold'—see *P. Strobus* 'Hillside Winter Gold'

P. *Strobus* × *P. Ayacahuite*

Introduced in 1993–94 by Buchholz & Buchholz nursery of Gaston, OR.

P. *sylvestris* L.

SCOTS PINE. SCOTCH PINE. SCOTS or SCOTCH FIR. NORTHERN PINE. DEAL WOOD. From much of the Old World temperate zone, Atlantic to Pacific oceans. The most extensively distributed *Pinus*. The name *sylvestris* from Latin *silvestris* means wild, of the woods or forests; not cultivated. Despite the name, it is very commonly cultivated. In North America since <1752. Naturalized in places. Foliage sage-green or in some cultivars lovely bluish. Bark orange or red-tinged. Needles 2 per bundle, 1"–4½" long. Cones 1"–3" long. Habit varies from squat and bushy to tall and slender. Records: to 157' tall in NE Poland, Estonia and

Latvia; 128' × 16'1½" Inverary, Scotland (1950; aged 290); 108' × 17'5" Belladrum, Highland, Scotland (1987); 106' × 4'3" Monroe, WA (1988); 64' × 15'6" × 76' Lenawee County, MI (1983); 60' × 18'1" Spye Park, Wiltshire, England (<1961); 60' × 15'10" × 62' Nevada, IA (1986); 50 × 12'0" × 48' Rock County, WI (1979); trunks to 19'0" around have been noted.

P. *sylvestris* 'Aurea'

GOLDEN SCOTS PINE. Introduced in 1875 by William Barron & Son, Elvaston nursery, Borrowash, near Derby, England. Extremely rare in North America. In contemporary commerce. Needles bright gold in winter. Looks sickly in summer. Growth slow. Records: 88½' × 3'3" Glentanar, Aberdeenshire, Scotland (1987); 42½' × 5'3" Ardargie, Tayside, Scotland (1988).

P. *sylvestris* 'Auvergne'—see *P. sylvestris* 'French Blue'

P. *sylvestris* 'Fastigiata'

COLUMNAR SCOTS PINE. SENTINEL PINE. Described in 1856; *P. sylvestris* 'Pyramidalis' of 1850 may be the same. In North American commerce since ≤1920; common only since the 1980s. Growth slow; habit narrowly upright. Records: 52' × 4'0" Dryburgh Abbey, Selkirk, Scotland (1984); 32' × 2'10" × 13' Sidney, B.C. (1994; *pl.* ca. 1963); 30' × 1'7" × 8' Seattle, WA (1993; *pl.* 1957).

P. *sylvestris* 'French Blue'

= *P. sylvestris* 'Auvergne'

Nurseries who import seeds from Europe find those from south-central France (Auvergne) yield bluer-needled, more attractive trees than most other locales, and since ≤1980 have used the names 'French Blue' or 'Auvergne' to market such seedlings.

P. *sylvestris glauca* 'Mount Vernon Blue'—see *P. sylvestris* 'Mount Vernon Blue'

P. *sylvestris* 'Mitsch Weeping'

Introduced in 1978–79 by Mitsch nursery of Aurora, OR. "Occurred in a MUGO PINE bed but looks like *P. sylvestris*. Upright weeping like WEEPING NORWAY SPRUCE." Much broader than tall unless staked.

P. *sylvestris* 'Mount Vernon Blue'

= *P. sylvestris glauca* 'Mount Vernon Blue'

Introduced ≤1958 by Wells nursery of Mt. Vernon, WA. Common. A grafted selection described as "very blue" or "bright blue" or "striking blue."

P. sylvestris 'Watereri'
('Wateriana')

Discovered ca. 1865 by Anthony Waterer senior. Introduced by Knap Hill nursery, near Woking, Surrey, England. Common. Begins life as a stout conic bush, and eventually becomes a giant shrub or globose tree about 20'–30' tall and wide.

P. tuberculata—see P. attenuata

P. tabulæformis Carr.

= *P. sinensis* Mayr 1906, non Lamb. 1832
= *P. Wilsonii* Shaw
= *P. funebris* Kom.
= *P. mongolica* hort.

CHINESE PINE. CHINESE HARD PINE. CHINESE RED PINE. From N and north-central China; wild but not certain to be native in Korea. Introduced in 1862 by R. Fortune to England; in 1919 by E. Wilson to the Arnold Arboretum. Very rare. At least in the past, some nurseries supplied *P. Thunbergii* (JAPANESE BLACK PINE) under the name *P. tabulæformis*. Indeed, the latter does resemble *P. Thunbergii*, but sometimes the trunk shows reddish like *P. densiflora* (JAPANESE RED PINE). In habit and persistence of cones it presents much variation. The name *tabulæformis* refers to its frequent habit of developing a broad crown of wide spreading branches. Bark usually dark gray, sometimes partly pale reddish. Needles 2 (3) per bundle, 3½"–7" long. Cones 1½"–2½" long, lustrous yellow, then nut brown, finally fading gray; usually very persistent. Records: to 80' × 10'0" in the wild; 69' × 2'7" Wind River, WA (1990); 64' × 3'9" Portland, OR (1989); 36' × 5'3" Tacoma, WA (1992); 33' × 5'0" Seattle, WA (1988).

P. Tæda L.

LOBLOLLY PINE. OLDFIELD PINE. NORTH CAROLINA PINE. SHORTLEAF PINE. FRANKINCENSE PINE. From the southeastern U.S. Except in the South, rarely cultivated for ornament. The epithet *Tæda* is from an ancient Latin name for a resinous PINE tree or PINE torches in general—for which the timber of this species is well suited and was much used. Needles (2) 3 per bundle, 5"–10" long, bright green. Cones 2"–6" long. One of the first trees to occupy grounds exhausted by cultivation. Tolerates wetter conditions than do most PINES. LOBLOLLY refers to the moist depressions on which the tree is usually found in the wild. Records: to 182' tall says the American Forestry Association; 163' × 14'8" near Urania, LA (1980; 165 years old); 147' × 15'8" Watten, AR (1974); 135' × 21'5" King William County, VA (1986).

P. taurica—see P. nigra var. Pallasiana

P. Thunbergii Parl. ex DC. 1868, non Lamb. 1824

= *P. Thunbergiana* Franco
= *P. Massoniana* S. & Z. 1842, non Lamb. 1803
= *P. tabulæformis* hort., non Carr.

JAPANESE BLACK PINE. Japanese: *Kuro-matsu*. *O-matsu*. From Japan, S Korea. Named after Carl Peter Thunberg (1743–1828), Swedish physician, pupil of Linnæus. Introduced in 1852 by Siebold to Holland. Common in cultivation. Tolerates seaside conditions. Slender silky white buds and spring "candles" contrast delightfully with its rich dark green foliage. Needles 2 per bundle, 3"–5¾" long. Cones 1½"–3" long, sometimes dozens per cluster. The Japanese consider this species male, and *P. densiflora* (JAPANESE RED PINE) female. It has little save the name in common with AUSTRIAN BLACK PINE (*P. nigra*), being far more informal and lithe-looking. Records: to 130' × 20'6" in the wild; 90' × 7'4" Portland, OR (1993).

P. Thunb. 'Angelica's Thunderhead'—see P. Thunb. 'Thunderhead'

P. Thunbergii 'Iseli Golden'

Introduced ≤1982 by Cœnosium nursery: "Tree with golden new growth." The name refers to Iseli nursery of Boring, OR.

P. Thunb. 'Ja-no-me-matsu'—see P. Thunb. 'Oculus-draconis'

P. Thunbergii Majestic Beauty™ PP 5078 (1983)

= *P. Thunbergii* 'Monina'

Introduced in 1983 by Monrovia nursery of California. Cutting-grown. Smog resistant. Salt tolerant. Green even in cold weather. Denser foliage than normal.

P. Thunbergii 'Monina'—see P. Thunb. Majestic Beauty™

P. Thunbergii 'Oculus-draconis'

= *P. Thunbergii* 'Ja-no-me-matsu'

DRAGON EYE PINE. Described in 1890. Extremely rare—much more so than the *P. densiflora* banded cultivar. Possibly a proportionately a dwarfish tree. Needles, besides being gold-banded, are extra stout—to 6⅝" long.

P. Thunbergii 'Ogon'

Introduced ≤1986. Small upright tree. Needles bright gold—best in spring and summer.

P. Thunbergii 'Shirago-kuro-matsu'—see P. Thunb. 'Variegata'

P. Thunbergii 'Suiken'

Origin unknown. In commerce ≤1989. Extremely rare. Needles amazingly thick, bluish-green, twisted.

P. Thunbergii 'Thunderhead'

= P. Thunbergii 'Angelica's Thunderhead'

Selected by Wm. Devine of Angelica nursery of Kennedyville, MD. Introduced ≤1980. Compact if not dwarf, with striking white buds and long dark green needles.

P. Thunbergii 'Variegata'

= P. Thunbergii 'Shirago-kuro-matsu'

In California commerce ≤1887. Named officially in 1890. Extremely rare. Some needles yellow, others partly so.

P. Torreyana Parry ex Carr.

TORREY PINE. SOLEDAD PINE. DEL MAR PINE. Extremely rare in the wild: from coastal S California, near the mouth of the Soledad River of San Diego County and (ssp. insularis Haller) Santa Rosa Island 175 miles away. Discovered in Soledad Canyon in 1850 by C. Perry. In 1853, John Torrey (1796–1873), botanist at Columbia University—sent specimens of this species to France. Named after him in 1855. In California commerce since 1858–59. Almost never grown elsewhere. A rags to riches story: it is rare, small and often crooked in the wild; large, prized and exuberant in cultivation. Of monumental size, with a hefty trunk, rounded and airy crown, and grayish needles. Needles 5 per bundle, 7"–13" long, coarse and rough. Cones 4"–6" long and *wide*, chocolate brown; seeds very large, to 1" long. Records: 147' × 15'8" New Plymouth, New Zealand (≤1982); 133' × 13'4" × 70' Sacramento, CA (1989); 126' × 20'5" × 130' Carpinteria, CA (1993; *pl.* 1888; "The Wardholm Tree").

P. tuberculata—see P. attenuata

P. uncinata Mill. ex Mirb.

= P. montana var. rostrata Ant.
= P. montana var. uncinata (Mill.) Heer
= P. Mugo var. rostrata (Ant.) Gord.
= P. Mugo ssp. rostrata (Ant.) E. Murr.
= P. Mugo ssp. uncinata (Mill.) Domin

MOUNTAIN PINE. GIANT MUGO PINE. From mountains in parts of Europe. Introduced to cultivation between 1779 and 1840. In North American commerce ≤1918. Very rarely listed by nurseries, but once planted commonly in parts of the north. Essentially a treelike MUGO PINE (P. Mugo). Needles 2 per bundle, 1"–3" long. Cones 1½"–2¾" long, with scales markedly thick and knobby compared to those of P. Mugo. Dark and homely. Records: to 80' × 9'6" in the wild; 65½' × 5'3" Cambridge, England (1989); 62' × 3'8" Seattle, WA (1987); 56' × 9'8" Patterdale, Cumbria, England (1985).

P. virginiana Mill.

= P. inops Soland. 1789, non Bong. 1833

VIRGINIA PINE. JERSEY PINE. SCRUB PINE. POVERTY PINE. From the eastern U.S., Long Island, New York, to NE Mississippi. Uncommon in cultivation except in the southeast. Usually scraggly, yet grows well on heavy, clayey, impoverished land, though not on sandy light soils. Needles 2 per bundle, 1½"–3" long. Cones 1½"–3" long. Records: 120' × 8'6" Chambers County, AL (1989); trunks to 9'5" around in S Indiana.

P. virginiana 'Wate's Golden'

Introduced ≤1982. Outstanding gold color in winter. Tree slow; small.

P. Wallichiana A.B. Jacks.

= P. Griffithii McClelland 1854, non Parl. 1868
= P. excelsa Wall. ex D. Don 1824, non Lam. 1778
= P. nepalensis de Chambr., non J. Forbes, non Royle

HIMALAYAN (WHITE) PINE. BHUTAN PINE. BLUE PINE. From the Himalayas, E Afghanistan to N Burma. Nathaniel Wallich (1786–1854), Danish surgeon and botanist with the East India Company, superintendent of the Calcutta Botanic Garden; travelled widely in India and Burma, introduced this pine to England in 1823. William Griffith (1810–1846), was a botanist of genius stature. A species much like *P. Strobus* (EASTERN WHITE PINE) but wider, airier, with larger cones and longer needles. Needles 5 per bundle, 4"–8" long, more or less droopy. Cones 6"–13" long, slender. Records: to 165' × 17'0" in the wild; 126' × 10'10" Tikokino, New Zealand (≤1982); 121' × 11'9" Abbeyleix, County Leix, Ireland (1985); 112'

× 15'9" Bicton, Devon, England (1968); 99' × 6'6" Tacoma, WA (1990); 96' × 10'8" Easton, MD (1990); 92' × 8'8" Delaware County, PA (1980).

P. Wallichiana 'Frosty'

Introduced ≤1982. Graceful needles variegated frosty white. Lovely in winter, but in autumn can look ill: yellow, blue and white.

P. Wallichiana 'Morton'

Introduced ≤1992 by Buchholz & Buchholz nursery of Gaston, OR. Selected because it is cold-hardy at Morton Arboretum of Lisle, IL.

P. Wallichiana 'Mulfordiana'—see P. Wallichiana 'Zebrina'

P. Wallichiana 'Zebrina'

= P. Wallichiana 'Mulfordiana'

Raised in 1874 by Croux & Fils nursery of Sceaux, France. Described in 1889. Rare. Needles barred (zebra-like), marked an inch below the apex with (2) 5 (7) creamy-yellow bands, otherwise green and gold.

P. Wangii var. kwangtungensis—see P. kwangtungensis

P. Wilsonii—see P. tabulæformis

Pirus spp.—see Pyrus spp.

Pistacia

[ANACARDIACEÆ; Cashew Family] 9–10 spp. of trees and shrubs, evergreen or deciduous, leaves usually compound. Name from ancient Latin pistacia, the PISTACHIO TREE, in turn from Greek pistake, ultimately Persian pista or Arabic fustuq. Male and female flowers on separate trees; the males are dense clusters of stamens, the females airier and less conspicuous, blooming slightly later. Related genera include Cotinus (SMOKE TREE), Rhus (SUMACH), and Schinus (PEPPER TREE).

P. atlantica Desf.

MT. ATLAS PISTACHIO. MT. ATLAS MASTICH. From the Canary Islands, N Africa, SE Europe, through the Near East to W Pakistan. The epithet atlantica means from the Atlas mountains. Introduced to European cultivation in 1790. Named in 1800. In North America ≤1910; in commerce here ≤1918–19. Very rare overall, although reseeding in parts of California's Sacramento Valley. Used primarily as a P. vera rootstock because it resists nematodes, and increases yields and growth. Cold-hardy (tolerates -20°F), drought-tolerant, with handsome foliage which stays green late into fall then drops without lively colors. Leaves compound, of 5–9 (11) untoothed leaflets, smoky gray-blue, the central stem narrowly winged. Fruit borne in clusters 2"–5½" long, resinous nutlets ¼"–⅓" long; they can be crushed for an oil. The tree tends to form a broad, dense, low crown. Records: to 60' tall in the wild; 49½' × 5'4" × 57½' Los Angeles, CA (1993; pl. 1954); 46' × 19'8" Turkey (1993).

P. chinensis Bge.

CHINESE PISTACHE. CHINESE PISTACHIO. GITTERWORT. From China, Taiwan, and the Philippines. Introduced to cultivation ca. 1890. In North American commerce ≤1914. Common. Naturalized in E Texas and parts of California. Leaves compound, of 8–16 leaflets, strongly odorous when crushed, smelling like SMOKE TREE (Cotinus) or SWEETGUM (Liquidambar) leaves. Fall color variable; ranges from fiery crimson to lemon yellow. When young it is slow growing, sometimes lopsided, and can look stubby in winter. Flowers from March into May. Berries thin-fleshed, hard, inedible, ca. ¼" wide, and somewhat flattened; first green, then yellow, next red and finally metallic blue when fully ripe. Records: to 100' × 16'0" in China; 76' × 6'5" Sacramento, CA (1989); 75' × 7'7½" × 83½' Davis, CA (1993; pl. 1933).

P. chinensis 'Keith Davey' PP 2277 (1963)

A specimen 30 years old, selected in 1957 by the Saratoga Horticultural Foundation of California. Introduced in 1958. Named after Keith L. Davey (1907–1987), founder of Davey Tree Surgery Company in northern California. Sturdy branching structure; fruitless; dramatic orange-red fall color. Rare because it is difficult to propagate and grows slower than seedlings.

Pistacia texana Swing.

TEXAS PISTACHE. AMERICAN PISTACHIO. WILD PISTACHIO. From S Texas (rare) and NE Mexico (common). Named in 1920. Almost never cultivated <1964. Largescale propagation has occurred since the mid-1980s. Foliage airy, evergreen or tardily deciduous. Leaves 2"–4" long, of (8) 10–16 (18) leaflets, lovely wine-red when young. Fruit dark reddish-brown, ¼" long. Hardy to 5°F. Usually multitrunked. Record: 39' × 4'3" × 46' Val Verde County, TX (1975).

P. vera L.

PISTACHIO. GREEN ALMOND. From SW and central Asia. Introduced by a London apothecary to England in 1570. In North America since 1853–54. Grown in California orchards for the edible nuts; not planted for ornament because it is wholly lacking in pizazz. In Latin, *vera* means true. Leaves usually trifoliate, with rarely only one, or 5–7 leaflets. Flowers in April. A small bushy tree with a dense, round crown. Thrives in dry climates, as with the OLIVE TREE (*Olea europæa*). Recorded to 30' tall. Wind-pollinated; some female cultivars are 'Kerman', 'Lassen' and 'Red Aleppo'; the common male pollinator is 'Peters'.

Planera

[ULMACEÆ; Elm Family] A genus of only the following species, a deciduous tree. Named in 1791 after Johann Jacob Planer (1743–1789), German botanist and physician at Erfurt. Closely related genera are *Aphananthe*, *Celtis* (HACKBERRY), *Ulmus* (ELM), and *Zelkova*.

P. acuminata—see Zelkova serrata

P. aquatica (Walt.) F. J. Gmel.

WATER ELM. PLANER TREE. From the SE United States, growing primarily where water is abundant. Introduced to cultivation in 1816. Exceedingly rare. Considering how obscure and far-removed from glamor this species is, it is wonderful to relate that its first scientific name was *Anonymos aquaticus*, in 1788. Leaves 1"–3" long, lopsided, roughish. Flowers and fruit insignificant. Usually a small tree. Records: 106' × 15'3" × 96'

New Bern, NC (1983); 72' × 8'3" Windsor Castle, Berkshire, England (1972; now dead).

P. carpinifolia—see Zelkova carpinifolia

P. crenata—see Zelkova carpinifolia

P. Davidii—see Hemiptelea Davidii

P. japonica—see Zelkova serrata

P. Keaki—see Zelkova serrata

P. Richardii—see Zelkova carpinifolia

Platanus

[PLATANACEÆ; Planetree or Sycamore Family] 6–9 spp. of immense deciduous trees, featuring mottled bark and MAPLE-like leaves. Grown for shade. Greek *platys*, ample or broad; alluding to the spreading branches or palmate leaves. With *Platanus*, the two major considerations are size and anthracnose. Being monumental, these trees need much space, and have the strength to buckle concrete and enter sewers easily. Anthracnose is a fungal blight that disfigures the trees in early summer, but rarely proves fatal. Although the leaves are MAPLE-like in shape, they are short-stemmed, the base of each stem swollen and hollow, fitting over the leaf bud. The fruit are conspicuous dry seedballs, dangling on a stem. The bark of some specimens is ghostly white and very attractive. Fall color yellow-brown.

P. × acerifolia (Ait.) Willd.

= P. × hybrida Brot.
= P. × intermedia hort.
= P. × hispanica Mill. ex Muenchh.
= P. orientalis hort. (in part), non L.
= P. orientalis var. acerifolia auct.
(P. orientalis × P. occidentalis)

HYBRID PLANE(TREE). HYBRID SYCAMORE. LONDON PLANE(TREE). EUROPEAN SYCAMORE. Hybrids between ORIENTAL PLANETREE and AMERICAN SYCAMORE first appeared in Europe in the 1600s, possibly as early as ca. 1645 at Tradescant's garden, south of London, England. Such hybrids are highly variable. The habit of calling them all by the name LONDON PLANETREE is like calling all dogs collies. The oldest specimens in London may be those in Berkeley Square, planted in 1789; it was not extensively planted there until 1811. The tallest trees of any kind (more than 130') in central London are of this kind. The clone originally called LONDON PLANE was in time superseded by cultivar 'Pyramidalis' anyway. Be that as it may, the name LONDON PLANE is here to stay. The hybrids achieved their fame by easily tolerating adverse urban conditions such as the stifling black soot of industrial London. They have become cosmopolitan urban trees, and are very common in North America. Their immensity proves awkward in tight quarters. In late spring they shed millions of tiny hairs, causing irritation to people who must breathe near them. Leaves more deeply lobed than those of *P. occidentalis*, less lobed than those of *P. orientalis*; commonly ca. 9" wide. Most seedballs (1"–2" wide) are in pairs, some are single or in trios or more. Records: 180' × 13'1" Spain (in the 1980s); 160' × 18'10" Bryanston, Dorset, England (1983); 150' × 20'5" Philadelphia County, PA (1980); 117' × 20'2" Walla Walla, WA (1993); 115' × 30'2" Ely Cathedral, Cambridge, England (1990).

P. × acerifolia 'Bloodgood'

In 1798, James Bloodgood founded a nursery on Long Island, NY, which lasted until 1919. Well before 1900 this cultivar was being propagated by cuttings, but wasn't named until ca. 1900 by Meehan nursery of Pennsylvania. It is common.

P. × acerifolia 'Columbia'

Originated as an intentional cross in 1970 at the U.S. National Arboretum. Named and introduced in 1984. Common. Resists anthracnose on the East Coast, not on the West Coast. Leaves deeply lobed. Seedballs usually 2–3 per stem. Good mildew resistance.

P. × acerifolia 'Kelseyana'

= *P. occidentalis* 'Kelseyana'
= *P. occidentalis* 'Kelsey'
= *P. occidentalis* 'Aureo-variegata'

Introduced <1899 by F.W. Kelsey nursery of New York. Very rare. Leaves variegated golden-yellow.

P. × acerifolia 'Liberty (Island)'

Originated as an intentional cross in 1968 at the U.S.

National Arboretum. Named and introduced in 1984. Uncommon. Leaves not as deeply lobed as in *P. × acerifolia* 'Columbia'. Seedballs usually 1–2 per stem. Good resistance to mildew and anthracnose.

P. × acerifolia Metroshade™

= *P. × acerifolia* 'Metzam'

Introduced in 1993 by Lake County nursery of Perry, OH. "The most vigorous growing." Disease resistant.

P. × acerifolia 'Metzam'—see P. × acerifolia Metroshade™

P. × acerifolia 'Pyramidalis'

= *P.* 'Pyramidalis'

The form presently most common in London; known there since 1850; described in 1856. Although much planted in North America, its name has been unused for the most part. In 1957–58 Scanlon nursery of Ohio began selling it, or at any rate something called 'Pyramidalis'. Scanlon said: "This fine pyramid makes available a form infinitely more practical than the wide-spreading umbrageous form of the species." The problem is, 'Pyramidalis' *is* the wide-spreading umbrageous form, with a short, massive trunk that soon divides into widely spreading, stout forks. The real LONDON PLANE is the taller, elegant form, with pretty bark. 'Pyramidalis' trunks are swollen, burly, dark and brutish; their upper limbs show some pale green to mustard-colored bark. Leaves shallowly lobed. Records: 105' × 15'7" and 99' × 16'6" × 106' Walla Walla, WA (1993).

P. × acerifolia 'Suttneri'

Cultivated <1896 in Europe. Introduced to North America in 1965 by the Arnold Arboretum. Exceedingly rare but in commerce. Leaves variegated creamy-white. Record: 70' × 8'3" Puttenham, Surrey, England (1978).

P. × acerifolia 'Yarwood'

Originated at the University of California, Berkeley, as an otherwise unremarkable specimen resistant to powdery mildew. Named in 1978 after Dr. Cecil E. Yarwood, plant pathologist. Very common. Leafs-out much later than most *Platanus*. Leaves relatively large.

P. × hispanica—see P. × acerifolia

P. × hybrida—see P. × acerifolia

P. × intermedia—see P. × acerifolia

P. mexicana Moric.

From NE Mexico; possibly also native in Guatemala. Named in 1837. Rare in cultivation; sold only in the southwestern U.S. Leaves to 8" wide, with 3–5 deep lobes; margins untoothed; whitish-wooly beneath. Seedballs 1–2 per stem, 1½" wide. Recorded to 115' × 15'6" in the wild.

P. mexicana Alamo™

Introduced ≤1986 by Lone Star Growers of San Antonio, TX.

P. occidentalis L.

AMERICAN SYCAMORE. EASTERN (U.S.) SYCAMORE. AMERICAN PLANE(TREE). BUTTONBALL TREE. BUTTON-WOOD. From the central and eastern United States, far S Ontario, and parts of Mexico. Common in the wild and in cultivation. The epithet *occidentalis* means western; from Latin *occidere*, to descend, referring to the setting sun. Named SYCAMORE by English immigrants reminded by its broad MAPLE-like leaves of their SYCAMORE (*Acer Pseudoplatanus*). Leaves broad and large (commonly to 14" × 16"), with conspicuous stipules. Seedballs (buttonballs) 1 (rarely 2) per stem, 1"–1½" wide. The most massive (not the tallest) tree east of the Rockies. Generally a woodland species, it does not thrive in cities as do its hybrid offspring; very hurt by anthracnose. Records: to 190' tall says A. Lounsberry; 176' × 33'4" Indiana (<1875); 166' × 14'4" Congaree Swamp, SC (1978); 161' × 24'4" Adrian, MI (1979); 150' × 42'3" Green County, IN (≤1915); 150' × 17'2" Magnolia, DE (1978); 144' × 25'5" New Windsor, MD (1990); 130' × 17'8" Tyler County, TX (1972); 129' × 48'6" Jeromesville, OH (1982); 120' × 29'4" Bucks County, PA (1981); a trunk 62'0" around in Gibson County, IN (<1882).

P. occidentalis 'Aureo-variegata'—see P. × acerifolia 'Kelseyana'

P. occidentalis var. glabrata (Fern.) Sarg.

TEXAS SYCAMORE. From Iowa to Texas and N Mexico. Compared to typical *P. occidentalis*, leaves usually smaller and more deeply lobed. In Texas and southern Californian commerce ≤1958. Highly resistant to root rot, alkalinity, heat and drought. Leaves green and nearly hairless (i.e., glabrate) beneath.

P. occidentalis 'Howard' PP 5359 (1984)

GOLDEN SYCAMORE. Discovered as a seedling and patented (at age two) by D. Howard of Burgaw, NC. In commerce ≤1987; extremely rare. New leaves lemon-yellow, with more green as they age. Growth slower than typical.

P. occid. 'Kelsey' or 'Kelseyana'—see P. × acerifolia 'Kelseyana'

P. orientalis L.

ORIENTAL PLANE(TREE). Persian: *Chinar* or *Dulb*. From the Balkan Peninsula and SW Asia, eastward to the Himalayas. The most enormous shade tree of southeastern Europe and Asia Minor. Rare in North America, although historically the name *P. orientalis* has been used by U.S. nurseries for hybrids (*P. × acerifolia*). The epithet *orientalis* means eastern; from Latin *oriens*, rising or originating, referring to the rising sun. Some botanists think that practically no purebred *P. orientalis* were planted in North America before the 1950s, and that specimens so called were hybrids which merely look like *P. orientalis*. The present writer's examination of the Seattle arboretum's 1954 Turkish-imported *P. orientalis* and the 1904 Olmsted-planted ones, revealed no clear difference—the 1904 specimens may be hybrid segregates, but in a practical sense they wholly resemble the bona fide Old World trees. Leaf deeply lobed, to ca. 12" wide, remaining later in fall than those of hybrids. Seedballs (2) 3–4 (6) per stem, ca. 1"–1⅓" wide; borne with greater frequency than those of most hybrids, or *P. occidentalis* specimens. Compared to hybrids the foliage is more droopy and lighter. Records: 164' × 102'11" Armenia (n.d.); 134' × 12'3" Woodstock Park, Kent, England (1982); 70' × 28'3" Rycote, Oxfordshire, England (1983); 92' × 11'4" Seattle, WA (1993; *pl.* ca. 1904); 82' × 23'6" × 210' Corsham Court, Wiltshire, England (1989); 75' × 6'7" Seattle, WA (1994; from 1954 Turkish seed).

P. orientalis var. acerifolia—see P. × acerifolia

P. orientalis 'Autumn Glory'

Introduced ≤1973 by Duncan & Davies nursery of New Zealand. Exceedingly rare in North America. Fall color superior. Very susceptible to powdery mildew in California.

P. orientalis Majestic Beauty™

Originated from seeds imported from the Sochi Arboretum on the Black Sea of Russia in 1971. Huntington Gardens of San Marino, CA, gave cuttings to Monrovia nursery in 1974. From 1980 until 1987 Monrovia sold the cultivar, saying it had "scarlet color and leaf drop all at once," and resisted anthracnose.

P. 'Pyramidalis'—see *P.* × *acerifolia* 'Pyramidalis'

P. racemosa Nutt.

CALIFORNIA SYCAMORE. WESTERN SYCAMORE. Spanish: *Aliso.* From California and Baja California. Named in 1845. Introduced to cultivation in 1870. Common in California nurseries. Leaves deeply lobed, very fuzzy beneath, 6"–12" (18") wide. Once in a while (cold winters?) the foliage turns deep gold in fall. Highly susceptible to anthracnose. Seedballs bristly, 2–7 per stem (hence the epithet *racemosa*), ¾"–1¼" wide. Records: to 125' tall says P. Standley; 116' × 27'0" × 158' near Santa Barbara, CA (1945— washed away in a 1969 flood); a trunk 29'7" around in Santigo Canyon, Los Angeles County (<1884); a trunk 17'10" around at Carpinteria, CA (1993—the "Portola Sycamore").

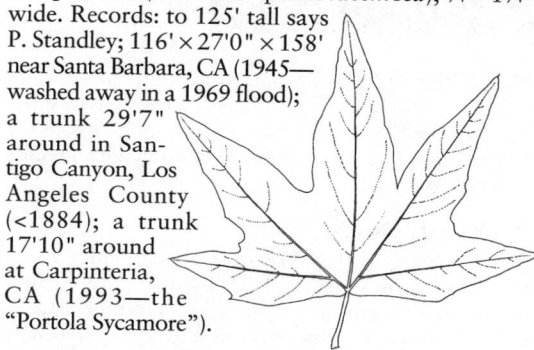

P. racemosa Wrightii—see *P. Wrightii*

P. Wrightii S. Wats.

= *P. racemosa* Wrightii hort.

ARIZONA SYCAMORE. From southwestern New Mexico, Arizona, and northwestern Mexico. Named in 1875 after Charles Wright (1811–1886), U.S. plant collector who obtained the first specimen in 1851. Introduced to cultivation in 1900. Rarely grown until the 1980s, when several major wholesale tree nurseries in S California propagated it. Leaves heart-shaped at the base; have 3–5 (7) deep lobes; can turn russet or bright yellow in fall. Seedballs 1–4, relatively smooth, not bristly. Records: 120' × 25'1" Animas Canyon, AZ (<1993); 114' × 23'7" × 116' Sierra County, NM (1981); 90' × 20'11" × 98' near Patagonia, AZ (1969).

Platycarya

[JUGLANDACEÆ; Walnut Family] 1–2 spp. of little known WALNUT relatives. From Greek *platys,* broad, and *karyon,* a nut; in allusion to the bracts covering the fruits, or the winged nutlets. Related genera are *Carya* (HICKORY and PECAN), *Juglans* (WALNUT), and *Pterocarya* (WINGNUT).

P. strobilacea S. & Z.

From China, Korea, Japan, Taiwan, and Viet Nam. Introduced to England in 1845 by R. Fortune. Extremely rare in North America; in commerce, but mostly only in botanic gardens. Leaves compound, of 7–17 leaflets with sharp and strongly incurved teeth; green late into November, eventually yellowing. Flowers yellowish, from late June to mid-July. Fruits woody, conelike (*strobilacea* means cone-like) and suggestive of those of teasel; 1"–1½" long. Bark rough, gray, fissured. Usually a large shrub or elegant small tree. Records: to 80' × 8'2" in the wild; 65' × 5'3" Paris, France (1982; *pl.* 1897).

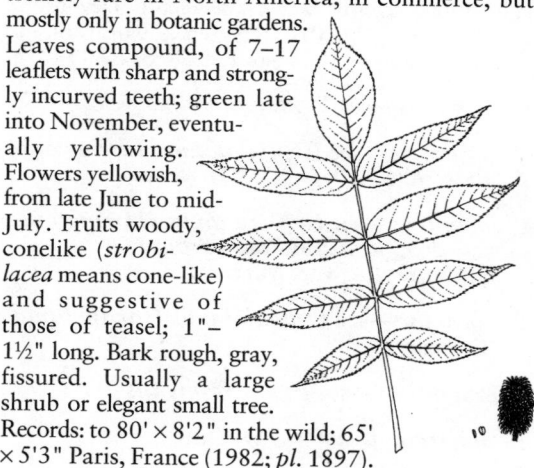

Platycladus orientalis*—see *Thuja orientalis

Podocarpus

[PODOCARPACEÆ; Podocarp Family] 90–100 spp. of coniferous evergreens grown for their decorative foliage. From Greek *podos* or *pous,* a foot, and *karpos,* a fruit: "foot-fruit" because of the long fleshy fruit-stalk of the species first described. Nearly all species are cold-tender; some are grown as houseplants. The only related genus in this volume is *Saxegothæa.*

Podocarpus andinus Poepp. *ex* Endl.

= *Prumnopitys elegans* Phil.
= *Prumnopitys andina* (Poepp. *ex* Endl.) De Laub.

PLUM FRUITED YEW. PLUM FIR. From S Chile, SW Argentina. (The name *andinus* means of the Andes. The generic name *Prumnopitys* is from *Prumnos*, Greek for the extreme or last, and *pitys*, a PINE.) Introduced in 1860 by R. Pearce from Valdivia to Veitch nursery of England. In North American commerce ≤1930. Extremely rare here. Needles paler than those of YEW (*Taxus*), ½"–1½" long. Male and female flowers usually on separate trees. Fruits called mountain grapes in Chile; yellowish-white, plum-like, edible. A bright green, fine-textured tree. Often shrubby in cultivation. Records: 71' × 4'3" Bicton, Devon, England (1968); 61' × 9'10" Tregrehan, Cornwall, England (1988); 35' tall at San Francisco, CA (1993).

P. chinensis—see P. macrophyllus

P. coraianus—see Cephalotaxus Harringtonia 'Fastigiata'

P. japonicus—see Cephalotaxus Harringtonia var. *drupacea* and Podocarpus macrophyllus var. Maki

P. koraiana—see Cephalotaxus Harringtonia 'Fastigiata'

P. longifolius—see P. macrophyllus

P. macrophyllus (Th.) D. Don

= *P. chinensis* hort.
= *P. longifolius* hort. *ex* Sieb.
= *P. sinensis macrophylla* hort.

YEW PINE. JAPANESE PODOCARP. LONGLEAF PODOCARP. YEW PODOCARP. SOUTHERN YEW. BUDDHIST PINE. From China, S Japan, and the Ryukyus. *Macrophyllus* from Greek *makro*-, large, and *phyllon*, a leaf. Introduced to Britain in 1804 by Captain Kirkpatrick of the East Indies Company. Introduced to the U.S. in 1862 by G.R. Hall. In commerce here ≤1888. Common. Leaves willowy, 3"–8" long, up to ½" wide. Fruit pea-sized, egg-shaped, powder-blue, borne on swollen, edible red stalks "like tiny red gum drops"; ripe in October-November. Usually a large, dense shrub in cultivation. Growth slow. Versatile: tolerates sun or shade, clipping, and container existence. Records: to 82' × 12'6" in the wild; 40' tall in Santa Barbara, CA; 20' × 4'0" × 30' Sacramento, CA (1989).

P. macrophyllus var. Maki Sieb. *ex* Endl.

= *P. japonicus* hort. *ex* Sieb.

Absolutely shrubby. Leaves only 1½"–3½" long, proportionately narrower. Several variegated cultivars were imported from Japan in the 1860s.

P. sinensis macrophylla—see P. macrophyllus

Poliothyrsis

[FLACOURTIACEÆ; Flacourtia Family] A genus of only the following species. From Greek *polios*, grayish white or hoary, and *thyrsos*, a panicle—from the color of the flower clusters. Related genera include *Azara* and *Idesia*.

P. sinensis Oliv.

PEARL-BLOOM TREE. From West-central China. Introduced in 1908 by E. Wilson to the Arnold Arboretum. Common in the wild, extremely rare in cultivation—but being promoted. A slender, loosely branched tree of an open, airy habit. Bark gray, deeply furrowed in age, like that of a BLACK OAK. Leaves vary considerably in size and shape, toothing and hairiness. When unfolding in spring they are downy and red-tinted. At maturity commonly to 7" × 3½"; stem to 2" long, red; leaf tip often markedly curved; underside coated with very short, inconspicuous hairs. Flowers small, in clusters 4"–8" long, not especially showy, but fragrant, yellowish-white to nearly white, in July–September. Seedpod ½"–¾" long, splitting into 3 and releasing many winged seeds. Records: 49' × 3'9" Caerhays, Cornwall, England (1971; now dead); 40' × 3'0" Glasnevin Botanic Garden, County Dublin, Ireland (1987); 36' × 1'11" Newcastle House, Glamorgan, Wales, (1991).

Poncirus

[RUTACEÆ; Rue Family] A genus of only 2 species, thorny, deciduous small trees. From *poncire*, the French name of a kind of CITRON. Citron, a town in Judæa, gave rise to the generic name *Citrus*. No *Citrus* species and hybrids are as cold-hardy as *Poncirus*, but some are far more hardy than is commonly known. (See catalogs of Woodlanders nursery of Aiken, NC, and Oregon Exotics, of Grants Pass, OR.) Related genera include *Fortunella*, *Phellodendron*, *Ptelea*, *Tetradium*, and *Zanthoxylum*.

P. trifoliata (L.) Raf.
= *Citrus trifoliata* L.
= *Ægle sepiaria* DC.

TRIFOLIATE ORANGE. HARDY ORANGE. BITTER ORANGE. THORNBUSH. LEMONBUSH. BENGAL QUINCE. From China and Korea. Named in 1763 (Latin *tri*, three, and *folium*, a leaf). Introduced from Japan to Holland by Siebold ca. 1844, and from China to England by R. Fortune in 1851. In North America long before 1869. Common here; naturalized in places. Used as a rootstock, it at once adds hardiness to *Citrus* trees and dwarfs them. Used for hybridizing, it also confers hardiness (it withstands -20°F). Crosses with the SWEET ORANGE (*C. sinensis*) are known as CITRANGES (× *Citroncitrus*), are hardier than regular *Citrus*, and also used as rootstocks. Used for ornament, *Poncirus* presents a unique appearance. Twigs deep green and stoutly thorny. A shrub or broad, small tree, it can be used as a hedge. Leaves emerge luminous yellow-green in spring, mature to glossy bright green; trifoliate; dropping yellow in fall. Flowers white and fragrant in April–May; 1½"–2" wide, of 4–7 petals. Fruit 1"–2½" wide, deep jade to emerald green, next rusty dark green, becoming rusty yellow, then soft yellow, finally bronzy-apricot; fuzzy, thick-skinned, seedy, and scant with juice—used as fuel rather than food in China. It is fragrant and ornamental. Records: to 35' tall says D. Wyman; 26' × 1'7" ×24' Harrisburg, PA (1968); 18' × 3'4" × 24' Annandale, VA (1986); 14' × 4'2" × 15' Aiken County, SC (1984).

P. trifoliata 'Monstrosa'
FLYING DRAGON. Japanese: *Hiryu*. Cultivated in China for centuries. Dwarf, in no sense a tree; branching contorted. Hardy to ca. -15°F.

Populus

[SALICACEÆ; Willow Family] 30–40 spp. of deciduous trees characterized by fast, rank growth. Nearly all in the temperate northern hemisphere. Male and female flowers on separate trees, in catkins. The genus comprises ASPENS, COTTONWOODS and POPLARS. *Populus* is the ancient Latin name of the POPLAR (conjectured from *arbor-populi* of the Romans, or the tree of the people; a POPLAR was much planted in Roman cities). POPLAR was the liberty tree of the French Revolution. In traditional China, POPLAR is one of the five official trees of mourning—especially for common people. A characteristic of many *Populus* species is the way the leaves rustle in the gentlest of breezes, because of their flattened leaf stems. L.H. Bailey wrote "The ripple of its foliage recalls the play of wavelets on a pebbly shore." Fall color is almost entirely pure yellow. Although *Populus* are easily propagated (except ASPENS), luxuriously leafy, and make handsome shade trees in a hurry, they present problems. The cottony seed-fluff released by females is messy. Bacterial canker attacks most species. Fast growth and relatively short life seem to go hand in hand. Greedy roots gobble garden space and can conquer sewers. Still, if planted in suitable locations, many POPLARS are excellent ornamental landscape trees. For the most part they have been planted on the prairies and Great Plains, where their role in shelterbelts is invaluable. They are also much planted for their tough, lightweight wood. Identification is difficult, experts disagree and confusion reigns. A closely related genus is *Salix* (WILLOW).

P. '44–52'—see P. × Petrowskiana 'Walker'

P. × acuminata Rydb.
= *P. coloradensis* Dode
(*P. angustifolia* × *P. deltoides* ssp. *monilifera*)

SMOOTHBARK COTTONWOOD or POPLAR. LANCELEAF COTTONWOOD. MOUNTAIN COTTONWOOD. Named in 1893 (for leaves that taper into a long narrow point; from Latin *acumen*, a sharp point). Introduced to cultivation in 1898. Common. A widespread hybrid between NARROWLEAF COTTONWOOD (*P. angustifolia*) and PLAINS COTTONWOOD (*P. deltoides* ssp. *monilifera*), ranging from Alberta and Saskatchewan south to New Mexico. Leaves ca. 4" × 2", glossy dark above, dull green beneath; yellow in fall. A round-topped tree, recorded to 80' × 8'4".

P. × acuminata 'Andrewsii'

= P. × Andrewsii Sarg.

= P. × Jackii 'Andrewsii'

A male clone named in 1913 after its introducer, Darwin Maxon Andrews (1869–1938), of Rockmont nursery, Boulder, CO. Long commercially extinct.

P. afghanica—see P. nigra 'Afghanica'

P. alba L.

WHITE POPLAR. SILVER POPLAR. SNOWY POPLAR. WOOLY POPLAR. WHITE ASPEN. ABELE. From N Africa and west-central Asia. Rarely cultivated in its typical version; mostly represented by cultivars 'Nivea' (female) and 'Pyramidalis' (male). The name ABELE derives from Dutch *Abeel* (applied to P. × canescens) in turn from Latin *albus*, white, in reference to the white leaf undersides and pale-colored young bark. Records (doubtless some specimens cited are really P. × canescens, GRAY POPLAR, which often is called WHITE POPLAR; others are the clone 'Nivea'): 140' × 21'3" Troyes, France (1882); 131' × 13'1" Jarogniewice, Poland (≤1973); 124' × 19'8" Chelmno, Poland (≤1973); 96' × 20'11" × 79' Fond du Lac, WI (1961); 93' × 21'11" × 86' St. Charles, IL (1992); 90' × 25'3" × 97' Onawa, IA (1985); 86' × 19'0" × 112' south of Chaveroix, MI (1979).

P. alba var. acerifolia—see P. alba 'Nivea'

P. alba var. arembergica—see P. alba 'Nivea'

P. alba 'Argentea'—see P. alba 'Nivea'

P. alba var. Bolleana—see P. alba 'Pyramidalis'

P. alba var. canescens—see P. × canescens

P. alba 'Fastigiata'—see P. alba 'Pyramidalis'

P. alba macrophylla—see P. × canescens 'Macrophylla'

P. alba 'Nivea'

= P. alba 'Argentea'

= P. alba var. acerifolia (Lodd.) Loud.

= P. alba var. arembergica (Lodd.) Loud.

= P. × canescens 'Nivea'

SILVER POPLAR. Named in 1789. 'Nivea' is Latin for snowy, referring to the dense felt of white hairs covering the leaf underside. The most common P. alba clone. Female; catkins light green. Usually sold just as "P. alba."

Customarily leaning, suckering from the roots, its lower trunk dark and chunky, upper portion pale creamy-gray. Often making MAPLE-shaped leaves (of 3–5 lobes) which lead people to call it SILVER MAPLE. The leaves on moderate twigs 1½"–3½"; on strong suckers, to 6¾".

P. alba 'Picardi'—see P. × canescens 'Macrophylla'

P. alba 'Pyramidalis'

= P. alba f. pyramidalis (Bge.) Dipp.

= P. alba var. pyramidalis Bge.

= P. alba var. Bolleana (Lauche) Otto

= P. Bolleana Lauche

= P. alba 'Fastigiata'

= P. alba 'Roumi'

PYRAMIDAL WHITE POPLAR. BOLLEANA (WHITE) POPLAR. BOLLE POPLAR. SILVER LOMBARDY POPLAR. Origin cloudy; found in 1841 apparently growing wild in the mountains between Bokhara and Samarkand. Named in 1854. Introduced to western Europe and the U.S. ca. 1872. Common. The 1878 *Bolleana* name is likely after Carl August Bolle (1821–1909). A male clone (female equivalents may exist in the wild). Bark smoky-cream colored. Habit fastigiate in youth, broadening to form a gigantic goblet. The leaves are not so white beneath, nor so MAPLE-like (except on young vigorous shoots and root-suckers) as those of 'Nivea'; in fact they far more resemble those of GRAY POPLAR (P. × canescens); commonly 2½"–3½" long. Records: 125' × 10'6" Butchart Gardens, B.C. (1972); 119' × 17'7" × 57' Vashon, WA (1992); 110' × 21'7" × 67' Vashon, WA (1992); 101' × 16'3" × 81' Seattle, WA (1987).

P. alba 'Raket'

ROCKET POPLAR. Raised in Holland <1956, an intentional cross of a wild P. alba and the clone 'Pyramidalis'. In European commerce since 1972. In North American commerce ≤1979. More common in Canada than the U.S. Habit very narrow. Leaves more silvery than those of 'Pyramidalis'.

P. alba 'Richardii'

GOLDLEAF WHITE POPLAR. Originated ca. 1910 in the Netherlands. Described in 1912; named after Richard, nurseryman of Naarden-bussum (near Amsterdam). Exceedingly rare in North America; here ≤1916. Compared to P. alba 'Nivea' it is much slower, less vigorous, shorter-lived, with many of its leaves bright yellow above. Record: 72' × 5'3" Lisle, IL (1986; *pl.* 1946).

P. alba 'Roumi'—see *P. alba* 'Pyramidalis'

P. alba var. *tomentosa*—see *P. tomentosa*

P. 'Andover'
(*P. nigra* var. *betulifolia* × *P. balsamifera* ssp. *trichocarpa*)

ANDOVER POPLAR. Bred intentionally in Maine. Described in 1934. Rare. Named after Andover, Maine. Record: 118' × 6'10" Thorp Perrow, Yorkshire, England (1990; *pl.* 1950).

P. × *Andrewsii*—see *P.* × *acuminata* 'Andrewsii'

P. 'Androscoggin'
(*P. Maximowiczii* × *P. balsamifera* ssp. *trichocarpa*)
= *P.* 'N.E. 41'

ANDROSCOGGIN POPLAR. Bred intentionally in Maine. Described in 1934. Named after the Androscoggin River. Common. Male. Leaves 6"–8" × 3¼"–4⅞"; stem 2⅜"–4". Record: 103' × 5'6" United Kingdom (1978; *pl.* 1958).

P. angulata—see *P. deltoides* and *P. deltoides* 'Carolin'

P. angulata 'Cordata'—see *P. deltoides* 'Cordata'

P. angulata var. *missouriensis*—see *P. deltoides*

P. angustifolia (James *ex* Long) Torr.
= *P. fortissima* Nels. & Macbr.

NARROWLEAF COTTONWOOD or POPLAR. WILLOWLEAF POPLAR. From SW Canada to Mexico, mostly in the Rocky Mountains. Named in 1823 (*angustifolia* means narrow-leaved; from Latin *angustus*, narrow, and *folium*, a leaf). Introduced to cultivation ≤1890. Common and easily distinguished. In the BALSAM POPLAR group. Twigs slender. Leaves WILLOW-like, to 7" × 1¾"; finely toothed, green on both sides. Bark pale green when young. Its hybrids with *P. deltoides* are called *P.* × *acuminata*. Records: 105' × 15'6" × 55' near Mancos, CO (1967); 79' × 26'2" × 80' Malheur County, OR (1973).

P. arizonica—see *P. Fremontii*

P. atheniensis—see *P. tremuloides*

P. Baileyana—see *P.* × *Jackii*

P. balsamifera L. (cf. *P. deltoides*)
= *P. Tacamahacca* Mill.

BALSAM POPLAR. EASTERN BALSAM POPLAR. HACKMATACK. TACAMAHAC. From Alaska to Newfoundland, across Canada and the N–NE United States, dipping farther south in the Rockies (into Colorado). Cultivated since 1689. Seldom planted. Name from Latin *balsamum*, balsam, and *ferre*, to bear. HACKMATACK and TACAMAHAC are native American names. Known by its dark, shiny foliage and fragrant, sticky buds. Leaves green above, whitish and stained rusty beneath; to 6" × 4". A tall, narrow-crowned tree. Records: to 150' × 22'0" in NW Canada says J. Kirkwood; 138' × 13'7" Champion, MI (1984); 128' × 13'9" × 57' Michigan (1994); 105' × 16'5" Sandwich, NH (1984); 98' × 17'0" South Egremont, MA (1968).

P. balsamifera 'Aurora'—see *P.* 'Candicans Aurora'

P. balsamifera 'Balm of Gilead'—see *P.* 'Candicans'

P. balsamifera var. *Michauxii* (Dode) Henry
= *P. balsamifera* var. *subcordata* Hylander
= *P. Tacamahacca* var. *Michauxii* (Dode) Farwell

HEARTLEAF BALSAM POPLAR. Named in 1905 after French naturalist François André Michaux (1770–1855). Horticulturists don't bother to distinguish this variety, but it warrants mention here because it is likely one parent of the widely-planted BALM OF GILEAD (*P.* 'Candicans'). Leaves slightly hairy beneath, round or heart-shaped at the base, commonly ca. 3" × 2¾".

P. balsamifera 'Mojave Hybrid'—see *P.* 'Mojave Hybrid'

P. balsamifera var. *suaveolens*—see *P. Simonii* 'Fastigiata'

P. balsamifera var. *subcordata*—see *P. balsamifera* var. *Michauxii*

P. *balsamifera* ssp. *trichocarpa* (T. & G. *ex* Hook.) Brayshaw

= *P. trichocarpa* T. & G. *ex* Hook.

BLACK COTTONWOOD. WESTERN BALSAM POPLAR. OREGON BALSAM POPLAR. BLACK BALSAM POPLAR. ROTTENWOOD. BALM. From S Alaska to NW Mexico. Named in 1852 (Greek *tricho*, hairy, and *karpos*, fruit). Introduced to cultivation in 1892. Very rarely cultivated, even within its native range, growing too enormous. The tallest *Populus*, a towering, imposing tree of immense vigor, its trunk less massive and crown less broad than that of *P. deltoides*. Differs from typical *P. balsamifera* in seed-capsules trilobed and hairy instead of bi-lobed and hairless; also suckers from the roots less frequently. Male catkins to 5" long. Leaves commonly ca. 5" long, to 15½" × 10⅜". Records: to 230' tall says J.K. Henry; 188' × 13'7" Olympic National Park, WA (1988); 180' × 20'6" Goldstream Park, B.C. (cut 1985); 155' × 26'3" Willamette Mission State Park, OR (1984); 147' × 30'2" near Salem, OR (1969); 142' × 30'0" Skumalasph Island, B.C. (1992); 101' × 32'6" near Haines, AK (1965).

P. 'Bassano'

The offspring of a *P. deltoides* which had been pollinated by a RUSSIAN POPLAR (i.e., a *P. laurifolia* or hybrid thereof). Grown somewhat in the Canadian prairie region.

P. *benzoifera pendula*—see *P. tremuloides* 'Pendula'

P. × *Bernardii*—see *P.* × *Jackii* 'Northwest'

P. × *berolinensis* (K. Koch) Dipp.
(*P. laurifolia* × *P. nigra*)

BERLIN POPLAR. Originated at the Berlin Botanic Garden; named in 1865. In North America ≤1890. Previously much cultivated in the prairie regions, now uncommon in commerce. The male parent was LOMBARDY POPLAR (*P. nigra* 'Italica'), so it is very narrow, yet not strictly fastigiate. A female clone; cotton not very messy. Leaves diamond-shaped, 1½"–4" long (to 6½" on sucker shoots), pale greenish-white beneath, with short, inconspicuous hairs; stem hairy. Records: 109' × 12'1½" × 55' La Ferme, Québec (<1994); 108' × 10'9" Prested Hall, Essex, England (1977); 98' × 11'10" Sobolice, Poland (≤1973); 90' × 8'8" × 55' Tacoma, WA (1993).

P. × *berolinensis* 'Certinensis'

= *P.* 'Certinensis'

CERTINES POPLAR. In German commerce ≤1885. Probably arose in France, because Certines is a town ca. 35 miles NW of Lyon. In North America ≤1890; sold here ≤1927. Male; catkins to 4¾" long. Habit much broader than that of typical *P.* × *berolinensis*. Twigs round, beige, hairy. Leaves to 4¾" long, broader than those of the female (typical) *P.* × *berolinensis* and rounded at the base; stems hairy. Flushes early in spring and drops its leaves early in fall—quite the first POPLAR to turn yellow in Seattle—in late September. Record: 115' × 8'6" × 54' Seattle, WA (1988).

P. × *berolinensis* 'Frye'

= *P.* 'Frye'

FRYE POPLAR. Bred intentionally in Maine. Described in 1934 (after the Frye, Maine, nursery of the Oxford Paper Company).

P. × *berolinensis* 'Rumford'

= *P.* 'Rumford'

RUMFORD POPLAR. Bred intentionally in Maine. Described in 1934. Named after Rumford, Maine, home of the Oxford Paper Company.

P. × *berolinensis* 'Strathglass'

= *P.* 'Strathglass'

STRATHGLASS POPLAR. Bred intentionally in Maine. Described in 1934.

P. *betulifolia*—see *P. nigra* var. *betulifolia*

P. *Bolleana*—see *P. alba* 'Pyramidalis'

P. *brevifolia*—see *P. Simonii*

P. 'Brooks No. 1'

= *P.* 'Griffin'
= *P. deltoides* 'Griffin'
= *P.* × *petrowskiana* 'Griffin'
?[*P. deltoides* ssp. *monilifera* × (*P. deltoides* × *P. laurifolia*)]

GRIFFIN POPLAR. Originated as a chance seedling of a *P. deltoides* ssp. *monilifera* (PLAINS COTTONWOOD), the pollen parent a RUSSIAN POPLAR (i.e., a *P. laurifolia* or hybrid thereof). Six male clones were selected <1960 by E. Griffin at Brooks research station of Alberta. No. 1 is very early to flush and defoliate, and cannot tolerate early autumn or late spring frosts, so is not suited to the Canadian prairies. Leaf triangular, as wide as long, stem pink and finely hairy, sometimes with glands. Resists leaf rust, but is highly susceptible to canker and borers.

P. 'Brooks No. 2'

Origin as above. Common in W Canada; most common of the six Brooks clones. Narrowly pyramidal. Very cold-hardy. Low shade resistance. A good ornamental for cold, dry zones.

P. 'Brooks No. 3'

Origin as above. Very rare. Poorly suited to Canadian prairie life.

P. 'Brooks No. 4'

Origin as above. Uncommon. Of limited use on Canadian prairies.

P. 'Brooks No. 5'

Origin as above. Rare. Of moderate use on Canadian prairies.

P. 'Brooks No. 6'

Origin as above. Not as common as 'Brooks No. 2' but more common than the others. Of moderate use on Canadian prairies.

P. 'Brunkild'

In commerce ≤1979 in Montana.

P. × canadensis Moench. 1785, non Michx. fil. 1813

=*P. × euramericana* Guinier
(*P. deltoides* × *P. nigra*)

HYBRID BLACK POPLAR. Since the 1700s, crosses have occurred between the common eastern North American COTTONWOOD (*P. deltoides*) and Europe's BLACK POPLAR (*P. nigra*). As a whole, such offspring are tough and possess proverbial hybrid vigor. Widely planted for wood production, their role as ornamentals is minor. Most of the cultivars are male (even though they may have feminine names). They are distinguished not so much by leaf characteristics as by overall form, rate of growth and time of flushing. ASPEN-like when young, they soon grow into dramatic, picturesque giants, reaching truly awe-inspiring proportions with advanced age. Some bear long colorful catkins in spring; "jewelled tassels" W. Jepson called them. Others have new leaves unfolding a bright red-orange at the same time. Leaves more or less triangular and conspicuously toothed, usually without glands, 2"–4" (6") long or wide.

P. × canadensis 'Aurea'—see P. × canadensis 'Serotina Aurea'

P. × canadensis 'Casale'

In commerce during the 1980s in California.

P. × canadensis 'Eugenei'

= *P. × Eugenei* Sim.-Louis *ex* K. Koch
= *P. deltoides Eugenei* hort.
= *P. carolinensis* hort. (in part; cf. *P. deltoides*), non Moench
= *P. carolina* hort. (in part; cf. *P. deltoides*)

CAROLINA POPLAR (in part; cf. *P. deltoides*). (PRINCE) EUGENE'S POPLAR. Originated in 1832 at Simon-Louis nursery near Metz, France, from *P. × canadensis* 'Regenerata' pollinated by LOMBARDY POPLAR (*P. nigra* 'Italica'). A male clone, by far the most common cultivar in its class. In the early 1900s it was grossly overplanted in many American cities. But its roots can readily heave concrete or invade sewers, and its branches are prone to storm breakage, so it has been banned from streetside planting in many cities. The name CAROLINA POPLAR is used both for this cultivar and for specimens (clonal or seedlings) of *P. deltoides*. The original 'Eugenei' has, according to European descriptions, a narrow crown, and smaller leaves than those of related cultivars. The leaf stem rarely bears glands (unlike *P. deltoides*). Many such trees have been planted in North America. In some locales, however, they became outnumbered by a clone originally called NORWAY POPLAR (*P.* 'Norway'), but sold as an "improved" CAROLINA POPLAR. Records: 150'×25'0" the original specimen in France (1913); 141' × 14'0" Colesborne, Gloucestershire, England (1984; *pl.* 1903); 124' × 16'5" Walla Walla, WA (1988); 113' × 18'7" Blaine, WA (1988).

P. × canadensis 'Gelrica'

= *P.* 'Gelrica'

DUTCH POPLAR. Said to be *P. canadensis* 'Marilandica' × *P. canadensis* 'Serotina' (same parentage as *P. × canadensis* 'Regenerata'). Originated ca. 1865 in Holland. Extremely rare in North America until the 1960s. Grown primarily in Canada. Male. Similar to *P. × canadensis* 'Serotina' but with paler (whitish) bark; leaves flush a fortnight earlier. Very late to defoliate.

P. × canadensis 'Imperial'

= P. 'Imperial'

Introduced ≤1979 by the USDA Soil Conservation Service. In commerce. Male. Broadly columnar to narrowly pyramidal; 50'–120' tall. Very cold-hardy.

P. × canadensis 'Incrassata'

= P. incrissata canadensis hort.

Origin unknown. Believed to be a BLACK POPLAR hybrid, first named in 1905, when said to be a female with leaves to 2¼" long and wide, thick, and deeply heart-shaped. Tested in Canada in 1951, and found a poor performer at Indian Head, Saskatchewan. Listed ≤1991 by Siebenthaler nursery of Dayton, OH.

P. × canadensis 'Marilandica'

= P. × marilandica Bosc ex Poir.

MAY POPLAR. A seedling of a BLACK POPLAR (P. nigra) pollinated by P. × canadensis 'Serotina' about 1800, in Holland or France. Named in 1816 (mistakenly believed to have come from Maryland). In French commerce ≤1838. Extremely rare in North America. Leaves glossy, light, and wave in the wind very prettily, shining like thousands of miniature mirrors on an airy, open crown not so heavy or breakage-prone as on 'Eugenei' and 'Robusta'. Clear light yellow fall color in mid-October, followed by the more golden color of P. × canadensis 'Eugenei'. Alas, it is female, and its catkins can lengthen to 8¾", releasing much sterile cotton in June. Young leaves minutely hairy and slightly coppery but very soon green. Records: 131' × 19'4" Peper Harrow, Surrey, England (1987); 115' × 17'0" Kew, England (1974; pl. ca. 1846); 100' × 9'6" and 82' × 10'10" Seattle, WA (1988).

P. × canadensis 'Prairie Sky'

= P. 'Prairie Sky'

(P. nigra 'Afghanica' × P. deltoides ssp. monilifera) Bred at Morden research station of Manitoba. Selected in 1978. Introduced ≤1993. Tall, narrow. Male. Highly canker-resistant. Hardier than most clones in the canadensis group.

P. × canadensis 'Regenerata'

= P. × regenerata Henry

= P. eucalyptus hort.

RAILWAY POPLAR. From a nursery at Arcueil, near Paris, France, in 1814. Likely a seedling of P. × canadensis 'Marilandica' pollinated by P. × canadensis 'Serotina'. Called by the French Peuplier Regeneré. Commonly planted along certain British railways. Extremely rare in North America. Female, with catkins to 6¾" long, most of which drop well before ripening their cotton. Leaf often subcordate at base. A darker foliage mass than P. × canadensis 'Marilandica' has, and a taller, narrower tree, with redder leaves in spring. Records: 131' × 14'5" Boultham Park, Lincolnshire, England (1983); 125' × 15'0" Harnham Road, Salisbury, Wiltshire, England (1984); 111' × 13'0" Tacoma, WA (1988); 109' × 12'10" Seattle, WA (1988).

P. × canadensis 'Robusta'

= P. × robusta (Sim.-Louis) Schneid.

= P. deltoides 'Robusta'

= P. vernirubens Henry

GIANT POPLAR. A male that arose ca. 1885–1890 at the French nursery of Simon-Louis, as a seedling of an eastern U.S. COTTONWOOD (P. deltoides 'Cordata') pollinated by P. nigra 'Plantierensis'. Named in 1904. Common in North America. One of various clones sold as COTTONLESS COTTONWOOD. Earliest to flush of the canadensis group; very pronounced coppery young growth. From the male parent it inherited the hairy twigs which distinguish it from most canadensis clones. Records: to 136' × 16'0" in Europe; 122' × 11'0" Tacoma, WA (1988); 85' × 11'10" Seattle, WA (1988).

P. × canadensis 'Serotina'

= P. × serotina Hartig

BLACK ITALIAN POPLAR. Probably originated in France in the early 1700s, from an eastern U.S. COTTONWOOD pollinated by a BLACK POPLAR (P. nigra). It was planted in Switzerland, then Italy, finally in England, where it was called the BLACK ITALIAN POPLAR. Very rare in North America. Its relatively late leafing is a key distinguishing feature, and accounts for the 1775 name serotina (Latin for late-coming). A broad-crowned tree of immense size. Records: 151' × 17'5" Abbeyleix, County Leix, Ireland (1985); 150' × 21'0" Fairlawne, Kent, England (1976); 125' × 22'6" Chelsworth, Suffolk, England (1976); 105' × 12'0" Ottawa, Ontario (1975); 102' × 10'2" Tacoma, WA (1993); 98' × 11'4" Seattle, WA (1988).

P. × canadensis 'Serotina Aurea'

= P. × canadensis 'Aurea'

= P. × canadensis 'Van Geertii'

= P. deltoides 'Aurea'

= P. deltoides aurea van Geert

GOLDEN POPLAR. The Belgium nurseryman van Geert found this ca. 1867 as a sport on a 'Serotina' POPLAR, and in 1872 introduced it to commerce. Described in 1876. Sold in North America ≤1888. Uncommon. Young foliage bright yellow. Slower and denser than typical 'Serotina'. Records: 108' × 10'9" Osterley

Park, Hounslow, London, England (1982); 99' × 12'1" near Puyallup, WA (1992); 88½' × 12'4" Manor Park, Aldershot, Hampshire, England (1989).

P. × canadensis 'Van Geertii'—see P. × canadensis 'Serotina Aurea'

P. 'Candicans'

= *P.* × *gileadensis* Roul.
= *P.* × *Jackii* 'Gileadensis'
= *P. balsamifera* 'Balm of Gilead'
= *P. ontariensis* Desf. *ex* Loud.
= *P. candicans* auct. (in part)

BALM OF GILEAD. HYBRID TACAMAHAC. ONTARIO POP-LAR. Origin unknown. Probably a hybrid from ca. 1755, or a sport of *P. balsamifera*. The 1789 epithet *candicans* means whitish; from Latin *candidus*, meaning bright white or hoary-white; in reference to the leaf undersides. Common in North America since the Colonial period, especially in Rhode Island, Massachusetts and New Hampshire. Presently scarcely in commerce. A sterile female, making loads of cotton. Nurseries selling COTTONLESS COTTONWOODS under the name *P. candicans* are really selling male clones of *P.* × *canadensis* or other kinds. The real BALM OF GILEAD has an agreeable balsam fragrance in spring, handsome, dark foliage, is fast-growing and tolerant of poor sites, but its abundant cotton is objectionable, and it suckers madly. Leaves differ from those of *P. balsamifera* in being quite hairy, broader and more coarsely toothed; commonly 5½" × 4", very dark green above, whitish beneath. Catkins ca. 6" long. A broad, irregular tree. Records: 97' × 7'0" Syon House, London, England (<1964); 89' × 11'11" × 78' near Cornell, MI (1959); a trunk nearly 31'0" around at Newburgh, NY (≤1881).

P. 'Candicans Aurora'

= *P.* × *candicans* 'Variegata'
= *P. balsamifera* 'Aurora'

AURORA POPLAR. Introduced in the 1920s by Treseder nursery of Truro, Cornwall, England, who obtained their stock from a garden in north Devon. Named 'Aurora' in 1954, after the goddess of dawn, because of its colorful spring foliage. Introduced to North America in 1966 by the Arnold Arboretum. In commerce here since the 1980s; very rare. Young foliage splashed creamy white and pink. Sometimes grown as a foliage plant in perennial borders, and pruned to the ground each winter, resulting in leaves as large as 11" × 10". Records: 75' × 3'9" Wisley, Surrey, England (1983); 62' × 5'0" Cockington Court, Devon, England (1984).

P. × candicans 'Mojave Hybrid'—see P. 'Mojave Hybrid'

P. × candicans 'Variegata'—see P. 'Candicans Aurora'

P. × candicans 'White'—see P. 'White'

P. × canescens (Ait.) Sm.

= *P. alba* var. *canescens* Ait.
(*P. alba* × *P. tremula*)

GRAY or GREY POPLAR. In botanical Latin, *canescens* means grayish-white, hoary. Common in North America since the 1800s. Frequently misidentified as WHITE POPLAR (*P. alba*). Contemporary nurseries almost never list this under its proper name. Leaves roundish, 2"–3¼", with a few big teeth (suggesting *P. grandidentata*), gray-hairy only when young. Records: to 164' tall says R. Meikle; 151' × 19'0" Birr Castle, County Offaly, Ireland (1990); 125' × 18'4" × 170' near Weston, MO (1960); 95' × 21'3" × 90' near Florida, OH (1950); 87' × 13'6" × 74' Olympia, WA (1993).

P. × canescens 'Macrophylla'

= *P. alba macrophylla* hort.
= *P. macrophylla* hort. (in part)
= *P.* × *canescens* 'Picard'
= *P. Picardi* hort.
= *P. alba* 'Picardi'

PICART'S or PICCART'S POPLAR. Origin unknown. Greek *macro*, large, and *phyllon*, leaf. In Dutch commerce since ≤1914–15. In North America since at least 1939, when imported from England by the Arnold Arboretum. In commerce here ≤1980. Rare. Forest Farm nursery of Williams, OR, supplies the following description: Large (up to 6") leaves provide fine yellow or red fall color; creamy gray bark; long, wooly male catkins in late winter; distinctive and decorative; vigorous and fast.

P. × canescens 'Nivea'—see P. alba 'Nivea'

P. × canescens 'Pendula'

WEEPING GRAY POPLAR. Origin shrouded in mystery. J. Paxton says this was introduced to England from North America in 1820. J. Loudon lists *P. alba* 'Pendula' under his section of varieties referable to *P. alba* or *canescens*, saying F. Mertens (d. 1831) described it. Neither of these early references is certain to apply to the male clone given botanical legitimacy (as *P. canescens* f. *pendula* Dipp.) in 1892. The extent of its occurrence in North America is unknown, but it has been in commerce and somewhat planted, though extinct commercially for decades, at least under its proper name. Doubtless it has been confused with *P.* 'Pseudograndidentata' and / or *P. tremula* 'Pendula'. Records: 82' × 6'2" and 54' × 8'9" Seattle, WA (1988).

P. × *canescens* 'Picard'—see *P.* × *canescens* 'Macrophylla'

P. × *canescens* 'Tower'

TOWER POPLAR. An intentional cross of *P. alba* × *P. tremula* 'Erecta'. Introduced in 1979 by W. Ronald of Morden research station, Manitoba. Male. Common. Easier to propagate than the erect ASPEN cultivar. Leaves glossy green above, furry white beneath. Fall color rich yellow.

P. carolina—see *P.* × *canadensis* 'Eugenei' and *P. deltoides*

P. carolinensis—see *P.* × *canadensis* 'Eugenei' and *P. deltoides*

P. cathayana Rehd.
= *P. suaveolens* auct. (in part), non Fisch. (cf. *P. Maximowiczii*)

CATHAY POPLAR. MONGOLIAN POPLAR. From northwest China to Manchuria and Korea. Introduced in 1908 by E. Wilson. Named in 1931, after an old name for China. In North American commerce sparingly, perhaps chiefly from the late 1940s into the late 1950s. It has been confused with *P. Maximowiczii* (a very rare and bolder species) and *P. Simonii* (a common, finer-textured species). Bark attractively pale (whitish-gray). Leaves ca. 4" × 2¾"; hairless. Twigs stout and round. Male catkins short, ≤2⅜" long. Female catkins up to nearly 8" long at maturity. Records: to 100' × 10'0" in Szechuan; 85' tall at Hillier Arboretum, Hampshire, England (1990); 62' × 3'5" Seattle, WA (1994; *pl.* 1971).

P. cathayana var. *Schneideri* Rehd.

From Yunnan, China. Named in 1931 after botanist Camillo Karl Schneider (1876–1951). Not recognized in horticulture, or even by most botanists. Twigs, buds and leaves finely hairy. Leaves not subcordate. Some specimens of what were presumed to be typical *P. cathayana* were examined by the writer, and they would seem to be referrable to this variety. They had leaves dark green above, whitish-green or perhaps gray-green beneath; bluntly toothed; the base broadly rounded to subcordate; the underside hairy if closely examined—a unique sort of appressed pubescence of white hairs by the base of the midrib. Sticky buds. Twigs first green, then gray on sunny side, brown on shady side; round. Leaves to 4" × 2¾"; stems grooved, to 2⅜" long.

P. 'Certinensis'—see *P.* × *berolinensis* 'Certinensis'

P. charkowiensis—see *P. nigra* 'Charkowiensis'

P. coloradensis—see *P.* × *acuminata*

P. 'Cordeniensis'

MORDEN POPLAR. A *P. balsamifera* hybrid introduced <1968 by Morden research station of Manitoba. Rare. Male. Very early to flush and defoliate, it is hurt by early autumn or late spring frosts. Susceptible to canker and leaf rust. Leaf nearly twice as long as wide, grayish-green beneath, finely toothed.

P. deltoides Bartr. *ex* Marsh.
= *P. angulata* Ait.
= *P. angulata* var. *missouriensis* Henry
= *P. virginiana* Foug.
= *P. carolinensis* Moench.
= *P. carolina* hort. (in part; cf. *P.* × *canadensis* 'Eugenei')
= *P. balsamifera* L. (in part)

EASTERN COTTONWOOD. SOUTHERN COTTONWOOD. NECKLACE POPLAR. From the Gulf Coast to Massachusetts, central Illinois and Ohio, to east Texas and Oklahoma. Named from *Delta*—Δ—4th letter of the Greek alphabet, and -*oides*, resemblance; leaf shaped like a triangle. A variable, widespread species; trees from the north bear smaller leaves, commonly 3"–5" long and wide; trees from the south bear larger leaves, commonly 5"–9" long. The trunk tends to fork low into massive arms making a broad crown. Records: to 190' tall says H. Fowells; 170' × 18'9" Wabash County, IL (<1875); 137' × 26'3" × 158' Wayne, MI (<1979); 132' × 31'1" Grundy County, IL (1984); 110' × 29'6" Seneca, WI (1987); 96' × 35'0" × 121' Gosper County, NE (1991); 85' × 36'1" × 121' Minidoka Dam, ID (1991); 78' × 34'1" × 126' Tama County, IA (1979).

P. deltoides 'Aurea'—see *P.* × *canadensis* 'Serotina Aurea'

P. deltoides aurea van Geerti—see *P.* × *canadensis* 'Serotina Aurea'

P. deltoides 'Carolin'
= P. angulata hort.

CAROLINA POPLAR (of Europe, not of North America). Presumably a male mutant of a southern U.S. COTTONWOOD (P. deltoides) that originated ca. 1750 in SW Europe. Its chief difference is that the catkin scales are merely coarsely toothed, not deeply divided as in its relatives. Twigs usually strongly angled. Leaves longer than broad. 'Cordata' is a similar female clone. Both do well in hot climates and stay green late into fall.

P. deltoides 'Cordata'
= P. angulata 'Cordata'

Described officially in 1861, in France. Like P. deltoides 'Carolin' except female, with greenish leaf stems (not reddish), and more cold-hardy.

P. deltoides Eugenei—see P. × canadensis 'Eugenei'

P. deltoides 'Griffin'—see P. 'Brooks No. 1'

P. deltoides 'Mighty Moe'
Introduced <1990 by the Nebraska agricultural experiment station, Lincoln. In commerce. A male clone.

P. deltoides ssp. monilifera (Ait.) Eckenwalder
= P. deltoides var. occidentalis Rydb.
= P. occidentalis (Rydb.) Britt. ex Rydb.
= P. monilifera Ait.
= P. Sargentii Dode
= P. texana Sarg.

(GREAT) PLAINS COTTONWOOD. NORTHERN COTTONWOOD. TEXAS COTTONWOOD. WESTERN BROADLEAF COTTONWOOD. From the Great Lakes and prairie provinces, south to the Texas panhandle. The 1789 name monilifera means necklace-bearing; from Latin monile, a necklace, and ferre, to yield or bear (referring to the elongated seedpods). Cultivated ≤1908; commonly sold and planted only within or near its native range. Leaves usually wider (ca. 4") than long, not as large as those of typical P. deltoides, usually with 2 glands at the base, and with fewer and coarser teeth. Twigs yellowish. Buds often hairy. Record: 120' × 29'8" × 93' near Hygiene, CO (<1967); ca. 1972, the same tree was claimed to be 105' × 36'0" × 93'.

P. deltoides var. occidentalis —see P. deltoides ssp. monilifera

P. deltoides 'Robusta'—see P. × canadensis 'Robusta'

P. deltoides 'Siouxland'
= P. 'Siouxland'

COTTONLESS COTTONWOOD. Introduced <1965 by the South Dakota experiment station. Common. Resistant but not immune to leaf rust. Leaves slightly larger than average. Golden in fall.

P. deltoides 'Walker'—see P. × Petrowskiana 'Walker'

P. deltoides ssp. Wislizeni (S. Wats.) Eckenwalder
= P. Wislizeni (S. Wats.) Sarg.
= P. Fremontii var. Wislizeni S. Wats.
= P. Fremontii ssp. Wislizeni (S. Wats.) E. Murr.

RIO GRANDE COTTONWOOD. From the southwest U.S.—El Paso, Texas, north to NE Arizona, E Utah and W Colorado. Named in 1878 for its discoverer, Friedrich Adolph Wislizenus (1810–1889), German-born physician of St. Louis, MO, who made an important plant collection in northern Mexico in 1846–47. A common shade tree in New Mexico. Unlike typical P. deltoides, young leaves hairless, have no glands, are broader, with fewer and coarser teeth; floral stems longer, and buds hairy. Record: 110' × 28'6" × 127' near Fort Davis, TX (1976).

P. dilatata—see P. nigra 'Italica'

P. 'Dunlop'—see P. × Petrowskiana 'Dunlop'

P. elegans—see P. nigra 'Elegans'

P. eucalyptus—see P. × canadensis 'Regenerata'

P. × Eugenei—see P. × canadensis 'Eugenei'

P. × euramericana—see P. × canadensis

P. fastigiata—see P. nigra 'Italica'

P. fortissima—see P. angustifolia

P. Fremontii S. Wats.
= P. arizonica Sarg. misapplied

FREMONT COTTONWOOD. VALLEY COTTONWOOD. WESTERN COTTONWOOD. From the SW United States, and Mexico. Named in 1875 after John Charles Frémont (1813–1890), a politician, explorer, soldier, and discoverer of this species. Cultivated commonly in its native range. Young leaves minutely hairy on both sides on the whole surface, the stem more clearly so; to 4" wide, more or less triangular, with rounded teeth. Records: 113' × 19'7" near Aztec, NM (1967); 94' × 34'10" × 103' near Patagonia, AZ (1970); 87' × 37'10" × 102' Old Fate McCauley Ranch, NM (1986).

P. Fremontii var. *Wislizeni*—see *P. deltoides* ssp. *Wislizeni*

P. Fremontii 'Zappetini'
Named after George Zappetini, owner of a nursery in California's Central Valley. In commerce ≤1989.

P. 'Frye'—see *P.* × *berolinensis* 'Frye'

P. 'Gelrica'—see *P.* × *canadensis* 'Gelrica'

P. × *generosa*—see *P.* × *Jackii* 'Generosa'

P. 'Geneva'
(*P. Maximowiczii* × *P. berolinensis* 'Certinensis')
GENEVA POPLAR. Bred intentionally in Maine. Described in 1934. Strongly resembles *P. Maximowiczii* but is easier to propagate from cuttings, and more cold-hardy. A clone of the same parentage is *P.* 'Oxford'.

P. × *gileadensis*—see *P.* 'Candicans'

P. græca—see *P. grandidentata* and *P. tremuloides*

P. græca var. *pendula*—see *P.* 'Pseudograndidentata'

P. grandidentata Michx.
= *P. tremula* ssp. *grandidentata* (Michx.) A. & D. Löve
= *P. græca* hort. (in part; cf. *P. tremuloides*)
BIGTOOTH ASPEN. LARGETOOTH ASPEN. CANADIAN ASPEN. From northeastern North America. Named in 1803. Seldom cultivated. Young leaves heavily white-felted, at maturity nearly hairless, dark and dull, 2"–6" long, with few (5–12, rarely to 16 per side), big teeth; stem flattened. Records: 132' × 8'9" Marquette, MI (1984); 102' × 11'8" Estill County, KY (1980); 93' × 17'10" Walker, NY (1973); 66' × 14'5" Caroline County, MD (1989).

P. grandidentata var. *pendula*—see *P.* 'Pseudograndidentata'

P. 'Griffin'—see *P.* 'Brooks No. 1'

P. heterophylla L.
SWAMP COTTONWOOD. RIVER COTTONWOOD. BLACK COTTONWOOD. DOWNY POPLAR. From the eastern U.S., in swamps and bottomlands. Named in 1753 (*heterophylla* means differently or diversely leaved; from Greek *heteros*, different, and *phyllon*, a leaf). Rarely cultivated. Leaves large (to 8" × 5"), dull above, more or less downy beneath, parchment-textured, subtly toothed. Bark on old trees becomes coarse and shaggy like on some HICKORIES (*Carya* spp.). Related Chinese species are *P. lasiocarpa* and *P. Wilsonii*. Records: 140' × 27'11" × 108' Medina, OH (1991); 130' × 17'0" × 120' St. Matthews, OH (1982).

P. 'Highland'
Introduced <1988 by Highland nursery of Greeley, CO. Male. To 50' tall or more; upright oval shape, compact, with dark wavy green leaves. Bark light colored, much like that of *P.* × *acuminata*. Disease resistant.

P. 'H.P. 101'—see *P.* 'Red Caudina'

P. 'H.P. 510'
Origin and attributes unknown. In U.S. commerce <1979.

P. hudsonica—see *P. nigra* var. *betulifolia*

P. 'Idaho'
= *P. idahoensis* hort.
Origin and attributes unknown. In U.S. commerce <1967–68.

P. idahoensis—see *P.* 'Idaho'

P. 'Imperial'—see *P.* × *canadensis* 'Imperial'

P. incrissata canadensis—see *P.* × *canadensis* 'Incrassata'

P. italica—see *P. nigra* 'Italica'

P. × *Jackii* Sarg.
= *P. Baileyana* Henry
(*P. deltoides* × *P. balsamifera*)
Intermediate between its parents. Cultivated since 1900. Named in 1913 after John George Jack (1861–1949), Canadian professor of dendrology. Record: 105' × 8'11" Lisle, IL (1986; *pl.* 1925).

P. × *Jackii* 'Andrewsii'—see *P.* × *acuminata* 'Andrewsii'

P. × Jackii 'Generosa'

= P. × generosa Henry

Originated as an intentional 1912 cross of P. deltoides 'Cordata' × P. balsamifera ssp. trichocarpa at Kew, England. Named in 1914. Sparingly in North American commerce during the 1920s and '30s; long extinct commercially. High disease susceptibility. Both male (2"–3" catkins) and female (catkins to 6" at maturity) clones exist. Early to flush, very rapid growth. Twigs hairless or hairy; leaf stems nearly round, sometimes minutely hairy; leaves 4"–13" long. If P. trichocarpa is maintained as a species distinct from P. balsamifera, then 'Generosa' must be placed under the binomial P. × generosa. Record: 138' × 10'8" Albury Park, Sussex, England (1986).

P. × Jackii 'Gileadensis'—see P. 'Candicans'

P. × Jackii 'Northwest'

= P. 'Northwest'

NORTHWEST POPLAR. Originated in central North Dakota. Introduced <1940 by Northwest nursery of Valley City, ND. Commonly used in shelter plantings in Canada's prairie provinces. Male. Young bark light creamy-gray. Very late to flush and defoliate. Resists leaf rust, but is canker-prone. Twigs and buds like those of P. balsamifera; leaves show influence of P. deltoides: broadly egg-shaped, boldly toothed, midrib sparingly hairy, stem reddish and finely hairy. Grows to 90' tall quickly, and has been criticized as being too large for most needs. The name NORTHWEST POPLAR has also been applied to a cross of P. deltoides ssp. monilifera × P. tremuloides. In 1966 the binomial P. × Bernardii Boivin was published to designate such hybrids. The type specimen was at Prairie nursery, Estevan, Saskatchewan, and dated from ca. 1928.

P. × Jackii 'Saskatchewan'

= P. 'Saskatchewan'

Found on the bank of S Saskatchewan River, near Saskatoon, Saskatchewan. Distributed <1940 by the forest nursery station of Indian Head, Saskatchewan. Male. Late to flush and early to defoliate. Leaf triangular, longer than wide, whitish beneath, stem pink and sparingly hairy, glands sometimes present.

P. 'Kelman'

Origin and attributes unknown. In U.S. commerce <1987–88.

P. 'Kingston'

Origin and attributes unknown. In U.S. commerce ≤1979.

P. koreana Rehd.

KOREAN POPLAR. From Korea, part of the U.S.S.R., and possibly Hokkaido. Introduced to cultivation in 1918 when E. Wilson sent cuttings to the Arnold Arboretum. Named in 1922. Extremely rare in North America. Leafs out early—mid-March, the foliage then a lovely apple-green and very fragrant. Drops early, too. Leaves 3"–6" (8") long, rough-textured and matte above, whitish beneath. Closely related to (if not a mere version of) P. Maximowiczii, which has larger leaves. Exceptional cold-hardiness. Records: to 100' tall in the wild; 80' × 6¼" Lisle, IL (1986; pl. 1923); 56' × 4'5½" Seattle, WA (1994; pl. 1955).

P. lasiocarpa Oliv.

CHINESE NECKLACE POPLAR. From China. Named in 1890 (Greek lasios, hairy, and karpos, fruit, because its seed-capsules are wooly hairy). Introduced in 1900 by E. Wilson for Veitch nursery of England. Extremely rare in North America. One of its cultivated clones is almost the only bisexual Populus, with catkins sometimes bearing both sexes of florets. A great tree to plant if you want to offend prim neighbors. Leaves the largest in the genus, coarse, and rattle in the breeze; heart-shaped, to 15" × 9¾" (12"); stem to 5½" long, reddish. Stout shoots, wooly while young, as are the greenish undersides of the big floppy leaves. Female catkins to 12¼" long in May–June, releasing their messy fluff in early July. Bark dark and flaky. Tree gaunt. Closely related to P. heterophylla and P. Wilsonii. Records: 85' × 7'9" Bath Botanic Garden, Avon, England (1984); 76' × 8'9" Combe House Hotel, Devon, England (1978); 40' × 2'6" Seattle, WA (1995; pl. 1968).

P. macrophylla—see P. × canescens 'Macrophylla'

P. 'Maine'

(P. 'Candicans' × P. berolinensis)

MAINE POPLAR. Bred intentionally in Maine. Described in 1934.

P. 'Majestic'

From the University of Wisconsin. In U.S. commerce <1987–88. Pyramidal habit; male; grows fast and resists diseases.

P. mandschurica—see *P. songarica*

P. × marilandica—see *P. × canadensis* 'Marilandica'

P. Maximowiczii Henry
= *P. suaveolens* auct. (in part), non Fisch. (cf. *P. cathayana*)

JAPANESE POPLAR. From NE Asia to N Japan. Named after Carl Johann Maximowicz (1827–1891). Introduced to cultivation between 1878 and 1890. In North American commerce ≤1931. Rare. Leaves flush early in spring; to 6⅛" × 4¼"; with a distinctive twist at the apex; heart-shaped at the base; in late October turning dirty green or fair yellow. Male catkins reddish. Female catkins 7"–15" long, releasing cotton in June and July (or as late as September). Bark pale gray, smooth for many years. Twigs usually hairy. In the BALSAM POPLAR group. Very closely related to *P. koreana*. Records: to 164' tall in Manchuria says A.D. Woeikoff; 100' × 20'0" in Korea; 78' × 5'9" Headfort, County Meath, Ireland (1966); 75' × 7'0" Birr Castle, County Offaly, Ireland (1985); 72' × 5'1" Seattle, WA (1993; *pl.*1964).

P. 'Mojave Hybrid'
= *P. balsamifera* 'Mojave Hybrid'
= *P. × candicans* 'Mojave Hybrid'

Discovered in the desert near California City. Said to be the issue of BALM OF GILEAD (? *P.* 'Candicans') crossed with a male COTTONLESS COTTONWOOD. In U.S. commerce ≤1968. Sold as a COTTONLESS COTTONWOOD, primarily in California and the Southwest.

P. monilifera—see *P. deltoides* ssp. *monilifera*

P. 'N.E. 17'
The initials N.E. stand for the Northeast Experiment Station, which took on in 1937 the POPLAR breeding program in Maine initiated in 1924 by Dr. E.J. Schreiner. In commerce ≤1991. Male. Narrow, columnar, to 60' tall and 25' wide.

P. 'N.E. 41'—see *P.* 'Androscoggin'

P. 'N.E. 47'—see *P.* 'Oxford'

P. 'N.E. 308'
In commerce ≤1991. Male. Narrow, columnar, to 60' tall and 25' wide; exceptionally fast growing.

P. nigra L.
BLACK POPLAR. From the far NW of Africa, through Europe to W Siberia and the Caucasus. Very rare in North America in its typical form, which does not sucker from the root, however burry and sprouty its dark trunk may be. Named BLACK POPLAR to distinguish it from WHITE POPLAR (*P. alba*). Leaves shiny green on both sides, triangular to diamond-shaped, 1"–3" (4½"). Records: to 131' × 46'0" Dijon, France (1890s; *pl.* ca. 1400); 131' × 22'4" Turkey (1991); 105' × 16'6" × 87' Sandwich, NH (1984).

P. nigra 'Afghanica'
= *P. thevestina* Dode
= *P. nigra* 'Thevestina'
= *P. nigra* var. *thevestina* (Dode) Bean
= *P. nigra* var. *afghanica* Aitch. & Hemsl.
= *P. afghanica* (Aitch. & Hemsl.) Schneid.
= *P. usbekistanica* Kom. 'Afghanica'
?= *P. nigra* ssp. *afghanica* 'Özbekistanica'

GHOST POPLAR. TEBESSA POPLAR. AFGHAN POPLAR. ALGERIAN BLACK POPLAR. Named in 1880, based on material from Afghanistan. Cultivated in France since 1903. The *thevestina* name dates from 1905. Introduced to North America <1930s. Common here; sold often as an "improved" LOMBARDY POPLAR (*P. nigra* 'Italica'). Slender and upright like the LOMBARDY POPLAR but the bole round rather than fluted, and clean rather than besprouted; bark whitish-gray rather than yellowish-brown; leaves not heart-shaped, and have inferior fall color; smaller in stature, and female. Records from Seattle, WA: 118' × 8'0" × 27' (1995) and 104' × 10'7" × 32' Seattle, WA (1993).

P. nigra ssp. *afghanica* 'Özbekistanica'—see *P. nigra* 'Afghanica'

P. nigra var. *betulifolia* (Pursh) Torr.
= *P. nigra* ssp. *betulifolia* (Pursh) W. Wettst.
= *P. betulifolia* Pursh
= *P. hudsonica* Michx. fil.
(*betulæfolia*)

ENGLISH BLACK POPLAR. MANCHESTER POPLAR. EAST ANGLIAN POPLAR. From Britain and W Europe. Cultivated since 1790 in England; introduced to North America <1800. Rare here. Named in 1814 (*betulifolia* from genus *Betula*, BIRCH, and Latin *folium*, a leaf). The English names reflect the tree's British cultivation. Unlike typical *P. nigra*, it has densely hairy twigs; leaf stems normally hairy. Typical BLACK POPLAR of S Europe and W Asia has hairless or very slightly hairy twigs. Overall this variety is a spreading tree with burry trunk. Rarely sends up root suckers. Leaves to ca. 3¼" long and wide. The name MANCHESTER POPLAR refers to a widely planted male clone. Records: 125' × 16'9" Leighton Hall, Shropshire, England (1985); 97' × 24'4" Longnor Hall, Shropshire, England (1985).

P. nigra 'Charkowiensis'
= *P. charkowiensis* Schröd.

A 1902 account reports "several years ago, in the nursery of Herr. J.J. Gabeschtoff, not far from Charkow [Kharkov], Russia, a new POPLAR arose as a chance seedling." Introduced to commerce in 1907–1908 by Späth nursery of Germany. Extremely rare in North America. Very vigorous, broader than LOMBARDY POPLAR. Young twigs and leaves sparsely covered with short hairs. Female. Record: 80' × 6'9" Glasnevin, Dublin, Ireland (1966).

P. nigra 'Elegans'
= *P. elegans* hort.

SLENDER LOMBARDY POPLAR. Introduced in the late 1800s by Ellwanger & Barry nursery of Rochester, NY. Described in 1894. Young twigs and leaf stems hairy, with a handsome reddish tint. Leaves small, light-colored, and very versatile in a breeze. Habit narrowly upright. Male. Its relative abundance in North America, and distinctiveness from the male version(s) of *P. nigra* 'Plantierensis', are unknown.

P. nigra 'Italica'
= *P. nigra* var. *italica* (Muenchh.) Koehne
= *P. nigra* var. *pyramidalis* (Borkh.) Spach
= *P. pyramidalis* Salisb.
= *P. fastigiata* Desf.
= *P. italica* (Muenchh.) Moench
= *P. dilatata* Ait.

LOMBARDY POPLAR. PYRAMIDAL POPLAR. MORMON TREE. A mutant thought to have originated from a BLACK POPLAR in Italy in the late 1600s or early 1700s. In North America since 1784. Very common and familiar. The universal spire tree. A male clone. Called MORMON TREE because it is at once upright, and was planted frequently in early Mormon settlements. Records: 157' × 13'4" Akaroa, Canterbury, New Zealand (≤1982; *pl.* ca. 1860); 142' × 28'0" × 65½' Seattle, WA (1994; *pl.* ca. 1905); 115' × 36'1½" Opotiki, New Zealand (≤1982; *pl.* ca. 1890).

P. nigra 'Plantierensis'
(*P. nigra* var. *betulifolia* × *P. nigra* 'Italica')

DOWNY LOMBARDY POPLAR. Originated ≤1880, when 15 seedlings were raised at the Simon-Louis nursery at Plantières, near Metz, France; introduced commercially in 1884–85; named in 1904. The name is not clonal, as at least one clone of each sex was distributed, although the male predominately. Young shoots and leaves sparsely downy. More leafy and vigorous than typical LOMBARDY POPLAR. Its relative abundance in North America, and distinctiveness from *P. nigra* 'Elegans', are unknown.

P. nigra var. pyramidalis—see P. nigra 'Italica'

P. nigra var. thevestina—see P. nigra 'Afghanica'

P. nigra 'Volga'—see P. 'Volga'

P. 'Noreaster'
In U.S. commerce <1990. A sterile female.

P. 'Northwest'—see P. × Jackii 'Northwest'

P. 'Norway'
= *P. sanfolia* hort.

NORWAY POPLAR. SUDDEN SAWLOG. Origin and affinities unknown. Perhaps introduced from Russia in the late 1800s or early 1900s, it was greatly popular in the 1920s, and in many locales superseded the CAROLINA POPLAR (*P.* × *canadensis* 'Eugenei'), being faster and "improved." Called NORWAY POPLAR because many were planted by Norwegian settlers in Minnesota.

P. obtusata fastigiata—see P. Simonii 'Fastigiata'

P. occidentalis—see P. deltoides ssp. monilifera

P. ontariensis—see P. 'Candicans'

P. 'Oxford'
= *P.* 'N.E. 47'
(*P. Maximowiczii* × *P. berolinensis* 'Certinensis')

OXFORD POPLAR. Bred intentionally in Maine. Described in 1934. Named after the Oxford Paper Company of Rumford, Maine. A clone of the same parentage is 'Geneva'.

P. pekinensis—see P. tomentosa

P. × *Petrowskiana* (Schröd. *ex* Reg.) Schneid.

= *P.* 'Petrowskyana'
(*P. deltoides* × *P. laurifolia*)

RUSSIAN POPLAR. Raised in Russia ca. 1880 at the garden of the Imperial Agricultural Institute at Petrowskoje-Rasumowskoje (near Moscow). Described in 1889; in Canada ≤1890. Any number of hybrids have been called RUSSIAN POPLARS. The common denominator seems to be genes of *P. laurifolia*. Both male and female clones have long been distributed in Canada under this name, but the female is now commercially extinct, because it made too much fluff, and its roots were too greedy. Leaves to 6" × 4"; pale beneath.

P. × *Petrowskiana* 'Dunlop'

= *P.* 'Dunlop'

A seedling from an open-pollinated RUSSIAN POPLAR (i.e., a *P. laurifolia* or hybrid thereof). Selected by R.H. Dunlop from an established shelterbelt on a farm near Conquest, Saskatchewan. Introduced ca. 1951. Still sold. Straight, strong; resists leaf rust but gets canker. Both sexes exist but the male is more common. Leaf slightly longer than wide, downy on the midrib, margins and stem.

P. × *petrowskiana* 'Griffin'—see *P.* 'Brooks No. 1'

P. × *Petrowskiana* 'Walker'

= *P.* 'Walker'
= *P.* '44–52'
= *P. deltoides* 'Walker'

Originated ca. 1947 by J. Walker of Indian Head, Saskatchewan. In commerce. Female. Of very rapid growth. Narrow. Rust-resistant. Late to flush and very late to defoliate, intolerant of early fall and late spring frosts. Leaf diamond-shaped, nearly as wide as long.

P. Picardi—see *P.* × *canescens* 'Macrophylla'

P. 'Prairie Sky'—see *P.* × *canadensis* 'Prairie Sky'

P. Przewalskii—see *P. Simonii*

P. 'Pseudograndidentata'

= *P. tremula* var. *pseudograndidentata* (Dode) Aschers. & Graebn.
= *P. grandidentata* var. *pendula* hort., non Loud.
= *P. pseudograndidentata* Dode
= *P. græca* var. *pendula* hort.
?(*P. grandidentata* × *P. tremula*)

Origin unknown. Probably a hybrid. First mentioned ≤1868 in France. A pendulous clone commonly planted in North America from ca. 1870 until the early 1900s. Long commercially extinct. It may be confused with *P.* × *canescens* 'Pendula'. Leaves shaped much like those of *P. tremula*, but thicker and larger, 2¾"–4½" wide. Male; florets with only 5 stamens.

P. pyramidalis—see *P. nigra* 'Italica'

P. 'Red Caudina'

= *P.* 'H.P. 101'

Origin unknown. In North American commerce <1980. Common. Leaves reddish when young, maturing large, triangular, dark green, leathery textured, stem red-tinged. Habit slender, pyramidal. Male.

P. × *regenerata*—see *P.* × *canadensis* 'Regenerata'

P. × *robusta*—see *P.* × *canadensis* 'Robusta'

P. 'Rochester'

(*P. Maximowiczii* × *P. nigra* 'Plantierensis')

ROCHESTER POPLAR. Bred intentionally in Maine. Described in 1934.

P. 'Roxbury'

(*P. nigra* × *P. balsamifera* ssp. *trichocarpa*)

ROXBURY POPLAR. Bred intentionally in Maine. Described in 1934. Record: 128' × 9'10" Thorp Perrow, Yorkshire, England (1990; *pl.* 1950).

P. 'Rumford'—see *P.* × *berolinensis* 'Rumford'

P. sanfolia—see *P.* 'Norway'

P. Sargentii—see *P. deltoides* ssp. *monilifera*

P. 'Saskatchewan'—see *P.* × *Jackii* 'Saskatchewan'

P. × *serotina*—see *P.* × *canadensis* 'Serotina'

P. Simonii Carr.

= *P. Przewalskii* Maxim.
= *P. suaveolens* var. *Przewalskii* (Maxim.) Schneid.
= *P. brevifolia* Carr. *ex* Schneid.

SIMON POPLAR. CHINESE POPLAR. From north China, and Korea. Discovered by Gabriel Eugène Simon (1829–1896) in 1862 and introduced to France the same year. In North America ≤1890; extremely rare—the male clone

'Fastigiata' has been sold by many nurseries as "*P. Simonii*." In the BALSAM POPLAR group. Leaves diamond-shaped, small (1½"–5" long). Record: 75' × 3'9" Oliwa, Poland (≤1973).

P. Simonii 'Fastigiata'
= *P. obtusata fastigiata* hort.
= *P. balsamifera* var. *suaveolens* hort., non Loud.

CHINESE LOMBARDY POPLAR. FLAGPOLE POPLAR. BLUE POPLAR. Introduced from China to the U.S. in 1913 by F. Meyer (possibly earlier, via France). In commerce here since 1914–15. Officially described in 1916. Common; often sold as "*P. Simonii*." Although the branches certainly ascend strongly, in no fair sense does this compare with the truly columnar LOMBARDY POPLAR or similar *P. nigra* cultivars. In age it sprawls out. Records: 67' × 9'4" × 47' Newhalem, WA (1993); 49' × 10'4" × 51' west of Royal City, WA (1993).

P. Simonii var. manshurica —see P. songarica

P. Simonii 'Pendula'
WEEPING SIMON POPLAR. Officially described in 1916. Extremely rare in North America. A large, elegantly pendulous tree. Male; catkins slender, 2½"–3¼" long. Many were planted during the 1920s and '30s in Seattle, WA, the largest 101' × 8'10" × 56' (1995) and 69' × 12'10" × 66' (1988).

P. 'Siouxland'—see P. deltoides 'Siouxland'

P. 'SK 17'
The initials "SK" stand for horticulturist Dr. Frank Leith Skinner (1882–1967), of Dropmore nursery, Manitoba. Attributes unknown. In commerce ≤1979.

P. 'SK Weeping'
Attributes unknown. In commerce ≤1979.

P. songarica Dode (nom. nud.?)
= *P. mandschurica* hort., ?non Nakai 1924
?= *P. Simonii* var. *manshurica* (Nakai) M. Kitagawa
= *P.* 'Sungarica'

MANCHURIAN POPLAR. From central Asia probably. Perhaps a hybrid. Dropmore nursery of Manitoba obtained this (male clone) from Kew, England, in 1948. It suffered no leaf rust or canker, so was introduced commercially in 1967–68. Very rare, but still sold in Canada sparingly as late as 1987. It has also been sold in Montana. In the BALSAM POPLAR group. Buds sticky and resinous. Habit somewhat similar to that of *P. × berolinensis* (i.e., narrow-crowned). Cat-

kins reddish-brown, very attractive. Twigs slightly angled, with loose, tawny fuzz. Leaves thick, dark green and shiny above, pale greenish-white beneath, 2"–3¼" long, rounded at the base, subtly edged with fine teeth; minutely and persistently hairy on both sides, especially beneath. Records: 95' × 8'1" Seattle, WA (1992, *pl.* 1967); 40' × 6'10" Dropmore, Manitoba (1965; *pl.* 1948).

P. 'Strathglass'—see P. × berolinensis 'Strathglass'

P. 'Sungarica'—see P. songarica

P. suaveolens—see P. cathayana and P. Maximowiczii

P. suaveolens var. Przewalskii—see P. Simonii

P. Tacamahacca—see P. balsamifera

P. Tacamahacca var. Michauxii—see P. balsamifera var. Michauxii

P. texana—see P. deltoides ssp. monilifera

P. thevestina—see P. nigra 'Afghanica'

P. tomentosa Carr.
= *P. pekinensis* L. Henry
= *P. alba* var. *tomentosa* (Carr.) Wesm.
?(*P. alba* × *P. tremula* var. *Davidiana*)
?(*P. alba* × *P. adenophylla*)

CHINESE WHITE POPLAR. From N and central China. Not known in the wild, but clones of both sexes are planted; it is used as a street-tree in Peking. Introduced to France by Simon in 1867. Named that year (*tomentosa* in Latin means densely wooly with soft, matted hairs). Introduced to North America by F. Meyer in 1914. Leaves broad, usually flat-based or shallowly cordate; not as deeply lobed as *P. alba* 'Nivea' or 'Pyramidalis' sucker shoots. On old trees, the leaves become hairless at maturity; sucker leaves are hairiest. The largest leaves are 6"–9" long. Record: 115' × 8'3½" × 55' Davis, CA (1993; male; *pl.* in mid-1950s).

P. tremula L.
EUROPEAN ASPEN. From NW Africa, Europe, to N China. Almost never planted in North America, except in cultivars. The Latin *tremere*, to quiver, gave rise to the name *tremula*, used for this

species. It often root-suckers. Leaves small and thin, roundish and coarsely toothed; 1"–3". Usually a small tree. Records: to 164' tall says V. Komarov; 98' × 18'4" Nowa Wies, Poland (≤1973); 92' × 18'8" Geneva, Switzerland (≤1967).

P. tremula 'Columnaris'—see P. tremula 'Erecta'

P. tremula 'Erecta'
= P. tremula 'Columnaris'

SWEDISH COLUMNAR ASPEN. Introduced in 1911 in Sweden. Name published in 1916. Introduced to North America in 1939 by the Arnold Arboretum. Difficult to propagate. Common here only since the mid-1970s. Male. Distinctly columnar. Young leaves light to dark maroon red, maturing green.

P. tremula ssp. grandidentata—see P. grandidentata

P. tremula 'Pendula'

WEEPING EUROPEAN ASPEN. First described in 1787. Nearly extinct in North American commerce since the 1940s. Strongly pendulous; topgrafted. Male; catkins profuse.

P. trem. var. pseudograndidentata—see P. 'Pseudograndidentata'

P. tremula 'Pyramidalis'

Cultivated in England since 1907. Introduced to North America in 1926 by the Arnold Arboretum. Not known in commerce. Possibly synonymous with P. tremula 'Erecta'.

P. tremula ssp. tremuloides—see P. tremuloides

P. tremuloides Michx.
= P. tremula ssp. tremuloides (Michx.) A. & D. Löve
= P. atheniensis Ludwig, non K. Koch
= P. græca Loud., non Ait. (cf. P. grandidentata)

QUAKING ASPEN. ASPEN POPLAR. TREMBLING ASPEN. AMERICAN ASPEN. MOUNTAIN ASPEN. CANADIAN ASPEN. GOLDEN ASPEN. QUIVER-LEAF. ASPE. From most parts of the continent: the widest range of any tree species in North America, occurring from Alaska to Newfoundland to Mexico. Commonly cultivated. Named in 1803 (Latin tremula (the EUROPEAN ASPEN), and Greek -oides, resemblance). Graceful and slender, its trembling leaves are fascinating to watch on a windy day. Its brilliant autumn yellow is famous. Leaves 1"–4½" long and wide, glossy, with flattened stems. Distinguished from P. tremula by having numerous comparatively sharp tiny teeth instead of few blunt bold teeth, and having a sharp, drawn-out apex; its bark is also paler and more beautiful. Colony-forming, some clone clumps in northern Alberta might have began life 4–6,000 years ago. Usually a small, slender tree in cultivation. Records: to 120' tall; 109' × 10'2" Ontonagon County, MI (1983); 86' × 11'8" north of Fort Klamath, OR (1974); 85' × 12'1½" New Richmond, Québec (<1994); 70' × 11'6" Santa Fe National Forest, NM (1965).

P. tremuloides 'Bethel Spire'

Introduced <1991. Grown by several major tree nurseries in the western U.S. Uniform upward sweeping branches forming a teardrop canopy. Deep green foliage contrasts with whitish green bark. Yellow to orange fall color.

P. tremuloides 'Kaibab'

Introduced <1991. Possibly named after Kaibab National Forest of Arizona. Grown by several major tree nurseries in the western U.S. Distinctive white bark. Denser than 'Bethel Spire' with more delicate branching; leaves more elongated and lighter green. An occasional bronze hue in the golden yellow fall color.

P. tremuloides 'Pendula'
= P. benzoifera pendula hort.

PARASOL DE ST. JULIEN. WEEPING AMERICAN ASPEN. One account says this was discovered in 1865 by an employee of Messrs. Baltet at St. Julien, near Troyes, France. That is incorrect. It was known as early as 1838 (as P. benzoifera pendula Tausch), and was in U.S. commerce ≤1854. Very rare here. A pendulous female, topgrafted. The name PARASOL DE ST. JULIEN has also been applied to P. × canescens 'Pendula', P. 'Pseudograndidentata', and P. tremula 'Pendula'.

P. tremuloides 'Perfection'

Introduced ≤1991 by Progressive Plants, Sandy, UT: "Exceptional symmetry (the classical natural look); internode spacing identical from top to bottom of head. One of the finest individuals of literally millions of seedlings observed."

P. trichocarpa—see *P. balsamifera* ssp. *trichocarpa*

P. tristis Fisch.

WEEPING POPLAR. BROWN-TWIG POPLAR. Originated <1831 in central Asia or Siberia, but not known in a wild state. Named in 1841 (in Latin, *tristis* means sad, hence weeping or pendulous). In North America ≤1896; sold here since ≤1937. Rare here; largely limited to Canada. Exceptional cold-hardiness. Can be planted north of the Arctic Circle in some places. Performs poorly in mild-winter areas. In the BALSAM POPLAR group, but immune to leaf rust that disfigures *P. balsamifera*. Compared to *P. Simonii* 'Pendula' it has darker, heavier foliage that dances less readily in the breeze; teeth sharper; drops its leaves much sooner in autumn. Leaves commonly ca. 4" × 2"; sucker leaves to 8¼" × 5". Male; catkins (1½") 2½"–3½" long; 14–57 stamens per floret. Growth slow for a POPLAR; sometimes only a large shrub. Record: 52' × 5'7" × 49' Seattle, WA (1989).

P. usbekistanica 'Afghanica'—see *P. nigra* 'Afghanica'

P. vernirubens—see *P.* × *canadensis* 'Robusta'

P. virginiana—see *P. deltoides*

P. 'Volga'

= *P. nigra* 'Volga'

Origin and attributes unknown. In commerce since ≤1907 (when sold by Teas' nursery of Carthage, MO). It may be a renaming of *P.* × *berolinensis*. Hardy in Minnesota and South Dakota.

P. 'Volunteer'

An open-pollinated seedling from a RUSSIAN POPLAR (i.e., a *P. laurifolia* hybrid). Tested in 1951 at the Forest nursery station of Indian Head, Saskatchewan. Female. Often multitrunked. Very early to flush and late to defoliate. Resists canker and leaf rust. Leaf twice as long as wide, grayish-green beneath, finely toothed, glandless, stem pink and hairy. Buds very gummy.

P. 'Walker'—see *P.* × *Petrowskiana* 'Walker'

P. 'Wheeler'

An open-pollinated seedling selected by W. Kerr from the farm of Sigurd Wheeler at Rosthern, Saskatchewan. Related to *P. balmsamifera*. Tested in 1951 at the Forest nursery station of Indian Head, Saskatchewan, and found not suited for the Canadian prairies. Slow growing. Male. Leaf twice as long as wide, subtly toothed.

P. 'White'

= *P.* × *candicans* 'White'

Sold as WHITE COTTONLESS COTTONWOOD by L.E. Cooke nursery of Visalia, CA, from at least 1957 to 1981. Bark white. Does well in the Mojave Desert.

P. Wilsoni Schneid.

From central and W China. Named in 1916 after the great plantsman Ernest Henry Wilson (1876–1930). Wilson had introduced it in 1907. In North American commerce ≤1931. Extremely rare. Only a female clone is cultivated; difficult to strike by cuttings, so usually grafted. Leaves dull bluish-green above, pale whitish-gray beneath; very large (to 9" × 7"; stem to 6" long). Twigs purplish. Closely related to *P. heterophylla* and *P. lasiocarpa*. Records: to 82' × 5'0" in the wild; 60' × 5'0" Annesgrove, County Cork, Ireland (1968).

P. Wislizeni—see *P. deltoides* var. *Wislizeni*

Prumnopitys andina—see *Podocarpus andinus*

Prumnopitys elegans—see *Podocarpus andinus*

Prunus

[ROSACEÆ; Rose Family] About 400 spp. of widely distributed trees and shrubs. *Prunus* is the ancient Latin name of the EUROPEAN PLUM (i.e., *Prunus* × *domestica*). A highly varied genus, consisting of ALMONDS, APRICOTS, CHERRIES (mostly), PEACHES, PLUMS, and CHERRY LAURELS. Some botanists prefer a narrower view, and so divide *Prunus* into several genera, thereby making the genus *Prunus* refer exclusively to PLUMS.

P. 'Accolade'

= *P.* × *subhirtella* 'Accolade'

?(*P. Sargentii* × *P. subhirtella*)

ACCOLADE CHERRY. Originated ca. 1945 at Knap Hill nursery, Woking, Surrey, England. Introduced in 1952. In North America ≤1963. Rare except in the maritime Pacific Northwest. Flowers dark pink in the bud stage, opening soft pink, in clusters of 2–4, each blossom 1"–1½" wide, semi-double (12–15 petals) in March or April, before the leaves appear. Almost no fruit is produced. Leaves to 5½" long, lightly hairy on both sides; edged with fine, sharp teeth. Habit broad and low, forming a large, vigorous crown, with long slender twigs inclined to droop gently. The crown of foliage is open and airy. Records: 26' × 2'6" × 39' and 23' × 2'9" × 47' Seattle, WA (1993; *pl.* 1967).

P. *æquinoctialis*—see P. *pendula* var. *ascendens*

P. 'Allred'
('Alfred')
= *P. cerasifera* 'Allred'

ALLRED PLUM is a hybrid seedling of *P. cerasifera* 'Pissardii' from Amity, AR. Discovered in 1939, and introduced to commerce in 1941 by Ross R. Wolfe's nursery of Stephenville, TX. Planted primarily in the Midwest. Sold as a dual-purpose tree: ornamental and fruitful. Strong and productive. Leaves large, summer color neither red nor purple, but bronzy. The other parent of this hybrid was perhaps a JAPANESE PLUM (*P. salicina*), but 'Allred' flowers are borne on hairy stems unlike those of nearly all PLUM blossoms, Japanese varieties included. Flowers white. Plums freely borne, 1¼" wide, with red skin and pulp, ripening early.

P. 'Amabilis'
= *P. serrulata* 'Amabilis'
= *P. serrulata* 'Higurashi' ('Higurashe')
= *P. serrulata* f. *amabilis* Miyoshi
= *P. Lannesiana* f. *higurashi* Wils.

In the SATO ZAKURA group. The 'Higurashi' name means "twilight." The *amabilis* name in Latin means pleasing or attractive. In North American commerce at least during the 1930s. Extremely rare. Tree upright, cup-shaped, to 18' tall. Flowers deep pink. Flowers in clusters of 2–4 on short stout stems; whitish-pink (the centers almost white, the edges of outer petals deep pink or even red); 1½"–2" wide, 25–30 petals; inodorous; sepals toothed. Young foliage brownish- or yellowish-green.

P. 'Amanogawa'
= *P. serrulata* 'Amanogawa'
= *P. Lannesiana* f. *amanogawa* Wils.
= *P. Lannesiana* f. *erecta* (Miyoshi) Wils.
= *P. serrulata* f. *erecta* Miyoshi

= *P. serrulata* 'Pyramidalis'

WHITE COLUMN CHERRY. APPLE BLOSSOM CHERRY. In the SATO ZAKURA group. Name means "celestial river" or "milky way." Introduced to the U.S. in 1906 by D. Fairchild. Common. Fastigiate, its stout knobby twigs and branches all grow straight upward after the fashion of LOMBARDY POPLAR. Flowers slightly fragrant, single or semi-double, of (5) 9 (15) petals, very pale pink or practically white. Young foliage slightly yellowish-bronze. Records: 38' × 4'7" × 32' Seattle, WA (1993); 28' × 2'6" × 13' Tacoma, WA (1992).

P. 'Amayadori'
= *P. serrulata* 'Amayadori'
= *P. serrulata* f. *dilatata* Miyoshi
= *P. Lannesiana* f. *amayadori* (Koidz.) Wils.

In the SATO ZAKURA group. In North American commerce at least during the 1940s and '50s. Extremely rare. Tree umbrella-shaped, large (to 50' tall). Buds light red or pink. Flowers white (or faintly tinged pink at the tips), semi-double (10–15 petals), and strongly fragrant. Young foliage weak bronzy-green. Resembles *P.* 'Shirotae' but has smaller flowers.

P. *americana* Marsh.

AMERICAN PLUM. RED PLUM. YELLOW PLUM. AUGUST PLUM. From central and eastern North America. The most widely distributed and cultivated of North American native PLUMS. Shrubby or a small tree, with root suckers forming thorny thickets. Fragrant white flowers in April or May give rise to plums ¾"–1⅜" (larger in cultivars), red (or yellow) skinned with yellowish pulp. Leaves sharply toothed, 2"–4" long, yellow to red in fall. As a rootstock it confers cold-hardiness, but can sucker. Ornamentally it is fair, but not as appreciated as certain other of its relatives, including some of its many hybrids. Records: 48' × 3'3" × 36' Florida (1994); 35' × 3'3" × 27' Gainesville, FL (≤1993); 35' × 3'0" × 35' near Lakeville, MI (1972); 30' × 3'2" × 37' Alachua County, Fl (1992); 29' × 5'0" × 33' near Steyer, MD (1949); 28' × 3'10" × 28' Marion, VA (1985).

P. *americana* var. *lanata*—see P. *mexicana* and P. *nigra*

P. *americana* 'Newport'—see P. 'Newport'

P. *americana* var. *nigra*—see P. *nigra*

P. × *Amygdalo-persica*—see P. × *persicoides*

P. *Amygdalus*—see P. *dulcis*

P. Ansu—see *P. Armeniaca* var. *Ansu*

P. apetala (S. & Z.) Fr. & Sav.

CLOVE CHERRY. From Japan. Named in 1843 (meaning "without petals"). Introduced by E. Wilson in 1914. Exceedingly rare in North America. A few cultivars exist in Japan. Blooms slightly before the leaves emerge. Flowers in April, 1–3 per bud, ⅝"–¾" wide, nodding, white or pinkish-white. Fruit black, sweet, ⅓". A shrubby small tree 15'–26' tall. Related to *P. incisa* (FUJI CHERRY).

P. 'Ariake'

= *P. serrulata* 'Ariake'
= *P. serrulata* f. *candida* Miyoshi
= *P. Lannesiana* f. *ariake* (Koidz.) Wils.
= *P. serrulata* 'Candida'
= *P. Lannesiana* 'Candida'
('Ariyake')

In the SATO ZAKURA group. The name means "dawn." Imported to the U.S. in 1912 as part of the Potomac planting. Exceedingly rare. Flowers remarkably like those of *P.* 'Ojochin' at first glance (pink buds open to single or with a few extra petals, whitish, to 2" wide). 'Ariake' differs in having less wrinkled petals, less pink, not so freely produced. 'Ariake' is less tree-like, with branches likely to arise from near the base of the trunk. But it can grow 20' tall and wide. Young foliage bronzy-green.

P. arkansana—see P. mexicana

P. Armeniaca L.

= *Armeniaca vulgaris* Lam.

APRICOT TREE. From E Manchuria and Korea. *Armeniaca* is one of the ancient Latin names for the APRICOT TREE, introduced to Italy by way of Armenia. In North America by 1735. Common; grown for its edible fruit. Closely related to PEACH (*P. Persica*), but has firmer fruit of richer flavor, and roundish leaves. Moreover, it is a stouter tree of larger size. Flowers appear in early spring before the leaves, are hurt often by frosts; nearly stalkless, extremely pale pink, ¾"–1¼" wide, as attractive as those of most *Prunus*. The familiar soft, lightly fuzzy fruit ripens orange-red in summer. As ornamentals, APRICOT TREES are not desirable, needing annual care to stay vigorous and healthy, while the tree's form and the texture of its foliage are only of average appeal. Few ornamental cultivars exist; most attributed to this species rightly are of the JAPANESE APRICOT, *P. Mume*. An extremely rare cousin is BRIANÇON APRICOT, *P. brigantina*. A hybrid is *P.* × *dasycarpa* (BLACK APRICOT). APRICOTS can grow tall and wide, although most are kept pruned to 15' or less. Records: 55' × 6'2" in the U.S.S.R.; 48' × 6'4" × 47' Pinckney, MI (<1979); 45' × 8'10" × 52' Wishram, WA (1986; *pl.* ca. 1867).

P. Armeniaca var. Ansu Maxim.

= *P. Ansu* (Maxim.) Kom.
= *Armeniaca Ansu* (Kom.) Kostina

Introduced to Western cultivation in 1880. Named in 1883 after the Japanese vernacular *Anzu*. Most APRICOTS cultivated for their fruit in Japan, Korea and E China are this kind; better adapted to a maritime climate. Very rare in North America. Looks similar to typical APRICOT. Pink buds open to white flowers usually in pairs instead of singly borne. Leaves pointier. Fruit redder and hairier.

P. Armeniaca 'Charles Abraham'

= *P. Mume* 'Charles Abraham'

Introduced ≤1937 in California. Commercially extinct since the 1940s. Named after Charles Christian Abraham (1851–1929) of the Western nursery, San Francisco, CA. Abraham might have secured it from an old Chinese temple garden. He disliked "great, blowzy flowers developed horticulturally from species." The cultivar was not introduced until after his death precisely because it is such a thing. Very large deep red buds open to masses of very double flowers, rich pink shaded carmine.

P. Armeniaca var. mandshurica Maxim.

= *P. mandshurica* (Maxim.) Koehne
= *Armeniaca mandshurica* (Maxim.) Skovorts.

MANCHURIAN APRICOT. From Manchuria, Korea, and adjacent Russia. Named in 1883. Cultivated in the West since 1900 in Germany. Rare in North America. The first APRICOT to bloom and ripen. Flowers in April, pinkish, 1¼" wide, on stalks ⅛"–½" long; self-fertile. Leaves more elongate, coarsely and sharply toothed. Fruits rounded, yellow, 1" wide. E. Wilson reported its distinctive large size and thick, corky, black bark. Most authors call it a shrubby small tree 12'–16' tall; the *Flora of the U.S.S.R.* says to 49' × 4'7".

P. Armeniaca var. mandshurica 'Mandan'

Introduced <1980 by Mandan research station of Mandan, ND. Flowers pinker than average.

P. 'Asagi'

= *P. serrulata* 'Asagi'
= *P. serrulata* f. *luteoides* Miyoshi

In the SATO ZAKURA group. Very rare. A synonym of *P.* 'Ukon' for all practical purposes, but its pale yellow flowers are single, the earliest of the several yellow cultivars to open. See also *P.* 'Gyoiko'.

P. 'Asahi'
= *P. serrulata* 'Asahi'

In the SATO ZAKURA group. Sold in the late 1920s and early '30s by W.B. Clarke and other California nurseries. Long commercially extinct. Paul Russell says it is much like *P.* 'Shiro-fugen' except the young foliage is green, not coppery-red.

P. 'Asahi-botan'
= *P. serrulata* 'Asahi-botan'
?= *P. Lannesiana* 'Asahi-yama'

In the SATO ZAKURA group. Introduced ≤1929 by Wohlert nursery of Narberth, PA. Extremely rare. A distinct dwarf, similar to *P.* 'Jeanne Wohlert'; flowers arranged in the same hyacinth-like bottlebrush formation. Flowers semi-double, fragrant, delicately blush-pink colored. A bush, branching from the ground up. Very slow.

P. avium L.
= *Cerasus avium* (L.) Moench
= *C. sylvestris* Lund.
= *C. nigra* Mill.

MAZZARD (CHERRY). WILD SWEET CHERRY. MERRY TREE. GEAN. From central and S Europe, N Africa, Caucasia, NW Iran, across Asia to the Russian Far East. The epithet *avium* is from Latin *avis*, bird. GEAN is of French origin. CHERRY is derived from Greek. A robust woodland tree. Common and fully naturalized in North America, where it has been cultivated since <1600. Compared to its SWEET CHERRY fruiting cultivar progeny, MAZZARD differs in being leaner, taller, with smaller, less choice fruit. Its seedlings are the most frequently used rootstock for grafting of various fruiting and flowering CHERRY TREES. Rarely suckers except in woodland settings. Pure white (very rarely tinged with pink) flowers ca. 1" wide, barely before the leaves in spring; fruit ripens in early summer, red, purple or black. Autumn leaf color usually yellow, but can be a rainbow of green, yellow, orange and red. Records: to 110' tall says L. Brimble; 102' × 7'4" Priors Mesne, Gloucestershire, England (1976); 100' × 5'6" Seattle, WA (1993); 82' × 21'11" × 71' West Chester, PA (1989); 56' × 18'10" × 84' Eugene, OR (1989; *pl.* 1937).

P. avium 'Decumana'
= *P. avium* 'Nicotianæfolia'
= *P. avium* 'Macrophylla'
= *P. avium* 'Mamillaris'

BIGLEAF MAZZARD. Originated in France. The 1808 Latin word *decumana* has reference to a tenth, or tithe—the relation to this cultivar is unknown. In North America ≤1896. Exceedingly rare. Leaves very large, to 8"–12" long; flowers proportionate.

P. avium 'Flore Pleno'—see *P. avium* 'Plena'

P. avium 'Macrophylla'—see *P. avium* 'Decumana'

P. avium 'Mamillaris'—see *P. avium* 'Decumana'

P. avium 'Multiplex'—see *P. avium* 'Plena'

P. avium 'Nicotianæfolia'—see *P. avium* 'Decumana'

P. avium 'Pendula'

WEEPING MAZZARD. Cultivated in Europe since 1825. Extremely rare in North America. Usually topgrafted to make a small mounded tree. Branches stiffly pendulous. Foliage orange-red in autumn. Flowers pale pink.

P. avium 'Plena'
= *P. avium* 'Flore Pleno'
= *P. avium* 'Multiplex'

DOUBLE FLOWERED MAZZARD. Cultivated in France <1700. In North American commerce ≤1910. Uncommon. Identical to the regular MAZZARD except for 1½" wide flowers with up to 30–40 petals rather than the customary 5 (*plena* in Latin means full or plump; having extra petals). Awkwardly large, this cultivar is admirably tough and cold hardy. Record: 51' × 6'6" × 53' Seattle, WA (1993).

P. avium var. *regalis*—see *P.* × *Gondouinii*

P. avium 'Rosea Pendula'—see *P.* 'Kikushidare-zakura'

P. avium 'Scanlon'—see *P.* × *Gondouinii* 'Schnee'

P. avium 'Schnee'—see *P.* × *Gondouinii* 'Schnee'

P. azoricus—see *P. lusitanica* ssp. *azorica*

P. 'Beni-torano-o'
= *P. serrulata* 'Beni-torano-o'
= *P. Lannesiana* f. *benitoranowo* Wils.
= *P. serrulata* f. *formosissima* Miyoshi

In the SATO ZAKURA group. Name means "pink tigertail." In North America since <1916. Extremely rare. Don't confuse with *P.* 'Torano-o'. Very similar to *P.* 'Yedo-zakura' (some say identical). Flowers usually with <10 petals, rosy-pink; clustered near ends of branches.

P. 'Bennishi'

= *P. serrulata* 'Bennishi'

In the SATO ZAKURA group. Sold during the 1930s by Bobbink & Atkins nursery of Rutherford, NJ. Attributes unknown.

P. 'Berry'—see P. Cascade Snow™

P. × blireiana André

(*P. cerasifera* 'Pissardii' × *P. Mume* 'Alphandii')
BLIREIANA PLUM. DOUBLE-PINK JAPANESE PLUM. DOUBLE-ROSE CHERRY PLUM. BLIREIANA FLOWERING-PLUM. DOUBLE CHERRY-PLUM. It has been called PINK PARADISE in England. Among the best-known purpleleaf trees. Originated ca. 1895 as a chance seedling at La Croix (near Bléré), France. First flowered in April, 1901; in commerce 1905. 'Blireiana' has never been out of commerce and is sold wherever ornamental PLUM TREES are available. Flowers very early in spring, vivid pink, fragrant, double (ca. 22 petals) and profuse. No other PURPLELEAF PLUM cultivar has flowers with so many petals and stamens. Leaves unfold deep reddish purple, turn bronze at maturity, and ultimately dark green with purplish spots on top; proportionately broader and duller than those of most PURPLELEAF PLUMS. Habit chaotic, congested, and twiggy. The trunk develops unsightly warts and burls. It is as if the cream-of-the-crop genetics went into flowers, leaving only the dregs for the rest of the tree. Naturally dwarf; trunks are no more than 10" through or 20' tall, and both of these figures are the rare exception. Since the trunk is so short and ugly, some propagators topgraft 'Blireiana' on CHERRY PLUM trunks. Fruit almost never set; the plums are lightly fuzzy-skinned.

P. × blireiana 'Moseri'

= *P. Moseri* hort.
= *P. Pissardii Veitchii* hort.

Of the same origin as the preceding, MOSER PLUM grows larger and is more open, with paler flowers of only 15 petals opening slightly later and yielding fruit more readily. Its leaves are larger and less hairy.

'Moseri' is often misidentified or rather, under-identified, as BLIREIANA PLUM. It has been sold as "light-pink *blireiana*." Named for the Moser family, prominent nursery proprietors at Versailles. In North American commerce since ≤1911. Record: 27' × 4'7" × 33' Puyallup, WA (1993).

P. × blireiana 'Newport'—see P. 'Newport'

P. brigantina Villars

= *Armeniaca brigantiaca* (Vill.) Pers.

BRIANÇON APRICOT. From SE France. Named in 1779. In North America since ≤1896. Extremely rare. Essentially confined to collections and botanic gardens. Flowers ¾" wide, pinkish or white, in crowded tufts of 2–4 during April. Leaves hairy above and beneath, 1½"–3¼" long, jaggedly toothed. Fruit golden-yellow, smooth, ¾"–1" long, freestone, flavor mild and spritely; ripe early September. Unlike *P. Armeniaca* (COMMON APRICOT) and *P. Mume* (JAPANESE APRICOT), it has sharp, elongated buds, and much more importantly, is essentially disease free, which is why it is included in the present volume. A bushy small tree with slender green twigs and CHERRY-like bark; to 20' tall.

P. campanulata Maxim.

= *P. cerasoides* var. *campanulata* Koidz.

FORMOSAN CHERRY. TAIWAN CHERRY. CRIMSON CHERRY. The literal translation of its scientific name is BELL-FLOWERED CHERRY. From S China, Taiwan, and the Ryukyus. Named in 1883. Introduced to Western cultivation in 1899; to North America in 1915; sold here since ≤1923. Noted for its deep pink or red floral display in earliest spring. The most successful FLOWERING CHERRY in southern California. In the northern states and Canada it has scarcely been tested, so the limits of its cold hardiness need study. Flowers bell-shaped, usually clear red, solitary or few (2–4) per cluster, pendulous, ½"–¾" wide, with slender stems. Leaves high-gloss, hairless or lightly hairy beneath; sharply toothed; to 6⅞" × 2⅞" and identical to those of *P. cerasoides* (not in this volume) or perhaps less hairy and larger. Fruit red, ½"–⅝" long. Tree to 33' × 6'0, often narrowly erect in habit. Its hybrids include *Prunus* 'Kursar', *P.* 'Okamé', *P.* 'Shosar'; possibly *P.* 'Pink Cloud' and *P.* 'Wadae'.

P. campanulata 'Plena'

Origin unknown. Introduced to the U.S. from England in 1949 by the Arnold Arboretum. Exceedingly rare. Flowers small, red, double.

P. caroliniana (Mill.) Ait.

= *Laurocerasus caroliniana* (Mill.) M.J. Roem.

CAROLINA LAUREL. CAROLINA LAURELCHERRY. SOUTHERN LAUREL. WILD ORANGE. MOCK ORANGE. AMERICAN CHERRY-LAUREL. From the SE United Sates coastal plain. A broadleaf evergreen of lush, elegant texture and sparkling foliage. Cold hardy, it can be planted well beyond its original native range. In U.S. commerce since ≤1771. Common. Flowers in small tight clusters, fragrant, white, in late winter or early spring. Leaves glossy, bright green, and smooth, to 5¾" × 1⅞", sometimes with a few short sharp teeth. Cherries small, black, dry, inedible; can be messy. Bark smooth, dark gray. Closely related to *P. Laurocerasus* (ENGLISH LAUREL) from SE Europe, larger in every respect. Records: 55' × 9'10" × 48' near Eutawville, SC (1954); 48' × 10'2" × 35' Lake Houston State Park site, TX (1985); 47' × 10'7" × 55' Lakeland, FL (1987).

P. caroliniana Bright 'n Tight™

= *P. caroliniana* 'Monus'

('Brite & Tite')

Introduced in 1961 by Monrovia nursery of California. Compact medium-size shrub or small tree.

P. caroliniana 'Cherry Ruffle'

Discovered ca. 1988 alongside a road in North Carolina. Registered in 1990 by Flowerwood nursery of Loxley, AL. Flowers prominent, pink, as are the leaf edges and stems. Leaves slightly twisted and somewhat upright.

P. caroliniana 'Monus'—see P. caroliniana Bright 'n Tight™

P. Cascade Snow™

= *P.* 'Berry'

In the SATO ZAKURA group. Originally imported from a Japanese nursery by Rae Selling Berry (1881–1976) of Portland, OR. Its Japanese cultivar name was lost (possibly it is *P.* 'Shirayuki'); the clone was therefore renamed and introduced to commerce in 1994–95 by Schmidt nursery of Boring, OR. Pale pink buds open to pure white, single flowers, weakly scented, 1½"–1¾" wide, in short-stemmed clusters of (2) 3 (4). The individual flowerstems are lightly hairy, the sepals slightly toothed. Young leaves bronzy.

P. cerasifera Ehrh.

= *P. Myrobalana* (L.) Loisel.

= *P. domestica* var. *myrobalan* L.

CHERRY PLUM. MYROBALAN (PLUM). FLOWERING PLUM.

From Eurasia; an ancient hybrid race. From Latin *Cerasus*, a CHERRY TREE, and *ferre*, to bear, hence cherry-bearing. This species derives from *P. divaricata* (not in this volume), a thorny, bushy little tree with small yellow fruit. CHERRY PLUM does not grow wild except when it escapes from cultivation, which it does freely. The tree is larger than *P. divaricata*, less spiny with little sharp twigs; its fruit is larger (ca. ⅞"–1⅓") and can be green, orange, red or purple as well as yellow; its leaves are larger and wider. In other words, CHERRY PLUM is a tame or lush version of *P. divaricata*. Some botanists make *P. cerasifera* and *P. divaricata* synonymous, reasoning that these two names constitute one species with wild and cultivated manifestations. CHERRY PLUM is primarily used as a rootstock, but selections of it are highly valued ornamentally, and in some cases for the fruit. The name MYROBALAN derives from Greek *myron*, unguent, perfume, and *balanos*, acorn. Flowers white, small but profuse and very welcome in their early spring bloom. Leaves small (to 2⅝" × 1½"), thin, closely and finely toothed; larger in most cultivars. Twigs slender compared to those of most PLUM TREES. Record: 40' × 11'4" × 54' Big Lake, WA (1993).

P. cerasifera 'Allred'—see P. 'Allred'

P. cerasifera 'Asplenifolia'—see P. cerasifera 'Diversifolia'

P. cerasifera 'Atropurpurea'—see P. cerasifera 'Pissardii'

P. cerasifera 'Blaze'—see P. cerasifera 'Nigra'

P. cerasifera 'Diversifolia'

= *P. cerasifera* 'Asplenifolia'

Date of origin possibly 1925. Extremely rare in North America for decades, this cultivar was offered almost exclusively by Hillier's nursery of England, as: "The cut-leaf *P. Pissardii*, leaves narrow and deeply lobed," or "Leaves bronze-purple, varying in shape from ovate to lanceolate, often irregularly lobed or toothed. Flowers white. A sport of 'Pissardii'."

P. cerasifera 'Dwarf Purple Pony'—see P. cerasifera Purple Pony™

P. cerasifera 'Feketiana'—see P. cerasifera 'Pendula'

P. cerasifera 'Frankthrees'—see P. Mt. St. Helens™

P. cerasifera 'Hessei'

Even among PURPLELEAF PLUMS 'Hessei' is a freak. G. Krüssmann best describes it: "Shrub, small, slow growing; leaves narrow, irregularly incised and partly deformed, usually dark brown, teeth usually yellow or greenish, occasionally also yellow on a portion of the leaf blade. Developed around 1906 by Hesse of Weener, W. Germany." The raiser, Hermann Albrecht Hesse (1852–1937), had an important nursery career and distributed numerous plants. *Hillier's Manual of Trees and Shrubs* says of 'Hessei': "A medium-sized shrubby form with leaves pale green on emerging, becoming bronze-purple and mottled creamy white. Flowers snow-white, crowding the slender purple shoots in late March." Rare but available in Europe; virtually unknown in North America. A comparatively early North American nursery reference to it is the 1931 catalog of L. Coates nursery of San José, CA: "A dwarf slow growing plum with purple leaves margined white." Besides 'Hessei', another variegated PURPLELEAF PLUM cultivar is *P. cerasifera* 'Purpusii' (a tree).

P. cerasifera 'Hollywood'—see P. 'Hollywood' and P. 'Spencer Hollywood' and P. 'Trailblazer'

P. cerasifera 'Krauter's Vesuvius'

= *P. cerasifera* 'Vesuvius' (in part)

KRAUTER'S VESUVIUS PURPLELEAF PLUM. Introduced by Carl Krauter of Krauter nursery, Bakersfield, CA. The earliest mention of the tree is in 1956. It spread quickly in cultivation. Not only has it become far more widely planted than the original *Prunus* 'Vesuvius' of L. Burbank, but is the most common PURPLELEAF PLUM in the southwestern U.S. Many writers fail to note the differences between the original hybrid 'Vesuvius' and Krauter's purebred CHERRY PLUM version. 'Krauter's Vesuvius' looks like *P. cerasifera* 'Thundercloud'. There is no doubt of its genetic validity as a separate individual clone, but seeing one or the other, it is impossible to know which it is. The youngest leaves of 'Krauter's Vesuvius' are deeper red and less bronzy-purple than those of 'Thundercloud', but this difference is observable only for a week or two in a nursery where both trees are together for comparison. 'Krauter's Vesuvius' thrives better in the hot, dry Southwest.

P. cerasifera 'Lindsayae'

Miss Nancy Lindsay introduced this cultivar from Iran to England in the 1930s. It bears pink, single flowers, green leaves on a strong, broad crown, and produces few plums—golden with a red blush; weakly flavored; large for *P. cerasifera*. Almost unknown in North America, though mature specimens in Victoria, British Columbia, are handsome enough to prove that the rarity of the tree has nothing to do with its lack of merit. Records from Victoria: 49½' × 4'9½" × 42' (1993) and 36' × 5'0" × 40' (1992).

P. cerasifera Mt. St. Helens™—see P. Mt. St. Helens™

P. cerasifera 'Newport'—see P. 'Newport'

P. cerasifera 'Nigra'

= *P. cerasifera* 'Blaze'

The first printed work containing the cultivar name 'Nigra' was the 1916 *Standard Cyclopedia of Horticulture* by L.H. Bailey. The sole extent of Bailey's treatment of 'Nigra', however, is "very dark purple leaves." The brevity and vagueness of this mention make it worthless, as many clones have "very dark purple leaves." The 1917 edition of *Johnson's Gardener's Dictionary* cites 'Nigra' as having been introduced in 1908. Whether contemporary nursery stock dubbed 'Nigra' is the same as stock that Bailey (*et al.*) originally intended is impossible to certify. 'Nigra' as sold currently, represents *P. cerasifera* with some of the darkest leaves, but the clone also differs in bearing pink flowers which open some 2 or 3 weeks later in spring than those of 'Pissardii'. 'Nigra' is more densely compact compared to its otherwise similar kin *P. cerasifera* 'Thundercloud', 'Krauter's Vesuvius', and 'Woodii'. It may further differ from these similar taxa in making fewer plums. Though 'Nigra' is a major clone (or name, anyway) in Canada, Europe, and Australia, it has been grown relatively little in the U.S. (in commerce here ≤1936). In England, a fancy nursery name for 'Nigra' is 'Blaze'. Dr. B.K. Boom suggested that the "Nigra" of European commerce was really 'Woodii' and the authentic 'Nigra' of U.S. origin was rarely grown. If cultivar names were treated according to the rigorous rules applied to scientific names, 'Nigra' would be instantly disallowed as ambiguous.

P. cerasifera 'Othello'

= *P.* 'Othello'

OTHELLO PLUM. A seedling of *P. cerasifera* 'Pissardii', with darker leaves whose fruit ripens earlier than normal. Originated by L. Burbank of Santa Rosa, CA, who sold the rights in 1905 to Vaughan's Seed Store of Chicago and New York. Sold for decades after its introduction, but during the last 30 years seldom or never offered for sale, at least under its proper name. Presumably of average growth and form.

P. cerasifera 'Pendula'
= P. cerasifera 'Feketiana' or 'Feketeana'

WEEPING CHERRY PLUM. Cultivated in Germany since 1864; first named officially in 1901. Very rarely grown in North America. A greenleaved cultivar despite having been erroneously cited in some sources as purpleleaved. White flowers in March, on strongly drooping, green twigs. Varies according to its rootstock, from a dense, dripping top-grafted mop-head to a large, stout-trunked, wide tree. It might be confused with the 'Weeping Santa Rosa' JAPANESE PLUM (P. salicina).

P. cerasifera 'Pissardii'
= P. cerasifera 'Atropurpurea'
= P. Pissardi(i) or Pissarti(i)

PISSARD PLUM. PURPLELEAF PLUM. COPPER PLUM. The first PURPLELEAF PLUM. Found ca. 1878 by Monsieur Pissard, head gardener to the shah of Persia (Iran). In 1880, Pissard sent it to France. The novelty tree boomed in popularity, was sold widely (in U.S. commerce ≤1885), and soon the original clonal 'Pissardii' was "diluted" by an undocumented combination of seedling variants, sports, and later imports from Persia. Today it is an uncertain matter to know and describe the pure, original 'Pissardii' clone. Though dark-leaved, it was not as dark or as persistently so as were some of its seedlings. Its flowers were white, not pink. It was fruitful, with plums of red skin and flesh. Various seedlings have exhibited darker flowers, later blooming, darker leaves, larger leaves, cut or variegated leaves, hairy twigs, darker or larger plums, sometimes with yellowish flesh. For long after its introduction, 'Pissardii' was often thought of as a large shrub rather than a tree, and most older North American nursery catalogs included it in the shrub section. Records: 48' × 7'4" × 57' Seattle, WA (1987); 44' × 9'1" × 47' Victoria, B.C. (1989).

P. cerasifera 'Pissardii Rosea'—see P. cerasifera 'Rosea'

P. cerasifera 'Pissardii Rubra'

In the 1939 catalog of W.B. Clarke nursery of San José, CA. The description only reads: "A form of [P. cerasifera 'Pissardii'] with somewhat ruddier foliage."

P. cerasifera 'Purple Flame'

PURPLE FLAME PLUM. Originated by L. Burbank ca. 1922; introduced commercially in 1931 by Stark Bro's nursery of Missouri. Stark sold the clone until the early 1970s: "Height 15'–20'. Before the colorful wine red foliage appears, the tree is a mass of pink blushed white blooms with deep red at the throat. Small red plums, which are good to eat, follow." Likely the clone had been offered exclusively by Stark, so probably only individuals scattered around the U.S. obtained specimens. How this clone differs from P. 'Allred', P. cerasifera 'Othello', and other PURPLELEAF PLUMS whose fruit is considered a major asset is still unknown. It may be an extra-narrow tree, as is suggested by its name "flame."

P. cerasifera Purple Pony™
= P. cerasifera 'Dwarf Purple Pony'

PURPLE PONY PLUM. A seedling from Merced, CA, in the late 1950s; from an open-pollinated P. cerasifera 'Krauter's Vesuvius'. Named because of its dwarfhood, full purple color in the summer, and total fruitlessness. Registered ≤1972 by L.E. Cooke nursery of Visalia, CA. Rarely seen in nurseries outside of California. Semi-dwarf with "outstanding purple foliage that holds its color from spring to leaf drop." A scant producer of single pink blossoms: one per bud, or rarely, a few pairs. The flowers are borne primarily near the tree top, and appear with rather than before the unfolding leaves. The sepals do not reflex strongly, as on nearly all other CHERRY PLUM seedlings, and the flowerstalks are comparatively short. The tree's foliage is very dark and persistently so. In this respect it is like P. cerasifera 'Nigra' and other cultivars; however, its leaves are comparatively narrower and less hairy. The features exhibited by 'Purple Pony' suggest it is a hybrid, but it may be an aberrant, nonhybridized CHERRY PLUM seedling. Record: 17' × 2'4" × 19' Los Angeles, CA (1993; pl. 1974).

P. cerasifera 'Purpusii'

PURPUS' PLUM. Best described by G. Krüssmann: "New growth green, then becoming red-brown, later with yellow and pink zoning along the midrib. Introduced into the trade by Hesse of Weener, W. Germany in 1908." Flowers white. Named after Joseph Anton Purpus (1860–1933), who worked at the botanic gardens of Darmstadt, Hesse, Germany. Offered by the Hesse nursery for decades. Rarely imported into North America. The name is sometimes misspelled and more often mistaken for meaning "purple." In brief, 'Purpusii' is a variegated PURPLE-LEAF PLUM—like *P. cerasifera* 'Hessei' (which see) in this respect, but the latter is bushy.

P. cerasifera 'Rosea'

= *P. cerasifera* 'Pissardii Rosea'

The name 'Rosea' has been applied to various cultivars of *Prunus*, including two PURPLELEAF PLUMS—one of them the true clone (see *Prunus* 'Rosea'). The incorrect usage began when the famous Wayside Gardens nursery of Mentor, OH, offered *Prunus Pissardii rosea*, from at least 1944 to 1972. The clone actually sold by Wayside was likely *P. cerasifera* 'Nigra' or 'Woodii'.

P. cerasifera 'Spaethiana'—see P. cerasifera 'Woodii'

P. cerasifera 'Stribling Thundercloud'—see P. 'Vesuvius'

P. cerasifera 'Thundercloud'

THUNDERCLOUD PLUM. The first use of this name, spelled as two words, was in 1919 by L. Burbank of Santa Rosa, CA. In recent decades a 'Thundercloud' clone has become the most widely planted PURPLELEAF PLUM in North America. The use of the name was not widespread in the 1920s and '30s. Catalogs and books cite conflicting information: the flowers are sometimes listed as white, but normally (and more recently) as pink. More than one clone has gone under the name. It seems impossible to know if the tree sold by hundreds of nurseries today is Burbank's. The 'Thundercloud' in contemporary commerce is an unhybridized *P. cerasifera* with dark leaves, pink flowers, and purplish plums, inside and out. It cannot be easily distinguished from 'Krauter's Vesuvius', 'Nigra', and 'Woodii'. Records: 34' × 3'5" × 27' and 30' × 5'4" × 39' Seattle, WA (1988).

P. cerasifera 'Vesuvius'—see P. cerasifera 'Krauter's Vesuvius' and P. 'Vesuvius'

P. cerasifera 'Woodii'

= *P. cerasifera* 'Wood's Variety'
= *P. cerasifera* 'Spaethiana'

Named for or by the English nursery founded by William Wood (1781–1863), in Maresfield, East Sussex, England. Introduced to the U.S. from France in 1931 by the Arnold Arboretum. Extinct in commerce. Practically identical to *P. cerasifera* 'Nigra'.

P. cerasifera 'Wood's Variety'—see P. cerasifera 'Woodii'

P. cerasoides var. campanulata—see P. campanulata

P. Cerasus L.

= *Cerasus communis* Poit. & Turp.
= *Cerasus vulgaris* Mill.
= *Cerasus acida* Ehrh.
?(*P. avium* × *P. fruticosa*)

PIE CHERRY. SOUR CHERRY. TART CHERRY. Not truly wild; originated in the Near East; long naturalized in Europe and parts of North America. *Cerasus* is the classical Latin name of the CHERRY TREE, from *Kerasos*, later Kerasund or Keresoon, then Kerasun or Giresun, a town in Turkey, whence the CHERRY was brought to Rome by the general Lucullus in [73?] 68 B.C.—but maybe CORNELIAN CHERRY (*Cornus mas*) was meant. Very commonly grown for its delicious fruit. With its white flowers, dark glossy leaves and bright red fruit, the tree is beautiful—but only certain cultivars are planted for ornament. Much smaller, even shrubby, compared to SWEET CHERRY (*P. avium*). Often suckers from the roots. Record: 41' × 11'9" × 53' Windsor, CT (1988).

P. Cerasus 'Globe'—see P. × Gondouinii 'Schnee'

P. Cerasus 'Rhexii'

= *Cerasus vulgaris dupliciflora* Lobel

Cultivated in Europe <1581. In North American commerce ≤1910 (likely much earlier). Very rare here. Flowers 1¼"–1½" wide, with ca. 60 petals; pure white except green in the center.

P. Cerasus 'Roseo-plena'—see P. 'Hokusai'

P. Cerasus 'Schnee'—see P. × Gondouinii 'Schnee'

P. Cerasus 'Semperflorens'

= *Cerasus semperflorens pendula* hort.

ALL SAINTS' CHERRY. EVERBLOOMING CHERRY. Cultivated in Europe <1623. In North American commerce ≤1891. Exceedingly rare. Topgrafted; weeping somewhat from a wide, roundish crown. Flowers late, borne singly all summer long, not showy. Cherries red.

P. 'Choshu-hizakura'

= *P. serrulata* f. *splendens* Miyoshi
= *P. serrulata* 'Choshu-hizakura'
= *P. Lannesiana* f. *chosiuhizakura* (Koidz.) Wils. ('Choshiu-hizakura')

In the SATO ZAKURA group. Name means "red" or

"pink cherry of Choshu." Buds purple-red. Flowers nearly single, of 5–7 (9) petals, deep rosy-pink, 1⅝"–2" wide, in loose clusters of 2–4 (6); sepals untoothed, wine-colored. Young foliage reddish-brown or coppery-red. Record: 30' × 3'10" × 36' Seattle, WA (1993).

P. × cistena (Hansen) Koehne
(cistina)
= P. 'Crimson Dwarf'
(P. Besseyi × P. cerasifera 'Pissardii')

CISTENA PLUM. DWARF RED SAND CHERRY. PURPLELEAF SAND CHERRY. HANSEN'S PURPLE PLUM. PURPLE BUSH PLUM. DWARF REDLEAF PLUM. An intentional hybrid made <1906 by N. Hansen of Brookings, SD. The female parent is WESTERN SAND-CHERRY (not in this volume), a bush with tiny fruit. Cistena means baby in the Sioux language. Introduced in 1910. Common. The most cold-hardy and dwarf PURPLELEAF PLUM. Leaves 1½"–3" long, hairless, purple. Flowers fragrant, white, in April and May. Fruit sparingly produced, small, dark purple, of poor quality. Naturally a shrub, sometimes trained into tree form. Record: 13' × 1'8½" × 23' Yakima, WA (1994).

P. × cistena Big Cis™ PP 5003 (1983)
= P. × cistena 'Schmidtcis'

A sport found ca. 1975 and put into commerce by Schmidt nursery of Boring, OR. More robust, with larger leaves and faster growth.

P. × cistena 'Schmidtcis'—see P. × cistena Big Cis™

P. communis—see P. × domestica and P. dulcis

P. 'Crimson Dwarf'—see P. × cistena

P. 'Curtis Bok'
= P. serrulata 'Curtis Bok'

In the SATO ZAKURA group. Introduced <1942 by Wohlert nursery of Narberth, PA. Long extinct commercially. Named by Wohlert for his neighbor the judge. A variation of P. 'Kwanzan' described as deep rosy-pink.

P. cyclamina Koehne
CYCLAMEN CHERRY. From central China. Discovered in 1889–90 by A. Pratt. Introduced in 1907 by E. Wilson for the Arnold Arboretum. Named in 1912. Extremely rare in North America. Heavily promoted since ca. 1980 by the Arnold Arboretum. Blooms in early to mid-April, before P. Sargentii. Flowers pale rose, 1¼"–2⅜" wide, shortly stalked. Young foliage bronze to coppery-red. Fruit dull purple-red, peasized, ripe in late June or early July. Fall color poor. Record: 30' tall and 40' wide at Arnold Arboretum (1980; pl. 1930).

P. 'Daikoku'
= P. serrulata 'Daikoku'
= P. serrulata 'Beni-fugen' (wrongly—this is properly a synonym of P. 'Fugenzo')

In the SATO ZAKURA group. Introduced in 1899. Named in England in 1916. In North American commerce since ≤1935. Uncommon. Named after one of the 7 Japanese gods of prosperity. Daikoku is generally depicted as a fat and jovial god accompanied by a huge sack of rice. Since the flowers of this cultivar look somewhat opulent, the name of this deity seems appropriate. Habit erect when young, ultimately spreading; to 30' tall. Buds dark purplish-red, thick, truncate. Flowers of 40–50 petals, purplish-pink, darkest in the center, with leafy carpels in the flower center; 2"–2½" wide, in loose, long-stalked drooping clusters; late in the season. Young foliage yellowish-green.

P. × dasycarpa Ehrh.
= Armeniaca dasycarpa (Ehrh.) Borkh.
(P. Armeniaca × P. cerasifera)

BLACK APRICOT. PURPLE APRICOT. From SW & Central Asia, where it has been cultivated for centuries for the edible fruit. Introduced to England between 1781 and 1790 by C. Loddiges' nursery. Named in 1791 (dasycarpa from Greek, meaning very hairy-fruited). Exceedingly rare in North America, but more than one selection is in commerce among fruit enthusiasts. More frost-resistant than APRICOT. Twigs olive-red or purplish, hairless, thin. Leaves PLUM-like, 1½"–2½" long. Flowers white or pink tinged, ¾" wide, mid-April to early May. Fruit 1½" wide, purple-red to violet-black, velutinous-hairy, juicy, sour, apricot-flavored. A small tree, to 20' tall.

P. Davidiana (Carr.) Franch.
= Persica Davidiana Carr.
= Amygdalus Davidiana (Carr.) C. de Vos

DAVID'S PEACH. CHINESE WILD PEACH. From N China. Possibly the PEACH (P. Persica) was derived from this species. Introduced in 1865 to France by the Basque Jesuit, Jean Pierre Armand David (1826–1900). Named in 1872. In North American commerce ≤1900. Uncommon. Used as a rootstock in China. Flowers white or light pink, 1" wide, very early in spring—in January sometimes, or as late as mid-March. Leaves very slender and sharp, to 5¾" × 2"; jaggedly toothed; pale glaucous beneath with red venation. Fruit small (1"–1¼" wide), yellowish, dry and inedible. Recorded by F. Meyer to 50'–60' tall in the wild.

P. Davidiana 'Alba'

Named in 1872. In North American commerce ≤1910. Rare. White flowers.

P. Davidiana 'Rosea'

In North American commerce ≤1918. Very rare. Flowers pink. Probably this is the typical color form of P. Davidiana.

P. Davidiana 'Rubra'

Named in 1887. In North American commerce ≤1910. Very rare. Flowers bright rosy-red.

P. demissa—see P. virginiana

P. × domestica L.

= P. communis Huds. 1762, non Arcang. 1882
= P. sativa Rouy & Camus
?(P. cerasifera × P. spinosa)

EUROPEAN PLUM. COMMON PLUM. PRUNE PLUM. GARDEN PLUM. Unknown in the wild; from Iran and Asia Minor; of complex hybrid origin. Cultivated for its edible fruit in North America since ≤1638; very common. Flowers in April, white, ¾"–1" wide. Leaves 1½"–3" long, bluntish, more or less hairy. Fruit to 3" long, bluish-black, purple, red or greenish; when dried called prunes. A root-suckering shrub or small tree. Record: 45' × 7'9" × 41' Reed College, Portland, OR (1976). A second Portland tree, claimed in 1993 to be the champion, is really P. cerasifera (CHERRY PLUM).

P. × domestica var. insititia (L.) Fiori & Paol.

= P. × domestica ssp. insititia (L.) Schneid.
= P. insititia L.

BULLACE. The 1755 name insititia means grafted, i.e. cultivated. Twigs densely downy; branches often thorny. Fruit ¾"–1", usually rounded or broadly ellipsoid, usually dark purple, can be greenish. Usually a large shrub. Has been considered intermediate between typical P. domestica and P. spinosa (BLACKTHORN). A cultivated version is DAMSON (originating near Damascus), a small tree, fruit 1"–2" long, always dark purple. A second cultivated version is MIRABELLE, bearing round, yellow fruit.

P. domestica var. myrobalan—see P. cerasifera

P. × domestica 'Plantierensis'

('Plantieri')

Presumably from Plantières, near Metz, France. Cultivated since the 1630s in England. In North America ≤1896. Exceedingly rare here. Flowers semi-double. Fruit violet.

P. × dropmoreana F.L. Skinner (nom. nud.)

DROPMORE CHERRY. Bred in 1952 by F.L. Skinner's nursery in Dropmore, Manitoba, in a colchicine experiment which crossed (P. Cerasus 'Kozlov' × P. pennsylvanica) × P. Maackii. Introduced in 1954. Fruit extremely bitter. The seeds are fertile, their offspring used as cold-hardy rootstock for SOUR CHERRY cultivars. The DROPMORE CHERRY itself, says J. Searles, makes profuse single white flowers in May; has showy CHERRY-like shiny bark; and semi-glossy foliage turning yellow in fall.

P. dulcis (Mill.) D.A. Webb

= P. Amygdalus Batsch
= P. communis (L.) Arcang. 1882, non Huds. 1762
= Amygdalus communis L.

ALMOND TREE. From N Africa to Syria. Famous and much cultivated for its edible kernels or nuts. Until 1967, known as P. Amygdalus (from amysso or amusso, to lacerate, referring to the corrugated or fissured shell of the nut). Dulcis means sweet. As a nut-producer it is mainly grown in California, where the two chief cultivars are 'Mission' and 'Nonpareil'. Usually self-incompatible, so mixed plantings prevail. With greater strength and disease-resistance than the closely related and showier PEACH (P. Persica), ALMONDS are worthy as ornamental flowering trees in regions where they receive sufficient winter-chill. In some locales their floral display is in danger of being wrecked by late spring frosts. Flowers white or palest pink, 1"–1½" wide. Leaves 2"–4" long, narrow and shiny, subtly toothed, of poor and late fall color: weak yellow with much green. Fruit like a small, thin-fleshed, green peach. Record: 38' × 5'11" × 31' The Dalles, OR (1989).

P. dulcis 'Alba Plena'

DOUBLE WHITE ALMOND. Described in 1903 in Germany. Extremely rare in North America. Flowers double, pure white.

P. dulcis 'Pendula'

WEEPING ALMOND. Cultivated in Europe since ca. 1548; officially named in 1865. Extremely rare in North America. Pendulous habit.

P. dulcis 'Roseoplena'

= *Amygdalus communis* 'Flore Pleno'
= *Amygdalus communis* 'Flore Roseo Pleno'
= *Amygdalus communis* 'Double Pink'

DOUBLE PINK ALMOND. Described in 1792 in Austria. In North American commerce ≤1890; rare here. Flowers double, pale pink, in April or May (late for an ALMOND). Fruitless or nearly so. Tree compact, round-topped, usually ca. 15' tall. Both leaves and fruit (when made) suggest this clone has some PEACH (*P. Persica*) genes, so is probably best referred to as a cultivar of *P. × persicoides*. Record: 30' × 5'10" × 29' Seattle, WA (1992).

P. × effusa—see P. × Gondouinii

P. × effusa 'Schnee'—see P. × Gondouinii 'Schnee'

P. emarginata (Dougl. ex Hook.) Eaton

= *P. prunifolia* (Greene) Schafer
= *P. mollis* (Dougl. *ex* Hook.) Walp., non Torr.
= *Cerasus mollis* Dougl. *ex* Hook.
= *C. emarginata* Dougl. *ex* Hook.
= *C. erecta* Presl

BITTER CHERRY. QUININE CHERRY. FIRE CHERRY. WESTERN PIN CHERRY. From B.C. to New Mexico. Named in 1832 (*emarginata* refers to the shallow notches in the petals). Introduced to cultivation in the 1860s. Extremely rare in commerce, even within its native range. Very slender in trunk and limb. A weak, short-lived tree with nondescript flowers, bitter red fruit, pale yellow fall color. Closely related to *P. pennsylvanica* (FIRE CHERRY). Records: 103' × 6'6" × 38' Toledo, WA (1974); 62' × 9'5" × 56' near Gardiner, OR (1975); 50' × 9'8" × 45' Bowen Island, B.C. (1981).

P. 'Frankthrees'—see P. Mt. St. Helens™

P. fruticosa f. shojo—see P. 'Shojo'

P. 'Fudan-zakura'

= *P. serrulata* 'Fudan-zakura'
= *P. Lannesiana* f. *fudanzakura* (Koidz.) Wils.
= *P. serrulata* f. *semperflorens* Miyoshi
= *P. serrulata* 'Shiki-zakura'
= *P. pubescens sakura* hort.
= *P. Leveilleana* 'Fudan-zakura'

In the SATO ZAKURA group. Name means "continuous cherry." It has been exceedingly rare in North America; in commerce ≤1930s, then largely neglected until the 1990s. A small tree, of a broad vase-like crown with slender shoots. Buds soft pink. Flowers white, single (or nearly so), 1⅓"–1½" wide, either blooming sporadically between late November and late-April, or simply blooming much earlier than the other SATO ZAKURA (February); easily forced. Young foliage coppery-red or reddish-brown. Winter buds smaller than those of most SATO ZAKURA. Leaves broad (to 4½" × 2⅝"), sharply doubly toothed, not glaucous; hairy on both surfaces. Leafstems short (≤½" long), conspicuously large-glanded, hairy, with prominent large dissected, even leaflike stipules. Young shoots hairless. (Japanese books note hairless leaves, so must refer to a different clone than that grown in the West.)

P. 'Fugenzo'

= *P. serrulata* 'Fugenzo'
= *P. serrulata* 'Kofugen'
= *P. serrulata* 'James (H.) Veitch'
= *P. serrulata* f. *classica* Miyoshi (in part)
= *P. serrulata* f. *albo-rosea* Mak., non Wils. (cf. *P.* 'Shirofugen')
= *P. serrulata* f. *fugenzo* Mak. (in part)
= *P. serrulata* 'Beni-fugen' (cf. 'Daikoku')

In the SATO ZAKURA group. Name means "fugen elephant" (the petal tips are curved like an elephant nose) or "goddess on a white elephant." Known by ≤1400s; introduced to England in 1878 by J.H. Veitch. In North American commerce since ≤1901. Commonly listed by nurseries until recently. Tree moderately strong, broadly rounded; often with interwoven branching. Less vigorous than *P.* 'Kwanzan' and with a flat-headed growth habit; tree less leggy and gaunt. Crimson buds have sharply toothed sepals curled characteristically. Flowers 1⅞"–2½" wide, double, (16) 25–30 (50) petals, deep pink, usually with 2 (rarely only 1) tiny leafy carpels in the middle. Among the last to bloom in spring. Young foliage with a hint of bronze. Record: 21' × 4'9" × 31' Seattle, WA (1993; *pl.* 1941).

P. 'Fuku-rokuju'

= *P. serrulata* 'Fuku-rokuju'
= *P. serrulata* f. *contorta* Miyoshi
= *P. Lannesiana* f. *fukurokuju* Wils.

In the SATO ZAKURA group. 'Fuku-rokuju' means "genius of good fortune and long life" (or "wealth"). The name *contorta* refers to the much-wrinkled petals. Planted in 1912 along the Potomac; some also elsewhere in Washington, D.C. Exceedingly rare in North America. Habit stiffly upright, slowly making a well-rounded compact crown. Buds deep carmine-pink. Flowers very pale pink, almost white in the center, semi-double (ca. 15–20 petals), 2" wide; in clusters of 2–4 in large globular masses at or near the ends of branches. Main floral stems relatively short and thick. Sepals nearly always untoothed. Young foliage bronzy-green. Leaf often roundish and blunt. *P.* 'Tanko-shinju' ('Pink Pearl') is very similar, differing chiefly in broader sepals, possibly pinker flowers; habit more spreading. Also similar is *P.* 'Hokusai'.

P. × *Gondouinii* (Poit. & Turp.) Rehd.
= *P.* × *effusa* (Host) Schneid.
= *P. avium* var. *regalis* (Poit. & Turp.) Bailey
(*P. Cerasus* × *P. avium*)

SOUR CHERRY / SWEET CHERRY hybrids, such as DUKE or ROYAL CHERRIES, are given this binomial. The name commemorates a gardener named Gondouin, who raised such a tree ca. 1760 at the royal gardens at Choisy, near Paris.

P. × *Gondouinii* 'Schnee'
= *P. Cerasus* 'Schnee'
= *P. Cerasus* 'Globe'
= *P.* × *effusa* 'Schnee'
= *P. avium* 'Schnee'
= *P. avium* 'Scanlon'

SCHNEE CHERRY. Originated ca. 1910–1920 by Wilhelm Pfitzer of Stuttgart, Germany. *Schnee* is the German word for snow. Scanlon nursery of Ohio, sold this as a topgrafted (on MAZZARD CHERRY, *P. avium*), globular tree from 1959 onward. Grows larger than many SOUR CHERRIES. Flowers single, white, mostly sterile. Fruit ca. ½" long, darkest purple. Leaves hairless above, with scattered long pale hairs below. Definitely more MAZZARD-like in both leaf and fruit, showing SOUR CHERRY influence in the tree size and form, as well as in the flowers.

P. 'Gosho (-zakura)'
('Goshio-zakura', 'Gosio-zakura', 'Gozio-zakura')
= *P. serrulata* 'Gosho (-zakura)'
= *P. serrulata* f. *radiata* Miyoshi
= *P. Lannesiana* f. *gosiozakura* (Koidz.) Wils.

In the SATO ZAKURA group. Name means "five stems" —referring to the floral clusters. In North American commerce during the 1930s and '40s. Very rare; long commercially extinct. Tree upright, spreading; to 18' tall. Buds deep rosy-red. Flowers in short-stemmed, rather stiff clusters of 2–6 (commonly 5); semi-double (ca. 18–20 petals), pale pink, deeper at the margins and beneath; to 2" wide; sepals not toothed, reddish-brown. Similar to *P.* 'Tanko-shinju'.

P. 'Gozanoma-nioi'
= *P. serrulata* 'Gozanoma-nioi'
= *P. serrulata* 'Ozu Mako'
= *P. Lannesiana* f. *gozanomanioi* Wils.

In North America ≤1916. Very rare. Sold from at least 1941 to 1958 by Kingsville nursery of Maryland. Flowers single, white, to 1¼" wide, very fragrant. Similar to *P.* 'Taki-nioi'.

P. 'Gyoiko'
('Gioiko')
= *P. serrulata* 'Gioiko' or 'Gyoiko'
= *P. serrulata* 'Tricolor'
= *P. serrulata* f. *tricolor* Miyoshi
= *P. Lannesiana* f. *gioiko* (Koidz.) Wils.

In the SATO ZAKURA group. Name means "the imperial yellowish costume." Cultivated in the West since ca. 1903. In North American commerce since ≤1931. Uncommon. Tree upright like *P.* 'Ukon' and *P.* 'Kwanzan'. Very similar to 'Ukon'. Flowers ca. 1½" wide, semi-double (11–20 petals), pale yellow (a shade darker than 'Ukon') with green stripes which later turn cerise; with age more or less uniformly pinkish. Young foliage greenish-brown or reddish-brown.

P. 'Hally Jolivette'
?(*P. subhirtella* × *P. apetala*)

HALLY JOLIVETTE CHERRY. PINK MIST CHERRY. Bred in 1941 at the Arnold Arboretum, named and introduced in 1944. Rare until the late 1950s; uncommon since. Named after Dr. Hally Jolivette Sax (1884–1979). A twiggy bush or very small tree. Natural bonsai. Often topgrafted on trunks of BIRCHBARK CHERRY (*P. serrula*). Flowers pure white; paired or in trios; double (15–24 petals); in March. Twigs very slender, scantily hairy. Leaves a great deal like those of *P. incisa*; 1"–2¼" long, deeply toothed, lightly hairy on both sides.

P. 'Hata-zakura'
= *P. serrulata* 'Hata-zakura'
= *P. serrulata* f. *vexillipetala* Miyoshi
= *P. Lannesiana* f. *hatazakura* (Koidz.) Wils.

In the SATO ZAKURA group. Name means "flag cherry" (refers to the enlarged and folded floral filaments). In North American commerce ≤1939. Very rare. Branches ascending. Buds pink. Flowers fragrant, single (usually) or semi-double, small, white or pink-flushed; early. Young foliage bronzy-brown.

P. 'Hillieri'

= *P.* × *Hillieri* hort.
?(*P. Sargentii* × *P. incisa* or *P. yedoensis*)

HILLIER CHERRY. A seedling of *Prunus Sargentii* from the Arnold Arboretum, raised <1928 by Hillier nursery of England. *P. incisa* was first suggested as its male parent, but the latest word from Hillier suggests *P.* × *yedoensis*. Introduced to North America ≤1946, but extremely rare here. Mauve-pink buds open to blush-pink or whitish flowers, 1"–1¼" wide, borne 2–3 together. Young foliage bronze; leaves hairy above, the veins hairy beneath. Mature leaves exquisitely sharply toothed, otherwise resembling *P. Sargentii* in shape, size (to 4⅛" × 2½"), and in being pale beneath. A broad-crowned tree, more elegant in texture than *P.* × *Juddii*, with more long shoots. Similar flowers and foliage to *P.* 'Spire'. Record: 30' × 8'5" × 56' Seattle, WA (1993).

P. × Hillieri 'Spire'—see P. 'Spire'

P. 'Hillier Spire'—see P. 'Spire'

P. 'Hisakura'

= *P. serrulata* 'Hisakura'
= *P. serrulata* f. *unifolia* Miyoshi
= *P. serrulata* f. *hisakura* Koehne
= *P. serrulata* 'Ichiyo'
= *P. Lannesiana* 'Hisakura'
('Hizakura')

In the SATO ZAKURA group. In North American commerce since ≤1931. Uncommon. The name 'Hizakura' (meaning "red" or "pink cherry") is used in contemporary Japan for the clone described as follows. Its vernacular *Ichiyo* means "one-leaved"—referring to the green carpel(s), either normal or leaflike, which is (or are) often conspicuous in the flower center. 'Hisakura' has long been incorrectly called 'Ichiyo' in the West, where the name 'Hisakura' has been used for *P.* 'Choshu-hizakura' and *P.* 'Kwanzan' and possibly for others. Tree strong, to 25' tall, broadly spreading with a rounded crown. Buds carmine. Flowers double (15–50 petals), frilled; pale pink at first, soon pure white except for pink tinges on margins and undersides, 1½"–2" wide, in small clusters of 2–4, with long slender stems; sepals with occasional teeth. Young foliage bronzy- or yellowish-green, soon green.

P. 'Hokusai'

= *P. serrulata* 'Hokusai'
= *P. serrulata* 'Rosea'
= *P. serrulata* 'Rosea-plena'
= *P. Cerasus* 'Rosea-plena'

= *Cerasus flore roseo pleno* hort.

In the SATO ZAKURA group. Imported to Holland ca. 1866 by Siebold. Named in 1925 after the famous Japanese artist Hokusai Katsushuka (1760–1849). In North American commerce since ≤1929. Rare. Tree wide spreading; vigorous. Flowers profuse, semi-double (7–20 petals), pale pink with an "orange," "apricot," or "mushroom" tinge, 1⅔"–2" wide, in loose, long-stemmed clusters of (3) 4–6. Young foliage pale-bronze. Similar to *P.* 'Fuku-rokuju'. Record: 24' × 6'11" × 57' Tacoma, WA (1990).

P. 'Hollywood'

= *P. cerasifera* 'Hollywood'
(*P. cerasifera* 'Pissardii' × *P. salicina*)

HOLLYWOOD PLUM. A chance seedling that originated ca. 1932 in Modesto, CA, found by L.L. Brooks. Introduced to commerce in 1936. Its relative abundance is difficult to state because several clones go under the same name, notably *P.* 'Spencer Hollywood' and *P.* 'Trailblazer'. All cultivars called HOLLYWOOD PLUM feature purplish foliage and good crops of edible fruit. The original 'Hollywood' is notable for its very early blooming and ripening. On the West Coast it blooms in February and March, and ripens its plums in June and July. Pale pink buds open to white flowers. Leaves widest above the middle. Plums 1½"–2" (2½"), red inside and out.

P. 'Horaisan'

= *P. serrulata* 'Horaisan'
= *P. Lannesiana* f. *horaisan* (Koidz.) Wils.

In the SATO ZAKURA group. Sold during the late 1930s and '40s by Kohankie nursery of Painesville, OH. Extremely rare. Flowers white, semi-double.

P. 'Horinji'

= *P. serrulata* 'Horinji'
= *P. serrulata* f. *horinji* (Koidz.) Wils.
= *P. serrulata* f. *decora* Miyoshi
= *P. serrulata* 'Kabuto-zakura' of Ingram
= *P. Lannesiana* 'Decora'

In the SATO ZAKURA group. Name is of an ancient Buddhist temple in Kyoto. Introduced to the West ca. 1905. In North American commerce since ≤1934. Rare. Tree small, with stout, stiffly ascending branches, sparsely furnished with foliage; to 18' tall and 12' wide. Buds mauvy-pink. Flowers 1¾"–2" wide, flattish, almost white in center with pinker margins; semi-double (12–20 petals); in large drooping clusters of 2–6; sepals and calyx dark purplish-brown. Blooms over a unusually long period. Young foliage greenish-brown. Leaves long and narrow.

P. *hortulana* Bailey

HORTULAN PLUM. The name WILD GOOSE PLUM is partly used for this species, but mostly for the closely related, more southerly *P. Munsoniana* (not in this volume). From parts of the Upper Midwest, Ohio to Oklahoma. Named *hortulana* in 1892 because it was first noticed through the work of horticulturists, who had grown it for fruit long before it was named by botanists. Many fruiting cultivars exist; it is not grown for ornament. Actually, rather than a pure species, *P. hortulana* may be best regarded as a name applicable to various hybrids involving *P. americana* and *P. angustifolia*. Flowers small (mostly ≤½" wide), white, mostly in April before the leaves emerge. Plums ¾"–1¼", bright red or yellowish-red to pure gold, slightly bloomy. A small tree, not suckering from the root or thicket-forming. Record: 27' × 2'9" × 30' Van Meter State Park, MO (1972).

P. 'Hosokawa'

= *P. serrulata* 'Hosokawa'
= *P. serrulata* 'Hosokawa-nioi' ('Hesokawanoi', 'Hosakawanoi')
= *P. serrulata* f. *hosokawa-nioi* Miyoshi
= *P. Lannesiana* f. *hosokawa* Wils.
= *P. Lannesiana* 'Hosokawa-odora'

In the SATO ZAKURA group. Named after Lord Hosokawa, a Japanese nobleman. In North American commerce ≤1931. Very rare. Tree spreading, to 15' tall. Buds faintly pink. Flowers single or nearly so, pure white, fragrant, to 1½" wide in rather long-stemmed clusters of 3–6; sepals sharply toothed. Young foliage yellowish-brown, soon green. See also *P.* 'Ruth Wohlert'.

P. 'Hosokawa-beni'

= *P. serrulata* 'Hosokawa-beni'

('Hasokawa-beni', 'Hosokawa-teni', 'Hozokawa-beni')

In the SATO ZAKURA group. In North American commerce ≤1931. Very rare. Described by P. Wohlert as upright, of SUGAR MAPLE form. Flowers midseason, fragrant, blush or pale pink, semi-double.

P. *ilicifolia* (Nutt. *ex* H. & A.) D. Dietr.

= *Cerasus ilicifolia* Nutt. *ex* H. & A.

HOLLYLEAF CHERRY. EVERGREEN CHERRY. ISLAY. MOUNTAIN HOLLY. From coastal California, Napa County southward. Cultivated since the Spanish period in California. Scarcely ever grown elsewhere. The name *ilicifolia* means HOLLY-leaved; from genus *Ilex*, holly, and *folium*, a leaf. Leaves evergreen, HOLLY-like, 1"–2" long. Flowers in 1"–3" clusters. Cherries purple, red or reddish-yellow (rarely pure yellow); the pit big and pulp thin. A shrub or small tree. Some nurseries offer it in either bush form or trained as trees. Records: 56' × 7'10" × 45' Jolon, CA (1993); 33' × 4'0" × 44' Davis, CA (1992; *pl.* ca. 1938).

P. *ilicifolia* var. *integrifolia*—see *P. Lyonii*

P. *ilicifolia* ssp. *Lyonii*—see *P. Lyonii*

P. *ilicifolia* var. *occidentalis*—see *P. Lyonii*

P. *ilicifolia* × P. *Lyonii*

Some California horticulturists say most plants sold as *P. Lyonii* are really hybrids. Skylark nursery of Santa Rosa has sold these hybrids since ≤1980.

P. × *incam* or *incamp*—see *P.* 'Okamé'

P. *incisa* Th. *ex* J.A. Murr.

FUJI CHERRY. MAME CHERRY. PIGMY CHERRY. CUTLEAF CHERRY. From Japan; grows abundantly at the base of Mt. Fuji. The name *Mame* signifies dwarf or pygmy, alluding to the tree's habit. The 1784 epithet *incisa* refers to the sharply and delicately toothed leaves. Grown in North America since <1910. Uncommon. Twiggy large shrubs or small trees 8'–30' tall. Leaves purplish or reddish when unfolding, hairy above and below on the veins; to 3⅛" × 1⅝"; the margins incised with deep, sharp teeth. Flowers in March, April or early May, pure white or pale pink, small (¾"–1" wide), solitary or in pairs or rarely trios; stems relatively short; petals dropping all too soon, but the calyx is red, showy and persistent. Fruit purple-black or pure black, not so shiny as those of HIGAN, YOSHINO or SARGENT CHERRIES; ¼"; flavor okay. Most of the following cultivars have not been noted in North American commerce, but may be present, or introduced soon.

P. *incisa* 'February Pink'

Introduced in 1956–57 by Hillier nursery of England. Name self-explanatory.

P. *incisa* 'Hilling's Weeping'

Introduced ≤1964–65 by George Jackman & Son nursery of England. Slender branches hang vertically giving the outline of an inverted U. Abundant dainty white flowers. Topgrafted.

P. incisa 'Midori'—see *P.* 'Yamadei'

P. incisa 'Moerheimi'—see *P.* 'Moerheimi'

P. incisa 'Oshidori'

Cultivated in Japan ≤1985. Flowers quite double (35–40 petals), pale pink.

P. incisa 'Pendula Alba'

Introduced ≤1990 by Weston nursery of Hopkinton, MA. Pendulous branching. Unless it is pre-1959 the Latin cultivar name is illegitimate.

P. incisa 'Plena'

Cultivated in Japan. Flowers semi-double, pale pink.

P. incisa f. *serrata* (Koidz.) Wils.

= *P. incisa* var. *serrata* Koidz.

Named in 1915. By 1938 some botanists insisted the name isn't warranted; that seedlings vary. Nor is *serrata* included in J. Ohwi's 1965 *Flora of Japan*. Be that as it may, this entity was named on the supposition that its leaf teeth are less finely doubly-toothed. In cultivation it makes a larger tree, that could pass for a *P.* × *subhirtella* except the flowers are only borne singly or in pairs, and the calyx tube is hairless and only slightly constricted. Records: 25' × 2'10" × 34½' Seattle, WA (1993; *pl.* 1950); 23' × 3'0" × 26½' Victoria, B.C. (1993).

P. incisa 'Yamadei'

= *P. incisa* var. *Yamadei* Mak.
= *P. incisa* 'Zansetsu'
= *P. incisa* 'Midori'

MIDORI CHERRY. Japanese: *Midori-zakura* (GREEN CHERRY), *Ryokugaku-zakura* (GREEN-CALYX CHERRY). Collected at the foot of Mt. Fuji in April 1916. Named that year after Hanjiro Yamade, director of Gotenba Agricultural High School. Introduced to North America ≤1917. Extremely rare, but in commerce. Young growth an attractive pale bright green with no red tint. Flowers snow-white, green in the center instead of red. Fruit red, of inferior flavor; stem longer and less hairy than that of typical *P. incisa*.

P. incisa 'Zansetsu'—see *P. incisa* 'Yamadei'

P. insititia—see *P.* × *domestica* var. *insititia*

P. jamasakura Sieb. *ex* Koidz.

= *P. serrulata* var. *spontanea* (Maxim.) Wils.
= *P. mutabilis* Miyoshi
= *P. Sargentii* ssp. *jamasakura* (Sieb.) Ohwi

JAPANESE HILL CHERRY. From approximately the S half of Japan. Named in 1830 (a Latinization of the Japanese name meaning HILL CHERRY). Very popular in Japan. Introduced to Western cultivation in 1893. Extremely rare. In Japan it never hybridizes with *P. Sargentii*, but *P. jamasakura* × *P. verecunda* occurs. Overall more variable than *P. Sargentii*. *P. jamasakura* has the same distinctively pale waxy leaf undersides as its familiar relative SARGENT CHERRY, but narrower leaves (to 4¼" × 2"), more gently and gradually pointed, edged by much finer teeth that are usually only single. Leafbuds markedly long, narrow and with jagged scale tips. Pink buds open to pale pink or white flowers, showy against the bronze- or coppery young foliage. Flowers partly borne in umbels (as in *P. Sargentii*) of 3–4, but usually are arranged on a common stalk (peduncle). The first large JAPANESE CHERRY to bloom in spring; well into leafage when *P. Sargentii*, *P. verecunda* (KOREAN HILL CHERRY) and *P. speciosa* blossom. Fruit ⅓", purplish-black, bitter. Compared to SARGENT CHERRY, this species is more refined in branching and leaf, but offers less dramatic floral display—being paler and more diaphanous. Its fall color is not as superb, being pastel yellows, oranges and reds, with the pale undersides of the fallen leaves affording a lively contrast. Records: to 82' × 20'4" in the wild; 58' × 6'0" × 55' Seattle, WA (1993); 48' × 10'5" × 59' Vancouver, WA (1993).

P. jamasakura 'Plena Pendula'—see *P.* 'Kiku-shidare-zakura'

P. jamasakura var. *verecunda*—see *P. verecunda*

P. 'Jeanne Wohlert'

= *P. serrulata* 'Jeanne Wohlert'

In the SATO ZAKURA group. Introduced in 1929–30 by Wohlert nursery of Narberth, PA. Named after one of Wohlert's daughters. Very rare; commercially extinct since 1940s. Tree very dwarf, tending to branch directly from the ground. Flowers semi-double, delicately tinted light pink, on short stems. Similar to *P.* 'Asahi-botan'.

P. 'Jo-nioi'

= *P. serrulata* 'Jo-nioi'
= *P. serrulata* f. *affinis* Miyoshi
= *P. Lannesiana* f. *jonioi* Wils.

In the SATO ZAKURA group. Name means "supreme fragrance," or "elegant fragrance," or "snow on the mountains." Introduced to Western cultivation ca. 1900. In North American commerce ≤1939. Rare.

Tree strong, can grow 36' tall and wide. Buds slender, pinkish. Flowers deliciously fragrant, single or nearly so, pure white, 1½" wide, in short-stalked clusters of 3–5; purple-brown sepals. Comparatively worthless except for fragrance. Young foliage bronzy-green. P. 'Taki-nioi' has longer stalked clusters of slightly smaller flowers, and is a small, flattened tree that blooms later.

P. × *Juddii* E.S. Anders.
(*P. Sargentii* × *P. yedoensis*)

JUDD CHERRY. Raised at the Arnold Arboretum in 1914 as a seedling from one of W. Bigelow's original 1890-introduced SARGENT CHERRY trees. Named in 1935 after William Henry Judd (1888–1946), who worked at the Arnold Arboretum for more than 30 years. In commerece ≤1963; very rare. Greatly resembles *P. Sargentii* in its broad, abruptly pointed leaves displaying brilliant deep red fall color. Flowers whitish or palest pink, borne in umbels (as in *P. Sargentii*) of 2–6, or arranged on an exceedingly short common stalk (peduncle), of essentially hairless parts (stems can have a few scattered, long, pale hairs). Flowers accompanied by bronzy, lightly hairy young foliage. Fruit can be set, but often either aborts or gets taken by birds before it matures. Tree large, broad and dense. Its only practical difference from typical *P. Sargentii* is the paler flowers. Of a technical nature, the slightly hairy leaves (to 4⅜" × 2½") are not quite so waxy pale beneath, and are more consistently doubly-serrated (*P. Sargentii* leaves are somewhat simply toothed occasionally). Thus, rather than a proven hybrid, JUDD CHERRY may be a hairy variation of SARGENT CHERRY officially titled *P. Sargentii* f. *pubescens* (Tatew.) Ohwi. Record: 35' × 5¼" × 45' Seattle, WA (1994; *pl.* 1940).

P. 'Kaido'
= *P. serrulata* 'Kaido'

In the SATO ZAKURA group. Introduced ≤1934 by, but not originated by, W.B. Clarke nursery of San José, CA. Clarke nursery obtained its specimen ca. 1920, as an unknown cultivar. Commercially extinct since 1950s. Named after *Malus Halliana*, which the Japanese call *Kaido*. Flowers almost the exact counterpart of the KAIDO CRABAPPLE with the same lovely shade of pure pink. Blooms profusely. Flowers semi-double (5–15 petals), of medium size. Growth very slow, erect. Leaves turn red in autumn.

P. 'Kankakee'
= *P.* 'Kankakee Newport'

KANKAKEE PURPLELEAF PLUM. Origin not known; in commerce ≤1991–92. Likely associated with Kankakee nursery of Aroma Park, IL, which has been in business for 3 generations. Said to differ from typical NEWPORT PLUM (*P.* 'Newport') in being pyramidal.

P. 'Kiku-shidare-zakura'
= *P. serrulata* 'Kiku-shidare-zakura'
= *P. serrulata* 'Cheal's Weeping Cherry'
= *P. serrulata* 'Clarke's Weeping Cherry'
= *P. serrulata* 'Wohlert's Weeping Cherry'
= *P. serrulata* 'Double Pink Weeping'
= *P. serrulata* 'Pendula'
= *P. serrulata* 'Pendula Flore Plena'
= *P. serrulata* 'Rosea Pendula'
= *P. serrulata* f. *rosea* Wils.
= *P. jamasakura* 'Plena Pendula'
?= *P. avium* 'Rosea Pendula'

In the SATO ZAKURA group. Name means "weeping chrysanthemum cherry." Introduced ca.1900 to England. In North American commerce since ≤1930s. Common. A small tree, arching and more or less weeping from a topgraft. Tends to be gawky and thinly furnished. Flowers medium-sized, extremely double, with 50–70 (110) petals, dark pink. Young foliage faintly bronze, very soon green. Leaves dark, narrower than those of most SATO ZAKURA (to 4⅜" × 1⅜") and exceptionally glossy; prominently edged with incised teeth; stem rich red.

P. 'Kiku-zakura'
= *P. serrulata* 'Kiku-zakura'
= *P. serrulata* f. *chrysanthemoides* Miyoshi

In the SATO ZAKURA group. Exceedingly rare in North America. Name means "chrysanthemum cherry." Tree shrubby, slow and remaining small; habit erect. Flowers late-blooming, soft pink, 1⅝" wide, tightly double (ca. 200 petals). Young foliage bronzy-green.

P. 'Kirin'
= *P. serrulata* 'Kirin'
= *P. serrulata* f. *kirin* (Koidz.) Wils.
= *P. serrulata* f. *atrorubra* Miyoshi
= *P. Lannesiana* 'Kirin'

In the SATO ZAKURA group. Grown in North America <1940 but exceedingly rare. According to E. Wilson, "flowers large, rose, very double, late." C. Ingram says: "nothing more than a slower-growing, broad-crowned form of *P.* 'Kwanzan', with an inflorescence correspondingly more compact and tightly bunched." H. Warren adds it blooms slightly earlier; T. Everett adds the flowers are not as deep colored. The name 'Kirin' is used in Japan for a small tree, paler-flowered than *P.* 'Kwanzan', with 21–50 petals, toothed sepals and 2 tiny leaflike carpels in the middle; young foliage bronzy.

P. 'Kokonoye (-sakura)'
('Kokonoe')
= *P. serrulata* 'Kokonoye (-sakura)'
= *P. serrulata* f. *kokonaye* Wils.
= *P. serrulata* f. *homogena* Miyoshi
= *P. Lannesiana* 'Homogena'

In the SATO ZAKURA group. Exceedingly rare in North America. Flowers early; semi-double or double, soft pink, 1¾" wide, profuse. Tree very small: one more than 50 years old was 10' tall and 18' wide.

P. 'Kurama-yama'
('Kurama-tama')
= *P. serrulata* 'Kurama-yama'

In the SATO ZAKURA group. Name means "Mt. Kurama" of Japan. In North American commerce ≤1934. Very rare. Grows very slow and is compact; of upright habit, to 20' tall. Buds deep pink. Flowers double (ca. 35 petals), to 2" wide, light pink in the center, strongly stained cerise toward the frilled margins; sepals large, often sharply toothed. Differs from *P.* 'Daikoku' in its broader sepals and in having a tuft of ca. 7 petals in the middle. Young foliage pale brownish-green. Leaves often blunt at the apex.

P. 'Kursar'
(*P. nipponica* var. *kurilensis* × *P. campanulata*)
KURSAR CHERRY. Bred ca. 1930, and named (*P. kurilensis* × *P. Sargentii*) by C. Ingram of England. The breeder later determined the pollen parent was not *P. Sargentii* after all, but *P. campanulata*. Introduced to commerce in the 1950s. Extremely rare in North America. Flowers vivid pink, in March or early April. Young foliage reddish-bronze. Mature leaves dark, persistently hairy on both sides, finely toothed; orange in fall. Twigs hairless.

P. 'Kwanzan'
= *P. serrulata* 'Kwanzan'
= *P. serrulata* f. *purpurascens* Miyoshi
= *P. serrulata* f. *sekiyama* (Koidz.) Wils.
= *P. serrulata* 'Kanzan' or 'Kansan'
= *P. serrulata* 'Sekizan'
= *P. serrulata* 'Sekiyama'
= *P. Lannesiana* 'Sekiyama'

In the SATO ZAKURA group. Both the 'Kwanzan' and 'Sekiyama' names refer to the same sacred mountain in China. Introduced to the West ca. 1913. The most common of all SATO ZAKURA. Tree strong and massive; more cold-hardy than most SATO ZAKURA. Flowers large, double, with 20–30 (50) petals, dark rosy-pink, fading in time; sepals untoothed. Young foliage dark bronzy-red. Leaves very large. Fall color can be pleasing peachy-orange from a distance. Records: 50' × 5'1" × 41' Sultan, WA (1993); 39' × 9'4" × 55' Sumner, WA (1992). Being so widely cultivated, with so many synonyms, there is considerable variation in vigor, color and time of blooming in stock from nurseries. For example, *P.* 'Masu-yama' is paler; *P.* 'Yae-kanzan' is an unusually double form. 'Kwanzan' is sometimes sold wrongly as *P. serrulata* 'Hisakura' ('Hizakura'), or 'Oh-nanden'.

P. lanata—see *P. nigra*

P. Lannesiana (Carr.) Wils.
= *Cerasus Lannesiana* Carr.
= *P. serrulata* var. *Lannesiana* (Carr.) Mak.

This name, given in 1872 to honor M. Lannes of Montebello, Italy, is much used by Japanese horticulturists. Contemporary western botanists dismiss it. The application in Japan is to ornamental FLOWERING CHERRIES which have been in Japanese termed *Sato zakura*, and in Western horticulture, cultivars of *P. serrulata*.

P. Lannesiana f. *albida*—see *P. speciosa*

P. Lannesiana 'Albo-rosea'—see *P.* 'Shiro-fugen'

P. Lannesiana f. *amanogawa*—see *P.* 'Amanogawa'

P. Lannesiana f. *amayadori*—see *P.* 'Amayadori'

P. Lannesiana f. *ariake*—see *P.* 'Ariake'

P. Lannesiana 'Asahi-yama'—see *P.* 'Asahi-botan'

P. Lannesiana f. *benitoranowo*—see *P.* 'Beni-torano-o'

P. Lannesiana f. *botanzakura*—see *P.* 'Moutan'

P. Lannesiana 'Bullata'—see *P.* 'Ojochin'

P. Lannesiana 'Candida'—see *P.* 'Ariake'

P. Lannesiana f. *caudata*—see *P.* 'Torano-o'

P. Lannesiana f. *chosiuhizakura*—see *P.* 'Choshu-hizakura'

P. Lannesiana 'Decora'—see *P.* 'Horinji'

P. Lannesiana f. *erecta*—see *P.* 'Amanogawa'

P. Lannesiana f. *fudanzakura*—see *P.* 'Fudan-zakura'

P. Lannesiana f. *fukurokuju*—see *P.* 'Fuku-rokuju'

P. Lannesiana f. *gioiko*—see *P.* 'Gyoiko'

P. Lannesiana f. *gosiozakura*—see *P.* 'Gosho (-zakura)'

P. Lannesiana f. *gozanomanioi*—see *P.* 'Gozanoma-nioi'

P. Lannesiana f. *grandiflora*—see *P.* 'Ukon'

P. Lannesiana f. *hatazakura*—see *P.* 'Hata-zakura'

P. Lannesiana f. *higurashi*—see *P.* 'Amabilis'

P. Lannesiana 'Hisakura'—see *P.* 'Hisakura'

P. Lannesiana 'Homogena'—see *P.* 'Kokonoye (-sakura)'

P. Lannesiana f. *horaison*—see *P.* 'Horaison'

P. Lannesiana f. *hosokawa*—see *P.* 'Hosokawa'

P. Lannesiana 'Hosokawa-odora'—see *P.* 'Hosokawa'

P. Lannesiana f. *jonioi*—see *P.* 'Jo-nioi'

P. Lannesiana 'Kirin'—see *P.* 'Kirin'

P. Lannesiana f. *mikurumakaisi*—see *P.* 'Mikuruma-gaeshi'

P. Lannesiana f. *moutan*—see *P.* 'Moutan'

P. Lannesiana 'Nobilis'—see *P.* 'Yedo-zakura'

P. Lannesiana f. *ohsibayama*—see *P.* 'Ohsibayama'

P. Lannesiana f. *ojochin*—see *P.* 'Ojochin'

P. Lannesiana 'Sekiyama'—see *P.* 'Kwanzan'

P. Lannesiana f. *senriko*—see *P.* 'Senriko'

P. Lannesiana 'Shirayuki'—see *P.* 'Shirayuki'

P. Lannesiana 'Shirotae'—see *P.* 'Shirotae'

P. Lannesiana f. *sirotae*—see *P.* 'Shirotae'

P. Lannesiana f. *speciosa*—see *P. speciosa*

P. Lannesiana f. *sumizome*—see *P.* 'Sumizome'

P. Lannesiana 'Superba'—see *P.* 'Shogetsu'

P. Lannesiana f. *takinioi*—see *P.* 'Taki-nioi'

P. Lannesiana 'Taoyame'—see *P.* 'Tao-yoma (-zakura)'

P. Lannesiana f. *temari*—see *P.* 'Temari'

P. Lannesiana 'Washinowo'—see *P.* 'Washi-no-o'

P. Lannesiana f. *wasinowo*—see *P.* 'Washi-no-o'

P. Lannesiana f. *yayeakebono*—see *P.* 'Yae-akebono'

P. Lannesiana f. *yedozakura*—see *P.* 'Yedo-zakura'

P. Laurocerasus L.
= *Cerasus Laurocerasus* (L.) Loisel.
= *Padus Laurocerasus* (L.) Mill.
= *Laurocerasus officinalis* Roem.
ENGLISH LAUREL. CHERRY LAUREL. LAUREL CHERRY. From SE Europe and adjacent Asia, to N Iran. Cultivated since 1558 in Italy. The 1753 name *Laurocerasus* means laurel-cherry, referring to its evergreen LAUREL-like leaves, and CHERRY-like fruit. Introduced to North American commerce ≤1871. Very common. Leaves bright green, 6"–9" long. Flowers white, in 3"–6½" long clusters, sometime between March and late May. Fruit a purplish-black cherry, ripe in fall, taken

by birds (and if not, making a mess). In its typical form this species is moderately cold-hardy, but its very cold-hardy cultivars are mere shrubs. Records: 45' × 18'10" (at 1½') × 101' Shelton Abbey, County Wicklow, Ireland (ca.1830; *pl.* ca. 1740); 44' × 2'6" × 48' Seattle, WA (1990); 32' × 8'0" × 43' Seattle, WA (1988).

P. *Laurocerasus* 'Bertinii'—see P. *Laurocerasus* 'Magnoliæfolia'

P. *Laurocerasus* 'Camelliæfolia'
('Camelliifolia')
Named officially in 1901. In North America ≤1895; sold here ≤1925. Extremely rare. Leaves contorted and twisted. A freak. The name *camelliæfolia* means *Camellia*-leaved; from genus *Camellia*, and *folium*, a leaf.

P. *Laurocerasus* 'Latifolia'—see P. *Laurocerasus* 'Magnoliæfolia'

P. *Laurocerasus* 'Macrophylla'—see P. *Lauro.* 'Magnoliæfolia'

P. *Laurocerasus* 'Magnoliæfolia'
= P. *Laurocerasus* 'Macrophylla'
= P. *Laurocerasus* 'Latifolia'
= P. *Laurocerasus* 'Bertinii'
= P. *Laurocerasus* 'Versaillensis'
Originated <1869 at Versailles, France. Likely raised by Pierre Bertin (1800–1891). In North American commerce ≤1893. Very rare. Leaves extraordinarily large, to 12¾" × 5". Not as cold-hardy as some smaller-leaved cultivars. Excellent for tropical effect. The name *magnoliæfolia* means *Magnolia*-leaved; from genus *Magnolia*, and *folium*, a leaf. Record: 38' tall and 64' wide Seattle, WA (1993; *pl.* 1951).

P. *Laurocerasus* 'Versaillensis'—see P. *Lauro.* 'Magnoliæfolia'

P. *Leveilleana*—see P. *verecunda*

P. *Leveilleana* 'Fudan-zakura'—see P. 'Fudan-zakura'

P. *lusitanica* L.
= *Laurocerasus lusitanica* (L.) Roem.
= *Padus lusitanica* (L.) Mill.
PORTUGAL LAUREL. From Spain, Portugal, Morocco and SW France. Introduced in 1648 to the Oxford Botanic Garden. In North American commerce since ≤1871. Common. Naturalized in places on the Pacific Coast. A broadleaf evergreen. Leaves notably dark and lustrous, 2"–5⅞" long, with purplish-red stems. Flowers in slender long clusters in May and June; very fragrant (HAWTHORN-scented). Cherries small, reddish-purple, repulsively bitter. Unless pruned it is a mere shrub, however giant. Records: to 70' tall in the wild; 59' × 3'4" × 35' Tacoma, WA (1992); 47' × 9'4" × 55' Tukwila, WA (1992); 45' × 12'6" × 51' Tukwila, WA (1992).

P. *lusitanica* ssp. *azorica* (Mouill.) Franco
= P. *lusitanica* ssp. *Hixa* (Willd.) Franco
= P. *azoricus* hort.
Native to the Canary Islands and the Azores. *Hixa* or *Hija* is a vernacular name. Introduced to English cultivation ≤1846. In North American commerce ≤1888; extremely rare here. Accounts vary regarding its distinctions from typical P. *lusitanica*. Most accounts say that it is smaller, has broader, less dark, thicker leaves (to 5½" × 2⅞"), and fewer flowers in shorter upright clusters. The twigs are thicker. Briefly, it is squatter, less dark and less elegant. In San Francisco it can bloom from February into June.

P. *lusitanica* ssp. *Hixa*—see P. *lusitanica* ssp. *azorica*

P. *lusitanica* 'Variegata'
Described officially in 1865. In North America ≤1895; sold here ≤1931. Extremely rare. Leaves variegated creamy-white and green. Shrubby.

P. *Lyonii* (Eastw.) Sarg.
= P. *ilicifolia* ssp. *Lyonii* (Eastw.) Raven
= P. *ilicifolia* var. *integrifolia* Sudw.
= P. *ilicifolia* var. *occidentalis* Brandegee
CATALINA CHERRY. From Santa Rosa, Santa Cruz, Anacapa, Santa Catalina, and San Clemente Islands of California, and NW Mexico. Named after William Scrugham Lyon (1852–1916), U.S. forester and horticulturist who discovered it (likely in 1884). Cultivated almost exclusively in California. Many plants offered in the trade are hybrids with the close relative P. *ilicifolia*. CATALINA CHERRY is a tree, more compact than P. *ilicifolia*. Leaves 3"–6" long, usually smooth-edged. Cherries larger, darker (purple or black), better-tasting (fruit growers seek selections with smaller pits). Handsome but subject to whitefly; fruit messy. Records: 75' × 4'8½" San Marino, CA (≤1939); 41' × 10'0" × 55' Catalina Island, CA (1993); 38' × 6'5½" × 42' Davis, CA (1992; *pl.* 1941).

P. *Maackii* Rupr.

= *Padus Maackii* (Rupr.) Kom.

GOLDBARK CHERRY. MONGOLIAN GOLDBARK BIRD CHERRY. GOLDBARK CHOKECHERRY. AMUR CHOKE-CHERRY. MANCHURIAN CHERRY. From Manchuria, Korea, NE U.S.S.R. Named in 1857 after Richard Karlovich Maack (1825–1886), Russian naturalist and explorer. Introduced in 1878 to the Arnold Arboretum here from St. Petersburg. In commerce here ≤1931 (in the early 1900s, *P. Padus* var. *commutata* was sold as *P. Maackii*). Uncommon until the 1980s. Prized for cold-hardiness and attractive honey-brown bark. Flowers small, white, in elongated clusters beginning in late March. Fruits tiny, shiny, black and bitter. Colors yellow and defoliates earlier than most CHERRIES. Closely related to *P. Padus*. Records: 62' × 4'9" Cluny Gardens, Tayside, Scotland (1985); 40' × 3'8" × 39' Spokane, WA (1988; *pl.* 1954); 36' × 7'7" Westonbirt, Gloucestershire, England (1988).

P. *Maackii* 'Amber Beauty'

A 1968 Dutch introduction. Not yet in North American nurseries. Ascending branches and lovely amber bark.

P. *Mahaleb* L.

= *Cerasus Mahaleb* (L.) Mill.

MAHALEB CHERRY. PERFUMED CHERRY. ST. LUCIE CHERRY. ROCK CHERRY. From Europe, SW and central Asia. Introduced in 1714 from Austria to England. *Mahaleb* from the Arabic name *Mahhlab*. J. Loudon relates that the center of pipe-making was in the Vosges mountains of eastern France, in the neighborhood of the Abbey of St. Lucie. MAHALEB CHERRY wood was made into pipe-tubes, not bowls. Common in North America since the 1850s; naturalized in places here. Above all it is used as a CHERRY rootstock. Compared to its chief rival for this use (MAZZARD; *P. avium*), it is generally inferior, being more cold-hardy and drought-tolerant, but shorter-lived and absolutely intolerant of wet or heavy soils. As an ornamental, it offers glossy, dark, healthy foliage, and perfumed tiny white clustered flowers in late April to mid-May. Leaves 1½"–2½" long, broad; green into November. Cherries black, ¼" long. Records: to 50' tall; 46' × 7'10" Poland (≤1973); 44' × 9'9" × 52' Davis, CA (1994).

P. *mandshurica*—see *P. Armeniaca* var. *mandshurica*

P. 'Masu-yama'

= *P. serrulata* 'Masu-yama'
= *P. serrulata* f. *masuyama* Wils.

In the SATO ZAKURA group. In North American circulation <1942. Exceedingly rare. Said to be like *P.* 'Kwanzan' but paler-flowered, with a "somewhat different habit of growth."

P. 'Meigetsu'

= *P. serrulata* 'Meigetsu'
= *P. serrulata* f. *meigetsu* Wils.
= *P. serrulata* f. *sancta* Miyoshi

In the SATO ZAKURA group. In North American commerce ≤1941. Extremely rare. Flowers single or semi-double, white changing to blush. Name means "full moon."

P. *melanocarpa*—see *P. virginiana*

P. *mexicana* S. Wats.

= *P. arkansana* Sarg.
= *P. americana* var. *lanata* Sudw.—misapplied

MEXICAN PLUM. BIG-TREE PLUM. INCH PLUM. From the south-central U.S. and NE Mexico. Named in 1882. Introduced to cultivation in 1910. Widely grown in central and eastern Texas and Louisiana. Flowers ½"–1" wide, white fading to pale pink; February–March. Leaves 2½"–4¾" long, sharply toothed; sometimes feltlike textured above; sometimes yellowing in fall. Plums ¾"–1¼" long, (yellow to) mauve to purplish-red, bloomy. Records: to 46' tall says C. Sargent; 26' × 5'0" × 34' Irving, TX (1981); 15' × 5'3" × 24' Hood County, TX (1991).

P. *mexicana* Bright Star™

Introduced <1986 by Lone Star Growers, San Antonio, TX.

P. 'Mikuruma-gaeshi'

= *P. serrulata* 'Mikuruma-gaeshi'
= *P. serrulata* 'Kirigayatsu'
= *P. serrulata* f. *diversifolia* Miyoshi
= *P. serrulata* 'Mitchell's Single Pink'
= *P. Lannesiana* f. *mikurumakaisi* (Koidz.) Wils.

In the SATO ZAKURA group. Incorrectly called *P. serrulata* 'Temari'. The name means "the royal carriage returns." In North American commerce since ≤1912. Rare. Sidney B. Mitchell (1878–1951), of Berkeley, CA, distributed stock of his specimen before its proper name was known. Tree stiffly upright; long ascending branches covered with short flowering spurs (like on *P.* 'Okiku'). In age, habit decidedly spreading. Blooms ca. 10 days before *P.* 'Kwanzan'.

Buds pointed, deep carmine-pink, sepals untoothed. Flowers single, rarely with an extra petal or two, lightly fragrant, profuse, very pale pink or white above, pinker below, 1½"–2¹⁄₁₆" wide, flat, in short-stemmed clusters of 2–4. Young foliage bronzy-green. Fruit often formed, pea-size, blackish-purple, no good to eat, yet viable. Record: 21' × 4'4" × 39' Seattle, WA (1993).

P. × Miyoshii 'Ambigua'—see P. 'Taizan-fukun'

P. 'Moerheimi'
= P. incisa 'Moerheimi'
= P. × yedoensis 'Moerheimi'
Raised ca. 1930, from imported Japanese seeds, first offered in 1937–38 by B. Ruys Royal Moerheim nursery of Dedemsvaart, Holland. Introduced to the U.S. by the Arnold Arboretum in 1938. Extremely rare here. Small weeping tree of wide-spreading, dome-shaped habit. Soft pink buds open in late March and early April to profuse, elegantly drooping ⅞" single white flowers.

P. mollis—see P. emarginata

P. Moseri—see P. × blireiana 'Moseri'

P. 'Moutan'
= P. serrulata 'Moutan'
= P. serrulata f. Moutan Miyoshi
= P. serrulata 'Botan (-zakura)'
= P. Lannesiana f. moutan (Koidz.) Wils.
= P. Lannesiana f. botanzakura Wils.
Name means "peony cherry." In North American commerce ≤1930. Very rare. Tree small, with a flat wide crown. Flowers pale pink fading to white, semi-double (6–15 petals), to 2" wide, in short-stalked clusters of 3–5; sepals strongly toothed. Young foliage bronzy- or yellow-green.

P. 'Mrs. A.E. Wohlert'
= P. serrulata 'Mrs. A.E. Wohlert'
In the SATO ZAKURA group. Introduced ca. 1940 by Wohlert nursery of Narberth, PA. Named after A.E. Wohlert's wife. Very rare; extinct commercially since 1940s. A sport of P. 'Kwanzan' showing greater brilliancy.

P. Mt. St. Helens™ PP 4987 (1988)
= P. 'Frankthrees'
= P. cerasifera 'Frankthrees'
= P. cerasifera Mt. St. Helens™
MT. ST. HELENS PLUM. A sport of P. 'Newport' found ca. 1975 and put into commerce ca. 1981 by Schmidt nursery of Boring, OR. More robust; leaves larger, of richer purple color. Faster growth.

P. 'Muckle'—see P. × nigrella

P. Mume (Sieb.) S. & Z.
JAPANESE APRICOT. JAPANESE FLOWERING APRICOT. JAPANESE PLUM TREE (see also P. salicina). From China, Korea, and a variety in Taiwan. Named by Siebold in 1828 (Mume or ume is Japanese vernacular), and introduced by him to Holland between 1841 and 1844. In North America since ≤1911. Uncommon here; all 40 cultivars cited below are little known and very rare unless noted, and include half a dozen not known in North America, to serve as a stimulation and to show the range of variation. In Japan P. Mume is the Royal Crest, is widely cultivated (more than 300 cultivars), and greatly beloved. Usually a low bushy tree to 15' tall; can be twice as tall and just as wide (see P. Mume 'Dione'). Flowers pale pink (varying much in cultivars), often richly fragrant with spicy odor suggesting a carnation. Blooms usually in February–March. The flowering dates supplied below are mostly from W.B. Clarke nursery of San José, CA. Leaf to 4½" × 2⅞", with fine teeth, usually sharp, and a characteristic pinched apex. In a nomenclatural sense, typical P. Mume has its leaf hairy on both sides, yellowish-green. But this is actually rare. The more common form, technically termed var. tonsa, has a quite or nearly hairless leaf except near the base of the midrib beneath; the leaf is also narrower, and gray-green colored. Fruit yellow to orange or red, 1"–1½", fuzzy-skinned, cling-stone; usually poor quality as food, and messy if not eaten. Picked green and pickled, the fruit is esteemed in Japan.

P. Mume 'Alba'
Described in 1885. In North American commerce ≤1958. Flowers white. As traditionally defined, 'Alba' is a vague name that might apply to any number of clones.

P. Mume 'Alba-plena'
Described in 1903. In North American commerce ≤1958. Flowers delicate rose in bud, opening pure white; semi-double.

P. Mume 'Alphandii'
= P. Mume 'Flore Pleno' (in part)
= P. Mume 'Roseo Plena'
Introduced in 1860 by Siebold to Holland; to France in 1878. Described in 1885. In North American commerce ≤1948. Flowers semi-double, rosy-pink.

Named after Jean Charles Adolphe Alphand (1817–1891) French garden architect and horticulturist.

P. Mume 'Augustus'

Flowers clear pink, 1⅓" wide.

P. Mume 'Beni-chi-dori'

('Beni-Shidare', 'Beni-shidon', 'Beni-shidori')

In U.K. commerce ≤1957. Flowers strongly fragrant, double, "vivid magenta carmine" or "rich madder pink."

P. Mume 'Bonita'

Probably came from Japan but was named in 1940 by W.B. Clarke nursery of San José, CA. Still in commerce. Named after one of Clarke's three daughters. Flowers double, deep red, deliciously fragrant. Leaf barely hairy. Tree somewhat dwarf.

P. Mume 'Brittania'

In North American commerce ≤1954–55. Flowers single red, very early.

P. Mume 'Charles Abraham'—see P. Armeniaca 'Charles Abraham'

P. Mume 'Contorta'

In North American commerce ≤1987.

P. Mume 'Dawn'

= P. Mume 'Musashinono'

Originally from Japan and is said to be known there as 'Musashi-nono' but was named 'Dawn' ≤1929 by W.B. Clarke nursery of San José, CA. Still in commerce; among the commonest of all. Flowers ca. 1½" wide, rich clear pink, very double. Petals exquisitely ruffled; delightfully fragrant. Blooms first week February. Leaf hairless. Tree somewhat dwarf.

P. Mume 'Dione'

A specimen received in 1959 at the Los Angeles arboretum has hairy leaves, and measures 28½' × 3'5" × 27½' (1993).

P. Mume 'Double Red'

Likely 'Splendens' renamed. In North American commerce ≤1934. Flowers semi-double, light red.

P. Mume 'Early Double Pink'

In North American commerce ≤1934. Blooms a week or two before 'Dawn' but is somewhat similar.

P. Mume 'Early Double Red'

In North American commerce ≤1934.

P. Mume 'Early Double White'

In North American commerce ≤1941. Blooms much earlier than 'Rosemary Clarke'.

P. Mume 'Flore Pleno'—see P. Mume 'Alphandii'

P. Mume 'Flore Roseo Pleno'

In U.K. commerce ≤1917. Flowers double, rose-pink. May be an alternate name for 'Alphandii'.

P. Mume 'Jitsugetsuse'

In U.K. commerce ≤1957. Flowers pale rose.

P. Mume 'Kobai'

In North American commerce ≤1991. Flowers variously described as "double, light pink, profuse;" "semi-double, red;" "vivid rose-pink;" "single, pink."

P. Mume 'Matsubara Red'

('Matsubana Red')

In North American commerce ≤1970. Flowers red, early, ⅞" wide, semi-double; calyx blood-red. Young foliage reddish. Leaf hairless. Twigs purple.

P. Mume 'Mme. Dorbon'

In North American commerce ≤1931. Flowers large, double, bright shell-pink; blooming midseason.

P. Mume 'Musashinono'—see P. Mume 'Dawn'

P. Mume 'No. 207'

Introduced to North American commerce ≤1939 by W.B. Clarke nursery of San José, CA. Flowers double, soft pink; with beautifully ruffled and reflexed petals.

P. Mume 'No. 209'

Origin as above. Flowers double, soft pink—by far the earliest double Mume (mid-December onwards), lasting 2 months.

P. Mume 'No. 210'

Origin as above. Flowers double, pink, rather small but with fine color. Possibly the best early pink. Blooms January 1st.

P. Mume 'O-moi-no-mama'
('O-moi-no-wac')
In U.K. commerce since ≤1957. Flowers semi-double, some white, some pink.

P. Mume 'Peggy Clarke'
Introduced to North American commerce in 1941 by W.B. Clarke nursery of San José, CA. Still in commerce. Named after one of Clarke's three daughters. Flowers double, deep rose, medium-sized, somewhat cupped; calyx red; extremely long stamens. Blooms 2 weeks after 'Rosemary Clarke' and has smaller flowers. Leaves hairless.

P. Mume 'Pendula'
= P. Mume 'Weeping Pink'
Described in 1848 by Siebold. In North American commerce ≤1931. Flowers single or semi-double, pale pink. Branching pendulous. Leaf hairless.

P. Mume 'Pink Glow'
In North American commerce ≤1989. Flowers pink.

P. Mume 'Præcox'
In North American commerce ≤1934. Flowers single, white; blooming among the earliest of all flowering fruit trees—usually on New Year's Day.

P. Mume 'Rosebud'
In North American commerce ≤1989. Flowers large, semi-double, light pink.

P. Mume 'Roseglow'
In North American commerce ≤1987.

P. Mume 'Roseo Plena'—see P. Mume 'Alphandii'

P. Mume 'Rosemary Clarke'
Introduced to North American commerce in 1938 by W.B. Clarke nursery of San José, CA. Still in commerce. Named after one of Clarke's three daughters. Flowers 1⅛"–1½" wide, semi-double (ca. 16 petals), snow white; rosy-red calyx; intensely fragrant.

P. Mume 'Rubra Plena'—see P. Mume 'Splendens'

P. Mume 'Shira Kagi'
In North American commerce ≤1928.

P. Mume 'Splendens'
= P. Mume 'Rubra Plena'
Described in 1903. Flowers double, red. Likely also sold as 'Double Red'.

P. Mume 'Tojibai'
In to North American commerce ≤1987. Flowers white, intensely fragrant, very early (late November).

P. Mume var. tonsa Rehd.
In a nomenclatural sense, typical P. Mume has its leaf hairy on both sides, yellowish-green. But this is actually rare. The more common form, in 1921 technically named var. tonsa, has a quite or nearly hairless leaf except near the base of the midrib beneath. The leaf is also narrower, inclined to be broad-cuneate, gray-green colored. In botanical Latin the term tonsa means shaven, hence becoming hairless.

P. Mume 'Viridicalyx'
Described in 1908 in Japan. Calyx green (in Latin viridis is green).

P. Mume 'W.B. Clarke'
In North American commerce ≤1980. Named after California nurseryman Walter Bosworth Clarke (1876–1953). Flowers double, pink. Leaves hairless. Habit weeping. Doubtless a renaming of one of the two following cultivars.

P. Mume 'Weeping Double Pink No. 201'
Introduced to North American commerce ≤1939 by W.B. Clarke nursery of San José, CA. Flowers fully double, pure peach-blossom pink, blooming about a week or 10 days earlier than 204.

P. Mume 'Weeping Double Pink No. 204'
Introduced to North American commerce ≤1939 by W.B. Clarke nursery of San José, CA. Flowers fully double, pink, blooming about a week or 10 days later than 201.

P. Mume 'Weeping Pink'—see P. Mume 'Pendula'

P. Mume 'Weeping Red'
In North American commerce ≤1934. Flowers red. Growth rapid. Long slender branches which droop irregularly. Blooms after 'Early Double Pink' and before 'Dawn'.

P. Mume 'Weeping White'

In North American commerce ≤1934. Flowers white. Branching pendulous.

P. Mume 'Whiskers'

In North American commerce ≤1989. Flowers light red.

P. Mume 'Yara'

In North American commerce ≤1928.

P. mutabilis—see P. jamasakura

P. Myrobalana—see P. cerasifera

P. 'Newport'

= P. cerasifera 'Newport'
= P. americana 'Newport'
= P. × blireiana 'Newport'
= P. Newportii hort.
(P. 'Omaha' PLUM × P. cerasifera 'Pissardii')

NEWPORT PLUM. Bred in 1913 at the Minnesota State Fruit-Breeding Farm. Named (after a town in Minnesota) and introduced in 1923. Common. Remarkably cold-hardy for a PURPLELEAF PLUM. Also well suited to wet soils. Flowers small (⅝" wide), dull white to pale pink; sweetly fragrant. Leaves 2"–3⅓" long dark purple all summer, attractively reddish in autumn. Branching broad and elegant. See also P. 'Kankakee' and P. Mt. St. Helens™. Records: 25' × 6'0" × 31' Sumner, WA (1993); 24' × 6'8" × 29' Puyallup, WA (1993); 18' × 5'1" × 35' Seattle, WA (1988).

P. 'New Red'

= P. serrulata 'New Red'

In the SATO ZAKURA group. In North American commerce ≤1929. Rare. Very similar to P. 'Kwanzan' but has petaloid projections on the stamens (longer than the filaments). Flowers 2" wide, sepals green, slightly flushed red; untoothed. Young foliage bronze. Some writers claim 'New Red' is identical to P. 'Kwanzan'.

P. nigra Ait.

= P. americana var. nigra (Ait.) Waugh
= P. lanata (Sudw.) Mackenzie & Bush
= P. americana var. lanata Sudw.

CANADA PLUM. HORSE PLUM. RED PLUM. WILD PLUM. From Maine to Illinois to SE Manitoba. Named nigra (Latin for black) from the dark branches. Not cultivated for ornament, and seldom grown for its fruit. Flowers larger than those of its close relative P. americana, ¾"–1¼" wide, often pink. Fruit usually darker. Tree more cold-hardy. Some botanists have pointed out that P. nigra is merely the northward version of P. americana. As one goes north, the tree decreases in size and its flowers become pinker. Even in the South a cold winter can make P. americana flowers pink. Record: 51' × 4'2" × 48' near Utica, MI (1972).

P. nigra 'Princess Kay'

Discovered by Catherine (Kay) Nylund in 1974 in the wild near Grand Rapids, Itasca County, northern Minnesota. Registered in 1985; introduced in 1986. Common in the Midwest. Blooms freely when young; the showy double, white flowers contrast well with the dark bark in early May. Some red plums ripen in August.

P. × nigrella W.A. Cummings

= P. 'Muckle'
(P. nigra × P. tenella)

MUCKLE PLUM. Bred <1949 by Robert M. Muckle of Clandeboye, Manitoba. Named and introduced (after Muckle's death) in 1952. Very rare. Flowers 1½" wide, bright purplish-pink, single or semi-double (10% have ten petals); sterile. A shrub or dwarf 10' tall tree.

P. 'Oh-nanden'

= P. serrulata f. ohnanden (Koidz.) Wils.
= P. serrulata 'Oh-nanden'

In the SATO ZAKURA group. Name means "avalanche" or "snowslide." In North America since <1930. Exceedingly rare. Flowers like those of P. 'Kwanzan' but paler; sepals untoothed; petals ca. 42–47. Young foliage apple-green. Some dismiss 'Oh-nanden' as a synonym of P. 'Kwanzan'.

P. 'Ohsibayama'

= P. serrulata 'Ohsibayama'
= P. Lannesiana f. ohsibayama (Koidz.) Wils.
= P. serrulata f. planifolia Miyoshi
('Oshibayama')

In the SATO ZAKURA group. Sold during the 1940s and '50s by Kingsville nursery of Maryland. Extremely rare. Flowers single or semi-double, blush-pink to white.

P. 'Ojochin'

= P. serrulata 'Ojochin'
= P. serrulata f. bullata Miyoshi
= P. serrulata 'Senriko' sensu Ingram
= P. serrulata 'Morni-jigare'
= P. Lannesiana f. ojochin (Koidz.) Wils.
= P. Lannesiana 'Bullata'

In the SATO ZAKURA group. The name means "large paper lantern." In North American commerce since <1930. Uncommon. Tree strong, to 30' tall or more, broadly spreading or rounded. Compared to *P.* 'Ariake' it is a better-shaped tree, branching from 3 or 4 feet above the base and developing a broad, compact crown; much more floriferous. Flowers weakly fragrant, single or semi-double, 5–10 (13) large wrinkled petals, whitish with a hint of pink, borne as many as 8 per cluster. Each flower up to 2¼" wide, much like those of *P.* 'Tai Haku'. Young foliage bronzy-green, many leaves rounded instead of long-tipped. Leaves large, to 10⅛" × 4⅜". Record: 25' × 4'5" × 28' Fircrest, WA (1993).

P. 'Okamé'

= *P.* × *incam* hort.
= *P.* × *incamp* hort.
(*P. incisa* × *P. campanulata*)

OKAMÉ CHERRY. Bred ca. 1930 by C. Ingram of England. In North America since ≤1946. Named officially in 1947. In North American commerce ≤1963–64. The Morris Arboretum has promoted OKAMÉ CHERRY heavily since 1977. Flowers very early, bright pink, small but profuse, in pairs or trios; calyx red. Leaves to 3⅛" × 1½", the margins incised with sharp teeth; stipules very long and jagged. Fall color handsome yellow-orange to orange-red. Tree bushy and twiggy; small, ≤25' tall. Twigs hairless, red when young. Record: 24½' × 2'½" × 20' Seattle, WA (1994; *pl.* 1950).

P. 'Okiku (-zakura)'

= *P. serrulata* 'Okiku (-zakura)'

In the SATO ZAKURA group. Name means "large chrysanthemum." Don't confuse with *P.* 'Kiku-zakura'. Exceedingly rare in North America; here since <1924. Tree of stiff upright habit; gaunt and disease-prone; of poor habit; like *P.* 'Yae-akebono'. Flowers in clusters along the branches, semi-double (19–22 petals), pale pink, 2" wide; sepals finely toothed; often a leafy carpel. Young foliage bronzy-green.

P. 'Oshibayama'—see P. 'Ohsibayama'

P. 'Oshokun'

= *P. serrulata* 'Oshokun'
= *P. serrulata* f. *conspicua* Miyoshi

In the SATO ZAKURA group. Name of a famous Chinese courtesan noted for her surpassing beauty. Exceedingly rare in North America. Tree lacks vigor and has ugly form, but the flowers are exceptionally attractive. Buds deep carmine. Flowers single, lovely pure blush-pink, in short-stemmed clusters with strong CRABAPPLE perfume. Young foliage brownish-green.

P. 'Osibayama'—see P. 'Ohsibayama'

P. 'Othello'—see P. cerasifera 'Othello'

P. Padus L.

= *P. racemosa* Lam.
= *Padus racemosa* (Lam.) Gilib.
= *Cerasus Padus* (L.) DC.

BIRD CHERRY. EUROPEAN BIRD CHERRY. MAYDAY TREE. CLUSTER CHERRY. HACKBERRY. HAGBERRY. From Eurasia. Long grown in North America; common. *Padus* from Greek *pados*, a tree. Capitalized because it was an old generic name. Leaves flush forth cheerfully bright green in early spring; large and not as pointed or coarsely toothed as those of most CHERRIES; invested with charm by the accompanying petite, but numerous and fragrant, pure white flowers in clusters 3"–6" long. The name BIRD CHERRY is apt: the small, black fruit is repulsively bitter to humans, yet relished by birds. Also called MAYDAY TREE because of the normal time of bloom—although a "harbinger" strain (var. *commutata*) can bloom in mid-March. Closely related to *P. virginiana* (CHOKECHERRY). Foliage more coarse and dull. Flowers larger. Seeds rough unlike those of *P. virginiana*. Bark gray, rough and unlike that of most CHERRIES. Prone to aphids and disfiguring black knot disease. Records: see *P. Padus* 'Warereri'; 63' × 6'10" × 67' Christchurch, New Zealand (1970); 54' × 3'8" Stanwood, WA (1993); 43' × 5'8" Tacoma, WA (1993).

P. Padus 'Albertii'

The name suggests that it was originally associated with Johann Albert von Regel (1845–1908) of the St. Petersburg Botanic Garden. Cultivated in Canada ≤1899. Introduced to North American commerce ≤1970–71 (when offered by Scanlon nursery of Ohio). Uncommon. Strong growing, floriferous. Habit compact; in age broad-crowned.

P. Padus 'Berg'

= *P. Padus* Rancho®

Associated with Clayton V. Berg's Valley nursery of Helena, MT. Introduced to commerce ≤1970–71 (when offered by Scanlon nursery of Ohio). Rare. Young foliage green, quickly turning reddish-purple as in *P. virginiana* 'Schubert'. Habit compact; usually sold topgrafted to make a globular tree to ca. 30' tall and 25' wide.

P. Padus 'Colorata'
('Coloratus')

The best known purplish BIRD CHERRY cultivar. Discovered in 1953 in Smaland Province of Sweden. Received an Award of Merit from the Royal Horticultural Society of England in 1974. Offered by some Canadian wholesale nurseries since ≤1979, but scarce if present at all in the U.S. nursery trade. A small tree distinguished by its dark purple twigs, bronzy-colored young foliage, and flowers that are deep pink in the bud, opening pink. In summer the leaves are dark green above with purple veins, lurid pale glaucous gray-purple beneath, and overall the tree has a murky green appearance.

P. Padus var. commutata Dipp.

HARBINGER BIRD CHERRY. From NE Asia. Introduced to cultivation in 1890. Named in 1893 (Latin, meaning "changed"). In the early 1900s, sold erroneously as *P. Maackii* in North America. Many trees sold as typical *P. Padus* are actually this variety. Leaves coarsely toothed, nearly green instead of grayish beneath; unfolding very early in spring.

P. Padus 'Dropmore'

Sold by Dropmore nursery of Manitoba from 1967 until 1973. Very free-flowering, with 4"–5" long flower clusters. Habit compact. Leaves absolutely hairless.

P. Padus 'Grandiflora'—see P. Padus 'Watereri'

P. Padus 'June Scanlon'

Originated by Scanlon nursery of Ohio. *Trees* magazine, January-February 1970: "wait till you see *P. Padus* 'June Scanlon'. Iridescently purplish foliage, black bark, and shellpink flowers like LILY-OF-THE-VALLEY, a superb little tree, looks like it will go to 16–18'. A chance seedling but how lovely—it had to have a good name." Named for Mrs. Scanlon, June S. Faulds. Edward H. Scanlon's obituary in a 1976 *Trees* magazine mentions SCANLON PINK BIRDCHERRY, *P. Padus* 'Scanlon', calls it PP 3107 (1972). Apparently this clone either remained unpropagated, or was renamed.

P. Padus 'Pendula'

WEEPING BIRD CHERRY. Originated in 1849 in France. Described officially in 1875 in Germany. Exceedingly rare in North America. Branches pendulous.

P. Padus 'Plena'

DOUBLE FLOWERED BIRD CHERRY. Cultivated in 1890 in Germany; in 1896 in Canada. Described officially in 1906. Very rare in North America. Flowers double (*plena* in Latin means full or plump; having extra petals), large and long-lasting.

P. Padus 'Purple Queen'

Similar to but darker than 'Colorata'. A younger selection, also of European origin, and like 'Colorata', it makes a smaller tree than typical *P. Padus*. May be just a nursery trade name for 'Colorata'.

P. Padus 'Purpurea'

In North American commerce ≤1985–86. An obscure name. May be a nursery name for *P. Padus* 'Colorata' or 'June Scanlon' or another BIRD CHERRY clone. J. Searles writes: "purplish-green foliage and dark purple flowers." Handy nursery of Portland, OR, writes: "slightly pyramidal; both new and old growth is dark burgundy. Unlike any other BIRD CHERRIES, this bears dark purple clusters of flowers; 30' tall."

P. Padus Rancho®—see P. Padus 'Berg'

P. Padus 'Scanlon'—see P. Padus 'June Scanlon'

P. Padus 'Spaethi'

Presumably introduced by Späth nursery of Germany. Described in 1940. Flowers larger (ca. ¾" wide) than those of typical *P. Padus*. Rare in North America. Records: 44' × 3'4" × 27' and 40' × 5'1" × 40' Seattle, WA (1988).

P. Padus Summerglow®
= *P. Padus* 'Wandell'

Originated by Willet N. Wandell of Urbana, IL. Introduced ≤1987–88 by Femrite nursery of Aurora, OR. Foliage reddish-purple all summer. Like *P. virginiana* 'Schubert' but larger (to 50' tall, 35' wide), and does not sucker from the root.

P. Padus 'Wandell'—see P. Padus Summerglow®

P. Padus 'Watereri'

= *P. Padus* 'Grandiflora'

Raised <1914 by Waterer's Knap Hill nursery of Woking, Surrey, England. Introduced to the U.S. in 1923 by the Arnold Arboretum. Rare. Larger than typical in growth, leaves and flower clusters (to 8" long). A rank grower. Record: 88' × 6'3" Hergest Croft, Herefordshire, England (1985).

P. 'Pandora'

?(*P. subhirtella* 'Rosea' × *P. yedoensis*)

PANDORA CHERRY. Raised and introduced ≤1939 by Waterer nursery of Bagshot, Surrey, England. In North America ≤1942; sold here since ≤1963–64. Rare. Palest pink or actually quite white flowers, 1¼" wide, in clusters of 2–4. Shoots slender and hairless. Leaves extremely finely toothed (even incised), to 3¾" × 1⅝", sparsely hairy, very dark green; fall color yellow with hint of pink. Tree vigorous and elegant, less burly and sprouty than *P. × yedoensis*. Crown light, with angular branches holding slender long shoots. May be a *P. incisa* hybrid. Record: 51' × 4'0" Tacoma, WA (1992).

P. 'Paul Wohlert'

= *P. serrulata* 'Paul Wohlert'

In the SATO ZAKURA group. Introduced in 1925 by Wohlert nursery of Narberth, PA. Named after Wohlert's son. Uncommon; extinct commercially since ca. mid-1960s. Semi-dwarf, of spreading habit. Buds red. Flowers semi-double, deep pink; very early, fragrant.

P. pendula Maxim.

= *P. × subhirtella* 'Pendula'
= *P. × subhirtella* 'Ito-zakura'
= *P. × subhirtella* 'Shidare (higan) zakura'

WILD WEEPING (HIGAN) CHERRY. WEEPING SPRING CHERRY. From Japan. A naturally pendulous tree of large size. Ellwanger & Barry nursery of Rochester, NY, listed in 1846–47 *Cerasus pendula*, which is probably this tree. Parsons nursery of Flushing, NY, obtained 15 FLOWERING CHERRY varieties in March 1862, including this, from G.R. Hall. Flowers vary from nearly white to pale pink. Leaves to 5¼" × 1½", finely and sharply toothed. Records: 48' × 8'10" × 51' Walla Walla, WA (1993); 47½' × 12'6" Japan (1994); 46' × 8'7" × 38' Portland, CT (1988); 41' × 7'0" × 37' Seattle, WA (1989); 33' × 8'5" × 54' Kent, WA (1992).

P. pendula var. ascendens Mak.

= *P. × subhirtella* var. *ascendens* (Mak.) Wils.
= *P. × subhirtella* 'Ascendens'
= *P. × subhirtella* 'Beni-higan' (in part)
= *P. × subhirtella* 'Shiro-higan' (in part)
= *P. pendula* f. *ascendens* (Mak.) Ohwi
= *P. æquinoctialis* Miyoshi

EQUINOX CHERRY. WILD SPRING CHERRY. From China, Korea, and Japan. Cultivated in the West since ca. 1916. Rare. Used as a rootstock. A tall tree, not pendulous. Leaves longer and narrower than those of *P. × subhirtella* (HIGAN CHERRY). Flowers white or palest pink, small. Records: to 80' × 20'0" in Japan; 57' × 4'8" Woodinville, WA (1993); 52' × 6'9" Woodinville, WA (1992); 34' × 6'10" × 53' Lakewood, WA (1993).

P. pendula 'Eureka Weeping'

= *P. × subhirtella* 'Eureka Weeping'
= *P. × subhirtella* 'Ito-shidare'

EUREKA WEEPING (HIGAN) CHERRY. Named (likely after Eureka, CA) in the 1920s by W.B. Clarke nursery of San José, CA. Flowers palest pink, turning white. Topgrafted and maintaining a mushroom-like, pendulous habit, gaining little height beyond the point it was grafted. The name, if not the clone, is extinct in commerce. 'Eureka Weeping' may be the clone also known as 'Pendula Rosea'—a pale pink weeping cultivar of *P. pendula*.

P. pendula 'Fukubana'

= *P. × subhirtella* 'Fukubana'
= *P. × subhirtella* 'Momi-jigari'
= *P. × subhirtella* 'Roseo-plena'
= *P. × subhirtella* 'Flore Plena'
= *P. × subhirtella* 'Spring Glory'
= *P. serrulata* 'Fukubana'

DOUBLE PINK HIGAN CHERRY. Named in 1908 in Japan. Cultivated in California since <1927. Very rare; likely out of commerce since the 1970s. 'Momi-jigari' means "excursion to view red autumn maple leaves." The last HIGAN to bloom in spring. Red buds like those on *Malus floribunda* open to profuse, deep pink double flowers, usally less than 1" wide, of 12–21 sharply cleft petals, lasting a long time in spring, gradually fading to pale pink. Unlike most HIGAN cultivars, the calyx tube is slightly or not constricted, but is conspicuously reddish. Flowers (2) 3 (4) per cluster. Leaves relatively small, to 3⅜" × 1¼".

P. pendula 'Park Weeping'
= P. × subhirtella 'Park Weeping'
= P. × subhirtella 'Beni-shidare'

PARK WEEPING (HIGAN) CHERRY. PINK WEEPING HIGAN CHERRY. Imported for 1915 Panama Pacific exposition of San Francisco. Introduced in the 1920s by W.B. Clarke nursery of San José, CA. Propagated from a tree in Golden Gate Park's Japanese Tea Garden. The name, if not the clone, is extinct in commerce. Flowers deeper pink than those of P. pendula 'Eureka Weeping'. Although topgrafted and definitely weeping, the tree gradually gains height. How this clone differs from P. pendula 'Pendula Rubra' is unknown.

P. pendula 'Pendula Plena Rosea'
= P. × subhirtella 'Pendula Plena Rosea'
= P. × subhirtella 'Sendai Ito-zakura'
= P. × subhirtella 'Endo-zakura'
= P. × subhirtella 'Totsu-zakura'
= P. × subhirtella 'Double Park Weeping'
= P. × subhirtella 'Yae Shidare-higan'
= P. × subhirtella 'Yae Beni-shidare'

DOUBLE WEEPING (HIGAN) CHERRY. DOUBLE PARK WEEPING CHERRY. Introduced from Japan to England in 1928. In North American commerce since ≤1937. Common since the 1950s. Flowers dark pink, double, ⅞" wide, blooming later than the single-flowered cultivars. Tree invariably topgrafted. Record: 18' × 5'9" × 31' Puyallup, WA (1993).

P. pendula 'Pendula Rosea'
= P. × subhirtella 'Pendula Rosea'

This name is not in general usage. It would appear to apply to a clone like the following except with paler flowers. See also P. pendula 'Eureka Weeping'.

P. pendula 'Pendula Rubra'
= P. × subhirtella 'Pendula Rubra'
= P. × subhirtella 'Pendula Lanceolata'

PINK WEEPING (HIGAN) CHERRY. Common. Usually sold as 'Pendula'; compared to typical seedling-grown P. pendula, this has smaller, coarser leaves, and pinker flowers that open a bit later in spring. Some of the flower clusters are pedunculate. Always topgrafted, forming a small tree. Record: 26' × 8'5" × 40' Camas, WA (1993).

P. pendula 'Stellata'
= P. × subhirtella 'Stellata'
= P. × subhirtella 'Beni-hoshi'
= P. × subhirtella 'Pink Star'

STAR FLOWERED SPRING CHERRY. CLARKE'S SPRING CHERRY. Originated as a seedling discovered in San Francisco's Golden Gate Park Tea Garden. Introduced ≤1934 by W.B. Clarke nursery of San José, CA. Rare but still in commerce. Dark pink buds open to pale pink, tightly clustered single flowers, to 1⅜" wide, as many as 10 per bud, with an extremely long season of bloom in spring. The name refers to the petal edges rolled inwards so as to accentuate the starlike appearance. It produces pea-size, black, very shiny cherries of adequate flavor, quite like those of the WEEPING HIGAN. Record: 25' × 5'3" × 33' Seattle, WA (1992; pl. 1940).

P. pennsylvanica L. fil.

FIRE CHERRY. WILD RED CHERRY. NORTHERN PIN CHERRY. PIGEON CHERRY. BIRD CHERRY. From much of North America, although not in the Deep South or Southwest. Seldom cultivated. A short-lived pioneer species. Flowers small, white, 2–10 per cluster, usually in April and May. Leaves sharp and slender. Fruit translucent red, ¼"–⅓". Its western counterpart is P. emarginata (BITTER CHERRY). Records: to 91' tall in the Great Smoky Mountains; 85' × 5'11" Great Smoky Mountains National Park, TN (1982); 80' × 6'8" Gilmer County, GA (1982).

P. pennsylvanica 'Jumping Pond'
A Canadian selection from <1980. Dwarf, with drooping branches.

P. pennsylvanica 'Liss'
Fruit three times larger than typical.

P. pennsylvanica 'Stockton Double'
Discovered near Stockton, Manitoba by Mrs. M.N. Badhan. Introduced in 1929 by Morden research station. Extremely rare. Flowers double. Habit compact, rounded. Foliage dark green, then brilliant red in fall.

P. Persica (L.) Batsch
= Persica vulgaris Mill.
= Amygdalus Persica L.

PEACH. COMMON PEACH. From China. Persica derives from malum persicum (apple of Persia) the Greek and Roman name of the PEACH, which refers to its introduction to Europe from Iran (Persia). Capitalized because it was an old generic name. Brought to Florida by Spaniards or French Huguenots in the late 1500s, and immediately went wild. Can bear fruit when only three years old. A 1776 ad offered a double-flowered cultivar. To date, more than 2,000 fruiting cultivars have been named. The first named cultivar in the U.S. is 'Oldmixon' (ca. 1730). On the other hand, ORNAMENTAL PEACHES in general have suffered a decline in popularity from their status a few decades ago; the 71 cultivars be-low include some not definitely known to be in North America. PEACH trees are short-lived, small, and subject to leaf-curl and other ailments. They require much sunshine, and annual or semi-annual hard pruning. Some of the cultivars, in full bloom, offer an unbeatable floral display. Flowers typically pink, can be white or red; in spring before the leaves appear. Leaves slender, 4"–9" long, often curved. Records: 39' × 3'9" Paris, France (1982; *pl.* 1910); 18' × 13'9" Japan (1994); 18' × 6'0" × 32' Morrisville, VA (1986).

P. Persica 'Ackerman Redleaf'—see *P. Persica* 'Royal Redleaf'

P. Persica 'Alba'
= *P. Persica* 'White'

WHITE FLOWERING PEACH. Described in 1833 in England. Flowers white.

P. Persica 'Alboplena'
= *P. Persica* 'Double White'
= *P. Persica* 'Flore Albo Pleno'

DOUBLE WHITE FLOWERING PEACH. Introduced to England in 1849. Very common. Flowers semi-double, large (ca. 2" wide), snow-white, showing yellow stamens. Blooms before 'Icicle'.

P. Persica 'Alboplena Pendula'—see *P. Persica* 'Double White Weeping'

P. Persica 'Alma Stultz'
AZALEA FLOWERIED NECTARINE. Originated as a seedling raised by L. Burbank of Santa Rosa, CA. Sold in 1904 to Joseph Asbury Johnson. Named in 1956 (after Johnson's daughter, Mrs. O.M. Stultz (1893–1965), longtime director of the Audubon Center of Southern California), and introduced in 1957 by Los Angeles nurseryman T. Payne. Still in commerce. Flowers azalea-like, 2" wide, delicate rosy white shading to deep pink at the base of the petal; deliciously fragrant.

P. Persica 'Altair' PP 1022 (1951)
Introduced by Armstrong nursery of Ontario, CA. Flowers double, pink, blooming in late February in southern California. Fruit white-fleshed, freestone, ripe in mid-August in southern California.

P. Persica 'Atropurpurea'—see *P. Persica* 'Foliis Rubris'

P. Persica 'Aurora'
Originated and introduced (in 1937) by W.B. Clarke nursery of San José, CA. The best of 500 seedlings. Flowers semi-double, open-flared so the stamens show, very soft pastel pink, blooming early. Rapid, quite vigorous. Moderate crop of white skinned, white-fleshed, freestone peaches. (Plant Patent 1245 was issued in 1954 to a fruiting cultivar also named 'Aurora'; it had been selected in 1951 and introduced in 1952.)

P. Persica 'Bloodleaf'—see *P. Persica* 'Foliis Rubris'

P. Persica 'Blushing Bride'—see *P. Persica* 'Early Double White'

P. Persica 'Bonfire' P.A.F.
Raised in 1984 and selected in 1988 at the University of Arkansas. Introduced in 1992. Dwarf. Leaves red. Flowers double, showy, pink. Fruit small, poor.

P. Persica 'Burbank (Double Pink)'
= *P. Persica* 'Double Pink Late'
= *P. Persica* 'Roseo-plena Tardiva'

Presumably originated by plant breeder and nurseryman Luther Burbank (1849–1926) of Santa Rosa, CA; perhaps introduced in 1915. In California commerce since ≤1931. Common. Long thought the standard of excellence in a mid-season double pink PEACH. Flowers double, opening flat, ca. 2" white, clear pink. Flowers slightly larger and deeper pink than those of 'Klara Mayer'. An especially long blooming season.

P. Persica 'Burbank's Orchid' PP 290 (1938)
= *P. Persica* 'Orchid'

Originated by Luther Burbank of Santa Rosa, CA. Introduced in 1939 by Stark Bro's nursery of Louisiana, MO. Flowers large, double, pink. Fruit small, white-fleshed, freestone.

P. Persica 'Burbank's Santa Rosa' PP 291 (1938)

= P. Persica 'Santa Rosa'

Exactly as preceding except flowers crimson.

P. Pers. 'California (Double) Red'—see P. Pers. 'Camelliæflora'

P. Persica 'Cambridge Carmine'—A synonym of P. Persica 'Cardinal' or 'Magnifica' or 'Russel's Red'

P. Persica 'Camelliæflora'

= P. Persica 'California (Double) Red'
= P. Persica 'Late Double Red'
= P. Persica 'Double Red Late'
= P. Persica 'Rubra-plena Tardiva'

Described in 1858 in Belgium. In North American commerce since ≤1910. Common. Flowers very double, large, with ruffled petals; deep, rich red; the latest red to bloom.

P. Persica 'Candy Stick'—see P. Persica 'Peppermint Stick'

P. Persica 'Cardinal'

?= P. Persica 'Cambridge Carmine'

Origin unknown; probably from England. In commerce ≤1958 there, as well as in Germany, Canada, and the U.S. Flowers semi-double or double, vivid red. Similar to if not identical to 'Magnifica' and 'Russel's Red'. (A fruiting cultivar bred in 1941 was also named 'Cardinal'.)

P. Persica 'Carnea Flore Plena'—see P. Persica 'Duplex'

P. Persica 'Caryophyllus'—see P. Persica 'Dianthiflora'

P. Persica 'Cascade'

Introduced ≤1975 in New Zealand. Flowers double, ice-white like those of 'Iceberg' but branches gracefully weeping from a 6' topgraft.

P. Persica 'Cerise'—see P. Persica 'Double Cerise'

P. Persica 'Charming'—see P. Persica 'Prince Charming'

P. Persica 'Chrysanthemum'

Originated in South Carolina. Introduced ≤1906 by Fruitland nursery of Augusta, GA, which sold it through 1926–27. Later offered by W.B. Clarke nursery of San José, CA. Long commercially extinct. Flowers large, light pink, the center quilled like a chrysanthemum.

P. Persica 'Clara Meyer'—see P. Persica 'Klara Mayer'

P. Persica 'Crimson Cascade' (original name; see below)

Introduced ≤1966–67 in England. Flowers double, crimson. Branches weeping.

P. Persica 'Crimson Cascade' (registered name; see above)

Raised in 1978 and selected in 1981 at the University of Arkansas. Introduced in 1992. Vigorous. Extremely weeping. Leaves dark red fading to greenish-red by midsummer. Flowers double, showy, dark red. Fruit small, poor. It should be renamed, since its name was already taken.

P. Persica 'Daily News 2-Star' PP 1156 (1952)

The Daily News Stars series were the first FRUITING-FLOWERING PEACHES on the market. Developed by Dr. W.E. Lammerts. Introduced ≤1952 in California. Flowers large, single, deep-pink. Fruit red-skinned, white-fleshed, semi-freestone. Ripens in June. In proper locations has red and yellow fall color.

P. Persica 'Daily News 3-Star' PP 1092 (1952)

As the preceding. Still in commerce in early 1980s. Flowers large, single, dark pink. Fruit excellent, red-skinned, yellow-fleshed, free-stone. Ripens in early August.

P. Persica 'Daily News 4-Star' PP 1093 (1952)

As the preceding. Still in commerce in early 1980s. Flowers large, single, salmon-pink. Fruit deep red-skinned, white-fleshed, free-stone. Ripens in mid-June. In proper locations has red and yellow fall color.

P. Persica 'Dianthiflora'

= P. Persica 'Caryophyllus'
= P. Persica 'Dianthiflora Plena'

Described in 1858 in Belgium. Extremely rarely, if ever, offered in North American commerce. Flowers semi-double, pink.

P. Persica 'Dianthiflora Plena'—see *P. Persica* 'Dianthiflora'

P. Persica 'Double Cerise'

= *P. Persica* 'Cerise'

Introduced in California ≤1931. Out of commerce since the 1940s. Flowers double, opening very deep pink and changing to cerise or almost claret-colored; the last of all to bloom.

P. Persica 'Double Delight' PP 1787 (1958)

Originated in Ontario, CA by H.C. Swim, of Armstrong nursery. Selected in 1949. Introduced in 1957. Flowers large, semi-double (14–18 petals), delicate shell-pink; in late March. Fruit large, moderately red-blushed; flesh yellow; free-stone; ripe in mid-July. Tree vigorous. (Blooms 10 days after 'Saturn' and ripens later, too.)

P. Persica 'Double Maroon'

Introduced in 1934 by W.B. Clarke nursery of San José, CA. Long extinct commercially. A pure red flowered sport of *P. Persica* 'Woodside'.

P. Persica 'Double Pink'—see *P. Persica* 'Duplex'

P. Persica 'Double Pink Early'

In California commerce since ≤1931. As *P. Persica* 'Duplex' (double, pink) but earlier to bloom.

P. Persica 'Double Pink Late'—see *P. Persica* 'Burbank'

P. Persica 'Double Pink Weeping'

= *P. Persica* 'Weeping Double Pink'
= *P. Persica* 'Weeping Pink'

PINK WEEPING PEACH. Introduced in 1938 by W.B. Clarke nursery of San José, CA. "For several years we've grown red and white double weepers, but couldn't find any double pink. So we bred one." Common. Flowers very fully double, pink. Branches pendulous; topgrafted.

P. Persica 'Double Red'—see *P. Persica* 'Rubro-plena'

P. Persica 'Double Red Early'

= *P. Persica* 'Early Red'
= *P. Persica* 'Early Double Red'

Introduced <1931 in California. Common. Though it blooms 10 days later than 'San José Pink' it is still 10 days before all other cultivars. Flowers good-size, semi-double, slightly loose, rather light clear red.

P. Persica 'Double Red Late'—see *P. Persica* 'Camelliæflora'

P. Persica 'Double Red Weeping'

= *P. Persica* 'Rubra-plena Pendula'

In California commerce since ≤1931. Uncommon. Flowers very fully double, red. According to W.B. Clarke, the "color is very rich and entirely distinct from that of the erect reds." Topgrafted; branches pendulous.

P. Persica 'Double White'—see *P. Persica* 'Alboplena'

P. Persica 'Double White Early'—see *P. Pers.* 'Early Double White'

P. Persica 'Double White Weeping'

= *P. Persica* 'Alboplena Pendula'

In North American commerce since ≤1934. Uncommon. Flowers semi- to fully double, pure white. Branches pendulous; topgrafted.

P. Persica 'Duke of Edinborough'

Presumably from England. In British Columbia commerce ≤1953–54. Long commercially extinct. Flowers double, red.

P. Persica 'Duplex'

= *P. Persica* 'Rosea-plena' or 'Roseo-pleno'
= *P. Persica* 'Rosea Flore-pleno'
= *P. Persica* 'Flore Pleno'
= *P. Persica* 'Flore Roseo Pleno'
= *P. Persica* 'Multiplex'
= *P. Persica* 'Double Pink'
= *P. Persica* 'Carnea Flore Plena'

DOUBLE PINK PEACH. Cultivated <1636 in France. Described officially in 1770 in England. Very common. Flowers double, pink. Cultivars of the same theme include 'Burbank' and 'Klara Mayer'.

P. Persica 'Dwarf Mandarin'

= *P. Persica* 'Mandarin'

Introduced in 1940 by W.B. Clarke nursery of San José, CA. Several dwarf cultivars were imported from China. "A great favorite among the Chinese for growing in pots and tubs." Available in several colors: white, pale pink, pink, red, and variegated pink and white (all double). Sold topgrafted at 1' or 2'. Ultimate height ca. 5' tall.

P. Persica 'Early Double Red'—see *P. Persica* 'Double Red Early'

P. Persica 'Early Double White'
= P. Persica 'Double White Early'
= P. Persica 'Blushing Bride'

Introduced in 1937 by W.B. Clarke nursery of San José, CA. Common. Originally called 'Blushing Bride' because many of the flowers showed a slight blush. This became less noticeable with propagation so that by 1941 nearly all the flowers were simply pure white. Still in commerce. Flowers large, double, usually pure white, but some marked with soft rose, or occasionally entirely rose; early to bloom—a week or so before 'Iceberg'.

P. Persica 'Early Red'—see P. Persica 'Double Red Early'

P. Persica 'Edward H. Rust'

Introduced ≤1948 by, but not originated by, W.B. Clarke nursery of San José, CA. E.H. Rust (1863–1944) was a California nursery friend of Clarke's. Long extinct commercially. Flowers white.

P. Persica 'Fastigiata'—see P. Persica 'Pyramidalis'

P. Persica 'Flore Albo Pleno'—see P. Persica 'Alboplena'

P. Persica 'Flore Pleno'—see P. Persica 'Duplex'

P. Persica 'Flore Roseo Pleno'—see P. Persica 'Duplex'

P. Persica 'Flore Sanguineo Pleno'—see P. Persica 'Russel's Red'

P. Persica 'Flory (Dwarf)'

Raised from a seed brought from north China in 1938, by Carl R. Flory (1884–1981) of Modesto, CA. Introduced ≤1945. Sold until at least the late 1960s. Tree dwarf, 2'–6' tall. Flowers very large, double, showy bright red, swathing the branches. Fruit small, white-fleshed, freestone; ripening in late August; bland. Leaves long, willowy and very attractive.

P. Persica 'Foliis Purpureis'—see P. Persica 'Foliis Rubris'

P. Persica 'Foliis Rubis'—see P. Persica 'Foliis Rubris'

P. Persica 'Foliis Rubris'
= P. Persica 'Foliis Rubis'
= P. Persica 'Foliis Purpureis'
= P. Persica 'Atropurpurea'
= P. Persica 'Rubrifolia'
= P. Persica 'Purpurea'
= P. Persica 'Bloodleaf'

BLOODLEAF PEACH. The first Prunus purplish-leaf variant. Originated in Mississippi during the 1860s. In commerce since 1871. Exported quickly to Europe and there renamed P. Persica 'Foliis Rubris' in 1873. Flowers single, pale pink. Leaves beet-red while young, fading to bronzy-green above. Fruit small, red-skinned, white-fleshed. In the United States, BLOODLEAF PEACH has become a general vernacularism applied to any red- or purplish-leaved PEACH. Other, younger PURPLELEAF PEACH cultivars are 'Rancho Redleaf' and 'Royal Redleaf'. Actually red-leaved PEACH seedlings are commonly raised (by the thousands) to use for grafting.

P. Persica 'Gen Bei'

Introduced <1935 in California. Long commercially extinct. Very slow growing. Flowers variegated pink and white.

P. Persica H6818031—see P. Persica 'Harrow Candifloss'

P. Persica 'Harrow Candifloss'
= P. Persica H6818031

Originated in 1968 at Harrow research station of Harrow, Ontario. An open-pollinated seedling. Selected in 1973, introduced in 1980. Flowers profuse, 1¼"–1⅝" wide, 15 petals plus 1–5 petaloid parts in the middle; medium pink, becoming dark in the center with age. One of the first cold-hardy, late-blooming PEACHES for Canada.

P. Persica 'Harrow Frostipink'

As preceding but flowers light pink. Tree hardier.

P. Persica 'Harrow Rubirose'

As preceding but flowers deep-rose to red, and slightly smaller.

P. Persica 'Helen Borchers'

Introduced in 1939 by W.B. Clarke nursery of San José, CA. Very common. Parentage unknown; it may be a 'Klara Mayer' seedling. Helen (d. 1961) was the wife of Walter B. Borchers (a Clarke nursery employee for at least 20 years). Flowers profuse, double, unusually large (to 2½" wide), clear pink (without the harsh tones of rose so common in PEACHES), petals ruffled and incurved. Blooms late, in the north during May instead of April. Unlike 'Klara Mayer', it makes a healthy, vigorous tree to 25' tall and 30' wide. Thought by many the finest of all.

P. Persica 'Iceberg'
?= *P. Persica* 'Icicle'

Introduced in 1938 by W.B. Clarke nursery of San José, CA. Very common in commerce until at least the late 1950s. Flowers profuse, very large, snow white, semi-double or double. Early blooming. By far the best white—one of the finest of any color.

P. Persica 'Icicle'
= *P. Persica* 'White Double Late'

Since ≤1962–63, Oregon and California nurseries have used this name for a double, white PEACH. Except that some say it blooms late, there is every reason to suppose 'Icicle' is a synonym of 'Iceberg'.

P. Persica 'Jeanne Wohlert'
Introduced ≤1941 by Wohlert nursery of Narberth, PA. Named after one of A.E. Wohlert's daughters. Long commercially extinct. Its attributes unknown.

P. Persica 'Jerseypink'
Bred at Rutgers University of New Brunswick, NJ. Selected in 1985. Released in 1990. Flowers numerous, large, double, rich pink, late. Fruit sparse, to 2⅜", cling-stone.

P. Persica 'Klara Mayer'
('Klara Meyer', 'Clara Meyer')

Introduced in 1891 by Späth nursery of Germany. In North American commerce <1931. Uncommon, especially since the 1960s. Flowers densely double, peach-pink, almost 2" wide, very full and tufted with ruffled petals. A twiggy, slow growing tree. Some fruit produced; of medium size and good flavor.

P. Persica 'Late Double Red'—see P. Persica 'Camelliæflora'

P. Persica 'Lilian Burrows'
Introduced ≤1961 in England. Not known in North America. Tree of shapely habit. Flowers double, 2" wide, delicate pink, with pink and white stamens.

P. Persica 'Lord Baldwin'
Discovered in Virginia by Dr. J.T. Baldwin. Introduced ≤1981 by Bountiful Ridge nursery of Princess Anne, MD. Flowers deep rose-pink, abundant, lasting

as long as a month. Fruit small, but very decorative and edible. Habit distinctly upright.

P. Persica 'Magnifica'
?= *P. Persica* 'Cambridge Carmine'

Probably imported from Japan. Introduced ≤1894 by Veitch nursery of England. Flowers 1½"–1¾" wide, semi-double or double, bright carmine-red or crimson. Habit lax and spreading; semi-pendulous branches. Similar to if not same as 'Cardinal' and 'Russel's Red'.

P. Persica 'Mandarin'—see P. Persica 'Dwarf Mandarin'

P. Persica 'McDonald Red'
Found and introduced by Mr. J.E. McDonald of Martinsburg, WV. Introduced ≤1981 by Bountiful Ridge nursery of Princess Anne, MD. Flowers bright red, fully double, large, profuse. Fruitless.

P. Persica 'Multiplex'—see P. Persica 'Duplex'

P. Persica 'Orchid'—see P. Persica 'Burbank's Orchid'

P. Persica 'Palace Peach'
Introduced ≤1946 in England; not known to be in North America. Flowers dark crimson, semi-double, 1" wide.

P. Persica 'Pendula'
WEEPING PEACH. Described in 1839 in Europe. This name, without indication of floral color, is seldom used. Nurseries tend to specify whether their WEEPING PEACHES bear pink, red, white or variegated flowers. Nearly all such cultivars are double.

P. Persica 'Peppermint' PP 5147 (1983)
Patented by Sam S. Skrhak of McGregor TX. Sold in Texas. Flowers double, red and white. Considering the following cultivar and its 'Peppermint' synonym used as early as 1955, it is incredible that this cultivar could have been allowed its name.

P. Persica 'Peppermint Stick'
= *P. Persica* 'Peppermint'
= *P. Persica* 'Candy Stick'
= *P. Persica* 'Variegated'

Probably a selection of the 1858 cultivar 'Versicolor'. Introduced in 1933 by W.B. Clarke nursery of San José, CA. Common. Flowers double, mostly white, plentifully marked with vivid red stripes, but also has some pink with red stripes and here and there a few clear red. Strong growth, making a large tree. Comes partly true from seed.

P. Persica 'Pink Cascade' (original; see below)

Introduced ≤1968 by Stark Bro's nursery of Louisiana, MO. Likely no more than 'Double Pink Weeping' renamed.

P. Persica 'Pink Cascade' (registered name; see above)

Raised in 1978 and selected in 1981 at the University of Arkansas. Introduced in 1992. Vigorous. Extremely weeping. Leaves dark red fading to greenish-red by midsummer. Flowers double, showy, pink. Fruit small, poor. It should be renamed, since its name was already taken.

P. Persica 'Pink Charming'—see P. Persica 'Prince Charming'

P. Persica 'Prince Charming'

= P. Persica 'Pink Charming'
= P. Persica 'Charming'

Origin unknown. By 1958 it was being sold in Canada, England, Germany and the U.S. Flowers double, large, rosy-red. Small tree of upright habit.

P. Persica 'Purpurea'—see P. Persica 'Foliis Rubris'

P. Persica 'Pyramidalis'

= P. Persica 'Fastigiata'
= P. Persica 'Upright'

Described in 1871. Extremely rare in North America. Narrowly upright habit.

P. Persica 'Rancho Redleaf' PP 1440 (1955)

Discovered in 1949 in Bakersfield, CA. Selected in 1954. Introduced ≤1956 by Del Rancho Fortuna nursery of McFarland, CA. Still in commerce; used as an ornamental and as a rootstock (75% of its seedlings are red-leaved). Flowers large, extremely double, radiant pink, swathing the branches from trunk to tip. Leaves deep red, wine-colored, holding fairly well into the summer before bronzing. Confusion with 'Royal Redleaf' has occurred.

P. Persica 'Red Pep'

Introduced in 1939 by W.B. Clarke nursery of San José, CA. Name an abbreviation for 'Red Peppermint Stick'. 'Peppermint Stick' always produces some clear red flowers, and occasionally a shoot will show only

this color. As these flowers appear later than 'Double Red Early' and before 'Camelliæflora', it seemed worthwhile to breed them out by bud selection. This was carried out for several generations until finally everything but red was eliminated.

P. Persica 'Rosea Flore-pleno'—see P. Persica 'Duplex'

P. Persica 'Rosea-plena' or 'Roseo-pleno'—see P. Persica 'Duplex'

P. Persica 'Roseo-plena Tardiva'—see P. Persica 'Burbank'

P. Persica 'Royal Redleaf'

= P. Persica 'Ackerman Redleaf'

A chance seedling discovered in 1938. Introduced ca. 1940 by Ackerman nursery of Bridgman, MI. Very rare until ca. 1955. Flowers large, pink, single. Leaves red. Fruit medium-sized, sweet, red-skinned, white-fleshed, free-stone, ripening in mid-August.

P. Persica 'Rubra'—see P. Persica 'Rubro-plena'

P. Pers. 'Rubra-plena Pendula'—see P. Pers. 'Double Red Weeping'

P. Persica 'Rubra-plena Tardiva'—see P. Persica 'Camelliæflora'

P. Persica 'Rubrifolia'—see P. Persica 'Foliis Rubris'

P. Persica 'Rubro-plena'

= P. Persica 'Semi-plena Rubra'
= P. Persica 'Sanguinea Plena'
= P. Persica 'Splendens'
= P. Persica 'Double Red'
= P. Persica 'Rubra'

RED FLOWERING PEACH. Imported in the 1840s to Europe from China. Described in 1854. Flowers semi-double or double, red. Common. Derivative cultivars include 'Burbank's Santa Rosa', 'Camelliæflora', 'Cardinal', 'Double Red Early', 'Duke of Edinborough', 'Magnifica', 'McDonald Red', 'Palace Peach', and 'Russel's Red'.

P. Persica 'Russel's Red'

= P. Persica 'Flore Sanguineo Pleno'
?= P. Persica 'Cambridge Carmine'

Raised by L.R. Russel nursery of Windlesham, England <1933. In North America since ≤1940. Flowers large, semi-double or double, bright carmine-red or crimson. Fairly vigorous constitution. Habit twiggy and bushy-headed. Similar to if not identical to 'Cardinal' and 'Magnifica'.

P. Persica 'Sanguinea Plena'—see P. Persica 'Rubro-plena'

P. Persica 'San José Pink'

Introduced <1934 by W.B. Clarke nursery of San José, CA. Seldom sold since the late 1950s. Flowers earliest of all (ca. 10 days before 'Double Red Early' and 3 weeks before most kinds), double, pink, medium-sized—not as fine as those of later-blooming cultivars.

P. Persica 'Santa Rosa'—see P. Persica 'Burbank's Santa Rosa'

P. Persica 'Saturn' PP 1485 (1956)

Originated in Ontario, CA by H.C. Swim, of Armstrong nursery. Selected in 1949. Introduced in 1955. Still in commerce in the mid-1980s. Flowers large, semi-double (14–16 petals), deep pink; in late March. Fruit large; flesh yellow; free-stone; ripe in late July. Tree large, vigorous. Low chilling requirement.

P. Persica 'Seedling No. 16'

Introduced in 1939 by W.B. Clarke nursery of San José, CA. Long extinct commercially. Grows slowly, blooms sparsely. Flowers are enormous, well-colored and beautifully formed with ruffled petals surpassing all others in size at least.

P. Persica 'Semi-plena Rubra'—see P. Persica 'Rubro-plena'

P. Persica 'Splendens'—see P. Persica 'Rubro-plena'

P. Persica 'Tom Thumb' PP 306 (1938)

Discovered during the late 1920s in Argentonsur-Creuse (Indre), France. Introduced ca. 1938 by Stark Bro's nursery of Louisiana, MO. Long commercially extinct. Flowers "rather attractive." Fruit poor. Tree naturally dwarf.

P. Persica 'Upright'—see P. Persica 'Pyramidalis'

P. Persica 'Variegated'—see P. Persica 'Peppermint Stick'

P. Pers. 'Variegated Weeping'—see P. Pers. 'Versicolor Weeping'

P. Persica 'Versicolor'
= P. Persica 'Versicolor A'

Described in 1858 in Belgium. In North American commerce since ≤1931. Flowers semi-double, medium sized, white striped and splashed rosy-red; occasionally solid rosy-red or white. It reverts easily to red. Evidently the forerunner of 'Peppermint Stick'. How the two are to be distinguished is not known.

P. Persica 'Versicolor A'—see P. Persica 'Versicolor'

P. Persica 'Versicolor B'

Introduced ≤1934 by W.B. Clarke nursery of San José, CA. Attributes unknown.

P. Persica 'Versicolor Weeping'
= P. Persica 'Variegated Weeping'

Introduced ≤1934 by W.B. Clarke nursery of San José, CA. Flowers colored like those of 'Peppermint Stick' but single. Branches pendulous.

P. Pers. 'Weeping Double Pink'—see P. Pers. 'Double Pink Weeping'

P. Persica 'Weeping Pink'—see P. Persica 'Double Pink Weeping'

P. Persica 'Wendle Weeping'—see P. Persica 'Windle Weeping'

P. Persica 'White'—see P. Persica 'Alba'

P. Persica 'White Double Late'—see P. Persica 'Icicle'

P. Persica 'White Glory'

An ornamental NECTARINE selected in 1960 as a seedling of 'S-37' PEACH at Sandhills research station of Jackson Springs, NC. Registered in 1984. Flowers abundant, large, showy, white. Tree of weeping habit. Suggested for topgrafting at 6'–7'. A 15 year old specimen was 13' tall and 15' wide. Fruit few, 1¼"–1⅝", astringent.

P. Persica 'Windle Weeping'
('Wendle Weeping')

Introduced ≤1945–46 in England. Not known in North America. Flowers single to semi-double, purplish-pink. Leaves broad. Habit semi-pendulous.

P. Persica 'Woodside'

Introduced ≤1934 by W.B. Clarke nursery of San José, CA. Extremely rare; extinct commercially.

Flowers early-midseason, double, very large, opening very widely, variegated: ground color soft silvery-pink lightly marked with red. Although the variegation is not pronounced and is a secondary matter, the the flower's ground color and appearance is charming. Named in honor of the Woodside Garden Club. A pure red flowered sport from 'Woodside' is 'Double Maroon'.

P. × persicoides Dalla Torre & Sarnth.

= *P. × Amygdalo-persica* (West.) Rehd.
= *Amygdalus Amygdalo-persica* West.
= *Amygdalus hybrida* Poit. & Turp.
(*P. dulcis × P. Persica*)

HYBRID ALMOND TREE. First recorded ca. 1623 in Switzerland, ALMOND-PEACH hybrids have been in California since the early 1850s as chance seedlings. More cold-hardy than purebred ALMOND trees, they are used as rootstocks, for ornament and for nut-production. The 1909 epithet *persicoides* is from *Persica*, PEACH tree, and Greek *oides*, resemblance. Always beautiful in bloom; sometimes with edible nuts. Differ from purebred PEACH (*P. Persica*) in being larger, stronger trees with shorter, less glossy, less curved leaves, and in producing greenish, thin-skinned, smaller fruit. Compared to ALMOND (*P. dulcis*), the hybrids have pink flowers, bloom later in spring, and the leaves are larger. Generally the hybrids more resemble the ALMOND parent, and the cultivars are almost universally sold as ALMONDS. See *P. dulcis* 'Roseoplena'.

P. × persicoides 'Hall's Hardy'

Selected by Mr. Hall of Coffeyville, KS. Introduced ca. 1925. Common: the best known fruiting clone. Self-fertile, hardy, pink-flowering. Indistinguishable from 'Pollardii' either coincidentally or because they are one clone.

P. × persicoides 'Pollardii'

= *P. Pollardii* hort. *ex* Rehd.

Originated in Creswick, Victoria, Australia, ca. 1864. Named after a Mr. Pollard of Ballaret, Victoria. The only clone that has been much grown for ornament. Presently not widely cultivated in North America, little known and unavailable in wholesale sizes and quantities. Flowers 1½"–2" wide, pale pink, in (late February) March or early April; self-fertile. Nuts ripen in late summer or early fall. Hardy, less disease-prone than PEACHES, and more attractive than ordinary ALMONDS. The sticky nuts can be borne in such quantity as to be a nuisance unless they are desired as food.

Leaves dark, shiny green, very finely toothed, free of leaf-curl disease (the bane of PEACHES); to 5⅞" × 1⅞"; stem to ⅝" long, grooved, purplish, often with several glands. Indistinguishable from 'Hall's Hardy' either coincidentally or because they are one clone. Record: to 30' tall in England; 25' × 6'6" Seattle, WA (1989; *pl.* 1950).

P. 'Pink Cloud'

= *P. serrulata* 'Pink Cloud'

In the SATO ZAKURA group. Originated as a chance seedling at the Huntington Gardens of San Marino, CA. Named and distributed in the 1980s. In commerce ≤1991. Liable to be confused nominally with *P. × subhirtella* 'Rosy Cloud'. Almost certainly a *P. speciosa* selection; possibly a hybrid involving *P. campanulata*. Has a low chill-need. Tree vigorous, to more than 40' tall. Flowers profuse, light pink, single; early; clustered on a hairless common stalk. Sepals red (like on *P.* 'Okamé'). Fruit longer than wide, with very swollen stems. Leaves hairless, to 5" × 2½", very finely sharply toothed. Stipules long, delicately fringed.

P. 'Pink Perfection'

= *P. serrulata* 'Pink Perfection'

In the SATO ZAKURA group. Raised in 1935 by Waterer, Sons & Crisp nursery of Bagshot, England. A seedling of *P.* 'Shogetsu', the pollen parent thought to be *P.* 'Kwanzan'. In North American commerce since ≤1959–60. Uncommon; grown mostly in the maritime Pacific Northwest. Tree broadly vase-shaped. Buds light red. Flowers pink, in April-May, double (ca. 30 petals). Young foliage pale bronze. Record: 20' × 3'5" × 35' Tacoma, WA (1993).

P. Pissardi(i) or Pissarti(i)—see P. cerasifera 'Pissardii'

P. Pissardii Veitchii—see P. × blireiana 'Moseri'

P. Pollardii—see P. × persicoides 'Pollardii'

P. 'Poumeria-zakura'

= *P. serrulata* 'Poumeria-zakura'
('Poumaria'; 'Prunaria Sakura')

In the SATO ZAKURA group. Sold during the 1930's by B.O. Case nursery of Vancouver, WA. As described by Case: Tree rather dwarf, very upright, blooms at same time as the FRUITING CHERRIES and by contrast makes them "look like 15¢." Flowers entirely double, pinkish old-rose blended with creamy-white.

P. prunifolia—see *P. emarginata*

P. pubescens sakura—see *P.* 'Fudan-zakura'

P. racemosa—see *P. Padus*

P. 'Rosea'

= *P. cerasifera* 'Rosea'
= *P. spinosa* 'Rosea'
(*P. cerasifera* 'Nigra' × *P. spinosa*)

Raised by B. Ruys Royal Moerheim nursery of Dedemsvaart, Holland. Introduced ≤1954–55. Not known in North America. Also called "Sloepink" in Britain. A kind of PURPLELEAF PLUM.

P. 'Rosy Morn'

= *P. serrulata* 'Rosy Morn'

In the SATO ZAKURA group. Sold ≤1941 by Wohlert nursery of Narberth, PA. Flowers heavy; lighter pink than those of *P.* 'Kwanzan'.

P. 'Royal Burgundy' PP 6520 (1989)

= *P. serrulata* 'Royal Burgundy'

In the SATO ZAKURA group. A mutation from *P.* 'Kwanzan' discovered by Frank Parks of Speer and Sons nursery, Woodburn, OR. In commerce since <1990. Leaves purplish-black; their fall color reddish-orange.

P. 'Ruth Wohlert'

= *P. serrulata* 'Ruth Wohlert'

In the SATO ZAKURA group. Introduced in 1929–30 by Wohlert nursery of Narberth, PA. Named after one of A.E. Wohlert's daughters. Very rare; commercially extinct since 1950s. Tree dwarf. Wohlert described it as like *P.* 'Hosokawa' but more vigorous. Flowers double, blush pink.

P. salicina Lindl.

= *P. triflora* Roxb.

JAPANESE PLUM. ORIENTAL PLUM. SALICINE. From China, but long grown in Japan, and called *Sumomo* there. Described in 1828 (*salicina* means resemblance of the leaves to those of *Salix*, the WILLOWS). Introduced to Vacaville, CA, in 1870 by D.E. Hough; the first fruit ripened in Berkeley, CA, 1876, on nurseryman John Kelsey's trees. Although handsome, this species and its numerous cultivars rank as fruit-producers primarily; their ornamental role is wholly incidental. Compared to its counterpart EUROPEAN PLUM (*P.* × *domestica*), it is earlier to bloom, with more slender leaves. It can have attractive fall color as well. *Prunus Mume* (JAPANESE APRICOT) has also been called

"Japanese plum" in artistic and literary traditions. Records: to 40' tall in the wild; 26' × 5'3" × 25' Tacoma, WA (1990); 20' × 7'7" × 37' Woodland, WA (1993).

P. Sargentii Rehd.

= *P. serrulata* var. *sachalinensis* (F. Schmidt) Wils.
= *P. serrulata* 'Sargentii'

SARGENT CHERRY. YAMA CHERRY. NORTH JAPANESE HILL CHERRY. From N Japan, Korea, Sakhalin. Named for Charles Sprague Sargent (1841–1927), great American tree expert. Introduced via seeds sent to the Arnold Arboretum in 1890 by Dr. W.S. Bigelow. Common. Variable: flowers typically rosy-pink (rarely white), 1"–1½" wide, on stalks to 1⅝" long, borne in clusters of 2–3. Leaves notably wide (to 6⅛" × 3¼"), abruptly pointed, sharply toothed; pale waxy beneath, utterly hairless except in f. *pubescens* (see below), on red stems. Cherries repulsively bitter, black, ⅓" wide. Fall color superb red, with some green. Bark handsomely dark. Records: to 80' × 12'6" in the wild; 45' × 3'11" Puyallup, WA (1993); 36' × 7'1" × 43' Seattle, WA (1992; *pl.* 1940); 22' × 7'6" × 38' West Hartford, CT (1988).

P. Sargentii 'Columnaris'

COLUMNAR SARGENT CHERRY. Raised at the Arnold Arboretum in 1914 as a seedling from one of W. Bigelow's original 1890-introduced SARGENT CHERRY trees. Named in 1939. Registered in 1949. Common. Not strictly columnar except while young, but branching is very narrowly upright.

P. Sargentii ssp. *jamasakura*—see *P. jamasakura*

P. Sargentii f. *pubescens* (Tatew.) Ohwi

Lightly hairy leaves or flowerstalks. Ornamentally identical to typical *P. Sargentii*.

P. Sargentii 'Rancho' PP 2065 (1961)

RANCHO COLUMNAR SARGENT CHERRY. Introduced between 1956 and 1959 by Scanlon nursery of Ohio. Either an outright renaming of 'Columnaris' or so similar as to be practically identical. More than one strongly upright *P. Sargentii* clone exists. Documentation about them is too vague to enable distinguishing them nominally. Some nurseries that list "*P.*

Sargentii" are not actually selling random seedlings, but grafted narrow-crowned clones better for streetside planting.

P. Sargentii 'S. Edwin Muller'

Selected in 1930. Registered in 1952 by H.J. Hohman of Kingsville nursery, Maryland. Long commercially extinct. Flowers when young, well before the leaves appear.

P. sativa—see P. × domestica

P. SATO ZAKURA
(formerly called *P. serrulata* cultivars)

Until the 1980s, the JAPANESE FLOWERING CHERRIES collectively known as SATO ZAKURA (meaning village or cultivated cherries), were treated by Westerners as cultivars of *P. serrulata*. But this is incorrect according to botanical rules, as the tree first named *P. serrulata* is not the parent of any of the trees usually placed under its banner. The SATO ZAKURA are of mixed parentage; some are purebred *P. speciosa* cultivars, others hybrids. They have been grown in North America since 1862 when G.R. Hall brought 15 double-flowered cultivars from Japan. In 1903, the U.S. Bureau of Plant Industry received 30 cultivars, in 1904 an additional 50 arrived from the Yokohama nursery; in 1906 D. Fairchild brought 25. By 1933 at least 45 cultivars were in the U.S., and Paul Russel treated 40 of them fully in his book *Oriental Flowering Cherries*. The present volume treats 75. The cultivars bloom at different times from early March through late May, with large petals pure white to creamy-yellow and all shades of pink, usually semi-double or double-flowered and usually scentless. The twigs are stout, leaves large, and branches few. The young foliage is more often than not bronze rather than pure green in color. Early in this century the naming of cultivars was done differently, so Wilson and Miyoshi used *formæ* designations for what are in today's practice cultivars. Hence, upon seeing a combination such as *P. serrulata* f. *amabilis* Miyoshi, the reader should translate *P.* 'Amabilis'. Experts disagree on correct cultivar names for some clones (as well as orthography), and regrettably the only way to ensure understanding is to cite a horde of synonyms.

P. 'Senriko'

= *P. serrulata* 'Senriko'
= *P. serrulata* f. *picta* Miyoshi
= *P. Lannesiana* f. *senriko* (Koidz.) Wils.

In the SATO ZAKURA group. Name means "one thousand miles scent." Sold during the 1940s and '50s by Kingsville nursery of Maryland. Extremely rare. Flowers pale pink passing to white; almost single; very large; fragrant. Sometimes *P.* 'Choshu-hizakura' has gone under this name, as has *P.* 'Ojochin'.

P. serotina Ehrh.

= *Padus serotina* (Ehrh.) Borkh.

WILD BLACK CHERRY. BLACK CHERRY. RUM CHERRY. CABINET CHERRY. WHISKEY CHERRY. From central and eastern N America, Mexico, Guatemala. Commonly planted as a shade tree; naturalized well beyond its original range. The epithet *serotina* is Latin for late-coming, referring to the time of blooming, or fruit ripening. Flowers white, small, after the leaves, in clusters 4"–6" long. Fruit ⅓"–½", purplish-black, edible. Fall color yellow to orange-red; late. Twigs and leaves stink when bruised. The largest of all *Prunus*. Invaluable for timber. Records: 145' × 12'7" Great Smoky Mountains National Park, TN (1994); 138' × 15'1" × 128' Washtenaw County, MI (1983); 114' × 23'9" × 93' Van Buren County, MI (1972).

P. serotina 'Pendula'

WEEPING BLACK CHERRY. Described in 1882. In commerce ≤1888 by Th. B. Meehan nursery of Dresher, PA. Rare. Commercially extinct.

P. serotina 'Silver Cloud'

Found in Brooks, Alberta, in 1973. Registered in 1985. The large, cream-to-white lenticels are reminiscent of clouds on brown-purple bark. Moderately showy in bloom.

P. serrula Franch.

= *P. serrulata* 'Tibetica'

BIRCHBARK CHERRY. CELLOPHANE BARK CHERRY. RED-BARK CHERRY. TIBETAN CHERRY. From W China, Tibet. Named in 1890. Introduced in 1908 by E. Wilson. Until promoted beginning in 1963–64 by Scanlon nursery of Ohio, extremely rare in North America. Still uncommon in general. Leaves slender, 2"–5" long, remain green late in fall and drop without showy color. Floral display ho-hum. Grown for splendid bark: bright reddish-brown, glossy and peeling, absolutely unmistakable. Often used as a stock trunk atop which other CHERRIES are grafted. Records: to 60' tall in the wild; 49' × 3'5" Edinburgh, Scotland (1985); 46' × 3'7" Tacoma, WA (1992); 37' × 4'10" × 41' Milton, WA (1992); 34½' × 5'4½" × 37'

Aurora, OR (1993); 33' × 6'3" Crathes Castle, Tayside, Scotland (1987).

P. serrulata Lindl.
= *P. serrulata* 'Alba Plena'
= *P. serrulata* 'Serrulata'

DOUBLE CHINESE CHERRY. Introduced in 1822 from Canton to Europe. Very rare in North America. Tree small, flat-topped. Young foliage green. Flowers white, double, inodorous. (Since the 1980s it has been incorrect to list the numerous JAPANESE FLOWERING CHERRIES as cultivars under *P. serrulata*. They are treated generally under P. SATO ZAKURA, with 75 individual entries easily found alphabetically under the cultivar name, as for example, *P.* 'Ojochin'—not *P. serrulata* 'Ojochin').

P. serrulata f. *affinis*—see *P.* 'Jo-nioi'

P. serrulata 'Akebono'—see *P.* × *yedoensis* 'Akebono'

P. serrulata 'Alba Plena'—see *P. serrulata*

P. serrulata f. *albida*—see *P.* 'Shirotae' and *P. speciosa*

P. serrulata 'Albo Rosea'—see *P.* 'Shiro-fugen'

P. serrulata f. *albo-rosea*—see *P.* 'Fugenzo' and *P.* 'Shiro-fugen'

P. serrulata 'Amabilis'—see *P.* 'Amabilis'

P. serrulata f. *amabilis*—see *P.* 'Amabilis'

P. serrulata 'Amanogawa'—see *P.* 'Amanogawa'

P. serrulata 'Amayadori'—see *P.* 'Amayadori'

P. serrulata f. *ambigua*—see *P.* 'Taizan-fukun'

P. serrulata 'Anenome'—see *P.* 'Shumei (-zakura)'

P. serrulata f. *arguta*—see *P.* 'Washi-no-o'

P. serrulata 'Ariake'—see *P.* 'Ariake'

P. serrulata 'Asagi'—see *P.* 'Asagi'

P. serrulata 'Asahi'—see *P.* 'Asahi'

P. serrulata 'Asahi-botan'—see *P.* 'Asahi-botan'

P. serrulata f. *atrorubra*—see *P.* 'Kirin'

P. serrulata 'Autumn Glory'—see *P. verecunda* 'Autumn Glory'

P. serrulata 'Beni-fugen'—see *P.* 'Daikoku' and *P.* 'Fugenzo'

P. serrulata 'Beni-torano-o'—see *P.* 'Beni-torano-o'

P. serrulata 'Bennishi'—see *P.* 'Bennishi'

P. serrulata 'Beni Higan'—see *P.* × *subhirtella* 'Beni Higan'

P. serrulata 'Beni Hoshi'—see *P. pendula* 'Stellata'

P. serrulata 'Bizarre'—see *P.* 'Shibori'

P. serrulata 'Botan (-zakura)'—see *P.* 'Moutan'

P. serrulata f. *bullata*—see *P.* 'Ojochin'

P. serrulata 'Candida'—see *P.* 'Ariake'

P. serrulata f. *candida*—see *P.* 'Ariake'

P. serrulata f. *cataracta*—see *P.* 'Taki-nioi'

P. serrulata f. *caudata*—see *P.* 'Torano-o'

P. serr. 'Cheal's Weeping Cherry'—see *P.* 'Kiku-shidare-zakura'

P. serrulata 'Choshu-hizakura'—see *P.* 'Choshu-hizakura'

P. serrulata f. *chrysanthemoides*—see *P.* 'Kiku-zakura'

P. serr. 'Clarke's Weeping Cherry'—see *P.* 'Kiku-shidare-zakura'

P. serrulata f. *classica*—see *P.* 'Fugenzo' and *P.* 'Shiro-fugen'

P. serrulata f. *conspicua*—see *P.* 'Oshokun'

P. serrulata f. *contorta*—see *P.* 'Fuku-rokuju'

P. serrulata 'Curtis Bok'—see *P.* 'Curtis Bok'

P. serrulata 'Daikoku'—see *P.* 'Daikoku'

P. serrulata f. *decora*—see *P.* 'Horinji'

P. serrulata f. *dilatata*—see *P.* 'Amayadori'

P. serrulata f. *diversifolia*—see *P.* 'Mikuruma-gaeshi'

P. serrulata 'Double Pink Weeping'—see *P.* 'Kiku-shidare-zakura'

P. serrulata 'Edo-zakura'—see *P.* 'Yedo-zakura'

P. serrulata f. *erecta*—see *P.* 'Amanogawa'

P. serrulata *flore luteo pleno*—see *P.* 'Ukon'

P. serrulata f. *formosissima*—see *P.* 'Beni-torano-o'

P. serrulata 'Fudan-zakura'—see *P.* 'Fudan-zakura'

P. serrulata 'Fugenzo'—see *P.* 'Fugenzo'

P. serrulata f. *fugenzo*—see *P.* 'Fugenzo'

P. serrulata 'Fujizan'—see *P.* 'Shirotae'

P. serrulata 'Fukubana'—see *P. pendula* 'Fukubana'

P. serrulata 'Fuku-rokuju'—see *P.* 'Fuku-rokuju'

P. serrulata 'Gioiko'—see *P.* 'Gyoiko'

P. serrulata f. *globosa*—see *P.* 'Temari'

P. serrulata 'Gosho (-zakura)'—see *P.* 'Gosho (-zakura)'

P. serrulata 'Gozanoma-nioi'—see *P.* 'Gozanoma-nioi'

P. serrulata f. *grandiflora*—see *P.* 'Ukon'

P. serrulata 'Gyoiko'—see *P.* 'Gyoiko'

P. serrulata 'Hakuyuki'—see *P.* 'Shirayuki'

P. serrulata 'Hasokawa-beni'—see *P.* 'Hosokawa-beni'

P. serrulata 'Hata-zakura'—see *P.* 'Hata-zakura'

P. serrulata 'Hesokawanoi'—see *P.* 'Hosokawa'

P. serrulata 'Higantakura'—see *P.* × *subhirtella* 'Flore Pleno'

P. serrulata 'Higatekuri'—see *P.* × *subhirtella* 'Flore Pleno'

P. serrulata 'Higurashi'—see *P.* 'Amabilis'

P. serrulata 'Hisakura'—see *P.* 'Hisakura'

P. serrulata f. *hisakura*—see *P.* 'Hisakura'

P. serrulata 'Hokusai'—see *P.* 'Hokusai'

P. serrulata f. *homogena*—see *P.* 'Kokonoye (-sakura)'

P. serrulata 'Horaisan'—see *P.* 'Horaisan'

P. serrulata 'Horinji'—see *P.* 'Horinji'

P. serrulata f. *horinji*—see *P.* 'Horinji'

P. serrulata 'Hosokawa'—see *P.* 'Hosokawa'

P. serrulata 'Hosokawa-beni'—see *P.* 'Hosokawa-beni'

P. serrulata 'Hosokawa-nioi'—see *P.* 'Hosokawa'

P. serrulata f. *hosokawa-nioi*—see *P.* 'Hosokawa'

P. serrulata 'Ichiyo'—see *P.* 'Hisakura'

P. serrulata 'James (H.) Veitch'—see *P.* 'Fugenzo'

P. serrulata 'Jeanne Wohlert'—see *P.* 'Jeanne Wohlert'

P. serrulata 'Jo-nioi'—see *P.* 'Jo-nioi'

P. serrulata 'Kabuto-zakura'—see *P.* 'Horinji'

P. serrulata 'Kaido'—see *P.* 'Kaido'

P. serrulata 'Kanzan' or 'Kansan'—see *P.* 'Kwanzan'

P. serrulata 'Kiku-shidare-zakura'—see *P.* 'Kiku-shidare-zakura'

P. serrulata 'Kiku-zakura'—see *P.* 'Kiku-zakura'

P. serrulata 'Kirigayatsu'—see *P.* 'Mikuruma-gaeshi'

P. serrulata 'Kirin'—see *P.* 'Kirin'

P. serrulata f. *kirin*—see *P.* 'Kirin'

P. serrulata 'Kofugen'—see *P.* 'Fugenzo'

P. serrulata 'Kojima'—see *P.* 'Shirotae'

P. serrulata 'Kokonoe'—see *P.* 'Kokonoye (-sakura)'

P. serrulata 'Kokonoye (-sakura)'—see *P.* 'Kokonoye (-sakura)'

P. serrulata f. *kokonaye*—see *P.* 'Kokonoye (-sakura)'

P. serrulata 'Kurama-yama'—see *P.* 'Kurama-yama'

P. serrulata 'Kwanzan'—see *P.* 'Kwanzan'

P. serrulata var. *Lannesiana*—see *P.* *Lannesiana*

P. serrulata f. *longipes*—see *P.* 'Shogetsu'

P. serrulata f. *luteoides*—see *P.* 'Asagi'

P. serrulata f. *luteo-virens*—see *P.* 'Ukon'

P. serrulata 'Mangetsu'—see *P.* 'Ukon'

P. serrulata 'Masu-yama'—see *P.* 'Masu-yama'

P. serrulata f. *masu-yama*—see *P.* 'Masu-yama'

P. serrulata 'Meigetsu'—see *P.* 'Meigetsu'

P. serrulata f. *meigetsu*—see *P.* 'Meigetsu'

P. serrulata 'Mikuruma-gaeshi'—see *P.* 'Mikuruma-gaeshi'

P. serrulata 'Mitchell's Single Pink'—see *P.* 'Mikuruma-gaeshi'

P. serrulata 'Miyako'—see *P.* 'Shogetsu'

P. serrulata 'Morni-jigare'—see *P.* 'Ojochin'

P. serrulata 'Mount Fuji'—see *P.* 'Shirotae'

P. serrulata 'Moutan'—see *P.* 'Moutan'

P. serrulata f. *Moutan*—see *P.* 'Moutan'

P. serrulata 'Mrs. A.E. Wohlert'—see *P.* 'Mrs. A.E. Wohlert'

P. serrulata 'Mt. Fuji'—see *P.* 'Shirotae'

P. serrulata 'Naden'—see *P.* × *Sieboldii*

P. serrulata 'New Red'—see *P.* 'New Red'

P. serrulata f. *nivea*—see *P.* 'Shirayuki'

P. serrulata f. *nobilis*—see *P.* 'Yedo-zakura'

P. serrulata 'Oh-nanden'—see *P.* 'Oh-nanden'

P. serrulata f. *ohnanden*—see *P.* 'Oh-nanden'

P. serrulata 'Ohsibayama'—see *P.* 'Ohsibayama'

P. serrulata 'Ojochin'—see *P.* 'Ojochin'

P. serrulata 'Okiku (-zakura)'—see *P.* 'Okiku (-zakura)'

P. serrulata 'Oku-miyako'—see *P.* 'Shogetsu'

P. serrulata 'Oshibayama'—see *P.* 'Ohsibayama'

P. serrulata 'Oshima-zakura'—see *P.* *speciosa*

P. serrulata 'Oshokun'—see *P.* 'Oshokun'

P. serrulata 'Osibayama'—see *P.* 'Ohsibayama'

P. serrulata 'Ozu Mako'—see *P.* 'Gozanoma-nioi'

P. serrulata 'Paul Wohlert'—see *P.* 'Paul Wohlert'

P. serrulata 'Pendula'—see *P.* 'Kiku-shidare-zakura'

P. serrulata 'Pendula Flore Plena'—see *P.* 'Kiku-shidare-zakura'

P. serrulata f. *picta*—see *P.* 'Senriko'

P. serrulata 'Pink Cloud'—see *P.* 'Pink Cloud'

P. serrulata 'Pink Perfection'—see *P.* 'Pink Perfection'

P. serrulata f. *planifolia*—see *P.* 'Ohsibayama'

P. serrulata 'Poumeria-zakura'—see *P.* 'Poumeria-zakura'

P. serrulata 'Prunaria Sakura'—see *P.* 'Poumeria-zakura'

P. serrulata var. *pubescens*—see *P. verecunda*

P. serrulata var. *pubescens* 'Taizan-fukun'— see *P.* 'Taizan-fukun'

P. serrulata f. *purpurascens*—see *P.* 'Kwanzan'

P. serrulata f. *purpurea plena*—see *P.* 'Yae-murasaki (-zakura)'

P. serrulata 'Pyramidalis'—see *P.* 'Amanogawa'

P. serrulata f. *radiata*—see *P.* 'Gosho (-zakura)'

P. serrulata 'Rosea'—see *P.* 'Hokusai'

P. serrulata f. *rosea*—see *P.* 'Kiku-shidare-zakura'

P. serrulata 'Rosea Pendula'—see *P.* 'Kiku-shidare-zakura'

P. serrulata 'Rosea-plena'—see *P.* 'Hokusai'

P. serrulata 'Rosy Cloud'—see *P.* × *subhirtella* 'Rosy Cloud'

P. serrulata 'Rosy Morn'—see *P.* 'Rosy Morn'

P. serrulata 'Royal Burgundy'—see *P.* 'Royal Burgundy'

P. serrulata 'Ruth Wohlert'—see *P.* 'Ruth Wohlert'

P. serrulata var. *sachalinensis*—see *P. Sargentii*

P. serrulata f. *sancta*—see *P.* 'Meigetsu'

P. serrulata 'Sargentii'—see *P. Sargentii*

P. serrulata 'Sekiyama'—see *P.* 'Kwanzan'

P. serrulata f. *sekiyama*—see *P.* 'Kwanzan'

P. serrulata 'Sekizan'—see *P.* 'Kwanzan'

P. serrulata f. *semperflorens*—see *P.* 'Fudan-zakura'

P. serrulata 'Senriko'—see *P.* 'Ojochin' and *P.* 'Senriko'

P. serrulata 'Serrulata'—see *P. serrulata*

P. serrulata 'Shibori'—see *P.* 'Shibori'

P. serrulata 'Shiki-zakura'—see *P.* 'Fudan-zakura'

P. serrulata 'Shimidsu(ii)'—see *P.* 'Shogetsu'

P. serrulata 'Shiratama (-zakura)'—see *P.* 'Shiratama (-zakura)'

P. serrulata 'Shirayuki'—see *P.* 'Shirayuki'

P. serrulata 'Shiro-fugen'—see *P.* 'Shiro-fugen'

P. serrulata 'Shirotae'—see *P.* 'Shirotae' and *P.* 'Shogetsu'

P. serrulata 'Shirotama (-zakura)'—see *P.* 'Shiratama (-zakura)'

P. serrulata 'Shogetsu'—see *P.* 'Shogetsu'

P. serrulata 'Shojo'—see *P.* 'Shojo'

P. serrulata 'Shosar'—see *P.* 'Shosar'

P. serrulata 'Shumei (-zakura)'—see *P.* 'Shumei (-zakura)'

P. serrulata 'Sirayuki'—see *P.* 'Shirayuki'

P. serrulata f. *sirayuki*—see *P.* 'Shirayuki'

P. serrulata 'Sirotae'—see *P.* 'Shirotae'

P. serrulata f. *splendens*—see *P.* 'Choshu-hizakura'

P. serrulata var. *spontanea*—see *P. jamasakura*

P. serrulata f. *subfusca*—see *P.* 'Sumizome'

P. serrulata 'Sumizome'—see *P.* 'Sumizome'

P. serrulata f. *superba*—see *P.* 'Shogetsu'

P. serrulata 'Tai Haku'—see *P.* 'Tai Haku'

P. serrulata 'Taizan-fukun'—see *P.* 'Taizan-fukun'

P. serrulata 'Takasago'—see *P.* × *Sieboldii*

P. serrulata 'Taki-nioi'—see *P.* 'Taki-nioi'

P. serrulata 'Tanko-shinju'—see *P.* 'Tanko-shinju'

P. serrulata 'Tao-yoma (-zakura)'—see *P.* 'Tao-yoma (-zakura)'

P. serrulata 'Temari'—see *P.* 'Temari'

P. serrulata 'Tibetica'—see *P. serrula*

P. serrulata 'Torano-o'—see *P.* 'Torano-o'

P. serrulata 'Tricolor'—see *P.* 'Gyoiko'

P. serrulata f. *tricolor*—see *P.* 'Gyoiko'

P. serrulata 'Ukon'—see *P.* 'Ukon'

P. serrulata 'Umineko'—see *P.* 'Umineko'

P. serrulata f. *unifolia*—see *P.* 'Hisakura'

P. serrulata f. *versicolor*—see *P.* 'Yae-akebono'

P. serrulata f. *vexillipetala*—see *P.* 'Hata-zakura'

P. serrulata 'Victory'—see *P.* 'Shiro-fugen'

P. serrulata f. *viridiflora*—see *P.* 'Ukon'

P. serrulata 'Wase-miyako'—see *P.* 'Wase-miyako'

P. serrulata 'Washi-no-o'—see *P.* 'Washi-no-o'

P. serrulata f. *wasinowo*—see *P.* 'Washi-no-o'

P. serrulata f. *Watererii*—see *P.* × *Sieboldii*

P. serr. 'Wohlert's Weeping Cherry'—see *P.* 'Kiku-shidare-zakura'

P. serrulata 'Yae-akebono'—see *P.* 'Yae-akebono'

P. serrulata 'Yae-kanzan'—see *P.* 'Yae-kanzan'

P. serr. 'Yae-murasaki (-zakura)'—see *P.* 'Yae-murasaki (-zakura)'

P. serrulata 'Yedo-zakura'—see *P.* 'Yedo-zakura'

P. serrulata 'Yoshino'—see *P.* × *yedoensis*

P. serrulata 'Yukon'—see *P.* 'Ukon'

P. 'Shibori'
= *P. serrulata* 'Shibori'
= *P. serrulata* 'Bizarre'

In the SATO ZAKURA group. In North American commerce in the 1930s. Exceedingly rare. A curiosity. Flowers small, very double, mixed green and white petals.

P. 'Shiratama (-zakura)'
= *P. serrulata* 'Shiratama (-zakura)'
('Shirotama')

In the SATO ZAKURA group. Sold ≤1935 by W.B. Clarke nursery of San José, CA. Extremely rare; commercially extinct since the 1950s. Tree of medium to large size and spreading habit; very healthy. Flowers single, pure white (or nearly so); early and profuse.

P. 'Shirayuki'
= *P. serrulata* 'Shirayuki'
= *P. serrulata* f. *sirayuki* (Koidz.) Wils.
= *P. serrulata* f. *nivea* Miyoshi
= *P. serrulata* 'Sirayuki'
= *P. serrulata* 'Hakuyuki'
= *P. Lannesiana* 'Shirayuki'

In the SATO ZAKURA group. Discovered near Arakawa River in Tokyo, April 1909 by M. Miyoshi. Name means "white snow." Extremely rare in North America (but see *P.* Cascade Snow™). Tree large, of upright habit. Buds pink-tinged. Flowers single (or nearly so), white, scentless, very early; in clusters of 3–4; sepals toothed. Young foliage light brown.

P. 'Shiro-fugen'
= *P. serrulata* 'Shiro-fugen'
= *P. serrulata* f. *albo-rosea* Wils., non Mak. (cf. *P.* 'Fugenzo')
= *P. serrulata* f. *classica* Miyoshi (in part)
= *P. serrulata* 'Albo Rosea'
= *P. serrulata* 'Victory'
= *P. Lannesiana* 'Albo-rosea'

In the SATO ZAKURA group. Name means "white god" or "white red." The Japanese common name for this cultivar is *Fugenzo*. Imported to the U.S. by D. Fairchild in 1906. Common. Tree broad and strong, with relatively slender twigs. Buds deep pink. Flowers large, double (20–36 petals), first soft pink, then white, then fading pink-cerise in age. Two (or as many as five) tiny leaflike carpels in the middle. Late-blooming compared to most SATO ZAKURA. It has a habit of blooming again, sparsely, in mid-June or early July. Young foliage coppery-red. Record: 38' × 7'6" × 49' Vancouver WA (1993).

P. 'Shirotae'

= *P. serrulata* 'Shirotae'
= *P. serrulata* 'Mt. Fuji' or 'Mount Fuji'
= *P. serrulata* 'Sirotae'
= *P. serrulata* 'Kojima'
= *P. serrulata* f. *albida* Miyoshi
= *P. serrulata* 'Fujizan' says A.E. Wohlert
= *P. Lannesiana* f. *sirotae* (Koidz.) Wils.
= *P. Lannesiana* 'Shirotae'

In the SATO ZAKURA group. Name means "snow white" or "snowflake." Introduced to Western cultivation ca. 1905. Common. Sometimes *P.* 'Shogetsu' is supplied under this name. Usually a vigorous, very strongly spreading tree, wide and low. It may be recognized any time of year by its flat-topped, horizontal growth. Flowers lightly fragrant, semi-double, 5–11 petals, pure white (except for sometimes a faint pink blush when first opening), appearing earliest of all: early March. Young foliage green. Leaves edged by delicate long-fringed teeth. Records: 37' × 5'10" × 51' Seattle, WA (1990; *pl.* 1940); 21' × 7'8" × 43' Seattle, WA (1987).

P. 'Shogetsu'

= *P. serrulata* 'Shogetsu'
= *P. serrulata* f. *superba* Miyoshi
= *P. serrulata* 'Shimidsuii' or 'Shimidsu (-zakura)'
= *P. serrulata* f. *longipes* hort., non Miyoshi
= *P. serrulata* 'Oku-miyako' hort. angl., non Miyoshi
= *P. serrulata* 'Miyako' hort. (in part)
= *P. serrulata* 'Shirotae' hort. (in part)
= *P. Lannesiana* 'Superba'

In the SATO ZAKURA group. Name means "moonlight thru pine branches," or "moon hanging low over a pine," or "fairy queen." Introduced to Western cultivation after 1900. In North American commerce ≤1931. Common. Tree weak, delicately drooping, wide-spreading. Buds apple-pink. Flowers double (20–30 petals), large (to 2⅜" wide), white, with 1 or 2 tiny leaflike carpels in the middle. They are long-stemmed (to 2¾") and dangle in clusters altogether ca. 6" long, blooming late in spring and long persisting, fading to pale pink near the end of their tenure. Young foliage green. Some say 'Shogetsu' / 'Superba' is different than 'Shimidsu' / 'Oku-miyako' / *longipes*. If so, they are very similar and have become inextricably mixed in commerce. Records: 17' × 2'6" × 40' Rockport, WA (1993); 13' × 5'4" × 29' Tacoma, WA (1992).

P. 'Shojo'

= *P. serrulata* 'Shojo'
= *P. fruticosa* f. *shojo* (Koidz.) Hara
= *P.* × *yedoensis* f. *shojo* (Koidz.) Wils.

In the SATO ZAKURA group. Extremely rare. Flowers large, semi-double or double, rosy-pink. Similar to *P.* 'Taizan-fukun'.

P. 'Shosar'

= *P. serrulata* 'Shosar'
(*P. incisa* × *P. campanulata*) × *P. Sargentii*

SHOSAR CHERRY. Bred by C. Ingram in England. In North American commerce ≤1990. Extremely rare. Tree narrowly upright, broadly fastigiate; strong. Flowers single, 1½" wide, deep cerise-pink—like those of *P. Sargentii* but 2–3 weeks earlier. Flowerstems and calyx deep red. Fall color usually good.

P. 'Shumei (-zakura)'

= *P. serrulata* 'Shumei (-zakura)'
= *P. serrulata* 'Anenome'

In the SATO ZAKURA group. Introduced ≤1934 by W.B. Clarke nursery of San José, CA. Long extinct commercially. Flowers pink, semi-double.

P. × Sieboldii (Carr.) Wittm.

= *P. serrulata* 'Takasago'
= *P. serrulata* 'Naden' hort. p.p., non Miyoshi, non Mak.
= *P. serrulata* f. *Watererii* Mak.
(*P. apetala* × *P. speciosa*)

NADEN CHERRY. Japanese: *Naden* or *Musha Zakura*. The Takasago name refers to a classical song that praises the cherry blossoms of Takasago Island (Taiwan). Others say Takasago means "Good health and long life." Often considered in the SATO ZAKURA group. Imported to Holland from Japan by Siebold ca. 1862–64. Named in 1866 after Philipp Franz Balthasar von Siebold (1796–1866). Siebold lived in Japan from 1823 to 1830, and introduced many Japanese plants to Europe. In North American commerce ≤1880. Common. More cold-hardy than most

SATO ZAKURA. Flowers medium sized, single or (usually) semi-double (9–15 petals), pale pink, borne in compact clusters like snowballs; fragrant. Occasionally the flowers and leaves develop at the same time, in which event the flowers are paler, almost white, and more nearly single, with longer common stalks (peduncles). Young foliage yellow-brown to reddish-bronze, coated on both sides with persistent, fine hairs. Growth very slow; congested and twiggy. Record: 24' × 4'6" × 40' Seattle, WA (1993).

P. Simonii Carr.

APRICOT PLUM. From N China; unknown in the wild. Introduced to Western cultivation in 1863. Named in 1872, after Eugène Simon (1848–1924), who introduced it from China to France. In North American commerce ≤1892. Exceedingly rare. Invaluable for fruit-breeding; but for itself, despised and rejected as an ornament. Closely related to *P. salicina* (JAPANESE PLUM). Leaves long and narrow. Fruit 2" wide, brick-red, with yellow pulp, cling-stone. A small, narrow tree.

P. 'Snofozam'—see P. Snow Fountains®

P. Snow Fountains®
= *P.* 'Snofozam'

SNOW FOUNTAINS® CHERRY. Introduced ca. 1985 by Lake County nursery of Perry, OH. Common. Flowers white. Rather than topgrafted and completely pendulous as most cultivated WEEPING CHERRIES, this is naturally weeping, and builds itself up. Leaves to 3⅜" × 1½".

P. 'Snow Goose'
= *P.* × *subhirtella* 'Snow Goose'
(*P. speciosa* × *P. incisa*)

SNOW GOOSE CHERRY. Raised by A. Doorenbos of Holland. Named in 1970. In North American commerce since ≤1990. Rare. Flowers pure white. Foliage bright green. Differs from *P.* 'Umineko' in having a broader crown and larger leaves which appear after the flowers.

P. speciosa (Koidz.) Ingram
= *P. serrulata* f. *albida* (Mak.) Mak.
= *P. serrulata* 'Oshima-zakura'
= *P. Lannesiana* (Carr.) Wils. var. *speciosa* (Koidz.) Mak.
= *P. Lannesiana* f. *speciosa* (Koidz.) Koehne
= *P. Lannesiana* f. *albida* (Mak.) Wils.

OSHIMA CHERRY. From Japan. Introduced to Germany in 1909. Rare in North America. Highly variable. Flowers white or pink, to 1⅝" wide, in loose clusters of 3–7. Usually fragrant. Young foliage any color, often green. Leaves with delicate long teeth, like fringes. Some SATO ZAKURA cultivars are simply selections rather than hybrids of this species. Tree large, wide, vigorous. Records: 44' × 3'6" × 46' and 35' × 7'4" × 40' Seattle, WA (1990).

P. 'Spencer Hollywood'
= *P. cerasifera* 'Hollywood' (in part)

SPENCER HOLLYWOOD PLUM. Named and introduced (ca. 1960?) by S.J. Rich nursery of Hillsboro, OR. Named after the people who originally supplied it to the Rich nursery. Rare except in the maritime Pacific Northwest. A fruitful, naturally dwarf PURPLELEAF PLUM. Flowers pale pink, lightly fragrant. Leaves glossy dark greenish above, purplish beneath. Plums abundant, often breaking limbs with their weight; egg-shaped, red-skinned, purple-red inside; freestone. Ripens late July and August. The original 'Hollywood' PLUM is no dwarf, and ripens its crop much earlier. 'Spencer Hollywood' is routinely sold as 'Hollywood'.

P. spinosa L.

BLACKTHORN. SLOE. From Europe, N Africa, W Asia. A bushy, spiny little tree or large suckering shrub. Flowers small, white. Fruit a bluish-black miniature plum. Seldom sold in North America, and scarcely considered an ornamental tree. Its fruit, while no good to eat, is visually pleasing. A few of its cultivars are rarely planted. For its hybrids, the BULLACE and DAMSON, see *P.* × *domestica* var. *insititia*.

P. spinosa 'Flore Pleno'—see P. spinosa 'Plena'

P. spinosa 'Plena'
= *P. spinosa* 'Flore Pleno'

Origin unknown, likely in S France. Described officially in 1770. In North American commerce ≤1888. Extremely rare here. Almost invariably bushy. Flowers fully double, pure white.

P. spinosa 'Purpurea'

Introduced in 1903 in France. In North American commerce ≤1948. Extremely rare. Less spiny than typical *P. spinosa*. Foliage purplish. Flowers pink. A large shrub or small tree. Possibly a hybrid with a purpleleaf cultivar of CHERRY PLUM (*P. cerasifera*).

P. spinosa 'Rosea'—see P. 'Rosea'

P. 'Spire'

= P. 'Hillier Spire'
= P. × Hillieri 'Spire'

SPIRE CHERRY. Raised in 1937 at Hillier nursery of England, as a seedling from P. 'Hillier'. Introduced in 1956. Sold in North America since ≤1963–64. Uncommon. Tree narrow vase-shaped, to 30'–40' tall. Flowers pale pink. Young foliage reddish-purple. Fall color brilliant red.

P. × subhirtella Miq.

= P. × subhirtella 'Subhirtella'
= P. × subhirtella 'Beni-higan' (in part)
(P. pendula var. ascendens × P. incisa)

HIGAN CHERRY. ROSEBUD CHERRY. CULTIVATED HIGAN. SPRING CHERRY. Unknown in the wild; of natural hybrid origin in Japan. Named in 1865. As typically described (in the botanic sense), this was received by the Arnold Arboretum from the Botanic gardens of Tokyo in 1894. A small tree 20'–30' tall, often wider; not coming true from seeds—but grown widely in Japan from cuttings. Leaves 1½"–3" long, deeply toothed and lightly hairy. Buds pale pink. Flowers from early March to early April, white, to 1½" wide, in clusters of (2) 3–4 (5); calyx tube and flowerstems scantily, barely hairy. Twigs slender and hairy. Cherries black, very shiny, ca. ⅓" long. SPRING CHERRY is a literal rendering of the Japanese Higan Zakura. The name 'Beni-higan' (literally, PINK HIGAN) has been used for at least three different trees, but it would seem most commonly for this one—it logically should apply to 'Rosea'. Seven cultivars previously listed under subhirtella are now known to be either wholly P. pendula or more nearly akin to it. Whether pendulous or not, P. pendula clones have longer, narrower, more finely toothed leaves than those of P. × subhirtella. Record: 37' × 13'6" × 63' Timonium, MD (1972).

P. × subhirtella 'Accolade'—see P. 'Accolade'

P. × subhirtella 'Ascendens'—see P. pendula var. ascendens

P. × subhirtella var. ascendens—see P. pendula var. ascendens

P. × subhirtella 'Ascendens Plena'—see P. × subhirtella 'Flore Pleno'

P. × subhirtella 'Ascendens Rosea'—see P. × subhirtella 'Rosea'

P. × subhirtella var. ascendens 'Rosea Flore Plena'—see P. × subhirtella 'Atsumori'

P. × subhirtella 'Atsumori'

= P. × subhirtella var. ascendens 'Rosea Flore Plena' (in part)

DOUBLE PALE PINK HIGAN CHERRY. Imported in 1940 to Victoria, B.C., from K. Wada nursery of Japan. Name means "apple blossom." Slower than P. pendula 'Fukubana'; upright, with paler, larger (1"–1⅜" wide) flowers. Red buds open apple-blossom pink, fade to pale pink or almost white (the color of 'Autumnalis Rosea'); 15–17 petals; in age with with purplish calyces and filaments. (2) 3 (4) per cluster, stems to 1½" long. Leaves unfold clear green rather than the bronze of 'Fukubana'; inferior fall leaf color to 'Fukubana'. Tree dwarfish, erect; leaves typical. Minimal brown-rot. Perhaps less cold-hardy than some cultivars.

P. × subhirtella 'Autumnalis'

= P. × subhirtella 'Jugatsu-zakura'

AUTUMN FLOWERING CHERRY. WINTER FLOWERING CHERRY. Grown in Japan since the 5th century. Cultivated in the West since 1900. Rare in North America; most trees so called are P. × subhirtella 'Autumnalis Rosea'. 'Jugatsu-zakura' means "October bloomer." Flowers borne in fall, winter or spring; white or ever so faintly pink, double (14–16 petals), on stems to 1½" long.

P. × subhirtella 'Autumnalis Rosea'

Cultivated in North America ≤1940. Common. Usually sold as P. × subhirtella 'Autumnalis'. Fall flowers faintly pink, spring flowers deeper pink; 14–19 petals. Leaves to 3½" × 1½"; rough with hairs on the upper surface. Records: 36' × 3'6" × 29' and 29' × 5'6" × 40' Seattle, WA (1990)

P. × subhirtella 'Beni-higan'—see P. pendula var. ascendens and P. × subhirtella and P. × subhirtella 'Rosea'

P. × subhirtella 'Beni-hoshi'—see P. pendula 'Stellata'

P. × subhirtella 'Beni-shidare'—see P. pendula 'Park Weeping'

P. × subhirtella 'Double Park Weeping'—see P. pendula 'Pendula Plena Rosea'

P. × sub. 'Endo-zakura'—see P. pendula 'Pendula Plena Rosea'

P. × *sub.* 'Eureka Weeping'—see *P. pendula* 'Eureka Weeping'

P. × *subhirtella* 'Flore Plena'—see *P. pendula* 'Fukubana'

P. × *subhirtella* 'Flore Pleno'
= *P.* × *subhirtella* 'Ascendens Plena'
= *P.* × *subhirtella* 'Totsuka-shidare'
= *P.* × *subhirtella* 'Wohlert's Double'
= *P. serrulata* 'Higantakura' or 'Higatekuri'

DOUBLE WHITE HIGAN CHERRY. In North American commerce since ≤1931. Uncommon. Mauvy-pink buds open to double (14–22 petals) flowers, palest pink fading essentially white, 1"–1⅛" wide, in clusters of (2) 3 (4). Usually topgrafted. Exhibits the *P. incisa* end of the foliage trait range.

P. × *subhirtella* 'Fukubana'—see *P. pendula* 'Fukubana'

P. × *subhirtella* 'Ito-shidare'—see *P. pendula* 'Eureka Weeping'

P. × *subhirtella* 'Ito-zakura'—see *P. pendula*

P. × *subhirtella* 'Jugatsu-zakura'—see *P.* × *subhirtella* 'Autumnalis'

P. × *subhirtella* 'Momi-jigari'—see *P. pendula* 'Fukubana'

P. × *subhirtella* 'Park Weeping'—see *P. pendula* 'Park Weeping'

P. × *subhirtella* 'Pendula'—see *P. pendula*

P. × *sub.* 'Pendula Lanceolata'—see *P. pendula* 'Pendula Rubra'

P. × *subhirtella* 'Pendula Plena Rosea'—see *P. pendula* 'Pendula Plena Rosea'

P. × *subhirtella* 'Pendula Rosea'—see *P. pendula* 'Eureka Weeping' and *P. pendula* 'Pendula Rosea'

P. × *subhirtella* 'Pendula Rubra'—see *P. pendula* 'Pendula Rubra'

P. × *subhirtella* 'Pink Cloud'—see *P.* × *subhirtella* 'Rosy Cloud'

P. × *subhirtella* 'Pink Star'—see *P. pendula* 'Stellata'

P. × *subhirtella* 'Rosea'
= *P.* × *subhirtella* 'Ascendens Rosea'
= *P.* × *subhirtella* 'Beni-higan' (in part)

PINK SPRING CHERRY. Very rare. Flowers clear shell-pink, with reddish calyx, unlike those of typical *P.* × *subhirtella*. The name 'Beni-higan' (literally, PINK HIGAN) has been used for at least three taxa, but it would seem most logically should be restricted to 'Rosea'. A sport of 'Rosea' is 'Whitcomb'.

P. × *subhirtella* 'Rosy Cloud' PP 4540 (1980)
= *P.* × *subhirtella* 'Pink Cloud'
= *P. serrulata* 'Rosy Cloud'
(*P. subhirtella* 'Autumnalis' × *P. pendula* 'Pendula Plena Rosea')

Introduced ca. 1980 by Princeton nursery of New Jersey. Common. Flowers pink, large, double. Tree upright spreading.

P. × *subhirtella* 'Roseo-plena'—see *P. pendula* 'Fukubana'

P. × *sub.* 'Sendai Ito-zakura'—see *P. pendula* 'Pendula Plena Rosea'

P. × *subhirtella* 'Shidare (higan) zakura'—see *P. pendula*

P. × *subhirtella* 'Shiro-higan'—see *P. pendula* var. *ascendens* and *P.* × *yedoensis*

P. × *subhirtella* 'Snow Goose'—see *P.* 'Snow Goose'

P. × *subhirtella* 'Spring Glory'—see *P. pendula* 'Fukubana'

P. × *subhirtella* 'Stellata'—see *P. pendula* 'Stellata'

P. × *subhirtella* 'Stricta'
Imported from Japan to Victoria, B.C. Not known in commerce. Branching sinuous, forming a compact crown with clouds of curved twigs. Flowers 2–3 per cluster, with 5 irregular white petals. Leaves typical.

P. × *subhirtella* 'Subhirtella'—see *P.* × *subhirtella*

P. × *sub.* 'Totsu-zakura'—see *P. pendula* 'Pendula Plena Rosea'

P. × *subhirtella* 'Totsuka-shidare'—see *P.* × *subhirtella* 'Flore Pleno'

P. × *subhirtella* 'Whitcomb'
≠ *P.* × *subhirtella* 'Rosea'

WHITCOMB CHERRY. Believed to be a sport of *P.* × *subhirtella* 'Rosea'. Originally planted ca. 1913 in the garden of David Whitcomb (1879–1966), who lived northwest of Seattle; propagated ca. 1925–30. Until the 1980s, rarely grown outside of the maritime Pacific Northwest (where it is common). Flowers single (or a few semi-double), deep pink, blooming in late winter or earliest spring, before the other HIGAN cultivars. Tree larger than *P.* × *subhirtella* 'Rosea' and blooms earlier, but otherwise similar. Leaves similar to those of 'Autumnalis Rosea' but darker, finer-toothed, less hairy, with more veins, and usually larger (to 4¾" × 2¼"). Compared to 'Autumnalis Rosea' the flowers are later to bloom, single, the petals wider and darker pink, the sepals don't reflex, the pedicels are shorter. Records: 39' × 3'6" × 36' Seattle, WA (1990); 30' × 7'0" × 55' Seattle, WA (1993); 27' × 8'1" × 51' Seattle, WA (1993).

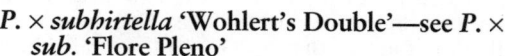

P. × *subhirtella* 'Wohlert's Double'—see *P.* × *sub.* 'Flore Pleno'

P. × *sub.* 'Yae Beni-shidare'—see *P. pendula* 'Pendula Plena Rosea'

P. × *sub.* 'Yae Shidare-higan'—see *P. pendula* 'Pendula Plena Rosea'

P. 'Sumizome'
= *P. serrulata* 'Sumizome'
= *P. serrulata* f. *subfusca* Miyoshi
= *P. Lannesiana* f. *sumizome* Wils.

In the SATO ZAKURA group. Name means "inky dye"—referring to shadows cast on the ground. At least three clones have been called 'Sumizome'. The following description is based on the Arnold Arboretum clone grown in England, and presumably marketed in the late 1930s and '40s by Kohankie nursery of Paineville, OH. Tree wide spreading, like *P.* 'Shiro-fugen'. Flowers a little later than on *P.* 'Hokusai', of similar soft pink, 1¾"–1⅞" wide, semi-double (12–14 petals), strongly HAWTHORN-scented. Young foliage bronzy-green.

P. 'Tai Haku'
= *P. serrulata* 'Tai Haku'

In the SATO ZAKURA group. Name means "great white cherry." All specimens in Japan had died, but one dating from 1900 remained alive in England and saved the variety from extinction. In North American commerce since ≤1934. Uncommon. A strong tree, up to 40' tall. Buds palest pink. Flowers single, pure white, to 2½" wide (largest of any SATO ZAKURA). Young foliage deep copper. Leaves large, to 9⅜" × 4", with attractively fringed teeth on the edges. Records: to 40' tall in England; 29' × 3'7" × 37' Tacoma, WA (1992).

P. 'Taizan-fukun'
= *P. serrulata* 'Taizan-fukun'
= *P. serrulata* f. *ambigua* (Miyoshi) Ingram
= *P. serrulata* var. *pubescens* 'Taizan-fukun'
= *P.* × *yedoensis* 'Taizan-fukun'
= *P.* × *Miyoshii* 'Ambigua'
('Taisen-fukon')

In the SATO ZAKURA group. Name means "god of Taizan Mountain" (in China). In North American commerce <1934. Uncommon. Tree erect and flaring vase-like; small. Flowers pale pink, double (36–49 petals), small (1⅛"–1⅞" wide), on scantily hairy stems ca. 1" long; scentless. Floral parts, young twigs and leaves lightly hairy. Young foliage bronze. Leaves small for SATO ZAKURA, underside shiny, stem hairy, fall color brilliant reddish, purple and yellow. Differs from YOSHINO CHERRY (*P.* × *yedoensis*) in bearing smaller, thinner, less glossy leaves; blooming later, and is less hairy.

P. 'Taki-nioi'
= *P. serrulata* 'Taki-nioi'
= *P. serrulata* f. *cataracta* Miyoshi
= *P. Lannesiana* f. *takinioi* Wils.

In the SATO ZAKURA group. In North America <1919; in commerce here ≤1934. Rare. Name means "fragrant cloud" or "fragrance of a waterfall or cascade." Tree strong, flattened and broad. Buds pink-tinged. Flowers to 1¼" wide, pure white, single, in clusters of 3–4 (6); very fragrant; blooming late (for a single-flowered cultivar), in May. Young foliage reddish-bronze. Fall color yellow to orange. A similar cultivar is *P.* 'Gozanoma-nioi'.

P. 'Tanko-shinju'
= *P. serrulata* 'Tanko-shinju'

In the SATO ZAKURA group. Name means "pink pearl"

or "two people commit suicide in a coal mine." In North America since ≤1920; named here; in commerce since ≤1929. Uncommon; commercially extinct. Vigorous, vase-shaped at first, ultimately a spreading 25' tall tree. Buds mauve-pink. Flowers fluffy, of ca. 10–17 twisted petals, broadly rounded, only notched once; very pale pink at center, often with a pink eye in age, deep pink at margins; to 2" wide, in long drooping clusters of 2–6 as globular masses bunched towards ends of branches. The clusters are markedly long-stalked. Sepals untoothed. Young foliage bronzy. Similar to P. 'Fuku-rokuju'.

P. 'Tao-yoma (-zakura)'

= P. serrulata 'Tao-yoma (-zakura)'
= P. Lannesiana 'Taoyame'
('Taoyame')

In the SATO ZAKURA group. Imported <1929 from Japan to England. In North American commerce ≤1959. Very rare. Tree broad-topped, of medium vigor. Flowers soft shell pink fading to practically white, semi-double (5–14 or rarely 20 petals), in clusters of 4–6; blooming early. Young foliage coppery or purplish-brown. Record: 24' × 3'0" × 39' Seattle, WA (1993; pl. 1959).

P. 'Temari'

= P. serrulata 'Temari'
= P. serrulata f. globosa Miyoshi
= P. Lannesiana f. temari (Koidz.) Wils.

In the SATO ZAKURA group. Name means "ball," referring to flower clusters. Tree broadly rounded, of moderate strength. Buds deep red. Flowers double, (15) 20–25 (30) petals, pale pink, with some leafy carpels in the center; in compact, heavy balls. Young foliage tardy to appear, very faintly bronze, essentially green. Leaves often rounded at apex. Records: 26' × 3'6" × 31' and 22' × 4'7" × 39' Seattle, WA (1993)

P. 'Torano-o'

= P. serrulata 'Torano-o'
= P. serrulata f. caudata Miyoshi
= P. Lannesiana f. caudata (Miyoshi) Nemoto

In the SATO ZAKURA group. Name means "tigertail." Don't confuse with P. 'Beni-torano-o'. Very rare. In U.S. commerce from at least 1931 to 1958. Flowers in clusters of 3–8, small (to 1½" wide), single (or nearly so), white. Young leaves yellowish-green. Habit upright-spreading; of moderate size.

P. 'Trailblazer' PP 1586 (1957)

= P. cerasifera 'Hollywood' (in part)

TRAILBLAZER PLUM. Originated ca. 1947 in Portland, OR. Introduced in 1955. Uncommon. A PURPLELEAF PLUM valued as much for the edible fruit as for the form and foliage. Confused with P. 'Hollywood'. Flowers rather small (⅝"–1" wide), whitish. Leaves greenish above, purplish beneath. Plums red, 1½"–2" long, ripe from late July into September. Crown open and spreading, not markedly upright. Record: 22' × 5'0" × 25' Walla Walla, WA (1993).

P. triflora—see P. salicina

P. 'Ukon'

= P. serrulata 'Ukon' ('Yukon')
= P. serrulata flore luteo pleno hort.
= P. serrulata f. grandiflora Wagner
= P. serrulata f. luteo-virens Miyoshi
= P. serrulata f. viridiflora Mak.
= P. serrulata 'Mangetsu'
= P. Lannesiana f. grandiflora (Wagner) Wils.

In the SATO ZAKURA group. Name means "yellowish." Cultivated in the West since ca. 1903. In North American commerce since ≤1920s. Common. Also called the GREEN CHERRY. Tree tall, rounded and strong; more cold-hardy than most SATO ZAKURA. Flowers semi-double, with 5–14 petals, at first creamy-white or pale yellow with green tones, fading to red in the center. Young foliage light bronzy-green. Fall color can be purple or rusty-red. P. 'Gyoiko' is similar, with slightly smaller, darker, more double, later flowers. P. 'Asagi' is a 'Ukon' synonym for all practical purposes. Records: 42' × 4'9" × 36' Tukwila, WA (1993); 32' × 5'3" × 48' Tacoma, WA (1992); 29' × 4'5" × 53' Seattle, WA (1992).

P. 'Umineko'

= P. serrulata 'Umineko'
('Umeniko', 'Umineka')
(P. speciosa × P. incisa)

UMINEKO CHERRY. Bred in England by C. Ingram; named ≤1928. In North America since ≤1942; in commerce here ≤1979–80. Rare. Name means "seagull" in Japanese. Tree vigorous. Habit very upright when young; to 25' tall or more. Flowers pure white, 1"–1¼" wide, cup-shaped, in April. Leaves large, bright green. A clone of the same parentage from Holland is P. 'Snow Goose'.

P. verecunda (Koidz.) Koehne
= P. serrulata var. pubescens (Mak.) Wils. (in part)
= P. jamasakura var. verecunda Koidz.
= P. Leveilleana Koehne

KOREAN HILL CHERRY. From China, Korea, and Japan. Introduced to the West in 1907. Named in 1912 (in Latin meaning shy or bashful). In North American commerce during the 1930s; extremely rare here. A close cousin of SARGENT CHERRY, differing in blooming later in spring, pure white or at least much paler pink; leaves narrower (to 6" × 2⅜"), greener beneath, with slightly finer teeth, and conspicuous hairs on the leafstems and flowerstems. Fruit the same size as that of SARGENT CHERRY, deepest purple or pure black, usually not as repulsively flavored. Fall color can be gold as well as red. The related JAPANESE HILL CHERRY is P. jamasakura. Records: to 65' tall in the wild; 60' × 7'11" × 53' Newhalem, WA (1993; pl. in 1930s).

P. verecunda 'Autumn Glory'
= P. serrulata 'Autumn Glory'

Selected by C. Ingram of England for consistently superb fall color (intense vivid scarlet); named in 1969 by Hillier's nursery; introduced ≤1971–72. In North American commerce since ≤1990. Rare.

P. 'Vesuvius'
= P. cerasifera 'Vesuvius' (in part)
= P. cerasifera 'Stribling Thundercloud'

VESUVIUS PLUM. Originated by L. Burbank of Santa Rosa, CA. Introduced in 1907. A hybrid of uncertain background; no evidence of CHERRY PLUM (P. cerasifera) in its appearance. Uncommon. Grossly confused with P. cerasifera 'Krauter's Vesuvius'. Of value for foliage, its white 1" flowers are poor, being both scanty and inconspicuous, and having to compete with the emerging leaves. Foliage handsome dark glossy purple. Fruit seldom made. Tree small, of flaring vase form, the trunk forking low. Record: 28' × 6'5" × 30' Arlington, WA (1992).

P. virginiana L.
= P. demissa (Nutt.) D. Dietr.
= P. melanocarpa (A. Nels.) Rydb.
= Padus virginiana (L.) Mill.
= Cerasus demissa Nutt.

CHOKECHERRY. COMMON CHOKECHERRY. From most of North America. Well known where native, but seldom cultivated elsewhere. Closely related to the Old World BIRD CHERRY (P. Padus). Differs from BIRD CHERRY by being smaller, with smaller flowers, opening later in spring, and often it root suckers. Fruit ¼"–½", usually dark reddish purple, sometimes amber, yellow, or black; often acceptable for eating, especially if cooked; raw it is often astringent. Leaves usually glossy above; vary in hairiness and size (maximum 6" × 3½"). A slender large shrub or small tree. Records: 73' × 4'6" Kootenai County, ID (1991); 70' × 2'5" Clark Fork, ID (1987); 67' × 5'9" × 63' Ada, MI (1979).

P. virginiana 'Bailey's Select'—see P. virginiana 'Canada Red'

P. virginiana 'Boughen's Yellow'
Selected <1975 by W.J. Boughen of Boughen nursery, Valley River, Manitoba. Fruit yellow, large, mild enough to eat fresh. A handsome ornamental in fruit season because its clustered yellow cherries hang like clusters of yellow grapes. If it is the same as P. virginiana 'Boughen Sweet Chokecherry', it was introduced as early as 1923.

P. virginiana 'Canada Red'
= P. virginiana 'Bailey's Select'
= P. virginiana 'Red Select'

Registered in 1979. Common. A sport of P. virginiana 'Schubert' selected and introduced by Bailey nursery of St. Paul, MN. Grows faster, foliage darker red, trunk straighter, with well distributed branches, making a full rounded crown.

P. virginiana 'Copper Schubert'—see P. virg. 'Schubert Copper'

P. virginiana 'Mini-Schubert'
Introduced <1990. J. Searles says "a densely compact small size tree with red foliage. It is an excellent candidate for formal lollipop-shaped trees."

P. virginiana 'Red Select'—see P. virginiana 'Canada Red'

P. virginiana 'Robert'
Selected in 1984 by L. Lee of Barrhead, Alberta. Named after Robert Simonet, who supplied the seed. Publicized since 1993. Leaves red-purple. Cherries large, mild tasting, in compact clusters.

P. virginiana 'Schubert'
('Shubert')

PURPLELEAF CHOKECHERRY. Introduced in 1943 by Oscar H. Will nursery of Bismarck, ND. Common.

Selected by Lawrence Schubert from thousands of seedlings. Leaves green at first, then dark purple. In mid-May, when half the foliage is greenish and half purplish, it looks awkward. In June, when 90% of the crown is purple, the occasional spurt of bright green new growth or root suckers makes an odd presence. The leaves recall PURPLE BEECH leaves. Lawyer nursery of Plains, MT, reports that 'Schubert' CHOKE-CHERRY, when seed-grown, yields "approximately 60–70% true-to-type plants with purple color." This fact explains why the original 'Schubert' clone, like 'Pissardii' PLUM, has been somewhat lost in the flood of its progeny. The clone *P. virginiana* 'Canada Red' has eclipsed 'Schubert'.

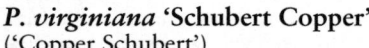

P. virginiana 'Schubert Copper'
('Copper Schubert')

A hybrid of 'Mission' and 'Schubert' from Beaverlodge nursery of Beaverlodge, Alberta. Registered in 1976. Rare. Foliage coppery-green. Fruit red, not astringent.

P. virginiana 'Sharon'

Named ≤1982. A small, neat purpleleaf cultivar.

P. virginiana 'Spearfish'

From Spearfish, in the Black Hills of South Dakota. Introduced in 1924 by N. Hansen. Rare. Fruit yellow.

P. 'Wadae'
= *P.* × *Wadai* hort. Jap.
?(*P. subhirtella* × *P. campanulata*)
?(*P. subhirtella* × *P. pseudocerasus*)

WADA CHERRY. Originated in Japan; of garden origin. In North America since ≤1950. Not known to have been in commerce here; exceedingly rare. Flowers in early March, solid pink, in clusters of 2–4 upon a short common stalk (peduncle). Some say "scented like ripe peaches." Tree small, gaunt and open. Trunk peely, warty, slender. Overall, an inelegant, disease-prone, twiggy little tree, that suckers profusely from the trunk, the sprouts reddish when young. Twigs pale gray. Leaves usually at most 3¼" × 2"; rich green, wrinkled, slightly rough-hairy above; green late into November.

P. × *Wadai*—see *P.* 'Wadae'

P. 'Wase-miyako'
= *P. serrulata* 'Wase-miyako'

In the SATO ZAKURA group. Sold during the 1940s and '50s by Kingsville nursery of Maryland. Very rare. Tree vigorous. Carmine-pink buds open to palest pink or whitish flowers; semi-double (13–17 petals), ca. 1¾" wide, delicately scented or scentless; in loosely held, long-stemmed clusters of 4–7; sepals subtly toothed. Young foliage greenish. Record: 44' × 3'8½" Seattle, WA (1994; *pl.* 1949).

P. 'Washi-no-o'
= *P. serrulata* 'Washi-no-o'
= *P. serrulata* f. *arguta* Miyoshi
= *P. serrulata* f. *wasinowo* Ingram
= *P. Lannesiana* f. *wasinowo* (Koidz.) Wils.
= *P. Lannesiana* 'Washinowo'

In the SATO ZAKURA group. Name means "eagle's tail" (may refer to the ragged petal edges). In North American commerce ≤1931. Extremely rare. Paul Russel called it a slightly improved OSHIMA CHERRY (*P. speciosa*) with larger flowers and smaller stature. Rare. Tree vigorous, upright like *P.* 'Kwanzan'. Buds shell-pink. Flowers essentially single, white, 1½" wide, faintly fragrant; early; calyx reddish-green. Young foliage pale bronzy-green or brownish-bronze. Fall color rich yellow.

P. 'Yae-akebono'
= *P. serrulata* 'Yae-akebono'
= *P. serrulata* f. *versicolor* Miyoshi
= *P. Lannesiana* f. *yayeakebono* Wils.

In the SATO ZAKURA group. In North American commerce ≤1949. Exceedingly rare. Tree small, disease-prone. Flowers fragrant, semi-double (12–16 petals), pink, to 1¾" wide, 3–5 per cluster. Young foliage bronzy-green. No relation to *P.* × *yedoensis* 'Akebono'. Resembles *P.* 'Okiku-zakura'.

P. 'Yae-kanzan'
= *P. serrulata* 'Yae-kanzan'

In the SATO ZAKURA group. Introduced ≤1934 by W.B. Clarke nursery of San José, CA. Rare; out of commerce since ca. 1960. Similar to *P.* 'Kwanzan' but has about double the number of petals, making flowers very full and slightly larger.

P. 'Yae-murasaki (-zakura)'
= *P. serrulata* 'Yae-murasaki (-zakura)'
= *P. serrulata* f. *purpurea plena* Miyoshi

In the SATO ZAKURA group. Name means "double purple." G. Chadbund points out it *ought* to mean "semi-double, bluish rose-pink." In North American commerce ≤1941. Very rare. Slow growing; at length to 15'–18' tall; wide crowned. Flowers profuse, purplish-pink, to 1¼" wide; semi-double (8–14 petals); sepals slightly toothed, narrow; stiff, short-stemmed clusters of 2–4 (5). Young foliage pale reddish-brown.

P. × yedoensis Matsum.

= P. × subhirtella 'Shiro-higan' (in part)
= P. serrulata 'Yoshino'
?(P. speciosa × P. pendula var. ascendens)
?(P. speciosa × P. subhirtella)

YOSHINO CHERRY. POTOMAC CHERRY. Originated by a man called Ito at Somei (presently Tokyo) in the late Edo era (i.e. <1867). Named officially in 1901. In 1902 seeds were introduced to the Arnold Arboretum. In 1912 trees were planted at Potomac Park of Washington, D.C. Now common and well known. Flowers pale pink or white, in stemless or shortly stalked (especially on flowers from trunk sprouts) clusters of 3–6, the flowerstems usually quite hairy. Leaves to 5⅝" × 2½". Cherries black, shiny, ca. ½" long; bitter. Tree large, burry-trunked. Records: 55' × 12'0" × 56' Chevy Chase, MD (1990); 41' × 9'6" × 65' Seattle, WA (1993).

P. × yedoensis 'Afterglow' PP 5730 (1986)

Introduced ≤1985 by Princeton nursery of New Jersey. Common. An exceptionally vigorous seedling of P. × yedoensis 'Akebono', with rich pink flowers that do not fade to white. More cold-hardy than ordinary YOSHINO CHERRY.

P. × yedoensis 'Akebono'

= P. × yedoensis 'Daybreak'
= P. serrulata 'Akebono'

AKEBONO CHERRY. DAYBREAK CHERRY. Selected in 1920 by W.B. Clarke nursery of San José, CA. Introduced ca. 1925. Common. More cold-hardy than typical P. × yedoensis. A smaller tree bearing larger, pinker flowers, in full bloom a bit later in spring, making a denser display. (Paul Russel notes that Clarke's 'Akebono' is not same as that of M. Miyoshi, but the latter's clone is not cultivated except in Japan.) Record: 28' × 6'5" × 47' Seattle, WA (1992).

P. × yedoensis 'Daybreak'—see P. × yedoensis 'Akebono'

P. × yedoensis 'Ivensii'

Raised from seed in 1925 by Hillier nursery of England. Named to commemorate nursery manager Arthur J. Ivens (1897–1954). Introduced to the U.S. in 1937 by the Arnold Arboretum. Extremely rare here. Sold in the 1960s by Scanlon nursery of Ohio. Small, vigorous and weeping; long tortuous branches. Flowers pink in the bud, open snow-white, ca. ¾" wide.

P. × yedoensis 'Moerheimi'—see P. 'Moerheimi'

P. × yedoensis 'Pendula'—see P. × yedoensis f. perpendens

P. × yedoensis f. perpendens Wils.

= P. × yedoensis 'Shidare-Yoshino'
= P. × yedoensis 'Pendula'

WEEPING YOSHINO CHERRY. Introduced to North America in 1910 from Japan. Named in 1924. In commerce here <1934. Uncommon. Flowers smaller than those of typical P. × yedoensis, and appearing earlier in spring. Leaves also smaller (to 3¾" × 2"). Branches weeping. Habit dwarfish. More than one clone exists.

P. × yedoensis 'Shidare-Yoshino'—see P. × yedoensis f. perpendens

P. × yedoensis f. shojo—see P. 'Shojo'

P. × yedoensis 'Taizan-fukun'—see P. 'Taizan-fukun'

P. 'Yedo-zakura'

= P. serrulata 'Yedo-zakura'
= P. serrulata 'Edo-zakura'
= P. serrulata f. nobilis Miyoshi
= P. Lannesiana 'Nobilis'
= P. Lannesiana f. yedozakura Wils.
('Edo-zakura')

In the SATO ZAKURA group. Name means "yedo cherry." In North American commerce since ≤1931. Uncommon. Tree to 18' tall, of slow to moderate growth. Buds carmine. Flowers 1¾"–2½" wide, in short-stemmed clusters of 2–5, forming globular masses; pale pink in center, deeper at edges; of 8–26 ruffled petals; carpel sometimes leaflike; sepals small, serrate. Young foliage brownish-green. Some say P. 'Beni-torano-o' is a synonym.

Pseudocydonia

[ROSACEÆ; Rose Family] A genus of only the following species. From Greek *pseudes*, false, and genus *Cydonia*, QUINCE TREE.

P. sinensis (Dum.-Cours.) Schneid.
= *Malus sinensis* Dum.-Cours.
= *Cydonia sinensis* (Dum.-Cours.) Thouin
= *Chænomeles chinensis* Koehne
= *Pyrus cathayensis* Hemsl. (in part)

CHINESE QUINCE. PERFUME QUINCE. Chinese: *Suan-Li-Kan. Mu Kua* (wooden gourd). From China. Introduced to Western cultivation ≤1800. Named in 1811. In North American commerce ≤1888. Long very rare in commerce; in the 1990s mass-produced by Princeton nursery of New Jersey. A large shrub or small tree of handsome form, crisp foliage (semi-evergreen, with warm glowing orange-red tones in November) and superb bark. To be at its peak form it requires pruning, which can be a prickly job. It is, like the shrubby FLOWERING QUINCES (*Chænomeles*), easily "scorched" badly by fireblight. Tardily deciduous; semi-spiny. Peeling bark is attractively mottled and encourages caressing, at its best in May and June as the trunk expands. Flowers palest pink, in (late March) April–May. Fruit immense (to 7" long and 4" wide), light green for months, finally pure yellow, waxy skinned, tough fleshed, with pleasing fragrance but no food value. The great plant breeder L. Burbank of Santa Rosa, CA, began working with this species in 1884; he released in 1885 a cultivar called '**Hong Kong**' with fruit "of immense size, often weighing over two pounds." He followed it with '**Elephant**' in 1919. These two cultivars are long lost. Handy nursery of Portland, OR, has topgrafted bushy FLOWERING QUINCES (*Chænomeles*) onto *Pseudocydonia* trunks. Records: to 50' × 6'3" in the wild; 36' × 3'11" × 36' Sacramento, CA (1989); 34' × 3'3" × 28' Seattle, WA (1990).

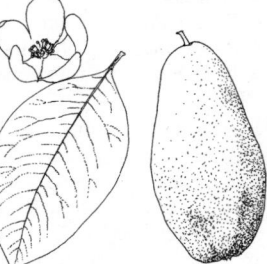

Pseudolarix

[PINACEÆ; Pine Family] A genus of only the following species, a Chinese deciduous conifer, prized for its lush, delicate foliage. From Greek *pseudes*, false, and genus *Larix*, LARCH TREE.

P. amabilis (Nels.) Rehd.
= *Pseudolarix Kaempferi* auct. (in part)
= *Larix Kaempferi* auct. (in part)
= *Chrysolarix amabilis* (Nels.) H.E. Moore
= *Larix amabilis* Nels.

GOLDEN LARCH. CHINESE GOLDEN LARCH. From China, mostly in the southeast. There called *Ching Sung* (GOLDEN PINE, because of the needles). Introduced to the West in 1852 when R. Fortune sent potted plants to Britain. In 1853 Fortune found wild specimens and sent seeds. A specimen in Belgium, of independent origin, is said to have been planted by Siebold ca. 1840. In any case, *Pseudolarix* has been in North America since ≤1859, and thrives, but is rare in most locales and at best uncommon. The epithet *amabilis* in Latin means pleasing or attractive. Needles unusually wide for a LARCH, 1¼"–3" long, golden in fall. Cones 2½"–3" long, like miniature globe artichokes, breaking up when ripe. Habit often very broad. Records: to 150' × 10'0" in the wild; 90' × 7'5" West Hartford, CT (1988); 85' × 8'0" Philadelphia, PA (ca. 1985); 75½' × 8'10" Carclew, Cornwall, England (1989); 57' × 7'11" Wellesley, MA (1980); 42' × 7'4" × 55' Arnold Arboretum, MA (1980; *pl.* 1891).

P. Kaempferi—see *Pseudolarix amabilis*

Pseudotsuga

[PINACEÆ; Pine Family] 4–8 spp. of coniferous evergreens known as DOUGLAS FIRS; only one species common in cultivation. *Pseudotsuga* derives from the uncouth combination of a Greek word (*pseudes*; false) with a Japanese (*tsuga*; HEMLOCK TREE), indicating the relation of these trees with the HEMLOCKS. Cones pendulous, with conspicuously protruding narrow, forked bracts.

P. Douglasii—see *Pseudotsuga Menziesii*

P. macrocarpa (Torr.) Mayr

BIGCONE DOUGLAS FIR. LARGECONE DOUGLAS FIR. BIGCONE SPRUCE. From S California mountains. Discovered in 1858; named in 1860 (Greek *macro*, large, and *karpos*, fruit). In California commerce ≤1893. Exceedingly rare. It doesn't transplant well and is not as ornamental or cold-hardy as *P. Menziesii*. Needles dark, glossy green, to 3" long. Cones 4"–7½" long, of substantial texture and tougher than those of *P. Menziesii*. Very few trees are as tolerant of drought. Records: 173' × 21'7" Angeles National Forest, CA (1944); 120' × 24'0" Los Padres National Forest, CA (1964).

P. Menziesii (Mirb.) Franco

= *P. mucronata* (Raf.) Sudw.
= *P. taxifolia* (Lam.) Britt. *ex* Sudw.
= *P. Douglasii* (Lindl.) Carr.

DOUGLAS FIR. From British Columbia to Mexico. The most important timber tree in the United States. Archibald Menzies (1754–1842), Scots physician and naturalist, discovered it in 1792 on Nootka Sound. In 1825, another Scot, David Douglas (1798–1834), rediscovered it and in 1826 sent seeds to England. The State Tree of Oregon, this species also made Washington "the Evergreen State." It coats the hillsides and valleys of millions of square miles in the maritime Pacific Northwest. Needles ¾"–1½" long. Cones 2"–4½" long. Bark in age becomes dark brown and deeply corky. One of the world's largest trees. Its great height and the habit of shedding its lower branches in storms makes large specimens awkward if not dangerous in confined spaces in cities or near dwellings. Records: 415' × 44'0" Lynn Valley, B.C. (1902); 393' × 50'6" Mineral, WA (1906); 326' × 36'6" Coos County, OR (1991); 326' × 21'1" Olympic National Park, WA (1988); 242' × 41'2" Port Renfrew, B.C. (1985); 205' × 45'5" Olympic National Park, WA (1985); a trunk 56'6" around at Conway, WA (n.d.).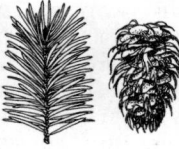

P. Menziesii 'Astro Blue'

= *P. Menziesii* 'Compacta Glauca'

Introduced in 1968 by Vermeulen nursery of New Jersey; listed as 'Compacta Glauca' until 1971. Of dense, broad pyramidal form with ascending branches. Foliage light blue. A cultivar of *P. Menziesii* ssp. *glauca*.

P. Menziesii 'Big Flats'

Selected in 1955 by Big Flats nursery of New York. Still in commerce. A cultivar of *P. Menziesii* ssp. *glauca*. Vigorous. Branches pendant. Needles long and glaucous.

P. Menziesii 'Carnefix Weeping'—see *P. Menz.* 'Idaho Weeping'

P. Menziesii 'Coeur d'Alene'

Selected in Coeur d'Alene, ID. In commerce <1990. A cultivar of *P. Menziesii* ssp. *glauca*. Very cold hardy. Tight pyramidal habit. Needles gray.

P. Menziesii 'Compacta Glauca'—see *P. Menziesii* 'Astro Blue'

P. Menziesii 'Fastigiata'

This name was first used ≤1850 by Knight & Perry nursery of London, England. But the clone designated then is not the only one sold as 'Fastigiata' in North America. Since 1913, a *P. Menziesii* ssp. *glauca* seedling from Rochester, NY, has circulated as 'Fastigiata' (or may sometimes be sold as 'Glauca Fastigiata'). It is narrow with short upright branches. Besides the Rochester clone, another 'Fastigiata' (perhaps the original clone from England) has short green needles, is compact, and markedly erect.

P. Menziesii ssp. glauca (Beissn.) E. Murr.

= *P. Menziesii* var. *glauca* (Beissn.) Franco

ROCKY MOUNTAIN DOUGLAS FIR. INTERIOR DOUGLAS FIR. COLORADO DOUGLAS FIR. INLAND DOUGLAS FIR. BLUE DOUGLAS FIR. Discovered in Colorado in 1862 and introduced soon after. A mountainous, inland subspecies, more commonly cultivated than the typical or coastal version, being more cold-hardy. Foliage comparatively glaucous. Cones with more prominent bracts. Tree tends to be stouter, broader and of slower growth. Records: 209' × 18'5" Clearwater County, ID (1991); 173' × 19'8" Umatilla National Forest, WA (1992); 158' × 23'6" Ochoco National Forest, OR (1984); 140' × 24'7" Deschutes National Forest, OR (1981).

P. Menziesii 'Glauca Fastigiata'—see *P. Menziesii* 'Fastigiata'

P. Menziesii 'Glauca Pendula'

Raised from Colorado seeds by Simon-Louis nursery of Metz, France. Name published in 1891. In North American commerce ≤1986. Rare. Pyramidal, branches horizontal; branchlets weeping; needles gray-green. A cultivar of *P. Menziesii* ssp. *glauca*.

Pseudotsuga Menziesii 'Graceful Grace'

In commerce ≤1982. Needles glaucous and unusually long. Growth fast. Leader irregularly works its way upward without needing to be staked; lateral branches hang down.

P. Menziesii 'Hess's Select Blue'

Possibly originated by Hess nursery of Cedarville (before then Mountain View), NJ. In commerce ≤1980. Needles vivid glaucous blue—the brightest blue of any DOUGLAS FIR.

P. Menziesii 'Hillside Gold'

Selected ca. 1970 at Hillside Gardens of Lehighton, PA. In commerce ≤1982. Extremely rare. A "tree with a golden cast."

P. Menziesii 'Idaho Weeping'

= *P. Menziesii* 'Pendula Idaho'
= *P. Menziesii* 'Carnefix Weeping'

Found by Warren Carnefix in the mountains of Idaho. Named ca. 1989 in Oregon. In commerce ≤1992. A cultivar of *P. Menziesii* ssp. *glauca* but needles not especially glaucous. Less weeping but hardier than the coastal green kind ('Pendula'). Variable, either of upright habit with a curving, twisting leader and pendulous branches, or grows wider than tall.

P. Menziesii 'Marshall'

Originated ca. 1930 in Colorado. Introduced by Marshall nursery of Arlington, NE. Registered in 1963. Densely pyramidal form. A cultivar of *P. Menziesii* ssp. *glauca*. One planted in 1972 at the Morton Arboretum, Lisle, IL, was only 7½' tall and 5½' wide in 1986.

P. Menziesii 'Pendula'

= *P. Menziesii* 'Skagit Falls'

WEEPING DOUGLAS FIR. Discovered by Sisson in valleys and slopes of Mt. Shasta. Name published in 1853 in France. In North America ≤1924. Rare. Doubtless both the original clone and 'Glauca Pendula' have circulated under this name. Foliage green. Crown naturally pendulous and irregular. Growth slower than typical but it is no dwarf. Records: 39' × 2'9" Seattle, WA (1988); 38' × 3'7" Tukwila, WA (1992).

P. Menziesii 'Pendula Idaho'—see *P. Menziesii* 'Idaho Weeping'

P. Menziesii 'Roger's Weeping'

In commerce ≤1986. Grows flat on the ground unless staked.

P. Menziesii 'Skagit Falls'—see *P. Menziesii* 'Pendula'

P. Menziesii 'Skyline'

('Skylands')

Discovered as a mutation by O. Solburger. In commerce ≤1992. A cultivar of *P. Menziesii* ssp. *glauca*. Gaunt snakebranch habit. Growth slow but not dwarf. Can grow 15' tall in 30 years. Foliage light blue.

P. Menziesii 'Slavinii'

Discovered in 1914 among seedlings at Cobb's Hill Reservoir of Rochester, NY. Named in 1932 after horticulturist Bernard Henry Slavin (1873–1960). Very rare. Semi-dwarf, conical, broad at base, distinctly narrowed towards the top. Needles somewhat crowded, ½"–¾" long.

P. mucronata—see *Pseudotsuga Menziesii*

P. taxifolia—see *Pseudotsuga Menziesii*

Ptelea

[RUTACEÆ; Rue Family] 3–4 (12) spp. of shrubs or small trees, all North American or Mexican. An ancient Greek name for ELM, transferred by the botanist Linnæus to this genus on account of the similarity of the winged seeds. Related genera include *Fortunella* (KUMQUAT), *Phellodendron* (CORK TREE), *Poncirus* (TRIFOLIATE ORANGE), *Tetradium*, and *Zanthoxylum*.

P. trifoliata L.

HOP TREE. WAFER ASH. STINKING ASH. TREE TREFOIL. SHRUBBY TREFOIL. SKUNK BUSH. POTATOCHIP TREE. PRAIRIE GRUB. WINGSEED. SWAMP DOGWOOD. PICKAWAY ANISE. From much of North America—S Ontario to Mexico. Fairly common in cultivation. Usually a shrub; rarely a small tree. Leaves can be large (to 7") or small, soft with persistent felt beneath, or essentially hairless; dotted with glands and weakly to strongly fragrant. In any case they are *trifoliate* (Latin *tri*, three, and *folium*, a leaf) just like the leaves borne by common bean plants in the vegetable garden. Flowers tiny, pale greenish-white, from early May into

July, depending on locale and year. Seeds ⅔"–1", pale, wafer-like, ornamental if not striking. The name HOP TREE came about when the seeds were used as hop substitutes. Records: 45' × 3'11" × 27' Bamffshire, Scotland (1835); 36' × 2'9" × 40' Ada, MI (1979); 34' × 4'5" × 27' Hartford, CT (1991).

P. trifoliata 'Aurea'

GOLDEN HOP TREE. Origin uncertain. B. Boom says 1853 in Germany. A. Rehder says <1886. In North American commerce ≤1890. Described officially in 1892. Very rare. Foliage golden. Growth consistently shrubby.

Pterocarya

[JUGLANDACEÆ; Walnut Family] 6–11 spp. of deciduous trees, all Asian. From Greek *pteron*, a wing or feather, and *karyon*, a nut; in allusion to the winged seeds; hence the name WINGNUT. Leaves compound like those of WALNUT trees (*Juglans*), stay green late into autumn, then drop with no coloration. Dangling, showy, chainlike clusters of small winged, inedible seeds ("nuts" only in a botanic sense). Like POPLARS (*Populus*), they are gross feeders, thirsty, grow amazingly fast and require much room. Often they are multitrunked, and suckering. They may be coarse and graceless, but are commanding in their large size. Sometimes the foliage is glossy and handsome, and the dangling seed-clusters are always interesting. They are too little known for one species (or hybrid) to be declared superior to the rest as an ornamental. Related genera include *Carya* (HICKORY and PECAN), *Juglans* (WALNUT) and *Platycarya*.

P. caucasia—see P. fraxinifolia

P. fraxinifolia (Lam. ex Poir.) Spach
= *P. caucasia* C.A. Mey.
= *Juglans fraxinifolia* Lam. *ex* Poir.

CAUCASIAN WINGNUT. From SW Asia. Introduced to cultivation in 1782. Named in 1798, from genus *Fraxinus* (ASH), and Latin *folium*, a leaf. In North America ≤1891; in commerce here ≤1907. Extremely rare. Scanlon nursery of Ohio praised this lavishly, especially the 12"–20" seed chains. "Anyone with any sort of an artistic sense will embrace this tree with loving appreciation." Leaves 8"–25" long; leaflets (7) 15–27 (41). Records: 125' × 13'0" Abbotsbury, Dorset, England (1986); 115' × 18'4" Melbury Park Dorset, England (1982); 85' × 19'11" Lacock Abbey, Wiltshire, England (1987); 84' × 9'7" × 68' Bel Air, MD (1990); a trunk 21'6" around in Cave Hill Cemetery, Louisville, KY (ca. 1980).

P. japonica—see P. stenoptera

P. rhoifolia S. & Z.

JAPANESE WINGNUT. From Japan. Japanese: *Sawagurumi*. Named in 1845, from Latin *rhus, rhois*, the SUMACH (genus *Rhus*), and *folium*, a leaf, because of the leaf resemblance. Introduced in 1888. Exceedingly rare. Leaves 8"–20" long; leaflets 11–21. Records: to 100' tall in the wild; 72' × 6'4" Singleton Abbey, West Glamorgan, Wales (1982); 69' × 19'10" × 90' Vineland, Ontario (ca. 1982).

P. sinensis—see P. stenoptera

P. stenoptera C. DC.
= *P. sinensis* hort. *ex* Rehd.
= *P. japonica* hort. *ex* Dipp.

CHINESE WINGNUT. From China, where it pioneers on floodplains, gulches, and river isles. Introduced in 1860 by Siebold to Holland. Named in 1862 (Greek *stenos*, narrow, and *pteron*, a wing or feather). In North America ≤1896; sold here ≤1920. Rare. The hardiest species according to the Morton Arboretum; other sources have indicated to the contrary. Easily distinguished by its narrow seed wings. Leaves 8"–15" long; leaflets 11–25; stem winged. Records: 98½' × 15'0" Paris, France (1982; *pl.* 1895); 87' × 9'6" × 73' Philadelphia, PA (1980); 85' × 9'6" Dyffryn, Glamorgan, Wales (1988); 77' × 11'3" Berkeley, CA (1989; *pl.* 1935).

Pterostyrax

[STYRACACEÆ; Storax Family] 3–4 spp. of deciduous trees, all in eastern Asia. From Greek *pteron*, a wing or feather, and genus *Styrax*. So named because of the winged seeds of *P. corymbosa*. Prized for their fragrant, attractive white flowers in late spring. Related genera include *Halesia* (SILVERBELL), *Rehderodendron*, and *Styrax* (SNOWBELL).

P. corymbosa S. & Z.
= *Halesia corymbosa* Nichols.

SMOOTHBARK EPAULETTE TREE. LITTLE EPAULETTE TREE. From E China and Japan. Named in 1839. Introduced in 1850. In North American commerce ≤1887. Very rare. Leaf recalls that of YULAN (*Magnolia denudata*) in size and shape: to 7¾" × 4½"; minute pinhead-like teeth dot the margins. Scurfy twigs, buds and leaf surfaces. Fall color golden-yellow, coloring after *P. hispida* is naked. Flowers white, in 3"–5" clusters of 20–30, from early May into June; lemony or soapy-scented. Bark taut and smooth. Record: 55' × 4'5" × 41' Seattle, WA (1989).

P. hispida S. & Z.
= *Halesia hispida* (S. & Z.) Mast.

EPAULETTE TREE. FRAGRANT EPAULETTE TREE. WISTERIA TREE. From China and Japan. Named in 1846 (Latin meaning provided with stiff or bristly hairs). Introduced in 1862 to Russia, in 1875 to Western Europe. In North American commerce ≤1888. Uncommon. Young seedclusters of June and July are bristly and do suggest the name EPAULETTE TREE aptly. BOXELDER (*Acer Negundo*) female seeds hang in a somewhat similar way. Bark corky and furrowed as on *Halesia* (SILVERBELL). Leaves long and pointy, to 11½" × 6". Twigs hairless, slightly glaucous. Flowers fragrant, creamy white, in 4"–10" hanging clusters from late May into June. Despite the name WISTERIA TREE, the flowers are more like those of the shrub genus *Deutzia*. Seeds with bristly hairs. Tree often multitrunked and suckering from the base. Records: to 56' × 6'6" in the wild; 53' tall × (multitrunked) × 60' wide Seattle, WA (1993; *pl.* 1948).

P. psilophylla Diels *ex* Perk.

SMOOTHLEAF EPAULETTE TREE. From W Hupeh, China. Named in 1907 (Greek *psilo*, bare or bald, and *phyllon*, a leaf). Sold ≤1993 by Piroche Plants of Pitt Meadows, B.C. Recorded to 65½' tall in the wild. A specimen of independent origin raised from seed in 1983 is 23' × 1'0" (1994) and very vigorous in Seattle. Its habit and foliage are almost identical to *P. corymbosa*, but leaves (to 7½" × 3⅞") slightly less hairy. Recorded to 82' tall in the wild.

Pyrus

(*Pirus*)

[ROSACEÆ; Rose Family] 20–30 (60) spp. of Old World trees. From *pirum* or *pyrum*, a pear, and *pirus* or *pyrus*, A PEAR TREE; the ancient Latin names. Many other *Pyrus* names have been applied to members of *Malus* (CRABAPPLE), *Sorbus* (MOUNTAIN ASH), etc. As ornamentals, PEARS have been planted in large quantity only in recent decades. Identification of many species and hybrids is difficult. The flowers are always small, creamy-white or white (rarely pinkish), in spring, in clusters, and do not even begin to show the delightful diversity in color, size and scent of those borne by *Malus* (CRABAPPLES). The fruit is almost never decorative, or is but fleetingly or barely so. It is primarily for summer foliage that most PEARS are valued in the landscape; some have outstanding fall color as well.

P. × *adstringens*—see *Malus* × *adstringens*

P. aldenhamensis—see *Malus* × *purpurea* 'Aldenhamensis'

P. americana—see *Sorbus americana*

P. angustifolia—see *Malus angustifolia*

P. Aria—see *Sorbus Aria*

P. × *arnoldiana*—see *Malus* × *arnoldiana*

P. × *atrosanguinea*—see *Malus* × *atrosanguinea*

P. aucuparia—see *Sorbus aucuparia*

P. baccata—see *Malus baccata*

P. baccata cerasifera—see *Malus* × *robusta*

P. baccata var. *mandshurica*—see *Malus baccata* var. *mandshurica*

P. betulæfolia Bge.
(*betulifolia*)

BIRCHLEAF PEAR. From N China. Named in 1835, from genus *Betula* (BIRCH), and Latin *folium*, a leaf. Introduced to France ca. 1865 by Simon. Introduced to North America ca. 1882 by E. Bretscheider. In commerce here since ≤1940s. Uncommon. Leaves coarsely and sharply toothed, bright green above, silvery-green beneath. Juvenile leaves can be lobed. Fruit green-brown, ≤½", 2 (3) seeded, without grit cells. Records: to 65½' tall in Anhwei, China (1925); ca. 50' tall × 5'3" × 60' China (1982).

P. betulæfolia Dancer™ PP 7033 (1989)
= *P. betulæfolia* 'Southworth'
= *P. betulæfolia* 'Paradise'

Introduced by Discov-Tree Research of Oquawka, IL. In production by several major wholesale tree nurseries. The long leafstem permits "dancing in the slightest breeze." Good fireblight resistance. Fruit sparse.

P. betulæfolia 'Paradise'—see *P. betulæfolia* Dancer™

P. betulæfolia 'Southworth'—see *P. betulæfolia* Dancer™

P. × *Bretschneideri* Rehd.
(*P. pyrifolia* × *P. betulæfolia*)

From N China. Introduced to North America ca. 1882 by Emil Bretscheider (1833–1901). Exceedingly rare. Named in 1915. Leaves finely and sharply toothed. Fruit variable, can be 1⅛" long; usually yellow. The 1993 catalog of Lake County nursery of Perry, OH, says "35' tall, slender oval crown; ⅓" yellowish-brown fruit." Record: 38' tall at Lisle, IL (1986; *pl.* 1922).

P. brevipes—see *Malus brevipes*

P. Calleryana Decne.

CALLERY PEAR. FLOWERING PEAR. From China, Taiwan, Viet Nam, and Japan. Collected in 1858 by the missionary Joseph Maxine Marie Callery (1810–1862); named in 1872. In 1908 introduced by E. Wilson to the Arnold Arboretum from Hupeh, China. Common in cultivation. Naturalized in Maryland. Flowers in March and April. Leaves subtly toothed, hairless or scantily hairy when young, 1½"–3" long, usually glossy and attractive all summer. Fall color often superb, from late October, November and into mid-December. Fruit ½"–⅝", 2 (3) seeded, with grit cells. Branches can be somewhat thorny; most cultivars are thornless. Record (see also *P. Calleryana* 'Bradford'): 55' × 8'6" × 50' Philadelphia, PA (1980).

P. Calleryana Aristocrat™ PP 3193 (1972)

Selected in 1969 from seedlings planted in 1966 by W.T. Straw of Carlisle nursery, Independence, KY. Introduced in 1973–74. Common. Leaves narrow, glossy, wavy, cupped, brilliant purple-red to orange in fall. Narrow branch crotches resist storm breakage. Grows fast. Of open, broad, horizontal habit yet strongly pyramidal form overall. More fruitful than many cultivars. Good disease resistance, except very fireblight susceptible.

P. Calleryana 'Autumn Blaze' PP 4591 (1980)

Selected in 1969 at Oregon State University, Corvallis. Originally called "Oregon Pear Rootstock 250." Introduced in 1980. Common. Right-angle lateral branches form a broad crown. Fruit sparse, persistent. More cold-hardy than most cultivars. Fall color relatively early, brilliant red. Somewhat thorny.

P. Calleryana 'Bradford'

BRADFORD PEAR. Selected from seeds purchased in Nanking, China, in 1919 (not, as is usually stated, from 1918 F. Meyer seeds). Named for Frederick Charles Bradford (1887–1950), former director of the USDA Plant Introduction Station of Glenn Dale, MD. Introduced ca. 1950. Name published in 1963 (though in use before then). Common, but less planted now than formerly, because it often splits in age, and better cultivars are now sold. Branches thornless. Wider crowned than many newer cultivars. Fall color late, brilliant red-crimson. Some nurseries have sold seedlings under this name. Record: 59' × 4'8" × 62' Bowie, MD (1990).

P. Calleryana Burgundy Snow™
= *P. Calleryana* 'Bursnozam'

Introduced ≤1991 by Lake County nursery of Perry, OH. "To 40' tall. By far the heaviest blooming of our ornamental pears; pure white flowers burgundy-centered; ⅞" cinnamon fruit."

P. Calleryana 'Bursnozam'—see *P. Calleryana* Burgundy Snow™

P. Calleryana 'Capital'

Originated in Glenn Dale, MD, as a 1960 seedling from an open-pollinated 'Bradford' PEAR. Selected by the USDA in 1969. Described and introduced in 1981. Common. Crown narrow, said to grow to 18' tall and 4' wide, then broaden to ca. 35' tall and 12' wide. Bright purplish-red or bronzy-red fall color. Fruits are small and inoffensive. Fireblight resistant. Branches thornless.

P. Calleryana Chanticleer® PP 2489 (1965)

= *P. Calleryana* 'Cleveland Select'
= *P. Calleryana* 'Select'
= *P. Calleryana* 'Glen's Form'

Selected in 1959 by Scanlon nursery of Ohio. The original specimen was on public property as a street-tree in Cleveland. Marketed as "the pear, Chanticleer, something to crow about." Introduced in 1965. Common. Very tightly narrow pyramidal; formal. The several synonyms cited have not been used exclusively for one clone, because while most "Chanticleer" trees are narrow pyramidal trees, some are practically columnar. Fall color usually red-purple.

P. Calleryana 'Cleprizam'—see *P. Calleryana* Cleveland Pride®

P. Calleryana Cleveland Pride®

= *P. Calleryana* 'Cleprizam'

Introduced ≤1991 by Lake County nursery of Perry, OH. "To 30' tall. Salmon-pink new leaves; rich burgundy in fall; ¼" tan fruit. Good urban sreet tree." The name refers to the royalties, which are dedicated to scholarships for Cleveland children.

P. Calleryana 'Cleveland Select'—see *P. Calleryana* Chanticleer®

P. Calleryana 'DTR101'—see *P. Calleryana* Pzazz™

P. Calleryana 'Earlyred'

= *P. Calleryana* 'Simpson Red'

Introduced ≤1988 by Simpson nursery of Vincennes, IN.

P. Calleryana var. *Fauriei*—see *P. Fauriei*

P. Calleryana Frontier™

= *P. Calleryana* 'Fronzam'

Introduced ≤1991 by Lake County nursery of Perry,

OH. "To 35' tall. Hardiest of our pears; ⅞" tan fruit; very upright; foliage dark midnight-green."

P. Calleryana 'Fronzam'—see *P. Calleryana* Frontier™

P. Calleryana Gladiator™

= *P. Calleryana* 'Gladzam'

Introduced ≤1991 by Lake County nursery of Perry, OH. "To 40' tall. Most vigorous of our pears; ⅞" tan fruit."

P. Calleryana 'Gladzam'—see *P. Calleryana* Gladiator™

P. Calleryana 'Glen's Form'—see *P. Calleryana* Chanticleer®

P. Calleryana f. *graciliflora* Rehd.

Named in 1920 at the Arnold Arboretum, where it had been raised from seeds obtained in 1907 in Hupeh, China. Introduced to commerce ≤1940 by W.B. Clarke nursery of San José, CA. Exceedingly rare. Compared to typical *P. Calleryana*, flower clusters are distinctively looser and more slender; flower smaller (¾" wide), with pink rather than purple anthers. Record: 38' × 2'1" Lisle, IL (1986; *pl.* 1924).

P. Calleryana 'Mepozam'—see *P. Calleryana* Metropolitan™

P. Calleryana Metropolitan™

= *P. Calleryana* 'Mepozam'

Introduced ≤1991 by Lake County nursery of Perry, OH. "To 45' tall and 35' wide. Extremely vigorous; for use in large spacious areas; ⅞" tan fruit."

P. Calleryana 'Orchard Park'

Introduced ≤1993 by Schichtel nursery of Orchard Park, NY. Said to grow 30' tall and 15' wide.

P. Calleryana Princess™

Introduced in 1976 by Scanlon nursery of Ohio. The parent tree then ca. 28' tall and wide. "A better round form than 'Bradford' PEAR and considerably hardier." Fall color orange to red. Apparently selected from a street-tree in Cleveland. Still in commerce but uncommon.

P. Calleryana Pzazz™

('Pizazz')
= *P. Calleryana* 'DTR101'

Introduced ≤1986 by Discov-Tree Research of Oquawka, IL.

P. Calleryana 'Rancho'

Selected in 1959 by Scanlon nursery of Ohio. Introduced in 1964–65. Out of commerce. Broadly columnar and formal, at least while young, then broadly pyramidal. Fall color plum, 10 days before *P. Calleryana* 'Chanticleer'.

P. Calleryana 'Redspire' PP 3815 (1975)

Introduced in 1975 by Princeton nursery of New Jersey. Common. A 'Bradford' PEAR seedling that goes dormant earlier in fall, escaping damage from early frosts. Larger flowers, but fewer of them. Narrow-oval crown. Fall color crimson and purple. Very fireblight susceptible.

P. Calleryana 'Select'—see P. Calleryana Chanticleer®

P. Calleryana 'Simpson Red'—see P. Calleryana 'Earlyred'

P. Calleryana 'Stone Hill'

Origin and attributes disputed. W. Wandell credits it to Ed Shelte, and equates it with *P. Calleryana* Chanticleer® and 'Cleveland Select'. Several major wholesale tree nurseries offer it.

P. Calleryana Trinity® PP 4530 (1980)

= *P. Calleryana* 'XP-005'

Introduced 1971–72 by Handy nursery of Portland, OR. Common. Crown rounded. Flowers profuse. Leaves very glossy, orange to red in fall. Fruit very sparse, to ⅝" long.

P. Calleryana Valiant® PP 8050 (1992)

= *P. Calleryana* 'Valzam'

Introduced ≤1991 by Lake County nursery of Perry, OH. "A shorter, more compact 'Cleveland Select' selection, among first to show fall color—crimson red; ¼" tan fruit."

P. Calleryana 'Valzam'—see P. Calleryana Valiant ®

P. Calleryana 'Whitehouse'

Selected in 1969 from open-pollinated *P. Calleryana* 'Bradford' seed, at Glenn Dale, MD. Named after Dr. William Edwin Whitehouse (1893–1982), USDA horticulturist and plant explorer; one of the men responsible for introducing 'Bradford'. Described in 1977; introduced in 1978. Common. Narrow-pyramidal, becoming oval. Early purple-red fall color, long persisting. Fruit sparse, at least when not planted near other PEARS.

P. Calleryana 'XP-005'—see P. Calleryana Trinity®

P. cathayensis—see Pseudocydonia sinensis

P. 'Charlottae'—see Malus coronaria 'Charlottae'

P. communis L.

COMMON PEAR TREE. EUROPEAN PEAR. DOMESTIC PEAR. ORCHARD PEAR. From Europe, W Asia; of unknown, partly hybrid origin. Possible parents include: *P. pyraster*, *P. salvifolia*, *P. nivalis*, *P. austriaca*. Grown for fruit, not ornament. Introduced to North America <1600. Berckmans' nursery in 1861 had 1,300 cultivars for sale! Flowers in March or April. Leaves subtly toothed, dark and glossy, 2"–4" long, hairy when young. Fruit 1¾"–5½" long, 5 seeded, with grit cells, calyx persists. Giant old PEARS can bear as many as 150 bushels per year. Records: 108' × 5'9" Zawada, Poland (≤1973); 75' × 9'9" × 70' Leslie County, KY (1987); 65' × 7'0" × 60' London, England (≤1920); 59' × 14'6" × 56' Lowden, WA (1990); 57' × 11'10" × 50' Wayne County, MI (1976); 48' × 17'8" × 52' Essex County, Ontario (1979).

P. coronaria—see Malus coronaria

P. cratægifolia—see Malus florentina

P. Cydonia—see Cydonia oblonga

P. × Dawsoniana—see Malus × Dawsoniana

P. diversifolia—see Malus fusca

P. discolor—see Sorbus discolor

P. domestica—see Sorbus domestica

P. 'Dropmore'

('Pioneer' PEAR × *P. ussuriensis*)

Introduced ≤1958 by Dropmore nursery of Manitoba. Sold by that firm until 1968.

P. × Eleyi—see Malus × Eleyi

P. Fauriei Schneid.

= *P. Calleryana* var. *Fauriei* (Schneid.) Rehd.

KOREAN FLOWERING PEAR. KOREAN PEA PEAR. From Korea. Named in 1906, after Père Urbain Faurie (1847–1915), French missionary in Japan, Taiwan and Korea. Introduced in 1918 by E. Wilson. Since the 1980s, the name at least has been common in commercial listings, but often the clones supplied are mislabeled, being really *P. Calleryana*. Authentic *P. Faurei* differs from CALLERY PEAR as follows: leafs-out before blooming; flowers appear later in spring, are smaller, fewer per cluster; fruit without grit cells; tree broad, shrubby and never thorny; defoliates much earlier in fall. Fruit ca. ⁹⁄₁₆" long, first olive green with prominent beige dots, and firm; then black inside and out, soft, with 2–3 seeds; tart. Leaves small (to 2³⁄₈" × 1¹⁄₂"), finely hairy beneath. Fall color reddish. Records: to 35' tall and wide in the wild; 20' × 1'10" × 25¹⁄₂' Seattle, WA (1994; *pl.* 1968).

P. florentina—see *Malus florentina*

P. floribunda—see *Malus × floribunda*

P. floribunda atrosanguinea—see *Malus × atrosanguinea*

P. fusca—see *Malus fusca*

P. germanica—see *Mespilus germanica*

P. × Halliana—see *Malus × Halliana*

P. × Hartwigii—see *Malus × Hartwigii*

P. heterophylla—see *Malus × heterophylla* and *Pyrus Regelii*

P. hupehensis—see *Malus hupehensis*

P. intermedia—see *Sorbus intermedia*

P. intermedia var. latifolia—see *Sorbus × latifolia*

P. ioensis—see *Malus ioensis*

P. ioensis texana Blanco™—see *Malus ioensis* Blanco™

P. Kaido—see *Malus × micromalus*

P. kansuensis—see *Malus kansuensis*

P. Kawakamii—see *P. taiwanensis*

P. Lemoinei—see *Malus × purpurea* 'Lemoinei'

P. × magdeburgensis—see *Malus × magdeburgensis*

P. Malus—see *Malus × domestica*

P. Malus 'Pendula'—see *Malus* 'Elise Rathke'

P. Malus var. sylvestris—see *Malus sylvestris*

P. microcarpa var. robusta—see *Malus × robusta*

P. × micromalus—see *Malus × micromalus*

P. Niedzwetskyana—see *Malus Sieversii* 'Niedzwetskyana'

P. nivalis Jacq.
= *P. nivea* hort.

SNOW PEAR. SNOW TREE. From central and SE Europe. Named in 1774 (Latin for snowy, referring to the wooly white hairs on the young shoots and leaves). Cultivated since 1800. Introduced to North American commerce ≤1963–64 (the year Scanlon nursery of Ohio offered it). Exceedingly rare. A small, round-topped tree. Leaves 2"–3" long, subtly toothed or untoothed, wooly-white when young. Fruit to 2¹⁄₄" long, 5 seeded, with grit cells; calyx persists. Records: to 65¹⁄₂' tall in the wild; 39' × 2'10¹⁄₂' Lisle, IL (1986; *pl.* 1935).

P. nivea—see *P. nivalis*

P. Parkmanii—see *Malus × Halliana* 'Parkmanii'

P. × platycarpa—see *Malus × heterophylla*

P. Prattii—see *Malus Prattii*

P. prunifolia—see *Malus prunifolia*

P. pulcherrima—see *Malus × floribunda*

P. pumila—see *Malus × domestica*

P. × purpurea—see *Malus × purpurea*

P. pyrifolia (Burm. fil.) Nakai
= *P. serotina* Rehd.
= *P. sinensis* auct., non Decne., Poir., Lindl.

ORIENTAL PEAR TREE. JAPANESE PEAR. CHINESE PEAR. PEKING PEAR. APPLE PEAR. ASIAN PEAR. SAND PEAR. From China. Originally named *Ficus pyrifolia* (the PEAR-leaf FIG) in 1768. The East Asian edible PEAR. Introduced to North America ca. 1840. Common as a food plant, not planted for ornament. Still, some cultivars can have breathtaking orange fall color. Flowers earlier in spring than EUROPEAN PEAR (*P. communis*), but if pollinated by early-blooming European trees, hybrid offspring can be produced (such as cultivars 'Kieffer' and 'LeConte'). Fruit roundish, 1¾" wide or more, 5 seeded, with grit cells confined to the core. Leaves 3"–6" long, finely, sharply toothed. Recorded to 50' tall in the wild.

P. pyrifolia var. *culta* (Mak.) Nakai

Cultivars with superior fruit go under this general name. Hence virtually all *P. pyrifolia* specimens sold. Record: 40' × 4'10" × 47' Mountlake Terrace, WA (1993).

P. Regelii Rehd.

= *P. heterophylla* Reg. & Schm. 1878, non (Spach) Steud. 1841

From E Turkestan, on dry stony slopes. Discovered <1878 by Johann Albert von Regel (1845–1908), physician, plant explorer. Introduced ca. 1891 by Dr. Dieck of Zoeschen, Germany. Named after Regel in 1939. Exceedingly rare in North America; here since ≤1896. Fruit ¾"–1⅓" long and wide, 5 seeded, with grit cells, very tart and sticky; calyx persists. Leaves highly variable, subtly to coarsely toothed, often very deeply and elegantly lobed; hairless except when young, shiny. A shrub or small 40' tree. Thorns abundant, slender. Tree extremely drought-tolerant.

P. Regelii Angel Wing®

Introduced ≤1988–89 by Pacific Coast nursery of Portland, OR. Uncommon. "Dense light green willowy leaves. Large pinkish-white flowers." Valued for elegant gray-green summer foliage, as its fall color is negligible.

P. Ringo—see *Malus prunifolia* var. *Rinki*

P. Ringo var. *Kaido*—see *Malus* × *micromalus*

P. × *robusta*—see *Malus* × *robusta*

P. salicifolia Pall.

WILLOWLEAF PEAR. SILVER PEAR. From SW Asia (wrongly cited also in SE Europe). In 1780 its discoverer P.S. Pallas introduced it to Britain by sending seeds to J. Banks. In North America ≤1863. Very rare until the late 1980s, when the clone 'Pendula' became popular. The tree is always somewhat loosely pendulous. Perhaps more than one 'Pendula' clone has circulated. The following description is based on wild *P. salicifolia* specimens: A shrub or small tree ca. 30' tall. Thorns abundant. Leaves narrow (*salicifolia* from genus *Salix*, WILLOW, and Latin *folium*, a leaf),

to 3½" × ¾", untoothed, silvery with hairs, recalling from a distance RUSSIAN OLIVE (*Elæagnus angustifolia*). Grows on dry stony sites; drought and frost resistant; has abundant root-suckers. Fruit sweet but has grit cells, is globose or pear-shaped, to ¾" (1³⁄₁₆") long, 5 seeded, downy at first, then hairless, golden or yellow-brown; calyx persists; stem thick, shorter than the body of the fruit. Cultivated trees tend to produce larger fruit and fewer, if any, thorns, so may be hybrids. Moreover, seedlings from cultivated *P. salicifolia* specimens, says M. Hadfield, "produce almost without exception common wild PEARS." A specimen of so-called *P. salicifolia* raised from seed (from Kew, England) at the Seattle arboretum, has leaves as large as 4" × 1½" and yellow fruit to 2¼" × 1¾". Seedlings of this Seattle tree make green, roundish, hairless leaves. Records: 46' tall at Holland Park, London, England (≤1984); 45' × 4'0" Victoria Park, London, England (≤1920).

P. salicifolia 'Argentea Pendula'—see *P. salicifolia* 'Pendula'

P. salicifolia 'Glauca Pendula'—see *P. salicifolia* 'Pendula'

P. salicifolia 'Pendula'

= *P. salicifolia* 'Argentea Pendula'
= *P. salicifolia* Silver Frost®
= *P. salicifolia* 'Silver Cascade'
= *P. salicifolia* 'Silfrozam'
= *P. salicifolia* 'Glauca Pendula'

WEEPING WILLOWLEAF PEAR. Cultivated since 1854 in Germany. Probably in North American commerce in the late 1800s, certainly ≤1905. Only common since ca. 1984. This clone (or these clones if indeed several exist) is/are the common manifestation of *P. salicifolia*. Flowerbuds red-tipped, open creamy-white. Fruit greenish-yellow, pear-shaped, to ca. 1½" long. Topgrafted to make a small, sprawling tree wider than tall. Records: 36' × 4'0" East Bergholt Place, Suffolk, England (1972); 18' × 2'5" × 20' Vancouver, B.C. (1994).

P. salicifolia 'Silfrozam'—see *P. salicifolia* 'Pendula'

P. salicifolia 'Silver Cascade'—see *P. salicifolia* 'Pendula'

P. salicifolia Silver Frost®—see *P. salicifolia* 'Pendula'

P. Sargentii—see *Malus Sargentii*

P. Scheideckeri—see *Malus* × *Scheideckeri*

P. serotina—see *P. pyrifolia*

P. serrulata Rehd.
From central China. May be a hybrid between *P. Calleryana* and *P. pyrifolia*. Introduced in 1907. Named in 1915. Sold during the 1940s by Kohankie nursery of Painesville, OH. Extremely rare. Fruit roundish, ½"–¾" wide, ripening brown. In early November the leaves are yellow, rosy and green. The epithet *serrulata* refers to the finely, sharply toothed leaves (2"–4½" long). Record: 26' × 1'4" × 18' Lisle, IL (1986; *pl.* 1972).

P. Sieboldii—see *Malus Sieboldii*

P. sikkimensis—see *Malus sikkimensis*

P. sinensis—see *P. pyrifolia* and *P. ussuriensis*

P. Smithii—see × *Cratæmesplius Smithii*

P. Sorbus—see *Sorbus domestica*

P. Soulardii—see *Malus* × *Soulardii*

P. spectabilis—see *Malus spectabilis*

P. spectabilis floribunda Scheideckeri—see *Malus* × *Scheideckeri*

P. spectabilis var. *Kaido*—see *Malus* × *micromalus*

P. × *sublobata*—see *Malus* × *sublobata*

P. sylvestris—see *Malus sylvestris*

P. taiwanensis Iketani & Ohashi
= *P. Kawakamii* Hay.—misapplied
EVERGREEN PEAR. From Taiwan. Named in 1911 after Takiya Kawakami (1871–1915). But in 1993 botanists declared that the name *P. Kawakamii* of B. Hayata, as originally applied, was only a synonym of *P. Calleryana*, so therefore a new name was needed: *P. taiwanensis* (of Taiwan—the only *Pyrus* endemic there). In California commerce since ≤1923, but only common since ca. 1940. Primarily represented by a grafted clone, grown less now than formerly because it is fireblight-prone. A low, wide, leaderless tree of irregular shape. Bark thick, dark, deeply checked. Leaves thick, stiff, strongly glossy, teeth sharp and jagged, margin wavy; to 4" × 2⅞"; stem to 1⅞" long. Semi-deciduous, defoliating in January in cold regions. Flowers 1³⁄₁₆" wide, can bloom sporadically beginning in November, mostly appear January–March. Fruit small (¾"–1³⁄₁₆" long) and sparse; usually without viable seeds in the common clone. Record: 37½' × 3'2" × 24' Redlands, CA (1993).

P. theifera—see *Malus hupehensis*

P. Toringo—see *Malus Sieboldii*

P. toringoides—see *Malus toringoides*

P. transitoria—see *Malus transitoria*

P. Tschonoskii—see *Malus Tschonoskii*

P. ussuriensis Maxim.
= *P. sinensis* Decne. 1871–72, non Lindl. 1826
USSURI PEAR. MANCHURIAN PEAR. HARBIN PEAR. From NE China, Korea, the Ussuri region of the Russian Far East, and Japan. Introduced to cultivation in 1855 in St. Petersburg, Russia. Named in 1857. Introduced to Canada ≤1897; to the U.S. in 1908 by N. Hansen of South Dakota. Initially used as a very cold-hardy rootstock, hardier than *P. betulæfolia* or *P. Calleryana*. Sold for its intrinsic value as a landscape tree since ≤1927 in Manitoba. Still very rarely grown for ornament, and valued only where *P. Calleryana* is too cold-tender. Foliage handsome, but fruit relatively large and messy, the branches can be thorny, and the tree grows too large for many sites. Fruit highly variable in size, ⅝"–2½", 5 seeded, with grit cells; calyx persists; dull dingy green or golden-green, apple-shaped; pulp crisp and sweet, flavor can be delicious. Leaves hairy when young, coarsely and sharply toothed; fall color pale orange, reddish or rich bronze and purple. The first PEAR to bloom in spring. Records: to 98½' tall in Manchuria; 75' tall and wide in Korea; trunks to 14'0" around; 52' × 5'3" × 60' Lisle, IL (1986; *pl.* 1926); 37' × 7'6" × 55' Glastonbury, CT (1988).

P. ussuriensis var. *champali* hort.
Introduced ≤1940 by W.B.Clarke nursery of San José, CA. Long commercially extinct, and nothing known of it other than Clarke's description: "bears white flowers in large rounded clusters, which at a distance look much like those of Snowball; brilliant orange and red fall color."

P. ussuriensis 'McDermand'
A seed-grown cultivar—minimal variation observed in offspring. Released in 1990 by the U.S. Soil Conservation Service. Originated ultimately with seeds N. Hansen brought in 1924 from near Harbin, Manchu-

ria. In 1954, Dr. John McDermand, with the S.C.S. in Bismarck, ND, obtained seeds of this background from Morden, Manitoba, and after testing the offspring, found the selection worth recommending for windbreaks, wildlife value, etc. Fruit tends to be 1⅛"–1½" and ripe in September.

P. ussuriensis 'MorDak'—see P. ussuriensis Prairie Gem

P. ussuriensis Prairie Gem®

= P. ussuriensis 'MorDak'

Introduced by North Dakota State University of Fargo. In commerce ≤1991. Described by Bailey nursery of St. Paul, MN, as "more rounded than USSURI PEAR, with thick, leathery leaves, of golden-yellow fall color. 25' tall." Fruit ca. 1⅓" and only produced if a different tree pollinates it. Good fireblight resistance. Crown dense, even, and oval.

P. Van Eseltinei—see Malus 'Van Eseltine'

P. Veitchii—see Malus yunnanensis var. Veitchii

P. yunnanensis—see Malus yunnanensis

P. Zumi—see Malus × Zumi

Quercus

[FAGACEÆ; Beech Family] 500–600 spp. of widely distributed trees known as OAKS. Quercus is the ancient Latin name. OAKS can be evergreen or deciduous, shrubby or monumentally large. Their wood is usually strong, has been invaluable for shipbuilding and other important purposes. The bark of some species has been important in tanning and for cork. OAKS frequently possess a branching pattern of horizontal and twisting limbs evocative of grand strength. Since the genus is so large, much variation exists. The flowers are wind-pollinated and usually go unnoticed by most people. The only constant feature is the reproductive unit, a cupped nut called the acorn (from "ac cern" = oak corn). At least in North America, OAKS are often classified in three general categories. WHITE OAK acorns usually mature in one year, and the leaf lobes (if any) are comparatively blunt; the bark is usually pale; the young foliage in spring is often pinkish, red or bronzy; some species in the WHITE OAK

group are called CHESTNUT OAKS because of their leaf shape. RED or BLACK OAK acorns usually mature in two years, the leaf lobes are bristly; the bark is usually dark; the young foliage in spring is often yellowish; and all species are American; some species in the RED OAK group are called LAUREL or WILLOW OAKS because of their leaf shape. LIVE OAKS are evergreen, and belong to either the WHITE or RED groups. The following pages treat a total of 60 species and 6 hybrids. The group counts are: 20 LIVE, 16 regular WHITE, 8 CHESTNUT WHITE, and 16 RED species. Several small-scale U.S. nurseries offer seedlings of some dozen or two additional species. POISON OAK is neither a tree nor a Quercus. Related genera include: Castanea (CHESTNUT), Castanopsis, Chrysolepis, Fagus (BEECH), Lithocarpus, and Nothofagus (SOUTHERN BEECH).

Q. acuminata—see Q. Muhlenbergii

Q. acuta Th.

= Q. lævigata Bl.
= Cyclobalanopsis acuta (Th.) Oerst.

JAPANESE RED OAK (from the Japanese name Akagashi). JAPANESE EVERGREEN OAK. From China, Korea, and Japan. Introduced ca. 1878 by C. Maries to Veitch nursery of England. In North American commerce ≤1900. Uncommon. Grown mostly in the Southeast. The hardiest Japanese evergreen OAK; even hardier than the American native Q. virginiana (LIVE OAK). Nurseries have confused it with Q. glauca (RING-CUPPED OAK). Leaves to 8" × 3", unlobed and untoothed, matte or glossy dark green above, dull yellowish-green beneath, with 8–11 pairs of veins; apex elegantly narrowed (hence the name acuta). Acorns crowded on a spike; ¾" long; cup ringed. Records: to 80' tall in the wild; 49' × 5'3" Killerton, Devon, England (1984); 46' × 6'9" Caerhays, Cornwall, England (1984).

Q. acutissima Carruth.

= Q. serrata S. & Z., non Th. ex J.A. Murr.

SAWTOOTH OAK. BRISTLE TIPPED OAK. JAPANESE CHESTNUT OAK. From the Himalayas, China, Korea, and Japan. Introduced in 1833 by Siebold to Holland. To New Zealand ≤1857; to England ca. 1862. Possibly in North American commerce ≤1887, but confused with Q. glandulifera (KONARA OAK), so uncertainty reigns. Very rare until the 1950s; common since the 1980s, especially in the Southeast (promoted there partly because turkeys love eating its acorns). A broad-crowned tree. Leaves CHESTNUT-like, to 7" × 2½", with 12–19 parallel vein pairs ending in bristly teeth (acutissima from Latin acutus, sharp, and the superlative -*issima*—very sharply pointed). Late to turn color in fall and not known for autumnal beauty: usually dark gold and pale brown—some California specimens turn bright yellow. Acorns squat, to 1"; cups with loose, spreading scales. Records: to 115' tall in Japan; 75½' × 7'9" Highnam Court, Gloucestershire, England (1988); 72' × 12'6" in Japan (1994); 69' × 2'10½" Seattle, WA (1993; *pl.* 1948); 58' × 7'9" × 53' Cambridge, MA (1994); 52' × 7'4" × 42' Lisle, IL (1986; *pl.* 1933); 48' × 6'5" × 54' College Park, MD (1990); 45' × 6'2" × 62' Davis, CA (1992; *pl.* 1964).

Q. acerifolia—see *Q. Shumardii* var. *acerifolia*

Q. agrifolia Née

CALIFORNIA LIVE OAK. COAST LIVE OAK. HOLLY(-LEAVED) OAK. From California, Baja California. Named in 1801, meaning literally *field*-leaved; likely a mistake for *aqui*-folia (HOLLY-leaved). Introduced to cultivation in 1849 by K. Hartweg. Familiar and commonly cultivated in California (Oakland was named for it) and to a minor extent in coastal Oregon and Washington. Leaves HOLLY-like, stiff, evergreen, convex, thick, unlobed, spiny-toothed, to 3½" × 1¾" (yet often much smaller). Acorns slender, to 1⅝" long. Fast-growing and broad. Can be shrubby. Records: 108' × 24'10" × 129' Chiles Valley, Napa County, CA (1951); 90' × 26'0" × 132' CA (1981); 87' × 30'9" × 123' 4 miles west of Gilroy, CA (1924); 85' × 29'2" × 127' near Gilroy, CA (1976); 59' × 27'2" × 60' Green Valley, CA (1993); 50' tall and 200' wide at Hillsborough, CA (1938).

Q. alba L.

WHITE OAK. AMERICAN WHITE OAK. RIDGE WHITE OAK. FORKLEAF OAK. STAVE OAK. From the central and eastern U.S. and S Ontario and Québec. Named *alba* (from Latin for white) because of its bark. As G. Emerson explained in 1850: "The bark on the trunk is of a very light ash-color, whence it is universally known, and always called the white oak." Common in cultivation, well known and greatly revered. No other North American OAK has so many famous and historic specimens on record. The State Tree of Connecticut, Iowa and Maryland. Wood extraordinarily valuable and widely used.

Leaves usually pinkish as they unfold in spring; at maturity to 9" × 5½", deeply and gently lobed; pale beneath. Fall color purplish-red. Acorns to 1¼" long. Records: 182' × 14'6" West Feliciana Parish, LA (<1921); 150' × 18'0" Lower Wabash Valley, IN (<1875); 150' × 26'8" Madison County, NC (<1945); 149' × 15'3" × 98' Annapolis, MD (1990); 121' × 19'8" × 134' West Allegan, MI (1979); 108' × 32'2" × 160' Wye Mills State Park, MD (1972).

Q. aquatica—see *Q. nigra*

Q. arizonica Sarg.

ARIZONA (WHITE) OAK. ARIZONA LIVE OAK. From Arizona, New Mexico, Texas, Mexico. Almost never cultivated. Leaves oval, evergreen; matte dark green or blue-green above; pale yellow-gray, felted and strongly veined beneath; short-stemmed; to 4" × 2⅜", unlobed, weakly spine-toothed, tough. Acorns to 1" long. Records: to 60' × 12'6" says C. Sargent; 45' × 8'4" × 56' Santa Cruz County, AZ (1993); 37' × 11'11" × 36' the Research Ranch, AZ (1971).

Q. bambusæfolia—see *Q. myrsinæfolia*

Q. bicolor Willd.
= *Q. platanoides* Sudw.
= *Q. Prinus* var. *tomentosa* Michx.

SWAMP WHITE OAK. From the northern half of the central and eastern U.S., and extreme SE Canada. Commonly cultivated. In the WHITE OAK group. Leaves usually dark green and glossy above, pale and more or less felty beneath (hence the name *bicolor*); to 7¾" × 5½", with 5–10 shallow lobes or coarse teeth which are relatively sharp for a WHITE OAK. Fall color yellow-brown, orange or red. Acorns to 1½" long, on stalks to 4" long. A rounded tree with flaky bark, and often many twiggy tufts giving it an untidy look. Records: 139' × 19'4" × 134' Grosse Isle, MI (1986—exaggerated? The same tree was only 108' × 17'7" × 82' in 1992); a trunk 27'6" around near Bedford, PA (ca. 1930).

Q. × *bimundorum* Palm.
(*Q. robur* × *Q. alba*)

Named in 1948, based on specimens seen from Cambridge, MA (1917), near Boston, MA (1923), and near Horsham, PA (1936). The Latin name means of two (*bi-*) worlds (*mundus*)—the Old (*Q. robur*, ENGLISH OAK) and the New (*Q. alba*, WHITE OAK). This hybrid is not cultivated except in the following clone.

Q. × bimundorum Crimson Spire™
= Q. 'Crimschmidt'
= Q. Crimson Spire™

Introduced ca. 1993 by Schmidt nursery of Boring, OR. Columnar. Fall color red.

Q. borealis—see Q. rubra

Q. Buckleyi Nixon & Dore
= Q. Shumardii var. texana (Buckl.) Ashe p.p.
= Q. texana Buckl. 1873, non 1860

TEXAS RED OAK. From central Texas hill country, often on dry limestone ridges, extending north into central Oklahoma. Long known as Q. texana (which see); renamed in 1985, after Texan botanist Samuel Botsford Buckley (1809–1884). Introduced to cultivation in 1894. In U.S. commerce ≤1905. Uncommon; grown mostly in Texas. In the RED OAK group. Leaf deeply, sharply lobed, to 5½" × 5¼", scarlet in late autumn. Acorns to ¾" long. Tree often multitrunked, usually <35' tall. Bark furrowed. Record: 80' × 12'6" Mother Neff State Park, TX (1972).

Q. californica—see Q. Kelloggii

Q. Canbyi Trel.
From NE Nuevo León, Mexico. Named in 1924, after William Marriott Canby (1831–1904). Extremely rare; offered since ≤1990 by some Texas nurseries. Lone Star Growers nursery of San Antonio has marketed it as SIERRA OAK™. In the RED OAK group. Leaf vaguely recalls that of PIN OAK (Q. palustris) but much smaller and much less lobed, more or less evergreen; thin, shiny, scalloped with bristle-tipped teeth, size highly variable, from 2" × ½" to 4¼" × 1¾"; underside has hair-tufts in vein intersections. Acorns small. Tree of broad, open habit, to 50' tall or more.

Q. Castanea—see Q. Muhlenbergii

Q. castaneæfolia C.A. Mey.
(castaneifolia)

CHESTNUTLEAF OAK. PERSIAN OAK (also applied to Q. macranthera). From SW Asia. Introduced to cultivation ca. 1846. Extremely rare in North America. Praised in England as among the finest and fastest of OAKS. Leaves CHESTNUT-like (genus Castanea, CHESTNUT, and Latin folium, a leaf), to 7½" × 3", with 10–14 parallel vein pairs. Acorns to 1½" long; cup shaggy-scaled. Records: 105' × 22'0" Kew, England (1989; pl. ca. 1846); 76' × 8'7½" × 65' Davis, CA (1993; pl. 1963).

Q. Cerris L.
TURKISH OAK. TURKEY OAK. BITTER OAK (acorns particularly bitter). Turkish: Anadol Palamud Ag. From central and S Europe to SW Asia. Introduced to England in 1735. Cerris is from the ancient Latin name for this tree, cerrus. A rugged, impressive but not colorful or especially distinctive species. Planted in earlier decades of the 20th century; extremely rare in North American commerce since the 1980s. Escaped, if not naturalized, in some locales. In the WHITE OAK group. Leaves sharply toothed or shallowly lobed, usually fine-sandpaper textured above, downy beneath; to 6" × 3"; fall color late and unremarkable. Acorns to 1¼" long; cups large and bristly-fringed. Records: 141' × 25'10" Knightshayes, Devon, England (1987); 107' × 5'9" Seattle, WA (1987; pl. ca. 1909); ca. 90' × 14'5" × 111' Carclew, Cornwall, England (1928); 73' × 14'7" × 89' Philadelphia, PA (1980); 65' × 26'5" Chertsey, Surrey, England (1965); 64' × 16'6" × 77' Hartford, CT (1987).

Q. Cerris 'Variegata'
Origin shrouded in mist. B.K. Boom says this tree's proper name is 'Argenteovariegata', and it was named in 1864 in Germany. But J. Loudon of England mentions an 1836 catalog of C. Loddiges and Sons nursery listing 'Variegata'. Also there is an 1867 description of 'Aureovariegata', which may or may not be the same clone. The contemporary clone circulated as 'Variegata' has leaves variegated yellow as they unfold, becoming creamy-white at maturity. A small lovely tree, exceedingly rare. In North America ≤1968, although nearly all seem to date from the mid-1980s or more recently.

Q. chinensis—see Q. variabilis

Q. chrysolepis Liebm.
CANYON LIVE OAK. CAÑON LIVE OAK. GOLDCUP OAK. MAUL OAK. IRON OAK. From SW Oregon, California, Baja California, Nevada, Arizona, New Mexico, and Texas. Named in 1854 (from Greek chryso, gold, and lepis, a scale—it has golden-scaled acorn cups and leaf undersides). In California commerce since ≤1871. Uncommon in cultivation there, and very rarely grown in maritime Washington. The most variable western OAK, in size, leaf and acorn; the most widely distributed California OAK. Wood very valuable, strong and hard, used for maul heads. Leaves to 4"

× 2"; evergreen, dark above, golden (especially when young) or pale powder-blue beneath; unlobed, either untoothed or spiny-edged. Acorns usually 1"–2" long—some are the largest in California. A dense and dark-foliaged tree of commanding size. Records: 110' × 17'3" near Ukiah, CA (<1910); 82' × 20'9" × 75' Angeles National Forest, CA (≤1988); 72' × 33'8" × 81' Cleveland National Forest, CA (1993); 60' × 36'3" × 130' Angeles National Forest, CA (1944).

Q. *chrysolepis* ssp. *tomentella*—see Q. *tomentella*

Q. *coccinea* Muenchh.

SCARLET OAK. From the eastern U.S. Common in cultivation. Latin *coccineum* means scarlet, referring to the fall color. In the RED OAK group. Much like BLACK OAK (Q. *velutina*), but with lighter-green, thinner, leaves (to 8¼" × 6⅝"), with remarkably slender, deep, sharp lobes. Famous for deep red fall color. Intermediate in texture between its close cousins Q. *palustris* (PIN OAK) and Q. *rubra* (RED OAK). Acorns to 1" long. Records: 181' × 20'3" Lower Wabash Valley, IN (<1875); 150' × 17'10" × 128' Colbert County, AL (1978); 126' × 16'1" Fort Washington, MD (1990); 117' × 20'3" × 126' Hillsdale County, MI (1991).

Q. *coccinea* 'Knap Hill'—see Q. *coccinea* 'Splendens'

Q. *coccinea* 'Splendens'
= Q. *coccinea* 'Knap Hill'

Introduced ≤1893 by Knap Hill nursery of England. Imported to North America in 1929 by the Arnold Arboretum. In commerce here since ≤1948. Very rare. Superior fall color. A. Mitchell points out the leaves are larger than those of typical SCARLET OAK, and the undersides bear tufts of hairs at the vein intersections. Less cold-hardy than typical Q. *coccinea*: in Victoria, B.C., specimens with trunks 5"–6" thick were killed in the cold of 1968–69. Records: 92' × 7'4" London, England (1985); 79' × 8'10" Knap Hill nursery, Surrey, England (1989).

Q. *conferta*—see Q. *Frainetto*

Q. 'Crimschmidt'—see Q. × *bimundorum* Crimson Spire™

Q. Crimson Spire™—see Q. × *bimundorum* Crimson Spire™

Q. *cuneata*—see Q. *falcata*

Q. *cuspidata*—see *Castanopsis cuspidata*

Q. *Daimio*—see Q. *dentata*

Q. *darlingtonensis*—see Q. *hemisphærica*

Q. *densiflora*—see *Lithocarpus densiflorus*

Q. *dentata* Th. *ex* J.A. Murr.
= Q. *Daimio* K. Koch

DAIMYO OAK. DAIMIO OAK. (JAPANESE) EMPEROR OAK. From Mongolia, China, the S Kuriles, Korea, and Japan. Introduced to Western cultivation in 1830. Brought to North America by G.R. Hall in 1862. Extremely rare. In the WHITE OAK group. Remarkable for giant leaves, to 20" × 11¾", with bluntly rounded lobes (hence the name *dentata*) or deep undulations; downy beneath. Fall color tawny to russet. Acorns squat, ¾", in shaggy-scaled cups. Growth usually slow, crown often gaunt. Records: to 98½' tall in Japan; 75½' × 10'0" × 63' Seattle, WA (1995; *pl.* ca. 1932); 47' × 9'5" × 40' Philadelphia, PA (1975; *pl.* 1876).

Q. *dentata* 'Pinnatifida'
From Japan. Described in 1875. In North American commerce ≤1887. Exceedingly rare but in commerce. Leaves deeply dissected into narrow, crisped lobes.

Q. *digitata*—see Q. *falcata*

Q. *diversifolia*—see Q. *rugosa*

Q. Douglasii H. & A.

BLUE OAK. From California's hot, dry foothills. Named in 1840, ten years after specimens were collected by the famous Scots plant-collector David Douglas (1798–1834). Cultivated sparingly in California; scarcely ever elsewhere. In the WHITE OAK group. Leaves distinctively bluish; golden-brown fall color; to 3½" × 2"; unlobed or shallowly lobed, sinuately toothed to nearly untoothed. Acorns ¾"–1½" long. Record: 94' × 20'3" × 48' Alameda County, CA (1974).

Q. 'Dropmore'

(*Q. macrocarpa* × *Q. mongolica*)

Introduced in 1957 by Dropmore nursery of Manitoba. Extremely rare; long out of commerce. Fast growing and cold-hardy.

Q. edulis—see Lithocarpus edulis

Q. ellipsoidalis E.J. Hill

NORTHERN PIN OAK. JACK OAK. From the Great Lakes region—SE North Dakota to NW Ohio. Named in 1899 (for its ellipsoidal acorns). Introduced to cultivation in 1902. Extremely rare. Sold in the late 1980s by Siebenthaler nursery of Dayton, OH. In the RED OAK group. Rather than a species in the conventional sense, it may be a hybrid swarm originating from PIN OAK (*Q. palustris*) and BLACK OAK (*Q. velutina*), possibly with some influence of RED OAK (*Q. rubra*). Leaves to 5" × 4", sharply lobed, of unspectacular, late russet-red fall color. Acorns to ¾" long, in deep cups. Records: 86' × 11'7" × 93' Oakland County, MI (1978); 79' × 12'8" × 159' Lamham, MD (1983); 73' × 13'9½" Fairfield, WI (1984).

Q. Emoryi Torr.

EMORY OAK. From Texas, New Mexico, Arizona, and mountains of NW Mexico. Named in 1848 after its discoverer, William Hemsley Emory (1811–1887), leader of two military and scientific expeditions in the Southwest, and a Major General in the Civil War. Twigs felty. Leaves evergreen, short-stemmed, glossy rich green on both sides, thick, scarcely hairy, HOLLY-like but usually only weakly prickly; to 4" × 1¼". Acorns to ¾" long. Records: 84' × 12'4" × 84' Greenback Valley, AZ (1966); 73' × 16'6" × 98' Santa Cruz County, AZ (1976); 56' × 15'6" × 92' Santa Cruz County, AZ (1993); 43' × 20'6" × 68' Empire Ranch, AZ (1986). One planted in 1973 at Aurora, OR, remained unhurt in cold that severely injured *Q.*

agrifolia (CALIFORNIA LIVE OAK) and *Q. Suber* (CORK TREE): 40½' × 2'11½" × 27' (1993).

Q. Engelmannii Greene

ENGELMANN OAK. MESA OAK. MESA BLUE OAK. PASADENA OAK. EVERGREEN WHITE OAK. One of California's rarest OAKS. From SW California, Santa Catalina Island, and N Baja California. Named in 1889 after George Engelmann (1809–1884), German-American physician and botanist of St. Louis, MO. Very rarely cultivated, even in California. Leaves evergreen, distinctly bluish-green, usually narrow (to 4" × 1½"), bluntish, slightly uneven or weakly spiny on the margin. Acorns to 1¼" long, slender, the cup deep. Handsome native specimens thrive at the Los Angeles arboretum. Record: 78' × 10'9" × 100' Pasadena, CA (1990).

Q. falcata Michx.

= *Q. triloba* Michx.
= *Q. digitata* (Marsh.) Sudw.
= *Q. cuneata* auct., non Wangh.

SOUTHERN RED OAK. TURKEYFOOT OAK. SPANISH OAK. From the southeastern U.S., with a few more northerly populations. Not commonly cultivated. In the RED OAK group. Fall color not the fine red of many other RED OAKS. The name SPANISH OAK (not limited to this species) might have originated when settlers were reminded somehow of an OAK in Spain. The epithet *falcata* means sickle-shaped, referring to many of the leaf lobes. Leaves drooping, to 12" × 7"; base rounded, lobes sharp, slender, the central one notably long and narrow; densely hairy beneath. Acorns ½" long and wide. Record: 135' × 28'0" × 141' Harwood, MD (1983).

Q. falcata var. pagodæfolia Ell.

= *Q. pagodæfolia* (Ell.) Ashe
= *Q. pagoda* Raf.
(*pagodifolia*)

CHERRYBARK OAK. BOTTOMLAND RED OAK. SWAMP RED OAK. SWAMP SPANISH OAK. Cultivated about as frequently as typical *Q. falcata*. Often considered a distinct species. Usually grows larger, is hairier. The epithet *pagodæfolia* means with leaves shaped like the outline of a pagoda. Leaves broadly wedge-shaped at the base, whitish beneath. Bark flaky, resembling that of BLACK CHERRY (*Prunus serotina*). Records: to 130' tall; 124' × 27'0" × 136' Sussex County, VA (1991); 110' × 28'6" × 108' Virginia (1994); 105' × 27'0" × 140' South Mills, NC (1989).

Q. *Farnetto*—see Q. *Frainetto*

Q. *femina*—see Q. *robur*

Q. *Frainetto* Ten.
= Q. *conferta* Kit.
= Q. *Farnetto* Ten.
= Q. *pannonica* Booth *ex* Gord.

HUNGARIAN OAK. ITALIAN OAK. From Italy to the Black Sea. Named *Frainetto* in 1813, an error for *Farnetto*, an Italian name. Cultivated since 1800 in Holland; introduced to Britain by Lawson nursery of Edinburgh in 1838. In North American commerce ≤1888. Exceedingly rare. In the WHITE OAK group. Leaves notably variable; in Western Europe a grafted clone is grown (Hillier nursery of England proposes the name 'Hungarian Crown' for it), featuring leaves beautifully doubly-lobed, dark green, to 9¾" × 5½", very short-stemmed, hairy on both sides. Acorns ca. ¾" long. A large tree of handsome form, splendid foliage, impressive strength and no obvious faults. Records: to 131' tall in SW Asia; 115' × 12'6" Stratfield Saye, Hampshire, England (1986); 98' × 17'9" Buxted Park, Sussex, England (1990).

Q. *Frainetto* Forest Green®
= Q. *Frainetto* 'Schmidt'

Introduced ≤1989 by Schmidt nursery of Boring, OR. The only clone of Q. *Frainetto* commonly grown in North America.

Q. *Frainetto* 'Schmidt'—see Q. *Frainetto* Forest Green®

Q. *Gambelii* Nutt.
= Q. *utahensis* (A. DC.) Rydb.

UTAH WHITE OAK. ROCKY MOUNTAIN WHITE OAK. COLORADO OAK. From mountains of the southwestern U.S., and far northern Mexico. Named in 1848 after William Gambel (1821–1849) American naturalist who collected it in 1844 in the southern Rockies. Introduced to cultivation in 1894. In U.S. commerce ≤1925. Uncommon. In the WHITE OAK group. Leaves to 7" × 4", variable but usually deeply and bluntly lobed recalling Q. *alba* (WHITE OAK) in shape, and sometimes Q. *macrocarpa* (BUR OAK). Fall color yellow, orange and red. Acorns to ⅞" long. Often only a tall shrub or small tree. Records: to 75' tall; 47' × 18'3" × 85' Gila National Forest, NM (1954).

Q. *Garryana* Dougl. *ex* Hook.

OREGON WHITE OAK. WESTERN WHITE OAK. PACIFIC POST OAK. GARRY OAK. From S British Columbia to central California. Named in 1839 after Nicholas Garry (1781?–1856), an officer of the Hudson's Bay Company. Introduced to cultivation in 1873. Rarely cultivated, even within its native range. In the WHITE OAK group. Foliage remarkably dark, and the pale, deeply chunky gray bark a gratifying contrast. Twigs stout, hairy like the buds. Leaves to 6½" × 5"; lobes can be mildly pointed although not bristle-tipped. Fall color muted, rarely a memorable warm red-brown. Acorns plump, to 1¼" long. Records: to 150' tall say E. Sheldon and T. Howell; 122' × 25'2" × 133' El Dorado County, CA (1991); 120' × 25'6" near Mendocino National Forest, CA (1944); 93' × 20'7" × 106' Woodland, WA (1990).

Q. *glandulifera* Bl.
= Q. *serrata* Th. *ex* J.A. Murr., *nom. ambig.*

KONARA OAK (from *Ko-nara*, one of several Japanese names). From China, Korea, Japan, and the S Kuriles. Named in 1850, from Latin *glandula*, gland, and *ferre*, to bear. Introduced to Russian cultivation in 1864. Brought to North America in 1893 by the Arnold Arboretum. Extremely rare. Young spring growth reddish. Foliage green late into fall. Fall color mixed green, orange and red, sometimes brilliant. Leaves show baffling variation in size, shape and hairiness. Usually small and vaguely CHESTNUT-like yet proportionately broader; pale beneath, usually with a light silvery sheen of fine hairs. Vary from 2"–10" long and to 5⅜" wide; edged with 6–14 gland-tipped teeth per side; stem ¼"–1⅛" long. Twigs slender. Acorns to ½" long, short-stalked. Records: to 82' × 9'10" in the wild; 62' × 6'6" Kew, England (1984; *pl.* 1893).

Q. *glauca* Th. *ex* J.A. Murr.
= *Cyclobalanopsis glauca* (Th.) Oerst.

RING CUPPED OAK. JAPANESE BLUE OAK. BLUE JAPANESE OAK. From the Himalayas, China, Korea, Japan, the Ryukyus, and Taiwan. The commonest OAK in Japan, existing in many cultivars; often used in hedging. Introduced to Western cultivation in 1804. Uncommon. In North American commerce ≤1958. Evergreen. Leaves red-bronze when young in spring; yellow-green all winter—no justification for the name BLUE (the Japanese name *Ara-kashi* means ROUGH OAK.) Leaves to 6¼" × 2⅞", elliptic, toothed at least near the apex, with an abrupt drip-tip; glaucous and inconspicuously silky-haired beneath; 8–13 pairs of prominent parallel veins; stem yellowish. Acorns ¾" long; cup ringed. A formal-looking giant shrub or small tree with upward-swept branches, drooping leaves. Records: to 82' × 9'10" in the wild; 36' × 4'3" Caerhays, Cornwall, England (1984); 25½' × 2'2" × 23½' Seattle, WA (1994; *pl.* 1937).

Q. glaucoides Mart. & Gal.

From central and S Mexico. Named in 1843 (*glaucous*, and Greek *-oides*, resemblance—appearing to be coated with a grayish bloom). Extremely rare in cultivation; sold in Texas. Leaves evergreen; reddish when young, with yellowish hairs; maturing thick and glaucous green, to 6" × 3⅛", short-stemmed, margins undulate, untoothed or each side set with 1–7 broad and subtle teeth. Acorns to ¾" long, usually long-stalked. A small tree, usually ≤16' tall, reported at most 33' tall. See also *Q. Laceyi*.

Q. hemisphærica Bartr. ex Willd.

= *Q. laurifolia* auct., non Michx.
= *Q. laurifolia* 'Darlington'
= *Q. darlingtonensis* hort.

LAUREL OAK. DARLINGTON OAK. From the southeast U.S., only on well-drained ground. Commonly cultivated there since ca. 1816, at first largely through the efforts of W.O. Woods of Darlington, SC (where the tree was originally not native). In texture and foliage similar to WILLOW OAK (*Q. Phellos*) but with thicker, larger, more or less evergreen leaves. Frequently confused with SWAMP LAUREL OAK (*Q. laurifolia*), and some botanists unite these two species. Leaves slender, acute and minutely bristle-tipped (or blunt) at the apex; to 5" × 2" but commonly no more than 4" × 1". Bark deeply ridged, thick and dark. A large, round-headed tree. Record: 84' × 20'0" × 102' Darlington, SC (1958). (Some records listed under *Q. laurifolia* are probably actually *Q. hemisphærica*.)

Q. × heterophylla Michx. fil.
(*Q. Phellos* × *Q. rubra*)

BARTRAM OAK. BURRIER'S OAK. The original specimen of this hybrid grew on land owned by John Bartram (1699–1777), on the Schuylkill River near Philadelphia, PA. It was described botanically in 1812 (Greek *heteros*, different or other, and *phyllon*, a leaf). Although cultivated as early as 1783 in Belgium and 1822 in France, it has remained extremely rare in North America, being largely limited to arboreta and botanic gardens. It was in commerce here even in the 1800s, and it occurs spontaneously in cultivation sometimes. In the RED OAK group, and intermediate between its parents. Leaves to 7" × 3⅛". Record: 96' × 13'5" Marshalltown, Chester County, PA (1980).

Q. × hispanica Lam.
= *Q. pseudosuber* Santi
(*Q. Cerris* × *Q. Suber*)

EXETER OAK. DEVONSHIRE OAK. SPANISH OAK. The *hispanica* name was given in 1783 because it was originally thought that this hybrid came from Gibraltar, Spain. The cross does occur in the wild. Best known of many variable offspring is LUCOMBE OAK ('Lucombeana'), which arose from a *Q. Cerris* (TURKISH OAK) acorn sown in 1762 in William Lucombe's nursery at Exeter, Devonshire, England. After dying at age 98, Lucombe (1696–1794) was buried in a coffin made from the wood of his famous hybrid OAK. *Q.* × *hispanica* was introduced to the U.S. in 1830, and was in California commerce ≤1854; it has remained exceedingly rare. A specimen in Seattle has made seedlings which appear identical to itself. Leaves dark green and shiny, semi-evergreen, to 5" × 2", ovate, coarsely and sharply toothed or shallowly lobed. Bark somewhat corky. Records: 118' × 14'6" Peper Harrow, Surrey, England (1987); 82' × 25'0" Exmouth, Devon, England (1990).

Q. hypoleuca—see Q. hypoleucoides

Q. hypoleucoides A. Camus
= *Q. hypoleuca* Engelm. 1876, non Miq. 1855

SILVERLEAF OAK. WHITELEAF OAK. From the southwestern U.S., and northern Mexico. The 1932 epithet *hypoleucoides* means *hypoleuca*, and Greek *-oides*, resemblance—like *Q. hypoleuca*. Foliage evergreen, varies from comparatively fine-textured and dense, to consisting of fewer, longer leaves (to 8½" × 1¾"). In any case they are WILLOW-shaped, usually untoothed, thick and leathery, dark matte green above and startling white beneath except for greenish veins. Acorns to ⅝" long. Tree usually sparse, with upswept branches. Records: 73' × 8'1" Cochise County, AZ (1991); 69' × 10'3" × 52' Arizona (1994); 48' × 7'8" Pinos Altos, NM (1987); 42' × 4'11" Seattle, WA (1992).

Q. Ilex L.

HOLM OAK. HOLLY OAK. (THE) HOLM. From the Mediterranean region to the W Himalayas. *Ilex* is the classic Latin name for this tree. HOLM and HOLLY both evolved from the Middle English *holin*, meaning prickly. Cultivated in northwestern Europe since the 1500s. In California commerce ≤1858; now common along the Pacific Coast, from SW British Columbia to San Diego, reseeding if not naturalized in many locales. Excellent for seaside planting. One of the hardiest evergreen

OAKS. Leaves leathery, very dark green above, more or less felted and often gray beneath; the sides often rolled under; juvenile trees have HOLLY-like teeth. Leaf size usually 3" × 1" but can reach 5" × 2¼" on sucker shoots. Acorns to 1½" long, with a peculiar, thin but deep cup of close scales. The mature tree becomes monumental, but its dark color and density are forbidding. Alan Mitchell expresses it "unchanging gloom throughout the year." Simply thinning the excess foliage does wonders, making the tree airy and cheerful. Records: to 131' tall in Spain, where it is very common; 104' × 9'7" × 72' Sacramento, CA (1989; *pl.* 1870); 80' × 24'0" Chilham Castle, Kent, England (1983; *pl.* ca. 1619); 70' × 20'8" × 96' New Zealand (≤1982; *pl.* <1878); 47' × 7'0" × 55' Bainbridge, WA (1989); 46' × 28'3" Westbury Court, Gloucestershire, England (1986).

Q. Ilex 'Fordii'

PYRAMIDAL EVERGREEN OAK. Raised by Lucombe and Pince's nursery in Exeter, England. Named after Exeter nurseryman William Ford (1760–1829). Described in 1843. In North American commerce ≤1910. Exceedingly rare. Habit markedly fastigiate and narrow; leaves slender.

Q. Ilex var. *phillyræoides*—see *Q. phillyræoides*

Q. imbricaria Michx.

SHINGLE OAK. NORTHERN LAUREL OAK. From the eastern U.S. Name from Latin *imbrex*, a tile; hence imbricate or overlapping, from the use of the wood by early settlers of Illinois for shingles. D. Browne in 1832 asserted: "In the country of Illinois where it attains much greater dimensions, it is employed for shingles, probably for want of a better species, for the wood is inferior to that of the willow oak, which it nearly resembles." Uncommon in cultivation, being devoid of glamor, majesty or bright color, yet easily cultivated. In the RED OAK group. Leaves LAUREL-like in shape, but deciduous; to 8" × 3', downy beneath. Fall color golden brown or russet red. Acorns squat, to ⅔". Records: 110' × 11'3" near Waynesburg, PA (1980); 104' × 16'8" Cincinnati, OH (1989); 97' × 11'0" × 84' Hartford, CT (1987); 81' × 19'1" × 81' Wayne County, OH (1982).

Q. Kelloggii Newb.

= *Q. californica* (Torr.) Cooper

CALIFORNIA BLACK OAK. From central Oregon to N Baja California. Discovered in 1846 by K. Hartweg. Named in 1857 after Albert Kellogg (1813–1887), California physician and botanist. In California commerce ≤1871. Not commonly cultivated, even in its native land. In the RED OAK group. Compared to *Q. velutina*, the BLACK OAK of the East, this West Coast native has smaller leaves, is less colorful in fall, and its bark is slower to become conspicuously rough. Leaves to 10" × 6", sharply, elegantly lobed, persistently finely hairy. Young growth in March or April prettily reddish or purplish. Fall color brown, rosycrimson or orange-gold. Acorns massive, to 1½" long, best tasting of those in California; the cup deep. Records: to 130' tall; 124' × 28'2" × 115' below Galice, OR (1972); 80' × 32'10" near Marial, OR (1944).

Q. Laceyi Small

LACEY OAK. SMOKY OAK. CANYON OAK. ROCK OAK. TEXAS BLUE OAK. From limestone soils of south-central Texas and NE Mexico. Named in 1901 for the man who made it known to science, Howard Lacey of Lacey's Ranch near Kerrville, TX. Previously regarded as a mere variation of *Q. glaucoides* (a Mexican evergreen). Cultivated in Texas and the adjacent Southwest. Young leaves peach-pink; summer color striking smoky bluish-gray; golden in late fall. Leaves to 8¼" × 4¼" but commonly half that size; hairless; untoothed to shallowly (rarely deeply) lobed. Acorns to 1" long, short-stalked. Record: 58' × 8'11" × 96' Blanco County, TX (1989).

Q. lævigata—see *Q. acuta*

Q. laurifolia Michx.

= *Q. obtusa* (Willd.) Pursh
= *Q. rhombica* Sarg.

SWAMP LAUREL OAK. DIAMOND LEAF OAK. From the southeastern U.S., thriving in heavy soils and poor drainage. Common in cultivation. Tolerates even the wet clays of Houston, TX. Leaves thin, tardily deciduous, blunt at the apex, diamond-shaped, usually widest at the middle, to 5⅓" × 2⅓". The epithet *laurifolia* from genus *Laurus*, and Latin *folium*, a leaf. Acorns to ¾" long. Bark gray and scaly. Very similar to WATER OAK (*Q. nigra*). Confused with *Q. hemisphærica* (LAUREL OAK). Records: 148' × 20'9" Congaree Swamp, SC (1976); 102' × 19'5" × 116' Waycross, GA (1970); 93' × 22'3" × 122' Marengo County, AL (1993); a trunk 24'6" around at Highlands Hammock, FL (1935).

Q. laurifolia 'Darlington'—see *Q. hemisphærica*

Q. lobata Née

CALIFORNIA VALLEY OAK. CALIFORNIA WHITE OAK. WATER OAK (a local name of ranchers and farmers). MUSH OAK (because of its rot-prone posts). WEEPING OAK. From California, favoring moist, fertile soil in hot valleys. In commerce there ≤1871; scarcely ever planted elsewhere. Named in 1801 (from Greek *lobos*, the lobe of the ear, in reference to the leaf margin). In the WHITE OAK group. Because of the tree's great size and shape, yet comparatively small leaves on an elegant crown, it has been called the AMERICAN ELM OF CALIFORNIA. Leaves deeply bluntly lobed, finely hairy, commonly to 4" × 2", at most 6" × 3¼". Fall color late and poor. Acorns large, to 2½" long × 1⅛" wide. One of the largest of all OAKS. Records: 178' tall near Visalia, CA (ca. 1900); 163' × 29'0" × 99' south of Covelo, CA (1984); 158' × 29'2" × 125' Gridley, CA (1985); 96' × 28'3" × 153' near Chico, CA; the Hooker Oak (1944; fell 1977); trunks to 43'6" around once existed.

Q. lyrata Walt.

OVERCUP OAK. SWAMP POST OAK. WATER WHITE OAK. From the SE United States, in moist ground. Uncommon in cultivation. The epithet *lyrata* refers to its slender, lyre-shaped leaves (to 10" × 4¾"). In the WHITE OAK group; closely related to *Q. macrocarpa* (BUR OAK). Fall color yellow, orange or scarlet. Acorn highly distinctive, ¾"–1½" wide, almost wholly enclosed by the cup. Records: 156' × 21'6" × 120' Lewiston-Woodville, NC (1987); 148' × 22'4" Richland County, SC (1983); 130' × 22'9" Queen Anne, MD (1990).

Q. macranthera Fisch. & Mey. *ex* Hohen.

CAUCASIAN OAK. PERSIAN OAK (also applied to *Q. castanæfolia*). From dry mountains of the Caucasus and Transcaucasus, and N Iran. Named in 1838 (Greek *macro*, large, and *anthos*, a flower—referring to the showy anthers). Introduced to cultivation ≤1873. Exceedingly rare in North America. In the WHITE OAK group. Twigs stout and densely shaggy with long yellowish-gray hairs initially; leaves bold and handsome, golden-brown in fall. Leaves very dark green, persistently hairy beneath, to 10¼" × 7¼"; short-stemmed. The lobing recalls that of *Q. dentata* (DAIMYO OAK) and *Q. Frainetto* (HUNGARIAN OAK). Acorns 1" long. Drought resistant. Records:

102' × 8'6" Westonbirt, Gloucestershire, England (1988; *pl.* 1878); 85' × 10'5" Melbury, Dorset, England (1989).

Q. macrocarpa Michx.

BUR OAK. MOSSYCUP OAK. PRAIRIE OAK. From central and eastern North America. Commonly cultivated. The State Tree of Illinois. In the WHITE OAK group. Greek *macro*, large, and *karpos*, fruit—acorns to 2½" (even 3⅛" in Texas) long and wide. Called BUR OAK because the acorn cup is rough, shaggily fringed near its rim, and almost envelopes the acorn like a bur. Leaves often large (to 15" × 8"), deeply lobed, usually with a giant terminal portion and very narrow "waist." Fall color varies from dismal gold-brown to purple-red. Twigs often with corky ridges. A rugged, imposing tree, very cold-hardy; rejoices in hot summers, deep soil and ample moisture. Records: to 180' × 53'0" in the primeval forest; 165' × 22'0" Lower Wabash Valley, IN (<1875); 143' × 21'4" × 114' Big Oak State Park, MO (1950); 132' × 25'1" × 184' near Thorn Creek, IL(<1990); 106' × 22'0" × 124' Berrien County, MI (1975); 95' × 26'6" × 102' Paris, KY (1980).

Q. marilandica Muenchh.

= *Q. nigra* Wangh., non L.

BLACKJACK (OAK). BARREN OAK. From the central and eastern U.S., often on barren ground; a "SCRUB OAK." Rarely cultivated. In the RED OAK group. Leaves brazenly bold and unconventional, usually 6" long and wide, to 11¾6" × 10½"; widest near apex and uniquely pear-shaped. Fall color yellow, tawny, dark rusty-red, or brown. Acorns to 1" long. Usually short-trunked, with drooping branches. Records: 90' × 8'7" × 80' Greenville, SC (1991); 67' × 9'5" × 72' Caddo Parish, Louisiana (1985); 53' × 13'0" × 78' Grant County, OK (1980).

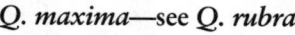

Q. maxima—see *Q. rubra*

Q. Michauxii Nutt.

= *Q. Prinus* auct., non L.

SWAMP CHESTNUT OAK. BASKET OAK. COW OAK. From the southeastern U.S. The naturalist François André Michaux (1770–1855) first described it. Very rarely cultivated. Leaves CHESTNUT-like, unlobed, widest above the middle, to 10" × 6", with softly rounded large teeth. Fall color pinkish-red to rich crimson. Acorns to 1½" long, sweet, relished by cattle. Bark pale gray, thin and scaly. Wood made into baskets. Tree tolerates wet soil. Records: 200' × 16'5" × 148' Fayette County, AL (1989); 152' × 19'8" × 111' Wayne County, NC (1987); 122' × 22'7" × 123' Myrtle Grove, MD (1972; now dead); trunks to 31'6" around once existed.

Q. minor—see Q. stellata

Q. mongolica Fisch. ex Turcz.

MONGOLIAN OAK. From much of NE Asia, although scarce in Mongolia. Cultivated since 1835 in Germany. Named in 1838. Extremely rare in North America. Leaves CHESTNUT-like; to 8" × 6"; the base with two tiny ear-like lobes; stem short (to ¼"). Records: to 120' × 16'0" in the wild; 27' × 6'5" × 38' Philadelphia, PA (1980).

Q. mongolica var. grosserrata (Bl.) Rehd. & Wils.

From Japan, Sakhalin and the S Kuriles. Introduced to the Arnold Arboretum in 1893 by C. Sargent. Rehder and Wilson doubted whether grosserrata is even varietally distinct from typical Q. mongolica; they said the "number of veins (11–16 pairs per leaf) has no significance." Leaves to 12" × 7". Fall color greenish-yellow to bright red. Acorns ¾" long. Record: 61' × 7'7" Arnold Arboretum (1972).

Q. montana—see Q. Prinus

Q. Muhlenbergii Engelm.
(Muehlenbergii)
= Q. acuminata (Michx.) Sarg., non Roxb.
= Q. Castanea Willd. April 1801, non Née March 1801
= Q. prinoides Willd. var. acuminata (Michx.) Gl.

CHINQUAPIN (CHINKAPIN) OAK. YELLOW CHESTNUT OAK. From New England to NE Mexico. Named after Gotthilf Henry Ernest Mühlenberg (1753–1815), Pennsylvania minister and botanist. Uncommon in cultivation, but adaptable to many diverse sites. Leaves CHESTNUT-like, to 9¼" × 5⅛"; very pale beneath; stem often yellowish. Fall color golden. Acorns small (to ¾") but sweet (hence the name CHINQUAPIN OAK). Records: to 160' × 31'6" in the primeval forest; 130' × 15'10" Cross County, AR (≤1960); 120' × 17'11" × 132' Ann Arbor, MI (1991); 100' × 19'4" × 103' Breckinridge County, KY (1988); 84' × 20'5" × 120' Berks County, PA (1989); 72' × 21'11" × 62' Ross County, OH (1971).

Q. myrsinæfolia Bl.
(myrsinifolia)
= Q. bambusæfolia Fort., non Hance
= Cyclobalanopsis myrsinæfolia (Bl.) Oerst.

BAMBOO LEAF OAK. JAPANESE LIVE OAK. CHINESE EVERGREEN OAK. From S China, Korea, Japan, and Laos. Named in 1850 (from genus Myrsine, and Latin folium, a leaf). Introduced to Western cultivation in 1854 by R. Fortune. Uncommon in North America, and very frequently mislabeled says B. Yinger. Leaves evergreen, purplish-red when young, at maturity long, narrow, drooping; to 5¾" × 1⅞"; inconspicuously sharply and shortly toothed near apex; pale green above, glaucous-blue beneath; hairless. Acorns to ¾" long; cup ringed. Usually dense and shrubby. Records: to 82' × 18'4" in the wild; 60' × 2'6" Leonardslee, Sussex, England (1985); 44' × 3'4" × 31' Redmond, WA (1988).

Q. nigra L., non Wangh. (see Q. marilandica)
= Q. aquatica Walt.

WATER OAK. 'POSSUM OAK. DUCK OAK. From the southeastern U.S. Common in cultivation. In the RED OAK group. Tardily deciduous or essentially evergreen. Leaves often narrowed at the base and widest above the middle, pear-shaped, sometimes shallowly three-lobed near the apex; shinier underneath than on the top side; to 7½" × 3½". Acorns to ¾" long. Growth rapid. Records: 133' × 13'4" × 100' Lincoln Parish, LA (1983); 110' × 20'2" × 122' Currituck County, NC (1983); 97' × 22'9" × 117' Monroe County, AL (1987); ?' × 26'0" × 120' Toddsburg, VA (ca. 1930).

Q. Nuttallii—see Q. texana

Q. obtusa—see Q. laurifolia

Q. pagoda—see Q. falcata var. pagodæfolia

Q. pagodæfolia—see Q. falcata var. pagodæfolia

Q. palustris Muenchh.

PIN OAK. From the central and eastern U.S. (not in the South), and S Ontario. Very commonly cultivated. The name palustris is Latin, meaning of the swamps or marshes. In the RED OAK group. Slender in all respects: trunk, limb, branch, twig, leaf—only the tiny squat acorns belie the name PIN OAK. Leaves thin and glossy, to 6" × 5¼", sharply deeply lobed. Fall color bright red. Crown often narrow and dense with numerous slender drooping branches. Acorns squat, ½" long. Records: 135' × 16'0" × 135' Saint Davids, PA (1955); 134' × 17'4" × 99' near Smithland, KY (1972); 92' × 23'3" × 104' Buckingham County, VA (1976); 81' × 22'0" × 99' Hope, IN (1981).

Q. palustris 'Crownright' PP 2936 (1969)

Introduced by Princeton nursery of New Jersey. Common. Habit relatively upright and narrow, appropriate for streetside planting.

Q. palustris 'Mills Variegated' PP 2899 (1969)

Patented by Foster Mills of Groveport, OH. Not known to be in commerce. Leaves variegated with ivory flecks.

Q. palustris 'Sovereign' PP 2662 (1966)

Selected by D.P. Cole of Mentor, OH. Mass-produced ≤1958. Commercially extinct; replaced by 'Crownright'. Habit upright.

Q. pannonica—see Q. Frainetto

Q. pedunculata—see Q. robur

Q. petræa (Matt.) Liebl.
= Q. sessiliflora Salisb.

DURMAST OAK. SESSILE OAK. From Europe, W Asia. Exceedingly rare in North America. Closely related to ENGLISH OAK (Q. robur). The name petræa (from Latin petra, rock) means growing in stony or rocky places—as on mountains where Q. robur (ENGLISH OAK) is unsuccessful. DURMAST is an English name used since the 1700s, of obscure origin. In the WHITE OAK group. Greatly variable in leaf size and shape; leaves 3"–5" long or at most 7" × 4¾", green late into fall. Acorns much like those of Q. robur, ENGLISH OAK, to 1¼" long, but shortly stalked (hence the name SESSILE OAK to contrast with the long-stemmed acorns of Q. robur). Records: 141' × 15'2" Whitfield, Herefordshire, England (1984); 85½' × 10'3½" × 79½' Seattle, WA (1994); 82' × 32'9" Shobdon, Herefordshire, England (1989); 78' × 11'4" × 82' Vancouver, B.C. (1992); 69' × 36'9" near Powis Castle, Wales, England (1989).

Q. petræa 'Columna' or 'Columnar'—see Q. × rosacea 'Columna'

Q. petræa 'Insecata'
= Q. petræa 'Laciniata' (in part)
= Q. robur 'Laciniata' (in part)

= Q. petræa 'Laciniata Crispa'

Originally described in 1893. Introduced in 1928–29 by Hesse nursery of Germany. Extremely rare in North America. Leaves more or less irregularly incised and lobed, often very narrow and drawn-out in length.

Q. petræa 'Laciniata'—see Q. petræa 'Insecata'

Q. petræa 'Laciniata Crispa'—see Q. petræa 'Insecata'

Q. petræa f. mespilifolia (Wallr.) Rehd.

Originally described in 1822; cultivated since 1843 in France. Exceedingly rare in North America. A considerable percentage of acorns breed true. The name mespilifolia from genus Mespilus, MEDLAR, and Latin folium, a leaf. Leaves narrow, mostly untoothed and unlobed, to 8" × 1⅝". Records: 80' × 9'8" Leicestershire, England (1985); a trunk 13'1" around at Sledziejowice, Poland (≤1973).

Q. petræa 'Purpurea'
= Q. petræa 'Rubicunda'

Cultivated since 1877 in the Netherlands. Described in 1884. In North American commerce ≤1910. Exceedingly rare. Growth slow. Young leaves brownish-purple, later dark reddish gray-green with red veins.

Q. petræa 'Rubicunda'—see Q. petræa 'Purpurea'

Q. Phellos L.

WILLOW OAK. PEACH OAK. PIN OAK. From the southeastern U.S. Commonly cultivated. Phellos is an ancient Greek name of the CORK TREE, Q. Suber, and for some reason Linnæus applied it to this species. In the RED OAK group. Leaves distinctively WILLOW-like or narrow (to 7" × 1⅝"). Fall color weak yellow. Acorns ½" long. A fine-textured OAK of increasing favor in landscaping. Records: 158' × 17'8" Congaree Swamp, SC (1978); 135' × 25'3" Queenstown, MD (1983; now dead); 112' × 23'3" × 114' Oxford, MD (1990); 92' × 19'4" × 124' St. Mary's City, MD (1990).

Q. phillyræoides A. Gray
= Q. Ilex var. phillyræoides (A. Gray) Franch. (phillyreoides)

UBAME OAK. Japanese: Uba-me-gashi. From China, Korea, Japan, and the Ryukyus. Named in 1859 from genus *Phillyrea*, and Greek *-oides*, resemblance. Introduced to Western cultivation in 1861 by R. Oldham. Leaves evergreen, bronzy or maroon when young. Mature leaves to 3" long; bright yellow-green and spoon-shaped; can be inconspicuously toothed, especially near apex; glossy beneath. Twigs olive-green overlaid with beige scurf. Acorns ⅝" long. Dense shrub or small tree. Records: to 50' tall in the wild; 34' × 4'11" × 35' Seattle, WA (1992).

Q. *phillyræoides* 'Emerald Sentinel'

Selected in the 1980s at North Carolina State University. "In our trials this species has been the most cold hardy and consistently evergreen of all the evergreen oaks." Growth rapid; to 5' per year. Raised easily from cuttings.

Q. *platanoides*—see Q. *bicolor*

Q. *polymorpha* Cham. & Schlecht.

From mountains of E Mexico and Guatemala; and a grove near Devil's River, Val Verde County, TX. Named in 1830 (from Greek *poly*, many, and *morphe*, form or shape). Cultivated in France <1877. Common in Texas cultivation since ca. 1983. Lone Star Growers nursery of San Antonio has trademarked the name MONTERREY OAK™. Monterrey is Mexico's third largest city. Leaves recalling those of a PEAR; evergreen, to 4½" × 3¾", commonly only 3" × 1¼"; untoothed or with subtle teeth near the apex; thick, smooth, dark green or bluish-green, stem ca. ½" long. Acorns to 1" long. Tree recorded to 60' tall. The largest native Texan specimen said to be ca. 26' × 15'6" (≤1992).

Q. *prinoides* var. *acuminata*—see Q. *Muhlenbergii*

Q. *Prinus* L., non auct. (see Q. *Michauxii*)
= Q. *montana* Willd.

CHESTNUT OAK. ROCK CHESTNUT OAK. TANBARK OAK. From the eastern U.S. and S Ontario. Common in cultivation. *Prinus* from *prinos*, an ancient Greek name of the HOLM OAK, Q. *Ilex*. G. Emerson explained the name ROCK CHESTNUT OAK in 1850: "It grows naturally and flourishes on the steep sides of rocky hills, where few other trees thrive, and where the other kinds of oak can hardly get a foothold." D.J. Browne says the bark is remarkably like that of the CHESTNUT (*Castanea*). As regards leaves, several other species of *Quercus* more closely resemble CHESTNUT. Leaves to 11" × 5", with 6–12 big blunt teeth per side. Fall color yellowish to dull orange.

Acorns to 1½" long, dark brown and shiny. Records: to 130' tall; 102' × 14'8" × 73' Huntingdon County, PA (1977); 95' × 22'4" × 82' Northport, NY (1985); 65' × 18'6" × 117' Suffield, CT (1985).

Q. *Prinus* var. *tomentosa*—see Q. *bicolor*

Q. *pseudosuber*—see Q. × *hispanica*

Q. *pseudoturneri*—see Q. × *Turneri* 'Pseudoturneri'

Q. *reticulata*—see Q. *rugosa*

Q. *rhombica*—see Q. *laurifolia*

Q. *rizophylla*—see Q. *rysophylla*

Q. *robur* L.
= Q. *pedunculata* Ehrh.
= Q. *femina* Mill.

ENGLISH OAK. BRITISH OAK. COMMON OAK. PEDUNCULATE OAK. TRUFFLE OAK. From Europe, N Africa, and the Caucasus. Extremely common in North American cultivation; wild and weedy in some locales. The epithet *robur* is an ancient Latin name for either an OAK or its timber, denoting the strength or hardness of its wood. This is the OAK of Druids, of mistletoe, and yule logs, of Robin Hood's cudgel and King Arthur's round table. In the WHITE OAK group. Leaves variable, small, bluntly lobed, often buggy and always lacking showy fall color. Two extreme populations have been noted, at least in the Old World: Dry southern specimens make hairy, firm, deeply lobed leaves (to 5" × 3"); trees in moister northern regions make thinner, less lobed, and larger (to 8" long) leaves. Acorns to 1⅜" long, on 1"–5" long stalks, hence the name PEDUNCULATE OAK (in contrast to SESSILE OAK, Q. *petræa*). Despite its ho-hum color and plain foliage, ENGLISH OAK is tough as nails, easily raised, and, after about 100 years, awe-inspiring. Records: to 150' tall; 138' × 15'2" Abbotsbury, Dorset, England (1986); 102' × 14'10" × 89' Olympia, WA (1993); 98' × 15'3" × 104' Sidney, B.C. (1988; *pl.* 1914; now dead); 87½' × 20'10" × 109½' Rotorua, New Zealand (≤1982; *pl.* 1863); 85' × 15'10" × 93½' North Bend, OH (≤1989; *pl.* ca. 1857); 82' × 28'0" Turkey (1991); 81' × 12'11" × 76' MI (1976); 75' × 16'11" × 72' Philadelphia County, PA (1980); a trunk

39'8" around at Bowthorpe, Lincolnshire, England (1965; ca. 600 years old).

Q. robur Attention!® PP 6746 (1989)
= Q. robur 'Wandell'

Introduced by Willet N. Wandell of Urbana, IL. A clone of Q. robur f. fastigiata.

Q. robur 'Concordia'

GOLDEN ENGLISH OAK. CONCORD OAK. Introduced ca. 1843 by Van Geert's nursery of Ghent, Belgium. In North American commerce ≤1888; very rare here. Growth slow, often shrubby. Leaves bright yellow-golden, especially in early summer. In late November, those leaves still persisting are a paper-bag brown. Records: 52' × 2'7" Szczepow, Poland (≤1973); 41' × 2'8½" × 32' Seattle, WA (1993; pl. 1947); 36' × 5'6" Wilton House, Wiltshire, England (1987); 33' × 3'3" Wirty, Poland (≤1973).

Q. robur 'Cristata'

CLUSTER OAK. Originated in Savernake Forest, Wiltshire, England. Named in 1917 (Latin for crested or plumed). Extremely rare in North America; offered since ≤1980 by Vermeulen nursery of New Jersey. A freak. Leaves small, clustered together, twisted and folded, very lopsided. Breeds 50% true when raised from acorn. Record: 36' × 2'6" Talbot Manor, Norfolk, England (1978).

Q. robur f. fastigiata (Lam.) Schwarz

COLUMNAR ENGLISH OAK. FASTIGIATE ENGLISH OAK. CYPRESS OAK. UPRIGHT ENGLISH OAK. Originated <1783. Described in 1785. Very common in cultivation. Grows narrowly upright like a wavy, irregular LOMBARDY POPLAR (Populus nigra 'Italica'). Precise shape depends on age, growing conditions, and whether grown from acorn or graft. It breeds more or less true; clones exist. Record: 99' × 10'10" × 52' Port Coquitlam, B.C. (1992).

Q. robur 'Foliis Variegatis'—see Q. robur f. variegata

Q. robur 'Laciniata'

CUTLEAF ENGLISH OAK. From ≤1888 until at least 1910, North American nurseries listed this name. It must be considered a general term applied to various clones with deeply lobed and dissected leaves. The accepted modern names for such clones sold include: Q. petræa 'Insecata'; Q. robur 'Asplenifolia', 'Filicifolia', and 'Pectinata'.

Q. robur 'Matterhorn' PP 3706 (1975)

Selected by M. Baron of Lansing, MI. Introduced by Schmidt nursery of Boring, OR. A clone of Q. robur f. fastigiata.

Q. robur 'Michround'—see Q. robur Westminster Globe™

Q. robur 'Pendula'

MOCCAS WEEPING OAK. Described in 1838 based on a large specimen at Moccas Court, Herefordshire, England. In North American commerce ≤1888. Whether the stock now sold as 'Pendula' is the same clone is not known. The original tree and its descendents grow to at least medium-size, with drooping branches. See also 'Pendula Dauvessei'. Records: 92' × 15'3" Whitfield, Herefordshire, England (1984); 75' × 8'2" × 40' Bucks County, PA (1980); 49' × 9'6" Matejki, Poland (≤1973).

Q. robur 'Pendula Dauvessei'

DAUVESSE'S WEEPING OAK. Likely originated or introduced by D. Dauvesse's nursery in France. Described in 1879. In North American commerce ≤1891. Long commercially extinct (unless it has been sold as 'Pendula'). Fast, with long slender pendulous branches.

Q. robur 'Pyramich'—see Q. robur Skymaster™

Q. robur 'Rosehill' PP 6539 (1989)

Introduced by Rosehill Gardens of Kansas City, MO. Rare. Habit broadly columnar. Resists powdery mildew.

Q. robur 'Salicifolia'

WILLOWLEAF ENGLISH OAK. Origin unknown (salicifolia means WILLOW-leaved; from genus Salix, WILLOW, and Latin folium, a leaf). Possibly a synonym of a clone called 'Holophylla'. Extremely rare in North America. Leaves to 4¼" × 1¼", utterly unlobed, and blunt. Record: 22' × 2'1" × 27' Lisle, IL (1986; pl. 1960).

Q. robur Skymaster™ PP 3707 (1975)
= Q. robur 'Pyramich'

Selected by M. Baron of Lansing, MI. Introduced ca. 1981–82. Narrow pyramidal form. Light acorn crops.

Q. robur Skyrocket™

Introduced ca. 1989 by Schmidt nursery of Boring, OR. A clone of Q. robur f. fastigiata.

Q. robur f. variegata (West.) Rehd.

= Q. robur 'Foliis Variegatis'

Named officially in 1770, but known much earlier; a 1602 *Survey of Cornwall* says: "there groweth an Oke, bearing leaves speckled with white, as does another, called Painter's Oke." Over the years at least 6 variegated cultivars have been named: 'Albomarmorata', 'Argenteomarginata', 'Argenteopicta', 'Argenteovariegata', 'Aureobicolor', and 'Maculata'. One or more has been in North American commerce since ≤1853. Though more than one clone has circulated, the least rare is irregularly white-edged, its leaves usually deformed. Sold as SILVER-VARIEGATED OAK. Record: 98½' × 14'11" Dupplin Castle, Tayside, Scotland (1983).

Q. robur 'Wandell'—see Q. robur Attention!®

Q. robur Westminster Globe™ PP 3708 (1975)

= Q. robur 'Michround'

Selected by M. Baron of Lansing, MI. Registered ca. 1980. Introduced by Schmidt nursery of Boring, OR. Habit rounded. Extremely heavy acorn crops.

Q. robur 'Willamette'

Introduced ca. 1991 by Handy nursery of Portland, OR (at the north end of the Willamette Valley). Densely fastigiate habit. A clone of Q. robur f. *fastigiata*.

Q. × rosacea Bechst.

(Q. petræa × Q. robur)

HYBRID ENGLISH OAK. Not cultivated except the following clone.

Q. × rosacea 'Columna'

= Q. petræa 'Columna'
= Q. petræa 'Columnar'

(Q. petræa 'Muscaviensis' × Q. robur f. fastigata)

Originated ca. 1935 in Germany. Introduced in 1939–40 by Hesse nursery there. In North American commerce since ≤1958; rare. Habit strongly upright if not columnar. Leaves long, narrow and unlobed or weakly lobed.

Q. rubra L.

= Q. maxima (Marsh.) Ashe
= Q. borealis Michx. fil.

RED OAK. COMMON RED OAK. NORTHERN RED OAK. EASTERN RED OAK. From central and eastern North America. Extremely common in cultivation. Latin: *ruber*, red. New Jersey's State Tree. Fall color to dark red or brownish, rarely orange. Leaves matte, variable in depth of lobes, sharply tipped; to 14½" × 9". Acorns plump, to 1¼" long, cup often shallow. Habit usually stout, big-limbed and broad-spreading. Growth rapid. Records: 165' × 15'7" Pope, IL (1987); 150' × 19'0" Wabash County, IL (<1882); 132' × 15'2" Grays River, WA (1990); 127' × 23'7" × 128' near Riverside, MI (1978); 98' × 26'6" × 102' Massachusetts (1982); 88' × 26'3" × 88' Ashtabula County, OH (1970); 66' × 30'4" × 89' Rochester, NY (1987).

Q. rubra 'Aurea'

= Q. rubra 'Sunshine'
= Q. rubra 'Lutea'

Discovered ca. 1878 in Holland; introduced commercially in 1880. Introduced to North America ≤1896; extremely rare here. Leaves yellow, at least in early summer. May scorch in hot summer regions. Growth far less robust than typical seedlings. Breeds partly true from acorn; more than one clone may go under the name 'Aurea'. Hillier nursery of England proposes the name '**Limelight**' for the Continental European 'Aurea'. The Arnold Arboretum imported 'Aurea' from Germany in 1965, and that accession may in circulation. Records: 66' × 4'1" Port Coquitlam, B.C. (1994); 44' × 6'0" Adaremanor, County Limerick, Ireland (1975).

Q. rubra 'Limelight'—see Q. rubra 'Aurea'

Q. rubra 'Lutea'—see Q. rubra 'Aurea'

Q. rubra 'Sunshine'—see Q. rubra 'Aurea'

Q. rugosa Née

= Q. diversifolia Trel.
= Q. reticulata Humb. & Bonpl.

NETLEAF OAK. From Arizona, New Mexico, Texas, Mexico, and Guatemala. Named in 1801. Introduced to cultivation in 1833. Extremely rare. Although cold-hardy in many areas, it is often slow, bushy and coarse. Foliage evergreen; often dull. Leaves droopy, thick, convex, often rough (rugose) and veiny, to 7" × 4", widest above the middle, unlobed, coarsely and shallowly sharp-toothed; stem to ¼" long. Young leaves in April red hairy above, felty whitish- or golden beneath; mature leaves also turn red as they fall. Acorns to 1" long, borne 2–6 (11) on a slender stem 1½"–5" long. Records: to 60' tall in Mexico; 42' × 5'1" × 26½' Berkeley, CA (1993; *pl.* 1969); 38' × 7'0" × 36' Big Bend National Park, TX (1983).

Q. *rysophylla* Weatherby
(*rizophylla*; *ryzophylla*; *risophylla*)

MEXICAN LOQUAT LEAVED OAK. From mountains of NE Mexico. Named in 1910 (and spelled as cited above). Cultivated in Texas since ≤1983. Extremely rare but exciting and likely to be grown wherever possible. Leaves evergreen, short-stemmed, unlobed, with minute bristly teeth; to 9¾" × 3". Well named LOQUAT-LEAF OAK for color, shape and stiff texture; but unlike the LOQUAT (*Eriobotrya japonica*), the leaves are scarcely hairy. Usually a small tree; at most 82' tall.

Q. *Schneckii*—see Q. *Shumardii*

Q. *serrata*—see Q. *acutissima* and Q. *glandulifera*

Q. *sessiliflora*—see Q. *petræa*

Q. *Shumardii* Buckl.
= Q. *Schneckii* Britt.

SHUMARD RED OAK. SHUMARD OAK. LEOPARD OAK. SPOTTED OAK. From the central and eastern U.S., mostly in the south. Named in 1860 after Benjamin Franklin Shumard (1820–1869); State geologist of Texas. Introduced to cultivation in 1897; rare or at best uncommon until the 1980s. A. & S. Wasowski report that in eastern Texas two other species are often mistakenly marketed as this species. In the RED OAK group. Leaves much like those of SCARLET OAK (*Q. coccinea*), but usually with conspicuous tufts of orange-brown, felty hairs in the vein intersections beneath; to 8¾" × 6". Moreover, SHUMARD OAK colors later in fall or stays green late into winter. Acorns to 1¼" long. Records: to 226' × 25'1" in primeval conditions; 190' × 20'9" × 88' Tennessee (1994); 181' × 20'3" Lower Wabash Valley, IN (<1921); 155' × 20'0" × 116' Congaree Swamp, NC (1984); 97' × 21'9" × 105' Lake Providence, LA (1975).

Q. *Shumardii* var. *acerifolia* Palmer
= Q. *acerifolia* (Palmer) Stoynoff & Hess

MAPLELEAF OAK. Very rare: from Magazine Mountain, Logan County, AR. Named in 1927 (genus *Acer*, MAPLE, and Latin *folium*, a leaf). Promoted as a good ornamental since the late 1980s. In 1990 Stoynoff & Hess proposed that it merits (separate) species status. A shrub or small tree, often multi-trunked; at most 50' tall. Leaves look like those of a SUGAR MAPLE (*Acer saccharum*), wider than long, 5 (7) lobed; to 5½" × 7¼" but usually only 2" × 3½". Fall color bright red. Acorns much smaller than those of typical *Q. Shumardii*.

Q. *Shumardii* 'Royal Flush' PP 4149 (1977)
Discovered as a chance seedling. Introduced in 1984 by Schmidt nursery of Boring, OR. Young leaves retain a deep maroon color until early summer.

Q. *Shumardii* var. *texana*—see Q. *Buckleyi*

Q. *stellata* Wangh.
= Q. *minor* (Marsh.) Sarg.

POST OAK. IRON OAK. BOX WHITE OAK. ROUGH OAK. From the central and eastern U.S. Very rarely cultivated. The epithet *stellata* means starlike, referring to the leaf shape or (less likely) to its star-shaped hairs. In the WHITE OAK group. G. Emerson explained in 1850: "In the Southern States, it is called Post oak, and is preferred to all other kinds of wood, on account of its durability, when used as posts." Called ROUGH OAK from the roughness of its leaves. Leaves shiny and intensely dark above, hairy beneath, to 8⅜" × 6¾"; remarkably wide, boldly lobed, comparatively "cross-like" in outline with dominant middle lobes. Fall color dull yellow or brown. Acorns to 1" long. D. Browne said in 1850: "They are very sweet, and form a delicious food for squirrels and wild turkeys; hence the tree is sometimes called Turkey Oak." In modern parlance the name TURKEY OAK is applied by writers to *Q. lævis* (not in this volume). Often shrubby. Records: 108' × 9'10" Wood County, TX (1989); 96' × 15'2" × 104' Red River Parish, LA (1984); 85' × 19'8" × 88' Surry County, VA (1987).

Q. *Suber* L.
CORK TREE. CORK OAK. From the W and central Mediterranean region. Introduced ≤1699 from France to England. Planted in 1847 in Virginia, Georgia and other southern states. In California since ca. ≤1856; now very common there. *Suber* is an ancient Latin name for this tree. The unusual spongy bark can be 12" thick on old specimens and is the cork used for dart boards, bottle stoppers, floats, etc. Foliage evergreen, dull and dusty-looking. Leaves to 5⅞" × 4", prickly. Acorns to 1¼" long, the cup deep and its uppermost scales fringed loosely. In Seattle, freezes do not kill this species, but snow loads wreak havoc with its crown. Records: 85' × 8'3" × 67' Sacramento, CA (1989); 81' × 18'0" × 88½' Napa, CA (1994); 75' × 16'2" × 88' Davis, CA (1992); trunks to 25'0" around in the Old World.

Q. *texana* Buckl. 1860, non 1873
= *Q. Nuttallii* Palmer

NUTTALL OAK. RED RIVER OAK. SMOOTHBARK RED OAK. From SE Missouri to SE Texas and Alabama, on heavy soils and poorly drained bottomlands. Introduced to cultivation ≤1923; seldom in commerce until the 1980s; grown primarily in the Southeast. Named originally in 1860, then in 1927 after Thomas Nuttall (1786–1859), British-American botanist and ornithologist. In 1985 botanists pointed out that this was the real *Q. texana*, while the tree previously called *Q. texana* had to be renamed *Q. Buckleyi*. In the RED OAK group. Similar to PIN OAK (*Q. palustris*) and SCARLET OAK (*Q. coccinea*), but with larger acorns (¾"–1½" long). Leaves thin, sharply lobed, to 9" long, dark above; paler and shinier beneath, with conspicuous hair tufts in vein intersections. Fall color late and spectacular red. Bark only slightly furrowed. Records: to 130' tall; 118' × 23'4" × 85' West Feliciana Parish, LA (1988); 110' × 21'8" × 96' Washington County, MS (1984).

Q. *tinctoria*—see *Q. velutina*

Q. *tomentella* Engelm.
= *Q. chrysolepis* ssp. *tomentella* (Engelm.) E. Murr.

ISLAND LIVE OAK. From islands off California and Baja California. The rarest OAK of California. Named in 1877. In cultivation since 1930 but extremely rare. Leaves evergreen, minutely tomentose; to 4⅛" × 2", recalling those of TAN OAK (*Lithocarpus densiflorus*). Acorns to 1½" long. Recorded to 65½' × 11'0" in the wild. May grow taller in garden conditions. Rapidly forms a lovely dark green, dense, flame-shaped crown. Likely too cold-tender for anywhere outside the mild Pacific Coastal strip (needs testing).

Q. *triloba*—see *Q. falcata*

Q. × *Turneri* Willd.
(*Q. Ilex* × *Q. robur*)

Q. × *Turneri* 'Pseudoturneri'
= *Q. pseudoturneri* Willd.

TURNER'S OAK. Raised <1780 by Spencer Turner (1728–1776) of Holloway Down, Essex, England. In North America since ≤1891. Extremely rare. Among the hardiest of evergreen OAKS; leaves drop as the buds open in spring. Leaves ca. 4¾" × 2⅜". The many specimens in Vancouver, B.C., are topgrafted and form gaunt, rounded trees of singular appearance and little beauty. Usually broad and low. Records: 87' × 12'0" Eastnor Castle, Herefordshire, England

(1984); 72' × 17'0" Kew, England (1989; *pl.* ca. 1865); 39' × 7'10" × 55' Vancouver, B.C. (1992).

Q. *utahensis*—see *Q. Gambelii*

Q. *variabilis* Bl.
= *Q. chinensis* Bge. 1835, non Abel 1818

CHINESE CORK OAK. ORIENTAL OAK. CHINESE OAK. From China, Japan, Korea, and Taiwan. Introduced in 1861 by R. Fortune to England. In North American commerce ≤1948 (when offered by Kohankie nursery of Painesville, OH). Extremely rare. Because of its leaves it looks much like a corky-barked CHESTNUT (*Castanea*). Leaves to 8½" × 3¼", very pale beneath, edged with fine bristly teeth. Fall color golden. Acorns squat, ca. ¾" wide; sweet; cups large, with loose tentacle-like scales. Records: 108' × 5'2" Anhwei, China (1925); 85' × 3'10" Seattle, WA (1990; *pl.* 1937); 61' × 7'0" × 63' Hartford, CT (1987); 56' × 14'9" Japan (1994).

Q. *velutina* Lam.
= *Q. tinctoria* Bartr.

BLACK OAK. YELLOW OAK. DYER'S OAK. QUERCITRON (OAK). From much of central and eastern North America. Uncommon in cultivation. In the RED OAK group. The epithet *velutina* means velvety; from the young foliage and the buds. The Latin *tinctoria* pertains to dyeing, for which this tree was much used. D. Browne explained in 1850: "From the cellular integument of the black oak is obtained *quercitron*, of which great use is made in dyeing wool, silk and paper hangings. This substance was first prepared as a dye by Dr. Bancroft; he has given it the name of *quercitron*, by which it is now universally recognized." Bark dark, notably rough near the tree base; orange or bright yellow inner bark. Buds large, fuzzy, as are the young leaves in spring. Leaves perplexingly variable, often bold, sharply lobed and bristle-tipped, to 12" × 10". Fall color dull red, or orange brown, or attractively brooding red-brown. Acorns 1" long. Records: to 165' × 34'6" in the primeval forest; 131' × 20'7" × 137' St. Clair County, MI (1988); 84' × 25'8" × 95' East Granby, CT (1988); 80' × 20'7" × 140' Lloyd Neck, NY (1972).

Q. *virens*—see *Q. virginiana*

Q. virginiana Mill.

= *Q. virens* Ait.

LIVE OAK. SOUTHERN LIVE OAK. LOUISIANA LIVE OAK. From the far south of the U.S.; Mexico, and Cuba. Commonly cultivated. Along with EVERGREEN MAGNOLIA (*Magnolia grandiflora*) it may be considered the unofficial tree symbol of the Deep South. An extraordinarily wide-crowned tree, often pictured dripping with Spanish moss in old avenues. Leaves evergreen, narrow, to 5" × 2½", unlobed, sparsely if at all toothed. Acorns to 1" long, slender. Records: 87' × 33'10" × 135' Teche, LA (1932); 78' × 35'0" × 168' near Hahnville, LA (1950; dead 1967); 55' × 36'7" × 132' near Lewisburg, LA (1976).

Q. virginiana Heritage®

Introduced ≤1979 by Storm nursery of Fremont, TX. "The most adaptable and fastest."

Q. Wislizenii A. DC.

INTERIOR LIVE OAK. SIERRA LIVE OAK. From California and Baja California. Discovered by J. Frémont in 1844. Named in 1864 after Friedrich Adolph Wislizenus (1810–1889), German-born physician of St. Louis, MO, who collected specimens in 1851. Introduced to cultivation in 1874; uncommon and essentially limited to the Pacific Coast. Leaves evergreen, HOLLY-like, wide, flat, lustrous, variably spiny-toothed; to 4⅔" × 2" but commonly only 2½" × 1¼". Acorns to 1⅝" long. Crown varies from dense to open and airy. Small-leaved shrubby variants exist. Records: to 100' tall; 89' × 22'4" × 68' near Stockton, CA (1982).

Raphiolepis Majestic Beauty™—see *Eriobotrya deflexa* × *Raphiolepis indica*

Raphiolepis 'Montic'—see *Eriobotrya deflexa* × *Raphiolepis indica*

Rehderodendron

[STYRACACEÆ; Storax Family] 9 or 10 spp. of deciduous trees, all east Asian. Named after distinguished tree expert Alfred Rehder (1863–1949), who worked at the Arnold Arboretum from 1898 to 1940. Related genera include *Halesia* (SILVERBELL), *Pterostyrax* (EPAULETTE TREE), and *Styrax* (SNOWBELL TREE).

R. macrocarpum H.H. Hu

REHDER TREE. From China—at 7–10,000' elevation on Mt. Omei, a sacred mountain in Szechuan. Discovered by F.T. Wang in 1931; named in 1932 (Greek *macro*, large, and *karpos*, fruit). Seeds sent by Dr. Hu to the Arnold Arboretum in 1934. Exceedingly rare in cultivation. Sold in tiny sizes in small quantity by specialty nurseries. Leaves long and pointy (to 8" × 2¾"), finely toothed, shiniest on undersides; stems red, as are the young twigs. In woodland conditions, many leaves still hang, greenish, into November. In the open, pastel orange-red fall color prevails in mid-October. Flowers during May, in clusters of 4–6, each a white bell 1" wide, with yellow stamens. Fragrance variously described as MOCK ORANGE, strong LEMON-like, or MAGNOLIA-like. Fruit dry and woody, to 3¼" long and 1½" wide, 1–2 seeded, dull red-brown in September. The fruit, although curious, are not things of beauty, and can be objected to as litter. A slender small tree. Records: to 65½' tall in the wild; 39' × 3'7" Trewithen Garden, Cornwall, England (1987; *pl.* ca. 1935); 38' × 3'1" Seattle, WA (1994; *pl.* 1957).

Retinispora obtusa—*Chamæcyparis obtusa*

Retinispora pisifera—*Chamæcyparis pisifera*

Retinospora ericoides—*Chamæcyparis thyoides* 'Ericoides'

Retinospora filicoides—*Chamæcyparis obtusa* 'Filicoides'

Retinospora 'K. & C.'—*Chamæcyparis pisifera* 'Boulevard'

Retinospora leptoclada—*Chamæcyparis thyoides* 'Andelyensis'

Retinospora obtusa—*Chamæcyparis obtusa*

Retinospora pisifera—*Chamæcyparis pisifera*

Retinospora plumosa—*Chamæcyparis pisifera* f. *plumosa*

Retinospora squarrosa—*Chamæcyparis pisifera* f. *squarrosa*

Retinospora Veitchii—*Chamæcyparis pisifera* 'Squarrosa Veitchii'

Rhamnus

[RHAMNACEÆ: Buckthorn Family] 125–160 spp. of widely distributed shrubs and trees, deciduous or evergreen. Known as BUCKTHORNS in English. *Rhamnos* is the ancient Greek name of a thorny shrub (probably *R. cathartica*). BUCKTHORNS are usually shrubby, and virtually none are remarkable for floral beauty or showy fruit. The handsome foliage and excellent hardiness of some species has kept them from oblivion, yet their sudden disappearance would find few mourners. They are no more glamorous than muskoxen. Nine species are native in North America, and two more naturalized here. The unrelated SEA BUCKTHORN is *Hippophaë rhamnoides*. Two genera related to *Rhamnus* include *Hovenia* (JAPANESE RAISIN TREE) and *Ziziphus* (JUJUBE).

R. Alaternus L.

ITALIAN BUCKTHORN. MEDITERRANEAN BUCKTHORN. From the Mediterranean region. Cultivated since 1605 in the Netherlands. In North America practically limited to the Pacific Coast, and not common. *Alaternus* is the ancient Latin name of this species, adopted from Dioscorides, of unknown etymology. An evergreen shrub, or trained tree to 25' tall; of bright, cheerful aspect. It sometimes suckers from the roots. Leaves to 3⅞" × 1⅞", glossy rich green, very finely toothed. Flowers inconspicuous, March into June. Berries ¼", black. Drought-tolerant; best on well-drained soil. Hurt by severe freezes. Records: 46½' × 1'5¼" San Francisco, CA (1995); a trunk ca. 4'0" around in San Diego, CA (1994).

R. Alaternus 'Argenteo-variegata'
= *R. Alaternus* 'Variegata'
= *R. Alaternus* 'Foliis Argenteis'

Described in 1770, but known much earlier. In California ≤1908. Extremely rare. Leaves edged creamy-white. More cold-tender than typical *R. Alaternus*. Smaller, but can reach at least 15' tall.

R. Alaternus 'Foliis Argenteis'—see R. Alat. 'Argenteio-variegata'

R. Alaternus John Edwards™
Originated by the John Edwards nursery of East Palo Alto, CA. Introduced ≤1962 by the Saratoga Horticultural Foundation of California. A treelike clone.

R. Alaternus 'Variegata'—see R. Alaternus 'Argenteo-variegata'

R. cathartica L.

EURASIAN BUCKTHORN. COMMON BUCKTHORN. HART'S THORN. WAY THORN. PURGING BUCKTHORN. RAM THORN. EUROPEAN BUCKTHORN. HIGHWAY THORN. RHINE BERRY. RAIN BERRY. From Europe, west and north Asia, N Africa. Long commonly cultivated in North America; naturalized, even weedy, in many places since the 1800s. Somewhat used for hedging. Named from Greek *kathartikos*, cleansing or purging (its ripe fruit was used to prepare purgatives). In 1968 the name BUCKTHORN was explained by H.L. Edlin: "the short shoots bear flowers and berries each year, but they elongate very slowly. As the scars of each successive fruit cluster accumulate, the short shoot becomes corrugated, and soon the shoot looks just like the rough base of the antler of a roe-buck. Hence the tree really is the *buck's horn thorn*, shortened nowadays to buckthorn." A tough, hardy species, but thorny and devoid of particular attractions, prettiest when its tender spring greenery emerges to contrast with the rough blackish bark. Leaves to 3" long, egg-shaped, bright green, finely toothed, hairless, often with 3 main veins from the base. Flowers pale greenish, tiny, in May and June. Foliage dark. Leaves can remain green into November, then drop while a plain yellowish-green color. Dyes from the bark and berries yield variously green, purple, yellow or brown. Berries glossy black, ripe in fall. Records: 61' × 3'9" × 65' Ann Arbor, MI (1972); 32' × 4'6" × 34' State College, PA (1954).

R. Frangula L.
= *Frangula Alnus* Mill.

ALDER BUCKTHORN. GLOSSY BUCKTHORN. BREAKING BUCKTHORN. BERRY BEARING ALDER. BLACK DOGWOOD. BUTCHER'S PRICK TREE. GUNPOWDER TREE (the best source for gunpowder charcoal). From western Eurasia. Common in North America, and wild in some places, favoring moist sites. Less treelike than *R. cathartica*. Not thorny. Called ALDER BUCKTHORN because it frequently occurs with ALDERS (*Alnus*) in wet ground. *Frangula* is an old generic name for this species, from Latin *frangere*, to break, perhaps referring to the brittleness of its twigs. Leaves to 3" long, untoothed, with 8–12 pairs of parallel veins. Fall color deep yellow. Berries showy red, then black, ¼"–⅓". Record: 34' × 1'1" × 19' Oakland County, MI (1976).

R. Frangula 'Asplenifolia'
= *R. Frangula* 'Laciniata'

In North America since ≤1888. Described officially in 1892. Uncommon. In commerce ≤1939. Leaves of regular length and gloss but only ¼" wide, if that. In Latin, *aspleniifolius* means with leaves like the frond of the SPLEENWORT FERN. Shrubby, at most 15' tall.

R. Frangula 'Columnaris' PP 1388 (1955)
= *R. Frangula* 'Tallcole'

TALLHEDGE®. Originated as a seedling found in 1936 in Bedford, OH. Introduced by Cole nursery of Painesville, OH. Very common. Often disease-prone and short-lived. Grows ca. 12'–15' tall, in a tightly narrow form.

R. Frangula 'Laciniata'—R. Frangula 'Asplenifolia'

R. Frangula 'Tallcole'—R. Frangula 'Columnaris'

R. Frangula Tallhedge®—R. Frangula 'Columnaris'

R. Purshiana DC.
= *Frangula Purshiana* (DC.) Cooper

CASCARA (BUCKTHORN). CÁSCARA SAGRADA. SACRED BARK TREE. OREGON BEARWOOD. BITTERBARK. COFFEE-TREE. CHITTIM. CHITTAM. From British Columbia to Montana and California. Named in 1825 after Frederick Traugott Pursh (1774–1820), U.S. botanist, who first described this species in 1814. Introduced to cultivation in 1870. Very rare; of interest for wildlife value and medicinal use (laxative; alleviates arthritis), but too dull to be used ornamentally. Leaves to 8" × 3", with 10–17 pairs of parallel veins. Fall color pure yellow in woods; mixed yellow, orange, red, purplish and green in exposed sites. Saplings in woods remain evergreen. Berries black, ½" wide, coffee-flavored; ripe from late August through October. Bark smooth and gray (looks like that of *Ailanthus*, TREE OF HEAVEN). Branches upswept, forming a neat, oval crown. Supremely shade-tolerant. Short-lived. Records: 70'×2'10" Blaine, WA (1988); 60'×9'5" Rockport, WA (<1945); 51'×8'8" Gold Bar, WA (1992).

Rhamnus Zizyphus—see Ziziphus Zizyphus

Rhaphiolepis Majestic Beauty™—see Eriobotrya deflexa × Raphiolepis indica

Rhaphiolepis 'Montic'—see Eriobotrya deflexa × Raphiolepis indica

Rhus

[ANACARDIACEÆ; Cashew Family] 150–200 spp. of groundcovers, vines, shrubs or trees, deciduous or evergreen. The generic name *Rhus* is derived from the ancient Greek (*rhous*) and Latin (*rhus*) name of *R. coriaria*, MEDITERRANEAN SUMACH (not in this volume); maybe from Celtic *rudh*, red, in allusion to the color of the fruit and leaves of some species in autumn. The common name SUMAC(H) is from *summâq*, the Arabic name of the plant (akin to Turkish *summak* or *somak*), The chief historic use of most SUMACHS was as a tannin source. In contemporary landscape design they supply troublefree toughness, wildlife value and dramatic foliage of flamboyant fall color. They thrive in poor, dry soil and demand only sufficient sunlight. Drawbacks of some species include short lifespans, weedy rootsuckering, or poisonous sap. POISON IVY (*R. radicans*), POISON OAK (*R. diversiloba*, *R. Toxicodendron*) and POISON SUMACH (*R. vernix*) are three unholy members of this genus, but only the latter is a tree, and its dreadful nature bars it from ornamental horticulture. It would be swell if plant-breeders could raise poison-free stock. All eight *Rhus* species treated below are deciduous and bear pinnately-compound leaves with flaming fall color, except *R. lancea* (AFRICAN SUMACH), and all bear male and female flowers on separate plants. Genera related to *Rhus* include *Cotinus* (SMOKE TREE), *Pistacia* (PISTACHIO), and *Schinus* (PEPPER TREE).

R. americana—Cotinus obovatus

R. chinensis—Rhus javanica var. chinensis

R. copallina L.

FLAMELEAF SUMACH. SHINING SUMACH. DWARF SUMACH. WINGED SUMACH. BLACK SUMACH. MOUNTAIN SUMACH. UPLAND SUMACH. From central and eastern North America, and W Cuba. Commonly cultivated. Similar to *R. glabra* (SMOOTH SUMACH) and *R. typhina* (STAGHORN), but sleeker, with its leafstems winged. Leaflets 9–23. Shoots finely hairy. Fall color rich shiny purple or deep red. The epithet *copallina* derived from *copal*, a Mexican Indian name for a white resin; it was thought that this species afforded a copal like that of commerce. Usually a shrub. Records: 55' × 2'7" × 22' Grenada County, MS (1974); 49' × 2'11" × 19' Marion County, TX (1986).

R. cotinoides—*Cotinus obovatus*

R. Cotinus—*Cotinus Coggygria*

R. glabra L.

SMOOTH SUMACH. SCARLET SUMACH. SLEEK SUMACH. VINEGAR TREE. From at least a part of every one of the 48 contiguous States, and parts of Canada and Mexico. A suckering shrub or rarely shortlived small tree. Twigs stout, pithy, hairless and whitish-bloomy. Leaflets 11–31. Fall color brilliant red. Flowers small, dingy pale yellow-green, in prominent clusters during early summer. Seedcones can be taken at maturity, soaked in water, and a pink lemonade-like beverage made; the same applies to STAGHORN SUMACH (*R. typhina*, which can be viewed as a furry version of *R. glabra*). Records: 45' × 2'6" Homochito National Forest, MS (≤1951); 42' × 1'11" Akron, AL (1976); 26' × 3'2" × 27' Walla Walla, WA (1993).

R. glabra 'Laciniata'

CUTLEAF SMOOTH SUMACH. Discovered near Philadelphia, PA. Cultivated since ca. 1850. Named officially in 1863 in France. In North American commerce ≤1888. Once common, it has declined in popularity, being less cold-hardy than typical *R. glabra*, and inclined to revert to normal foliage. Fall color excellent red. See *R.* × *pulvinata*.

R. glabra 'Morden Selection'

Presumably from Morden research station of Manitoba. Introduced ≤1991–92 by Bailey nursery of St. Paul, MN. "Good dark leaves, attractive bright red seed clusters. Slower and smaller than regular." Said to attain only 6' in height, which is not tree-scale at all.

R. Henryi—*R. Potaninii*

R. hirta—*R. typhina*

R. × *hybrida*—*R.* × *pulvinata*

R. javanica L. var. *chinensis* (Mill.) Yamazaki

= *R. chinensis* Mill.
= *R. Osbeckii* (DC.) Decne. *ex* Steud.
= *R. semi-alata* Murr.

CHINESE SUMACH. JAVA SUMACH. [CHINESE] NUT-GALL TREE. CHINESE PLUME TREE. From temperate E Asia. Introduced to Western cultivation in the 1700s. Rare in North America. In China it is the host of the nut gall insect. Leaflets 7–17, coarsely toothed, the stem winged—most developed near the end of the leaf. Handsome red fall color. Flowers the most showy of SUMACHS, in whitish plumes, in August-September. Fruits densely hairy, red-yellow. Tree usually short-trunked, round-headed 15'–20' tall; sometimes absolutely shrubby, but seldom suckering. Record: 24' × 1'11" Seattle, WA (1990; *pl.* 1956).

R. javanica var. *chinensis* 'September Beauty'

Introduced ≤1986 by Dr. E. Orton of Rutgers University, New Jersey. A male clone. Flower clusters large, to 22" long × 20" wide.

R. lancea L. fil.

AFRICAN SUMACH. WILLOW SUMACH. From South Africa, in the arid interior region, where it is called *kareeboom* (KAREE TREE). Named in 1781. Introduced to the U.S. ca. 1916. The only South African species in this volume. Widely planted in southern California and the Southwest, especially in desert areas. Tolerates drought, heat, and poor soil. Cold-hardy to about 12°–14°F. Tree evergreen, with a broad, airy crown of light sprays that flutter prettily in the breeze. Bark dark, rough, with orange fissures. Foliage delicate and lacy, WILLOW-like. Leaves trifoliate, dark shiny green, hairless; leaflets to 6" long. The name *lancea*, Latin for a light spear or lance, refers to the leaflet shape. Flowers tiny and greenish, in January–February. Its tiny beige fruits recall radish seeds; ripe in June. Male specimens are more vigorous and upright. Recorded to 35' × 12'6" × 61'.

R. Osbeckii—*R. javanica* var. *chinensis*

R. Potaninii Maxim.

= *R. Henryi* Diels
= *R. sinica* hort., non Diels

CHINESE VARNISH TREE. POTANIN SUMACH. From central and W China. Discovered in 1885 by the Russian scholar Grigory Nicolaevich Potanin (1835–1920). Introduced to English cultivation in 1902 by E. Wilson for Veitch nursery. In North America ≤1916. Extremely rare here, but undeservedly so. Leaflets 5–11, hairy both sides; coarsely toothed (Rehder and Wilson say on young plants the leaflets are deeply toothed, on adults, untoothed). Fall color can be mixed green, orange, and some soft gold; or soft shades of red or purple. Flowers showy in handsome whitish clusters, May through early July. Fruit red, hairy, tiny. Usually a low, rounded and bushy tree. Little or no poisonous sap. Records: to 82' tall in the wild; 79' × 8'2" Mount House, Alderley, Gloucestershire, England (1986; *pl.* ca. 1940).

R. × *pulvinata* Greene

= R. × *hybrida* Rehd.
(R. *glabra* × R. *typhina*)

HYBRID SUMACH. The Latin name means pillow or cushion, and why it was applied to this SUMACH is anyone's guess. Cultivated since 1893 in Germany. Ignored in North America. It occasionally occurs in the wild, and has been propagated commercially, although virtually never sold under its correct name. A cutleaf clone commonly sold in Europe as R. *glabra* 'Laciniata' was renamed 'Red Autumn Lace' in 1994.

R. *semi-alata*—R. *javanica* var. *chinensis*

R. *sinica*—R. *Potaninii*

R. *trichocarpa* Miq.

JAPANESE SUMACH. From Japan, the S Kuriles, Korea, and China. Named in 1866 (Greek *tricho*, hairy, and *karpos*, fruit). Introduced in 1890 by C. Sargent to the Arnold Arboretum. Extremely rare. Usually a shrub; can be a small tree 25' × 1'9". Leaflets 9–17, untoothed, softly hairy, riotously colored in autumn. Flowers tiny, greenish-yellow, in inconspicuous drooping axillary clusters, May into July. Fruit yellowish, rough, whitish underneath its skin.

R. *typhina* L.

= R. *hirta* (L.) Sudw., non Engelm.

STAGHORN (SUMACH). FUZZY SUMACH. VELVET SUMACH. HAIRY SUMACH. VIRGINIAN SUMACH. From eastern North America. Very commonly cultivated. A large suckering shrub forming thickets, or small, generally leaning tree. Bold and colorful. Leaflets 11–31; red, scarlet or orange in fall. The specific epithet means like *Typha*, the CATTAIL PLANT, from its velvety branches. The name STAGHORN refers to the young horns of a stag. Branches stout, densely velvety and pithy. Winter aspect gaunt. Flowers greenish, tiny, in congested clusters during the summer. Female specimens make prominent, furry seed-cones (sometimes called "bobs"), ripening crimson or maroon, to 8" long. Records: 61' × 4'2" Camp Hill, AL (1985); 49' × 2'5" Orchard Lake, MI (1979); 42' × 3'7" ×36' Gatlinburg, TN (1984).

R. *typhina* 'Dissecta'

= R. *typhina* f. *dissecta* (Rehd.) Reveal
= R. *typhina* 'Laciniata' of J.W. Manning 1900, non Wood 1877

CUTLEAF SUMACH. FERNLEAF SUMACH. SHREDDED LEAF SUMACH. Discovered ca. 1892 in Vermont. Introduced ca. 1898. Very common. Tree smaller than typical R. *typhina*. Leaflets dissected elegantly. Fall color orange-red.

R. *typhina* 'Laciniata'

Discovered in 1846. Described in 1877. Almost never cultivated—confused nominally with R. *typhina* 'Dissecta'. Leaves and bracts more or less laciniate; inflorescence often partly transformed into contorted bracts.

R. *vernicifera*—R. *verniciflua*

R. *verniciflua* Stokes

= R. *vernicifera* DC.
= R. *vernix* Th. *ex* J.A. Murr. 1784, non L. 1753
= *Toxicodendron vernicifluum* (Stokes) F. Barkley

VARNISH TREE. CHINESE LACQUER VARNISH TREE. LACQUER TREE. From the Himalayas and China. Much cultivated in Japan (sap made into black Japan lacquer). Introduced to Western cultivation in 1829 by Siebold to Holland (B.K. Boom claims 1766 in France). Unknown in England before 1862. In North American commerce ≤1887. Extremely rare here. A bold, robust tree, with poisonous sap. Leaflets 5–19, untoothed, velvety beneath to virtually hairless. Flowers greenish-white, tiny, sweetly fragrant, in inconspicuous drooping clusters, May into July. Fruit yellow, shiny, hairless, ¼"–⅓". One of the first trees to color in autumn. Fall color varies, can be green with some yellow and red. The 1812 epithet *verniciflua* is Greek-derived, from *vernix*, varnish, and *fluo*, to flow—flowing with varnish. This species yields the glossy lacquer used for polished woodenware in Japan. Records: to 100' tall in China; 70' × 7'3" Westonbirt, Gloucestershire, England (1982); 42' × 8'4" Witham Hall, Lincolnshire, England (1983).

R. *vernix*—R. *verniciflua*

Robinia

[LEGUMINOSÆ; Pea Family] 4 spp. of deciduous trees or shrubs, all North American, called LOCUSTS. Some botanists split *Robinia* into as many as 20 species. The genus is homogeneous as a group, but distinguishing species, varieties and hybrids is daunting. Named after the French arborists and herbalists Jean (1550–1629) and Vespasien Robin (1579–1662). The best known species (*R. Pseudoacacia*, BLACK LOCUST) was cultivated in France by 1635 (as *Acacia Americana Robini*). Leaves pinnately compound, healthy lush green, with negligible fall color. Flowers showy, pea-like, white, pink or purplish. Seedpods elongated, flattish, and dry at maturity. Branches often thorny, always brittle. Roots usually sucker. Trees thrifty, easily pleased, pollution-tolerant. Of great value in ecologic/wildlife plantings. The following account is weak on details, and some cultivated pink-flowering LOCUST trees seem not referrable to any cited clone, yet were clonally distributed. Hence there are insufficient clonal names for the trees which have been planted. A related genus is *Laburnum* (GOLDENCHAIN), with yellow flowers. The HONEY LOCUSTS are genus *Gleditsia*.

R. × *ambigua* Poir.
= *R.* × *dubia* Foucault 1813, non Poir. 1804
= *R.* × *intermedia* Soul.-Bod.
= *R.* × *hybrida* Audib. *ex* DC.
(*R. Pseudoacacia* × *R. viscosa*)

HYBRID LOCUST. Originated as a *R. viscosa* (CLAMMY LOCUST) seedling in France. First flowered in 1812; named in 1816. In North American commerce ≤1851. The original clone is more like *R. Pseudoacacia* (BLACK LOCUST) than *R. viscosa* (CLAMMY LOCUST), and has pale pink flowers. This cross likely occurs in the wild. Leaflets 11–21. Pods to 3" (4") long.

R. × *ambigua* 'Bella-rosea'
= *R. Pseudoacacia* var. *bella-rosea* hort.
= *R. bella-rosea* Nichols.–Mottet.
= *R. amoena* hort. *ex* K. Koch

Originated in 1860 in Leiden, Holland. Very rare in North America. More like *R. viscosa* than *R. Pseudoacacia*. Twigs viscid, spiny. Leaflets 13–21. Flowers deep rosy-pink.

R. × *ambigua* 'Bella Rosa Pink Cascade'—see *R.* 'Casque Rouge'

R. × *ambigua* 'Decaisneana'
= *R. Pseudoacacia* 'Decaisineana'
= *R. decaisneana* hort.

PINK LOCUST. Originated <1860 in France. Named in 1863, likely after Joseph Decaisne (1807–1882), French botanist. Common in North American cultivation, although far less frequently sold now than in the past. Young twigs gummy-feeling. Leaflets 13–21. Flowers pink, slightly larger than those of *R. Pseudoacacia*. Pods to 3⅛" long, often with viable seeds. A definite tree with a ramrod-straight, hefty trunk. Records: 74' × 8'0" and 68' × 8'11" Seattle, WA (1988).

R. × *ambigua* 'Decaisneana Rubra'—see *R.* × *Slavinii* 'Hillieri'

R. × *ambigua* 'Idahoensis'
= *R. idahoensis* hort.
= *R. Pseudoacacia* var. *idahoensis* hort.

IDAHO LOCUST. Introduced in 1938 by Porter-Walton nursery of Salt Lake City, UT. Very common in cultivation, especially in the western U.S. More than one clone has been sold as IDAHO LOCUST. Leaflets 9–15. Flowers showy purplish-pink, in 4½" (8") long, glandular-hairy clusters of up to 12; commences blooming after *R.* × *Slavinii* 'Purple Robe', from late May and June into early July. Young growth hairy. Spiny. Grows 30'–40' tall.

R. amoena—see *R.* × *ambigua* 'Bella-rosea'

R. bella-rosea—see *R.* × *ambigua* 'Bella-rosea'

R. Bessoniana—see *R. Pseudoacacia* 'Bessoniana'

R. Boyntonii—see *R. hispida*

R. breviloba—see *R. neomexicana*

R. 'Cascade Rouge'—see *R.* 'Casque Rouge'

R. 'Casque Rouge'
= *R.* 'Cascade Rouge'
= *R. Pseudoacacia* 'Pink Cascade'
= *R. Pseudoacacia* 'Casque Rouge'
= *R.* × *ambigua* 'Bella Rosa Pink Cascade'
= *R.* × *Margaretta* 'Pink Cascade'

Origin unknown. Some European sources say "U.S. ca. 1934." In North American commerce ≤1959–60. Very rare until ca. 1992 when Duncan & Davies nursery of New Zealand began marketing it. The French *casque rouge* translates red helmet. The oldest name may be 'Pink Cascade'. A Dutch article in 1982 said *R.* × *Slavinii* Purple Crown™ was synonymous with this. Leaflets 13–17. Flowers resemble those of IDAHO LOCUST (*R.* × *ambigua* 'Idahoensis'). Perhaps less spiny than IDAHO. Crown low and rounded.

R. contorta—see *R. Pseudoacacia* 'Tortuosa'

R. decaisneana—see *R.* × *ambigua* 'Decaisneana'

R. × *dubia*—see *R.* × *ambigua*

R. Elliotii—see *R. hispida*

R. fastigiata—see *R. Pseudoacacia* 'Pyramidalis'

R. fertilis—see *R. hispida* var. *fertilis*

R. fertilis 'Monument'—see *R. hispida* 'Monument'

R. glutinosa—see *R. viscosa*

R. × *Hillieri*—see *R.* × *Slavinii* 'Hillieri'

R. hispida L.
= *R. Elliotii* (Chapm.) Ashe
= *R. nana* Elliot 1822
= *R. Boyntonii* Ashe

ROSE ACACIA. BRISTLY LOCUST. MOSS LOCUST. From the southeastern U.S. Commonly cultivated. An aggressively suckering shrub, to 16' tall; a tangled small tree only if trained or topgrafted. The epithet *hispida* means beset with stiff or bristly hairs. Botanists studying *Robinia* reported in 1984 that this species consisted of an aggregate of sterile clones. Twigs and pods hispid to nearly hairless. Leaflets (7) 9–13 (19). Flower clusters (3) 4–11 (15) flowered; flowers can be scentless but are always lovely; pink (rarely white) to rosy-purple; in May, June, and July—sometimes into September.

R. hispida var. *fertilis* (Ashe) Clausen
= *R. fertilis* Ashe

From mountains of North Carolina and Tennessee. Cultivated since ca. 1900. Named in 1923. Pods abundant, 2"–3½" long, very bristly, red and highly ornamental when young; brown in winter.

R. hispida 'Flowering Globe'

FLOWERING GLOBE LOCUST. Introduced ≤1955 by Scanlon nursery of Ohio, as *R. Pseudoacacia* × *R. hispida* 'Macrophylla'. Whether or not that parentage is correct, this clone is obviously a *R. hispida* hybrid or form. Still in commerce. Invariably topgrafted on *R. Pseudoacacia* trunks. Grows to ca. 18' tall, with a globular, rather loose head. Leaflets 11–19. Some small thorns in addition to sparse bristles. Flowers in heavy, dark pink 8"–10" clusters in mid-June.

R. hispida var. *inermis*—see *R. hispida* 'Macrophylla'

R. hispida var. *Kelseyi* (Cowell *ex* Hutch.) Isely
= *R. Kelseyi* Cowell *ex* Hutch.

KELSEY LOCUST. An alleged native of Tennessee mountains. Harlan Page Kelsey (1872–1959) discovered it wild in his Massachusetts nursery, and introduced it to cultivation in 1900. Rare. Named in 1902. Some botanists studying *Robinia* reported in 1984 that KELSEY LOCUST was known only in cultivation, a self-fertile *R. hispida* clone, essentially hairless, with narrow leaflets (bright light brown when young), and handsome red pods covered with sticky purple hairs. A large shrub or slender small tree.

R. hispida 'Macrophylla'
= *R. macrophylla* Schrad. *ex* DC.
= *R. hispida* var. *inermis* Kirchn.

SMOOTH ROSE ACACIA. Cultivated <1825 in France. Since ≤1934 sold as a topgraft on *R. Pseudoacacia* trunks. Uncommon. Not bristly or scarcely so; flowers and leaflets larger (Greek *makro*, large, and *phyllon*, a leaf) than on typical *R. hispida*. Flowers lavender-pink, very pretty.

R. hispida 'Monument'
= *R. hybrida* 'Monument'
= *R. fertilis* 'Monument'

MONUMENT LOCUST. Introduced ≤1940 by W.B. Clarke nursery of San José, CA. Common during the 1950s. Seldom sold since the mid-1960s. Clarke believed it a hybrid of *R. hispida* var. *Kelseyi* and *R. hispida* 'Macrophylla', and said it grows erect, so need not be topgrafted. Europeans call it a compact clone of *R. hispida* var. *fertilis*. Scanlon nursery of Ohio offered 'Monument' as a small tree, and said its flowers have a better rose-pink color than those of IDAHO LOCUST (*R.* × *ambigua* 'Idahoensis') and are larger; and the reddish tomentum of its branches distinguishes it. Leaflets 11–13.

R. × *Holdtii* Beissn.
(*R. neomexicana* × *R. Pseudoacacia*)

First known ca. 1890 in Frederick Von Holdt's (b. 1860) garden in Colorado. Named in 1902. Not intentionally sold by nurseries, this hybrid tends to pop up when *R. neomexicana* seedlings are raised. Flowers vary from blush-white to deep pink. Likely most record specimens cited as *R. neomexicana* are actually hybrids. A definite hybrid record is: 60' × 7'0" × 52½' Seattle, WA (1994; *pl.* 1957).

R. × *hybrida*—see R. × *ambigua*

R. *hybrida* 'Monument'—see R. *hispida* 'Monument'

R. *hybrida* 'Wisteria'—see R. 'Wisteria'

R. *idahoensis*—see R. × *ambigua* 'Idahoensis'

R. *inermis*—see R. *Pseudo.* 'Inermis' and R. *Pseudo.* 'Umbraculifera'

R. × *intermedia*—see R. × *ambigua*

R. *Kelseyi*—see R. *hispida* var. *Kelseyi*

R. *luxurians*—see R. *neomexicana*

R. *macrophylla*—see R. *hispida* 'Macrophylla'

R. × *Margaretta*—see R. × *Slavinii*

R. × *Margaretta* 'Pink Cascade'—see R. 'Casque Rouge'

R. *nana*—see R. *hispida* and R. *Pseudoacacia* 'Umbraculifera'

R. *neomexicana* Gray
= *R. luxurians* (Dieck) Schneid.
= *R. Rusbyi* Woot. & Standl.
= *R. breviloba* Rydb.
= *R. subvelutina* Rydb.

NEW MEXICO LOCUST. (SOUTH)WESTERN LOCUST. ROSE LOCUST. From mountains of the southwestern U.S. and northern Mexico. Named in 1854. Cultivated since 1882. Uncommon. Suckering shrub or small tree. Leaflets 9–21 (25). Flowers densely clustered, pale pink. Pods hairless or glandular-hispid, 2⅜"–4" × ⅓" wide. Readily crosses with *R. Pseudoacacia* (see *R.* × *Holdtii*), so likely some of these records are hybrids: 77' × 5'4" × 14' Coconino National Forest, AZ (1985); 70' × 5'3" Kew, England (1981); 40' × 1'2" × 10' Prescott National Forest, AZ (1974); 23' × 7'5" × 19' Lincoln National Forest, NM (1981).

R. *Pseudoacacia* L.
(*Pseudacacia*)

BLACK LOCUST. FALSE ACACIA. PEA FLOWER LOCUST. YELLOW LOCUST. WHITE LOCUST. GREEN LOCUST. SILVER CHAIN. WHYA TREE. From parts of the central and eastern U.S.; long commonly cultivated, now widely naturalized in much of North America and elsewhere. One of the world's most adaptable, tough, distinctive and familiar trees. Wood very valuable. Attacked by borers in much of North America; not in the West. Spreads by root suckers and seeds. Named in 1753, *Pseudoacacia* being an old generic name meaning FALSE ACACIA. Called LOCUST since North American missionaries thought it was the pod of this species which was the "locusts and wild honey" of John the Baptist. The tree's dark and rugged trunk supports an open, elegant head of healthy green foliage. Branches armed with short paired thorns, at most 1⅓" long. Leaflets (7) 9–19 (25). Flowers showy, white, fragrant, in drooping clusters to 8" long, from May into early July. Pods 2"–5" (6") × ½", purple-brown, flat and hairless, with 4–14 seeds; in early August the reddish pods are pretty. Only 3 of the 18 following cultivars originated in North America; many more cultivars exist (or used to) in Europe. Records: 120' × 8'0" Great Smoky Mountains National Park, TN (1974); 109' × 14'9" Walla Walla, WA (1993); 103' × 16'6" Richmond, MA (1969); 96' × 23'4" Dansville, NY (1974); 96' × 18'5" Hillsdale County, MI (1979).

R. *Pseudoacacia* 'Angustifolia—see R. *Pseudoacacia* 'Microphylla'

R. *Pseudoacacia* 'Appalachia'—see R. *Pseudoacacia* f. *rectissima*

R. *Pseudoacacia* 'Aurea'
Originated ca. 1859 in Germany; named in 1864. Rare in North America. Foliage pale yellow at least in early summer, becoming light green. See also *R. Pseudoacacia* 'Frisia' and 'Dean Rossman'. Records: 80' × 5'6" Moor Park, Ludlow, Shropshire, England (1962); 63' tall and 38' wide at Lisle, IL (1986; *pl.* 1960).

R. Pseudoacacia var. *bella-rosea*—see *R.* ×
  ambigua 'Bella-rosea'

R. Pseudoacacia 'Bessoniana'
= *R. Bessoniana* hort.

Originated ca. 1859 in Germany; named officially in
1886. Uncommon in North America. Resembles *R.
Pseudoacacia* 'Umbraculifera' but has a well-developed
trunk of its own, and slenderer branches forming a
more open, ovoid crown. Mostly thornless. Flowers
sparse. Leaflets relatively few, often only 5. Likely
some nurseries have sold 'Umbraculifera' as 'Bessoniana'. Record: a trunk 16'9" around in Czechoslovakia (1988).

R. Pseudoacacia 'Casque Rouge'—see *R.*
  'Casque Rouge'

R. Pseudoacacia 'Crispa'

Named in 1825 in France. In North American commerce ≤1851. Extremely rare. Thornless. Leaflets
more or less undulately curled. Nurseryman J. Breck
wrote in 1851: "very singularly curious and elegant
leaves, each being curiously and uniformly contorted."

R. Pseudoacacia 'Dean Rossman'

Discovered as a chance six-year old seedling in 1984
by Dean Michael Rossman of Mahopac, NY. Registered in 1990. Leaves pale yellow, the color better and
more persistent in summer than on *R. Pseudoacacia*
'Frisia'. Thorns fewer and smaller than typical.

R. Pseudoacacia 'Decaisneana'—see under *R.*
  × *ambigua*

R. Pseudoacacia 'Elegantissima'—see *R.*
  Pseudo. 'Microphylla'

R. Pseudoacacia f. *erecta*—see *R. Pseudo.*
  'Monophylla Fastigiata'

R. Pseudoacacia 'Fastigiata'—see *R.*
  Pseudoacacia 'Pyramidalis'

R. Pseudoacacia Fibermaster®

Introduced ≤1991 by Better Trees, Inc., of St. John's,
MI. A seed-propagated cultivar selected because most
individuals grow with relatively few breakage-prone
forking trunks.

R. Pseudoacacia 'Frisia'

Discovered by W. Jansen ca. 1935 in a former nursery
at Zwollerkerspel, Holland. Named after Friesland

Province. In North American commerce since ≤1958.
Becoming common where the climate permits it to
thrive. Leaves bright yellow all summer; red thorns;
much better than *R. Pseudoacacia* 'Aurea', but see *R.
Pseudoacacia* 'Dean Rossman'. Record: 72' × 7'6"
Auburn, WA (1992).

R. Pseudoacacia 'Globosum'—see *R. Pseudo.*
  'Umbraculifera'

R. Pseudoacacia 'Heterophylla'—see *R.*
  Pseudoacacia 'Unifoliola'

R. Pseudoacacia 'Idahoensis'—see *R.* ×
  ambigua 'Idahoensis'

R. Pseudoacacia 'Inermis'
= *R. inermis* Mirb., non de Vos

THORNLESS LOCUST. Raised in France; named in 1804
(*inermis* in Latin means unarmed; without thorns).
Thornless or nearly so. Tree vigorous and full-sized.
Leaves extra large. Frequently *R. Pseudoacacia* 'Umbraculifera' is called 'Inermis' incorrectly.

R. Pseudoacacia inermis globosa—see *R.
  Pseudo.* 'Umbraculifera'

R. Pseudoacacia 'Macrophylla'

Introduced ≤1824. Greek *makro*, large, and *phyllon*,
a leaf. In North American commerce ≤1851. A specimen received in 1950 by the Seattle arboretum from
Morton Arboretum of Lisle, IL (as 'Amorphæfolia'—
a small-leaf cultivar), may be 'Macrophylla'—it bears
leaves as long as 17", leaflets to 3¼" × 1⅝", and pods
to 5½" × ¾".

R. Pseudoacacia 'Microphylla'
?= *R. Pseudoacacia* 'Angustifolia'
?= *R. Pseudoacacia* 'Elegantissima'
?= *R. Pseudoacacia* 'Mimosæfolia'

Originated in 1813 in England. Described in 1830
(Greek *micro*, very small, and *phyllon*, leaf). Very
rare in North America. Several clones similar to this
were once cultivated, but they are very difficult to tell
apart. Tree has a delicate textural quality like that of
Gleditsia triacanthos (HONEY LOCUST). Leaflets ca. 1"
× ¼". Small to medium-sized (to 40' × 30' wide), slow
tree; rarely flowers when young. At maturity it flowers and sets pods.

R. Pseudoacacia 'Mimosæfolia'—see *R.
  Pseudo.* 'Microphylla'

R. Pseudoacacia 'Monophylla'—see R. Pseudoacacia 'Unifoliola'

R. Pseudoacacia 'Monophylla Fastigiata'

= R. Pseudoacacia f. erecta Rehd.

Originated ca. 1880 by Dr. G. Dieck of Germany as a seedling of R. Pseudoacacia 'Unifoliola'. Named in 1885. Very rare in North America. Habit narrow, full sized. Leaflets reduced in number and increased in size, especially the terminal one (monophylla from Greek monos, one, and phyllon, a leaf). Record: 71½' × 4'11" Seattle, WA (1994; pl. 1960).

R. Pseudoacacia 'Ohio Prostrate'

Origin unknown, <1966. Extremely rare. Topgrafted at 6' to weep.

R. Pseudoacacia 'Pendulifolia'

Originated ca. 1860 in Germany; described in 1864. Extremely rare in North America. Leaves drooping. Apt to be confused with R. Pseudoacacia 'Rozynskiana' (a much more striking clone). Record: 50' × 5'0" Seattle, WA (1994; pl. 1950).

R. Pseudoacacia 'Pink Cascade'—see R. 'Casque Rouge'

R. Pseudoacacia 'Purple Robe'—see R. 'Purple Robe'

R. Pseudoacacia 'Pyramidalis'

= R. fastigiata hort.
= R. Pseudoacacia 'Fastigiata'

FASTIGIATE LOCUST. PYRAMIDAL LOCUST. Originated ca. 1839 in France. Named in 1845. Uncommon in North America. Habit fastigiate and columnar; thornless (a few short thorns of some strong shoots); fewer flowers than typical. Records: 67' × 4'8" × 25' Seattle, WA (1992; pl. 1965).

R. Pseudoacacia f. rectissima (Raber) stat. nov.

= R. Pseudoacacia var. rectissima Raber

SHIPMAST LOCUST. Cultivated on Long Island, NY, since early 1700s. Named officially in 1936 (from Latin recta, straight, and the superlative -issima— very straight or straightest). Several clones exist, one named 'Appalachia' in 1956. Trunk very straight and columnar; bark less deeply furrowed; crown narrow; smaller branches; fewer flowers; nearly sterile; rarely makes pods.

R. Pseudoacacia 'Rozynskiana'

('Rozynskyana', 'Rosynskiana')

WEEPING BLACK LOCUST. Discovered ≤1896 in Count Zamoyski's nursery at Podzamcze, central Poland, where it had been produced and sold already at the turn of the century. Introduced to western European cultivation in 1903 by Späth nursery of Germany. In North American commerce ≤1940. Extremely rare. Still available, as by Arborvillage nursery of Holt, MO. Looks superficially like a WEEPING WILLOW. Leaf to 19½" long with 15–21 drooping loosely placed leaflets. Flowers very profuse. Similar to but far more distinctive than R. Pseudoacacia 'Pendulifolia'. Records: 80' × 6'0" Nymans, Sussex, England (1985); 65' × 4'0" Mirfield, Yorkshire, England (1989); a trunk 7'10" around in Brooklyn, NY (1972).

R. Pseudoacacia 'Semperflorens'

PERPETUAL BLACK LOCUST. Originated in France; described in 1871. Name means ever-flowering; from Latin semper, always or ever, and florens, blooming. It blooms intermittently all summer. In North American commerce ≤1888. Extremely rare. The name has been misapplied to some pink-flowered recurrent bloomers. Under this name ≤1918 L. Coates nursery of California sold "a variety which seems to have originated on our grounds. Rose-pink flowers in dense clusters almost continuously from June to September. Branches smooth." A specimen labeled 'Semperflorens' at VanDuesen gardens of Vancouver, B.C., is podless. Any sterile Robinia, incapable of setting pods, might easily bloom in vain all summer long.

R. Pseudoacacia 'Tortuosa'

= R. contorta hort.

TWISTED LOCUST. Originated <1810. Described in 1813 in France. In North American commerce ≤1851. Very rare. Short zigzag-twisted branches, short stature, slow growth; usually few-flowered. Records: 62' × 6'0" Edinburgh, Scotland (1985); 55' × 9'9" Kew, England (1981); 42' × 4'8" Puyallup, WA (1993).

R. Pseudoacacia 'Umbraculifera'

= R. Pseudoacacia inermis globosa hort.
= R. Pseudoacacia 'Inermis' (in part—incorrectly)
= R. Pseudoacacia 'Globosum'
= R. nana hort., non Elliot 1822
= R. inermis de Vos, non Mirb.

MUSHROOM LOCUST. GLOBE LOCUST. PARASOL LOCUST. Originated in France or Austria <1810. Described in 1811 (Latin umbraculum, umbrella, and ferre, to bear). Commonly cultivated. A thornless, trunkless, spherical large shrub; rarely produces flowers. Usually sold topgrafted, as are the following records. Records: 38' × 7'4" × 23' Walla Walla, WA (1993); 26' × 5'8" × 32' Tacoma, WA (1990).

R. Pseudoacacia 'Unifoliola'

= R. Pseudoacacia 'Monophylla'
= R. Pseudoacacia 'Heterophylla'

SINGLELEAF LOCUST. Imported (as 'Monophylla') to Boston in 1850 by nurseryman J. Breck. For all that, the usual account of this clone is that it a arose in France ca. 1855, when raised by Deniaux of Brain-sur-l'Authion, Maine-et-Loire (according to Carrière) or, Angers (according to Talou) and was put in commerce by Lebigot of Angers ca. 1859 (the year it was officially described). Extremely rare in North America. Likely to be confused with R. Pseudoacacia 'Monophylla Fastigiata'. Leaflets 1–7, large. Record: 62' × 5'9" Leamington, Warwick, England (1971).

R. Purple Robe™ PP 2454 (1964)

= R. × Slavinii Purple Robe™
= R. Pseudoacacia Purple Robe™
(R. ambigua 'Decaisneana' × R. hispida 'Monument')

An intentional cross by W. Silva of California. Common; replacing IDAHO LOCUST (R. × ambigua 'Idahoensis'). Grows rapidly. Bronzy-red new foliage. Flowers large, violet-purple, by April 20th—well before those of other Robinia. Leaflets 17–21. Described as thornless but some specimens labeled Purple Robe™ bear thorns like those of typical R. Pseudoacacia. Said to grow 35'–50' tall.

R. Rusbyi—see R. neomexicana

R. × Slavinii Rehd.

= R. × Margaretta Ashe
(R. Pseudoacacia × R. hispida)

First raised in 1915 in Rochester, NY, and named in 1921 after Bernard Henry Slavin (1873–1960), the horticulturist who gathered the seed (from a R. hispida var. Kelseyi) from which the tree was raised. This hybrid is locally spontaneous in the eastern U.S. Very rarely offered in commerce. Not known to bear pods.

R. × Slavinii 'Hillieri'

= R. × Hillieri hort.
= R. × ambigua 'Decaisneana Rubra'

COMPACT PINK LOCUST. Raised ca. 1930 by Hillier nursery of England; named in 1933. In North America ≤1953; extremely rare. An elegant small rounded tree; slightly fragrant lilac-pink flowers in June. Leaflets 9 usually.

R. × Slavinii Purple Crown™ PP 7731 (1991)

Patented by Wm. Flemmer, III, of Princeton nursery, New Jersey. Sold mostly on the West Coast. Said to grow 20'–30' tall; rich purple flowers in early June; few pods; foliage open. A Dutch article in 1982 equated R. 'Casque Rouge' with this.

R. × Slavinii Purple Robe™—see R. Purple Robe

R. subvelutina—see R. neomexicana

R. viscosa Vent.

= R. glutinosa Simms

CLAMMY LOCUST. GUMMY ACACIA. From the SE United States in mountains of west North Carolina, possibly adjacent South Carolina and Tennessee. Named in 1799 (viscosus in Latin means sticky). Cultivated ≤1818 in Cambridge, MA. In commerce ≤1841 and once commonly planted, rarely sold now. It often hybridizes. Leaflets (11) 13–21 (27). Flowers pink to rose-purple (rarely creamy-white), inodorous, in dense clusters well after those of R. Pseudoacacia. Pods (commonly not formed) 2"–3½" long, very slender, thinly covered with reddish glandular hairs. Floral parts, twigs and pods glandular and sticky, especially when young. Thorns weak and usually tiny (to ½"). A large shrub or small tree. Bark less dark and more flaky than that of R. Pseudoacacia. Records (the first likely a hybrid or a graft on R. Pseudoacacia): 59' × 10'4" Futog, Serbia (ca. 1948); 45' tall at Croome, Worcestershire, England (1830s, when 30 years old); 42' × 4'0" Borde Hill, Sussex, England (1968); 33' × 3'3" Sidney, B.C. (1973; pl. 1926); 28' × 4'9" Kew, England (1928); a trunk 4'10" around at Duncan, B.C. (1995).

R. 'Wisteria'

= R. hybrida 'Wisteria'

Introduced ≤1940 by W.B. Clarke nursery of San José, CA. Attributes unknown. Long extinct commercially, at least under this name.

Rulac Negundo—Acer Negundo

Sabal

[PALMÆ or ARECACEÆ; Palm Family] 14–16 (20) spp. of New World PALMS. All need much light. The 1763 name *Sabal* is of uncertain origin; maybe a South American name for one of the species. The hardiest species may be *S. minor*, but it is usually a mere shrub. The other PALM genera in this volume are *Butia, Ceroxylon, Chamærops, Nannorrhops, Trachycarpus,* and *Washingtonia.*

S. Palmetto (Walt.) Lodd. *ex* J.A. & J.H. Schult.

CABBAGE PALMETTO. CAROLINA PALMETTO. COMMON PALMETTO. From North Carolina to Florida, near the coast; also Cuba and the Bahamas. The State Tree of South Carolina. Common in cultivation. No PALM can tolerate as wide a range of conditions—pure beach sand, sour muck, clay; can be transplanted when 80' tall; hardy to near 0°F. Named in 1788, from the Spanish common name *palmetto*, a "small palm." D.J. Browne explained in 1832: "The base of the leaves, when tender, is eaten with oil and vinegar; and resembles the artichoke and cabbage in taste, whence is derived the name of Cabbage Tree. But to destroy a vegetable which has been a century in growing, to obtain three or four ounces of a substance neither richly nutritious nor peculiarly agreeable to the palate, would be pardonable only in a desert which was destined to remain uninhabited for ages." Frond to 8' wide, with 40–95 segments. Blossoms mostly in July, but June through August. Fruit ⅓"–½" wide. Seedlings can be weedy. Records: 90' × 3'9" × 14' Highland Hammock State Park, FL (1965); 62' × 5'10" × 30' Brunswick, GA (1991).

Salisburia adiantifolia—Ginkgo biloba

Salix

[SALICACEÆ; Willow Family] 300–500 spp. of shrubs and trees known as WILLOWS (SALLOWS, and OSIERS), distributed from the arctic to the subtropics, sea-level to alpine summits. *Salix* is an ancient Latin name. WILLOWS are usually deciduous, and are characteristically pioneer species needing much sun and tolerating soaking wet soil. The leaves are often long and slender. Stipules, small rudimentary leaves by the leafstems, are usually present. Male and female flowers are in catkins on separate plants. Male florets each bear from (1) 2 to 12 stamens, usually with yellow anthers. Female florets ripen tiny capsules which release minuscule seeds, sent airborne by cottony tufts. WILLOWS have a reputation for being difficult to identify, because there are so many, they are so prone to hybridizing, and can be inherently variable. They also have a reputation for being rapid-growing, short-lived, brittle, buggy, greedy, and inappropriate for gardens.

An objective review finds they are a varied lot, often fascinating, and not necessarily so bad as one might fear. Any tree lover ought to be able to learn the names of those species native in his or her locale. Often the presence of insect galls, and sometimes of certain fungal diseases, serves as a helpful indicator, being species-specific. It is said the New World has about 100 *Salix* species; everyone knows WILLOWS. But not even one native American WILLOW species is common in ornamental planting; we plant foreigners and hybrids. Excepting the unrivaled WEEPING WILLOWS, some of our natives are just as pretty as any foreigners, but we must take the time to select the best clones and plant them in the right places.

A completely unscientific, but fairly practical classification of landscape WILLOW trees, yields four groups: WEEPING WILLOWS, SHADE-TREE WILLOWS, PUSSY WILLOWS, and "everything else." The latter category is smallest and includes WILLOWS grown primarily for colorful winter twigs, as well as small trees with pretty foliage. Many tree WILLOWS are kept shrubby on purpose, so their lengthy whiplike twigs can display maximum winter color, or can be harvested for basketry. Drawing the line between shrubby and treelike WILLOWS is especially problematic. WILLOWS in cultivation are usually raised from cuttings rather from seed, so are prevailingly clones. The most closely related genus is *Populus* (POPLARS, ASPENS and COTTONWOODS).

S. alba L.

WHITE WILLOW. EUROPEAN WHITE WILLOW. HUNTINGDON WILLOW. From Europe, NW Africa, W Asia. Named in 1753. Introduced to North America in colonial times (≤1775) and widely naturalized, mostly in its varieties. Extinct commercially except in its cultivars. The typical form of WHITE WILLOW is a large shade tree of fine texture; valued in Europe for timber as well. Twigs greenish. Leaves silky-hairy, 2"–4" long. Records: 100' × 21'0" Northampton, MA (<1987); 98' × 19'5" Hanover, NH (1985); 85' × 23'6" near Winona, OH (<1945); 60' × 26'2" × 110' near Ashtabula, OH (<1961); a trunk 28'5" around at Prague, Czechoslovakia (1985)

S. alba f. *argentea*—see *S. alba* var. *sericea*

S. alba 'Aurea Pendula'—see *S.* × *sepulcralis* 'Chrysocoma'

S. alba 'Britzensis'

CORALBARK WILLOW. SCARLET WILLOW. REDTWIG WILLOW. Raised from seed by Späth nursery at Britz, near Berlin, Germany. In cultivation ≤1878. A male clone of *S. alba* var. *vitellina*. Similar to and confused with the 1840 *S. alba* 'Chermesina'. The name 'Britzensis' has been applied to more than one clone. All have in common attractive winter twig color. Nurseries describe this color variously; here is a selection from a dozen nursery catalogs: bright flame (Meehan 1900–01); deep red (Elm City 1903); like *Cornus sibirica* (Ellwanger & Barry 1910); salmon (Andorra 1915); bright red (Bobbink & Atkins 1921); bronze (Princeton 1924); bronzy-yellow (Andorra 1927–28); reddish-bronze (E & F 1929); brilliant red (O. Will 1933); brilliant orange-scarlet (Hillier 1938); brilliant sealing-wax red (Jackman 1950–51); bright copper-orange (Sunningdale 1957). Obviously some specimens of *S. alba* 'Cardinalis' and 'Chermesina' have been sold as 'Britzensis'. Twig color alone will not suffice in identifying WILLOW clones. We must also know the sex, and the tree's shape and vigor.

S. alba var. *calva*—see *S. alba* var. *cærulea*

S. alba var. *cærulea* (Sm.) Sm.

= *S. cærulea* Sm.
= *S. alba* var. *calva* G.F. Mey.
(*cærulea, cerulea*)

BLUE WILLOW. CRICKETBAT WILLOW. Leaves not remaining hairy (unlike typical *S. alba*), and conspicuously glaucous beneath. Branching habit strongly upright although in no sense columnar. Cultivated primarily via a female clone found ca. 1780 in NW Suffolk, England. Named in 1812. The Latin *cæruleus* means heavenly blue. Grown extensively in English plantations for wood, prized for making cricketbats since it is light, resilient and strong. More common in North America than typical *S. alba*, less common than *S. alba* var. *vitellina*. Prone to disfiguring fungal diseases, and not especially ornamental, it has long been out of commerce. Recorded to 135' × 20'0".

S. alba 'Cardinalis'

= *S. cardinalis* hort.

BELGIAN RED WILLOW. CARDINAL WILLOW. A cultivar of *S. alba* var. *vitellina*. Cultivated since the 1880s, mostly for basketry twigs. A narrowly conical small tree to 20' tall, like *S. alba* 'Britzensis' but female, with narrower leaves.

S. alba 'Chermesina'

CARMINE-TWIG WILLOW. Found near Braunschweig in Germany. Described in 1840 (Greek *kermesina* means carmine-red). A cultivar of *S. alba* var. *vitellina*. Confused and wrongly equated with *S. alba* 'Britzensis'. Twigs carmine-red in winter. Other sources have described the twig color as vivid scarlet, bright red, or even orange—which underscores the mixing up with 'Britzensis', 'Chrysostela' etc. Although North American nurseries have listed 'Chermesina', apparently mostly the clone has circulated as one of those sold as 'Britzensis'. It may be practically impossible to describe these clones in unambiguous fashion.

S. alba 'Chrysostela'

Described in 1930 (meaning column of gold, from Greek *chryso-*, golden, and *stela*, column). In British nurseries since ≤1943. A cultivar of *S. alba* var. *vitellina*. Broadly columnar habit. Winter twigs golden, reddish towards their tips. Male. Catkins to 2⅞" long at most.

S. alba 'Pyramidalis'

A cultivar of *S. alba* var. *vitellina*. Not known in North America, but could be here. It sounds similar to *S. alba* 'Britzensis', 'Cardinalis', 'Chermesina' and 'Chrysostela'. The 1971 *Yearbook* of the International Dendrology Society says it was found ca. 1920 by A. Wróblewski in Podole, Poland. A 65' tall, wide column, with very vivid red or yellow-red, shiny twigs.

S. alba 'Regalis'—see *S. alba* var. *sericea*

S. alba var. *sericea* Gaud.

= *S. regalis* hort. *ex* K. Koch
= *S. alba* 'Regalis'
= *S. alba* var. *sibirica* hort.
= *S. alba* var. *splendens* (Bray *ex* Opiz) Anderss.
= *S. alba* f. *argentea* Wimm.

SILVER WILLOW. ROYAL WILLOW. Cultivated in Europe since the early 1800s. The *sericea* name dates from 1830 and means silky. In North American commerce ≤1908. Uncommon. Foliage densely and persistently silvery-hairy, making the tree distinctively silvery, looking from a distance like an enormous RUSSIAN OLIVE (*Elæagnus angustifolia*). Twigs greenish-brown underneath gray hairs. Several clones are cultivated. In England the prevalent one is less robust than typical WHITE WILLOW. In North America, a female prevails (catkins to 2½" long), and has no trouble growing 100' tall. Possibly this clone is the one N. Hansen imported from Russia in the early 1900s. Records: 96' × 10'4" × 85' Seattle (1995; *pl.* 1954); 82' × 10'10" Belton Park, Lincolnshire, England (1978); 65' × 9'3" × 79' Seattle (1987; *pl.* 1954).

S. alba var. *sibirica*—see *S. alba* var. *sericea*

S. alba 'Snake'—see *S.* 'Snake'

S. alba var. *splendens*—see *S. alba* var. *sericea*

S. alba 'Tristis'—see *S.* × *sepulcralis* 'Chrysocoma'

S. alba var. *vitellina* (L.) Stokes
= *S. vitellina* L.
= *S. aurea* Salisb.

GOLDEN WILLOW. (RUSSIAN) YELLOW WILLOW. Cultivated ≤1623 in Switzerland. Named in 1753 (egg-yolk yellow shoots, from Latin *vitellus*, egg yolk). Very common in North America and vegetatively naturalized here. Clones of both sexes occur. Twig color varies from lemon-yellow to orange-yellow (golden) or red. Seen from afar, as across a lake, the white leaf undersides fluttering in the wind make the tree stand out; then in winter the warm-colored twigs highlight the landscape like daubs of bright paint on a dark canvas. Leaves much less hairy than those of typical *S. alba*. Male catkins 2½"–4⅜" long. Records: 133' × 25'1" × 142' New Hudson, MI (1991); 83' × 28'7" × 132' Jackson County, MI (1971); 58' × 30'7" × 96' near Commerce, MI (1959).

S. alba 'Vitellina Pendula Nova'—see *S.* × *sepulcralis* 'Chrysocoma'

S. amplifolia—see *S. Hookeriana*

S. amygdalina—see *S. triandra*

S. amygdaloides Anderss.

PEACHLEAF WILLOW. ALMONDLEAF WILLOW. From much of interior North America, centered in the Great Plains. Named in 1858 (from *S. amygdalina* and Greek *-oides*, resemblance). Cultivated since 1895. Not generally in commerce or cultivation; least rare perhaps in the Canadian prairie region. Twigs

hairless, yellowish-brown to reddish-brown, usually not especially brittle. Leaves to 6" × 1⅝", or at most 9" × 2"; not glossy above, but pale beneath; stipules small and fleeting. Records: 92' tall in Chaska, MN (<1986); 83' × 13'0" Bend, OR (1972); 67' × 23'8" × 80' Union County, OR (1975); 58' × 34'9" × 82' West Allis, WI (1989); 56' × 8'0" × 95' Walla Walla, WA (1993).

S. atrocinerea—see *S. cinerea* var. *atrocinerea*

S. aurea—see *S. alba* var. *vitellina*

S. babylonica L.
= *S. Napoleonis* hort.

BABYLON WEEPING WILLOW. CHINESE WEEPING WILLOW. From W China, not Babylon. When this species was named in 1738, it was believed to be the one referred to in Psalm 137: "By the waters of Babylon, there we sat down, yea, we wept, when we remembered Zion. We hanged our harps, upon the willows in the midst thereof." Introduced to western Europe from Turkey in the late 1600s; in England ≤1730. In North American commerce ≤1790. Long common. One of the world's most celebrated and distinctive trees. Napoleon's prized WEEPING WILLOW came from Britain and was planted in 1810 by General Beatson on St. Helena Island. It succumbed to a storm at about the time Napoleon died (1821). But cuttings were planted around the grave. Many nurseries subsequently sold "*Salix Napoleonis*" to eager buyers. True BABYLON WEEPING WILLOW is somewhat cold-tender, and although common and naturalized in the southeast U.S. (occurring in both sexes), it is relatively rare on the West Coast (mostly a female clone), and nonexistent in cold regions northward. Trees of the north called *S. babylonica* are simply its hybrids: *S.* × *pendulina*, *S.* × *sepulcralis* (and their crosses with other species). Twigs greenish, olive-golden or reddish-brown. Leaves 2"–6" long × ⅓"–¾" wide, lightly hairy when young; glaucous beneath; stem hairy. Female catkins narrow, 1"–2" long; ovary short-staked, hairless. Records (the first two may be hybrids): 134' × 17'11" × 76' Westminster, MD (1990); 114' × 24'3" × 106' Asheville, NC (1987); 52' × 11'5" × 64' Steilacoom, WA (1992).

S. babylonica 'Annularis'
= *S. babylonica* 'Crispa'

RINGLEAF WILLOW. RAM'S HORN WILLOW. SCREWLEAF WILLOW. HOOPLEAF WILLOW. Cultivated since 1827 in Belgium. Named 'Annularis' in 1829 and 'Crispa' in 1838. In North American commerce ≤1841.

Uncommon. Leaves curled in strong hoops as its names suggest. A female clone. Not as weeping or vigorous or cold-hardy as typical *S. babylonica*. Record: 58' × 7'11" × 57' Tacoma, WA (1990).

S. babylonica 'Aurea'—see *S.* × *sepulcralis* 'Chrysocoma'

S. babylonica 'Crispa'—see *S. babylonica* 'Annularis'

S. babylonica dolorosa—see *S.* × *pendulina* 'Blanda'

S. babylonica 'Navajo'—see *S. Matsudana* 'Navajo'

S. babylonica var. pekinensis—see *S. Matsudana*

S. babylonica 'Snake'—see *S.* 'Snake'

S. babylonica 'Tortuosa'—see *S. Matsudana* 'Tortuosa'

S. babylonica 'Umbraculifera'—see *S. Matsudana* 'Umbraculifera'

S. basfordiana—see *S.* × *rubens* 'Basfordiana'

S. × blanda—see *S.* × *pendulina* 'Blanda'

S. × blanda 'Fanick'—see *S.* × *pendulina* 'Fan-Giant'

S. × blanda Fan Willow™—see *S.* × *pendulina* 'Fan-Giant'

S. brachystachys—see *S. Scouleriana*

S. bullata—see *S. fragilis* 'Bullata'

S. caprea L.
= *S. præcox* Salisb.
= *S. discolor* 'French Pink' (in part—cf. *S. cinerea*)
GOAT WILLOW. FRENCH (PINK) PUSSY WILLOW. FLORIST'S WILLOW. GREAT SALLOW. SALLY. From Europe, and all across Russia to the Far East. The name *caprea* is Latin for a goat, but its application to this species is of obscure significance. Maybe the tree's foliage was used for goat fodder, or its wooly catkins resemble a goat's

beard. Long cultivated in North America, but often plants so called are really *S. cinerea* (GRAY WILLOW). Comparatively difficult to strike from cuttings. Grown for its showy late winter catkins. Twigs thick, hairy when young, becoming hairless and reddish-brown or yellow-green within the first year. Tolerates dry soils, being in England often on sandy slopes, old slag heaps and drier situations than most WILLOWS. Leaves to 6⅛" × 3½" but commonly half that size or less. Usually a shrubby small tree. Records: 75' tall Bialowieza National Park, Poland (1974); 69' × 5'0" Moniack Glen, Highland, Scotland (1987); 52½' × 11'10" Ardross Castle, Highland, Scotland (1989).

S. caprea 'Kilmarnock'
= *S. caprea* 'Pendula' (for the most part)
= *S. kilmarnocki* hort. (for the most part)
WEEPING GOAT WILLOW. KILMARNOCK WILLOW. WEEPING PUSSY WILLOW. Discovered on the bank of the Ayr River in Scotland. Introduced in 1853 by Thomas Lang of Kilmarnock, Ayrshire. In North American commerce ≤1884. Uncommon. A mophead, dense weeping tree little taller than the point at which it is topgrafted. Male; its female counterpart is *S. caprea* 'Weeping Sally'. Record: 20' × 6'3" × 20' Sidney, B.C. (1993).

S. caprea 'Pendula'—see *S. caprea* 'Kilmarnock' & 'Weeping Sally'

S. caprea 'Tricolor'—see *S. cinerea* 'Variegata'

S. caprea 'Variegata'—see *S. cinerea* 'Variegata'

S. caprea 'Weeping Sally'
= *S. caprea* 'Pendula' (to a lesser degree)
= *S. kilmarnocki* hort. (to a lesser degree)
Cultivated ≤1880. Named in 1976 by Roy Lancaster. The female counterpart to *S. caprea* 'Kilmarnock'. More vigorous, but less effective in flower, and branches less steeply pendulous.

S. cardinalis—see *S. alba* 'Cardinalis'

S. caudata—see *S. lucida* ssp. *caudata*

S. cærulea—see *S. alba* var. *cærulea*

S. × chrysocoma—see *S.* × *sepulcralis* 'Chrysocoma'

S. cinerea L.
= *S. discolor* 'French Pink' (in part—cf. *S. caprea*)
GRAY WILLOW. GRAY SALLOW. From Europe, W Asia,

and N Africa. Common in North America since the 1800s, even naturalized in some places. Usually misidentified as *S. caprea* or *S. discolor*, and called FRENCH PINK PUSSY WILLOW. Nurseries almost never list it under its proper name. The Latin epithet *cinerea* means ashy, in reference to the twig color. Twigs densely hairy, often for the first two years. Peeling the bark off two-year old twigs reveals unique raised stripes or ridges on the wood. Leaves similar to those of *S. caprea* but hairier, smaller (especially narrower), to 4⅛" × 2"; hairy beneath; very short-stemmed. Catkins to 2" long. Usually a shrub.

S. cinerea var. *atrocinerea* (Brot.) O. de Bolòs & J. Vigo

= *S. cinerea* ssp. *oleifolia* (Sm.) Macreight
= *S. atrocinerea* Brot.

RUSTY SALLOW. COMMON SALLOW. From Britain to Portugal, even NW Morocco. By far the commonest WILLOW in the lowland British Isles. Uncommon in North America. Differs from typical *S. cinerea* in several respects. Much more treelike. Hairs rusty, with tiny black glands—most noticeable on vigorous shoots in early autumn. Twigs become hairless, dark reddish-brown. Leaves less hairy. Stipules small and fleeting instead of big and persistent. The 1804 name *atrocinerea* is from the Latin prefix *atro*, very dark, and *cinerea*, ashy—because it is a conspicuously darker-looking variety. The name *oleifolia* means OLIVE-leaved—from genus *Olea*, OLIVE, and Latin *folium*, a leaf.

S. cinerea ssp. *oleifolia*—see *S. cinerea* var. *atrocinerea*

S. cinerea 'Tricolor'—see *S. cinerea* 'Variegata'

S. cinerea 'Variegata'

= *S. caprea* 'Tricolor'
= *S. caprea* 'Variegata'
= *S. cinerea* 'Tricolor'

Named in 1770. Long present in North America but always rare. Leaves small; variegated yellow, white and green. A male clone. Young shoots and leaves reddish.

S. cœrulea—see *S. alba* var. *cœrulea*

S. contorta—see *S. Matsudana* 'Tortuosa'

S. cordata var. *mackenzieana*—see *S. eriocephala* ssp. *mackenzieana*

S. daphnoides Vill.

VIOLET WILLOW. EUROPEAN VIOLET WILLOW. From Europe to N Scandinavia, also the Himalayas and central Asia. Named in 1786 (genus *Daphne*, and Greek *-oides*, resemblance). Cultivated since 1796 in Germany; 1820 in Switzerland, 1829 in England. In North America ≤1863. Extremely rare. In July, shoots green, leaf undersides powder-blue. The autumn/early winter twigs very attractively violet-bluish bloomed. Leaves 2"–6" long, to 1" wide, glossy green above, dusty blue below. Attractive catkins. At least in the British Isles, males tend to form a broadly spreading crown; females are usually columnar and taller; in Seattle exactly the opposite has occurred. Records: to 60' tall; 57' × 5'1" Glasnevin, Ireland (1974; *pl.* 1934); 48' × 4'10" (male) and 41' × 6'11" (female) Seattle, WA (1994; *pl.* 1960).

S. decipiens—see *S. fragilis* 'Decipiens'

S. 'Diamond'—see *S. eriocephala* ssp. *mackenzieana*

S. discolor Muhl.

PUSSY WILLOW. SILVER PUSSY WILLOW. AMERICAN PUSSY WILLOW. GLAUCOUS WILLOW. BOG WILLOW. From much of northern North America. Named in 1803, meaning different- or parti-colored (leaves green above, glaucous white beneath). True *S. discolor* is essentially a shrub, rarely 20' tall, not commonly cultivated. But its name is universally applied by nurseries to cultivated PUSSY WILLOWS of various species and hybrids, including: *S. caprea*, *S. cinerea*, *S. Hookeriana*, *S. × sericans*—virtually any small tree grown for handsome early spring catkins. The catkins open ca. 1 week after those of *S. caprea*, and are less compact. Twigs hairy when young, soon bald or nearly so. Leaves to 5" × 1½", usually no more than 4" × 1⅓"; sparsely silky when young. Records (all suspect as to identity): 47' × 4'6" × 33' Clinton County, MI (1983); 40' × 5'2" × 45' Wilmington, MA (1972); 25' × 6'2" × 48' Jamestown, RI (1983).

S. discolor 'French Pink'—see *S. caprea* and *S. cinerea*

S. dolorosa—see *S. × pendulina* 'Blanda'

S. 'Dropmore Weeping Willow'

(*S. amygdaloides* × *S. pendulina* 'Blanda')

Originated in 1956 at Dropmore nursery of Manitoba. Extremely rare; not in commerce.

Populus nigra 'Italica'
LOMBARDY or
PYRAMIDAL POPLAR
4/3   Page 479
The universal spire tree,
an extremely common
male clone.

Populus Simonii
'Pendula'
WEEPING SIMON POPLAR
4/3   Page 481
Large, gracefully pendulous,
fine-textured shade trees.

Populus tremuloides
QUAKING ASPEN
11/17   Page 482
Acclaimed for smooth gray
bark, whispering leaves,
and golden fall color.

Populus tristis
WEEPING or BROWN-
TWIG POPLAR
5/13   Page 483
Obscure and seldom heard
of except in northern
prairie locales.

Prunus Armeniaca
APRICOT TREE
3/10   Page 485
As lovely in flower as
when laden with its
luscious orange fruit.

Prunus avium 'Plena'
DOUBLE FLOWERED
MAZZARD (CHERRY)
3/-   Page 486
Double flowers last longer
than regular ones, and set
no messy fruit.

Prunus × *blireiana*
BLIREIANA FLOWERING
PLUM
2/26   Page 487
A semidwarf hybrid whose
fragrant flowers are
followed by purplish leaves.

Prunus × *blireiana*
'Moseri'
MOSER PLUM
3/10   Page 487
Larger growing, less dense,
with paler flowers than
typical *Prunus* × *blireiana*.

Prunus cerasifera
CHERRY or
MYROBALAN PLUM
3/17   Page 488
Snow-white blossoms in
early spring on a ruggedly
handsome trunk.

Prunus cerasifera
'Krauter's Vesuvius'
'KRAUTER'S VESUVIUS'
PURPLELEAF PLUM
4/4   Page 489
Intense purple leaves were
preceded by profuse pink
flowers.

Prunus cerasifera
'Thundercloud'
'THUNDERCLOUD'
PURPLELEAF PLUM
3/20   Page 491
Very similar to 'Krauter's
Vesuvius' PURPLELEAF PLUM,
but not as dark.

Prunus 'Choshu-hizakura'
'CHOSHU-HIZAKURA' CHERRY
3/22   Page 491
Its Japanese name means red
cherry of Choshu.

Prunus 'Hally Jolivette'
'HALLY JOLIVETTE'
CHERRY
3/27   Page 495
Topgrafted on a trunk of
BIRCHBARK CHERRY (*Prunus
serrula*).

Prunus 'Hillieri'
HILLIER CHERRY
10/29   Page 496
Fiery fall color; pale pink
spring flowers.

Prunus incisa f. *serrata*
FUJI, MAME, or PIGMY
CHERRY
4/3   Page 497
A very compact, often
shrubby little tree.

Prunus jamasakura
JAPANESE HILL CHERRY
3/9   Page 498
Rarely cultivated in the
Western World, this
species grows larger than
most flowering cherries.

Prunus × *Juddii*
JUDD CHERRY
3/23   Page 499
Very similar to *P. Sargentii*,
but with pale flowers.

Prunus 'Okamé'
OKAMÉ CHERRY
3/14   Page 508
Twiggy, compact, and
early to bloom, it can have
pretty fall color as well.

Prunus pendula
WILD WEEPING HIGAN
CHERRY
3/17   Page 510
A naturally pendulous tree.
Usually grafted cultivars
are sold.

Prunus Persica 'Icicle'
ICICLE FLOWERING
PEACH
3/25   Page 516
Double, white blossoms
early in spring.

Prunus Persica
'Double Pink Weeping'
WEEPING FLOWERING
PEACH
3/27   Page 514
Many WEEPING PEACH cultivars
exist, most being low and
broad.

Prunus Sargentii
SARGENT CHERRY
4/3   Page 520
Acclaimed for flowers, red
fall color, and sturdy form.

Prunus 'Shiro-fugen'
'SHIRO-FUGEN' CHERRY
4/-   Page 526
Long-lasting pale pink
flowers contrast with
coppery-red young leaves.

Prunus 'Shirotae'
'SHIROTAE' (or 'MT. FUJI')
CHERRY
3/22   Page 527
Snow-white flowers on a
strongly horizontal crown.

Prunus 'Shogetsu'
'SHOGETSU' CHERRY
4/20   Page 527
Dangling, frilled white flowers of uncommon elegance.

Prunus × *Sieboldii*
NADEN CHERRY
4/11   Page 527
Profuse, heavy floral balls.

Prunus 'Spencer Hollywood'
'SPENCER HOLLYWOOD' PLUM
7/6   Page 528
First-rate for flowers, purple foliage and lovely edible plums.

Prunus × *subhirtella*
HIGAN, ROSEBUD, or SPRING CHERRY
3/27   Page 529
An early-blooming petite tree, wholly superseded in commerce by its flashier offspring.

Prunus × *subhirtella* 'Whitcomb'
WHITCOMB CHERRY
3/10   Page 531
Solid clouds of pure pink blossoms early in the year.

Prunus 'Ukon'
'UKON' CHERRY
4/15   Page 532
Odd yellowish-green flowers.

Prunus 'Wadæ'
WADA'S CHERRY
3/8   Page 534
Exceedingly rare; lovely in
bloom but disease-prone.

Prunus × yedoensis f.
perpendens
WEEPING YOSHINO
CHERRY
3/8   Page 535
A little mop very unlike
regular YOSHINO CHERRY.

*Pseudocydonia
sinensis*
CHINESE QUINCE
4/1   Page 536
Exquisite multicolored
peeling bark, fascinating
big yellow-green fruit.

*Pseudotsuga
Menziesii*
DOUGLAS FIR
11/4   Page 537
The signature tree of the
northern Pacific coast
region.

Pseudotsuga Menziesii
ssp. *glauca*
ROCKY MOUNTAIN
DOUGLAS FIR
6/15   Page 537
Much hardier than typical
DOUGLAS FIR, and more widely
planted in the Eastern States
and Provinces.

Pseudotsuga Menziesii
'Pendula'
WEEPING DOUGLAS FIR
1/-   Page 538
A grotesquely irregular tree
with sagging limbs guaranteed to raise eyebrows.

Pyrus Calleryana
CALLERY or FLOWERING
PEAR
11/18   Page 541
Fair white flowers in spring,
inconsequential fruit,
glorious fall color.

Quercus agrifolia
CALIFORNIA or COAST
LIVE OAK
7/28   Page 548
One of many evergreen OAKS,
it has HOLLY-like leaves.

Quercus coccinea
SCARLET OAK
10/8   Page 550
Glowing warm red; a
majestic shade tree of the
eastern U.S.

Quercus Garryana
OREGON WHITE OAK
8/29   Page 552
Rugged, pale trunks
contrast well with
amazingly dark foliage.

Quercus lobata
CALIFORNIA VALLEY
or WHITE OAK
4/29   Page 555
One of the largest OAK
species, with great character,
though dull fall color.

Quercus petræa
DURMAST or SESSILE
OAK
9/22   Page 557
Exceedingly rare in North
America, but common in
its native Europe.

Quercus robur
ENGLISH OAK
8/26   Page 558
The OAK of Robin Hood, very common in cultivation and growing wild in some places here.

Quercus robur 'Concordia'
GOLDEN ENGLISH OAK
6/4   Page 559
Very rare; a sunny splash in early summer; slow growing.

Quercus rubra
RED OAK
10/5   Page 560
Its fall color can be gold, red, or brown.

Quercus Suber
CORK TREE
3/26   Page 561
Bark from this species is harvested commercially for cork.

Rhamnus cathartica
EURASIAN BUCKTHORN
3/22   Page 564
Though pretty in spring, and troublefree, it is weedy in many places now, spread by birds.

Rhus lancea
AFRICAN SUMACH
7/1   Page 566
Thrives in the arid Southwest and California; grown for its sparking evergreen foliage.

Rhus typhina
STAGHORN SUMACH
10/19   Page 567
Reliable flaming fall color
on a shrubby tree.

Robinia hispida
ROSE ACACIA, BRISTLY
or MOSS LOCUST
6/17   Page 569
A tangled, suckering shrub
that must be pruned or
grafted to be a small tree.

Robinia pseudoacacia
BLACK LOCUST or
FALSE ACACIA
5/15   Page 570
Dark, rugged trunk and
limbs contrast picturesque-
ly with the airy foliage.

Robinia pseudoacacia
'Frisia'
GOLDEN BLACK LOCUST
7/12   Page 571
Not for the faint of heart,
it remains gold all summer
long.

Robinia viscosa
CLAMMY LOCUST
7/11   Page 573
Old-fashioned and now
rarely sold, a meritorious
small tree, its pink flowers
tightly clustered.

Salix babylonica
'Annularis'
RINGLEAF WILLOW
2/28   Page 576
Each leaf is curled into
a hoop or spiral.

Salix Matsudana
'Tortuosa'
CORKSCREW WILLOW
3/27   Page 582
Twisted limbs, twigs and
leaves; now sold in similar
gold and redtwig variations.

Salix Scouleriana
SCOULER PUSSY WILLOW
10/18   Page 584
A widely distributed native
of Western North America;
the largest of PUSSY WILLOW
species.

Salix × sepulcralis
SEPUCHRAL WEEPING
WILLOW
5/6   Page 585
Most trees called "*Salix
babylonica*" are actually
hybrids.

Sambucus nigra
EUROPEAN
BLACK ELDER
6/14   Page 586
Much folklore surrounds
this dark little tree and its
pure black berries.

Sambucus nigra
'Marginata'
VARIEGATED BLACK
ELDER
5/13   Page 587
Good for a bright splash
in a shady corner.

Sapium sebiferum
CHINESE TALLOW TREE
5/30   Page 588
ASPEN-like foliage with
dependably rich fall color
even in hot areas.

Sassafras albidum
SASSAFRAS
10/11   Page 588
Fall color often brilliant
yellow to bright orange or
red.

Schinus Molle
PEPPER TREE
7/29   Page 589
Colorful, distinctively beautiful, and tough as nails—
only severe cold kills it.

Schinus polygamus
5/30   Page 590
Cold-hardy but rather
homely; this small South
American native is little
grown.

*Sciadopitys
verticillata*
UMBRELLA PINE
2/16   Page 590
From Japan, a REDWOOD
relative with dark green
needles in attractive
"umbrella" whorls.

Sequoia sempervirens
COAST REDWOOD
10/5   Page 591
Earth's tallest trees
presently are of this species.

*Sequoiadendron
giganteum*
SIERRA REDWOOD or
GIANT SEQUOIA
3/15   Page 592
More massive but less lofty
than COAST REDWOOD.

Sophora japonica
CHINESE SCHOLAR TREE
or (JAPANESE) PAGODA
TREE
8/20   Page 593
A LOCUST relative valued
for creamy-white late
summer flowers.

Sorbus commixta
JAPANESE
MOUNTAIN ASH
10/17   Page 600
Reddish-purple fall color
and bright red berries.

Sorbus decora
SHOWY MOUNTAIN ASH
9/14   Page 600
Weighty masses of lovely
berries are quickly gobbled
by birds.

Sorbus Forrestii
FORREST
MOUNTAIN ASH
11/14   Page 601
White berries remain well
into winter since birds
ignore them.

Sorbus hupehensis
HUPEH MOUNTAIN ASH
10/5   Page 601
Pinkish-white berries and
bluish-green leaves.

Sorbus scopulina
WESTERN
MOUNTAIN ASH
9/15   Page 605
A dwarf montane species
rarely grown in the lowlands.

Sorbus 'Wilfrid Fox'
'WILFRID FOX'
WHITEBEAM
8/31   Page 607
Silver foliage and few fruit
on a slender upswept
crown.

Stewartia monadelpha
ORANGEBARK or
TALL STEWARTIA
Page 608
With bark so pretty year-
round, the summer flowers
and fall leaf color become
almost unnecessary.

*Stewartia
pseudocamellia*
JAPANESE or
COMMON STEWARTIA
10/26   Page 608
Peely bark, good fall color,
and abundant white flowers
in June.

Styrax Obassia
BIGLEAF
SNOWBELL TREE
6/4   Page 610
A slender, small Japanese
native that grows best in
woodland conditions.

Syringa reticulata
JAPANESE TREE LILAC
9/14   Page 612
White PRIVET-like flowers
in June quite unlike those
of common lilac flowers,
precede the subtle fall
color.

*Taiwania
cryptomerioides*
FORMOSAN REDWOOD
or TAIWAN CEDAR
6/3   Page 612
Little known in cultiva-
tion, needing ample room,
moisture, and a mild
climate.

Tamarix chinensis
'Plumosa'
TAMARISK
8/20   Page 613
This clone is not one of the
weedy SALTCEDAR species
of TAMARISKS.

Taxodium distichum
BALD CYPRESS
10/19   Page 614
Native in swampy low
grounds, these titanic trees
often produce "knees"
with their roots.

Taxus baccata 'Fastigiata'
and 'Fastigiata Aurea'
IRISH YEW
6/19   Page 616
Both regular and golden IRISH YEWS
afford formal effects.

Taxus brevifolia
PACIFIC YEW
4/29   Page 617
Planted rarely because it is
very slow and scrawny; in
age it becomes impressive.

Tetradium Daniellii
BEEBEE TREE
10/19   Page 620
Formerly called *Euodia*, this
is a highly variable east
Asian species.

Thujopsis dolabrata
HIBA ARBORVITÆ
1/17   Page 632
Bold, lizard-like scaly
foliage densely set on
a slow-growing long-lived
tree.

Tilia cordata
LITTLELEAF LINDEN
3/27   Page 634
Winter through summer
flowertime sees this at its
best; its autumnal phase is
not memorable.

Tilia cordata 'Rancho'
'RANCHO' LITTLELEAF
LINDEN
7/24   Page 635
Flowers (and seeds) of *Tilia*
species are wholly unmistakable.

Tilia 'Euchlora'
CRIMEAN LINDEN
10/7   Page 636
Less aphid-prone and
better for planting than
most *Tilia*.

Tilia × flavescens
'Dropmore'
'DROPMORE' BASSWOOD
6/19   Page 637
A cold-hardy BASSWOOD
hybrid from Canada.

Tilia × Moltkei
'Spectabilis'
SPECTACULAR LINDEN
1/2   Page 638
Long commercially extinct;
old specimens remain as
silent testimonials to this
clone's value.

Torreya californica
CALIFORNIA NUTMEG
TREE
10/19   Page 642
Luxurious masses of dark,
sharp needles, which stink
if crushed.

Trachycarpus Martianus

4/2   Page 643

If it proves as cold-hardy as its commonly grown cousins this should replace them.

Trachycarpus Wagnerianus

3/31   Page 643

A dwarf version of the very common *Trachycarpus Fortunei*.

Ulmus lævis

EUROPEAN WHITE ELM

5/14   Page 658

One of the ELMS once planted before the Dutch Elm Disease scourge.

Ulmus pumila

SIBERIAN ELM

11/4   Page 663

Widely planted in the past, but being replaced by stronger, long-lived ELMS.

Umbellularia californica

OREGON MYRTLE or CALIFORNIA LAUREL

7/20   Page 666

A broadleaf evergreen of potent fragrance, gargantuan size, and precious wood.

Xanthoceras sorbifolia

YELLOW-HORN

3/29   Page 667

A shrubby tree with charming flowers, glossy, delicate leaves, and edible seeds.

S. *Elæagnos* Scop.
= *S. rosmarinifolia* Host 1797, non L. 1753
= *S. incana* Schrank 1789, non Michx. 1803

ROSEMARY WILLOW. HOARY WILLOW. ELEAGNUS WIL-LOW. SAGE WILLOW. From central & S Europe and western N Africa to W Asia. Cultivated in France since 1762; in England since 1820. In North American commerce since the 1800s; uncommon. The 1772 epithet *Elæagnos* is derived from a Greek name (see genus *Elæagnus*). Leaves to 5" × ⅞"; gray-green above, wooly-white beneath; no stipules. Varies from a shoulder-high shrub to a tree. Records: to 52½' tall; 23' × 3'3" Greece (1994).

S. *Elæagnos* ssp. *angustifolia* (Cariot) Rech. fil.
= *S. rosmarinifolia* hort., non L. 1753,
    non Hook. 1839

From S France, Spain. More frequently cultivated, but usually as "*S. Elæagnos.*" The name *angustifolia* means narrow-leaved; from Latin *angustus*, narrow, and *folium*, a leaf. Leaf to 4¾" × ½". An airy, elegant little tree or large shrub of silvery-gray leaves and pinkish twigs. Record: 18½' × 7'3" × 30' Seattle, WA (1995).

S. × *elegantissima*—see S. × *pendulina* 'Elegantissima'

S. *eriocephala* ssp. *mackenzieana* (Hook.) Dorn
= *S. prolixa* Anderss.
= *S. mackenzieana* (Hook.) Barr. *ex* Anderss.
= *S. cordata* Muhl. var. *Mackenzieana* Hook.
= *S. rigida* Muhl. var. *Mackenzieana* (Hook.) Cronq.
= *S.* 'Diamond'

MACKENZIE WILLOW. POST WILLOW. DIAMOND WILLOW ("Trunk conspicuously marked by peculiar diamond-shaped places of arrested wood-growth at the base of lateral branches which have been starved or crowded out."—J.S. Shoemaker). From W Canada, the U.S. Rockies, south to New Mexico, west into California mountains and foothills. Discovered <1833. Named in 1838 after the Mackenzie River—in turn after Alexander Mackenzie (1755–1820), Scots trader and explorer. In U.S. commerce (as *S.* 'Diamond') ≤1900, and as late as 1952; mostly if not solely in the West. A tall shrub or small slender tree, to 30' tall. Twigs greenish-brown, densely velvety at first, becoming brown and hairless. Leaves hairless, dark and shiny above, pale beneath; to 4" × 1½".

S. × *erythroflexuosa*—see S. 'Golden Curls'

S. × *excelsior*—see S. × *rubens*

S. 'Flame'
Introduced ≤1990 by Bergeson nursery of Fertile, MN. Named for its orange-red twigs. Dense, oval-shaped shrub to 20' tall. Branches curl upward and inward. (It may be a renaming of one of the confused *S. alba* var. *vitellina* redtwig clones.)

S. *flavescens*—see S. *Scouleriana*

S. *fragilior*—see S. × *rubens* 'Latifolia'

S. *fragilis* L.
CRACK WILLOW. BRITTLE WILLOW. SNAP WILLOW. RED-WOOD WILLOW (because of the salmon wood color). From central Europe and SW Asia. Cultivated in North America since ≤1800s, naturalized in some locales. Almost never listed by nurseries. Outnumbered by *S. alba* and the hybrid *S.* × *rubens*. Twigs an unexciting greenish-brown, very brittle (but no more so than some of its hybrids or certain other species). You can flick your finger and snap off twigs with the lightest pressure, or let strong winds make a mess of them for you. Leaves turn dirty golden-green and drop earlier in fall than those of *S. alba* or the hybrid *S.* × *rubens*. Less easily rooted from cuttings. Growth slower than for its hybrids or *S. alba*. Trunk short, crown broad. Records (British *Salix* expert R.D. Meikle says typical *S. fragilis* never grows more than ca. 50' tall, and the claimed heights of 80'–90' can only apply to the clone 'Russelliana' or to hybrids): 122' × 25'5" × 124' Macomb County, MI (1979); 110' × 25'9" × 153 Beverly Hills, MI (1985); 72' × 15'11" × 67' Montréal, Québec (<1994); 41½' × 6'4" × 53½' Seattle, WA (1994; *pl.* 1958).

S. *fragilis* 'Bullata'
= *S. fragilis* var. *sphærica* Hryniew.
= *S. bullata* hort.

Introduced in 1906 by Späth nursery of Germany. In North American commerce ≤1915–16. Extremely rare. Crown spherical and smaller than that of typical *S. fragilis*. Record: 21' × 3'1" × 26½" Seattle, WA (1994; *pl.* 1969).

S. *fragilis* 'Decipiens'
= *S. decipiens* Hoffm.

WHITE WELSH WILLOW. WHITE DUTCH WILLOW. BEL-GIAN RED WILLOW. Named in 1791, meaning deceptive. Not known in the wild; a male clone grown for basketry. Extremely rare in North America. A small tree. Winter twigs yellowish or red, shiny ("varnished crimson"). Leaves hairless, coarsely toothed, short, to 3½" × 1". Catkins only ⅝"–1⅛" long.

S. *fragilis* var. *latifolia*—see S. × *rubens* 'Latifolia'

S. *fragilis* 'Russelliana'
= S. × *rubens* 'Russelliana'
= S. *Russelliana* Sm. 1804, non Willd. 1806

DUKE OF BEDFORD'S WILLOW. BEDFORD WILLOW. LEICESTERSHIRE WILLOW. DR. JOHNSON'S WILLOW. Originated ca. 1800 in Leicestershire, England; named in 1804 after John Russell, the 6th Duke Of Bedford (1766–1839), a keen WILLOW enthusiast. The favorite tree of Dr. Samuel Johnson (1709–1784), was (by report) a specimen of this kind, 49' × 11'10" × 63' (Lichfield, England, 1781). In North American commerce ≤1850. Rare, at least nominally—it may be cultivated simply as "S. *fragilis*." In England it is very common and its timber the most valuable of any WILLOW. Female; catkins to 2¾" long. Twigs bright olive-brown. Leaves coarsely toothed, to 6⅞" × 1½", very sparsely silky, becoming hairless; slightly glaucous beneath. Grows larger than typical S. *fragilis*.

S. *fragilis* var. *sphærica*—see S. *fragilis* 'Bullata'

S. *franciscana*—see S. *lasiolepis*

S. 'Golden Curls'
= S. × *erythroflexuosa* Ragonese
= S. × *sepulcralis* 'Erythroflexuosa'
= S. *Matsudana* 'Golden Curls'
= S. *Matsudana* 'Tortuosa Aurea Pendula'
= S. 'Tortuosa Aurea Pendula'
(S. *Matsudana* 'Tortuosa' × S. *sepulcralis* 'Chrysocoma')

GOLDEN CORKSCREW WILLOW. Originated in 1961 in Argentina; in North American commerce by 1972. Becoming common. Weeping, with golden, twisted twigs. The name *erythroflexuosa* from Greek *erythros*, red, and *flexuosa*, twisted. This epithet seems more applicable to S. Scarlet Curls®, so there may have been confusion in its application.

S. *Gooddingii* Ball
= S. *nigra* var. *vallicola* Dudley

SOUTHWESTERN BLACK WILLOW. CALIFORNIA BLACK WILLOW. DIXIE BLACK WILLOW. From Kansas south to Texas and northern Mexico, west into California. Named in 1905, likely after Leslie Newton Goodding (1880–1967), botanist of the USDA. Some experts

view S. *Gooddingii* as a synonym of S. *nigra*. It differs from S. *nigra* in having paler (yellowish-gray) twigs and in floral details (ovaries sometimes hairy). Leaves to 7" long, the same shade of green or gray-green on both sides; stipules small and fleeting. Usually grows 20'–45' tall. Not commonly cultivated; sold by native-plant nurseries for soil stabilization and revegetation. Records (likely the same tree): 93' × 24'0" × 117' Smartville, CA (1969); 75' × 23'0" × 103' near Smartville, CA (1972).

S. *Hookeriana* Barratt
= S. *amplifolia* Cov.
(*Hookerana*)

BEACH PUSSY WILLOW. COAST PUSSY WILLOW. SHORE PUSSY WILLOW. HOOKER PUSSY WILLOW. From E Siberia, and S Alaska to NW California; strictly coastal. Discovered ca. 1826 by J. Scouler. Named in 1839 after William Jackson Hooker (1785–1865), British botanist. Introduced to cultivation in 1891. Twigs stout and fuzzy. Leaves to 7" × 3", dark glossy green above, thickly felted beneath; stipules rarely present and always very small and fleeting. A premier PUSSY WILLOW on account of its bold texture and robustness. Male catkins to 4" long and when fully fluffed-out nearly 2" wide. Records: 48' × 4'0" × 27' near Cannon Beach, OR (1964); 42' × 9'10" × 40' near Cannon Beach, OR (≤1956); 32' × 4'3" × 27' Warrenton, OR (1975); 28' × 3'2" × 43' Tacoma, WA (1991).

S. *Hookeriana* 'Clatsop'
Presumably from Clatsop County of NW Oregon. As described by Forest Farm nursery of Williams, OR: a stout-branching 5'–20' shrub selected by the Soil Conservation Service for revegetation use; showy 4" catkins.

S. *incana*—see S. *Elæagnos*

S. *kilmarnocki*—see S. *caprea* 'Kilmarnock' and 'Weeping Sally'

S. *lasiandra*—see S. *lucida* ssp. *lasiandra*

S. *lasiandra* var. *caudata*—see S. *lucida* ssp. *caudata*

S. lasiandra var. *lancifolia*—see *S. lucida* ssp. *lasiandra*

S. lasiandra 'Nehalem'—see *S. lucida* 'Nehalem'

S. lasiandra 'Roland'—see *S. lucida* 'Roland'

S. lasiolepis Benth.
= *S. franciscana* von Seem.

ARROYO PUSSY WILLOW. WHITE(LEAF) WILLOW. CALIFORNIA PUSSY WILLOW. From Washington and Idaho to northern Mexico. Often the only WILLOW on the banks of summer-dry arroyos. Discovered in 1846 by K. Hartweg near Monterey, CA. Named in 1857 (from Greek *lasios*, hairy, and *lepis*, a scale—referring to the shaggy white hairy floral scales). Very rarely cultivated, mostly planted for native revegetation projects. Leaves dark dull green above, pale powder-blue or whitish and thinly hairy beneath; to 6" × 1¼". Generally a large multitrunked shrub, its two-toned foliage a lovely sight. Records: to 50' × 4'8" says C. Sargent; 27' × 3'7" × 20' Wallowa County, OR (1975); 20' × 3'3" × 34½' Berkeley, CA (1994).

S. lasiolepis 'Rogue'
Presumably from the Rogue River of SW Oregon. As described by Forest Farm nursery of Williams, OR: A large shrub or small tree, 6'–20' tall. Selected by the Soil Conservation Service. Long narrow leaves on yellow stems. Bark smooth.

S. laurifolia—see *S. pentandra*

S. 'Licks'
(*S. babylonica* × *S. lucida* ssp. *lasiandra*)
Introduced ≤1893 by Sherwood Hall nursery of Menlo Park, CA. Long commercially extinct. Claimed parentage unconfirmed.

S. lucida Muhl.
SHINING WILLOW. SHINY WILLOW. AMERICAN BAY WILLOW. From northeastern N America, in wet sites. Named in 1803 (*lucida* in Latin means shining—referring to its leaves and twigs). Introduced to cultivation in 1811. Rarely grown. Closely related to *S. pentandra* (BAY WILLOW) but has narrower leaves with drawn-out tips, and obvious stipules. Twigs very glossy, usually hairless. Leaves to 5½" × 1¾", long tapered at apex; dark glossy green above, paler beneath; stipules large. Usually a shrub or small tree ca. 20' tall. Records: 70' × 8'2" Winnipeg, Manitoba (<1986); 66' × 6'11" Glasnevin, Ireland (1974); 60' × 7'6" × 58' Traverse City, MI (1972); 48' × 8'5" × 48' Warrenton, VA (1981).

S. lucida ssp. caudata (Nutt.) E. Murr.
= *S. caudata* (Nutt.) Heller
= *S. lasiandra* var. *caudata* (Nutt.) Sudw.

ROCKY MOUNTAIN BLACK WILLOW. From much of the Rocky Mountain region. Named in 1843, *caudata* meaning tailed, referring to the very long tapered leaf-tips. The common name compares it to the eastern *S. nigra* (BLACK WILLOW). Leaves smaller and thicker than those of typical *S. lucida*; green, not glaucous beneath. Otherwise essentially as *S. lucida* ssp. *lasiandra*.

S. lucida ssp. lasiandra (Benth.) E. Murr.
= *S. lasiandra* Benth.
= *S. lasiandra* var. *lancifolia* (Anderss.) Bebb
= *S. Lyallii* (Sarg.) Heller

PACIFIC BLACK WILLOW. WESTERN BLACK WILLOW. LANCELEAF WILLOW. WHIPLASH WILLOW. From much of western North America, mostly the West Coast. Named in 1857 (the Greek *lasiandra* meaning with shaggy stamens). Introduced to cultivation in 1883. Exceedingly rarely grown. Leaves to 14" × 2½"; glaucous beneath. Records: to 85' tall; 82' × 7'4" × 31' Cowichan Lake, B.C. (1986); 79' × 6'6" × 40' Seattle, WA (1993); 74' × 8'9" × 55' Grants Pass, OR (1972).

S. lucida 'Nehalem'
= *S. lasiandra* 'Nehalem'

A cultivar of *S. lucida* ssp. *lasiandra*. Likely from Nehalem River of Clatsop County, OR. As described by Forest Farm nursery of Williams, OR: a multi-stemmed 5'–30' shrub that withstands flooding and dry conditions.

S. lucida 'Roland'
= *S. lasiandra* 'Roland'

A cultivar of *S. lucida* ssp. *lasiandra*. A male clone released in 1986 after being observed for 10 years by the Alaska Department of Natural Resources. Branching dense; leaves large; strong growing; resistant to diseases and insects.

S. lutea—see *S. × sepulcralis* 'Chrysocoma'

S. Lyallii—see *S. lucida* ssp. *lasiandra*

S. mackenzieana—see *S. eriocephala* ssp. *mackenzieana*

S. Matsudana Koidz.
= *S. babylonica* var. *pekinensis* Henry

PEKING WILLOW. HANKOW WILLOW. From China, Manchuria, E Siberia, and Korea. Named in 1915 after Sadahisa Matsuda (1857–1921), Japanese botanist. Aside from its non-weeping branching, *S.*

Matsudana is so similar to *S. babylonica* (BABYLON WEEPING WILLOW) that it can scarcely be regarded as a distinct species. *S. Matsudana* and its three cultivars (below) might most properly be referred to as *S. babylonica* var. *pekinensis*, but since "*S. babylonica*" is already the most loosely applied name in the world of WILLOWS, more often than not used for hybrids, any additional tinkering would be like throwing oil on a bonfire. *S. Matsudana* was introduced to Western cultivation in 1905 when the Arnold Arboretum received cuttings (of a female clone) from Dr. J.G. Jack. In North American commerce ≤1930s. Rare. Performs well in comparatively dry sites, considering it's a WILLOW. A shade tree, not pendulous (or barely so in great age). Twigs yellowish-green, sometimes green or olive. Leaves flush early in spring; to 4¾" × 1", bright green above, glaucous beneath; stipules large. Female catkins ½"–1¼" long. Record: 44' × 7'11" × 61' Seattle, WA (1992).

S. *Matsudana* 'Globosa'—see S. *Matsudana* 'Umbraculifera'

S. *Matsudana* 'Golden Curls'—see S. 'Golden Curls'

S. *Matsudana* 'Navajo'
= *S.* 'Navajo'
= *S. umbraculifera* hort. (in part)
= *S. babylonica* 'Navajo'

NAVAJO GLOBE WILLOW. Origin unknown. In commerce ≤1967–68. Grown mostly in the Southwest and California, often in desert areas. Similar to *S. Matsudana* 'Umbraculifera' but hardier, larger, to 70' tall and wide.

S. *Matsudana* 'Snake'—see S. 'Snake'

S. *Matsudana* 'Tortuosa'
= *S. contorta* hort.
= *S. tortuosa* hort.
= *S. babylonica* 'Tortuosa'

CORKSCREW WILLOW. TWISTED HANKOW WILLOW. DRAGON'S CLAW WILLOW. RATTLESNAKE WILLOW. CONTORTED WILLOW. DRAGON'S MOUSTACHE WILLOW. CURLY WILLOW. TWISTED WILLOW. Introduced to North America in 1923 when the Arnold Arboretum received cuttings (of a female clone) from China. Named in 1924 (Latin *tortuosa* means full of crooks or turns). In commerce ≤1930s. Very common. Strikingly twisted, bent, curled branches, twigs and leaves make this clone unmistakable. Its hybrids include S. 'Golden Curls' and

Scarlet Curls®. Records: 75' × 16'1" × 67' Riverside, CT (1987); 66' × 8'4" Niagara Falls, Ontario (1976); 56' × 12'10" × 71' Grandview, WA (1993); 40' × 10'3" × 45' Skagit City, WA (1988).

S. *Matsudana* 'Tortuosa Aurea Pendula'—see S. 'Golden Curls'

S. *Matsudana* 'Umbraculifera'
= *S. Matsudana* 'Globosa'
= *S. umbraculifera* hort. (in part)
= *S. babylonica* 'Umbraculifera'

GLOBE WILLOW. Introduced to Western cultivation in 1906 when the Arnold Arboretum received cuttings from F. Meyer. Named in 1925 (Latin *umbraculum*, umbrella, and *ferre*, to bear). In commerce ≤1948. Grown mostly in the Southwest. A dense, round-headed 40' tree, growing wider than tall. See also *S. Matsudana* 'Navajo'.

S. *Napoleonis*—see S. *babylonica*

S. 'Navajo'—see S. *Matsudana* 'Navajo'

S. *nigra* Marsh.

BLACK WILLOW. From much of central and eastern N America, primarily on riversides and floodplains. Named *nigra* in 1785 after its dark brown to blackish scaly bark. Hardy under trying conditions, rapid growing, but not commonly planted, being utterly common in the wild and taken for granted. Twigs brittle, sparsely hairy or (usually) hairless, brown to reddish-brown. Leaves to 7½" × 1", green on both sides but paler beneath; fall color light yellow (or dropping green); stipules usually small and fleeting. The largest native North American *Salix*. Records: to 140' tall; 114' × 31'7" × 136' Traverse City, MI (≤1991); 96' × 26'11" × 116' Washtenaw County, MI (1984).

S. *nigra* var. *vallicola*—see S. *Gooddingii*

S. 'Niobe (Weeping)'—see S. × *sepulcralis* 'Chrysocoma'

S. 'North Star'
A hybrid offered ≤1931 by Pioneer nursery of Monrovia, CA. Long extinct commercially. Origin and attributes unknown.

S. *Nuttallii*—see S. *Scouleriana*

S. × *pendulina* Wender.
(*S. fragilis* × *S. babylonica*)

WEEPING CRACK WILLOW. Originated in Germany in the early 1800s. Named in 1831. Habit strongly weeping. Twigs pale brown, hairless. Catkins female or bisexual; ovary short-stalked, hairless.

S. × *pendulina* 'Blanda'
= *S.* × *blanda* Anderss.
= *S. Petzoldii* hort. *ex* Scheele
= *S. babylonica dolorosa* hort.
= *S. dolorosa* hort. (in part)

WISCONSIN WEEPING WILLOW. Originated in Germany. Named and introduced commercially in 1867 (Latin *blanda* means charming). In North American commerce since <1884. Common. A large tree, not strongly weepy. More cold-hardy than purebred *S. babylonica*. Twigs green. Young twigs and leaves scarcely hairy. Leaves glossy green above, glaucous beneath; stem hairless. Female; ovaries distinctly stalked, hairless. Records: 62' × 6'7" Glasnevin, Dublin, Ireland (1987); 53' × 10'6" × 80' Christchurch, New Zealand (1970).

S. × *pendulina* 'Elegantissima'
= *S.* × *elegantissima* K. Koch

THURLOW WEEPING WILLOW. Originated ca. 1860 in Germany. Named in 1871 (Latin *elegans*, elegant, and the superlative *-issima*—very elegant or most elegant). In North American commerce since ≤1906. Common. Probably named after Thomas C. Thurlow (1832–1909), founder of Cherry Hill nursery, West Newbury, MA. A large weepy tree. More cold-hardy than purebred *S. babylonica*, broader and less pendulous. Twigs yellow-brown. Leaves to 5¼" × ⅞". Female; catkins to 2½" long; ovaries short-stalked, hairy towards base. Some botanists have called this name a synonym of *S. babylonica*, others say it is 'Blanda' renamed. Certainly North American nurseries and arboreta have mixed up the various WEEPING WILLOWS. Quick study will not suffice; until someone spends a few years doing a thorough investigation, all names and descriptions are best regarded as provisional. Record: 37' × 6'4" × 56½' Seattle, WA (1994; *pl.* 1966); 36' × 12'5" Kings Meadow, Reading, Berkshire, England (1988).

S. × *pendulina* 'Fan-Giant'
= *S.* × *blanda* Fan Willow™
= *S.* × *blanda* 'Fanick'

FAN GIANT BLUE WEEPING WILLOW™. Introduced ≤1967–68 by L.E. Cooke nursery of Visalia, CA. Borer and blight resistant. To 50' tall. Young shoots and leaves hairless.

S. *pentandra* L.
= *S. laurifolia* Wesm.

BAY (LEAVED) WILLOW. LAUREL (LEAVED) WILLOW. SWEET BAY WILLOW. From N & C Europe, W Asia. Named from Greek *penta*, 5, and *andros*, male, referring to the 5 stamens. Actually each male floret has (4) 5–8 (12) stamens. Closely related to *S. lucida* (SHINING WILLOW). Long cultivated in North America, and escaped in some locales. Common. Prized for its clean glossy foliage and great hardiness. Leaves to 5¼" × 2"; can be as dark and shiny as any tree leaves; stipules usually not seen—tiny and fleeting. Twigs dark reddish-brown, glossy, hairless. The names allude to the leaf appearance, not fragrance. Catkins appear relatively late, in May or even June; males are more attractive, their catkins bright yellow, long and showy. Records: to 70' tall; 59' × 5'10" Bournemouth, Devon, England (1985); 52½' × 10'2" × 46½' Alma, Québec (<1994); 52' × 23'1" × 38' Red Deer, Alberta (n.d.; *pl.* ca. 1906); 45' × 8'0" × 54' Wellesley, MA (1983); 43' × 10'3" × 63' Seattle, WA (1993).

S. *Petzoldii*—see S. × *pendulina* 'Blanda'

S. *Piperi* Bebb

PIPER PUSSY WILLOW. From NW Washington to 40 miles N of San Francisco, CA; always in wet soil. Named in 1895 after Charles Vancouver Piper (1867–1926), the botanist who in 1889 collected the type specimens in Seattle, WA. Introduced to cultivation in 1898. Extremely rarely planted, even in its native range. Best called a variety of *S. lasiolepis*, it is so similar, even being galled in identical fashion, and of equal ornamental value. *Salix* expert G.W. Argus thinks it unworthy of specific recognition, and a mere synonym of *S. Hookeriana*. Leaves dark green and glossy above, powder-blue beneath, scarcely hairy when very young; commonly no more than 4½" × 1⅜" but as large as 7" × 2". Record: 30' × 4'5" × 48' Seattle, WA (1994).

S. *præcox*—see S. *caprea*

S. 'Prairie Cascade'
(*S. pentandra* × *S. pendulina* 'Blanda')

Originated in 1956 at Dropmore nursery of Manitoba. Introduced in 1981 by Morden research station of Manitoba. Common. A hardy WEEPING WILLOW for the north.

S. prolixa—see *S. eriocephala* ssp. *mackenzieana*

S. regalis—see *S. alba* var. *sericea*

S. rigida var. *mackenzieana*—see *S. eriocephala* ssp. *mackenzieana*

S. rosmarinifolia—see *S. Elæagnos* and *S. Elæag.* ssp. *angustifolia*

S. × rubens Schrank
= *S.* × *viridis* Fries
= *S. Russelliana* Willd. 1806, non Sm. 1804
= *S.* × *excelsior* Host

HYBRID WHITE WILLOW. ROCHESTER WILLOW. From Europe, where it is probably the most frequent of all *Salix* hybrids; commoner and more widespread than pure *S. fragilis* (CRACK WILLOW) and more commonly cultivated. Although now extremely rarely listed by North American nurseries, it was somewhat widely planted in the past, largely as "*S. fragilis*." Named in 1789, the Latin *rubens* meaning red or blush. The name ROCHESTER WILLOW may reflect its having been sold ≤1892 by Ellwanger & Barry nursery of Rochester, NY. Twigs greenish (to golden or red in crosses with *S. alba* var. *vitellina*). Foliage elegant, high-gloss, supplying a large, billowy fine-textured crown. Leaves commonly 5" × 1" but to 10" × 2" on strong sucker shoots; glossy pure green above, bluish-green beneath. Records: 92' × 14'1" Bath, Avon, England (1988); 76' × 11'11" × 66' Seattle, WA (1988).

S. × rubens 'Basfordiana'
= *S. basfordiana* Scaling *ex* Salter
(*S. fragilis* × *S. alba* var. *vitellina*)

BASFORD WILLOW. Found ca. 1863 by basketeer William Scaling of Basford, Nottinghamshire, England. In North American commerce ≤1915. Almost never listed by name, it exists in old plantings here and there. A male clone. Twigs glossy yellowish-orange or partly tipped brick-red. British *Salix* expert R.D. Meikle calls it "easily the most beautiful of all our tree willows." Leaves bright glossy green, slender, to 5⅞" × ¾". Catkins to 4" long.

S. × rubens 'Latifolia'
= *S. fragilior* Host
= *S. fragilis* var. *latifolia* Anderss.

Named ≤1828. In Latin, *latifolia* means broad-leaved (from *latus*, broad, and *folium*, a leaf). In North America ≤1899, but very rare. A male clone. Twigs glossy olive-brown. Leaves coarsely toothed, to 4¾" × 1½"; thinly hairy while young. Catkins 1½"–2½" long, rather stout, and often forked.

S. × rubens 'Russelliana'—see S. fragilis 'Russelliana'

S. × rubens 'Sanguinea'
= *S. sanguinea* Scaling

Found <1870 in the French Ardennes by basketeer William Scaling of Basford, Nottinghamshire, England. Not known in North America, but it may be here, possibly grown under another name. A female clone; catkins 1¼"–1⅝" (2⅜") long. Twigs glossy bright red. Leaves small, ca. 3⅛" × ⅝", thinly hairy while young. A small tree.

S. rugosa—see *S.* × *sericans*

S. Russelliana—see *S. fragilis* 'Russelliana' and *S.* × *rubens*

S. × *Salamonii*—see *S.* × *sepulcralis*

S. sanguinea—see *S.* × *rubens* 'Latifolia'

S. 'Scarcuzam'—see *S.* Scarlet Curls®

S. Scarlet Curls®
= *S.* 'Scarcuzam'

Introduced ≤1987 by Lake County nursery of Perry, OH. Becoming common. A small vigorous tree (said to grow 30' tall) with twisted golden branches, scarlet winter twigs, and curly leaves. See also *S.* 'Golden Curls'.

S. Scouleriana Barratt ex Hook.
= *S. flavescens* Nutt. 1842, non Host 1828
= *S. brachystachys* Benth.
= *S. Nuttallii* Sarg.

SCOULER PUSSY WILLOW. WESTERN PUSSY WILLOW. FIRE WILLOW. MOUNTAIN WILLOW. From much of western N America. Named in 1838 after John Scouler (1804–1871), Scots naturalist and physician who discovered it in 1825 at the mouth of the Columbia River. Introduced to cultivation in 1918. Rarely planted. Highly variable, it ranges from sea-level to 10,000 feet elevation, from waterlogged bogs to dry hillsides; from a straggling bush 2' tall to a tree more than 80' tall (largest of all PUSSY WILLOWS). The finest specimens are handsome for catkins, summer foliage and form. Fall color of mottled green, yellow-orange and bronze can also be attractive. Leaves immensely variable, but at most to 6" × 2¼", generally widest above the middle and relatively bluntish for a WIL-LOW; often rusty-hairy. Records: 82' × 2'8" Anacortes, WA (1988); 64' × 12'0" Maury Island, WA (1993); 53' × 19'5" × 45' Willamina, OR (1974); 49' × 21'0" × 34' Sidney, B.C. (1989).

S. × *sepulcralis* Simonk.
= S. × *Salamonii* Carr. *ex* Henry
(S. *babylonica* × S. *alba*)

SALAMON WEEPING WILLOW. SEPUCHRAL WEEPING WILLOW. Originated <1864 on property of the Baron de Salamon at Manosque, Basse-Alpes, France. Introduced commercially in 1869 by Simon-Louis nursery of Metz, France. In North American commerce ≤1888. Common. Likely often travels under other names. Although originally a female clone ('Salamonii'), it has vegetatively escaped if not naturalized in some locales. The name in Latin pertains to a tomb or sepulchral associations such as mourning. Twigs olive-green, weeping but far less so than those of S. *babylonica*. Catkins sometimes androgynous, to 2" long; ovaries hairless, unstalked. Leaves to 6½" long and less than 1" wide, staying green late into fall or winter. Records: 88' × 10'10" × 65' Seattle, WA (1990); 85' × 12'0" × 87' Seattle, WA (1988); 83' × 14'11" × 75' Fife, WA (1990).

S. × *sepulcralis* 'Chrysocoma'
= S. *alba* 'Tristis' hort., non S. *alba* var. *tristis*
   (Ser.) Koch
= S. *alba* 'Vitellina Pendula Nova'
= S. *alba* 'Aurea Pendula'
= S. 'Niobe (Weeping)'
= S. *lutea* hort.
= S. *babylonica* 'Aurea'
= S. × *chrysocoma* Dode
(S. *babylonica* × S. *alba* var. *vitellina* 'Tristis')

GOLDEN WEEPING WILLOW. NIOBE WEEPING WILLOW. Introduced in 1888 by Späth nursery of Germany. In North America ≤1906. Very common. The 1908 *chrysocoma* name is from Greek *chryso*, golden, and *kome*, hair—a fanciful and apt reference to this tree's long golden weeping twigs. The frequently used but incorrect epithet *tristis* is Latin for sad or mournful (the proper 'Tristis' is a rare female, less pendulous clone). The NIOBE name was given <1907 by N.E. Hansen of South Dakota. Twigs bright yellow-golden, striking in late winter. Leaves to 7" × 1", coloring yellow and dropping earlier in fall than those of typical S. × *sepulcralis*. Male; catkins 1½"–2" long in April or May (female flowers occasionally appear). Records: 128' × 21'2" × 123' Grosse Point, MI (1985); 117' × 22'7" × 116' Detroit, MI (1979); 86'

× 28'8" × 93' Hartland, MI (1991); 63' × 23'9" × 81' Lemonweir, WI (1985).

S. × *sepulcralis* 'Erythroflexuosa'—see S. 'Golden Curls'

S. × *sericans* Tausch *ex* A. Kern
= S. × *Smithiana* auct., non Willd. 1809
= S. *rugosa* hort., non Sér. 1815
(S. *caprea* × S. *viminalis*)

BROAD LEAVED OSIER. HYBRID PUSSY WILLOW. From Europe. Sold there since the early 1800s as S. *rugosa*; usually sold as S. *Smithiana*, commemorating Sir James Edward Smith (1759–1828), British botanist. The Latin *sericans* name dates from 1860 and means silky. In North America commerce ≤1915. Very rare. Originally grown for coarse basketry, it is a vigorous PUSSY WILLOW with large showy male catkins and good disease resistance. Leaves distinctly long, slender and sharply pointed, to 7" × 1½" (or more on heavily pruned trees), lightly hairy beneath; veining conspicuous. Record: 35' × 8'0" Seattle, WA (1988; *pl.* 1958).

S. × *Smithiana*—see S. × *sericans*

S. 'Snake'
= S. *alba* 'Snake'
= S. *babylonica* 'Snake'
= S. *Matsudana* 'Snake'
(S. *alba* var. *sericea* × S. *Matsudana* 'Tortuosa')

Introduced ≤1990. Described as a new and improved S. *Matsudana* 'Tortuosa'. Said to grow only 12' tall—scarcely believable given its cited parentage. Young leaves finely hairy on both sides.

S. *tortuosa*—see S. *Matsudana* 'Tortuosa'

S. 'Tortuosa Aurea Pendula'—see S. 'Golden Curls'

S. *triandra* L.
= S. *amygdalina* L.

ALMOND LEAVED WILLOW. FRENCH WILLOW (J. Loudon says FRENCH WILLOW is a male clone with larger, broader leaves). From temperate Eurasia. The 1753 name *triandra* refers to its male florets having 3 stamens; the equally old *amygdalina* name means ALMOND-like in reference to its leaves. In North America ≤1863; extremely rare here as a landscape plant, but used in basketry, where female clones are favored. A shrub or 30' tree. Twigs pale brown, glossy. Leaves to 6" × 1⅝", hairless except when young. Catkins late, as with S. *lucida* (SHINING WILLOW) and *S. pentandra* (BAY WILLOW). C. Newsholme judges it "An outstandingly attractive, hardy, vigorous willow with exceedingly good glossy foliage and a spectacular display of prolific, fragrant, 'candle-like', golden male-catkins. Deserves much wider recognition as a garden shrub."

Salix umbraculifera—see *S. Matsudana* 'Navajo' and 'Umbraculifera'

S. × *viridis*—see *S.* × *rubens*

S. vitellina—see *S. alba* var. *vitellina*

S. 'Wentworth'
= *S. wentworthi* hort.

Origin unknown. In North American commerce between at least 1915 and 1957. Catalogs checked from five nurseries manage between them only this description: "tall, rapid, upright, with reddish bark." In other words, probably a renaming of a redtwig clone of a *Salix alba* var. *vitellina* or hybrid thereof.

S. wentworthi—see *S.* 'Wentworth'

Sambucus

[SAMBUCACEÆ; Elder Family (or CAPRIFOLI-ACEÆ; Honeysuckle Family)] 20–40 spp. of mostly deciduous shrubs and small trees, called ELDERS. *Sambucus* is an ancient Latin name of *S. nigra*, maybe in turn from the Greek *sambuke*, a musical instrument. Stout pithy twigs bear opposite pairs of big pinnately compound leaves, which stink when bruised, and lack showy fall color. Flowers creamy-white, followed by numerous small berries beloved by birds. Rank-growing, coarse-textured, and shrubby in general, ELDERS excite little interest among tree lovers. Some attain tree size, but unless pruned are usually suckering gigantic shrubs, gawky in winter. Preferring rich, moist soil, they tolerate trying conditions, and are very cold-hardy. Every one of the 48 contiguous States has at least one species of ELDER. The folklore surrounding *S. nigra*, and its value in medicinal and culinary spheres, renders it a prized species for those in the know. Ornamentally it is by far the most variable species. ELDER should not be confused with ALDER (*Alnus*). The BOXELDER is *Acer Negundo*. Two shrub genera related to *Sambucus* are *Lonicera* (HONEYSUCKLE) and *Viburnum*.

S. cerulea Raf.
= *S. glauca* Nutt.
?= *S. mexicana* Presl *ex* DC.
(*cærulea*, *cœrulea*)

BLUE ELDER. BLUEBERRY ELDER. From S British Columbia to Mexico. Named in 1838 (Latin *cæruleus* means heavenly- or sky-blue). Introduced to cultivation in 1850. Extremely rarely sold. Creamy-white flowers in flat clusters from May into July. Powder-blue glaucous bloom coats the berries, which are very small, numerous, highly decorative in fall and early winter, and good to eat. Leaflets 5–9 (13), slender. Adapted to sunny, dry conditions; drought-tolerant. Records: to 50' tall at most; 48' × 5'2" Brush Prairie, WA (1993); 45' × 7'7" Salem, OR (1973; *pl.* 1947); 40' × 11'5" San José, CA (1979).

S. glauca—see *S. cerulea*

S. mexicana—see *S. cerulea*

S. nigra L.

BLACK ELDER. EUROPEAN BLACK ELDER. DEVIL'S WOOD. BOWER or BOUR or BOOR TREE. From Europe, SW Asia, W Siberia, and N Africa. Long cultivated, and of long-suffering constitution, shade-tolerant and left alone by most bugs and diseases, it persists in old gardens and parks, although is almost never sold any more, especially in its typical version. Remarkable for rapid growth while young, it slows much in age. Creamy-white flowers are showy in flat clusters 6"–12" wide from May into July. Foliage very dark, and berries jet black, hence the epithet *nigra*. Leaflets (3) 5–7 (9). The shiny black berries on red-stemmed clusters in fall are a rich spectacle. ELDER wine, made from the flowers or berries, is famous for its medicinal virtues. At least 20 cultivars have been named. Records: 50' × 7'4" Florence Court, County Femanagh, Ireland (1836; *pl.* 1786); 28' × 4'2" × 20' Seattle, WA (1992).

S. nigra 'Albovariegata'—see *S. nigra* 'Marginata'

S. nigra 'Aurea'
= *S. nigra* 'Foliis Luteis'

GOLDENLEAF ELDER. Cultivated since ≤1826 in England. In North American commerce ≤1890.

Common in the 1930s; subsequently rarely sold. Foliage golden.

S. nigra 'Foliis Argenteis'—see *S. nigra* 'Marginata'

S. nigra 'Foliis Luteis'—see *S. nigra* 'Aurea'

S. nigra 'Foliis Purpureis'—see *S. nigra* f. *porphyrophylla*

S. nigra 'Guincho Purple'—see *S. nigra* f. *porphyrophylla*

S. nigra f. *laciniata* (L.) Zab.

PARSLEYLEAF ELDER. FERNLEAF ELDER. CUTLEAF ELDER. Known since the 1500s; described officially in 1753. In North American commerce ≤1890. Very rare. Leaflets deeply slashed and elegantly lacelike.

S. nigra 'Marginata'

= *S. nigra* 'Variegata' (in part)
= *S. nigra* 'Albovariegata' (in part)
= *S. nigra* 'Foliis Argenteis'

Cultivated since the 1800s in England. In North American commerce ≤1890. Rare. Leaflets margined yellowish at first, fading to creamy-white. Great for brightening a dark shady spot in a garden.

S. nigra f. *porphyrophylla* E.C. Nelson

= *S. nigra* 'Foliis Purpureis'
= *S. nigra* 'Purpurea'

PURPLELEAF ELDER. Known since the 1950s in England. Named in 1986 (from Greek, meaning purple, and *phyllon*, a leaf). In North America ≤1974. Very rare. Two or three clones exist, all with their leaves more or less brooding purplish, at least in early summer. One called '**Guincho Purple**' originated at Guincho, Helen's Bay, County Down, Ireland.

S. nigra 'Purpurea'—see *S. nigra* f. *porphyrophylla*

S. nigra 'Variegata'—see *S. nigra* 'Marginata'

Sapindus

[SAPINDACEÆ; Soapberry Family] 12–13 spp. of mostly tropical or subtropical trees and shrubs. From Latin *sapo*, soap, and *indus*, Indian, referring to the detersive properties of the fruit pulp, and soapy use of the first species known to Europeans, a native of the West Indies and tropical America. Related genera include *Koelreuteria* (GOLDEN RAIN TREE), and *Xanthoceras* (YELLOW-HORN).

S. Drummondii H. & A.

WESTERN SOAPBERRY. WILD CHINA TREE (comparing it to *Melia Azedarach*). From the southwestern U.S., and northern Mexico, in dry, poor soil. Discovered by Thomas Drummond (1780–1835), Scots botanical explorer in North America in 1833–34. Named in 1838. Cultivated since 1900, primarily in Texas. A tough and adaptable, pest-free tree. Form rounded. Bark scaly, reddish-brown. Leaves pinnately-compound, like those of the PECAN tree, 8"–15" long, of 8–18 untoothed leaflets; fall color lovely golden yellow. Male and female flowers on separate trees; tiny, yellowish-white, in 6"–10" long clusters during May and June; males are showier but females make the fruit—a translucent yellow-orange ½" berry (used in earlier times for washing clothes). Records: 72' × 7'6" × 59' Coyle, OK (1984); 62' × 10'6" × 67' Corpus Christi, TX (1993); 56' × 8'11" × 67' Pickens County, AL (1989).

S. Mukorossi Gaertn.

CHINESE SOAPBERRY. SOAP NUT TREE. From the Himalayas, N India, China, Korea, Taiwan, and the Ryukyus. Named in 1788, from the Japanese name *Mukuroji*. Introduced to Western cultivation in 1877. Extremely rare; in commerce at least as seedlings by small specialty nurseries. Cold-hardiness varies depending on where the seeds were obtained; some stock is cold-tender. Rehder and Wilson call it "one of the noblest of Chinese trees," forming a "wide-spreading head of massive branches." Bark smooth, gray, recalling that of *Fagus* (BEECH). Foliage bright green; fall color late, rosy and gold or pure, attractive yellow. Leaves 8"–27" long. Leaflets 6–16, untoothed, hairless or minutely hairy. Flowers very small, yellowish-green, in terminal clusters 5"–14" long, in spring or early summer, and even on one tree can be male, female or bisexual. Berries ⅓"–¾" wide, shiny yellowish to golden-brown, ripe in late fall or early winter; each containing a hard black seed. Fruit used as soap; seeds made into rosaries and beads. Records: to 82' × 16'5" in the wild; 32½' × 2'7" × 25½' Davis, CA (1994; *pl.* 1964).

Sapium

[EUPHORBIACEÆ; Spurge Family] ca. 100 spp. of trees and shrubs, mostly tropical and subtropical. From *sapinus*, a name used by the Roman naturalist Pliny for a resinous PINE or FIR. Though *Sapium* is not coniferous, its wounded stem exudes a greasy sap. A related genus is *Mallotus*.

S. sebiferum (L.) Roxb.
= *Stillingia sebifera* Michx.
= *Croton sebiferum* L.

CHINESE TALLOW TREE. CHINESE CANDLENUT TREE. POPCORN TREE (the bright white clusters of seeds hang on after the leaves fall). From China. The 1753 epithet *sebiferum* means wax- or tallow-bearing (from Latin *sebum*, tallow, and *ferre*, to yield or bear). Cultivated near Savannah, GA, ca. 1785. In commerce by the 1920s. Now naturalized in parts of the southern U.S. from North Carolina to SE Texas. Heat-loving; drought-tolerant. Performs well on any soil. Young growth red tinged. Leaves heart-shaped, 1"–3", suggestive of those of ASPENS (*Populus* spp.); sap white. Flowers catkin-like, in July, delicate yellow. Sterile specimens are often preferred for ornamentals. Fall color orange-yellow or glowing red in November. In China the seeds' whitish waxy coat is used to obtain vegetable tallow used for candles and soaps. Tree usually small. Records: to 80' × 12'0" in China; 56' × 9'5" × 44' Evangeline Parish, LA (1977); 52' × 10'0" × 86' Travis County, TX (1978); 51' × 11'7" × 72' Polk County, TX (1987).

Sassafras

[LAURACEÆ; Laurel Family] 2–3 spp. of deciduous trees. The name *Sassafras* was likely adapted by Spanish or French settlers from a native American name used in Florida. Related genera include *Apollonias*, *Cinnamomum* (CAMPHOR TREE), *Laurus* (BAY LAUREL), *Lindera*, *Neolitsea*, *Persea*, and *Umbellularia* (OREGON MYRTLE).

S. albidum (Nutt.) Nees
= *S. officinale* Nees & Eberm.
= *S. variifolium* (Salisb.) Ktze.
= *Laurus Sassafras* L.
= *L. albida* Nutt.

SASSAFRAS. SMELLING STICK. CINNAMON WOOD. AGUE TREE. MITTENLEAF. TEA TREE. SALOOP. From the central and eastern U.S., and extreme S Ontario. The name *albidus* means nearly white, referring to the glaucous bloom sometimes present on the leaf undersides. A common, well known tree, distinctive in appearance as well as its odor and taste. Formerly valued primarily for medicinal and culinary uses (dried powdered leaves added to soups afford mucilage like eggplant; roots have been used to flavor root beer). An ornamental small tree. Touchy about transplanting, once successfully established it is is largely pest-free and undemanding; very adaptable. Usually slender and short-branched in the woods; in the open it can be broad and burly. Its varied leaf shapes are pleasing. Fall color often brilliant yellow to bright orange or red. Females make bright blue berries on red stems. Root-suckering can be a nuisance, and the branches are brittle. Flowers tiny, yellow-green, from April into June. Records: 130' × 11'1" × 38' Montgomery County, PA (1980); 100' × 17'3" × 68' Owensboro, KY (1972); 89' × 13'9" × 77' Lakeside, MI (1979); trunks can be over 19'0" around.

S. officinale—see S. albidum

S. Tzumu (Hemsl.) Hemsl.
CHINESE SASSAFRAS. From central and E China. Introduced in 1900 by E. Wilson for Veitch nursery of England. Named in 1891 after a Chinese vernacular. Exceedingly rare in North America. Leaves very

large, to 11" × 6⅛"; stems to 3⅜" long. Less cold-hardy and less fragrant than *S. albidum*. Male and female flowers on the same tree, yellow, in early April. Berries black with a glaucous bloom, stem orange-red. Fall color orange, red and purplish in late autumn. Recorded to 115' × 16'5" in the wild.

S. variifolium—see *S. albidum*

Saxegothæa

[PODOCARPACEÆ; Podocarp Family] A genus of one species. H.R.H. Prince Albert of (the Prussian Province) Saxe-Coburg-Gotha (1819–1861), Prince Consort to Queen Victoria, and "a great patron of horticulture," permitted this genus to bear one of his names. A related genus is *Podocarpus*.

S. conspicua Lindl.

PRINCE ALBERT'S YEW. Araucarian: *Mañío Lahuán*. From S Chile and Argentina. Introduced in 1847 by Wm. Lobb to Veitch nursery of England. The 1851 epithet *conspicua* means remarkable (may allude to Lindley's having characterized the tree as being remarkable in its YEW-like habit, JUNIPER-like fruit, *Podocarpus* male flowers, *Dacrydium* seeds, etc.). Exceedingly rare; it offers nothing particularly outstanding, and to thrive needs the precious combination of mild winters and ample summer moisture without excessive heat. In other words, the maritime West Coast. Can perform well even in deep shade. Foliage YEW-like, the wide needles to 1⅛" long, hard and curved, dark green above, pale bluish beneath. Fruit ⅓"–¾" wide, rounded, vaguely like a JUNIPER berry but with prickly blue-green scales; 6–12 seeds. Records: to 131' tall in the wild; 59' × 5'8" Woodhouse, Lyme Regis, Dorset, England (1982); 44' × 6'0" Castlewellan, County Down, Ireland (1982).

Schinus

[ANACARDIACEÆ; Cashew Family] 27–30 spp. From Greek *schinos*, the MASTIC TREE, *Pistacia Lentiscus*, which this genus resembles in its resinous juice. Related genera include *Cotinus*, (SMOKE TREE), *Pistacia* (PISTACHIO), and *Rhus* (SUMACH).

S. dependens—see *S. polygamus*

S. Molle L.

PEPPER TREE. CALIFORNIA PEPPERTREE. PERU PEPPERTREE. PERUVIAN MASTIC TREE. PERUVIAN PEPPER TREE. From the American tropics and subtropics: Brazil, Peru, Chile, and N Argentina, ascending to 12,750' elevation in the Andes. The epithet *Molle* is from the old Peruvian (Quechua) name *Mulli*. Seeds were found in adobe bricks of a mission at La Soledad, CA, founded in 1791, but 1830 is the only conclusive date for its introduction to California. Naturalized there and in S Texas. Very well known. A broadleaf evergreen of willowy aspect, cold-hardy only to ca. 10°F. Good drainage is essential for best performance. Male and female flowers usually on separate trees. Leaves compound; leaflets 14–60, shiny; powerfully fragrant when touched. Fruit peppercorn-sized, light pink to rose-red, berry-like, conspicuous in fall and winter. Called PEPPER TREE because the seeds were once used to adulterate pepper. They also were used to make a traditional beer in Peru. Although the tree is beautiful, drought-tolerant, and withstands drastic pruning, its sap hurts car paint, it harbors the black scale *Citrus* pest, it is brittle and has messy berries, its roots invade sewers and break walks, its flowers contribute to hayfever, it is subject to oak root fungus, and it can be weedy. Records: to 130' tall in Peru; 70' × 14'0" Moor Park, CA (ca. 1980); 54' × 30'0" × 75' San Juan Capistrano, CA (1969); 47' × 26'10" × 83' Santa Barbara, CA (1972).

Schinus Molle 'Shamel'

Found in 1941 by plant physiologist Dr. Archibald Dixon Shamel (1878–1956) of Riverside, CA. Very pendant, dense, dark foliage. Male. Growth rapid.

S. polygamus (Cav.) Cabr.

= S. dependens Ort.

From western South America. Mapuche (Chilean): *Huingán*. Spanish: *Incienso*. Introduced to European cultivation in 1790. Named in 1795; the Greek *polygamus* suggesting the tree can bear both unisexual and bisexual flowers, but normally a given tree is male or female. Once widely planted in California; tested in the 1960s as a street-tree; now quite rare in commerce. Much hardier than *S. Molle*, and both less dramatic and less troublesome. Spiny. Leaves evergreen, not compound, leathery, usually untoothed, variably fragrant, to 2⅜" × ¾" but they vary a great deal and are usually narrower. Flowers very small but abundant, greenish-white, in late spring. Berries dull dark grayish-purple or black. Tolerates heat, drought and considerable frost. Often only a shrub; can be a dense, rounded, twiggy tree. Records: to 30' tall; 27½' × 3'10" × 34' Davis, CA (1994).

Sciadopitys

[TAXODIACEÆ; Bald Cypress Family] Only one species in the genus, a coniferous evergreen. From Greek *skias* or *skiados*, an umbrella or parasol, and *pitys*, a FIR or PINE. Literally the PARASOL or UMBRELLA PINE, in allusion to the whorls of broad needles.

S. verticillata (Th.) S. & Z.

UMBRELLA PINE. JAPANESE UMBRELLA PINE. PARASOL PINE. From Japan. Japanese: *Koya-maki*. Named in 1784. Introduced to Western cultivation by various people between 1853 and 1862. Now fairly common in those regions where it grows well. Dislikes lime soils. Prized for rich green, pleasingly billowy evergreen foliage. Needles wide, flat and grooved, 3"–6" long, in umbrella-like whorls (hence the epithet *verticillata*). Cones pliable,

egg-shaped, 2"–4" (5") long. Bark dark red-brown, soft and fibrous. Slow growing in cultivation. Usually dense and narrowly conical; often multitrunked. Records: to 150' tall in Japan; 75' × 5'3" Benenden School, Kent, England (1986); 67½' × 5'0" Wanganui, New Zealand (≤1982); 54' × 7'5" Everett, WA (1987).

S. verticillata 'Aurea'

Originated in Japan. Introduced to Western cultivation in 1888 by F.L. Temple to San Francisco. Extremely rare. Needles yellow. Probably the same as *S. verticillata* 'Variegata'.

S. verticillata 'Joe Kozey'

Selected by the University of Connecticut. Introduced ≤1986. A clone featuring dominant central leader growth, making a taller than usual specimen in a given number of years.

S. verticillata 'Ossorio's Gold'

Originated at Alfonso Ossorio's estate on Long Island, NY. Introduced ≤1990 by Cœnosium Gardens nursery of Lehighton, PA. Slow (4"–8" growth yearly). Needles golden, long.

S. verticillata 'Variegata'

Originated in Japan. Introduced to Western cultivation in 1859 by Siebold to Holland. Sent to the U.S. in 1861 by G.R. Hall. Extremely rare. Some needles pale yellow, some half yellow, some green. Likely the same as *S. verticillata* 'Aurea'.

S. verticillata 'Wintergreen'

Selected, introduced (≤1979) and named (≤1981) by the University of Connecticut. Foliage stays bright green in winter, not bronzing (as many specimens do).

Sequoia

[TAXODIACEÆ; Bald Cypress Family] A genus of only the following species, the COAST REDWOOD, a coniferous evergreen. Sequoyah (Sequoiah) a.k.a. George Guess (1770–1843), son of a European trader and Cherokee woman, was raised as an Indian in Georgia, and invented a Cherokee alphabet or syllabary in 1826. The name *sequoia* means 'possum, a Cherokee epithet for a half-breed. For DAWN REDWOOD see *Metasequoia*.

S. gigantea—see *Sequoiadendron giganteum*

S. sempervirens (D. Don) Endl.

COAST REDWOOD. COMMON REDWOOD. CALIFORNIA REDWOOD. From foggy, coastal SW Oregon and N California. First named as a *Taxodium* (BALD CYPRESS) in 1824, the epithet *sempervirens* meaning evergreen; from Latin *semper*, always or ever, and *virens*, green. Introduced to the St. Petersburg botanic garden in 1840; in 1843 K. Hartweg sent seeds to Britain. In 1847 S. Endlicher described the genus *Sequoia*. Cultivated in North America since <1851. Long famous as generally the world's tallest trees—rivaled only by some anomalous EUCALYPTS and DOUGLAS FIRS. Foliage YEW-like, the needles short and wide (≤1¼" long), arranged in dense flat sprays. Cones ¾"–1¼" long. Most ornamental when planted in groves or moist valleys; out in the open, it hogs space and often looks unkempt. Unsightly suckers often surround the base. Records: 372' × 52'5" "The Dyerville Giant" Humboldt Redwoods State Park (1972—fell March 1991 when 377' tall); 363' × 53'2" "Giant Tree" Humboldt Redwoods State Park (1989—once likely 415' tall); 313' × 70'5" × 101' "Newton Tree" Prairie Creek Redwoods State Park (1993—33,700ft³); 233' × 72'3" "Westridge Giant" Prairie Creek Redwoods State Park (1993—top snapped; tree aged well over 2,000 years).

S. sempervirens 'Adpressa'

= *S. sempervirens* 'Albo-spica'

Raised by A. Leroy, nurseryman of Angers, France. Named in 1867. Very rare in North America; in largescale production since ≤1977 by Mitsch nursery of Aurora, OR. Tree dense, pyramidal, wispy-looking. Shoots much narrower and slenderer; young tips creamy-white. Needles much smaller than typical, bluer, and uniformly directed forward (*adpressus* means pressed against or on). Growth slow. Often kept as a shrub by pruning. Record: 92' × 10'6" Gloucestershire, England (1984).

S. sempervirens 'Albo-spica'—see *S. sempervirens* 'Adpressa'

S. sempervirens 'Aptos Blue'

Introduced ≤1975 by the Saratoga Horticultural Foundation of California. Common. Dense lush typical green (not at all pale powder blue) foliage in flat sprays; needles large and wide. Branches nearly horizontal, slightly upright.

S. sempervirens 'Argentea'

SILVER REDWOOD. Introduced commercially in 1936 by W.B. Clarke nursery of San José, CA. Normal growth rate and shape, but foliage bright silvery-green.

S. sempervirens 'Cantab'

= *S. sempervirens* 'Prostrata' (in part)

Originated <1920 as a witches'-broom on a tree in England's Cambridge Botanic Garden. Propagated in the 1930s and '40s; named 'Cantab' ≤1953 (abbreviation of *Cantabrigia*, the Latinized name of Cambridge). In North America ≤1958. Rare. Varies from a congested shrub ('Prostrata') to fully treelike, albeit denser in habit and slower-growing than typical. Needles broad, short (ca. ½" long × ⅕" wide), very glaucous. Record: 49' × 2'10½" × 23' Seattle, WA (1994; *pl.* 1960).

S. sempervirens 'Filoli'

Introduced ≤1990 by the Saratoga Horticultural Foundation of California. Very rare. Selected at Filoli Gardens of Woodside, CA. Foliage bluish.

S. sempervirens 'Glauca'

Named in 1874 in England. As cultivated there 'Glauca' is a rare clone with bluish-gray needles, shorter (ca. ½" long) than typical. But North American nurseries have likely applied this name (since ≤1895) to any of several similar selections. W.B. Clarke nursery of San José, CA, said in 1936: "often seen in the Santa Cruz mountains. Pronounced bluish tint that makes it less somber."

S. sempervirens 'George Itaya'

Introduced ≤1975 by the Saratoga Horticultural Foundation of California. Very rare. Growth not robust. Crown narrow, not dense. Foliage reminiscent of *Cryptomeria* in having the twig ends closely clustered and upright. Somewhat similar to 'Los Gatos'.

S. sempervirens 'Henderson Blue'

Introduced ≤1975 by the Saratoga Horticultural Foundation of California. Foliage strikingly pale blue. Best kept as a shrub and pruned hard, because its crude habit and profuse cones are unsightly. Needles large, to 1½" × ¼". Very slow-growing.

S. sempervirens Kenwood™

Originated by Wapumne nursery of California and sold ≤1993. Foliage blue.

Sequoia sempervirens 'Los Altos'

Introduced ≤1975 by the Saratoga Horticultural Foundation of California. Common. Coarse, dark shiny green foliage. Branches long, slightly arching upward. Crown wide; not especially dense. Less cold-hardy than the other cultivars.

S. sempervirens 'Los Gatos'

Introduced ≤1975 by the Saratoga Horticultural Foundation of California. Rare. Branches distinctly upswept; crown open.

S. sempervirens Majestic Beauty™
= *S. sempervirens* 'Monty'

Introduced ≤1981 by Monrovia nursery of California. Said to bear delicate, glaucous blue-green foliage on horizontal branches and pendulous branchlets.

S. sempervirens 'Monty'—see *S. sempervirens* Majestic Beauty™

S. sempervirens 'Prostrata'—see *S. sempervirens* 'Cantab'

S. sempervirens 'Santa Cruz'

Introduced ≤1975 by the Saratoga Horticultural Foundation of California. Rare. Tree of regular conical silhouette, with twig sprays held in a dense, slightly drooping fashion.

S. sempervirens 'Santa Rosa'

Introduced ≤1975 by the Saratoga Horticultural Foundation of California. Common. Branches long, straight or slightly ascending. Foliage of moderate density; soft-textured; branchlets drooping; needles thin, light grassy- or sea-green above, vividly whitish beneath. Looks like *Metasequoia* (DAWN REDWOOD).

S. sempervirens 'Simpson's Silver'

Introduced in 1994 by the Saratoga Horticultural Foundation of California. Selected from a tree of Simpson Timber Company of Korbel, CA. Simpson had found it near Long Prairie Creek in 1975. Needles strikingly light blue above, silvery-blue beneath. Growth rapid. Full pyramidal form.

S. sempervirens 'Soquel'

Introduced ≤1975 by the Saratoga Horticultural Foundation of California. Common. More compact than most cultivars, more elegant, less coarse than typical, and suckers less. Branches short, horizontal or slightly ascending to form a light, narrow crown.

Foliage bluish-green, upswept in spiky tufts. Needles shorter than those of the other Saratoga cultivars.

S. sempervirens 'Woodside (Blue)'
?= *S. sempervirens* 'Filoli'

Introduced <1988. Uncommon. Foliage handsome pale glaucous blue. Growth normal.

Sequoiadendron

[TAXODIACEÆ; Bald Cypress Family] A genus of only the following species, a coniferous evergreen closely related to *Sequoia*.

S. giganteum (Lindl.) Buchh.
= *Sequoia gigantea* (Lindl.) Decne. 1854, non Endl. 1847
= *Wellingtonia gigantea* Lindl.

SIERRA REDWOOD. GIANT SEQUOIA. MAMMOTH TREE. BIGTREE. From the high-elevation western slopes of the Sierra Nevada Range in California. The most massive of all trees. Discovered in 1833 by trapper-explorer Zenas Leonard, whose notes were not published until 1839. Generally, John Bidwell is credited as the first European to see these trees, in 1841. The hunter A.T. Dowd was next, in the spring of 1852, while chasing a wounded grizzly bear. Dowd brought publicity upon the trees. William Lobb brought seedlings and seeds to England in late autumn 1853. The species was being sold in California ≤1858. Long since world-famous as earth's largest tree, and grown wherever possible. Unlike *Sequoia sempervirens* (COAST REDWOOD), the *Sequoiadendron* doesn't sucker, and is a much more handsome tree as an open-grown ornamental, with its greatly swollen red trunk and neat pyramidal shape. It is also more cold-hardy. Only honey fungus seems to kill it, although many trees are struck by lightning and thereafter nearly cease height growth. Foliage bluish-green, sharply scaly and cord-like. Cones 1½"–3¾" long. The British call it *Wellingtonia*, after their Duke of Wellington (1769–1852). The tallest and stoutest examples in the British Isles are: 170½' × 28'11" Castle Leod, Strathpeffer, Scotland (1986; *pl.* 1854); 118' × 35'6" Cluny Garden, Tayside, Scotland (1988). On the U.S. East Coast, remarkable examples include: 81' ×

13'7" Bristol, RI (1986); 80' × 11'0" Tyler Arboretum, Media, PA (ca. 1987). British Columbia and Washington State both have examples more than 150' tall. Some centuries-old California giants are: 290' × 75'6" Round Medow (1981); 285' × 39'4" one of the Three Graces (1971); 275' × 83'3" General Sherman (1975); 269' × 93'0" Boole (<1980); 267' × 90'11" General Grant (<1980); 247' × 84'3" Bull Buck (1975). Specimens over 350' tall once existed, but presently the tallest known are ca. 295'.

S. giganteum 'Aureo-variegatum'
= S. giganteum 'Aureum'
= S. giganteum 'Hartland'

Raised ca. 1856 by Mr. R. Hartland of the Lough nursery, County Cork, Ireland. In 1875 G. Gordon described it as having ca. ⅓ of its branchlets pale golden yellow when young, gradually changing to a delicate, permanent straw color. Other accounts add that it is slower than typical. Extremely rare. Record: 88½' × 11'2" Cerne Abbey, Dorset, England (1989).

S. giganteum 'Aureum'—see S. giganteum 'Aureo-variegatum'

S. giganteum 'Glaucum'

Named in 1860. In North American commerce ≤1925. Long very rare; since the 1990s becoming more readily available. As tall as typical, but slenderer and less dense (even gaunt-looking); attractive pale bluish foliage. Record: 119' × 16'6" × 40' Tacoma, WA (1992).

S. giganteum 'Hartland'—see S. giganteum 'Aureo-variegatum'

S. giganteum 'Hazel Smith'

Originally obtained ca. 1960 as a seedling, by Don & Hazel Smith (owners of Watnong nursery of Morris Plains, NJ). Don died in 1984, Hazel in 1985; this clone was in commerce ≤1988. Exceptionally cold-hardy. Distinctly more uniform, pyramidal habit and bluer foliage than most.

S. giganteum 'Pendulum'

Introduced in 1863 by Lalande, nurseryman of Nantes, France. Described in 1871. In North American commerce ≤1907. Uncommon. Can be a tall pillar 3' wide, its branches wholly pendulous, or a leaning freak, flopping and sprawling about. Records: 105' × 8'7" Bodnant Gardens, Gwynedd, Wales (1989; pl. 1890); 44' × 2'9" × 12' Seattle, WA (1992); 36' × 7'2" × 32' Seattle, WA (1987).

S. giganteum 'Variegatum'

Mentioned in 1867 in France; cultivated in England ≤1868. In 1875 G. Gordon described it as having ca. ¼ of its branchlets delicate straw colored. Other accounts call it white-variegated. Extremely rare. Since 1992–93, Stanley & Sons nursery of Portland, OR, has sold a clone "equally green and yellow" that "sometimes burns on the yellow foliage." Since ≤1994, Buchholz & Buchholz nursery of Gaston, OR, has sold a "rich butter yellow" clone under this name; it may actually be 'Aureo-variegatum'.

Simaba quassioides—see Picrasma quassioides

Sophora

[LEGUMINOSÆ; Pea Family] 50–80 spp. of quite variable habit (trees, shrubs and herbs), hardiness and distribution. Latinized from the Arabic name sufayra, given to an allied plant with pea-shaped flowers, possibly of this genus.

S. japonica L.
= Styphnolobium japonicum Schott

CHINESE SCHOLAR TREE. (JAPANESE) PAGODA TREE (said to grow around temples). From China, Korea, and Viet Nam. Known in China as "Tree of Success in Life," and planted there on graves of higher officials; scholars were graced with Koelreuteria trees. Introduced to Western cultivation ca. 1747 when seeds were sent to France by Fr. d'Incarville, a Jesuit in China. In England ≤1753; in North America ≤1811. Common. Tolerates heat, cold, drought, poor soil, dust, smoke, rocky ground and whatnot. Given poor conditions however, it may be ugly, as it often is in S California. Leaves pinnately compound; leaflets 7–19. Prized for its late summer display of small creamy-white flowers in profuse clusters. In China the flowerbuds have been used to dye silk yellow. Seedpods 2"–3½" long, constricted between the seeds; soapy if crushed; often messy and slippery on walks. Twigs greenish; stink if bruised. Records: to 100' × 20'0" in China; 90' × 11'7" Essex, CT (1985); 88' × 16'5" London, England (1982); 84' × 10'3" × 101' Monroe, MI (1979); 78' × 16'6" × 98' Montgomery County, PA (1978); 77' × 16'8" × 99' Edgartown, MA (1986).

Sophora japonica 'Columnaris'
? = *S. japonica* 'Pyramidalis'

Described in 1907 in Germany. In North America ≤1956. Extremely rare. Habit columnar. Possibly sold as 'Pyramidalis' by Scanlon nursery of Ohio ≤1958.

S. japonica 'Contorta Pendula'—see *S. japonica* f. *pendula*

S. japonica 'Foliis Variegatis'—see *S. japonica* 'Variegata'

S. japonica 'Halka' PP 7554 (1991)
Originated by Chester J. Halka of Englishtown, NJ. Propagation rights assigned to Schmidt nursery of Boring, OR.

S. japonica f. *pendula* (Lodd. *ex* Sweet) Zabel
= *S. japonica* 'Tortuosa'
= *S. japonica* 'Contorta Pendula'

WEEPING CHINESE SCHOLAR TREE. Introduced <1827 in England. In North American commerce ≤1832. Uncommon. Normally doesn't bloom. Makes a tight hump or mop of contorted branches and weeping branchlets. More than one clone goes under the name 'Pendula'. In Europe a very rare clone is larger than the prevailing sort, less dense, and bears flowers. Records: 82' × 18'3" Philadelphia County, PA (1980); 33' × 6'6" Knap Hill Nursery, Surrey, England (n.d.); 29½' × 4'5" × 34' Seattle, WA (1994; *pl.* 1961); 14' × 3'6" × 17½' Lower Hutt, New Zealand (≤1982; *pl.* ca. 1843).

S. japonica 'PNI 5625'—see *S. japonica* Regent®

S. japonica 'Princeton Upright' PP 5524 (1985)
Selected as a seedling at Princeton nursery of New Jersey. Introduced ≤1986. Common. Distinctly upright branching. Highly resists twig dieback. Resists bark canker.

S. japonica 'Pyramidalis'—see *S. japonica* 'Columnaris'

S. japonica Regent® PP 2338 (1964)
= *S. japonica* 'PNI 5625'

Introduced by Princeton nursery of New Jersey. Common. Vigorous, fast; branching upright. Leaf-hopper resistant. Exceptionally glossy dark foliage. Large clusters of long-lasting flowers; blossoms at an earlier age than typical.

S. japonica 'Tortuosa'—see *S. japonica* f. *pendula*

S. japonica 'Variegata'
= *S. japonica* 'Foliis Variegatis'

Described ≤1838 in England. In North America ≤1966 (introduced that year by the Arnold Arboretum). Exceedingly rare. Foliage creamy-white variegated. Records: 56' × 5'11" (1982; *pl.* 1927) and 46' × 6'6" Paris, France (1982; *pl.* 1907).

S. japonica 'Violacea'
Introduced to cultivation in 1858 in France. In North American commerce ≤1888. Extremely rare. Flowers flushed purplish, blooming very late in the season.

Sorbus

[ROSACEÆ; Rose Family] 85–120 (250) spp. of trees and shrubs. From the ancient Latin name of *S. domestica*: *sorbus*. MOUNTAIN ASHES and WHITEBEAMS are small, from shrub-sized to 80' tall. All are deciduous; most display attractive fall color. Generous flattish ELDER-like clusters of small creamy-white flowers appear April to June, giving rise to berries, usually red but of varied colors and sizes, mostly unpalatable raw, but sometimes tasty; never toxic. Many of the species are able to reproduce from seed as genetically identical individuals, a process called apomixis. In the following pages, 23 species bear pinnately-compound leaves, as do regular ASH trees (*Fraxinus* species): these comprise the MOUNTAIN ASHES proper. An additional 9 species bear ALDER-like leaves, and are usually called WHITEBEAMS. Finally, 3 hybrids bear intermediate shaped leaves: *S. × hybrida*, *S. × Meinichii*, and *S. × thuringiaca*. Unfortunately, *Sorbus* don't flourish in most of North America. They either resent long growing seasons, or summer heat, or dryness, or succumb to fireblight or insect borers. However, they thrive in SW British Columbia and the maritime Pacific Northwest.

S. alnifolia (S. & Z.) K. Koch
= *Micromeles alnifolia* (S. & Z.) Koehne

ALDER WHITEBEAM. DENSEHEAD MOUNTAIN ASH. KOREAN MOUNTAIN ASH. ATSUKI PEAR (from the Japanese name *Azuki-nashi*). From China, Manchuria, Ussuri, Korea, Japan, and Taiwan. Introduced to Holland in 1860 by Siebold, but little known until marketed by Späth nursery of Germany in 1892. That same year C. Sargent sent seeds from Japan to the Arnold Arboretum. The epithet *alnifolia* means ALDER-like leaves; from genus *Alnus*, ALDER, and Latin *folium*, a leaf. HORNBEAM (*Carpinus*) leaves are also similar. Since its leaves don't even remotely resemble those of ASHES, the recently much-used name KOREAN MOUNTAIN ASH (also applied to *S. commixta*) seems inapt. Leaves 1½"–4" long, with 6–10 (12) vein pairs. Unlike those of other cultivated species, these leaves are shiny, crisp and not wooly. Beauty, and resistance to insect borers, have ensured this species a major role in ornamental horticulture. It flowers freely, is shapely, blazes in glorious yellow or golden fall color, and produces pretty reddish-pink berries that hang well even after the leaves drop. Some specimens are tightly fastigiate, others rounded, both with very slender twigs. Maximum reported height is 70' but most are half as tall or less. Bark smooth and somewhat like that of a BEECH (*Fagus*).

S. alnifolia 'Red Bird' PP 3400 (1973)
Selected by Princeton nursery of New Jersey. Narrow columnar. Abundant translucent red berries; fall color rich golden yellow.

S. alnifolia 'Skyline'
Selected in 1962 by Hillier nursery of England. Columnar.

S. alnifolia 'Upright'
In the 1960s Scanlon nursery of Ohio sold this clone, of an upright shape with a rounded head and beautiful fiery orange fall color. The same clone has likely been sold as 'Erecta' by Handy nursery of Portland, OR.

S. americana Marsh.
= *Pyrus americana* auct., non DC.

AMERICAN MOUNTAIN ASH. ROUNDWOOD. MISSEY-MOOSEY. From NE North America; southward only on mountains. In cultivation, usually small, of stiff habit; slow; and of much weaker constitution than *S. aucuparia*. Seldom planted now, it was planted more commonly in earlier decades of this century.

Sometimes nurseries have sold *S. decora* under the name *S. americana*. Leaves 6"–12" long; leaflets (9) 11–19, yellowish in fall. Buds sticky, hairless. Flowers very small, ⅛"–¼" wide. Berries to ⁵⁄₁₆" wide. Records: 71' × 3'6" × 62' Leelanau County, MI (1978); 62' × 6'8" × 40' West Virginia State Park (1979); 42' × 7'11" × 26' Albany, NY (1972); 40½' × 8'7" × 42' Beauport, Québec (<1994).

S. americana 'Belmonte'
From Belmonte Arboretum, Wageningen, Holland; named in 1964. In the Canadian nursery trade since ≤1975. Selected because of its upright branching structure and density. Some trees going under this name in England were actually *S. commixta*.

S. americana var. decora—see S. decora

S. americana 'Dwarfcrown'—see S. americana Red Cascade™

S. americana 'Nana'—see S. aucuparia 'Fastigiata'

S. americana Red Cascade™ PP 4157 (1977)
= *S. americana* 'Dwarfcrown'

J. Frank Schmidt & Son nursery of Boring, OR, registered this cultivar in 1980 erroneously as a *S. tianschanica* selection. It differs little if at all from ordinary *S. americana*, but offers uniformity, being a clone.

S. amurensis Koehne
AMUR MOUNTAIN ASH. From NE Asia. Introduced in 1907, but little known. It may prove to be only a variant of *S. pohuashanensis*, or merely an Amur River basin subspecies of *S. aucuparia*. It has been ignored partly because of an inaccurate claim that it is less cold-hardy than *S. aucuparia*, but no better-looking. But in Montana, *S. amurensis* doesn't suffer from sunscald, where *S. aucuparia* often does. The *Flora of the U.S.S.R.* describes it as a tree to 26' tall; leaf to 8¼" long, of 11–15 leaflets; berries ¼"–⅓" wide, bright red.

S. 'Apricot Queen'
= *S. aucuparia* 'Apricot Queen'
= *S. cashmiriana* 'Apricot Queen'
= *S. discolor* 'Apricot Queen'

An *S. aucuparia* hybrid originated ca. 1950 by Lombarts nursery of Zundert, Holland; introduced 1957–58. First sold by North American nurseries ca. 1965. Apricot-colored berries.

595

S. *Aria* (L.) Crantz

= *Pyrus Aria* (L.) Ehrh.
= *Cratægus Aria* L.

WHITEBEAM. WHITE WILD-PEAR. WHITELEAF TREE. (RED) CHESS-APPLE. CUMBERLAND HAW. LOTE TREE. SEA-OULER. From Europe and N Africa. *Aria* was the ancient Greek Theophrastus' name for this species. To say "the White Beam tree" is to unwittingly say "the White Tree tree"—since *béam* is the Old English word for tree (cognate with German *baum*). Though the white leaf undersides are exquisite in spring, and the red berries lovely in autumn, the inconsequential floral display and inconsistent fall color (yellow to biscuit-brown or russet usually, instead of flaming orange or red), have doomed WHITEBEAM to second-class status. It has seldom been offered in North American nurseries. The leaf, green above, with white fuzz beneath, is shaped like that of an ALDER (*Alnus*); to 5" × 3⅝"; stem to 1⅛" long; 8–15 vein pairs. Berries red, ½"–⁹⁄₁₆" long, with scattered white hairs; of fair flavor. Records: to 80' tall; 75' × 5'3" Alexandra Park, Hastings, Sussex, England (1983); 70' × 9'0" Castle Ashby, Northamptonshire, England (1983); 38½' × 4'8" × 38½' Victoria, B.C. (1994).

S. *Aria* 'Angustifolia'—see S. *Aria* f. *longifolia*

S. *Aria* 'Aurea'

From Späth nursery of Germany in 1893, 'Aurea' had very narrow yellow leaves. Superseded by 'Chrysophylla' whose wider leaf retains its color better, and is still narrower than normal (variable in size and shape, but a typical example 5½" × 2¾").

S. *Aria* 'Chrysophylla'

A variant with deep yellow, narrow leaves introduced ≤1897 by Späth nursery of Germany. An improvement on 'Aurea' because the yellow lasts throughout the season. Greek *chryso-*, golden, and *phyllon*, leaf.

S. *Aria* 'Decaisneana'

= S. *Aria* 'Majestica'

MAJESTIC WHITEBEAM. GREAT WHITEBEAM. The original grew in the French horticulturist Lavallée's Arboretum Segrez in 1858. Likely named after Joseph Decaisne (1807–1882), French botanist. The Metz nursery of Simon-Louis offered it in 1879. Generally acclaimed as the best WHITEBEAM variant. Larger twigs, buds, leaves (to 7" × 4") and fruit (to ⅝" long). In North America ≤1896; sold here since ≤1940. Record: 68' × 7'0" Westonbirt, Gloucestershire, England (1975).

S. *Aria* 'Edulis'—see S. *Aria* f. *longifolia*

S. *Aria* 'Gigantea'

GIANT WHITEBEAM arose in Holland ca. 1934 as an S. *Aria* seedling; selected by Jacques Lombarts and listed in the 1953–54 catalog of Lombarts nursery of Zundert. Like S. *Aria* 'Decaisneana' but with still larger (to 9¾" × 6") and more lobulate leaves, and larger fruit (to ⅔"–¾" long). This may not yet be present in North America.

S. *Aria* 'Latifolia'—see S. × *latifolia*

S. *Aria* f. *longifolia* (Pers.) Rehd.

NARROWLEAF WHITEBEAM variants were first described in 1783 by the French botanist Lamarck. More than one clone has been brought into cultivation. Some bear not only relatively slender leaves, but larger, better-tasting or juicier berries—such as 'Edulis', cultivated by 1809 in Germany. Described as slenderest-leaved of all, 'Angustifolia' was recorded by 1827. 'Salicifolia' has been applied to a stiffly fastigiate clone with leaves to 9½" × 4" and tasty red ¾" long berries, imported to Seattle from Poland in 1972. But Hillier's 'Salicifolia' is "graceful in habit, with lax branches." And the scientific name S. *Aria* var. *salicifolia* Myrin *ex* Hartm., is said to be an 1838 synonym for a shrubby northern European species related to S. *Aria*, with narrow leaves, and berries ⅝" wide: S. *rupicola*. None of these variants has been widely grown in N America.

S. *Aria* 'Lutescens'

= S. *Aria* 'Sulphurea'

Introduced <1885 by Simon-Louis nursery of Metz, France. Neat conical habit good for street-tree usage. Leaf slightly smaller than average for S. *Aria*, to 4" long; twigs sometimes purplish. In North American commerce since ≤1917; likely our most widely planted *Aria* cultivar. Has been called GOLDBEAM but this manufactured name, if it is to be suffered at all, would better fit S. *Aria* 'Chrysophylla'.

S. *Aria* 'Magnifica'

Hesse nursery of Germany raised this from seed and described it in 1916. Very rare. Listed in 1991 by Greer nursery of Eugene, OR. It may actually be a hybrid with HIMALAYAN WHITEBEAM (S. *cuspidata*).

Vigorous. Leaf to 5" × 3" and is last of the *S. Aria* cultivars to drop in the fall. Berries ½", bright red, not abundant.

S. Aria 'Majestica'—see *S. Aria* 'Decaisneana'

S. Aria 'Salicifolia'—see *S. Aria* f. *longifolia*

S. Aria 'Sulphurea'—see *S. Aria* 'Lutescens'

S. Aria 'Wilfrid Fox'—see *S.* 'Wilfrid Fox'

S. × arnoldiana Rehd.

ARNOLD MOUNTAIN ASH. Raised at the Arnold Arboretum in 1907 from seed of *S. pekinensis* received in 1902 from Germany. Named in 1920. Usually *S. pekinensis* is cited as a synonym of *S. discolor*—a white-berried Chinese species. But ARNOLD MOUNTAIN ASH is described as a pink-berried hybrid between *S. discolor* and *S. aucuparia*. The matter may not be so simple, however. The tree that gave the seed from which *arnoldiana* was raised, might itself have been a hybrid, such as *S. discolor* × *S. pohuashanensis*. In any case, *S. arnoldiana* has been distributed very little. In Seattle, it blooms earlier than most *Sorbus*, bears (11) 13–19 leaflets and handsome pink berries.

S. × arnoldiana 'Kirsten Pink'—see *S.* 'Kirsten Pink'

S. × arnoldiana 'Old Pink'—see *S.* 'Old Pink'

S. aucuparia L.

= *Pyrus aucuparia* (L.) Gaertn.

COMMON MOUNTAIN ASH. EUROPEAN MOUNTAIN ASH. ROWAN. ROAN. WITCHEN TREE. WITCHWOOD. FOWLER'S SERVICE-TREE. QUICKBEAM. QUICKEN. From Europe, N Africa, W Asia, and Siberia. The epithet *aucuparia* derives from Latin *avis*, a bird, and *capere*, to catch, either from the use of the tree's shoots to make birdlime or because the berries were used as bait in fowlers' traps. Called MOUNTAIN ASH because it is found higher in mountains of Scotland (to 3,200') than any other tree, especially the lowland-loving common ASH (*Fraxinus excelsior*), which is similar in leaf shape. ROWAN is from Old English *raun*—in reference to its red berries and maybe its fall color.

Imported to Williamsburg, VA <1752, this species has been the most widely planted *Sorbus* in North America, and often comes up wild. It has always been common in nurseries in regions where it will grow. Leaf to 9" long; leaflets (9) 11–17 (19). Buds hairy. Berries orange, turning usually to red-orange or pure red, about ⅜" wide. Bark reminiscent of BIRCH (*Betula*) or CHERRY (*Prunus*), in its polished, horizontal, peeling way. Records: 85' × 6'3" Bremerton, WA (1995); 78' × 3'9" Seattle, WA (1993); 58' × 8'4" Kitchener, Ontario (1975); 43' × 10'3" × 39' Seattle, WA (1988).

S. aucuparia 'Apricot Queen'—see *S.* 'Apricot Queen'

S. aucuparia 'Asplenifolia'

= *S. aucuparia* var. *laciniata* hort., non Hartm.

CUTLEAF MOUNTAIN ASH. From Germany. Named by 1853, but described officially in 1869. Although common in Europe, it has been rare in N America; some Midwest and Ontario nurseries listed it since ≤1960. Possibly a fixed juvenile form with its leaflets extra deeply toothed; fernlike. Latin *asplenifolius* means "leaves like the frond of the spleenwort"—that is, fernlike. Leaflets very downy, and sometimes bear 1–2 distinct small lobes at the base.

S. aucuparia 'Beissneri'

= *S. aucuparia* 'Dulcis Laciniata'

After Ludwig Beissner (1843–1927), German dendrologist. Originated ca. 1890 in the Erzgebirge border region of Germany and Bohemia. Very rare in North America. Like *S. aucuparia* 'Edulis' but with honey-colored bark, especially lovely when wet, and leaflets extra-deeply toothed, even to the point of being lobed, splendid yellow in fall.

S. aucuparia 'Black Hawk'

Introduced in the 1960s by Matt Tures Sons nursery of Huntley, IL. Widely grown since the 1980s. Tree strong and columnar. Berries large and orange. Leaves thick, dark, and sun-scald resistant.

S. aucuparia 'Brilliant Yellow'—see *S.* 'Brilliant Yellow'

S. aucuparia Cardinal Royal™ PP 3114 (1972)

= *S. aucuparia* 'Michred'

Introduced by Dr. Milton Baron of Michigan State University. Propagation rights assigned in the 1970s to Schmidt nursery of Boring, OR. Common. Compared to average *S. aucuparia*, this clone is vigorous and bears much larger clusters of showy red berries coloring early.

S. aucuparia 'Cherokee'

Introduced in the 1960s by Matt Tures Sons nursery of Huntley, IL. A strong, columnar tree with large orange berries and thick dark leaves that resist sunscald; narrower than the otherwise similar clone 'Black Hawk', and less well known.

S. aucuparia 'Cole's Columnar'

A narrowly columnar clone with bright fruit. Introduced ≤1957 by Cole nursery of Painesville, OH.

S. aucuparia 'Columbia Queen'

From 1964 to 1975, Scanlon nursery of Ohio marketed this clone, "a very vigorous grower with a cone-shaped head, very dark foliage and brilliant red heavy clusters of berries." It is denser and narrower than most seedlings. The name Columbia may refer to the river of that name, as the tree was first grown by Handy nursery of Portland, OR. Rarely grown in recent years.

S. aucuparia 'Dulcis'—see S. aucuparia 'Edulis'

S. aucuparia 'Dulcis Laciniata'—see S. aucuparia 'Beissneri'

S. aucuparia 'Edulis'
= S. aucuparia 'Dulcis'
= S. aucuparia 'Moravica'

MORAVIAN MOUNTAIN ASH. This name has been applied (both clonally by horticulturists, and varietally by botanists) to trees with better-tasting, usually larger berries. Such trees were in cultivation in Germany ≤1800, but the first clone to be extensively circulated, from Bohemia, dates from 1887. Specimens were in Canada by 1887. Niels Hansen collected seeds from big-fruited trees in Russia in 1906, and introduced them to the U.S. in 1910. Since the 1960s, a few Canadian and northern U.S. nurseries have offered 'Edulis'. Compared to regular trees, the leaflets are larger (to 3⅞" × 1⅛"), nearly hairless, and are toothed only in their upper halves; the berries taste less repulsive, although are still poorly flavored unless cooked, and nowhere near the best that *Sorbus* offers. The original cloned 'Edulis' also features purplish leafstalks; widely spaced, narrow leaflets, extreme hardiness, vigor and upright habit. A good ornamental even if one doesn't eat its berries.

S. aucuparia 'Fastigiata'

FASTIGIATE MOUNTAIN ASH. COLUMNAR MT.-ASH. UPRIGHT MT.-ASH. *S. aucuparia* seedlings vary in growth habit from columnar to broadly rounded. The name 'Fastigiata' has been applied to more than one clone. The first so described was raised in 1838 by Mr. Hodgkin of Dunganstown nursery, County Wicklow, Ireland. But by the early 1900s another clone became more prominent. In Europe this was sold variously as *S. americana* 'Nana' or *S. decora* 'Nana' or *S. scopulina*. These names all suggest a North American origin. A most likely theory is that the tree is a cross of *S. aucuparia* and *S. decora*. In any case, the mystery clone called in recent decades *S. aucuparia* 'Fastigiata' is a very slow, coarse, stout-twigged tall shrub or small tree. Its tight compact habit and lovely large berries are desirable, but the crude twigs and foliage are drawbacks. Introduced to North America ≤1957 when the Arnold Arboretum imported it from England. In recent years Canadian nurseries, as well as Handy of Portland, OR (as DWARF COLUMNAR MT.-ASH), and Sherman, of Iowa, have listed it. Narrow clones that might be sold as 'Fastigiata' are: 'Cherokee', 'Cole's Columnar', and 'Wilson'.

S. aucuparia 'Fifeana'—see S. aucuparia 'Fructu Luteo'

S. aucuparia 'Fructu Luteo'
= S. aucuparia 'Xanthocarpa'
= S. aucuparia 'Fifeana'

YELLOWBERRY MOUNTAIN ASH. Of unknown, but European origin <1838; berries orange-yellow. Introduced to North America ≤1894. Rare.

S. aucuparia 'Kirsten Pink'—see S. 'Kirsten Pink'

S. aucuparia var. laciniata—see S. aucuparia 'Asplenifolia'

S. aucuparia var. Meinichii—see S. × Meinichii

S. aucuparia 'Michred'—see S. aucuparia Cardinal Royal™

S. aucuparia 'Moravica'—see S. aucuparia 'Edulis'

S. aucuparia 'Pendula'

WEEPING MOUNTAIN ASH. Known in Germany ≤1853; described officially in 1864. In effect a sideways sprawler lacking apical dominance, it is topgrafted, making a crude, broad, weeping tree. Usually flowers and fruits sparsely. Long grown in North America, but rarely in recent years. One grower remarked, its "branches all seem to have a mind of their own." Record: 17' × 5'1" × 31' Lynnwood, WA (1993).

S. aucuparia 'Pink Pagoda'—see S. hupehensis 'Pink Pagoda'

S. aucuparia 'Rosedale'

Origin unknown but likely North American. Listed since ≤1953–54 by B.C. nurseries, as a strong upright tree with disease-resistant large deep green leaves, and little or no fruit.

S. aucuparia 'Rossica'

RUSSIAN MOUNTAIN ASH. From the Kiev region of Russia, put into commerce by Späth nursery of Germany in 1898. Soon superseded by 'Rossica Major' and is intermediate between that clone (see below) and normal trees. Trees *sold* as 'Rossica' are more likely to be 'Rossica Major'. Several nurseries since the 1950s (e.g., Braun, Cannor, Connon, Manten, Massot, Schichtel) have listed the former, but the latter name is rarely encountered.

S. aucuparia 'Rossica Major'

Like 'Rossica' which it has largely replaced, this was a Späth introduction, in 1903. Also from the Kiev vicinity. Like 'Edulis' it is large-fruited (to over ⅝" long); though the leaflets are similarly longer and relatively broader than normal, they are *hairy* beneath, slightly puckered, and *more* toothed. The tree is very hardy and vigorous, its branches tightly ascending.

S. aucuparia 'Sheerwater Seedling'

Originated near Sheerwater stream at Woking, Surrey, England. Nurseryman Rowland Jackman put it in commerce <1955. The Arnold Arboretum imported it to the U.S. in 1965. Its attributes are vigor, a tight, upswept egg-shaped crown, and abundant large clusters of berries that color red early—in July. Some Canadian nurseries have offered it since the 1980s.

S. aucup. 'Warleyensis'—see S. pohuashanensis, & S. Wilsoniana

S. aucuparia 'Wilson'

WILSON COLUMNAR MOUNTAIN ASH. Introduced ca. 1960 by Scanlon nursery of Ohio. A tight columnar selection. What may be an example planted ca. 1962 in Seattle was 48' × 6'6" × 23' in 1992.

S. aucuparia 'Xanthocarpa'—see S. aucuparia 'Fructu Luteo'

S. 'Brilliant Yellow'

= S. aucuparia 'Brilliant Yellow'

An S. aucuparia hybrid originated ca. 1950 by Lombarts nursery of Zundert, Holland; introduced 1957–58. First sold by North American nurseries ≤1968–69. Listed in 1990 and 1991 by Lake County nursery of Perry, OH—not in their 1993 catalog. Bright yellow berries—more brilliant and in larger clusters than those of S. aucuparia 'Fructu Luteo'.

S. 'Carpet of Gold'

An S. aucuparia hybrid originated ca. 1950 by Lombarts nursery of Zundert, Holland; introduced 1957–58. First sold by North American nurseries ≤1962. Tree fastigiate. Berries orange-yellow.

S. cashmiriana Hedl.

KASHMIR MOUNTAIN ASH. From the W Himalayas, in and near Kashmir. Described in 1901. Introduced to England in 1934, and from there imported to the Arnold Arboretum in 1949. It stands out with pinkish-tinged flowers, and showy, comparatively large snow-white berries (½"–⅝"), but is often short-lived in cultivation. Leaf 3½"–7⅞" long; 13–19 leaflets, of variable fall color—dull yellowish to russet or bright red. Reported up to 40' tall but usually half that height or less. First widely promoted in North America by Scanlon nursery of Ohio in the 1970s, and subsequently offered largely by his licensed growers, as small seedlings in limited quantity.

S. cashmiriana 'Apricot Queen'—see S. 'Apricot Queen'

S. cashmiriana 'Kirsten Pink'—see S. 'Kirsten Pink'

S. 'Charming Pink'

An S. aucuparia hybrid originated ca. 1950 by Lombarts nursery of Zundert, Holland; introduced 1957–58. First sold by North American nurseries ≤1968–69. Listed in 1990 by Lake County nursery of Perry, OH. Pink berries.

S. *commixta* Hedl.

= *S. japonica* (Maxim.) Koehne, non Sieb., non (Decne.) Hedl.

JAPANESE MOUNTAIN ASH. KOREAN MOUNTAIN ASH. From Japan, Sakhalin, the S Kuriles, and Korea. Introduced first in 1880, then in 1906. Though in the U.S. nursery trade by the 1920s, rarely grown in North America. By no means the only *Sorbus* in Japan, this is the major one, significant in horticulture. It is variable and its name *commixta* likely refers to the consternation of botanists attempting to delineate its proper place in the cosmos. In Western cultivation it is found in various manifestations under different names. Closely related to *S. americana*, it is more robust and treelike (easily to 30'–50' tall). Leaf to 12" long; 11–15 (17) leaflets, often glossy, usually rich red or purplish-red in fall. Buds long, slender, reddish-purple with little or no hair. Record: 41½' × 3'1" Victoria, B.C. (1994).

S. *commixta* 'Embley'

= *S.* 'Embley'
= *S. discolor* hort. UK, non (Maxim.) Maxim.

CHINESE SCARLET MOUNTAIN ASH. In 1890, some Arnold Arboretum seed of "*S. discolor*" made its way to Britain. An especially good seedling grown at Embley Park, Romsey, Hampshire, was marketed by Hillier nursery and named in 1971. 'Embley' differs in its markedly slender leaflets, not glossy, that color better, later, and last longer—"flaming scarlet." Record: 56' × 5'3" Sheffield Park, Sussex, England (1974).

S. *commixta* var. *rufoferruginea* Shirai *ex* Schneid.

= *S. rufoferruginea* (Shirai *ex* Schneid.) Schneid.

FLAMEBERRY MOUNTAIN ASH. Named in 1906, and introduced to cultivation in 1915, this variety is hairier than ordinary *S. commixta*, but not much different horticulturally. Its prime attraction is its lovely dark red fall color. *Sorbus* expert Hugh McAllister says it's somewhat intermediate between *S. aucuparia* and *S. commixta*: "Other than its notable fall color, only its reddish conical buds with rusty hairs distinguish it from *S. aucuparia*." The Japanese botanist J. Ohwi asserts that it differs from *S. commixta* in that its flower clusters and leaf undersides are coated with long soft brown hairs.

S. *commixta* var. *rufoferruginea* 'Longwood Sunset'

From Longwood Gardens of Kennett Square, PA, introduced in 1990. The original specimen was grown by P. Hill in 1964 from seeds collected from a cultivated specimen in Japan. Selected as a replacement for *S. aucuparia*, being heat-tolerant, disease-resistant, with rich burgundy fall color and plentiful orange berries.

S. *Conradinæ* hort., non Koehne—see *S. pohuashanensis*

S. 'Coral Beauty'

An *S. aucuparia* hybrid originated ca. 1950 by Lombarts nursery of Zundert, Holland; introduced 1957–58. First sold by North American nurseries ≤1966. Large, apricot colored berries.

S. *decora* (Sarg.) Schneid.

= *S. sambucifolia* hort., non (Cham. & Schlecht.) Roem.
= *S. americana* hort. (in part), non Marsh.
= *S. americana* var. *decora* (Sarg.) Sarg.
= *S. scopulina* Hough, non Greene
= *Pyrus sitchensis* Robinson & Fernald, non (Roem.) Piper

SHOWY MOUNTAIN ASH. ELDERLEAF MOUNTAIN ASH. From S Greenland to Wisconsin. Traditionally this many-named species has been described by how it differs from its associate, *S. americana*. It has blackish, slightly hairy buds; leaflets (7) 11–17, broader and less pointy; flowers larger and open later; larger berries (to nearly ½"). In fact its name *decora* means handsome or showy and refers to the fruit—the large heavy clusters are striking in September as they bend the branches with their ripened weight, much more memorable than the fall leaf coloration. But birds eat the berries very quickly. Usually forms a shrub or small robust tree to about 20'–25', often slow growing. Valued for cold-hardiness, and for being, overall, a prettier species than *S. americana*. Records: 58' × 4'9" × 32' Mackinac County, MI (1975); 27' × 5'3" × 33' Pembroke, Ontario (1977).

S. *decora* 'Nana'—see *S. aucuparia* 'Fastigiata'

S. *discolor* (Maxim.) Maxim., non hort. UK (cf. *S. commixta* 'Embley')

?= *S.* × *pekinensis* Koehne—see *S.* × *arnoldiana*
= *Pyrus discolor* Maxim.

SNOWBERRY MOUNTAIN ASH. From N China. Emil

Bretschneider, physician in Peking, is said to have introduced this species from China to the Arnold Arboretum sometime between 1866–1884, likely in 1880. Thence it was introduced to England in 1882–83. But plants raised in Europe from Bretschneider's seeds turned out to be *S. pohuashanensis*. Still other plants called *S. discolor* later proved to be *S. commixta*. True *S. discolor* was introduced to Britain from Späth nursery of Germany in 1903. In short, this species has confused people, and it has been cultivated relatively seldom in its authentic state. Leaf 6" long; leaflets 11–15 (17), vivid red in fall. Berries white, ⅜" long. The 1859 name *discolor* is derived from Latin, meaning "having two colors"—particolored or different colored: the leaflets are green on top and pale beneath.

S. discolor 'Apricot Queen'—see S. 'Apricot Queen'

S. discolor 'Kirsten Pink'—see S. 'Kirsten Pink'

S. domestica L.

= *Pyrus domestica* (L.) Sm.
= *Pyrus Sorbus* Gaertn.

THE TRUE SERVICE. WHITTY PEAR TREE. THE SORB TREE. SERVICE TREE. From S & E Europe, N Africa, and SW Asia. Rare in North America's nursery trade, less so on the West Coast, where it was available commercially ≤1854. Enormous size, and large fruit, set it apart. Leaves recall those of *S. aucuparia*, being 5"–9" long, of 11–21 leaflets. Its fruit has been classed into apple-like, pear-like, and berry-like. Unripe fruit is pale green, becoming greenish-yellow, eventually with an orange blush (in a rare cultivar bright glossy red), to 1½" long. Until soft it is astringent. When soft, and beginning to brown, it drops, making a slippery mess from late September into mid-November. In some specimens the fruits are only in pairs or trios, in others they're borne in clusters of as many as 14. The name *domestica* is from Latin *domus*, as this species was the edible *soruum* cultivated in ancient Latin civilization. When eaten at the perfect stage they are pleasantly pear-like. Regarding its role in ornament, the fruit, being so big, yet dull, is a liability. The tree can be distinguished even in winter by its brown bark fissured into rough scales, and its slender, green,

shiny, sticky buds. Records: 79' × 9'4" Paris (1982; *pl.* 1817); 78' × 4'5" × 37' Seattle, WA (1993; from 1949 seed); 77' × 10'8" Woodstock, County Kilkenny, Ireland (1904); 77' × 9'5" × 61' Edmonds, WA (1992; *pl.* ca. 1920); 45' × 14'2" × 50' Verrières, France (±1835).

S. 'Embley'—see S. commixta 'Embley'

S. fennica—see S. × hybrida

S. Folgneri (Schneid.) Rehd.

= *Micromeles Folgneri* Schneid.
= *Aria Folgneri* (Schneid.) H. Ohashi & Iketani

FOLGNER'S CHINESE WHITEBEAM. From C & SW China. Introduced ca. 1901 by E. Wilson to Veitch nursery of England. An elegant, distinctively sinuous tree; poised, not staid. Its slender leaves (to 6¼" long), silvery-hairy beneath, are remarkable for waiting so long to assume fall color—in mid-November, the last *Sorbus* still greenish. The belated color change is to rich red or orange. Berries ½"–¾" long, first clear orange but turning pinkish if not red in part. This has not been offered by major North American nurseries. Excellent examples dating from 1948 in Seattle are still a far cry from the record sizes in England: 66' × 3'4" Caerhays Castle, Cornwall (1985); 60' × 6'6" Leonardslee, Sussex (1984).

S. Forrestii McAll. & Gillh.

= *S. Prattii* Hand.-Mazz., non Koehne

FORREST MOUNTAIN ASH. From SW China. Introduced in 1921 from Yunnan province by George Forrest (1873–1932), this species went unnamed until 1980. Before then it was grown under other names. A white-fruited species, it is related to *S. hupehensis* but has larger flowers and berries (*S. aucuparia*-sized) ripening rather later than those of many other species—early October. Forrest said it was a shrub 25'–40' tall. Specimens grown in Seattle since 1945 are burly, suckery small trees, superb in mid-November with their white fruit. Leaflets (13) 15 (19).

S. glabrescens—see S. hupehensis

S. grandidentata—see S. × thuringiaca 'Quercifolia'

S. hupehensis Schneid.

= *S. laxiflora* Koehne
= *S. glabrescens* (Cardot) Hand.-Mazz.

HUPEH MOUNTAIN ASH. From central and W China. Named in 1906. Introduced by E. Wilson in 1910.

Some botanists make fine distinctions, and split what horticulturists call HUPEH MOUNTAIN ASH into several species, differing in minor ways. Leaf bluish-green, 4"–7" (10") long; leaflets (9) 11–15 (17); fall color variously yellow-orange or dark red. Berries usually pink-tinged, sometimes essentially milk-white; small, firm and long-lasting. Records: 51' × 5'1" Borde Hill, Sussex, England (1989); 49' × 6'2" SW Kansu, China (1925); 49' × 3'8" Seattle, WA (1994); 33' × 4'9" Caerhays, Cornwall, England (1984).

S. hupehensis Coral Fire®

Introduced ≤1987–88 by Pacific Coast nursery of Portland, OR. A clone featuring red leaf stems, coral-red berries and bright red fall color. Fireblight resistant.

S. hupehensis 'Pink Pagoda'

= *S. aucuparia* 'Pink Pagoda'

The original specimen of this clone, at the University of British Columbia's Asian Garden, was selected in 1985 and named and introduced in 1988. It bears mostly 11–13 leaflets. Berries first dark pink, especially at the ends, fading to almost white, then darkening again in winter; last longer into winter than those of most *Sorbus*.

S. × *hybrida* L.

= *S. Meinichii* hort. (in part), non (Lindeb. *ex* Hart.) Hedl.
= *S. pinnatifida* hort. (in part–cf. *S.* × *thuringiaca*)
= *S. fennica* (Kalm) Fries

FINNISH WHITEBEAM. From S & SW Scandinavia, a tetraploid apomict cross of *S. aucuparia* and either *S. obtusifolia* or *S. rupicola*. Exceedingly confused with *S.* × *thuringiaca* (*S. aucuparia* × *S. Aria*) that reproduces by amphimixis and is therefore more variable. Though cultivated since 1797 in Germany, probably 99% of trees called *S.* × *hybrida* are really either *S.* × *thuringiaca* (which see) or are *S. aucuparia* × *S. intermedia*. Leaf to 5¾" × 3¼"; of (2) 4 (6) free leaflets and one huge, much lobed portion that makes most of the leaf. Berries red, ½"–⅝" wide, sweet. Records: 60' × 3'3" Westonbirt, Gloucestershire, England (1980); 39' × 5'5"

Grignon, France (1894); 35' × 3'2" Seattle, WA (1994; *pl.* 1945); 34' × 3'9" Newcastle House, Glamorganshire, Wales (1980).

S. × *hybrida* f. *fastigiata*—see *S.* × *thuringiaca* 'Fastigiata'

S. × *hybrida* 'Gibbsii'

A clone named after being exhibited in 1920 by the Hon. Vicary Gibbs (1853–1932), of Aldenham, Hertfordshire, England. The Arnold Arboretum introduced it to the U.S. in 1925. But it has rarely if ever been sold in nurseries here. Scarcely different from *S.* × *hybrida*, but of more compact and shapely habit; with slightly larger berries (to ¾" wide), darker red. Leaf to 6⅜" × 3¾". Records: 35' × 5'3" East Bergholt Place, Suffolk, England (1972); 26½' × 2'3" Vancouver, B.C. (1994; *pl.* 1978).

S. × *hybrida* 'Leonard Springer'—see *S.* × *thuringiaca* 'Leonard S.'

S. × *hybrida* var. *Meinichii*—see *S.* × *Meinichii*

S. × *hybrida* 'Pyramidalis'—see *S.* × *thuringiaca* 'Fastigiata'

S. × *hybrida* 'Quercifolia'—see *S.* × *thuringiaca* 'Quercifolia'

S. intermedia (Ehrh.) Pers.

= *S. scandica* (L.) Fries, non Coste
= *S. suecica* (L.) Krok *ex* Hartm.
= *Pyrus intermedia* Ehrh.

SWEDISH WHITEBEAM. In Sweden called *Oxel*. From N Europe. A tetraploid apomict, long cultivated; likely of hybrid origin but of uncertain parentage. Leaves intermediate between those of *S. Aria* and *S. torminalis* (or *S. aucuparia*); grayish beneath, to 4¾" × 3⅛"; stem 1¼"–2" long; 5–9 vein pairs. A strong, tough species, air-pollution tolerant, floriferous, with good yellow fall color and consistent crops of ½" wide red berries. Fairly well known in North American cultivation, but grown less in recent decades than it was 75 years ago. Records: 75' × 9'8" Newby Hall, N Yorkshire, England (1982); 46' × 5'5" × 39' Tacoma, WA (1988); 26' × 9'10" × 36' Tacoma, WA (1990); a trunk 13'1" around at Okolice Salina, Poland (≤1973).

S. intermedia 'Skandia'

Braun nursery of Mt. Hope, Ontario, offered this in the 1980s and early 90s. Likely it is just plain *S.*

intermedia. The catalog says: "30'; slow-growing; young leaves gray-green; orange fruit; fireblight resistant."

S. japonica—see *S. commixta*

S. 'Joseph Rock'

ROCK MOUNTAIN ASH. Joseph Francis Charles Rock (1884–1962), Austrian linguist and plant collector; collected *Sorbus* seed in Yunnan, China, and sent it to Edinburgh in 1932. Some of the seeds went to the Wisley gardens of Surrey, England. One seedling there proved so different from the others, it was propagated and named 'Joseph Rock'. The original tree was 50' × 3'3" (1985). Despite its lovely looks, it is fireblight-prone. Some of its seedlings look very much like it, and some have in turn been named, for example 'Sunshine'. One *Sorbus* expert believes 'Joseph Rock' is a cultivar of *S. Rehderiana*. Tree is dainty in its parts; compact, slender of trunk. Leaf 4"–8" long, of (5) 15–19 (21) leaflets, purplish in autumn. Numerous very small (to ⅜" wide) shiny, dark yellow berries make a pleasing contrast. In North America since ≤1965, the oldest and finest of our few specimens are likely found in B.C. and W Washington. One at the University of B.C. Asian Garden measures 38' × 1'10" × 22' (1993). Cannor nursery of B.C. has grown it.

S. 'Kirsten Pink'

= *S. aucuparia* 'Kirsten Pink'
= *S. × arnoldiana* 'Kirsten Pink'
= *S. cashmiriana* 'Kirsten Pink'
= *S. discolor* 'Kirsten Pink'

KIRSTEN PINK MOUNTAIN ASH. One of 23 *S. aucuparia* hybrids originated ca. 1950 by Lombarts nursery of Zundert, Holland; introduced 1958. Overall, much like *S. aucuparia* but far less robust, with pink berries. First sold in North American nurseries in 1965. But at least two clones go under the name 'Kirsten Pink' and we need to find out which is correctly named. One has largely untoothed leaflets, and plump soft berries; the other has leaflets sharply toothed to their bases, with smaller, firmer, paler, narrow, shiny berries. Since at least 7 (besides 'Kirsten Pink') Lombarts hybrid cultivars produce more or less pink berries, asking "will the real 'Kirsten Pink' please stand up?" is no easy matter.

S. × latifolia (Lam.) Pers., s.l.

= *S. Aria* 'Latifolia' hort.
= *Pyrus intermedia* var. *latifolia* (Lam.) DC.

SERVICE TREE OF FONTAINEBLEAU. CORNISH WHITEBEAM. From Europe, a hybrid of *S. Aria* (or a related species) and *S. torminalis*. First noted in France's forest of Fontainebleau (south of Paris) early in the 18th century. Offered by North American nurseries from the 1940s into the 1960s, but scarcely at all since then. *S. × paucicrenata* is similar. Large, WHITEBEAM-like leaves serve as a golden backdrop in October for large, orange-brown, speckled berries. Leaf 3"–6" long, quite wide, as the epithet *latifolia* implies; with 6–10 vein pairs. Given ideal conditions, the tree is powerful; although the largest measured recently are smaller, the all-time champion was 75' × 11'0" at Oakley Park, Cirencester, Gloucestershire, England (1906).

S. × latifolia var. *parumlobata*—see *S. × paucicrenata*

S. laxiflora—see *S. hupehensis*

S. megalocarpa Rehd.

= *Aria megalocarpa* (Rehd.) H. Ohashi & Iketani

From W China. Introduced in 1908 and 1910 by E. Wilson. Exceedingly rare. A small tree or large shrub. Twigs stout. Buds large (to ¾"), glossy, sticky, very pointed, green and brown, breaking forth as early as February to reveal yellowish flowers that appear before the leaves unfold (usually April in Seattle). Leaves emerge salmon-pink to purplish-red colored, and at maturity look amazingly like those of MAZZARD CHERRY (*Prunus avium*), being large (up to 10" × 4½"; stem to 1" long, finely toothed, with 12–20 vein pairs), turning reddish with some yellow, or russet, in autumn, dropping in November to reveal the dull fruits, which can be 1⅓" long (*megalocarpa* means big-fruited). The berries hang firmly to the twigs, are speckled brown, and can look ugly. We are accustomed to discarding fruit when it turns brown. But these have sour, tangy, delicious bright green flesh inside. They hang on the tree into early January, even in freezing temperatures, still edible and a treat.

S. megalocarpa var. *cuneata* Rehd.

Wilson made only one collection of this variant, from a tree in W Szechuan province in October 1910. It differs in being more vigorous, with narrowed (i.e., cuneate) leaf-bases, and smaller fruit, only ⅝" long.

S. × Meinichii (Lindeb. *ex* Hartm.) Hedl.

= *S. aucuparia* var. *Meinichii* Lindeb. *ex* Hartm.
= *S. hybrida* var. *Meinichii* (Lindeb. *ex* Hartm.) Rehd.
= *S. × thuringiaca* 'Meinichii'

MEINICH MOUNTAIN ASH. From Norway. A tetraploid apomict named in 1879 after Norwegian amateur botanist and government official Hans Thomas Meinich (1817–1878), who had made the tree known to science. In cultivation since 1904 when the Earl of Ducie imported it from Norway to England. In North America since ≤1947. Clearly derived largely from *S. aucuparia*. The other parent possibly *S. × hybrida*. A small tree. Leaf consists of 8–12 free leaflets with a larger, lobed terminal leaflet. Berries scarlet. To an extent, *S. × hybrida* has been grown wrongly under the *Meinichii* name; *S. × thuringiaca* variants (e.g., cultivar 'Leonard Springer') with numerous leaflets have also been confused with it. Until someone obtains samples from the various nurseries selling *Meinichii* to compare critically, it is anyone's guess whether they're uniform, or correctly labeled.

S. 'Old Pink'

= *S. × arnoldiana* 'Old Pink'

An *S. aucuparia* hybrid originated ca. 1950 by Lombarts nursery of Zundert, Holland; introduced 1957–58. Imported to the U.S. by the Arnold Arboretum in 1965. Sold in Canada since 1967.

S. × paucicrenata (Ilse) Hedl.

= *S. latifolia* var. *parumlobata* (Irm. *ex* Düll) Schneid.

Reportedly grown since 1866 in England, this hybrid or "microspecies" from the Alps and eastern Germany is believed to be *S. Aria* × (*S. Aria* × *S. torminalis*). It sets few fruit, and overall resembles *S. latifolia*. During the 1960s Scanlon nursery of Ohio offered it, because *S. Aria* gets fireblight; this does not. Scanlon wrote of *S. × paucicrenata*: "Light green elliptic leaf somewhat silvery underneath; sparsely-produced tile-colored berries."

S. pekinensis—see S. discolor and S. × arnoldiana

S. pinnatifida—see S. × hybrida and S. × thuringiaca

S. pohuashanensis (Hance) Hedl.

= *S. Conradinæ* hort., non Koehne
= *S. aucuparia* 'Warleyensis' (in part—cf. *S. Wilsoniana*)

POHUA (SHAN) MOUNTAIN ASH. From N China. Discovered in 1874. Introduced by E. Bretschneider in 1882 to the Arnold Arboretum. The status of this species in North American cultivation is poorly known: some trees so sold may actually be either hybrids or other species altogether. At any rate, some nurseries have listed *pohuashanensis*, correctly or otherwise. Botanically, it has been called a northern Chinese subspecies of *S. aucuparia*. Horticulturally, it has been called *the best* Chinese MOUNTAIN ASH. It is more slender and hairy than *S. aucuparia*, and often has conspicuous persistent stipules under the flower clusters. Leaf to 7" long; leaflets 11–15. A form grown by Valley nursery of Helena, MT, produces a natural lollipop-shaped tree. Some small-scale nurseries promote this species for use as an edible-fruit tree. Record: 40' × 1'10" Buckingham Palace, London, England (1987).

S. Prattii Koehne

PRATT MOUNTAIN ASH. From W China. Likely named for the English naturalist Antwerp E. Pratt, who arrived in China in 1887 as a private, amateur plant collector, and found this species in 1889–90. Introduced by E. Wilson in 1910 to the Arnold Arboretum. A large shrub or small tree to 25' tall, with white (a tinge of pink sometimes) ¼"–⁷⁄₁₆" wide berries. Leaf to 5½"(7½") long; leaflets (15) 21–33; yellowish fall color. Well known in England, rare in North America, although in the nursery trade to a very limited extent since the 1950s. Some trees sold as *S. Prattii* are really *S. Forrestii* (q.v.).

S. quercifolia—see S. × thuringiaca 'Quercifolia'

S. 'Red Copper Glow'

An *S. aucuparia* hybrid originated ca. 1950 by Lombarts nursery of Zundert, Holland; introduced 1957–58. First sold by North American nurseries ≤1966. Abundant berries described variously as fleshy pink or bright scarlet with coral and copper overtones.

S. 'Red Tip'

An *S. aucuparia* hybrid originated ca. 1950 by Lombarts nursery of Zundert, Holland; introduced 1957–58. First sold by North American nurseries ≤1966. A narrowly-upright small tree of slow growth. Berries white with a bright red cheek.

S. Rehderiana Koehne

REHDER MOUNTAIN ASH. From W China and Tibet. Introduced by E. Wilson in 1908 to the Arnold Arboretum. Named after Alfred Rehder (1863–1949), great tree and shrub expert. A small, slender tree, late to bloom, with small long-lasting berries of various colors: pink, yellow or creamy-white. Rust-colored hairs on the buds, young shoots and leaves (of 15–19 leaflets). Berries pale with age. *S.* 'Joseph Rock' (q.v.) is likely a variant of it.

S. 'Rowancroft Pink Coral'

Originated from seed collected in Ottawa's Dominion Arboretum by the accomplished Canadian plant breeder Isabella Preston. Introduced ≤1960s by Rowancroft nursery of Meadowvale, Ontario.

S. rufoferruginea—see S. commixta var. rufoferruginea

S. sambucifolia—see S. decora and S. scopulina

S. Sargentiana Koehne

SARGENT MOUNTAIN ASH. From W China. Introduced by E. Wilson to the Arnold Arboretum in 1908 or 1910. Named for Charles Sprague Sargent (1841–1927), great American tree expert. Rarely grown in North America. A bold species with leaves so large as to recall SUMACH (*Rhus*) or WALNUT (*Juglans*): to 13" long; of (7) 9–11 (13) leaflets, the largest up to 6" × 1⅞" (terminal one smallest), sharp-toothed, especially near the apex; pale below with a pink midrib, prominent venation; stipules persistent, large; buds red, glossy, huge and sticky—like a HORSE-CHESTNUT (*Æsculus Hippocastanum*). Fall color late but spectacular (usually red). Berries tiny, produced in enormous clusters of sometimes more than 200. The species is represented in cultivation mostly by a grafted, unnamed clone that tends to grow slowly into a broad, low tree. Records: 42' × 3'9" Westonbirt, Gloucestershire, England (1982); 30' × 5'3" Trewithen, Cornwall, England (1985); 25' × 2'10" × 16' Vancouver, B.C. (1993; *pl.* 1978).

S. Sargentiana 'Warleyensis'— see S. Wilsoniana

S. scandica—see S. intermedia

S. scopulina Greene

(*S. scopulina* also used for *S. aucuparia* 'Fastigiata' & *S. decora*)
= *S. sambucifolia* Rydb., non (Cham. & Schlecht.) Roem.

WESTERN MOUNTAIN ASH. From western N America. Introduced in 1917. A shrubby tree. The typical form has 11–15 (17) leaflets; var. *cascadensis* (G.N. Jones)

C.L. Hitchc. has 9–11 (13) with redder fruit. The berries color earlier than those of most species grown in Seattle, and are gone first (by mid-August), leaving an early, dreadful late-summer leaf-coloration, a dirty "fall" color. Apparently the species cannot adapt to a long growing season, but it has value in the brief growing season of the Rocky Mountain region (the epithet *scopulina* derives from the Latin *scopulus*—a rock or cliff; in reference to the tree's habitat). Record: 14' × 2'0" × 19½' (1993) Spokane, WA.

S. semipinnata—see S. × thuringiaca

S. suecica—see S. intermedia

S. 'Sunshine'

SUNSHINE MOUNTAIN ASH. A seedling of *Sorbus* 'Joseph Rock', selected in 1968 by Hillier nursery of England. Yellow berries; 15–17 leaflets. As conjectured with 'Joseph Rock', this may be an *S. Rehderiana* cultivar. Listed in 1990 by Cannor nursery of Chilliwack, B.C.

S. × thuringiaca (Ilse) Fritsch

= *S. pinnatifida* hort. (in part—cf. *S. × hybrida*)
= *S. semipinnata* (Roth) Hedl., non Borbas
= *S. × hybrida* hort., non L.
(*S. Aria* × *S. aucuparia*)

BASTARD SERVICE TREE. From W and C Europe. Grown since 1803 in Germany. Routinely confused with *S. × hybrida* (which has a broader leaf and a larger, rounder, redder berry). Most authors mistakenly describe this taxon under the name *S. × hybrida*, or call the two synonymous. In fact, *Sorbus × thuringiaca* is common and robust, while *S. × hybrida* is rare and of ordinary constitution. Few nurseries label this tree properly. Leaf to 8¼" × 3½"; 8–12 (14) vein pairs; of unremarkable fall color, at best an adequate yellow. Records: 72' × 7'10" St. Clere House, Kent, England (1987); 56' × 9'8" × 53' Brush Prairie, WA (1993).

S. × thuringiaca 'Fastigiata'

= *S. hybrida* f. *fastigiata* Rehd.
= *S. × hybrida* 'Pyramidalis'

Introduced <1910 by the English nursery of Messrs. Backhouse of York. Its branches ascend tightly, but ultimately form a broad dome, so it's not a columnar tree at all. Common; hopelessly confused with *S. × thuringiaca* 'Quercifolia'.

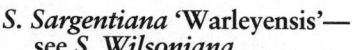

S. × *thuringiaca* 'Leonard Springer'

SPRINGER MOUNTAIN ASH. Named after Leonard A. Springer of Holland. Introduced ≤1938 by Lombarts nursery of Zundert, Holland. Much like *S. × Meinichii*. Leaf consists of 8–10 free leaflets topped by several fused together into a larger terminal leaflet; overall the leaf is shorter than that of *Meinichii*. Since the leaf shape of 'Leonard Springer' is intermediate between *S. × thuringiaca* & *S. aucuparia*, this cultivar should probably be segregated as *S.* 'Leonard Springer'. In any case, it makes heavy bunches of orange-red ½"–⅝" long fruit; and is of more spreading habit than other *S. × thuringiaca* forms. Rarely cultivated in North America. Nurseries offered it in the 1960s. Ed Scanlon said it made attractive but bitter red berries birds will not eat.

S. × *thuringiaca* 'Meinichii'—see *S. × Meinichii*

S. × *thuringiaca* 'Quercifolia'

= *S. × hybrida* 'Quercifolia'
= *S. quercifolia* hort. *ex* Hedl.
= *S. grandidentata* hort.
(*S. Aria* f. *longifolia* × *S. aucuparia*)

OAKLEAF MOUNTAIN ASH. Grown since the late 1700s. The most common form of *S. × thuringiaca*—scarcely different from 'Fastigiata'. Its pyramidal form is so perfect it almost looks sheared. Berries orange-red, to ½" long. Fireblight resistant.

S. *tianschanica* Rupr.

(*tianshanica*)

TURKESTAN MOUNTAIN ASH. From high mountains of Kashmir, Afghanistan and Turkestan. Named in 1869, after the Tien-shan mountain range of central Asia. Introduced from Russia in 1895; in Canada by 1899. Not in general cultivation. Since the 1950s or earlier, Fairview Evergreen nursery of Pennsylvania, and others, have wrongly sold *S. americana* under this name. Authentic TURKESTAN MOUNTAIN ASH is a shrub or small 25' tree that flushes and blooms early (flowers ⅝"–1" wide), ripens rather few, large (to ⁷⁄₁₆" wide) red berries early (late June onward), defoliates early (in August and early September), with ugly color. Leaves dark, rich shiny green, 4"–6" (8⅝") long; leaflets (9) 11–13 (15), to 2½" × ⅞". The tree, or shrub, may indeed be useful as an ornamental where severe climates and short growing seasons prevail. Frank Meyer, the USDA's premier plant explorer early in this century, saw the species in its mountainous homeland in 1910: "after scaling a dangerous, dry mountain, we arrived at a beautiful but cold lake at 10,000 feet altitude; this lake is fed from the eternal snows on the mountains around. The soil in these high regions is sterile and the growing season very short, for the snow melts away in early May and returns again at the beginning of September. Still one finds there masses of a mountain ash (*S. tianshanica*)." Seattle's largest: 17' × 3'2" × 19' (1993).

S. *tianschanica* 'Dwarfcrown'—see *S. americana* Red Cascade™

S. *tianschanica* Red Cascade™—see *S. americana* Red Cascade™

S. *torminalis* (L.) Crantz

WILD SERVICE TREE. CHEQUER TREE—in Kent and Sussex, England. From Europe, N Africa, and SW Asia. Probably because it is neither as spectacular nor as manageable in size as other species, this has rarely been grown for ornamental use. During the 1940s and '50s, several Ohio nurseries sold it. "Service" is derived from *Sorbus*, as this species was the wild SERVICE in contrast to its cultivated counterpart *S. domestica*. The fruit of both species was valued for eating. The epithet *torminalis* is thought to derive from Latin *tormina*, "the gripes"—maybe the berries were used as a remedy for this complaint (colic). A large tree with lobed, MAPLE-like leaves 3"–5" (6") long and almost as wide, utterly unlike those of any other *Sorbus*. Its squat green buds are also most unusual for a *Sorbus*. Furthermore, it can form root suckers, and the bark is shaggy. Though the fruits are not showy, ripening drab brown, the fall color can be supreme: lovely pastel carmine, or yellow, even brilliant gold or sometimes crimson. Its beauty is real, but subtle. A clone selected for superior fall color could be valuable for park usage. As for size, a most unlikely 150' height is recorded by F.K. Makins; specific records: 87' × 7'6" Gatton Manor, Surrey, England (1977); 65' × 13'9" Udimore Old Parsonage, Sussex, England (1984); 85' × 12'5" Hall Place in Kent, England (1985); 53' × 4'8" × 47' Seattle, WA (1992; *pl.* 1949).

S. 'Upright Yellow'

An *S. aucuparia* hybrid originated ca. 1950 by Lombarts nursery of Zundert, Holland; introduced 1957–58. First sold by North American nurseries ≤1966.

S. *Vilmorinii* Schneid.

VILMORIN MOUNTAIN ASH. From W China. Though unnamed until 1906, this species had been introduced in 1889 to the French nurserymen Henry Lévêque de Vilmorin (1843–1899) and Maurice Lévêque de Vilmorin (1849–1918) by the missionary Delavay, who traveled extensively in China. Rare; Wayside nursery of Mentor, OH, offered it in 1958–59. A shrub or small tree of delicate build, so bushy it is sometimes topgrafted on an *S. aucuparia* trunk to make a little tree. Berries crimson, fading to pink, then almost white. Leaf 4"–6" long; leaflets (11) 19–25 (31), dark red or purple in fall. Record: 25' × 3'9" Borde Hill, Sussex, England (1968; *pl.* 1914).

S. 'White Wax'

Originated by Hillier nursery of England. Sold by Girard and Wayside nurseries of Ohio ca. 1966–68. A shrubby, slow-growing tree. Leaflets 19–23. Berries pure white, sometimes as many as 100 per cluster. May be a selection of *S. Vilmorinii*, or, less likely, of *S. Prattii*.

S. 'Wilfrid Fox'

= *S. Aria* 'Wilfrid Fox'
(*S. Aria* × *S. cuspidata*)

WILFRID FOX WHITEBEAM. From Surrey, England <1920. Named in 1964 by Harold Hillier. Dr. Wilfrid Stephen Fox (1875–1962) founded Winkworth Arboretum near Godalming, Surrey, just before World War II, and was an enthusiastic arboriculturist who had a special interest in fall color. When young, 'Wilfrid Fox' is columnar, excellent for tight spaces. Eventually it may grow round-headed—or else *two* clones are going under its name. Notable for large leaves, that drop late and for setting few fruit. Leaf to 8⅝" × 4⅞"; stem to 1½" long; 12–15 vein pairs; in fall remaining green and yellow-green, leafy, when *S. Aria* is essentially bare and *S.* × *latifolia* wholly so. Berries sparse, colored orange-red like unripe tomatoes, ⅝"–¾" long. 'Wilfrid Fox' has not yet made its way into North American nurseries, but surely will. Record: 47' × 3'1" × 29' Seattle, WA (1993; *pl.* 1966).

S. *Wilsoniana* Schneid.

= *S. Sargentiana* 'Warleyensis' (in part)
= *S. aucuparia* var. *warleyensis* hort. (in part—see *S. pohuashanensis*)

WILSON MOUNTAIN ASH. From central China. Named in 1906 after the famed plant explorer Ernest Henry Wilson (1876–1930). According to *Sorbus* expert H. McAllister, maybe the closely related *S. Sargentiana* is best regarded as a variety of *S. Wilsoniana*. But certainly trees grown as *S. Sargentiana* 'Warleyensis' are *S. Wilsoniana*, which compared to *S. Sargentiana* is more vigorous, with thinner twigs, and smaller leaflets. However, most trees called *S. Wilsoniana*, in the UK at least, are really *S. glabrescens* [i.e, a *S. hupehensis* variation]. The designation *warleyensis* refers to Warley Place, near Brentwood in Essex, England—the garden of Ellen Willmott (1858–1934). From *Sorbus* seed collected in China, the best seedling was exhibited by Miss Willmott in October 1931, and won an Award of Merit. See also *S. pohuashanensis* for another tree grown as 'Warleyensis'.

S. *Zahlbruckneri* Schneid.

= *Aria Zahlbruckneri* (Schneid.) H. Ohashi & Iketani

From China. Named in 1906, presumably after Alexander Zahlbruckner (1860–1938). Imported from England to North America ca.1960 by Scanlon nursery of Ohio. Scanlon offered it commercially ca. 1963–75. A fireblight-free WHITEBEAM, of slender build, recalling *S. Folgneri*, but with smaller, less hairy leaves. Record: 48' × 2'4" Seattle, WA (1994; *pl.* 1959).

Sterculia platanifolia—see *Firmiana simplex*

Stewartia

(*Stuartia*)

[THEACEÆ; Tea Family] 6–10 spp. of shrubs or small trees, all but one deciduous. Named after John Stuart (1713–1792), 3rd Earl of the Isle of Bute; a patron of Botany. Flowers showy, white petals cupped around yellowish-orange or darker stamens. Fall color often bright. Bark of several species flaky and attractively warm colored. Best in woodland settings. Related genera include *Camellia* (not in this volume), *Franklinia* and *Gordonia*.

S. gemmata—see *S. sinensis*

S. × *Henryæ* Li
(*S. monadelpha* × *S. pseudocamellia*)

HYBRID STEWARTIA. Named in 1964 after Mrs. J. Norman Henry (Mary G. Henry) and her daughter Josephine Henry, of Gladwyne, PA, in whose garden it was first discovered. The cross might well have originated in other places as well. Nurseries have partly distributed this hybrid as "*S. sinensis*." Since ≤1985 it has been sold true to name. The original Henry specimen was described as more floriferous than either parent. Fall color can be rich red and purple. In Seattle, specimens of this cross have neither the lovely cinnamon bark of *S. monadelpha*, nor the large flowers of *S. Pseudocamellia*, and are comparatively plain.

S. × *Henryæ* 'Skyrocket'
Registered in 1992 by Mrs. J.W. (Polly) Hill of Martha's Vineyard, MA, who raised it from a seed collected in 1960 at the Scott Arboretum, Swarthmore PA. Bark has handsome many-colored marbling. Flower size ranges midway between the two parents, at ca. 2" wide. Very vigorous.

S. *koreana*—see *S. Pseudocamellia* 'Korean Splendor'

S. *monadelpha* S. & Z.
ORANGEBARK STEWARTIA. TALL STEWARTIA. Japanese: *Hime-shara*. From S Japan, and Quelpaert Island of S Korea. Named in 1841 (Greek *monos*, one, and *adelphos*, brother—for its fused stamens). Introduced to cultivation ca. 1903. In North American commerce ≤1936–37. Uncommon. A slender species. Flowers small, 1"–1½" wide. Leaves to 5½" × 2⅜"; bright rose and cheerful purple in fall. Bark showy cinnamon-orange, very uplifting when viewed in winter, especially against a backdrop of glossy deep evergreen foliage. The largest species. Records: to 80' × 9'6" in the wild; 41' × 2'11" × 35' Seattle, WA (1990; *pl.* 1945).

S. *ovata* (Cav.) Weatherby
= *S. pentagyna* L'Hérit.

ALLEGHENY STEWARTIA. SUMMER DOGWOOD. MOUNTAIN CAMELLIA. From the SE United States. Named in 1788 (ovate or egg-shaped leaves). In commerce since ≤1888. Uncommon. Blooming in July and into August after the other species are done; flowers 3" wide. Leaves noticeably larger and wider than those of other species, to 9" × 4". Fall color purplish-bronze to golden, bright orange or red. Bark plain. Often a shrub; can be a small tree of floppy, heavy habit. Records: 27' × 7" × 13' Onconee County, SC (1970); 25' × 1'8" × 17' Seattle, WA (1992; *pl.* 1941); 25' × 1'3" × 16' Great Smoky Mountains National Park, TN (1982).

S. *ovata* f. *grandiflora* (Bean) Kobuski
WILLIAMSBURG CAMELLIA. Named in 1914 in England (*grandiflora* means large flowered; from Latin *grandis*, large, and *floris*, a flower). Occurs sporadically throughout the range of the species, but is common near Williamsburg, VA. Flowers often 4"–4½" (not 3") wide, sometimes with purplish (not yellow-orange) filaments, and often extra petals (5–8 total, not merely 5).

S. *ovata* 'Red Rose'
Registered in 1992 by Mrs. J.W. (Polly) Hill of Martha's Vineyard, MA, who raised it from a seed collected in 1968 from the wild stand at Williamsburg, VA. Stamens red, anthers yellow.

S. *ovata* 'Royal Purple'
Same origin as 'Red Rose'. Stamens purple, anthers yellow. "In colonial times the Royal Governor lived in the Palace in Old Williamsburg so I included the word Royal in memory of that period."

S. *ovata* 'White Satin'
Same origin as 'Red Rose'. Stamens white, anthers yellow.

S. *pentagyna*—see *S. ovata*

S. *Pseudocamellia* Maxim.
COMMON STEWARTIA. JAPANESE STEWARTIA. DECIDUOUS CAMELLIA. Japanese: *Natsu-tsubaki*. From Japan. Introduced to the West in 1860 by Siebold to Holland, and in 1862 by T. Hogg to New York. Named in 1867 (Greek *pseudes*, false, and genus *Camellia*). By far the most common *Stewartia* in cultivation. Flowers are small balls of cotton in the bud stage, opening to "silk" camellia-like blossoms 2½"–3" wide (or more). Leaves 1⅓"–4" long. Fall color orange-red to deep burgundy. Bark handsomely mottled and flaking. Often only a large shrub. Records: 56' × 4'7" Killerton, Devon, England (1985); 45' × 3'5" Puyallup, WA (1992).

608

S. Pseudocamellia 'Ballet'

= *S. Pseudocamellia* var. *koreana* 'Ballerina'

Registered by Mrs. J.W. (Polly) Hill of Martha's Vineyard, MA, who raised it from a seed collected in 1966 from the Arnold Arboretum. First flowered 1980. More graceful spreading branches than any of its siblings. Flowers to 3½" wide instead of the usual 3⅛". Fall color soft orange-tan.

S. Pseudocamellia 'Cascade'

Introduced ≤1991–92 by Gossler Farm nursery of Springfield, OR. Discovered as a cascading plant. Tips droop and main trunk branches very low. After 25 years only 15' tall.

S. Pseudocamellia var. koreana—see S. Pseudo. 'Korean Splendor'

S. Pseudocamellia var. koreana 'Ballerina'—see S. Pseudocamellia 'Ballet'

S. Pseudocamellia 'Korean Splendor'

= *S. Pseudocamellia* var. *koreana* (Nakai *ex* Rehd.) Sealy

= *S. koreana* Nakai *ex* Rehd.

KOREAN STEWARTIA. From S Korea. The cultivar name 'Korean Splendor' was registered in 1975 to designate a seed-grown population (not a clone) from E. Wilson's 1917 Korean introduction of *S. Pseudocamellia*. Flowers more saucer-shaped (less cup-shaped); fall color orangish (never maroon and purplish); prolonged blooms in June and July. Bark less showy. Branches often more fastigiate. Record: 39' × 3'11" × 47' Stamford, CT (1986).

S. Pseudocamellia 'Milk and Honey'

Registered in 1992 by Mrs. J.W. (Polly) Hill of Martha's Vineyard, MA, who raised it from a seed collected in 1966 from the Arnold Arboretum. First flowered 1980. More graceful, spreading branches than any of its siblings. Flowers to 4" wide instead of the usual 3⅛".

S. rostrata Spong.

From E China. Introduced to the U.S. in 1936 (as "*S. sinensis*") from Lushan Botanic Garden of China. Exceedingly rare. Named in 1974 for its distinctive, persistent seed capsules, 1" long, ⅝" wide (in Latin, *rostrata* means beaked). Leaves to 6" × 2½", rubbery-feeling; wet glossy look, very short-stemmed. Flowers much like those of *S. Pseudocamellia*. Bark rough, gray and nothing special. Records: to 40' tall in the wild; several ca. 23'–25' tall in Seattle, WA (1994).

S. serrata Maxim.

Japanese: *Hikosan-hime-shara*. From S Japan. Introduced to Western cultivation <1915. In North American commerce ≤1940s. Rare. The first *Stewartia* to flush in spring, and to bloom (in early May): red sepals against creamy swelling balloon-like petals; done by early June. Small tree; dark green foliage; abundant 2"–2½" flowers. Leaves to 3¾" × 1⅛", dull above, shiny beneath; stem red. Bark plain brown. Best in woodland conditions; apt to get sunburned if exposed. Records: to 40' tall; 25' × 1'7" Seattle, WA (1994; *pl.* 1954).

S. sinensis Rehd. & Wils.

= *S. gemmata* Chien & Cheng

From central & E China. Introduced in 1901 by E. Wilson for Veitch nursery of England. Extremely rare in North America. Some trees sold as *S. sinensis* are actually *S.* × *Henryæ* or *S. rostrata*. Twigs fuzzy. Leaves to 4" long, matte above, dark and reticulate, the underside paler, shiny and hairless except the midrib. Flowers 1½"–2" wide. Bark lovely, smooth and reddish. Records: to 60' tall in China; 56' × 3'2" Trewithen, Cornwall, England (1987); 46' × 3'10" Tilgate Park, Sussex, England (1988).

Stillingia sebifera—see Sapium sebiferum

Stranvæsia Davidiana—see Photinia Davidiana

Stuartia—see Stewartia

Styphnolobium japonicum—see Sophora japonica

Styrax

[STYRACACEÆ; Storax Family] 100–130 spp. of widely distributed trees and shrubs. Ancient Greek name of *S. officinalis*, in turn from the Arabic name *Assturak*. Grown mostly for their sweet-scented white flowers of early summer. Fall color usually ordinary yellow. Related genera include *Halesia* (SILVERBELL), *Pterostyrax* (EPAULETTE TREE), and *Rehderodendron* (REHDER TREE).

S. Hemsleyanus Diels
(*S. Hemsleyana*)

From central & W China. Introduced in 1900 by E. Wilson. Named in 1901 after William Botting Hemsley (1843–1924), Keeper of the Kew Herbarium. Exceedingly rare in North America. Found in a few arboreta and major parks. A slender, slow growing small tree. Closely related to and much like *S. Obassia*, but has exposed buds, flowers upright to spreading rather than horizontal to drooping, and, above all, is more showy in flower and less dumpy looking. Leaves to 9" × 6". Records: 39' × 2'0" Wakehurst Place, Sussex, England (1989); 36' × 2'9" Bodnant, Gwynedd, Wales (1981); 32½' × 1'8" Seattle, WA (1994; *pl.* 1948).

S. japonicus S. & Z.
(*japonica*)

JAPANESE SNOWBELL TREE. JAPANESE SNOWDROP TREE. JAPANESE STORAX. From Japan, Korea, the Ryukyus, China, Taiwan, and the Philippines. Introduced to Western cultivation in 1862. Common. A short knobby trunk gives rise to broad branches bearing dense, fine foliage. Covered with ¾" bell-like white flowers in late May and June. Leaves ca. 3" long, dark, glossy; yellow in fall. Fruit an acrid, hard, felty little gray-green berry. Sometimes only a large shrub. Records: 49' × 2'9" × 33' Seattle, WA (1990); 37' × 7'10" × 43' Montgomery County, PA (1980); 35½' × multitrunked × 48' Arnold Arboretum, MA (1991; *pl.* 1892); 27' × 5'6" × 33' Vancouver, B.C. (1989).

S. japonicus 'Benibana'

In Japan this name is applied to pink-flowered seedlings. What North Americans now call 'Pink Chimes' was imported as 'Benibana'.

S. japonicus 'Carillon'
= *S. japonicus* 'Pendula'
= *S. japonicus* 'Shidare'

Introduced ≤1977 by Shibamichi nursery of Kawaguchi City, Japan. Introduced to the U.S. in 1978 by B. Yinger. Sold mostly through mail-order nurseries. Essentially a shrub, wider than tall, of slightly pendulous habit. May eventually grow into a tree.

S. japonicus 'Crystal'

A selected seedling grown at North Carolina State Arboretum from seeds collected in Korea in 1985. Distributed to nurseries in 1992. Cuttings easily rooted. Upright, subfastigiate habit. Foliage very dark. Flowers with 2–9 petals and dark purple stems.

S. japonicus 'Emerald Pagoda'
= *S. japonicus* 'Sohuksan'

A selected seedling grown at North Carolina State Arboretum from seeds collected in 1985 on Sohuksan Island, off SW Korea. Named 'Emerald Pagoda' in 1992. Columnar habit. Leaves dark, leathery, to 6" long. Flowers to 1½" wide or more, with 2–8 petals and spicy, pungent fragrance.

S. japonicus 'Issai'

Introduced from Japan to the U.S. in 1982 by B. Yinger. Free-flowering. Fast growth.

S. japonicus 'Kusan'

Discovered by Dr. R. Ticknor in Aurora, OR. Introduced ≤1991 by Roslyn nursery of Dix Hills, NY. A compact globe, slow; to 11' tall and wide in 10 years.

S. japonicus 'Pendula'—see *S. japonicus* 'Carillon'

S. japonicus 'Pink Charm'—see *S. japonicus* 'Pink Chimes'

S. japonicus 'Pink Chimes'
= *S. japonicus* 'Rosea'
= *S. japonicus* 'Pink Charm'

Introduced ≤1976 by Shibamichi Kanjiro nursery of Angyo, Japan. Introduced (as 'Benibana') to the U.S. in 1977–78 by B. Yinger. (Likely previously introduced by the U.S. National Arboretum.) Flowers delicate pink; bell-shaped.

S. japonicus 'Rosea'—see *S. japonicus* 'Pink Chimes'

S. japonicus 'Shidare'—see *S. japonicus* 'Carillon'

S. japonicus 'Sohuksan'—see *S. japonicus* 'Emerald Pagoda'

S. Obassia S. & Z.

BIGLEAF SNOWBELL TREE. FRAGRANT SNOWBELL TREE. From N China, Manchuria, Korea, and Japan. Named in 1835, after a Japanese vernacular. Introduced in 1860 by Siebold to Holland. In North American commerce ≤1887. Uncommon, but becoming readily

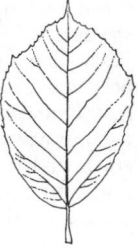

available in the maritime Pacific Northwest. Leaves large, even recalling *Catalpa*, up to 10½" × 9"; dull, roundish, and fuzzy. The leaf stems hide the buds. Flowers white, in early May in drooping clusters 4"–8" long. Best in woodland conditions. Usually a slender tree with bold foliage. Records: *56' × 2'9"* Wakehurst Place, Sussex, England (1980); *52' × 3'6"* Ladham House, Goudhurst, Kent, England (1975); 50' × 1'10" Seattle, WA (1990); 40' × 3'5" × 50' Portland, OR (1989).

Svida or ***Swida alternifolia*—see *Cornus alternifolia***

Svida or ***Swida controversa*—see *Cornus controversa***

Svida or ***Swida Walteri*—see *Cornus Walteri***

Syagrus capitata*—see *Butia capitata

× Sycoparrotia

(*Parrotia* × *Sycopsis*)

[HAMAMELIDACEÆ; Witch-Hazel Family] 1 bigeneric hybrid. Name from genus *Sycopsis*, an evergreen large shrub, and genus *Parrotia* (PERSIAN IRONWOOD).

S. semidecidua Endr. & Anl.

Raised in Switzerland about 1950. Named in 1968. In North American commerce ≤1986. Rare. In November it is indeed semideciduous, half yellowish-green. Part bush, part tree, part deciduous, part evergreen. Leaves to 6" × 2⅝", dark green, glossy, borne in attractive tabular layers. Flowers not showy, consisting of bright yellow stamens with red anther tips.

Syringa

[OLEACEÆ; Olive Family] 20–30 spp. of mostly deciduous shrubs called LILACS; a few small trees. Leaves opposite. Named from Greek *syrinx*, a tube, pipe or reed, referring to hollow stems of *Philadelphus* (MOCK ORANGE), a shrub genus to which the name was originally applied. LILAC is from the Arabic *Lîlag* and Turkish *Leylak*. The following two species are PRIVET-like in certain ways, bear creamy-white early-summer flowers, and are rather unlike the familiar shrubby LILACS. Other genera in the OLEACEÆ include: *Chionanthus* (FRINGETREE), *Fraxinus* (ASH), *Ligustrum* (PRIVET), *Olea* (OLIVE), *Osmanthus*, and *Phillyrea*.

***S. amurensis*—see *S. reticulata* var. mandshurica**

S. amurensis* var. *japonica*—see *S. reticulata

S. japonica*—see *S. reticulata

S. pekinensis Rupr.

= *Ligustrina pekinensis* (Rupr.) Dieck

CHINESE TREE LILAC. PEKING LILAC. From N China mountains. Introduced to Western cultivation in 1881 by E. Bretschneider who sent seeds to England from Peking, and in 1882 to the Arnold Arboretum. A specimen first flowered at the Arnold Arboretum in 1889. In commerce ≤1909. Uncommon. On some specimens the bark is handsome cinnamon-brown, peeling in CHERRY-like strips; on some it is deeply corrugated. Twigs slender. Leaves 2"–4"; hairless (or sparsely hairy), usually relatively narrowed at the base; stem to 1" long. Flowers yellowish-white in nodding, loose 3"–6" clusters in June. Usually shrubby, graceful. Not as cold-hardy as *S. reticulata*. Records: 40' × 5'7" × 41' Kenosha, WI (1988); 25' × 3'11" × 30' Ottawa (1978; *pl.* 1902).

***S. pekinensis* 'DTR 124'—see *S. pekinensis* Summer Charm™**

***S. pekinensis* 'Morton'—see *S. pekinensis* Water Tower®**

S. pekinensis 'Pendula'

Originated as a seedling from the Arnold Arboretum. Introduced <1888 by F.L. Temple of Shady Hill nursery, Cambridge, MA. It was sold topgrafted in the 1890s, but almost disappeared from horticulture by the 1950s. Branches moderately pendulous.

Syringa pekinensis Summer Charm™
= *S. pekinensis* 'DTR 124'

Introduced ≤1993–94 by Discov-Tree Research of Oquawka, IL. Reliably upright and of pleasing tree form. Flowers well annually. Foliage relatively fine-textured.

S. pekinensis Water Tower®
= *S. pekinensis* 'Morton'

Selected at the Morton Arboretum of Lisle, IL. Named in the 1990s (after the Chicago Water Tower, a historically significant structure that survived the "Great Chicago Fire"). The clone features a graceful upright habit and CHERRY-like, exfoliating bark.

S. reticulata (Bl.) Hara
= *S. amurensis* var. *japonica* (Maxim.) Fr. & Sav.
= *S. japonica* Maxim. *ex* Decne.
= *Ligustrina reticulatum* Bl.

JAPANESE TREE LILAC. GIANT TREE LILAC. Japanese: *Hashidoi*. From Japan. Named in 1855. Introduced to Western cultivation by W.S. Clark who sent seeds to the Arnold Arboretum in 1876. Common. Twigs shiny brown. Bark often CHERRY-like. The expanding bright greenery in early spring affords a lovely sight. Leaves 3"–8"; hairy beneath at least while young, rounded or broadly wedge-shaped at the base; stem to 1" long. Flowers yellowish-white in dense 8"–24" clusters from May to July; odor powerful. Records: 40' × 7'0" × 21' Montgomery County, PA (1980); 37' × 6'11 × 28' St.-Hyacinthe, Québec (<1994); 35' × 5'10 × 27' Shawano, WI (1973); 25' × 4'5" × 41' Wellesley, MA (1983); 23' × 6'2" × 36' Wethersfield, CT (1987).

S. reticulata 'Chantilly Lace'
Originated in 1980 at John Herrmann nursery of Limehouse, Ontario. Registered in 1986. Leaves edged creamy-yellow; central portion blotched dark and light green. Prone to sunburn.

S. reticulata 'Ivory Silk'
Introduced ≤1978 by Sheridan nursery of Ontario. Common. Sturdy, more compact 20' (not 30' as the type) oval growth habit. Large clusters of fragrant flowers in early July, even when young. CHERRY-like bark. Less prone to chlorosis.

S. reticulata var. *mandshurica* (Maxim.) Hara
= *S. amurensis* Rupr.

AMUR LILAC. MANCHURIAN LILAC. From Manchuria and Korea. Introduced to cultivation in 1855. Named in 1857. Rarely cultivated. A sturdy shrub or small tree (to 50' tall in the wild). Flushes early in spring. Leaves hairless, rounded or subcordate at the base, 2"–6" long, stems stout and short. Flower clusters 4"–6" long, in June.

S. reticulata 'Regent'
Introduced ≤1990 by Princeton nursery of New Jersey. Habit upright. Exceptionally vigorous.

S. reticulata 'Summer Snow'
Introduced ≤1989 by Schichtel nursery of Orchard Park, NY. Habit compact, rounded, to 20' tall and 15' wide. Flowers profuse, in large clusters.

S. reticulata 'Upright'
Origin unknown. Not in commerce. One planted in 1976 at Aurora, OR, has the narrow fastigiate habit of a LOMBARDY POPLAR (*Populus nigra* 'Italica'): 23' × 2'1½" × 9' (1993).

Taiwania

[TAXODIACEÆ; Bald Cypress Family] 1–2 spp. of immense East Asian coniferous evergreens related to the California REDWOODS. Named after Taiwan.

T. cryptomerioides Hay.
FORMOSAN REDWOOD. TAIWAN CEDAR. From the western slopes of Mt. Morrison, Taiwan. Discovered by N. Konishi in 1904 on the west slope of Mt. Morrison at 6–8,000' elevation. Named in 1906 (*cryptomerioides* from genus *Cryptomeria*, JAPANESE RED CEDAR, and Greek *-oides*, resemblance). In 1918 E. Wilson sent 4 plants to the Arnold Arboretum. Exceedingly rare; virtually never in commerce. Mature foliage and cones (½" long) not yet seen in cultivation. Young specimens indeed recall *Cryptomeria* (JAPANESE RED CEDAR) but are more glaucous with prickly awl-like needles ¼"–⅞" long. Adult foliage has smaller leaves, only ⅕"–¼" long. Records: to 260' × 31'0" in the wild; 59' × 3'10" × 20' San Marino, CA (1993); 40' × 2'11" Berkeley, CA (1993; *pl.* 1974); 29' × 1'10½" Seattle, WA (1994; *pl.* 1969).

T. cryptomerioides var. Flousiana (Gaussen) Silba

= T. Flousiana Gaussen

From SW & C China and NE Burma in subtropical monsoon and humid regions. First collected in 1912. Named in 1939, after Fernande Flous, a French botanist. In North America ≤1949. Even rarer than typical T. cryptomerioides. Said to be the tallest Chinese tree, attaining 250' × 37'7". Wood was used to make coffins. This species has been confused with the so-called COFFIN JUNIPER (Juniperus recurva var. Coxii). Differs from the Taiwan species in bearing longer needles, softer, greener. May be more cold-hardy.

T. Flousiana—see T. cryptomerioides var. Flousiana

Tamarix

[TAMARICACEÆ; Tamarisk Family] 50–54 spp. of fine-textured Old World large shrubs or small trees, called TAMARISKS or SALT CEDARS. Tamarix is an ancient Latin name, maybe after a river, or it may be an African or Hebrew word—there is much conjecture but no certainty. This genus features delicate foliage recalling that of Asparagus, and lovely pink flowers. Tough and tolerant of adverse conditions such as along sea coasts, in salty soil, and in deserts. Some species have become serious weeds in certain locales. Great confusion exists in naming and identification. Close examination of the minute scale-like leaves and tiny flowers is needed for precise naming. The following account intentionally includes some shrubby cultivars because they are so misunderstood. Any clone cited can be trained to tree form, but left alone is usually a wide bush. The bark is often handsome red-brown, shreddy, CEDAR-like. Some clones are most ornamental and floriferous if kept as heavily pruned shrubs. In cold northern regions the climate keeps them shrubby.

T. æstivalis or 'Aestivalis'—see T. chinensis 'Rosea'

T. chinensis Lour.

= T. pentanda hort., non Pall.
?= T. ramosissima Ledeb.

SUMMER FLOWERING TAMARISK. SALT CEDAR. SALT SHRUB. ROSE TAMARISK. FLOWERING CYPRESS. From China and temperate E Asia. Named in 1790. Introduced to cultivation in 1827. (Whether the T. ramosissima named in 1829 by Ledebour should be considered a synonym or a closely related species is disputed.) A problem species in California. Offered by few nurseries, except in its cultivars. Foliage blue-green. Flowers showy rose-pink, from June through September. Records: 44' × 7'3" × 45' Albuquerque, NM (1967); 34' × 12'6" × 38' Columbus, NM (1981).

T. chinensis 'Cheyenne Red'

Introduced ≤1980 in the Midwest. Out of commerce. Flowers darker than typical. 'Rubra' is similar.

T. chinensis 'Pink Cascade' PP 1275 (1954)

= T. Odessana 'Pink Cascade'

Raised by Jackman nursery of Surrey, England. Gulf Stream nursery of Wachapreague, VA, imported this and patented it. Offered by Wayside nursery in 1955. Common. A shrub of great vigor. Flowers slightly richer pink than those of 'Rosea'; July into September.

T. chinensis 'Plumosa'

= T. juniperina Bge.
= T. plumosa hort. ex Carr.
= T. japonica hort. ex Dipp.

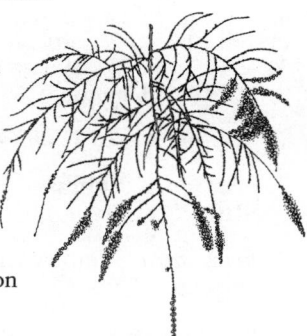

Named in 1833. Introduced to cultivation ca. 1856 when Siebold sent it to Holland. In North American commerce ≤1892. Relatively rare. Flowers less showy, but foliage very fine, bright green, on long elegant plumes.

T. chinensis 'Rosea'

= T. ramosissima 'Rosea'
= T. æstivalis hort.
= T. hispida æstivalis hort.
= T. 'Aestivalis'

Raised in the late 1800s by Chenault nursery of Orleans, France. Common. Flowers rosy-pink.

T. chinensis 'Rubra'

= T. ramosissima 'Summer Glow'
= T. pentandra hort. 'Rubra'
= T. pentandra hort. 'Summer Glow'
= T. hispida æstivalis rubra hort.
= T. 'Summer Glow'

Originated ca. 1935 in France. Common since the

1940s. A darker-flowered (deep carmine) sport of 'Rosea'.

Tamarix hispida æstivalis—see *T. chinensis* 'Rosea'

T. hispida æstivalis rubra—see *T. chinensis* 'Rubra'

T. japonica—see *T. chinensis* 'Plumosa'

T. juniperina—see *T. chinensis* 'Plumosa'

T. Odessana 'Pink Cascade'—see *T. chinensis* 'Pink Cascade'

T. parviflora DC.
= *T. tetandra* hort., non Pall.

SPRING FLOWERING TAMARISK. SMALLFLOWER TAMARISK. From SE Europe; possibly also native in Spain and Algeria. Named in 1828 (*parviflora* from Latin *parvus*, small, and *floris*, flower). Common in cultivation since 1853. Flowers tiny but profuse, smothering the tree, fluffy pink, from March into June; petals and sepals usually 4 (vs. 5 in *T. chinensis*). The spent flowers are temporarily an ugly brown color before the delicate green foliage eclipses them. Records: 44' × 5'9" × 20' Princess Anne, MD (1972); 31' × 3'2" × 31' Washtenaw County, MI (1976); 14' × 4'8" × 22' Hampton, VA (1986).

T. pentanda—see *T. chinensis*

T. pentandra 'Rubra'—see *T. chinensis* 'Rubra'

T. pentandra 'Summer Glow'—see *T. chinensis* 'Rubra'

T. plumosa—see *T. chinensis* 'Plumosa'

T. ramosissima—see *T. chinensis*

T. ramosissima 'Rosea'—see *T. chinensis* 'Rosea'

T. ramosissima 'Summer Glow'—see *T. chinensis* 'Rubra'

T. 'Summer Glow'—see *T. chinensis* 'Rubra'

T. tetandra—see *T. parviflora*

Taxodium

[TAXODIACEÆ; Bald Cypress Family] 2 (or 3) spp. of large New World conifers, deciduous or evergreen, called BALD CYPRESSES. *Taxodium* from Greek *taxos*, YEW TREE (genus *Taxus*), and *-oides*, signifying resemblance or external appearance—as the foliage is similar. The only tree that might be confused with *Taxodium* is DAWN REDWOOD, *Metasequoia*. BALD CYPRESSES offer stately shade trees with soft, fine foliage, warm red-brown bark, and a strong constitution.

T. ascendens Brongn.
= *T. distichum* var. *imbricarium* (Nutt.) Croom
= *T. imbricarium* (Nutt.) R.M. Harper
= *Cupressus disticha* var. *imbricaria* Nutt.

POND CYPRESS. From the Coastal Plain, SE Virginia to Louisiana. Named in 1818. Seldom cultivated. Less cold-hardy than *T. distichum*, smaller, with shorter needles (⅕"–½") closely held against the twigs. Often gaunt overall, although up close the foliage is fine. The name *ascendens* refers to the posture of the deciduous branchlets, not to the habit of the tree, and *imbricarium* refers to the closely overlapping needles. Fall color usually golden-yellow. Usually markedly slender in cultivation, with short branches. Knees rarely produced, and short. Record: 135' × 23'8" near Newton, GA (1969).

T. ascendens 'Nutans'
= *T. distichum* var. *nutans* (Ait.) Sweet 1827, non Carr. 1867
= *Cupressus disticha* var. *nutans* Ait.
= *Glyptostrobus lineatus* (Poir.) Druce, non auct.

PENDANT POND CYPRESS. Named in 1789 (*nutans* means nodding, in reference to the branchlets). Branches pendulous at ends. Branchlets very slender and pendant, more obviously so in fall than in spring.

T. ascendens 'Prairie Sentinel' PP 3548 (1974)

Discovered in 1968 in White County, IL, by Earl Cully of Cully nursery, Jacksonville, IL. Registered in 1971. Unusually short branches and narrow habit.

T. distichum (L.) Rich.
= *Cupressus disticha* L.

BALD CYPRESS. COMMON BALD CYPRESS. DECIDUOUS CYPRESS. LOUISIANA CYPRESS. SOUTHERN CYPRESS. SWAMP CYPRESS. MARSH CYPRESS. GULF CYPRESS. SABINO TREE. From the S United States, essentially. Common in swamps. State Tree of Louisiana. Can live 1,300 years. Renowned for durable, rot-resistant wood. A 1905 article said "The name BALD CYPRESS is given it from the broad, spreading, angular branches at the extreme top of the trees, reaching out over the tops of all its fellows of the swamp, its trunk being bare of limbs throughout its length until these spreading arms are reached." Peculiar conical excrescences from the roots sometimes form and are known as CYPRESS knees; they can reach 14' in height. Needles flat, ½"–¾" long, borne in two ranks along twigs (hence the epithet *distichum*). Fall color late, golden- or purplish-brown. Bark soft, fibrous reddish-brown. Trunks often widely buttressed. Records: to 150' tall; 146' × 18'9" Lower Wabash Valley, IN (<1875); 140' × 61'4" Weakley County, TN (1951); 138' × 38'3" Windsor, NC (1977); 83' × 53'8" W Feliciana Parish, LA (1981).

T. distichum var. *imbricarium*—see *T. ascendens*

T. distichum 'Mickelson'—see *T. distichum* Shawnee Brave®

T. distichum 'Monarch of Illinois' PP 3547 (1974)

Discovered in 1962 in Pittsfield, IL, by Earl Cully of Cully nursery, Jacksonville, IL. The original specimen was ca. 130 years old, 90' tall and 65' wide. Because of its unusually wide branching habit it was registered ca. 1968–69.

T. distichum var. *nutans*—see *T. ascendens* 'Nutans' and *T. distichum* 'Pendens'

T. distichum 'Pendens'

= *T. distichum* var. *nutans* Carr. 1855, non (Ait.) Sweet 1827
= *T. distichum pendulum* Horsey 1925, non (Endl.) Carr. 1867

Originally named in 1855. Named 'Pendens' in 1939. Branchlets slender, drooping. Needles usually more widely separated than normal. Cones relatively large, to 1½" long. Habit very graceful, distinctly pyramidal.

T. distichum pendulum—see *T. distichum* 'Pendens'

T. distichum Shawnee Brave® PP 3551 (1974)
= *T. distichum* 'Mickelson'

Discovered in 1968 in Johnson County, IL, by Earl

Cully of Cully nursery, Jacksonville, IL. Registered in 1971. Tight pyramidal form with abundant relatively short branches. Central trunk straight. Grows rapidly.

T. imbricarium—see *T. ascendens*

T. mucronatum Ten.

MONTEZUMA BALD CYPRESS. MEXICAN CYPRESS. Mexican-Spanish: *Ahuehuete*. *Sabino*. From extreme S Texas, Mexico, and Guatemala. Named in 1853 (Latin *mucro*, a sharp point, and -*atum*, provided with). Cultivated in Mexico since long before the Spanish conquest; the National Tree there. Introduced to Europe in 1838. Grown in California since ≤1905. Rare; mostly sold in Texas. Compared to *T. distichum*, foliage evergreen or briefly deciduous; needles shorter; cones slightly larger, to 1½" long. Branches often strongly pendent. Flowers in autumn (not spring like *distichum*). Less cold-hardy (Oikos nursery of Kalamazoo, MI, says hardy to -22°F). Records: to 175' tall; 135' × 117'6" × 150' "El Arbol de Tule" at El Tule south of Oaxaca in southern Mexico (1982); 95' × 14'5" × 67' Sacramento, CA (1989); 84' × 14'6" × 65' San Marino, CA (1993; *pl.* 1912); 45' × 20'4" × 79' Hidalgo County, TX (1991).

Taxus

[TAXACEÆ; Yew Family] (3) 7–10 spp. of coniferous evergreens known as YEWS. *Taxus* is an ancient Latin name, from the Greek *taxos*, YEW TREE, in turn perhaps from *taxon*, a bow—its wood was used to make bows. Shrubs or small trees. Shade tolerant. Foliage very dark and usually dense. The attractive red berries of late summer and fall partly surround a poisonous seed. Of the following species, only female and bisexual specimens make fruit. The most closely related genus in this volume is *Torreya* (NUTMEG TREE).

T. baccata L.

ENGLISH YEW. COMMON YEW. From Europe, N Africa, SW Asia. D. Wyman says it was present in New England ≤1638. E. Wilson says some were planted in New Jersey in 1713. Common; reseeding in places (birds help disperse it). Nurseries no longer offer the typical seedlings; cultivars and *T.* × *media* clones have replaced it. In northern Europe YEW symbolizes death and immortality. Some specimens are aged more than 1,500 years. A dark, dense tree, usually with a short thick trunk. Useful for hedging and topiary. The heavy, close-grained wood was used for English longbows. Needles ½"–1½" long, often shiny above; gradually tapered to a point. Berries (*baccata* means berry-bearing in Latin) ½" long, dark coral-red. Not as cold-hardy as *T. cuspidata* or its hybrids (*T. × media*). Records: 106' tall in eastern Georgia; 95' × 9'2" Belvoir Castle, Leicestershire, England (1987); 65' × 9'6" Princeton, NJ (ca. 1980); 64' × 35'0" Tandridge, Surrey, England (1984); 56' × 14'0" × 58' Carmichael, MD (1972); 49' × 15'3" × 50' Queenstown, MD (1990); 47' × 13'10" × 59' Puyallup, WA (1992); trunks to 65' around once existed.

T. baccata 'Adpressa'

= *T. brevifolia* hort., non Nutt.
= *T. tardiva* hort.

SHORTLEAF YEW. A female, that arose ca. 1828 at Dickson nursery of Chester, England. Introduced ca. 1838 by Knight and Perry nursery of Chelsea. In North American commerce ≤1888. Uncommon. Some specimens are largely male. Needles short (hence the name *brevifolia*), densely set (in botanical Latin *adpressus* means pressed against or on), dark bluish-green. Usually a shrub. Record: 36' × 6'5" Alexandra Park, Sussex, England (≤1985).

T. baccata f. *aurea* (Nels.) Pilg.

GOLDEN YEW. Known since the 17th century. Described officially in 1866. Common. A collective name for seedlings or cultivars in which the foliage is more or less yellowish. Color usually most developed at needle tips and margins. Often the spring growth is bright golden, but gradually fades to green. Usually a dense shrub, sometimes a small tree. Seedlings vary considerably in habit. Both male and female forms exist. Record: 52' × 8'0" Westonbirt, Gloucestershire, England (1982).

T. baccata 'Crowderi'—see *T. baccata* 'Erecta'

T. baccata 'Dovastoniana'

('Dovastonii')
= *T. baccata horizontalis* hort.
= *T. imperialis* hort. *ex* Hoopes

DOVASTON YEW. WEST FELTON YEW. Essentially male, technically monoecious, having one female branch. Usually the female is grown. To hold soil near a sandy well, John Dovaston planted a seedling he'd bought for sixpence from a cobbler ca. 1776 at West Felton, Shropshire, England. In North American commerce ≤1888. Once common here, rare in nurseries since early 1980s. Branches lengthy and horizontal, with dark foliage attractively draping them. Records: 56' × 12'3" the original tree (1983); 43' × 12'3" × 50' Christchurch, New Zealand (≤1982; *pl.* <1884).

T. baccata 'Erecta'

= *T. baccata* 'Crowderi'
= *T. stricta* hort., non *T. baccata* 'Stricta' of Lawson 1836
= *T. stricta* Gord. 1875
= *T. baccata fastigiata* hort. (in part), non Loudon
= *T. pyramidalis* Knight, non hort.
?= *T. baccata* f. *pyramidalis* Carriere 1855
?= *T. baccata* var. *pyramidalis* hort. *ex* Laws. 1851

FULHAM YEW. BROOM ENGLISH YEW. An IRISH YEW (*T. baccata* 'Fastigiata'), seedling, named in 1838. Well known in North American commerce ≤1868. Now essentially out of the nursery trade. Male, originally, but otherwise similar females have been sold under this name. Close erect formal habit but less compact and broader than IRISH YEW, with shorter needles (ca. ⅝") of paler green; possibly hardier. Usually bushy; can be 25' tall. *T. baccata* 'Overeynderi' is similar.

T. baccata 'Erecta Aurea'

Introduced ≤1880 by Wm. Barron & Son's Elvaston nursery of Borrowash, near Derby, England. In North American commerce ≤1925. Extremely rare. Needles rich golden, without green stripes. Otherwise like 'Erecta'.

T. baccata 'Fastigiata' (cf. *T. baccata* 'Erecta')

= *T. baccata* 'Hibernica'
= *T. pyramidalis* hort., non Knight
= *T. fastigiata* Lindl.
= *T. hibernica* hort.
= *T. baccata* 'Stricta' of Lawson 1836

IRISH YEW. FLORENCE COURT YEW. About 1760, Mr. Willis, farmer of County Fermanagh, Ireland, found two plants of this form on his farm in the mountains above Florence Court. After planting one in his own garden, he took the other to Mount Florence, the seat of the Earl of Enniskillen. The variety became commercially available when cuttings were supplied to the London nursery of Lee and Kennedy. Commonly cultivated and familiar. In recent years, however, comparatively rare in much of the north, replaced by *T. × media* cultivars. Female. Habit strongly fastigiate and upright, making a dense column. Needles whorled. Often no more than a bush. Records: 63½' × 10'9" Hawkes Bay, New Zealand (≤1982); 62' ×

10'10" Culzean Castle, Strathclyde, Scotland (1984); 37' tall in Seattle, WA (1988).

T. baccata 'Fastigiata Argentea'—see T. bacc. 'Fastigiata Variegata'

T. baccata 'Fastigiata Aurea'

GOLDEN IRISH YEW. Named in 1866. Like IRISH YEW but slower, less common, young growth deep golden-yellow. Also female; hardier.

T. baccata 'Fastigiata Aureomarginata'

FISHER'S GOLDEN YEW. Raised ca. 1880 by Fisher & Son & Sibray, Handworth nursery, of Sheffield, England. Rare. Male. Young needles edged bright golden yellow, especially on upper surfaces.

T. baccata 'Fastigiata Variegata'

= T. baccata 'Fastigiata Argentea'

Named in 1851. Rare. Young needles striped and edged silvery-white or with pale straw-colored blotches. Possibly some nurseries have sold 'Fastigiata Aureomarginata' under this name.

T. baccata 'Fructo-luteo'

= T. baccata 'Lutea'
= T. baccata 'Xanthocarpa'

YELLOWBERRY YEW. Discovered ca. 1817 by Mr. Whitlaw of Dublin, near Glasnevin, Ireland. But it seems to have been neglected till 1833 when it was noticed on the grounds of Clontarf Castle, whence cuttings were distributed. Named 'Fructo-luteo' in 1838, but most authors prefer the 1847 'Lutea' name. All its names mean the same thing. Extremely rare in North America and commercially extinct.

T. baccata 'Hibernica'—see T. baccata 'Fastigiata'

T. baccata horizontalis—see T. baccata 'Dovastoniana'

T. baccata 'Lutea'—see T. baccata 'Fructo-luteo'

T. baccata 'Overeynderi'

An IRISH YEW (T. baccata 'Fastigiata'), seedling raised ca. 1860 by C.G. Overeynder (1838–1915) of Boskoop, Holland. Out of commerce since the 1970s. Male. Branches erect. Like 'Erecta' but smaller in growth (to ca. 16' tall), twig size and needles (¾"). Less hardy than 'Erecta' but more hardy than IRISH YEW.

T. baccata f. pyramidalis—see T. baccata 'Erecta'

T. baccata var. pyramidalis—see T. baccata 'Erecta'

T. baccata 'Robusta'—see T. × media 'Robusta'

T. baccata 'Stricta'—see T. baccata 'Fastigiata'

T. baccata 'Xanthocarpa'—see T. baccata 'Fructo-luteo'

T. brevifolia Nutt.

PACIFIC YEW. WESTERN YEW. OREGON YEW. From Alaska to central California. Discovered in 1825 by D. Douglas on the Columbia River. Named in 1849 (Latin brevis, short, and folium, a leaf). In commerce this name has usually been misapplied to T. baccata 'Adpressa' or T. cuspidata 'Nana' (a bush). Introduced to English cultivation in 1854. In North American commerce ≤1871. Almost never offered true to name until recently. Of recent celebrity status because it yields taxol, an anticancer agent. Awkwardly slow-growing, usually scant of foliage. Only its lovely peeling reddish bark is first-rate. Needles not necessarily short (to 1½" long), usually dull green and abruptly pointed. Berries ⅓" wide, translucent orange-red, the seed protruding or nearly so. Records: to 90' tall say E. Sheldon and T. Howell; 84' × 7'7" and 77' × 9'4" Capilano River, B.C. (1991); 38' × 10'2" × 55' Seattle, WA (1988); 54' × 15'0" Gifford Pinchot National Forest, WA (1988).

T. columnaris Adamsi—see T. × media 'Adams'

T. cuspidata S. & Z.

JAPANESE YEW. Japanese: Ichii. From Korea, NE China, SE U.S.S.R., and Japan. Named in 1846 (cuspidate needle tips). Introduced to England in 1854–55 by R. Fortune. The dwarf 'Nana' first reached North America in 1861–62; the tree version (called 'Capitata' in nurseries) was introduced in 1892. Common. Hardier than T. baccata. Needles wide. Records: 82' × 13'1" Japan (1994); 36' × 8'4" × 33' Wellesley, MA (1983); 23' × 4'10" × 28' Kenosha, WI (1988); trunks to 16'5" around in the wild.

T. cuspidata 'Adamsii'—see T. × media 'Adams'

T. cuspidata 'Columnaris'—see *T. × media* 'Adams'

T. cuspidata 'Fastigiata'—see *T. × media* 'Hicksii'

T. cuspidata 'Robusta'—see *T. × media* 'Robusta'

T. cuspidata 'Stovekenii'—see *T. × media* 'Stovekenii'

T. fastigiata—see *T. baccata* 'Fastigiata'

T. hibernica—see *T. baccata* 'Fastigiata'

T. Hicksii—see *T. × media* 'Hicksii'

T. imperialis—see *T. baccata* 'Dovastoniana'

T. × media Rehd.
(*T. baccata* × *T. cuspidata*)

HYBRID YEW. First raised ca. 1903 and distributed ca. 1920 by T.D. Hatfield, superintendent of Hunnewell Pinetum of Wellesley, MA. Named in 1923. Very common in commerce. Many cultivars. Prized for hardiness and shade tolerance. Usually shrubby, or at any rate, treated as a shrub. In time, some clones attain tree size.

T. × media 'Adams'
= *T. cuspidata* 'Adamsii'
= *T. cuspidata* 'Columnaris'
= *T. × media* 'Columnaris'
= *T. columnaris Adamsi* hort.

Introduced <1962 by Adams nursery of Springfield, OH. Uncommon, even rare since the 1980s. Male. Columnar when young; to 10'–25' tall.

T. × media 'Anthony Wayne' PP 1617 (1957)
Raised in 1943 by Hess nursery of Wayne, NJ. Female. Rare; sold by conifer specialty nurseries. Strongly ascending irregular flame shape; vigorous. Foliage yellowish-green.

T. × media 'Columnaris'—see *T. × media* 'Adams'

T. × media 'Costich'
= *T. × media* 'Hicksii No. 2'

Selected by C.S. Sargent in the early 1900s. Like *T. × media* 'Hicksii' but growth is more rapid, narrower. Male. Extremely rare; out of commerce. Inferior in hardiness and growth rate to *T. × media* 'Stovekenii'. The 'Costich' name dates from 1976.

T. × media 'Hicksii'
= *T. cuspidata* 'Fastigiata'
= *T. Hicksii* hort.

Introduced in early 1900s by Henry Hicks (1870–1954) of Hicks nursery of Westbury, Long Island. Officially named in 1923. Very common. Female. Erect; fastigiate.

T. × media 'Hicksii No. 2'—see *T. × media* 'Costich'

T. × media 'Hiti'
A selected *T. cuspidata* seedling from Hiti nursery of Pomfret, CT, ca. 1925. Some say it is purebred *T. cuspidata*. Others say it is practically the same as *T. × media* 'Stovekenii'. Rare. Male. 15'–20' tall; much broader than 'Hicksii'.

T. × media 'H.M. Eddie'
Introduced ≤1986, likely in British Columbia. Discovered by and named after nurseryman Henry M. Eddie (1881–1953) of Vancouver. Dark green year-round. Conical tree to 20' tall.

T. × media 'Jeffreyi Pyramidalis'—see *T. × media* 'Kelseyi'

T. × media 'Kelseyi'
= *T. × media* 'Jeffreyi Pyramidalis'

BERRYBUSH YEW. Propagated from plants on a small estate in Locust Valley, Long Island, by nurseryman John Vermeulen. Vermeulen's nursery introduced it in 1928 as 'Vase Shape' and later changed the name to honor New York nurseryman Frederick Wallace Kelsey (1850–1935). Common. Female. Erect or strongly ascending branches, yet becoming broad; dark and dense. To 15' tall. Berries abundant, late-maturing.

T. × media 'Pilaris'
PILLAR YEW. Introduced in 1947 by Vermeulen nursery of New Jersey. Uncommon; offered by conifer specialist nurseries. Male, narrow columnar shape like IRISH YEW (*T. baccata* 'Fastigiata').

T. × media 'Pyramidalis'
PYRAMIDAL YEW. Introduced in 1946 by Vermeulen nursery of New Jersey. Uncommon; offered by conifer specialist nurseries. Female, with upright branching.

T. × *media* 'Pyramidalis Robusta'—see *T.* × *media* 'Robusta'

T. × *media* 'Robusta'
= *T.* × *media* 'Pyramidalis Robusta'
= *T. cuspidata* 'Robusta'
= *T. baccata* 'Robusta'
OBELISK YEW. Introduced in 1946 by Vermeulen nursery of New Jersey. Uncommon; offered by conifer specialist nurseries. Male, robust, straight and strong; columnar, dense. Dark green.

T. × *media* 'Sentinalis'
SENTINEL YEW. Introduced in 1947 by Vermeulen nursery of New Jersey. Uncommon; offered by conifer specialist nurseries. Female, tight narrow columnar form. Bright green.

T. × *media* 'Stovekenii'
= *T. cuspidata* 'Stovekenii'
Selected ca. 1932 as a seedling *T. cuspidata* by Mr. Stoveken, foreman of the A.N. Pierson nursery of Cromwell, CT. Rare since the 1960s. Male. Vigorous, fastigiate; broadly columnar. Considered one of the hardiest and very best narrow columnar YEWS, superior in many aspects to 'Hicksii' and 'Costich'. Can be 20' tall in 30 years.

T. × *media* 'Stricta'
= *T.* × *media* 'Stricta Viridis'
SENTINEL YEW. Introduced in 1946 by Vermeulen nursery of New Jersey. Rare since the early 1980s; not even offered by Vermeulen. Male, narrowly erect, compact.

T. × *media* 'Stricta Viridis'—see *T.* × *media* 'Stricta'

T. nucifera—see *Torreya nucifera*

T. pyramidalis—see *T. baccata* 'Erecta' and *T. baccata* 'Fastigiata'

T. stricta—see *T. baccata* 'Erecta'

T. tardiva—see *T. baccata* 'Adpressa'

Tetracentron

[TETRACENTRACEÆ; Spur Leaf Family] Only one species in the genus. From Greek *tetra*, four, and *kentron*, a spur, referring to the four spur-like appendages of the fruit. The affinity of this Family is disputed. The nearest relatives may be *Cercidiphyllum* (KATSURA), *Euptelea*, *Magnolia* or *Trochodendron* (WHEEL TREE).

T. sinense Oliv.
SPUR LEAF. From C & SW China, Nepal, Burma, SE Tibet, (and the Himalayas), favoring moist slopes and bottomlands. Named in 1889. Introduced in 1901 by E. Wilson for Veitch nursery of England. In North America ≤1912. Extremely rare. Sold in small sizes by mail-order nurseries. A reptilian sort of tree. Bark nearly smooth. At least on young specimens there is a striking gap between the branch and leaves, which makes the trees look thirsty. Leaves borne on obvious spurs; "wrinkled" with prominent veins, to 5⅝" × 4"; fall color dreadful—ho-hum yellow or dirty golden bronze and murky purple. Stipule-like growths are semi-thorny, rather fascinating but quick to fall. Buds slender, hornlike. Records: to 131' × 19'8" in the wild; 52' × 4'3" Nymans, Sussex, England (1985); 30' × 2'6½" Seattle, WA (1994; *pl.* 1962).

Tetradium

= *Euodia*, hort., p.p.
= *Evodia*, hort., p.p.
[RUTACEÆ; Rue Family] 9 spp. of trees or shrubs from the Himalayas east to Japan and south to Java and Sumbawa. The genus *Tetradium* was named in 1790, from Greek *tetradion*, quaternion, since the flowers and fruit parts usually occur in fours. Leaves opposite, pinnately compound, fragrant when bruised. Bark smooth, pale brown or gray like that of a BEECH (*Fagus*) or HOLLY (*Ilex*). Valued as shade trees with attractive small whitish flowers in large clusters during summer. Good honey trees. Related genera include *Phellodendron* (AMUR CORK TREE), *Ptelea* (HOPTREE), and *Zanthoxylum*. In 1981, six *Euodia* species were

transferred to *Tetradium Daniellii*. *Tetradium* differs from a narrow interpretation of *Euodia* (from Greek *euodes*, a sweet scent; referring to that of the leaves) in being more temperate in distribution, with more leaflets than the ≤3 of *Euodia*. That *E. Daniellii* and *E. hupehensis* are practically identical is no news to tree experts. But *E. velutina* can be very dissimilar. To suddenly relabel every *Euodia* in cultivation as *Tetradium Daniellii*, while not maintaining any subspecific, varietal or cultivar names for distinctive populations, results in a species so bafflingly variable that its extreme manifestations are as follows: on one end, a tree with (3) 5 dark glossy green, broad leaflets; on the other end, one with 11–13 dull, velvety, medium green, narrow leaflets. But in 1981, T.G. Hartley, the botanist who studied these trees wrote: "This may appear to be an overly conservative interpretation of this species [*Tetradium Daniellii*], but in the study of a large number of herbarium specimens of obviously closely inter-related plants here assigned to it, I have not found sufficient morphologic discontinuity in any of the variable characters, or sufficiently distinct combinations of various character states to warrant recognition of more than a single taxon." Nonetheless, even allowing that an unbroken continuum of *Tetradium Daniellii* forms exist in the wild, horticulturists are free to name—as cultivars—any ornamentally distinctive populations; we are free to choose the best clones and promote them.

Tetradium Daniellii (Benn.) Hartley

= *Euodia Daniellii* (Benn.) Hemsl.
= *Euodia Delavayi* Dode
= *Euodia Henryi* Dode
= *Euodia hupehensis* Dode
= *Euodia velutina* Rehd. & Wils.
= *Euodia vestita* W.W. Smith

BEEBEE TREE. From SW China, northeast to Korea. Discovered in China in 1861 by William Freeman Daniell (1818–1865), a British army surgeon. Introduced to North America when the Arnold Arboretum received Korean seeds in 1905 from Dr. L.J.G. Jack. In commerce ≤1927. Uncommon. Leaves 6"–18" long; leaflets (3) 5–9 (13), entirely hairless to remarkably soft and velvety, broadly egg-shaped to lancelike. Flowers in ELDERBERRY-like clusters 2"–6¼" across, from June into September. Flowers whitish, or tinged yellow or pinkish. Seed clusters can ripen a raspberry color, and are strongly odorous. Seeds black, tiny and shiny (the name BEEBEE TREE was coined to refer to them). Fall color often ugly green and dull yellow. Records: 79' × 10'3" Glendoick, Tayside, Scotland (1986); 75' × 9'10" Philadelphia, PA (1988); 65' × 9'0" Philadelphia, PA (1980); 59' × 5'10" Seattle, WA (1988; *pl.* 1931); a trunk 10'5" around at Roslyn Estates, Long Island, NY (1972).

Thuja

(*Thuia, Thuya*)

[CUPRESSACEÆ; Cypress Family] 6 spp. of coniferous evergreens. The Latin common name ARBORVITÆ dates from ≤1558; it was given in France to *Thuja occidentalis*, the first tree introduced from Canada to the Old World. In Latin *arbor* is tree, and *vitæ* life. The name refers to the tree's use to cure scurvy afflicting Jacques Cartier's explorers in the 1530s. The relieved explorers called it *L'arbre de vie*. North Americans usually call the trees CEDARS. *Thuja* derives from Greek *thyia* or *thya*, an ancient name used by Theophrastus (370–288 B.C.) for some resin-bearing evergreen, possibly a JUNIPER. Maybe related to *thuon*, a sacrifice; the resin used as an incense in Eastern sacrifices. *Thuja* foliage is scaly, in flat sprays, with numerous raisin-sized cones. The bark is fibrous and reddish-brown, and its wood rot-resistant, lightweight and fragrant. The only very closely related genus is *Thujopsis* (HIBA ARBORVITÆ). *Thuja* is of major importance in horticulture. Unfortunately nurseries often used to act as if the genus consisted of one species only, so the history and synonyms of the cultivars are especially difficult to unravel. Partly for this reason the splitting of *Thuja* into two genera (*Thuja* and *Platycladus*) is not adopted in this volume. A broadly defined genus can include two "sections" or "subgenera."

T. aurea—see *T. orientalis* f. *aurea* and *T. plicata* 'Aurea' and *T. plicata* 'Zebrina'

T. caucasica—see *T. occidentalis* 'Wareana'

T. dolabrata—see *Thujopsis dolabrata*

T. elegantissima—see *T. occidentalis* 'Elegantissima' and *T. orientalis* 'Elegantissima'

T. fastigiata—see *T. occidentalis* 'Fastigiata'

T. gigantea—see *T. plicata*

T. gigantea 'Albomaculata'—see *T. plicata* 'Zebrina'

T. gigantea 'Aureovariegata'—see *T. plicata* 'Zebrina'

T. 'Golden Lobbi'—see *T. plicata* 'Zebrina'

T. 'Goldspot'—see *T. occid.* 'Aureovariegata' and *T. plicata* 'Zebrina'

T. japonica—see *T. Standishii*

T. 'Giganteoides'

Discovered in Scandinavia in the 1930s. Rare and little known in North America, but recently publicized. Possibly a cross of *T. occidentalis* and *T. plicata*. It more closely resembles *T. plicata*. Vigorous; grows ca. 3' per year; withstands ice and snow; foliage dark green all year.

T. koraiensis Nakai

KOREAN ARBORVITÆ. KOREAN THUYA. From Korea and NE China, preferring warm, rainy conditions. E. Wilson, who sent seeds from Korea to the Arnold Arboretum in 1917, reported this as a slender tree 30' × 2'6", or a sprawling irregular shrub on Korean mountains. Unique also is the shockingly white underside of its new growth. Shrubby and slow-growing. In North American commerce since 1930s, but extremely rare. Records: 42' × 2'3" Hergest Croft, Herefordshire, England (1980; *pl.* 1925); to 30' × 3'0" in China.

T. Lobbii—see *T. plicata*

T. Lobbii 'Aurea'—see *T. plicata* 'Zebrina'

T. Menziesii—see *T. plicata*

T. occidentalis L.

ARBORVITÆ. AMERICAN ARBORVITÆ. NORTHERN WHITE CEDAR. EASTERN WHITE CEDAR. TREE OF LIFE. From eastern North America. Cultivated since the 1530s in France (or at any rate ≤1560s). Commonly cultivated, especially

as an evergreen hedge plant in the Midwest. Very cold-hardy. Typical wild specimens are usually gaunt and far inferior to the best cultivars, which are numerous: some absolute dwarves, others fully tree-sized, and many intermediate between shrubs and trees; 60 are in this volume. In winter the foliage often bronzes, so cultivars which stay green are prized. Crushed foliage smells acrid, like tansy. Records: 125' × 15'6" Natural Bridge, VA (1944); 113' × 18'0" Leelanau County, MI (1975).

T. occidentalis 'Ada'

Introduced in 1972 by Vermeulen nursery of New Jersey. Fine compact rounded column. Sturdy branches hold up under snow loads. Grows quickly. Good green color all year.

T. occidentalis 'Alba'

= *T. occidentalis* 'Albospica'
= *T. occidentalis* 'Albospicata'
= *T. occidentalis* '(Queen) Victoria' (in part)

QUEEN VICTORIA ARBORVITÆ. SILVER TIPPED ARBORVITÆ. Originated <1875 in H.E. Maxwell's nursery, Geneva, NY. Published in 1875. Commercially extinct. Pyramidal, free-growing. Tips of young branchlets white. The name (for Queen Victoria of England; 1819–1901), has also been applied to *T. occidentalis* 'Columbia'.

T. occidentalis 'Albospica'—see *T. occidentalis* 'Alba'

T. occidentalis 'Albospicata'—see *T. occidentalis* 'Alba'

T. occidentalis 'Albovariegata'—see *T. occidentalis* 'Argentea'

T. occidentalis 'Argentea'

?= *T. occidentalis* 'Albovariegata'
= *T. occidentalis* 'Variegata Argentea'
= *T. occidentalis* 'Variegata'

Originally named 'Variegata' in 1770 in England. Never common in North America; long extinct in commerce. An unstable white-variegated form. Whole branches can be silvery-whitish. The name 'Albovariegata' was published officially in 1909 in Germany and may refer to a more stable white-variegated clone.

T. occidentalis 'Aurea'

= *T. occidentalis* 'Variegata Aurea'
= *T. occidentalis* 'Mastersii Aurea'

BUSHGOLD EASTERN ARBORVITÆ. Name officially published in Europe in 1866 (maybe even 1855). A broad shrub or small tree of golden yellow foliage. "Aurea" has been often misapplied to *T. occidentalis* 'Lutea' (GEORGE PEABODY ARBORVITÆ), and less often misapplied to *T. occidentalis* 'Aurea Americana'.

T. occidentalis 'Aurea Americana'
= *T. occidentalis* 'Brinckerhoffii'
= *T. occidentalis* 'Aurea' (in part)
Originated <1859 by D. Brinckerhoff nursery of Fishkill Landing, NY. Commercially extinct, perhaps <1900. Young shoots yellow, becoming bright green.

T. occidentalis 'Aurea Maculata'—see *T. occid.* 'Aureovariegata'

T. occidentalis 'Aurea Spicata'—see *T. occidentalis* 'Aureospicata'

T. occidentalis 'Aureospicata'
?= *T. occidentalis* 'Elegantissima' (q.v.)
= *T. occidentalis* 'Semperaurea'
= *T. occidentalis* 'Semperaurescens'
= *T. occidentalis* 'Spicata Aurea'
= *T. occidentalis* 'Aurea Spicata'
= *T. plicata* 'Aurea' (in part)
= *T. plicata* 'Semper-aurea'
= *T. plicata* 'Semperaurescens'
Origin unknown. Possibly in California commerce ≤1887 (as *Thuja aurea*—a name also used for *T. orientalis* f. *aurea* and *T. plicata* 'Aurea' and *T. plicata* 'Zebrina'). Named 'Aureospicata' in 1891 in Germany. 'Semperaurea' is a 1923 name meaning ever golden. Still in commerce, largely in Canada. Pyramidal, dense, narrow, vigorous. Foliage thick, luxurious (as *T. plicata*), shiny green, golden-yellow tipped, yellowish-brown in winter. In age the tree loses much of its yellow, and all of it except on the sunniest side. Records: 75½' × 6'0" Westonbirt, Gloucestershire, England (1981); 72' × 9'3" Whittingehame, East Lothian, Scotland (1987); 55' × 6'7" × 20' Burlington, WA (1992).

T. occidentalis 'Aureovariegata'
= *T. occidentalis* 'Wareana Aurea'
= *T. occidentalis* 'Wareana Aureovariegata'
= *T. occidentalis* 'Wareana Variegata'
= *T. occidentalis* 'Plicata Aurea'
= *T. occidentalis* 'Aurea Maculata'
= *T. occidentalis* 'Goldspot' (in part)
= *T. plicata variegata* Carr.
= *T. Wareana variegata* hort.
= *T.* 'Goldspot' (in part)
GOLDSPOT ARBORVITÆ. GOLDEN SIBERIAN ARBORVITÆ. Of French origin. Named ≤1865. Gordon's 1875

description: "a portion of its leaves and lesser sprays of a pale yellow, intermixted all over the plant in a variegated manner, and a less robust habit." Other writers tend to say golden or golden yellow. These names have been applied to more than one clone, in large part (especially by Oregon and Washington nurseries) to the gold-variegated *T. plicata* 'Zebrina'.

T. occidentalis 'Brandon'
From the Patmore nursery of Brandon. Manitoba. In commerce ≤1940. Common. Dense columnar form. Very cold-hardy.

T. occidentalis 'Brinckerhoffii'—see *T. occid.* 'Aurea Americana'

T. occidentalis 'Buchananii'
Introduced ≤1887 by Parsons nursery of Flushing, NY. Almost commercially extinct since the 1930s. Narrow, gaunt and starved-looking: scanty slender twigs bear drooping, dull grayish-green foliage with few cones.

T. occidentalis 'Burrowii'
Origin unknown. In commerce ≤1906. Extremely rare, long commercially extinct. Foliage yellow.

T. occidentalis 'Canadian Gold'
Origin unknown. Sold ≤1993 by Wells nursery of Mt. Vernon, WA. Foliage bright yellow year-round. This clone may be something else renamed, but is not the same as *T. plicata* 'Canadian Gold'. Since the cultivar names are (stupidly) identical, the two clones will no doubt become mixed in commerce.

T. occidentalis 'Carlson's Gold'
Origin unknown. D & M nursery of Portland, OR, sold it ≤1990.

T. occidentalis 'Carman Columnar'
= *T. occidentalis* 'Carmen'
Imported from Holland. Named in mid-1960s, and introduced ≤1974 by Aubin nursery of Carman, Manitoba. Out of commerce. Erect compact conical habit. Medium green. Slow. Hardy.

T. occidentalis 'Carmen'—see *T. occidentalis* 'Carman Columnar'

T. occidentalis 'Columbia'
= *T. occidentalis* '(Queen) Victoria' (in part)
SILVERTIP ARBORVITÆ. Introduced ≤1887 by Parsons nursery of Flushing, NY. Common until ca. 1950; now extremely rare in commerce. Of strong habit,

similar to typical specimens. Foliage broad, with a beautiful silvery variegation, more pronounced in winter. The name (for Queen Victoria of England; 1819–1901), has also (mostly?) been applied to *T. occidentalis* 'Alba'.

T. occidentalis 'Columnaris'—see *T. occidentalis* 'Fastigiata'

T. occidentalis 'Compact American'
('Compacta Americana')

Introduced ≤1948. Presumably the name is simply shorthand for COMPACT AMERICAN ARBORVITÆ and is thus a synonym of 'Compacta'; or, less likely it may compare this clone to a European or Canadian compact cultivar. Since ≤1991 Lake County nursery of Perry, OH, has been selling under this name "a 30' tall and 10' wide compact pyramid with good deep green color."

T. occidentalis 'Compacta'
= *T. occidentalis* 'Parsons'

PARSONS' ARBORVITÆ. Presumably introduced ≤1894 by Parsons nursery of Flushing, NY. Broadly pyramidal or oval, dense and slow. Foliage light green. Very hardy. A 1926 catalog remarked that nurseries sold various plants (rather than one clone) as 'Compacta', and this trend has continued. For example, in 1947 a clone called 'Compacta Erecta' was introduced by Westminster nursery of Maryland.

T. occid. 'Compacta Americana'—see *T. occid.* 'Compact American'

T. occidentalis 'Compacta Erecta'—see *T. occidentalis* 'Compacta'

T. occidentalis 'De Groot's Spire'

Introduced ≤1985 by Sheridan nursery of Ontario. Named for Constant De Groot, nursery propagator. A narrow column. Foliage fine, medium-green with slight winter browning. Growth slow.

T. occidentalis var. *densa*—see *T. occidentalis* 'Wareana'

T. occid. 'Douglas Spiralis'—see *T. occid.* 'Douglasii Pyramidalis'

T. occidentalis 'Douglasii Aurea'

Raised <1918 by D. Hill nursery of Dundee, IL. Common until ca. 1970; now very rarely sold. Broadly pyramidal, vigorous; to 50' tall; branches spreading; sprays yellow, grading to yellowish-green at the base; golden yellow, bronzed in winter. Faster growth than *T. occidentalis* 'Lutea' and darker yellow.

T. occidentalis 'Douglasii Pyramidalis'
= *T. occidentalis* 'Douglas Spiralis'
= *T. occidentalis* 'Pyramidalis Douglasii'

DOUGLAS PYRAMIDAL ARBORVITÆ. Originated <1855 by Robert Douglas (1813–1897) of Douglas nursery, Waukegan, Il. Common; still in commerce. Very dense, narrowly pyramidal with crowded, twisted and frond-like foliage on short upswept branches. Bronzy in winter. Vigorous. Confused with *T. occidentalis* 'Spiralis' (and indeed the two may be the same). Record: 55' × 4'9" × 25' Walla Walla, WA (1993).

T. occidentalis 'Elegantissima'
= *T. elegantissima* hort. (in part)

GOLDTIP ARBORVITÆ. Origin unknown. In North American commerce <1917. Still sold, from the South into Canada. Tree expert A. Rehder thought this a synonym of *T. occidentalis* 'Lutea', but nursery catalog descriptions uniformly dispute that judgement. Maybe some specimens sold as 'Elegantissima' were indeed 'Lutea'. 'Elegantissima' more likely is a synonym of *T. occidentalis* 'Aureospicata'. Narrowly pyramidal. Foliage shiny dark green, the sprays yellow-tipped, changing to brownish in winter.

T. occidentalis 'Emerald (Green)'—see *T. occidentalis* 'Smaragd'

T. occidentalis 'Endean'

Originated and introduced by Endean nursery of Richmond, Ontario. Named officially in 1949. Very rare; extinct in commerce. Pyramidal, open; branches stout, erect, shining gray; branchlets stout, at first green, later light yellow; leaves light green.

T. occidentalis 'Europe Gold'
('Eurogold')

Originated in Holland. Introduced in 1974. In B.C. commerce since the early 1980s. An intense yellow (best color in winter), flame-shaped bushy small tree.

T. occidentalis 'Fastigiata'
= *T. occidentalis* 'Pyramidalis'
= *T. occidentalis* 'Columnaris'
= *T. occidentalis* 'Stricta'
= *Thuja fastigiata* hort.
= *Thuja pyramidalis* hort.

PYRAMIDAL ARBORVITÆ. Named in 1865 in Germany.

A wholly inapplicable name, as is the 1867 'Stricta'. The 1892 'Columnaris' is best, but nurseries prefer the 1907 name 'Pyramidalis'. The dates just cited are the officially recognized dates of publication, and "Pyramidalis" was in commercial use <1907. In any case this clone (or these clones, probably) is ubiquitous. Used for screens, hedges, and foundation plantings. Columnar or very narrowly pyramidal, with very short branches bearing moderately dense foliage and many cones. Brownish in winter. Gradually being replaced by cultivars greener in winter. Record: 43' × 5'10" × 12' Sedro Woolley, WA (1988).

T. occidentalis 'Filicoides'

FERNLEAF ARBORVITÆ. Named officially in Germany in 1891 (means fernlike; from Latin *filix*, fern, and Greek -*oides*, resemblance). In North American commerce ≤1916, and as late as 1958. Densely branched narrowly pyramidal. Ultimate branchlets short and regularly pinnately arranged. Similar to *T. occidentalis* 'Douglasii Pyramidalis' and 'Spiralis'.

T. occidentalis 'Filifolia'—see T. occidentalis 'Filiformis'

T. occidentalis 'Filiformis'

?= *T. occidentalis* 'Filiformis Pendula'
?= *T. occidentalis* 'Filifolia'

THREADLEAF ARBORVITÆ. Named officially in Germany in 1901 (having threads or filaments; from Latin *filum*, thread, and *forma*, form). In North American commerce ≤1888 (if 'Filifolia' is a synonym). In any case, still in commerce, but rare. A shrub, slowly reaching 10'-25'. Varies from short and dense mounds to gaunt, more upright growth, as influenced by rootstock or growing conditions. Secondary branchlets long, filamentous or whipcord-like, erect with drooping tips; shoots only slightly ramified—the stout long terminal branchlets up to 2' long without a lateral twig.

T. occidentalis 'Filiformis Pendula'—see T. occidentalis 'Filiformis'

T. occidentalis 'George Peabody'—see T. occidentalis 'Lutea'

T. occidentalis 'George Washington'

= *T. occidentalis* 'Washingtoni Aurea'

Introduced ≤1948 by Sherwood nursery of Gresham, OR. Still in commerce. The name has been partly misapplied to *T. plicata* 'Zebrina'. Sherwood says: "Exceedingly bright golden all year. Similar in shape and color to 'George Peabody' but much showier."

Doty & Doerner nursery of Portland, OR (1957–58): "Pyramidal, compact. Strong lemon-yellow variegation." A specimen seen labeled 'George Washington' at Mitsch nursery of Aurora, OR, in 1992, was similar to *T. plicata* 'Zebrina'.

T. occidentalis 'Goldspot'—see T. occidentalis 'Aureovariegata' and T. plicata 'Zebrina'

T. occidentalis 'Harrisonii'

Described officially in 1902. Long extinct commercially. Neat little tree with the entire foliage tipped almost pure white.

T. occidentalis 'Hetz' Wintergreen'

= *T. occidentalis* 'Wintergreen'
≠ *T. occidentalis* 'Lombarts' Wintergreen' (q.v.)

A *T. occidentalis* "Pyramidalis" seedling. Introduced ≤1950 by F.C. Hetz & Sons Fairview Evergreen nursery of Fairview, PA. In North America ≤1953. Common. Narrow pyramidal; vigorous; to 30' tall and 6' wide. Foliage coarser than on other pyramidal cultivars. Dark green even in winter.

T. occidentalis 'Holmstrup'

Originated by nurseryman A.M. Jensen of Holmstrup, Denmark; introduced ≤1951. In North American commerce ≤1967. Common. Very columnar; compact, very slow to 10'-15'; in effect a dwarf PYRAMIDAL ARBORVITÆ (*T. occidentalis* 'Fastigiata'). Bright green year-round.

T. occidentalis 'Hoopseii'

Named after Josiah Hoopes (1832–1904), author of *Book of Evergreens*. In commerce ≤1888. Long commercially extinct. Broad-pyramidal or dome shaped; dense. Foliage coarse, light green.

T. occidentalis 'Lake St. John'

From Brandon, Manitoba, research station. Extinct commercially.

T. occidentalis 'Lobbi Atrovirens'—see T. plicata 'Atrovirens'

T. occidentalis 'Lobbi Aurea'—see T. plicata 'Zebrina'

T. occidentalis 'Lombarts' Wintergreen'

Introduced ≤1965 by Lombarts nursery of Zundert, Holland. Not known in North American commerce. Not the same as 'Hetz' Wintergreen'. Described by Hillier nursery of England as a small to medium-sized columnar tree; green year-round.

T. occidentalis 'Lutea'

= T. occidentalis 'George Peabody'
= T. occidentalis 'Aurea'—misapplied; see T. occidentalis 'Aurea'
= T. occidentalis 'Elegantissima'—misapplied; see T. occidentalis 'Elegantissima'

GEORGE PEABODY ARBORVITÆ. Originated <1870 in Henry E. Maxwell's nursery of Geneva, NY. Common. A bright yellow narrow conical tree. Over the years, nurseries have selected improved sports and kept selling them under the original name, or under slight variants (e.g., T. occidentalis lutea 'Bobbink & Atkins' and T. occidentalis lutea 'Mary Corey'). Records: 66' × 4'9" Little Hall, Canterbury, England (1984); 58' × 5'6" Dochfour, Inverness-shire, Scotland (1981).

T. occidentalis lutea 'Bobbink & Atkins'—see T. occid. 'Lutea'

T. occidentalis lutea 'Mary Corey'—see T. occidentalis 'Lutea'

T. occidentalis 'Lutescens'—see T. occid. 'Wareana Lutescens'

T. occidentalis 'Malonyana'

From the park of Count Ambrózy-Migazzi at Malonya (now Mlynany), Czechoslovakia. Dates from the late 1800s; named in 1913 in Germany. In North America, but not known in commerce, at least not under its proper name. Columnar, CYPRESS-like, very vigorous; to 65' tall. Foliage dark green even in winter.

T. occidentalis 'Martini'

Introduced ≤1954–55 by Tingle nursery of Pittsville, MD. Extinct in commerce. Vase-shaped.

T. occidentalis 'Masonic'

Introduced <1990 by nurseryman C. Berg of Helena, MT. A columnar selection from the west side of Helena's Masonic Temple.

T. occidentalis f. Mastersii Rehd.

= T. plicata Endl. 1847 p.p., Parl., Beissn. 1891; non D. Don 1824
= T. occidentalis var. plicata Wells 1865, Masters 1897, non Hoopes 1868

MOSS ARBORVITÆ. CURLED-LEAF ARBORVITÆ. Introduced to England sometime between 1781 and 1790 by Conrad Loddiges. A seed-grown strain, never widely sold, and long out of commerce, or being sold under other names. The name Mastersii dates from 1939, and was given in honor of Maxwell Tylden Masters (1833–1907), English botanist and conifer authority. It was Masters who in 1897 first cleared up the confusion surrounding this form and the authentic Thuja plicata (WESTERN RED CEDAR). A small dense tree with short branches. Branchlet systems rigid, much flattened, and taking an erect and parallel position like those of T. orientalis. Foliage distinctly glandular, brownish-dark green above, bluish-green beneath. See also T. occidentalis 'Wareana' (SIBERIAN or WARE ARBORVITÆ).

T. occidentalis 'Mastersii Aurea'—see T. occidentalis 'Aurea'

T. occidentalis 'Meehani'

MEEHAN'S GOLDEN ARBORVITÆ. Introduced ≤1888 by Thomas B. Meehan nursery of Dresher, PA. Still being sold in 1905. "Broader than the common form [i.e., T. occidentalis 'Aurea' or 'Lutea']. Tips edged with golden tint."

T. occidentalis 'Mission'—see T. occidentalis 'Techny'

T. occidentalis 'Nigra'

WINTERGREEN ARBORVITÆ. Introduced <1933. Common. Narrowly pyramidal. Dark green even in winter. To 25'–50' tall.

T. occidentalis 'Pacific Gold'

In Pacific Northwest commerce ≤1993.

T. occidentalis 'Parsons'—see T. occidentalis 'Compacta'

T. occidentalis 'Pendula'

Raised ca. 1857 at Standish nursery of Bagshot, Surrey, England. In North American commerce since ≤1890; now uncommon. Slender ascending branches and pendulous branchlets of blue-green foliage (grayer in winter) set on an upright but tortuous small tree to 15'–25' tall.

T. occidentalis var. plicata—see T. occidentalis f. Mastersii

T. occidentalis 'Plicata Aurea'—see T. occidentalis 'Aureovariegata'

T. occidentalis 'Pyramidalis'—see T. occidentalis 'Fastigiata'

T. occid. 'Pyramidalis Douglasii'—see T. occid. 'Douglasii Pyra.'

T. occidentalis 'Pyramidalis Improved'

Introduced ≤1975 by Mitsch nursery of Aurora, OR. Discontinued in 1980–81 in favor of *T. occidentalis* 'Smaragd'.

T. occidentalis 'Pyramidalis Spiralis'—see *T. occidentalis* 'Spiralis'

T. occid. 'Queen Victoria'—see *T. occid.* 'Alba' and 'Columbia'

T. occidentalis 'Riversii'

RIVERS' ARBORVITÆ. Named ≤1891, maybe after English nurseryman Thomas Rivers (1798–1877). Rare; out of commerce since ca. 1960s. Dense, broadly pyramidal large shrub or small tree. Vigorous. Foliage rich bright (yellowish-) green.

T. occidentalis 'Robusta'—see *T. occidentalis* 'Wareana'

T. occidentalis 'Rosenthali'

ROSENTHAL ARBORVITÆ. Described in 1884. Likely after Austrian nurseryman R.C. Rosenthal (*fl.* 1882–1888). In North American commerce ≤1915. Commonly sold until the 1990s. Very slow growing, compact, broadly columnar. Foliage glossy, dark.

T. occidentalis 'Semperaurea'—see *T. occidentalis* 'Aureospicata'

T. occidentalis 'Semperaurescens'—see *T. occid.* 'Aureospicata'

T. occidentalis 'Sherman(ii)'

A 1931 *Thuja occidentalis* 'Wareana' sport from Sherman nursery of Charles City, IA. Introduced in 1934; still in commerce. Foliage very dark green, of much heavier texture than other types of ARBORVITÆ. Broad pyramidal 25'–30' tall.

T. occidentalis 'Sherwood Column'

Introduced ≤1968 by Sherwood nursery of Gresham, OR. Columnar. Foliage thick, soft, dense, holds its green well in winter.

T. occidentalis 'Sherwood Frost'

Introduced ≤1968 by Sherwood nursery of Gresham, OR. Cone-shaped, very dense. Vigorous and fast. Foliage bright green, almost tufted, the tips covered with a minute variegation in such a manner that the whole tree appears to be covered with frost, making a beautiful contrast to the rich green base color.

T. occidentalis 'Sherwood Moss'

Introduced ≤1968 by Sherwood nursery of Gresham, OR. Cone-shaped semi-dwarf tree. Dense, symmetrical, yet informal in appearance. Bright green in summer, violet-hued in winter. Foliage feathery, almost moss-like.

T. occidentalis 'Sherwood Plumespire'

Introduced ≤1968 by Sherwood nursery of Gresham, OR. Spirelike column. Foliage very dark, exceedingly soft, moss-like, plume-like, feathery, bright green in summer, soft violet in winter.

T. occidentalis var. *sibirica*—see *T. occidentalis* 'Wareana'

T. occidentalis 'Skybound'

Originated as a seedling raised in 1956 by by R.M. Boughen of Valley River nursery, Manitoba. First sold in 1966. Rare. Conical dense erect tree with a tendency to produce multiple trunks. Foliage tight, dark green, not fading in winter. Very hardy.

T. occidentalis 'Smaragd'

= *T. occidentalis* 'Emerald (Green)'

Selected by D.T. Poulsen, nurseryman of Kelleriis, Denmark. Introduced in 1950. In North America ≤1962; in commerce here ≤1973–74. Common. Densely compact columnar-conical form, to at least 10' tall. Bright emerald green all year.

T. occidentalis 'Spicata Aurea'—see *T. occidentalis* 'Aureospicata'

T. occidentalis 'Spiralis'

= *T. occidentalis* 'Pyramidalis Spiralis'

Origin unknown. Maybe an improved version of *T. occidentalis* 'Douglasii Pyramidalis'. Introduced ≤1888 by Thomas B. Meehan nursery of Dresher, PA. Still being sold. Compact narrowly pyramidal. Upright branches with very close-set short branchlets; the branchlet-systems concave and twisted, suggesting a spiral arrangement if seen from above. Record: 42½' × 2'3" Sotterley Hall, Suffolk England (1985).

T. occidentalis 'Stricta—see *T. occidentalis* 'Fastigiata'

T. occidentalis 'Sudworthii'

Introduced ≤1992 by Iseli nursery of Boring, OR. Similar to *T. occidentalis* 'Lutea' (GEORGE PEABODY ARBORVITÆ). Form broadly upright. Foliage yellow, with a hint of orange in winter. The Latinized name is illegitimate unless it was applied <1959.

T. occidentalis 'Sunkist'

Introduced <1968 in Boskoop, Holland. In North American commerce <1990. A large shrub or small tree. Foliage yellowish.

T. occidentalis 'Techny'

= *T. occidentalis* 'Mission'

Discovered <1956 at Mission Gardens of Techny, Il. Introduced commercially ≤1967. Common. Fast. Very winter hardy. Very dark green even in worst winters. 10'–25' tall.

T. occidentalis 'Unicorn'

Originally selected in 1964 by C. De Groot. Introduced ≤1975 by Sheridan nursery of Oakville, Ontario. Common in Canadian commerce in the 1980s; still sold. Columnar, dense. Foliage very dark green, becoming dark olive.

T. occidentalis 'Variegata'—see T. occidentalis 'Argentea'

T. occidentalis 'Variegata Argentea'—see T. occidentalis 'Argentea'

T. occidentalis 'Variegata Aurea'—see T. occidentalis 'Aurea'

T. occidentalis 'Vervæneana'

VERVÆNE ARBORVITÆ. Raised ca. 1855 by Domien Vervæne (ca. 1810–1870), of Ledeberg, near Ghent, Belgium. Described in 1862. In North American commerce ≤1906; common. Densely pyramidal, a large shrub or eventually small tree to 50' tall. Branches slender; branchlets crowded, spreading, fine; color varies from light yellow and green, to wholly green or wholly pale yellow, and dull bronzy in winter; very distinct.

T. occidentalis 'Victoria'—see T. occid. 'Alba' and 'Columbia'

T. occidentalis 'Viridis'

?= *T. occidentalis* 'Viridissima'

Introduced <1891, probably in Europe. Extremely rare in North America, at least under the name cited. A compact narrow-pyramidal tall tree with lustrous dark green foliage (*viridis* is Latin for green).

T. occidentalis 'Viridissima'—see T. occidentalis 'Viridis'

T. occidentalis 'Wareana'

= *T. occidentalis* 'Robusta'
= *T. occidentalis* var. *sibirica* Hoopes
= *T. occidentalis* var. *densa* Gord.
= *T. caucasica* hort.
= *T. tatarica* hort.
= *T. Wareana* hort., non Booth

SIBERIAN ARBORVITÆ. WARE ARBORVITÆ. Raised ca. 1827 by nurseryman G. Weare (not Ware) or his father James Weare (fl. 1790s–1830s), of Coventry, Warwickshire, England. (Ascription to Thomas Ware is erroneous.) In North America <1852. Very common. Low, dense, broadly pyramidal; stout branched. Foliage thick, bright green. Closely allied to *T. occidentalis* f. *Mastersii* but usually more robust and with heavier foliage. Very hardy. Growth slow. Maximum 26' tall.

T. occidentalis 'Wareana Aurea'—see T. occid. 'Aureovariegata'

T. occid. 'Wareana Aureovariegata'—see T. occid. 'Aureovariegata'

T. occidentalis 'Wareana Lutea'—see T. occid. 'Wareana Lutescens'

T. occidentalis 'Wareana Lutescens'

= *T. occidentalis* 'Lutescens'
= *T. occidentalis* 'Wareana Lutea'

Introduced ca. 1880 by Hesse nursery of Germany. In North American commerce ≤1903. Still in commerce, just barely. Similar to *T. occidentalis* 'Wareana' but more compact, and foliage pale yellow or golden at first.

T. occidentalis 'Wareana Variegata'—see T. occid. 'Aureovariegata'

T. occid. 'Washingtoni Aurea'—see T. occid. 'George Washington'

T. occidentalis 'Watnong Gold'

A sport of the shrub *T. occidentalis* 'Ellwangeriana Aurea Nana'. Originally selected in 1964 by Watnong nursery of Morris Plains, NJ. Introduced ≤1968. Registered in 1973. Common. Tall, compact column. Gold even in winter.

T. occidentalis 'Wintergreen'—see T. occid. 'Hetz' Wintergreen

T. occidentalis 'Yellow Ribbon'

Introduced in Holland in 1981. In North American commerce in the 1990s. Young growth orange-yellow. Columnar, slow, to at least 10' tall and 3' wide.

T. occidentalis 'Zebrina'—see T. plicata 'Zebrina'

T. orientalis L.

= *Biota orientalis* (L.) Endl.
= *Platycladus orientalis* (L.) Franco

ORIENTAL ARBORVITÆ. CHINESE ARBORVITÆ. CHINESE THUYA. BOOKLEAF CYPRESS (from its parallel foliage sprays). ORIENTAL CEDAR. From China, Burma, Korea, and possibly NE Iran. Plant explorer E. Wilson reported never finding it wild in China, only planted, including enormous old specimens. Introduced to Europe ca. 1700. Named in 1753. In North America since ≤1818. Very common. Highly adaptable, tolerating much heat and dryness as well as cold. Seedlings vary from dark green to golden yellow, fine to coarse, dense to loose. *T. orientalis* is called a separate genus by some botanists (a valid scientific viewpoint but horticulturally a headache). The 1832 alternate generic name *Biota* still crops up in some nurseries, as does the 1842 *Platycladus,* from Greek *platys* broad, and *cladus* flattened (or *klados*, a branch). Foliage relatively weakly scented; in strongly vertical sprays. Cones larger than those of the other species, and fleshy-looking; seeds thick and unwinged. Records: to 80" × 38'0" in China; 59' × 8'4" Edgewood, MD (1972); 52' × 6'4" Pencarrow, Cornwall, England (1970); 52' × 5'0" Penjerrick, Cornwall, England (1959); 47' × 6'6" Highnam, Over, near Gloucester, England (1970).

T. orientalis 'Anita'

Introduced ≤1931 by Griffing nursery of Beaumont, TX. Bright green, pyramidal, medium-sized.

T. orientalis f. aurea (Carr.) Rehd.

= *T. aurea* hort. (in part)

GOLDEN ORIENTAL ARBORVITÆ. As presently used, *aurea* is a group name to indicate any seedling or cultivar with foliage more or less golden, even if only in spring. The name dates from <1850, but nurseries have mostly used it as part of a conjunction ('Aurea Bonita', 'Aurea Conspicua', 'Aurea Elegantissima', 'Aurea Nana', 'Aurea Pyramidalis'). Both dwarf and tree-size forms exist.

T. orientalis 'Aurea Conspicua'—see T. orientalis 'Conspicua'

T. orientalis 'Aurea Elegantissima'—see T. orient. 'Elegantissima'

T. orientalis 'Bakeri'

= *T. orientalis* 'Baker's Pyramid'
= *T. orientalis* 'Baker's Hybrid'
= *T. orientalis* 'Baker's Green Spire'
= *T. orientalis* 'Pyramidalis Bakeri'

Origin unknown. In U.S. commerce ≤1928–29. Common; still sold. Broad pyramidal, compact, to 15'–25' tall. Foliage rich light green. Adapted to hot dry localities.

T. orientalis 'Baker's Green Spire'—see T. orientalis 'Bakeri'

T. orientalis 'Baker's Hybrid'—see T. orientalis 'Bakeri'

T. orientalis 'Baker's Pyramid'—see T. orientalis 'Bakeri'

T. orientalis 'Beverlyensis'

BEVERLY HILLS ARBORVITÆ. GOLDEN COLUMN ARBORVITÆ. Originated in CA <1917 (the year published in L.H. Bailey's *Cyclopedia*). Common. Compact narrow pyramidal. Golden young foliage. Rapid; to 15'–20' tall. E. Lord & J. Willis say it has similar shape to 'Elegantissima' but longer and more fernlike (instead of roundish or oval) leaf-sprays.

T. orientalis 'Blue Cone'

= *T. orientalis* 'Conica Glauca'

Originated <1938 by Howard's Montopolis nursery of Austin, TX. Still in commerce. Symmetrical pyramidal shape; to 15' tall or more. Dense bluish-green foliage.

T. orientalis 'Blue Green'

Origin unknown. In U.S. commerce ≤1928–29. Sold by Southern nurseries until at least 1930. Extinct in commerce, or renamed.

T. orientalis 'Bluespire'

= *T. orientalis* 'Howardi'

Originated <1938 by Howard's Montopolis nursery of Austin, TX. Much grown in Texas, at least into the mid-1980s. Columnar, compact, to 12' tall or more. Foliage bluish-green.

T. orientalis 'Burtoni'

Introduced ≤1954–55 (when offered by Monrovia nursery of California). Columnar. Green.

T. orientalis 'California Golden'

Introduced ≤1931 by Griffing nursery of Beaumont, TX. Pyramidal. Foliage gold. Similar to 'Aurea Conspicua' but doesn't hold bright yellow in winter.

T. orientalis 'Columnaris'—see *T. orientalis* 'Columnaris Stricta'

T. orientalis 'Columnaris Stricta'

= *T. orientalis* 'Columnaris'

Introduced ≤1938 (when offered by Overlook nursery of Crichton, AL). Still in commerce in 1958; now extinct. Narrow compact columnar. Green.

T. orientalis 'Conica Glauca'—see *T. orientalis* 'Blue Cone'

T. orientalis 'Conspicua'

= *T. orientalis* 'Aurea Conspicua'

GOLDSPIRE ARBORVITÆ. Raised <1902 by nurseryman P.J. Berckmans (1830–1910) of Augusta, GA. Common. This should be known as BERCKMANS ARBORVITÆ but another cultivar (bushy 'Aurea Nana') became very popular under that name. 'Conspicua' differs in being slenderer, more erect, with less distinctly vertical sprays. Foliage light green tipped with intense gold.

T. orientalis 'Elegantissima'

= *T. orientalis* 'Aurea Elegantissima'
= *T. elegantissima* hort. (in part)

YELLOW COLUMN ARBORVITÆ. Raised in 1858 by Rollison's nursery of Tooting, England. In North America <1870. Common. Pyramidal to 20' tall; compact and narrow at first, but when 100 years old rather broad, floppy and showing its age. Branches erect and stout; fan-shaped sprays bright gold-tipped in spring, greenish-yellow in summer, bronzy-green in winter. Record: 35' × 4'2" × 37' Seattle, WA (1987).

T. orientalis 'Goodwin'

Found as a seedling ca. 1950 by Paul M. Goodwin, nurseryman of Kingfisher, OK. Commercially extinct. Dense symmetrical ovoid form. Deep green even in winter. Extra hardy.

T. orientalis 'Gordon'

Introduced ≤1931 by Griffing nursery of Beaumont, TX. Uniform pyramidal. Gray-green.

T. orientalis 'Gracilis'—see *T. orientalis* 'Nepalensis'

T. orientalis 'Green Cone'

Introduced ≤1985 (when offered by Aldridge nursery of Von Ormy, TX). Dark green. Does well in hot, dry places.

T. orientalis 'Holmani'

Introduced ≤1954–55 (when offered by Monrovia nursery of California). Compact, upright, medium height. Deep green.

T. orientalis 'Howardi'—see *T. orientalis* 'Bluespire'

T. orientalis 'Hudgins'

Introduced ≤1931 by Griffing nursery of Beaumont, TX. Very compact. Blue-green, feathery foliage.

T. orientalis 'Kallay Gold'

Introduced ≤1958 (when offered by Kallay Bros. nursery of Painesville, OH).

T. orientalis 'Maurieana'—see *T. orientalis* 'Murray'

T. orientalis 'Murray'

?= *T. orientalis* 'Maurieana'

Introduced ≤1931 by Griffing nursery of Beaumont, TX. Compact upright. Fine green.

T. orientalis 'Nepalensis'

= *T. orientalis* 'Gracilis'

NEPAL ARBORVITÆ. DIANA ARBORVITÆ. Named in 1847. Out of commerce. Of slender, graceful, compact, ascending habit.

T. orientalis 'Pyramidalis'

= *T. orientalis* 'Stricta'
= *T. orientalis* 'Tatarica'

GREEN SPIRE ARBORVITÆ. Cultivated since ca. 1820 in Europe. Long common in North America. Tall, narrowly fastigiate shrub or small tree, to 30' tall. Bright green. Cones relatively small.

T. orientalis 'Pyramidalis Bakeri'—see *T. orientalis* 'Bakeri'

T. orientalis 'Rochester'

Likely selected by B.H. Slavin of Rochester, NY. In commerce ≤1958. Commercially extinct. Similar to the usual form, but hardier.

T. orientalis 'Roena'

Introduced ≤1931 by Griffing nursery of Beaumont, TX. Tall, cone-shaped pyramidal. Light green.

T. orientalis 'Sibyl'

Introduced ≤1931 by Griffing nursery of Beaumont, TX. Compact, broad-based, tapering to the top. Leaves close-fitting, blue-green.

T. orientalis 'Sikes'

Introduced ≤1931 by Griffing nursery of Beaumont, TX. Tall, very narrow pyramidal. Good substitute for ITALIAN CYPRESS (*Cupressus sempervirens*). Bright green.

T. orientalis 'Stricta'—see T. orientalis 'Pyramidalis'

T. orientalis 'Tatarica'—see T. orientalis 'Pyramidalis'

T. orientalis 'Texarkana Glauca'—see T. orientalis 'Texana Glauca'

T. orientalis 'Texas Blue'—see T. orientalis 'Texana Glauca'

T. orientalis 'Texana Glauca'

= *T. orientalis* 'Texas Blue'
?= *T. orientalis* 'Texarkana Glauca'

TEXAS BLUE ARBORVITÆ. Origin unknown. In U.S. commerce ≤1927. No longer sold. Tall, pyramidal, fast growing. Foliage loose, pale blue-green, feathery.

T. orientalis 'Thornhill'

Introduced ≤1931 by Griffing nursery of Beaumont, TX. Upright, compact. Dark green all year.

T. orientalis 'Wintergreen'

Introduced ≤1931 by Griffing nursery of Beaumont, TX. Tall pyramidal. Rich dark green all year.

T. plicata Donn ex D. Don 1824, non Endl. 1847 p.p.

= *T. Menziesii* Dougl. *ex* Endl.
= *T. gigantea* Nutt., non Carr.
= *T. Lobbii* hort. *ex* Gord.

WESTERN RED CEDAR. PACIFIC RED CEDAR. GIANT ARBORVITÆ. SHINGLE CEDAR. CANOE CEDAR. GIANT CEDAR. From S Alaska to N California, east to Montana. Named in 1824 (plicate, folded into plaits, perhaps suggested by the flattened twigs with regularly arranged scale-like leaves, or by the buttressed trunk). Introduced to cultivation in 1853 by William Lobb (1809–1864) to Veitch nursery of England. Common. The Official Tree of British Columbia. For cultivated trees long ago sold as "*T. plicata*," see *T. occidentalis* f. *Mastersii*. Foliage fruity-smelling when crushed, sweeter than that of *T. occidentalis*. The largest member of the CYPRESS family. Records: 277' × 30'5" Sqwaka Valley, B.C. (1980); 194' × 62'0" Cheewhat Lake, B.C. (1988); 178' × 61'0" south of Forks, WA (1977); 159' × 63'5" Quinault Lake, WA (1993); 130' × 66'1" Kalaloch, WA (1954); a trunk 76'0" around at 1'6" measured by D. Kinsey (1906).

T. plicata 'Atrovirens'

= *T. occidentalis* 'Lobbi Atrovirens'

Originated <1874 by nurseryman R. Smith of Worcester, England. In North America ≤1898; sold here ≤1921. Common. Habit typical. Keeps bright shiny green color year round.

T. plicata 'Aurea'

= *T. aurea* hort. (in part)

Cultivated since the 1860s in England. Most trees sold under this name are actually *T. plicata* 'Zebrina'; some are *T. occidentalis* 'Aureospicata'. A 1900 description from Veitch nursery of England: "a large proportion of the foliage and young growths light yellow, most conspicuously in the short lateral growths of the terminal shoots." Briefly, 'Aurea' is tinted old-gold, while 'Zebrina' has zebra-like stripes of alternating green and creamy-gold. 'Aurea' is very rare; 'Zebrina' common.

T. plicata 'Aureovariegata'—see T. plicata 'Zebrina'

T. plicata 'Canadian Gold'

Introduced ≤1980–81 by Mitsch nursery of Aurora, OR. A fast, broad pyramidal tree. Foliage evenly bright gold on sunny side; 'Sunshine' very similar. Both this and 'Sunshine' are unattractive bronze in January unlike *T. occidentalis* 'Canadian Gold'.

T. plicata 'Columnaris'—see T. plicata 'Fastigiata'

T. plicata 'Excelsa'

?= *T. plicata* 'J. Timms & Co.'

Found in a Berlin cemetery in 1904 and introduced ≤1947–48 by J. Timm nursery of Elmshorn, Germany. In North American commerce ≤1968–69. Much used for hedging in British Columbia. Compact; narrow; branches strongly ascending. Foliage heavy, glossy dark green even in winter.

T. plicata 'Fastigiata'
= T. plicata 'Columnaris'
= T. plicata 'Pyramidalis'
= T. plicata 'Stricta' says Hillier's
Named in 1867 in France. Narrowly columnar like LOMBARDY POPLAR (*Populus nigra* 'Italica'). In North America ≤1899; sold here ≤1927. Rare. See *T. plicata* 'Hogan'.

T. plicata 'Gracilis'
Described in 1867 in Europe. Extremely rare. Sprays finer, with smaller leaves. A loose and irregular shrub or small tree.

T. plicata 'Gracilis Aurea'
In North American commerce ≤1927 (when offered by California nursery of Niles, CA). Very rare; commercially extinct. Described by California nursery as "Very distinct; small, of fairly loose spreading habit. The golden-tipped branches are fine and delicately pendulous." Conifer specialist P. den Ouden said of it (1965): "Pyramidal, loose, open, slow. Sprays flimsy, curved, irregular, yellow-tipped. Very tender." One in Seattle has very fine foliage, of a pale color, and it produces few or no cones; its habit is of a huge shrub: 25½' × 4'3" × 27½' (1994).

T. plicata 'Green Pyramid'—see T. plicata 'Striblingi'

T. plicata 'Green Sport'—see T. plicata 'Watnong Green'

T. plicata 'Hogan'
Named after Hogan Road of Gresham, OR. In commerce ≤1948, almost exclusively in Oregon and Washington. Seed-grown; not a clone. Often the name *T. plicata* 'Fastigiata' is misapplied. Tree densely compact with a narrower silhouette. Such trees are common in Washington and Oregon.

T. plicata 'J. Timms & Co.'—see T. plicata 'Excelsa'

T. plicata 'Leei'—see T. plicata 'Zebrina'

T. plicata 'Lobbie Goldspot'—see T. plicata 'Zebrina'

T. plicata 'Magnifica Aurea'
In North American commerce ≤1927 (when offered by California nursery of Niles, CA). Exceedingly rare; commercially extinct. Attributes unknown.

T. plicata 'Pyramidalis'—see T. plicata 'Fastigiata'

T. plicata 'Semper-aurea' or 'Semperaurescens'—see T. occidentalis 'Aureospicata'

T. plicata 'Stribling(i)'
= T. plicata 'Green Pyramid'
In California commerce ≤1966–67. Doubtless named after Stribling's nursery of Merced, CA. Dense, narrow column useful for screening. Dark green. Sounds very much like *T. plicata* 'Excelsa'.

T. plicata 'Stricta'—see T. plicata 'Fastigiata'

T. plicata 'Sunshine'
Origin unknown; in Oregon commerce ≤1986. Looks like *T. plicata* 'Canadian Gold' and also reportedly originated in Canada. Said to be brighter gold.

T. plicata variegata—see T. occidentalis 'Aureovariegata'

T. plicata 'Virescens'
Introduced ≤1990–91 by Mitsch nursery of Aurora, OR. The name, being Latinized, is invalid, being long past the 1959 cutoff date. Habit looks typical, but perhaps narrower than usual; foliage bright glossy green all year.

T. plicata 'Watnong Green'
= T. plicata 'Green Sport'
Selected in 1960s by Watnong nursery of Morris Plains, NJ. In largescale nursery production ≤1980 (as 'Green Sport'). Renamed 'Watnong Green' in 1988–89. Broad, fast pyramid. Superb green all year.

T. plicata 'Zebrina'
= T. aurea hort. (in part)
= T. plicata 'Aurea' (in part)
= T. plicata 'Aureovariegata'
= T. Lobbii 'Aurea'
= T. gigantea 'Aureovariegata'
= T. gigantea 'Albomaculata'
= T. occidentalis 'Zebrina'
= T. occidentalis 'Goldspot' (in part)
= T. 'Goldspot' (in part)
= T. occidentalis 'George Washington' (in part)
?= T. 'Golden Lobbi'
?= T. occidentalis 'Lobbi Aurea'
?= T. plicata 'Lobbie Goldspot'
?= T. plicata 'Leei'
ZEBRA CEDAR. Origin unknown; likely Holland in the 1860s. Named 'Zebrina' ca. 1900 (from Portuguese

zibru, and Latin *zebra*). Grown previously and subsequently under other names. In North American commerce it has been sold as 'Zebrina' rarely (mostly since the 1980s). But under other names it has long been common, on the West Coast at least. Foliage variegated with bands of green and golden-yellow. Tree vigorous, broadly pyramidal. *T. plicata* 'Aurea' is tinted old-gold, while 'Zebrina' has zebra-like stripes of alternating green and creamy-gold. 'Aurea' is very rare; 'Zebrina' common. Over the years some sports of 'Zebrina' have been selected. For example, in 1979–80 Massot nursery of Richmond, B.C., said: "Our selection is brighter and richer gold; a definite improvement." Since ≤1987, '(Zebrina) Extra Gold' has been circulating in Europe. Records: 95' × 8'6" Castlehill, Devon, England (1989); 76' × 12'2" × 51' Olympia, WA (1993); 73' × 10'7" × 65' Woodinville, WA (1989); 65' × 13'7" × 40' Renton, WA (1992).

Thuja pyramidalis—see *T. occidentalis* 'Fastigiata'

T. Standishii (Gord.) Carr.

= *T. japonica* Maxim.

JAPANESE ARBORVITÆ. JAPANESE THUYA. Japanese: *Kurobe. Nezo-ko.* From Japan. Introduced in 1860–61 by R. Fortune for John Standish (1814–1875), nurseryman of Bagshot, then at Ascot, Berkshire, England. In North America ≤1874. Uncommon. Foliage nonglandular, dull, with a faint piney odor— A. Mitchell asserted in 1985: "its subtle blend of lemon, eucalyptus and balsam is the most sublime aroma in the garden." Cones small. Records: to 115' × 18'0" in Japan; 79' × 7'2" Tregrehan, Cornwall (1979); 65' × 9'11" Powerscourt, County Wicklow, Ireland (1989); 58' × 6'10½" Port Coquitlam, B.C. (1994).

T. tatarica—see *T. occidentalis* 'Wareana'

T. Wareana hort., non Booth—see *T. occidentalis* 'Wareana'

T. Wareana variegata hort.—see *T. occidentalis* 'Aureovariegata'

Thujopsis

(*Thuyopsis*)

[CUPRESSACEÆ; Cypress Family] Only one species in the genus. From Genus *Thuja*, and Greek *-opsis*, resemblance.

T. borealis—see *Chamæcyparis nootkatensis*

T. dolabrata (L. fil.) S. & Z.

= *Thuja dolabrata* L. fil.

HIBA ARBORVITÆ. HIBA CEDAR. DEERHORN CEDAR. BATTLE AXE CEDAR. LIZARD TREE. Japanese: *Asunaro.* From Japan. Named in 1781 (from Latin *dolabra* = a pick axe, mattock or hatchet). Introduced to Western cultivation between 1853 and 1861. Uncommon. Densely foliated. Foliage *Thuja*-like but far more substantial. The English names allude to its bright green, scaly foliage. Cones to ¾" long. Hates dry conditions. Needs shade in hot, sunny regions. Often only a shrub or multi-trunked small tree; suited for hedging. Slow growing. Records: to 100' × 9'5" in Japan; 82' × 5'0" Woodstock, County Kilkenny, Ireland (1989); 69' × 8'10" Tregrehan, Cornwall (1987); 47' × 3'11" Tacoma, WA (1989).

T. dolabrata var. *Hondai* Mak.

From N Japan. Named in 1901, likely after Siroku Honda (b. 1866). More cold-hardy, larger growing, and denser than the typical form. Cones globular (not broadly ovoid), and lacking prominent prickles. Very rare in cultivation; in botanic gardens and arboreta.

T. dolabrata 'Variegata'

Introduced by Siebold to Holland in 1859, and by R. Fortune to England in 1861. Extremely rare in North America; least so in the maritime Pacific Northwest. Branchlets partly cream- or white-variegated. Much prone to reverting to nearly all green. Record: 52' × 2'5" Seattle, WA (1987).

Thuya—see *Thuja*

Tilia

[TILIACEÆ; Linden Family] 30–45 spp. of deciduous trees known as LINDENS, LIMES or BASSWOODS; from the northern hemisphere. *Tilia* is an ancient Latin name. Possibly related to Greek *ptilon* (wing), after the winglike bract of the flower clusters. Prized for shade. Leaves heart-shaped, usually lopsided at the base, finely and sharply toothed. The creamy flowers, though small, appear in great abundance in summer, are fragrant, and beloved by bees; some people make tea from them. The ensuing little berry-sized fruits are like tiny nutlets in a thin husk, borne on a most peculiar winged papery-textured narrow bract. LINDENS have been widely planted as street-trees. In spring and early summer they are charming, then aphids and inadequate moisture cause them to look ratty, yet they are strong and don't die easily. The North American native species are much less adapted to trying urban streetside conditions, but are magnificent in parklike settings. All species appreciate rich, moist soil, but *T. tomentosa* (SILVER LINDEN) is superb and largely unaffected by aphids even in dryish sites. Fall color on most species is adequate yellow at best, but usually poor, dull brown or wan yellow. Seed-raised specimens may be less prone to unsightly burls and trunk sprouts, and grow taller than vegetatively-grown specimens.

T. alba pendula—see *T. tomentosa* 'Pendula'

T. alba spectabilis—see *T.* × *Moltkei* 'Spectabilis'

T. americana L.
= *T. glabra* Vent.
= *T. neglecta* Spach

BASSWOOD. AMERICAN BASSWOOD or LINDEN. WHISTLE-WOOD. WHITTLEWOOD. LINN. BEE TREE. WICKYUP. MONKEYNUTS TREE. From eastern North America. Common in cultivation. Trunk smooth-barked until large; often surrounded by suckers bearing immense leaves. Leaves green or yellowish-green above, green beneath, more or less hairless, 4"–10" long. "Basswood" is derived from bast-wood, because the bark fibers were once widely used and economically significant.

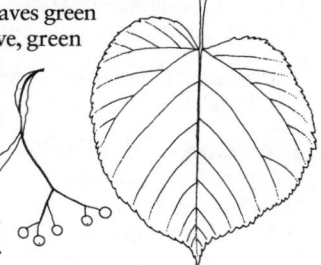

See also *T. heterophylla*. Records: to 140' tall; 135' × 11'8" Marquette County, MI (1981; aged 237 years); 122' × 20'9" Cincinnati, OH (1987); 94' × 24'4" Montgomery County, PA (1980).

T. americana 'American Sentry'—see *T. americana* 'Sentry'

T. americana 'Bailyard'—see *T. americana* Frontyard™

T. americana 'Capitol'
Introduced ≤1991–92.

T. americana Continental Appeal™—see *T. heterophylla* Continental Appeal™

T. americana 'Dakota'
Introduced <1980 by Ben Gilbertson of Kindred, ND. Not in commerce. Roundheaded.

T. americana 'Douglas'
Selected in 1970 by nurseryman R.G. Klehm of South Barrington, IL. Introduced in 1985. Rare. Branching upright. Foliage luxuriant deep green.

T. americana 'Fastigiata'
= *T. americana* 'Pyramidalis'

PYRAMIDAL AMERICAN LINDEN. Named in 1931. The original specimen then ca. 20 years old in Genesee Valley Park of Rochester, NY. In commerce since ≤1940s; still sold. Distinctly pyramidal when young. Under the same name, Bailey nursery of St. Paul, MN, has sold (since ≤1991) what they call their own selection.

T. americana Frontyard™
= *T. americana* 'Bailyard'

Introduced in 1994–95 by Bailey nursery of St. Paul, MN. "Excellent, symmetrical branching habit."

T. americana var. *heterophylla*—see *T. heterophylla*

T. americana ssp. *heterophylla*—see *T. heterophylla*

T. americana Legend™
= *T. americana* 'Wandell'

Introduced ≤1988 by Willet N. Wandell of Urbana, IL. "Excellent branching habit; broad pyramidal." Foliage "superior green."

T. americana 'Lincoln'

Selected in 1970 by nurseryman R.G. Klehm of South Barrington, IL. Introduced in 1985. Rare. Branching upright; habit slender. Foliage light green.

T. americana 'Macrophylla'

= *T. macrophylla* hort. *ex* V. Engler
= *T. mississippiensis* hort. *ex* Rehd.

BIGLEAF BASSWOOD. Named in 1862 (from Greek *makro-*, large, and *phyllon*, a leaf) in Germany. In North American commerce ≤1891. Very rare; extinct commercially. Leaves huge, commonly 12"–15".

T. americana pendula—see T. tomentosa 'Pendula'

T. americana 'Pyramidalis'—see T. americana 'Fastigiata'

T. americana 'Redmond'

= *T.* × *euchlora* 'Redmond'

Discovered in Fremont, NE, in the early 1920s by nurseryman C. Matthew Redmond. Introduced in 1927 by Plumfield nursery of Fremont. The name 'Redmond' is said to date from only 1942. Common nationally since the 1950s. Pure *T. americana*, despite often being miscalled a hybrid.

T. americana 'Rosehill'

Origin unknown (likely Rosehill Gardens of Kansas City, MO). Introduced ≤1987–88. Grown by several major wholesale tree nurseries. Said to be "improved."

T. americana 'Sentry'

= *T. americana* 'American Sentry'

Introduced <1991 by McKay nursery of Waterloo, WI. Habit uniform, symmetrical. Branches silver when young.

T. americana 'Wandell'—see T. americana Legend™

T. argentea—see T. tomentosa

T. asplenifolia—see T. platyphyllos 'Laciniata'

T. australis—see T. heterophylla

T. Continental Appeal™—see T. heteroph. Continental Appeal™

T. cordata Mill.

= *T. parvifolia* Ehrh. *ex* Hoffm.

LITTLELEAF LINDEN. SMALL LEAVED LINDEN. WINTER LINDEN (in contrast to SUMMER LINDEN, *T. platyphyllos*). MALE LINDEN (in contrast to FEMALE LINDEN, *T. platyphyllos*). From Europe, and the Caucasus. Commonly grown in North America. Leaves 1½"–3" (4⅜") long and wide, cordate (heart-shaped) at the base, dark green above, blue-green beneath, with orange-brown tufts of fuzz at the junction of blade and stem. Seeds small, downy, smooth or faintly ribbed; soft. Records: to 138' tall in the wild; 132' × 12'3" Tottenham House, Savernake, Wiltshire, England (1984); 96'×13'0" Arlington, WA (1992); 81' × 14'9" Avon, WA (1988); 79' × 17'0" Forde Abbey, Dorset, England (1988); 78' × 15'3" Queenstown, MD (1990); a trunk 27'3" around at Czarny Potok (N. Sacz), Poland (≤1973); a trunk 29'8" around at Frasnes, Belgium (≤1992).

T. cordata 'Alley'

Named ≤1990s. Origin and attributes unknown. Sold in 1980s by Beaver Creek nursery of Poplar Grove, IL.

T. cordata 'Baileyi'—see T. cordata Shamrock™

T. cordata 'Bicentennial'

= *T. cordata* 'XP110'

Introduced (as *T. cordata* 'XP110') in 1962–63 by Scanlon nursery of Ohio. Renamed 'Bicentennial' in 1976. Still in commerce. Tight pyramidal habit. Branch crotch angles more acute than those of *T. cordata* 'Rancho'.

T. cordata Chancellor® PP 2712 (1967)

= *T. cordata* 'Chancole'

Introduced in 1965–66 by Cole nursery of Painesville, OH. Still in commerce. Habit relatively upright, narrow and compact.

T. cordata 'Chancole'—see T. cordata Chancellor®

T. cordata Corinthian®

= *T. cordata* 'Corzam'

Introduced in 1987 by Lake County nursery of Perry, OH. Still in commerce. Compact narrow pyramid form; evenly spaced limbs. Small, thick leaves.

T. cordata 'Corzam'—see *T. cordata* Corinthian®

T. cordata 'De Groot'
Introduced in 1973 by Sheridan nursery of Ontario. Common. Named for Constant De Groot, long-time propagator at Sheridan nursery. Sturdy, compact, slow. Leaves small and dark.

T. cordata Fairview™ PP 3259 (1972)
Selected in 1969. Introduced in 1973 by McGill nursery of Fairview, OR. Common. Normal habit but stronger branching, rapid growth. Leaves slightly larger than usual. Record: 47½' × 3'7" × 33' Aurora, OR (1993; *pl.* 1975).

T. cordata 'Firecracker'
Introduced ≤1991 by Willoway nursery of Avon, OH. Leafs out about two weeks later than most cultivars. Broad pyramid form with good branching habit. Flowers abundant, in late June.

T. cordata 'Glenleven'—see *T.* × *flavescens* 'Glenleven'

T. cordata 'Green Globe'
Originated in 1960 as a seedling. Introduced in 1983 by Sheridan nursery of Ontario. Crown round and compact. Sold topgrafted. See also *T. cordata* 'Lico'.

T. cordata Greenspire® PP 2086 (1961)
= *T. cordata* 'PNI 6025'

Introduced in 1961 by Princeton nursery of New Jersey. Common. Wm. Flemer, III, says it resulted from a <1953 cross between the best *T. cordata* in Boston's park system and a very fine selection from Germany. Distinctive small leathery leaves. Grows rapidly into a narrow, tidy oval form. Strong straight trunk and radial branching. Highly susceptible to trunk damage from winter sunscald or mechanical damage.

T. cordata 'Handsworth'—see *T. platyphyllos* 'Handsworth'

T. cordata 'June Bride' PP 3021 (1971)
Introduced in 1971 by Manbeck nursery of New Knoxville, OH. Common. Substantially pyramidal habit and a semihorizontal, very even branching habit around the straight central leader. Leaves small and glossy. Exceptionally floriferous (hence the name).

T. cordata 'Lico'
Introduced ≤1977 in Holland; in North American commerce ≤1987. Uncommon. A topgrafted, globular dwarf. See also *T. cordata* 'Green Globe'.

T. cordata 'Morden'
Originated in 1954 as a seedling from Sheridan nursery of Ontario. Named in 1969 at Morden research station of Manitoba. Still in commerce. Exceptional cold-hardiness.

T. cordata 'Norbert'—see *T. cordata* Prestige®

T. cordata Norlin™
= *T. cordata* 'Ronald'

Introduced ≤1990 by Jeffries nursery of Manitoba. Named after Wilbert G. Ronald. Growth rapid. Broad pyramidal form, with strong branches. Sunscald resistant. Dark green leaves resist leaf gall and leaf spot effectively in the Northern Plains.

T. cordata 'Olympic'
Introduced ≤1970–71 by Schmidt nursery of Boring, OR. Still in commerce. Broad and symmetric branching habit. Leaves glossy; late to fall.

T. cordata 'PNI 6025'—see *T. cordata* Greenspire®

T. cordata Prestige® PP 6745 (1989)
= *T. cordata* 'Norbert'

Introduced by Discov-Tree Research of Oquawka, IL. Few seeds made. Rapid growth. Good branching habit.

T. cordata 'Prestige'—see *T. heterophylla* Continental Appeal™

T. cordata 'Pyramidalis'
Introduced ≤1949–50 by Kohankie nursery of Painesville, OH. Commercially extinct. Habit narrowly pyramidal.

T. cordata Rancho™ PP 2092 (1961)
Discovered in 1952. Introduced in 1961 by Scanlon nursery of Ohio. Still in commerce. Broad, dense pyramidal habit with upright branching. Leaves small, very dark. Flowers profusely.

T. cordata 'Ronald'—see *T. cordata* Norlin™

T. cordata Salem®

Introduced in 1973–74 by Handy nursery of Portland, OR. Still in commerce. Upsweeping branches form a rounded crown. Brilliant deep green foliage.

T. cordata Shamrock™

= T. cordata 'Baileyi'

Introduced in 1987 by Bailey nursery of St. Paul, MN. Similar to T. cordata Greenspire® but stouter branched with a less dense, more open canopy. Leaves slightly larger. More vigorous.

T. cordata 'Sheridan'

Sold by Sheridan nursery of Ontario in the 1990s as SHERIDAN HYBRID LINDEN, "heads dense, foliage dark." If it is indeed a hybrid, it does not belong under T. cordata. But nurseries sometimes use the word "hybrid" loosely.

T. cordata 'Spaethi'—see T. × flavescens

T. cordata 'Swedish Upright'

Introduced in 1906 by A. Rehder from Sweden to the Arnold Arboretum. Named in 1963. Not in commerce. Tight pyramidal form; lateral branches at right angles, lower ones pendulous.

T. cordata 'Tures(ii)'

Introduced <1992 by Matt Tures Sons nursery of Huntley, IL. Fast growing, straight-trunked, tall pyramidal form.

T. cordata 'XP110'—see T. cordata 'Bicentennial'

T. dasystyla—see T. 'Euchlora'

T. 'Euchlora'

= T. × euchlora K. Koch
= T. × europæa 'Euchlora'
= T. × vulgaris 'Euchlora'
= T. dasystyla hort. (in part), non Stev. 1831
?= T. × europæa var. dasystyla
    Loud. 1838 p.p.
?(T. platyphyllos ssp. caucasica
    × T. cordata)

CRIMEAN LINDEN. CAUCASIAN LINDEN. From the Caucasus-Crimea region, certainly a hybrid but of debated origin. Introduced ca. 1860 (as T. dasystyla) by Booth's Flottbeck nursery near Hamburg, Germany. Named (from Greek eu, good, and chloros, green) in 1866. Long in North

America, but only common since the 1980s. Leaves 2"–4", glossy bright green; clear yellow late in fall. Seeds football-shaped, fuzzy, strongly ribbed; usually scantily borne, and sterile. Twigs apple-green. Grafted or grown from cuttings. In age the crown is dumplinglike and not as lofty as many other Tilia. Records: 69' × 6'0" Westonbirt, Gloucestershire, England (1988); 69' × 4'9" and 59' × 7'6" Seattle, WA (1988; pl. ≤1916); 52½' × 8'3" Kew, England (1987; pl. 1872).

T. × euchlora Laurelhurst™—see T. × europæa 'Laurelhurst'

T. × euchlora 'Redmond'—see T. americana 'Redmond'

T. × europæa L. p.p., emend. Sm.

= T. × vulgaris Hayne
= T. hybrida Bechst.
= T. intermedia DC.
(T. platyphyllos × T. cordata)

EUROPEAN LINDEN. COMMON LIME (of England). EUROPEAN BASSWOOD. From Europe. In Williamsburg, VA <1724. Rare in North America. Nurseries have employed the name frequently, but usually supplied T. cordata (LITTLELEAF LINDEN) or T. platyphyllos (BIGLEAF LINDEN). This hybrid is nearer to T. platyphyllos in looks. It can produce fertile seed. In Europe it is common, being easily transplanted and tolerant of ill usage such as mal-pruning. Excellent old specimens are in New England. The tallest recorded Tilia. Records: 151' × 12'6" Duncombe Park, Hemsley, Yorkshire, England (1972); 143' × 16'5" Gatton Park, Surrey, England (1979); 118' × 31'0" Stanway, Gloucestershire, England (1982); 112' × 12'4" Ellicott City, MD (1990); 86' × 15'8" West Hartford, CT (1987); a trunk 17'6" around in Germantown, PA (1970).

T. × europæa alba Parmentieri—see T. tomentosa 'Pendula'

T. × europæa 'Aurea'—see T. platyphyllos 'Aurea'

T. × europæa var. dasystyla—see T. 'Euchlora'

T. × europæa 'Euchlora'—see T. 'Euchlora'

T. × europæa 'Gocrozam'—see T. × europæa Goldcrown®

T. × *europæa* Goldcrown®
= *T.* × *europæa* 'Gocrozam'
Introduced ≤1991 by Lake County nursery of Perry, OH. Leaf bright golden-yellow when young, on reddish stems; green with age.

T. × *europæa* 'Grandiflora'—see *T. platyphyllos*

T. × *europæa* 'Koningslinde'—see *T.* × *europæa* 'Pallida'

T. × *europæa* 'Laciniata Rubra'—see *T. platyphyllos* 'Laciniata'

T. × *europæa* 'Laurelhurst'
Introduced ≤1988–89 by Moller's nursery of Gresham, OR. In 1993-94 they switched the name to *T.* × *euchlora* Laurelhurst™. In Laurelhurst Park of Portland, OR, there is a *T.* × *europæa*. Maybe it was the specimen propagated by Moller's. Their catalog says the "parent tree came from Europe ca. 1920."

T. × *europæa* 'Pallida'
= *T. vulgaris pallida* hort.
ROYAL LINDEN. KAISER LINDEN. Described in 1844. In North America ≤1933; in commerce since <1958; very rare until recently; still uncommon. Twigs and buds reddish-brown in autumn and winter. Leaves large, green above, yellowish-green beneath. This is the tree of Berlin's celebrated street Unter den Linden; twigs reddish in winter. A similar but apparently not identical clone, perhaps cultivated only in Europe, is 'Koningslinde' (Dutch Royal Linden).

T. × *europæa* 'Wratislaviensis'
= *T.* 'Wratislaviensis'
GOLDEN LINDEN. Possibly a sport of *T.* × *europæa* 'Pallida'; raised ≤1898 at Breslau, Poland. Described in 1904. In North America since ≤1965 (the year imported by the Arnold Arboretum). In commerce ≤1985–86. Rare. At least some nurseries have supplied it topgrafted at 7', saying it stays small and partly weeps. New shoots and young leaves bright yellow early, greenish in midsummer.

T. × *flavescens* A. Br. *ex* Döll
= *T. Spaethii* Schneid.
= *T. cordata* 'Spaethi'
(*T. americana* × *T. cordata*)
Originated <1836 in Germany. Named in 1843 (Latin meaning yellowish—possibly referring to the flowers). In North American commerce ≤1939 (when

sold by Princeton nursery of New Jersey). Extremely rare.

T. × *flavescens* 'Dropmore'
Introduced in 1955 by Dropmore nursery of Manitoba. Still in commerce. A seedling of *T. cordata* (LITTLELEAF LINDEN) that looks so much more like *T. americana* (BASSWOOD) that its stated parentage is questionable. It looks like a BASSWOOD, but is immune to the mite that disfigures the native BASSWOOD, it tolerates drier soil, and grows faster than either parent. Seeds small, faintly ribbed, fuzzy, hard; usually with viable seeds.

T. × *flavescens* 'Glenleven'
= *T. cordata* 'Glenleven'
A seedling of a *T. cordata* that was pollinated intentionally with *T. americana*. Introduced in 1962–63 by Sheridan nursery of Ontario. Common; often sold as a *T. cordata* cultivar. Vigorous; grows fast. Narrow-crowned. Seeds few, BASSWOOD-sized and hard.

T. × *flavescens* 'Wascana'
A 1971 seedling of an open-pollinated *T.* × *flavescens* 'Dropmore'; selected in 1978 by W.G. Ronald of Morden research station, Manitoba; named and introduced in 1982. Not common. Hardier, faster, and with a wider and stronger branching habit than 'Dropmore'.

T. glabra*—see *T. americana

T. grandifolia*—see *T. platyphyllos

***T. heterophylla* Vent.**
= *T. Michauxii* Nutt.
= *T. monticola* Sarg.
= *T. venulosa* Sarg.
= *T. australis* Small
= *T. americana* var. *heterophylla* (Vent.) Loud.
= *T. americana* ssp. *heterophylla* (Vent.) E. Murr.
WHITE BASSWOOD. From the S Appalachian region, primarily. The 1800 name *heterophylla* means differently or diversely leaved (from Greek *heteros*, different, and *phyllon*, a leaf). Leaves densely whitish-hairy beneath, commonly 7"–12" long. Seeds large, fuzzy, not ribbed; fairly hard. There are specimens quite intermediate between this species and *T. americana*. Records: 119' × 11'1" Great Smoky Mountains National Park, TN (1994); 101' × 12'0" Henderson County, NC (1986); 87' × 14'8" Bowie, MD (1990); 58' × 15'4" Monticello, GA (1972).

T. heterophylla Continental Appeal™ PP 3770 (1975)

= *T. americana* Continental Appeal™
= *T.* Continental Appeal™
= *T. heterophylla* 'Prestige'
≠ *T. cordata* Prestige®

Introduced by Wandell nursery of Urbana, IL. Rare. Dark, vigorous compact crown. Leaves handsome white beneath.

T. heterophylla 'Prestige'—see T. heteroph. Continental Appeal™

T. hybrida—see T. × europæa

T. × intermedia—see T. × europæa

T. kiusiana Mak. & Shiras.

KYUSHU LINDEN. From S Japan. Japanese: *Hera-no-ki*. Named in 1900 after Kyushu Island. Introduced to the West in 1930. Almost nonexistent in North American commerce: in the early 1970s it was sold topgrafted by Scanlon nursery of Ohio. Leaves narrow for a *Tilia*, to 3" × 1¼" (2"); short-stemmed. A large shrub or small tree; bark shaggy. Records: to 50' tall in Japan; 23' × 1'6" Westonbirt, Gloucestershire, England (1983).

T. laciniata—see T. platyphyllos 'Laciniata'

T. macrophylla—see T. americana 'Macrophylla'

T. Michauxii—see T. heterophylla

T. mississippiensis—see T. americana 'Macrophylla'

T. × Moltkei Späth *ex* Schneid.

= *T.* 'Moltkei'
(*T. americana* × *T. tomentosa*)

MOLTKE LINDEN. Originated in Germany ca. 1875. Introduced to commerce in 1883 by Späth nursery of Germany. Very rare in North America. The pollen parent was possibly *T. tomentosa* 'Pendula'. Another suggested parentage is *T. americana* × *T. heterophylla*. Named after Field Marshall Count H.K.B. von Moltke (1800–1891). Resembles *T. americana* more than *T. tomentosa*, especially in its susceptibility to leaf-eating insects. Records: 102' × 9'6" Westonbirt, Gloucestershire, England (1988); 54' × 9'2" Lisle, IL (1986; *pl.* 1929).

T. × Moltkei 'Spectabilis'

= *T. tomentosa* 'Spectabilis'
= *T. × spectabilis* Dipp., non Host
= *T. alba spectabilis* hort.
= *T. vulgaris alba superba* hort.

SHOWY LINDEN. SPECTACULAR LINDEN. Introduced in 1893 by G. Dieck of Zoschen, Germany. Said to be a seedling of *T. tomentosa*. Others say it is a purebred *T. americana*. Very rare; commercially extinct since the early 1930s. The name *spectabilis* in Latin means worth seeing, notable or remarkable. Leaves large (to 7½" × 6"), dark green above, paler gray-green beneath. Record: 69' × 7'7½" Seattle, WA (1990; *pl.* 1893).

T. mongolica Maxim.

MONGOLIAN LINDEN. From N China, Mongolia, and the Russian Far East. Introduced to the West by E. Bretschneider, sometime between 1863 and 1882. In commerce ≤1906. More popular in Canada than the U.S. Rare. Usually propagated by grafting rather than raised by seed. The prevalent clone is a small tree, rarely 40' tall, with droopy habit. Leaves 1½"–3¾" long, with unique large, bold teeth (lobes). Flushes earlier in spring than most *Tilia*. Bare before other *Tilia* in fall. Turns ugly gold in Seattle, but can be striking bright yellow in early September in Alberta, Canada. Seeds football-shaped, downy, indistinctly ribbed; usually sterile. Records: 80' height estimated at Angers, France (1973); 62' × 5'2" Kew, England (1979; *pl.* 1904); 43' × 3'4" Seattle, WA (1993; *pl.* 1963).

T. monticola—see T. heterophylla

T. 'Mrs. Stensson'—see T. × varsaviensis 'Mrs. Stensson'

T. neglecta—see T. americana

T. Oliveri Szysz.

CHINESE SILVER LINDEN. From central China. Named in 1890 after Daniel Oliver (1830–1916), one-time Keeper of England's Kew Herbarium. Introduced in 1900 by E. Wilson for Veitch nursery of England. In North American commerce at least between 1939 and 1950, when sold by Kohankie nursery of Painesville, OH. Extremely rare. Leaves 3"–8" long, dark green above, pure white felty-hairy beneath; stem 1"–3" long. Twigs hairless. Records: 92' × 6'0"

Westonbirt, Gloucestershire, England (1990); trunks to 13'0" around in the wild.

T. parvifolia—see T. cordata

T. 'Petiolaris'—see T. tomentosa 'Pendula'

T. petiolaris 'Chelsea Sentinel'—see T. toment. 'Chelsea Sentinel'

T. platyphyllos Scop.
= T. grandifolia Ehrh.
= T. × europæa 'Grandiflora'

BIGLEAF LINDEN. BROAD LEAVED LINDEN. LARGE LEAVED LINDEN. SUMMER LINDEN (in contrast to WINTER LINDEN, T. cordata). FEMALE LINDEN (in contrast to MALE LINDEN, T. cordata). DUTCH LINDEN. From Europe and SW Asia. Long common in North American cultivation, although usually sold as T. × europæa. Now nurseries rarely list it, preferring T. cordata (LITTLE-LEAF LINDEN). Leaves large (platyphyllos from Greek platys, wide or broad, and phyllon, a leaf), thin, and lightly hairy, remaining green later in fall than those of T. cordata. The leaf size is only large (to 5"–7" long and wide) relative to T. cordata; many other Tilia leaves are as big or bigger. Twigs persistently lightly hairy. Flowers earliest of Tilia, in (late May) June, with strong, sweet perfume. Seeds big, densely fuzzy, very hard. Records: to 135' tall in Europe; 121' × 14'9" Scone Palace, Perthshire, Scotland (1981); 100' × 16'3" Titley Court, Herefordshire, England (1970?); 96' × 7'2" Tacoma, WA (1987); 72' × 12'6" Oxford, MD (1972); 70' × 14'4" Skagit City, WA (1987); 46' × 24'4" Pitchford Hall, Shropshire, England (1984); trunks to 44'0" around in Europe.

T. platyphyllos 'Asplenifolia'—see T. platyphyllos 'Laciniata'

T. platyphyllos 'Aurea'
= T. × europæa 'Aurea'

GOLDTWIG LINDEN. Originated in Europe <1838. In North American commerce ≤1853–54. Twigs golden-yellow in winter. See also T. platyphyllos 'Handsworth'.

T. platyphyllos 'Corallina'—see T. platyphyllos 'Rubra'

T. platyphyllos 'Fastigiata'
= T. platyphyllos 'Pyramidalis'

'Fastigiata' was A. Rehder's 1940 name for what had been known otherwise as 'Pyramidalis' since <1864 in Germany. Unfortunately other trees had also received that older name, so Rehder felt it ambiguous. F. Santamour thinks 'Pyramidalis' is the best name. Uncommon in North America and out of commerce. The trunk gives rise to several ascending forks which in time gently splay out.

T. platyphyllos 'Fastigiata Laciniata'—see T. platyphyllos 'Laciniata'

T. platyphyllos 'Handsworth'
= T. cordata 'Handsworth'

Originated by Fisher and Holmes' nursery at Handsworth, Sheffield, England. In North American commerce ≤1888. Rare. Most trees here date from scions obtained in 1952 by the Arnold Arboretum. Twigs greenish-yellow in winter. Leaves narrower than usual and only weakly heart-shaped at the base, if at all. See also T. platyphyllos 'Aurea'.

T. platyphyllos 'Laciniata'
= T. asplenifolia hort.
= T. laciniata hort. ex Courtois
= T. × europæa 'Laciniata Rubra'
= T. platyphyllos 'Laciniata Rubra'
= T. platyphyllos 'Fastigiata Laciniata'
?= T. platyphyllos 'Asplenifolia'
('Lacinia')

CUTLEAF EUROPEAN LINDEN. PYRAMIDAL CUTLEAF LINDEN. Cultivated since ≤1835 in Europe. Long grown in North America (since ≤1853), but uncommon. Tightly conical; leaves small, elegantly deeply lobed and toothed. Floriferous. Twigs reddish. Smaller than typical. Records: 85' × 6'1" Drumkilbo, Tayside, Scotland (1986); 56' × 5'0" Tarrytown, NY (ca. 1980); 50' × 9'4" Jardine Hall, Dumfries, Scotland (1985). (Whether 'Asplenifolia' as originally described is a synonym of 'Laciniata' is unknown. J. Loudon wrote "in the Bollwyler Catalogue of Baumann for 1838, we have T. aspleniifolia nova, which, we presume, is a subvariety of T. europæa laciniata." In any case, there appears to be only one CUTLEAF LINDEN clone circulating in North America, regardless of the fact that more than one name has been affixed to it.)

T. platyphyllos 'Laciniata Rubra'—see T. platyphyllos 'Laciniata'

T. platyphyllos 'Örebro'

Originated in 1935 from a park in Örebro, Sweden. Described in 1939. In North America since ≤1966. Rare. Bright red twigs, shapely narrow, fastigiate crown. A specimen sold to the Seattle arboretum in 1966 is neither fastigiate or red twigged, being quite typical looking, except stays green remarkably late into autumn. Street-trees planted in Seattle match it. This clone may really be 'Delft' or 'Paul Kruger' from the Netherlands. Record: 21' × 1'2" Lisle, IL (1986; *pl.* 1966).

T. platyphyllos 'Pyramidalis'—see *T. platyphyllos* 'Fastigiata'

T. platyphyllos 'Rubra'

= *T. platyphyllos* 'Corallina'

REDTWIG LINDEN. Originated ca. 1755 in France; described officially in 1770. Long cultivated in North America. Out of commerce since perhaps the 1930s. Twigs red in winter.

T. Spaethii—see *T.* × *flavescens*

T. × *spectabilis*—see *T.* × *Moltkei* 'Spectabilis'

T. tomentosa Moench

= *T. argentea* Desf. *ex* DC.

SILVER LINDEN. (EUROPEAN) WHITE LINDEN. From SE Europe, SW Asia. Introduced from Hungary to England in 1767 by J. Gordon, nurseryman at Mile End. Long grown in North America. Common. Twigs white-hairy when young. Leaves thick, round, abruptly pointed, dark green above, densely white fuzzy (tomentose) beneath, 3"–6" long and wide. The contrasting color makes the foliage handsome, especially when fluttering in a gentle breeze. More drought-tolerant and less buggy than most *Tilia*. Flowers narcotic to bees. Crown very dense; usually distinctly rounded at the apex, whether the tree is short or tall. Records: 125' × 19'6" Montgomery County, PA (1980); 120' × 10'1" Port Coquitlam, B.C. (1992); 115' × 14'10" Tortworth Court, Gloucestershire, England (1986); a trunk 21'1" around at Eatons Neck, NY (1972).

T. tomentosa 'Brabant'

Originated ca. 1930 in the Dutch village of Hoeven in Brabant. Named in 1970. In North American commerce ≤1989–90. Foliage especially aphid-resistant. Branching erect, broadly conical.

T. tomentosa 'Chelsea Sentinel'

= *T. petiolaris* 'Chelsea Sentinel'

Originated at the Royal Hospital of Chelsea, England. Named and introduced in 1987–88 by Hillier nursery of England. In North American commerce ≤1991–92. Broadly columnar, semi-pendant.

T. tomentosa 'Erecta'

Introduced ≤1994 by Arborvillage nursery of Holt, MO. "Narrow growing form with striking foliage." The cultivar name, being Latin yet post-1959, is invalid.

T. tomentosa Green Mountain®

= *T. tomentosa* 'PNI 6051'

Introduced <1990 by Princeton nursery of New Jersey. Dense, rounded form. Leaves dark lustrous green above, frosty silver beneath. Rapid growth to 50'–70' high, 40' wide.

T. tomentosa 'Pendula'

= *T.* 'Petiolaris' hort., non *T. petiolaris* DC.
= *T. alba pendula* hort.
= *T. americana pendula* hort.
?= *T.* × *europæa alba* Parmentieri hort.

SILVER PENDENT LIME. PENDENT WHITE LIME. WEEPING (WHITE) LINDEN. Origin unknown, European, <1840. Long cultivated in North America, but rare. Pendent branches forming a lofty dome. Leafstems long, often 2½". Records: 130' × 15'9" Villanova, PA (1980); 121' × 12'10" Hall Place, Kent, England (1985); 110' × 17'5" Swarthmore College, PA (1987).

T. tomentosa 'PNI 6051'—see *T. tomentosa* Green Mountain®

T. tomentosa 'Princeton'

Named in 1983, and introduced ≤1990 by Princeton nursery of New Jersey. Vigorous. Uniform oval form.

T. tomentosa 'Sashazam'—see *T. tomentosa* Satin Shadow™

T. tomentosa Satin Shadow™

= *T. tomentosa* 'Sashazam'

Introduced <1990 by Lake County nursery of Perry, OH. The catalog description does not indicate any distinguishing features, and sounds like ordinary *T. tomentosa*. Maybe more compact than usual.

T. tomentosa 'Spectabilis'—see *T.* × *Moltkei* 'Spectabilis'

T. tomentosa Sterling® PP 6511 (1988)

= *T. tomentosa* 'Wandell'
= *T. tomentosa* 'Sterling Silver'

Introduced by Willet N. Wandell of Urbana, IL. Common. Symmetrical broad pyramid. Disease resistant. The leaves resemble those of *T. heterophylla* or *T.* × *Moltkei* with their thinly gray-hairy undersides.

T. tomentosa 'Sterling Silver'—see *T. tomentosa* Sterling®

T. tomentosa 'Wandell'—see *T. tomentosa* Sterling®

T. 'Varsaviensis'

= *T.* × *varsaviensis* Kobendza
= *T.* 'Mrs. Stensson'
?(*T. platyphyllos* × *T. tomentosa*)

WARSAW LINDEN. Originated ca. 1900 in the botanic gardens of Warsaw, Poland. Named in 1951. Name registered in 1965. Not known in commerce. Renamed in 1965 after Mrs. J. Stensson, landscape architect of Oakville, Ontario, who introduced it from Europe. Twigs olive-brown or dark raspberry color, very hairy when young, later hairless. Leaves 2½"–4" long, abruptly pointed, stem slender; very hairy on both sides in spring, becoming shiny above, gray-hairy beneath; staying green late into fall. Slow, and not especially vigorous.

T. venulosa—see *T. heterophylla*

T. × *vulgaris*—see *T.* × *europæa*

T. vulgaris alba superba—see *T.* × *Moltkei* 'Spectabilis'

T. × *vulgaris* 'Euchlora'—see *T.* 'Euchlora'

T. vulgaris pallida—see *T.* × *europæa* 'Pallida'

T. 'Wratislaviensis'—see *T.* × *europæa* 'Wratislaviensis'

Toona

[MELIACEÆ; Mahogany Family] 6–7 spp. All from the Old World. Related closely to the New World *Cedrela*. The name *Toona* is an Indian vernacular, first used as a scientific name in 1803. The only related genus in this volume is *Melia* (CHINABERRY).

T. sinensis (A. Juss.) M. Roem.

= *Cedrela sinensis* A. Juss.
= *Cedrela Toona* Roxb. *ex* Rottl.
= *Ailanthus flavescens* Carr.

CHINESE CEDAR. CHINESE TOON. From Pakistan, India, China, Tibet, Burma, Nepal, Indonesia and Malaysia. Known to science since 1743 thanks to the Jesuit d'Incarville; introduced to France in 1861 by G.E. Simon. In North American commerce ≤1884. Uncommon. A gaunt tree that can sucker rampantly. Bark shaggy. Leaves onion-odored, compound, to 28" long, of 10–32 leaflets, toothed or untoothed. The young leaves are esteemed as a vegetable in China. Leaves paper-like in spring, vividly pink or rose, then ivory (at least in maritime climates), turning green all summer. Fall color can be clear lemon yellow, but is commonly washed-out yellow of no beauty. Flowers in large pendulous sprays, fragrant, white (or slightly lavender), in June or July, attractive to bees. Fruit a 1" long woody capsule opening to bell shape in late fall to release winged seeds. Records: to 98' × 10'9" in the wild; 88' × 7'0" Hergest Croft, Herefordshire, England (1985); 66' × 8'3" Wakehurst Place, Sussex, England (1973); 67' × 7'7" × 74' Germantown, PA (1980); 46' × 5'4" × 37' Hartford, CT (1987); a trunk 7'10" around at Southampton, Long Island, NY (1972).

T. sinensis 'Flamingo'

Raised in Australia <1930. Imported to New Zealand that year, by H. Wright of Avondale. Introduced to commerce in the 1950s. Named 'Flamingo' in 1981. Cultivated in the Northern Hemisphere since ≤1982. New growth showy pink, fading to creamy, then green.

Torreya

[TAXACEÆ; Yew Family (or CEPHALOTAXA-CEÆ; Plum Yew Family)] 4–7 spp. of coniferous evergreens known as NUTMEG TREES (not to be confused with the unrelated tropical tree from which the spices nutmeg and mace are obtained). Named in 1838 after John Torrey (1796–1873), distinguished North American botanist at Columbia University. Overall, YEW-like but more formal, with larger needles supplying a more substantial effect. They need sufficient summer moisture, if not rich soil or partial shade. In dry exposed sites, they are terribly stunted and yellow. If cutting-grown, they will also be very slow and usually remain bushy and multitrunked. To be best they should be raised from seed and given woodland conditions. Isolated specimens rarely if ever set fruit.

T. californica Torr.
= *Tumion californicum* (Torr.) Greene
CALIFORNIA NUTMEG TREE. CALIFORNIA TORREYA. STINKING CEDAR. STINKING YEW. From central California. Introduced to cultivation in 1851 via Wm. Lobb to Veitch nursery of England. Sold in California since ≤1859, but very rarely. Needles very sharp with spiny tips, stiff, 1"–2" (3½") long; dark polished green on above, much paler and duller yellow-green beneath. Crushed needles stink. Fruit 1"–1½" long, green or streaked purple. Tree has a luxurious, droopy look. Records: 141' × 14'10" near Mendocino, CA (1944; 250 years old when cut in 1982); 96' × 20'11" × 68' Swanton, CA (≤1993).

T. grandis Fort. *ex* Lindl.
From China. Discovered and introduced to England by R. Fortune in 1855. Exceedingly rare and little known. Offered in 1993 by Piroche Plants nursery of Pitt Meadows, B.C.

T. nucifera (L.) S. & Z.
= *Taxus nucifera* L.
JAPANESE NUTMEG TREE. JAPANESE TORREYA. Japanese: *Kaya*. From Japan and Korea. Named in 1753 (Latin *nux, nucis*, a nut, and *ferre*, to yield or bear. Hence nut-bearing). Introduced to England in 1764 by Capt. T. Cornwall. In North America ≤1873.

Rare. Needles ¾"–1¼" (1½") long, ⅛"+ wide, dark, glossy, usually curved; sweetly fragrant when bruised. Fruit to 1" long, pale green, the seed edible. Records: to 115' tall in the wild; 82' × 24'3" Japan (1994); 63' × 7'11" Sacramento, CA (1989); 50' × 6'0" Swarthmore, PA (ca. 1980); 35' × 11'0" × 25' Philadelphia, PA (1975; *pl.* ca. 1876).

T. nucifera 'Gold Strike'
Introduced by Shibamichi nursery of Kawaguchi City, Japan. Brought to North America in 1977 by B. Yinger. Many or most shoots variegated bright yellow.

T. taxifolia Arn.
FLORIDA TORREYA. STINKING CEDAR. From Decatur County of SW Georgia to NW Florida. Discovered in 1833 by H.B. Croom, a planter and amateur botanist of North Carolina. Named in 1838 (genus *Taxus*, YEW tree, and Latin *folium*, a leaf). Cultivated since ≤1863. Extremely rare in the wild and under attack by a fungal blight since the late 1950s. Needles (¾") 1"–1½" (1¾") long, and stink unlike the sweet piney sent of *T. nucifera*. Also they are less dark (more yellowish-green), usually more gradually tapered to their tips, and stiffer, more prickly to handle. Record: nearly 60' tall × 9'4" × 52' Norlina, NC (1974).

Toxicodendron altissimum—see *Ailanthus glandulosa*

Toxicodendron vernicifluum—see *Rhus verniciflua*

Toxylon pomiferum—see *Maclura pomifera*

Trachycarpus

[PALMÆ or ARECACEÆ; Palm Family] 4 (6) spp. of slender small PALMS of eastern Asia, amazingly cold-hardy. From Greek *trachys*, rough, and *karpos*, a fruit—the fruits of some species are roughly felted with hairs. Flowers bright yellow. The following three species are summarized thus: *T. Fortunei* is common and well known; *T. Wagnerianus* is, in effect, a mere dwarf version of it; *T. Maritanus* is exceedingly rare and far bolder—its cold-hardiness needs to be verified. A high level of inaccuracy in labeling at both nurseries and botanic gardens prevails.

Other PALM genera in this volume are: *Butia, Ceroxylon, Chamærops, Nannorrhops, Sabal,* and *Washingtonia.*

T. excelsus—see *T. Fortunei*

T. Fortunei (Hook.) Wendl.
= *T. excelsus* Wendl.
= *T. Takil* hort. (in part)
= *Chamærops excelsa* Mart., non Th.
= *Chamærops Fortunei* Hook.

CHINESE FAN PALM. WINDMILL PALM. CHUSAN PALM. HEMP PALM (bark fibers useful). From China, N Burma, and NE India; cultivated in S Japan (*Shurochiku* or *Wa-juro*). Named in 1860 after Robert Fortune (1812–1880), who saw it on Chusan Island of S China, and sent it to England in 1849. It had already been introduced by Siebold to Holland in 1818. In North America since ≤1858–59. Common; the most reliable cold-hardy PALM tree known thus far, though some others may be prove as hardy after testing. It reseeds freely in Seattle. Trunk shaggy with brown fibers. Fronds "fan-like," ca. 2½'–4' wide, of 30–40 (50) segments which are usually pendulous. Male and female flowers usually on separate trees; in May or early June. Fruit looks like blueberries or grapes but are dry and contain big bony seeds. Records: 50' tall at Menlo Park, CA (1938; *pl.* 1903); 49' × 2'8" Trebah, Cornwall, England (1987); 43' × 2'3" Berkeley, CA (1993); 38' × 1'9" Tacoma, WA (1991); 26' × 3'11" Penrose, Cornwall, England (1984).

T. humilis—see *Chamærops humilis*

T. khasianus—see *T. Martianus*

T. Martianus (Wall.) Wendl.
= *T. khasianus* (Griff.) H. Wendl.
= *Chamærops Martiana* Wall.

From Nepal, NE India, and Burma, up to 7,800' elevation. Introduced to cultivation by N. Wallich ca. 1817. Named after Karl Friedrich Philipp von Martius (1794–1868), professor at Munich, PALM specialist. In California commerce ≤1880 (at least nominally). Extremely rare; most PALMS so called are really other species. Trunk smooth, slender. Fronds the largest and least deeply cut in the genus, at least 4' wide; rigid; bluish-green; (30) 47–75 segments; stem to 3' long. Records: to 50' tall in the wild; 30' × 1'7" and one trunk 1'9½" around at San Marino, CA (1993).

T. nepalense—see *T. Wagnerianus*

T. nepalensis—see *T. Wagnerianus*

T. Takil—see *T. Fortunei* and *T. Wagnerianus*

T. Wagnerianus Becc.
= *T. Takil* hort. (in part)
= *T. nepalensis* hort.
= *T. nepalense* hort.

Probably a variety of *T. Fortunei.* Not known in the wild. Cultivated in Japan (*To-juro*) and the United States (since ≤1890). Uncommon. Like *T. Fortunei* but smaller. Fronds small (1½'–2¼'), relatively more pointed than rounded in silhouette, rigid, more deeply divided into 33–50 segments, shorter-stemmed (to 34"). Trunk fibers looser. Flower clusters *very* densely arranged. Recorded to 33' tall.

Trochodendron

[TROCHODENDRACEÆ; Wheel Tree Family] Only one species in the family, a broadleaf evergreen. From Greek *trochos,* a wheel, and *dendron,* a tree; the flowers are star-like, or like the radii of a wheel because of the spreading stamens.

T. aralioides S. & Z.
WHEEL TREE. WHEEL-STAMEN TREE. BIRDLIME TREE. From S Korea, Japan, the Ryukyus, and Taiwan. Named in 1838 (from genus *Aralia,* and Greek *-oides,* resemblance—in respect to its inflorescence). Cultivated in England since <1894. In North American commerce ≤1954; very rare. Usually a slender large shrub or small tree. Best in woodland conditions. Leaves recall those of MOUNTAIN

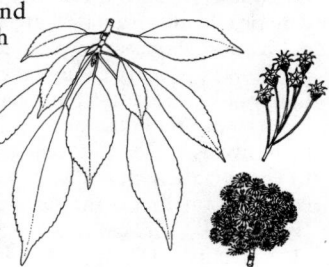

643

LAUREL (*Kalmia latifolia*), whorled and dark, to 6¼" × 2¾"; stem to 3½" long. Flowers from (late March) late April into June, small, greenish-yellow, more interesting than showy. Seed-capsules pale green and vaguely button-like. Records: to 80' × 20'7" in Taiwan; 46' × 5'6" Arduaine, Strathclyde, Scotland (1986); 32½' tall (multitrunked) Seattle, WA (1994; *pl.* 1941).

Tsuga

[PINACEÆ; Pine Family] 9–11 (14) spp. of coniferous evergreens, called HEMLOCKS. *Tsuga* is Japanese and means the mother tree. The various poison hemlocks are weedy herbs (*Cicuta* and *Conium* spp.) in the parsley family (UMBELLIFERÆ or APIACEÆ). The name HEMLOCK TREE was used as early as 1663 (in a book by Englishman John Josselyn). HEMLOCKS tend to be comparatively delicate, shade tolerant, and prefer woodland conditions, or in any case loathe dry, hot summers. For landscape designs where the formal symmetric look of FIRS (*Abies*) and SPRUCES (*Picea*) is too stiff, HEMLOCKS may well lend a graceful touch. The needles are short, blunt and usually not stiff; the cones mostly thimble-sized or less usually; the leading tip of the trees droops. The genus as a whole has few cultivars, but *T. canadensis* sports variants freely, many of them dwarfish. The 1984 book *Cultivated Hemlocks* by John C. Swartley details the history and attributes of the cultivars. Six species are more or less important in cultivation, as indicated below. The several others, all Chinese and Himalayan, are little known, but may prove valuable and are being sold by a few conifer specialist nurseries.

T. Albertiana—see *T. heterophylla*

T. canadensis (L.) Carr.

EASTERN HEMLOCK. COMMON HEMLOCK. CANADIAN HEMLOCK. HEMLOCK SPRUCE. From eastern North America. Pennsylvania's State Tree. Very common in cultivation. Pioneers despised its wood (it does make good, hard pavers), though they valued the bark for tanning. EASTERN HEMLOCK has played a major role in horticulture. In the primeval forest, specimens live as long as 969 years, as did one in Cambria County, PA. Needles and cones the smallest in the genus. Needles (⅙") ¼"–⅓" (⅝") long. Cones ½"–¾" (1"). Records: 159' × 11'10" Joyce Kilmer

Park, TN (1994); 123' × 18'8" Aurora, WV (1979); 100' × 19'11" Great Smoky Mountains National Park, TN (1972).

T. canadensis 'Albo-spica'

= *T. canadensis* 'Albospicata'
= *T. canadensis* 'Argentea'

Cultivated since ≤1875. Still in commerce. Young shoots white tipped. Slow growing; a large shrub, or sometimes eventually a small tree. The newer cultivar 'Summer Snow' is superior. Next to it, 'Albo-spica' can look washed-out. See also 'LaBar's White-Tip'.

T. canadensis 'Argentea'—see *T. canadensis* 'Albo-spica'

T. canadensis 'Ashfield Weeper'—see *T. canadensis* f. *pendula*

T. canadensis 'Atrovirens'

Introduced ≤1890 by Parsons nursery of Flushing, NY. The Latin means deep green. Usually if not always, 'Hicks' is sold incorrectly under this name.

T. canadensis 'Aurea'

Named in 1866. Still in commerce (nominally), but extremely rare. Superseded in fact if not in name by newer, better cultivars such as 'Everitt Golden' and 'Golden Splendor'. Slow-growing but not dwarf. Young branchlet tips soft golden-yellow, fading yellowish-green to green.

T. canadensis 'Bradshaw'

Selected in 1936 from nursery seedlings by H.J. Hohman of Kingsville nursery, Kingsville, MD. Out of commerce. Pyramidal, compact, bright green. Slow.

T. canadensis 'Brookline'—see *T. canadensis* f. *pendula*

T. canadensis 'Classic'

Introduced ≤1986. Broad pyramidal, upright. Twisted branches laden with dark green needles having silvery undersides.

T. canadensis 'Compacta'—see *T. canadensis* 'Hiti'

T. canadensis 'Dawsoniana'

Selected in 1927 by Henry S. Dawson, owner of Eastern nursery of Holliston, MA, from plants grown in the Hunnewell arboretum of Wellesley, MA. Still sold. Compact, bushy. Needles broad, short, obtuse, bright medium green.

T. canadensis 'Elm City'—see *T. canadensis* f. *pendula*

T. canadensis 'Everitt Golden'

Found in 1918 on an exposed slope near Eaton, NH, by Samuel A. Everitt of Huntington, NY. Common; sometimes incorrectly sold as 'Aurea'. A stiff, coarse textured semi-dwarf tree; branches upreaching. Needles closely set, not two-ranked, golden yellow in spring and early summer, then greenish-yellow and finally bronze in late fall. Dense, stubby; quite unlike 'Golden Splendor'.

T. canadensis 'Fremdii'

Found in a large stock of HEMLOCKS at Rye, NY, in 1887 by Charles Fremd (b. 1834); propagated in 1897 and introduced in Holland by P. Koster of Boskoop. Common. A dense, slow, dark pyramidal large shrub or small tree. Needles crowded, broad and short.

T. canadensis 'Geneva'

A seedling from Geneva, NY. Named officially in 1965. Growth compact, very slow: 38' tall by 30' wide in 1973, when 110 years old. Needles short, ¼"–⁷⁄₁₆".

T. canadensis 'Golden Splendor'

Introduced in 1979–80 by Mitsch nursery of Aurora, OR, who said: "from Joe Cesarini of Phyto Ecology. Upright, fast; tolerates full sun better than other GOLDEN HEMLOCKS." More bright and vigorous than 'Aurea' or 'Everitt Golden'.

T. canadensis 'Harmon'

Discovered in 1920s at the LaBar Rhododendron nursery of Stroudsburg, PA. Named after Russell Harmon, manager there. Columnar, broad, dense, compact; medium green. The original tree 17' tall by 20' wide in 1971.

T. canadensis 'Hicks'

Introduced <1965 by Hicks nursery of Westbury, NY. Usually sold incorrectly as *T. canadensis* 'Atrovirens'. Pyramidal, slow; spreading branches; dense foliage. Needles large, tinged yellow all year.

T. canadensis 'Hiti'

= *T. canadensis* 'Pomfret'

Found ca. 1940 in Pomfret, CT, by E.B. Baker, manager of the Hiti nursery. Has been incorrectly distributed as 'Compacta'. Was commonly sold in the 1950s. Dense, narrow pyramidal large shrub or small tree; very hardy. Similar to 'Fremdi' but less compact and branches more upright; inner branches not drooping; needles less crowded, longer, conspicuously bluish beneath.

T. canadensis 'Horsford Contorted'

= *T. canadensis* 'Pigtail'

William C. Horsford (1910–1989) of Vermont, profiled in the Summer 1989 American Conifer Society *Bulletin*, "comes from a long line of plantsmen." He supplied 40,000 HEMLOCK seedlings a year to one Connecticut nursery. The site of 'Horsford Contorted' had "a number of contorted upright growing plants." Horsford and G. Williams of Wolcott, VT, "propagated the bush form that was contorted." Slow; it may eventually become a small tree. Extremely twisted fulvous reddish twigs, branches, and needles too; needles often yellow-tipped.

T. canadensis 'Humphrey Welch'

Discovered by Richard Bush of Canby, OR; in commerce ≤1991. An airy little tree; quarter-inch needles. Named after the well known British conifer expert.

T. canadensis 'Hussii'

Found in 1900 by John F. Huss (b. 1849), Superintendent of Parks at Hartford, CT. A very slow tree, not wholly dwarf—to 17' tall in 40 years. Thick branches and short, twiggy branchlets.

T. canadensis 'Jan Verkade'—see *T. canadensis* f. *pendula*

T. canadensis 'Jenkinsii'

Charles Francis Jenkins (1865–1951) started a HEMLOCK arboretum in Germantown, PA in 1931, and this seedling from Towson nursery of Maryland was his "most distinctive and unusual." Named by L.H. Bailey in 1933. The original died in 1940. Rare in cultivation. Narrow pyramidal but open growth and a straight leader. Needles short and dainty, ca. ⅜" long, on slender graceful branches. Record: 48' × 2'4" × 25' Seattle, WA (1993; *pl.* 1948).

T. canadensis 'Julians'—see *T. canadensis* 'Slenderella'

T. canadensis 'Kelsey's Weeping'—see *T. canadensis* f. *pendula*

T. canadensis 'Kingsville'

= *T. canadensis* 'Kingsville Fastigiate'

Found as a seedling in 1936 by H.J. Hohman of Maryland's Kingsville nursery; introduced ≤1946 . By the late 1950s the original was 18' tall and 3½' wide. Branches very short. When not clipped, however, the clone becomes rather typical; now out of commerce.

T. canadensis 'Kingsville Fastigiate'—see T. canadensis 'Kingsville'

T. canadensis 'LaBar White-Tip'

Originated ≤1945 at LaBar Rhododendron nursery of Stroudsburg, PA. An irregular bushy tree; the original 23' tall by 24' wide in 1970. White young growth that changes to dark green. The absolute shrub 'Gentsch White' foliage is less dark and less vividly white. Some nurseries have sold 'LaBar White-Tip' incorrectly as 'Albo-spica'.

T. canadensis f. macrophylla Beissn.

Cultivated since ≤1870, but rarely since the 1950s. Several clones with larger needles than typical, commonly ⅝"–¾". Greek *macro*, large, and *phyllon*, a leaf. Growth varies from slow and shrubby to treelike.

T. canadensis f. microphylla (Lindl.) Beissn.

Cultivated since 1864 (Greek *micro*, small, and *phyllon*, a leaf). Several clones have been distributed, including shrubs such as 'Parvifolia'. Needles commonly no more than ¼".

T. canadensis 'New Gold'

Introduced ≤1985–86 by Mitsch nursery of Aurora, OR. Typical but bright gold in early summer, green by winter.

T. canadensis f. pendula Beissn.

= *T. canadensis* 'Sargentii' (in part)

WEEPING HEMLOCK. As used presently, *pendula* is a collective name that embraces any weeping HEMLOCK cultivars or seedlings. Some botanists have preferred to limit the usage of the name to what it was intended to designate in 1877, the year it was officially published. Parsons nursery of Flushing, NY, had a clone for sale by 1873; specimens were in cultivation even earlier, by the 1860s. Cultivars include: **'Ashfield Weeper'**, **'Brookline'**, **'Elm City'**, **'Jan Verkade'**, **'Kelsey's Weeping'**, **'Valentine'** and **'Wodenethe'**. Several of these comprise the much beloved SARGENT WEEPING HEMLOCKS (named after Henry Winthrop Sargent (1810–1882), Fishkill Landing, New York, an indefatigable enthusiast for testing the success of conifers in the cold climate he lived in). Generally they are groundcovers, broad shrubs, or, after many decades, small trees, at most over 19' tall and twice as wide.

T. canadensis 'Pigtail'—see T. canadensis 'Horsford Contorted'

T. canadensis 'Pomfret'—see T. canadensis 'Hiti'

T. canadensis 'Pyramidalis'—see T. cana. 'Vermeulen's Pyramid'

T. canadensis 'Sargentii'—see T. canadensis f. pendula

T. canadensis 'Slenderella'

= *T. canadensis* 'Julians'

Introduced ≤1984 by Mitsch nursery of Aurora, OR. Mitsch says it came from Longwood Gardens of Kennett Square, PA. Vigorous; of open habit. Needles only ca. ¼" long, light green.

T. canadensis 'Stranger'

The original tree, from David S. Stranger (b. 1871), in Cherry Hill nursery of Newbury, MA, was 13' tall in 1938. A compact tree as broad as tall; slow. Needles broad and thick. Endures wind well.

T. canadensis 'Summer Snow'

Introduced ≤1983–84 by Mitsch nursery of Aurora, OR. Dark green foliage with lovely white tips. Much more attractive than 'Albo-spica' and larger than the shrubby 'Gentsch White'.

T. canadensis 'Valentine'—see T. canadensis f. pendula

T. canadensis 'Vermeulen's Pyramid'

= *T. canadensis* 'Pyramidalis' (in part)

Collected in the wild ca. 1915. Introduced in 1941 (listed as 'Pyramidalis' until 1960) by Vermeulen nursery of New Jersey. Rapid, tall, slender compact pyramidal dense habit. To 15' tall and 5' wide in eight years.

T. canadensis 'Westonigra'

Discovered in the early 1940s in a field at Gillette nursery of Southwick, MA. Grown from cuttings and grafts for many years. Compact yet rapid growing and upright; exceptionally dark foliage. Seedlings breed 75–95% true. Sold since ca. 1948 by Weston nursery of Hopkinton, MA.

T. canadensis 'Wodenethe'—see *T. canadensis* f. *pendula*

T. caroliniana Engelm.

CAROLINA HEMLOCK. From the S Appalachian mountains. Named and first cultivated in 1881; in commerce ≤1888. Common in cultivation. It does not transplant well. Needles bright green, ⅓"–¾" long. Cones 1"–1½" long, the scales elongate as on *T. heterophylla*. Records: to 140' tall at Linville Falls, NC (1974); 101' × 9'9" Linville Falls, NC (1966); 88' × 11'7" Burke County, NC (1972); 74' × 10'6" Tacoma, WA (1990).

T. caroliniana 'Arnold's Pyramid'

Originated as a seedling raised at the Arnold Arboretum. Named in 1949. Distributed in 1956. Exceedingly rare. Densely pyramidal shape, 25' tall, 15' wide when 32 years old.

T. caroliniana 'LaBar Weeping'

Discovered in North Carolina. Cultivated ≤1967. Essentially a groundcover it is so weeping. Very slow, dense.

T. diversifolia (Maxim.) Mast.

NORTHERN JAPANESE HEMLOCK. Japanese: *Kometsuga* (means RICE or WHITE HEMLOCK—from the gray-white needle undersides). From central and N Japan. Introduced to England in 1861 by J.G. Veitch. The 1868 Latin name *diversifolia* means diverse-leaved. Uncommon in North America. Most here are low bushy trees, often multitrunked. Many have been grown from rooted cuttings. Perhaps a shrubby garden race had originally been introduced. HEMLOCK expert C. Jenkins judged *T. diversifolia* far more interesting and ornamental than its darker peer *T. Sieboldii*. The first HEMLOCK to flush in spring. Flowers tiny but showy pale lavender (not yellowish-white and small as in *T. canadensis*). Needles plump, ¼"–⅝" long. Cones wide. Smaller, more colorful, and hardier than *T. Sieboldii*. Records: to 130' × 9'6" in Japan; 70' × 3'6" Leonardslee, Sussex, England (1979); 59' × 8'3" Abercairney Castle, Tayside, Scotland (1986); 34' × 3'3" × 30' Seattle, WA (1992); 30' × 3'3" Philadelphia, PA (1980).

T. heterophylla (Raf.) Sarg.
= *T. Albertiana* (A. Murr.) Sénécl.

WESTERN HEMLOCK. WEST COAST HEMLOCK. PACIFIC HEMLOCK. From S Alaska to N California west of the Cascade Mountains, and the N Rocky Mountains. Named in 1830 (Greek *heteros*, different or other,

and *phyllon*, a leaf). Introduced to cultivation in 1851 by J. Jeffrey to Britain. Rarely cultivated except somewhat in its native range, not because it lacks beauty, but because it is ill-adapted elsewhere. Needles ¼"–¾" long. Cones ¾"–1⅛" long. The largest HEMLOCK, a slender tower of lush, elegant beauty. It can live 800 years. Records: to 259' tall; 248' × 10'3" Vancouver Island, B.C. (1983); 241' × 22'6" Hoh River, WA (1988); 163' × 28'5" Enchanted Valley, WA (1993; top broken).

T. heterophylla 'Sixes River'

Found in the 1980s by Blue Diamond nursery of Winston, OR. Discovered in Oregon on a 75' tall tree which had one cascading limb. Introduced in 1985–86 by Mitsch nursery of Aurora, OR. Very unusual and quite pronounced curve at each joint. Growth fast.

T. Mertensiana (Bong.) Carr.
= *Hesperopeuce Mertensiana* (Bong.) Rydb.

MOUNTAIN HEMLOCK. ALPINE HEMLOCK. From mountains, S Alaska to central California. Named in 1832–33 after Karl Heinrich Mertens (1795–1830), German physician and naturalist, who discovered it at Sitka, Alaska in 1827. Introduced to British cultivation in 1851 by J. Jeffrey from Mt. Baker, WA, and in 1854 by Wm. Murray from Mt. Scott, B.C. Almost never cultivated in North America except sparingly in its native range, often from trees collected in the wild. Needles whorled around the twigs instead of more or less evenly parted into two ranks as the other species. Cones the largest of all, 1½"–3" long. Foliage varies from pure green to gray-blue, the pale ones sold as 'Glauca' sometimes. Grows slower in cultivation than *T. canadensis*, *T. caroliniana*, or *T. heterophylla*. Excellent as a dense, small tree for tight spaces or containers. A planted specimen seen 65' × 7'6" is outstandingly large. Wild trees attain great sizes only after centuries. Records: to 200' tall say E. Sheldon and T. Howell; 194' × 13'1" Olympic National Park, WA (1988); 113' × 23'3" Alpine County, CA (1972)

T. Sieboldii Carr.

SOUTHERN JAPANESE HEMLOCK. From S Japan (where called *Tsuga* or *Toga*), and Korea. Introduced to the West ca. 1850 when sent to Holland by Philipp Franz Balthasar von Siebold (1796–1866), well known early authority on Japanese plants. Slightly more common in North American cultivation than its peer *T. diversifolia*. Twigs shiny and hairless. Needles broad and blunt, ⅓"–1" long. Cones ¾"–1¼" long. Foliage and bark dark. It thrives in the Piedmont unlike *T. caroliniana* or *T. canadensis*.The last HEM-LOCK to flush in spring. Grows faster than *T. diversifolia*. Still, usually very slow and often shrubby. Records: 130' × 12'0" in Japan; 75½' × 4'1" Culzean Castle, Strathclyde, Scotland (1989); 65½' × 8'11" Ochtertyre, Tayside, Scotland (1989); 50' × 7'5" Philadelphia, PA (1980).

Tumion californicum—see *Torreya californica*

Ulmus

[ULMACEÆ; Elm Family] 18–45 spp. of deciduous trees called ELMS. All from the temperate northern hemisphere. Fine foliaged trees valued for shade and handsome form. *Ulmus* is the ancient Latin name. ELM flowers are tiny and give rise to papery winged seeds; mostly they appear before the trees leaf out in spring, but 3 species flower and seed in autumn. The leaves are lopsided, veiny, sharply toothed, and short-stemmed. Fall color is normally yellow. Dutch Elm Disease (DED) is caused by the fungus *Ceratocytis ulmi* (a.k.a. *Ophiostoma ulmi*), and has killed millions of trees. It orginated in Belgium, ca. 1900–1905, but received its name since it was first studied by Dutch scientists. In the early 1900s, seedling ELMS were planted extensively, especially as street trees. Since the 1930s, DED has devastated our ELMS, so in the 1980s and '90s emphasis is on planting clonal hybrids or cultivars of *U. parvifolia* and other disease-resistant ELMS. ELM classification and identification is difficult. Clonal identification of landscape ELMS is very chancy now, and will grow virtually impossible as more selections are planted. For some European cultivars not yet in North American commerce, see the *Journal of Arboriculture* May 1995. Related genera include *Aphananthe*, *Celtis* (HACKBERRY), *Planera* (WATER ELM), and *Zelkova*.

U. Accolade™
= *U.* 'Morton'
(*U. japonica* × *U. Wilsoniana*)
Raised in 1924. Selected at the Morton Arboretum of Lisle, IL. Named in 1986. Introduced in the 1990s. Graceful vase-shaped habit. Vigorous. Resists DED,

elm leaf miner, elm leaf beetle. Leaves deep glossy green. Good yellow fall color.

U. alba—see U. americana

U. alata Michx.
WINGED ELM. CORK ELM. WAHOO. From the SE United States. Named in 1803, the Latin meaning winged. Very rarely cultivated. Twigs can be densely hairy or hairless, but are always hairy near the buds. Usually even the young twigs are corky, with two broad narrow wings. Leaves small, 1¼"–2½" (3¾") long; vein pairs 11–14; smooth or rough above, downy beneath. Dull yellow fall color. Winged seeds small (¼"–⅜") and hairy. Usually a small slender tree of no particular charm, and lacking the dignified grandeur of many ELMS. Records: 118' × 11'3" Torreya State Park, FL (1989); 114' × 11'0" × 112' Fanning Springs, FL (1983); 105' × 14'6" Madison County, AL (<1945); 97' × 15'5" Richmond County, NC (1991).

U. americana L.
= *U. alba* Raf.

WHITE ELM. AMERICAN (WHITE) ELM. GRAY ELM (from its bark; to distinguish it from RED ELM). SOFT ELM (refers to the wood). WATER ELM (it favors moist sites). From central and eastern North America. Very common, the greatest and most beloved of ELMS. Previously extensively planted. Variable in crown shape. The most celebrated of its varied silhouettes is vase-like, with fine weeping branch extremities. Leaves and twigs hairy or hairless. Leaves 3"–6" long. Leaf bases not especially lopsided for an ELM; often the two sides meet in close proximity. Leaf veins tend to be close, numerous and straight, in 13–18 pairs. Winged seeds small (⅜"–½"), fringed with fine hairs. Records: to 180' × 41'0" in old growth forests; 160' × 24'7" × 147' near Trigonia, TN (1951); 145' × 21'2" Wisconson (died 1968); 144' × 16'6" × 72' Congaree Swamp, SC (<1978); 125' × 23'8" × 122' Southampton County, VA (1985; died 1988); 97' × 30'3" × 147' Wethersfield, CT (1944; died 1950); 92' × 26'5" × 102' Center White Creek, NY (1974).

U. americana 'American Liberty'

= U. americana 'Libertas'

= U. 'Liberty'

Bred in 1968–70, its parentage largely U. americana. "A mixture of six clones with typical upright vase-shaped crowns and a high degree of resistance to DED." Introduced in 1983 by the University of Wisconsin, Madison.

U. americana 'Ascendens'

Described in 1930, based on a specimen 76' tall and 17' wide in Seneca Park of Rochester, NY. In commerce as late as 1958. Very columnar. Lateral branches quite small and fastigiate. Bark much less furrowed than usual. Leaves to 5½" × 3⅜", hairy both sides. Flowers not seen in 25 years of observing. Does not lose its upright habit (unlike U. americana 'Columnaris').

U. americana 'Augustine (Ascending)'

Selected in the 1920s at Normal, or Bloomington, IL. Heavily marketed from 1949 into the 1950s. Columnar form with ascending branches. Leaves large. Record: 62' × 5'3" × 30' Lisle, IL (1986; pl. 1948).

U. americana 'Aurea'

Found in Vermont and introduced in the late 1800s by F.L. Temple nursery of Cambridge, MA. Still in commerce in the early 1920s. Leaves yellow. The name U. americana var. aurea has been applied incorrectly to U. glabra 'Lutescens' also.

U. americana 'Beebe's Weeping'

= U. fulva 'Pendula'

From a tree found wild near Galena, IL, by Mr. E. Beebe. Described in 1889 by T. Meehan in Garden and Forest. Probably long extinct in commerce.

U. americana 'Brandon'—see U. americana 'Patmore'

U. americana 'Columnaris'

Discovered by J. Dunbar at Conesus Lake, Livingston County, NY. In commerce during the 1940s and '50s. When described by A. Rehder in 1921, the original was 65½' tall and 20' wide. Upright branches forming a rather wide columnar head, the top flattened, ending in many branches of nearly equal height. It tends with age to lose its distinctive upright habit. Leaves relatively broad, to 3" wide, scabrous above, softly hairy on the veins beneath; stem very short, <⅛". Record: 72' × 5'6" × 27' Lisle, IL (1986; pl. 1929).

U. americana 'DED-Free' PP 3108 (1972)

Patented by Wm. Flemer, III, of Princeton nursery of New Jersey. In commerce ≤1980 to a very limited extent. The name refers to its resistance to Dutch Elm Disease.

U. americana 'Delaware'—see U. 'Delaware #2'

U. americana 'Exhibition'—see U. americana 'Patmore'

U. americana 'Fastigiata'

Origin unknown. Whether this is a nursery name for any especially narrow colunar clone (such as one also called 'Fiorei' for example), or a group name, it doesn't seem to have any official published description. Records of trees so called: 92' × 7'7" × 45' Lisle, IL (1986; pl. 1926); 88' × 7'10" × 35' Tacoma, WA (1990).

U. americana 'Great Plains'

Selected by Mr. L.P. Wedge of Will nursery, Bismarck, ND. Introduced ≤1942. "An unusually handsome, grafted one for boulevard planting."

U. americana 'Hamburg'—see U. 'Hamburg'

U. americana 'Harbin'—see U. pumila 'Dropmore'

U. americana 'Independence' PP 6227 (1988)

A seedling of U. americana 'Moline' raised by Dr. E. Smalley at the University of Wisconsin. It is one of the several clones collectively known as 'American Liberty'. Vigorous. Resists DED.

U. americana 'Jackson'

Selected at Wichita, KS. In commerce ≤1994. Resists DED. Branching pattern suggests a WHITE OAK (Quercus alba).

U. americana 'Jefferson'—see U. 'Jefferson'

U. americana 'Kimley'

From a large finely pendulous specimen found near Oshawa, Ontario. Introduced ≤1957 by Sheridan nursery of Ontario.

U. americana 'Klehmii'

From a tree in Arlington Heights, IL, grafted by Charles Klehm. Introduced ≤1929 by Naperville nursery of Naperville, IL. Fine vase-shape.

U. americana 'Lake City'

Introduced ≤1938 (the year sold by Will nursery of Bismarck, ND). Commonly planted into the 1960s. Will says: "A hardy selection of fine shape, especially adapted to street planting where the trees must be uniform." Not columnar, but branching upright, forming a broad top. Leaves larger than those of *U. americana* 'Moline'.

U. americana 'Libertas'—see U. 'American Liberty'

U. americana 'Littleford'

Selected ca. 1915 at Hinsdale, IL. Likely named after nurseryman F.J. Littleford. First sold in 1927. Still in commerce until at least the late 1950s. Branching upright, crown rather narrowly vase-shaped. Leaves larger than usual. Record: 52' tall by 28' wide at Lisle, IL (1986; *pl.* 1943).

U. americana 'Minneapolis Park'

Selected by the parks department of Minneapolis, MN. In commerce ≤1958 and sold at least into the mid-'60s. Especially suited for boulevard planting.

U. americana 'Moline'

The original was planted in 1903 at Moline, IL. Propagated since 1916; in commerce ≤1928. Very common into the 1960s. The original died in 1962 from DED (it is highly susceptible). Crown narrow when young but when fully grown rather open, the main trunk upright but older branches horizontal and in time drooping. Very vigorous and fast. Leaves large, often 7" × 4".

U. americana 'Morden'

Selected in 1939 by Morden research station of Manitoba. Introduced ≤1948 by Patmore nursery of Brandon, Manitoba (see also 'Brandon' and 'Exhibition'). Sold into the 1950s, perhaps even early '60s. Tolerant of ice storms. Very hardy. Grows rapidly but is rather coarse.

U. americana 'Patmore'

= *U. americana* 'Brandon (Ascending)'
= *U. americana* 'Exhibition (Boulevard)'

Selected from seeds obtained near Brandon, Manitoba. Introduced ≤1952 by Patmore nursery of Brandon. Still in commerce. Upright narrow vase shape; branches densely covered with small twigs.

U. americana f. pendula (Ait.) Fern.

WEEPING AMERICAN ELM. Described in 1789 in England. More than one clone (e.g., 'Beebe's Weeping'); sold sparingly in the 1930s, likely much earlier also. Generally full-sized, vase shaped form with long and very slender branches strongly pendulous at their ends.

U. americana pendula SCAMPSTON WEEPING ELM—see U. glabra 'Scampstonensis'

U. americana 'Princeton'

Selected in 1922 by Princeton nursery of New Jersey. Still sold. Vigorous. Leaves large, leathery, resisting leaf beetle damage. Crown similar to that of *U. americana* 'Moline' but with a slightly more spreading top. Resists DED.

U. americana 'Queen City'

Selected ca. 1944 on Lake Shore Boulevard of Toronto, Ontario. Introduced ≤1949. Sold at least until 1958. Symmetrical, vase-shaped, dense. Bark relatively smooth.

U. americana 'Sheyenne'

D. Hoag wrote in 1965 that this clone was "enjoying widespread success" in the upper Midwest.

U. americana 'Urnii'—see U. americana 'Vase'

U. americana 'Vase'

= *U. americana* 'Urnii'
= *U. vaseyi* hort.

From ≤1921 through at least the late 1950s, these names, representing more than one clone, have been applied to "vase-shaped" specimens of *U. americana*. They were especially sold by Ohio nurseries.

U. americana 'Washington'

On July 3, 1775, General George Washington assumed command of the Continental Army, under this ELM, at Cambridge, MA. After the revolutionary war and Washington was elected first president, the tree became popular. The original died in 1923 but scions have been distributed and sold widely. There is nothing intrinsically remarkable about this clone; sentimental value alone justifies it. (Note, nurseries also sometimes sell *U.* 'Washington' as *U. americana* 'Washington'.)

U. angustifolia var. cornubiensis—see U. minor var. cornubiensis

U. asplenifolia—see U. glabra 'Crispa'

U. 'Bea Schwarz'—see *U.* × *hollandica* 'Bea Schwarz'

U. 'Belgica'—see *U.* × *hollandica* 'Belgica'

U. 'Boulevard'—see *U.* 'Rosehill'

U. 'Buisman'—see *U.* × *hollandica* 'Christine Buisman'

U. 'Camperdownii'—see *U. glabra* 'Camperdownii'

U. campestris—see *U. glabra* and *U. minor* var. *vulgaris*

U. campestris var. *aurea*—see *U. glabra* 'Lutescens'

U. campestris clemmeri—see *U.* × *hollandica* 'Klemmer'

U. campestris var. *concavifolia*—see *U.* × *hollandica* 'Webbiana'

U. campestris var. *cornubiensis*—see *U. minor* var. *cornubiensis*

U. campestris 'Foliis Variegatis'—see *U. minor* 'Argenteo-variegata'

U. campestris Klemmeri—see *U.* × *hollandica* 'Klemmer'

U. campestris var. *latifolia*—see *U.* × *hollandica* 'Hollandica'

U. campestris var. *major*—see *U.* × *hollandica* 'Hollandica'

U. campestris marmorata—see *U. minor* 'Variegata'

U. campestris monumentalis—see *U. minor* var. *sarniensis*

U. campestris 'Purpurea'—see *U.* 'Purpurea'

U. campestris var. *stricta*—see *U. minor* var. *cornubiensis*

U. campestris var. *umbraculifera*—see *U. minor* 'Umbraculifera'

U. campestris vegeta—see *U.* × *hollandica* 'Vegeta'

U. campestris Wheatleyi—see *U. minor* var. *sarniensis*

U. carpinifolia—see *U. minor*

U. carpinifolia 'Christine Buisman'—see *U.* × *hollandica* 'Ch. B.'

U. carpinifolia var. *cornubiensis*—see *U. minor* var. *cornubiensis*

U. carpinifolia 'Dampieri'—see *U.* × *hollandica* 'Dampieri'

U. carpinifolia 'Gracilis'—see *U. minor* 'Gracilis'

U. carpinifolia f. *sarniensis*—see *U. minor* var. *sarniensis*

U. carpinifolia var. *umbraculifera*—see *U. minor* 'Umbraculifera'

U. carpinifolia 'Variegata'—see *U. minor* 'Variegata'

U. carpinifolia 'Webbiana'—see *U.* × *hollandica* 'Webbiana'

U. carpinifolia 'Wredei'—see *U.* × *hollandica* 'Wredei'

U. 'Cathedral' PP 8683 (1994)
(*U. japonica* × *U. pumila*)
Originated by the University of Wisconsin. In commerce ≤1991. Of the same parentage as *U.* 'New Horizon' but not as hardy. Good DED resistance. Excellent tolerance of verticillium wilt disease. Resists elm leaf miner.

U. 'Charisma'
(*U.* Accolade™ × *U.* 'Vanguard')
Named in 1994 at the Morton Arboretum of Lisle, IL. Foliage notably deep glossy green.

U. chinensis—see *U. parvifolia*

U. 'Christine Buisman'—see *U.* × *hollandica* 'Christine Buisman'

U. 'Commelin'—see *U.* × *hollandica* 'Commelin'

U. 'Coolshade'
(*U. rubra* × *U. pumila*)
Originated in 1946 at Sarcoxie nursery of Missouri.

Introduced ≤1951. Growth rapid yet stocky and compact, resisting breakage from ice. Foliage dark green. See also *U.* 'Improved Coolshade'.

U. cornubiensis—see *U. minor* var. *cornubiensis*

U. crassifolia Nutt.
CEDAR ELM. BASKET ELM. SOUTHERN ROCK ELM. RED ELM. From the south-central U.S. and extreme NE Mexico. Named in 1837 (Latin *crasse*, thick, and *folium*, a leaf). Cultivated since 1876, but sparingly and almost wholly within its native range. Leaves small, very rough, sandpaper-textured above, rough-hairy below, 1"–2" (to 2¼" × 1⅛" but usually <1½" × ¾"); stem ¼"–½" long; vein pairs (8) 9–11. Twigs hairy, can be corky. Golden-yellow fall color, or evergreen in far south Texas. The least cold-hardy native ELM. Flowers and seeds (hairy) appear in autumn. Records: 118' × 8'6" Silver River, FL (1986); 94' × 15'11" Bryan, TX (1969); 82' × 11'4" × 85' Catahoula Parish, LA (1984).

U. crenata—see *Zelkova carpinifolia*

U. 'Dampieri'—see *U.* × *hollandica* 'Dampieri'

U. Dampieri aurea—see *U.* × *hollandica* 'Wredei'

U. 'Danada'
(*U. japonica* × *U. Wilsoniana*)
Originated in 1924 at the Morton Arboretum of Lisle, IL. Named for Dan and Ada Rice, namesakes of the Danada Forest Preserve near the arboretum. Introduced in 1994. Habit graceful. Young leaves red-tinted. Resists DED.

U. Davidiana Planch.
From NE Asia. Named in 1872 after Jesuit naturalist Jean Pierre Armand David (1826–1900). Extremely rare in cultivation. Much confused with *U. japonica*. Seeds hairy in the center; *U. japonica* has hairless seeds. Twigs can be corky-winged. Leaves to 4" long. Tolerates alkaline soils. Recorded to 90' tall.

U. Davidiana var. *japonica*—see *U. japonica*

U. 'Delaware #1'—see *U.* 'Urban'

U. 'Delaware #2'
= *U. americana* 'Delaware'
Originated in 1940 in North Dakota. Released in the early 1980s by the USDA research station of Delaware, OH. In commerce ≤1985–86. An *U. americana* hybrid. Highly resists DED.

U. densa—see *U. minor* 'Umbraculifera'

U. Dippeliana f. *Dampieri*—see *U.* × *hollandica* 'Dampieri'

U. effusa—see *U. lævis*

U. foliacea—see *U. minor*

U. foliacea 'Dovæi'—see *U. glabra* 'Dovæi'

U. foliacea 'Monumentalis'—see *U. minor* var. *sarniensis*

U. foliacea var. *stricta*—see *U. minor* var. *cornubiensis*

U. foliacea var. *umbraculifera*—see *U. minor* 'Umbraculifera'

U. foliacea 'Variegata'—see *U. minor* 'Variegata'

U. foliacea var. *Wheatleyi*—see *U. minor* var. *sarniensis*

U. foliacea 'Wredei'—see *U.* × *hollandica* 'Wredei'

U. 'Fremont'—see *U.* 'Hamburg Hybrid'

U. 'Frontier'
(*U. minor* × *U. parvifolia*)
Hybridized in 1971 by the USDA research station of Delaware, OH. Had not flowered as of February 1990, when released to nurseries. Tolerant of Elm Yellows and DED. Leaves average 2⅛" × 1¼". Red-purple fall color.

U. fulva—see *U. rubra*

U. fulva 'Pendula'—see *U. americana* 'Beebe's Weeping'

U. glabra Huds.
= *U. scabra* Mill.
= *U. montana* Stokes
= *U. campestris* L. (in part)
WYCH ELM. SCOTCH ELM. MOUNTAIN ELM. BROAD LEAVED ELM. From Europe, N and W Asia. Uncommon in North America. WYCH is likely akin to Old English *wican*, to yield or bend, in reference to the pliant branches of this or any of several other trees.

The 1762 name *glabra* (smooth) refers to the bark. Leaves 3"–7" long, usually rough above, some are completely smooth; vein pairs (10) 13–18 (21); very short-stemmed. Winged seeds (⅝") ¾"–1". Rarely suckers; twigs never corky. A massive domed tree. Records: 164' tall in Bargas, Cantabria, Spain, (≤1988); 134½' × 12'4" Castle Howard, Yorkshire, England (1985); 120' × 16'0" Sacramento, CA (1982); 111' × 14'5" Tacoma, WA (1987); 92' × 22'4" Brahan House, Scotland (1982); 88' × 19'7" × 99' Riverside, CT (1988); a trunk 25'0" around at Monks Eleigh, Suffolk, England (<1964).

U. glabra 'Asplenifolia'—see U. glabra 'Crispa'

U. glabra 'Atropurpurea'
≠ *U.* 'Purpurea'

Known since 1881 in Germany. In commerce there since ≤1887. Exceedingly rare in North America. Leaves dark purple.

U. glabra 'Bea Schwarz'—see U. × hollandica 'Bea Schwarz'

U. glabra 'Camperdownii'
= *U.* × *vegeta* 'Camperdownii'
= *U.* 'Camperdownii'

CAMPERDOWN ELM. UPSIDE DOWN ELM. UMBRELLA ELM. Originated <1850 at Camperdown House, 3 miles NW of Dundee, Scotland. Described officially in 1864. In North American commerce since the 1870s. Common. A strongly weeping tree grown as a topgraft. Branching tortuous, rootlike, slowly increasing in height as the zigzag twigs form a densely leafy bower. Leaves large, to 8" × 6½" but usually ca. 6¾" × 4½" with 13–17 vein pairs; harshly hairy; abruptly short pointed from the "broad shoulders." Winged seeds conspicuous pale green before drying pale tan; to 1" long. Records: 30' × 6'4" London, England (1967); 28' × 8'1" × 33' St.-André-de-Kamouraska, Québec (<1994); 24' × 8'8" × 42' Corvallis, OR (1989); 24' × 7'7" × 32' Wilmot, WI (1963); 23' × 8'5" × 35' Ottawa, Ontario (1975); 21' × 6'9" × 35' Puyallup, WA (1993); a trunk 9'9" around in Monroe, WI (1971).

U. glabra 'Cornuta'
= *U. tridens* Hartig
= *U. montana* var. *laciniata* hort., non Trautv.

HORNED ELM. Originated ca. 1835 in France. Exceedingly rare in North America. At least the larger leaves bear 3 or 5 long projections or lobes, forming a broad and "armed" apex (in Latin, *cornuta* means horned). Leaves particularly harsh above, very hairy beneath; vein pairs 17–20. Twigs in autumn red-brown, rough with short hairs. Compare *U. glabra* var. *laciniata*.

U. glabra 'Crispa'
= *U. asplenifolia* hort.
= *U. glabra* 'Asplenifolia' hort. *ex* Rehd.
= *U. glabra* 'Urticifolia'

FERNLEAF ELM. Known <1800 in Europe. Exceedingly rare in North America. Leaves narrow, with incised, twisted and incurved teeth. Growth slow.

U. glabra 'Dovæi'
= *U. montana* 'Dovæi'
= *U. foliacea* 'Dovæi'
('Dovei')

Introduced in 1868 by A. Leroy of France. Sold from ≤1907 to at least as late as 1939 in North America. Vigorous. Well-shaped upright habit. Suited for avenues. Bark smooth. Leaves large.

U. glabra 'Exoniensis'
= *U. montana* var. *fastigiata* Loud.
= *U. glabra* var. *fastigiata* hort., non Kirchn.
= *U. glabra* 'Pyramidalis'
= *U. glabra* 'Fordii'

EXETER ELM. FORD'S ELM. Propagated <1826 by nurseryman William Ford (1760–1829), of Exeter, England. Branching fastigiate and twiggy; very dense. Much planted in Europe; DED-resistant. Leaves very harsh and dark, smaller than usual, ca. 4" long; 11–13 vein pairs. Some leaves are twisted and do not open fully, enfolding one side of the shoot. Record: 72' × 11'10" Preston Hall, Lothian, Scotland (1987).

U. glabra var. fastigiata—see U. glabra 'Exoniensis'

U. glabra 'Fordii'—see U. glabra 'Exoniensis'

U. glabra 'Horizontalis'
= *U. glabra* 'Pendula'
= *U. montana* var. *pendula* Loud., non hort.

WEEPING WYCH ELM. TABLETOP ELM. HORIZONTAL ELM. SPREADING ELM. Discovered ca. 1816 in Perth nursery of Scotland. Very rare in North America.

Branches stiffly splaying and drooping, herring-bone pattern, making an erratic spreading crown, partly pendulous. Either trained up on its own roots, or topgrafted. Leaves average ca. 5¾" × 4" with 12–14 vein pairs, smooth and essentially hairless. The only specimen known to the writer has never flowered or set seeds, unlike the 'Camperdown' cultivar that does so yearly. Records: 65½' × 4'1" Gray House, Tayside, Scotland (1986); 52½' × 7'9" Geneva, Switzerland (≤1967); 42' × 7'10" Cambridge, East Anglia, England (1973); 39' × 9'8" Bath, Avon, England (1984); 21' × 5'4" × 30' Philadelphia, PA (1980); 44' × 8'8" × 66' Christchurch, New Zealand (1970).

U. glabra var. laciniata Trautv.

= *U. laciniata* (Trautv.) Mayr

MANCHURIAN ELM (also applied to *U. pumila*). From NE Asia—far from the typical *U. glabra* population. Named in 1859. Introduced to cultivation in 1900. Very rare; a tree more freakishly intriguing than ornamental. Leaves horridly rough-hairy, 3"–7" long, widest near the apex, with 3–5 jagged lobes; very unequal at the base; vein pairs 12–13. Usually a shrub or slender small tree, 30'–50' tall, at most 80' × 9'0". Twigs sparingly hairy when young; pale yellowish-brown or gray-brown in autumn. Compare *U. glabra* 'Cornuta'.

U. glabra 'Lutescens'

= *U. montana* 'Lutescens'
= *U. scabra* var. *lutescens* Dipp.
= *U. americana* var. *aurea* hort. (in part)
?= *U. campestris* var. *aurea* hort.

GOLDEN WYCH ELM. Originated in Germany ca. 1885. Described in 1892. Exceedingly rare in North America; least so in Canada. Promoted since ≤1992 by Duncan & Davies nursery of New Zealand. Usually has a short-boled, broad bushy crown. Foliage golden, especially in spring. Sometimes sold incorrectly as *U. procera* 'Louis van Houtte' (not in this volume; a cultivar with a much smaller leaf). Records: 101' × 8'0" Munches, Dumfries, Scotland (1985); 43' × 8'0" × 56' Vancouver, B.C. (1992).

U. glabra 'Pendula'—see U. glabra 'Horizontalis'

U. glabra 'Purpurea'—see U. 'Purpurea'

U. glabra 'Pyramidalis'—see U. glabra 'Exoniensis'

U. glabra 'Scampstonensis'

= *U. scampstoniensis* hort. *ex* Steud.
= *U. americana pendula* SCAMPSTON WEEPING ELM

SCAMPSTON ELM. Originated <1810 at Scampston Hall, Yorkshire, England. Probably a hybrid. Possibly in part a commercial synonym of *U. glabra* 'Camperdownii'. Popular in British and American commerce in the 1870s. Long out of commerce. A topgrafted weeping tree.

U. glabra 'Urticifolia'—see U. glabra 'Crispa'

U. glabra 'Superba'—see U. × hollandica 'Superba'

U. Green King®

= *U. pumila* Green King®
= *U. pumila* 'Neosho'
= *U. pumila* "Broadleaf Hybrid"
= *U. pumila* "Field's New Hybrid Elm"

Discovered as a sport in 1938–39 by Neosho nursery of Missouri. Renamed Green King® in 1960 by H. Field nursery of Shenandoah, IA. One can infer that it was sold as a cross between *U. americana* and *U. pumila*—but it may be *U. rubra* × *U. pumila*. Other prairie nurseries also sold trees of this reported parentage as early as 1940.

U. 'Groeneveld'—see U. × hollandica 'Groeneveld'

U. 'Hamburg'

= *U. 'Hamburg Hybrid'*
= *U. americana* 'Hamburg'
(*U. pumila* × *U. rubra* or *U. americana*)

Originated at Plumfield nursery of Fremont, NE. Selected ca. 1932. Introduced ≤1948 by Inter-State nursery of Hamburg, IA. D. Hoag wrote in 1965 "it appears to be identical to trees introduced for trial as 'Fremont' and 'Rgeth' and there is a direct possibility that one hybrid is masquerading under the three names."

U. 'Hollandica'—see U. × hollandica 'Hollandica'

U. × hollandica Mill.

(*U. minor* × *U. glabra*)

HYBRID ELMS. DUTCH ELMS. From Europe. Named in 1768, by an Englishman: the trees were well known in Holland. Distinguishing the following cultivars is often difficult, since so many original descriptions were vague, and so many collections of labeled specimens were killed by DED. Likely some of the 17 cultivars cited below have parentage other than *U. minor* × *U. glabra*. Usually hybrids look intermediate between *U. minor* (SMOOTHLEAF ELM) and *U. glabra* (WYCH ELM). Sometimes they resemble one of the parents. They have hairless or sparsely hairy twigs; the leaf undersides have inconspicuous to moderately obvious hair tufts, and the vein pairs number (13) 14–17 (21). The highly variable *U. minor*, in contrast, has hairless or very hairy twigs; the leaf undersides have moderately obvious to quite showy hair tufts, and the vein pairs number (9) 12–14 (17). Usually the hybrid leaves are larger (often 3"–5") and have more teeth (*U. minor* has <110 teeth) as well. On a practical level, the hybrids are bolder looking, sucker less, and tend to grow larger.

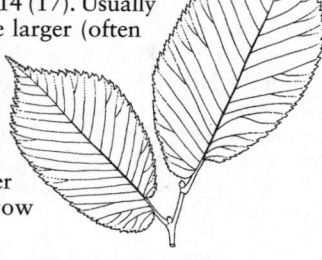

U. × *hollandica* 'Bea Schwarz'
= *U.* 'Bea Schwarz'
= *U. glabra* 'Bea Schwarz'

Selected ca. 1945 in the Baarn research station of Holland by Dr. J.C. Went of the Dutch Elm Committee. Named after Marie Beatrice Schwarz, a Dutch botanist who studied DED. Described and released in 1948. Never became popular; of poor form, slow growth.

U. × *hollandica* 'Belgica'
= *U.* 'Belgica'
= *U. montana* var. *hollandica* Huberty
?= *U. latifolia* hort.
?= *U.* × *hollandica* 'Latifolia'

BELGIUM ELM. BELGIAN ELM. HOLLAND ELM. The "DUTCH" ELM of the Netherlands (*Hollandse Iep*), not of England. Originated in 1694 in Belgium. In North American commerce ≤1893, and until at least 1948. Strongly resembles *U. glabra* (WYCH ELM) but young shoots more slender and become hairless by fall, leaves narrower. Tree massive, to 120' × 13'0"; straight-trunked; broad-crowned. Bark rough. Leaves 3"–6" long; 14–18 vein pairs; rough above, softly hairy beneath; stem <¼" long. Very DED-susceptible.

U. × *hollandica* 'Christine Buisman'
= *U. procera* 'Christine Buisman'
= *U. carpinifolia* 'Christine Buisman'
= *U. minor* 'Christine Buisman'
= *U.* 'Christine Buisman'

= *U.* 'Buisman'

Selected for disease resistance at the Willie Commelin Scholten Laboratory at Baarn research station of Holland. From an ELM population raised from seed collected in 1928 in Madrid, Spain. Released to nurseries in 1937. Imported to North America in 1938; commonly sold in the 1950s and '60s; still in commerce. Named after Christina J. Buisman (d. 1937), Dutch plant pathologist who studied DED. It has a spreading habit with pendulous lateral branches. Accounts vary as to its susceptibility to coral-spot fungus (*Nectria cinnabarina*). Leaves 2"–3" long, the base very oblique; hair tufts in vein intersections beneath. Some say this clone has undesirable bushy growth and shape, and is susceptible to cold injury. Recorded to 90' tall.

U. × *hollandica* 'Commelin'
= *U.* 'Commelin'

Hybridized in 1940–41 at a genetics lab at Wageningen, Holland; selected at Baarn research station. Described in 1959. Released in 1961. Named after pioneer Dutch botanists Jan (1629–1692) and his nephew Caspar (1667–1731) Commelin (Commelijn). Although resistant to the original strain of DED, it falls prey to a more aggressive strain of the late 1960s. Similar to *U.* × *hollandica* 'Vegeta' but narrower-crowned, with darker gray branches, duller and brown branchlets, smaller leaves (to 4") with fewer veins (9–12 pairs), and short-hairy undersides.

U. × *hollandica* 'Dampieri'
= *U. Dippeliana* f. *Dampieri* (Kirchn.) Schneid.
= *U. minor* 'Dampieri'
= *U.* 'Dampieri'
= *U. carpinifolia* 'Dampieri'

Originated in Belgium. Described in 1863. Extremely rare in North America; sold until the late 1940s. Medium-sized and narrow-pyramidal, broadening slightly in age. Twigs short, slender, hairless. Leaves crowded on short branchlets, bright green, firm, only slightly lopsided at the base, to 2½" long, short-stemmed, almost hairless on both sides except tufts of hairs beneath; margins deeply toothed and wrinkled. Resists DED.

U. × *hollandica* 'Dampieri Aurea'—see *U.* × *hollandica* 'Wredei'

U. × *hollandica* 'Dauvessei'

Originated <1877 and likely named after D. Dauvesse's nursery in France. Branches ascend to form a broadly pyramidal or conical crown. Shoots more or less hairy. Leaves rarely more than 4" × 2¼" (to 5" long); base very lopsided; softly hairy beneath; stem to ¼" long. Seed near apex of wing.

U. × hollandica 'Dumont(ii)'

DUMONT ELM. Discovered by a gardener ca. 1865 on the estate of M. Dumont at Tournay, Belgium. Described in 1892 in France. Sold as late as 1931 in North America; exceedingly rare here. Very similar to U. × hollandica 'Belgica' but much narrower, regular pyramidal crown; branches ascending. Very vigorous; trunk straight. Leaves also smaller.

U. × hollandica 'Groeneveld'

= U. 'Groeneveld'
('Groeneveldt')

Selected for DED-resistance at the Bosbouw research station of Holland. One parent was the same seedling of SMOOTHLEAF ELM which was used in the production of U. × hollandica 'Christine Buisman'; the other was a WYCH ELM clone. Released in 1963. Still in North American commerce. Resembles U. × hollandica 'Commelin' but with a tighter upright habit, slower growing and shorter. Crown dark, dense, narrowly oval, well and regularly branched. Very DED-resistant. Not for wet soil. Thought likely to grow ca. 50' tall.

U. × hollandica 'Hollandica'

= U. major Sm.
= U. × hollandica 'Major'
= U. 'Hollandica'
= U. montana var. gigantea hort.
= U. campestris var. latifolia hort.
= U. campestris var. major (Sm.) Planch.

The "DUTCH" ELM of England, not the Netherlands. Originated ca. 1680. The name DUTCH ELM derives from a tradition that the tree was introduced to England from the Netherlands about the time of the accession of William III (1689). In the Netherlands, however, it is regarded as Engelse Iep, ENGLISH ELM. The name Ulmus major dates from 1814. North American nurseries have distributed this under various names; it has been confused with U. × hollandica 'Belgica' and ENGLISH ELM (U. minor var. vulgaris). Silhouette is distinctive amongst ELMS in being open and scraggy. Trunk short and stout. Bark shallowly fissured, finely flaky and red-brown. The main branches are crooked or sinuous, and often pendulous at the ends. From a distance it can be confused with an OAK (Quercus). Twigs and root suckers often corky-winged. Leaves relatively broad, and in trimmed hedges can be confused with ENGLISH ELM but usually differ in

having over 120 marginal teeth. Young shoots slightly hairy. Leaves 2½"–6" long, one side cordate at the base and developed farther down the stem than the other side, which is tapered. Upper side dark shiny green, hairless or nearly so; underside bright green, with hair tufts; 10–15 vein pairs; stem ¼"–⅜" long. Winged seed ¾"–1" long; seed near the notch. Recorded to 120' × 18'10.

U. × hollandica 'Klemmer'

= U. campestris clemmeri hort.
= U. campestris Klemmeri hort.

KLEMMER ELM. From Belgium. Cultivated <1877. Described in 1891. In North American commerce until the late 1940s. Tall, narrowly conical with ascending branches. Relatively smooth-barked. Young shoots hairy. Leaves 2"–4" long; stem to ⅜" long; margins somewhat crinkled; hairless yet rough above, finely hairy beneath; ca. 12 vein pairs. Seed near notch of wing.

U. × hollandica 'Latifolia'—see U. × hollandica 'Belgica'

U. × hollandica 'Major'—see U. × hollandica 'Hollandica'

U. × hollandica 'Pendula'—see U. × hollandica 'Smithii'

U. × hollandica 'Pioneer'

= U. 'Pioneer'

Hybridized in 1971 by the USDA research station of Delaware, OH. Released in 1983. Common. Leaves average 4⅕" × 2¼". Crown densely round-oval. Fast and vigorous. High resistance to DED.

U. × hollandica 'Pitteursii'

= U. scabra var. macrophylla hort.

Discovered <1848 on the Pitteurs estate in St. Troud (St. Truiden), Belgium. Extremely rare in North America. Tree vigorous—one season's growth in the nursery can be 6'–9' long. Leaves very large, 5"–8" long, rough and hairy; convex. Crown broadly oval.

U. × hollandica 'Purpurascens'—see U. 'Purpurea'

U. × hollandica 'Smithii'

= U. × hollandica 'Pendula'
= U. 'Smithii'
= U. montana var. pendula hort., non Loud.
= U. pendula W. Masters 1831, non Willd. 1811

DOWNTON ELM. Raised in 1810 at Smith's nursery of

Worcester, England. From Nottinghamshire seeds. Mr. Knight of Downton Castle purchased some of the seedlings, and one turned out to weep. Described in 1831. Known only in Europe; likely introduced to North America at some time. Small tree. Branches ascending at first, shoots elegantly pendulous. Young shoots more or less hairy, becoming corky. Leaves tough, elliptic, to 3½" long; very unequal at the base, shiny, smooth and hairless above, sparsely hairy beneath; coarsely double-toothed; 14–16 vein pairs; stem ⅓" (W.J. Bean says ¾") long. Winged seed ¾"; the seed above the middle.

U. × *hollandica* 'Superba'

= U. *præstans* Schoch *ex* Beterams
= U. *glabra* 'Superba'
= U. *montana superba* hort.

BLANDFORD ELM. Apparently raised in England in the early 1800s, either by Masters nursery of Canterbury, or by Gill of Blandford. But described in 1848 in Belgium. In North American nurseries between at least 1910 and 1931. Narrowly conical form. Bark smooth and grayish. Young shoots hairless, somewhat glossy, gray-brown. Leaves 3"–5" long; base very lopsided; hairless and smooth above, with small hair tufts beneath; 15–18 vein pairs; stem to ⅜" long. Winged seed ⅝"–¾", the seed nearly in the middle.

U. × *hollandica* 'Vegeta'

= U. × *vegeta* (Loud.) Lindl.
= U. *Huntingdoni* hort.
= U. *campestris vegeta* hort.
= U. 'Vegeta'

HUNTINGDON ELM. CHICHESTER ELM (without justification, according to M. Hadfield). Raised ca. 1750 from seed of an *U. minor* near an *U. glabra* in Hinchingbrook Park, Cambridgeshire, England, by the nurserymen Ingram & Wood, at Brampton, a few miles south-west of Huntingdon. Named *vegeta* in 1823 (Latin meaning thriving or vigorous). To judge from its presence in nursery catalogs this has been the most common older *hollandica* clone sold in North America. Tall, with a short trunk, usually forked; open-crowned, main branches erect, later more outspread and nodding. Root suckers few, not corky. Bark rough. Twigs hairless or only slightly hairy, olive-green and somewhat glossy. Leaves light green, 3"–6" long; doubly and sharply toothed; base very lopsided; smooth and hairless above, with obvious hair tufts beneath; (12) 14–18 vein pairs; stem to ⅓" long. Winged seed to 1" long, the seed in upper half of wing. Fairly fertile; seedlings have been sold as

HUNTINGDON ELMS. Records: 143' × 28'3" Oxford, England (<1911; W.J. Bean says this almost certainly antedated the true HUNTINGDON ELM, but was very similar); 110' × 15'10" and 93' × 17'7" Bressingham, East Anglia, England (1973).

U. × *hollandica* 'Webbiana'

= U. *minor* 'Webbiana'
= U. *carpinifolia* 'Webbiana'
?= U. *campestris* var. *concavifolia* hort. *ex* Loud.

Origin cloudy. If 'Webbiana' is the same as *U. campestris* var. *concavifolia* it originated <1838; otherwise it was raised shortly before 1869, when Simon-Louis nursery of France offered it. Introduced to North America ≤1899; extremely rare here. Said to be like CORNISH ELM (i.e., a very narrow-crowned tree), but with leaves folded longitudinally. Leaves to 3" long; roughish above, folded lengthwise.

U. × *hollandica* 'Wredei'

= U. × *hollandica* 'Dampieri Aurea'
= U. *Dampieri aurea* hort.
= U. *minor* 'Wredei'
= U. *foliacea* 'Wredei'
= U. *carpinifolia* 'Wredei'

GOLDEN ELM. WREDE ELM. Raised as a sport of *U. × hollandica* 'Dampieri' ca. 1875 by Inspector Wrede at Alt-Geltow, near Potsdam, Germany. In North American commerce ≤1910 and still sold as of 1991. DED-resistant. Narrowly pyramidal crown; to 60' tall. Small, wide, shiny, bright golden leaves.

U. 'Homestead'

U. *pumila* × [(U. *hollandica* 'Vegeta' × U. *minor*) × (U. *pumila* var. *pinnato-ramosa* × U. *minor* 'Hoersholmiensis')]

Hybridized in 1970 by the USDA research station of Delaware, OH. Released in 1983. Common. Leaves average 2¾" × 1⅓"; coated with close fine hairs beneath; 13–17 vein pairs; fall color late, straw yellow. Very rapid growth. Densely pyramidal. Highly resists DED.

U. *Huntingdoni*—see U. × *hollandica* 'Vegeta'

U. 'Improved Coolshade' PP 1747 (1958)

(U. *pumila* × U. *rubra*)
= U. 'Primus'

Originated at Sarcoxie nursery of Missouri. Replaced their *U.* 'Coolshade'. Fast, breakage-resistant growth.

U. 'Independence'—see U. *americana* 'Independence'

U. 'Jacan'—see *U. japonica* 'Jacan'

U. japonica (Rehd.) Sarg. 1907, non Sieb. 1830

= *U. Davidiana* var. *japonica* (Rehd.) Nakai
= *U. pumila* var. *suberosa* Turcz.

JAPANESE ELM. From NE Asia and Japan. Introduced to the West in 1895 when seeds were sent to the Arnold Arboretum from Sapporo, Japan. In commerce ≤1931. Rare. High DED-resistance. Tolerates alkaline soils. Its broad-crowned habit can resemble *U. americana*. Twigs can be corky, can be hairy. Leaves rough, at length can be smooth and glossy above; 3"–5" long; stem <¼" long; 7–13 (16) vein pairs. Fall color gold or russet. Winged seed hairless, to ¾" long. Records: to 110' × 19'8" in the wild; 83' × 11'4" × 68' Amherst, MA (1983).

U. japonica 'Discovery'

Raised from seeds collected at Morden research station of Manitoba. Selected in 1985. Registered in 1994 by Prairie Shade nursery of Portage La Prairie, Manitoba. Habit distinctly upright, compact vase-shaped.

U. japonica 'Jacan'

= *U.* 'Jacan'

Released and registered in 1977–78. Selected by Morden research station of Manitoba. Vase-shaped, DED-tolerant; to 50' tall.

U. japonica 'Mitsui Centennial'

Raised at Morden research Station of Manitoba; selected in 1976; named and introduced in 1980–81 to mark the centennial of Mitsui nursery of Japan. More common in Canada than the U.S. Fast growing. Exceptionally cold-hardy. Resists DED.

U. 'Jefferson'

= *U. americana* 'Jefferson'

Selected by Dr. H.V. Webster, plant physiologist with the U.S. National Park Service. Named in 1993. Parentage unknown, except partly *U. americana*. DED resistant.

U. 'Kansas'

= *U.* 'Kansas Hybrid'

Introduced ≤1961 by Kansas nursery of Salina, KS. Commercially extinct. A seedling of a *U. pumila*, showing hybrid vigor; raised in the late 1930s. Habit upright. Leaves dark, large and shiny. Growth rapid; drought- and cold-hardy.

U. Keaki—see *Zelkova serrata*

U. laciniata—see *U. glabra* var. *laciniata*

U. lævis Pall.

= *U. pedunculata* Fouq.
= *U. effusa* Willd.

EUROPEAN WHITE ELM (comparing it to its close cousin AMERICAN WHITE ELM, *U. americana*). FLUTTERING ELM (long-stalked flowers flutter in the breeze). HUNGARIAN ELM. RUSSIAN ELM. SPREADING ELM. From central and SE Europe to W Asia. Named *lævis* (Latin for smooth) in 1784. Cultivated since 1800 in Germany. Virtually never listed by North American nurseries, unless it has traveled under incorrect names. Common in Washington cities. Twigs persistently hairy. Leaves softly hairy beneath, mildly rough above, broad and abruptly pointed, to 4¼" × 2⅝"; 12–16 vein pairs; stem ≤ ¼" (in Russia, twigs can be hairless, leaves can be less fuzzy below, to 5" × 3½"; up to 18 vein pairs). Winged seeds almost identical to those of *U. americana*, but rounder, less oval. A tall densely leafy tree with a fluted trunk often with burls of short sprouts. Although of commanding size and delicate foliage texture, its branching pattern is too plain to excite the admiration afforded some more distinctive species. Insects which skeletonize other ELM leaves in Seattle ignore those of this species. Records: 113' × 10'7" × 55' Spokane, WA (1988); 87' × 15'8" × 86' Fall City, WA (1992; *pl.* 1920); 84' × 11'7" × 101' Everett, WA (1988); a trunk 23'0" around at Role (Koszalin), Poland (≤1973).

U. latifolia—see *U.* × *hollandica* 'Belgica'

U. 'Liberty'—see *U. americana* 'American Liberty'

U. 'Lincoln' PP 5015 (1983)

(*U. pumila* × *U. rubra*)

Selected ca. 1958. Patented by Samuel E. Clegg of Plainfield, IL. Tree features horizontal branching with a central leader, glossy foliage, and substantial DED-resistance.

U. major—see *U.* × *hollandica* 'Hollandica'

U. minor Mill., s.l.
= *U. carpinifolia* Gledit.
= *U. foliacea* Gilib.
= *U. nitens* Moench

SMOOTHLEAF ELM. EUROPEAN FIELD ELM. NARROWLEAF ELM. SMOOTH ELM. FEATHERED ELM. From Europe, N Africa, SW Asia. Named in 1768, this is Europe's common and highly variable ELM. The leaves are not necessarily smooth, nor narrow, they can be nearly round; mostly they are ≤ 2¾" long, rarely more than 3½". Often it is difficult to tell hybrids from pure-bred *U. minor* variants. Usually hybrids (treated under *U.* × *hollandica*) bear larger leaves, or at any rate the leaves usually have more vein pairs and more teeth. Most *U. minor* variations root-sucker, and those with corky twigs are often called CORK ELM. Records: to 140' tall in the wild; 103' × 13'4" and 97' × 14'2" Walla Walla, WA (1990); 69' × 15'6" Kippenross House, Tayside, Scotland (1987); 60' × 11'7" × 96' Princess Anne, MD (1990); a trunk 28'4" around in Spain (≤1988).

U. minor ssp. angustifolia—see U. minor var. cornubiensis

U. minor 'Argenteo-variegata'
= *U. procera* 'Argenteo-variegata'
= *U. campestris* 'Foliis Variegatis'

SILVER ENGLISH ELM. Known since 1677 in England. A sport of the ENGLISH ELM with leaves striped and splashed silvery, creamy or golden. Leaves rather roundish, lobulate, to 2¾" × 2⅜", with white fuzz by the midrib beneath; barely rough above; 8–9 vein pairs. Smaller and weaker than typical ENGLISH ELM; to ca. 80' tall. Apt to be confused with *U. minor* 'Variegata' (leaves elongated). Both are extremely rare in North America.

U. minor 'Christine Buisman'—see U. × hollandica 'Christine B.'

U. minor var. cornubiensis (West.) Richens
= *U. minor* ssp. *angustifolia* (West.) Stace
= *U. angustifolia* (West.) West. var. *cornubiensis* (West.) Melv.
= *U. carpinifolia* Gledit. var. *cornubiensis* (West.) Rehd.
= *U. campestris* var. *stricta* Ait.
= *U. campestris* var. *cornubiensis* West.
= *U. foliacea* var. *stricta* (Ait.) Rehd.
= *U. cornubiensis* hort.

CORNISH ELM. From Cornwall, W Devonshire, and S Dorset, England (also Brittany, says Hillier). A gaunt, narrowly erect tree. About the last ELM to leaf out in spring. Young twigs more or less hairy or only hairy near buds. Leaves somewhat leathery, 2"–2¾" long; dark and smooth above; stem ⅓" long; vein pairs 10–12. Winged seed narrow, ca. ⅝" long. Records: to 121' × 11'11" Wilton House, near Salisbury, England (≤1961); 97' × 7'3" × 43' Seattle, WA (1987); a trunk 26'0" around at Rosuic on Goonhilly Downs, Cornwall, England (1928).

U. minor 'Dampieri'—see U. × hollandica 'Dampieri'

U. minor 'Gracilis'
= *U. minor* 'Umbraculifera Gracilis'
= *U. carpinifolia* 'Gracilis'

Introduced in 1897–98 by Späth nursery of Germany. It originated there as a branch sport on *U. minor* 'Umbraculifera', and is very similar but of more rounded habit, with thinner branches and smaller leaves. Never flowers or sets seeds. Records: 42' × 6'6" × 40' Seattle, WA (1993; *pl.* <1946); 29' × 6'10½" × 26' Spokane, WA (1993).

U. minor 'Koopmannii'

Introduced to Germany in 1883 by O. Lauche from Turkestan. Named after botanist Karl Koopmann, who reported seeing mighty specimens in Turkestan cemeteries. Introduced to commerce in 1885 by Späth nursery of Germany. Very similar to *U. minor* 'Umbraculifera' but with an oval (not round) head, just as dense. Can be shrubby in cultivation. Young shoots paler, often corky. Leaves 1"–1⅜" long; more grayish-green and lightly hairy beneath; stem ≤¼" long.

U. minor var. lockii (Druce) Richens
= *U. Plottii* Druce

LOCK ELM. PLOT ELM. SMALL LEAVED ELM. From central England. In 1911, the botanist G.C. Druce published the name *U. Plottii* because he believed that this was the ELM described by the English antiquary and naturalist Robert Plot (1640–1696) in 1677—but it wasn't. So PLOT ELM is a poor name. The name LOCK ELM refers to the locking and binding of saws and tools when working the tough timber. Extremely rare in North America. Twigs sparingly, minutely hairy at first. Leaves 1⅜"–1¾" (2¾") long; only slightly lopsided, often heart-shaped at the base;

doubly sharply toothed with usually less than 70 teeth; 7–11 vein pairs. At first the leaves are dull green above and slightly rough; densely hairy beneath. Later they are quite smooth above, and practically hairless beneath except for conspicuous axillary tufts. Winged seed ⅜"–⅝" long. A slender, loosely branched tree to ca. 100' tall with a distinctively drooping "ostrich-feather" leader. Branches weak, drooping at ends. Root suckers freely. Twigs not normally corky. Has a habit of developing lateral shoots on only one side of the twig.

U. minor 'Monumentalis'—see U. minor var. sarniensis

U. minor 'Purpurea'—see U. 'Purpurea'

U. minor var. sarniensis (Loud.) Druce
= U. carpinifolia f. sarniensis (Loud.) Rehd.
= U. × sarniensis (Loud.) H. Bancr.
= U. campestris Wheatleyi Simon-Louis
= U. campestris monumentalis hort. U.S.A., non Rinz
= U. Wheatleyi (Bean) Druce
= U. foliacea 'Monumentalis'
= U. foliacea var. Wheatleyi Rehd.
= U. minor 'Monumentalis'

GUERNSEY ELM. WHEATLEY ELM. JERSEY ELM. MONUMENT ELM. From the Channel Islands. Some say native only in Guernsey, and introduced to the other Channel Islands; Hillier says likely from N France. Cultivated since ≤1836. Uncommon in North America. A dense narrowly pyramidal tree. Much more spire-like, usually larger, tidier and more graceful than CORNISH ELM (U. minor var. cornubiensis). Does not aggressively sucker. Leaves broader than those of CORNISH ELM, 1½"–2½" long; very dark and glossy above, with inconspicuous hair tufts beneath; vein pairs 10–15. Bark has no ridges, but is in rectangular plates like ENGLISH ELM (U. minor var. vulgaris). Records: to 125' × 18'0" in the British Isles; 110' × 15'4" Jordans, Ardingly, Sussex, England (1973); 105' × 8'8" × 47' Port Coquitlam, B.C. (1992); 102' × 13'0" × 63' Bellingham, WA (1993).

U. minor 'Umbraculifera'
= U. carpinifolia var. umbraculifera (Trautv.) Rehd.
= U. foliacea var. umbraculifera (Trautv.) Rehd.
= U. campestris var. umbraculifera Trautv.
= U. densa Litv.
= U. turkestanica Regel

GLOBE ELM. From Turkestan. Described in 1873 (Latin umbraculum, umbrella, and ferre, to bear).

Cultivated since 1875 in Germany. In North American commerce ≤1910 and until at least 1969. In nature this must be considered a botanical variety, although in Western cultivation it prevails as a clone. It is often planted in dry SW and Central Asia. A densely twiggy, broad-crowned small tree, good for formal effect. Twigs slender. Leaves 1¼"–3" long; base rather symmetrical; somewhat rough above; stem ≤⅓" long. Winged seeds small, ca. ⅓". See also U. minor 'Gracilis' and U. minor 'Koopmannii'.

U. minor 'Umbraculifera Gracilis'—see U. minor 'Gracilis'

U. minor 'Variegata'
= U. campestris marmorata hort.
= U. carpinifolia 'Variegata'
= U. foliacea 'Variegata'

TARTAN ELM. More than one clone has been so called, beginning as early as ca. 1772 in France. The leaves of the most common of these rare clones are creamy-white variegated, especially near the margins; to 3¼" × 1⅝", with white hair tufts beneath; smooth above; 11–15 vein pairs; stem to ⅜" long. See also U. minor 'Argenteo-variegata' (leaves roundish). Record: 85' × 10'10" × 73' Portland, OR (1991).

U. minor var. vulgaris (Ait.) Richens
= U. procera Salisb.
= U. campestris L., pro parte

ENGLISH ELM. HEDGEROW ELM. From England, traditionally. Exact origin uncertain: probably an ancient introduction from NW Spain to S England in the latter Bronze Age. Introduced to the U.S. <1752. First planted on the Boston common in 1780. Common here, at least nominally—some North American stock called ENGLISH ELM differs from the true English clone in having larger leaves (3½"–5"), elliptic rather than roundish, less hairy, more veins (10–18); larger and more numerous seeds. The ENGLISH ELM of England's leaves are 2"–3⅝" (4") long, rough above, with (9) 10–12 vein pairs. Suckers very numerous; sometimes corky. Records: to 165' tall in Europe; 150' × 20'0" Northampton, Gloucestershire, England (died 1895); 141' tall at Syon House, Middlesex, England (1964); 136' × 15'4" × 81' Sacramento, CA (1995); 127' × 25'2" Berlin, MD (ca. 1980); 124' × 19'11" × 107' Towson, MD (1972); 120' × 20'0" Washington, D.C. (1981); 114' × 16'3" Puyallup, WA (1993); 80' × 23'1" × 90' Wellesley, MA (1984); 30' × 27'10" Carshalton, Surrey, England (1964).

U. minor 'Webbiana'—see U. × hollandica 'Webbiana'

U. minor 'Wredei'—see *U.* × *hollandica* 'Wredei'

U. montana—see *U. glabra*

U. montana 'Dovæi'—see *U. glabra* 'Dovæi'

U. montana var. *fastigiata*—see *U. glabra* 'Exoniensis'

U. montana var. *gigantea*—see *U.* × *hollandica* 'Hollandica'

U. montana var. *hollandica*—see *U.* × *hollandica* 'Belgica'

U. montana var. *laciniata*—see *U. glabra* 'Cornuta'

U. montana 'Lutescens'—see *U. glabra* 'Lutescens'

U. montana var. *pendula*—see *U. glabra* 'Horizontalis' and *U.* × *hollandica* 'Smithii'

U. montana 'Purpurea'—see *U.* 'Purpurea'

U. montana superba—see *U.* × *hollandica* 'Superba'

U. 'Mops'

Released ≤1993, when described by Lake County nursery of Perry, OH, as being "35' tall by 25' wide, an upright, compact oval; twigs distinctly winged; topgrafted at 4'." See *U. pumila* 'Mophead'.

U. 'Morton'—see *U.* Accolade™

U. 'New Horizon' PP 8684 (1994)
(*U. japonica* × *U. pumila*)

Originated by Dr. E. Smalley at the University of Wisconsin. Released in 1990. Highly disease-resistant. Relatively slow. Large dark leaves.

U. nitens—see *U. minor*

U. parvifolia Jacq.
= *U. chinensis* Pers.

CHINESE ELM. LACEBARK ELM. CHINESE PAPERBARK ELM. From China, Korea, Japan, and Taiwan. Introduced to Western cultivation in 1794; named in 1798 (from Latin *parvus*, small, and *folium*, a leaf). In North American commerce ≤1828, now common and re-seeding in places here. Prized for its fine foliage and uniquely handsome mottling bark, as well as DED-resistance. Sometimes evergreen or nearly so in warm-winter regions; elsewhere variable fall color—sometimes impressive red, but in most cases persisting green leaves give way slowly to patchy yellowing and prolonged leaf fall. Cold hardiness and bark beauty also vary considerably. Leaves to 2½" × ⅞"; vein pairs 10–15 (19). Flowers and seeds (hairless, ⅓"–½") appear in autumn. Records: 95' × 14'9" Philadelphia, PA (1988); 89' × 8'11" × 76' Sacramento, CA (1989); 62' × 15'4" × 64' Philadelphia, PA (1980); 53' × 11'0" × 59' Baltimore, MD (1990).

U. parvifolia 'A. Ross / Central Park' PP 6983 (1989)
(*U. parvifolia* 'Across Central Park')

A tree planted <1873 in New York City's Central Park. The name honors Arthur Vining Ross. In propagation ≤1987 by New York Parks Department. Selected for cold-hardiness. Fall color "mimosa yellow."

U. parvifolia Allee™ PP 7552 (1991)
= *U. parvifolia* 'Emerald Vase'
= *U. parvifolia* 'Emer II'

A chance seedling from near Athens, GA. Patented by John H. Barbour. Promoted since 1989; introduced in 1992. The original measured 70' × 9'2" × 59' (1988; age ca. 50 years). Leaves typical, with subdued yellow fall color. Suffers no leaf scorch or dieback.

U. parvifolia Athena™ PP 7551 (1991)
= *U. parvifolia* 'Emer I'
= *U. parvifolia* 'Emerald Isle'

A chance seedling from near Athens, GA. Promoted since 1989; introduced in 1992. The original measured 32' × 7'4" × 54' (1988, when aged ca. 50 years). Pretty bark. Leaves dark and thick. Symmetrical crown. Fall color bronzy-brown and not pleasing.

U. parvifolia 'Brea'—see *U. parvifolia* 'Drake'

U. parvifolia 'Burgundy'

Named ≤1989, when the original was estimated 7–8 years old. Rounded form. Fall color wine-red in November.

U. parvifolia 'Catlin'

Selected ca. 1950 as a bud sport by John Catlin of La Canada, CA. Introduced ≤1980 (year offered by Olle Olsson nursery of Monrovia, CA). Little known. More or less a dwarf; to ca. 15' tall. Leaves very small, ≤½" long.

U. parvifolia 'Corkbark'

= U. parvifolia 'Corticosa'

Introduced to the U.S. from Japan in 1973; in commerce here ≤1989; very rare. Especially corky bark. Can be a mere shrub, or 20' tree.

U. parvifolia 'D.B. Cole'

Introduced ≤1991–92 by Arborvillage nursery of Holt, MO: "Smaller; dense head; outstanding bark."

U. parvifolia 'Drake'

= U. parvifolia 'Brea'

Introduced in California ≤1952. Common. Branching upswept, not very pendulous. Foliage evergreen, or nearly so at least in southern California. Not among the more cold-hardy cultivars.

U. parvifolia 'Dynasty'

Raised in 1968 by the United States National Arboretum. Released in 1984–85. Bark not as ornamental as many. Foliage ordinary. Chosen since it is deciduous, with attractive red fall color, cold-hardy and has a well-formed, vase-shaped, small crown.

U. parvifolia 'Elsmo'

Released in 1990 by the USDA Soil Conservation Service in Missouri. A seed-propagated cultivar featuring excellent form, cold-hardiness, dense foliage, and resistance to phloem necrosis disease.

U. parvifolia 'Emer I'—see U. parvifolia Athena™

U. parvifolia 'Emer II'—see U. parvifolia Allee™

U. parvifolia 'Emerald Isle'—see U. parvifolia Athena™

U. parvifolia 'Emerald Vase'—see U. parvifolia Allee™

U. parvifolia 'Golden Rey' PP 7240 (1990)

Discovered as a seedling by retired nurseryman Bruce Rey. Introduced by Warren & Son nursery of Oklahoma City. Young leaves primrose-yellow, changing to nearly chartreuse. Leaves yellow all summer, deepening to yellow-gold in fall.

U. parvifolia 'Hallelujah'

Introduced ≤1993–94 by Arborvillage nursery of Holt, MO: "Our selection out of a block of USDA seedlings. Fastest; excellent bark and foliage. Cold hardy."

U. parvifolia 'King's Choice' PP 5554 (1985)

A seedling 11 years old in 1989, which was twice as large as its siblings. Selected by Hampstead, MD nursery owner Benjamin J. King, when he was 80 years old. Propagated by tissue culture. Introduced in 1991. Fall color dull yellow.

U. parvifolia 'Milliken'

Originated in Spartanburg, SC. Named ≤1993. "Large, billowy white oak form with attractive exfoliating bark."

U. parvifolia 'Ohio'

Selected <1990 by A.M. Townsend, of the United States National Arboretum. Said to have originated at the research station of Delaware, Ohio—hence its name. Introduced to commerce in 1991–92. Parent tree 40' tall in 28 years. Fall color grayish-red.

U. parvifolia 'Pathfinder'

Raised in 1963 at Delaware, OH, by the USDA. Registered in 1990. Introduced to commerce in 1991. Fall color distinctive brilliant red. Resists DED and leaf-beetles.

U. parvifolia 'Pendens'

Raised in California ca. 1920, from seeds received from China. Not cultivated, at least under this 1945 name. Long slender branches and branchlets.

U. parvifolia 'Prairie Shade'

Released in 1985 by Oklahoma State University at Stillwater. Chosen from ca. 800 seedlings planted in 1973. Easily raised from cuttings unlike most cultivars. Anthracnose resistant. Untouched by leaf beetles. Hardier than 'Drake', 'Sempervirens' and 'True Green'. Can endure -35°F.

U. parvifolia 'Red Fall'

Selected by S. Bieberich of Sunshine nursery, Clinton, OK. Named ≤1993. Red fall color.

U. parvifolia 'Sempervirens'

= U. sempervirens hort.

EVERGREEN ELM. Introduced ≤1935 by W.B. Clarke nursery of San José, CA. Common. Leaves small, evergreen or nearly so. Less cold-hardy than the fully deciduous cultivars. The epithet sempervirens means evergreen; from Latin semper, always or ever, and virens, green.

U. parvifolia 'State Fair'

Named in the 1990s for the State Fairgrounds of

Oklahoma City, OK. Crown globe-shaped, dense. Bark pretty.

U. parvifolia 'The Thinker'
Selected by M. Hayman at the University of Louisville, KY. Crown rounded, bark attractive. Named ≤1993 (it grows near Auguste Rodin's famous statue).

U. parvifolia 'True Green'
Commonly grown in California since ≤1971. Leaves very dark and glossy; held late into winter. Less cold-hardy than are the fully deciduous cultivars.

U. 'Patriot'
(U. 'Urban' × U. Wilsoniana 'Prospector')
Hybridized in 1980 by the U.S. National Arboretum. Selected and named in 1993. High DED resistance. Resists elm leaf beetle.

U. pedunculata—see U. lævis

U. pendula—see U. × hollandica 'Smithii'

U. 'Pioneer'—see U. × hollandica 'Pioneer'

U. 'Plantyn'
(U. glabra 'Exoniensis' × U. Wallichiana) × U. minor

Selected 1962 at Wageningen, Holland. Named after Christoffel Plantyn (Plantijn) who encouraged the 16th century Dutch botanists Dodoens and Lobel and printed their herbals. Released in 1975. Rare in North America; not known to be in nurseries.

U. Plottii—see U. minor var. lockii

U. præstans—see U. × hollandica 'Superba'

U. 'Primus'—see U. 'Improved Coolshade'

U. procera—see U. minor var. vulgaris

U. procera 'Argenteo-variegata'—see U. minor 'Arg.-variegata'

U. procera 'Christine Buisman'—see U. × hollandica 'Christine B.'

U. pumila L.
SIBERIAN ELM. CHINESE ELM. MANCHURIAN ELM. From central Asia, N China, Mongolia, E Siberia, and Korea. Introduced to France ≤1771. The botanically typical form of the species is a small-leaved shrub (hence the 1753 name pumila meaning dwarf) of E Siberia and Mongolia. But the kind in N China, Manchuria and Korea is a tree and is the form generally cultivated since ca. 1905. During the 1930s this became extremely popular and was extensively planted, valued for quick growth, cold-hardiness, heat-tolerance, ability to thrive on poor soil, and handsome foliage retaining a good green color into fall. Its brittleness, often short lifespan and weedy seedlings are drawbacks, and it has been roundly condemned by many. Although it may be the least desirable ELM, some of its cultivars are serviceable trees and possess toughness that mocks many of the prettier ELMS. The leaves are small for an ELM, though bigger (and coarser) than those of U. parvifolia. Twigs gray, only scantily hairy. Leaves small, to 2½" (3") × 1¼"; not conspicuously lopsided; vein pairs 10–13 (16). Winged seeds roundish, ⅜"–⅝". Records: 146' × 18'10" × 112' Detroit, MI (1991); 122' × 14'9" × 147' Oakland County, MI (1987); 85' × 18'6" × 95' Philadelphia, PA (1980); 80' × 17'4" × 75' Bath, NH (1967); 70' × 19'1" Philadelphia, PA (ca. 1980)

U. pumila "Broadleaf Hybrid"—see U. Green King®

U. pumila 'Chinkota'—see U. pumila 'Dropmore'

U. pumila 'Dropmore'
= U. pumila 'Chinkota'
= U. pumila 'Harbin'
= U. pumila 'Manchu'
= U. americana 'Harbin'

Raised from seeds collected by Mr. Ptitsin in the Harbin region of Manchuria/Siberia. Named 'Dropmore' in 1953 but introduced earlier under different names as follows: "Harbin strain" by Skinner nursery of Dropmore, Manitoba (≤1951); "Manchu" by H.D. Stewart nursery of Sutherland, Saskatchewan (≤1951); "Chinkota" by South Dakota research station of Brookings (≤1955). Seed-raised, and primarily remarkable for superior cold-hardiness. Still in commerce into the late 1980s.

U. pumila "Field's New Hybrid Elm"—see U. Green King®

U. pumila Green King®—see U. Green King®

U. pumila 'Harbin'—see U. pumila 'Dropmore'

U. pumila 'Mophead'

?= *U.* 'Mops'

Sold ≤1980s by Connon nursery of Ontario. See *U.* 'Mops'.

U. pumila 'Manchu'—see U. pumila 'Dropmore'

U. pumila 'Mr. Buzz'

Selected <1990 by Westerveldt nursery of Selm, AL. Not in commerce. Dense, dark; vigorous.

U. pumila 'Neosho'—see U. Green King®

U. pumila 'Park Royal'

Selected, and introduced ≤1967 by Sheridan nursery of Ontario. Still in commerce. To 60' tall; straight trunked, symmetrical, and "good" growth rate.

U. pumila 'Pendula'

Described in France in 1845. Whether the clone so called in 1990s commerce is identical is not known.

U. pumila 'Pyamidalis Fiorei'

Selected ca. 1950 and introduced ≤1957 by Charles Fiore nursery of Prairie View, IL. Strictly pyramidal.

U. pumila var. suberosa—see U. japonica

U. 'Purpurea'

= *U.* × *hollandica* 'Purpurascens'
= *U. montana* 'Purpurea'
= *U. glabra* 'Purpurea'
= *U. minor* 'Purpurea'
= *U. campestris* 'Purpurea'
= *U.* × *sarniensis* 'Purpurea'

PURPLE ELM. Originated in Belgium ≤1863. In North American commerce ≤1880. Exceedingly rare in North America. Young leaves tinged purple, to 2½" long. Confusion exists concerning the several PURPLE-LEAF ELMS. This one is most likely a hybrid. A tall slender tree. See also *U. glabra* 'Atropurpurea'. Record: 106' × 7'5" × 41' Port Coquitlam, B.C. (1992).

U. racemosa—see U. Thomasii

U. 'Regal' PP 5335 (1984)

U. hollandica 'Commelin' × (*U. minor* × *U. minor* 'Hoersholmiensis')

Originated by Dr. E.B. Smalley of the University of Wisconsin. Released in 1983. Common. Columnar. High DED-resistance. Vigorous; hardy. Leaves to 4¾" × 2⅜"; stem to ⅝" long.

U. 'Rgeth'—see U. 'Hamburg Hybrid'

U. 'Rosehill'

= *U.* 'Boulevard'

Selected in 1951 by Rosehill Gardens of Kansas City, MO. Believed to be *U. pumila* × *U. rubra*. Introduced ≤1958–59 by Willis nursery of Ottawa, KS.

U. rubra Muhl.

= *U. fulva* Michx.

SLIPPERY ELM. MOOSE ELM. INDIAN ELM. SWEET ELM. RED ELM. GRAY ELM. From central and eastern North America. Named *rubra* in 1793 for its rusty-red buds (easily recognized in winter by the iridescent red hairs on the twigs and buds). Not commonly cultivated. Once highly valued for the sweet, slippery inner bark used medicinally. Rather coarse and wolf-like. Fall color dull yellow. Twigs hairy. Leaves to 5⅝" (8") × 3⅜"; stem ¼" long; (10) 14–19 vein pairs. Winged seeds large ½"–¾", the middle hairy. Records: 134' × 13'3" Porcupine Mountains State Park, MI (<1979); 116' × 21'2" Henderson, KY (1962); 115' × 22'2" Big Oak Tree State Park, MO (1982); 100' × 20'0" × 119' Sugar Grove, OH (1989).

U. 'Sapporo Autumn Gold' PP 3780 (1975)

(*U. pumila* × *U. japonica*)

Raised from a *U. pumila* seed imported in 1958 from the Hokkaido Botanic Garden of Sapporo, Japan. The parent was doubtless pollinated by an *U. japonica*. Named by Dr. E.B. Smalley of the University of Wisconsin; released in 1973; still in commerce. Twigs moderately hairy. Young growth tinged red. Leaves not lopsided at the base, to 4" × 2⅛"; vivid semi-transparent pale greenish-yellow in fall. High DED-resistance. With age the tree develops a strong central trunk.

U. × sarniensis—see U. minor var. sarniensis

U. × sarniensis 'Purpurea'—see U. 'Purpurea'

U. scabra—see U. glabra

U. scabra var. lutescens—see U. glabra 'Lutescens'

U. scabra var. macrophylla—see U. × hollandica 'Pitteursii'

U. scampstoniensis—see U. glabra 'Scampstonensis'

U. sempervirens—see U. parvifolia 'Sempervirens'

U. serotina Sarg.

SEPTEMBER ELM. SOUTHERN RED ELM. From the southeastern U.S. Named in 1899 (Latin for late) because it flowers in fall. Introduced to cultivation in 1903, the last North American ELM to become known; long confused with *U. Thomasii*. Extremely rarely cultivated. Twigs hairless, often golden-brown; can be irregularly corky-ridged; buds hairless. Leaves tinged yellow-brown, narrow, to 4⅞" × 2", with (even for an ELM) very short stems; sandpaper-textured to smooth and shiny above, always softly hairy beneath; vein pairs (15) 18–22. Flowers and seeds appear in autumn (hence SEPTEMBER ELM), dangling in clusters to 2", of as many as 22 seeds, silvery with hairs. Usually a small tree. Records: 150' × 8'9" × 64' Colbert County, AL (1985); 71' × 8'2" × 70' Monroe County, MI (1976).

U. 'Smithii'—see *U. × hollandica* 'Smithii'

U. Thomasii Sarg.

= *U. racemosa* Thomas 1831, non Borkh. 1800
ROCK ELM. (AMERICAN) CORK ELM. HICKORY ELM. CLIFF ELM. From central and eastern North America. Named in 1902 after David Thomas (1776–1859,) its discoverer, a U.S. civil engineer and horticulturist, who first named it. Cultivated since 1875, but never commonly sold. Often grows on dry rocky slopes, yes, but called ROCK ELM for its very hard wood. Twigs hairless or densely hairy; buds hairy. Older twigs usually corky. Leaves smoothish or somewhat rough above, soft-downy beneath, averaging ca. 3¾" × 2⅛"; stem to ¼" long; vein pairs straight and numerous, (15) 19–21 (22). Bright yellow in fall. Winged seeds long-stemmed, hairy, ⅓"–¾". Records: 117' × 16'10" × 122' Cassopolis, MI (1989); 103' × 19'10" near Atchison, Kansas (≤1955).

U. tridens—see *U. glabra* 'Cornuta'

U. turkestanica—see *U. minor* 'Umbraculifera'

U. 'Urban'

= *U.* 'Delaware #1'
(*U. hollandica* 'Vegeta' × *U. minor*) × *U. pumila*
Hybridized in 1956 by the USDA research station of Delaware, OH. Released to some wholesale nurseries in 1972. Selected for form and DED-resistance. Leaves to 2¾" × 2⅜"; late to drop in autumn.

Vigorous—one planted in Aurora, OR, in 1975, grew 45' tall and 28' wide in 10 years.

U. 'Vanguard'

(*U. japonica* × *U. pumila*)
Raised in 1980 at the Morton Arboretum of Lisle, IL. Named in 1992. "Superior."

U. vaseyi—see *U. americana* 'Vase'

U. 'Vegeta'—see *U. × hollandica* 'Vegeta'

U. × vegeta—see *U. × hollandica* 'Vegeta'

U. × vegeta 'Camperdownii'—see *U. glabra* 'Camperdownii'

U. 'Washington'

Selected by Dr. H.V. Webster, plant pathologist with U.S. National Park Service. Introduced ≤1985–86. Valued for DED-resistance. It has been confused with *U. americana* 'Washington', so a name change has been proposed.

U. Wheatleyi—see *U. minor* var. *sarniensis*

U. 'Willis'

Selected by a Mr. Minnick of Kansas City, MO. Believed to be *U. pumila* × *U. rubra*. Introduced ≤1958–59 by Willis nursery of Ottawa, KS. Leaves large, resembling those of *U. americana*. Growth very fast.

U. Wilsoniana Schneid.

WILSON ELM. From W China. Discovered by the great plantsman Ernest Henry Wilson (1876–1930) in 1900; introduced by him to the Arnold Arboretum in 1910. Named in 1912. Not in commerce except as the following cultivar. Leaves rough above, downy beneath; vein pairs numerous, 16–22. Recorded to 80' × 9'5" in the wild.

U. Wilsoniana 'Prospector'

Originated as a seedling in 1963, planted ca. 1965 in Delaware, OH. Selected in 1980 for evaluation; released in 1990. Tolerates elm leaf beetles, Elm Yellows and DED. Leaves average 4½" × 3⅓", orange-red when young. Crown dense. Yellow fall color.

Umbellularia

[LAURACEÆ; Laurel Family] Only one species in the genus, a fragrant broadleaf evergreen. From Latin *umbellula* (diminutive of *umbella*), a small umbrella, in reference to the flower clusters. Most closely related to BAY LAUREL (*Laurus nobilis*).

U. californica (H. & A.) Nutt.

= *Laurus regia* Dougl.
= *Oreodaphne californica* Nees

OREGON MYRTLE. CALIFORNIA LAUREL. CALIFORNIA BAY. PEPPERWOOD. From SW Oregon and California. Introduced to British cultivation in the 1820s. Named in 1833. In North America it is cultivated mostly in California, Oregon and further north on the Pacific Coast. An immense, dense, dark green globe. Leaves HOLLY-like but wholly toothless, spineless and intensely aromatic; to 5" × 1½". The odor of crushed leaves is not trifling; one of the strongest of all leaf scents. Flowers tiny, yellowish, borne January into late May. Fruit olive-like. Tolerates shade, drought, hard pruning and frost. Wood pleasantly scented and highly valuable. Drawbacks as a street-tree include its broad habit, huge size, and susceptibility to scale. Records: to 175' tall says C. Sargent; 150'×33'11" north of Pepperwood, CA (1973); 100' × 50'0" Santa Barbara, CA (n.d.); 88' × 41'9" Rogue River, OR (1978).

U. californica 'Claremont'

Selected <1981 from Fresno County, CA. Extremely rare. Leaves very broad, finely hairy beneath. Cutting-grown.

Virgilia lutea—see *Cladrastis kentukea*

Vitex

[VERBENACEÆ; Verbena Family] 250–270 spp. of mostly subtropical and tropical trees and shrubs, deciduous or evergreen. *Vitex* is an ancient Latin name, akin to *viere*, to bind or twist; the flexible branches were used in basketry. The following species is prized for its flowers and fragrance. A related genus is *Clerodendrum*.

V. Agnus-castus L.

CHASTE TREE. MEXICAN LAVENDER. MONK'S PEPPER TREE. SAGE TREE. ABRAHAM'S BALM. INDIAN SPICE. HEMP TREE. LAVENDER TREE. From the Mediterranean region to central Asia. Cultivated since antiquity; in England since 1570. *Agnus-castus* is a Middle English name from Latin *agnus*, lamb, and *castus*, chaste. The tree was thought to be an anti-aphrodisiac. J.C. Loudon, paraphrasing Pliny's account of CHASTE TREE, explained in 1838 "the Athenian matrons, during the festival in honor of Ceres, called Thesmophoria, when they were dressed in white robes, and enjoined to preserve the strictest chastity, strewed their beds with it." While only a perennial or small shrub in the Midwest and parts of the Northeast, this species is a hardy small tree in the south and much of the Pacific Coast. Leaves opposite, compounded into 5–7 slender leaflets, dark green above, gray-green beneath, highly sage-scented when crushed. Flowers lavender-blue (pink, or white), in slender spikes during late summer and fall. Bark chunky, like *Sambucus cerulea* (BLUE ELDER). Heat and sun-loving; drought-tolerant. Records: 65' tall at Padua, Italy (1938; *pl.* 1550); 30' × 4'10" × 36' Richland County, SC (1984); 22' × 5'1" ×29' Brownwood, TX (1982); 19' × 7'7" × 41' San Antonio, TX (1991).

Volkameria japonica—see *Clerodendrum trichotomum*

Washingtonia

[PALMÆ or ARECACEÆ; Palm Family] 2 spp. of North American native PALMS, named after George Washington (1732–1799). Other PALM genera in this volume are: *Butia, Ceroxylon, Chamærops, Nannorrhops, Sabal,* and *Trachycarpus.*

W. filifera (Linden *ex* André) Wendl.

CALIFORNIA WASHINGTONIA. CALIFORNIA FAN PALM. DESERT FAN PALM. HARDY FANLEAF PALM. COTTON PALM (fronds fringed with creamy cotton-like threads). HULA PALM. PETTICOAT PALM (its fan-shaped leaves bend down at maturity to form a petticoat of thatch). From low desert canyons of mountains in S California, SW Arizona, and N Baja California. The 1874 name *filifera* is from Latin *filum*, thread, and *ferre*, to bear—thread-bearing: the frayed frond edges have threadlike fibers. Withstands considerable cold in the desert, but needs sand or good drainage elsewhere. A California landmark species; its heavy, thick, very tall trunk is surmounted by a tuft of fronds. Fronds 3'–6' wide, of ca. 50–70 segments; the stem 3'–5' long, usually very spiny edged. Old fronds are usually removed, since they are haven for pigeons and rats, and a fire hazard. Records: 101' × 8'9" × 22' and 83' × 10'0" × 21' Sacramento, CA (1989; *pl.* 1870); 67' × 11'0" × 19' Hollywood, CA (≤1993). The closely related *W. robusta* is less cold-hardy, taller and much slenderer, with smaller fronds.

Wellingtonia gigantea—see *Sequoiadendron giganteum*

Xanthoceras

[SAPINDACEÆ; Soapberry Family] 1 or 2 spp. of deciduous shrubs or small trees. From Greek *xanthos*, yellow and *keras*, horn. There are yellow horn-like appendages (projecting glands) between the petals. Related genera include *Koelreuteria* (GOLDEN RAIN TREE) and *Sapindus* (SOAPBERRY).

X. sorbifolia Bge.

YELLOW-HORN. SHINYLEAF YELLOW-HORN. CHINESE FLOWERING CHESTNUT. HYACINTH SHRUB. POPCORN SHRUB (flowers resemble popped corn). From N China. Cultivated since the 1820s in Russia. Named in 1833 (Latin *Sorbus*, MOUNTAIN ASH, and *folium*, a leaf). Introduced from China to France in 1866. In North American commerce shortly thereafter. Uncommon. Prized for its flowers and elegant bright green foliage. Usually a spindly shrub, rarely a small tree; can form colonies by root suckering. Leaves, flowers, seeds are all edible. Leaves recall MOUNTAIN ASH (*Sorbus*), being pinnately compound, 5"–12" long, of 9–17 shiny leaflets. Flowers in April and May, the 6"–10" tall clusters like those of HORSE CHESTNUT (*Æsculus Hippocastanum*), white, first with yellowish-green, then red centers. The fruit is an easily-cracked capsule to 2½", containing edible ½" nuts. Bark like BLACK LOCUST (*Robinia Pseudoacacia*). Heat-loving; very cold-hardy and drought tolerant. Often short-lived. It can bloom the third year raised from seed. Records: to 26' tall at most; 23' × 1'0" Trengwainton, Cornwall, England (1987); 13' × 2'11" Paris, France (1982).

Xanthoxylum—see *Zanthoxylum*

Zanthoxylum

(*Xanthoxylum*)
[RUTACEÆ; Rue Family] ca. 150–250 spp. of shrubs and trees, deciduous or evergreen, usually pungently aromatic; mostly tropical and subtropical. From Greek *xanthos,* yellow, and *xylon,* wood (the heartwood of some species is yellow). Valued for neat foliage and sometimes showy fruit. The cold-hardy species are extremely rarely cultivated, little known, and yet intriguing. They tend to be pest-free, elegant, and thorny. Few trees possess such piercing odor. Since many are mere shrubs, and none are commonly grown, the following species is included as being most treelike, and native. Several East Asian species are occasionally sold in small sizes by specialty nurseries. Related genera include: *Fortunella* (KUMQUAT), *Phellodendron* (CORK TREE), *Poncirus* (TRIFOLIATE ORANGE), and *Tetradium.*

Z. Clava-Herculis L.

HERCULES' CLUB. TOOTHACHE TREE. SOUTHERN PRICKLY ASH. TINGLE TONGUE. PEPPERBARK. From the Coastal Plain, Virginia to E Texas, usually in poor sandy soil. Flowers greenish, in April and May. Leaves to 15" long; leaflets 5–19, hairless, shiny above, dull beneath, crudely toothed and lopsided. A slender small tree. Branches spiny; trunk pale gray, with corky little "rhinoceros horns." Should not be confused with *Aralia spinosa,* another "HERCULES' CLUB." The chewed bark was a toothache remedy that tingles on the tongue. Records: 65' × 2'7" × 20' Gainesville, FL (1993); 51' × 4'2" × 28' Jasper County, TX (1993); 50' × 2'7" × 32' Sam Houston National Forest, TX (1982); 38' × 7'6" × 59' Little Rock, AR (1961).

Zelkova

[ULMACEÆ; Elm Family] 4–6 spp. of deciduous trees. The 1842 name is an adaption of *Zelkoua,* the Cretan common name. Related genera include: *Aphananthe, Celtis* (HACKBERRY), *Planera* (WATER ELM), and *Ulmus* (ELM).

Zelkova acuminata—see *Zelkova serrata*

Z. carpinifolia (Pall.) K. Koch

= *Z. crenata* Spach
= *Ulmus crenata* hort. Paris *ex* Desf.
= *Planera crenata* Desf.
= *Planera Richardii* Michx.
= *Planera carpinifolia* (Pall.) P. Watson

CAUCASIAN ELM. From the Transcaucasian forests of Armenia and W Georgia, and bordering N Iran and NE Anatolia. Introduced to France in 1760. Named in 1788 (Latin *Carpinus,* HORNBEAM tree, and *folium,* a leaf). In North American commerce ≤1854, but extremely rare here. Unlike *Z. serrata,* this species is susceptible to Dutch Elm Disease (DED). As cultivated in the British Isles it usually has a giant bushy upswept crown on a stout short trunk, smooth and BEECH-like. Twigs persistently hairy. Leaves to 4½" × 2"; coarsely toothed; very short-stemmed; vein pairs 6–8 (13). Fall color yellow. Often suckers from the root. Records: to 115' × 31'0" in Turkey; 115' × 23'0" Madrid, Spain; 115' × 7'10" Wardour House, Wiltshire, England (1977); 88½' × 22'10" Worlingham, Suffolk, England (1990); 56' × 8'5" Enumclaw, WA (1992).

Zelkova crenata—see *Zelkova carpinifolia*

Zelkova Davidiana—see *Hemiptelea Davidiana*

Zelkova Keaki—see *Zelkova serrata*

Z. serrata (Th.) Mak.

= *Z. acuminata* (Lindl.) Planch.
= *Z. Keaki* (Sieb.) Maxim.
= *Corchorus serratus* Th.
= *Planera acuminata* Lindl.
= *Planera japonica* Miq.
= *Planera Keaki* (Sieb.) Kirchn.
= *Ulmus Keaki* Sieb.

COMMON ZELKOVA. SAWLEAF ZELKOVA. Japanese: *Ke(y)aki.* From Korea, Japan, Taiwan, and maybe China. Named in 1794. Introduced to the West in

1830 by Siebold to Holland. Cultivated in North America since 1862. Common. Flowers minute, inconspicuous, in spring. Valued for branching habit and foliage. Leaves to 5¼" × 2½"; surface often quite rough; vein-pairs 8–15 (23); teeth vary from subdued and appressed to sharp and jagged (serrate). Fall color forgettable yellow to warm, soft orange or rusty-red, rarely purplish. Bark often handsomely mottled and flaky. Records: to 164' × 31'6" in Japan; 101' × 26'0" Ruakura, New Zealand (1980; *pl.* ca. 1925); 84' × 16'0" Ardmore, PA (1980); 65' × 14'0" Washington, D.C. (ca. 1980).

Z. serrata Autumn Glow®

Introduced ≤1990–91 by Femrite nursery of Aurora, OR. Habit compact, small. Excellent fall color.

Z. serrata 'Goshiki'

Originated in Japan. Imported to North America in 1978 by B. Yinger; in commerce here, but very rare. Leaves variegated pink, white, cream or pale yellow.

Z. serrata Green Vase® PP 5080 (1983)

Introduced by Princeton nursery of New Jersey. Common. Taller and less broad than *Z. serrata* 'Village Green'. Fall color yellow-orange.

Z. serrata 'Green Veil'

= *Z. serrata* 'Pendula'
= *Z. serrata* 'Shidare'

Originated in Japan, long ago. Imported to North America in 1978 by B. Yinger; in commerce here, but very rare. The 'Green Veil' name dates from 1983. Gracefully weeping, narrow tree.

Z. serrata 'Halka' PP 5687 (1986)

Growth rapid. Crown habit approaches the cherished vase shape exemplified by *Ulmus americana*.

Z. serrata 'Illinois Hardy'

Introduced in 1993–94 by Princeton nursery of New Jersey. "Survived a particularly harsh winter in northern Illinois that killed all the other zelkovas around it."

Z. serrata 'Parkview'

Origin not known. Very rare. Described by M. Dirr as of "good vase shape."

Z. serrata 'Pendula'—see Z. serrata 'Green Veil'

Z. serrata 'Shidare'—see Z. serrata 'Green Veil'

Z. serrata 'Spring Grove'

Introduced ≤1988–89. Originated in Spring Grove Cemetery of Cincinnati, OH. Handsome dark foliage; wine-red fall color.

Z. serrata Village Green™ PP 2337 (1964)

Introduced by Princeton nursery of New Jersey. Common. Rounded crown. Fall color rusty-red. Hardier than most seedlings.

Ziziphus

(*Zizyphus*)

[RHAMNACEÆ; Buckthorn Family] 40–86 (150) spp. of mostly tropical and subtropical trees and shrubs. *Ziziphus* is ancient Latin, from *zizyphon*, the ancient Greek name of *Z. Lotus*. Derived possibly from Persian *zizafun*. Related genera include *Hovenia* (JAPANESE RAISIN TREE) and *Rhamnus* (BUCKTHORN).

Z. Jujuba—see Z. Zizyphus

Z. vulgaris—see Z. Zizyphus

Z. Zizyphus (L.) Karst.

= *Z. Jujuba* Mill. 1768, non Lam. 1789
= *Z. vulgaris* Lam.
= *Rhamnus Zizyphus* L.

COMMON JUJUBE. CHINESE DATE. From SE Europe and much of Asia. Named in 1753 (*Jujuba* is the Middle Latin name, maybe derived from Arabic or Malayan). Introduced to South Carolina in 1837. Now naturalized in parts of the South. Grown more for its edible fruit than as an ornamental. Probably 100 fruiting cultivars exist in China; a handful are grown here, the best known 'Lang' and 'Li'. Thrives in hot, dry, alkaline conditions, where it can tolerate great cold. Pouts in wet, clayey soils and cool summers. Leaves dark and glossy, ¾"– 3" long. Flowers tiny but abundant (March–June), yellowish-green with intense fragrance of grape soda. Trunk rugged, like that of BLACK LOCUST (*Robinia Pseudoacacia*). Wild specimens are usually thorny;

cultivars usually slightly thorny, if at all. Sometimes root-suckers. Bears when young. Fruit "datelike," variable in color (usually reddish-brown), shape (oval, rounded, or pear-shaped) and size (½"–3"). Ripe between August and December. Records: to 50' × 10'0" in the wild; 43' × 4'10" × 34' Ft. Worth, TX (1989); 35½' × 3'9" × 29' Indio, CA (1993; *pl.* 1920 or later).

Zizyphus—see *Ziziphus*

Statistics

The trees included in this volume can be divided into various categories. First, a breakdown by quantity in the standard hierarchical system.

Full entries:

Species	950
Subspecies	36
Varietates	159
Formæ	95
Hybrids (with × symbol)	120
Cultivars	3,540
SUBTOTAL	4,900

Taxa mentioned in passing:

Species	10
Varietates	1
Cultivars	167
SUBTOTAL	178
GRAND TOTAL	5,078

Genera with the most taxa:

Acer (MAPLE)	446
Malus (APPLE, CRABAPPLE)	415
Ilex (HOLLY)	389
Prunus (CHERRY, PLUM, etc.)	371
Magnolia (MAGNOLIA)	241
Cornus (DOGWOOD)	193
Juniperus (JUNIPER)	182
Pinus (PINE)	168
Chamæcyparis (CYPRESS)	136
Ulmus (ELM)	135
Picea (SPRUCE)	128
Fraxinus (ASH)	126
Populus (POPLAR, COTTONWOOD)	115
Thuja (ARBORVITÆ, CEDAR)	109
Quercus (OAK)	103
Cratægus (HAWTHORN)	102

Species according to geographic origin:

Asia	424
Canada and the U.S.A.	305
Europe and North Africa	141
Australia	32
South America	23
Mexico	22
New Zealand	5
South Africa	1

List of genera arranged by family

This book contains 72 families and 198 genera. Sometimes botanists disagree on which family to assign certain genera to. For example, *Davidia* (DOVE TREE) has been placed variously under DAVIDIACEÆ, CORNACEÆ, or NYSSACEÆ. Some families also have alternate names, as FABACEÆ for LEGUMINOSÆ, ARECACEÆ for PALMÆ. Such matters are usually noted in individual generic introductions throughout this book, and are omitted from the following tabulation. Hybrid genera are included.

ACERACEÆ; Maple Family
 Acer
 Dipteronia

AGAVACEÆ; Agave Family
 Cordyline

ANACARDIACEÆ; Cashew Family
 Cotinus
 Pistacia
 Rhus
 Schinus

ANNONACEÆ; Custard Apple Family
 Asimina

AQUIFOLIACEÆ; Holly Family
 Ilex

ARALIACEÆ; Aralia Family
 Aralia
 Kalopanax

ARAUCARIACEÆ; Araucaria Family
 Araucaria
 BETULACEÆ; Birch Family
 Alnus
 Betula

BIGNONIACEÆ; Bignonia Family
 Catalpa
 × *Chitalpa*

BUXACEÆ; Box Family
 Buxus

CAPRIFOLIACEÆ; Honeysuckle Family
 Sambucus

CARPINACEÆ; Hornbeam Family
 Carpinus
 Ostrya

CELASTRACEÆ; Bittersweet Family
 Euonymus
 Maytenus

CEPHALOTAXACEÆ; Plum Yew Family
 Cephalotaxus

CERCIDIPHYLLACEÆ; Katsura Family
 Cercidiphyllum

CORNACEÆ; Dogwood Family
 Cornus

CORYLACEÆ; Hazel Family
 Corylus

CUPRESSACEÆ; Cypress Family
 Austrocedrus
 Calocedrus
 Chamæcyparis
 × *Cupressocyparis*
 Cupressus
 Fitzroya
 Fokienia
 Juniperus
 Thuja
 Thujopsis

CYATHEACEÆ; Tree Fern Family
  Dicksonia

DAPHNIPHYLLACEÆ; Daphniphyllum Family
  Daphniphyllum

DAVIDIACEÆ; Dove Tree Family
  Davidia

EBENACEÆ; Ebony Family
  Diospyros

EHRETIACEÆ; Ehretia Family
  Ehretia

ELÆOCARPACEÆ; Elæocarpus Family
  Elæocarpus

ELÆAGNACEÆ; Eleagnus Family
  Elæagnus
  Hippophaë

ERICACEÆ; Heath Family
  Arbutus
  Oxydendrum

EUCOMMIACEÆ; Eucommia Family
  Eucommia

EUCRYPHIACEÆ; Eucryphia Family
  Eucryphia

EUPHORBIACEÆ; Spurge Family
  Mallotus
  Sapium

EUPTELEACEÆ; Euptelea Family
  Euptelea

FAGACEÆ; BEECH Family
  Castanea
  Castanopsis
  Chrysolepis
  Fagus
  Lithocarpus
  Nothofagus
  Quercus

FLACOURTIACEÆ; Flacourtia Family
  Azara
  Idesia
  Poliothyrsis

GINKGOACEÆ; Ginkgo Family
  Ginkgo

HAMAMELIDACEÆ; Witchhazel Family
  Liquidambar
  Parrotia
  × *Sycoparrotia*

HIPPOCASTANACEÆ; Horse Chestnut Family
  Æsculus

ILLICIACEÆ; Illicium Family
  Illicium

JUGLANDACEÆ; Walnut Family
  Carya
  Juglans
  Platycarya
  Pterocarya

LAURACEÆ; Laurel Family
  Apollonias
  Cinnamomum
  Laurus
  Lindera
  Neolitsea
  Persea
  Sassafras
  Umbellularia

LEGUMINOSÆ; Pea Family
  Acacia
  Albizia
  Caragana
  Cercis
  Cladrastis
  Gleditsia
  Gymnocladus
  + *Laburnocytisus*
  Laburnum

Maackia
Robinia
Sophora

LYTHRACEÆ; Loosestrife Family
Lagerstrœmia

MAGNOLIACEÆ; Magnolia Family
Liriodendron
Magnolia
Manglietia
Michelia

MELIACEÆ; Mahogany Family
Melia
Toona

MORACEÆ; Mulberry Family
Broussonetia
Cudrania
Ficus
Maclura
Morus

MYRICACEÆ; Wax Myrtle Family
Myrica

MYRTACEÆ; Myrtle Family
Eucalyptus

NYSSACEÆ; Tupelo Family
Nyssa

OLEACEÆ; Olive Family
Chionanthus
Fraxinus
Ligustrum
Olea
Osmanthus
Phillyrea
Syringa

PALMÆ; Palm Family
Butia
Ceroxylon
Chamærops
Nannorrhops

Sabal
Trachycarpus
Washingtonia

PINACEÆ; Pine Family
Abies
Cedrus
Keteleeria
Larix
Picea
Pinus
Pseudolarix
Pseudotsuga
Tsuga

PLATANACEÆ; Planetree Family
Platanus

PODOCARPACEÆ; Podocarp Family
Podocarpus
Saxegothæa

PROTEACEÆ; Protea Family
Embothrium

RHAMNACEÆ; Buckthorn Family
Hovenia
Rhamnus
Ziziphus

ROSACEÆ; Rose Family
Amelanchier
Cotoneaster
+ *Cratægomespilus*
Cratægus
× *Cratæmespilus*
Cydonia
Eriobotrya
Malus
Mespilus
Photinia
Prunus
Pseudocydonia
Pyrus
Sorbus

RUBIACEÆ; Madder Family
Emmenopterys

RUTACEÆ; Rue Family
Fortunella
Phellodendron
Poncirus
Ptelea
Tetradium
Zanthoxylum

SABIACEÆ; Sabia Family
Meliosma

SALICACEÆ; Willow Family
Populus
Salix

SAPINDACEÆ; Soapberry Family
Koelreuteria
Sapindus
Xanthoceras

SCROPHULARIACEÆ; Figwort Family
Paulownia

SIMAROUBACEÆ; Quassia Family
Ailanthus
Picrasma

STERCULIACEÆ; Chocolate Family
Firmiana

STRACACEÆ; Storax Family
Halesia
Pterostyrax
Rehderodendron
Styrax

TAMARICACEÆ; Agave Family
Tamarix

TAXACEÆ; Yew Family
Taxus
Torreya

TAXODIACEÆ; Bald Cypress Family
Athrotaxis
Cryptomeria
Cunninghamia
Glyptostrobus
Metasequoia
Sciadopitys
Sequoia
Sequoiadendron
Taiwania
Taxodium

TETRACENTACEÆ; Spur Leaf Family
Tetracentron

THEACEÆ; Tea Family
Franklinia
Gordonia
Stewartia

TILACEÆ; Linden Family
Tilia

TROCHODENDRACEÆ; Wheel Tree Family
Trochodendron

ULMACEÆ; Elm Family
Aphananthe
Celtis
Hemiptelea
Planera
Ulmus
Zelkova

VERBENACEÆ; Verbena Family
Clerodendrum
Vitex

Glossary of horticultural and botanical terms

Explanations and definitions of terms refer to the senses intended in this book: other writers sometimes use the words differently. All words shown in BOLD SMALL CAPITALS are glossary entries. Tree names are shown in REGULAR SMALL CAPS.

ALTERNATE (of leaves): The way leaves are arranged in relation to one another on twigs is called alternate unless the leaves are OPPOSITE one another (as in MAPLES for example) or whorled around the twigs (as in most conifers).

ANTHERS: The pollen-bearing tips of STAMENS; the male floral organs.

ARBORESCENT: Tree-like. A little-used synonym is *dendroid*.

ARBORETUM: Collection of planted trees (and often shrubs). Plural: *arboreta*.

AROUND (of trunks): The circumference or girth of a trunk, equivalent to someone's waist measurement. Measurements are generally taken at 4½' above the average soil level at the base of the trunk. In Great Britain and parts of Canada at 5 feet, about 1½ meters.

BACKCROSS (of hybrids): When an offspring of a cross (*i.e.* hybridization) is in turn crossed with one of its parents, the action and the resulting "incestuous" progeny is called a backcross. The result is a HYBRID with significantly more of its genetic background coming from one parent than from the other.

BINOMIAL: The genus and species scientific name considered together.

BISEXUAL: Producing both female and male reproductive organs. Most trees are bisexual. In this book the term is usually employed if specific individual trees, in being bisexual, are anomalous compared to the majority of their kind. For example, most individual OSAGE ORANGE trees (*Maclura pomifera*) are either male or female; few are bisexual. *Hermaphroditic* is a synonym.

BLOOM: 1) A thin, powdery or waxy layer on the skin of a fruit, or other plant part; easily rubbed off, making the surface shiny instead of dull. 2) The flower, or period of flowering.

BOTANIST: One who seriously studies plants, usually with a scientific approach. One who particularly studies or deals with trees may be called a dendrologist or an arborist. See also HORTICULTURAL.

BRACT: A reduced or modified leaf, which can be PETAL-like and showy, or utterly inconspicuous.

BROADLEAF EVERGREEN: An evergreen tree or shrub other than those known as CONIFERS. For example, most *Ilex* (HOLLY), and *Magnolia grandiflora*.

BUDDING: A form of GRAFTING.

CALYX: A collective term for the SEPALS.

CATKIN: An elongated, usually slender, limp, drooping, fleeting floral organ. Most catkin-bearing trees produce conspicuous male catkins whose role is releasing POLLEN to fertilize separate female floral organs. Technical terms for catkins are *strobile* or *ament*. An English name for some is *lamb's tail*. Common trees producing them include: ALDER (*Alnus*), BIRCH (*Betula*), HAZEL (*Corylus*), WALNUT (*Juglans*), WILLOW (*Salix*).

CLONE: A reproduction genetically identical to its source, having been reproduced/propagated vegetatively rather than sexually. A person desiring a 'Gravenstein' APPLE TREE doesn't plant a seed to get one—it won't work—but instead grows the cloned CULTIVAR 'Gravenstein' via grafting, cuttings or other asexual reproductive methods.

COMPOUND (of leaves): Most leaves are simple. Compound ones consist of a number of LEAFLETS sharing one central stalk that arises from one leafbud. See LEAFLETS.

CONIFER: A generally cone-bearing, needled or scalelike-foliaged evergreen tree or shrub, for example: CEDARS (various genera), FIRS (*Abies*), PINES (*Pinus*), SPRUCES (*Picea*); also the berry-bearing JUNIPERS (*Juniperus*) and YEWS (*Taxus*); and some are deciduous, as BALD CYPRESS (*Taxodium*), LARCH (*Larix*), and DAWN REDWOOD (*Metasequoia*).

CORDATE: Heart-shaped. Usually in reference to leaf bases.

COROLLA: Collective term for PETALS.

CROSS: A hybrid.

CULTIVAR: See the Introduction, p. xvii.

CUTTINGS: A cutting is an example of clonal (= asexual or vegetative) propagation (see CLONE). For example, nurserymen snip off twigs of LEYLAND CYPRESS (× *Cupressocyparis Leylandii*), root them, and sell them—as LEYLAND CYPRESS trees, not as "rooted cuttings." Trees so grown are sometimes marketed as "own root" stock. Root-cuttings as well as twig-cuttings are sometimes used to propagate certain trees, such as *Populus alba* (WHITE POPLAR). To take "slips" is to take cuttings.

DOUBLE (of flowers): Flowers with extra PETALS—sometimes just a few, sometimes dozens—that appear fuller, fluffier and showier than the "single" or normal ones. They usually set less fruit than normal plants, or none. Often the STAMENS and STYLES are converted into PETALS. Common roses are doubled, as are many JAPANESE FLOWERING CHERRY trees, and plenty of others. "Semi-double" is intermediate between single and fully double.

DOWNY: Softly hairy.

ENDEMIC: A plant native only in a given location is said to be endemic to that place.

EXFOLIATING: Peeling away in thin layers, as does BIRCH bark.

FASTIGIATE: Unusually slender and compact HABIT, narrower than a typical tree-form. Useful for planting where space is severely limited or where a strong vertical accent is sought.

FILAMENTS: The slender "legs" or stems of STAMENS, bearing the ANTHERS.

FLORET: a very small flower, usually one of many in some sort of cluster, for example a CATKIN.

FOUNDATION-PLANTING: Trees or shrubs planted near a house foundation—that is, by the walls—to mollify the transition from flat earth to vertical walls, to hide an ugly foundation or otherwise to beautify or accent the house.

GALLS: Swellings of various kinds, caused by certain insects. Galls can be found on virtually any parts of susceptible trees: bud, leaf, twig, flowerbud, fruit... They vary so much that entire books are devoted to their growth and appearance.

GLABROUS: Devoid of hairs. The opposite of PUBESCENT.

GLAND: Tiny secreting cells. A glandular plant part is often sticky or resinous, sometimes only microscopically so.

GLAUCOUS: Covered with a pale BLOOM, usually appearing dull powdery blue.

GRAFTING: A method of propagating plants by attaching one kind of plant onto another closely related kind. There are varied motives for grafting and different ways of doing it. Plant-propagation books go into much detail about it. See BUDDING, CLONE, ROOTSTOCK.

HABIT: Characteristic manner of growth. For example, narrow, broad, weeping, upswept, horizontal.

HARDY: More or less tolerant of cold, trying winters. Every place has certain hardy plants. Virtually any plant that consistently makes it through the winter outdoors without suffering significant injury, is called hardy. Those that do not are called "semi-hardy" or TENDER.

HORTICULTURAL: The adjectival form of horticulture, a fancy word for gardening. It has to do with growing, caring for, studying and teaching about plants. See also BOTANIST. The abbreviation *hort.* found after some names in this book, indicates names used by gardeners and nurserymen but not officially sanctioned by science.

HYBRID: A mule, a cross. When two closely related but *separate species* of plants or animals interbreed (in nature or in cultivation), their progeny is called hybrid. Among the commonly grown hybrid trees are: most JAPANESE FLOWERING CHERRIES (*Prunus*), REDFLOWER HORSE CHESTNUT (*Æsculus × carnea*), SAUCER MAGNOLIA (*Magnolia × Soulangiana*), FRASER PHOTINIA (*Photinia × Fraseri*), LONDON PLANE (*Platanus × acerifolia*), virtually all PLUM trees (*Prunus*), almost all of the WEEPING WILLOWS (*Salix babylonica* offspring). Scientific names of hybrids are frequently but by no means invariably marked with an × or an x if the proper symbol is not available.

JUVENILE: An immature stage noticeably different from the adult phase. Certain CONIFERS especially, exhibit significant juvenile foliage. *Eucalyptus* and a few other non-CONIFERS do too.

LANGUAGE OF FLOWERS: A code of symbolic meanings given to plants. A great fad in Victorian times, it fell into disfavor and is now largely forgotten and little known. Hundreds of plants, from mosses and mushrooms to flowers, fruits and trees, were given more or less appropriate meanings, affectations, keywords, sentiments. A bouquet of flowers could thus convey a complicated message.

LAYERING: A method of vegetative or asexual plant propagation wherein a branch is made to root by being placed in contact with soil or some other rooting-medium such as peat moss.

LEADER: The tip twig of a tree.

LEAFLETS: "Little leaves" borne together forming one COMPOUND leaf. See also PALMATELY COMPOUND and PINNATELY COMPOUND.

LENTICEL: A bumpy little dot that serves as a breathing pore on a twig. The relative abundance and shape of lenticels help identify some trees in winter.

MIDRIB: The main vein of a leaf, running down the middle. The leafstem or PETIOLE is a continuation of the midrib.

NATURALIZED: A species not native in a given locale, but growing wild there, reproducing side by side with the natives.

OLD-GROWTH: Unlogged old trees being left or ignored or preserved—as opposed to second- or third-growth trees that follow logging, forest fires or slides.

OPEN-GROWN: A tree having full "elbow room" with plenty of sunlight and exposure to wind, as opposed to growing tall and skinny due to competition, as in a forest or in a densely-planted landscape.

OPPOSITE (of leaves): When leaves are opposite one another on the twigs, rather than ALTERNATE or whorled. MAPLE (*Acer*) is a good example of a tree with opposite leaves.

ORIGINAL (of English names): Tree names sometimes come to signify other trees, related or unrelated. Sometimes a different tree has nearly usurped the usage of an old name. For example, modern tree-writers often ignore the fact that the "Scots Pine" was originally *the* "Fir" tree. Now the name "Fir" is applied to other trees. Hence, any tree mentioned as original in this book is the tree first known under a particular name, whether or not it is still called by that name.

OVARY: The female floral part that consists of the future fruit and seeds in embryonic form. Usually a tiny swollen bulb in the middle of the flower, with a protruding beak (STYLE) that terminates in the STIGMA. The POLLEN from the male floral organs (STAMENS) must come in contact with the OVARY'S STIGMA for fertilization to take place.

PALMATELY COMPOUND (of leaves): A kind of COMPOUND leaf with the LEAFLETS radiating from one point on the main leafstem.

PEDICEL: The flowerstem, which ultimately becomes the fruit's stem.

PETAL: The attractive and usually colorful wing-like floral appendages that delight our eyes.

PETIOLE: The leafstem or leafstalk.

PINETUM: A collection of PINES and PINE-like trees, as an ARBORETUM is a general collection of trees, and a palmetum a collection of PALMS.

PINNATELY COMPOUND (of leaves): A kind of COMPOUND leaf: the main leafstem is lined by two rows of LEAFLETS. ASH (*Fraxinus*) and WALNUT TREES (*Juglans*) are good examples of trees bearing such leaves.

PISTIL: The name given collectively to the female floral organs: OVARY, STYLE, and STIGMA.

POLLEN: Yellowish, sporelike dust produced on ANTHERS that sit atop the STAMENS of the flowers. Pollen serves as the male portion in reproduction. *Pollination* is the process by which pollen is transferred by bees or some other source to the STIGMA. For *fertilization* to occur, the pollen must make its way down through the style or beak to the OVARY'S inner recesses.

PUBESCENT: Hairy, fuzzy, wooly, in any degree, ranging from a few scattered, short, microscopic hairs to thick wooly fuzz as on a peach. The opposite of GLABROUS.

REVERT: When a plant with some kind of abnormality—such as VARIEGATION, or dwarfish stature or weeping habit—wholly or partly returns to producing normal or typical growth.

ROOTSTOCK: The roots used by plant propagators for BUDDING or GRAFTING cultivars. For example, an APPLE TREE (*Malus × domestica*) can be obtained in dwarf, semi-dwarf, or STANDARD sizes depending on what kind of rootstock is used.

RUGOSE: Rough and wrinkly, as some leaf surfaces.

SEMI-EVERGREEN: Also called sub-evergreen or partial-evergreen. A tree retaining its leaves, or many of them, very late in autumn or even well into winter, yet not fully evergreen as most HOLLIES (*Ilex* spp.) are for example.

SEPAL: Green or occasionally reddish PETAL equivalents that are comparatively inconspicuous, hidden beneath the showy PETALS on the outside of the flower. Instead of being very delicate-textured, colorful, and broad like PETALS, sepals are usually narrow, small and plain. A collective term for the sepals is CALYX.

SERRATE: Having sharp teeth (as on a saw).

STAMENS: The male floral organs, each consisting of a threadlike FILAMENT topped by ANTHERS that bear the POLLEN.

STANDARD: Two meanings: 1) Relating to trees that are routinely offered by nurseries in several sizes, "standard" refers to normal or average size, as opposed to dwarf or semi-dwarf size; 2) Such plants routinely sold by nurseries either in shrub form *or* tree form, are called "standards" when grown in tree form: a single trunk with a definite crown. Examples: FRASER PHOTINIA (*Photinia × Fraseri*), BAY LAUREL (*Laurus nobilis*), SERVICEBERRY (*Amelanchier*).

STIGMA: The tip of the OVARY, serving as the sticky destination of POLLEN.

STIPULE: Tiny leaf-like appendages at the junction of the leafstem and the twig. Not invariably present. PLANETREES or SYCAMORES (*Platanus* spp.) have prominent stipules.

STREET-TREE: A tree planted alongside a street, usually in a planting strip of lawn between the street and sidewalk. The term is also used for trees planted in traffic-diverting circles or triangles.

STYLE: The beak of the OVARY; the tapering neck between the OVARY proper and the STIGMA.

SUCKER: Usually vertical, fast-growing, strong shoots that pop up variously from roots, trunks or branches of (usually heavily-pruned) trees. They commonly have extra-large leaves, and, at least to begin with, do not bear flowers or fruit. As a general rule, they are considered undesirable eyesores minimized by pruning in the growing season as opposed to dormant-season pruning.

TAXONOMY: The science of classification.

TENDER: Prone to being hurt or killed in a given climate's winter. We usually tend to call tender those trees that have a reasonable chance of growing here, but that are certainly not HARDY. Tender can also apply to plants that don't have a prayer of being grown here except in a greenhouse.

TOPPED: A tree is topped when its top is decapitated by wind, lightning, or humans. Legitimate reasons for tree-topping exist in certain cases, but in general it is a practice too often abused, done poorly or for the wrong reasons. Often cited as an abominable crime by extremists on the conservative end of the spectrum.

TOPIARY: The art of vegetative sculpture. Just as people shave poodles, or brush, comb, and curl their own hair into various artificial forms, so clippers and shears can be used to shape trees and shrubs.

TRIFOLIATE: Three LEAFLETS, as a three-leaf clover.

VARIEGATION: Two or more colors appearing together in a leaf, such as green and yellow, or green and white and pink.

WITCHES'-BROOMS: Abnormally congested, twiggy masses growing in tree crowns like cancerous mutations. There are various causes. Some kinds of trees never get them, others frequently do. When plant enthusiasts propagate them the result is often a dwarfed version of the normal tree, quite suitable in small-scale gardens or rockeries.

Suggested Reading

No bibliography of sources will be listed. It would require more than 30 pages to cite every reference examined, which would prove more of a nuisance than an asset to most users. Certain specialized books, catalogs or articles are recommended in appropriate places in the tree entries themselves.

If you would like to learn about a tree not listed in this book, begin with:

1) Books

- Bailey, Liberty Hyde. 1914–1917. *Standard Cyclopedia of Horticulture*. New York: MacMillan.

- Bailey, Liberty Hyde Hortorium staff. 1976. *Hortus Third*. New York: MacMillan.

- Bean, William J. 1970–1988. *Trees and Shrubs Hardy in the British Isles*. 7th ed., and Supplement. 5 vols. Rev. by D.L. Clarke, chief ed. London: John Murray.

- Boom, B.K. 1965. *Flora der Cultuurgewassen van Nederland*, Deel I *Nederlandse Dendrologie*. 5th ed. Wageningen: H. Veenman & Zonen.

- Hillier, H.G., P.H.B. Gardner, and Roy Lancaster. 1991. *Hillier Manual of Trees and Shrubs*. 6th ed. Newton Abbot, England: David & Charles.

- Huxley, A., et al. 1992. *The New Royal Horticultural Society Dictionary of Gardening*. 4 vols. London: The Macmillan Press; New York: The Stockton Press.

- Krüssmann, Gerd. 1986. *Manual of Cultivated Broad-Leaved Trees and Shrubs*. 3 vols. Originally published as *Handbuch der Laubgehölze* (1978). Translated by Michael E. Epp. London: B.T. Batsford; Portland, Oregon: Timber Press.

- Lewis, John. 1987–1992. *The International Conifer Register*. 3 vols. (thus far) London: The Royal Horticultural Society.

- Rehder, Alfred.1940. *Manual of Cultivated Trees and Shrubs Hardy in North America*. 2nd ed. New York: MacMillan. Reprinted in 1986 by Timber Press of Portland, OR.

2) Nursery catalogs

Often the only sources of information about newly introduced trees. One can find collections of nursery catalogs at horticultural libraries.

3) Periodicals

- American Conifer Society *Bulletin*

- *American Nurseryman*

- Journal of *Arboriculture*

- *Arnoldia*

- *Avant Gardener*

- *Dendroflora*
- The (Royal Horticultural Society) *Garden*
- Holly Society *Journal*
- *HortScience*
- International Dendrology Society *Yearbook*
- IPPS (International Plant Propagators Society) *Proceedings*
- *Magnolia* (Journal of the Magnolia Society)
- The *New Plantsman*.

4) Computer databases and networks

Increasingly playing a major role and should be consulted.

INDEX OF VERNACULAR NAMES

A

Abele: *Populus alba* - 468
Abeto: *Abies Pinsapo* - 8
Abraham's Balm: *Vitex Agnus-castus* - 666
Acacia, Bailey: *Acacia Baileyana* - 11
    Black: *Acacia melanoxylon* - 12
    Blackwood: *Acacia melanoxylon* - 12
    Catkin: *Acacia floribunda* - 12
    Everblooming: *Acacia rhetinodes* - 12
    False: *Robinia Pseudoacacia* - 570
    Fernleaf: *Acacia Baileyana* - 11
    Gummy: *Robinia viscosa* - 573
    Persian: *Albizia Julibrissin* - 69
    Pink: *Albizia Julibrissin* - 69
    Purpleleaf: *Acacia Baileyana* f. *purpurea* -11
    Rose: *Robinia hispida* - 569
    Rose (Smooth): *Robinia hispida* 'Macrophylla' - 569
    Screwpod: *Acacia pravissima* - 12
    Thorny: *Gleditsia triacanthos* - 228
Acalocote: *Pinus Ayacahuite* - 440
Ague Tree: *Sassafras albidum* - 588
Aka-ezo-matsu: *Picea Glehnii* - 431
Aka-gaeshi: *Quercus acuta* - 547
Aka-matsu: *Pinus densiflora* - 443
Al-arzah: *Fitzroya cupressoides* - 209
Alder, American Gray: *Alnus rugosa* - 73
    Berry-bearing: *Rhamnus Frangula* - 564
    Black: *Alnus glutinosa* - 71
    California: *Alnus rhombifolia* - 72
    Common: *Alnus glutinosa* - 71
    European: *Alnus glutinosa* - 71
    European Gray: *Alnus incana* - 71
    European Green: *Alnus viridis* - 73
    European White: *Alnus incana* - 71
    Hawthorn-leaf: *Alnus glutinosa* 'Incisa' - 71
    Hazel: *Alnus rugosa* - 73
    Hoary: *Alnus rugosa* - 73
    Hybrid: *Alnus* × *Spaethii* - 73
    Italian: *Alnus cordata* - 70
    Japanese: *Alnus japonica* - 72
    Mountain: *Alnus tenuifolia* - 73
    Neapolitan: *Alnus cordata* - 70
    Oregon: *Alnus rubra* - 72
    Red: *Alnus rubra* - 72
    Royal: *Alnus glutinosa* 'Imperialis' - 71
    Sierra: *Alnus rhombifolia* - 72
    Sitka: *Alnus sinuata* - 73
    Slide: *Alnus sinuata* - 73
    Smooth: see *Alnus rugosa* - 73
    Speckled: *Alnus rugosa* - 73
    Tag: *Alnus rugosa* - 73
    Thinleaf: *Alnus sinuata* - 73
    Thinleaf: *Alnus tenuifolia* - 73
    Upright European: *Alnus glutinosa* f. *pyramidalis* - 71
    Weeping Gray: *Alnus incana* 'Pendula' - 72
    Western: *Alnus rubra* - 72
    White: *Alnus rhombifolia* - 72
Alerce or Alerze: *Fitzroya cupressoides* - 209
Alligator Tree: *Liquidambar Styraciflua* - 310
Almond: *Prunus dulcis* - 493
    Double Pink: *Prunus dulcis* 'Roseoplena' - 494
    Double White: *Prunus dulcis* 'Alba Plena' - 493
    Green: *Pistacia vera* - 462
    Hybrid: *Prunus* × *persicoides* - 519
    Weeping: *Prunus dulcis* 'Pendula' - 493
Anacua: *Ehretia Anacua* - 190
Anacuita: *Ehretia Anacua* - 190
Anadol Palamud Ag: *Quercus Cerris* - 549
Anagua or Anaqua: *Ehretia Anacua* - 190
Angelica Tree, Chinese: *Aralia chinensis* - 78
    Japanese: *Aralia elata* - 78
Anise Tree, Japanese: *Illicium anisatum* - 270
Aniseed Tree: *Illicium anisatum* - 270
Apple Tree: *Malus* × *domestica* - 360
Apple, Argyle: *Eucalyptus cinerea* - 194
    Chinese: *Malus prunifolia* var. *Rinki* - 383
    Common: *Malus* × *domestica* - 360
    Crab: *Malus* spp. - 347
    Cultivated: *Malus* × *domestica* - 360
    Custard: *Asimina triloba* - 82
    Edible: *Malus* × *domestica* - 360
    European Wild: *Malus sylvestris* - 399
    Golden: *Cydonia oblonga* - 186
    Hedge: *Maclura pomifera* - 315
    Magdeburg: *Malus* × *magdeburgensis* - 376
    Orchard: *Malus* × *domestica* - 360
    Plum-leaved: *Malus prunifolia* - 383
    'Possum: *Diospyros virginiana* - 189
    Turkey: *Cratægus mollis* - 165
    Turkestan: *Malus Sieversii* 'Niedzwetskyana' - 393
Apricot, Black: *Prunus* × *dasycarpa* - 492
    Briançon: *Prunus brigantina* - 487
    Common: *Prunus Armeniaca* - 485
    Fruiting: *Prunus Armeniaca* - 485
    Japanese: *Prunus Mume* - 504
    Manchurian: *Prunus Armeniaca* var. *mandshurica* - 485
    Purple: *Prunus* × *dasycarpa* - 492
Ara-kashi: *Quercus glauca* - 552

C

Gowen: *Cupressus Goveniana* - 182
Green Column: *Chamæcyparis Lawsoniana* 'Erecta
   Viridis' - *119*
Green Pyramid: *Chamæcyparis Lawsoniana* 'Erecta
   Viridis' - *119*
Gulf: *Taxodium distichum* - *614*
Hinoki: *Chamæcyparis obtusa* - *125*
Italian: *Cupressus sempervirens* - *185*
Kashmir: *Cupressus cashmeriana* - *182*
Lawson: *Chamæcyparis Lawsoniana* - *117*
Leyland: × *Cupressocyparis Leylandii* - *177*
Louisiana: *Taxodium distichum* - *614*
MacNab: *Cupressus MacNabiana* - *183*
Marsh: *Taxodium distichum* - *614*
Mediterranean: *Cupressus sempervirens* - *185*
Mendocino: *Cupressus Goveniana* var. *pigmæa* - *183*
Mexican: *Taxodium mucronatum* - *615*
Min: *Cupressus Chengiana* - *182*
Modoc: *Cupressus Bakeri* - *181*
Monterey: *Cupressus macrocarpa* - *183*
Moss Sawara: *Chamæcyparis pisifera* f. *squarrosa* - *128*
Nootka: *Chamæcyparis nootkatensis* - *123*
Ovens: × *Cupressocyparis Ovensii* - *180*
Patagonian: *Fitzroya cupressoides* - *209*
Pillar: *Cupressus sempervirens* - *185*
Plume Sawara: *Chamæcyparis pisifera* f. *plumosa* - *128*
Pond: *Taxodium ascendens* - *614*
Prickly: *Juniperus formosana* - *283*
Pygmy: *Cupressus Goveniana* var. *pigmæa* - *183*
Roman: *Cupressus sempervirens* - *185*
Rough Barked Arizona: *Cupressus arizonica* - *180*
Sawara: *Chamæcyparis pisifera* - *127*
Scarab: *Chamæcyparis Lawsoniana* 'Allumii' - *117*
Silver: *Chamæcyparis pisifera* f. *squarrosa* - *128*
Siskiyou: *Cupressus Bakeri* var. *Matthewsii* - *181*
Sitka: *Chamæcyparis nootkatensis* - *123*
Smooth Arizona: *Cupressus arizonica* var. *glabra* - *181*
Southern: *Taxodium distichum* - *614*
Stinking: *Chamæcyparis nootkatensis* - *123*
String Sawara: *Chamæcyparis pisifera* f. *filifera* - *127*
Sulphur Moss: *Chamæcyparis pisifera* 'Squarrosa
   Sulphurea' - *129*
Sulphur Sawara: *Chamæcyparis pisifera* 'Sulphurea' - *129*
Swamp: *Taxodium distichum* - *614*
Taiwan: *Chamæcyparis formosensis* - *117*
Threadbranch Sawara: *Chamæcyparis pisifera* f. *filifera*
   - *127*
Tsangpo: *Cupressus gigantea* - *182*
Twisted: *Chamæcyparis obtusa* 'Coralliformis' - *125*
Veitch Moss: *Chamæcyparis pisifera* 'Squarrosa
   Veitchii' - *129*
White: *Chamæcyparis thyoides* - *129*
White Variegated Lawson: *Chamæcyparis Lawsoniana*
   f. *albospica* - *117*
Wintergolden Lawson: *Chamæcyparis Lawsoniana*
   'Stewartii' - *123*

Yellow: *Chamæcyparis nootkatensis* - *123*
Young's Gold Hinoki: *Chamæcyparis obtusa* 'Youngii' - *127*

D

Dahoon: *Ilex Cassine* - *257*
   Myrtle: *Ilex Cassine* var. *myrtifolia* - *257*
   Narrowleaf: *Ilex Cassine* var. *angustifolia* - *257*
   Yellowberry: *Ilex Cassine* f. *Lowei* - *257*
Date of Trebizond: *Diospyros Lotus* - *188*
Date Plum: *Diospyros Lotus* - *188*
Date, Chinese: *Ziziphus Jujuba* - *669*
   Trebizond: *Elæagnus angustifolia* - *190*
Deal Wood: *Pinus sylvestris* - *458*
Deer Wood: *Ostrya virginiana* - *419*
Deodar: *Cedrus Deodara* - *105*
Devil's Walking Stick: *Aralia spinosa* - *79*
Devil's Wood: *Sambucus nigra* - *586*
Dill-seed Tree: *Pinus Pinaster* - *453*
Dogwood: *Cornus* spp., *Euonymus europæus* - *199*
   Aurora®: *Cornus florida* × *C. Kousa* Aurora® - *143*
   Bigleaf: *Cornus macrophylla* - *148*
   Black: *Rhamnus Frangula* - *564*
   Blue-fruited: *Cornus alternifolia* - *135*
   Blue: *Cornus alternifolia* - *135*
   Cherry: *Cornus mas* - *148*
   Chinese Kousa: *Cornus Kousa* var. *chinensis* - *145*
   Constellation®: *Cornus florida* × *C. Kousa* Constellation®
     - *143*
   Double Flowered: *Cornus florida* f. *pluribracteata* - *140*
   Eastern: *Cornus florida* - *137*
   Eddie's White Wonder: *Cornus florida* × *C. Nuttallii*
     'Eddie's White Wonder' - *143*
   Evergreen: *Cornus capitata* - *135*
   Evergreen Kousa: *Cornus capitata* ssp. *angustata* - *136*
   Flowering: *Cornus florida* - *137*
   Galaxy®: *Cornus florida* × *C. Kousa* Galaxy® - *143*
   Giant: *Cornus controversa* - *136*
   Hongkong: *Cornus hongkongensis* - *144*
   Japanese: *Cornus Kousa* - *144*
   Korean: *Cornus coreana, Cornus Kousa* - *136, 144*
   Kousa: *Cornus Kousa* - *144*
   Male: *Cornus mas* - *148*
   Mexican Flowering: *Cornus florida* ssp. *Urbiniana* - *142*
   Pacific: *Cornus Nuttallii* - *150*
   Pagoda: *Cornus alternifolia* - *135*
   Pink: *Cornus florida* f. *rubra* - *141*
   Red: *Cornus florida* f. *rubra* - *141*
   Ruth Ellen®: *Cornus florida* × *C. Kousa* Ruth Ellen® - *143*
   Stardust®: *Cornus florida* × *C. Kousa* Stardust® - *143*
   Stellar Pink®: *Cornus florida* × *C. Kousa* Stellar Pink® - *143*
   Stellar® series: *Cornus florida* × *C. Kousa* - *143*
   Summer: *Stewartia ovata* - *608*
   Swamp: *Ptelea trifoliata* - *538*

E

F

G

Bee: *Nyssa sylvatica* - 416
Black: *Nyssa sylvatica* - 416
Blue: *Eucalyptus globulus* - 195
Bog: *Eucalyptus Kitsoniana* - 196
Broad Leaved Kindling Bark: *Eucalyptus Dalrympleana* - 195
Broad Leaved Ribbon: *Eucalyptus Dalrympleana* - 195
Cabbage: *Eucalyptus pauciflora* - 196
Cider: *Eucalyptus Gunnii* - 195
Cotton: *Nyssa aquatica* - 416
Funnel Fruited: *Eucalyptus coccifera* - 194
Ghost: *Eucalyptus pauciflora* - 196
Jounama Snow: *Eucalyptus pauciflora* ssp. *Debeuzevillei* - 197
Mount Buffalo: *Eucalyptus Mitchelliana* - 196
Mountain: *Eucalyptus Dalrympleana* - 195
Mountain White: *Eucalyptus Dalrympleana* - 195
Omeo: *Eucalyptus neglecta* - 196
Omeo Round Leaved: *Eucalyptus neglecta* - 196
Red: *Liquidambar Styraciflua* - 310
Round Leaved Snow: *Eucalyptus Perriniana* - 197
Silver Dollar: *Eucalyptus cinerea* - 194
Small Leaved: *Eucalyptus parvula* - 196
Snow: *Eucalyptus pauciflora*, *Eucalyptus pauciflora* ssp. *niphophila* - 196, 197
Sour: *Nyssa sylvatica* - 416
Southern Blue: *Eucalyptus globulus* - 195
Spinning: *Eucalyptus Perriniana* - 197
Starleaf: *Liquidambar Styraciflua* - 310
Sweet: *Liquidambar Styraciflua* - 310
Tasmanian Blue: *Eucalyptus globulus* - 195
Tasmanian Snow: *Eucalyptus coccifera* - 194
Tingaringy or Tingiringi: *Eucalyptus glaucescens* - 195
Tupelo: *Nyssa sylvatica* - 416
Upland Yellow: *Nyssa sylvatica* - 416
Urn: *Eucalyptus urnigera* - 198
Urn Fruited: *Eucalyptus urnigera* - 198
Urn Pod: *Eucalyptus urnigera* - 198
Water: *Nyssa aquatica* - 416
Wolgan Snow: *Eucalyptus Gregsoniana* - 195
Gunpowder Tree: *Rhamnus Frangula* - 564
Gutta Percha Tree: *Eucommia ulmoides* - 198

H

Hack Tree: *Celtis occidentalis* - 110
Hackberry: *Celtis* spp., *Prunus Padus* - 109, 508
Chinese: *Celtis sinensis* - 110
Common: *Celtis occidentalis* - 109
European: *Celtis australis* - 109
Hybrid: *Celtis* Magnifica™ - 109
Lowland: *Celtis lævigata* - 109
Mediterranean: *Celtis australis* - 109
Netleaf: *Celtis reticulata* - 110
Northern: *Celtis occidentalis* - 109

Southern: *Celtis lævigata* - 109
Western: *Celtis reticulata* - 110
Hackmatack: *Larix laricina*, *Populus balsamifera* - 306, 469
Hagberry: *Prunus Padus* - 508
Hana-kaede: *Acer pycnanthum* - 48
Hanakaido: *Malus Halliana* - 367
Hana-no-ki: *Acer pycnanthum* - 48
Handkerchief Tree: *Davidia involucrata* - 187
Hara-momi: *Picea polita* - 434
Hardtack: *Ostrya virginiana* - 419
Harewood, English: *Acer Pseudoplatanus* - 46
Harewood, Gray: *Acer Pseudoplatanus* - 46
Harlequin Glory Bower: *Clerodendrum trichotomum* - 134
Harry Lauder's Walking-stick: *Corylus Avellana* 'Contorta' - 152
Hart's Thorn: *Rhamnus cathartica* - 564
Hashidoi: *Syringa reticulata* - 612
Hauchiwa-kaede: *Acer japonicum* - 21
Haw, Apple: *Cratægus opaca* - 168
Blue: *Cratægus brachyacantha* - 158
Cumberland: *Sorbus Aria* - 596
May: *Cratægus opaca* - 168
Southern Summer: *Cratægus æstivalis* - 156
Summer: *Cratægus flava* - 161
Hawmedlar: × *Cratæmespilus grandiflora* - 174
Hawthorn, Allegheny: *Cratægus intricata* - 162
Altai Mountain: *Cratægus altaica* - 157
Apple: *Cratægus æstivalis* - 156
Asian: *Cratægus pinnatifida* var. *major* - 171
Autumn Glory: *Cratægus* 'Autumn Glory' - 157
Azarole: *Cratægus Azarolus* - 157
Biltmore: *Cratægus intricata* - 162
Black: *Cratægus Calpodendron*, *Cratægus Douglasii* - 158, 160
Blue: *Cratægus orientalis*, *Cratægus orientalis* 'Blue Hawthorn' - 168, 169
Blueberry: *Cratægus brachyacantha* - 158
Blueleaved: *Cratægus orientalis* 'Blue Hawthorn' - 169
Broadleaf Cockspur: *Cratægus* × *persimilis* 'Prunifolia' - 170
Canby Cockspur: *Cratægus crus-galli* var. *Canbyi* - 159
Carrière: *Cratægus* × *Lavallei* - 164
Cerro: *Cratægus erythropoda* - 161
Chinese Bigleaf: *Cratægus pinnatifida* var. *major* - 171
Chocolate: *Cratægus erythropoda* - 161
Cockspur: *Cratægus crus-galli* - 159
Common: *Cratægus monogyna* - 166
Dotted: *Cratægus punctata* - 171
Double Pink / Red English: *Cratægus lævigata* 'Rosea Flore Pleno' - 164
Double Scarlet Contorted English: *Crat. lævigata* 'Salisburifolia' - 164
Double Scarlet English: *Cratægus lævigata* 'Paul's Scarlet' - 163
Double Very Pale Pink English: *Cratægus lævigata* 'Masekii' - 163
Double White English: *Cratægus lævigata* 'Candidoplena' - 162

I

J

K

L

M

N

O

Chinese Cork: *Quercus variabilis* - 562
Chinese Evergreen: *Quercus myrsinæfolia* - 556
Chinkapin: *Quercus Muhlenbergii* - 556
Chinquapin: *Quercus Muhlenbergii* - 556
Cluster: *Quercus robur* 'Cristata' - 559
Coast Live: *Quercus agrifolia* - 548
Colorado: *Quercus Gambelii* - 552
Columnar English: *Quercus robur* f. *fastigiata* - 559
Common: *Quercus robur* - 558
Concord: *Quercus robur* 'Concordia' - 559
Cork: *Quercus Suber* - 561
Cork (Chinese): *Quercus variabilis* - 562
Cow: *Quercus Michauxii* - 555
Cypress: *Quercus robur* f. *fastigiata* - 559
Daimio or Daimyo: *Quercus dentata* - 550
Darlington: *Quercus hemisphærica* - 553
Dauvesse's Weeping: *Quercus robur* 'Pendula Dauvessei' -559
Devonshire: *Quercus × hispanica* - 553
Diamond-leaf: *Quercus laurifolia* - 554
Duck: *Quercus nigra* - 556
Durmast: *Quercus petræa* - 557
Dyer's: *Quercus velutina* - 562
Emory: *Quercus Emoryi* - 551
Emperor: *Quercus dentata* - 550
Engelmann: *Quercus Emoryi* - 551
English: *Quercus robur* - 558
English (Columnar): *Quercus robur* f. *fastigiata* - 559
English (Cutleaf): *Quercus robur* 'Laciniata' - 559
English (Fastigiate): *Quercus robur* f. *fastigiata* - 559
English (Golden): *Quercus robur* 'Concordia' - 559
English (Hybrid): *Quercus × rosacea* - 560
English (Upright): *Quercus robur* f. *fastigiata* - 559
English (Willowleaf): *Quercus robur* 'Salicifolia' - 559
Evergreen Japanese: *Quercus acuta* - 547
Evergreen White: *Quercus Emoryi* - 551
Exeter: *Quercus × hispanica* - 553
Fastigiate English: *Quercus robur* f. *fastigiata* - 559
Forkleaf: *Quercus alba* - 548
Garry: *Quercus Garryana* - 552
Goldcup: *Quercus chrysolepis* - 549
Golden English: *Quercus robur* 'Concordia' - 559
Holly: *Quercus agrifolia, Quercus Ilex* - 548, 553
Holly-leaved: *Quercus agrifolia* - 548
Holm: *Quercus Ilex* - 553
Hungarian: *Quercus Frainetto* - 552
Interior Live: *Quercus Wislizenii* - 563
Iron: *Quercus chrysolepis, Quercus stellata* - 549, 561
Island Live: *Quercus tomentella* - 562
Italian: *Quercus Frainetto* - 552
Jack: *Quercus ellipsoidalis* - 551
Japanese Blue: *Quercus glauca* - 552
Japanese Chestnut: *Quercus acutissima* - 547
Japanese Emperor: *Quercus dentata* - 550
Japanese Evergreen: *Quercus acuta* - 547
Japanese Live: *Quercus myrsinæfolia* - 556
Japanese Red: *Quercus acuta* - 547

Konara: *Quercus glandulifera* - 552
Lacey: *Quercus Laceyi* - 554
Laurel: *Quercus hemisphærica* - 553
Laurel (Northern): *Quercus imbricaria* - 554
Laurel (Swamp): *Quercus laurifolia* - 554
Leopard: *Quercus Shumardii* - 561
Live (Arizona): *Quercus arizonica* - 548
Live (California): *Quercus agrifolia* - 548
Live (Canyon): *Quercus chrysolepis* - 549
Live (Coast): *Quercus agrifolia* - 548
Live (Interior): *Quercus Wislizenii* - 563
Live (Island): *Quercus tomentella* - 562
Live (Japanese): *Quercus myrsinæfolia* - 556
Live (Louisiana): *Quercus virginiana* - 563
Live (Sierra): *Quercus Wislizenii* - 563
Live (Southern): *Quercus virginiana* - 563
Lucombe: *Quercus × hispanica* 'Lucombeana' - 553
Mapleleaf: *Quercus Shumardii* var. *acerifolia* - 561
Maul: *Quercus chrysolepis* - 549
Mesa (Blue): *Quercus Emoryi* - 551
Mexican Loquat-leaved: *Quercus rysophylla* - 561
Moccas Weeping: *Quercus robur* 'Pendula' - 559
Mongolian: *Quercus mongolica* - 556
Monterrey™: *Quercus polymorpha* - 558
Mossycup: *Quercus macrocarpa* - 555
Mush: *Quercus lobata* - 555
Netleaf: *Quercus rugosa* - 560
Northern Laurel: *Quercus imbricaria* - 554
Northern Pin: *Quercus ellipsoidalis* - 551
Nuttall: *Quercus texana* - 554
Oregon White: *Quercus Garryana* - 552
Oriental: *Quercus variabilis* - 562
Overcup: *Quercus lyrata* - 555
Pacific Post: *Quercus Garryana* - 552
Pasadena: *Quercus Emoryi* - 551
Peach: *Quercus Phellos* - 557
Pedunculate: *Quercus robur* - 558
Persian:*Quercus castaneæfolia,Quercus macranthera* -549,555
Pin: *Quercus palustris, Quercus Phellos* - 556, 557
'Possum: *Quercus nigra* - 556
Post: *Quercus stellata* - 561
Post (Pacific): *Quercus Garryana* - 552
Post (Swamp): *Quercus lyrata* - 555
Prairie: *Quercus macrocarpa* - 555
Pyramidal Evergreen: *Quercus Ilex* 'Fordii' - 554
Quercitron: *Quercus velutina* - 562
Red (Bottomland): *Quercus falcata* var. *pagodæfolia* - 551
Red (Common): *Quercus rubra* - 560
Red (Eastern): *Quercus rubra* - 560
Red (Japanese): *Quercus acuta* - 547
Red (Northern): *Quercus rubra* - 560
Red (Shumard): *Quercus Shumardii* - 561
Red (Smoothbark): *Quercus texana* - 562
Red (Southern): *Quercus falcata* - 551
Red (Swamp): *Quercus falcata* var. *pagodæfolia* - 551

Red (Texas): *Quercus Buckleyi* - 549
Red River: *Quercus texana* - 562
Ridge White: *Quercus alba* - 548
Ring-cupped: *Quercus glauca* - 552
Rock: *Quercus Laceyi* - 554
Rock Chestnut: *Quercus Prinus* - 558
Rocky Mountain White: *Quercus Gambelii* - 552
Rough: *Quercus stellata* - 561
Sawtooth: *Quercus acutissima* - 547
Scarlet: *Quercus coccinea* - 550
Sessile: *Quercus petræa* - 557
Shingle: *Quercus imbricaria* - 554
Shumard Red: *Quercus Shumardii* - 561
Sierra™: *Quercus Canbyi* - 549
Sierra Live: *Quercus Wislizenii* - 563
Silver-variegated: see *Quercus robur* f. *variegata* - 560
Silverleaf: *Quercus hypoleucoides* - 553
Smoky: *Quercus Laceyi* - 554
Smoothbark Red: *Quercus texana* - 562
Southern Red: *Quercus falcata* - 551
Spanish: *Quercus falcata, Quercus × hispanica* - 551, 553
Spanish (Swamp): *Quercus falcata* var. *pagodæfolia* - 551
Spotted: *Quercus Shumardii* - 561
Stave: *Quercus alba* - 548
Swamp Chestnut: *Quercus Michauxii* - 555
Swamp Laurel: *Quercus laurifolia* - 554
Swamp Post: *Quercus lyrata* - 555
Swamp Red: *Quercus falcata* var. *pagodæfolia* - 551
Swamp Spanish: *Quercus falcata* var. *pagodæfolia* - 551
Swamp White: *Quercus bicolor* - 548
Tan: *Lithocarpus densiflorus* - 314
Tanbark: *Lithocarpus densiflorus, Quercus Prinus* - 314, 558
Texas Blue: *Quercus Laceyi* - 554
Texas Red: *Quercus Buckleyi* - 549
Truffle: *Quercus robur* - 558
Turkish: *Quercus Cerris* - 549
Turkey: *Quercus Cerris* - 549
Turkeyfoot: *Quercus falcata* - 551
Turner's: *Quercus × Turneri* - 561
Ubame: *Quercus phillyræoides* - 557
Upright English: *Quercus robur* f. *fastigiata* - 559
Utah White: *Quercus Gambelii* - 552
Water: *Quercus lobata, Quercus nigra* - 555, 556
Water White: *Quercus lyrata* - 555
Weeping: *Quercus lobata* - 555
Western White: *Quercus Garryana* - 552
White: *Quercus alba* - 548
White (Arizona): *Quercus arizonica* - 548
White (Box): *Quercus stellata* - 561
White (California): *Quercus lobata* - 555
White (Oregon): *Quercus Garryana* - 552
White (Rocky Mountain): *Quercus Gambelii* - 552
White (Swamp): *Quercus bicolor* - 548
White (Utah): *Quercus Gambelii* - 552
White (Water): *Quercus lyrata* - 555
White (Western): *Quercus Garryana* - 552

Whiteleaf: *Quercus hypoleucoides* - 553
Willow: *Quercus Phellos* - 557
Yellow: *Quercus velutina* - 562
Yellow Chestnut: *Quercus Muhlenbergii* - 556
Ohatsuki-icho: *Ginkgo biloba* var. *epiphylla* - 226
Old Man's Beard: *Chionanthus virginicus* - 131
Oilnut: *Juglans cinerea* - 271
Oleaster: *Elæagnus angustifolia* - 190
Oleaster, Bohemian: *Elæagnus angustifolia* - 190
Olive: *Olea europæa* - 416
    Common: *Olea europæa* - 416
    Holly: *Osmanthus heterophyllus* - 418
Olive, Russian: *Elæagnus angustifolia* - 190
    Tea (Hardy): *Osmanthus × Fortunei* - 418
    Tea (Holly-leaf): *Osmanthus heterophyllus* - 418
    Wild: *Elæagnus angustifolia, Halesia carolina, Nyssa aquatica* - 190, 234, 416
O-matsu: *Pinus Thunbergii* - 459
Omorika: *Picea Omorika* - 433
Oneberry: *Celtis occidentalis* - 110
Onigurumi: *Juglans ailantifolia* - 270
Oni-momiji: *Acer diabolicum* - 17
Open-arse: *Mespilus germanica* - 407
Opossum Tree: *Liquidambar Styraciflua* - 310
Opossum Wood: *Halesia carolina* - 234
Orange, Bitter: *Poncirus trifoliata* - 467
    Hardy: *Poncirus trifoliata* - 467
    Mock: *Prunus caroliniana* - 488
    Osage: *Maclura pomifera* - 315
    Trifoliate: *Poncirus trifoliata* - 467
    Wild: *Prunus caroliniana* - 488
Osage Orange: *Maclura pomifera* - 315
    Thornless: *Maclura pomifera* f. *inermis* - 316
Osier, Broad-leaved: *Salix × sericans* - 585
    Green: *Cornus alternifolia* - 135
Osmanthus, Chinese: *Osmanthus armatus* - 417
    Common: *Osmanthus heterophyllus* - 418
    Hybrid: *Osmanthus × Fortunei* - 418
O-urajiro-no-ki: *Malus Tschonoskii* - 401
Oyama-renge: *Magnolia Sieboldii* - 338
Oyamel: *Abies religiosa* - 9
O-zumi: *Malus × Zumi* - 404

P

Pagoda Tree, Japanese: *Sophora japonica* - 593
Palm Lily: *Cordyline australis* - 134
Palm, California Fan: *Washingtonia filifera* - 667
    Chinese Fan: *Trachycarpus Fortunei* - 643
    Chusan: *Trachycarpus Fortunei* - 643
    Cotton: *Washingtonia filifera* - 667
    Desert Fan: *Washingtonia filifera* - 667
    Dracena: *Cordyline australis* - 134
    Dwarf Fan: *Chamærops humilis* - 130

Pine, Afghan: *Pinus brutia* var. *eldarica* - 441
  Aleppo: *Pinus halepensis* - 446
  Alpine Whitebark: *Pinus albicaulis* - 439
  Ancient: *Pinus longæva* - 449
  Apache: *Pinus Engelmannii* - 444
  Arizona: *Pinus ponderosa* var. *arizonica* - 454
  Arizona Longleaf: *Pinus Engelmannii* - 444
  Arkansas: *Pinus echinata* - 444
  Armand: *Pinus Armandii* - 440
  Arolla: *Pinus Cembra* - 442
  Austrian Black: *Pinus nigra* - 450
  Balkan: *Pinus leucodermis, Pinus Peuce* - 448, 453
  Beach: *Pinus contorta* - 443
  Bhutan: *Pinus Wallichiana* - 460
  Big: *Pinus Lambertiana, Pinus ponderosa* - 448, 454
  Bigcone: *Pinus Coulteri* - 443
  Bird's-eye: *Pinus contorta* - 443
  Bishop: *Pinus muricata* - 450
  Black: *Pinus nigra* - 450
  Black (Austrian): *Pinus nigra* - 450
  Black (Common): *Pinus nigra* - 450
  Black (Corsican): *Pinus nigra* var. *corsicana* - 451
  Black (Crimean): *Pinus nigra* var. *Pallasiana* - 451
  Black (European): *Pinus nigra* - 450
  Black (Japanese): *Pinus Thunbergii* - 459
  Black (Turkish): *Pinus nigra* var. *Pallasiana* - 451
  Black Hills Ponderosa: *Pinus ponderosa* var. *scopulorum* - 454
  Black Sea: *Pinus brutia* var. *Pityusa* - 442
  Blackjack: *Pinus ponderosa* - 454
  Blue: *Pinus Wallichiana* - 460
  Blue Linber: *Pinus flexilis* 'Glauca' - 445
  Bordeaux: *Pinus Pinaster* - 453
  Border White: *Pinus strobiformis* - 456
  Bosnian: *Pinus leucodermis* - 448
  Bosnian Redcone: *Pinus leucodermis* - 448
  Bournemouth: *Pinus Pinaster* - 453
  Brazilian: *Araucaria angustifolia* - 79
  Bristlecone: *Pinus aristata* - 439
  Brutian: *Pinus brutia* - 441
  Buddhist: *Podocarpus macrophyllus* - 466
  Bull: *Pinus ponderosa* - 454
  Bur: *Pinus pungens* - 454
  Calabrian: *Pinus brutia, Pinus nigra* var. *corsicana* - 441, 451
  Calabrian Cluster-pine: *Pinus brutia* - 441
  California White: *Pinus monticola* - 450
  Canton Water: *Glyptostrobus pensilis* - 232
  Chile or Chilean: *Araucaria araucana* - 79
  Chilghoza: *Pinus Gerardiana* - 446
  Chinese: *Pinus tabulæformis* - 459
  Chinese Hard: *Pinus tabulæformis* - 459
  Chinese Red: *Pinus tabulæformis* - 459
  Chinese Water: *Glyptostrobus pensilis* - 232
  Chinese White: *Pinus Armandii* - 440
  Chir: *Pinus Roxburghii* - 456
  Cluster: *Pinus Pinaster* - 453

  Coast: *Pinus contorta* - 443
  Colorado Bristlecone: *Pinus aristata* - 439
  Columnar Scots: *Pinus sylvestris* 'Fastigiata' - 458
  Coulter: *Pinus Coulteri* - 443
  Cow's Tail: *Cephalotaxus Harringtonia* var. *drupacea* - 111
  David's: *Pinus Armandii* - 440
  Del Mar: *Pinus Torreyana* - 460
  Digger: *Pinus Sabiniana* - 456
  Dragon Eye (Black): *Pinus Thunbergii* 'Oculis-draconis' - 459
  Dragon Eye (Red): *Pinus densiflora* 'Oculis-draconis' - 444
  Dragon Eye (White): *Pinus parviflora* 'Oculis-draconis' - 453
  Dwarf Mountain: *Pinus Mugo* - 450
  Eastern White: *Pinus Strobus* - 456
  Eilar: *Pinus brutia* var. *eldarica* - 441
  Emodi: *Pinus Roxburghii* - 456
  European Black: *Pinus nigra* - 450
  Fingercone: *Pinus monticola* - 450
  Foothill: *Pinus Sabiniana* - 456
  Foxtail: *Pinus aristata, Pinus Balfouriana* - 439, 440
  Frankincense: *Pinus Tæda* - 459
  Georgia: *Pinus palustris* - 452
  Ghost: *Pinus Sabiniana* - 456
  Giant Mugo: *Pinus uncinata* - 460
  Gigantic: *Pinus Lambertiana* - 448
  Ginger: *Chamæcyparis Lawsoniana* - 117
  Golden Dragon-eye: *Pinus parviflora* 'Oculus-draconis' - 453
  Golden Scots: *Pinus sylvestris* 'Aurea' - 458
  Gray: *Pinus Banksiana, Pinus Sabiniana* - 441, 456
  Graybark: *Pinus leucodermis* - 448
  Great Basin Bristlecone: *Pinus longæva* - 449
  Greek Stone: *Pinus Peuce* - 453
  Guangdon(g): *Pinus kwantungensis* - 448
  Hard: *Pinus palustris* - 452
  Hard (Chinese): *Pinus tabulæformis* - 459
  Heart: *Pinus palustris* - 452
  Heavy: *Pinus ponderosa* - 454
  Heldreich: *Pinus Heldreichii* - 447
  Herzegovinian: *Pinus leucodermis* - 448
  Hickory: *Pinus aristata, Pinus pungens* - 439, 454
  Hill: *Pinus palustris* - 452
  Himalayan (White): *Pinus Wallichiana* - 460
  Horncone: *Pinus Banksiana* - 441
  Hudson Bay: *Pinus Banksiana* - 441
  Idaho White: *Pinus monticola* - 450
  Insignis: *Pinus radiata* - 454
  Italian Stone: *Pinus Pinea* - 453
  Jack: *Pinus Banksiana* - 441
  Japanese Black: *Pinus Thunbergii* - 459
  Japanese Red: *Pinus densiflora* - 443
  Japanese Table: *Pinus densiflora* 'Umbraculifera' - 444
  Japanese Umbrella: *Pinus densiflora* 'Umbraculifera', *Sciadopitys verticillata* - 444, 590
  Japanese White: *Pinus parviflora* - 452
  Jeffrey: *Pinus Jeffreyi* - 447
  Jelecote: *Pinus patula* - 453
  Jersey: *Pinus virginiana* - 460

Goldleaf White: *Populus alba* 'Richardii' - 468
Gray: *Populus* × *canescens* - 473
Griffin: *Populus* 'Brooks No. 1' - 470
Hybrid Black: *Populus* × *canadensis* - 470
Italian Black: *Populus* × *canadensis* 'Serotina' - 472
Japanese: *Populus Maximowiczii* - 478
Korean: *Populus koreana* - 477
Lombardy: *Populus nigra* 'Italica' - 479
Lombardy (Chinese): *Populus Simonii* 'Fastigiata' - 481
Lombardy (Downy): *Populus nigra* 'Plantierensis' - 479
Lombardy (Silver): *Populus alba* 'Pyramidalis' - 468
Lombardy (Slender): *Populus nigra* 'Elegans' - 479
Maine: *Populus* 'Maine' - 477
Manchester: *Populus nigra* var. *betulæfolia* - 478
Manchurian: *Populus songarica* - 481
May: *Populus* × *canadensis* 'Marilandica' - 472
Mongolian: *Populus cathayana* - 474
Morden: *Populus* 'Cordeniensis' - 474
Narrowleaf: *Populus angustifolia* - 469
Necklace: *Populus deltoides* - 474
Northwest: *Populus* × *Jackii* 'Northwest' - 477
Norway: *Populus* 'Norway' - 479
Ontario: *Populus* 'Candicans' - 473
Oxford: *Populus* 'Oxford' - 479
Picart's: *Populus* × *canescens* 'Macrophylla' - 473
Piccart's: *Populus* × *canescens* 'Macrophylla' - 473
Prince Eugene's: *Populus* × *canadensis* 'Eugenei' - 471
Pyramidal: *Populus nigra* 'Italica' - 479
Pyramidal White: *Populus alba* 'Pyramidalis' - 468
Railway: *Populus* × *canadensis* 'Regenerata' - 472
Rochester: *Populus* 'Rochester' - 480
Rocket: *Populus alba* 'Raket' - 468
Roxbury: *Populus* 'Roxbury' - 480
Rumford: *Populus* × *berolinensis* 'Rumford' - 470
Russian: *Populus* × *Petrowskiana* - 480
Silver: *Populus alba, Populus alba* 'Nivea' - 468, 468
Silver Lombardy: *Populus alba* 'Pyramidalis' - 468
Simon: *Populus Simonii* - 480
Simon (Weeping): *Populus Simonii* 'Pendula' - 481
Slender Lombardy: *Populus nigra* 'Elegans' - 479
Smoothbark: *Populus* × *acuminata* - 467
Snowy: *Populus alba* - 468
Strathglass: *Populus* × *berolinensis* 'Strathglass' - 470
Tebessa: *Populus nigra* 'Afghanica' - 478
Tower: *Populus* × *canescens* 'Tower' - 474
Tulip: *Liriodendron Tulipifera* - 312
Weeping: *Populus tristis* - 483
Weeping Gray: *Populus* × *canescens* 'Pendula' - 473
Weeping Simon: *Populus Simonii* 'Pendula' - 481
White (Chinese): *Populus tomentosa* - 481
White: *Populus alba* - 468
Willowleaf: *Populus angustifolia* - 469
Wooly: *Populus alba* - 468
Yellow: *Liriodendron Tulipifera* - 312
'Possum Wood: *Diospyros virginiana* - 189
Potatochip Tree: *Ptelea trifoliata* - 538

Prairie Grub: *Ptelea trifoliata* - 538
Prick Timber: *Euonymus europæus* - 199
Prick Wood: *Euonymus europæus* - 199
Prickly-ash, Southern: *Zanthoxylum clava-Herculis* - 668
Prickly Castor-oil Tree: *Kalopanax pictus* - 295
Pride of India: *Koelreuteria paniculata, Melia Azedarach* - 297, 406
Princess Tree: *Paulownia tomentosa* - 421
Privet, Chinese: *Ligustrum lucidum* - 309
    Crinkleleaf: *Ligustrum lucidum* 'Recurvifolium' - 309
    Glossy: *Ligustrum lucidum* - 309
    Japanese: see *Ligustrum* - 308
    Mock: *Phillyrea latifolia* - 423
    Shining: *Ligustrum lucidum* - 309
    Silverleaf: *Ligustrum lucidum* 'Excelsum Superbum' - 309
    Tree: *Ligustrum lucidum* - 309
Prune: *Prunus* × *domestica* - 493
Puzzle Monkey: *Araucaria araucana* - 79

Q

Quickbeam: *Sorbus aucuparia* - 597
Quicken: *Sorbus aucuparia* - 597
Quickthorn: *Cratægus monogyna* - 166
Quince, Bengal: *Poncirus trifoliata* - 467
    Chinese: *Pseudocydonia sinensis* - 536
    Common: *Cydonia oblonga* - 186
    Fruiting: *Cydonia oblonga* - 186
    Perfume: *Pseudocydonia sinensis* - 536
Quiverleaf: *Populus tremuloides* - 482

R

Rain Berry: *Rhamnus cathartica* - 564
Raisin Tree, Japanese: *Hovenia dulcis* - 235
Ram Thorn: *Rhamnus cathartica* - 564
Raoul: *Nothofagus procera* - 415
Rattle Box: *Halesia carolina* - 234
Raulí: *Nothofagus procera* - 415
Rauol: *Nothofagus procera* - 415
Redbay: *Persea Borbonia* - 422
    Swamp: *Persea Borbonia* var. *pubescens* - 422
Redbird Tree: *Cercis canadensis* - 113
Redbud, California: *Cercis occidentalis* - 115
    Chinese: *Cercis chinensis* - 114
    Common: *Cercis canadensis* - 113
    Eastern: *Cercis canadensis* -113
    European: *Cercis Siliquastrum* - 115
    Mexican: *Cercis canadensis* var. *texensis* - 114
    Oklahoma: *Cercis* 'Oklahoma' - 115
    Texas: *Cercis canadensis* var. *texensis* - 114
    Texas White: *Cercis canadensis* var. *texensis* 'Texas White' - 114

S

T

U

V

Y

Z